EYEWITNESS HISTORY

The Progressive Era

Faith Jaycox

Facts On File, Inc.

NOTE ON PHOTOS

Many of the illustrations and photographs used in this book are old, historical images. The quality of the prints is not always up to modern standards, as in some cases the originals are damaged. The content of the illustrations, however, made their inclusion important despite problems in reproduction.

The Progressive Era

Copyright © 2005 by Faith Jaycox
Maps copyright © 2005 by Facts On File, Inc.

Facts On File, Inc.
132 West 31st Street
New York NY 10001

Library of Congress Cataloging-in-Publication Data
Jaycox, Faith.
    The Progressive Era / Faith Jaycox.
      p. cm. — (An eyewitness history)
    Includes bibliographical references (p.) and index.
    ISBN 0-8160-5159-3 (acid-free paper)
    1. Progressivism (United States politics) 2. United States—Politics and government—1865–1933. 3. Progressivism (United States politics)—Sources. 4. United States—Politics and government—1865–1933—Sources. I. Title. II. Series.
    E661.J395 2005
    973.8—dc22
                                      2004012363

Text design by Joan M. Toro
Cover design by Cathy Rincon
Maps by Dale Williams

Printed in the United States of America

VB JT 10 9 8 7 6 5 4 3 2 1

This book is printed on acid-free paper.

CONTENTS

PREFACE

During the three decades between 1890 and 1920, the United States entered the modern era and considered how best to meet the challenges it presented. The nation had a newly urban and diverse society, new technological capabilities, and a new industrial economy that had grown with astonishing speed in the 25 years following the Civil War. Equally important, the nation had new status in the world and notably enlarged power in the international community. Faced with so much change in so short a time, many Americans found they were no longer entirely sure of their nation's identity. They embarked on a voluble reconsideration of many fundamental questions, not least of which was the meaning of social cohesion and social responsibility in a culture long committed to individual rights and limited government.

Some of the conclusions the nation arrived at by 1920, it is now clear, were wrong at best—none more so than the adoption of laws to enforce racial segregation and to disenfranchise African Americans. But other decisions, formalized in legislation or expressed through civic institutions, had positive effects. One change, women's suffrage, doubled the number of enfranchised American citizens with one stroke—the largest single expansion of voting rights, and thus democracy, since the nation's founding. These and other changes that occurred from 1890 to 1920 were wide and deep. Many mark a watershed in American historical development and continue to influence America's journey a century later.

These crucial decades take their familiar label, the Progressive Era, from reformers and reform-minded people who were called progressives. Over the last half century historians have debated at great length who the progressives were, what they actually accomplished, and even whether the concept of progressivism has any clearly definable meaning whatsoever. Today historians understand progressivism to have been a persuasion with heterogeneous and sometimes even contradictory advocates and programs. During the era itself, however, people who called themselves progressives believed they were participating in a definable "progressive movement." That movement, they believed, was reclaiming a decent society from the forces of economic rapaciousness by expanding the role of collective social action and reclaiming a decent politics—and even democracy—from the forces of corruption that had seized it.

Just as historians do not agree about the nature of progressivism, they do not all assign the same time boundaries to the Progressive Era. This volume begins in 1890, a year in which the frontier was declared closed in the West and literate Americans were shocked by the exposé of eastern city slums in Jacob Riis's best-selling *How the Other Half Lives.* It ends in 1920. Traditionally many histories of the Progressive Era ended in 1917, when America entered World War I. More recently, in recognition of new scholarship that has established the pivotal role women played in reform, many historians have chosen 1919, the year Congress passed a Constitutional amendment giving women the right to vote. But in fact it was 1920 before women's suffrage was ratified by the last necessary state—a requirement for enacting an amendment to the Constitution, which in the recent era the proposed Equal Rights Amendment failed to meet. In 1920 women voted in a presidential election for the first time, Prohibition began, and the census showed that the majority of Americans (51 percent) now lived in urban areas. Very quickly, the great reform era ended in the roar of the twenties.

Like all methods of organizing historical evidence, a chronological format permits the emphasis of some kinds of information while making other emphases more difficult. This volume makes use of chronology as an opportunity to track the step-by-step development of several reform movements at the heart of progressivism, such as the beginning of conservation initiatives and the movement to end child labor. It also follows the development of events leading to the four Progressive Era amendments to the U.S. Constitution: the establishment of income tax, direct election of senators, prohibition of liquor, and women's suffrage. It traces the movement for "direct democracy" (which included not only the direct election of senators but also primary elections and the recall of elected officials), a good example of reforms so taken for granted today that it is difficult to think of them as reforms at all. Yet like all such changes they were momentous and debatable to the people who chose to enact them. Another major development covered in this volume is the emergence of America as a world power, both economically and militarily, at a time when most of Europe was ruled by powerful sovereigns and knew only limited democracy.

Some other issues proved more difficult to present in a chronological format. One was the emergence of a mass or consumer society with greater leisure time, an important cultural change during the progressive decades. Two representative topics related to that change, however—the development of motion pictures and of the first professional sport, baseball—are followed in detail. Also difficult to assign to specific moments in time were important and widespread changes in philosophies and ways of thinking—not least of which was the eclipse of belief in the all-powerful individual by the belief that people are creatures of their environment. These changes in attitude have been touched upon in presenting topics to which they are particularly relevant. The fine arts, including literature, are treated briefly but most popular arts and culture are not covered.

One of the most distinguishing traits of the Progressive Era was the rise of large cities. But even at the end of the era America remained a sprawling and varied nation where some 49 percent of the population still lived in rural areas. *The Progressive Era* attempts to give some attention to all places and groups in the narrative, in the eyewitness documents, and in the photos selected to illustrate them. The Eyewitness Testimony has been chosen to give the reader an idea of the range of points of view, experiences, and arguments that existed at the time. Some documents are highly opinionated, some are personal, and some official. No one document, of course, tells the whole story.

ACKNOWLEDGMENTS

One of the pleasures of writing a book is the opportunity to interact with researchers in many places. For their courtesy and assistance in locating and providing specific material I am indebted to Barbara Dunn of the Hawaiian Historical Society; Nancy Sherbert of the Kansas State Historical Society; W. C. Burdick at the National Baseball Hall of Fame and Museum, Cooperstown, New York; Patricia McSchlosser of Bainbridge Island, Washington; and Rebekah Johnston of the Historical Society of Western Pennsylvania, who remembered me when new material surfaced six months later. The photo research team at the Arizona Historical Society, Tucson, and staff at the Reference Section, Library of Congress Prints and Photographs Division, provided exceptional assistance. Very special thanks are due to Beth Weinhardt of the Westerville, Ohio, Public Library, who went to extraordinary lengths to locate and provide images from the Anti-Saloon League collection housed there. I benefited from being able to use the comprehensive collection of the Minnesota Historical Society Library; the Hennepin County, Minnesota, Library System, Edina and Southdale Branches, also made materials available to me on interlibrary loan. I am especially indebted to the Minneapolis Public Library System. While I was at work on this project much of its excellent historical collection was moved to temporary locations or storage facilities and the main library building torn down in preparation for constructing a new one. Throughout it all Teresa Mercier and other staff members at the Linden Hills Branch went out of their way to locate materials and make them accessible to me—on an almost daily basis at some points—and always with unfailing good cheer. The library system's public relations staff also aided my requests on several occasions. Last but hardly least it is my pleasure to offer thanks to the staff of Facts On File, especially editor Nicole Bowen and Laura Shauger, who guided the process and when necessary tweaked it with great skill and patience.

INTRODUCTION

During the decades from 1890 to 1920 America experienced sweeping change in every area of politics, society, and culture. The previously rural-dwelling nation moved to town in large numbers, while back on the farm agriculture became decisively mechanized. Large numbers of new immigrants arrived, many from cultures that differed markedly from that of their adopted nation. The automobile appeared, the Wright brothers flew, the skyscraper soared, jazz was born, modern art was put on display, motion pictures were invented, and the first World Series was played (1903, Boston defeated Pittsburgh). Mass newspapers began to offer sensational news-as-entertainment. Women left their homes to serve and to reform the larger community, and even more shockingly they took to the streets to demand the right to vote. Schooling lengthened and new professions developed while old ones organized themselves into powerful national associations. The consumer movement began. The divorce rate rose.

The surrender of the Plains Indians was completed at Wounded Knee and with or without their consent all Native Americans were made U.S. citizens, obligating many to accept individual homestead allotments. The western frontier closed, the last of the 48 continental states was added to the union, and a new movement to conserve natural resources began. The "New South" began to industrialize but also eroded African-American political rights and segregated the races in all aspects of social life. Race riots and lynchings stained many areas of the nation, *Plessy v. Ferguson* and its watchword "separate but equal" became the law of the land, the NAACP was founded, and the Great Migration of African Americans from the South (where almost all lived in 1890) to northern industrial cities occurred. Working people struggled to deal with newly hazardous, uncertain, and oppressive conditions of labor. Modern labor unions began to grow. Strikes often ended in violence and in 1912 almost a million American men—6 percent of the electorate—voted for the Socialist Party. Americans faced as never before the fearful spectacle of class animosity.

Politics changed as well between 1890 and 1920. The raucous, mass participation party politics of the 19th century came to an end. Modern interest groups formed around specific issues and began to use sophisticated means to interject their demands into policy making. Voting rates dropped, never to recover. The power of the presidency increased significantly. Four amendments to the Constitution were enacted, one of them establishing the modern income tax. And far from least important, America forsook its isolation from world affairs. The nation displayed its rebuilt navy by sailing it around the world, fought the Spanish-American War, acquired a foreign empire, and eventually entered the Great War in Europe. Yet following the "war to make the world safe for democracy" abroad, the era ended with turbulence at home—spurred by racial issues, labor issues, and fears on the part of many ordinary people that America was threatened from within by revolutionaries like those who declared a communist government in Russia in 1919.

THE GREAT REFORM ERA

Amid these dizzying changes progressivism emerged. Progressives were reformers and supporters of reform who undertook a multiplicity of efforts to alleviate the dysfunction, or the corruption, or the economic injustice, or the human suffering that had accompanied America's explosion of industrial growth, urbanization, and new ways of life. Most prominent progressives—from settlement house workers to municipal reformers to conservationists to trustbusters—had personally observed these changes and the problems they brought within their own lifetimes. They had been born into a 19th-century world in which "the state and society were nothing; the individual was everything," as progressive historians Charles and Mary Beard put it succinctly.[1] As the 20th century approached, however, they found themselves confronting a world in which the individual—and even democracy itself—appeared to have been swallowed whole by a huge new economy and a new way of life. Progressives were divided on many points and even on many goals. But they were united in their conviction that only collective social action on behalf of "the people"—a group they constantly referred to but never defined—could counterbalance new accretions of private power. Slowly, many came to accept the idea that only an active and finally an enlarged government—and especially an enlarged national government—could revitalize and protect traditional democratic values.

Progressives did not all think alike. They ran a gamut from proponents of moderate adjustments to proponents of extreme change—and there were also, of course, both conservatives to the right of progressives and radicals to the left who took exception to the progressive stance and to reforms. Yet many Americans were clearly dissatisfied with existing conditions. They were outraged by the behavior of the trusts and the powerful businessmen who had manipulated the traditional language of individual rights to assume unprecedented control over the economy and even the government itself. They were horrified by the sufferings of the new and primarily immigrant working poor and the indecent conditions in which they were forced to lived. They were angered by the political malfeasance they could see before their own eyes and outraged more by the revelations of investigative reform journalists called muckrakers. Waves of public anger swept over the nation one after the other during the progressive decades, followed by a rising tide of reform initiatives. Most initiatives began in scattered municipalities in the 1890s. Over time the voluntary civic groups interested in social reform efforts began to form associations to find strength in numbers, and some civic groups slowly changed into quasi-official and later even official arms of government. Those interested in political reform moved on from the cities to tackle state level corruption. After Theodore Roosevelt became a so-called accidental president in 1901 upon the assassination of William McKinley, reformers unexpectedly had a symbol and a kindred spirit in the White House itself. Reform began to take on a national framework. By the end of the first decade of the 20th century countless reform initiatives were at high tide and washing across the land.

HISTORIANS AND THE PROGRESSIVES

In spite of these events, the question that has most vexed historians for many years has been whether or not a progressive movement actually existed. During the Progressive Era itself, to be sure, people of a progressive persuasion thought of themselves as an identifiable group. Most progressive-minded people shared a vocabulary. They believed their reform efforts would protect "the people" from "selfish interests" or "antisocial" individuals. They spoke of their goals as increasing "democracy" and "fairness." So self-conscious were they, in fact, that by 1915 their first history, Benjamin Parke DeWitt's *The Progressive Movement,* was already rolling off the presses.

The early historians of progressivism were progressives themselves. They saw progressivism as a democratic movement of ordinary Americans, determined to repossess the power accrued by ruthless corporations, corrupt politicians, and misapplied wealth. The validity of that view, however, has been a matter of disagreement among historians since the 1950s and remains an implied question in most historical writing about the Progressive Era today. Historians have argued at length about which group really led progressive change and what its motives really were. They have argued over whether progressive accomplishments were indeed progressive, in the ordinary sense of that word as forward-looking, liberal, and inclusive, or whether those accomplishments were in fact very conservative and even dominated by the business interests they purported to oppose. Historians have argued intensely over whether progressives meant what they said: Did they truly seek greater justice for all Americans or did they simply seek greater control over those who were less powerful or culturally different, and to what extent did they achieve either?

Early historians of progressivism saw many connections between progressivism and farm-based populist sympathies. In the 1950s, however, historians began to see progressivism as a creation of the urban middle and upper middle classes. They also ceased viewing it as a democratic movement, describing it instead as an attempt by relatively privileged people to maintain their own leadership and power. The landmark work of this school of thought was Richard Hofstadter's *The Age of Reform* (1955). Like many of the historians who would follow him, Hofstadter often seemed less interested in the very real social and economic problems the progressives addressed than in the psychological motives that spurred them to action. He maintained that progressives were members of the traditional 19th-century American leadership class—ministers, lawyers, business and property owners in towns and cities of modest size throughout the nation. They became reformers, he said, because they had lost status to the newly wealthy, nationally powerful elite, which had been created by the potent economic development of the late 19th century. Progressives were, he continued, Protestant and comfortably middle-class people threatened on one side by ruthless wealth and on the other by the culturally and religiously different immigrants arriving from eastern and southern Europe. Hofstadter's thesis, called the status revolution theory, was quickly questioned by other historians in some very important ways. Most important, the characteristics he ascribed to progressives, several studies showed, were also shared by conservatives—and in fact did nothing to distinguish progressives from most civic leaders at any other point on the political spectrum. Other studies showed and continue to show that people who worked for reform were a socially varied lot and sometimes included working people and immigrants themselves. Nonetheless, the change in relative socioeconomic power that Hofstadter pointed out was real enough, and even today the status revolution theory has not completely disappeared from historical writing about progressivism.

By the 1970s, however, some historians had begun to make different arguments about progressivism and to identify different groups as the leading force of the movement. Some pointed out that progressives did not think of themselves as an old and declining leadership class but instead as a rising "new middle class." The new middle class was made up of new professionals and experts who were confident they could solve the problems of their changing and sometimes chaotic society by applying scientific expertise and by organizing people, institutions, and government in efficient new ways. At the same time other historians began to argue that it was businessmen themselves, not professionals and experts, who led the progressive movement. Some even argued that reform was actually a tool of conservatives. According to their interpretation, reform was used not to increase democracy but to forestall the radical democratic demands that seemed to threaten from many quarters. Many other historians began to debunk specific reform movements, making unfavorable comparisons between what progressives said they were doing and what it appeared to a later generation that they had actually accomplished.

Faced with such conflicting interpretations, historians took another look at the era and began to view progressivism as a different kind of phenomenon—one that did not have a single group of leaders and was not a *movement* as that word is ordinarily understood. The many groups and individuals who claimed the title *progressive* clearly did not all have the same goals and sometimes they even clashed fundamentally. Many historians came to agree that it was misleading to speak of such widespread but varied reform initiatives as a unified, goal-oriented "movement." Some pointed out that reformers working for specific goals often formed alliances with other groups and individuals to find solutions for large problems. But those alliances were not permanent and new, different ones might come together for the next reform effort. Progressivism had so many faces, some historians pointed out, because many groups—professionals, businessmen, labor or immigrant activists, clubwomen, even the middle class or "the people"—contributed to most reform initiatives. Often, the results they achieved were a matter of compromise and negotiation and pieces cobbled together from several different agendas.

Today, historians who write about the Progressive Era usually work in discrete subfields such as economic, political, or social history. They usually focus on specific events or specific places instead of searching for one overarching interpretation or identifying one group as the leaders of progressivism. One important development in recent years has come from the field of women's history. Many studies have refocused attention on the important role that women and voluntary women's organizations played in achieving many kinds of reforms during the Progressive Era. Nonetheless, most historians today assume that the progressive stance was pluralistic. Some, in fact, have even suggested that its real unifying element was an attempt to find processes to solve the new conflicts of pluralism and group strife itself. In any case, recent histories have made a welcome return to acknowledging the seriousness of the problems America faced during the progressive decades and the legitimacy of efforts made by progressive-minded people to solve them.

1

An Era Ends, An Era Opens
1890–1893

AN ERA ENDS FOR NATIVE AMERICANS ON THE PLAINS

By the end of the 1880s, Native American groups on the western plains faced dire poverty. Shortly after the Civil War, they had been forced to accept the establishment of a large reservation in the Dakotas and smaller reservations elsewhere. Federal management of these reservations was disastrous. White agents were ill-informed at best and often corrupt. The Indians' situation was rendered desperate by the rapid, wanton destruction of the buffalo, their traditional source of food and other resources. By the 1880s fewer than 1,000 buffalo remained of the 15 million that had roamed the plains in 1860. Inflamed by these calamitous changes, Indians on the plains had engaged in almost continuous hostilities and outright wars with the United States after 1865.

Faced with this situation, federal officials adopted a new Indian policy. They decided to dissolve traditional tribal organizations, convert Indians into land-owning small farmers, and incorporate them into U.S. citizenship and society. The Dawes Severalty Act of 1887 called for the transfer of collectively owned tribal land to individual American Indian owners, in 160-acre plots. The Bureau of Indian Affairs (BIA) began to prepare Native Americans for assimilation into the majority culture. In cooperation with religious and philanthropic organizations, the bureau encouraged Indian children to attend special boarding schools, hoping to separate them from their tribal customs and languages, communal ties, and traditional rituals. Many supporters of these policies were reformers driven by humanitarian zeal in the face of Indian suffering. Others were, as always, merely anxious to appropriate more Indian land for non-Indian settlement.

Many tribes, already living on the verge of starvation and now unmistakably faced with the end of their way of life, turned to religion to understand their situation. Some underwent a spiritual revival. In 1889 the prophet Wovoka, a Northern Paiute (Numu) in Nevada, had a vision in which whites had disappeared and the buffalo reappeared. He began to preach that Indians were to prepare for this change by living in peace among themselves and performing a ritual circle dance to encourage their ancestors to return. Wovoka quickly gained followers. Representatives of many tribes came to observe him. Throughout 1890 the five-day dance ritual spread rapidly across the plains, especially among the Arapaho, Cheyenne, and Lakota.

In the Dakotas among the Lakota, reservation agents interpreted the Ghost Dance (as whites named it) as preparation for war. They ordered it stopped.

1

These Miniconjou Lakota, photographed in 1891, were among the few surviving members of Chief Big Foot's band after the massacre at Wounded Knee Creek, South Dakota. *(Library of Congress, Prints and Photographs Division, LC-USZ62-22972)*

The Lakota leader was Sitting Bull (Tatanka-Iyotanka) from the Hunkpapa band of Lakota. He had led the defeat of George Armstrong Custer at the Battle of Little Bighorn in 1876 and was revered by many other Indian groups as a military and spiritual chief. Sitting Bull was unbowed and continued to resist U.S. plans for assimilation—even after a sojourn in Canada, two years as a prisoner of war, a stint with Buffalo Bill's Wild West Show, and a drought and a sweep of epidemic illness among the Sioux (Dakota, Lakota, Nakota) in 1889–90. Government officials at the Standing Rock Indian Agency believed he would encourage his people to resist the Ghost Dance prohibition. On December 14, 1890, officials ordered the reservation police to arrest Sitting Bull. (Reservation police were also Indians, trained by the U.S. government. They are also called Indian police.) A scuffle broke out between the police, led by Lieutenant Henry Bullhead, and supporters of Sitting Bull. Shots rang out. Sitting Bull was killed, as was his son Crow Foot, six other supporters, and six Indian police.[1]

The death of Sitting Bull was only a prelude. Two weeks later, the Seventh Cavalry pursued a group of about 350 Miniconjou Lakota, led by Big Foot, as they attempted to flee. Soldiers rounded them up at Wounded Knee Creek, South Dakota, where the Indian band attempted to surrender. On December 29, as soldiers were disarming the Indians, a shot again rang out. The soldiers responded with their new machine guns, killing 153 Indian men, women, and children and wounding another 44. Twenty-five soldiers were also killed. The massacre at Wounded Knee was the last major armed conflict between the Plains Indians and the U.S. government. It has come to symbolize the end of Indian warfare—as well as the end of the traditional Indian way of life—in the American West.

THE FRONTIER CLOSES

In presenting the results of the 1890 census, the superintendent of the U.S. Census declared the American frontier closed. "Up to and including 1880 the country had a frontier of settlement, but at present the unsettled area has been so broken into isolated bodies of settlement that there can hardly be said to be a frontier line," he wrote in his introduction to the census statistics. "In the discussion of its extent, the westward movement, etc., it cannot, therefore, any longer have a place in the census reports."[2]

While the East was transforming into an urban, industrial powerhouse in the decades after the Civil War, the American West had undergone an equally consequential change. During and after the war, the federal government actively encouraged new settlement west of the Mississippi. Although some white Americans had moved into the West earlier, the new flood of settlement dwarfed all previous migrations. One line of settlement pushed west, and another pushed east from the Pacific coast. Most migrants were native-born Americans (including some African Americans), but by the end of the century they were joined by many new immigrants from Germany, Scandinavia, Czechoslovakia, and elsewhere.

In popular American belief, the imaginary line called the frontier had traditionally divided civilized society, with its farms, towns, and government, from an untamed, unsettled West. Some Americans cherished the idea of the West for its promise of free or cheap land where they could make a fresh start and improve their lot. Others cherished it as a place of rugged individualism and bold adventure, and still others for the grandeur of its landscapes and the spiritual renewal they inspired. The passing of the frontier only magnified the importance of the West in popular belief. It occurred at the very moment when profound economic and social changes seemed to have shaken America to its foundations. Many people feared that mammoth corporations and burgeoning cities were swallowing up the traditional American way of life that the frontier symbolized.

Three years after the frontier was declared closed, the American Historical Association met at the World's Columbian Exposition in Chicago. A young historian from the University of Wisconsin, Frederick Jackson Turner, presented a memorable essay entitled "The Significance of the Frontier in American History." The most important factor in American development, he argued, was "the existence of an area of free land, its continuous recession, and the advance of settlement westward." Unlike other historians, Turner did not believe that American institutions and values could be understood by studying their European roots. It was the frontier, he believed, that was responsible for both American individualism and democracy. "And now," he concluded, "four centuries from the discovery of America, at the end of a hundred years of life under the Constitution, the frontier has gone, and with its going has closed the first period of American history."[3]

WESTERN MYTHS AND REALITIES

The Turner thesis or frontier thesis, as Frederick Jackson Turner's ideas came to be called, described a belief about national identity that was, and continues to be, cherished by many Americans. It also influenced how historians thought about American history for many years. But today most historians dispute the Turner thesis. They argue that the realities of the West and western development were far more complex than the thesis grants. For one thing, although settlements were indeed scattered throughout the American West by 1890, a significant amount of land remained in the public domain. In fact, four times as many homesteads were claimed after 1890 as before.

In addition, the frontier thesis does not account for the important role of large business corporations, wage labor, and government aid in developing the West. Family farms and ranches did dominate the prairie and the Great Plains, but other regions of the West developed very differently. In the Pacific Northwest from northern California through Washington state, large lumber corporations existed by 1890. Elsewhere in California, large-scale fruit and vegetable farming abounded and relied on seasonal wage laborers. In the mountainous regions of seven different western states, mining was the important industry, and by 1890 some miners were even unionized. Throughout the West, the largest business of all in America in 1890, the railroads, tied existing communities together and made it possible for many new ones to develop,

These orange pickers, photographed in Los Angeles in the mid 1890s, were agricultural wage workers. The newly invented refrigerated boxcar made it possible to ship fresh fruit coast to coast. *(Library of Congress, Prints and Photographs Division, LC-USZ62-78372)*

while transporting farm products, raw materials, and finished goods as well as people. The U.S. government, for its part, had provided extensive subsidies in the form of land grants to railroad corporations to underwrite their growth.

Historians also point out that the American West had never been all vacant land. Most parts had long been inhabited by people who were not U.S. settlers. Even in 1890 more than 500 designated Native American reservations existed, scattered from the Mississippi to the Pacific. The 250,000 remaining Native Americans, both on and off reservation lands, were themselves divided into many culture and language groups. In addition, because much of the American Southwest had been part of the Mexican Republic prior to 1848, long-established Spanish-speaking communities existed from Texas to California and as far north as Colorado. By 1890, most of the Southwest was dominated by Anglos, or English-speakers, but exceptions still existed. Traditional Hispanic culture still remained strong in south Texas and in New Mexico territory, where Spanish-speaking residents were a majority and some remained large landholders.

THE URBAN WEST

The advance of the frontier and the development of western cities went hand in hand. More than half of post–Civil War western migrants did not move to isolated frontier homesteads. Instead, they moved to the towns or cities that served as centers of trade and government. By 1890 Salt Lake City, Utah, Portland, Oregon, and Seattle, Washington, all had populations nearing 45,000; Denver, Colorado, had more than 100,000. The California city of Los Angeles, with a population of more than 50,000 and exceptionally determined civic boosters, was growing by leaps and bounds. The West also had a large metropolis, San Francisco, California, with almost 300,000 people by 1890. San Francisco was the financial, commercial, and manufacturing center for the entire trans–Rocky Mountain west and home to powerful capitalists and entrepreneurs. The Bank of California headed by William Ralston had its headquarters there, as did several mining companies and the Southern Pacific Railroad, run by entrepreneurs like Leland Stanford, Collis Huntington, and others.

San Francisco and other West Coast cities were also home to people of Asian descent, especially Chinese. Chinese immigrants, who began arriving around 1850, had worked in mining, then railroad building, then agriculture throughout the West. In many places where they resided, they had been subjected to extensive discrimination, anti-Chinese agitation, and outright violence. The Chinese Exclusion Act of 1882 had banned additional immigration for 10 years and prevented Chinese already in the United States from becoming citizens. By 1890, however, Chinese people had established distinctive and somewhat independent sections called Chinatowns, in San Francisco and some other western cities (as well as in New York). While most Chinese were unskilled laborers and servants, some established small businesses. A few were successful merchants; their organization, the Six Companies, worked to advance Chinese interests in the larger society.

THE CONSERVATION ERA BEGINS

As the frontier closed and cities multiplied, some Americans became increasingly concerned about the fate of natural areas, especially the spectacular wild spaces in the West. Some conservationists argued for preservation of these natural resources, and others argued for their active management—two different approaches that were destined to be increasingly incompatible.

Yosemite Valley, for example, had been set aside for protection by the state of California, but conservation activists believed the state had been remiss in its oversight. In 1890 they succeeded in having Yosemite National Park established. (The first American national park, Yellowstone, had been established in 1872.) In the new national park, the U.S. Army was given responsibility for preventing abuses such as commercial logging. A year later in 1891, a bill now known as the Forest Reserve Act was passed. The act made it possible for the president to remove large tracts of forest land from the public domain, preventing the land from being opened, claimed, sold, or granted to individuals. The Forest Reserve Act was a rider belatedly added to a bill to revise land laws, and it slipped through Congress with less scrutiny than was customary. The act was destined to be increasingly important in the Progressive decades, however, and to effect major changes in United States land policy. Before President Benjamin Harrison's term ended in early 1893, he set aside 13 million acres. These reserves, in seven western states and Alaska, were the beginnings of the national forest system. The Alaska tract, called the Afognak Forest and Fish Culture Reserve, was also the earliest national wildlife refuge.[4] A related movement to preserve historic sites and Indian antiquities also began during these years.

Late in May 1892 a group of 27 men, organized by University of California scientists and outdoorsmen, met in San Francisco to found a group devoted to the preservation of Yosemite and the Sierra Nevada. They named themselves the Sierra Club. As president they chose one of the group, John Muir, a naturalist and writer who was one of the most influential conservationists of the era. Early members of the Sierra Club, like most conservationists of the day, were usually established, educated professionals, but rarely the wealthiest of Americans. Women were well represented among early conservationists.

Not all Americans supported the efforts of the early conservationists. In many localities businessmen wanted to use protected natural resources for profit, settlers wanted to claim homesteads, ranchers wanted to graze cattle and sheep, and local governments wanted more taxable acreage. All these interests attempted to block conservation efforts. Within a few months of the Sierra Club's founding, members found it necessary to act to protect Yosemite. California representative Anthony Caminetti, at the urging of special interests there, had introduced a bill in Congress to greatly reduce the park's size. Conservationists successfully prevented the bill from coming to a vote.[5]

AMERICA MOVES TO TOWN

Between the Civil War and 1890, the United States underwent a great transformation. Formerly a small, rural nation, whose ordinary people almost all earned their living from agriculture, it changed into a large nation with many city dwellers who earned their living in business and industry. Between 1860 and 1890, the population of America doubled, from 31.4 million to nearly 63 million. But cities grew much more quickly than rural areas. As late as 1870, only 21 cities had populations of more than 50,000. By 1890 three cities had more than a million residents

By the 1890s, Chinese people lived and worked throughout the West, often as miners, railroad workers, and agricultural workers. This 1891 photo, taken in South Dakota, shows the funeral service of High Lee. *(Library of Congress, Prints and Photographs Division, LC-USZ62-20140)*

(New York, Chicago, and Philadelphia), seven had more than 250,000 (Baltimore, Boston, Buffalo, Cincinnati, Cleveland, San Francisco, St. Louis), and two others were drawing close to the quarter-million mark (Pittsburgh, New Orleans). Fourteen additional cities had populations of more than 100,000, and 18 others more than 50,000. In sum, 44 cities had populations of more than 50,000, for a total of nearly 12 million Americans residing in cities of significant size. "The United States was born in the country," as eminent historian Richard Hofstadter wrote, "and has moved to the city."[6]

Many Americans had ambivalent feelings about the cities that were growing so rapidly. They were attracted—but also often alarmed—by the new urban culture that was changing their traditionally rural-minded nation. Americans moved from the countryside to the city primarily in search of employment. But they also came for the conveniences, opportunities, and marvels of an urban lifestyle—theaters, restaurants, large stores, organized sports, and most marvelous of all, electric lighting. They were joined there by wave after wave of new immigrants, who were entering the country in unprecedented numbers and often took up residence in cities. By 1890, several major cities—Chicago, New York, Milwaukee, Detroit—had populations of which more than 80 percent were either immigrants or the children of immigrants.

As cities mushroomed, so did urban problems. The new city dwellers overwhelmed housing and sanitary facilities, other public and social services, and municipal government itself, especially in the very largest towns. Fire and police protection was outpaced, schools were inundated, and street maintenance was for all practical purposes nonexistent. In 1890 most streets remained unpaved even in major cities. In Chicago, for example, of the 2,048 miles of existing streets only 629 miles were paved, much of that with wood. Unpaved streets were dusty when dry, muddy when wet, and deeply rutted when frozen, making it extremely difficult to clean them or to remove refuse—a major problem since horses powered much of the transportation on city streets. The most critically inadequate public service was sanitation. Both sewer lines and garbage disposal were sorely lacking. Even where sewer lines existed sewage was usually emptied untreated into the nearest body of water, as was industrial waste near factories. The water supply was constantly in danger of becoming contaminated, exposing urban dwellers to frequent illness and sometimes epidemic disease—one reason why the death rate in cities was much higher than in rural areas.

Overall in 1890, 35 percent of the total U.S. population was classified as urban. But city dwellers were not spread out evenly across the country. More than half of America's city dwellers lived in five states: Massachusetts, New York, Pennsylvania, Illinois, and Ohio. In contrast, less than 8 percent of southerners lived in towns. These differences made for important contrasts in regional problems and perspectives.

THE CITY REACHES OUTWARD AND UPWARD

Growing cities rapidly expanded outward, in rings around their centers. Earlier, in the "walking city" of preindustrial America (as historians call it), each neighborhood housed people of many income groups, as well as workshops, businesses, and other facilities. As cities grew, separate commercial and industrial sections developed—most of them increasingly dirty and noisy. Residential neighborhoods became more and more divided by economic status as

Cities grew rapidly in the late 19th century, becoming busier and more congested. A trolley, horse-drawn vehicles, and pedestrians crowd together on this Philadelphia street in the 1890s. *(Library of Congress, Prints and Photographs Division, LC-USZ62-91659)*

people with sufficient means escaped to new neighborhoods at the edges of town, with lawns, trees, fresh air, and better sanitation. The urban middle class was able to expand its housing opportunities primarily because of new transportation technology, especially the electric trolley. The electric trolley, or street railway, was introduced in Richmond, Virginia, in 1888 and within a decade had overtaken America. Trolleys did little to change the living options of the poor, however, because the poor could not afford the fares. They were left to squeeze into undesirable areas, usually near the factories where they worked.

As cities grew outward in the late 19th century they also expanded upward. The change was due to new building technology, vastly aided by the Otis Elevator Company's introduction of the first electric powered elevators in 1899. The time-honored method of construction was the masonry foundation, which limited the height a building could rise. In the late 1880s, architects began to experiment with iron or steel frames, which could rise much higher. By 1891 the new, tall, steel-framed buildings were being referred to as "skyscrapers." One of the most influential was the nine-story Wainwright building in St. Louis, designed by the great architect Louis Sullivan of Chicago and begun in 1890. The Wainwright building is considered the first to solve many problems central to the interior and exterior design of the new, tall buildings. Sullivan's rule was "form follows function." Unlike previous architects, he used strong vertical lines to unify the building while also emphasizing its height. He also arranged the interior offices around courts to allow for light and ventilation. Sullivan's student, Frank Lloyd Wright, later said that when Sullivan first showed him the design, he was immediately aware of its importance: "The 'skyscraper,' as a new thing beneath the sun, an entity with virtue, individuality, and beauty all its own, was born," he wrote.[7]

THE NEW IMMIGRANTS ARRIVE

The flow of immigrants to the United States, which had increased dramatically in the 1880s, continued to expand as the 1890s opened. Between 1890 and 1893, an average of about half a million newcomers arrived annually.

Prior to 1880, the vast majority of white immigrants came from the British Isles, Germany, and other nations of northern and western Europe. A modest number of immigrants, to be sure, had always come from southern and eastern Europe, even in colonial days. But as late as 1880 only 11 percent of all European immigrants came from those areas. By 1890 that number had risen to 36 percent; by 1893 to 45 percent; and by 1900 to 76 percent. (Census and immigration data defined southern and eastern Europe as Spain, Portugal, Italy, Greece, Turkey, Armenia, Poland, Romania, Bulgaria, Hungary, Russia, and the Baltic states of Estonia, Latvia, Lithuania, and Finland.) Like immigrants from northern and western Europe, who were also continuing to arrive in large numbers, southern and eastern Europeans hoped to improve their lot in life. Many were encouraged by so-called America letters sent home by relatives or friends. These letters painted a picture of America as a golden land of opportunity, a haven of religious freedom, or a refuge for the oppressed.

The new immigration, as historians call this change in the origins of immigrants, brought wave after wave of newcomers from cultures and nations whose institutions were very different from those of the United States. Most came from countries with no democratic political or social traditions, little public education, high birth and death rates, and few legal or political rights for ordinary individuals. As always, some of the new arrivals from all countries were educated or came from financially established families. But most of the new immigrants were very poor. Most came from rural and peasant backgrounds. Many were illiterate. The transition of these new immigrants to American life was destined to be slow, difficult, and often painful. Some headed for free homesteads in the West. But the majority settled in New York and other large

New immigrants from southern and eastern Europe formed ethnic neighborhoods, where some established a foothold in business. These bread peddlers are selling their wares on Mulberry Street, heart of New York's Italian neighborhood on the Lower East Side. Note the neighborhood shop for bicycles, which were extremely popular in the 1890s. *(Library of Congress, Prints and Photographs Division, LC-D401-1385)*

cities, where they provided the unskilled and semi-skilled industrial labor demanded by the expanding industrial economy. They formed ethnic neighborhoods where they continued to speak their own languages and practice some of their own customs and values. They founded churches or synagogues closely identified with their native language or ethnic group and established fraternal organizations to aid their compatriots. Some were able to establish small businesses.

The largest group in the new immigration was Italians. More than 4 million arrived in the half century prior to 1920. Most, especially the landless farm laborers or *contadini,* were driven from southern Italy and Sicily by dire poverty and overpopulation. The second-largest group was Slavic-speaking peoples, most from nations in the Austro-Hungarian Empire. Many were Polish-speaking; others were Bohemians (Czechs), Slovaks, or other smaller groups. Some came for economic opportunity and some came to escape forced military service or other forms of oppression at the hands of Germans or Russians. Many Slavs spread out through Pennsylvania into the Midwest, settling on farms or in cities like Pittsburgh, Detroit, and Chicago.

The third-largest group of new immigrants was from the census category called Russia and the Baltic States. It included some ethnic Russians, but the vast majority belonged to other ethnic minorities. The largest group of immigrants from Russia were Jews, who also made up a percentage of immigrants from other eastern European countries. For many years eastern European Jews had been victims of religious and ethnic persecution. In Russia, they were forced to live in an area on the western border called the Pale of Settlement. Beginning in the 1880s, they were victimized by pogroms, or violent mob attacks on their homes, businesses, and lives. More than a third of all eastern European Jews chose to leave their homes during this period, and 90 percent came to the United States. Sometimes entire communities migrated together, including professionals, businessmen, and religious leaders as well as ordinary workers.

Many other countries in the world, such as Argentina, Australia, New Zealand, and Canada, also experienced heavy immigration in this period. The United States, however, received by far the largest number of immigrants, from the greatest variety of nations and ethnic groups. People migrated from Mexico to the American Southwest and to New England and elsewhere from both French- and English-speaking Canada. (No written records were kept of these arrivals until 1908.) A few arrived from South America and island nations like Cuba. Immigration from Japan also slowly began to increase, and in 1891 topped 1,000 for the first time.

"THE RICH GET RICHER"

Between the Civil War and 1890, America underwent rapid, dramatic, and unprecedented economic growth. In a mere 25 years—far less than a lifetime—the United States became an industrial giant. By 1890 America led all other nations of the world in the value of the manufactured goods it produced—having pulled ahead of Great Britain, France, and Germany during those years. "With a stride that astonished statisticians," wrote eminent early-20th-century historians Charles and Mary Beard, "the conquering hosts of business enterprise swept over the continent."[8]

This astonishing economic growth was accompanied by an increasingly obvious gap between the rich and the poor. There was no tax on income at the time, and little tax on business. On the one hand, a new group of tremendously wealthy entrepreneurs and capitalists appeared. Although some were generous philanthropists, many also lived in what one historian calls "almost grotesque luxury."[9] Unlike the rich of preindustrial America, they displayed their wealth openly, even riotously. They maintained opulent city mansions and country estates, private yachts and private train cars. They spent dazzling sums on lavish balls and parties. And increasingly, the details of their lifestyle and social events were dangled before the public in the popular press.

On the other hand, a new army of poorly paid industrial wage workers had been created by the tremendous expansion of industry and manufacturing. In 1890 the population of the United States was twice as large as it had been in 1860, but the number of industrial workers was nearly four times as large. To be sure, the growing economy had raised the standard of living for most Americans, including some ordinary working people. But for industrial wage workers, prosperity was accompanied by alarming new conditions. The new economy made frequent and frightening swings from good times to bad. It was also accompanied by a new phenomenon in working families' lives: periodic urban industrial unemployment. In preindustrial America, workers in small factories were likely to live where they might have a small garden and cow. But the new industrial workers lived in crowded cities. Nothing except their uninsured weekly wages stood between them and starvation. And even in times of full employment, a large segment of the new industrial army did not prosper. Millions of fully employed people lived below what is now called the poverty line. Unskilled workers, as numerous social investigations revealed, could not support the bare minimum needs of a family unless their wives and children also worked for wages—and even then it was a daily struggle. In the teeming cities, the working poor lived in previously unthinkable squalor. But hard times were not limited to the city. In the countryside, many farmers also failed to share in the general prosperity of the late 19th century and were in increasing financial distress. "The system which makes one man a millionaire," wrote Knights of Labor union leader Terence Powderly, "makes tramps and paupers of thousands."[10]

By 1890, the new sense of distance between rich and poor rankled some Americans and frightened many more.

By the 1890s a new group of spectacularly wealthy people had appeared in America. This mansion, on New York's Fifth Avenue, was the home of Cornelius Vanderbilt. *(Library of Congress, Prints and Photographs Division, LC-D401-13098)*

Americans traditionally believed that class antagonism did not exist in American society, and that a natural "harmony of interests" held among the different economic groups. By 1890, however, some Americans had begun to grow fearful of the threat posed by the poor, and had begun to speak openly of "class conflict." Some well-to-do people merely used the term to express their fear that have-nots might try to take some of their new wealth. But many thoughtful Americans were increasingly concerned that new economic divisions threatened American democracy itself.

"HOW THE OTHER HALF LIVES"

In 1890, many middle- and upper-class Americans were shocked and appalled by Jacob Riis's *How the Other Half Lives: Studies Among the Tenements of New York*. Riis, a former police reporter and photographer (and himself a Danish immigrant), graphically portrayed the appalling conditions in the city's slums. Riis described the dark, dank alleys, the overcrowded apartments, and the plight of the urban poor who lived there. Using newly invented flash photography, he provided eye-opening and disturbing photographs of slum life as well. Riis was particularly concerned about the effect of such conditions on families. Tenements, he wrote, "above all . . . touch the family life with deadly moral contagion." Riis's book was the first well-known example of a new kind of investigative journalism destined to be very important during the Progressive Era. (It was later called "muckraking.") Investigative journalists like Riis dove into contentious social and political issues and wrote sensational exposés. They carried concern for problems they wrote about into cities and villages across the nation and helped to ignite many reform movements.[11]

A tenement was a substandard, badly maintained apartment building. Not all cities housed the poor exclusively in tenements. In Philadelphia, for example, they were more likely to live in decrepit, narrow row houses. But the tenements of New York—specially constructed or remodeled for the poor—came to symbolize the worst living conditions in America to much of the public. Typically, tenements were four- to six-story walk-ups with at least four families per floor. Many buildings had no central heating. Ventilation was inadequate because many rooms had no windows. Indoor plumbing was rare. Usually, outdoor and sometimes open privies were shared by all residents. Even those buildings with shared indoor facilities emptied sewage into alleys or courts, where garbage was also left to rot. Water often did not come into the buildings. It had to be pumped and carried indoors and up the flights of stairs by women for cooking, cleaning, laundry, or bathing.

Slums were not new in the late 19th century, but they were becoming larger and far more heavily populated. Because the housing shortage was so severe in burgeoning cities, landlords subdivided existing apartments into smaller units, squeezed in more tenants, and collected more rents. Many families had only one room. Making the problem more severe, the renters themselves (or, in some cities, working families who owned small homes) often took in boarders. The boarding system provided extra income and also provided housing for relatives and single people moving to the city. However, it contributed to population densities unknown before or since in American cities. And while the rural South and West were violent places in the late 19th century, the overcrowded city slums contributed more than their share to a tremendous growth in crime rates. The overall murder rate in America, for example, rose from 25 per million people in 1880 to more than 100 per million people in 1900. Many Americans increasingly associated crime not only with cities but also with the immigrant groups who lived there.

Traditionally, Americans believed that most poverty grew from individual character flaws, not from social and economic forces. They believed in self-reliance and worried that too much assistance would only make the poor more dependent. The Charity

Organization Society (COS), a national umbrella organization for traditional relief groups, for example, still insisted in 1890 that aid never be given without careful investigation into the individual recipient's "worthiness." But the traditional view of poverty was increasingly questioned, even by COS officials. Exposés like *How the Other Half Lives* made many thoughtful men and women wonder if any principle, moral or economic, could justify such terrible violations of conventional decency. They wondered if a new approach, and a new way of thinking about poverty, might be needed to relieve such squalid living conditions and desperate need.

THE SETTLEMENT HOUSE RESPONDS TO POVERTY

By the opening of the 1890s, young, college-educated men and women had begun a movement to found settlement houses in the worst slums of the burgeoning cities. In 1891 there were six settlement houses; by 1910 more than 400 would exist. Settlement workers moved into the slum neighborhoods they served. There, they opened a large building, often a run-down mansion, which served as a dormitory for them as well as space for services and activities offered to the neighborhood. The settlement house hoped to reach across the growing gulf of antagonism between rich and poor in late-19th-century America. In the often-quoted words of Jane Addams, settlements were founded "on the theory that the dependence of the classes on each other is reciprocal."

The first two settlement houses in America, University Settlement (1886) and College Settlement (1889) were opened on New York's Lower East Side. In 1889, Jane Addams and Ellen Gates Starr opened Hull-House on Halsted Street in Chicago. Its distinguished roster of workers and visitors soon made it the most famous of the settlements and an influential voice for reform. Addams herself, who wrote and lectured widely, eventually became known as the social philosopher of the movement and one of the most respected women in America. Another well-known settlement leader was Lillian Wald of New York. In 1893 she and Mary Brewster, both trained nurses, moved to the Lower East Side. Wald and Brewster pioneered the visiting or public-health nurse service and founded the Henry Street Settlement.

Settlement houses provided a wide range of services to immigrants and other urban poor—child care and kindergartens, sewing lessons, English lessons, public-health clinics, even public bathing facilities and housing for single women. They helped organize many neighborhood clubs to encourage cooperative efforts to improve the community and to introduce immigrants to democratic procedures and civic life. Settlement workers also took a new approach to poverty, called the environmental approach. Instead of focusing on financial aid to individuals, they focused on the social and economic problems of the neighborhood they served. They undertook countless investigations, collecting and compiling solid data on conditions in the neighborhoods—partly to understand the problems and partly to spur the public and government to action. As the historian of social welfare, Walter Trattner, puts it, "Residence, Research, and Reform were the 3 R's of the movement."[12]

The majority of the American settlement houses were secular or nonsectarian and privately supported, although many of the founders and workers were inspired by their religious belief. Some settlements had ties to Protestant denominations like the Congregationalists, Presbyterians, and Episcopalians, and the great majority of settlement workers were Protestants (Jane Addams was a Quaker). But there were also a significant number of Jewish settlement workers (Lillian Wald, for example) and by the movement's height about 25 houses were supported by Jewish philanthropy. The nonsectarian settlements also drew some Catholic workers, and in the later 1890s the first Catholic-sponsored settlement, St. Rose's, was founded on East 69th Street in New York by Marion Gurney. By 1915, 27 Catholic settlements or urban missions existed.

Many were led by nuns in a new religious order, Sisters of Our Lady of Christian Doctrine, founded by Gurney to undertake settlement and urban mission work.[13]

More than 90 percent of settlement workers were college educated and more than half had done graduate work as well. More than 75 percent were women. In addition to what the settlements accomplished for the poor, they also began to carve out a new profession, social work, for college-educated women, who had few options other than teaching in 1890. Historians often compare the attraction of settlement work for young, educated, and usually idealistic people to that of the Peace Corps during the 1960s. A few devoted their lives to it, but many more worked for only a few years before assuming other positions—sometimes very influential ones. Allen F. Davis, a historian of the settlement house movement, concludes that overall, churches and fraternal clubs probably had more impact on the urban poor than did the settlements. "But the settlements and their residents had a greater impact on the nation," he writes, because so many settlement workers became prominent organizers of reform movements in the years to follow.[14]

NEW BEGINNINGS IN AMERICAN LITERATURE

In 1893, a young journalist named Stephen Crane published a shocking novel set in the slums of New York, *Maggie, a Girl of the Streets*. He paid the costs of publication himself, because commercial publishers believed the novel to be indecent. *Maggie* sold few copies (and Crane's own family burned as many as they could find), but today it is considered the first major American work in a new literary movement called naturalism. Naturalist novels depicted human beings, including characters from the lower classes, in a brutal struggle for survival and often as victims of social or economic forces beyond their control—a view of life that contradicted the established view among editors and publishers that fiction should provide moral uplift. Many naturalist novels would be set, like Crane's, in the burgeoning new cities. Novelist Hamlin Garland, on the other hand, who grew up in Wisconsin, Iowa, and the Dakotas, began in *Main Travelled Roads* (1891) to depict the harsh and discouraging life of farmers in prairie states he called the Middle Border. Garland, who was a devotee of Henry George's single tax idea, also introduced political themes into his work.

A new era in women's writing in America began as well. In 1892 Charlotte Perkins Gilman published a short story, "The Yellow Wallpaper." It detailed the mental breakdown (which Gilman herself had suffered) of a young wife who is confined to her home and treated like a child. Some American critics were shocked by it; others praised it as a chillingly accurate portrayal of insanity. Since the 1880s, however, the British had been labeling fiction like Gilman's, which in fact questioned women's position in society, as "new woman fiction." It was destined to blossom in the coming progressive decades in both popular and serious writing. Gilman herself would become a theorist of a more radical movement called, after about 1910, feminism.

AMERICA CONSIDERS A NEW ROLE ON THE WORLD STAGE

Prior to 1890, American foreign relations were guided by the spirit of isolationism. The United States was protected from external threat by the Atlantic and Pacific Oceans. It remained focused on its own development, settlement, and problems—and was little interested in foreign affairs.

After 1890, however, American policymakers began to envision a more prominent role in world affairs. Many conditions had changed. The United States had become one of the most powerful industrial nations in the world. Communications were much improved. Telegraph cables stretched across the Atlantic Ocean and crisscrossed many countries, while steam-powered ships cut ocean crossings to days rather than months.

Some Americans desired only to increase foreign trade. But an increasing number believed the United States ought to wield influence in the world, appropriate to its new power. Worldwide, older alliances and balances of power were in flux because Germany and Japan had also developed great new industrial strength. The Europeans and the Japanese were actively acquiring new colonies, especially in Africa and eastern Asia. Some Americans feared they would be put at a disadvantage if they did not join in the race.

American foreign policy began to show new signs of assertiveness. In addition, policy makers became more receptive to imperialism, the acquisition or wielding of authority over weaker, less developed nations around the globe. Of course, despite being isolationists, Americans had always been expansionists. Most accepted the idea of Manifest Destiny, holding that it was inevitable and probably part of the divine plan for Americans to spread across the continent and perhaps northward into Canada as well. (The term *Manifest Destiny* was coined in the 1840s by journalist John O'Sullivan, although the idea arrived with the earliest colonists.) By 1890 the United States had acquired Alaska, the Midway Islands, and an interest in Samoa. The step from Manifest Destiny to a new imperialism was not a long one.

An early sign of change was renewed interest in developing a powerful new American navy. After the Civil War, most American military troops had been decommissioned. Military and naval equipment gradually fell into very poor condition. Then, in 1890, Captain Alfred Thayer Mahan published a very influential book, *The Influence of Sea Power Upon History, 1660–1783.* Mahan was the president of the Naval War College. From his study of history, he concluded that strong navies had always determined the outcome of past European wars, and, therefore, America could be great only by developing its sea power. He argued for "looking outward," or extending American influence beyond the boundaries of the United States. He also supported cutting a canal across Central America and creating naval bases in both the Atlantic and Pacific. Mahan's writings impressed many prominent Americans. They convinced President Harrison and members of Congress of the need for a modern, steam-powered navy.

Thomas B. Reed, powerful Republican Speaker of the House from Maine. As chair of the House Rules Committee, he made many alterations in congressional procedure. *(Library of Congress, Prints and Photographs Division, LC-USZ62-96128)*

THE POLITICS OF STALEMATE

In 1890, the only major responsibilities of national officials in Washington were to conduct foreign policy, maintain the military, oversee Indian and land policy, preside over the treasury, and collect tariffs (taxes on imports and sometimes exports) to pay for these efforts. Other federal activities had slowly and gradually increased since the Civil War, but the only large government agency in existence in 1890 was the postal service. Despite growing concern about changes in American society, few Americans in 1890 expected or wanted the national government to operate any differently.

Local political contests were highly spirited at the time, but on the national scene, political balance and legislative stalemate were the orders of the day. Since the end of post–Civil War Reconstruction in 1877, Democrats and Republicans had divided the popular vote almost equally between them in presidential and congressional elections. Neither side could put through major policy changes even had they wanted to, and on the whole they did not want to—despite the tremendous social and economic change that America was experiencing.

The parties—whose principles and identities in 1890, it should be noted, differed in many ways from those they have today—did not favor identical approaches to the issues, of course. On the whole the Democrats (who were the overwhelmingly predominant party of the agricultural South) rejected any national intrusion into the economy or social behavior and strongly supported states' rights and local control. These principles were attractive not only to southern whites but also to some northern urbanites and many western farmers. Republicans, on the other hand (who were still identified as the party that had saved the Union in the Civil War), believed that thriving industrial development made for a prosperous nation. They accepted the idea of national action to encourage economic development and to maintain certain principles in national life, like public education or protection for the rights of African Americans. In 1890 the most discussed policy divide of all was over the tariff—the source of almost all the money used to run the government. Republicans favored high tariffs to protect American manufacturers. Democrats favored low tariffs to increase the supply of cheaper goods.

A BRIEF BREAK FROM STALEMATE: THE LEGISLATION OF 1890

In 1890, the president was Benjamin Harrison, a Republican. In the election of 1888, Harrison had bested the incumbent president, Grover Cleveland, a Democrat, in his bid for reelection. The Republicans also won majorities in the House and Senate—the first time since Reconstruction that one party controlled both Congress and the White House. President Harrison and Republican congressmen thought these results meant the American people wanted an end to political stalemate. The 51st Congress, which opened late in 1889 and ran through March 1891, saw the establishment of Reed's Rules. The powerful House Speaker Thomas B. Reed, Republican of Maine, did away with rules that formerly allowed the party in the minority to block legislation. A torrent of new legislation—and new spending—followed.

The Sherman Anti-Trust Act

To almost every American in 1890, the most startling and unsettling change since the Civil War was the rise of gigantic new business corporations. They were unprecedented in size and complexity, in the swift pace at which they grew, and in the power they could wield. With the help of investment bankers, resourceful entrepreneurs and industrialists increasingly reorganized into various combinations, agreements, pools or cartels, and trusts. Some grew by absorbing the companies that supplied them with raw materials. Andrew Carnegie, for example, owned not just Carnegie Steel but iron ore mines in the Midwest; factories that converted iron ore into iron bars; coal mines to supply blast furnaces; ships, docks, and warehouses to transport the raw materials to the factories and the steel to its markets. Others grew by swallowing their competitors. John D. Rockefeller, for example, formed a trust in the oil industry. Technically a stock swap, the trust required owners of individual companies to exchange their stock for stock in the trust itself; former owners collected a share of profits, but the trust's board of trustees took control of directing all of the companies. Either way, the huge new organizations enabled a tiny number of people to control materials, costs, prices, and most of all, competition. The result was usually a monopoly of the market by one or a few companies. Many prominent captains of industry held that in such business matters they owed nothing to the public, or to its ideas of ethics. As William Vanderbilt succinctly put it, "The public be damned."

By 1890, Americans used the terms *trust* and *monopoly* to refer to any large and powerful business organization. They were suspicious and angered by them all. By concentrating economic power in a few hands, they believed, the trusts were destroying the cherished American right of individual opportunity to compete and get ahead. Although Americans traditionally did not want or expect the government to interfere in free enterprise, many had come to view the trusts as a threat to the free-enterprise system itself. By 1890, 15 states had passed laws prohibiting combinations that destroyed competition, but entrepreneurs simply filed their legal incorporation papers in other states. Many Americans had come to believe that action by the federal government was necessary to curb the trusts and the powerful entrepreneurs and capitalists who formed them.

In response to growing public pressure, the 51st Congress with only one dissenting vote, quickly passed the Sherman Anti-Trust Act. It was named for Senator John Sherman, Republican of Ohio, who sponsored it. The act declared illegal "every contract, combination in the form of trust or otherwise, or conspiracy in restraint of trade or commerce among the several states, or with foreign nations." It also instructed the attorney general to file suits against trusts and monopolies in federal courts. The law proved difficult to enforce, however, partly because it was not very specific. Congress wrote it that way deliberately, many historians believe, to placate the public without actually challenging industrialists' power. During the two remaining years of President Harrison's administration, the Department of Justice lost seven of eight antitrust suits in federal courts. In the decade to follow, in fact, the law was more frequently and successfully used against labor unions than against big business.

The McKinley Tariff and the Federal Elections (Force) Bill

The Republican Party believed that its recent victories were due to its support for a high tariff to protect American manufacturers. In May 1890, the House of Representatives agreed on a new and even higher tariff than any yet passed. The bill was drafted by Representative William McKinley, Republican of Ohio, and sent to the Senate for consideration. The House then moved on to the federal elections bill, proposed by Representative Henry Cabot Lodge, Republican of Massachusetts. The federal elections bill permitted federal supervision of congressional elections to prevent fraud and disenfranchisement. Although it applied to all sections of the United States, its northern supporters intended it to protect African-American voting rights in the South. "This is the starting point and this is the goal," said Republican senator John Ingalls of Kansas. "Stack your guns, open your ballot boxes, register your voters, black and white." White southern Democrats derisively called it the Force Bill. In July the House also sent the federal elections bill on to the Senate.[15]

Both the McKinley tariff and the federal elections bill needed Senate approval. Democrats, who knew how anxious the Republicans were to pass the McKinley tariff, offered them a deal: Democrats would approve the tariff if Republicans would kill the federal elections bill. The deal was struck. The death of the federal elections bill marked the end of major national efforts to protect African-American rights in the South until the 1960s. The *New York Herald* said at the time, "The plain truth is that the North has gotten tired of the Negro."

THE SHERMAN SILVER PURCHASE ACT

In response to growing pressure from advocates called silverites, many of whom represented farm interests, the Sherman Silver Purchase Act was passed on July 15. (It, too, was named for Senator Sherman of Ohio.) The act required the government to purchase 4.5 million ounces of silver per month and to issue Treasury notes, a kind of paper money, to the sellers. One result of the act was to substitute the policy of bimetalism for the gold standard, under which only gold could back up the nation's paper currency. Under bimetalism either gold (a scarcer and more valuable metal) or silver (a more abundant but less valuable metal) could do so. But the Sherman Silver Purchase Act also gave the new Treasury notes important characteristics. Not only could they be redeemed for gold instead of the silver with which they had been purchased, but their value was to be calculated on an inflated silver-to-gold ratio of 16:1, or 16 times as much silver per dollar as gold. On the open market in 1890, silver was worth far less than that. Silver advocates pushed to retain the 16:1 ratio, which had been set by the government many decades earlier when silver was more valuable, because they wanted to increase the amount of paper money that could be issued under terms of the act. Their opponents, not unreasonably, feared that people would sell their silver to the government at the inflated price, then later demand more valuable gold for the Treasury notes they had received.

Controversies about money, the monetary system, silver, and bimetalism were destined to be extremely important in American politics in the 1890s. One question was whether paper money needed to be fully backed up and redeemable for specie, or valuable metals, at all. But a more momentous question to the public was whether that specie should be gold or silver or both. Today, it is difficult to grasp the great public emotion this question provoked. In large part, it was so prominent because silver-versus-gold came to operate as a symbol for two different systems of values, one rural-minded and one oriented to commercial growth and progress—an 1890s version of what today is sometimes called a "culture war." But the controversy over money and metal was nonetheless based on real economic issues that were important to ordinary people.

In the last quarter of the 19th century, prices fell and the value of money rose in America, a situation called deflation. Deflation occurred in part because the amount of money in circulation was declining, especially relative to the growing economy and population. During this deflationary period, the prices of farm products experienced an especially large fall (the price of manufactured goods fell too, but not as much). Farmers came to believe that increasing the amount of money circulating in America would help to raise agricultural prices, ease their financial difficulties, and reassert the proper importance of agrarian values in the new industrial America.

At the time, paper money was not usually issued by the government. Instead, it was issued by chartered national banks that by law had to back up the money they issued with gold—and because most national banks were located in the East, farmers in the West and South were inclined to blame "eastern banks" for their problems. Farm interests, therefore, wanted the national government itself to buy large amounts of silver and to issue silver-backed money. They also wanted the government to continue using the inflated 16:1 silver-to-gold ratio. Not surprisingly, farmers were joined by silver mining interests in the West, who wanted to sell their ores to the government at inflated prices. The silverites' catch phrase was "free and unlimited coinage of silver" or just "free silver." (*Free* in these phrases means "abundant.")

Gold standard advocates, or goldbugs, on the other hand, believed just as fervently that American currency should be backed by gold and gold only. The gold standard was respected worldwide and enabled American businessmen to sell products in international markets and to attract foreign investors. Goldbugs despised the notion of inflated currency in favor of what they called "sound money." They believed that bimetallism would cause people to refuse silver and hoard gold, thus depleting the nation's gold reserve. A depleted gold reserve, they believed, would decimate American prosperity at home and destroy its strength and respect in the world at large.

The Sherman Silver Act of 1890 doubled the amount of silver the U.S. Treasury had been permitted to purchase since 1878. Unfortunately, it alarmed goldbugs while failing to produce the results that silverites desired.

THE BILLION-DOLLAR CONGRESS AND THE RETURN OF STALEMATE

The 51st Congress passed hundreds of other bills, including large appropriations for modernizing the American navy and a generous pension bill for Union (but not Confederate) veterans of the Civil War. The Second Morrill Act, of 1890, provided additional funds for state colleges supported by land grants awarded in the Morrill Act of 1862. (These institutions are often called land grant colleges.) The Second Morrill Act, however, also required that colleges be established for African Americans in any state that refused to admit them to the existing state college. Under terms of the act, Georgia State Industrial College (later Savannah State) was established for blacks before the end of 1890; others soon followed in North Carolina and West Virginia.

The 51st Congress not only passed an unprecedented number of bills, it also spent an unprecedented amount of public money. It was soon labeled the Billion-Dollar Congress. Whenever Speaker of the House Reed was greeted with this label, he reportedly would reply, "This is a billion-dollar country." In the midterm congressional elections of November 1890, however, Americans voters registered their disapproval. (Midterm elections are congressional elections held in the middle of a four-year presidential term.) The Republican majority in the Senate was reduced, and its majority in the House of Representatives was lost to the Democrats. Balance and stalemate returned to Washington.[16]

WESTERN OKLAHOMA BECOMES A TERRITORY

In the late 19th century, most of the present state of Oklahoma—then called Indian Territory—was assigned to Native Americans as tribal groups. The Five Civilized Tribes, as the Cherokee, Chickasaw, Choctaw, Creek, and Seminole were known, occupied eastern Oklahoma. In western Oklahoma, the federal government had settled many smaller groups of Indians from the plains and other places. In the middle of Oklahoma was a section of so-called Unassigned Lands. As the American West filled with settlers, the federal government came under increasing pressure to open this section to non-Indian settlers. In 1889 it did. The first land run, or land rush, was held for some 2 million acres. In a land run, prospective settlers lined up at set spots under U.S. Cavalry oversight and at a signal raced to stake a homestead claim.

Meanwhile, under the terms of the Dawes Act, Congress had approved the transfer of most tribal lands to private, individual Indian ownership. Each Native American man, woman, and child was to receive an allotment, usually 160 acres, the standard size of a government homestead. However, the Dawes Act did not apply to the Five Tribes in eastern Oklahoma, who had a separate and distinctive relationship with the federal government. In eastern Oklahoma, no immediate change occurred. In western Oklahoma, however, allotment proceeded quickly. After all the Native Americans there had received an allotment, millions of surplus acres were left over. Additional large land runs were held in western Oklahoma in April 1892 (3.5 million acres) and September 1893 (6 million acres), as well as smaller ones in September 1891 and May 1895.[17]

The western half of Oklahoma received territorial status on May 2, 1890, when the Oklahoma Organic Act was passed. (An organic act establishes fundamental law or governmental structure.) The act also attached the panhandle, known as No Man's Land, to Oklahoma. By accident, the panhandle had previously been omitted from any territory's jurisdiction and had thus become a well-known outlaw's roost.

The eastern half of modern Oklahoma state continued to be called Indian Territory. It remained in possession of the Five Civilized Tribes. Most tribal members strongly preferred to live in accordance with their traditional values, and communal ownership of land was one of the most important. Traditionally, tribal citizens could use what land

and resources they needed to support a modest life. Only a very few were rich, but almost none were poor.

The realities of life in Indian Territory by 1890, however, were complex. The tribes had permitted railroads to build across their lands, connecting them to the rest of the nation. Since all tribal members held common rights to all of the land, any one could choose to lease plots to the settlers who arrived constantly, looking for a piece of land to farm. Large segments had been leased, cleared, and put under cultivation in this way. In addition, there were rich mineral deposits in the Indian lands, especially coal. Any tribal member could lease the coal-rich sections as well. Mining companies obtained these leases and brought in miners to do the labor, many of them from the new immigrant groups pouring into America at the time. A small number of Indians even acted as entrepreneurs themselves and amassed great individual wealth. Towns, businesses, and houses grew up on leased lands to accommodate the needs of the new farming and mining settlers. By 1890, about 180,000 people lived in Indian Territory, but less than 30 percent of them were Indian.[18]

The many non-Indian settlers, whom the Indians called intruders, made for an increasingly difficult political and civil situation. Non-Indians were required to pay yearly fees to the tribes, like taxes, to live and conduct business in their nations. But non-Indians had no voice or vote in the tribal governments, nor did they have state government, federal congressmen, or the right to vote for president. Corporations doing business were under no regulation whatsoever, and workers did not have even the minimal protections afforded elsewhere. Non-Indians could not attend tribal schools, but the tribes did not establish public schools. The traditionally minded tribal governments did not provide other services needed by a growing population either, such as road building, water lines, or fire protection. Law enforcement and justice were even greater problems. The Indian police and courts did not exercise either criminal or civil jurisdiction over people who were not tribal citizens. For non-Indians, a few federal marshals and distant federal courts in Arkansas were the only alternatives to vigilante action. Not surprisingly, as the number of settlers increased in Indian Territory, they put pressure on the federal government to take action. Many other Americans also agreed that the time had come to incorporate the Five Tribes fully into the United States.

In 1893, Congress established the Dawes Commission, named for its senior member and author of the Dawes Act, Senator Henry Dawes of Massachusetts. Its purpose was to negotiate with leaders of the Five Tribes to end their special forms of government, accept American citizenship, and transfer their tribal land to private, individual ownership. Negotiations, however, met with no success.

IDAHO AND WYOMING BECOME STATES

By law, a territory of the United States could be considered for statehood once its population reached 60,000—although Congress was sometimes known to aid or hinder admission depending on the political loyalties of its residents. In 1890, the Wyoming and Idaho territories were preparing for statehood.

Idaho had recently experienced serious regional divisions between its southern residents and its northern panhandle residents, as well as violence against its Chinese miners. But the most important political issue in Idaho was the hostility of many territorial residents to the Mormons, properly known as the Church of Jesus Christ of Latter-day Saints. (For more information on Mormons' distinctive beliefs, see below under Utah.) The Mormons had arrived in neighboring Utah in the 1840s with plans to establish communities throughout the Rocky Mountain West. While gold seekers rushed to the northern and western frontiers of future Idaho for its mining opportunities, the Mormons began to move up into its southeast corner to farm. In 1860 they founded the territory's first town at Franklin and eventually numerous other settlements. Other Idaho settlers, however, objected to the Mormon custom of voting in a bloc, and strongly disapproved of the Mormon belief that men had the right to take numerous wives. In 1885, the territorial legislature had established the Test Oath Act. It denied the right to vote or hold office to men who swore they were Mormons on the basis of their denomination's practice of polygamy, which was illegal. In July 1899, when Idaho held a convention in Boise to write a proposed state constitution, representatives included a similar test oath in it. The proposed constitution was overwhelmingly ratified by Idaho voters the following November.

Meanwhile Mormons fought the Test Oath Act the whole way to the Supreme Court. In February 1890, the act was upheld (*Davis v. Beason*). After the decision, Congress approved the Idaho constitution as voters approved it. On July 3, 1890, Idaho became the 43rd state.

In September 1889, Wyoming held a convention in Cheyenne to prepare its proposed state constitution. Disagreement quickly arose among the all-male representatives over voting rights for women. In Wyoming Territory, women had the full franchise, approved in 1869 by the all-male territorial legislature. Women voted, served on juries, and held territorial offices without incident; they also received equal pay for equal qualifications in the public schools. At the convention a few representatives opposed women's suffrage on principle, but more were concerned that Congress would not admit Wyoming to the union if the state constitution included it. The proposal to omit it, however, was soundly defeated. "If they will not let us in with this plank in our constitution," said delegate Charles H. Burritt, "we will stay out forever." Another forward-looking area of the Wyoming constitution concerned water rights. In 1890 most of America followed an English common law principle granting all landowners along a body of water a right to its uninterrupted flow. In the arid West, however, the scarcity of water was quickly introducing new political issues that were unknown in the East and South and that were destined to multiply. Wyoming, like Colorado and California before it, established the state's right to establish "priority of appropriation for beneficial use" of water and set up a system of state control.[19]

The Wyoming constitution was ratified by voters, a bill was approved by Congress, and signed into law by President Harrison on July 10, 1890, making Wyoming the 44th state—and the first and only state in 1890 to grant voting rights to women.

UTAH FAILS TO ACHIEVE STATEHOOD

By 1890, Utah Territory, which strongly desired statehood, had already made six unsuccessful attempts to be admitted to the union. A majority of Utah residents were Mormons and Congress had no desire to admit a Mormon-dominated state.

The 19th-century Mormons had a distinctive religion and culture. The belief that met the strongest disapproval of other Americans was, of course, polygamy, which Mormons called plural marriage. (One man was permitted to have numerous wives. Mormon beliefs did not, however, permit women to have more than one husband.) But many other aspects of 19th-century Mormon culture were also at odds with the beliefs of other Americans. Most important, the 19th-century Mormon community did not separate church and state. Men who had positions of leadership in the church also controlled civil government. These civil/religious leaders were not chosen democratically but were selected by those above them in the church hierarchy. These leaders placed a high value on political consensus. In the territorial legislature, for example, it was expected that after discussion had occurred, votes would be unanimous; on public questions, church leaders would instruct the populace how to vote. In many other areas of life as well, Mormons did not value or stress individualism as most other Americans did. Church leaders planned all aspects of their physical communities and the economy, always emphasizing group welfare. For example, Zion's Cooperative Mercantile Institution, or ZCMI, was a church-sponsored, cooperative system of stores at which all church members were strongly encouraged to shop.[20]

This church-ruled and group-oriented way of life was, of course, highly valued and strongly supported by Mormon adherents. But by 1890, Mormons were far from the only settlers in Utah. Many non-Mormons had arrived in the large westward migration after the Civil War, and after 1885 they averaged roughly a third of the overall population. Some men and a few women were drawn by gold and silver mining, railroad work, or a nearby military outpost. Among other newcomers were appointed territorial government officials, Jewish families, settlers of several Protestant denominations, and Catholic churchmen. These settlers, like most Americans, expected church and state to be separate and believed that individuals should make their own economic decisions. They resented the lack of public schools. They objected to the fact that Mormons did not include non-Mormon minorities in much of the political process of the territory. They were extremely suspicious about the lack of public disagreement in politics. Most of all, they were outraged by the practice of polygamy.

Although historians disagree about the exact number of polygamous Mormon marriages in the late 19th century, they were not a majority. In a study of one community, Utah historian Dean L. May found 10 percent of Mormon men had more than one wife, and about 25 percent of the total population lived in polygamous households.[21] After the Supreme Court upheld Idaho's Test Oath Act in 1890, the Cullom-Strubble bill was introduced into Congress to enable the use of a similar oath to disenfranchise Mormons nationwide. Alarmed, the Utah territorial legislature appropriated money to construct a public capitol and other buildings for civil government. It also established a tax-supported public school system.

"I have arrived at a point," wrote Mormon church president Wilford Woodruff in his diary on September 25, 1890, ". . . where I am under the necessity of acting for the temporal salvation of the Church. . . . and after praying to the Lord and feeling inspired, I have issued . . . [a] proclamation." The proclamation advised Mormons "to refrain from contracting any marriage forbidden by the laws of the land." Known as the Woodruff Manifesto, the proclamation was unanimously ratified by a general conference of Mormons on October 6. In private, some Mormon men continued to live and establish families with numerous women, to which local officials usually turned a blind eye.[22]

In 1891, the church's political branch, the People's Party, was disbanded. Soon, Utah Mormons and non-Mormons realigned within the Democratic and Republican Parties. In Washington, leaders of both parties began to look more favorably on the cause of statehood. On January 4, 1893, President Harrison granted amnesty to "all persons . . . who since November 1, 1890, have abstained from unlawful cohabitation, but upon the express condition that they shall in the future faithfully obey the laws of the United States."[23]

AGRICULTURAL DISTRESS

Between the end of the Civil War and 1900, the number of farms in America more than doubled. The new farms were established by both immigrants and native-born Americans, as they took up homestead claims across the Midwest, Great Plains, and Far West. Farm productivity—the yield of each acre of farmland—almost doubled as well.

During these same years, however, the nature of farming underwent many important changes. As railroads stretched across the country, farmers began to send crops to distant markets, allowing them to specialize more and grow large quantities of one cash crop. They bought new, drudgery-reducing—but expensive—agricultural machinery. To buy machinery, they became large debtors, taking out mortgages in the West and crop liens in the South. As debtors they were forced to rely on credit and interest rates set by bankers in the distant cities of the Northeast. As specialized growers they were also forced to rely on crop buyers in faraway cities (collectively called the commodity market, operating like the stock market) to set their prices. Prices even came to depend partly on international markets.

Some farmers in the near-Midwest and on the Pacific Coast adjusted successfully to the new conditions. A few, in fact, became very wealthy during the period. But the vast majority of farmers, especially in the plains and South, did not prosper. Especially distressing to farmers, the prices for farm products fell steadily. Corn, for example, fell from 78 cents a bushel to 23 cents by 1890, and wheat from $1.60 a bushel to under 50 cents. (Prices for most manufactured products were declining too, but not as sharply.) From the farmers' perspective, it took more bushels of corn to pay back every dollar borrowed for machinery in previous years, when prices were a bit higher. As prices fell, farmers tried to raise more and more crops to keep their incomes steady. But a larger supply in the markets only caused prices to fall more.

Understandably, many farmers did not fully fathom the new economic world in which they lived. Many could not believe that the problem was overproduction, pointing to the undernourished urban poor. It was puzzling, Kansas governor Lorenzo Dow Lewelling commented, that "there were hungry people . . . because there was too much bread." Especially in the West and South, many farmers came to believe they were at the mercy of distant and malicious forces.[24]

THE FARMERS "RAISE MORE HELL"

In the 1880s, three organizations called Farmers' Alliances had formed. The Northwestern Alliance began in the north-central Midwest. Another group, founded as the Southern Alliance in Lampasas, Texas, was renamed the National Farmers' Alliance and Industrial Union (NFA & IU) as it grew. A second southern group, the Colored Farmers' Alliance, was founded for African Americans, who numbered nearly half the farmers in the South. By 1890 it had well over a million members. Nationwide, farm women made up at least one-quarter of the alliances' membership and in many locals were full voting members and officers.

Alliances created a sense of community among isolated farmers by hosting social activities of many kinds from picnics to burial services. But alliances also developed a lecture circuit and a small army of speakers and writers to educate farmers about farm problems. They soon had more than 1,000 affiliated periodicals, with their own National Reform Press Association. Speakers and writers continually promoted the idea of cooperative ventures on the local scene and democratic oversight of big business on the national scene to solve farmers' problems.

By 1890, farm prices were at new lows. Mortgages, liens, and discontent were at a new high. During the winter of 1889–90, midwestern farmers famously heated their homes by burning corn, since the price of corn had fallen lower than the price of fuel. Mary Elizabeth Lease, a Kansan and a commanding alliance speaker, was soon quoted widely in newspapers urging farmers to "Raise less corn and more hell!"

As the midterm elections of 1890 approached, farmers began to agree on the need for direct political action. Some alliances organized local third parties, usually called People's (later Populist) Parties. They were especially strong in Kansas, Nebraska, the Dakotas, and Minnesota but also existed in Colorado and other parts of the West including California. In the South, however, political action was complicated by racial issues. Most white alliance members resisted cooperating with blacks to form a new third party, and black alliance members had good reason to be skeptical of white alliances. Instead, white alliance members tried to gain control of the local Democratic Party, which stood for white solidarity.

In the November elections, the People's Parties scored significant victories in the central Midwest. They elected many state legislators and sent a number of congressmen to Washington. The Kansas and South Dakota legislatures even elected populists to the Senate. (In 1890 senators were elected by state legislatures, not by popular vote.) Southern alliances seemed to be, if anything, even more successful working within the Democratic Party. The South elected four pro-alliance governors, eight pro-alliance state legislatures, and 44 congressmen and three senators who promised to support alliance goals.

In December 1890, NFA & IU representatives met again in Ocala, Florida. Alliance members issued 12 demands, known as the Ocala platform, which they believed would alleviate farmers' economic distress. One demand was a subtreasury plan to replace the hated, powerful eastern banks. Subtreasuries were to be federally operated depositories or banks that would make low-interest loans to farmers. The Ocala platform also called for government control—and in the last resort ownership—of communication and transportation, including railroads. Other demands were for free silver and a graduated income tax to replace tariffs and property taxes, which were thought to burden people of modest incomes unfairly. In the eyes of most Americans at the time, all of these demands were radical.

The idea of a third party continued to grow among alliance members, although southerners remained lukewarm about the idea. In May 1891, the Northwest Alliance organized a meeting in Cincinnati of more than 1,400 delegates from a wide variety of alliance, labor, and other reform groups. The group endorsed the idea of a national People's Party and began to mobilize. Soon after the Cincinnati meeting the better-known name for the party and its adherents, Populist, came into use, probably coined by Kansas representatives from the Latin word *populus,* or people.[25]

THE NEW SOUTH

In 1889, Henry Grady, editor of the *Atlanta Constitution,* received widespread publicity for a speech in Boston that popularized the term *the New South.* The term designated a plan for progress, modernization, and prosperity to rebuild the South, which was still suffering economically from the devastation of the Civil War. Grady and many other southern promoters wanted to encourage a less agricultural, more industrial, and more varied southern economy.

Southern industry did expand greatly in the late 19th century. New, modern textile mills multiplied in Georgia, North and South Carolina, and Alabama. The lumber industry prospered, with camps and small mills throughout the South. Coal mining expanded in the Appalachians. By 1890, the iron and steel industry had developed throughout the Lower South, using iron ore from northern Alabama. Birmingham, Alabama, where the industry was centered, grew from a cornfield in 1870 into a city of almost 40,000 people by 1890. Tobacco processing and cigarette production also grew. In 1890 tobacco entrepreneur and fierce competitor James B. Duke of North Carolina formed the American Tobacco Company. It controlled 90 percent of the nation's cigarette manufacturing. In many industries, however, northerners and northern capital dominated the new development.

Despite this growth, average income in the South remained at about half that in the North. For one thing, southern industrial workers received very low wages. In textiles and tobacco, a high percentage of southern factory workers were women, who were paid less than men. The textile industry also relied extensively on child labor, and children were paid the least of all. Average income also remained low because the New South, despite its new industries, still remained primarily agricultural—just like the Old South. Like farmers elsewhere in America, southern farmers experienced hard times in the late 19th century.

Southern farmers continued to rely heavily on cash crops, especially King Cotton. But cotton dropped from 11 cents a pound in 1875 to under 5 cents in 1894. Each year, more farmers lost their land and were forced into tenant farming. Tenancy took two forms. Tenants who owned their own tools and animals rented only land. The poorer sharecroppers, including most black farmers, had to rent not only land but also tools, a mule, and a small house. In return, they received a share of the crop, usually about half. Tenants, sharecroppers, and even small landowners all paid for supplies by using crop liens, or claims against a yet-to-be-grown crop. As prices declined, farmers often had nothing left for themselves after paying the landlord and merchants who had extended credit. Soon, they were not even able to pay their creditors, and fell further into debt each year. By 1900, about half of all white farmers and about three-quarters of all black farmers in the South would be tenants rather than landowners. Small merchants and landlords suffered as well.

BLACK DISENFRANCHISEMENT AND JIM CROW IN THE NEW SOUTH

Spokesmen for the New South upheld the idea of what they called racial cooperation. But like most other white southerners in the late 19th century, they did not accept the idea of black political participation or of integration, much less of racial equality. White southerners were determined to maintain their political and social domination of the black population, or white supremacy. They viewed the constitutional guarantees for African Americans enacted after the Civil War as a display of northern ill will, meant to humiliate the defeated Confederacy.

Prior to 1890, nonetheless, racial relations in the South were not all cut from the same cloth. The extent of black voting, political participation, and day-to-day segregation were local matters. In some places, African Americans began to lose their newly gained civil and political rights as soon as federal troops withdrew from the South in 1877, at the end of Reconstruction, usually by means of violence and intimidation. But elsewhere, they did vote. Some white Democrats even behaved like the political bosses in the urban, ethnic North, courting black votes and delivering them to the polls. At least one southern black served in each Congress until the turn of the century, and several state legislatures had black representatives into the 1890s. In some places blacks and whites rode in the same train cars, visited the same parks, and stayed in the same hospitals. Some established whites paternalistically supported black "uplift." "It is a great deal pleasanter," wrote a white Charleston newspaper editor in the late 1880s, "to travel with respectable and well-behaved colored people than with unmannerly and ruffianly white men."[26]

Beginning in 1890, however, a change occurred throughout the South. Whites began to seek formal ways to reduce the civil and social rights of African Americans. They began to pass statewide laws formalizing the separation of the races in all aspects of everyday life. They also began to adopt laws or other formal means of preventing African Americans from voting. One reason that whites pushed for legal disenfranchisement, historians believe, was the rise of discontent and populism among farmers. Well-established white leaders feared that poor black and white farmers might join together and, as a majority, demand significant change. Even if they did not, whites feared, competition for the farmers' vote would give African Americans strong bargaining power. White politicians were quick to exploit this imagined threat, which they called "Negro domination."

In 1890, Mississippi became the first state to prevent African Americans from voting by writing new laws that circumvented the U.S. Constitution. A state constitutional convention was convened to change the suffrage provisions instituted during Reconstruction. Although the majority of the population in Mississippi was black, only one African American, Isaiah Montgomery (founder of the all-black town

Mound Bayou), was in attendance. The president of the convention, S. S. Calhoon, did not mince words. "We came here to exclude the Negro," he declared. "Nothing short of this will answer."[27]

The major problem facing the Mississippi convention was the Fifteenth Amendment to the U.S. Constitution, passed in 1870. It gave men the right to vote regardless of "race, color, or previous condition of servitude." In order to avoid direct conflict, the new Mississippi suffrage provision did not mention "race." Instead, Mississippi imposed a poll tax on each voter, which had to be paid months in advance and later proven with a receipt. It imposed long residency requirements—an obstacle for sharecroppers, who often moved yearly. It also denied the vote to any person who could not read a section of the state constitution and explain its meaning to the examiner's satisfaction. All told, these new requirements disenfranchised many poor whites as well as blacks. But the literacy clause gave local examiners the power to pass whites but fail blacks if they chose—and in practice, they often did. These and other requirements were called the Second Mississippi Plan. (The so-called first Mississippi Plan of 1875 had been systematic terror and violence against blacks, used to enable white Democrats to regain control of the state from Reconstruction Republicans.)

Within the next two decades, six more southern states adopted both literacy and poll tax requirements and others adopted one or the other to prevent blacks and in some places poor whites from voting. White southerners also used an arsenal of other methods to restrict black voting, while still evading a court challenge on the basis of the Fifteenth Amendment. State legislatures gerrymandered voting districts. That is, they drew oddly shaped districts, either to confine all black voters to one district or to prevent a majority of black voters in any. They made polling places inaccessible by roadblocks and designed complicated ballots. If all else failed, outright fraud remained; ballot boxes were stuffed or votes were incorrectly counted. Violence against blacks also continued, especially near election times.

At the same time disenfranchisement was occurring, southern states also began to pass a network of laws to enforce the social segregation of black and white people. The segregation these laws established was called Jim Crow, after a well-known stereotypical black character in minstrel shows.

Again, there was a Constitutional roadblock—the Fourteenth Amendment. It requires the "equal protection of the laws" for all people in the United States and forbids the states to "abridge the privileges or immunities" of any citizen. On that basis African Americans often attempted to challenge discriminatory laws in the courts. In 1883, however, the U.S. Supreme Court had ruled in the *Civil Rights Cases* (109 US 3), a set of five cases heard and decided together, that the Fourteenth Amendment did not apply to private organizations or individuals. This ruling meant that states could permit private companies, groups, and facilities to discriminate or segregate freely, although the government could not legally allow discrimination in state matters like legal proceedings.

The first Jim Crow or segregation laws applied to railroads and required separate cars for black and white people. In 1890, a test case, *Louisville, New Orleans, and Texas Railroad v. Mississippi,* came before the Supreme Court. The Court ruled that a state could even require (not just permit) segregation in transportation facilities. By 1892, Louisiana, Alabama, Arkansas, Georgia, Tennessee, and Kentucky joined Mississippi, Florida, and Texas in requiring separate seating or facilities in trains, streetcars, and depots as well as steamboats and wharves.

In some places, of course, Jim Crow laws simply recognized established customs of segregation. But the change was nonetheless very significant and extremely alarming to African-American leaders. It indicated that discrimination would increase, rather than lessen, in the future. Worse, it gave the government's approval to discrimination and differential treatment of its citizens. Their fears were to prove correct. Jim Crow laws continued to increase and eventually required segregation in all sorts of facilities—hotels, restaurants, theaters, parks, prisons, hospitals, morgues, and even cemeteries. Many of the Jim Crow and voting requirement laws that were set in place in the Progressive Era were not successfully challenged and overturned until the Civil Rights movement of the 1960s.

IDA B. WELLS BEGINS THE ANTILYNCHING CRUSADE

At the same time that Jim Crow segregation and disenfranchisement were established in the South, lynchings became appallingly common. From 1890 to 1899 alone, an average of 187 people per year suffered death by lynching in the nation as a whole. More than 80 percent were in the South and some two-thirds of the victims were African American. Almost all were men, but a few women were also lynched. Lynchings occurred most frequently in states with the largest black populations: Mississippi, Alabama, Georgia, and Louisiana.

A few lynching victims, both black and white, had already been convicted of serious crimes. Some others had been arrested although not tried. These lynchings were organized and very public, carried out with the unspoken approval of local officials. Prisoners were seized from jail cells and hanged before a large crowd that had gathered specifically to watch. Most lynchings, however, were carried out by smaller groups and were less public and far less predictable. These lynch mobs would capture their victims and take them to a remote site, often torturing and mutilating them before murdering them. Their goal was to terrorize the black population. They blamed some of their victims for crimes. But some victims had done nothing more than transgress customs of deference demanded by whites, others had offended by achieving unusual success—and some were simply in the wrong place at the wrong time. "During these years," writes historian Kennell Jackson, "no Black American escaped the fear of lynching. Everyone lived near a lynching, or had read or heard of one, or had a relative or friend who had been caught by a mob."[28]

Many white southerners disapproved of lynching, mob violence, and the blatant scorn for law and order that they represented. Yet white police, courts, and juries almost never brought white perpetrators to justice for their grisly, murderous acts or their lawlessness.

Many African-American journalists and other leaders spoke out bravely against lynching. The most prominent antilynching crusader was Ida B. Wells (later Wells-Barnett), an African-American woman born in Mississippi in 1862. In 1891, she left her work as a rural teacher to help found the black newspaper *Free Press* in Memphis. A year later, three black grocery store owners were lynched in Memphis—primarily because of long-simmering resentment at their success. The triggering incident was a fight over marbles between black and white boys. One of the white boys was the son of a white grocer whose nearby store had lost much of its black business. A court fined the black children, then dismissed the claims of the white parents. Soon, a white mob attacked and destroyed the black grocery store; three white men were injured in the melee. The three black owners were arrested and put in jail. On the third night they were dragged from their cells and lynched.

Ida B. Wells knew the family of one of the victims, Thomas Moss, very well. After his death, she undertook to research every known recent incident of lynching in the South. Armed with this information, she sparked what became an international antilynching movement. Her courageous and impassioned articles describing the record of brutality soon led a mob to destroy her newspaper office, leaving behind a death threat. She moved to New York, then Chicago. She continued to work as a journalist and to publicize her campaign throughout the North and Europe.

AFRICAN AMERICANS RESIST DEFEAT

In 1890, when the total U.S. population was 63 million, there were 7.5 million African Americans in the United States. Nine out of every 10 lived in the South, and eight out of every 10 lived in a rural area.

In the North and West, home to only 10 percent of the African-American population in 1890, customary local discrimination and segregation certainly existed. But schools were usually integrated and no statewide attack was made on black voting rights. Some white colleges, and professional schools, admitted a few African-American students. In the North, a black middle class of skilled craftspeople, business owners, and professionals had existed for some time. In the West, blacks had served in army units and worked in ranching as cowboys for many decades; in the late 19th century more black women and families also joined the westward movement.

In the South, however, African Americans faced drastically limited opportunities, blatant injustice, and outright violence. The vast majority farmed for a living, many as tenants or sharecroppers. North or South, blacks were not usually hired for industrial work in 1890, although in the South tobacco processing, mining, iron and steel, and lumber sometimes offered a few opportunities. Despite all odds, however, a middle and professional class was also developing in the South. Some African Americans acquired property or established small businesses like blacksmith shops, barbershops, or hotels. Others entered professions, becoming teachers, nurses, doctors, journalists, or ministers. They trained at the black colleges established soon after the Civil War and supported primarily by white northern philanthropy, such as Atlanta University, Fisk, Howard, and Hampton Institute. North as well as South, a very few even achieved significant financial success.

While African Americans strongly objected to the imposition of Jim Crow laws, they themselves preferred some of their institutions, like churches, to be free from white oversight. According to historian Barbara Bair, the black church "was the strongest single institution of African-American self help" in the late 19th century.

The church was a very important institution in the lives of many African Americans. This photo shows congregants gathered outside a church in Georgia. It was included in a collection on "American Negro Life" compiled by W. E. B. DuBois for the Paris Exposition of 1900. *(Library of Congress, Prints and Photographs Division, LC-USZ62-103393)*

Long a center of spiritual life and social networks, the church was closely connected to almost every social welfare and educational effort blacks made. It also served as a training ground for leaders. As segregation increased, African Americans also organized to build schools and colleges, hospitals like Provident in Chicago (incorporated in 1891) and other institutions. These institutions offered black professionals control as well as employment.[29]

In 1890, T. Thomas Fortune, editor of the black newspaper *New York Age,* organized the Afro-American League to work for justice and black progress. The league opposed lynchings, supported political rights, and advocated the formation of black economic institutions like banks and other businesses to serve the black community. Other activists continued to promote emigration to Africa. African Methodist Episcopal (AME) bishop Henry McNeal Turner, for example, encouraged blacks to move to Liberia. (The republic of Liberia, on the west coast of Africa, was founded in 1822 by freed American slaves with the aid of the U.S. government and private philanthropy.) During 1891, Turner's letters describing a visit to Liberia were widely published in black newspapers. A few black people did leave the United States for Africa, but far more moved to the American west. Some established or moved to all-black towns or communities as far west as California, in search of both land and safety. Edwin P. McCabe, an African-American man who had served as auditor of Kansas, established the all-black town of Langston City, Oklahoma, after claiming land in the 1889 land run. His dream was to make Oklahoma an African-American state. The black southerners he had recruited as settlers continued to arrive and by 1910 had founded 25 towns in Oklahoma.

WOMEN ORGANIZE TO ENLARGE THEIR SPHERE

Throughout the 19th century, most Americans believed that women and men occupied separate spheres of life. Men, they believed, were suited for the public sphere of politics, business, and money-making. Women occupied the domestic sphere and even those who worked for wages, were assumed to be primarily suited for domestic labor. Women, most Americans believed, were inherently altruistic, motherly, and inclined to high moral character, natural qualifications for the maintenance of home and children. Women could sometimes extend their activities beyond the home without disapproval if their volunteer work or occupation related to children, the family, or religion. Otherwise, women who engaged in public activities outside the home could expect to meet obstacles and generate controversy. Nonetheless, in the late 19th century women's groups of many different kinds began to proliferate and expand energetically. Most were founded by middle- and upper-middle-class women (including middle-class African-American women) and began as self-culture or educational clubs. Some were for the benefit of less fortunate women, like the Women's Education and Industrial Union of Boston, although young urban working women also organized clubs to enhance their own lives. All of these groups helped to expand women's knowledge and, perhaps more important, gave them experience in organizing, working together, and speaking and acting publicly.

Beginning around 1890, local women's groups began to join together. Women's clubs were slowly expanding their interests to civic problems, and clubwomen believed that larger groups could exert more effective pressure for change. In 1890 Jane Cunningham Croly, a professional journalist, founded the General Federation of Women's Clubs to serve as a national alliance. Other groups of women organized nationally as well. The Daughters of the American Revolution (DAR) was founded in 1890, for example, to preserve the nation's history and promote civic values. Its first president was First Lady Caroline Scott Harrison, who undertook the first inventory and cataloging of historic objects in the White House. In an address to the DAR—the first

Caroline Scott Harrison, first lady of the United States until her untimely death during the campaign of 1892, undertook the first survey of historic objects in the White House. *(Library of Congress, Prints and Photographs Division, LC-USZ62-25798)*

public speech ever delivered by a first lady—she declared that the success of the nation's early struggle for freedom was partly "due to the character of the women of that era." In 1893, the Catholic Women's League was founded by Alice Timmons Toomey and others, and the National Council of Jewish Women was founded by Hannah Greenebaum Solomon and others. Both drew together many local social service groups. "Who is this new woman . . . ?" asked Solomon. "She is the woman who dares to go into the world and do what her convictions demand."[30]

The New York Consumers' League, founded in 1890 by Josephine Shaw Lowell, Dr. Mary Putnam Jacobi, Maud Nathan, and other influential New York women, was a distinctly activist group. The purpose of the league was to achieve reforms for working women in the new department stores rising in the larger cities. Department stores like Macy's in New York and Marshall Field's in Chicago offered a new concept of shopping—many different kinds of items under one roof. They also offered young working women a new kind of employment, as salesladies, which many found more desirable than other kinds of available work. However, early retail employees worked for very low pay under difficult conditions, such as 12- to 18-hour days with no stools to sit on behind the counters, six-day work-weeks, and no vacations. The Consumers' Leagues hoped to mobilize affluent patrons to effect improvement. They developed the White List, which named stores meeting Standards of a Fair House, and encouraged women to patronize them. (It was thus the opposite of a blacklist, which names establishments to be avoided.) The standards included acceptable wages, hours, sanitary conditions, respect for seniority, and refusal to employ children under 14. The first New York list of 1891 listed only eight acceptable stores. By 1893, league members had brought enough pressure to bear that they were able to expand the list to 24. Similar consumers' groups soon appeared in other eastern cities.[31]

WOMAN SUFFRAGE ADVOCATES UNITE

In the late 19th century, two national women's suffrage organizations existed. The National Woman Suffrage Association focused on winning a constitutional amendment for women's suffrage. The American Woman Suffrage Association worked for suffrage at the state level. In February 1890, they merged. The new organization was called the National American Woman Suffrage Association (NAWSA). Elizabeth Cady Stanton served as president until 1892, when she was replaced by Susan B. Anthony. Nearly half a century earlier, the first convention for women's rights had been held at Stanton's home in Seneca Falls, New York, and since then the two women had been dominant figures in the suffrage movement.

When NAWSA was founded in 1890 only one state, Wyoming, had complete woman suffrage. Nineteen other states and two territories gave women the right to vote in school elections and two other states permitted them to vote on tax or municipal issues. NAWSA immediately began to conduct state-level campaigns for suffrage, but the earliest ones were not successful. In 1893, however, NAWSA helped Colorado women mount a successful referendum for the vote. The Colorado Non-Partisan

Equal Suffrage Association, led by Denver newspaperwoman Ellis Meredith and other state women, secured the endorsement of the Populist governor, the Republican ex-governor, and 33 out of 44 newspapers in the state. Local brewers and saloon keepers—the primary financial backers of suffrage opposition in most places, primarily because women were strong supporters of temperance,—were caught off guard, perhaps because women totaled only about 30 percent of the population in frontier Colorado. By a 6,000-vote margin in a total tally of 65,000 votes, the men of Colorado gave women the franchise. "Oh how glad I am that at last we have knocked down our first state by popular vote," wrote Susan B. Anthony to Meredith.[32]

WCTU, THE LARGEST WOMAN'S ORGANIZATION

In 1890, the largest and most influential group working to advance women's causes was the Women's Christian Temperance Union, or WCTU. First organized in 1874, by 1890 it had groups in every state and territory and more than half of all U.S. counties. Its newspaper, the *Union Signal,* had almost 100,000 subscribers. The editor, Mary Allen West, was a professional journalist. Its publisher was the Woman's Temperance Publishing Association, a stock company open to women only, founded by Matilda Carse of Chicago in 1880. The company had its own plant and employed almost 100 women in clerical, editorial, printing, and administrative positions. By 1892 the WCTU had nearly 150,000 members—well over 200,000, counting the Young Women's branch—and was the largest organization of women in the world. In contrast, historian Ruth Bordin points out, the General Federation of Women's Clubs had 20,000 dues-paying members and NAWSA 13,000 at the time.[33]

The WCTU mobilized great support for expanding women's activities into the public sphere by emphasizing that women had a duty to protect home and children. Although some women abused alcohol, drinking and the saloons in which it occurred were considered male preserves. Alcohol abuse, on the other hand, was considered a problem from which women and children suffered and of which they were innocent victims. Alcohol abuse and the domestic violence it encouraged were serious problems in the late 19th century. However, activists also used the drunkard as a symbol to magnify the difficulties of women's second-class citizenship. By law and custom a woman was at her husband's mercy and completely dependent on him for support. She could divorce him only with great difficulty. She had little hope of obtaining adequate employment to support her family. In some places she still was not entitled to her own earnings if she did. By 1890, the WCTU supported equal and unlimited suffrage for women. They called it the "home protection ballot."

Frances Willard, the former dean of Evanston College for Women (absorbed into Northwestern University), served as president from 1879 till her death in 1898. Willard was an accomplished leader, organizer, and publicist who believed that true temperance reform required a "Do Everything" philosophy. Under her direction the WCTU became a wide-ranging social reform and political action group. WCTU projects included improving conditions for working women, aiding new immigrants, founding child care facilities, and improving the conditions of female prisoners. The WCTU also worked to eliminate the double standard of sexual behavior, raise the age of consent (set at 10 for girls in some states), and eliminate prostitution. Some members worked in the international peace movement.

In comparison with the other national women's groups, the WCTU was an inclusive organization. A few local groups had both black and white members—although white southern women objected to integration and Ida B. Wells objected to Willard's failure to make African-American rights a national WCTU concern. But African-American women usually organized and ran their own separate organizations, designated WCTU No. 2's. At least one Native American group also existed, in Oklahoma. The

WCTU was an officially ecumenical organization as well, although it was closely related to Protestant religious traditions. Some Catholic women belonged, and the WCTU exchanged representatives with the Catholic National Total Abstinence Union.[34]

Even the WCTU's membership, it should be pointed out, was smaller than the combined memberships of women's groups affiliated with their local churches or denominations. These groups, usually called missionary societies, had religious purposes. They did not organize together, however, and their activities rarely extended into reform. Other associations with close religious ties and many women members, especially the YWCA (founded in 1858) and the Salvation Army (founded in America in 1879), did engage in social service work. The YWCA especially assisted young women arriving in the city from rural areas, founding many boardinghouses and hotels. The Salvation Army—whose female workers were called slum sisters—actually took to the streets looking for the poorest of the poor to aid.[35]

WOMEN WORKERS AND PROFESSIONALS

In 1890, the primary occupation of the majority of adult women was the care of their families and homes. Only some 20 percent, the vast majority of them young and single, worked for wages outside their homes. Others worked for pay within their homes, caring for boarders or doing sewing or laundry for others—but unfortunately, census takers did not record their work, nor did they record the home-based labor of farm wives. More than half of the women who did work outside the home were in domestic service. Most of the others were engaged in either light industrial labor or in such new white collar occupations as saleslady, office worker, or telephone operator. Among educated and professional women, teaching was the primary occupation and nursing a second. A few women became doctors. A few also trained in law, although the right had to be won slowly on a state-by-state basis.

One profession in which women's advances had been impressive was journalism, where the plucky "stunt girls" had moved reporting by women onto the front page. The best known was Nellie (or Nelly) Bly, the pseudonym of Elizabeth Jane Cochrane. Bly successfully performed dangerous stunts like getting herself sent to prison or to an insane asylum in order to report firsthand on conditions there. By far her most famous stunt was her breakneck 72-day trip around the world. The voyage was publicized daily by her employer, the *New York World,* Bly arrived back in Manhattan on January 25, 1890, to a tumultuous welcome.

AMERICANS RESPOND TO INCREASING IMMIGRATION

When immigration began to increase and its sources began to shift to southern and eastern Europe, Americans assumed that the new wave of immigrants, like those before them, would learn English and blend into American ways of life. Some of the new immigrants, especially those who were young, did embrace American ways, and most others harbored a dream of becoming "real Americans." But most faced a very difficult transition, and they adjusted very slowly. As they clustered in ethnic neighborhoods in the growing cities, maintaining some of their traditions and their language, their slow acculturation was increasingly visible to other Americans. Old stock Americans, and even those whose own parents were immigrants, responded with increasing dismay and hostility. (*Old stock* is a term adopted by the U.S. Census in the 19th century to describe people born in America whose parents were also American-born.) Many began to speak of an immigrant problem. Some feared that the new immigrants could never be assimilated or Americanized. Some even feared that they posed a threat to the American way of life.

As fears about the newcomers grew, nativism grew as well. (Nativism is the practice of opposing immigration or immigrant cultures within an established nation, based on beliefs that immigrants and their cultures are inferior or threaten the established ways of life.) Some nativism, like that in earlier periods of American history, was based on simple prejudice. But some of the nativism in the late 19th century had a newer basis: the association that the public made between the new immigrants, disorder in the burgeoning cities, and corruption in urban politics. Based on this association, some Americans feared that the new immigrants could not understand or uphold democracy.

Some expressions of nativism were based in religious fears or objections. Most of the new immigrants from southern and eastern Europe were Catholic or Jewish. Although some Catholics and Jews had lived in and continued to immigrate to America since the earliest colonial days, a large majority of Americans in 1890 were Protestant. Some nativists disliked the growth of the Catholic Church in America because they feared its church officials would attempt to intervene in politics or the public schools. A few even imagined a conspiracy by the Vatican to undermine American democracy. In 1887, the American Protective Association (APA) was founded in Iowa to oppose immigration and encourage discrimination against Catholics in the workplace and in political offices. By 1893, it claimed to have half a million members.

On the other hand, at first many Americans welcomed the eastern European Jews. Although some anti-Semitism existed in America, many people viewed the eastern Europeans as refugees from religious persecution. As their numbers grew, however, their distinctive old-world customs and clothing increasingly made them a target for nativists. Eastern European Jewish culture also seemed remote and off-putting to old-stock American Jews—most of whom had German or Sephardic (Spanish or Portuguese) roots; many of whom belonged to Reform synagogues, a modern branch of Judaism founded in America; and some of whom were both financially and socially prominent. Most American Jews remained eager, however, to help the eastern Europeans escape oppression and immigrate to America.

Other expressions of nativism had economic grounds. Many working people feared the effects of high immigration on job availability, although they did not always object to the immigrants themselves. Labor leaders feared the leverage that immigration gave to employers. New immigrants were often willing to accept wages and conditions below the levels acceptable to established Americans, or even to work as strike breakers. They were harder for labor leaders to organize because they spoke so many different languages. Not surprisingly, labor protests against unrestricted immigration increased during years of economic hardship.

Ironically, in the minds of many middle-class Americans the labor unions themselves, and labor violence in particular, were un-American ideas that could be laid at the feet of recent immigrants. This belief was fixed in the public mind by the 1886 riot in Haymarket Square, Chicago. During a labor protest, a bomb had been thrown at a group of policemen, killing one and wounding others. The Haymarket affair was blamed on immigrant anarchists. A small number of new immigrants did, in fact, bring radical political ideas, like anarchism and Marxist socialism, to America. But in the public mind, these ideas were associated with all immigrants in general. As immigration increased this association helped raise fears among some people for the political stability of the nation.

Italian immigrants, while not usually considered political revolutionaries, were all assumed to be violent and to have connections to the Sicilian outlaw brotherhood, the Mafia. In October 1890, New Orleans police chief David Hennessy was shot to death shortly after confronting two warring Sicilian families. Nineteen Sicilians were indicted, including a 16-year-old boy. In March 1891, a jury acquitted 16 of them, having failed to agree on the remaining three. The next day an angry lynch mob broke into the prison, shooting nine of the men dead and hanging two others. The Italian government protested, demanding justice, and recalled its ambassador. Relations remained strained until the U.S. government paid an indemnity to Italy.

THE FEDERAL RESPONSE TO IMMIGRATION

By the 1890s, many American officials believed that a more formal means of oversee-ing entry into the United States was necessary. To date, each state with an entry port had a separate state commission to supervise the process, under general oversight of the Department of the Treasury. (Immigration was assigned to Treasury because it had jurisdiction over commerce with other nations at the time.) On March 3, 1891, Congress passed legislation establishing the office of Superintendent of Immigration within the Treasury Department. The act named 24 official ports of entry and also established inspection stations along the border of Mexico and Canada. But at all of these sites, the act gave the federal government jurisdiction to inspect arriving immi-grants. The act of 1891 decisively established the control of the federal government over the process of immigration to the United States. It was immediately challenged in the courts, but in January 1892, the Supreme Court declared that it was "constitutional and valid" (*Nishimura Ekiu v. United States*).

In 1892—a presidential election year—the 10-year Chinese Exclusion Act of 1882 was set to expire. Amid the growing concern about immigration in general, there was little debate in Congress over renewing it. In May 1892 Congress passed the Geary Act, named for Senator Thomas Geary, a Democrat from California. It extended Chi-nese exclusion for another 10 years, although categories of Chinese people such as merchants and students were still permitted to immigrate. More important, it also required all Chinese laborers already in the United States to obtain a certificate prov-ing they were legal residents—even if they had been born in this country. Unregis-tered Chinese could be deported and had no right to a trial. Many Americans disapproved of these requirements and officials in China were angered. The Geary Act was challenged in the courts but upheld by the Supreme Court in 1893 (*Fong Yue Ting v. United States*). In 1893, Congress amended the Geary Act to require Chinese mer-chants, who were exempt from other provisions, to prove their status by the testimony of "two credible witnesses other than Chinese."

ELLIS ISLAND OPENS

On April 18, 1890, the federal government closed Castle Garden, New York State's immigration receiving center at the tip of Manhattan, where the majority of immi-grants had long entered the United States. Under New York State oversight, however, Castle Garden had generated widespread complaints of abuse, corruption, and profi-teering. While Congress prepared to take control of immigration, an investigation veri-fied the complaints. Federal officials were temporarily directed to process newly arriving immigrants at the federal customs office, called the Barge Office, in lower Manhattan.

Meanwhile, Secretary of the Treasury William Windom searched for a site to build a new immigrant receiving center. He wanted to situate it on an island in New York Harbor, to give the government greater control and insulate new arrivals from hustlers and con men. He preferred Bedloe's (Liberty) Island, where the Statue of Liberty had been constructed in 1886, but settled for small Ellis Island immediately to the north. A two-story wood-frame reception center and other buildings were constructed. On New Year's Day 1892, Ellis Island received its first immigrants for processing.

Almost immediately after Ellis Island opened, however, accusations arose of faulty construction and financial deceit. Federal inspectors examined and approved the build-ings. Some Congressmen remained so suspicious, however, that they hired private architects to inspect them. The architects' report in May 1892 disclosed many serious defects in the wooden buildings. The main building, they concluded, "could not possi-bly last more than ten years, and probably not more than five." A House committee concluded in July 1892 that the Superintendent of Construction had been ineffectual and that the Treasury Department and Immigration Bureau had shown "recklessness in the handling of public money."[36]

THE HOMESTEAD STRIKE

The tremendous economic and industrial expansion after the Civil War created a demand for many new workers. As huge manufacturing firms arose and the use of machinery increased, however, the workday experience changed dramatically for most workers. Most continued to work six days a week, 12 or more hours a day, as was the custom. But the work was dirtier, physically harder and more exhausting, and far more dangerous. Accident rates expanded with the size of factories, although employers had no legal responsibility to compensate workers for severe injuries or even death. By the turn of the century some 30,000 workers were killed each year, and another quarter million were injured.

Other changes were also important. Machines began to set the pace of human work. They also made it possible to break complex jobs into simpler tasks. The work itself became more repetitive and more closely supervised, and highly skilled workers were increasingly demoted or eliminated. In addition, as companies increased in size, owners and supervisors ceased to have the personal connection to their workers that had distinguished smaller, independent concerns. The new entrepreneurs managed the new industrial workers like so much raw material—cutting wages and reducing hours whenever possible. They argued that doing so was part of free enterprise and that a worker just as freely accepted or rejected the job as offered.

Not surprisingly, American workers increasingly felt that they had lost their traditional dignity and freedom. They responded to the changes wrought by industrial expansion in the same way as businessmen had: by joining together. The first large national labor union, the Knights of Labor, had been founded in the 1870s. By 1890 it was in decline, its reputation tarred by violence. Another national union, the American Federation of Labor (AFL), founded in 1886 for skilled workers and led by Samuel Gompers, was on the rise. But in the early 1890s no union had the strength to match large employers, and even skilled workers lost many struggles to improve their lot.

In 1892, a significant strike occurred at Andrew Carnegie's Homestead Steel Works. Homestead, near Pittsburgh, was a town of 11,000 residents, 3,800 of whom were employed in Carnegie's steel mills. (In other words, almost every household had at least one employee there.) Many of the workers were highly skilled and owned modest homes. They held local government offices and considered themselves solid citizens. The vast majority were established Americans; fewer than 20 percent were new immigrants.

Carnegie's superintendent at Homestead was Henry Clay Frick. Frick decided that new steel-making technology made it possible to reduce the company's dependence on its highly skilled, expensive, and powerful workers—members of the Amalgamated Association of Iron, Steel, and Tin Workers, the largest union affiliated with the AFL. Frick forced workers to accept a series of wage decreases and finally announced he would no longer negotiate with the union. The union called a strike. "We do not propose that Andrew Carnegie's representatives shall bulldoze us," said John McLuckie, a steelworker, strike leader, and mayor of Homestead. "We have our homes in this town, we have our churches here, our societies and our cemeteries. We are bound to Homestead by all the ties that men hold dearest and most sacred."[37]

Frick erected 12-foot-high barbed wire fencing around the plant and shut it down on July 2, 1892. He engaged 300 armed Pinkerton Detective Agency guards to protect the strikebreakers he intended to hire. When the Pinkertons reached Homestead on river barges on July 6, they were met at the dock by a group of 10,000 steelworkers, their wives, and community sympathizers. Shots rang out, and a 12-hour battle ensued. Three Pinkertons and seven workers lay dead; many others were injured. But the Pinkertons were escorted out of town by the victorious strikers.

Big business, however, had grown powerful enough to bypass local control. At Frick's request the governor of Pennsylvania sent the entire 8,000-man state militia to keep order. Many strikers were arrested on various charges, although local juries refused to convict most of them. Then on July 23, Alexander Berkman, an anarchist from New York, attempted to assassinate Frick in his office. Although Berkman had no connection to the Homestead workers except in his own mind, the event destroyed public sympathy for the strike. By September, most departments of Carnegie's mill were operating, with strikebreakers for labor.

The strike dragged on, but on November 20 the union called an end to it. Frick sent a cable to Carnegie, who spent the strike in Scotland: "Our victory is now complete and most gratifying. Do not think we will ever have any serious labor trouble again." The largest and strongest skilled craft union in the nation had been crushed. Only some of the original workers were ever permitted to return to their jobs. For the next 20 years Carnegie's steelworkers worked brutally long hours for lower wages. The mill's profits skyrocketed, from $5 million in 1895 to more than $40 million in 1900.[38]

Shortly after the Homestead workers called off their strike, silver miners in Coeur d'Alene, Idaho, went on strike for similar reasons. Mine owners had installed machine drills, demoted skilled workers to shovelmen, and cut wages. Like Frick, the owners hired strikebreakers and called on the state militia and eventually the federal government for support. Armed fighting broke out and several hundred union workers were arrested, confined, and convicted on various charges.

SOCIAL CRITICS AND CRITIQUES IN THE EARLY 1890s

As conflicts and divisions in the new industrial society became more apparent and more alarming in the late 19th century, some social critics advanced far-reaching solutions—peaceful social cooperation, communal ownership, and even a classless society, ideas sometimes called utopian socialism. One such social critic was Edward Bellamy. His utopian novel *Looking Backward* (1888) was popular and influential with socially concerned, liberal-minded people. It inspired Nationalist Clubs throughout the nation in the early 1890s to promote Bellamy's vision of a cooperative society, in which businesses were nationalized and social problems like poverty and labor conflict were solved peacefully. Another movement was Christian Socialism. Adherents believed that socialism, or collective ownership, was inherent in Christian doctrine. A formal Christian Socialist organization was founded in Boston in 1889, although the movement had originated much earlier among Anglicans in England.

Many other critics and reformers also promoted the idea of a "cooperative commonwealth," a phrase coined by writer Laurence Gronlund in 1884. In a cooperative commonwealth, profits were returned to workers or were used for the good of society rather than the creation of individual wealth. The cooperative commonwealth idea greatly influenced the Populist movement, which promoted cooperative businesses owned jointly by the farmers or laborers who produced the goods. Another long-lived idea was the single tax, proposed by reformer Henry George in *Progress and Poverty* (1879). George argued that all social problems could be solved by taxing the extra appreciation in land values that was created by community growth, not by the efforts or improvements of the individual owner. Socially created value rightly belonged to the community, he argued, not to the private speculator.

Most of these social critics, however, usually continued to value traditional American beliefs like individual rights. Some even continued to value property rights and economic freedom, although they wanted the rights and benefits to be distributed more justly. Nonetheless, they argued that growing social problems could not be solved without fundamental changes in America's political and economic system. Their arguments were familiar to all reform minded Americans in the early 1890s, although most did not agree that such drastic changes were desirable.

The more radical doctrines of Marxism—socialism based in the ideas of Karl Marx and Frederich Engels—also gained adherents in the late 19th century as an industrial working class began to develop in America. (An industrial working class is a large group of workers who are employed for wages by the owners of large manufacturing businesses. Unlike independent craftsmen or employees of small workshops in the preindustrial era, they do not personally own the tools or machinery or other resources with which they work.) Marxism traveled to America with immigrants from Germany and other parts of Europe, where it was very familiar. Under capitalism, Marxists believed, a just society was not possible—partly because the large differences in wealth between workers and owners created such vast differences in political power. Marxists believed that conflict between the classes was inevitable and that it would eventually lead to the overthrow of capitalism, possibly by violence. Afterward, they believed, shared or collective ownership of the means of production would occur. In the early 1890s the small Socialist Labor Party, founded in the 1870s, was headed by Venezuelan-born Daniel De Leon. De Leon was a very orthodox Marxist and personally autocratic leader who believed that labor unions could not help the workingman.

THE ELECTION OF 1892

As the presidential election year dawned, angry farmers in the South and West were forming a third party, and the Democrats controlled Congress. Many Republican party leaders thought it was unwise for President Benjamin Harrison to run again as their candidate. The president was very independent, rarely dispensing the expected federal patronage to local political bosses, and was considered personally aloof. Nonetheless, when the Republicans met in convention in Minneapolis on June 7, they renominated Harrison on the first ballot. But they replaced the current vice president Levi P. Morton with a new candidate, Whitelaw Reid of New York.

The Democrats, who met in Chicago on June 21, nominated former president Grover Cleveland to run again as their candidate. As vice president they selected Adlai Stevenson of Illinois (father of the mid-20th-century presidential candidate of the same name). Cleveland, currently practicing law in New York, had won the popular vote by 100,000 in 1888 but lost the presidency in the electoral college. (In only two other American presidential elections, those of 1876 and 2000, has this situation occurred.) The former president was an obvious choice to oppose President Harrison, but southern and western Democrats worried that he would not appeal to angry farmers. Unlike many Democrats Cleveland wholeheartedly supported the gold standard and rejected free silver.

The new Populist Party was the last to hold its convention. On July 4 over 1,400 delegates streamed into Omaha. The preamble to the party's platform was written by Ignatius Donnelly of Minnesota, in urgent and sometimes apocalyptic prose: "We meet in the midst of a nation brought to the verge of moral, political, and material ruin," it opened. "The fruits of toil of millions are boldly stolen to build up colossal fortunes for a few, unprecedented in the history of mankind; and possessors of these, in turn, despise the Republic and endanger liberty." The platform, based on the Ocala demands of 1890, stressed three main points: an increased role for government in economic life, to counteract the monopolies of corporate capitalism; reform of money and the financial system, to end the control of eastern bankers; and reform of the political system to increase direct democracy. Populists wanted direct election of senators, direct primaries, and the initiative and referendum (which allow citizens themselves to propose legislation or vote to approve or disapprove legislation passed by officials). They also wanted a graduated income tax. The platform also contained several planks which Populists hoped would appeal to urban workers, whose support they hoped to gain.

The Populist platform outlined a genuinely radical, yet democratic, alternative to the economic and political system of 1892. The Populists did not reject either capitalism or industrialism. Instead, they wanted to reestablish democratic control over the nation's economic power. To do so, they believed, it was necessary for the national government to assume a new role in America, one far larger than it currently filled. To ensure that this expanded government would work properly, they also wanted to increase the average citizen's control over it by means of direct democracy. Many rank and file Populists probably did not fully embrace all of the more radical platform demands. ("The time has come," the platform famously stated, "when the railroad corporations will either own the people or the people must own the railroads.") But they did not believe that they were attacking traditional American beliefs and values—they believed, to the contrary, that they were restoring them. Although the platform explicitly spoke of class conflict, it drew from traditional American beliefs in free enterprise and in equal rights and from a long tradition of American social criticism.

Unfortunately for the Populists, they were not able to offer a strong alternative to the major party candidates in 1892. They settled for James B. Weaver, a former Union general residing in Iowa, who had run for president once before on the single-issue Greenback Party ticket. For vice president they nominated James G. Field, a former Confederate officer from Virginia.

Unlike either President Harrison or former president Cleveland, Weaver campaigned extensively. But the Populists faced formidable obstacles. In the South, Democrats fanned racial fears to keep whites loyal to the party. The Populist program did not appeal strongly to city-dwelling workers, who did not want to see food prices rise. Cleveland's victory was virtually assured after the untimely death of First Lady Caroline Scott Harrison on October 24, after which President Harrison withdrew completely from public appearances.

Cleveland won the election with 277 electoral votes to Harrison's 145. The Democrats also retained control of the House and won control of the Senate. But Weaver and the Populist Party tallied more than 1 million popular votes, the largest number to date for any third party in America. They carried Kansas and the silver-mining states of Colorado, Idaho, and Nevada and won the governor's office in Kansas and North Dakota.[39]

THE HAWAIIAN REVOLUTION

Since the early 19th century, American trading ships had stopped in at the Hawaiian Islands. Traders were followed by Christian missionaries and in the 1830s by permanent American and European planters, or landowners, who engaged primarily in sugar culture grown for export. Unfortunately, their coming repeated patterns of the European arrival in North America—a loss of indigenous population to disease and displacement of indigenous people from their traditional lands. Slowly, the traditional Native Hawaiian agricultural and fishing society was supplanted. In 1887 the United States was permitted to establish a naval base at Pearl Harbor.

In 1891, however, Queen Liliuokalani, an ardent Hawaiian nationalist, ascended the throne. She declared "Hawaii for the Hawaiians." On January 14, 1893, she abolished the Hawaiian constitution of 1887, which gave the vote only to men who owned a large amount of property. Her act also disbanded the legislature, which had many wealthy planters but few indigenous Hawaiians. Liliuokalani intended to provide a new constitution that would increase voting rights for Native Hawaiians. But to wealthy planters her suspension of the constitution was the last straw. At the time, their sugar farms were in dire straits because the McKinley Tariff of 1890 had put a tariff on Hawaiian sugar, which previously entered the United States duty-free. Many planters already secretly supported annexation to the United States. On January 17, they staged a coup and occupied government buildings. They were backed by a volunteer militia and 150 marines from the nearby warship *Boston*—authorized without White House approval by the U.S. minister to Hawaii, John S. Stevens. The queen surrendered under protest. Stevens raised the American flag on January 31 and declared the new Hawaiian republic a protectorate of the United States.

President Harrison, about to leave office, criticized Stevens's actions. But he decided to support a treaty of annexation, negotiated by a hasty delegation from the islands, mostly made up of American planters. When the new president, Grover Cleveland, and the newly elected, Democrat-controlled Senate took office, however, they refused to ratify the treaty. They began a series of investigations and negotiations that postponed annexation until 1898.

THE WORLD'S COLUMBIAN EXPOSITION OF 1893

Between the U.S. centennial in 1876 and World War I, Americans delighted in holding great expositions, sometimes called world's fairs. Expositions displayed continuing national growth and celebrated ever-increasing industrial and technological development—the "Progress of Civilization," as contemporaries often phrased it. Geared to adults, not children, expositions featured halls of machinery, new inventions, agricultural products, painting, sculpture, and exhibits by foreign nations.

The most important, influential, and wildly popular of these expositions was the Chicago World's Fair of 1893, officially known as the World's Columbian Exposition. It was planned to commemorate the 400-year anniversary of Christopher Columbus's arrival in the New World in 1492. It was officially dedicated in October 1892. In conjunction with the events, a National School Celebration was coordinated by the Boston-based children's magazine *Youth's Companion*. An editor, Francis Bellamy, wrote the Pledge of Allegiance in honor of the event, and the Federal Bureau of Education circulated it nationwide to schoolteachers. On October 12, 1892, more than 12 million public school children recited it for the first time. The Chicago fairgrounds opened to the public on May 1, 1893.

Many towns had competed fiercely for the honor of hosting the Columbian Exposition. All rivals were finally outbid by the civic, business, and monied leaders of Chicago, the second-largest city in America and determined to prove itself to the powerful East. Chicagoans reclaimed 700 acres of marshland along two miles of Lake Michigan shoreline. Director of Works Daniel H. Burnham, a prominent architect, organized architects and artists to create a new "city" of gleaming white buildings, as large as those in a real city. They were set in beautifully landscaped grounds designed by landscape architect Frederick Law Olmstead, Jr. A 60-foot Statue of the Republic by American sculptor Daniel Chester French presided over all. On a lagoon with its own wooded island was the much remarked Women's Building. A separate Board of Lady Managers had chosen M.I.T. graduate architect Sophia Hayden to design it; inside was a mural by the famous American impressionist painter Mary Cassatt.

In all, the fair had more than 400 buildings, designed in the Beaux-Arts style popular among cultured Americans at the time. Beaux Arts buildings resembled ornate classical temples, with many columns, statues, and other decorations that had symbolic meanings. Some forward-looking architects and critics—such as Louis Sullivan, who designed the fair's Transportation Building, or railroad station—did not approve of the style. But the public was awed. Everything—from the buildings and bridges down to statues and vases—was covered in a white plaster-like material resembling marble, quickly giving rise to the nickname "White City." At night the White City glowed with thousands of electric bulbs, the first large-scale demonstration of incandescent lamps for general lighting and an attraction in itself.

To the west of the White City, and carefully separated from it, was a mile-long recreational area called the Midway Plaisance. (It bequeathed the term *midway* to subsequent American fairs of all sizes.) There, visitors could find food and drink. They could view moving pictures in the kinetoscope unveiled by Thomas Edison or ride the huge, 2,000-passenger, 265-foot-tall mechanical wheel invented for the occasion by George Washington Ferris. They could also visit ethnic exhibits under the direction of the Department of Ethnology, such as a Persian Palace, an East Indian bazaar, a Hawaiian volcano, a Dahomey (Africa) Village—and the risqué belly dancer Little Egypt.

Throughout the year, the World's Congress Auxiliary, with 20 departments and 225 divisions, oversaw continual lectures and more than 130 national meetings of religious, educational, and intellectual organizations—including the American Historical Society, where Frederick Jackson Turner presented his frontier thesis. "When one sought rest at Chicago," remarked man of letters Henry Adams, "educational game started like rabbits from every building, and ran out of sight among thousands of its kind before one could mark its burrow." More than 300 women lectured at the World's Congress, including Susan B. Anthony, Jane Addams, and African-American novelist Francis Ellen Watkins Harper, who called the 1890s the Women's Era, a term that was much repeated.[40]

Antilynching crusader Ida B. Wells, however, declined to speak at the fair, to protest the scant representation of African-American life. African Americans were not excluded from attending the fair as visitors. They were, however, excluded from official representation in organizing the fair and even from the construction crews, despite petitions for a place on the committees or a separate building. Some African Americans independently organized a meeting day at the fair called Jubilee or Colored People's Day at which Frederick Douglass spoke, although black leaders disagreed over this approach. American Indians and their activities were displayed at the fair only in exhibitions designed by, and under control of, the ethnology department.

The Columbian Exposition caused a sensation among Americans that is hard to overestimate. Nearly 30 million people visited during its six-month run, most arriving by rail. "Sell the cookstove if necessary and come," wrote midwestern novelist Hamlin Garland to his parents. "You *must* see this fair."[41] The orderly and beautiful White City was an astonishing revelation to Americans of 1893—especially to those who were ambivalent about urban growth and alarmed by its problems. The real cities of 1893 were jumbled and ugly. They had grown as they would, the result of many individual decisions based on immediate utility. The White City, however, suggested that cities could not only achieve good public order but could even be beautiful, provided there was well-organized planning by experts and civic leaders. The Columbian Exposition gave rise to the City Beautiful movement, led by Burnham himself. Under its influence cities throughout America developed plans for better order and beautification in the coming decades.

Many commentators at the time, and many historians ever since, saw the fair as the symbol of a transitional moment in American history. Its grounds were planned to recapture the peace of an earlier, simpler America, yet its buildings were erected over skeletons of steel and its displays glorified machinery and technology. The fair opened on the brink of America's first industrial depression and continued as growing economic problems began to generate social unrest. It ended on October 28, 1893, one day after the five-term mayor of Chicago, Carter Harrison, was assassinated by a disappointed job seeker.

Depression

President Cleveland had barely taken office in March 1893 when the American economy began to shake and shudder. By the end of the year, it had collapsed into the most severe depression the nation had yet known, destined to last until 1897. "What a human downfall," wrote young Chicago reporter Ray Stannard Baker, "after the magnificence and prodigality of the World's Fair."[42]

The economic difficulties began in Britain and Europe. On May 6—five days after the Chicago World's Fair opened—the American stock market crashed. Railroads, the largest and most powerful industry in the nation, found they were overextended. One large railroad after another declared bankruptcy. The others ceased to prime the economy by ordering steel and other supplies—causing a domino effect of loss and failure in many associated companies. Farmers could not buy machinery because farm prices fell to even new lows. Banks began to call in their loans. "We are constantly hearing fresh evidence of the exceptional nature and severity of the industrial depression," wrote the *New York Commercial and Financial Advertiser* in August.[43] By the end of the year some 500 banks and 15,000 businesses, including more than 150 railroads, had failed. Even many factories that did not go out of business closed for a period, or cut back severely on the number of workers they employed, the hours they worked, and the wages they were paid. Unemployment rose drastically.

The causes of the depression were complex. But President Cleveland, like many other Americans, believed there was a simple explanation: the Sherman Silver Purchase Act. The president believed that ending the gold standard had undermined confidence. American gold reserves did in fact decline swiftly, as European investors demanded gold for American securities. Even ordinary Americans began to hoard it because the price of silver fell further and the silver in a silver-backed dollar was now really only worth about half a dollar in gold. The president called a special session of Congress to demand the Sherman Silver Purchase Act be repealed, despite the opposition of many in his own Democratic Party. While Congress pondered, a young Democratic congressman from Nebraska, William Jennings Bryan, held his colleagues in their seats for three hours with a passionate speech against repeal. With the help of Republican allies, however, the president prevailed and the Sherman Silver Purchase Act was repealed on November 1, 1893. But the Democratic Party suffered a very serious split over the issue, with many southerners and westerners voting against their own president.

CHRONICLE OF EVENTS

1890

Republican Benjamin Harrison is president; he became president in 1888 by vote of the electoral college, although incumbent president Grover Cleveland won the popular vote. The Republicans also have majorities in the House and Senate.

The population of the United States is 63 million. Population has doubled since 1860, when it was 31 million. Urban dwellers are 35 percent of the total population; in 1860 they were 20 percent. The North is more heavily urbanized than the South. New York, Chicago, and Philadelphia have populations of more than 1 million.

The director of the census announces that the American frontier has closed.

The Indian Ghost Dance ritual developed by Wovoka, a Nevada Paiute (Numu), spreads rapidly across the western plains.

The United States leads all other nations of the world in the value of the manufactured goods it produces. Tremendous economic growth since the Civil War has produced great new wealth, but industrialism has introduced new conditions and more uncertainty into the lives of workers. Some Americans are concerned about the newly evident divisions between rich and poor.

The new city residents have overwhelmed many city services in some places, and city neighborhoods are becoming increasingly divided by economic status.

The United Mine Workers of America (UMW) is founded from coal miners' locals, with connections to both the old Knights of Labor and the newer American Federation of Labor (AFL).

The first state law limiting men's working hours in private industry is passed in Ohio; it applies to railroads, where it is widely known that extremely long shifts increase accident rates.

Immigration is heavy. The source of European immigration is shifting, and about 36 percent is now from southern and eastern Europe. Historians call the movement from southern and eastern Europe the *new immigration* in distinction to the *old immigration* from northern and western Europe.

Jacob Riis's *How the Other Half Lives: Studies Among the Tenements of New York* is published, shocking many Americans. It is the first prominent example of investigative and exposé journalism later called muckraking.

Young, college-educated men and women are beginning to found settlement houses in the slums; there will be more than 400 by 1910.

In the West, San Francisco has a population of almost 300,000 people and is the region's financial, commercial, and manufacturing center. San Francisco and other West Coast cities are home to many Chinese people, who have established distinctive neighborhoods called Chinatowns. The Chinese Exclusion Act of 1882, however, has banned additional immigration for 10 years and prevented Chinese already in the United States from becoming citizens.

In the New South, industry has grown, but the region remains primarily agricultural. Birmingham, Alabama, which did not exist in 1879, has almost 40,000 people; it is the center of the New South's iron and steel industry.

Farmers are suffering as agricultural prices, increasingly dependent on world markets, continue to drop. Many have become debtors; especially in the South, many continue to lose their land, and tenant farming is on the rise.

Mississippi passes a new suffrage amendment intended to prevent black men from voting, although it also disenfranchises some poor whites. It does not mention race to avoid conflict with the Fourteenth Amendment. Instead it imposes a poll tax and a literacy requirement to be judged by local examiners. Within the next two decades many more southern states will follow suit.

The Supreme Court rules in *Louisville, New Orleans, and Texas Railroad v. Mississippi* that a state can require segregated transportation facilities. Laws requiring separation of the races in trains and many other facilities, called Jim Crow laws, will spread throughout the South after this date.

The Afro-American League, a forerunner of the NAACP, is organized.

A few African Americans emigrate to Africa, but far more move west, especially to Oklahoma, where some found all-black towns.

Women begin to found national organizations, such as the General Federation of Women's Clubs and the Daughters of the American Revolution (DAR). The Women's Christian Temperance Union (WCTU), a wide-ranging reform organization with chapters in every state of the nation, remains by far the largest women's group.

The New York Consumers' League, a women's group, is founded to work for improved conditions for sales clerks.

The two largest women's suffrage organizations merge to form the National American Woman Suffrage Association (NAWSA) and continue state level campaigns for suffrage.

America renews interest in developing a powerful new navy, spurred by Captain Alfred Thayer Mahan's *The Influence of Sea Power Upon History, 1660–1783.*

Architect Louis Sullivan's nine-story Wainwright Building in St. Louis, the first influential skyscraper, is completed.

January 25: Nellie Bly, a journalist for the *New York World,* arrives back in Manhattan after her breakneck 72-day trip around the world.

February 3: The Supreme Court in *Davis v. Beason* upholds the Idaho Test Oath Act, which effectively denies suffrage to all Mormons on the basis of the church's belief in polygamy,

April 18: Castle Garden, the old New York State immigration receiving center at the tip of Manhattan, closes after a Congressional investigation. Until January 1892 immigrants are processed at the Barge Office.

May 2: Oklahoma (formerly Indian Territory) becomes a territory.

Summer: Farmers Alliances throughout the Midwest and West work to form a third party to influence the November elections; in the South white alliance members attempt to gain influence in local Democratic politics.

June 27: The Dependent Pensions Act passes, extending benefits to Union veterans.

July 2: Congress passes the Sherman Anti-Trust Act in response to rising public anger about economic concentration and monopolies. Over the next decade it will be used most effectively as a weapon against labor unions, not business combinations.

July 3: Idaho is admitted as the 43rd state.

July 10: Wyoming is admitted as the 44th state, the first and only state granting women full suffrage.

August 19: Chickamauga, the first Civil War battlefield to be protected, is established as a National Military Park.

September: Wilford Woodruff, president of the Mormon church, urges his membership to observe civil marriage laws forbidding polygamy.

October 1: Yosemite National Park is established surrounding the Yosemite Valley reserve controlled by the state of California. The McKinley Tariff is passed.

November: In the midterm elections, Populists gain surprising victories in state legislatures and congressional elections throughout the Midwest; the South elects many pro–Farmers' Alliance Democrats. Nationally, American voters register their disapproval of the Billion Dollar Congress, reducing the Republican majority.

December: National Farmers Alliance & Industrial Union representatives meet in Ocala, Florida, and issue a platform of 12 demands to alleviate agricultural distress.

December 14: Government officials at the Standing Rock Indian Agency order the Indian police to arrest Sitting Bull, the revered Lakota chief; they believe he is using the Ghost Dance to encourage resistance among his people. During an ensuing scuffle shots ring out; Sitting Bull, his son Crow Foot, six other supporters, and six Indian police are killed.

December 29: The Seventh Calvary pursues 350 Miniconjou Lakota Indians to Wounded Knee Creek, South Dakota. The Indian band attempts to surrender, but when a shot is fired U.S. soldiers mow down some 200 men, women, and children in the snow. The massacre at Wounded Knee is the last major armed conflict between

The Wainwright Building in St. Louis introduced a new style for tall city buildings in 1890. Architect Louis Sullivan emphasized its height and made no attempt to disguise its use for business. *(Library of Congress, Historic American Buildings Survey, HABS MO,96-SALU,49-4)*

the Plains Indians and the U.S. government and symbolizes the end of the traditional Indian way of life in the American West.

1891

Queen Liliuokalani ascends the throne of Hawaii and declares "Hawaii for the Hawaiians."

March 3: In the most comprehensive immigration legislation to date, Congress decisively establishes control of immigration by the federal government. The act also establishes a superintendent of immigration and inspection stations along the border of Mexico and Canada.

The Forest Reserve Act authorizes set-asides that are the beginnings of the national forest system.

March 14: In New Orleans 11 Italians are lynched by an angry mob after a jury acquits them of murdering the chief of police.

May: Farmers Alliances and other reform groups meet in Cincinnati and endorse the idea of a national People's Party. Soon after, the term *Populist* comes into use, probably coined from the Latin word *populus,* or people.

May 15: Pope Leo XIII issues an encyclical, *Rerum Novarum,* condemning the exploitation of labor but also condemning socialism.

1892

Ida Wells Barnett begins an international antilynching movement when three black businessmen are lynched in Memphis, where she edits the *Free Press,* an African-American newspaper.

In New York, the City Club is founded to work for city government reform by prominent, reform-minded people such as August Belmont, John Jacob Astor, Cornelius Vanderbilt, J. P. Morgan, and Theodore Roosevelt. Within two years they will have seen to the establishment of Good Government Clubs in almost every part of the city, working class as well as affluent.

January: President Harrison threatens to declare war on Chile over an attack on American sailors in a saloon. War is averted at the last minute.

January 1: Ellis Island opens to process immigrants arriving through the Port of New York.

January 18: The Supreme Court declares the immigration act of 1891 "constitutional and valid" (*Nishimura Ekiu v. United States*).

February 22: Farmers Alliances meet again at St. Louis. Candidates adjourn to mobilize for a national nominating convention, with southerners in agreement.

May 5: Congress passes the Geary Act, extending Chinese exclusion for another 10 years and requiring all Chinese laborers to obtain a certificate proving the legality of their residence.

June 4: John Muir and others meet in the office of a San Francisco attorney, officially founding the Sierra Club, devoted to protecting the Sierra Nevada and other Pacific Coast natural areas.

June 7: The Republican convention convenes and renominates President Harrison, with Whitelaw Reid of New York as vice president.

June 21: The Democratic convention convenes and nominates former president Grover Cleveland, with Adlai Stevenson of Illinois as vice president.

July 2: Henry Clay Frick closes Andrew Carnegie's Homestead Steel Works because members of the powerful Amalgamated Association of Iron, Steel, and Tin Workers have called a strike. Frick engages 300 armed Pinkerton Detective Agency guards to protect the strikebreakers he intends to hire.

July 4: More than 1,400 Farmers Alliance and reform delegates meet in Omaha for the first convention of the Populist Party, officially called the People's Party, U.S.A. General James B. Weaver is nominated for president and James G. Field for vice president. The party's platform demands that government assume a larger role in counteracting big business on behalf of the people, as well as more direct democracy, money reform, and other issues.

July 6: The Pinkertons reach Homestead; they are met by a group of 10,000 steelworkers, their wives, and community sympathizers. Shots are fired; 12-hour battle ensues. Three Pinkertons and seven workers are killed, but the victorious strikers drive the Pinkertons out of town. The governor of Pennsylvania sends 8,000 state militia to reopen the plant.

July 23: Alexander Berkman, an anarchist from New York, attempts to assassinate Frick. Although he is not associated with the Homestead strikers, the event destroys public sympathy for them.

September: Most departments of Carnegie's Homestead steel mill are operating, with strikebreakers for labor.

October 12: In honor of the 400th anniversary of Columbus's arrival in the New World, 12 million public school children recite the Pledge of Allegiance for the first time. It has been composed for the occasion by magazine editor Francis Bellamy.

November: Cleveland wins the election; Democrats also retain control of the House and Senate. Weaver and the Populist Party tally more than 1 million popular votes, the largest number to date for any third party. Populists carry Kansas and the silver-mining states of Colorado, Idaho, and Nevada and win the governor's office in Kansas and North Dakota.

November 20: The union calls an end to the Homestead strike. The largest skilled craft union in the nation has been crushed.

1893

As new immigrants prove slow to adapt to American ways, nativism is on the rise. The anti-Catholic American Protective Association (APA) has half a million members.

In Chicago Florence Kelley of Hull-House establishes a children's playground, a new innovation in urban living. About the same time Lillian Wald opens a playground in New York at Henry Street Settlement. Soon after, small playgrounds appeared at other settlements in other large cities.

The Catholic Women's League and the National Council of Jewish Women are founded.

After a successful campaign by women's suffrage advocates, unsuccessfully opposed by the liquor industry, Colorado becomes the second state to give women the vote.

The Ohio Anti-Saloon League is founded at Oberlin; it is the forerunner of the National Anti-Saloon League organized two years later.

New Zealand becomes the first nation to grant women the right to vote.

January 4: President Harrison grants amnesty to Mormons who have abstained from polygamy since November 1890.

January 14: Queen Liliuokalani abolishes the Hawaiian constitution.

January 17: Hawaiian planters stage a palace coup, backed by a volunteer militia and 150 marines from the nearby warship *Boston,* authorized (without White House approval) by the U.S. minister to Hawaii, John S. Stevens. The queen surrenders under protest.

January 31: Stevens raises the American flag and declares Hawaii a protectorate of the United States.

February: President Harrison submits to the Senate a treaty to annex Hawaii.

March 3: As part of an Indian appropriations bill, the Dawes Commission is established to negotiate the transfer of lands from tribal to individual ownership with the Five Civilized Tribes of Oklahoma.

March 4: President Grover Cleveland takes office.

May 1: The World's Columbian Exposition, or Chicago World's Fair, opens to great public acclaim.

May 3: The Supreme Court upholds the Chinese Exclusion Act (*Fong Yue Ting v. United States*).

May 6: The stock market collapses, setting off a wave of business failures and the worst depression in American history to date.

July: A House investigating committee concludes that the wooden buildings on Ellis Island are badly constructed and that federal supervisors were remiss in oversight of construction.

July 12: Frederick Jackson Turner delivers his influential essay "The Significance of the Frontier in American History" to the American Historical Association meeting in Chicago.

October 28: The Chicago World's Fair ends, one day after the mayor of Chicago is assassinated by a disappointed job seeker.

November 1: Congress repeals the Sherman Silver Purchase Act at President Cleveland's insistence. The Democratic president believes it has caused the depression; his party suffers a serious split over the issue.

November 3: Congress again strengthens the Chinese Exclusion Act.

December 18: President Cleveland withdraws the Hawaiian annexation treaty.

EYEWITNESS TESTIMONY

. . . on the stock of my rifle is one hundred and twenty-six notches, each one representing a fine buffalo that has fallen to my own hand, while some I have killed with the knife and 45 colts, I forgot to cut a notch for. Buffalo hunting, a sport for kings, thy time has passed. Where once they roamed by the thousands now rises the chimney and the spire, while across their once peaceful path now thunders the iron horse, awakening the echoes far and near with bell and whistle, where once could only be heard the sharp crack of the rifle or the long doleful yelp of the coyote. . . .

With the march of progress came the railroad and no longer were we called upon to follow the long horned steers, or mustangs on the trail, while the immense cattle ranges, stretching away in the distance as far as the eye could see, now began to be dotted with cities and towns and the cattle industry which once held a monopoly in the west, now had to give way to the industry of the farm and the mill. To us wild cowboys of the range, used to the wild and unrestricted life of the boundless plains, the new order of things did not appeal, and many of us became disgusted and quit the wild life for the pursuits of our more civilized brother. I was among that number and in 1890 I bid farewell to the life which I had followed for over twenty years. . . .

Deadwood Dick, aka Nat Love, famous African-American cowboy, 1890, in Love, Life and Adventures *(1968), pp. 129–30.*

When you get home you must make a dance to continue five days. Dance four successive nights, and the last night keep up the dance until the morning of the fifth day, when all must bathe in the river and then disperse to their homes. You must all do in the same way.

I, [Wovoka], love you all, and my heart is full of gladness for the gifts you have brought me. When you get home I shall give you a good cloud which will make you feel good. I give you a good spirit and give you all good paint. I want you to come again in three months, some from each tribe there.

There will be a good deal of snow this year and some rain. In the fall there will be such a rain as I have never given you before.

Grandfather says, when your friends die you must not cry. You must not hurt anybody or do harm to anyone. You must not fight. Do right always. It will give you satisfaction in life. . . .

Do not tell the white people about this. Jesus is now upon the earth. He appears like a cloud. The dead are all alive again. I do not know when they will be here; maybe this fall or in the spring. When the time comes there will be no more sickness and everyone will be young again.

Do not refuse to work for the whites and do not make any trouble with them until you leave them. When the earth shakes do not be afraid. It will not hurt you.

I want you to dance every six weeks. Make a feast at the dance and have food that everybody may eat. Then bathe in the water. That is all. You will receive good words again from me some time. Do not tell lies.

Wovoka, Paiute religious leader, to the Cheyenne and Arapaho, 1890, as recorded by Arapaho Caspar Edson, in Mooney, "Ghost-Dance Religion" (1896), p. 781.

Thus arose a crisis, a seeming *impasse.* What was to do? Architects made attempts at solutions by carrying the outer spans of flood loads on cast columns next to the masonry piers, but this method was of small avail, and of limited application as to height. . . .

As a rule, inventions—which are truly solutions—are not arrived at quickly. They may seem to appear suddenly, but the groundwork has usually been long in preparing. . . .

So in this instance, the Chicago activity in erecting high buildings finally attracted the attention of the local sales managers of Eastern rolling mills; and their engineers were set at work. The mills for some time past had been rolling those structural shapes that had long been in use in bridge work. Their own ground work thus was prepared. It was a matter of vision in salesmanship based upon engineering imagination and technique. Thus the idea of a steel frame which should carry *all* the load was tentatively presented to Chicago architects.

The passion to *sell* is the impelling power in American life. Manufacturing is subsidiary and adventitious. But selling must be based on a semblance of service—the satisfaction of a need. The need was there, the capacity to satisfy was there, but contact was not there. Then came the flash of imagination which saw the single thing. The trick was turned; and there swiftly came into being something new under the sun. For the true steel-frame structure stands unique. . . .

. . . [T]he lofty steel frame makes a powerful appeal to the architectural imagination where there is any. . . . The appeal and the inspiration lie, of course, in the element of loftiness, in the suggestion of slenderness and aspiration, the soaring quality as of a thing rising from the earth as a unitary utterance.

Architect Louis Sullivan describes the birth of the steel-frame skyscraper among Chicago architects, ca. 1890, in his Autobiography of an Idea *(1926), pp. 311–13.*

When once I asked the agent of a notorious Fourth Ward alley how many people might be living in it I was told: One hundred and forty families, one hundred Irish, thirty-eight Italian, and two that spoke the German tongue. Barring the agent herself, there was not a native-born individual in the court. The answer was characteristic of the cosmopolitan character of lower New York, very nearly so of the whole of it, wherever it runs to alleys and courts. One may find for the asking an Italian, a German, a French, African, Spanish, Bohemian, Russian, Scandinavian, Jewish, and Chinese colony. Even the Arab, who peddles "holy earth" from the Battery as a direct importation from Jerusalem, has his exclusive preserves at the lower end of Washington Street. . . . A map of the city, colored to designate nationalities, would show more stripes than on the skin of a zebra, and more colors than any rainbow. The city on such a map would fall into two great halves, green for the Irish prevailing in the West Side tenement districts, and blue for the Germans on the East Side. But intermingled with these ground colors would be an odd variety of tints that would give the whole the appearance of an extraordinary crazy-quilt.

Jacob Riis, How the Other Half Lives *(1890), pp. 21, 25.*

I counted the other day the little ones, up to ten years or so, in a Bayard Street tenement that for a yard has a triangular space in the centre with sides fourteen or fifteen feet long, just room enough for a row of ill smelling closets [outhouses] at the base of the triangle and a hydrant at the apex. There was about as much light in this "yard" as in the average cellar. I gave up my self-imposed task in despair when I had counted one hundred and twenty-eight in forty families. . . . I have in mind an alley—an inlet rather to a row of rear tenements—that is either two or four feet wide according as the wall of the crazy old building that

The gap between rich and poor was becoming increasingly evident in America in the 1890s. Jacob Riis took this photo of a tenement family in "Poverty Gap," a tenement block in New York City on West 28th Street near the river. *(Library of Congress, Prints and Photographs Division, LC-USZ62-25686)*

gives on it bulges out or in. I tried to count the children that swarmed there, but could not. Sometimes I have doubted that anybody knows just how many there are about. Bodies of drowned children turn up in the rivers right along in summer whom no one seems to know anything about. When last spring some workmen, while moving a pile of lumber on a North River pier, found under the last plank the body of a little lad crushed to death, no one had missed a boy, though his parents afterward turned up. The truant officer assuredly does not know, though he spends his life trying to find out, somewhat illogically, perhaps, since the department that employs him admits that thousands of poor children are crowded out of the schools year by year for want of room.

Jacob Riis, How the Other Half Lives *(1890), pp. 179–80.*

In 1890 we had another crop failure. No rain to speak of. How the hot winds did blow and there was nothing raised but a little dried up fodder. Then we wondered again, how we would get thru the winter. But there was always some way provided. In 91 and 92 we had good crops, lots of good corn, but no market for it; 10-12-15 cents a bushel. As fuel was scarce, a good many burned corn that year. But it was very little corn we ever burnt. It seemed wicked to burn something that was needed for food.

Eva Hendrickson Klepper, a Nebraska pioneer farm wife, describes 1890 to 1892, in her memoirs, Jensen, ed., With These Hands *(1981), pp. 134–35.*

This is a nation of inconsistencies. The Puritans fleeing from oppression became oppressors. We fought England for our liberty and put chains on four million of blacks. We wiped out slavery and our tariff laws and national banks began a system of white wage slavery worse than the first.

Wall Street owns the country. It is no longer a government of the people, by the people, and for the people, but a government of Wall Street, by Wall Street, and for Wall Street.

The great common people of this country are slaves, and monopoly is the master. The West and South are bound and prostrate before the manufacturing East.

Money rules, and our Vice-President is a London banker. Our laws are the output of a system which clothes rascals in robes and honesty in rags.

. . . The politicians said we suffered from overproduction. Overproduction, when 10,000 little children, so statistics tell us, starve to death every year in the United States, and over 100,000 shopgirls in New York are forced to sell their virtue for the bread their niggardly wages deny them. . . .

Mary C. Lease, Populist orator, speech to Kansas farmers, 1890, in Freeman, Who Built America?, *vol. 2 (1992), p. 147.*

Lien laws were enacted in all the Southern States to help [white farmers] as well as the Negroes. The humane intent of these laws was to furnish a basis of credit. The man who had land could give a lien on that. Those who had live stock only could get their year's supplies on this security. Those who had neither land nor live stock could rent land and a mule, and could give a lien on the prospective crop to secure the landowner, and the merchant for the goods bought. This last lien enabled the Negroes to be independent of the white man's supervision. . . .

The share plan was a favorite with the Negroes. They were their own managers. The employer furnished the land, the mule, and necessary farm tools. He was responsible to the merchant for the supplies furnished the share worker. He generally received half the cotton and corn made by the Negro. The corn was in many cases less than the quantity furnished by the employer and consumed by the plow animal during the year.

How did this plan work? Generally speaking, it neither benefitted the Negro nor the white farmer. . . .

Mississippian Charles H. Otken describes sharecropping, ca. 1890, in his The Ills of the South *(1894), pp. 38–50.*

The Southern negro is in the country, not in the cities, and to know their wants, wishes, desires, and needs, you must go, among them, mingle with them, and hear and see for yourself[.] And when you say they have no desire to go to Africa, I say, who know the real condition of our race as well as any man who lives, a million at least of them desire to go somewhere. They want freedom, manhood, liberty, patriotism, or the right to protect themselves. At least a million of us have found out that this nation is a failure, that it either cannot or has no disposition to protect the rights of a man who is not white. Not a court in the nation has given a decision in favor of the black man in twelve years. The Supreme Court is an organized mob against the negro, and every subordinate court in the land has caught its spirit.

African emigration proponent Rev. Henry McNeal Turner, address given in Washington, D.C., 1890, in Boyd, ed., Autobiography of a People *(2000), p. 166.*

We were also early impressed with the curious isolation of many of the immigrants; an Italian woman once expressed her pleasure in the red roses that she saw at one of our receptions in surprise that they had been "brought so fresh all the way from Italy." She would not believe for an instant that they had been grown in America. She said that she had lived in Chicago for six years and had never seen any roses, whereas in Italy she had seen them every summer in great profusion. During all that time, of course, the woman had lived within ten blocks of a florist's window; she had not been more than a five-cent car ride away from the public parks; but she had never dreamed of faring forth for herself, and no one had taken her. Her conception of America had been the untidy street in which she lived and had made her long struggle to adapt herself to American ways.

Jane Addams describes her early experiences at Hull-House, ca. 1890, Twenty Years at Hull-House, *pp. 100–11.*

Section 241. Every male inhabitant of this state, except idiots, insane persons, and Indians not taxed, who is a citizen of the United States, twenty-one years old and upwards, who has resided in this state two years, and one year in the election district, or in the incorporated city or town in which he offers to vote, and who is duly registered, and who has never been convicted of bribery, burglary, theft, arson, obtaining money or goods under false pretenses, perjury, forgery, embezzlement, or bigamy, and who has paid, on or before the first day of February on the year in which he shall offer to vote, all taxes which may have been legally required of him, and which he has had an opportunity of paying according to law, for the two preceding years, and who shall produce to the officers holding the election satisfactory evidence that he has paid said taxes, is declared to be a qualified elector. . . .

Section 243. A uniform poll-tax of two dollars, to be used in aid of the common schools . . . is hereby imposed on every male inhabitant of this state between the ages of twenty-one and sixty years, except certain physically handicapped persons. . . .

Section 244. On and after the first day of January, A.D. 1892, every elector shall, in addition to the foregoing qualifications, be able to read any section of the constitution of this state; or he shall be able to understand the same when read to him, or give a reasonable interpretation thereof. . . .

Constitution of Mississippi, Article 12, passed 1890, Annotated Code . . . of Mississippi *(1892), p. 80.*

Section 1. Be it enacted by the General Assembly of the State of Louisiana, That all railway companies carrying passengers in their coaches in this State, shall provide equal but separate accommodations for the white, and colored races, by providing two or more passenger coaches for each passenger train, or by dividing the passenger coaches by a partition so as to secure separate accommodations; *provided* that this section shall not be construed to apply to street railroads. No person or persons, shall be permitted to occupy seats in coaches, other than the ones assigned to them on account of the race they belong to.

Section 2. Be it further enacted . . . , That the officers of such passenger trains shall have power and are hereby required to assign each passenger to the coach or compartment used for the race to which such passenger belongs; any passenger insisting on going into a coach or compartment to which by race he does not belong, shall be liable to a fine of twenty-five dollars or in lieu thereof to imprisonment for a period of not more than twenty days in the parish prison and any offi-cer of any railroad insisting on assigning a passenger to a coach or compartment other than the one set aside for the race to which said passenger belongs shall be liable to a fine of twenty-five dollars or in lieu thereof to imprisonment . . . ; and should any passenger refuse to occupy the coach or compartment to which he or she is assigned by the officer of such railway, said officer shall have power to refuse to carry such passenger on his train. . . .

Section 3. Be it further enacted . . . , [T]hat nothing in this act shall be construed as applying to nurses attending children of the other race. . . .

Acts of Louisiana, 1890, no. 111, pp. 152–54, reprinted in Green, ed., Equal Protection, *pp. 152–53.*

Somebody must say these things while there are still living witnesses to the social sequences of the period. What was known as 'hard liquor' begot violence in drinkers, and excited what was, for the women who made it, a violence of resistance. . . . I remember a pretty German woman who used to bring her three children to our house to be left until their father recovered from 'one of his spells.' I recall how she came one night with a great bloody bruise on her face, and my mother insisting on treating it with some sort of embrocation, and the unwiped tears on my mother's face while the two women kept up between them the pre-tense of a blameless accident. I remember the first woman who was allowed to speak in our church on the right of women to refuse to bear children to habitual drunkards. . . .

Autobiography of novelist Mary Austin, whose mother was a WCTU leader in Illinois, ca. 1890, Earth Horizon, *pp. 142, 145.*

She was slight and pretty, full of patience and tact unending and great charm for women. She had courage, and, within certain widely accepted limits of Protestantism, great liber-ality of thought. She had a statesmanly talent, and political intuition of wider range and greater spontaneity than any American woman I have ever known. . . . It was shown in the way in which she so successfully tied up the Union with other forward movements among women, or unob-trusively included them, or fended them off. A great many of her following were opposed on principle to Woman Suffrage, fought all attempts to ally it with the Woman's Christian Temperance Union. And it was as good as a play to watch the way in which Frances Willard circumvented and overrode them.

Mary Austin describes Frances Willard, ca. 1890, in her Earth Horizon, *pp. 142, 145.*

In Georgia, Mr. Grady's own state, the Negro's real wealth accumulated since the war, is $20 million. Its population of Negroes is 725,132. Twenty millions of dollars divided

Frances Willard, an astute organizer and politician, served as president of the Women's Christian Temperance Union (WCTU) from 1879 until her death in 1898. Under her leadership, the WCTU engaged in many reform activities. *(Library of Congress, Prints and Photographs Division, LC-USZ61-790)*

among that number will give to each person $27.58. Upon the same basis of calculation the total wealth of the Negro in the 15 Southern states, including the District of Columbia, is $146,189,834. The colored population of these states is 5,305,149. It seems an enormous sum. In those 15 states the Negro has, by the exceedingly friendly aid of their best friends, amassed a fortune of $1 a year. . . .

Again Mr. Grady says of the three essentials, iron, cotton, wood, that region has easy control. Make the list of essentials four, and add unpaid colored labor. He also says in cotton they have a fixed monopoly; in iron a proven supremacy; in timber, the reserved supply of the republic. They have also the Negro, the foundation of their institutions.

Rev. Joshua A. Brockett of St. Paul's A.M.E. Church, Cambridge, Massachusetts, responds to Henry Grady's famous New South speech in Boston, Philadelphia Christian Recorder, *January 16, 1890, reprinted in Adler, ed.,* Negro in American History *(1969), pp. 167–70.*

Only when a goodly rate of speed was attained was Miss Bly summoned to enter the special [train] car in which her journey was to be completed. There was cheering and applause. Everybody cheered. Old friends and newspaper co-laborers shook her hand, and she smiled glad, jolly smiles. Her sunburned face took on a new glow of delight. The mother awaited her in the state room, and through the throng of admiring friends she went to get the mother's welcoming kiss and rest in the maternal arms.

The door opened and all the men stepped back from it. That meeting was a sacred thing.

"Oh, Nellie!"

"Mother! I'm so glad!" Then the door closed. The rest of it was their secret and none would molest them.

Nellie Bly reaches Philadelphia, New York World, *January 25, 1890, quoted in Kroeger,* Nelly Bly *(1994), p. 172.*

The first amendment to the constitution, in declaring that congress shall make no law respecting the establishment of religion or forbidding the free exercise thereof, was intended to allow every one under the jurisdiction of the United States to entertain such notions respecting his relations to his Maker and the duties they impose as may be approved by his judgment and conscience, and to exhibit his sentiments in such form of worship as he may think proper, not injurious to the equal rights of others, and to prohibit legislation for the support of any religious tenets, or the modes of worship of any sect. The oppressive measures adopted, and the cruelties and punishments inflicted, by the governments of Europe for many ages, to compel parties to conform, in their religious beliefs and modes of worship, to the views of the most numerous sect . . . led to the adoption of the amendment in question. It was never intended or supposed that the amendment could be invoked as a protection against legislation for the punishment of acts inimical to the peace, good order, and morals of society. . . . However free the exercise of religion may be, it must be subordinate to the criminal laws of the country, passed with reference to actions regarded by general consent as properly the subjects of punitive legislation. . . .

Supreme Court Justice Stephen Field, delivering the opinion of the court in Davis v. Beason, *which upholds the disenfranchisement of Idaho Mormons, February 3, 1890, 133 US 333.*

I am unalterably opposed to female suffrage in any form. It can only result in the unsexing and degrading of the womanhood of America. It is emphatically a reform against nature. . . . I have no doubt that in Wyoming to-day women vote in as many [different] precincts as they can reach on horseback or on foot after changing their frocks and bustles. . . .

—*Representative Joseph Washington, Democrat of Tennessee*

I like a woman who is a woman and appreciates the sphere to which God and the Bible have assigned her. I do not like a man-woman. She may be intelligent and full of learning, but when she assumes the performance of the duties and functions assigned by nature to man, she becomes rough and tough and can no longer be the object of affection.

—*Representative William Oates, Democrat of Alabama*

House debate over admission of Wyoming as a women's suffrage state, March 1890, quoted in Harper, et al., eds., History of Woman Suffrage, *vol. 4, p. 999.*

The common statement that plural marriage debases husbands, degrades wives, and brutalizes offspring, is false. . . .

My father, Brigham Young, had fifty-six living children, all born healthy, bright, and without "spot or blemish" in body or mind. Thirty-one of the number were girls; twenty-five were boys. Seven died in infancy, three in childhood, seven more since reaching maturity. What bright memories we cherish of the happy times we spent beneath our father's tender watch-care, supplemented by the very sweetest mother-love ever given to mortals! . . . How pleasant were the seasons of evening prayer when ten or twelve mothers with their broods of children, together with the various old ladies and orphans who dwelt under the sheltering care of this roof, came from every nook and corner of the quaint, old-fashioned, roomy house at the sound of the prayer-bell. . . .

Defense of polygamy, "Family Life Among the Mormons, by A Daughter of Brigham Young," North American Review, *vol. 150 (March 1890), pp. 340–41.*

I have rejoiced to-day in the *manyness* of us more than in anything else. To-day I felt the joy of the vast intellectual wealth in us, and it has been like a shock of electricity. . . . We must learn sympathy, learn unity, learn the great lesson of organization. I am sure we never have begun to dream of what will yet appear. This club and other clubs reach out into the new life for women. It is certainly a new life. These clubs have made a new world, and we have got to adapt ourselves to it, and to educate the world around us.

Mary Eastman of the New England Woman's Club, address to the first meeting of the General Federation of Women's Clubs, March 20, 1890, in Wood, History of the General Federation, *p. 33.*

Legislation for protection [a protective tariff] is based upon the fundamental principle that the government has the right in some manner to take, without direct compensation, from one man or class of men part of his or their earnings and by law bestow it upon another man or class of men. It is precisely the basal principle of slavery. Slavery took by law all of a man's labor, returning only a livelihood measured by the humanity, the self-interest, and the will of the master. The protective tariff takes by law so much of a man's labor as is necessary to pay the difference caused by that tariff in the cost of necessary articles.

Representative William C. P. Breckinridge, Democrat of Kentucky, "Free Trade or Protection," North American Review, *vol. 150 (April 1890), p. 507.*

Heretofore the individual member [of the House of Representatives], of his own sweet will, has had the right to move to adjourn, to move to fix a day to adjourn to, to move for a recess, and to make any other motion he saw fit. He could do it even to the extent of stopping public business, and if seconded by one-fifth, or 20 per cent, of the members present, he could set in motion the roll-call, and he and his friends needed to rise in their places but twice in an hour, and the business of 60,000,000 people would be deadlocked, and four-fifths, or 80 per cent, of the members must look on idle, and useless, and paralyzed. Or if, on bill day, he wanted to wear out the day, he could put in the Revised Statutes for reenactment and have them read, and nobody could say him nay....

The right to walk in the street is guaranteed to everybody. That is what streets are for. Liberty of speech is a birth-right. Yet, if a party of swashbucklers should lock arms, and with loud and boisterous talk, or even in perfect silence, should sweep all other passengers off the sidewalk, how long would liberty of speech and the right of every citizen to walk the streets protect the band from the police?

Representative Thomas B. Reed, Republican from Maine and Speaker of the House, "Reforms Needed in the House," North American Review, *vol. 150 (May 1890), pp. 540–41.*

It would be difficult to put into words the hardships of this campaign ... in a new State through the hottest and dryest summer on record.... The Republicans refused seats to the ladies on the floor of their convention although Indians in blankets were welcomed. The Democrats invited the ladies to seats where they listened to a speech against woman suffrage by E. W. Miller, land receiver of the Huron district, too indecent to print, which was received with cheers and applause by the convention.... A big delegation of Russians came to this convention wearing huge yellow badges lettered, Against Woman Suffrage and Susan B. Anthony.

Unsuccessful campaign for women's suffrage, South Dakota, summer of 1890, described in Harper, et al., eds., History of Woman Suffrage, *vol. 4, pp. 555–56.*

The constitution of society, the necessity for the existence of society, the necessity of home government, which is the most important of all the parts of government, can only be preserved and perpetrated by keeping men in their sphere and women in their sphere.... In my judgment, Mr. President, the day that the floodgate of female suffrage is opened upon this country, the social organism will have reached the point at which decay and ruin begin.

—Senator John Reagan, Democrat of Texas Senate debate over admission of Wyoming as a woman suffrage state, June 1890, quoted in Harper et al., eds., History of Woman Suffrage, *vol. 4, pp. 1000, 1002.*

... it is the immoral influence of the ballot upon women that I deprecate and would avoid. I do not want to see her drawn into contact with the rude things of this world, where the delicacy of her senses and sensibilities would be constantly wounded by the attrition with bad and desperate and foul politicians and men. Such is not her function and is not her office; and if we degrade her from the high station that God has placed her in to put her at the ballot box ... we unman ourselves....

—Senator John Morgan, Democrat of Alabama Senate debate over admission of Wyoming as a woman suffrage state, June 1890, quoted in Harper et al., eds., History of Woman Suffrage, *vol. 4, pp. 1000, 1002.*

Our friends who cry out that the manufacturing system of America has been fostered long enough should never forget that the struggle which the American manufacturer has in competition with Europe is severe. His labor-cost is more than double that of his competitor. Mr. Clark and Mr. Coats, manufacturers of thread, have factories of similar character in the old land and in the new. They have both testified that their labor-cost in Newark and in Rhode Island is slightly more than double what it is abroad....

We have seen that the introduction of a new manufacturing industry is no child's play. It means ten to fifteen years of struggle and loss.... the only question for the legislator is, after examination and proof adduced, to determine how much, if at all, in each industry the import duties may be lessened, and whether, owing to errors in laws or in the construction thereof, changes in the other direction may be necessary.

Andrew Carnegie, "Summing Up the Tariff Discussion," North American Review, *vol. 51 (July 1890), pp. 59–61.*

Sec. 3. No person is permitted to vote, serve as a juror, or hold any civil office ... who is a bigamist or polygamist, or is living in what is known as patriarchal, plural or celestial marriage, or in violation of any law of this State, or of the United States, forbidding any such crime; or who, in any manner, teaches, advises, counsels, aids, or encourages any person to enter into bigamy, polygamy, or such patriarchal, plural, or celestial marriage, or to live in violation of any such law, or to commit any such crime; or who is a member of or contributes to the support, aid, or encouragement of any order, organization, association, corporation or secret society, which teaches, advises, counsels, encourages, or aids any person to enter into bigamy, polygamy or such patriarchal or plural marriage, or which teaches or advises that the laws of this State prescribing rules of civil conduct, are not the supreme law of the State....

State constitution of Idaho, accepted July 3, 1890, Article 6 disenfranchising Mormons, reprinted in Chronology and Documentary Handbook of the State of Idaho, *pp. 44–45.*

Section 1. The rights of citizens of the State of Wyoming to vote and hold office shall not be denied or abridged on account of sex. Both male and female citizens of this State shall equally enjoy all civil, political and religious rights and privileges.

Article 6, State constitution of Wyoming, accepted July 10, 1890, reprinted in Chronology and Documentary Handbook of the State of Wyoming *(1978), p. 48.*

Section 1. The water of all natural streams, springs, lakes or other collections of still water, within the boundaries of the State, are hereby declared to be the property of the State.

Section 2. There shall be constituted a board of control, to be composed of the State engineer and superintendents of the water divisions; which shall, under such regulations as may be prescribed by law, have the supervision of the waters of the State and of their appropriation, distribution and diversion, and of the various officers connected therewith. Its decisions to be subject to review by the Courts of the State.

Section 3. Priority of appropriation for beneficial uses shall give the better right. No appropriation shall be denied except when such denial is demanded by the public interests.

Article 8, State constitution of Wyoming, accepted July 10, 1890, reprinted in Chronology and Documentary Handbook of the State of Wyoming *(1978), pp. 54–55.*

Be it enacted . . ., That the Secretary of the Treasury is hereby directed to purchase, from time to time, silver bullion to the aggregate amount of four million five hundred thousand ounces, or so much thereof as may be offered in each month, at the market price thereof . . ., and to issue in payment for such purchases of silver bullion Treasury notes of the United States. . . .

SEC. 2. That the Treasury notes issued in accordance with the provisions of this act shall be redeemable on demand, in coin, at the Treasury of the United States, or at the office of any assistant treasurer of the United States. . . . That upon demand of the holder of any of the Treasury notes herein provided for the Secretary of the Treasury shall . . . redeem such notes in gold or silver coin, at his discretion, it being the established policy of the United States to maintain the two metals on a parity with each other upon the present legal ratio. . . .

Sherman Silver Purchase Act, July 14, 1890, U.S. Statutes at Large, 51st Congress, vol. 26, p. 289.

The first execution by electricity has been a horror. Physicians who might make a jest out of the dissecting room, officials who have seen many a man's neck wrenched by the rope, surgeons who have lived in hospitals and knelt beside the dead and dying on bloody fields, held their breaths with a gasp, and those unaccustomed to such sights turned away in dread.

The doctors say the victim did not suffer. Only his Maker knows if that be true. To the eye, it looked as though he were in a convulsive agony.

The current had been passing through his body for fifteen seconds when the electrode at the head was removed. Suddenly the breast heaved. There was a straining at the straps which bound him, a purplish foam covered the lips and was spattered over the leather head-band.

The man was alive. Warden, physicians, everybody, lost their wits. There was a startled cry for the current to be turned on again. Signals, only half understood, were given to those in the next room at the switchboard. When they knew what had happened, they were prompt to act, and the switch-handle could be heard as it was pulled back and forth, breaking the deadly current into jets. . . . One of the witnesses nearly fell to the floor. Another lost control of his stomach.

August 6, 1890: the New York World *describes the first death in the electric chair, of convicted murderer William Kemmler at Sing Sing prison, "The First Electrocide," August 7, p. 1.*

. . . [N]o money shall be paid out under this act to any State or Territory for the support and maintenance of a college where a distinction of race or color is made in the admission of students, but the establishment and maintenance of such colleges separately for white and colored students shall be held to be a compliance with the provisions of this act if the funds received in such State or Territory be equitably divided. . . . [T]he legislature of such State may propose and report to the Secretary of Education a just and equitable division of the fund to be received under this act between one college for white students and one institution for colored students . . .

Second Morrill Act, August 30, 1890, U.S. Statutes at Large, 51st Congress, vol. 26, p. 47.

Most people unacquainted with the behavior of mountain streams fancy that when they escape the bounds of their rocky channels and launch into the air they at once lose all self-control and tumble in confusion. On the contrary, on no part of their travels do they manifest more calm self-possession. Imagine yourself in Hetch Hetchy [Valley, California]. It is a sunny day in June, the pines sway dreamily, and you are shoulder-deep in grass and flowers. Looking across the valley through beautiful open groves you see a bare granite wall 1800 feet high rising abruptly out of the green and yellow vegetation and glowing with sunshine, and in front of it the fall, waving like a downy scarf, silver bright, burning with white sun-fire in every fiber. In coming forward to the edge of the tremendous precipice and taking flight a little hasty eagerness appears, but this is speedily hushed in divine repose. Now observe the marvelous distinctness and delicacy of the various kinds of sun-filled tissue into which the waters are woven. They fly and float and drowse down the face of that grand gray rock in so leisurely and unconfused a manner that you may examine their texture and patterns as you would a piece of embroidery held in the hand. It is a flood of singing air, water, and sunlight woven into cloth that spirits might wear.

John Muir describes Hetch Hetchy Valley, "Features of the Proposed Yosemite National Park," Century, vol. 40 (September 1890), p. 665.

The Southern Democrats declare that the enforcement of this or any similar law will cause social disturbances and revolutionary outbreaks. As the negroes now disfranchised certainly will not revolt because they receive a vote, it is clear, therefore, that this means that the men who now rule in those States will make social disturbances and revolution in resistance to a law of the United States. It is also not a little amusing to observe that small portion of the newspaper press which has virtue generally in its peculiar keeping, raving in mad excitement merely because it is proposed to make public everything which affects the election of the representatives of the people in Congress. There must be something very interesting in the methods by which these guardians of virtue hope to gain and hold political power when they are so agitated at the mere thought of having the darkness which now overhangs the places where they win their victories dispersed.

Senator Henry Cabot Lodge, Republican of Massachusetts, "The Federal Election Bill," North American Review, vol. 151 (September 1890), pp. 257–59.

Sir, it is no secret that there has not been a full vote and a fair count in Mississippi since 1875, that we have been preserving the ascendancy of the white people by revolutionary methods. In other words, we have been stuffing ballot boxes, committing perjury, and here and there in the state carrying the election by fraud and violence . . . No man

can be in favor of perpetrating the election methods which have prevailed in Mississippi since 1875 who is not a moral idiot.

A white delegate to the Mississippi Constitutional Convention, as reported in the Jackson Clarion-Ledger, *September 11, 1890, quoted in Skates,* Mississippi, *p. 123.*

We are not teaching polygamy or plural marriage, nor permitting any person to enter into its practice, and I deny that either forty or any other number of plural marriages have during that period been solemnized in our Temples or in any other place in the Territory. . . .

Inasmuch as laws have been enacted by Congress forbidding plural marriages, which laws have been pronounced constitutional by the court of last resort, I hereby declare my intentions to submit to those laws, and to use my influence with the members of the Church over which I preside to have them do likewise. . . . And I now publicly declare that my advice to the Latter-day Saints is to refrain from contracting any marriage forbidden by the law of the land.

Woodruff Manifesto, Wilford Woodruff, president of the Mormon church, September 26, 1890, available online at Center for Public Education and Information on Polygamy. URL: http://www.polygamyinfo.com/manfesto.htm.

To make sure that this law [the McKinley Tariff] shall not be repealed for some time to come, the Senate, the body most removed from popular elections, has had its membership increased by the creation of new States for purely partisan purposes. Idaho and Wyoming are admitted without sufficient population and with scarcely a pretence of fairness. Arizona and New Mexico are kept out, although possessing large populations, because they are not sure for the party in power. Idaho has 60,589 population, as against 153,076 in New Mexico. It can nullify the vote of New York in the Senate, and has about one-fifth the population of some Congress districts in that State and New Jersey. This, in the language of Mr. Speaker Reed, is "business."

Representative William McAdoo [1853–1930], Democrat of New Jersey, "What Congress Has Done," North American Review, vol. 151 (November 1890), p. 528.

The first session of the Fifty-first Congress was the longest but one, and the most extravagant in expenditures, ever convened. The appropriations which it made, including indefinite sums estimated at $2,000,000, aggregate in round numbers $465,500,000, being $15,000,000 in excess of the estimated revenues. . . .

For unseemly thrusts and controversies between the Chair and the members in their places, and between members on the floor, and the general exhibition of ill-nature, the session has been unprecedented. A conspicuous illustration of this was given by Republican members during the debate on [the tariff], when coarse vulgarity, vile epithets, and even physical blows were resorted to among themselves.

Representative J. C. Clements, Democrat of Georgia, "What Congress Has Done," North American Review, *vol. 151 (November 1890), pp. 530, 533.*

The children of the large Government boarding school were allowed to visit their parents on issue day, and when the parting moment came, there were some pathetic scenes. It was one of my routine duties to give written excuses from school when necessary on the ground of illness, and these excuses were in much demand from lonely mothers and homesick little ones. As a last resort, the mother herself would sometimes plead illness and the need of her boy or girl for a few days at home. . . . if nothing else could win the coveted paper, the grandmother was apt to be pressed into the service, and her verbal ammunition seemed inexhaustible.

Dr. Charles Eastman, medical doctor at the Pine Ridge Indian Agency and a Wahpeton Dakota, describes November 1890, in his From the Deep Woods, *pp. 76–84.*

Whether they will or no, Americans must now look outward. The growing production of the country demands it. An increasing volume of public sentiment demands it. The position of the United States, between the two Old Worlds and the two great oceans, makes the same claim, which will soon be strengthened by the creation of the new link [the Panama Canal] joining the Atlantic and Pacific. The tendency will be maintained and increased by the growth of the European colonies in the Pacific, by the advancing civilization of Japan, and by the rapid peopling of our Pacific States. . . .

Alfred Thayer Mahan, "The United States Looking Outward," Atlantic Monthly, *vol. 64 (December 1890), p. 822.*

THE OCALA DEMANDS

1. a. We demand the abolition of national banks.

b. We demand that the government shall establish subtreasuries or depositories in the several states, which shall loan money direct to the people at a low rate of interest, not to exceed two per cent per annum, on non-perishable farm products, and also upon real estate, with proper limitations upon the quantity of land and amount of money.

c. We demand that the amount of the circulating medium be speedily increased to not less than $50 per capita.

2. We demand that Congress shall pass such laws as will effectually prevent the dealing in futures of all agricultural and mechanical productions; providing a stringent system of procedure in trials that will secure the prompt conviction, and imposing such penalties as shall secure the most perfect compliance with the law.

3. We condemn the silver bill recently passed by Congress, and demand in lieu thereof the free and unlimited coinage of silver.

4. We demand the passage of laws prohibiting alien ownership of land, and that Congress take prompt action to devise some plan to obtain all lands now owned by aliens and foreign syndicates; and that all lands now held by railroads and other corporations in excess of such as is actually used and needed by them be reclaimed by the government and held for actual settlers only.

5. Believing in the doctrine of equal rights to all and special privileges to none, we demand—

a. That our national legislation shall be so framed in the future as not to build up one industry at the expense of another.

b. We further demand a removal of the existing heavy tariff tax from the necessities of life, that the poor of our land must have.

c. We further demand a just and equitable system of graduated tax on incomes.

d. We believe that the money of the country should be kept as much as possible in the hands of the people, and hence we demand that all national and state revenues shall be limited to the necessary expenses of the government economically and honestly administered.

6. We demand the most rigid, honest and just state and national government control and supervision of the means of public communication and transportation, and if this control and supervision does not remove the abuse now existing, we demand the government ownership of such means of communication and transportation.

7. We demand that the Congress of the United States submit an amendment to the Constitution providing for the election of United States Senators by direct vote of the people of each state.

The Ocala Platform, December 1890, Proceedings of the Supreme Council of the National Farmers' Alliance. *reprinted in Commager, ed.,* Documents of American History, *vol. 1, pp. 592–93.*

I said to Sitting Bull in an imploring way: "Uncle, nobody is going to harm you. The Agent wants to see you and then you are to come back,—so please do not let others lead you into any trouble." But the Chief's mind was made up not to go so the three head officers laid their hands on him. Lieut. Bullhead got a hold on the Chief's right arm, Shavehead on the left arm, and Red Tomahawk back of the Chief—pulling him outside. By this time the whole camp was in commotion—women and children crying while the men gathered all round us—said everything mean imaginable but had not done anything to hurt us. The police tried to keep order but was useless—it was like trying to extinguish a treacherous prairie fire. Bear that Catches in the heat of the excitement, pulled out a gun, from under his blanket, and fired into Lieut. Bullhead and wounded him. Seeing that one of my dearest relatives and my superior, shot, I ran up toward where they were holding the Chief, when Bear that Catches raised his gun—pointed and fired at me, but it snapped. Being so close to him I scuffled with him and without any great effort overcame him. . . . It was about this moment that Lieut. Bullhead fired into Sitting Bull while still holding him and Red Tomahawk followed with another shot which finished the Chief.

John Lone Man, member of the Indian police at Standing Rock Agency, describes December 14, 1890, as recorded by his relative Robert Higheagle, in Vestal, ed., New Sources, *pp. 49–52.*

In the morning the soldiers began to take all the guns away from the Big Foots. . . . Soldiers were on the little hill and all around, and there were soldiers across the dry gulch to the south and over east along Wounded Knee Creek too. The people were nearly surrounded, and the wagon-guns were pointing at them.

Some had not yet given up their guns, and so the soldiers were searching all the tepees, throwing things around and poking into everything. There was a man called Yellow Bird, and he and another man were standing in front of the tepee where Big Foot was lying sick. They had white sheets around and over them, with eyeholes to look through, and they had guns under these. An officer came to search them. He took the other man's gun, and then started to take Yellow Bird's. But Yellow Bird would not let go. He wrestled with the officer, and while they were wrestling, the gun went off and killed the officer. Wasichus and some others have said he meant to do this, but Dog Chief was standing right there, and he told me it was not so. As soon as the gun went off, Dog Chief told me, an officer shot and killed Big Foot who was lying sick inside the tepee.

Then suddenly nobody knew what was happening, except that the soldiers were all shooting and the wagon-guns began going off right in among the people.

Black Elk, an Oglala Sioux (later chief and holy man) who was at Wounded Knee, December 14, 1890, in Neihardt, ed., Black Elk Speaks, *pp. 260–61.*

[Republican] leaders, ever since the Civil War ended, have not only misrepresented the South with the view of keeping the Northern people hostile to her, but they have insisted that the South should be dealt with as if she were not loyal to the government. What is the Force bill but an effort to put the Southern people under bayonet rule and humiliate them? That the bill would be productive of race disturbances, and retard the South's prosperity, no thinking

man, who fully understands what the effect of the bill would be, for a moment doubts. There is no necessity for such a bill, but the attempt to pass it leads the Northern people to think there is.

Editorial, Savannah News, *December 20, 1890, reprinted in Nevins, ed.,* American Press Opinion, *p. 403.*

A majority of the thirty or more Indian wounded were women and children, including babies in arms. As there were not tents enough for all, Mr. Cook [Rev. Charles Cook, an Episcopal missionary and a Yankton Sioux] offered us the mission chapel, in which the Christmas tree still stood, for a temporary hospital. We tore out the pews and covered the floor with hay and quilts. There we laid the poor creatures side by side in rows, and the night was devoted to caring for them as best we could. Many were frightfully torn by pieces of shells, and the suffering was terrible. . . . In spite of all our efforts, we lost the greater

Dr. Charles Eastman, a Wahpeton Dakota and the physician at Pine Ridge Indian Agency, South Dakota, treated survivors of the Wounded Knee massacre. *(Library of Congress, Prints and Photographs Division, LC-USZ62-102275)*

part of them, but a few recovered, including several children who had lost all their relatives. . . .

On the day following the Wounded Knee massacre there was a blizzard. . . . On the third day it cleared, and the ground was covered with an inch or two of fresh snow. We had feared that some of the Indian wounded might have been left on the field, and a number of us volunteered to go and see. I was placed in charge of the expedition of about a hundred civilians, ten or fifteen of whom were white men. We were supplied with wagons in which to convey any whom we might find still alive. Of course a photographer and several reporters were of the party.

Fully three miles from the scene of the massacre we found the body of a woman completely covered with a blanket of snow, and from this point on we found them scattered along as they had been relentlessly hunted down and slaughtered while fleeing for their lives. Some of our people discovered relatives or friends among the dead, and there was much wailing and mourning. When we reached the spot where the Indian camp had stood, among the fragments of burned tents and other belongings we saw the frozen bodies lying close together or piled one upon another. I counted eighty bodies of men who had been in the council and who were almost as helpless as the women and babes when the deadly fire began, for nearly all their guns had been taken from them. A reckless and desperate young Indian fired the first shot when the search for weapons was well under way, and immediately the troops opened fire from all sides, killing not only unarmed men, women, and children, but their own comrades who stood opposite them, for the camp was entirely surrounded. . . . Although they had been lying untended in the snow and cold for two days and nights, a number had survived. Among them I found a baby of about a year old warmly wrapped and entirely unhurt. . . .

Dr. Charles Eastman, medical doctor at the Pine Ridge Indian Agency and a Wahpeton Dakota, describes December 29, 1890–January 1, 1891, in his From the Deep Woods, *pp. 109–14.*

This White List was distributed by circulating it in pamphlet form among the members and also by paying to have it appear as an advertisement in the leading newspapers. . . . Many of our members who had accounts with firms whose names did not appear on the list visited them and expressed themselves as unwilling to patronize any stores not on the White List of the Consumers' League. . . . The reaction, however, of the merchants, was sharp and quick. They did notice our advertisement and resented it. They treated the matter lightly at first; they pooh-poohed the absurd attempts of a handful of "busybodies" who were trying to revolutionize business methods. It never could be done; merchants who gave their entire time and thought to

their business knew better how to conduct that business than sentimental, visionary women who had no business training, and who allowed their hearts to run away with their heads. The Consumers' League, they contended, could not survive a year. . . .

Maud Nathan, a founder of the New York Consumers' League, 1890–91, Story of an Epoch-Making Movement, *pp. 28–30.*

The eagerness with which the women's clubs all over the country have taken up history, literature, and art studies, striving to make up for absence of opportunity and the absorption in household cares of their young womanhood, has in it something almost pathetic. But this ground will soon be covered. Is there not room in the clubs for outlook committees, whose business it should be to investigate township affairs, educational, sanitary, reformatory, and all lines of improvement, and report what is being done, might be done, or needs to be done, for decency and order in the jails, in the schools, in the streets, in the planting of trees, in the disposition of refuse, and the provision for light which is the best protection for life and property?

Jane Cunningham Croly, founder of the General Federation of Women's Clubs, speech at the council meeting held at the home of Mrs. Thomas Edison, 1891, quoted in Wood, History of the General Federation, *p. 46.*

Why do people look down on Working Girls? This is the question that we girls ask each other over and over again. . . .

Is it because we lack virtue? Are working girls, as a class, virtuous? Years ago, a man who know whereof he affirmed, wrote: "Not even the famed Hebrew maiden as she stood on the giddy turret, more sacredly guarded her honor than does many a half-starved sewing woman in the streets of New York.". . . It is true, there are exceptions, but has not the immoral working girl her rivals among a class of women who should be her teachers in all pure and noble living?

Is it because we work? What an absurd idea! People "look down" on us because we work? Why, the lawyer and the doctor and the clergyman and the professor and the merchant all work, and work hard, too, and every one looks up to them. "Of course," says a bright, young lady, "we expect men to work and support their families, but ladies do not work." Don't they? We have lady artists and musicians, lady doctors, lawyers and lecturers, trained nurses and teachers. If it isn't *work* that they are doing, what is it? "But," says the same young lady, "have you never discovered that there is a difference between brain work and manual labor?" Yes, we have discovered it, to our sorrow. The teacher considers herself superior to the sewing girl, and the sewing girl thinks herself above the mill girl, and the mill girl thinks the girl who does general housework a little beneath her, and Miss Flora McFlimsy, "who toils not, neither does she spin," thinks herself superior to them all.

Lucy Warner of the Working Girls Clubs, in their monthly
journal Far and Near, *January 1891, reprinted in Baxendall*
et al., eds., America's Working Women, *pp. 215–16.*

At present little remains to remind one of the condition of farmers during [my childhood.] They now generally occupy the great prairies of the West instead of the hills and valleys of the eastern States. They are no longer engaged in domestic farming. Like manufacturers and the operators of mines, they are producing articles for supplying the market. They buy almost as many things as do persons who live in towns. . . . They have given up raising small products for the supply of their tables, and as a consequence their grocery bills are large. As there are few trees in the prairie regions, and as the area occupied by forests in other parts of the country has been greatly reduced, farmers are compelled to purchase their fuel, which is generally bituminous coal, and to buy all the materials used in the construction of fences and buildings. . . .

The farmer of the present day has no necessity for bartering his products. . . . In many of the western States—Illinois, for instance—nine tenths of the farm houses are within five miles of railway stations. . . .

Rodney Welch, "The Farmer's Changed Condition,"
Forum, *vol. 10 (February 1891), pp. 692–93.*

[T]he President of the United States may, from time to time, set apart and reserve, in any State or Territory having public land bearing forests, in any part of the public lands wholly or in part covered with timber or undergrowth, whether of commercial value or not, as public reservations, and the President shall, by public proclamation, declare the establishment of such reservations and the limits thereof.

Forest Reserve Act, March 3, 1891, U.S. Statutes at Large,
51st Congress, vol. 26, p. 1103.

Be it enacted . . . That the following classes of aliens be excluded from admission to the United States, in accordance with the existing acts regulating immigration, other than those concerning Chinese laborers: All idiots, insane persons, paupers or persons likely to become public charges, persons suffering from a loathsome or a dangerous contagious disease, persons who have been convicted of a felony or other infamous crime or misdemeanor involving moral turpitude, polygamists, and also any person whose ticket or passage is paid for with the money of another or who is assisted by others to come. . . . but this section shall not be held to include persons living in the United States

from sending for a relative or friend who is not of the excluded classes . . .; Provided, That nothing in this act shall be construed to apply to or exclude persons convicted of a political offense. . . .

Sec. 7. That the office of superintendent of immigration is hereby created and established, and the President, by and with the advice and consent of the Senate, is authorized and directed to appoint such officer, whose salary shall be four thousand dollars per annum, payable monthly. The superintendent of immigration shall be an officer in the Treasury Department, under the control and supervision of the Secretary of the Treasury . . .

Sec. 8. . . . That the Secretary of the Treasury may prescribe rules for inspection along the borders of Canada, British Columbia, and Mexico so as not to obstruct or unnecessarily delay, impede, or annoy passengers in ordinary travel between said countries; Provided, That not exceeding one inspector shall be appointed for each customs district. . . .

Immigration Act of March 3, 1891, U.S. Statutes at Large,
51st Congress, vol. 26, pp. 1084–86.

But, Mr. Editor, can we do anything while the present parties have control of the ballot box, and we (the Alliance) have no protection? The greatest mistake, I see, is this: The wily politicians see and know that they have to do something, therefore they are slipping into the Alliance, and the farmers, in many instances, are accepting them as leaders; and if we are to have the same leaders, we need not expect anything else but the same results. The action of the Alliance in this reminds me of the man who first put his hand in the lion's mouth and the lion finally bit it off; and then he changed to make the matter better and put his head in the lion's mouth, and therefore lost his head.

Florida Colored Farmers' Alliance letter to the Washington
National Economist, *official journal of the National*
Farmers' Alliance, *March 7, 1891, reprinted in Aptheker, ed.,*
Documentary History of the Negro People, *pp. 808–09.*

In the violation of the ordinary routine of justice to which the citizens in complete and admirable self-control resorted yesterday, they were doing merely for law and for the administration of justice what law and the administration of justice had confessedly been unable to do for themselves. To vindicate law which had repeatedly been mocked and to reinstate oft-outraged justice again upon her throne, the people took defiant crime by the nape of the neck, and strangled it and threw it in the gutter. . . . The short, sharp, and decisive drama of yesterday had in it, moreover, a warning for another class besides the wretched and brutalized aliens who think they can import their secret assassination schemes into this country and graft them upon our free institutions, which stand before the world the high watermark of human liberty.

Editorial defending the lynching of 11 Italians, New Orleans Times-Democrat, March 15, 1891, reprinted in Nevins, ed., American Press Opinion, p. 405.

It has never been proved that the chief of police of New Orleans was assassinated either by the Italians who were murdered by the mob, or by any other Italians. The circumstantial evidence made it probable that the murder was committed by order of the Sicilian vendetta society, the Mafia, and on this unproved probability the spirit of vengeance was aroused to its highest pitch. . . . So the eleven prisoners were lynched yesterday on proof of being "dagos" and on the merest suspicion of being guilty of any other crime.

Editorial condemning the lynching, St. Louis Republic, March 15, 1891, reprinted in Nevins, ed., American Press Opinion, p. 404.

From Mrs. Felesberg we learned at once the more serious side of life in America. Mrs. Felesberg was the woman with whom we were rooming. A door from our room opened into her tiny bedroom and then led into the only other room where she sat a great part of the day finishing pants which she brought in big bundles from a shop, and rocking the cradle with one foot. She always made us draw our chairs quite close to her and she spoke in a whisper scarcely ever lifting her weak peering eyes from her work. When she asked us how we liked America, and we spoke of it with praise, she smiled a queer smile. "Life here is not all that it appears to the 'green horn,' she said." She told us that her husband was a presser on coats and earned twelve dollars when he worked a full week. Aunt Masha thought twelve dollars a good deal. Again Mrs. Felesberg smiled. "No doubt it would be," she said, "where you used to live. You had your own house, and most of the food came from the garden. Here you will have to pay for everything; the rent!" she sighed, "for the light, for every potato, every grain of barley. You see these three rooms, including yours? Would they be too much for my family of five?" We had to admit they would not. "And even from these," she said, "I have to rent one out."

Rose Gallup Cohen, who arrived in New York's Lower East Side from Russia, July 1891, in her Out of the Shadow, p. 73.

It was no easy task for me on the morning of that 7th of October, 1891, to believe my senses when I first experienced that well-nigh overwhelming feeling that I was really in the great city of New York. As our little party proceeded on across Battery Park up toward Washington Street, I felt the need of new faculties to fit my new environment. A host of questions besieged my mind. Was I really in New York? Was I still my old self, or had some subtle, unconscious transformation already taken place in me? Could I utter my political and religious convictions freely, unafraid of either soldier or priest? . . .

Nor did I have to wait very long for tangible evidence to convince me that America was the land of liberty and opportunity. On that very evening my eyes beheld a scene so strange and so delightful that I could hardly believe it was real. Sitting in the restaurant early in the evening we heard, approaching from the direction of "uptown," band music and the heavy tread of a marching multitude which filled the street from curb to curb. Someone, looking out of the window, shouted, "It is the laborers! They are on their way to Battery Park to hold a meeting and demand their rights." That was all that was needed for me to dash out with a few others and follow the procession to the near-by park.

I had heard in a very fragmentary way of the "united laborers" in Europe and America, but, while in Syria, and as a Turkish subject, it was almost beyond me to conceive of workingmen in collective moral and political action. . . . How I wished I could return to Syria just for a few hours and tell my oppressed countrymen what I had seen in America. . . .

Abraham Rihbany, an immigrant from Turkish-occupied Syria, October 1891, in his A Far Journey, pp. 180–86.

[The settlement house] movement [is] based, not only upon conviction, but upon genuine emotion, wherever educated young people are seeking an outlet for that sentiment of universal brotherhood, which the best spirit of our times is forcing from an emotion into a motive. These young people accomplish little toward the solution of this social problem, and bear the brunt of being cultivated into unnourished, oversensitive lives. . . . They feel a fatal want of harmony between their theory and their lives, a lack of coordination between thought and action. I think it is hard for us to realize how seriously many of them are taking to the notion of human brotherhood, how eagerly they long to give tangible expression to the democratic ideal. . . . Nothing so deadens the sympathies and shrivels the power of enjoyment, as the persistent keeping away from the great opportunities for helpfulness and a continual ignoring of the starvation struggle which makes up the life of at least half the race. To shut one's self away from that half of the race is to shut one's self away from the most vital part of it. . . .

Other motives which I believe make toward the Settlement are the result of a certain renaissance going forward in Christianity. . . . I believe that there is a distinct turning among many young men and women toward this simple acceptance of Christ's message. They resent the assumption that Christianity is a set of ideas which belong to the religious consciousness, whatever that may be. They insist that it cannot be proclaimed and instituted apart from the social life of the community and that it must seek a simple and natural expression in the social organism itself.

Jane Addams, "The Subjective Necessity for Social Settlements," speech to an Ethical Culture workshop in Massachusetts, 1892, Twenty Years at Hull-House, *pp. 115–16, 122.*

John laughs at me, of course, but one expects that in marriage. . . .

John is a physician, and *perhaps*—(I would not say it to a living soul, of course, but this is dead paper and a great relief to my mind)—*perhaps* that is one reason I do not get well faster.

You see he does not believe I am sick! And what can one do?

If a physician of high standing, and one's own husband, assures friends and relatives that there is really nothing the matter with one but temporary nervous depressions—a slight hysterical tendency—what is one to do?

My brother is also a physician, and also of high standing, and he says the same thing.

So I take phosphates or phospites—whichever it is, and tonics, and journeys, and air, and exercise, and am absolutely forbidden to "work" until I am well again.

Personally, I disagree with their ideas.

Personally, I believe that congenial work, with excitement and change, would do me good.

But what is one to do?

Charlotte Perkins Gilman, "The Yellow Wallpaper," 1892, pp. 9–10.

Woman should not, even by inference, or for the sake of argument, seem to disparage what is weak. For woman's cause is the cause of the weak; and when all the weak shall have received their due consideration, then woman will have her "rights," and the Indian will have his rights, and the Negro will have his rights, and all the strong will have learned at last to deal justly, to love mercy, and to walk humbly; and our fair land will have been taught the secret of universal courtesy which is after all nothing but the art, the science, and the religion of regarding one's neighbor as one's self, and to do for him as we would, were conditions swapped, that he do for us.

African-American educator Anna Julia Cooper, in her A Voice from the South *(1892), p. 117.*

A colored woman who had shown marked ability in drawing and coloring, was advised by her teacher, himself an artist of no mean rank, to apply for admission to the Cor-coran school [of art in Washington, D.C.] in order to study the models and to secure other advantages connected with the organization. She accordingly sent a written application accompanied by specimens of her drawings, the usual modus operandi in securing admission.

The drawings were examined by the best critics and pronounced excellent, and a ticket of admission was immediately issued together with a highly complimentary reference to her work. The next day my friend, congratulating her country and herself that at least in the republic of art no caste existed, presented her ticket of admission *in propria persona.* There was a little preliminary side play in Delsarte pantomine,—aghast—incredulity—wonder; then the superintendent told her in plain unartistic English that of course he had not dreamed a colored person could do such work, and had he suspected the truth he would never have issued the ticket of admission; that, to be right frank, the ticket would have to be cancelled,—she could under no condition be admitted to the studio.

Anna Julia Cooper, A Voice from the South *(1892), pp. 113–14.*

The more I reflect on the world, and the way its affairs are managed, the more I see that the right to vote in a democratic age is an acknowledgment by the States of the right of the citizen to have an opinion and a right to tender it for the guidance of her fellow citizens. . . . The voteless adult is nowhere, whose rights, whose individuality, whose common nature, even, are all held by suffrance, permitted rather than recognized, and as a consequence minimized beyond endurance.

Frances Willard, 1892 presidential address to the WCTU, quoted in Bordin, Woman and Temperance, *p. 120.*

In the year 1890 young Astor, a scion of the celebrated family which has so long been prominent in New York financial circles, was married. Both the groom and the bride represented millions of wealth and the wedding was an imposing and gorgeous affair. . . . the presents were valued at $2 million, and the couple and their attendants and a number of friends immediately departed on an expensive yachting cruise which was to cost them $10,000 a month to maintain . . .

About the time these princely entertainments were given, and in the same year with some of them, one of the metropolitan journals caused a careful canvass to be made of the unemployed of that city. The number was found to be *150,000 persons who were daily unsuccessfully seeking work within the city limits of New York.* Another 150,000 earn less than 60 cents per day. Thousands of these are poor girls who work from eleven to sixteen hours per day. In the year 1890, over 23,000 families, numbering about 100,000 people, were forcibly evicted in New York City owing to their inability to pay rent; and one-tenth of all who died in that city during the year were buried in the Potters Field....

Campaign tract of James Weaver, Populist nominee for president, 1892, in his Call to Action, *pp. 376–78.*

Hull-House was, we soon discovered, surrounded in every direction by home-work carried on under the sweating system....

The discoveries as to home work under the sweating system thus recorded and charted in 1892 (that first year of my residence) led to the appointment at the opening of the [Illinois State] legislature of 1893, of a legislative commission of enquiry into employment of women and children in manufacture, for which Mary Kenney and I volunteered as guides. Because we knew our neighborhood, we could and did show the commissioners sights that few legislators had then beheld; among them unparalleled congestion in frame cottages which looked decent enough, though drab and uninviting, under their thick coats of soft coal soot. One member of the Commission would never enter any sweatshop, but stood in the street while the others went in, explaining that he had young children and feared to carry them some infection.

This Commission had been intended as a sop to labor and a sinecure, a protracted junket to Chicago, for a number of rural legislators. Our overwhelming hospitality and devotion to the thoroughness and success of their investigation, by personally conducted visits to sweat-shops, though irksome in the extreme to the lawgivers, ended in a report so compendious, so readable, so surprising that they presented it with pride to the legislature.... The subject was a new one in Chicago. For the press the sweating system was that winter a sensation.

Florence Kelley describes her work as a Hull-House resident, 1892–1893, "I Go to Work," The Survey, *vol. 58 (June 1, 1927), 272.*

There were three big steamships in the harbor waiting to land their passengers and there was much anxiety among the newcomers to be the first landed at the new station. The honor was reserved for a little rosy-cheeked Irish girl. She was Annie Moore, 15 years of age, lately a resident of County Cork and yesterday one of the 148 steerage passengers landed from the steamship *Nevada.* . . . As soon as the gangplank was run ashore Annie tripped across it and hurried into the big building that almost covers the entire island. By a prearranged plan she was escorted to a registry desk which was temporarily occupied by Mr. Charles M. Henley, the former private secretary of Secretary Windom.... When the little voyager had been registered, Col. Weber [the commissioner of immigration] presented her with a $10 gold piece and made a short address of congratulations and welcome. It was the first United States

coin she had ever seen and the largest sum of money she had ever possessed....

Report of the first arrival at Ellis Island, "Landed on Ellis Island," New York Times, *January 2, 1892, p. 1.*

The isolation of every human soul and the necessity of self-dependence must give each individual the right to choose his own surroundings. The strongest reason for giving woman all the opportunities for higher education, for the full development of her faculties, her forces of mind and body; for giving her the most enlarged freedom of thought and action; a complete emancipation from all forms of bondage, of custom, dependence, superstition; from all the crippling influences of fear—is the solitude and personal responsibility of her own individual life. The strongest reason why we ask for woman a voice in the government under which she lives . . . is . . . because, as an individual, she must rely on herself....

How the little courtesies of life on the surface of society, deemed so important from man towards woman, fade into utter insignificance in view of the deeper tragedies in which she must play her part alone, where no human aid is possible!

. . . The talk of sheltering woman from the fierce storms of life is the sheerest mockery, for they beat on her from every point of the compass, just as they do on man, and with more fatal results, for he has been trained to protect himself, to resist, to conquer....

Elizabeth Cady Stanton, speech before the House Judiciary Committee, January 17, 1892, in Harper et al., eds., History of Woman Suffrage, *vol. 4, pp. 189–90.*

. . . it is necessary that the Columbian Exposition should not only bring together evidences of the amazing material productiveness which, within the century, has effected a complete transformation in the external aspects of life, but should force into equal prominence, if possible, corresponding evidences that the finer instincts of humanity have not suffered complete eclipse in this grosser prosperity, and that, in this head-long race, art has not been left entirely behind.

Architect Henry Van Brunt, "Architecture at the Columbian Exposition," Century, *vol. 44 (May 1892), p. 89.*

Sec. 6. And it shall be the duty of all Chinese laborers in the United States at the time of the passage of the act, and who were entitled to remain in the United States, to apply to the collector of internal revenue of their respective districts, within one year after passage of this act, for a certificate of residence, and any Chinese laborer, within the limits of the United States, who shall neglect, fail, or refuse to comply with the provisions of this act, or who, after one year from the passage hereof, shall be found within the jurisdiction of the United States without such certificate of residence, shall be deemed and adjudged to be unlawfully in the United States, and may be arrested by any United States customs official, collector of internal revenue or his deputies, United States marshal or his deputies, and taken before a United States judge, whose duty it shall be to order that he be deported from the United States . . . unless he shall clearly establish to the satisfaction of said judge that by reason of accident, sickness, or other unavoidable cause he has been unable to procure his certificate. . . . and by at least one credible white witness, that he was a resident of the United States at the time of the passage of this act. . . .

"Geary Act," May 5, 1892, U.S. Statutes at Large, 52nd Congress, v. 27, pp. 25–26.

Summer of 1892. I'm to meet the School Board.

We met.

The intent of the meeting was to notify me that "under no circumstances does the school board want to lose your services, but we ask you to change your mode of dress [that is, her nun's habit]."

I looked steadily at the Chairman and replied: "The Constitution of the United States gives me the same privilege to wear this mode of dress as it gives you to wear your trousers. Good-bye. . . ."

So this is the end of twenty-two years' work in Public School Number One, opened in 1870 when Trinidad [Colorado] was mostly governed by the best shotmen and sheriff's lead, mobs to hang murderers, and jail birds never come to trial, and the life of a man was considered a trifle compared to the possession of a horse. Jesuits and Sisters used every effort to quell the daily storms—while School Room Number One exerted an influence over the pupils—grown men and women—attending Room Number One that often astonished its teacher. . . . We supplied the school, building, janitor, and made repairs, and daily from the one story adobe building went forth cleaned hearts that had entered with murderous thoughts and designs; hearts filled to overflowing with the desire to get rich quick; hearts whose morality was fit companion to the beasts of the plains; and these spasmodically agitated hearts were quelled to calmness by her whose sole thought was peace—the path, to Heaven. . . .

Diary of Sister Blandina, a Catholic nun and teacher in a frontier school in southwest Colorado, summer 1892, in Segale, At the End of the Santa Fe Trail, p. 345.

We denounce the efforts of the Democratic majority of the House of Representatives to destroy our tariff laws by piecemeal, as manifested by their attacks upon wool, lead and lead ores, the chief products of a number of States, and we ask the people for their judgment thereon.

Republican party platform, adopted June 7, 1892, Platforms of the Two Great Political Parties, p. 87.

We call the attention of thoughtful Americans to the fact that after thirty years of restrictive taxes against the importation of foreign wealth, in exchange for our agricultural surplus, the homes and farms of the country have become burdened with a real estate mortgage debt of over $2,500,000,000, exclusive of all other forms of indebtedness; that in one of the chief agricultural States of the West there appears a real estate mortgage debt averaging $165 per capita of the total population, and that similar conditions and tendencies are shown to exist in other agricultural-exporting States. We denounce a policy which fosters no industry so much as it does that of the Sheriff.

Democratic party platform, adopted June 21, 1892, Platforms of the Two Great Political Parties, p. 80.

We contend that we have a legal right to the enjoyment of our property, and to operate it and control it as we please. . . . But for years our works have been managed. . . . by men [i.e. the union] who do not own a dollar in them. This will stop right here. The Carnegie Steel Company will hereafter control their works in the employment of labor.

Statement of the Carnegie Steel Company, July 2, 1892, quoted in Krause, The Battle for Homestead, p. 12.

. . . over the barge a fluttering white flag told the story that the Pinkertons sought for terms.

The spokesman of the Pinkertons announced that they would surrender if assured of protection from the mob.

They landed. Their arms were taken from them. With heads uncovered, to distinguish them from the mill hands, they passed along between two rows of guards armed with Winchesters. There were two hundred and fifty Pinkertons in line. . . .

Silently, sadly, and filled with fear, the disarmed Pinkertons, some bleeding, with bedraggled clothing, haggard and pale-faced, walked between their captors. Some held small bags with clothing. Alongside crowded the surging mass of hard-fisted men hurling epithets at them. For some time they walked thus, hoping for the shelter of the jail.

Now woman comes to the front!

One snatched a bag, tore from it a white shirt and waved it. This action was almost a signal to the brigade of women. They seized every bag and scattered the contents. With yells and shouts the crowd cheered the women. There was a fine humor here; to scatter the clothing of those who had come to scatter them.

Another woman threw sand into the eyes of a Pinkerton and cut him with a stone. Then, in spite of the guards, the women cast stones and missiles at the unprotected Pinkertons. The guards hurried them over the unlevel ground to the jail. . . .

And behind the high board fence, with the barbed wires charged with electricity, rest the mill hands waiting the developments of the future.

A reporter describes events at Homestead, Pennsylvania, July 6, 1892, Frank Leslie's Illustrated American, *July 16, 1892, available online at Strike at Homestead. URL: http://history.ohiostate.edu/projects/ HomesteadStrike1892/HistoryofSevenDays/ incident.htm.*

For an instant the sunlight, streaming through the windows, dazzles me. I discern two men at the further end of the long table.

"Fr——," I begin. The look of terror on his face strikes me speechless. It is the dread of the conscious presence of death. "He understands," it flashes through my mind. With a quick motion I draw the revolver. As I raise the weapon, I see Frick clutch with both hands the arm of the chair, and attempt to rise. I aim at his head. 'Perhaps he wears armor,' I reflect. With a look of horror he quickly averts his face, as I pull the trigger. There is a flash, and the high-ceilinged room reverberates as with the booming of cannon. I hear a sharp, piercing cry and see Frick on his knees, his head against the arm of the chair. I feel calm and possessed, intent upon every movement of the man. He is lying head and shoulders under the large armchair, without sound or motion. "Dead?" I wonder. I must make sure. About twenty-five feet separate us. I take a few steps toward him, when suddenly the other man, whose presence I had quite forgotten, leaps upon me. I struggle to loosen his hold. . . . Suddenly I hear the cry, "Murder! Help!" My heart stands still as I realize that it is Frick shouting. "Alive?" I wonder. I hurl the stranger aside and fire at the crawling figure of Frick. The man struck my hand,—I have missed!

Alexander Berkman describes his attempted murder of Henry Clay Frick, July 23, 1892, in his Prison Memoirs, *pp. 36–37.*

The right of any man to labor, upon whatever terms he and his employer agree, whether he belong to a labor organization or not, and the right of a person or corporation (which in law is also a person) to employ any one to labor in a lawful business is secured by the laws of the land.

In this free country these rights must not be denied or abridged. To do so would destroy that personal freedom which has ever been the just pride and boast of American citizens. Even the "moral suasion" which the members of labor organizations may use to prevent non-union men from accepting employment must not be carried too far or it may become intimidation and coercion, and hence be unlawful. We must recognize the fact that in this country every man is the architect of his own fortune.

Representative William C. Oates, chair of the House investigation committee, "The Homestead Strike," North American Review, *vol. 155 (September 1892), p. 362.*

If the great steel plant were not just where it is the town of Homestead would not be the flourishing place that it is. The establishment of that plant attracted workmen to the spot; they built homes, raised their families, and invested every dollar of their earnings there. Business men, professional men, and clergymen followed them, and a community of well-behaved, respectable citizens surrounds the steel works. The workmen by their labor made the steel works prosperous and great; on the other hand they made Homestead what it is. The men depend for their support on steady work, and the community back of them depends on their steady employment. Three parties are interested in this struggle, the Carnegie Steel Company, the employees of that concern, and the community. . . . The manager of the Carnegie Steel Company in asserting that he has the right to turn the makers of a prosperous town out of employment and out of the town,—for that naturally follows,—stands upon treacherous ground, for the makers of towns have equally as good a right to be heard as have the investors of money. . . .

Terence Powderly, head of the Knights of Labor, in "The Homestead Strike," North American Review, *vol. 155 (September 1892), pp. 372–73.*

The system which makes one man a millionaire makes tramps and paupers of thousands. The thousands go down to the brothels and slums, where they sprout the germs of anarchy and stand ready for any deed of desperation. The millionaire becomes more arrogant and unreasonable as his millions accumulate. . . . The employer who refuses arbitration fears for the justice of his cause. He who would acquire legitimately need not fear investigation; he who would steal must do it in the dark in order to be successful.

Terence Powderly, "The Homestead Strike," North American Review, *vol. 155 (September 1892), p. 373.*

I think all lawyers must agree
On keeping our profession free
From females whose admission would
Result in anything but good.

Because it yet has to be shown
That men are fit to hold their own.
In such a contest, I've no doubt,
We'd some of us be crowded out. . . .

Praise to the benchers who have stood
Against the innovating flood,
To save us and our ample fees
From tribulations such as these.
"The Law and the Lady," in Canadian humor magazine
Grip, vol. 39 (September 1892), p. 202.

At a signal from the Principal, the pupils, in ordered rank, hands to side, face the flag. Another signal is given; every pupil gives the Flag a military salute—right hand lifted, palm downward, to a line with the forehead and close to it. Standing thus, all repeat together, slowly, "I pledge allegiance to my Flag and the Republic for which it stands, one Nation, indivisible, with Liberty and Justice for all." At the words "to my Flag," the right hand is extended gracefully, palm upward, toward the Flag, and remains in this gesture until the end of the affirmation whereupon all hands immediately drop to the side.
The original Pledge of Allegiance, published anonymously but
attributed to Francis Bellamy, "National School
Celebration of Columbus Day: The Official Program,"
Youth's Companion, vol. 65 (September 8, 1892)
p. 446.

You might beseech a Southern white tenant to listen to you upon questions of finance, taxation, and transportation; you might demonstrate with mathematical precision that herein lay his way out of poverty into comfort; you might have him "almost persuaded" to the truth, but if the merchant who furnished his farm supplies (at tremendous usury) or the town politician (who never spoke to him excepting at election times) came along and cried "Negro rule!" the entire fabric of reason and common sense which you had patiently constructed would fall, and the poor tenant would joyously hug the chains of an actual wretchedness rather than do any experimenting on a question of mere sentiment. . . .

The white tenant lives adjoining the colored tenant. Their houses are almost equally destitute of comforts. Their living is confined to bare necessities. They are equally burdened with heavy taxes. They pay the same high rent for gullied and impoverished land.

They pay the same enormous prices for farm supplies. Christmas finds them both without any satisfactory return for a year's toil. Dull and heavy and unhappy, they both start the plows again when "New Year's" passes.

Now the People's Party says to these two men, "You are kept apart that you may be separately fleeced of your earnings. You are made to hate each other because upon that hatred is rested the keystone of the arch of financial despotism which enslaves you both. You are deceived and

blinded that you may not see how this race antagonism perpetuates a monetary system which beggars both.". . .
Georgia Populist Party leader Thomas E. Watson, "The Negro
Question in the South," Arena, vol. 6 (October 1892),
pp. 542–50.

A mere mob, collected upon the impulse of the moment without any definite object beyond the gratification of its sudden passions does not commit treason, although it destroys property and attacks human life. But when a large number of men arm and organize themselves by divisions and companies, appoint officers and engage in a common purpose to defy the law, to resist its officers, and to deprive any portion of their fellow citizens of the rights to which they are entitled under the constitution and laws, it is a levying of war against the state, and the offense is treason; . . . and it is a state of war when a business plant has to be surrounded by the army of the state for weeks to protect it from unlawful violence at the hands of men formerly employed in it . . .

We have reached the point in the history of the state when there are but two roads left us to pursue: the one leads to order and good government, the other leads to anarchy.
Edward H. Paxson, chief justice of the Pennsylvania Supreme
Court, to the Allegheny County Grand Jury considering
treason charges against Homestead strikers,
October 10, 1892, quoted in Burgoyne,
Homestead Strike, pp. 205–07.

After the procession of governors came what was to the more thoughtful among the multitude one of the most interesting features of the parade. Preceded by their own band, headed by their principal, and dressed in neat, new uniforms were several companies of Indian students from the industrial school at Carlisle in Pennsylvania. The leading company carried slates and school-books; the second, type galleys; the third, implements or products of agriculture, and the rest, such specimens or tools as represented their various pursuits. Halting in front of the grand stand, they performed a series of military evolutions with a rapidity and precision which won the applause of the observers. But how attractive soever this spectacle, it evoked as much of sadness as of interest, for here in this handful of boys, some of them the sole survivors of nations now swept from the earth, were represented the few who had availed themselves of this boon of education which the government extends to the offspring of its meanest citizens.
Historian Hubert Howe Bancroft describes the parade
celebrating the dedication of the World's
Columbian Exposition, October 20, 1892, in
The Book of the Fair, pp. 87–88.

Millions of Americans marveled at the elaborate buildings and carefully designed grounds of the 1893 Chicago World's Fair. This photo, taken by photographer Frances Benjamin Johnston, shows the Palace of Mechanic Arts and the Court of Honor Basin. *(Library of Congress, Prints and Photographs Division, LC-USZ62-116999)*

In practice, sweating consists of the farming out by competing manufacturers to competing contractors the material for garments, which, in turn, is distributed among competing men and women to be made up. The middleman, or contractor, is the sweater (though he also may be himself subjected to pressure from above) and his employees are the sweated or oppressed. He contracts to make up certain garments, at a given price per piece, and then hires other people to do the work at a less price. His profit lies in the difference between the two prices. In the process he will furnish shop room and machines to some, and allow others, usually the finishers, to take the work to their living and lodging rooms in tenements.

The sweater may be compelled to underbid his fellow contractor in order to get work, but he can count with a degree of certainty on the eagerness of the people who work for him to also underbid each other, so as to leave his margin of profit but little impaired. The system thrives upon the increasing demand for cheap, ready-made clothing, cheap cloaks, and cheap suits for children, which demand springs in turn from the rivalry of competing dealers and producers. Thus each class preys upon the other, and all of them upon the last and weakest. . . .

Explanation of "sweatshop labor," Illinois Bureau of Labor Statistics, Seventh Biennial Report, *1893, p. 359.*

The child led me over broken roadways, there was no asphalt, although its use was well established in other parts of the city,—over dirty mattresses and heaps of refuse . . . between tall, reeking houses whose laden fire-escapes, useless for their appointed purpose, bulged with household goods of every description. The rain added to the dismal appearance . . . intensifying the odors which assailed me from every side. Through Hester and Division streets we went to the end of Ludlow; past odorous fish-stands, for the streets were a market-place, unregulated, unsupervised, unclean; past evil-smelling, uncovered garbage-cans. . . . The child led me on through a tenement hallway, across a court where open and unscreened closets [outhouses] were promiscuously used by men and women, up into a rear tenement, by slimy steps whose accumulated dirt was augmented that day by the mud of the streets, and finally into the sickroom.

All the maladjustments of our social and economic relations seemed epitomized in this brief journey and what was found at the end of it. The family to which the child led me was neither criminal nor vicious. Although the husband was a cripple, . . . although the family of seven shared their two rooms with boarders,—who were literally boarders, since a piece of timber was placed over the floor for them to sleep on,—and although the sick woman lay on a wretched, unclean bed, soiled with a hemorrhage two days old, they were not degraded human beings, judged by any measure of moral values.

In fact, it was very plain that they were sensitive to their condition, and when, at the end of my ministrations, they kissed my hands . . . it would have been some solace if by any conviction of the moral unworthiness of the family I could have defended myself as a part of a society which permitted such conditions to exist. . . .

Lillian Wald describes her first case as a nurse on New York's Lower East Side, 1893, in her House on Henry Street, *pp. 4–7.*

Ascending a broad staircase, the visitor passes through a doorway, between two iron beams, into a cheerful looking apartment with plate glass windows, and on either side, rows of revolving chairs. Except that the windows are barred with iron gratings, and that above are other chambers poised in air, he would not know that he is already on one of the cars of the Ferris wheel; but so it is. Of these cars there are six and thirty, with iron, wood-covered frame, each 27 feet long, 13 in width, and 9 in height, with a weight of 13 tons and seating accommodation for 40 passengers. . . .

By night the trip is even more attractive; for the great wheel is ablaze with 2,500 electric lights attached to the outer rim, to the inner circle, to the spokes, the portals, the enclosing fence, and wherever else such lights could be placed to advantage. Far above the myriads of lamps that illumine the city of the Fair, towers this rainbow of revolving light, seen afar on the prairie and lake, like the bow of scientific promise set athwart the blackness of the night.

Historian Hubert Howe Bancroft describes G. W. Ferris's mechanical wheel, 1893, in his Book of the Fair, *p. 868.*

Stamping her foot forward, the dancer will move her shoulders up and down, increasing the contortions of her body, striking the castanets she carries, whirling sometimes, but more often stamping forward, each time to a posture nearer the floor, until, as she seems to expire in the excitement of the rapid music and cries of the musicians, other houris rise from their couch and take her place, or join her, waving long strips of illusion or lace in a graceful and rhythmic manner. No ordinary Western woman looked on these performances with anything but horror, and at one time it was a matter of serious debate in the councils of the Exposition whether the customs of Cairo should be faithfully reproduced, or the morals of the public faithfully protected.

Halsey C. Ives describes the dance of "Little Egypt" at the Chicago World's Fair, 1893, in his Dream City, *pages unnumbered.*

The exhibit of the progress made by a race in 25 years of freedom as against 250 years of slavery, would have been the greatest tribute to the greatness and progressiveness of American institutions which could have been shown the world. The colored people of this great Republic number eight millions—more than one-tenth the whole population of the United States. They were among the earliest settlers of this continent, landing at Jamestown, Virginia in 1619 in a slave ship, before the Puritans, who landed at Plymouth in 1620. They have contributed a large share to American prosperity and civilization. The labor of one-half of this country, has always been, and is still being done by them. The first credit this country had in its commerce with foreign nations was created by productions resulting from their labor. The wealth created by their industry has afforded to the white people of this country the leisure essential to their great progress in education, art, science, industry and invention.

Ida B. Wells, preface to her pamphlet The Reason Why the Colored American Is Not in the World's Columbian Exposition, *p. 4.*

I went to the fair at once and before I had walked for two minutes, a bewilderment at the gloriousness of everything seized me . . . until my mind was dazzled to a standstill. I studied nothing, looked at no detail, but merely got at the total consummate beauty and grandeur of the thing:— which is like a great White Spirit evoked by Chicago out of the blue water upon whose shore it reposes.

Diary entry of author Owen Wister, 1893, quoted in Trachtenberg, Incorporation of America, *p. 218.*

Not only do sailors know the wharves right well, but they know—often to their cost—the anything but healthful odours that emanate in certain places from under them; for much of the sewage of [San Francisco] is discharged not right out into the bay or ocean, but underneath the wharves. Witness Third Street, Clay Street, Brannan Street wharves, where the water is blackened by the filth, and foul air at low tide offends the noses of delicate persons. Can it be a matter for wonder that ships lying for some weeks near sewage discharged in great quantities not uncommonly have cases of typhoid and malaria. . . .

If ships along or near certain wharves are obliged to lie in such places, and suffer such odours, it has even been worse for the nasal organs this past year or two for the crews of those ships which have lain at anchor in Mission Bay, which is part of the Bay of San Francisco. The authorities are filling up a large area of depressed land adjoining the bay—presumably to make it possible for the children of men whose smelling organs may not be highly developed to eventually build for themselves houses in which to dwell. The material used for filling up this area, which is now mud and water, and to lay a good foundation for the saloons which will without doubt appear on the surface when it is sufficiently hardened, is the garbage of the city, and daily scores of carts find their way to this historic spot yclept [called] "The Dumps" and deposit their savoury burden. . . .

Memoirs of Rev. James Fell, ca. 1893, chaplain of the Seaman's Institute, British Merchant Seamen in San Francisco 1892–1898, *reprinted in Barker,* More San Francisco Memoirs, *pp. 279–80.*

The girl stood in the middle of the room. She edged about as if unable to find a place on the floor to put her feet.

"Ha, ha, ha," bellowed the mother. "Dere she stands! Ain' she purty? Lookut her! Ain' she sweet, deh beast? Lookut her! Ha, ha, lookut her!"

She lurched forward and put her red and seamed hands upon her daughter's face. She bent down and peered keenly up into the eyes of the girl.

"Oh, she's jes' dessame as she ever was, ain' she? She's her mudder's purty darlin' yit, ain' she? Lookut her, Jimmie! Come here, fer Gawd's sake, and lookut her."

The loud, tremendous sneering of the mother brought the denizens of the Rum Alley tenement to their doors. Women came in the hallways. Children scurried to and fro.

"What's up? Dat Johnson party on anudder tear?"

"Naw! Young Mag's come home!"

"Deh hell yeh say?"

Through the open door curious eyes stared in at Maggie. Children ventured into the room and ogled her, as if they formed the front row at a theatre. Women, without, bended toward each other and whispered, nodding their heads with airs of profound philosophy. A baby, overcome with curiosity concerning this object at which all were looking, sidled forward and touched her dress, cautiously, as if investigating a red-hot stove. Its mother's voice rang out like a warning trumpet. She rushed forward and grabbed her child, casting a terrible look of indignation at the girl.

From Stephen Crane's shocking novel about a New York tenement girl driven to prostitution, Maggie, A Girl of the Streets *(1893), pp. 47–48.*

When the Committee first offered [the Women's Building mural] to me . . . at first I was horrified, but gradually I began to think it would be great fun to do something I had never done before. The bare idea . . . put [French impressionist Edgar] Degas into a rage and he did not spare any criticism he could think of. I got up my spunk and said I would not give up the idea for anything. Now one only has to mention Chicago to set him off.

American artist Mary Cassatt, an expatriate who lived and worked in France, letter to a friend, early 1893, quoted in Weimann, Fair Women, *p. 205.*

At a meeting in Honolulu, late in the afternoon . . . a so-called committee of public safety, consisting of thirteen men. . . . was appointed "to consider the situation and devise ways and means for the maintenance of the public peace and the protection of life and property. . . ." [T]he committee addressed a letter to John L. Stevens, the American minister at Honolulu, stating that the lives and property of the people were in peril and appealing to him and the United States forces at his command for assistance. This communication concluded "we are unable to protect ourselves without aid, and therefore hope for the protection of United States forces." On receipt of this letter Mr. Stevens requested Captain Wiltse, commander of the U.S.S. Boston, to land a force "for the protection of the United States legation, United States consulate, and to secure the safety of American life and property." The well-armed troops, accompanied by two Gatling guns, were promptly landed and marched through the quiet streets of Honolulu to a public hall . . . just across the street from the Government building, and in plain view of the Queen's palace. . . .

While there were no manifestations of excitement or alarm in the city, and the people were ignorant of the contemplated movement, the committee entered the Government building, after first ascertaining that it was unguarded, and read a proclamation declaring that the existing government was overthrown, and a Provisional Government established in its place, "to exist until terms of union with the United States of America have been negotiated and agreed upon." . . .

Secretary of State W. Q. Gresham describes the Hawaiian revolution of January 14, 1893, in his report to President Cleveland October 18, available online at Kingdom of Hawai'i. URL: http://www.pixi.com/~kingdom/gresham.html.

I Liliuokalani, by the Grace of God and under the Constitution of the Hawaiian Kingdom, Queen, do hereby solemnly protest against any and all acts done against myself and the Constitutional Government of the Hawaiian Kingdom by certain persons claiming to have established a Provisional Government of and for this Kingdom. . . .

Now to avoid any collision of armed forces, and perhaps the loss of life, I do this under protest and impelled by said force yield my authority until such time as the Government of the United States shall, upon facts being presented to it, undo the action of its representatives and reinstate me in the authority which I claim as the constitutional sovereign of the Hawaiian Islands.

Queen Liliuokalani surrenders to the United States, January 17, 1893, from her Hawaii's Story, *p. 392.*

The overthrow of the monarchy was not in any way promoted by this government, but had its origin in what seems to have been a reactionary and revolutionary policy on the part of Queen Liliuokalani, which put in serious peril not only the large and preponderating interests of the United States in the islands but all foreign interests. . . .

President Benjamin Harrison to the U.S. Senate, February 15, 1893, in Richardson, ed., Messages and Papers of the Presidents, *vol. 9, p. 348.*

We, the people of the Hawaiian Islands, through the delegates of the branches of the Hawaiian Patriotic League of all districts throughout the kingdom, in convention assembled, take this mode of submitting our appeal and expressions of our unanimous wishes to the people of our great good friend, the Republic of the United States of America, with whom we always entertained most cordial relations, whom we have learned to look upon as our patrons and most reliable protectors, whose honor, integrity, and sense of justice and equity we have ever confidently relied [on] for investigation into grievous wrongs that have been committed against us as a people, against the person of our sovereign, and the independence of our land.

And while we are anxious to promote the closest and most intimate political and commercial relations with the United States, we do not believe that the time has yet come for us to be deprived of our nationality and of our sovereign by annexation to any foreign power.

And therefore we do hereby earnestly and sincerely pray that the great wrongs committed against us may be righted by the restoration of the independent autonomy and constitutional government of our Kingdom under our beloved Queen Liliuokalani, in whom we have the utmost confidence as a conscientious and popular ruler.

Joseph Nawaho, president of the Patriotic League, and 42 delegates, March 2, 1893, available online at Kingdom of Hawai'i. URL: http://www.pixi.com/ ~kingdom/petition1893.html.

The system of sewerage at the World's Fair is a combination of several methods of disposing of sewerage and will be given a thorough and lasting trial, which will settle for all time its claim as being the best solution of the problem of efficiently disposing of immense quantities of sewerage. It ingeniously combines the disinfectant and cremation methods, so as to leave absolutely no noxious residue. . . . every vestige of disease-producing waste is destroyed.

"Sewerage at the World's Fair," Manufacturer and Builder, Vol. 25 (June 1893), p. 136.

From the conditions of frontier life came intellectual traits of profound importance. The works of travelers along each frontier from colonial days onward describe certain common traits, and these traits have, while softening down, still persisted as survivals in the place of their origin, even when a higher social organization succeeded. The result is that to the frontier the American intellect owes its striking characteristics. That coarseness and strength combined with acuteness and inquisitiveness; that practical, inventive turn of mind, quick to find expedients; that masterful grasp of material things, lacking in the artistic but powerful to effect great ends; that restless, nervous energy; that dominant individualism, working for good and for evil, and withal that buoyancy and exuberance which comes with freedom—these are traits of the frontier, or traits called out elsewhere because of the existence of the frontier. Since the days when the fleet of Columbus sailed into the waters of the New World, America has been another name for opportunity, and the people of the United States have taken their tone from the incessant expansion which has not only been open but has even been forced upon them. . . . For a moment, at the frontier, the bonds of custom are broken and unrestraint is triumphant. There is not tabula rasa. The stubborn American environment is there with its imperious summons to accept its conditions; the inherited ways of doing things are also there; and yet, in spite of environment, and in spite of custom, each frontier did indeed furnish a new field of opportunity, a gate of escape from the bondage of the past; and freshness, and confidence, and scorn of older society, impatience of its

restraints and its ideas, and indifference to its lessons, have accompanied the frontier.

Frederick Jackson Turner, "The Frontier in American History," read at the meeting of the American Historical Association in Chicago, July 12, 1893, published in his Frontier in American History, pp. 37–38.

The enthusiasm awakened by [the Catholic Women's Congress at Chicago] drew a large body of Catholic women together, who organized a National League for work on the lines of education, philanthropy, and "the home and its needs"—education to promote the spread of Catholic truth and reading circles, etc.; philanthropy to include temperance, the formation of day nurseries and free kindergartens, protective and employment agencies for women, and clubs and homes for working-girls; the "home and its needs" to comprehend the solution of the domestic service question, as well as plans to unite the interests and tastes of the different members of the family. . . . The underlying idea of the league is that Catholic women realize that there is a duty devolving on them to help the needy on lines which our religious [nuns and priests] cannot reach, even were they not already so sadly overworked. . . . . Mankind has repeated the "Our Father" for well-nigh two thousand years, and yet the great body of humanity seems only now waking up to the fact that "*our* Father" implies a common brotherhood; that "no man liveth to himself alone"; that we are our brothers' keepers. Surely then, in the face of these great facts, it can only be through misapprehension of terms that the question is asked "Is there a public sphere for Catholic women?" . . . The great power of the age is organization, and nowhere is it more needed than among Catholic women, whose consciences and hearts are so keenly alive to evils that individuals find themselves powerless to overcome.

Alice Timmons Toomey, first president of the Catholic Women's League, "The Woman Question Among Catholics," Catholic World, Vol. 57 (August 1893), pp. 674–76.

On the one side stand the corporate interests of the United States, the moneyed interests, aggregated wealth and capital, imperious, arrogant, compassionless. On the other hand stand an unnumbered throng, those who gave to the Democratic party a name, and for whom it has assumed to speak. Work-worn and dust-begrimed, they make their mute appeal, and too often their cry for help beats in vain against the outer walls, while others, less deserving, gain access to legislative halls.

Congressman William Jennings Bryan, Democrat from Nebraska, speaks against repeal of the Sherman Silver Purchase Act, August 1893, quoted in Cashman, America in the Gilded Age, p. 244.

Our unfortunate financial plight is not the result of untoward events nor of conditions related to our natural resources, nor is it traceable to any of the afflictions which frequently check national growth and prosperity. With plenteous crops, with abundant promise of remunerative production and manufacture, with unusual invitation to safe investment, and with satisfactory assurance to business enterprise, suddenly financial distrust and fear have sprung up on every side. . . . Values supposed to be fixed are fast becoming conjectural, and loss and failure have invaded every branch of business.

I believe these things are principally chargeable to Congressional legislation touching the purchase and coinage of silver by the General Government. . . .

I earnestly recommend the prompt repeal of the provisions of the act passed July 14, 1890, authorizing the purchase of silver bullion, and that other legislative action may put beyond all doubt or mistake the intention and the ability of the Government to fulfill its pecuniary obligations in money universally recognized by all civilized countries.

President Cleveland's message to Congress urging repeal of the Sherman Silver Purchase Act, August 8, 1893, in Richardson, ed., Messages and Papers, *vol. 9, pp. 401–05.*

The practical and far-seeing policy of creating government forests and timber-land reserves must be popularized by campaigns of education, argument, and proof in the immediate region of the reserves. . . . Such reservations have been opposed in many sections by the very classes to be benefited and protected by the reserves. The average American, living only for the present day and the dollars of the moment, in this extravagant age of wood does not consider the lumberless condition of the next century. . . . The guarding of the water-supply is the only argument that appeals to Western settlers, and several Colorado valleys with empty flumes and irrigation ditches already offer object-lessons as to the effect of wholesale forest destruction on any watershed. . . .

Eliza Ruhamah Scidmore, "Our New National Forest Reserves," Century, vol. 6 (September 1893), pp. 792–93.

The Exposition itself defied philosophy. . . . the inconceivable . . . consisted in its being there at all. . . . since Noah's Ark, no such Babel of loose and ill-joined, such vague and ill-defined and unrelated thoughts and half-thoughts and experimental outcries as the Exposition, had ever ruffled the surface of the [Great] Lakes.

The first astonishment became greater every day. That the Exposition should be a natural growth and product of the Northwest offered a step in evolution to startle Darwin. . . . Critics had no trouble in criticising the classicism, but all trading cities had always shown traders' taste. . . . All trader's taste smelt of bric-á-brac; Chicago tried at least to give her taste a look of unity.

Bostonian historian Henry Adams damns the Chicago World's Fair with faint praise, September 1893, in his Education of Henry Adams, *pp. 339–40.*

With the sharp crack of a carbine in the hands of a sergeant of the Third Cavalry, followed by almost simultaneous reports from the weapons of the other soldiers stationed all along the line between Kansas and the Indian country, the greatest race ever seen in the world began to-day. It was on a race-track 100 miles wide, with a free field, and with a principality for the stake. . . . For a mile in the rear of the line, there was presented what appeared like a fine hedge fence, extending as far as the eye could reach along the prairie in both directions. But as the observer approached the fence it changed into a living wall. . . .

It was perhaps the maddest rush ever made. No historic charge in battle could equal this charge of free American people for homes. While courtesy had marked the treatment of women in the lines for many days, when it came to this race they were left to take care of themselves. Only one was fortunate enough and plucky enough to reach the desired goal ahead of nearly all her competitors. This was Miss Mabel Gentry, of Thayer, Neosho County, Kan., who rode a fiery little black pony at the full jump for the seven miles from the line to the town site of Kildare, reaching that point in seventeen minutes.

Third Oklahoma land rush, September 16, 1893, New York Tribune, September 17, reprinted in America: Great Crises, *vol. 10, pp. 22–24.*

I shan't go to Chicago [World's Fair], for economy's sake— besides I *must* get to work. But *every* one says one ought to sell all one has and mortgage one's soul to go there, it is esteemed such a revelation of beauty. People cast away all sin and baseness, burst into tears and grow religious, etc., under the influence!!

Philosopher William James to his brother, author Henry James, September 22, 1893, in James, Selected Letters, *p. 286.*

This was Woman's Day at the Exposition and ceremonies in the Woman's Building were going on all day. It has been a very cold day and I just could not stay in that cold Rotunda, so I went over to the Woman's Building and enjoyed myself with the other ladies . . . There was a Reception and Concert at night and we all stayed. . . . Before the entertainment was over we heard the dreadful news of the Assassination of Carter Harrison, the Mayor of Chicago. We could not believe it, but coming home it was all confirmed and papers were selling on the street telling about it. 'Tis a sad climax to the great World's Fair.

Sallie Sims Southall Cotten, North Carolina representative to the Board of Lady Managers, unpublished diary, October 28, 1893, quoted in Weimann, Fair Ladies, *p. 579.*

Where the application is made by a Chinaman for entrance into the United States on the ground that he was formerly engaged in this country as a merchant, he shall establish by the testimony of two credible witnesses other than Chinese the fact that he conducted such business before his departure from the United States, and that during such year he was not engaged in the performance of any manual labor, except such as was necessary in the conduct of his business as a merchant, and in default of such proof he shall be refused a landing.

Amendment of the Chinese Exclusion Act, November 3, 1893, U.S. Statutes at Large, 53rd Congress, vol. 28, p. 7.

It is charged against Populists that they favor paternalism in government. This is an error. They only demand that public functions shall be exercised by public agents, and that sovereign powers shall not be delegated to private persons or corporations having only private interests to serve. They would popularize government to the end that it may accomplish the work for which it was established—to serve the people, all the people, not only a few.

Kansas senator William Alfred Peffer, Populist, "The Mission of the Populist Party," North American Review, vol. 157 (December 1893), p. 666.

But for the notorious predilections of the United States minister for annexation, the Committee of Safety, which should be called the Committee of Annexation, never would have existed.

But for the landing of the United States forces upon false pretexts respecting the danger to life and property, the committee would never have exposed themselves to the pains and penalties of treason by undertaking the subversion of the queen's government.

But for the presence of the United States forces in the immediate vicinity and in position to afford all needed protection and support, the committee would not have proclaimed the Provisional Government from the steps of the government building.

And, finally, but for the lawless occupation of Honolulu under false pretexts by the United States forces, and but for Minister Stevens' recognition of the Provisional Government

Farming changed dramatically in the late 19th century as farmers purchased timesaving but expensive machinery. This threshing crew is using both a new steam-powered tractor and horse-drawn implements. The crew and family, with the women in their Sunday best, posed for a traveling photographer in North Dakota in the 1890s. *(Courtesy Minnesota Historical Society, SA4.6/p29, neg. 444)*

when the United States forces were its sole support and constituted its only military strength, the queen and her government would never have yielded to the Provisional Government....

President Grover Cleveland to the U.S. Senate, withdrawing the treaty to annex Hawaii, December 18, 1893, in Richardson, ed., Messages and Papers, *vol. 9, pp. 469–70.*

The widespread movement among the farmers to-day is their effort to adapt themselves and their occupation to the ever-changing environment, so that they shall be once more masters of the situation, receiving their due share of the product of American industry and exerting their due influence in the formation and development of national character. As a result of his industry the farmer has made food and the raw material of our factories produced from the soil more and more plentiful, of better quality and cheaper. Here we find an efficient cause of his pecuniary embarrassment; the supply of agricultural products has been increased beyond the demand, with the consequent fall of price. If the surplus of agricultural products was matched by a corresponding surplus of gold, of personal services, of means of transportation, and of the comforts, conveniences, and luxuries of life, such universal plenty would enrich all, beggaring none. But with over-production in agriculture, and monopolies of coal, of telephones, of electric railroads and of other essentials of modern civilization, the farmer finds himself at a great disadvantage.

Farmers have been content in the past to confine their labors to the production of wealth, leaving to others the control of those conditions which determine the distribution of this wealth. At last, however, they have awakened to the fact that the problems of distribution have not been successfully solved. They believe that they get too little for the product of their labor and others too much, that they must bear heavy burdens of society while they are at the same time practically debarred from the enjoyment of the advantages of the progressive culture of modern life.

C. S. Walker, "The Farmer's Movement," Annals of the American Academy of Political and Social Science, *vol. 4 (1893–94), p. 94*

2

"The Crisis of the '90s"
1894–1897

THE POLITICS OF THE DEPRESSION

As 1894 opened, the depression that began in 1893 continued unabated. America was beset by a widespread sense of disquiet. Businesses continued to fail. Industrial workers bitterly resented the refusal of the Cleveland administration to take any responsibility for alleviating their distress. Farmers were destitute. Millions of other middle-class and working Americans, who were neither farmers nor industrial workers, lived in fear that they too might soon lose their jobs. Those who remained financially secure worried about the economic situation—although some worried more about the general disquiet itself, believing it might be a symptom of serious political instability. Many more were alarmed at the suffering caused by America's first industrial depression and shocked at the divisions in American society that it had revealed.

In Washington, officials continued to focus on monetary policy. The drain on America's gold reserves continued, despite the repeal of the McKinley Silver Purchase Act. The gold reserve, which had been almost $200 million at the end of the 1880s, had sunk to $62 million by January 1894. President Cleveland was determined to raise it to no less than $100 million. According to law, if it was below that point, the country could not longer operate on a gold standard, or, as supporters called it, "sound money."

In desperation, the president turned to J. Pierpont Morgan to organize a sale of $50 million worth of government bonds to banks and the wealthy in return for gold. Morgan was the dominant American investment banker of the day. To the American public, he was also a symbol of Wall Street's excessive power and commonly labeled as head of the "money trust." Eventually, Morgan and his associates did succeed in stabilizing the gold supply. To do so, however, they had to float a second bond issue in November 1894 when reserves had shrunk to $42 million, and a third in February 1895. A fourth, in January 1896, was open to the public. Like all investment bankers, Morgan charged a hefty price for his services. Many ordinary Americans were angered at the bankers' handsome profit from national distress. Both the public and some political leaders showered President Cleveland with a new firestorm of criticism for being so preoccupied with the gold supply amid so much distress.

Meanwhile, the Democrats in Congress set to work on a hobbyhorse of their own: repeal of the Republican-sponsored McKinley Tariff. At the time, the tariff was the primary means of filling the federal treasury, but Democrats wanted to lower the rates. In February 1894, the House passed a bill sponsored by William L. Wilson of West Virginia, which lowered duties modestly. "We know that not all who march bravely in the parade are found in line when the musketry begins to rattle," he said in introducing the bill. "Reform is beautiful upon the mountain-top or in the clouds, but ofttimes very unwelcome as it approaches our own thresholds." The Senate soon proved him correct. Senators attached 634 amendments with special exceptions for their own local interests. Little overall reform remained and some rates were actually raised. President Cleveland denounced the final act, named the Wilson-Gorman Tariff. "The livery of Democratic tariff reform has been stolen and worn in the service of Republican protection," he wrote to one congressman. He refused to sign the bill, although he did not veto it. It became law without his signature.[1]

In addition to tariff reform, however, the Wilson-Gorman Act had another provision: a national income tax. It was proposed by Representative Benton McMillan of Tennessee and a fiery young congressman from Nebraska, William Jennings Bryan. An income tax was a long-time goal of farming interests and their Democratic congressmen, who wanted the tax to help fill the national treasury so that tariffs could be significantly lowered. Tariffs protected American industrialists and, many farmers believed, helped them accumulate wealth unfairly at the expense of consumers who had to purchase the goods they produced. Lowering the tariff was primarily seen as a way to make consumer goods cheaper for ordinary people, although some also saw it as a way to counter the new economy's increasingly vast differences in wealth. The Wilson-Gorman income tax, set at 2 percent of incomes over $4,000, was not designed to be a mass tax affecting almost everyone. The qualifying income would have limited tax liability to a tiny number of Americans in 1896, when the overall average income of farmers, wage earners, and salaried employees in manufacturing as well as teachers, ministers, and government and postal employees was $411.[2]

The income tax provision was extremely divisive in Congress. Not only Republicans but many conservative Democrats opposed the idea. Congress had levied taxes on income before, during the Civil War—but only as a wartime measure. Senator John Sherman of Ohio denounced it as "socialism, communism, devilism." But William Jennings Bryan supported it strongly. Opponents of the tax, he said during the congressional debate, "weep more because fifteen millions are to be collected from the incomes of the rich than they do at the collection of three hundred millions upon the goods which the poor consume." The income tax provision of the Wilson-Gorman Act faced a court challenge from its opponents almost immediately. In 1895 the Supreme Court declared it unconstitutional.[3]

WORKING PEOPLE IN THE DEPRESSION

For working people, 1894 was the most savage year of the depression that lasted from 1893 to 1897. Business collapses, layoffs, and wage cuts continued unabated. Although no central agency kept accurate employment statistics at the time, evidence of suffering abounded. Workers crowded around newspaper offices waiting for the employment want ads, then stormed the gates of factories looking to hire. Many men, called tramps, left their families and hopped freight train boxcars to search for work. Private charities were strained to the breaking point, and in some places the streets were crowded with the homeless. Newspapers published dramatic articles of people who committed suicide rather than starve or steal food. In New York, baker Louis Fleischmann gave away loaves of bread to those who lined up, popularizing the term *breadline*. On the opposite coast, a Tacoma philanthropist, A. V. Fawcett, hosted Christmas dinner for a thousand hungry children. Nationwide, as many as 3 million workers, or one out of every five, were probably unemployed; in manufacturing, the figure rose to one out of every three. In Chicago during 1893–94, two out of every five were unemployed, a total of

100,000. A young Chicago reporter (later a famous reform journalist), Ray Stannard Baker, wrote home to his father in Michigan, "There are thousands of homeless and starving men in the streets. I have seen more misery in this last week than I ever saw in my life before."[4]

Farmers suffered new miseries as well. Throughout the West and South, prices at the 1894 harvest dropped to a level below production costs. Foreclosures multiplied. In California, soup kitchens for agricultural workers were called Cleveland cafes. Julius S. Morton, Cleveland's secretary of agriculture, responded, "The intelligent, practical, and successful farmer needs no aid from the Government. The ignorant, impractical, and insolent farmer deserves none."[5]

Other federal government officials also seemed unconcerned with the obvious suffering, from the viewpoint of many Americans. Some local communities provided a small amount of work relief, but far from enough. In January 1894, Jacob S. Coxey, a successful businessman but ardent Populist from Massillon, Ohio, proposed a plan of national work relief. The program he envisioned would employ men to build public roads, financed by an issue of $500 million in paper money unbacked by gold reserves. Sympathetic congressmen like Populist senator William Peffer of Kansas introduced Coxey's "good roads" bill, but it did not have enough support for action to be taken. Coxey responded, "We will send a petition to Washington with boots on."

Coxey called on the unemployed to form "industrial armies" to march to Washington to demand relief. The unemployed responded nationwide—and throughout the country many other people cheered them on. "Coxey's men are going to Washington hoping to get what is left after the sugar trust and the other monopolists are given all they ask," wrote the *St. Louis Post-Dispatch*. Coxey's own group marched from Massillon on Easter Sunday, calling themselves the Commonweal of Christ, or Commonwealers. Journalists, some 40 of whom set out with the 125 marchers, dubbed them

"Coxey's Army" of unemployed men marched to Washington in April 1894, to press for aid to the unemployed during the depression. It was the first large demonstration of the kind called today a march on Washington. *(Library of Congress, Prints and Photographs Division, LC-USZ62-9803)*

This cartoon, "The Original 'Coxey Army,'" was published shortly after Coxey arrived in Washington. It portrays the heads of powerful trusts marching to the Capitol to demand government aid—a high, protective tariff. Andrew Carnegie, at the head of the line, holds a scroll that reads, "Help the Feeble Steel Industry." *(Library of Congress, Prints and Photographs Division, LC-USZ62-96769)*

Coxey's Army. As historian Carlos Schawantes notes, the industrial armies created "an unemployment adventure story that the press found irresistible." Press coverage helped focus the attention of America on industrial unemployment and on Coxey's idea of federal work relief.[6]

Along the way Coxey's Army picked up sympathizers. In many places they met enthusiastic receptions. As they marched through industrial towns north of Pittsburgh, for example, some 30,000 people turned out to cheer. About 500 marchers paraded into Washington on May 1, led by Coxey's teenaged daughter on a white horse, with Coxey, his wife, and their infant son in a carriage behind her. Government officials, however, viewed the march as a threat to law and order, as did some other conservative Americans. At the Capitol, where Coxey intended to deliver an address, armed police met and arrested him and other leaders. The marchers were herded into camps outside the city and clubbed if they resisted. Coxey was later convicted—of illegally walking on the grass.

Before the end of 1894, 17 industrial armies attempted similar marches. (The army from San Francisco included a teenaged Jack London, later a prominent American author.) Although in general women were excluded, a few did join and two were even elected leaders. The armies were not free from the racial and ethnic prejudices of the day, but Coxey himself welcomed all, and some African Americans marched with his group. More than 1,000 people in all eventually made it to Washington, the first time such a large number of protesters had done so.

THE PULLMAN STRIKE

The year 1894 was also a year of labor turmoil. In the wake of severe wage cuts, more than 1,400 strikes occurred. Many were accompanied by the eruption of violence. The strikes hit not only the East and Midwest but also the industrialized New South, where miners and dockhands added to the tally. The most important was a large railroad strike centered in Chicago.

In 1893, the American Railway Union (ARU) had been formed under the leadership of Eugene V. Debs. The ARU brought together many separate unions of skilled workers, such as engineers, conductors, and switchmen. It also opened its membership to unskilled workers and to women. It accepted any white worker (blacks were excluded) whose job had any connection to the railroad industry. Together, these workers formed one large industrial union, or a union that is industry-wide. By 1894 the ARU had 150,000 members, making it the largest single union in the country—fittingly, since railroads were the largest business. Not surprisingly, railroad management was alarmed at the ARU's growth. Managers immediately formed the General Managers Association (GMA), an organization of 24 companies whose lines passed through Chicago. The GMA agreed to meet the union head-on, together, at the first opportunity.

That opportunity came in the spring of 1894 when factory workers at the Pullman Palace Car Company, who had very recently joined the ARU, went out on strike. The company, located south of Chicago, manufactured luxuriously appointed sleeping, dining, and private Pullman cars for trains. Owner George M. Pullman had also built a thoroughly planned company town for his workers and managers. He rented them tidy brick rowhouses or apartments and sold them utilities as well. He considered Pullman, Illinois, a model solution to the problems of industrial workers. After the depression began, Pullman to his credit attempted to keep his plants open and his employees working, even accepting contracts at a loss. Despite that, more than half of the 5,800 Pullman workers were soon dismissed. The others received pay cuts—but no break at all in the rents or costs charged in company housing. Pullman refused to arbitrate either wages or rents, a stance which even many of his fellow capitalists found foolhardy. On May 11, Pullman workers walked out.

At first the strike, which included women workers such as the seamstresses and upholsterers who equipped the car interiors, was entirely peaceful. It garnered considerable sympathy and financial support in the Chicago community and beyond. Then in June, in a stroke of fateful timing, ARU representatives gathered in Chicago for a national convention. On June 21, the entire ARU voted to boycott, or refuse to handle, any train with Pullman cars attached. The next day the GMA agreed to fire any worker who joined the boycott. On June 26, the boycott began. It spread with lightning speed throughout the nation, as railroad workers in many places expressed not just sympathy but also their own deep anger at labor conditions. By the end of June, 150,000 ARU members—almost all the railway workers south and west from Chicago—were on strike. Rail traffic was paralyzed from the Atlantic coast to the Pacific.

Illinois governor John P. Altgeld and Chicago mayor John P. Hopkins maintained order, but both were known to be sympathetic to the workingman. The GMA quickly chose to go over Altgeld's head to the federal government, requesting armed troops to protect the 2,500 strikebreakers it had hired. President Cleveland's cabinet was divided, but Attorney General Richard Olney strongly supported intervention. Olney was a railroad lawyer before he assumed federal office and was still on retainer to several companies. On July 2, he obtained an injunction against the union. (An injunction is a court order demanding that someone either act or cease acting in a certain way, usually until a court can rule on a case.) It ordered all union members and officials to cease interfering with the conduct of 23 railroads. Olney argued that the strike was obstructing the delivery of the U.S. mail, and, in addition, was a conspiracy in restraint of trade that violated the Sherman Antitrust Act.

On July 4, President Cleveland ordered 2,000 armed U.S. marshals and federal troops to Chicago, over the protests of Governor Altgeld, to protect trains operated by strikebreakers. The companies themselves hired some 3,400 private guards. In the face of marshals, troops, guards, strikebreakers, and strikers, restraint dissolved. Violence escalated quickly, with local rowdies pitching in. On July 5, and for several nights thereafter, mobs destroyed over 600 railway cars and burned to the ground six buildings on the former grounds of the Chicago World's Fair. Soon the president sent another 14,000 state and federal troops to Chicago. In 27 other states where as many as a quarter million workers were now striking and boycotting, many other incidents of violence occurred as well. Throughout the nation, newspapers vilified Debs and competed with each other for sensationalist reporting and headlines: "Chicago at the Mercy of the Incendiary's Torch!" "Frenzied Mob Still Bent on Death and Destruction!" "Anarchists and Socialists Said to Be Planning the Destruction and Looting of the Treasury!" Although union leaders condemned the violence, more than 10 people were killed—none of them actually strikers—and many were injured. Nationwide, others also died in clashes connected to the strikes.

On July 10, Debs and other union leaders were arrested and jailed. Within a week the railroad strike and the ARU collapsed. Debs and 75 other leaders were indicted by a federal grand jury for contempt of court because they had disobeyed the injunction. On that basis, rather than for criminal activity, they were sentenced to prison by a judge. Some middle-class Americans were taken aback by imprisonment of union leaders for violating an injunction, without formal criminal charges or customary safe-guards for the accused.

The Pullman strike was far more extensive and far more violent than any con-flict between capital and labor ever before seen in America. In the words of legal historian John Papke, it "left the nation damaged, perplexed, and profoundly con-cerned about its future."[7] Most Americans had always considered labor violence to be much more deplorable than any action by a business owner, however tyrannical. Before Pullman, they often blamed labor problems on radical agitators. After Pull-man, they realized that the ordinary workingman's anger ran very deep, as did the division between capital and labor in the new industrial economy. Traditionally, Americans believed that ordinary, hard-working people could achieve sufficient means of self-support, and indeed that their opportunity to do so was one of the mainstays of democracy itself. If the new industrial economy had created a serious labor problem, therefore, the political consequences rippled widely. Not all Ameri-cans in 1893 drew the same conclusions from these events, but many were bewil-dered and frightened. Some socially concerned men and women became more interested in the plight of laborers, however, and began to reconsider the unregulated right of owners to determine the conditions of work.

The strike also had important consequences for American labor. All unions were temporarily weakened and the precedent of injunctions against strikers was set. And finally, the events at Pullman brought Eugene V. Debs to national prominence. After his release from jail, a cheering crowd of 100,000 people met the train that returned him to Chicago. But Debs, while pondering the political implications of his conviction during his imprisonment, had become a convert to socialism. He would soon emerge as the leader of the American socialist movement, a position he retained for the rest of the Progressive era.

WEALTH AGAINST COMMONWEALTH

Socially concerned Americans already disconcerted by the depression and labor tur-moil were further alarmed by journalists' revelations. In the opening years of the 1890s, rumblings appeared in the press that huge new corporations were indeed con-solidating economic power, as Americans suspected. Then in 1894 Henry Demarest Lloyd, a well-known reform journalist, published the powerful *Wealth Against Com-monwealth*. Lloyd amassed facts, dates, and statistics from official records to record the unsavory methods used by John D. Rockefeller and other great capitalists to eliminate competition and increase their personal economic control. Rockefeller, who incorpo-rated his Standard Oil Company in 1870, had perfected his control of the petroleum industry in 1879 by use of the trust, or control of many formerly competing compa-nies by one board of directors. After Congress passed the Sherman Anti-Trust Act in 1890, the Ohio State Supreme Court ordered the dissolution of the Standard Oil Trust in 1892. But Rockefeller, like all other powerful industrialists, found new ways to cir-cumvent the law. Like monopolies in other areas of industry, Standard Oil continued to grow.

"Corporations are grown greater than the State and have bred individuals greater than themselves," Lloyd wrote. "The naked issue of our time is with property becom-ing master instead of servant, property in many necessaries of life becoming monopoly of the necessaries of life." The size of the monopolies and the power of their owners—new things in American life—defied all social control, Lloyd argued, and threatened the American republic itself. Lloyd's well-documented book was largely ignored by conservatives, although Rockefeller reputedly paid a conservative economics professor to write rebuttals. But among socially concerned Americans of the 1890s, it was the most widely read exposé of an alarming dilemma: "Liberty produces wealth, and

This illustration is from William Hope Harvey's *Coin's Financial School,* a very popular work defending free silver. It compares the prosperity of 1872 under bimetallism with the financial distress of 1894 under monometalism, or the gold standard. *(Library of Congress, Prints and Photographs Division, LC-USZ62-93833)*

wealth destroys liberty," Lloyd wrote succinctly. "The corn of the coming harvest is growing so fast that, like the farmer standing at night in his field, we can hear it snap and crackle."[8]

THE MIDTERM ELECTION OF 1894

Amid the turmoil of 1894, midterm elections approached. Republicans were united in opposition to the Democrats, who had the misfortune of controlling the presidency during a depression. Among Democrats, however, disunity reigned. They had suffered a serious split over President Cleveland's insistence on the gold standard. The independent president had violated party loyalty on other issues as well. As a result, many Democrats appeared to oppose him more ferociously than did the Republicans. "He is an old bag of beef, and I am going to Washington with a pitchfork and prod him in his old fat ribs," proclaimed fellow Democrat, Governor Ben Tillman of South Carolina in his campaign speeches for a Senate seat. Tillman was thereafter known as Pitchfork Ben.

Democrats in the South and West were determined to wrest control of the party from President Cleveland and the northeastern conservatives who agreed with him. Their rallying cry, and their solution for all of America's problems, was "free silver!" or the abundant use of money backed by silver, whose value was highly inflated, in order to expand the money supply. Nebraska congressman William Jennings Bryan, an extremely powerful orator, traveled the South and West, pumping up the silver cause. "Silver conventions" were held, where many free copies of publications like *Coin's Financial School* by William H. Harvey were distributed. In Harvey's famous booklet of 1894, "Professor Coin" demonstrated that thanks to the gold standard, "the people are being reduced to poverty and misery; the conditions of life are so hard that individual selfishness is the only thing consistent with the instinct of self-preservation; all public spirit, all generous emotions, all the noble aspirations of man, are shriveling up and disappearing."[9] The gold standard was portrayed as the work of a conspiracy of eastern and English bankers; the Rothschilds, English bankers who were also Jewish, were described as an octopus stretching its tentacles around the globe.

The Populist Party agreed with the Democrats on silver but also ran a fervent campaign of its own. In response, white southern Democrats raised alarms of Negro domination if whites supported the third-party Populists. They also stepped up violence against blacks and committed outright fraud at the polls in places like Georgia. Despite these tactics, the Populists made gains in the South. Overall, they polled about one and a half million votes, a great increase over 1892. When the 54th Congress convened, the balance of power in the Senate was actually held by the six Populist senators. In the House, Democrats had suffered severe losses, with many prominent Democratic congressmen losing their seats.

COURT DECISIONS OF 1895

During early 1895, the Supreme Court handed down three decisions that raised further alarms among Americans already worried about divisions in the nation.

Under provisions of the Sherman Anti-Trust Act of 1890, the Justice Department brought suit against the American Sugar Refining Company (also called the E.C. Knight Company). The company, after purchasing four competitors, controlled more than 85 percent of sugar refining in America. The U.S. Constitution gives the federal government power to regulate business that crosses state lines, called interstate commerce. The Supreme Court held in *United States v. E.C. Knight,* however, that the Sherman Act did not apply to companies that were in business to manufacture a product and were only "indirectly" concerned with its later sale across state lines. The government's case, led by Attorney General Richard Olney, was not well presented and made some observers suspicious that the administration had little real interest in checking trusts and monopolies. The decision was a blow to the usefulness of the Sherman Act. After it was handed down, large business mergers began to multiply even faster.

In April and again at a rehearing in May, the Court declared the income tax established by the Wilson-Gorman Act of 1894 to be unconstitutional, by a vote of 5 to 4. The conservatives who brought the suit in *Pollock v. Farmers' Loan and Trust Company* rejoiced because they considered the tax a socialistic attack on private property. Many other Americans—especially farmers—saw the decision in *Pollock* as another triumph of the newly rich and powerful over the common people. The Constitution does not explicitly forbid tax on income, and the situation, arguments, and legal reasoning in *Pollock v. Farmers' Loan and Trust Company* were extremely convoluted. But after the decision, supporters of income tax realized it would be unlikely without a constitutional amendment. By December, supporters of the tax had unsuccessfully introduced the first of many attempts to pass such an amendment.

Also in May, the Court sustained the injunction obtained during the Pullman strike against Eugene V. Debs, in *In re Debs.* Debs was represented before the Supreme Court by the rising young lawyer Clarence Darrow. Darrow argued that in the face of huge new business combinations, workers had no choice but also to join and act together—but he argued to no avail.

CONSERVATION MOVEMENTS CONTINUE TO GROW

Despite the difficulties caused by the depression, conservation-minded Americans continued their efforts. Two important pieces of national legislation were achieved in the mid-1890s. The first, which pleased preservationists, was the National Park Protective Act of 1894. It protected the birds and animals in Yellowstone and established the principle that national parks would also be wildlife preserves, with hunting prohibited. The second was the Forest Management Act of 1897. It set up the administration of lumbering, mining, and grazing in the Forest Reserves (now called National Forests). It pleased those conservationists who preferred the managed use of natural resources. Before the end of his term President Cleveland added another 21 million acres to the reserves.

An important new conservation society was also founded. In 1888, George Bird Grinnell, a conservationist and editor of the popular nature journal *Forest and Stream,* had proposed a national society for the protection of birds. He suggested calling it the Audubon Society after famous ornithologist and artist John Audubon. Although the idea was very popular and several local clubs formed, Grinnell did not pursue the effort. In 1896, Harriet Lawrence Hemenway of Boston reignited the movement. She founded the Massachusetts Audubon Society and began a lasting movement. By the end of 1897 Audubon societies existed in 10 states. In the late 19th century, birds were widely killed to provide feathers for women's hats and other decorative objects. Many reform-minded conservationists championed bird protection, just as some today work to protect animals killed to make fur coats.

UTAH ACHIEVES STATEHOOD

In 1890, Mormons constituted more than two-thirds of the 211,000 residents of Utah, who also included 600 blacks, 3,400 Indians, and 800 people classified as *other,* probably Asians. In religious terms the Mormons were even more dominant, because 90 percent of Utah residents who belonged to any religious congregation at all belonged to the Mormon church.[10] Although Utahans had long desired statehood, United States officials objected to the Mormons' practice of polygamy and to their failure to separate church and state.

In 1890 and 1891, Mormons had disavowed polygamy and disbanded the church's political party. Early in 1894, President Cleveland restored civil rights to former polygamists who had presumably obeyed the law since 1890. On July 16, he signed the Utah Enabling Act, authorizing a constitutional convention to prepare for statehood.

Utah's convention of March 1895 drafted a constitution that provided for the separation of church and state. It also included an anti-polygamy clause, which (as required by the Enabling Act) could not be repealed without the consent of Congress. After much debate, the constitution also legalized suffrage and other equal rights for women. In November, the voters approved the document and elected their officials. The first state governor, Heber M. Wells, was a Mormon; the first congressman, Clarence E. Allen, was not; Utah's first U.S. senators were Frank J. Cannon, a Mormon, and Arthur Brown, a non-Mormon. On January 4, 1896, President Cleveland signed the proclamation making Utah the 45th state. Elaborate celebrations occurred throughout Utah.

AMERICA CONTINUES TO LOOK OUTWARD

The United States's willingness to act on the world stage continued to grow in the mid-1890s. In 1895–96, the nation teetered on the brink of war with Britain over a Venezuelan boundary dispute.

Venezuela and neighboring British Guiana, a British colony on the Atlantic coast of South America, had disagreed on their mutual border for many years. After gold was discovered on the boundary, the issue became more charged. Venezuela requested arbitration but Britain refused. In July 1895, Secretary of State Richard Olney notified Britain—in a letter not overly diplomatic—that America had the right to demand arbitration on Venezuela's behalf under the terms of the Monroe Doctrine. The doctrine, stated by President James Monroe in 1823, warned European powers against attempts to oppress or control independent nations in the Americas. If they did so, it would be viewed "as the manifestation of an unfriendly disposition toward the United States."

Britain failed to respond to Olney until November, at which time it denied the Monroe Doctrine was part of international law. Not deterred, President Cleveland requested and promptly received Congressional authorization to form a commission, determine the boundary, and if necessary send troops to enforce it. Meanwhile, Britain had encountered problems with the independent Boer Republics bordering its colony of South Africa, and Germany was threatening to aid the Dutch Boers. Britain did not want to be distracted by conflict with the United States, and agreed to arbitration.

Throughout the incident U.S. officials engaged in little consultation with Venezuela. President Cleveland's goal was not to forge closer relations with Latin America. Instead, he wanted to remind Old World nations—who were again racing to acquire new colonies elsewhere—that they were not welcome in the American hemisphere.

BOSSES, MACHINES, AND CORRUPTION

Between the Civil War and the end of the 19th century, corruption was rife at all levels of government in the United States—local, state, and federal. In part, corruption grew from the spoils system of job distribution. Few publicly funded jobs were filled competitively on the basis of qualifications, abilities, or merit. Instead, political party organizations and their officeholders at all levels had the authority to dispense the jobs to their loyal supporters. In 1883 the first limited civil service reforms had been passed, but in 1890 the president alone still controlled more than 100,000 appointments. The spoils system helped make political party organizations far more powerful in the 19th century than they are today.

Spoils, however, were only the tip of the corruption iceberg. Patronage and graft of many kinds existed—kickbacks from legitimate businessmen and hush money from those in illicit activities; profit from inside knowledge of future business or public projects; bribes for petty offices and for utility franchises worth millions; and last but not least, plain theft from city or state treasuries. While most political figures did refrain from outright thievery, almost none shared today's understanding of conflict of interest. Even men who were otherwise honorable saw no conflict in accepting financial rewards, gifts, commissions, or retainers from businesses and individuals whom they assisted.

By the 1890s, many Americans had become especially concerned about political corruption in the burgeoning cities. Big-city political organizations were called *machines* because their operations were so well oiled and powerful. The machines were impervious to the customary means of public control, in part because the hierarchy of bosses who ran them usually did not hold major elective offices. At the same time, these bosses indirectly controlled the existence and operation of crucial and often tax-supported services like transit, paving and street cleaning, utilities, police protection, and in some places even public schools. Bosses and machines were able to establish their invisible government primarily because rapid urban growth outstripped the capabilities of traditional, existing institutions of city government.

Bosses and machines obtained their financing chiefly from corrupt alliances with prosperous businessmen, who cut deals with them for prizes as large as the contract to construct a bridge or as small as the right to hang an awning on a storefront. But they maintained their power through voter support from poor and working men, who in the cities were often immigrants and their sons. Many of the men who rose in city machines were themselves first- or second-generation Americans. When poor or newly arrived families needed assistance, bosses stepped into the vacuum and provided aid with a human face. One local boss in New York, for example, made a point of knowing the birthdays of poor children in his district and presented them with shoes. Beginning in the ward (the smallest political division in a city, similar to a neighborhood in nonpolitical terms) and moving up the hierarchy to city hall, bosses located jobs, helped new immigrants obtain citizenship so they could vote, smoothed troubles with the police, and aided in financial emergencies. In return for their favors, party bosses expected—and got—voter loyalty to the party machine and its candidates for office. Where voter loyalty was not sufficient, they routinely committed election fraud.

Bosses and machines, some historians point out, gave poor and newly arrived urban Americans a modicum of political representation that otherwise they would not have had. In the eyes of many other Americans in the 1890s, however, responsible representative government in the cities seemed to have disappeared. To them, immigrant and other poor urban voters appeared to be trading their votes for personal favors, keeping machine candidates in power with no regard for traditional American ideas of public-spirited citizenship and no thought to the effects of corruption. In many cities, the cost of corruption was fast becoming insupportable. Desperately needed services, sanitation, building projects, transportation, and utilities continued to be sacrificed in the unsavory deals cut with businessmen and in money siphoned off to enrich the bosses. Although the poor supported the machines because they valued the individual aid they received, they themselves often suffered the most from deficiencies in public services.

THE CRUSADE FOR MUNICIPAL REFORM BEGINS

By the mid-1890s, anger at urban corruption—made more painfully evident by the depression—was rising throughout the nation. Civic leagues began to multiply in cities small and large to work for municipal reform. The reform-minded middle- and upper-class people who joined them aimed to revive the participation of honest, disinterested citizens in politics and government. They believed that it was possible to identify one overall public interest on many questions of civic life and that the public interest outweighed all competing party, individual, or special interests. In general, their goals were to weaken party machines and bosses, end corrupt deals between politicians and businessmen, and introduce nonpartisan administration into government. They hoped to achieve economy and efficiency, business principles that had enabled the prominent entrepreneurs to build powerful corporations so successfully. The end result, reformers hoped, would be vastly improved city services, the reduction of voting irregularities, the recovery of representative government, and perhaps lower taxes. Some reformers also hoped to find solutions for urban crime, vice, and other illegal activities. Civic leagues were often called Good Government Clubs. Their opponents mocked them as "goo-goos" for short.

In 1894, civic reformers in Philadelphia and New York issued a call for civic leagues to meet in a national conference. The first National Conference for Good City Government brought together figures like Theodore Roosevelt, reform lawyer Louis Brandeis, department store magnate Marshall Field, elder statesman Carl Schurz, and landscape architect Frederick Law Olmsted, Jr., as well as representatives of academic fields. These men organized a permanent National Municipal League to coordinate the efforts of local communities, influence public opinion, and develop model proposals. "After this convention," said Milwaukee reformer John A. Butler, "it will be felt everywhere that municipal reform is an assured and well-credited national movement, and men of first-rate ability and character will everywhere find it an honor to be associated with [the] cause." Within two years, more than 200 new local clubs had organized.[11]

The most dramatic example of civic league activity in the mid-1890s occurred in Chicago. In the late 19th century, building, supplying, and selling utilities and mass transit—including street trolleys, gas and electric lines, street lighting, and telephone service—was a private enterprise. An individual who could secure a utility or transit franchise from the government stood to reap a great fortune for it—sometimes hundreds of millions. Since these franchises were usually the most valuable prize officials and bosses had to offer, they were almost always beset by corrupt deal making. In 1895, wealthy utilities baron Charles Yerkes bribed the Illinois state legislature to pass a bill giving him the Chicago street trolley franchise for a century—without any payment to the city for the privilege. Governor Altgeld vetoed the bill. Yerkes funded a campaign to defeat Altgeld for reelection in 1897, while convincing the legislature to transfer its franchise-granting authority to the Chicago City Council, which he had long had in his pocket. This drama, however, aroused great anger in the city. A Municipal Voters League formed and rolled into action. By 1897, its supporters had elected enough members to city council to control it. They denied Yerkes his franchise. He later sold out and moved to New York.

In New York, a coalition of reformers managed to launch an investigation into the corruption of Tammany Hall, as New York City's Democratic machine was called, in early 1894. The governor, who was part of the machine, declined to fund the Lexow investigation (named for State Senator Clarence Lexow). Not to be deterred, reformers convinced the Chamber of Commerce to provide financing. The Lexow Committee built on the work of Rev. Charles Parkhurst, a Presbyterian minister. His interfaith City Vigilance League had been doggedly investigating New York City's underworld since 1892. The committee soon discovered that Tammany operated via extensive police corruption, including widespread shakedowns, voter intimidation and election fraud, collaboration with rent-racking landlords and strikebreaking employers, and maltreatment of new immigrants. The investigation led to a permanent nonpartisan police commission in New York, whose first chair was Theodore Roosevelt.

In the midst of the widely publicized Lexow investigation, reformers mobilized by New York's network of Good Government Clubs also launched an energetic campaign to elect a reform mayor. At the November election, polling places were monitored by more than 2,000 Good Government poll watchers. The reform candidate, wealthy merchant William L. Strong, won decisively. Strong promised to run the city with nonpartisan efficiency, and in many areas he succeeded. One of his most successful appointments was Colonel George Waring, Jr., a sanitary engineer and veteran of the Civil War. As head of the sanitation department, Waring reorganized sanitation workers along military lines, complete with white uniforms and parades through neighborhoods. He brought about a spectacular clean-up of city streets.

Another reform mayor who attracted national attention in the mid-1890s was Hazen S. Pingree, Republican mayor of normally Democratic Detroit from 1890 to 1897. Where New York's Strong emphasized the need for efficiency in municipal government, Pingree emphasized the need for social responsibility and social reform. Pingree, who also was a businessman, had wide support from both small business interests and communities of ethnic voters in Detroit. He ended corruption and introduced good management into city government. But he also entered the fray with utilities magnates to gain reduced rates for all citizens; improved the tax structure; put the unemployed to work on public projects; oversaw the construction of many new schools and parks; and lobbied for municipal ownership of utilities.

SETTLEMENT HOUSES AND REFORM IN THE URBAN SLUMS

The settlement house movement continued to flourish. By the mid 1890s, however, it had become clear to settlement workers that their programs for neighborhood residents did not touch the underlying conditions that had created the slum. Many workers began to lobby or take active roles in wider reform or social justice movements. They campaigned for better schools, public baths, and protections for working women and children. Their investigations increasingly taught them that many fully employed people could not maintain a decent standard of living and furthermore that working conditions in most industries were shockingly bad. Most settlement workers gave full support to labor causes and even labor organizing at a time when unions had few friends. And although at first settlement workers avoided local city politics they soon learned, in the words of historian Allen Davis, "that they had invaded a political world." Some even entered the fray against the bosses. "To keep aloof from it," Jane Addams eventually realized, "must be to lose one opportunity of sharing the life of the neighborhood." She had also learned that change was not likely to occur otherwise.[12]

One famous example was Addams's attempt to improve garbage collection in the Hull-House neighborhood, where slaughterhouses, livery stables, and residents alike dumped refuse in the streets and alleys. Hull-House investigators learned that the position of garbage inspector was a patronage job. It was held by one of boss Johnny Powers's corrupt cronies. Addams herself submitted a bid to the city to collect garbage in the ward. It was denied but generated so much publicity that the mayor appointed her as inspector instead. Addams and a young assistant, Amanda Johnson, devoted themselves to the job. But Powers fought back. He handed out patronage jobs to as many men associated with Hull-House programs as he could to buy their loyalty. Finally, he launched personal attacks on Johnson and had the City Council eliminate her job. In the meantime, however, the Hull-House workers had worked vast improvements. In one street, they removed 18 inches of solid, compacted garage, under which they discovered paving.

Settlement house workers played a large role in many other reform movements as well, often making great contributions by their knowledge and data collection, their important connections, and their ability to publicize issues. For example, they were in the vanguard of a movement to create designated, equipped, and supervised public playgrounds (which did not exist at the time) in densely packed tenement districts. The need for both parks and playgrounds was created by the growth of cities and city living, but in slum neighborhoods the lack of play space was particularly acute. The only possible place for children to play was in streets, which were dangerous and filthy and usually far from the eye of parents. "Nothing is now better understood," wrote Jacob Riis, "than that the rescue of the children is the key to the problem of poverty . . .; that a character may be formed where to reform it would be a hopeless task."[13] In 1893, Florence Kelley of Hull-House established the first playground in Chicago on land donated by a local slumlord after settlement house workers publicized his name. About the same time, a small playground was opened by Lillian Wald behind the Henry Street Settlement in New York. Soon after, small playgrounds appeared at other settlements in Chicago and New York, at College Settlement in Philadelphia, South End House in Boston, and many other places. Reformers in the playground movement also worked to open school property for play and recreation space after school hours, a goal first achieved in Boston in 1894, and to require that new city schools have an open-air playground, achieved in New York in 1895.

Settlement workers also maintained a high profile in the growing effort to improve slum housing, which many reform-minded people believed to be the worst social evil afflicting large cities. They knew the details of living conditions intimately and were always ready to testify when asked. In 1894 and 1895, the Department of Labor published two reports confirming that overcrowding existed in major cities but endorsing the solution of benevolent private and philanthropic development. Model tenements were occasionally built, but their improved design and sanitary facilities always priced them beyond the resources of the ordinary worker. The New York State Legislature also

As the number of city dwellers multiplied, many facilities and services were strained at the seams. As this photo by Jacob Riis shows, schools on New York's Lower East Side were so overwhelmed that some classes in the Essex Market School did not have desks. *(Library of Congress, Prints and Photographs Division, LC-USZ62-58027)*

commissioned an investigation of tenement housing in 1894. The lengthy report disclosed astonishing densities in some wards of Manhattan—worse than Bombay, India, considered the most overpopulated spot in the world. Public indignation increased when a journalist revealed that Trinity Church, one of the oldest and wealthiest of New York congregations, owned substandard housing. But the prominent were not alone in seeking the profits that could be made on slum housing. Tenement ownership was also a common route that ambitious newcomers themselves took to grow rich in America.

THE ANTI-LIQUOR MOVEMENT REVIVES

Since colonial days, when drinking rates were very high, crusades for personal temperance had been a part of American culture. Around 1840, per-person consumption of alcoholic beverages reached its highest point ever in America.[14] It spurred vigorous temperance and prohibition campaigns that successfully and drastically lowered drinking rates before the Civil War. But after the war, consumption began to rise again. Soon a new and vocal generation of temperance reformers appeared. In the late 19th century, however, both major political parties tried to avoid becoming embroiled in the issue on the national level. Both parties contained strong advocates of temperance and strong opponents. Both found that the liquor question sometimes divided party members by cultural or ethnic backgrounds or was otherwise internally divisive.

Despite the silence of the major parties, temperance reformers in the third-party Prohibition Party (founded 1869), the Women's Christian Temperance Union (founded 1874), and other temperance groups succeeded in keeping the issue before the public eye at the local and state level. Between 1880 and 1890, as a result of their campaigning, 18 states had voted on new prohibition amendments to their constitutions. Six approved them, although one quickly repealed. Eleven other states approved some form of local option laws, which permitted towns, counties, or even city precincts to limit or ban liquor sales, primarily by banning or refusing to license saloons. Nonetheless, in most places where liquor was outlawed, the law was not well enforced and extralegal saloons, called joints, flourished.

Despite these efforts, the consumption of alcohol continued to rise in the late 19th century. Saloons multiplied even faster than the booming population—especially in less affluent areas of the growing cities, where population density was high. In city neighborhoods of crowded tenements, saloons served as gathering places, which some historians refer to as poor men's clubs. Many customers were workingmen or members of some new immigrant groups, who traditionally considered alcoholic beverages an important part of sociability. Saloons were also multiplying because beer had become more popular than distilled liquor in America for the first time. Unlike liquor, beer was very perishable and could only be obtained on tap in saloons because bottling methods had not yet been perfected. Between 1880 and 1900, according to one estimate, the number of saloons doubled nationwide—although the city of Chicago had more saloons than 15 southern states added together.

As saloons multiplied, the liquor trade became far more competitive. Liquor manufacturers set saloon keepers up in business to stock their products—an attractive offer because it enabled people with little capital to establish a small business of their own. Saloon keepers competed with each other by offering free lunches and occasional free rounds of drinks. In addition to encouraging patrons to drink more, the fierce competition helped saloons gain a reputation for lawlessness. A few allowed vice, including gambling and prostitution, to flourish on their premises. Most of those that catered to workingmen violated long-established Sunday closing laws, because Sunday was the only day their customers were at leisure. On a March Sunday in 1894, for example, an investigation by the City Vigilance League found 2,960 open saloons in 19 districts in

New York City. Almost all saloons violated laws forbidding sales to minors, because children were customarily sent to fetch buckets of beer for factory workers' lunchtimes. "The law prohibiting the sale of beer to minors," Jacob Riis observed in *How the Other Half Lives,* "is about as much respected in the tenement-house districts as the ordinance against swearing."[15]

As Americans became more concerned about urban problems, many began to associate them with unregulated saloons. They saw saloons as a contributing cause of poverty and connected them to vice and violent public disorders. Most especially, they connected the saloon to urban political corruption. And in fact, although the causes of corruption were complex, the saloon was closely integrated into machine politics. Many local bosses and political aspirants actually owned saloons, and even those who did not used them as informal offices to meet with constituents, gather information, and dispense assistance. During elections, the role of the saloon was less benign. Bosses assembled and treated their loyal followers there—often immediately before they cast their votes—and in many cases used the saloons themselves as polling places.

By 1890, seven states maintained statewide prohibition—New Hampshire, Vermont, Maine, Kansas, Iowa, and the Dakotas. No other state joined the list for 17 years, but sentiment in favor of regulating liquor and the liquor interests was growing nonetheless. In some parts of the South, a dispensary system was initiated. In the dispensary system, the government acted as a liquor retailer. It purchased liquor from manufacturers and sold it to the citizens or saloon owners—but locked the dispensaries' doors on Sundays, holidays, and election days. First established in Athens, Georgia, in 1891, dispensaries were adopted as a statewide system in South Carolina in 1893 under Governor "Pitchfork Ben" Tillman. Local South Carolinians, however, resisted the special state liquor police (six people died in an 1894 shootout) and new forms of corruption developed in the dispensary system itself.

By the mid-1890s, a new, progressive response to the liquor question was evident nationwide. Like other emerging reform movements it was born from the new social concerns of Americans. Temperance had previously been considered a matter of personal and individual ethics, but the new reform movement was less concerned with reforming individuals who drank alcohol. Instead, it emphasized the effects on society of alcohol consumption and of malfeasance by the liquor trust, as manufacturers came to be called. In 1894, for example, the prestigious Committee of Fifty for the Investigation of the Liquor Problem was formed under the leadership of Seth Low, Columbia University professor and later reform mayor of New York. The committee proposed to study all aspects of the liquor question "scientifically" and "to secure a body of facts which may serve as a basis for intelligent public and private actions."

In 1895, the national Anti-Saloon League (ASL) was organized, headquartered in Ohio under the guidance of Howard H. Russell, a lawyer and ordained minister. The ASL was an independent political action group formed to oppose the liquor traffic and its center in the saloons. Its goal at the time was to enact local option laws. The ASL was a new kind of temperance organization. Although it engaged in politics, it was nonpartisan, or as it called itself, "omnipartisan." In any given campaign it focused on the lowest common denominator on which all temperance supporters could agree and favored practical politics—including political compromise. It did not insist on total abstinence among its supporters or its candidates. It backed

Many Americans thought political corruption was connected to saloons, as this cartoon illustrates. The saloon keeper/boss is distributing boodle, or graft, to the liquor commissioner, the judge, the police, and the councilmen. The cartoon was part of a flier distributed by the Anti-Saloon League. *(Courtesy Westerville, Ohio, Public Library, Anti-Saloon League Collection)*

HOW OUR PUBLIC WATCH DOGS ARE FED.

any candidate willing to support a given measure and directly urged supporters to cross party lines when necessary. It was also willing to work slowly. In 1894, for example, the Ohio Anti-Saloon League (the forerunner of the national ASL) drafted a model law to permit statewide local option. It was defeated, but the league used the opportunity to identify the major opponents in the Ohio legislature. In each following election, they targeted one or more opponents. Because of the ASL's approach, historian Jack Blocker calls it the "prototype of the political pressure group"—the first modern interest group formed to influence public policy on a single focused issue, while working outside of a major party organization. In contrast, the WCTU supported many different reforms, and the Prohibition Party functioned like the major political parties, supporting a comprehensive platform.[16]

The ASL began its growth into a national pressure group by assembling a professional, paid staff; emphasizing very careful organization, especially at the state level; and working through major Protestant denominational bodies, like Methodists, Presbyterians, and Baptists, who were known to have many sympathetic congregants. The ASL was an all-male organization. But the league worked closely with the WCTU and gave its support to the principle of women's suffrage, which WCTU president Frances Willard promoted as a means for women to protect their homes by deciding whether "the rum shop door" was opened or closed. As the liquor control movement regained steam in the mid-1890s, the WCTU itself began to focus more exclusively on prohibition, moving away from Willard's Do Everything reform philosophy.[17]

Most members of the ASL, the WCTU, and the Prohibition Party were Protestants. The temperance issue was also becoming important to American Catholics, however. At the parish level, temperance societies were organized and clergy oversaw pledges of abstinence. Temperance was, according to historian Jay Dolan, "the most enduring reform movement that Catholics sponsored in the nineteenth century."[18]

RELIGIOUS THOUGHT AND THE SOCIAL GOSPEL

In the 1880s, some Protestant theologians began to promote a new "social Christianity" or "applied Christianity". At the time, the majority of Protestant clergymen usually justified existing social and economic conditions as the inscrutable design of God and focused instead on individual morality and personal salvation. The new social Christianity held that Christian principles could and should be used to judge social and economic arrangements as a whole and furthermore that Christian belief called for social activism. Called the Social Gospel by the turn of the century, the movement was focused primarily on bettering life in the slums of the new industrial cities and achieving justice for the working poor. Richard Ely, a pioneering economist as well as an active Episcopalian lay leader, wrote, "It is as truly a religious work to pass good laws as it is to preach sermons; as holy a work to lead a crusade against filth, vice, and disease in slums of cities, and to seek the abolition of the disgraceful tenement-houses of American cities, as it is to send missionaries to the heathen." Ministers who worked with the poor also held that economic exploitation and terrible living conditions often made it impossible for the poor to achieve religious salvation. Rev. Walter Rauschenbusch, a young Baptist preacher working in a working-class German immigrant neighborhood in New York during the depression, commented, "One could hear human virtue cracking and crumbling all about." Rauschenbusch later became the most prominent of the Social Gospel theologians.[19]

By the mid-1890s, the Social Gospel was familiar in most Protestant theological seminaries. Many urban Protestant congregations, in addition, had also begun to support the institutional church movement, which opened church facilities for recreational and social welfare programs. In 1897, familiarity with the Social Gospel expanded greatly with the publication of a best-selling novel by a Congregational minister, Rev.

Charles M. Sheldon, entitled *In His Steps.* The novel portrayed a town whose inhabitants agreed to base their social actions for one year on the answer to a question: "What would Jesus do?" Over the next half century it sold millions of copies.

A parallel movement toward a social gospel began to have some influence in American Catholicism as well. In 1891, Pope Leo XIII's encyclical *Rerum Novarum* (Of new things) condemned the exploitation of labor: "A small number of very rich men have been able to lay upon the masses of the poor a yoke little better than slavery itself," the pope wrote. The encyclical urged support for labor unions and sanctioned government regulation of business in the interests of social justice, although it also upheld the rights of private property and criticized socialism. Among Catholic theologians in America, the social gospel did not flower until after the turn of the century. But clergy and laypeople, historian Mel Piehl points out, "had a long experience in coping with social problems before they began to reflect on them" because so many of the new immigrant and urban poor were Catholic congregants.[20]

In Jewish belief, a just community had always been an important doctrine. In the late 19th century, many American Jews responded to the increasing social problems in the industrial cities by increasing philanthropy, and some responded by entering the new profession of social work. Through the initiative of social workers, by the mid-1890s a federation movement was well under way to coordinate Jewish social welfare activities and philanthropies, which had grown so numerous as to be unwieldy. By the end of the decade a National Conference on Jewish Charities had been established.

Historians do not all agree on the extent to which religious beliefs influenced behavior in the Progressive Era. Arthur S. Link and Richard McCormick conclude, however, that the increased emphasis in faith communities on social and economic problems, while hard to evaluate, certainly "seared the consciences of millions of Americans, particularly in urban areas." It was one of several important influences on the rising interest in reform in the mid-1890s and in particular helped convince many Americans that reform was a moral as well as a practical necessity.[21]

THE PRESIDENTIAL CANDIDATES OF 1896

As the campaign of 1896 loomed, the depression still raged. A sense of crisis nagged at much of the country. Some Americans worried about the widespread corruption of democratic institutions. Some worried about the concentration of wealth and power. Some were outraged at the suffering caused by the cold-hearted pursuit of profit, and others worried more about the stability of society. But political party activists, it appeared, still worried the most about gold vs. silver.

The Republicans met first, on June 16 in St. Louis. Most party leaders had already joined with campaign manager Marcus A. Hanna, a wealthy industrialist, in support of William McKinley of Ohio. McKinley, in his second term as governor of Ohio, had formerly served in Congress for 15 years. A personally religious man of honorable personal reputation, he was also a good politician and a good public speaker. He was closely identified with the high protective tariff for which the Republicans stood, because the McKinley Tariff of 1890 carried his name. He enjoyed great support among rank and file Republicans. McKinley was elected on the first ballot. Garrett A. Hobart, a New Jersey lawyer and businessman, was nominated for vice president to add regional balance.

The proposed Republican platform contained a strong statement in favor of the gold standard. McKinley himself, however, had always skillfully avoided confronting the free-silver advocates head on. In fact, he had a reputation as a straddler on the issue among both goldbugs and silverites. He intended to campaign on the tariff, blaming the depression on reduced protection for American manufacturing in the Wilson-Gorman tariff passed by Democrats, and on the issue of political corruption. Before the convention McKinley had chosen the campaign slogan "The People Against the Bosses." Nonetheless, when the platform was presented to the delegates for approval, it was the gold plank that triggered a fight. Gold won, but it so angered delegates from western states that 24 of them walked out of the convention. Led by Senators Henry Moore Teller of Colorado, a former secretary of the interior and elder statesman of the Republican Party, and Frank Cannon of Utah, the next day they formed the Silver Republican Party.

The Democrats held a far more raucous convention in Chicago beginning July 7. Party leaders from the East still supported the gold standard—but free-silver mania had infected one state delegation after another throughout the West and South. Easterners were clearly outnumbered. Westerners and southerners cheered, whistled, whooped, and seized control of the convention and the party. They passed a platform that supported free silver, and for good measure they rejected almost all of President Cleveland's other policies as well. All they lacked was a candidate.

That candidate, Representative William Jennings Bryan of Nebraska, presented himself during a debate, with one of the most effective political speeches in American history. "I come to speak to you in defense of a cause as holy as the cause of liberty," he began, "the cause of humanity." It became known as the Cross of Gold speech because of its final passage: ". . . we will answer their demand for a gold standard by saying to them: 'You shall not press down upon the brow of labor this crown of thorns; you shall not crucify mankind upon a cross of gold.'" To strengthen his allusion to the crucifixion of Christ, Bryan stretched out his arms while delivering the final line. The audience was momentarily stunned silent, then burst into a demonstration that lasted half an hour.

The next day, on the fifth round of voting, 36-year-old Bryan became the youngest man ever nominated for president by a major party. Bryan was a Jeffersonian agrarian—that is, one who held to Thomas Jefferson's belief that independent farmers were the backbone of the American republic. To give the Democratic ticket balance Arthur Sewell of Maine, a banker who nonetheless opposed the gold standard, was nominated for vice president. Few eastern or conservative Democrats were placated. Commented the *New York World,* a usually Democratic paper, "The expected happened in the Chicago platform. The unexpected happened in the nomination for president. Lunacy having dictated the platform, it was perhaps natural that hysteria should evolve the candidate."[22]

To members of the Populist Party, of course, the unsettled condition of the nation in 1896 merely confirmed their beliefs. Had not their 1892 Omaha platform described a nation "brought to the verge of moral, political, and material ruin"? Nonetheless, by the time they met in St. Louis on July 24, they faced a serious quandary. Party leaders had anticipated that both Democrats and Republicans would nominate a gold-standard candidate. Then, they believed, support for their party would be swelled by all the unhappy reformers who supported free silver. But Bryan and the Democrats had stolen their thunder. If Populists nominated a candidate of their own, they would split and weaken the reform vote. If they endorsed Bryan, on the other hand, they risked demise as a distinctive party with a thoroughgoing program of reform.

As important as the silver issue was to Populists, many still did not want to abandon their overall platform. The 1896 platform retained all demands from 1892—and added new demands for good measure: public works projects for the unemployed and, more surprisingly, fair voting in the South (that is, an end to black disenfranchisement). But after much acrimony, the convention voted for fusion with the Democrats. (In fusion, two parties agree to support a single slate of candidates, in hopes of defeating another party.) Populists endorsed Bryan—and nominated their own candidate for vice president, Thomas E. Watson of Georgia. The convention was probably under the mistaken impression that Democrats would also agree to the principle of fusion, withdraw Sewell, and accept Watson on their ticket as well.

After the three conventions, dissension over monetary issues continued to split Democrats and Republicans. Silver Republicans, or the National Silver Party, eventually supported the Democratic nominee Bryan. Gold Democrats organized the National Democratic Party and nominated their own candidate. Other gold Democrats stayed in the party but worked quietly for Republican McKinley instead.

THE ELECTION OF 1896

The Democrats and Republicans both waged all-out campaigns, but they used very different tactics. Bryan, aware that his sonorous voice and persuasive oratory were his best assets, became the first presidential candidate to campaign throughout the country. "No man ever devoted himself more wholeheartedly or unselfishly to a presidential contest," writes historian Gilbert Fite.[23] Bryan traveled 18,000 miles by train to 26 states and more than 250 cities to present his case against the money power, as he called it. He drew unprecedented crowds, some of whom gathered at village depots in the middle of the night. Some citizens, to be sure, found this new way of campaigning undignified and unbefitting the office. But many more idolized Bryan. Many reformers and labor leaders campaigned for him, although his rural-minded emphasis did not overly impress urban workers. After the campaign of 1896, candidates began to be described as "running" for political office, rather than "standing" for office, the previous term of choice.

Republican William McKinley stayed home in Canton, Ohio, where he conducted a "front porch campaign." From his porch McKinley greeted trainloads of representative Republicans (some 750,000 in all) delivered by Mark Hanna's campaign organization. McKinley would deliver a short talk and answer prearranged questions. He specifically denounced the class and sectional conflicts emphasized by Bryan and instead stressed national unity. "The spirit of lawlessness," he said, "must be extinguished by the fires of an unselfish and lofty patriotism."[24] He downplayed religious divisions and de-emphasized divisive issues like temperance. He promised the ordinary working American a full dinner pail. The Republican Party blanketed the country with speakers, campaign buttons and gear, and 200 million pamphlets in 14 languages (total population at the time was under 70 million). Their overflowing treasury had been filled by business leaders who were terrified by Bryan. Republican campaign spending reached a new American record by far. Democrats had much, much less to spend—in part because many of their wealthy contributors and fund-raisers joined the gold Democrats.[25]

The spirited match between Bryan and McKinley sent voters to the polls in record numbers. In some states, turnout was as high as 95 percent. When the votes were counted, McKinley had won by more than 600,000 votes, or 51 percent, to Bryan's 46 percent, with 3 percent to third-party candidates. McKinley's win was the largest popular majority in two and half decades, and he carried 271 electoral votes to Bryan's 176. The total number of votes cast was so high, however, that Bryan actually received more votes than the winning candidate had received in 1892.

Republican campaign spending was not the sole reason for Bryan's defeat. Conservatives in both parties, aided by the press, associated him with both the radical Populist platform and the recent strikes and public disorder in the country. They painted him as a demagogue and rabble-rouser, if not an outright revolutionary. Many religious leaders even supported this view, despite Bryan's marked personal religiousness and upright family life. Although Bryan swept the agricultural South and West (excepting California and Oregon), he garnered little support among urban residents or industrial workers. Bryan appealed to a vision of America in which "prosperity in the city rested on prosperity in the farmlands," as he liked to put it. But McKinley appealed to the new realities of an urban, industrial nation.

1896 AS A TURNING POINT

Historians rank the election of 1896 as one of the most important in American history. It occurred amid the most serious conflict between economic interests, classes, and sections in the United States since the Civil War. The majority of Americans voted in favor of social stability, the industrial economy, and, many historians say, conservatism. Nonetheless, as the *New York World* conceded in its election postmortem, "But for the existence of real and grievous wrongs the elements of discontent . . . would have been powerless to control a party convention or to enlist even a respectable support for their cause. . . . There is no doubt that in this republic, based as it is upon simplicity and ideas of equality before the law, there are growing inequalities of privilege and increasingly offensive encroachments and vulgarities of the rich."[26] As it turned out, the enormous publicity the campaign gave to issues like monopoly and the concentration of wealth, monetary policy, the value of labor, and divisions among groups and classes of Americans marked a turning point. After 1896 many more Americans turned their energy to reimagining the idea of a public interest, and the reform-minded to crusading for new ways to improve the political system, the economy, and the everyday life of their communities.

The defeat of Bryan also drove some Americans further to the left. On January 1, 1897, popular labor leader Eugene V. Debs made an announcement to his moribund American Railway Union. "The issue is Socialism versus Capitalism," he said. "I am for Socialism because I am for humanity. We have been cursed with the reign of gold long enough. Money constitutes no proper basis of civilization. The time has come to regenerate society." Debs had studied socialist ideas while in jail for leading the 1893 railway strike, but it was the election of 1896 that convinced him a new radical movement was necessary. In June 1898 he formed the Social Democratic Party, opening an era of growing influence for socialism in America.[27]

After the defeat of Bryan in 1896, farm-centered radicalism ceased to be the cutting edge of the demand for reform. The Populist Party won a large number of local offices in 1896 and continued to function in some localities for the remainder of the Progressive Era. But as a national party, it declined quickly. Nonetheless, a long list of specific populist demands were to be enacted across the nation in the next two and half decades—the regulation of railroads and communications, direct democracy reforms, and shorter workdays, for example. Two of the demands—a graduated income tax and the direct election of senators—were enacted even though they required amendments to the U.S. Constitution, a far-from-easy task. Above all, the overriding idea behind the populist program was realized—a larger role for government in the economy and in many other aspects of American life in the name of reclaiming democracy for the ordinary person. These changes, however, were not accomplished by reformers who lived in the countryside, but rather by those who lived in the cities and who by 1896 were beginning to call their viewpoint "progressive." William Allen White, the well-known Kansas newspaper editor, later described progressivism as populism that had "shaved its whiskers, washed its shirt, put on a derby, and moved up into the middle class." Mary Elizabeth Lease also observed the similarities. "Note the list of reforms which we [populists] advocated that are coming into reality," she told a newspaper reporter in 1915 at the height of the progressive movement. "Brother, the times are propitious. The seed we sowed out in Kansas did not fall on barren ground."[28]

The election of 1896 also marked a decisive end to the era of political balance and legislative stalemate in Washington. The Republican Party began a long dominance of national politics that did not end until the depression of the 1930s, despite Democrat Woodrow Wilson's two terms in the White House from 1912 to 1920. At the same time, the era of vigorous local political contests and mass involvement by male voters drew to a close. Voter turnout at all levels began a slow decline, never to recover.

AFRICAN-AMERICAN WOMEN ORGANIZE

In 1895, Josephine St. Pierre Ruffin called for African-American women's clubs to meet together nationwide. Ruffin, a journalist and head of the Women's Era Club of Boston, was founder of a monthly journal, *The Women's Era*. The immediate catalyst for her call was an offensive attack on Ida B. Wells, and all black women in general, by a white male journalist from Missouri. Black women, he said, had "no sense of virtue" and were "altogether without character." African-American women had long endured accusations of sexual immorality by whites, and it was even one of the issues that Wells herself often addressed in her writings and lectures. "Too long have we been silent under unjust and unholy charges," said Ruffin.[29]

The convention, held in Boston in 1895, resulted in the formation of the National Association of Colored Women (NACW) in 1896. The NACW was the first national organization of African-American people. Mary Church Terrell of Washington, D.C., was elected president. Terrell, a former teacher who held bachelor's and master's degrees from Oberlin College, headed the organization until 1901.

Like the white clubwomen who organized nationally, black clubwomen who made up the NACW were middle class and relatively prosperous. They adopted as their motto "Lifting As We Climb." The NACW became very involved in education and child care issues, such as the establishment of kindergartens (a new educational innovation at the time) for black children. They supported many other self-help initiatives and worked for justice for African Americans, including efforts to end lynching. They also supported the women's suffrage and temperance movements.

BOOKER T. WASHINGTON EMERGES AS A LEADER

In February 1895, the great abolitionist leader and former slave Frederick Douglass died. The following September a very different African-American leader rose to national attention. On September 6, 39-year-old Booker T. Washington, head of the Tuskegee Institute in Alabama, took the stage at the Cotton States and International Exposition in Atlanta, Georgia. The audience of some 2,000 people at the opening ceremonies was mostly white, although some blacks sat in a separate section. They were about to hear a black man speak—an extremely rare event before a white audience in the South of 1895—and some whites voiced their disapproval.

Soon, however, whites were applauding. Blacks reportedly wept at the dignity of his presentation. Washington's brief, unpretentious, and characteristic speech opened with a story about sailors adrift at sea, who asked for water from a passing vessel. "Cast down your bucket where you are," they were told. When the sailors finally did, they discovered they had drifted into fresh and drinkable water. The story expressed Washington's belief that southern black people should not move North, West, or even to Africa. Instead, they should concentrate on improving their economic condition in the South. He also believed that if southern whites supported black economic progress, whites would benefit as well.

As Washington continued, he seemed to be making a bargain. If white leaders would enforce the law more justly and promote economic progress for blacks, he seemed to imply, African Americans would be willing to forgo immediate demands for equal political and social rights. This implied bargain, which came to be called the Atlanta Compromise, was summed up in the most famous line of Washington's speech. "In all things that are purely social we can be as separate as the fingers," he said, "yet one as the hand in all things essential to mutual progress."

Washington's speech was publicized and reprinted over and over again. Many white people praised his approach and soon identified him as the spokesman for African Americans in the United States. The editor of the *Atlanta Constitution,* for example, wrote in a widely reprinted editorial, "The whole speech is a platform upon which blacks and whites can stand with full justice to each other."[30] The vast of majority of black people, too, embraced Washington as a beloved leader. Many prominent blacks thought he was a masterful statesman and agreed with him that no other stance was possible in the South of 1895. Staunch white supremacists, of course, rejected even Washington's compromise as an acceptable role for black people.

From the outset, however, a few black intellectuals and leaders strongly disagreed with Washington's "accommodationist" approach to race relations. They preferred to confront injustices directly and publicly, which Washington never did. (Privately, however, he financed court cases challenging segregation.) They also opposed acquiescing to the loss of rights guaranteed by the Constitution in return for entry into "the all-powerful business and commercial world," as Washington called it. As Washington's national power grew over the next two decades and white southerners failed to live up to their end of the bargain, the number of his critics grew as well. Even today historians continue to disagree about the wisdom of Washington's choices. Yet as historians John Hope Franklin and Alfred Moss write, his influence "sometimes for better and sometimes for worse, was so great that there is considerable justification in calling the period the Age of Booker T. Washington."[31]

Washington's critics also disagreed with his philosophy of education. Washington was best known as the champion of industrial education (today usually called vocational or technical education.) Tuskegee students operated a farm, sawmill, foundry, print shop, furniture shop, and other enterprises and eventually built 54 of the 60 campus buildings. Tuskegee also offered academic education, and many students trained to be teachers there, but Washington stressed practical training for occupations currently available to blacks in the South. Critics believed this approach discouraged capable blacks from high aspirations and attainment, just as whites preferred. For his part, Washington believed that African Americans would not be able to achieve power in the South until they had achieved economic security.

Washington's Tuskegee was the first institution of higher education in America to have an all-black faculty and administration. In 1896 George Washington Carver joined the faculty. Carver was a gifted plant scientist educated at the State College of Agriculture in Iowa (now Iowa State University). Carver's goal was to help what Washington called "the man farthest down." His experiments quickly made the Tuskegee farm a showplace for successful agricultural methods. In his laboratories he developed hundreds of uses for the crops local farmers grew, but he also issued pamphlet after pamphlet with practical instructions and began a "movable agricultural school" using a wagon outfitted with agricultural equipment and exhibits. "The primary idea in all my work," he once said, "was to help the farmer and fill the poor man's empty dinner pail."[32]

Tuskegee provided many other outreach services to poor farmers in the area. In 1892, Washington invited local farmers to a gathering to determine, among other things, how Tuskegee students could "use their education in helping the masses of the colored people to lift themselves up."[33] Five hundred farmers arrived to attend the first Tuskegee Negro Conference (Washington had expected about 75), and the annual event continued to grow. The ordinary people who came from miles around spent the day discussing their situations, their problems, and their recommendations. Margaret Murray Washington, Washington's wife and a teacher at Tuskegee who always stressed equal opportunities for women, established additional outreach programs for women and mothers.

Black Intellectuals and the American Negro Academy

In 1895, William Edward Burghardt (W. E. B.) DuBois, later to be Washington's most prominent critic, became the first African American to earn a Ph.D. from Harvard. The same year he helped found the American Negro Academy (ANA) in Washington, D.C. The ANA was the first African-American learned society, or organization for scholars, intellectuals, and literary notables. One of its purposes was to study and disprove theories of racial inferiority and erroneous beliefs about African-American life and culture. Membership was by invitation only. The only woman invited to join was women's rights theorist and educator Anna Julia Cooper. Booker T. Washington was invited to the founding meeting but declined to attend.

Another founder of the ANA was poet Paul Laurence Dunbar, the first African-American literary figure to attain wide readership and fame among both white and black people. When Dunbar's second book of poetry was published in 1896, it was acclaimed by William Dean Howells, the most prominent white literary critic of the day. Howells arranged to have the book reprinted by a major publishing house as *Lyrics of a Lowly Life*. Most of Dunbar's poems dealt with African-American folk traditions and everyday life and attempted to capture black speech in dialect spellings. (Writing in the dialect of ordinary white folk was also a vogue among white writers at the time.) African Americans embraced Dunbar's poems and black schoolchildren frequently memorized them.

"Separate but Equal" Becomes the Law of the Land

As the 1890s progressed, white governments and courts in the South continued their attack on the citizenship rights of African Americans and the voting rights of black men. In 1896, South Carolina Democrats became the first to establish the white primary, which barred blacks from participating in the selection of party candidates to stand for election. Because Democrats almost always won general elections in the South, the party's process of choosing candidates was, in most cases, more important than the November election itself. But the Democratic Party claimed to be a private organization, and the Supreme Court had ruled private organizations exempt from the equal rights requirements of the Fourteenth Amendment. Thus, the party was legally able to restrict its conventions and primary elections to whites only. Soon, other southern states also adopted the tactic.

White governments in the South also continued to tighten Jim Crow restrictions, which enforced segregation of the races in public places. Throughout the nation, African-American leaders, newspaper editors, and ordinary citizens protested in various ways. One way was to challenge discriminatory laws through the courts, in the belief that they contradicted the Fourteenth and Fifteenth Amendments. Soon after the first Louisiana law requiring segregated train cars was passed in 1890, activists in New Orleans organized and raised money to fund a test case. A suit began in February 1892 but collapsed on a technicality.

In June 1892, the citizens' committee began another test case. Homer Plessy, who was one-eighth black and customarily regarded as white in public, agreed to be the subject. He sat in the white train car, told the conductor he was black, refused to move when told to, and was arrested. The railroad company had probably been informed of the event in advance and cooperated. Railroad companies were not enthusiastic about the separate car laws because they feared the laws would raise costs and be difficult to enforce.

To defend Plessy, the citizens' committee hired white lawyer Albion Winegar Tourgée. Tourgée, a resident of New York born in Ohio, had been a well-respected Republican appointee to the North Carolina courts during Reconstruction. In Louisiana criminal court, Plessy was declared guilty in a decision handed down by Judge John Ferguson. Following standard legal procedure, when Judge Ferguson's decision was appealed to higher courts, his name appeared as the defendant.

The case of *Plessy v. Ferguson* finally came before the United States Supreme Court in 1896. Tourgée and his team appealed to the Fourteenth Amendment, guaranteeing

JUSTICES OF THE
United States Supreme Court.

This composite shows the justices of the United States Supreme Court in 1896: Horace Gray, Rufus Peekham, Edward White, John Marshall Harlan, Henry Billings Brown, David Brewer, Stephen Field, George Shiras, Jr., and Chief Justice Melville Fuller. *(Library of Congress, Prints and Photographs Division, LC-USZ62-104541)*

the "equal protection of law," but also presented many other arguments. They questioned whether separate accommodations could be equal when one race held more power. They attacked the difficulty of defining exactly who was black and who was not. "Justice is pictured blind," argued Tourgée, "and her daughter, the Law, ought at least to be color-blind."[34]

On May 18, the Supreme Court handed down its decision in *Plessy v. Ferguson.* The Court upheld the decisions of the Louisiana courts and declared the separate car law to be constitutional, by a vote of 7 to 1. The court held that the separation of the races did not violate the U.S. Constitution, providing that accommodations were equal. It also held that laws requiring such separation were a reasonable use of state authority. Separate railroad cars were no more unreasonable, wrote Justice Henry Billings Brown for the majority, than the common practice of segregating children in schoolrooms. The Court rejected, on one hand, the assumption that "the enforced separation of the two races stamps the colored race with a badge of inferiority." On the other hand, it rejected the assumption that "social prejudices may be overcome by legislation." "If one race be inferior to the other socially," Brown concluded, "the Constitution of the United States cannot put them upon the same plane."

The lone dissenting justice, John Marshall Harlan, filed a vigorous and stinging dissent. One purpose of the constitutional amendments passed after the end of slavery, Justice Harlan wrote, was to prevent "the imposition of any burdens or disabilities that constitute badges of slavery or servitude." He pointed out that segregation was a slippery slope: "Why may not the State require the separation in railroad coaches of . . . Protestants and Roman Catholics?" Finally, he declared, "Our constitution is color-blind, and neither knows nor tolerates classes among citizens. . . . The law regards man as man."[35]

As Albion Tourgée had realized from the start, a Supreme Court ruling against Plessy would be far worse than no test case at all. *Plessy v. Ferguson* and its watchword "separate but equal" became the constitutional justification for all forms of segregation in America until 1954, when it was countermanded by a new decision, *Brown v. Board of Education.*

IDAHO JOINS THE SUFFRAGE COLUMN

In 1896, Idaho voters approved an amendment to their state constitution and became the fourth state to give women the right to vote, joining Wyoming, Colorado, and Utah. The campaign was conducted quietly under the direction of Carrie Chapman Catt, an Iowa teacher and newcomer to the national suffrage movement.

Elsewhere, the record was less encouraging in the mid-1890s. In 1894, the male voters of Kansas defeated a referendum to give women statewide suffrage, despite the fact that women had voted in municipal elections since 1887. In Massachusetts, a mock referendum on women's suffrage was defeated by a wide margin in 1896. (The referendum was a nonbinding vote intended by the legislature to serve as a kind of poll on the question.) In California men also voted down statewide women's suffrage in 1896, although by a small margin. In major California cities, the liquor interests had organized and financed a determined opposition. A majority of small-town and rural voters approved suffrage, analysis of the vote showed, but voters in the city—the site of the saloons—were responsible for the defeat. The California campaign marked the first time that women of substantial wealth, like Jane Lathrop Stanford and Phoebe Apperson Hearst, gave public and financial support to the suffrage movement.

Idaho was to be the last statewide suffrage victory until 1910. By 1897, however, in addition to the four suffrage states, women could vote in school elections in 22 other states and two territories. In four additional states they had municipal or tax-related voting rights.

THE BIRTH OF THE MOVIES

No one person invented moving pictures. In the late 19th century, many inventors in the United States, France, Britain, and Germany worked to develop cameras and projectors that could make pictures appear to move. The first person to market a viewing machine for them, however, was Thomas Edison, the prolific American inventor who had already given the world the phonograph, the telephone transmitter, and the electric lightbulb. Edison's machine, the Kinetoscope, was introduced at the Chicago World's Fair in 1893. It was an individual or peep show viewer. The customer looked into a large box, fitted with a magnifying lens and illuminated by an electric light, to view a movie about 90 seconds long. Edison's company also produced the movies for the Kinetoscope, using film manufactured by George Eastman's Kodak company. Kinetoscope parlors quickly popped up throughout the country.

Meanwhile, inventors continued to experiment with machines that could project moving pictures onto a large surface, allowing many people to view them at once. In 1895 and 1896 three projectors quickly followed each other. One was made by the Lumière brothers in France. Called the Cinématographe (from the Greek for *motion recorder*), it introduced words like *cinema* and *cinematography* into the language. The other inventors were Americans: W. K. L. Dickson, whose machine and company were called Biograph, and Thomas Armat. Armat's projector was purchased by Edison, named the Vitascope, and marketed under the Edison name.

Edison's Vitascope was the first to premiere moving pictures to a paying public audience in the United States. The event took place on April 23, 1896, at Koster and Bial's Music Hall, a vaudeville house, at Sixth Avenue and 23rd Street in New York. Vaudeville, a very popular theater entertainment during the Progressive decades, was a variety show. While some vaudeville catered to specific ethnic groups, some to the lowbrow, and some to the risqué, most drew a broad, middle-class, and respectable audience. Programs might feature 20 or more specialty acts, such as musicians, vocal groups, dancers, comedians, short dramatic scenes, magicians, jugglers, or animal acts. Edison's moving picture was introduced as the last act on the program, called the chaser. The audience marveled and the inclusion of motion pictures at the end of vaudeville programs quickly spread.

Today, when motion photography on screen and television is so much a part of everyday life, it is hard to imagine how astonished the first film audiences were to see pictures that moved. The earliest films "understandably exploited their visual amazement," writes film historian Gerald Mast. Films emphasized moving objects such as bicyclists racing or trains rushing. The best received at the Koster and Bial showing was *Rough Sea at Dover,* an English film of waves crashing. According to the trade publication *New York Dramatic Mirror,* "Some of the people in the front rows seemed to be afraid they were going to get wet, and looked about to see where they could run." Other popular early subjects were views of scenery or travelogues, brief comedies of filmed jokes or pranks, reenactment of historical scenes, and news events. But the beginning of the movies was also the birth of a new art form. Filmmakers soon began to develop greater storytelling and artistic technique.[36]

THE "YELLOW PRESS"

A few American newspapers had always carried overwrought stories of political scandal or lurid crime. But in the 1890s, some newspaper publishers intentionally took sensationalism to new heights. They wanted to create a regular new audience among the workaday Americans who rarely read the staid, highly literate, and more expensive traditional newspapers and journals. To compete for readers' attention, these publishers pioneered the use of large, multicolumn, melodramatic headlines and many illustrations. They developed new sections for sports, society, and fashion news. They championed causes and involved their readers in civic projects and promotional schemes. They encouraged reporters to expose corruption—which, conveniently enough, often meant highlighting sex and violence—and to exaggerate drama, emotion, and moral judgments in their stories. Balance, and sometimes truth, took a backseat.

The new journalism was pioneered by Joseph Pulitzer, who had purchased the struggling *New York World* in 1883 and built it into an enormously profitable and popular newspaper. He soon had many imitators. In 1895, California publisher William Randolph Hearst purchased the *New York Journal* and began to compete directly with Pulitzer. The competition drove the circulation of both papers to new heights.

When a revolution began in Cuba in 1895, both Pulitzer and Hearst saw a great opportunity. They hired the best reporters and illustrators they could find and sent them off with instructions to emphasize atrocities committed by Spain. When one illustrator, Frederick Remington (later a well-known artist of Western scenes), objected to drawing events that did not really occur, Hearst cabled, "You furnish the pictures and I'll furnish the war." By the end of 1897, both the *World* and the *Journal* occasionally topped a million in daily circulation, the largest yet seen anywhere in the world.[37]

Pulitzer's *World* had published the earliest comics in 1889. In early 1896, Richard Outcault's new cartoon, *Hogan's Alley,* debuted in the *World's* new Sunday comic section. Its main character was a slum-dwelling urchin soon called the Yellow Kid, because his dresslike garment was printed in bright yellow. The cartoon was wildly popular. By October, Hearst had stolen Outcault from Pulitzer; Pulitzer retaliated by simply hiring someone else to continue drawing the Kid for the *World*. The two rival Yellow Kids were publicized all over town. Almost immediately, traditional journalists began referring to the Pulitzer and Hearst style as the yellow press. Many people thought yellow journalism was offensive and ill-advised, catering to the worst in human nature. But its influence on newspaper journalism was permanent and continued to spread throughout the nation.

CUBA LIBRE!

Spain had once possessed an extensive empire in the Americas. By the late 19th century, however, its empire there had been reduced to the island colonies of Cuba and Puerto Rico. Cubans had long been struggling for independence, and in 1895 the insurrection flared anew. Cuba was suffering economic distress, partially caused by the high duty on Cuban sugar enacted in America's Wilson-Gorman tariff of 1894. But the underlying cause of the struggle was a long history of Spanish misrule and brutality.

Americans of Cuban descent, as well as a growing group of new emigrants whose communities centered in Florida, New York, and New Jersey, worked hard to publicize Cuba's plight. They created much popular sympathy for the goal of *Cuba libre,* or a free Cuba independent from Spain. The leader of the movement for independence was José Martí, a poet and intellectual as well as a brilliant organizer. He lived in exile in New

York, where he established the Partido Revolucionario Cubano (Cuban Revolutionary Party). Many Americans supported him because they equated a Cuban revolution against Spain to the American revolution against Britain in 1776. Other Americans, to the apprehension of Cuban patriots, thought Cuba had the potential to become part of America—even a state.

Fighting in Cuba began early in 1895, after U.S. officials intercepted a shipment of arms leaving Florida and tipped the insurrectionists' hand. Unfortunately, Martí was killed in battle on May 19. Martí had held strong democratic convictions and wanted effective civilian leadership. Without his active influence, however, the remaining leaders cast civil government in the shadows. On July 15, the insurgents declared a Republic of Cuba. They established a junta in New York, led by Tómas Estrada Palma. But the constitution they adopted in September left the miliary generals almost independent of civilian restraint.

Unfortunately, there were considerable atrocities on both the Cuban and Spanish sides. The Cuban military fought by means of guerrilla warfare. (In guerrilla warfare, small groups of fighters engage in constant unexpected skirmishes rather than direct confrontation with an opposing army.) In November Cuban general Máximo Gómez ordered the destruction of all plantations, refineries, factories, and railroads; workers who did not leave their jobs were shot as traitors to the Cuban cause. His goal was to destroy all sources of Spanish revenue, although Americans also owned and lost significant investments in Cuba. In response, Spain sent a new and brutal general, General Valeriano Weyler, in early 1896. He immediately established a policy called *reconcentración,* or reconcentration. The *pacíficos,* or civilian farm families in the countryside, were given a week to gather in hastily established camps with armed guards. Weyler hoped to flush out the guerrillas in this way because guerrilla fighters usually hide by blending into the civilian population. But by necessity or design, the camps were horrendously inadequate. Cubans by the thousands died of disease or malnutrition.

The sufferings of the Cuban civilians were widely publicized in America. Newspapers focused on the brutality of the Spanish and ignored that of the Cuban military. The struggle dragged on, and by the end of 1896 public sentiment in America increasingly favored U.S. military intervention. Some Americans had become outright imperialists, who frankly wanted to annex Cuba. Many others, however, saw intervention idealistically. They saw America as a protector of the weak and Cuba as a suffering neighbor who needed help to establish a democracy. Almost the only naysayers were businessmen and industrial leaders, who feared that war with Spain would interrupt the recovery from depression by again threatening the gold standard.

President Cleveland refused to intervene. When President McKinley took office in March 1897, he continued to curb the warmongers, although he did increase diplomatic efforts. Spain recalled General Weyler, modified the reconcentration policy, and by fall offered limited self-government to the Cubans. By the end of 1897, many Americans were hopeful that the Cuban crisis would be solved satisfactorily, without U.S. military action.

THE HAWAIIAN REPUBLIC

After the overthrow of Hawaiian Queen Liliuokalani in January 1893, Hawaii was governed by a provisional government, or PG. Leaders of the PG greatly desired annexation to the United States, but the Cleveland administration concluded that the majority of Hawaiians wanted the monarchy restored. When PG president Stanford Dole refused to consider the idea, however, President Cleveland chose not to intervene.

The PG organized an independent republic. Both the United States and Great Britain recognized the new Republic of Hawaii, although Queen Liliuokalani continued to protest. Voting rights in the republic were restricted to men who owned a certain amount of property or other wealth. Many Native Hawaiians, as well as most of the Japanese or Chinese immigrants who made up more than 25 percent of the population, remained disenfranchised.

Many Hawaiians of all ethnic backgrounds still supported the monarchy. During the fall of 1894, they planned an armed overthrow of the republic, importing contraband weapons from San Francisco. On January 6, 1895, the first skirmish occurred, but government troops squelched the rebellion in two weeks. Some 190 royalist rebels, including Liliuokalani herself, were brought to trial. Many were convicted, but sentences were commuted or reduced and all were freed by January 1, 1896. The former queen, sentenced to five years hard labor, was actually put under house arrest at Iolani Palace and in November 1896 restored to full freedom.

The success of the new republic in putting down the rebellion and its restraint in punishing the perpetrators raised its stature in the eyes of many Americans. In June 1897 officials of the Republic, believing the time was now right, drafted a request for annexation to the United States. Secretary of State John Sherman agreed to it, and President McKinley sent it to the U.S. Senate for ratification. In the fall, fact-finding delegations of pro- and anti-annexation congressmen visited the islands. During their visit, Hawaiians who opposed annexation held a large demonstration near the Iolani Palace grounds. A memorial to the U.S. president and Congress was read and approved. (A memorial is an informal diplomatic document which requests certain actions and presents supporting information.) It was delivered to Washington with thousands of signatures.

By the end of 1897, the Senate had not yet reached a decision on Hawaii. In fact, both houses of Congress debated the issue, even though only the Senate had authority to approve the treaty. American press and public opinion remained strongly divided. "The question of Hawaii's fate," historian Gavan Daws points out, "had become part of the larger question of the position of the United States in the world."[38]

IMMIGRATION CONTINUES TO STIR CONTROVERSY

During the depression years of 1894 to 1897, total immigration to the United States declined to an average of about 275,000 each year.

Americans continued to disagree about immigration policy, however. Many Americans still supported unrestricted immigration—including some very prominent people, such as Charles W. Eliot, the president of Harvard, and William James, the noted philosopher. Many ordinary Americans believed the nation should remain a land of opportunity for all. Others believed that immigrants fueled economic growth and prosperity. Many industrialists and businessmen supported immigration because they wanted labor that was cheap and plentiful—and easily replaceable in case of worker demands or strikes. An increasing number of Americans, however, feared that heavy immigration threatened the well-being of America and believed it should be limited in some way. In 1894 a group of prominent Bostonians, including congressmen, professors, and philanthropists, founded the Immigration Restriction League to work for changes in American policy. The league argued that only immigrants who were literate—that is, those who could read in their own native language—should be admitted to the United States. The league did not lobby to restrict immigration from any particular nation or religion. But a literacy test would have certainly excluded many of the new immigrants from southern and eastern Europe because they had a much higher illiteracy rate than those from northern and western Europe.

In February 1897, a bill passed both houses of Congress to restrict immigration by requiring a literacy test. The bill was vetoed by President Cleveland before he left office the following month.

ELLIS ISLAND BURNS

Shortly before midnight on June 14, 1897, fire broke out in the five-year-old receiving center on Ellis Island. Built of spruce and pine, it burned swiftly and collapsed within an hour. Nearly every other building on the island was destroyed as well. Incredibly, all of the employees and about 200 detained or hospitalized immigrants escaped unharmed. Most records were lost, however, some dating back to the 1850s.

Within a month, federal officials announced a design competition for new fire-proof buildings. Meanwhile, immigrants again were processed at the Barge Office on the tip of lower Manhattan, where normally only cabin class travelers passed through customs. The Barge Office was strained at the seams. Very quickly, old abuses reared their heads. Immigrants were mistreated and swindled by employees and preyed upon by local con artists. An extensive investigation led to several firings, but most officials believed the problems would disappear when the new Ellis Island building opened.

THE DEPRESSION OF THE 1890s ENDS

Shortly after the election of 1896, the American economy began to make a brisk recovery. Historians agree, however, that the credit does not belong to the newly elected President McKinley nor to the safeguarded gold standard. Part of the credit belongs to a sharp rise in prices for farm products in world markets, due to a decline in wheat harvests in Europe and elsewhere. Between 1896 and 1897 American farmers doubled their exports. The farmers, as it turned out, had been correct that a rise in agricultural prices would help lift the entire American economy. The inflation that farmers thought they wanted also began, destined to continue for many years—but ironically enough, it was caused by increased supplies of gold, not silver. Sensational new discoveries of gold were made in Australia, the Canadian Yukon, and Alaska, setting off dramatic new gold rushes. In the wake of the gold came an increased supply of money and new capital for industrial expansion. Soon, industrial production began to flourish again. During the summer of 1897, at President McKinley's request, Congress increased the tariff once again to give even more protection to American-made products. The Dingley Tariff (named for Representative Nelson Dingley of Maine) added duties to many goods that had previously entered America duty-free and raised duties on others to the highest point yet.

In the wake of economic recovery and reassuring leadership from President McKinley, the Crisis of the '90s, as many historians call the depression era, passed. Agrarian protest declined in the farmlands and labor turmoil lessened in the cities. But many Americans had been newly awakened to the sufferings of the vulnerable and the working poor. Others were more determined to rescue the democratic traditions that they saw floundering in a sea of business monopolies, corruption, and injustice. They plunged into new initiatives for reform.

CHRONICLE OF EVENTS

1894

The worst year of the 1893–97 depression is marked by protests, strikes, and violence throughout the country. Unemployment is most severe for industrial workers, but as many as 3 million are unemployed overall. Farm prices hit a new low.

Henry Demarest Lloyd's *Wealth Against Commonwealth* is published; it is a carefully documented exposé of Standard Oil and the power of big business.

Angered over urban political corruption, bosses, and machines, reform-minded urban residents have begun to form civic leagues. A permanent National Municipal League is organized to coordinate the efforts; the league movement will soon mushroom. In Detroit, reform mayor Hazen S. Pingree (1890–97) introduces honest government but also emphasizes social reform, working for lower utility rates, school construction, and unemployment relief.

Prominent Bostonians found the Immigration Restriction League and lobby for a literacy test for new immigrants.

Under the leadership of Seth Low, Columbia professor and later reform mayor of New York, a prestigious Committee of Fifty is formed to study all aspects of the liquor question "scientifically."

The U.S. Bureau of Labor publishes a report confirming that overcrowding exists in major cities but endorsing the solution of benevolent private and philanthropic development. The New York State Legislature also investigates tenement housing. The report discloses astonishing densities in some wards of Manhattan, arousing public indignation.

The Lexow Committee launches an investigation into New York's Tammany Hall, the Democratic machine. They soon uncover extensive police corruption; the investigation leads to a permanent nonpartisan police commission.

Boston becomes the first city to open its school property for supervised recreation after school hours, a major goal of the playground movement; by the end of the decade Chicago, San Francisco, and New York will as well.

January: Populist Jacob S. Coxey of Massillon, Ohio, proposes a plan of national work relief that would employ men to build public roads. Sympathetic Congressmen will introduce the "good roads" bill, but no action is taken. Coxey forms an industrial army of the unemployed and plans a march to Washington.

The gold reserve sinks to $62 million. President Cleveland asks investment banker J. P. Morgan to organize a sale of $50 million in government bonds to shore up the reserve. Many Americans are angered that the bankers profit from national distress. Three additional sales will be necessary.

February: The Dawes Commission begins meetings with leaders of the Five Civilized Tribes of Oklahoma. It meets great resistance to the idea of land division.

March 25, Easter Sunday: Coxey's Army leaves from Massillon, Ohio.

May 1: Coxey's Army of about 500 formally marches into Washington. Armed police arrest Coxey and other leaders for trespassing on the grounds of the Capitol. Before the end of 1894, 17 "industrial armies" attempt similar marches to demand government action for the unemployed; 1,000 marchers actually arrive in the city.

May 11: Workers at George M. Pullman's Pullman Palace Car Company outside Chicago go on strike. They are members of Eugene V. Debs's American Railway Union (ARU).

Summer: In the campaign for the upcoming congressional elections, Democrats are badly split; those in the South and West mount an extensive free-silver campaign in opposition to their own president's gold standard.

June 21: ARU representatives vote to boycott, or refuse to handle, any Pullman car or any train carrying a Pullman car.

June 26: The ARU boycott begins. The General Managers' Association (GMA) of railway executives fires men who participate and hires strikebreakers; the boycott and strikes spread with great rapidity throughout the nation. Within days American rail traffic is paralyzed. Some 250,000 railway workers participate.

July 2: Attorney General Richard Olney obtains an injunction against the ARU.

July 4: President Cleveland orders federal troops to Chicago; they will eventually number some 16,000. Violence erupts almost immediately, in Chicago and elsewhere.

In Hawaii, the provisional government adopts a constitution, creating the independent Republic of Hawaii. Voting rights are restricted and many indigenous people cannot vote.

July 5–8: Severe violence breaks out in Chicago; 600 railway cars are destroyed and six buildings are burned on the former world's fair grounds.

July 10: Debs and other union officials are arrested. The strike soon collapses and the ARU is destroyed. One week later Debs begins serving a six month jail term.

July 16: Utah's Enabling Act is signed, authorizing a state constitutional convention in preparation for statehood.

August: Congress passes the Wilson-Gorman tariff, which includes a modest income tax, the first ever passed by the federal government. President Cleveland is angered at the many special exceptions attached to the tariff and refuses to sign it; it becomes law without his signature. The income tax is soon challenged in the courts.

August 2: The Pullman works officially reopen.

September 25: President Cleveland restores the civil rights of disenfranchised Mormons who have given up polygamy.

November: In the midterm election, Democrats suffer severe losses; Populists make gains.

Reform candidate William L. Strong is elected mayor of New York after an energetic campaign by the Good Government clubs. He promises to run the city on businesslike principles.

1895

Charles and Frank Duryea establish the first American automobile manufacturing company. On Thanksgiving Day, their one-cylinder gasoline-powered buggy bests five other competitors to win America's first automobile race, from Chicago to Evanston, Illinois, and back.

New York City Council requires that any new city schools be built with an open-air playground, due largely to the tireless efforts of reformer and journalist Jacob Riis.

January 6: Hawaiians attempt an armed overthrow of the republic to reestablish the monarchy; it is squelched in two weeks. The republic's success and restraint raise its stature in American public opinion.

January 21: The Supreme Court rules in *United States v. E.C. Knight Co.* that the American Sugar Refining Company, which controls more than 90 percent of sugar manufacture, cannot be considered an illegal trust under the terms of the Sherman Anti-Trust Act.

February: An insurrection begins in Cuba, with the goal of independence from Spain. The headquarters of leader José Martí's Cuban Revolutionary Party is in New York, and many Americans are sympathetic to the revolution.

March: Utah's constitutional convention convenes; representatives approve the separation of church and state, outlaw polygamy, and grant the vote to women.

W. E. B. DuBois and others found the American Negro Academy (ANA), the first African-American learned society.

May 19: Cuban leader Martí is killed in battle.

May 20: After rehearing *Pollock v. Farmers' Loan and Trust Company,* the U.S. Supreme Court reaffirms its April decision; the income tax established in the Wilson-Gorman Act of 1894 is unconstitutional.

May 27: The Supreme Court upholds the injunction against Eugene Debs in *In re Debs.*

July 15: Cuban insurgents declare a republic; the constitution will give extensive power to military leaders.

July 20: The United States informs Britain that it has a right to intervene in the boundary dispute between Venezuela and British Guiana, due to the Monroe Doctrine.

September 6: Booker T. Washington, head of the Tuskegee Institute in Alabama, delivers a powerful speech at the Cotton States and International Exposition in Atlanta, Georgia, to an audience of both blacks and whites. He believes blacks should concentrate on economic progress. He also implies that blacks will forgo immediate demands for political and social rights if whites support their economic progress, a position later called the Atlanta Compromise. Most whites accept him as the African-American spokesman after this date; most blacks do as well, although a few intellectuals are very critical of his accommodationist approach. Black criticism will grow over the next decade.

November: General Máximo Gómez, head of the Cuban insurrection, orders the destruction of plantations and other sites that produce revenue for the Spanish; many Cuban workers who do not leave their jobs are shot.

November 26: Britain informs the United States that the Monroe Doctrine is not recognized in international law.

Booker T. Washington, born in slavery in Virginia, became the most prominent African-American leader in the 1890s. *(Library of Congress, Prints and Photographs Division, LC-USZ62-119924)*

December 17: President Cleveland asks Congress to authorize a commission to decide the Venezuelan boundary dispute, and enforce it if necessary, on the basis of the Monroe Doctrine; Congress quickly agrees.

December 18: The national Anti-Saloon League (ASL) is organized at a meeting in Washington, D.C., with headquarters in Oberlin, Ohio. It represents a new generation of temperance reformers who are politically astute. Extremely well organized with a paid staff, it is the first modern interest group. Temperance reform has revived because many Americans increasingly associate multiplying urban saloons and rising alcohol consumption with social problems like political corruption, vice, and poverty.

1896

The National Association of Colored Women (NACW) is formed, combining numerous smaller clubs.

Joseph Pulitzer's *New York World* and William Randolph Hearst's *New York Journal* do battle over a comic strip character called the Yellow Kid; the popular journalism they have pioneered gets the nickname the yellow press. They drive newspaper circulation to new heights by sensationalist reporting on the war in Cuba.

Paul Laurence Dunbar becomes the first African-American literary figure to attain wide readership among both white and black people when his *Lyrics of a Lowly Life* is published.

Idaho approves women's suffrage, the fourth state to do so. The next state victory will not come until 1910.

The first state law regulating men's hours in mining, a very dangerous occupation, is passed in Utah; it limits the working day to eight hours.

The first songs called rags or ragtime appear in sheet music, the primary means by which new music circulates at the time. Ragtime, a lively, syncopated music already familiar to black audiences, will be a direct antecedent of jazz.

January: J. P. Morgan organizes the fourth and final sale of bonds to stabilize the gold supply.

January 4: Utah becomes the 45th state.

February 10: Spanish general Valeriano Weyler arrives in Cuba and immediately begins a policy of reconcentration, forcing the civilian population into armed camps in an attempt to flush out the insurgents. The camps are wholly inadequate and Cubans will die by the thousands there. Their suffering is widely publicized in America.

April 23: The first public showing of a motion picture to a paying audience in America occurs at Koster and Bial's Music Hall in New York, at the end of a vaudeville program. It features Thomas Edison's Vitascope, a motion picture projector.

May 18: The Supreme Court hands down its decision in *Plessy v. Ferguson,* which began as a challenge to

This Republican campaign poster from the election of 1896 shows President William McKinley hoisted on a gold coin, stamped *sound money.* To illustrate his wide appeal, he is supported by workers, a white-collar employee, and a wealthy businessman. *(Library of Congress, Prints and Photographs Division, LC-USZ62-35595)*

Louisiana's Jim Crow law requiring segregated train cars. The Court upholds the doctrine of separate but equal by a vote of 7-1, declaring that segregation of the races does not violate the U.S. Constitution if accommodations are equal.

June 16–18: The Republican convention meets and nominates William McKinley for president. After a fight over the party platform's gold plank, western delegates walk out and form the Silver Republican Party.

July 7–11: The Democratic convention meets. Southern and western delegates pass a platform that supports free silver and rejects President Cleveland's other policies. William Jennings Bryan of Nebraska delivers his Cross of Gold speech in support of silver and is nominated for president.

July 23: The National Silver Party (the silver Republicans) meets in St. Louis.

July 24–26: The Populist convention meets; after much dissension delegates vote to also endorse Bryan but nominate their own candidate for vice president.

July through fall: Bryan campaigns nationwide, the first candidate to do so. McKinley conducts a front porch campaign, with supporters delivered by train to his home in Ohio to hear him speak. Bryan stresses agrarian ideas and the conflicts in American society; McKinley stresses the industrial economy and national unity. The Republicans have an unprecedented campaign treasury, stocked by businessmen frightened by what they believe to be Bryan's radicalism.

September 2: Gold Democrats hold a convention in Indianapolis to form a splinter National Democratic Party and nominate their own candidate for president.

November: Voters go to the polls in record numbers, and elect McKinley. Although Populists win many local offices, the party declines quickly after this date. The Republican Party establishes a national dominance that lasts until the 1930s; voter turnout declines nationwide after this election.

Hawaiian queen Liliuokalani is restored to full freedom by the republic and within a month leaves for the United States to continue pressing her case.

December: Popular Cuban general Antonio Maceo is killed, raising Spanish hopes for victory, but the war drags on.

1897

The American economy begins a brisk recovery. American farmers have doubled their exports due to crop failures abroad; the gold supply is increased by new discoveries of gold in the Alaskan Klondike and the Canadian Yukon, which set off dramatic new gold rushes.

Candidates supported by the Municipal Voters League of Chicago gain control of the city council and thwart the corrupt maneuvers of utilities baron Charles Yerkes to con-

trol it; it is one of the most spectacular civic league successes during the 1890s.

Rev. Charles M. Sheldon's novel *In His Steps: What Would Jesus Do?* popularizes the growing Protestant Social Gospel movement, which focuses on bettering life in the slums by applying Christian principles to society as a whole.

Great Britain passes a workmen's compensation law, which increases the interest of American reformers in the idea.

February: Congress passes a bill to restrict immigration by requiring a literacy test. President Cleveland vetoes it.

March 4: President William McKinley takes office

April 23: Choctaw and Chickasaw leaders come to terms with the Dawes Commission, the first of the Five Civilized Tribes of Oklahoma to do so.

Summer: Congress passes the Dingley Tariff at President McKinley's request; it is the highest to date.

June 14: The five-year-old receiving center on Ellis Island burns to the ground; all escape unharmed. Federal officials announced a design competition; immigrants are temporarily processed at the Barge Office in Manhattan.

June 16: Officials of the Hawaiian Republic draft a new treaty of annexation; it is sent to the U.S. Senate for ratification.

July 4: United Mine Workers (UMW) call a strike in coal fields from western Pennsylvania through Illinois.

September: The UMW coal strike is settled. The union wins higher wages and recognition. The victory is a new ray of hope for organized labor, which has suffered greatly in the depression.

October 8: Hawaiians hold a large demonstration against annexation while a congressional delegation is visiting.

November 20: Hawaiian protesters deliver a memorial to Congress. By the end of 1897 no action has yet been taken on the treaty.

December 6: In President McKinley's annual message to Congress he recommends against recognition of the Cuban insurgent government, hopeful that a solution with Spain will be found.

Eyewitness Testimony

Madame Hastings . . . inspired some awe, if not respect, by the vengeance she wreaked upon certain police officers, who; having a grudge against her, smashed her furniture during her enforced absence from her property. She reported them to Mayor Harrison in person, and their offense being proved, three policemen and one sergeant were dismissed from the force; from which it may be seen that the name and fame of Mary Hastings are as familiar to the administration as to the lawyers. . . . Madame . . . has plied her calling in Toronto, in British Columbia, in Denver, Portland, Oregon, in San Francisco, and has a wide and varied experience with the police wherever she has wandered. In San Francisco she was in prison for six months for conduct too scandalous even for Californians. On the whole she has the greatest terror of the police of the Dominion [Canada]. "When the English say you're to git, you've just got to git and that's all there is to it," she said mournfully, "you can't do anything with them; with our police it is different."

Of which there is no doubt. . . . The relations between the sporting houses and the police on their beats is intimate, not to say friendly. The house is at the absolute mercy of the officer, who can ruin its business by simply keeping it under constant observation, or he can, if he pleases, have it "pulled" every day in the week if his moral sense or his desire for vengeance should so prompt. The keeper of the house, if she is to live and thrive, must make friends with the policeman, and there is usually not the least difficulty in doing so. Tariffs vary in Fourth Avenue as in Washington, but Madame had succeeded in securing virtual protection at a blackmail scale of $50 per officer per week with free drinks, and occasional meals whenever the "cop" felt hunger or thirst. As there were four of them on duty, two by day and two at night, and they were often thirsty, it may be taken that this police "protection" cost the house $15.00 a week or $750 a year—an irregular license fee paid to private constables for liberty to carry on.

Crusading English journalist and reformer William Stead, in his If Christ Came to Chicago, *a widely read exposé of prostitution and vice (1894), pp. 38–39.*

Be it enacted by the General Assembly of the State of Louisiana, That all railway companies carrying passengers in this State shall upon the construction or renewal of depots at regular stations provide equal but separate waiting rooms in their depots for the white and colored races by providing two waiting rooms in each depot, provided that the requirements of this Act shall be fully complied with by the first day of January A.D. 1896. No person or persons shall be permitted to occupy seats or remain in a waiting room other than the one assigned to them on account of the race to which they belong.

Acts of Louisiana, 1894, no. 98, reprinted in Green, ed.,
Equal Protection (2000), pp. 156–57.

It is an astonishing proposition that a great nation is powerful enough to stop white moonshiners from making whiskey but is unable to prevent the moonshiners or any one else from murdering its citizens. It can protect corn but cannot protect life. It can prevent the sale of tobacco unless the seller pays a revenue to the government but it cannot protect its citizens at any price. It can go to war, spend millions of dollars and sacrifice thousands of lives to avenge the death of a naturalized white citizen slain by a foreign government on foreign soil, but cannot spend a cent to protect a loyal, native-born colored American murdered without provocation by native or alien in Alabama. Shame on such a government! The administration in power is *particeps criminis* with the murderers. It can stop lynching, and until it does, it has on its hands the innocent blood of its murdered citizens.

"How to Stop Lynching," editorial in the African-American journal, The Women's Era, *vol. 2, no. 2 (1894), p. 9.*

Such a national organization would not only be helpful to the active reformers, but would be very useful in arousing public interest, and thus bringing to the work of municipal reform the thing of which it stands most in need. . . . What is needed, before we can have in this country a genuine reform spirit, is a wide-spread and deep dissatisfaction with

In the 1890s, most African Americans lived in the South and farmed, often as sharecroppers or tenants. This family and their cabin, probably near Hampton, Virginia, were shot by photographer Frances Benjamin Johnston. *(Library of Congress, Prints and Photographs Division, LC-USZ62-68312)*

existing municipal rule. So far as our largest cities are concerned, the feeling ought to be something more than dissatisfaction—disgust rather, and a sense of degradation that as Americans we allow such travesties and libels upon popular government to continue.

Century on the proposed National Municipal League,
"Municipal Reform Suggestions," vol. 47
(February 1894), p. 631.

We stand here to-day to test these guaranties of our Constitution. We choose this place of assemblage because it is the property of the people. . . . Here rather than at any other spot upon the continent it is fitting that we should come to mourn over our dead liberties and by our protest arouse the imperiled nation to such action as shall rescue the Constitution and resurrect our liberties. . . . Up these steps the lobbyists of trusts and corporations have passed unchallenged on their way to committee rooms, access to which we, the representatives of the toiling wealth-producers, have been denied. . . . We are here on behalf of millions of toilers . . . whose opportunities for honest, remunerative, productive labor have been taken from them. . . . We are here to petition for legislation which will furnish employment for every man willing and able to work.

Jacob S. Coxey's "Address of Protest" which he was not
permitted to read on the steps of the Capitol, read into the
Congressional Record by Populist senator William Allen of
Nebraska, 53rd Congress, vol. 26, part 5, May 9, 1894,
p. 4512.

The attempt to affect United States legislation by organizing the unemployed into peaceful hosts and marching them, without previous furnishing of supplies, by the precarious means of begging their way for hundreds of miles, to the Capital appears to ordinary minds the height of absurdity. Yet notwithstanding . . . Coxey's first contingent is already in Washington, Kelly's from San Francisco at Des Moines, Ia.; Frye's, organized in Los Angeles, Cal., is in Pennsylvania; the Rhode Island body, calling itself a delegation of unemployed workmen, has passed New York; and many other companies under different designations are organizing, or have already accomplished miles en route. . . .

Kelly's [Charles T. Kelley's] contingent was called together from the unemployed in San Francisco. That city could hardly help furnishing a quota from the rougher element who are ready for any change. Some fifteen hundred joined at once. San Francisco . . . acted prudently and promptly in this Kelly case, to wit: to help the Kelly army at once across the bay to Oakland. The Oakland citizens, under instant stress, succeeded in procuring transportation from their city onward; and Californians sped their way as far as Ogden. Here the first difficulty with the railroads arose. A court decision, however, soon directed the railroad company

to return the men to California or take them somehow beyond the court's jurisdiction. The result was that the Union Pacific carried them as far as Omaha. By auxiliaries (women among them) Kelly's men passed across the Missouri. At Council Bluffs they were obliged to leave their box-cars. A large number of workmen from the mills and shops of Omaha and vicinity took a holiday and seized a Rock Island train for Kelly and his people. Wonderful to tell, Kelly declined to take advantage of this kindness unless he had the formal consent of the railway management. He said that his industrials were determined to break no law. . . .

The most significant feature of the Omaha and the Council Bluffs sojourn was the indorsement this Industrial Army received from prominent citizens . . .

Major-General O. O. Howard, "The Menace of 'Coxeyism,'
North American Review, vol. 158 (June 1894),
pp. 687–91.

We moved toward the mouths of the pits [furnaces], where a group of men stood with long shovels and bars in their hands. They were touched with orange light, which rose out of the pits. The pits looked like wells or cisterns of white-hot metal. The men signalled a boy, and the huge covers, which hung on wheels, were moved to allow them to peer in at the metal. They threw up their elbows before their eyes, to shield their faces from the heat, while they studied the ingots within.

"It takes grit to stand there in July and August," said my guide. "Don't it, Joe?" he said to one of the men whom he knew. The man nodded, but was too busy to do more. . . .

"But that isn't all. Those pits have to have their bottoms made after every 'heat,' and they can't wait for 'em to cool. The men stand by and work over them when it's hot enough to burn your boot-soles. . . ."

We went on into the boiler-plate mills, still noisier, still more grandiose in effect. . . . Everywhere in this enormous building were pits like the mouth of hell, and fierce ovens giving off a glare of heat, and burning wood and iron, giving off horrible stenches of gases. Thunder upon thunder, clang upon clang, glare upon glare! Torches flamed far up in the dark spaces above. Engines moved to and fro, and steam sissed and threatened. . . .

"How long do you work?" I asked of a young man who stood at the furnace near me.

"Twelve hours," he replied. "The night set go on at six at night and come off at six in the morning. I go on at six and off at six."

"For how much pay?"

"Two dollars and a quarter."

Novelist Hamlin Garland describes Carnegie's steel mill,
"Homestead and Its Perilous Trades," a nonfiction article for
McClure's, vol. 3 (June 1894), pp. 5, 8–9.

So far as I have been advised, the local officials have been able to handle the situation [the Pullman strike]. But if any assistance were needed, the State stood ready to furnish a hundred men for every one man required, and stood ready to do so at a moment's notice. Notwithstanding these facts the Federal Government has been applied to by men who had political and selfish motives for wanting to ignore the State Government . . .

At present some of our railroads are paralyzed, not by reason of obstruction, but because they cannot get men to operate their trains. For some reason they are anxious to keep this fact from the public, and for this purpose they are making an outcry about obstructions in order to divert attention. . . .

I repeat that you have been imposed upon in this matter. . . . I submit that local self-government is a fundamental principle of our Constitution. Each community shall govern itself so long as it can and is ready and able to enforce the law, and it is in harmony with this fundamental principle that the statute authorizing the President to send troops into States must be construed; especially is this so in matters relating to the exercise of the police power and the preservation of law and order.

John P. Altgeld, governor of Illinois, to President Cleveland, July 5, 1894, quoted in Browne, Altgeld of Illinois, *pp. 154–57.*

Federal troops were sent to Chicago in strict accordance with the Constitution and laws of the United States, upon the demand of the post office department that obstruction of the mails should be removed, and upon the representations of the judicial officers of the United States that the process of the Federal courts could not be executed through the ordinary means, and upon competent proof that conspiracies existed against commerce between the States.

President Grover Cleveland to Governor Altgeld, July 5, 1894, quoted in Browne, Altgeld of Illinois, *p. 159.*

A powerful conspiracy is at work over large sections of the country striving to subvert the government of law and to impose on the nation the decrees of the conspirators. . . . Eugene V. Debs and his fellow-demagogues long ago avowed that they would unite in an association the railway working-men of the country, so that all should obey a single will, promising them that a general suspension of traffic and intercourse ordered by its head would so evidently portend the utter ruin of the nation that the mere threat of it would extort from every community and every employer of labor compliance with its demands. They have prosecuted this plan with wonderful vigor, until now, believing that their organization is strong enough to defy opposition,

they have made a wanton display of their power, in order to terrorize society and show themselves its masters.

"Suppress the Rebellion," Harper's Weekly *editorial on the Pullman strike, July 14, 1894, available online at Railroad Extra. URL:http://www.railroadextra. com/sk94edit.Html.*

A hundred and fifty thousand railroad employees, their fellow members in the American Railway Union, sympathized with [the Pullman workers], shared their earnings with them, and after trying in every peaceable way they could conceive of to touch the flint heart of the Pullman company. Every overture being rejected, every suggestion denied, every proposition spurned with contempt—they determined not to pollute their hands and dishonor their manhood by handling Pullman cars and contributing to the suffering and sorrow of their brethren and their wives and babes. And rather than do this they laid down their tools in a body, sacrificed their situations and submitted to persecution, exile and the blacklist; to idleness, poverty, crusts and rags, and I shall love and honor these moral heroes to my latest breath.

There was more of human sympathy, of the essence of brotherhood, of the spirit of real Christianity in this act than in all the hollow pretenses and heartless prayers of those disciples of mammon who cried out against it, and this act will shine forth in increasing splendor long after the dollar worshipers have mingled with the dust of oblivion.

Had the carpenter of Nazareth been in Chicago at the time He would have been on the side of the poor, the heavy-laden and sore at heart, and He would have denounced their oppressors and been sent to prison for contempt of court under President Cleveland's administration.

Eugene Debs describes the ARU Pullman strike of June–July 1894, "The Federal Government and the Chicago Strike," published in the socialist newspaper Appeal to Reason, *August 1904, in his* Debs: His Life, Writing, and Speeches, *pp. 204–05.*

Q. Did the Pullman company during its years of prosperity ever voluntarily increase the wages of any class or of all classes of its employees?
A. Not specially on account of prosperous business. It has always paid its employees liberal wages. . . .
Q. But it has never increased the wages of its employees voluntarily?
A. Certainly it has not increased them any other way.
Q: It has never divided any of its profits with them in any shape or form?
A. The Pullman company divides its profits with the people who own the property. It would not have a right to

take the profits belonging to the people who own that property.

George Pullman testifies before the United States Strike Commission, convened August 1894, Report on the Chicago Strike of June–July 1894, *p. 554.*

Q. What is the basis of your objection to that union?
A. Our objection to that was that we would not treat with our men as members of the American Railway Union, and we would not treat with them as members of any union. We treat with them as individuals and as men.
Q. That is, each man as an individual, do you mean that?
A. Yes, sir. . . .
Q. Don't you think that the fact that you represent a vast concentration of capital, and are selected for that because of your ability to represent it, entitles him if he pleases to unite with all of the men of his craft and select the ablest one they have got to represent the cause?
A. As a union?
Q. As a union.
A. They have the right; yes, sir. We have the right to say whether we will receive them or not.

Thomas H. Wickes, vice president of the Pullman Company, testifying before the United States Strike Commission, convened August 1894, Report on the Chicago Strike of June–July 1894, *p. 621.*

In a large room sat the little slate-pickers. The floor slanted at an angle of forty-five degrees, and the coal, having been masticated by the great teeth, was streaming sluggishly in long iron troughs. The boys sat straddling these troughs, and as the mass moved slowly, they grabbed deftly at the pieces of slate therein. There were five or six of them, one above another, over each trough. The coal is expected to be fairly pure after it passes the final boy. The howling machinery was above them. High up, dim figures moved about in the dust clouds. . . .

Meanwhile they live in a place of infernal dins. The crash and thunder of the machinery is like the roar of an immense cataract. The room shrieks and blares and bellows. Clouds of dust blur the air until the windows shine pallidly afar off. All the structure is a-tremble from the heavy sweep and circle of the ponderous mechanism. Down in the midst of it sit these tiny urchins, where they earn fifty-five cents a day each. They breathe this atmosphere until their lungs grow heavy and sick with it. They have this clamor in their ears until it is wonderful that they have any hoodlum valor remaining. But they are uncowed; they continue to swagger. And at the top of the "breaker" laborers can always

be seen dumping the roaring coal down the wide, voracious maw of the creature.

Novelist Stephen Crane describes child laborers called breaker boys, "In the Depths of a Coal Mine," a nonfiction article for McClure's, *vol. 3 (August 1894), pp. 196–98.*

"The spectacle of men fighting for work . . ." My God! This is terrible! Battling for the privilege of working all day for enough to eat—and the next day go at it again; and so on until the earth rattles on their pine boxes.

Cannot the good God do something to relieve his wretched children? Or is this thing to go on forever? Why not give some good-hearted, honest man supreme power for four years, and let him improve God's world or blow it up. He could not make it much worse than it is, for the great mass of mankind.

A judicious hanging bee in Wall Street would be a good measure with which to begin the reformation.

Ignatius Donnelly in The Representative, *August 29, 1894, available online at 1896. URL: http:// iberia.vassar.edu/1896/depression.html.*

It is not fair and will not be fair to say that democracy has broken down in American cities until democracy shall have had a fair chance at self-government in our American cities, and that chance has no-where been given to the extent to which it is desirable. In other words, a city charter should give to the people of the city the largest degree of self-determination, both as to the form of government and as to the things which the government shall do.

Professor Edmund James, University of Pennsylvania, speaking at the National Municipal League's second Good City Government Conference, December 1894, Proceedings of the Second National Conference, *pp. 160–61.*

This action of the judicial power cannot be allowed to go without rebuke. It makes for the subversion of the most fundamental rights of American citizens. If Debs has been violating law, let him be indicted, tried by a jury, and punished; let him not be made the victim of an untenable court order and deprived of his liberty entirely within the discretion of a judge. The right of trial by jury for criminal offences lies at the bed-rock of free institutions. It cannot be denied without placing the liberty of every citizen in jeopardy. If the precedent now established is allowed to stand; there is no limit to the power which the judiciary may establish over the citizen.

Springfield Republican *comments on Debs's jail sentence for contempt, December 14, 1894, quoted in Andrews, "The Democracy Supreme,"* Scribner's, *vol. 19 (April 1896), p. 478.*

It is well that it should be understood that the present movement [for municipal reform] in New York City is first of all a moral movement, and has its grounds in the churches and the synagogues. A very large per cent. of every live current question is ethical in its ingredients, and falls, therefore, naturally and properly, within the jurisdiction of the church.

Rev. Charles Parkhurst, founder of the New York Vigilance League, "Facts for the Times," 1895, Tolman, ed., Municipal Reform, p. 17.

A great deal is done by the various charitable societies for the relief of distress, but as far as my observation goes the most effective charitable work is done by the poor themselves. Thousands of dollars are given away in the tenement districts every year by the inhabitants of the tenements, of which no charitable society makes a record. I have never related a peculiarly distressing case of poverty to a poor person but there was a ready response, and out of their own poverty the poor have ministered to these who were in need of relief. The children of our City Mission school, who come from the tenement-houses, contribute every Thanksgiving-Day from $80 to $100 for the poor in our immediate neighborhood. A club of fifty small boys and girls saved their pennies one year and bought thirty-five Thanksgiving dinners for the poor, consisting of chickens, potatoes, beans, turnips, and cabbages. The original plan was to have a head of cabbage go with each chicken, but the money gave out; this did not in any way disconcert the children, for they quickly served the difficulty by cutting a cabbage into four parts, and putting a quarter into each bag. The children worked from 7.30 to 11 P.M. distributing the provisions.

William T. Elsing, minister of the DeWitt Church in Rivington Street, "Life in New York Tenement Houses as Seen by a City Missionary," 1895, in Woods, ed., The Poor in Great Cities, p. 71.

The Committee prosecuted and succeeded in sending to the State penitentiary eight or ten men, some of them prominent officers of the city government, for fraud either in the administration of the government or in the elections. The Committee succeeded in having passed by the legislature the Election Bill, establishing registration of voters, and reserving one hundred feet each side of the polling-places....

—Citizens' Club of Cincinnati

...The saloons were becoming unbearable, and corrupting politics and officials increasing alarmingly, when a meeting was called June, 1894, to form an Anti-Saloon League. At the meeting it was voted to make it broader, and the name Citizens League was adopted. The growth has been rapid.

Men of all parties, creeds, and beliefs are coming in. Membership now numbers about one hundred and fifty—all strong, influential men. The chief object is against the saloon, because it is believed to be the center of vice, crime, and corruption in politics.

—Citizens' League of Norwalk, Connecticut

...The actual results accomplished have been the indictment by the grand jury of ten councilmen and the beginning of impeachment proceedings against the mayor. One councilman was found guilty.

—Citizens' Protective Association, New Orleans

Reports of various civic leagues throughout the United States for 1895, Tolman, ed., Municipal Reform, pp. 59, 62–63, 67, 80, 82.

The Hull-House Woman's Club . . . came together, however, in quite a new way that summer when we discussed with them the high death rate so persistent in our ward. After several club meetings devoted to the subject, despite the fact that the death rate rose highest in the congested foreign colonies and not in the streets in which most of the Irish American club women lived, twelve of their number undertook in connection with the residents, to carefully investigate the conditions of the alleys. During August and September the substantiated reports of violations of the law sent in from Hull-House to the health department were one thousand and thirty-seven. For the club woman who had finished a long day's work of washing or ironing followed by the cooking of a hot supper, it would have been much easier to sit on her doorstep during a summer evening than to go up and down ill-kept alleys and get into trouble with her neighbors over the condition of their garbage boxes. It required both civic enterprise and moral conviction to be willing to do this three evenings a week during the hottest and most uncomfortable months of the year. Nevertheless, a certain number of women persisted, as did the residents, and three city inspectors in succession were transferred from the ward because of unsatisfactory services. Still the death rate remained high and the condition seemed little improved throughout the next winter. In sheer desperation, the following spring when the city contracts were awarded for the removal of garbage, with the backing of two well-known business men, I put in a bid for the garbage removal of the nineteenth ward. My paper was thrown out on a technicality but the incident induced the mayor to appoint me the garbage inspector of the ward.

The salary was a thousand dollars a year, and the loss of that political "plum" made a great stir among the politicians. The position was no sinecure whether regarded from the point of view of getting up at six in the morning to see that the men were early at work; or of following the load-

Jane Addams, who founded Hull-House settlement in Chicago, participated in many reform movements and wrote widely about social justice issues. She was the best-known woman of the Progressive era. *(Library of Congress, Prints and Photographs Division, LC-USZ62-95722)*

ed wagons, uneasily dropping their contents at intervals, to their dreary destination at the dump; or of insisting that the contractor must increase the number of his wagons from nine to thirteen and from thirteen to seventeen, although he assured me that he lost money on every one and that the former inspector had let him off with seven; or of taking careless landlords into court because they would not provide the proper garbage receptacles; or of arresting the tenant who tried to make the garbage wagons carry away the contents of his stable.

Jane Addams describes garbage collection in Chicago in the mid-1890s, Twenty Years at Hull-House, *pp. 284–86.*

Wide open and unguarded stand our gates,
And through them presses a wild motley throng—
Men from the Volga and the Tartar steppes,
Featureless figures of the Hoang-Ho,
Malayan, Scythian, Teuton, Kelt, and Slav,
Flying the Old World's poverty and scorn;
These bringing with them unknown gods and rites,
Those, tiger passions, here to stretch their claws.
In street and alley what strange tongues are loud,
Accents of menace alien to our air,
Voices that once the Tower of Babel knew!
  O Liberty, white Goddess! Is it well
To leave the gates unguarded? . . .

Author and editor Thomas Bailey Aldrich's popular anti-immigrant poem "Unguarded Gates," Unguarded Gates *(1895), pp. 16–17.*

The Ewing Street Italian colony furnishes a large contingent to the army of bootblacks and newsboys; lads who leave home at 2.30 A.M. to secure the first edition of the morning paper, selling each edition as it appears, and filling the intervals with blacking boots and tossing pennies, until, in the winter half of the year, they gather in the Polk Street Night-School, to doze in the warmth, or torture the teacher with the gamin tricks acquired by day. For them, school is "a lark," or a peaceful retreat from parental beatings and shrieking juniors at home during the bitter nights of the Chicago winter.

There is no body of self-supporting children more in need of effective care than these newsboys and bootblacks. They are ill-fed, ill-housed, ill-clothed, illiterate, and wholly untrained and unfitted for any occupation. The only useful thing they learn at their work in common with the children who learn in school, is the rapid calculation of small sums in making change; and this does not go far enough to be of any practical value. In the absence of an effective compulsory school-attendance law, they should at least be required to obtain a license from the city; and the granting of this license should be in the hands of the Board of Education, and contingent upon a certain amount of day-school attendance accomplished.

Florence Kelley and Alzina P. Stevens, "Wage Earning Children," a chapter in Hull-House Maps and Papers *(1895), pp. 54–55.*

There is no improvement in the conditions under which the children work. Some of the boys act as butchers, sticking sheep, lambs and swine; others cut the hide from the quivering flesh of freshly stunned cattle; still others sort entrails, pack meat, and make the tin cans in which goods are shipped. In several places a boy has been found at work at a dangerous machine, *because his father had been disabled by it,* and keeping the place pending recovery depended upon the boy's doing the work during the father's absence.

Child labor in the Chicago stockyards, 1895, Illinois Inspector of Factories and Workshops, Annual Report, vol. 3, p. 11.

Not all or nearly all of the murders done by white men, during the past thirty years in the South, have come to light, but the statistics as gathered and preserved by white men, and which have not been questioned, show that during these years more than ten thousand Negroes have been killed in cold blood, without the formality of judicial trial and legal execution. And yet, as evidence of the absolute impunity with which the white man dares to kill a Negro, the same record shows that during all these years, and for all these murders, only three white men have been tried, convicted, and executed. As no white man has been lynched for the murder of colored people, these three executions are the only instances of the death penalty being visited upon white men for murdering Negroes. . . .

Ida Wells-Barnett, A Red Record, *1895, On Lynchings, p. 58.*

The competition among the sensational [newspapers] is very great. . . . The watch which they all keep up for something startling in the way of news is painful in its eagerness. War would, therefore, be a godsend to them. It would renew the rage for "extras," which attended the varying fortunes of our civil conflict. It would raise hundreds of journals out of want and anxiety, and, next to war, they welcome "the promise of war" . . . Hence every incident which can by any possibility lead to an international conflict is greatly magnified. Every blunder of a subordinate is attributed to the direct orders of a superior, and is converted into a deliberate insult. All foreign statesmen are made to plot against the United States, and concoct schemes for depriving us of something, or in some manner humiliating us. Apologies are treated as lies meant to throw us off our guard.

E. L. Godkin, editor of the prestigious journal The Nation, *"Diplomacy and the Newspaper," North American Review, vol. 160 (May 1895), pp. 575–76.*

[W]hat the [Sherman Anti-Trust] law struck at was combinations, contracts, and conspiracies to monopolize trade and commerce among the several states or with foreign nations; but the contracts and acts of the defendants related exclusively to the acquisition of the Philadelphia refineries and the business of sugar refining in Pennsylvania, and bore no direct relation to commerce between the states or with foreign nations. The object was manifestly private gain in the manufacture of the commodity, but not through the control of interstate or foreign commerce. It is true that the bill alleged that the products of these refineries were sold and distributed among the several states, and that all the companies were engaged in trade or commerce with the several states and with foreign nations; but this was no more than to say that trade and commerce served manufacture to fulfill its function.

Supreme Court Chief Justice Melville W. Fuller, writing for the majority in United States v. E.C. Knight Co., *January 21, 1895, 156 US 1.*

That there has been a growing sentiment in this country during the last few years in favor of more stringent laws regulating foreign immigration cannot have escaped the notice of any person who reads our newspapers and magazines. . . . The belief that a non-partisan, non-sectarian, and non-political organization is needed, which shall devote itself to this work, has led to the formation of the Immigration Restriction League. The objects of the league, which was started in Boston last July, are, as stated in its constitution: "To advocate and work for the further judicious restriction, or stricter regulation, of immigration, to issue documents and circulars, solicit facts and information, on that subject, hold public meetings, and to arouse public opinion to the necessity of a further exclusion of elements undesirable for citizenship or injurious to our national character. It is not an object of this league to advocate the exclusion of laborers or other immigrants of such character and standards as fit them to become citizens."

Robert De C. Ward, league officer, "An Immigration Restriction League," Century, vol. 49 (February 1895), p. 639.

[T]he Monroe Doctrine [was] the work of John Quincy Adams, a much greater man than the President whose name it bears. Washington declared that it was not the business of the United States to meddle in the affairs of Europe, and John Quincy Adams added that Europe must not meddle in the Western Hemisphere. As I have seen it solemnly stated recently that the annexation of Hawaii would be a violation of the Monroe Doctrine, it is perhaps not out of place to say that the Monroe Doctrine has no bearing on the extension of the United States, but simply holds that no European power shall establish itself in the Americas or interfere with American governments. . . .

There is a very definite policy for American statesmen to pursue in this respect if they would prove themselves worthy inheritors of the principles of Washington and Adams. We desire no extension to the south, for neither the population nor the lands of Central or South America would be desirable additions to the United States. But from the Rio Grande to the Arctic Ocean there should be but one flag and one country. Neither race nor climate forbids this extension, and every consideration of growth and national welfare demands it.

Henry Cabot Lodge, Republican senator from Massachusetts, "Our Blundering Foreign Policy," Forum, vol. 19 (March 1895), pp. 15–17.

It was said in argument that the passage of the statute imposing this income tax was an assault by the poor upon the rich, and by much eloquent speech this court has been urged to stand in the breach for the protection of the just rights of property against the advancing hosts of socialism. . . .

I may say, in answer to the appeals made to this court, to vindicate the constitutional rights of citizens owning large properties and having large incomes, that the real friends of property are not those who would exempt the wealth of the country from bearing its fair share of the burdens of taxation, but rather those who seek to have every one, without reference to his locality contribute from his substance, upon terms of equality with all others, to the support of the government.

Dissenting opinion of Supreme Court Justice John Marshall Harlan, Pollock v. Farmers' Loan and Trust Company, May 20, 1895, 158 US 601.

A most earnest and eloquent appeal was made to us in eulogy of the heroic spirit of those who threw up their employment, and gave up their means of earning a livelihood, not in defense of their own rights, but in sympathy for and to assist others whom they believed to be wronged. We yield to none in our admiration of any act of heroism or self-sacrifice, but we may be permitted to add that it is a lesson which cannot be learned too soon or too thoroughly that under this government of and by the people the means of redress of all wrongs are through the courts and at the ballot box, and that no wrong, real or fancied, carries with it legal warrant to invite as a means of redress the co-operation of a mob, with its accompanying acts of violence.

Supreme Court Justice David J. Brewer, writing for the majority in In re Debs, May 27, 1895, 158 U.S. 564.

If governmental control serves to stimulate the self-reliant energies of the people, if it opens up new avenues for private enterprise, if it equalizes and widens the opportunity for employment, if it prevents injustice, oppression, and monopoly, . . . then government is not socialistic but rather is supplementing the highest individualism.

University of Wisconsin economist John R. Commons in an article on the new progressive viewpoint, "Progressive Individualism," American Magazine of Civics, June 1895, quoted in Green, Language of Politics in America, p. 35.

O beautiful for halcyon skies,
   For amber waves of grain,
For purple mountain majesties
   Above the fruited plain!
     America! America!
   God shed his grace on thee
Till souls wax fair as earth and air
   And music-hearted sea!

Original words to "America the Beautiful," written by Wellesley professor Katherine Lee Bates after a trip to Pikes Peak, first published in The Congregationalist, July 4, 1895, available online at Virtual Falmouth. URL: http://www.fuzzylu.com/falmouth/bates/america.html.

To-day the United States is practically sovereign on this continent, and its fiat is law upon the subjects to which it confines its interposition. Why? It is not because of the pure friendship or good-will felt for it. It is not simply by reason of its high character as a civilized state, nor because wisdom and equity are the invariable characteristic of the dealings of the United States. It is because in addition to all other grounds, its infinite resources combined with its isolated position render it master of the situation and practically invulnerable against any or all other powers.

Secretary of State Richard Olney's letter to Britain's Lord Salisbury on the Venezuelan dispute, July 20, 1895, quoted in Dewey, National Problems, p. 306.

All Paris is talking of the prodigal extravagance of Rodman Wanamaker, the young son of ex-Postmaster General Wanamaker, of Philadelphia, who spent $20,000 this week on a single dinner to 22 guests. Even in this city of sumptuous dining it is doubtful whether so much money was ever squandered on a single feast. . . . Twenty-two of the finest equipages called at the same moment at the residences of the guests and brought them to the banquet hall. The decorations were marvelous. Luminous fountains planted upon great blocks of ice kept the air cool. It was not one dinner but 22 independent dinners, separately served, one to each guest. Each guest had before him a whole leg of mutton, a whole salmon, truffled fowl, a basket of peaches, and a double magnum of champagne, besides bottles of wine of sacred vintage and fabulous cost. After the banquet costly jewelry was distributed to the guests, among whom were a number of young titled Frenchmen. Paris newspapers speak of the banquet as magnificent, but in bad taste.

New York World, July 27, 1895, reprinted in Nevins, American Press Opinion, p. 414.

Now for the sake of the thousands of self-sacrificing young women teaching and preaching in lonely southern backwoods, for the noble army of mothers who have given birth to these girls, mothers whose intelligence is only limited by their opportunity to get at books, for the sake of the fine cultured women who have carried off the honors in school here and often abroad, for the sake of our own dignity, the dignity of our race, and the future good name of our children, it is "mete, right and our bounden duty" to stand forth and declare ourselves and principles, to teach an ignorant and suspicious world that our aims and interests are identical with those of all good aspiring women. Too long have we been silent under unjust and unholy charges. . . . It is not enough to try to disprove unjust charges through individual effort, that never goes any further. Year after year southern women have protested against the admission of colored women into any national organization on the ground of the immorality of these women. . . . Now with an army of organized women standing for purity and mental worth, we in ourselves deny the charge and open the eyes of the world to a state of affairs to which they have been blind, often willfully so, and the fact that the charges, audaciously and flippantly made, as they often are, are of so humiliating and delicate a nature, serves to protect the accuser by driving the helpless accused into mortified silence.

Josephine St. Pierre Ruffin, address to the first National Conference of Colored Women at Boston, July 29, 1895, The Women's Era, Vol. 2, no. 5 (1895), p. 14.

I have heard the great orators of many countries, but not even Gladstone himself could have pleaded a cause with more consummate power than did this angular Negro, standing in a nimbus of sunshine, surrounded by the men who once fought to keep his race in bondage. The roar might swell ever so high, but the expression of his earnest face never changed. . . .

A ragged, ebony giant, squatted on the floor in one of the aisles, watched the orator with burning eyes and tremulous face until the supreme burst of applause came, and then the tears ran down his face. Most of the Negroes in the audience were crying, perhaps without knowing just why.

Reporter James Creelman on Booker T. Washington's Atlanta address, New York World, September 18, 1895, quoted in Washington, Up from Slavery, pp. 240–41.

There will probably be a marked difference between what the next Congress will do and what the great mass of the people think it should do. The producing portion of the nation who feed, clothe and house the race, think that some of their long neglected natural rights should be declared and enforced, but no heed will be given to their convictions.

The floating signs indicate that a few bombastic assumptions of patriotism and a liberal number of Congressional bluffs at the gathering war clouds, with a profuse abuse of the State Department and the President, will usher in the session. . . . All the necessary declarations of belligerency will be unanimously adopted, the Monroe Doctrine will be re-declared with great acclamation, and much indignation will be expressed for the neglected past. Many other such pleasing matters will be attended to promptly that will not materially affect the industrial or business condition of the country.

Representative John C. Bell, Populist/Democrat of Colorado, "The Work of the Next Congress," North American Review, vol. 161 (December 1895), p. 663.

I am a farmer. When gold was worth half its present value I had $4000. I bought a $12,000 farm and gave a mortgage for $8,000 . . . For 4 years I paid my interest. During this time hundreds of mortgages have been foreclosed and hard working men have lost their all. Hundreds of others in this vicinity and all over New York State and New England are struggling like me to save their home. They are honest men. They do not wish to "debase" the currency nor to "repudiate their debts," but they find themselves confronted with a condition of things just the reverse of repudiation. . . . our farms have depreciated in value one half, or to tell the truth as it is the standard of value, gold have doubled thus obliging us to pay two dollars actual value for each dollar of our indebtedness as well as 12% interest instead of 6%. . . .

Volumes could be written of heartrending scenes of families driven from their home . . . and who do not know why the farm won't bring more than half it sold for a dozen years ago. The truth is real estate is worth as much now as then but the standard dollars is doubled in value.

Until that value is restored to its original place as compared with all commodities, it is a libel on the debtors of this country to accuse them of a desire to repudiate.

New York state farmer W. Chas. Maben to Grover Cleveland in defense of the free silver position, December 7, 1895, reprinted in De Novo, Selected Readings, pp. 123–24.

If a European power by an extension of its boundaries takes possession of the territory of one of our neighboring Republics against its will and in derogation of its rights, it is difficult to see why to that extent such European power does not thereby attempt to extend its system of government to that portion of this continent which is thus taken. This is the precise action which President Monroe declared to be "dangerous to our peace and safety," and it can make no difference whether the European system is extended by an advance of frontier or otherwise. . . .

I am . . . firm in my conviction that while it is a grievous thing to contemplate the two great English-speaking peoples of the world as being otherwise than friendly competitors in the onward march of civilization and strenuous and worthy rivals in all the arts of peace, there is no calamity which a great nation can invite which equals that which follows a supine submission to wrong and injustice and the consequent loss of national self-respect and honor, beneath which are shielded and defended a people's safety and greatness.

President Grover Cleveland's message to Congress on Venezuela, December 17, 1895, in Richardson, ed., Messages and Papers, *vol. 9, pp. 656, 658.*

I am very much pleased with the President's, or rather, with Olney's, message. . . . I do hope there will not be any backdown among our people. Let the fight [with Britain] come if it must; I don't care whether our seacoast cities are bombarded or not; we would take Canada.

Theodore Roosevelt, letter to Senator Henry Cabot Lodge on Cleveland's message of December 17, 1895, quoted in Smith, Rise of Industrial America, *p. 538.*

The situation seems to me this: An immense democracy, mostly ignorant and completely secluded from foreign influences and without any knowledge of other states of society, with great contempt for history and experience, finds itself in possession of enormous power and is eager to use it in brutal fashion against any one . . . who comes along . . . and is therefore constantly on the brink of some frightful catastrophe. . . .

E. L. Godkin on Cleveland's message, quoted in Smith, Rise of Industrial America, *p. 538.*

Liberty produces wealth, and wealth destroys liberty . . . Our bignesses—cities, factories, monopolies, fortunes, which are our empires, are the obesities of an age gluttonous beyond its powers of digestion. Mankind are crowding upon each other in the centres, and struggling to keep each other out of the feast set by the new sciences and the new fellowships. Our size has got beyond both our science and our conscience. The vision of the railroad stockholder is not far-sighted enough to see into the office of the General manager; the people cannot reach across even a ward of a city to rule their rulers; Captains of Industry "do not know" whether the men in the ranks are dying from lack of food and shelter; we cannot clean our cities nor our politics; the locomotive has more man-power than all the ballot-boxes, and the mill-wheels wear out the hearts of workers unable to keep up beating time to their whirl. If mankind had gone on pursuing the ideals of the fighter, the time would necessarily have come when there would have been only a few, then

only one, and then none left. This is what we are witnessing in the world of livelihoods. Our ideals of livelihood are ideals of mutual deglutition. We are rapidly reaching the stage where in each province only a few are left; that is the key to our times. Beyond the deep is another deep. This era is but a passing phase in the evolution of industrial Caesars, and these Caesars will be of a new type—corporate Caesars.

Henry Demarest Lloyd, Wealth Against Commonwealth *(1894), pp. 9–10.*

There is something in a very little experience of such places [slums] that blunts the perception, so that they do not seem so dreadful as they are; and I should feel as if I were exaggerating if I recorded my first impression of their loathsomeness. I soon came to look upon the conditions as normal, not for me, indeed, or for the kind of people I mostly consort with, but for the inmates of the dens and lairs about me. Perhaps this was partly their fault; they were uncomplaining, if not patient, in circumstances where I believe a single week's sojourn, with no more hope of a better lot than they could have, would make anarchists of the best people in the city. . . . I found them usually cheerful in the Hebrew quarter, and they had so much courage as enabled them to keep themselves noticeably clean in an environment where I am afraid their betters would scarcely have had heart to wash their faces and comb their hair. There was even a decent tidiness in their dress, which I did not find very ragged, though it often seemed unseasonable and insufficient. But here again, as in many other phases of life, I was struck by men's heroic superiority to their fate, if their fate is hard; and I felt anew that if prosperous and comfortable people were as good in proportion to their fortune as these people were they would be as the angels of light, which, I am afraid they now but faintly resemble.

Writer and critic William Dean Howells describes a visit to the Lower East Side of New York, in his Impressions and Experiences *(1896), pp. 138–39.*

For some unaccountable reason the weekly "doings of the yellow kid" became immensely popular with the readers of the *New York World*. Throughout the week these highly colored prints of the infant monster were distributed broadcast all over the city of New York and the country. Bushel baskets of them were daily carried to the towering dome of the *World* building, and from there thrown out to the four winds of heaven, which carried them away into distant regions, and the circulation of the *World* increased enormously.

Journalist Elizabeth Banks describes the cartoon wars of 1896, in her "American 'Yellow Journalism,'" The Living Age, *vol. 218 (Sept 3, 1898), p. 641.*

This advertisement for Joseph Pulitzer's *New York World* shows the wildly popular cartoon character, the Yellow Kid, who gave his name to yellow journalism. *(Library of Congress, Prints and Photographs Division, LC-USZ6-1862)*

Oh, dere's lots o' keer an' trouble
    In dis world to swaller down;
An' ol' Sorrer's purty lively
    In her way o' gittin' roun'.
Yet dere's times when I furgit 'em,—
    Aches an' pains an' troubles all,—
An' it 's when I tek at ebenin'
    My ol' banjo f'om de wall....
Paul Laurence Dunbar, "A Banjo Song," Lyrics of Lowly
Life (1896), pp. 42–43.

We wear the mask that grins and lies,
    It hides our cheeks and shades our
        eyes,—
This debt we pay to human guile;
With torn and bleeding hearts we smile,

And mouth with myriad subtleties.
Paul Laurence Dunbar, "We Wear the Mask," 1896,
Lyrics of Lowly Life, pp. 167–68.

We had a house of only two rooms. It was not adobe; it was made out of sticks. We called them *jacals.* I remember when I was eight years old, I had measles in the *jacalito.* I barely remember it as if in a dream, that skin, that is where they would lay me. There was only one bed and skins for all of us. Skins of goat or cow.

I never stepped inside a school. I learned how to read because my mother taught me. . . . One of my half brothers taught me how to write. When the school opened I was already too big to go. I was eleven.

When I was young, I helped make food and washed clothes but I also worked in the orchard and hoed weeds. . . .
Maria Duran, born to Mexican immigrants in 1888, describes
life in New Mexico in 1896–98, oral interview with Aracelli
Pando, New Mexico State University, in Jensen, ed.,
With These Hands, p. 121.

Article 1, Section 4. The rights of conscience shall never be infringed. The State shall make no law respecting an establishment of religion or prohibiting the free exercise thereof; no religious test shall be required as a qualification for any office of public trust or for any vote at any election; nor shall any person be incompetent as a witness or juror on account of religious belief or the absence thereof. There shall be no union of Church and State, nor shall any church dominate the State or interfere with its functions. No public money or property shall be appropriated for or applied to any religious worship, exercise or instruction, or for the support of any ecclesiastical establishment. No property qualification shall be required of any person to vote, or hold office, except as provided in this Constitution. . . .

Article 3, Ordinance. The following ordinance shall be irrevocable without the consent of the United States and the people of this State: First:—Perfect toleration of religious sentiment is guaranteed. No inhabitant of this State shall ever be molested in person or property on account of his or her mode of religious worship; but polygamous or plural marriages are forever prohibited.
Utah constitution, accepted by Congress January 1896,
available online at Utah's Road to Statehood. URL:
http://www.archives.utah.gov/exhibits/
Statehood/1896text.htm.

Guns were fired at daybreak. 10:00 a procession was formed, led by the Band of the Home Guards—followed by citizens, also a juvenile corps, or Bell Brigade.

At two o'clock the citizens met in the Social Hall and partook of a Pic Nic Dinner, then followed speech and Song, closing the day with a grand Inaugural Ball.

The day was all that could be desired. The weather was pleasant and all enjoyed themselves, there was nothing to mar the occasion, and it will be a day long to be remembered by the inhabitants of Kanab both old and young.

Rebecca Howell Mace, diary entry describing Utah's statehood celebration in remote Kanab on the Arizona border, January 6, 1896, quoted in May, Utah, *p. 129.*

If we are not striving for equality, in heaven's name for what are we striving? I regard it as cowardly and dishonest for any of our colored men to tell white people or colored people that we are not struggling for equality. . . . Yes, my friends, I want equality. . . . Now, catch your breath, for I am going to use an adjective: I am going to say we demand social equality. . . .

Rise, Brothers! Come let us possess this land. Never say: "Let well enough alone." Cease to console yourselves with adages that numb the moral sense. Be discontented. Be dissatisfied. "Sweat and grunt" under present conditions. Be as restless as the tempestuous billows on the boundless sea. Let your discontent break mountain-high against the wall of prejudice, and swamp it to the very foundation. Then we shall not have to plead for justice nor on bended knee crave mercy; for we shall be men. Then and not until then will liberty in its highest sense be the boast of our Republic.

John Hope, a professor and opponent of Booker T. Washington's views, speech to the black debating society of Nashville, February 22, 1896, reprinted in Meltzer, The Black Americans, *pp. 142–43.*

The question in which I am especially concerned is the question of open saloons on Sunday. . . . It has been thought right in the State of New York, since ever it was a State, to close all selling places on Sunday, and to allow the sale of actually necessary things only up to 10 o'clock. . . . And the demand comes to violate this, to keep one kind of shop open and one set of men at work; and the kind of shop is the most dangerous kind of shop; the shop where the week's earnings will be wasted; the shop where the tired worker up to Saturday night will unfit himself for the work which is to begin on Monday; the shop out of which proceed the brawls and quarrels which destroy the day of rest and desecrate the day of holiness, and fill the Monday court and the Monday prisons with criminals. It seems to me an insult to the intelligence of our American civilization. . . .

If it is said, "This is an interference with personal liberty," the answer is that personal liberty has to be interfered with if the person is doing wrong to himself or to his neighbor.

If, again, it is said that it makes unfair discrimination among classes, the answer is, that if this refers to clubs, there is no question but that the open bar of the club-house ought to be closed on Sundays, as much as the open bar of the saloon. But if it means to deprive the owners and members of a club of eating and drinking in their club-house on Sunday, then the argument proves too much, because that is in the nature of what a man does in his own house, whether rich or poor, and that the law does not touch.

Right Rev. William Croswell Doane, bishop of Albany, "Liquor and Law," North American Review *162 (March 1896), pp. 293–94.*

The statistics prepared by the committee [on immigration] show further that the immigrants excluded by the illiteracy test are those who remain for the most part in congested masses in our great cities. They furnish a large proportion of the population of the slums. The committee's report proves that illiteracy runs parallel with the slum population, with criminals, paupers, and juvenile delinquents of foreign birth or parentage, whose percentage is out of all proportion to their share of the total population when compared with the percentage of the same classes among the native born. . . .

Mr. President, more precious even than forms of government are the mental and moral qualities which make what we call our race. While those stand unimpaired all is safe. When those decline all is imperiled. They are exposed to but a single danger, and that is by changing the quality of our race and citizenship through the wholesale infusion of races whose traditions and inheritances, whose thoughts and whose beliefs are wholly alien to ours and with whom we have never assimilated or even been associated in the past, the danger has begun. . . . In careless strength, with generous hand, we have kept our gates wide open to all the world. If we do not close them, we should at least place sentinels beside them to challenge those who would pass through. The gates which admit men to the United States and to citizenship in the great Republic should no longer be left unguarded.

Senator Henry Cabot Lodge, Republican of Massachusetts, a longtime supporter of immigration restriction, to the Senate, March 16, 1896, Congressional Record, *54th Congress, vol. 28, pp. 2817, 2820.*

The first view showed two dancers holding between and in front of them an umbrella and dancing the while. The position of the umbrella was constantly changed, and every change was smooth and even, and the steps of the dancing could be perfectly followed.

Then came the waves, showing a scene at Dover pier after a stiff blow. This was by far the best view shown, and had to be repeated many times. As in the umbrella dance, there was absolutely no hitch. One could look far out to sea and pick out a particular wave swelling and undulating and growing bigger and bigger until it struck the end of the pier. Its edge then would be fringed with foam, and finally, in a cloud of spray, the wave would dash upon the beach. One could imagine the people running away.

New York Mail and Express reports the first commercial motion picture show on April 23, 1896, at Koster and Bial's Vaudeville House, April 24, p. 12, quoted in Musser, Emergence of Cinema, *p. 116.*

The common opinion as to the inability of Italian immigrants to assimilate is, I am frank to state, not shared by me. It must be admitted that Italians who come over in mature years, without education even in their own language, and during their sojourn in the United States move almost exclusively among their countrymen, find it exceedingly difficult to acquire even the rudiments of the national language; but such is the common experience with most other non-English speaking immigrants as well. On the other hand, we find that an Italian who has come here younger in years, or who has received a good education, becomes speedily a thorough American, even if his occupation brings him into contact mostly with his own countrymen. And children born in this country of Italian parents can scarcely be distinguished by their speech or their habits from the children of native Americans. The public schools of New York bear testimony to this statement. The Rev. Bonaventure Piscopo, of the Church of the Most Precious Blood (the largest Italian Roman Catholic Parish in the City of New York), is my authority for the statement that all the Italian priests, in their religious services, their Sunday schools, and even in their confessionals, are obliged to use the English if they hope to be understood at all by the second generation.

Dr. Joseph H. Senner, commissioner of immigration, "Immigration from Italy," North American Review, *vol. 162 (June 1896), pp. 655–56.*

The Republican party is unreservedly for sound money. It caused the enactment of a law providing for the redemption [resumption] of specie payments in 1879. Since then every dollar has been as good as gold. We are unalterably opposed to every measure calculated to debase our currency or impair the credit of our country.

Money plank of the Republican Party platform, adopted June 16–18, 1896, Platforms of the Two Great Political Parties, *p. 100.*

Recognizing that the money question is paramount to all others at this time, we invite attention to the fact that the Federal Constitution named silver and gold together as the money metals of the United States, and that the first coinage law passed by Congress under the Constitution made the silver dollar the monetary unit and admitted gold to free coinage at a ratio based upon the silver-dollar unit. . . .

We are unalterably opposed to monometallism which has locked fast the prosperity of an industrial people in the paralysis of hard times. Gold monometalism is a British policy, and its adoption has brought other nations into financial servitude to London. It is not only un-American but anti-American, and it can be fastened on the United States only by the stifling of that spirit and love of liberty which proclaimed our political independence in 1776 and won it in the War of the Revolution.

First plank of the Democratic Party platform (the "Chicago platform"), adopted July 7–11, 1896, Platforms of the Two Great Political Parties, *p. 92.*

Ah, my friends, we say not one word against those who live upon the Atlantic coast, but the hardy pioneers who have braved all the dangers of the wilderness, who have made the desert to blossom as the rose—the pioneers away out there, who rear their children near to Nature's heart, where they can mingle their voices with the voices of the birds—out there where they have erected schoolhouses for the education of their young, churches where they praise their Creator, and cemeteries where rest the ashes of their dead—these people, we say, are as deserving of the consideration of our party as any people in this country. It is for these that we speak. We do not come as aggressors. Our war is not a war of conquest; we are fighting in the defense of our homes, our families, and posterity. We have petitioned, and our petitions have been scorned; we have entreated, and our entreaties have been disregarded; we have begged, and they have mocked when our calamity came. We beg no longer; we entreat no more; we petition no more. We defy them.

. . . . .

You come to us and tell us that the great cities are in favor of the gold standard; we reply that the great cities rest upon our broad and fertile prairies. Burn down your cities and leave our farms, and your cities will spring up again as if by magic; but destroy our farms and the grass will grow in the streets of every city in the country.

. . . . .

Having behind us the producing masses of this nation and the world, supported by the commercial interests, the laboring interests, and the toilers everywhere, we will answer their demand for a gold standard by saying to them: You shall not press down upon the brow of labor this crown of thorns, you shall not crucify mankind upon a cross of gold.

William Jennings Bryan's Cross of Gold speech at the Democratic national convention, July 8, 1896, in his First Battle, *pp. 201–06 passim.*

William Jennings Bryan, the Democratic candidate for president in 1896, was a powerful orator. In his famous Cross of Gold speech, he stretched out his arms to remind his audience of the crucifixion of Christ. *(Library of Congress, Prints and Photographs Division, LC-USZ62-22703)*

The paramount issue at this time in the United States is indisputably the money question. . . . We are unalterably opposed to a single gold standard, and demand an immediate return to the constitutional standard of gold and silver, by restoration by this government, independently of any foreign power, of the unrestricted coinage of both gold and silver into standard money at a ratio of 16 to 1, and upon terms of exact equality as they existed prior to 1873; the silver coin to be a full legal tender equally with gold, for all debts and dues, public and private.

Platform of the National Silver Party (the silver Republicans), July 23, 1896, as published in the Burlington, Iowa, Weekly Hawkeye, *July 30, p. 7, reprinted in Porter and Johnson, eds.,* National Party Platforms, *p. 193.*

The manner in which the opponents of the Democratic ticket nominated at Chicago have begun their campaign must rouse the profoundest resentment of every American regardful of the interests and jealous of the honor of his country. The representatives of half of the American people have been denounced in delirious language as anarchists, cutthroats, and swindlers. This crusade has been one of reckless misrepresentation from the start. The libelers of the late convention know that the Chicago platform is not anarchical. In most respects it is inspired by enlightened progressiveness. The anarchical elements in the convention—Tillman and Altgeld—were distinctly frowned upon. . . . Nor is it possible with any more sincerity to call Mr. Bryan a demagogue. He follows the truth as he sees it, though it lead him to political destruction.

Lukewarm support for the Democratic ticket in Hearst's New York Journal, *July 13, 1896, the only New York newspaper to support Bryan, p. 10.*

Recent events have imposed upon the patriotic people of this country a responsibility and a duty quite as great as any since the civil war. Then it was a struggle to preserve the Government of the United States. Now it is a struggle to preserve the financial honor of the United States. Then it was a contest to save the Union. Now it is a contest to save the spotless credit of that Union. Then section was arrayed against section. Now men of all sections can unite, and will unite, to rebuke the repudiation of obligations and the debasement of our currency.

In this contest patriotism is above party and national honor more than any party name. The currency and the credit of the country are good now and must be kept good forever. . . .

One of William McKinley's front porch speeches, delivered July 11, 1896, Republican National Committee, Republican Campaign Text Book, *p. 201.*

We recognize that through the connivance of the present and preceding Administrations the country has reached a crisis in its National life, as predicted in our declaration four years ago, and that prompt and patriotic action is the supreme duty of the hour. . . .

The influence of European moneychangers has been more potent in shaping legislation than the voice of the American people. Executive power and patronage have been used to corrupt our legislatures and defeat the will of the people, and plutocracy has thereby been enthroned upon the ruins of democracy. To restore the Government intended by the fathers, and for the welfare and prosperity of this and future generations, we demand the establishment of an economic and financial system which shall make us masters of our own affairs and independent of European control. . . .

We demand the free and unrestricted coinage of silver and gold at the present legal ratio of 16 to 1, without waiting for the consent of foreign nations. . . .

People's Party (Populist) platform, adopted July 22–24, 1896, World Almanac, 1896, p. 94, reprinted in Porter and Johnson, eds., National Party Platforms, pp. 196–97.

With millions of others of your countrymen I congratulate you most heartily upon being the People's standard bearer in the great uprising of the masses against the classes. You are at this hour the hope of the Republic—the central figure of the civilized world. In the arduous campaign before you the millions will rally to your standard and you will lead them to a glorious victory. The people love and trust you—they believe in you as you believe in them, and under your administration the rule of the money power will be broken and the gold barons of Europe will no longer run the American government.

Eugene V. Debs, letter to William Jennings Bryan, July 27, 1896, in his Gentle Rebel: Letters of Eugene V. Debs (1995), p. 24.

What's the matter with Kansas? We all know; yet here we are at it again. We have an old mossback Jacksonian who snorts and howls because there is a bathtub in the statehouse; we are running that old jay for governor. We have another shabby, wild-eyed, rattle-brained fanatic who has said openly in a dozen speeches that "the rights of the user are paramount to the rights of the owner"; we are running him for chief justice, so that capital will come tumbling over itself to get into the State. . . . Then for fear some hint that the State had become respectable might percolate through the civilized portions of the nation, we have decided to send three or four harpies out lecturing, telling the people that Kansas is raising hell and letting the corn go to weeds.

Oh, this is a State to be proud of! We are a people who can hold up our heads! What we need is not more money, but less capital, fewer white shirts, and brains, fewer men with business judgment, and more of those fellows who boast that they are "just ordinary clodhoppers, but they know more in a minute about finance than John Sherman." . . .

William Allen White's anti-Populist editorial "What's the Matter With Kansas?" in the Kansas Emporia Gazette, August 15, 1896, widely reproduced by the Republican campaign, in White's, The Editor and His People, p. 247.

The action of the United States Court in the matter of the Debs Riot has been condemned by every Anarchist, every Socialist, every Communist, and every Populist in the country.

In suppressing this riot and demonstrating the power of the federal government to protect its own people and their rights President Cleveland performed an act which, in my judgment, will, in the centuries to come, do more for the preservation and maintenance of our institutions than any single act of any President since the close of the late Civil War.

Former senator Warner Miller, Republican from New York, "The Duty of the Hour," North American Review, vol. 163 (September 1896), pp. 365–66.

The problem that the Tuskegee Institute keeps before itself constantly is how to prepare . . . leaders. From the outset, in connection with religious and academic training, it has emphasized industrial or hand training as a means of finding the way out of present conditions. First, we have found the industrial teaching useful in giving the student a chance to work out a portion of his expenses while in school. Second, the school furnishes labor that has an economic value, and at the same time gives the student a chance to acquire knowledge and skill while performing the labor. Most of all, we find the industrial system valuable in teaching economy, thrift, and the dignity of labor, and in giving moral backbone to students. The fact that a student goes out into the world conscious of his power to build a house or a wagon, or to make a harness, gives him a certain confidence and moral independence that he would not possess without such training.

Booker T. Washington, "The Awakening of the Negro," Atlantic Monthly, vol. 78 (September 1896), p. 323.

This convention has assembled to uphold the principles upon which depend the honor and welfare of the American people in order that Democrats throughout the Union may unite their patriotic efforts to avert disaster from their country and ruin from their party. . . .

The experience of mankind has shown that by reason of their natural qualities gold is the necessary money of the large affairs of commerce and business, while silver is conveniently adapted to minor transactions, and the most beneficial use of both together can be insured only by the adoption of the former as a standard of monetary measure. . . .

Platform of the National Democratic Party (the gold Democrats), September 2, 1896, Proceedings of the Convention of the National Democratic Party, p. 64, reprinted in Porter and Johnson, ed., National Party Platforms, pp. 189—91.

Jacksonville, Fla., Sept. 10—At St. Augustine tonight James P. Weldman and Joe Allen quarreled while discussing the silver question. Allen drew a knife and cut Weldman, and the latter shot Allen twice, causing almost instant death. Both men leave families, and were active in politics.

Birmingham State Herald, September 11, 1896, available online at 1896: A Website of Political Cartoons. URL: http://iberia.vassar.edu/1896/currency.html.

Elaborate experiments in aerial locomotion are in progress at Dune Park, Northern Indiana, near Lake Michigan, under the direction of Mr. Octave Chanute. . . . A distance of 300 feet has been covered, at the height of say 30 feet from the ground, with less jar and shock than a ride in a rubber tired carriage. Two men carry the apparatus up the sand hill. At a height of 35 feet up the machine is lifted, and Mr. Hering fits himself under it and allows the wind to raise it. His arms fall over the bars provided. He makes two or three quick steps toward the lake, and the machine soars from the ground and darts through the air with a velocity described as rivaling that of an express train. The motion is horizontal, without any swaying motion. To stop the machine, the operator moves his body enough to tilt the apparatus slightly upward in front, when it coasts gradually and slowly to the ground. . . . The apparatus is modeled after the general form of an albatross, but has seven wings.

Report of glider experiments by aviation pioneers, "Aerial Flights," Scientific American, *vol. 75 (October 31, 1896), p. 329.*

Such important education is to be found in the clear reading of official reports, vital statistics, labor reports and annuals, tenement-house reports, police records, school reports, charity organization and institution year-books—such literature as may be had for the asking, yet is, in many ways, the important social, history-making literature of our times. . . .

Such reading as this suggests might be called "dry," mere skeletons of figures to be recognized only by people "interested in that sort of thing," literature not to be found in any but the specialist's library. But it is not dry; and even if so, it is a literature that concerns us all, more than any news compiled, and if awaiting readers now, will some day *force* the attention of the whole world. But read each figure a human being; read that every wretched unlighted tenement described is a *home* for people, men and women, old and young, with the strength and the weaknesses, the good and the bad, the appetites and wants common to all. Read, in descriptions of sweatshops, factories, and long-hour work-days, the difficulty, the impossibility of well-ordered living under the conditions outlined. Understanding reading of these things must bring a sense of fairness outraged, the disquieting conviction that something is wrong somewhere, and turning to your own contrasting life, you will feel a responsibility of the *how* and the *why* and the *wherefore.* Say to yourself, "If there is a wrong in our midst, what can I do? What is my responsibility? Who is to blame? Do I owe reparation?"

Settlement founder Lillian Wald, addressing the National Council of Jewish Women, November 1896, Proceedings of the First Convention, *reprinted in Appel, ed.,* The New Immigration, *pp. 26–27.*

Miles after miles of rich country went by as we gazed from the windows of the moving train, and all this vast extent of territory which we traversed belonged to the United States. . . . And yet this great and powerful nation must go across two thousand miles of sea, and take from the poor Hawaiians their little spots in the broad Pacific, must covet our islands of Hawaii Nei, and extinguish the nationality of my poor people, many of whom have now not a foot of land which can be called their own. And for what? In order that another race-problem shall be injected into the social and political perplexities with which the United States in the great experiment of popular government is already struggling? in order that a novel and inconsistent foreign and colonial policy shall be grafted upon its hitherto impregnable diplomacy?

Queen Liliuokalani's reflections during a train ride across the United States, December 1896, in her Hawaii's Story, *p. 310.*

Queen Liliuokalani ruled Hawaii until 1893, when she was unseated in a coup led by sugar growers, who hoped to make Hawaii an American dependency. In 1895 the queen's supporters made an unsuccessful attempt to regain control of the islands. *(Courtesy Hawaiian Historical Society, #4432)*

It is hard to believe that any one in his sober senses thinks the imprisonment of Debs a dangerous precedent. . . . Nobody in his right mind believes that there has been usurpation of the power by the courts, or that the power exercised is the source or beginning of peril to individual or collective rights. Out of all that had been done by the courts since the Government was founded there can be deduced no sound reason for depriving them of their accustomed and well-understood power to enforce respect and order in their presence, and to compel obedience to their writs and commands wherever lawfully sent.

William A. Woods, the federal judge who sentenced Eugene Debs to prison, writing in the 1897 Yale Law Review, quoted in Papke, The Pullman Case (1999), p. 94.

The part which women play in the yellow journalism of America is a very important one. There are almost as many women as men employed on the various staffs, and those who work on the space system sometimes earn more money than do the men—indeed, one of the good points of the yellow journalism is its tendency to recognize the equality of the sexes so far as the matter of pay is concerned. For the "exposures," which are constantly being undertaken by these journals, women, because of their acknowledged tactfulness, are more often employed than the men.

"Put a good woman on this!" shouts out the head editor to his assistant dozen of times a day. . . . When . . . I first took a position on a yellow journal, something over a year ago, I knew little or nothing of the sort of work that would be required of me as a "yellow woman journalist." I knew only that I needed money, and that I was offered by a yellow journal a good salary. My first inkling of what was expected of me came when I got my first assignment. I was asked to walk the streets of New York in the most dangerous part of the city, "allow" myself to become arrested as a disreputable women, spend a part of the night in jail with women of the street, and write up a brilliant account of the affair for the next morning's paper! . . .

This is an example of what is known in yellow journalism as a "moral exposure." . . . [The editor] has, so he says, "moral reasons" for sending out a young woman on a mission of that sort. He wants to reform New York!

Elizabeth Banks describes journalism in 1897, "American 'Yellow Journalism,'" The Living Age, vol. 218 (September 3, 1898), pp. 644–45.

"I want to know what Jesus would do in my case? I haven't had a stroke of work for two months. I've got a wife and three children, and I love them as much as if I was worth a million dollars. I've been living off a little earnings I saved up during the World's Fair jobs I got. I'm a carpenter by trade and I've tried every way I know to get a job.

You say we ought to take for our motto, 'What would Jesus do?' What would He do if He was out of work like me? I can't be somebody else and ask the question. I want to work. I'd give anything to grow tired of working ten hours a day the way I used to. Am I to blame because I can't manufacture a job for myself? I've got to live, and my wife and my children have got to live. But how? What would Jesus do? You say that's the question we ought to ask."

Mr. Maxwell sat there staring at the great sea of faces all intent on his, and no answer to this man's question seemed, for the time being, to be possible. "O God!" his heart prayed. "This is a question that brings up the entire social problem in all its perplexing entanglement of human wrongs and its present condition contrary to every desire of God for a human being's welfare. . . ."

Charles Sheldon, In His Steps, 1897, chapter 30, available online at Kansas Collection Books. URL: http://www.kancoll.org/books/sheldon/shchap30.htm.

In Cardenas, one of the principal seaport towns of the island, I found the pacificos [civilians] lodged in huts at the back of the town and also in abandoned warehouses along the water front. The condition of these latter was so pitiable that it is difficult to describe it correctly and hope to be believed.

The warehouses are built on wooden posts about fifty feet from the water's edge. They were originally nearly as large in extent as Madison Square Garden, but the half of the roof of one has fallen in, carrying the flooring with it, and the adobe walls and one side of the sloping roof and the high wooden piles on which half of the floor once rested are all that remain.

Some time ago an unusually high tide swept in under one of these warehouses and left a pool of water a hundred yards long and as many wide, around the wooden posts, and it has remained there undisturbed. This pool is now covered a half-inch thick with green slime, colored blue and yellow, and with a damp fungus spread over the wooden posts and up the sides of the walls.

Over this sewage are now living three hundred women and children and a few men. The floor be neath them has rotted away, and the planks have broken and fallen into the pool, leaving big gaps, through which rise day and night deadly stenches and poisonous exhalations from the pool below.

The people above it are not ignorant of their situation. They know that they are living over a deathtrap, but there is no other place for them. Bands of guerrillas and flying columns have driven them in like sheep to this city, and, with no money and no chance to obtain work, they have taken shelter in the only place that is left open to them.

With planks and blankets and bits of old sheet iron they have, for the sake of decency, put up barriers across these abandoned warehouses, and there they are now sitting on the floor or stretched on heaps of rags, gaunt and hollow-eyed. Outside, in the angles of the fallen walls, and among the refuse of the warehouses, they have built fireplaces, and, with the few pots and kettles they use in common, they cook what food the children can find or beg.

Journalist Richard Harding Davis, sent to Cuba by the New York Journal, *describes a Cuban "reconcentration" camp, January/February 1897, in his* Cuba in Wartime *(1897), pp. 48–50.*

The difficulties in the way of [research on alcohol use] are enormous. In matters which affect private character, truthful reports are proverbially hard to obtain. The accessible statistics are incomplete or inaccurate, or both. The effects of intemperance in promoting vice and crime are often mixed with the effects of many other causes, such as unhealthy occupations, bad lodgings, poor food, and inherited disabilities; and it is very difficult to disentangle intemperance as a cause from other causes of vice, crime, and pauperism. At every point connected with these investigations the studious observer encounters an intense partisanship, which blinds the eyes of witnesses and obscures the judgement of writers and speakers on the subject.

Charles W. Eliot, president of Harvard and member of the investigative group the Committee of Fifty, in his "A Study of American Liquor Laws," Atlantic Monthly, *vol. 79 (February 1897), pp. 178–79.*

At first most of the aldermen seemed to be bound hand and foot to the street-car companies; but half of them are elected every year, and we tried to select men who would stand by the people, and got them, if possible, to pledge themselves. When once pledged, it was pretty hard for them to go back on their word, but of course some had their price. Not until the second year was the Board of Aldermen really out of the grip of the street-car company. All this time we were fighting the company in the courts in regard to its franchise. It was a long, bitter fight, the case being taken from court to court. . . . While this struggle was going on, with decisions sometimes in our favor and sometimes in theirs, they were trying to get a new franchise, but I kept vetoing their measures, and it was pretty hard to pass anything over my veto. I used to stir up the public by sending out notices, and the people would pack the Council chamber and fairly terrify the Aldermen who wished to go back on their campaign promises. We even told them that we had plenty of rope there and would hang them. The newspapers, with the exception of one German paper, the "Abend-Post," were on the side of the street-car companies. When they published anything from me, they had it

put in such a light that it had an entirely different meaning. Once, when I issued a call for a mass-meeting to protest against a bill introduced in the Legislature to take away my appointive power, they refused to print the call, even when I offered to pay them for it. When the papers refused to publish my notices, I used to have bulletin-boards fastened with chains to four or five of the pillars about the City Hall. In this way I got a hearing.

Reform mayor Hazen Pingree of Detroit on his fight with the streetcar companies, in his "Detroit: A Municipal Study," Outlook, *vol. 55 (February 6, 1897), p. 438.*

Heretofore we have welcomed all who came to us from other lands, except those whose moral or physical condition or history threatened danger to our national welfare and safety. Relying upon the jealous watchfulness of our people to prevent injury to our political and social fabric, we have encouraged those coming from foreign countries to cast their lot with us and join in the development of our vast domain, securing in return a share in the blessings of American citizenship. . . .

It is said, however, that the quality of recent immigration is undesirable. The time is quite within recent memory when the same thing was said of immigrants who, with their descendants, are now numbered among our best citizens. . . .

The best reason that could be given for this radical restriction of immigration is the necessity of protecting our population against degeneration and saving our national peace and quiet from imported turbulence and disorder.

I can not believe that we would be protected against these evils by limiting immigration to those who can read and write in any language twenty-five words of our Constitution. In my opinion it is infinitely more safe to admit a hundred thousand immigrants who, though unable to read and write, seek among us only a home and opportunity to work, than to admit one of those unruly agitators and enemies of governmental control, who can not only read and write but delights in arousing by inflammatory speech the illiterate and peacefully inclined to discontent and tumult.

President Cleveland's veto of the immigration restriction act, March 2, 1897, in Richardson, ed., Messages and Papers, *vol. 9, pp. 757–59.*

At the southern end of the Lake Front will begin the Shore Drive, which, going above the Illinois Central Railway to the Lake, will extend over a stone bridge of the old Roman pattern to the first great outer concourse, and thence south seven and a half miles, to the lower end of Jackson Park. . . .

The driveway itself should be protected by a sea-wall, designed to express dignity as well as to afford security. Behind it should be a broad terrace, supporting seats made in the old Grecian pattern, so placed that the sitter might look out to sea. Next this wall should be a space, planted with tall shrubs, disposed partly to conceal and partly to reveal the Lake. Next this, a bicycle course and a greensward, covered with flowering plants. Next to this plantation should be an equestrian way, and west of it should be the great Avenue itself, with its broad green lawns and its rows of stately trees. Besides the Drive, on the west of it, should be another terrace, with here and there old Greek resting-places, some curved into the banks, out of which should flow fountains of water. The floor of this walk and of the recesses should be paved with small colored pebbles, in geometrical patterns. The wall itself, which is to be next west of the walk, should be built of long slivers of sparkling stone, like those encircling the Roosevelt farms that skirt along the Hudson, north of Poughkeepsie.

Architect Daniel Burnham describes his "City Beautiful" ideas for Chicago in a public meeting, April 1897, quoted in Moore, Daniel H. Burnham, vol. 2, p. 106.

The chief centre of corruption was the Police Department. No man not intimately acquainted with both the lower and humbler sides of New York life—for there is a wide distinction between the two—can realize how far this corruption extended. Except in rare instances, where prominent politicians made demands which could not be refused, both promotions and appointments towards the close of Tammany rule were made almost solely for money, and the prices were discussed with cynical frankness. There was a well-recognized tariff of charges, ranging from two or three hundred dollars for appointment as a patrolman, to twelve or fifteen thousand dollars for promotion to the position of captain. The money was reimbursed to those who paid it by an elaborate system of blackmail. This was chiefly carried on at the expense of gamblers, liquor sellers, and keepers of disorderly houses; but every form of vice and crime contributed more or less, and a great many respectable people who were ignorant or timid were blackmailed under pretence of forbidding or allowing them to violate obscure ordinances and the like. From top to bottom the New York police force was utterly demoralized by the gangrene of such a system, where venality and blackmail went hand in hand with the basest forms of low ward politics, and where the policeman, the ward politician, the liquor seller, and the criminal alternately preyed on one another and helped one another to prey on the general public.

Theodore Roosevelt, president of the reform New York Police Board, reports the Lexow Committee findings, in "Municipal Administration: The New York Police Force," Atlantic Monthly, vol. 80 (September 1897), p. 289.

. . . all at once I saw a thousand curious eyes turned upon me.

"What is it?" I asked the interpreter. "What did she say?"

He laughed. "'A reporter is here,' she says. She says to the people, 'Tell how you feel. Then the Americans will know. Then they may listen.'"

A remarkable scene followed. One by one men and women rose and in a sentence or two in the rolling, broad voweled Hawaiian made a fervent profession of faith.

"My feeling," declared a tall, broad shouldered man, whose dark eyes were alight with enthusiasm. "This is my feeling: I love my country and I want to be independent—now and forever."

"And my feeling is the same," cried a stout, bold-faced woman, rising in the middle of the hall. "I love this land. I don't want to be annexed."

"This birthplace of mine I love as the American loves his. Would he wished to be annexed to another, greater land?"

"I am strongly opposed to annexation. How dare the people of the Unites States rob a people of their independence?"

"I want the American government to do justice. America helped to dethrone Liliuokalani. She must be restored. Never shall we consent to annexation!"

"My father is American; my mother is pure Hawaiian. It is my mother's land I love. The American nation has been unjust. How could we ever love America?"

"Let them see their injustice and restore the monarchy!" cried an old, old woman, whose dark face framed in its white hair was working pathetically.

"If the great nations would be fair they would not take away our country. Never will I consent to annexation!"

"Tell America I don't want annexation. I want my Queen," said the gentle voice of a woman.

Journalist Miriam Michelson, reporting from Hawaii, "Many Thousands of Native Hawaiians Sign a Protest to the United States Government Against Annexation," San Francisco Call, September 30, 1897, available online. URL: http://www.hawaii-nation.org/sfcall.html.

[W]hat after all, am I? Am I an American or am I a Negro? Can I be both? Or is it my duty to cease to be a Negro as soon as possible and be an American? If I strive as a Negro, am I not perpetuating the very cleft that threatens and separates black and white America? Is not my only possible practical aim the subduction of all that is Negro in me to the American? Does my black blood place upon me any more obligation to assert my nationality than German, or Irish or Italian blood would? . . . Here, it seems to me, is the reading of the riddle that puzzles so many of us. We are Americans, not only by birth and by citizenship, but by our political ideals, our language, our religion. Farther than that, our Americanism does not go. At that point, we are Negroes, members of a vast historic race that from the very dawn of creation has slept, but half awakening in the dark forests of its African fatherland. We are the first fruits of this new nation, the harbinger of that black tomorrow which is yet destined to soften the whiteness of the Teutonic today.

W. E. B. DuBois, "The Conservation of Races," address to the first meeting of the American Negro Academy, March 1897, quoted in Lewis, W. E. B. Dubois, *pp. 172–73.*

There had been lots of gold brought out before, but when the steamer *Portland* came out [arriving in Seattle July 17, 1897], they advertised a ton of gold! Well, you know, a ton of gold sounds big! That is what started the gold rush—a ton of gold. Before the paper was cold on the print, hardly, the rush was started. All that gold! Each one thought they'd go in and grab off a piece. . . . The San Francisco *Call*, August 22, 1897, had a list of 31 boats on the way north from the west coast. Now that meant from California clear up. And there were 15,595 passengers on the boats. You know they were crowded.

Edith Feero Larson, whose family joined the Klondike gold rush, describes its start, summer 1897, quoted in Mayer, Klondike Women, *pp. 18–19.*

We take pleasure in answering thus prominently the communication below, expressing at the same time our great gratification that its faithful author is numbered among the friends of *The Sun:*

> I am 8 years old. Some of my little friends say there is no Santa Claus. Papa says, "If you see it in The Sun, it's so." Please tell me the truth, is there a Santa Claus?

Virginia O'Hanlon

Virginia, your little friends are wrong. They have been affected by the skepticism of a skeptical age. They do not believe except what they see. They think that nothing can be which is not comprehensible by their little minds. All minds, Virginia, whether they be men's or children's, are little. In this great universe of ours, man is a mere insect, an ant, in his intellect as compared with the boundless world about him, as measured by the intelligence capable of grasping the whole of truth and knowledge.

Yes, Virginia, there is a Santa Claus.

He exists as certainly as love and generosity and devotion exist, and you know that they abound and give to your life its highest beauty and joy. Alas! how dreary would be the world if there were no Santa Claus! It would be as dreary as if there were no Virginias. There would be no childlike faith then, no poetry, no romance to make tolerable this existence. We should have no enjoyment, except in sense and sight. The external light with which childhood fills the world would be extinguished. . . .

Journalist Francis P. Church, unsigned editorial, New York Sun, *Sept. 21, 1897, p. 6.*

3

America Becomes a World Power
1898–1901

AMERICA ON THE THRESHOLD OF A NEW ERA IN FOREIGN POLICY

At the end of the 19th century, the distribution of world power was very different than it would be at the end of the 20th. Great Britain was the strongest nation in the world, with an empire covering about one-fifth of the earth and a population of some 400 million. Most other western European nations also had colonies. Along with the Austro-Hungarian and Russian Empires, they kept a wary eye on the growing ambitions and strength of Germany and Japan.

The United States was little more than 100 years old. The young nation had developed great industrial power and economic strength, but it had not yet emerged as an actor on the world stage. Neither its officials nor its citizens had yet faced the dilemmas and conflicts of world power. As a consequence, idealism about America's role in the world was widespread in popular thought in the late 1890s, and sincerely believed. In the eyes of many Americans, rapid economic development confirmed a long held cultural belief—that America had a special mission in the world. That mission was to be a moral and model society, based in democracy, political freedom, representative institutions, unrestricted opportunity, and the value and rights of the individual. The nation's new economic strength, many Americans began to think, was the hand of providence or fate, working to enable the spread of American ideals among other peoples of the world.

Even in the 1890s, it is true, a significant group of Americans called anti-imperialists continued to prefer America's traditional commitment to isolationism. But the majority was beginning to see a larger role in the world as a new form of Manifest Destiny—holding that it was inevitable and probably part of the divine plan not only for Americans to spread across the continent and perhaps northward into Canada but even to spread across the globe. They believed expansionism was the appropriate policy for America and even a moral duty. Some expansionists, of course, had more complex motives. Some, particularly a younger, rising generation identified with the Republican Party, were unabashed nationalists who frankly thought expansionism was an important characteristic of any major power. This position was called the large policy. More aggressive nationalists like Assistant Secretary of the Navy Theodore Roosevelt and Senator Henry Cabot Lodge, who often supported expansion through military power and even war, were called *jingoes* and their policies *jingoism*.[1] "No national life is worth having," Roosevelt announced in an 1897 speech that was reprinted in newspapers from coast to coast, "if the nation is not willing . . . to stake everything on the supreme arbitrament of war . . . rather than to submit to the loss of honor and renown." Other expansionists had business interests and wanted to find new markets or investment opportunities. "American factories are making more than the American people can use; American soil is producing more than they can consume," said enthusiastic commercial expansionist Senator Albert Beveridge of Indiana in 1898. "Fate has written our policy for us," he continued, "We must get an ever increasing portion of foreign trade." Another articulate group of expansionists supported Christian missionary activity and hoped to see it increase in non–Christian nations.[2]

Complementing America's willingness to assume a new role in the world was the influence of Social Darwinism. Charles Darwin's influential theory of biological evolution (1859) had inspired social theorists to devise parallel interpretations of human history and society. One aspect of Social Darwinism was a justification for the ruthless accumulation of wealth by individuals, called "survival of the fittest." But by the 1890s Social Darwinism was more often used to explain the historical development of nations, cultures, and "races," as peoples of different nations or ethnic groups were commonly called at the time. Social Darwinists argued that world cultures exhibited three evolutionary levels of development: savagery, barbarism, and civilization. They believed that the industrialized nations of the United States and western Europe had evolved to the third, highest evolutionary stage called "civilization." Social Darwinists also explained why republican institutions and democracy had developed first and most strongly in Britain and the United States. They argued that people of English and Germanic descent (whom they called the Anglo-Saxon or Teutonic "races") had evolved a much greater capacity for self-government than other groups. Some also believed that Christianity was inseparable from the evolutionary stage of "civilization." The ideas of Social Darwinists were widely accepted by politicians, business leaders, religious leaders, and other popular opinion makers at the end of the 19th century. They held that nations that had reached "civilization" had a duty to be expansionists and bring law, order, and self-government to less evolved nations of the world.

Obviously, there were strongly ethnocentric and sometimes racist elements in Social Darwinist ideas. In February 1899—the same month that America approved the acquisition of the Philippines and began a long war there—a poem called "The White Man's Burden" appeared in *McClure's Magazine*. It was written by popular British author Rudyard Kipling to welcome America's new role as an imperialist nation. The poem was widely parodied by anti-imperialists and others who disagreed with its sentiments. But for good or ill, the phrase "white man's burden" immediately entered popular speech. It was a shorthand way to refer to ideas that, at the time, were accepted by many people as a worthy justification for expanding America's influence in the world.

THE SPANISH-AMERICAN WAR

In 1895, nationalists in Cuba, which was still a Spanish colony, had begun a revolution against Spain. Many Americans favored military intervention to aid the Cubans. At the end of 1897, however, it appeared that the conflict was moving toward a peaceful settlement and an autonomous government in Cuba.

As 1898 began, the situation in Cuba deteriorated. Both Spanish loyalists and Cuban nationalists openly resisted the new autonomous (but not independent) government that Spain had sanctioned for the island. Spanish brutality resumed and was widely reported in America. Then an unforeseeable event occurred. The Spanish minister to Washington, Enrique Dupuy de Lôme, wrote a letter to a friend in Cuba, confiding that the Spanish concessions of late 1897 had been granted merely to pacify the United States. He also confided his opinion that President McKinley was "weak and a bidder for the admiration of the crowd, besides being a would-be politician who tries to leave a door open behind himself while keeping on good terms with the jingoes of his party." De Lôme, of course, imagined his letter would be confidential, but it was intercepted by a Cuban sympathizer and delivered to the New York offices of the Cuban junta. On February 9, the letter was published in William Randolph Hearst's *New York Journal* under the sensational headline "The Worst Insult to the United States in Its History!" Other newspapers throughout the nation, which had also been following the war in Cuba in great detail, reprinted it. The letter caused a storm of popular indignation—especially the comments about President McKinley, despite the fact that his American critics said the same things about him. ("No more backbone than a chocolate eclair!" Assistant Secretary of the Navy Theodore Roosevelt huffed in a famous comment that luckily remained private.) President McKinley himself was more concerned about the revelation that Spain had no intention of significant reform in Cuba. Among both the public and the administration in Washington, sentiment in favor of intervention increased.[3]

De Lôme resigned immediately. But six days later a far more serious event took place. With the grudging approval of Spain, America had sent the warship *Maine* to dock in Havana's harbor in the event that Americans in Cuba should need to be evacuated quickly. On the evening of February 15, a massive explosion ripped through the *Maine*. Some 260 men out of a crew of 350 sailors, both white and African-American, were killed. The ship itself sank within minutes, leaving only tangled metal and masts visible above the water. Military men were inclined to think the explosion was an accident, probably in the coal-burning boilers that powered steamships at the time. But almost every newspaper in the country, many American citizens, and some officials assumed that the Spanish had used a mine, torpedo, or "infernal machine" (time bomb) to sink the *Maine*. "An act of dirty treachery on the part of the Spaniards," Roosevelt wrote to a friend.[4] "Whole Country Thrills with the War Fever Yet the President Says 'It Was an Accident'," said the *New York Journal,* offering a reward of $50,000 for information on the perpetrators. The *World* mounted a campaign to send its own deep-sea divers to investigate. "Remember the Maine!" became its cry.

In Madrid, U.S. diplomat General Stewart Lyndon Woodford, who opposed war, worked hard and skillfully to negotiate a peaceful settlement. But the public outcry for military intervention continued growing. In the Senate, a distressed Senator Redfield Proctor, Republican of Vermont, had reported back from an inspection tour of Cuba that the civilian population still faced appallingly bad conditions. Even many American businessmen, who had long opposed military action for fear it would upset the recovering economy, now favored it. President McKinley requested and received unanimous congressional approval of a $50 million military appropriations bill and ordered an inquiry of the *Maine* explosion. In late March, the Court of Inquiry reported that it could not identify the exact cause—but that it definitely came from outside the vessel. (Later studies also failed to pinpoint the cause, but the most recent concluded the most likely event was an internal explosion caused by the ship's boilers—and that even if it were sabotage, the Spanish government was not the perpetrator.)[5]

On March 27, the president demanded that Spain agree to an armistice; negotiate a peace with American arbitration; release civilians from the reconcentration camps immediately; and provide aid to displaced *pacificos,* or civilian farmers. Spain agreed to end the camps and to an

Putting a face on tragedy: The U.S.S. *Maine's* baseball team was photographed shortly before the ship was blown up in the Havana harbor. All but one of these young men died in the explosion. *(Library of Congress, Prints and Photographs Division, LC-USZ62-26149)*

armistice, but did not accept the idea of American mediation. Unsatisfied, President McKinley then asked Congress for a resolution of war. Public sentiment also ran strongly in favor of recognizing an independent Cuba, although the president did not request it. After a week of debate, on April 19, Congress passed a joint war resolution. It also acknowledged Cuban independence in the so-called Teller Amendment, named for its sponsor, Senator Henry Moore Teller of Colorado. The Teller Amendment announced that the United States had no interest in exercising authority over Cuba and intended "to leave the government and control of the island to its people." Although the Teller Amendment did not recognize the Cuban insurgents' government, it did forestall future annexation of Cuba.[6]

On April 22, President McKinley ordered a naval blockade of Cuba, considered an act of war under international law. Spain immediately severed diplomatic relations and declared war on April 24. On April 25 Congress formally recognized a state of war.

"A Splendid Little War"

The Spanish-American conflict lasted only 16 weeks, ending in August. John Hay, later secretary of state, called it "a splendid little war; begun with the highest motives; carried on with magnificent intelligence and spirit; favored by that Fortune which loves the brave." Many Americans agreed. The war was widely viewed as a humanitarian effort and enjoyed great popular approval and support. Even Republican senator George Hoar of Massachusetts, an outspoken anti-imperialist, said, "We cannot look idly on while hundreds of thousands of innocent human beings, women and children and old men, die of hunger close to our doors. . . . If guns and ships of war are ever to be used, they are to be used on such an occasion."[7]

The president called for 200,000 volunteers, but nearly a million young men offered to join the cause—including many who were highly educated or from prominent or wealthy families. Their enthusiasm was in marked contrast to attitudes during the Civil War. During the Civil War, some prominent public men, especially northern and western Democrats, had avoided service in the Union cause, and many wealthy men had legally purchased an exemption for themselves or their sons. As a result, the issue of draft avoidance had loomed large in many late 19th-century elections.

Theodore Roosevelt immediately resigned his position as assistant secretary of the navy and with his friend Dr. Leonard Wood formed the First Volunteer Calvary. The mounted regiment, an odd mixture of Ivy League graduates, cowboys, and even some Native Americans, was soon known as the Rough Riders. William Jennings Bryan headed the Third Nebraska Volunteers, called the Silver Battalion because so many participants were his political allies in the fight for free silver. Wall Street formed a volunteer unit. Congressman Joseph "Fighting Joe" Wheeler of Alabama, who had a distinguished military record in the Confederate army, accepted appointment as a U.S. Army general. Not only the well-established joined the war effort, however. Many communities and ordinary individuals also formed volunteer units.

Despite the martial enthusiasm, war preparations revealed many defects in the American military system of the late 1890s. The ill-prepared and poorly organized War Department had many difficulties mobilizing. The standing army, like the navy, had been permitted to shrink and decline after the Civil War. It had only 28,000 regulars. The War Department had to rely on state militias and volunteer units, but few had experienced military officers to lead them. "No words could describe to you the confusion and lack of system and the general mismanagement of affairs here," wrote Roosevelt to Henry Cabot Lodge while in Tampa awaiting transport to Cuba.[8] There were also serious supply problems. Available uniforms were completely unsuited for a tropical climate. Rifles were so lacking that many men had to train with wooden sticks. Provisioning was wholly inadequate and the discovery of "embalmed beef"—unscrupulously prepared canned meat—caused a popular uproar.

Another serious problem was racial tension. Four African-American units of the regular army usually served on the western frontier—the Ninth and Tenth Cavalries and the 24th and 25th Infantries. They had to be transported to Florida training camps to await transfer to Cuba. As the soldiers journeyed through the increasingly segregated South, many racial incidents occurred. In Tampa, site of the training camps, a riot occurred that resulted in many injuries. Nonetheless many black soldiers, whom the Cubans called "smoked Yankees," served with distinction in the war. Some received the Medal of Honor, although their units received little publicity or credit afterward. When the war began, the U.S. military had only one African-American commissioned officer—West Point graduate Charles Young. By the war's end he had been promoted to major. More than 100 other black soldiers had been appointed to the rank of first or second lieutenant, partly in response to pressure from African-American leaders to provide black officers for black regiments.

Most serious of all the military's problems was its inability to organize adequate sanitation, hygiene, and medical services for the tropics. Soon the troops suffered epidemics of malaria, typhoid, yellow fever, and dysentery. While fewer than 400 soldiers lost their lives from combat before the war ended, more than 10 times as many probably died from diseases during and after the war.[9]

When mobilization for the war began, all regular army hospital corpsmen were male recruits and lacked any formal medical training. Professional nursing schools for women, however, had existed in the United States since the 1870s. In April 1898, the surgeon general was authorized to employ nurses by contract. Many nurses immediately applied to serve. Under the direction of Dr. Anita Newcomb McGee, the Daughters of the American Revolution (DAR) served as an application review board for army nurses. Another group of nurses was organized and financed by a women's auxiliary of New York Presbyterian Hospital. Clara Barton, the founder of the American Red Cross—and 77 years old in 1898—outfitted a relief ship even before war was officially declared and personally led trained Red Cross nurses to Cuba.

Female nurses served with distinction in the Spanish–American War. This army ward hospital was set up in Kentucky to treat men injured in the war. *(Library of Congress, Prints and Photographs Division, LC-USZ62-96039)*

At first, some male military doctors resisted allowing women nurses to serve in field, or battle-site, hospitals. Soon, however, their objections were overcome by necessity and by the effective work of the nurses themselves. In August, an official Nurse Corps Division was created in the office of the surgeon general, headed by Dr. McGee, to coordinate all war nursing efforts. By mid-1899, when the first regulations for the Nurse Corps were published, more than 1,500 women had served as army nurses, and 6,000 more had applied. Among the nurses who served were some 280 nuns from the Sisters of Charity and several other Catholic and Episcopalian religious orders, including a community of Indian women from South Dakota. African-American nurses also served, recruited for the army by Namahyoke Sockum Curtis. Curtis sought black nurses who, like her, had recovered from yellow fever, were now immune, and could nurse patients with the disease.

By the war's end the army nurses had served in Cuba, Puerto Rico, Hawaii, and the Philippine Islands, on the hospital ship *Relief,* and on the mainland. Thirteen gave their lives in service. Another, 25-year-old Clara Maass, died while a volunteer in the yellow fever experiments conducted in Cuba by Major Walter Reed's team of doctors. One of the doctors, Dr. Jesse Lazear, also died, but the team proved conclusively in 1901 that the disease was carried by the *Aedes aegypti,* one of the more than 700 varieties of mosquito, leading to prevention of the disease.

THE WAR OPENS—AND CLOSES

Much to the surprise of Americans, the first battle of the Spanish-American War occurred not in Cuba but in the Philippine Islands. The Philippines, a large, mountainous archipelago, was strategically located southeast of Asia and its rich trading ports. It had been a Spanish colony for more than 300 years.

While the War Department struggled to mobilize the army, the navy had worked out its own strategic plans—primarily at the behest of Assistant Secretary Theodore Roosevelt, an ardent expansionist. In late February, six weeks before President McKinley asked for a declaration of war, Roosevelt had cabled the commander of the Pacific fleet, Commodore George Dewey. He told Dewey to be prepared to attack the Spanish fleet stationed in the Philippines, so it could not sail for Cuba in the event of war. At sunrise on May 1 Dewey sailed into Manila Bay. His seven vessels destroyed or captured 10 Spanish ships with only one American death. Dewey became an instant and widely celebrated popular hero and was immediately promoted to admiral.

In the Atlantic, a U.S. naval blockade stretched from Key West to Puerto Rico. A small Spanish fleet managed to elude it, however, and entered the harbor at Santiago, on the southern tip of Cuba. The navy soon arrived to block the fleet in. In Tampa, the still half-trained and half-supplied army troops scrambled onto ships for Cuba. Their mission was to capture the fortified hills that stood around the city of Santiago. In late June they seized Las Guásimas and on July 1 were victorious in two simultaneous battles at El Caney and San Juan Hill. During the battle at San Juan Hill, Roosevelt bravely led his Rough Riders and the Ninth and Tenth Cavalry units up nearby Kettle Hill, directly into Spanish fire. (Except for officers, the Rough Riders and cavalrymen were on foot, because the army had not yet managed to ship their horses to Cuba.) They took the site. Their victory made possible the attack on San Juan Hill itself, the closest fortified site to the city. In newspaper reports, the Rough Riders received the lion's share of attention. The colorful Colonel Roosevelt was soon portrayed as the hero of the entire battle.

With the hills surrounding Santiago in American hands, Spanish admiral Pascual Cervera attempted to evacuate his fleet from the harbor. His entire squadron was destroyed or driven ashore—with the loss of more than 400 Spanish lives and only one American. The news reached the United States on July 4, to great celebration.

Two weeks later the Spanish surrendered the city of Santiago. A week later American forces arrived at Spain's other island colony in the Atlantic, Puerto Rico. They occupied it with little opposition from defending Spanish forces. Soon Spain surrendered in the Philippines. On August 12 Spain and the United States agreed to an armistice and fighting was halted. The armistice with Spain ended Spanish control of Cuba, ceded Puerto Rico and Guam to the United States, and permitted U.S. occupation of Manila until a formal treaty could be negotiated.

HAWAII IS ANNEXED

After Dewey took Manila Bay, American officials quickly refocused their attention on Hawaii. If America was to have a naval base in the Philippines, the Hawaiian Islands now looked to be beneficial as a way station. In 1897, a treaty with leaders of the Hawaiian Republic, providing for annexation to the United States, had been buried in the Senate. Even now, annexationists feared, it could not win the necessary two-thirds majority in the Senate. They adopted a new strategy and proposed annexation by resolution—which required only a simple majority vote of both houses of Congress. The resolution passed. On July 7, President McKinley signed the bill. Queen Liliuokalani, who was still visiting in the United States, sadly returned to the islands. On August 12, the transfer of sovereignty was formally made.

THE TREATY OF PARIS

In the negotiations of a formal treaty to end the war, control of the Philippines was the only real question left to be decided. The Filipinos themselves, like the Cubans and Puerto Ricans, had been struggling for independence from Spain. Spain did not want to give up the islands, and at first the United States wanted only a naval base there. But Germany and other European nations, who were on the brink of an imperialist war on the Asian mainland, were also eyeing the Philippines. U.S. officials decided the situation was too unstable for an isolated naval base and demanded complete possession. Finally, Spain agreed to sell the islands to the United States for $20 million. The Filipinos themselves did not have a voice in the decision, although some had traveled to Paris in hopes of influencing the negotiations held there.

In December 1898 the Treaty of Paris was signed. For the United States, the treaty crossed a new line in the sand. America became a colonial power, in control of land whose residents were not self-governing. American poet Carl Sandburg, who had enlisted in the war at age 20, later wrote, "It was a small war, edging toward immense consequences."[10]

CAN A REPUBLIC BE AN EMPIRE? THE DEBATE OVER THE PHILIPPINES

Like all treaties with foreign powers, the Treaty of Paris still had to be ratified by the Senate. Both in the Senate and among the American public, the debate over the acquisition of the Philippines was fierce. Many Americans accepted U.S. influence in the nearby Caribbean islands of Cuba and Puerto Rico but still objected to making America a full-blown imperial power. The argument reflected two very different views of America's role in the world.

On one hand, a spirited anti-imperialist movement arose. In Boston, an Anti-Imperialist League formed and waged a vigorous publicity campaign against ratification of the treaty. League supporters included some of the most prominent citizens in America, such as former president Grover Cleveland, William Jennings Bryan, Mark Twain, Andrew Carnegie, E. L. Godkin (famous editor of the *Nation*), Samuel Gompers (head of the AFL), Senator "Pitchfork Ben" Tillman, Jane Addams, and the presidents of Harvard and Stanford. Anti-imperialists had a variety of motives. Many strongly opposed imperialism as a matter of principle. They believed that it was a contradiction of basic American values to deny self-government to others. "Is it possible that the Republic is to be placed in the position of the suppressor of the Philippine struggle for independence?" asked Andrew Carnegie. "Surely, that is impossible. With what face shall we hang in the school-houses of the Philippines our own Declaration of Independence, and yet deny independence to them?"[11] Other anti-imperialists wanted America to remain isolationist. They also objected to the expansion of a professional American military—which had traditionally been very small—that a larger role in the world would require. Some anti-imperialists feared colonial possessions would hurt American workers or American farmers by providing cheaper labor or cheaper agricultural products. Some reformers believed that America's resources should be used to solve the serious problems at home, not to govern distant colonies. Other anti-imperialists made racist arguments. They believed that the island residents were members of an inferior race, incapable of self-government, and unfit for participation in American institutions.

Defenders of the annexation of the Philippines were also a varied lot. Some sincerely believed that America had a duty to lift up less developed nations that labored under corrupt regimes or lacked self-government. Their goal was to extend the opportunity for democracy to others. Others, like Roosevelt, believed that imperialism would strengthen and energize the nation. Some businessmen saw an important way station that would enable them to enter lucrative trade in Asia. Militarists wanted naval stations to increase and protect America's military influence. Christian missionaries wanted to expand their work.

President McKinley, after considering the issue for a time, finally recommended approval of the treaty and annexation. A year later, in a much-quoted speech, he explained to a group of visiting Methodists how he had come to the decision. He told them that he spent "an agonizing night of prayer" over the Philippines' fate. He decided (with, he believed, divine guidance), that returning them to Spain would be "cowardly and dishonorable," and abandoning them to another European power "bad business." In his view the Filipinos were "unfit for self government." The only solution was to take the islands and "educate . . . and uplift and Christianize them, and by God's grace do the very best we could by them." The president misspoke about the Filipinos' religion—almost all had been converted to Catholicism centuries before by the Spanish, although a few practiced traditional religions and a very small percentage were Muslim. But he nonetheless summed up much pro-imperialist American thinking.[12]

The Senate continued to do battle over the treaty. Finally, ardent anti-imperialist William Jennings Bryan suggested a new strategy. The treaty should be ratified, he argued, and then America could and should grant the Philippines independence. Some other anti-imperialist senators were convinced by this argument. The treaty was ratified on February 6, 1899—by only one vote more than the required two-thirds majority. But events intervened and Bryan's strategy did not succeed. The night of February 4, hostilities had broken out between Filipino insurgents and American troops. The proposal to grant Philippine independence was quickly introduced by anti-imperialists in Congress but just as quickly defeated.

THE PHILIPPINE-AMERICAN WAR

At first many Filipinos, like many Cubans and Puerto Ricans, viewed the Americans as liberators and defenders of democratic freedoms. Some Filipinos had been struggling for independence from Spain since 1896 under the leadership of Emilio Aguinaldo. The 7 million residents of the islands, however, were also divided among themselves by tribal or ethnocultural identity and language. (There are 7,000 islands in the archipelago, although most people live on the 11 largest.)

Shortly after Dewey took Manila in May 1898, the U.S. Navy returned Aguinaldo from Hong Kong, where he was in exile, and encouraged his followers to aid in seizing the islands from Spain. Aguinaldo quickly organized local militias and *insurrectos* and had control of many important locations within a few weeks. "A little barefooted army seemed to grow up out of the ground," one American officer later wrote.[13] Aguinaldo and his supporters, however, did not wish to be taken over by America either. Aguinaldo declared the Philippines to be independent and himself interim dictator. By the end of July he had formed a detailed revolutionary government, in which voting rights were limited to *principales,* the propertied and educated business and political class. He also announced plans for a constitutional convention to form a republic. The United States did not recognize these acts.

Soon relations between U.S. officials and Filipino insurgents deteriorated. U.S. ground forces continued to expand their positions. They inflicted increasingly callous treatment and racist epithets on the Filipinos, who were dark-skinned—a troublesome issue for the many black American soldiers. In late November the Filipino revolutionary congress met as planned, adopted a constitution, and vowed to fight for independence. On January 1, 1899, Aguinaldo was declared president of the republic, but the United States did not recognize him or his government. Three days later, President McKinley's proclamation announcing American sovereignty was published.

On the night of February 4, 1899, American-Filipino tensions finally erupted into war. The bloody conflict was destined to last until July 1902. It cost America some 4,200 soldiers' lives in battle and $400 million. It also resulted in the deaths of at least 20,000 Filipino soldiers and at least 200,000 civilians in hostilities or by disease or famine.[14]

When the war began, it was officially called an insurrection, and U.S. activity was called pacification. The Filipino insurgents used guerrilla tactics. They discarded their uniforms, blended into the civilian population, and fought by hit and run, just as the Cuban insurgents had done. America, like Spain, soon discovered that it was not easy to fight a guerrilla war or to defeat *insurrectos.* The United States found itself exercising brutality against both insurgents and civilians—even establishing reconcentration camps just as Spain had done in Cuba. Whole villages were forced into camps while their homes and fields were burned. Captured Filipino fighters were sometimes tortured and executed. (Some Americans were eventually tried for such acts.) A general ordered his troops, "Kill everyone over the age of 10." The *insurrectos* committed just as many atrocities, often against other Filipinos who did not support them. But the conduct of the war, as well as the support of Filipinos for the *insurrectos,* varied from place to place on the islands. In some areas, there was little or no fighting.[15]

In March 1901, Aguinaldo was captured. He soon signed a document declaring his loyalty to the United States and asking his followers to cease fighting. Although sporadic hostilities continued (and would recur until 1916) American control of the islands was no longer in doubt. By 1901, however, the American public had been shaken by the reports of brutality. As the tales leaked out, becoming a public issue in 1902, the anti-imperialists at home believed their direst prediction had been confirmed—colonialism had corrupted American values. The *New York American* commented, "We have actually come to do the very thing we went to war to prevent." Many historians comment that the war marked the end of American innocence in world affairs, and some refer to it as "America's first Viet Nam."

CANADIANS ENTER AN IMPERIAL WAR

In October 1899, Great Britain went to war against the Boers (now called Afrikaners) in the British colony of South Africa. The Boers were descendants of early 17th-century Dutch settlers, who had established outlying, autonomous republics to evade British colonial control. The Afrikaners believed their independence was in jeopardy, and the British believed their security in South Africa was threatened when the Afrikaners sought German aid. The Boer War (now called the South African War) turned out to be, like the war in the Philippines, brutal.

Britain requested Canadian troops to aid the effort. Since Canada was part of the British Empire, the question of imperialism did not engage Canadians in the same way that it did Americans. Nonetheless, Canadian prime minister Wilfrid Laurier faced great opposition to the war, especially among French Canadians. As an attempted compromise, he raised volunteers but left their funding to Great Britain. English Canadians also organized many privately funded volunteer initiatives. It was the first time that Canadian soldiers served in an overseas war for the British Empire. The United States officially remained neutral.

Although the war went badly for the British at first, by the summer of 1900 the Boer armies had been defeated. In November, Britain proclaimed the annexation of the Boer republics. Immediately, the Afrikaners began to fight again, this time with guerrilla warfare. In response, the British criss-crossed the land with barbed wire and systematically laid waste to flush out the guerrillas. This tactic forced most civilians into refugee camps. Before the Boers signed a treaty in May 1902, the death toll from disease and poor conditions was staggering among both civilians and soldiers. The war caused great political controversy in Britain as well as in Canada, just as the Philippine War did in America.

GOVERNING AMERICA'S NEW EMPIRE

The Spanish-American and Philippine Wars marked the emergence of the United States as a major world power. They also marked the emergence of all the dilemmas and conflicts between idealism and self-interest that America's role in the world would continue to involve. For more than a century, the young nation had expanded across North America. Its continued expansion across oceans, however, was never free from debate among Americans—nor did it give rise to a clearly formulated, uniform policy for dependencies, as the nation chose to call its overseas possessions. In time, the United States reaffirmed its belief in self-determination, and by the mid-20th century, all dependencies had gained independence or self-government. In the meantime, the United States adopted a variety of strategies to govern them.

In the Philippines, President McKinley first established a commission to study conditions before the insurrection broke out. A second Philippine Commission in 1900, headed by William Howard Taft, developed a code of laws and a judicial system. In the summer of 1901, the president appointed Taft the first civilian governor of the islands. Taft proved to be able, effective, and popular. He soon granted much local autonomy, intended to teach islanders how to govern themselves and ready them for independence. (Independence was not granted, however, until 1946.) Taft also began the development of civil service and public health systems and the construction of many public improvements, such as roads, schools, and sanitation systems.

Cuba

The McKinley administration would not recognize the legitimacy of the government established by the Cuban insurgents. American military forces remained in Cuba until 1902, during which time the U.S. Army provided civil administration for the island. General Leonard Wood served as military governor. The army oversaw the building of many roads, schools, hospitals, and other public improvements.

In 1900, Cuban voters were finally permitted to hold a constitutional convention. The document they approved was modeled on the U.S. Constitution, but it did not make any reference to Cuba's relations with America. In response, Congress passed the Platt Amendment, attached to an army appropriations bill and named for Senator Orville H. Platt of Maine. The Platt Amendment made several demands of Cuba. Three were particularly important. First, Cuba was not to make any independent agreements with other foreign nations. Second, the United States was to be permitted to intervene, if necessary, to guarantee Cuban independence. Third, Cuba was required to lease naval stations to the United States. The present base at Guantánamo Bay was enabled by this demand.[16]

In the United States, public opinion was generally opposed to the Platt conditions, and many Cubans strongly resisted them. Finally, in June 1901, Cuban representatives reluctantly agreed. They appended the conditions to the constitution and later restated them in a treaty with the United States. Elections were held and Tomás Estrada Palma was elected as Cuba's first president. After his inauguration in early 1902, American military forces withdrew from the island. American capital remained in Cuba, however, and quickly came to dominate the Cuban economy. American investors bought many income-producing resources, such as sugar plantations, factories, and railroads, and usually held them as absentee owners.

Puerto Rico

The acquisition of Puerto Rico and its 950,000 residents met little controversy in the United States—ironically enough, since the island was destined to have a far closer relationship with America than did either the Philippines or Cuba. (Today Puerto Rico is a largely independent commonwealth whose residents are citizens of the United States. Since 1952, when it became primarily self-governing, its official name has been Estado Libre Asociado de Puerto Rico, or Free Associated State of Puerto Rico.)

Puerto Rico had been colonized by Spain soon after 1493, when Christopher Columbus landed there on his second voyage to America. Many among the indigenous Indian population soon succumbed to diseases and brutality, and the Spanish imported slaves from Africa to work sugar and later coffee plantations. Beginning in the early 19th century, Puerto Ricans had staged occasional insurgent uprisings against Spain. As a result, slavery had been abolished in 1873 and the island had gained representation in the Spanish parliament. Puerto Ricans continued to press for more independence, however, under leader Luis Muñoz Rivera. In 1897, they had been granted an autonomous (but not independent) government. The new government took effect only two months before the Spanish-American War was declared, and it lost its powers in the Treaty of Paris.

After the war ended, American military forces remained in Puerto Rico as they did in Cuba. A political division quickly developed over the continuing U.S. occupation. The Puerto Rican Republican Party saw U.S. domination as the best hope for new opportunities and new freedom, especially for the masses. The smaller Federal Party supported self-determination regardless. Disturbances between the two parties, called Las Turbas, marred the civil peace for four years after the conclusion of the Spanish-American War.

In 1900, Congress passed the Foraker Act, terminating military rule and establishing a formal colonial government. Under the Foraker Act, the governor was to be appointed by the president. A legislature with two houses was established, with the upper house or Executive Council appointed by the United States and the lower house or Chamber of Delegates elected by the Puerto Rican people. An elected resident commissioner was to sit in the U.S. House of Representatives as a nonvoting member and represent the island's interests. The Foraker Act also contained two important economic provisions, which are still in force today. One exempted the island from federal taxes, and the other established duty-free trade between Puerto Rico and the United States. The Foraker Act declared Puerto Ricans to be citizens of Puerto Rico but not of the United States.

Hawaii

In April 1900, Congress passed the Hawaii Organic Act, making the islands a territory of the United States, similar to territories such as Oklahoma on the mainland. Voters were entitled to elect a territorial legislature and a delegate to the House of Representatives, who could speak in debates but could not vote. Other officials were appointed, and Sanford Dole was appointed the first territorial governor. Among the 154,000 residents of the islands were many Chinese and Japanese immigrants. They were excluded from citizenship, although their Hawaiian-born children were not.

Native Hawaiians had full citizenship rights, however, and in fact were a voting majority. Some Native Hawaiians quickly formed a political party called Home Rule. They elected their leader, Robert W. Wilcox, as the congressional delegate, and won a majority in both houses of the territorial legislature. The first session was not promising. There was little cooperation between the Republican, Democrat, and Home Rule parties, nor between the Home Rulers and the governor. The Home Rulers insisted on speaking Hawaiian, not English. They attempted to pass numerous acts in support of Native Hawaiian culture—such as giving physicians' licenses to kahunas (priests who were also traditional healers). Many of the acts were considered objectionable and even frivolous by other delegates and in some cases were vetoed by Dole.

The economy of the islands remained dominated by sugar culture under control of a small group of white Hawaiian planters. The Hawaiian Sugar Planters Association (HSPA), founded in 1895, enabled sugar growers to act like a trust in regard to labor relations and the reduction of competition among themselves. The HSPA also immediately opened an agricultural experiment station, whose scientific and agricultural research greatly helped Hawaiian sugar compete in world markets. Coffee culture was slowly increasing as well, often in the hands of Japanese Hawaiians. The pineapple—not yet widely grown in the 1890s—also began to attract farmers. In 1901, James Drummond Dole incorporated the Hawaiian Pineapple Company.

Once Hawaii became an official U.S. territory, a significant change occurred in labor relations in the islands. Before 1900, most Japanese and Chinese immigrants were contract laborers who agreed in advance to work for a certain planter for a certain number of years, under stated wages and conditions, with no rights to move or work elsewhere. Contract wages were extremely low, and working conditions were often brutal. Under U.S. law, however, contract labor was illegal. When Hawaii became a territory, contract laborers became free laborers. Their discontent was immediately evident, with 20 strikes in the year 1900 alone. Over the next decade, plantation owners slowly began to improve conditions by means of the perquisite system. Instead of increased wages, plantation owners gave their laborers many fringe benefits, such as housing, medical services, and recreation facilities—but only as long as they remained on the plantation.

"DOES THE CONSTITUTION FOLLOW THE FLAG?"

The annexation of Hawaii and the acquisition of Cuba, Puerto Rico, the Philippines, and other islands did not end the debate over imperialism. The debate still included the familiar mix of principle, humanitarianism, self-interest, and sometimes racism, but it also contained a new question: Were these suddenly acquired lands an integral part of the American union? There were many pressing constitutional issues about their legal status and the civil and political rights of their residents. In public debate, the issues were summed up in the phrase, "Does the Constitution follow the flag?"

In the courts, many test cases were initiated and made their way to the Supreme Court for definitive rulings. On May 27, 1901, the Court handed down five decisions that, along with others to follow, became known collectively as the *Insular Cases*. (*Insular* means "relating to islands.") The issues in the cases were usually tangential and complicated; *Downes v. Bidwell,* for example, concerned tariffs on Puerto Rican goods. But out of the cases came rulings on a very fundamental question. The Court ruled that the Constitution as a whole did not automatically extend to a territory merely because the United States had sovereignty over it. Instead, said the Court, Congress had to vote to extend the Constitution. In the language of the court, the Constitution applied only in territories that had been "incorporated" into the United States by the vote of Congress. The Court did note that "fundamental" rights like due process, equal protection, or freedom of speech and religion extended even to "unincorporated" American dependencies. But the Court affirmed, in the *Insular Cases,* that Congress had the authority to govern overseas possessions as it wished. Said the fictional Irish American bartender Mr. Dooley, the popular creation of newspaper humorist Finley Peter Dunne, "No matter whether th' Constitution follows th' flag or not, th' Supreme Court follows th' illiction returns."[17]

AMERICA ESTABLISHES A FOREIGN POLICY FOR CHINA

America's new possessions in the Pacific held out the prospect of greatly increased trade in Asian markets, especially populous China. Unfortunately, the European imperial powers and Japan appeared to be on the verge of partitioning China into separate colonies. The Qing (Ch'ing) rulers were enfeebled and a brutal war with Japan (1894–95) had weakened the large nation. In different regions of China, Germany, Russia, France, Britain, and Japan claimed special, exclusive rights, certain kinds of authority, and usually a monopoly of trade. These areas were called "spheres of influence."

In September 1898, President McKinley acknowledged that the United States wanted to trade in China but wanted no special conditions. "Asking only the open door for ourselves, we are ready to accord the open door to others," he said.[18] This position was approved by anti-imperialists and Christian missionary interests, who were active in China and who vocally supported the preservation of China's sovereignty against spheres of influence. It was also approved by American businessmen, who pressured the State Department to act on their behalf. In September 1899, Secretary of State John Hay formally announced America policy via circular letter (letters with identical messages) to diplomats in Britain, Germany, Russia, Japan, Italy, and France. The letter and two that followed it became known as the Open Door Notes.

In the first note, Hay asked the powers to keep China trade open to all, even within their spheres of influence. Hay also asked that the Chinese nation itself retain all rights to set and collect tariffs, a way of insuring China's supremacy. The responses to his note were equivocal. Russia did not actually agree, Britain agreed only with conditions, and the other powers "agreed to agree" only if every other nation did. Nonetheless, Hay finessed the situation. He chose to label their responses assent. In a second note of March 1900, he announced that the Open Door policies were in effect and that America considered the agreement "final and definitive."

Almost immediately, the powers' intentions were put to a test. A secret society of Chinese nationalists and martial arts practitioners, Yihetuan (Yi Ho Ch'uan), or "righteous and harmonious fists," had gained adherents. They began an attempt to expel foreigners from the nation by force. The western nations called their insurgency the Boxer Rebellion. Roving gangs of Boxers first attacked Christian missions, slaughtering Catholic priests and nuns, Protestant missionaries and their families, and Chinese converts. (At the time there were an estimated 700,000 Catholic and 85,000 Protestant Chinese converts.) In June they entered Beijing (Peking), killing Christian Chinese and laying siege to the legations, or diplomatic staffs. For a month, the capital city was cut off from reliable outside contact. The Boxers also attacked the foreign community in Tianjin (Tientsin).

Secretary Hay quickly foresaw that the other powers would see an excuse to partition China when they rescued their citizens. To prevent it, he sent a third Open Door Note on July 3. It stated that America sought "permanent safety and peace" in China and the preservation of "Chinese territorial and administrative entity." He also dispatched American forces from the Philippines to join an international expeditionary force of 20,000, which rescued the diplomats on August 14. The American troops did not take part in further military operations, but in the following weeks the other powers suppressed the Boxer Rebellion elsewhere. Unfortunately, extensive destruction and looting also occurred. The number of people who died in the Boxer Rebellion is not accurately known. According to one estimate, more than 200 missionaries were murdered in the countryside, at least 200 foreigners died in the diplomatic quarter, and more died in Beijing's Catholic Peitang Cathedral compound. As many as 30,000 Chinese probably died.[19]

In the aftermath, Secretary Hay worked successfully to prevent the loss of territory by the Chinese nation. However, Dowager Empress Cixi (Tz'u-hsi), who was sympathetic to the Boxers, had actually declared war on the European powers, and China was subjected to harsh terms. Terms included the payment of huge indemnities totaling $333 million. The United States received $25 million but returned more than half to China when American claims were settled. In acknowledgment the Chinese government used it to create a fund to send students to the United States for education.

The policy formulated in the Open Door Notes remained the basis of American policy in Asia for the next 40 years. The last note affirmed America's intention to protect China from foreign partition, and from Japanese ambitions in particular, and was still important when World War II began. America's relationship with China nonetheless was conflicted, since Chinese workers were excluded from immigrating and Chinese Americans continued to be subjected to great discrimination.

THE ROOT REFORMS OF THE U.S. ARMY

As the Spanish-American War had revealed, United States military operations lacked effective organization and coordination. The Department of the Navy, headed by a cabinet-level secretary of the navy, operated separately from the army, which was headed by a cabinet-level secretary of war. (Neither the modern Department of Defense encompassing all military operations nor the Joint Chiefs of Staff existed.) Furthermore, the highest-ranking army officer, the commanding general, did not have any authority over army administration or supply operations. These matters were controlled in the office of the secretary of war by heads of various bureaus, who often held office for life and were very independent. Sometime rivalries developed between the commanding general and the secretaries themselves. In addition, there was no federal oversight at all of state militias (later called the National Guard).

In August 1899, President McKinley appointed Elihu Root as the new secretary of war. The president thought Root, a corporate attorney from New York, would be a good person to oversee the military governance of America's new island possessions. Root quickly realized other problems were equally pressing if America were to maintain its position as a new world power. He had no military background, but he had much experience with the organization and reorganization of corporations. He was also politically astute. He studied the issues thoroughly. He consulted with a rising group of reform-minded military officers. He conferred with congressmen. The changes he effected before he left office in 1904 came to be known as the Root reforms. Made with the approval of Congress, the Root reforms launched the transformation of the small, frontier-based 19th-century army into the modern American military system.

"An Act to Increase the Efficiency of the Permanent Military Establishment of the United States," better known as the Army Reorganization Act of 1901, was Root's first success. It increased the size of the standing army to about 90,000 and reorganized all branches. Medical services were expanded and the army nurse corps was officially established. In November 1901, Root announced his plan for the expansion and reorganization of military education, capped by a new Army War College. War colleges, an earlier European innovation, provided advanced training in command and strategy for officers at the highest levels. America's Naval War College had been established in 1888.

THE GREAT GOLD RUSH

While some Americans were heading south to fight Spain, others were heading north—in hopes of making their fortunes. In 1896, American-born George Washington Carmack and two Native companions, Skookum Jim and Kaa Goox, had made a significant gold strike in the Yukon. Carmack filed a claim on Rabbit (soon renamed Bonanza) Creek, a tributary of the Klondike River. In the summer of 1897, news of the strike finally reached the American mainland. The good news was given sensational front-page coverage. The publicity frenzy was augmented by railroad men, businessmen, and town boosters who stood to gain from a "stampede," as a gold rush was usually called at the time. And soon, a stampede was on. By the end of 1898, an estimated 100,000 to 200,000 men and women stampeders set out for the far north. About 50,000 completed the arduous trek to the Klondike goldfields. By the end of 1898, Dawson, Canada, established at the confluence of the Yukon and Klondike Rivers, had a population of more than 25,000.

Many of the stampeders had but a hazy idea of Alaska and were not even aware that the Klondike was in Canada. Most underestimated the difficulties of climate and terrain they were about to face. The difficult and dangerous Trail of '98 to the Klondike goldfields began at the Lynn Canal, a natural body of water jutting into the Alaskan panhandle. From there, stampeders followed the White Pass or the shorter but much steeper Chilkoot Pass (which in one two-and-a-half-mile stretch rises 1,600 feet) out of Dyea or Skagway. Once across the mountains, they built small river boats and proceeded 500 miles down the Yukon to their destination. Because the Canadian government required those entering the area to have a year's supply of food, stampeders often traveled with over a ton of equipment pulled by mules, horses, or dog teams. Some gave up the trek along the way, and many others were disappointed in their search for riches.

Some stampeders headed past the Klondike into Alaska, which soon yielded important strikes as well. The first, on the Seward Peninsula, resulted in a rush to Nome in 1899. The last great strike of the rush occurred in the Tanana Valley in 1902 and gave birth to the town of Fairbanks. The gold-rush settlements that sprang up overnight in Alaska soon gained reputations as lawless frontier communities filled with con men, claim jumpers, dance hall girls, and general disregard for conventional morality. In the Yukon, somewhat better order was maintained. The Yukon, officially attached to Canada's Northwest Territories until 1898, was overseen by a detachment of the Northwest Mounted Police or Canadian Mounties. The gold rush gave rise to many colorful legends, some of which distorted reality. Dance hall girls did exist, for example, but the majority of the women stampeders accompanied husbands, children, or other family members. Some women established small businesses that provided services like food, lodging, and laundry to the miners—one women toted her sewing machine over the trail and set up as a seamstress, for example—and a few became very wealthy. The stampeders also included African-American men and women.

By the end of 1899, the White Pass and Yukon Railroad was completed, making the journey far easier and mining areas far more accessible. Placer mining was soon worked out in Alaska and the Yukon. (Placers are easily accessible deposits, often in waterways, that can be unearthed or washed from gravel or sand by individuals without extensive equipment.) By 1900, large corporations had begun buying up individual claims. Soon, they began large-scale mining operations that depended on expensive machinery like dredges. As corporate, technological mining grew, the gold rush of 1898–1902 was increasingly celebrated in fiction and verse by writers like novelist Jack London and poet Robert Service. It came to be known as the last great frontier and the stampeders as the last, hardiest, and most individualistic of American pioneers.

AFTER THE GOLD RUSH

The gold rush of 1898–1902 refocused America's attention on Alaska. The United States still had little concrete idea of what to do with the enormous area, purchased in 1867 from Russia. The purchase had been very controversial because Alaska did not adjoin the lower states and seemed unlikely to be settled. It had been overseen first by the U.S. Army and then the U.S. Navy. In 1884, the Alaska Organic Act had designated it a district, not a territory, to evade the issue of future statehood. The Organic Act provided for a code of laws and a few appointed officials, including a governor and a district judge, but forbade a legislature or other forms of self-government. It made no provisions for law enforcement in most of the area. It did not allow the American residents to tax themselves for any services or improvements. It made no provisions for property ownership either, confirming the traditional use of the land by the Native Alaskan population. When the gold rush began, miner's codes—agreements among the residents on claim staking and rules of conduct—were the only real government in many Alaskan settlements.

Congress was now forced to reconsider the problem of Alaska. In 1890, the non-Native population was less than 4,300. By the end of the 1890s, it had grown to 30,450 and was now larger than the Native population of 29,500. Congress revised land laws, extending the Homestead Act to Alaska in 1898 and making it possible for railroads to obtain rights of way. It also allowed for the incorporation of towns. Incorporation made it officially possible for settlements to govern themselves by electing councils and mayors and by levying taxes for municipal improvements and schools. Congress also ordered moving the capital from Sitka to Juneau.[20]

Conservationists also became more interested in Alaska. During the summer of 1899, a distinguished group of scientists and conservationists explored and studied the coastline. Among the group were John Muir, George Bird Grinnell, John Burroughs, photographer Edward Curtis, artists, foresters, scientists, the chief of the U.S. Biological Survey, and members of railroad baron Edward H. Harriman's family, who funded the expedition. Fifteen volumes of their results were eventually published.

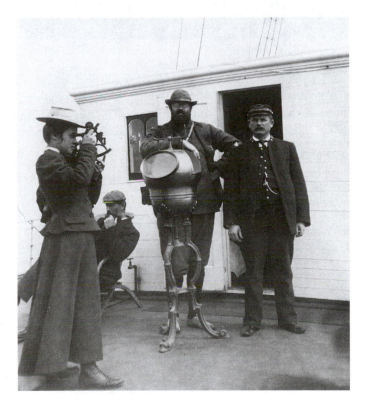

The Harriman expedition took a distinguished group of scientists and naturalists to explore and document Alaska in 1899. This photo was taken on board the expedition vessel by photographer Edward S. Curtis. The woman in the foreground is holding a sextant. *(Library of Congress, Prints and Photographs Division, LC-USZ62-130731)*

THE GOLD STANDARD ACT

The new discoveries of gold and the return of prosperity after the depression of the mid-1890s strengthened the position of goldbugs who supported a gold standard for the

FRED R. HAMLIN'S MUSICAL EXTRAVAGANZA

THE WIZARD OF OZ

· THE TIN MAN ·

In 1900, L. Frank Baum published *The Wonderful Wizard of Oz*, an instant classic. It was quickly turned into a successful musical, which this poster advertises. Baum was a populist, and some historians believe the story playfully symbolizes certain political issues—like the debate over the gold standard or "the Yellow Brick Road." *(Library of Congress, Prints and Photographs Division, LC-USZ62-130731)*

American monetary system. Supporters of free silver still existed, but public agitation on the silver issue had quieted. President McKinley decided that the time was right to make the gold standard a law. In early 1900, the Gold Standard Act was passed. It ended bimetallism by guaranteeing that U.S. notes or debts would be redeemed in gold.

ELLIS ISLAND REOPENS

As the depression lifted, immigration began to increase once again. By 1901, when 488,000 newcomers arrived, it had regained the pace of the early 1890s. One group whose numbers began to increased markedly were Armenians. From 1894 to 1896, the Armenians suffered the first of the barbaric massacres, which would continue until World War I, at the hands of the Ottoman Turks. Today, some historians refer to the period as the Armenian genocide. Many Armenians left their small nation for America. After 1898, many also emigrated to Canada's prairie provinces, following large group migrations of Dukhobors, a Russian-Armenian pacifist sect.

Although new Chinese immigrants were still excluded from the United States, in 1898 the Supreme Court handed down a decision that was very important to Chinese Americans. The Court ruled in *U.S. v. Wong Kim Ark* that a person born in the United States to resident alien parents was a citizen of the United States by right of birth—even if the parents themselves were denied the right of citizenship, as Chinese immigrants were. This decision helped extend the precedent that any person born in the United States was a citizen, regardless of ethnic or racial descent.[21]

On December 17, 1900, the reconstructed immigration processing station at Ellis Island opened to unanimous approval. The handsome, fireproof new reception center echoed the Beaux-Arts buildings of the Chicago World's Fair, although its exterior of red brick and light tan limestone was very different. When immigrants arrived at the building, they climbed a wide, sweeping staircase to the awe-inspiring Registry Room, with a three-story-high vaulted ceiling.

Not all newcomers to America were required to land at Ellis Island, however. Usually, those who had traveled in first- or second-class accommodations were examined on board ship, then permitted to enter the country. The majority of immigrants, however, traveled in steerage—the lowest-priced accommodations, very crowded and located very low in the ship. Steerage passengers were always taken to Ellis Island to pass through the inspection process.

Unfortunately, oversight of the immigration process did not always live up to the grand buildings designed for it. Accusations continued that immigrants were swindled at the money exchange, overcharged for food and railway tickets, and subjected to other abuses. In 1897, President McKinley appointed Terence Powderly, former head of the Knights of Labor, as commissioner-general of immigration (the new title for superintendent). Powderly took his job seriously and assigned a commission to investigate. As a result, 11 employees were fired in June 1900. Problems proved to be very entrenched, however, and followed the staff when they moved into the new facility on Ellis Island. In the summer of 1901 another scandal arose. Immigration inspectors were caught selling false citizenship papers to steerage passengers, allowing them to bypass Ellis Island and enter the country illegally.

REFORMERS BATTLE THE SLUM

Settlement workers, other urban reformers, and philanthropists continued their efforts to improve slum housing. In cities throughout the nation, studies of poor urban housing conditions were compiled. The most famous was done in New York. Lawrence Veiller, a former resident of University Settlement, and Robert DeForest, president of the Charity Organization Society (an information clearinghouse for other charity groups), formed a committee on tenement house reform in 1898. Under Veiller's leadership, they prepared a large exhibit of more than 1,000 photographs, maps, graphs, drawings of 200 tenement designs, even and a cardboard model of an entire tenement block. The New York Tenement House Exhibition, opening in February 1900, graphically demonstrated unbelievably crowded and unsanitary conditions in poor neighborhoods. More than 10,000 people viewed the exhibit in New York. Afterward it went on loan to many other cities and also had a great impact elsewhere.

The exhibit helped convince many influential New Yorkers of the need for reform. One was the reform-minded occupant of the governor's office, Theodore Roosevelt. Soon a bill establishing a New York State Tenement House Commission, drafted by Veiller, was passed. The commission held public hearings, then drafted a new housing code, adopted in 1901. As part of the legislation a Tenement Housing Department was established for the city. Enforcement would remain a long-term problem, and, as historian Robert Bremner writes, "although regulatory legislation might 'outlaw' bad houses, it did not provide good ones."[22] Nonetheless these actions began to alleviate some of the worst abuses in New York housing. For example, toilets and ventilation were now required in each apartment. Chicago passed a tenement law the following year, drawing on the research and recommendations of Hull-House, other Chicago settlements, and experts at the University of Chicago. During the following decade other large cities would begin to follow suit.

Reformers also continued their efforts to establish playgrounds in poor, crowded neighborhoods. Increasingly, reformers saw safe, supervised play areas as a way to counteract the influence of street culture and provide moral direction to children, which they believed would break the cycle of many social problems within the slums. As settlement founder Lillian Wald later wrote, the power to influence children "is given to those who play with, rather than to those who only teach them."[23] In New York, the Outdoor Recreation League was organized in 1898 by settlement workers, reformers, and many prominent citizens like Nicholas Murray Butler, president of Columbia University, literary giant William Dean Howells, and the tireless Jacob Riis. In 1899, a large league-funded playground, the beginning of Seward Park, opened on municipally owned land on the Lower East Side. As in cities elsewhere, however, New York politicians were still reluctant to consider playgrounds a municipal responsibility. The league battled to force the city to fund, staff, and maintain the popular site, a goal they achieved after reform mayor Seth Low took office in 1902.

Settlement founder Lillian Wald took an active role in reform issues throughout the Progressive Era. She initiated public-health nursing and school nursing services and was also active in the playground and child labor movements. *(Library of Congress, Prints and Photographs Division, LC-USZ62-15978)*

THE FIRST FEDERAL ANTI-POLLUTION LAW

In the crowded cities, the environmental problem of industrial waste continued to increase as factories grew in number, size, and production. Poor sanitation also remained a constant danger to public health. In the rivers that flowed by growing cities, water quality was clearly beginning to be affected by industrial wastes, sewage, and garbage dumping. Pittsburgh, for example, was rapidly developing one of the highest death rates in the world from diseases, such as typhoid fever and cholera, caused by impure water. In some cases, even the navigability of the waterways was blocked.

Some local activists and reformers intensified their efforts to improve conditions, and some local communities enacted regulations. But industrialists were often powerful enough to overcome local efforts. In 1899, when Congress passed the Rivers and Harbors Act, an appropriations bill for various waterway projects, it added a section forbidding discharging or dumping of certain kinds of wastes into rivers. The Rivers and Harbors Act was the first federal attempt to regulate pollution.

ORGANIZED LABOR REVIVES

Although organized labor did not fare well during the depression years of 1893 to 1897, as prosperity returned the labor movement began gaining strength. The largest national union, the American Federation of Labor (AFL), still had well over 250,000 members when the depression ended in 1897. By 1900 its membership had more than doubled, and it was becoming the dominant voice of labor. The AFL was primarily an association of skilled trade or craft groups. It also affiliated a few industry-wide or industrial unions, which accepted both skilled and unskilled workers in a given industry. Other unions together claimed another 300,000 members.

The AFL was led by Samuel Gompers, a former cigar maker born in England, from its formation in the 1880s until his death in 1924. Gompers accepted corporate industrialism and had no interest in utopian schemes, socialism, or radicalism. He supported bread-and-butter issues of higher wages, shorter hours, and better working conditions. In general Gompers's AFL had little interest in organizing unskilled workers, nor in organizing women workers. Most union officials and members believed that woman's role as homemaker was important and that workingmen should receive wages adequate to permit their wives to remain at home. Female labor, as the AFL newspaper commented, "is the knife of the assassin, aimed at the family circle."[24]

One exception was the International Ladies Garment Workers Union (ILGWU), founded in 1900 and affiliated with the AFL. Many of the workers who made "ladies' garments" were women themselves and the union had both men and women members. Because of the system of "sweating," or subcontracting clothing manufacture to the cheapest bidder, much of the work on women's clothing was done at home or in small sweatshops. Workers often toiled 70 hours a week for very low pay.

SOME GAINS FOR MINE WORKERS

Mining was the "most challenging and dangerous work" of the era, writes labor historian Daniel Nelson.[25] Mining communities were usually very isolated, and mines were exceptionally hazardous places. Hard-rock miners, who extracted minerals for the new industrial America (such as copper, for example, widely used in the expanding industries of telephone and electric wires), were primarily situated in the West and formed a union called the Western Federation of Miners. Coal miners were organized separately in the United Mine Workers of America (UMW). Coal was the product that made industrial America run. It was the main source of energy for trains, ocean-going ships, and many manufacturing operations including steel—not to mention heating and cooking in the typical American home. By the late 1890s, the UMW was the largest affiliate of the AFL. The UMW enrolled both skilled and unskilled workers, and both black and white members.

In the bituminous (soft) coal-mining region that stretched across the north central United States from Pennsylvania to Kansas, most coal companies were independent and relatively small. They chose to keep competition on an even keel by bargaining together with the miners. In 1898, the coal companies and the UMW established the so-called Central Competitive Field (CCF). CCF meetings were held periodically to negotiate wages and other issues in the region, although negotiations were often stormy and strikes sometimes still occurred. In anthracite (hard) coal-mining regions, the situation was very different. Most mining companies in anthracite regions were owned or controlled by large railroad trusts, which wanted dependable supplies for their engines. Pay was low, conditions were harsh, and company towns were closely supervised. Most hard-coal miners were unorganized in the late 1890s. Many were new immigrants from southern and eastern Europe, divided by language and sometimes ethnic animosities.

In 1899, an astute new leader, 28-year-old John Mitchell, was elected president of the UMW. Mitchell was personally charming, conservative, and conciliatory but also a keen tactician. He soon began the difficult task of organizing anthracite miners. In 1900, he called a strike in the eastern Pennsylvania anthracite coal fields. The union did not win recognition (company agreement that it could bargain for miners), but it did negotiate a 10 percent pay increase.

ANOTHER APPROACH TO LABOR-MANAGEMENT DISPUTES

In 1900, the National Civic Federation (NCF) was founded to find a peaceful resolution to the antagonism between labor and capital. The NCF grew from a civic federation organized by prominent citizens in Chicago in response to the violence of the 1894 Pullman strike. It brought together representatives of labor, capital, and the public. Among founding members were Samuel Gompers and John Mitchell; Senator Mark Hanna, an influential figure in the Republican Party; John D. Rockefeller and bankers August Belmont and J. P. Morgan; former president Grover Cleveland, Harvard president Charles Eliot, and prominent churchmen. Like most forward-looking progressive organizations, it accepted the permanence of large business combinations in the new industrial economy. But it also accepted the legitimacy of the unions—which many businesspeople still did not—and supported reform for workers, declaring "organized labor cannot be destroyed without debasement of the masses." The NCF held that both labor radicalism and business opposition to unions were against the public interest. Its supporters believed they could point the way to a new era in labor-management relations by offering NCF services to arbitrate disputes. Unfortunately, these sentiments were shared by only a tiny number of employers. But the NCF did raise the credibility of unions among the general public and publicized the need for reforms by holding national conferences, writing model programs, and lobbying.

BLACK DISENFRANCHISEMENT LENGTHENS ITS REACH

In 1898, Louisiana activated a new strategy to prevent African-American men from voting—the grandfather clause. In the eyes of many white southerners, the so-called Mississippi Plan to disenfranchise blacks had one drawback: it disenfranchised many poor whites as well. Louisiana's grandfather clause solved the problem. It exempted any man from literacy tests or other requirements if his father or grandfather had been legally entitled to vote on January 1, 1867. The exemption, of course, was designed to apply only to white men, because no black man had been entitled to vote in Louisiana before 1870 when the Fifteenth Amendment was passed. After Louisiana passed the grandfather clause, historians John Hope Franklin and Alfred Moss, Jr., write, "the pattern for constitutional disenfranchisement of blacks had been completely drawn." The grandfather clause was soon adopted by other southern states. The spread of various disenfranchisement strategies was clearly beginning to take a toll. In Louisiana, for example, the number of blacks registered to vote dropped from 130,344 in 1896 to 5,320 in 1900.[26]

From the point of view of middle- and upper-class whites in the South who would consider no alternative to white supremacy, the legal restriction of black voting was often interpreted as a civic reform measure. According to the reasoning of these white leaders, legal disenfranchisement would end corruption at the ballot box among white voters. In Virginia, birthplace of George Washington, Thomas Jefferson, and many American principles, for example, state leaders were embarrassed by the voting fraud routinely committed throughout the state to avoid counting black votes. They did not question the necessity of preventing blacks from voting. Instead, they called a constitutional convention in 1901 to do it legally. "By purging your electorate . . . ," said one representative, "you liberate the honest people of Virginia to demand honesty in elections."[27]

Established whites also justified Jim Crow, or segregation, laws as a kind of civic reform. They argued that separating the races in everyday life would lessen the temptation among white ruffians to flout the legal system by committing violence against blacks. In many southern court cases in the late 1890s, segregation in schools and public accommodations was upheld.

RACIALLY MOTIVATED VIOLENCE INTENSIFIES

Lynchings continued unabated, and in some cases were beginning to expand into rampages of destruction by whites. In February 1898, for example, a white mob attacked the home of the black postmaster of Lake City, South Carolina. The mob set the house on fire and shot into the flames. As the family tried to run from the house, members of the mob shot the postmaster and three of his children dead and wounded his wife and two other children. A delegation from Illinois accompanied Ida Wells Barnett, the most prominent antilynching advocate, to Washington to address President McKinley on the issue. The president expressed concern but took no action.

Race riots were also beginning to occur more frequently. They usually began when white mobs invaded black neighborhoods; of course, blacks usually attempted to defend themselves. In July 1900, a riot occurred in New Orleans after two policemen were killed, allegedly by Robert Charles, an African American. Charles was located by the police and shot. But for five days, with the support of local police, white mobs terrorized blacks and destroyed and looted property. When African Americans armed and resisted, the mayor called in the state militia. No white person was ever arrested for the destruction of property or even the deaths that occurred. In August 1900 a mob of whites, primarily Irish Americans, attacked blacks in the Tenderloin district of New York City after a white policeman was killed in a fight with a black man. The disturbance lasted three days. Other well-publicized incidents occurred in North Carolina, Georgia, Florida, and Illinois. African Americans continued to protest these actions. The National Afro-American Council, founded in 1899 to replace the moribund Afro-American League, called for blacks to observe a national day of prayer and fasting. In 1900 Representative George H. White, Republican of North Carolina, introduced an antilynching bill in Congress, but it did not come to a vote. Congressman White, the only remaining African American in the House of Representatives, left Congress in March 1901. No other African American would be elected for 28 years.

THE LAST YEARS OF INDIAN TERRITORY

After the western half of modern Oklahoma state became a territory in 1890, settlers immediately began working toward statehood. Although by 1900 the territorial population had reached 400,000—far more than necessary for statehood—they still had not achieved their goal. A major issue was the status of Indian Territory, the eastern half of modern Oklahoma. It remained in the hands of the Five Civilized Tribes. The Five Tribes were not eager to change their status. They had written constitutions, governments, courts, codes of law, and tribal schools. Most tribal members strongly preferred to remain as independent nations. But for many years, the tribes had been leasing much of their land to non-Indian settlers and industries. Towns and businesses had grown up. By 1900 the population of Indian Territory had grown to more than 390,000, but Indians were only 13 percent of the total.[28]

The Dawes Commission of 1893 met no success convincing tribal leaders to end their special forms of government, accept American citizenship, and transfer their tribal land to private, individual ownership. The federal government nonetheless ordered eastern Oklahoma surveyed and a census taken of Indian citizens. In 1898 Congress passed the Curtis Act, named for its author, Representative Charles Curtis of Kansas, a mixed blood Kaw Indian. The Curtis Act provided for the incorporation of towns in Indian territory and the establishment of public schools. It abolished all remaining tribal courts, established federal judicial districts, and made residents of Indian Territory subject to the legal code of Arkansas, the nearest state. It also provided for the forcible division of land if the Indians could not reach agreement with the federal government.

To prevent the forcible settlement, leaders of all five tribes did finally negotiate agreements. The agreed-upon allotment of land was complicated. Town sites and mineral-bearing lands were sold at auction, with proceeds and mineral rights reserved for the tribes. Unlike allotment procedures under the earlier Dawes Act, however, all remaining tribal lands were divided among tribal citizens instead of being parceled out in 160-acre plots. The amount each tribal citizen received varied, depending on the person's status as a full-blooded Indian, an Indian of mixed blood, a non-Indian who married an Indian, or a descendant of black slaves once held by the tribes. No land was left over to give to non-Indian homesteaders, although Indian owners could sell most of their allotted land if they chose. A new business called grafting quickly sprang up. Grafters developed unsavory, but borderline legal, means of obtaining land allotted to individual Indians. Allotments to children and the elderly were favorite targets.

The abrogation of the five tribal governments did not occur without extensive protest, however. In each nation, some people evaded the census, refused to claim their allotments, and returned all official documents. Opposition was especially strong among full-blooded Indian elders who cherished the traditional way of life. The most serious resistance, the Crazy Snake Rebellion, occurred in 1901. A group led by Chitto Harjo (whose name translates to Crazy Snake) attempted to establish a traditional Indian government over their fellow Creek by force. Federal authorities arrested and eventually tried 94, mostly elderly, Indians—who were convicted but set free on the condition of accepting their allotments. In the same year, Congress passed an act making all Native Americans of Indian Territory citizens of the United States.

A MODEL PROGRAM FOR MUNICIPAL REFORM

In 1888, Englishman James Bryce had published an admiring study of the United States, *The American Commonwealth,* that was widely read by literate Americans. Famously, however, Lord Bryce had declared, "There is no denying that the government of cities is the one conspicuous failure of the United States." Municipal reformers took Bryce's comment to heart. Reformer Brand Whitlock later wrote, "We quoted this observation so often that one might have supposed we were proud of the distinction."[29]

The first yearly meetings of the National Municipal League, however, revealed that the reformers themselves did not know or agree on what a good city government should look like. The league appointed a committee to propose a model program of municipal organization for the nation. It was published in 1900. The heart of the model program was diminishing the influence of political parties in municipal government. "City government must, to be efficient, be emancipated from the tyranny of the national and State political parties, and from that of the Legislature—the tool of the party," said Columbia professor and municipal reformer Frank Goodnow.[30] At the time, state legislatures had great power over conduct of government in the cities—which were, legally speaking, corporate bodies that existed because the state had given them a charter, and retained the power to amend it. (In contrast, the states and the federal government are social-compact bodies that exist because in theory the people themselves consent to be governed.) The Municipal League's model program called for home rule for all cities, or the right of city residents to adopt and amend their own city charters without state approval. Reformers saw home rule as more democratic, but also as a way to break the link between city and state political machines. As for that part of state oversight that was necessary or unavoidable, the model program proposed putting it in the hands of administrative bodies, composed of nonpartisan experts. By the turn of the century, only Missouri, Washington, California, and Minnesota had granted cities home rule statewide.

The model program also called for giving more power to mayors and city councils to lessen the power of nonelected bosses or, as it was usually phrased, to "make the lines of authority clear." But there were three essential corollaries to this reform. First, nonpartisan administrators appointed on the merit or civil-service system were to carry out the decisions made by the mayor and council. If the city council voted to build a bridge, for example, the administrators would select contractors and make other arrangements. Presumably, they would award contracts to the best companies, not to those who had purchased the influence of bosses or politicians. Second, the mayor and council were to be elected on a short ballot. The short-ballot reform called for changing many previously elected but minor positions to nonpartisan civil service appointments and for only a small number of city officials to be elected at one time. In addition, it called for city elections to be held separately from state or national elections. These reforms, it was believed, would focus city elections on important local issues and reduce the power of political machines. Third, and perhaps most important, the model program called for city council members to be elected at large. That is, council members were no longer to represent particular districts in the city. From the reformers' point of view, they would be less beholden to the ward bosses on whom the political machine rested and would be forced to appeal to the larger public interest.

The model program of the National Municipal League was widely publicized. It was not adopted wholesale in any city, but it clarified and focused the goals of municipal reformers. Throughout the nation, cities of many sizes would eventually enact parts of it. One issue the model program did not take a stand on was public ownership of city utilities such as streetcar lines and gas and electric services. In 1900, almost all were in private hands and were completely unregulated. But the movement for municipal control of utilities, often referred to as municipal socialism in 1900, was also becoming a very important question in municipal reform.

MUNICIPAL REFORM IN ACTION

Two reform mayors who gained office at the end of the 1890s illustrate what historians call the two strands of municipal reform in the Progressive Era: structural reform and social reform.[31] Structural reform refers to formal changes in the way political decision making occurs in a city—for example, instituting civil service rules, electing councilmen at large, or introducing principles of business efficiency into government operations. Social reform, sometimes called social justice reform, refers to changes that increase public services and amenities for all citizens and decrease the preferential treatment of powerful economic interests. Building public parks or controlling utility rates are examples of social reforms. Although some reform administrations emphasized structural reform and others social reform, the two kinds of reform almost always occurred together.

In San Francisco, the Republican bosses were under the thumb of the powerful Southern Pacific Railroad, memorably characterized by novelist Frank Norris as an octopus whose steel tentacles had a stranglehold on the city and state. In 1897, James D. Phelan, a Democrat, was elected mayor on a reform platform. Phelan quickly pushed through a new city charter with many structural reforms. The charter greatly increased the power of the mayor and provided for the citywide election of councilmen, called supervisors in San Francisco. It also gave city residents the powers of initiative and referendum. He also began the effort to create a municipally owned water system and other utilities. Phelan was, however, a strong supporter of excluding Asian immigrants from America.

In Toledo, Ohio, Samuel "Golden Rule" Jones took office as mayor in 1898. Jones, who immigrated from Wales as a child, was a successful manufacturer of drilling equipment before entering politics. He had earned his nickname by honest business dealings, humanitarian policies, and in particular, his fondness for the words of Jesus which Christians call the Golden Rule: "Do unto others as you would have others do unto you." Although Jones took office as a reformer, he was also the chosen candidate of the Republican machine. He soon found himself in a battle with party leaders, who wanted him to approve an unconscionable railroad franchise. He broke with the party and in 1899 ran as an independent, winning re-election and remaining mayor until his unexpected death in 1904. Like other famous Progressive Era mayors with a commitment to social reform, Jones enjoyed great support from ordinary people, including workers and immigrants, who were often accused of being the backbone of political machines and corrupt government. Ironically enough, Golden Rule Jones was often opposed by the Toledo Pastors' Union because he did not support anti-vice efforts.

During Jones's administration, Toledo established its first civil service system, relief programs for the poor, and a city park system and public playgrounds. Jones ordered park officials to replace "Keep off the Grass" signs with signs reading, "Citizens Protect Your Property." He instituted police and prison reforms and occasionally presided at police court, where he would dismiss cases against such offenders as prostitutes and vagrants. He did so, he said, because the poor "have no money, they have no counsel, and for petty offenses that are not offenses at all when committed by the rich, they are fined, imprisoned, disgraced and degraded."[31] Jones strongly advocated public ownership of utilities, although he was never successful in his campaign for a publicly owned power plant or control of streetcar fares. (The day after his death, stock in the privately franchised Toledo Street Railway jumped 24 points.) He was succeeded by a colleague and disciple, Brand Whitlock, who continued reform activities in Toledo for four more terms.

Prominent reform mayors filled an important role. Many had compelling personalities and attracted considerable press attention to their programs. They confirmed municipal reformers' belief that worthy, public-spirited individuals were necessary to put reform ideas into practice. "Good laws are important; good men to execute them are essential," wrote Clinton Rogers Woodruff, secretary of the National Municipal League, ". . . the municipal reform problem is in large part one of men."[32]

A Terrible Natural Disaster Leads to Municipal Reform

On September 8, 1900, a hurricane with winds of at least 120 miles per hour hit Galveston, Texas, which is located on a long, narrow island two miles off the Texas coastline. By the time evacuation was ordered, leaving was no longer possible. A steamship, tossed by the rough waters, had destroyed the bridges to the mainland. A storm surge, or tidal wave, more than 15 feet high swept across the island, completely submerging it. The wall of debris at its leading edge flattened buildings for some 15 blocks. When the surge subsided, 6,000 of Galveston's 38,000 residents had lost their lives (as well as more than 2,000 elsewhere on the island and on the mainland), thousand more were seriously injured, and as many as 10,000 were homeless. More than 2,600 homes had been swept away. Every resident of the city had suffered some loss. It was the worst natural disaster that the United States had ever experienced.

In the wake of the disaster, the old, corrupt city government was unable to function. At the request of a citizens' group, the governor of Texas appointed five businessmen to run the city and the rebuilding operations. The temporary commission was given both law-making and executive power, with each commissioner taking charge of one particular function or area. The plan was an overwhelming success and attracted much attention. Galveston permanently adopted the commission system of government, with commissioners subsequently elected, not appointed. Within a decade, more than 100 other cities had adopted it as well.

The Movement for Direct-Democracy Legislation

The American system of federal government, as designed by the Constitution, is a republic, or representative democracy. Another term is indirect democracy. This system enables citizens to influence important public laws and policies indirectly by debating them freely and by choosing the representatives or leaders who will actually determine and administer them. Direct democracy, on the other hand—for example, the New England town meeting— allows large numbers of citizens themselves to vote on laws, rather than permitting representatives to do it for them. The United States Constitution does not provide for direct democracy at the state or national level.

In the late 19th century, many reformers argued for increasing direct democracy in America. They believed that the ordinary citizen's ability to exert indirect influence, as the Constitution envisioned, had been lost because political corruption was so widespread. Most state legislatures, much of Congress, and many other officials appeared to be under the undisguised influence of special economic interests and trusts. Political party insiders and their machines had almost complete control over the selection of the candidates from whom the voters had to choose their representatives. These party insiders and bosses usually did not hold elective offices themselves, putting them beyond the reach of voters—but within easy reach of the interests.

If representatives almost universally abused the public trust, direct democracy reformers believed, representative democracy no longer worked and needed to be reformed. The solution, they said, was to give voters more direct power over important issues facing the state and national communities. Their goal was not to weaken representative government but to restore the influence of ordinary citizens by bypassing party bosses, special interests, and corruption.

One part of the crusade for direct democracy was the movement for direct legislation at the state level. The most popular measures were initiative and referendum. *Initiative* permits citizens to take the initiative to propose new laws or constitutional amendments by filing petitions signed by a certain percentage of voters. *Referendum* is the submission of a law to the voters for approval or rejection, either at the wish of the legislature itself or by request of citizens who have filed petitions. A third measure, *recall*, is the removal of a public official from office, usually after a special vote brought about by citizen petitions. Reformers in the Progressive Era did not invent initiative, referendum, and recall. All had been used informally at times in the American experience, and some states had always required a referendum to enact certain kinds of laws. Reformers, however, wanted to make them a widespread legal right.

Direct-democracy legislation had been advocated wholeheartedly by the Populist Party and small, radical reform groups in the early 1890s, "to restore the government of the Republic to the hands of the 'plain people,' with which class it originated," as the Populist platform of 1892 put it. At first, most other people dismissed tinkering with representative democracy and the Constitution as the work of cranks, if not dangerous radicals. Gradually, however, mainstream reform interests began to accept direct-democracy ideas. Women's suffrage advocates, prohibition advocates, and settlement workers, for example, all realized that direct legislation could advance measures avoided by political parties or opposed by entrenched interests. By 1895 Direct Legislation Leagues were active in New Jersey, South Dakota, Kansas, Michigan, Colorado, and Nebraska. In 1898, South Dakota became the first state to amend its state constitution to adopt initiative and referendum, and Utah followed in 1900. In Oregon, a direct legislation amendment was passed by two successive legislatures (as required by state law) in 1899 and 1901, then ratified by voters by an 11 to 1 margin.

THE MOVEMENT FOR DIRECT ELECTION OF SENATORS

The direct-democracy movement also included a demand for direct election of U.S. senators, although this could only be accomplished by an amendment to the Constitution. The Constitution provides for the election of U.S. senators by state legislators, not directly by the voters themselves. Unfortunately, most state legislatures were easily dominated, if not actually corrupted, by special interests. At times the elections became notorious. In 14 cases between 1891 and 1905, the process actually ground to a halt and some states went without a senator in Washington through at least one state legislative session. Between 1872 and the century's end, the Senate investigated 15 instances of outright bribery attempts in the election of senators by a state legislature. (In nearly 100 years prior to that date, there had been only one such case.) In 1899, for example, the Senate Committee on Privileges and Elections reported that Montana senator William A. Clark bought more than half of his votes in the state legislature. Clark himself admitted to a $140,000 "personal disbursement." He resigned when it appeared the Senate would expel him—only to have Montana's legislature return him to office in 1901.[33] Even where no actual corruption existed, many reform-minded people believed that most senators were too closely tied to corporate wealth and primarily represented its interests. The Senate, sprinkled with railroad, banking, lumber, coal, and mining barons, was popularly known as the Millionaire's Club. Beginning in 1893, proposals for a direct-election amendment to the Constitution were introduced in the House of Representatives in every new session.

THE MOVEMENT FOR DIRECT PRIMARY ELECTIONS

The third demand of the direct-democracy movement was for primary elections. In a primary election, voters select a party's candidates for office. In the convention system of selecting candidates that existed almost everywhere in the late 19th century, on the other hand, party insiders chose candidates with no opportunity for input from the average voter. Local party organizations held caucuses (meetings restricted to party members) to select delegates to the state convention. At the state convention, state delegates selected nominees for state office and delegates to the national convention.

Delegates to the national convention selected the party's candidate for president. Because political parties were traditionally considered voluntary associations, their activities were not under official governmental supervision. By the end of the 1890s, however, many states had passed some regulations to control widespread fraud in the convention system, usually at least requiring public notice of caucuses.

The idea of direct primaries gained popularity among the reform-minded as a means of limiting the power of political bosses and the ease with which special interests exerted influence in the convention system. The issue of primaries was especially important wherever one party was dominant because nomination was almost a guarantee of election. Throughout the last quarter of the 19th century, parties themselves sometimes held primary elections (among their members only) in many places in the West and South and in a few places in Pennsylvania. Progressive Era reformers, however, wanted to make primaries mandatory. They also wanted primary elections to be conducted under the same governmental oversight as general elections. In 1899 Minnesota became the first state in the nation to pass direct-primary legislation. The law applied only to Hennepin County, site of the state's largest city, Minneapolis, but in 1901 it was extended to the entire state. Florida and Oregon also passed primary legislation in 1901.

CHILD LABOR AND ITS FOES

One of the most prominent of all reform movements in the Progressive Era was the attack on child labor. Prior to the 1880s few voices were ever raised against the idea. Child labor was traditionally considered an economic boon for children and their families. It was also considered a morally valuable institution, one that prevented sins like idleness and taught virtues that put youngsters on the road to success. In 1890, the U.S. Census reported that more than one out of every six children between the ages of 10 and 15 was employed. The 1900 census counted some 1,750,000 employed children 15 or younger. Observers at the time, and historians today, believe that many child workers were not counted and that these figures are extremely conservative.

Throughout the 1890s, public concern about child labor became increasingly widespread. Settlement house workers brought the matter to public attention. Women's clubs took up the issue. The National Consumers' League (NCL) was especially active in the cause. The NCL had been organized in 1899 when the New York Consumers' League joined together with similar groups nationwide. It was headed by Hull-House alumna Florence Kelley, a licensed lawyer and tireless reformer. Until 1897 Kelley had been factory inspector for the state of Illinois, where she energetically publicized the conditions of child labor in the stockyards and sweatshops. Under her guidance, NCL chapters in all industrial cities made the publicity of children's working conditions a priority. Labor unions also joined the opposition to child labor.

Certain industries made extensive use of child labor and were the particular targets of public concern and early reform activity. One was anthracite coal mining. Young boys worked in the dark, dangerous coal mines, or in aboveground breakers, where they sat huddled over dusty, moving chutes of coal to pick out the slate and shale. A second industry was glass making, with factories spread across New Jersey, Pennsylvania, West Virginia, Ohio, and Indiana. Boys worked at various tasks in the furnace rooms, exposed to long hours of intense heat (usually a minimum of 100 degrees) and glaring light, to say nothing of the dangers of fumes, dust, burns, and broken glass. Girls did packing. Glass factories operated all night, when temperatures were cooler, and many children even worked the night shift. A third industry which made extensive use of child labor was textiles, especially in the South, where whole families were often employed. Most children worked as spinners, tending long rows of whirling bobbins to mend breaks in the thread. In 1900 one of every four cotton-mill workers was under the age of 15, and about half of them were less than 12. It was not even uncommon for six- and seven-year-olds to be employed. Canneries on the Atlantic and Gulf coasts also employed many children that young, along with their older siblings and parents. The children shucked oysters, picked shrimp, picked and processed fruits and vegetables—sometimes seven days a week, 16 hours a day. The final areas of particular concern were the so-called street trades in urban areas. Children roamed the streets selling newspapers, peddling, or working as messengers and delivery boys and girls.

Reformers in the Progressive Era objected to child labor for many different reasons. For one thing, industrial working conditions had become far more dangerous. The nation's children were being exploited, exhausted, sickened, and maimed in the nation's new industries, reformers pointed out, by the unrestrained greed of industrialists. Others attacked child labor because they saw it as an important cog in the larger wheel of poverty. It propped up a system of inadequate wages for adults and inadequate social supports for people in need. Even worse, by shortening or even barring school attendance, it perpetuated the cycle. Their reformers cited contemporary theories of psychological development and social evolution, holding that working children were prevented from developing properly from childhood to adulthood. Such children, they warned, might grow into adults unsuited and even threatening to democracy. And finally, many ordinary people, even those not otherwise engaged by reform movements, objected to the inhumanity of robbing children of healthy and happy childhoods.

The early campaigns were conducted at the state level. By 1900, 28 states had passed some minimal legislation, but most of the laws applied only to children employed in manufacturing or mining. Most did nothing more than raise the legal age of employment in factories to 10 and mines to 12, and perhaps limit working hours to 10 per day. Only eight states protected children from working after 10 P.M.

TEMPERANCE GAINS A DRAMATIC ADVOCATE

At the end of the 1890s, the major organized temperance groups with Protestant ties—the Prohibition Party, the Women's Christian Temperance Union (WCTU), and the Anti-Saloon League (ASL)—appeared to be accomplishing little. The ASL continued to do state-level organizing and had affiliates in 26 states by 1899, but it suffered from serious internal discord. Among Catholic clerics, however, temperance had become the "cause célèbre of moral reform," as historian Jay Dolan puts it. Many parishes sponsored temperance groups for men and women.[34]

The issue of liquor control remained a subject of public interest. For one thing, a new wave of antitrust sentiment was sweeping the nation, and concerns about a powerful liquor trust reawakened. At the request of Congress, in 1898 the commissioner of labor issued a report on the liquor traffic, or the production, consumption, distribution, and taxation of alcohol. *The Economic Aspects of the Liquor Problem* was statistical and did not attempt to look at either the social issues or the political influence of the industry. It did confirm, however, that the industry was becoming more concentrated and more heavily capitalized. In Canada, where citizens had the right to enact local option laws, Prime Minister Wilfrid Laurier held a national referendum on prohibition in 1898. The "drys" swept every province except Quebec; even nationwide, the overall vote was 278,000 in favor versus 264,000 opposed. Parliament took no action as a result of the referendum, however.

For several years, women in several states had once again begun demonstrating at local saloons, as they had done in the Women's Crusade of the 1870s that led to the founding of the WCTU. In dry states, liquor could not be manufactured or sold as

In 1900, Carry (or Carrie) Nation began a dramatic campaign to draw attention to the temperance cause, "smashing" illegal saloons in Kansas with her famous hatchet. This poster advertises a lecture by Nation. *(Courtesy Kansas State Historical Society)*

individual drinks. Under a Supreme Court ruling of 1888, however, dry states could not prohibit the sale of liquor brought into the state from elsewhere and sold as it was originally packaged; that is, by the bottle. In private clubs as well as "joints" (as illegal saloons were called), the dry law could be evaded—and usually was. Then, in the summer of 1900, the Women's Crusade was catapulted into the national spotlight. A Kansas woman, Carry Nation, decided to take direct and personal action against the joints in her officially dry state.

Nation was a physically imposing woman in her fifties. Her first husband, a doctor, had died of alcoholism at the age of 29. She believed she had been divinely called to promote temperance and enforce the liquor law. Nation began her work in Kiowa, Kansas, smashing, or vandalizing, three joints and daring officials to arrest her, since the saloons themselves were illegal. She was not arrested in Kiowa. But she was arrested six months later, when she and her followers expanded their campaign to the elegant Carey Hotel in Wichita. There she introduced her famous symbol, the hatchet. Before the end of her life in 1911, Nation and her followers, organized into bands called Home Defenders, had expanded the campaign of "hatchetation" to cities throughout the nation. Nation herself had been jailed some 30 times.

Temperance advocates welcomed the publicity about lax enforcement of liquor laws, but many disapproved of Nation's tactics. Among other problems, her pronounced activism violated widely held beliefs about appropriate behavior for women. "A woman must know a woman's place," Kansas governor William E. Stanley told her. "They can't come in here and raise this kind of disturbance." Nation herself was very clear about her motives. "You refused me the vote and I had to use a rock," she told the Kansas House of Representatives in 1901. The same year, Nation's second husband of 29 years, a lawyer, filed for divorce. "I married this woman because I needed someone to run my house," he said, claiming grounds of desertion. After the divorce Nation sold her house and used the money to establish a home for wives and children of alcoholics.[35]

THE CAMPAIGN AGAINST PROSTITUTION

During the Progressive Era, reformers conducted a national campaign against prostitution. Prostitution was not, of course, a new phenomenon. Prior to the Progressive Era it had sometimes been publically denounced, but also privately tolerated. It had even been regarded as a necessary evil—one that protected respectable women from immorality and even rape. Prostitutes themselves, however, had been viewed as thoroughly corrupt and unredeemable.

As cities began to mushroom after the Civil War, some observers urged the official regulation of urban prostitution by medical inspection and police oversight. Many large cities in Europe and Asia had adopted this approach, called the regulationist solution. But it was repugnant to most Americans. By 1890 it had met active opposition from groups such as religious interests, social purity crusaders (who encouraged sexual abstinence outside of marriage), women's rights advocates, and even civil libertarians. Some—especially the women's groups, who saw prostitution as a result of the sexual double standard as well as a moral issue—even tried to rehabilitate the prostitute herself.

Reformers began to call prostitution the social evil, and shortly after 1890, it began to attract new attention. Reformers believed that both prostitution and venereal disease were increasing rapidly. (Historians have no way of knowing if that is statistically true.) By 1900, reformers were also commenting on changes in the way prostitution was conducted. It was no longer small-scale, informal, and relatively unobtrusive, as it had been in the past, with prostitutes who worked either independently or for an independent madam. Instead, it had become a complex, commercialized, and well-organized business. It was intertwined not only with other vice activities but also with liquor interests, rental property interests, police, and politicians. Male procurers called cadets and pimps had become common. Obvious red-light districts had appeared in growing cities, usually in or near poor neighborhoods whose residents did not have enough political influence to stop them. Some districts, like Storyville in New Orleans, the Barbary Coast in San Francisco, the Tenderloin in New York, and the Levee in Chicago, gained national fame. Music blared and women sat in windows, gesturing to passersby. In some cities, directories were even published to list all the sporting houses and their specialties.

In 1900, prominent citizens and reformers in New York formed the Committee of Fifteen to study prostitution. Two years later they published *The Social Evil,* the first major report on urban vice. Vice reports, which presented statistics and surveyed the economic and political connections of prostitution in a city, quickly became a popular and powerful tool of antiprostitution reform groups. Like earlier antiprostitution reformers, progressives "frequently viewed prostitution with moral repugnance and attacked it with religious fervor," writes historian Ruth Rosen. Nonetheless, she continues, they began to stress the social factors that created and supported it. They investigated the relationship of prostitution to municipal corruption, to immigration, to the low wages paid to women, to the dangers that awaited both native-born country girls and immigrant girls from rural areas in the anonymous new industrial cities. Reformers were increasingly optimistic that prostitution could be greatly reduced if not eradicated, just as they believed of other socially created evils of the day.[36]

One integral part of the campaign against prostitution was the growing concern of the medical profession about venereal disease. By the opening of the 20th century many doctors believed it was a serious public health epidemic and they attributed it to prostitution. Sexually transmitted diseases were shrouded in secrecy in 1900—even medical publications used veiled terms—and doctors did not have authoritative information on the diseases' incidence. Nonetheless, some estimates by prominent doctors claimed that at least 60 percent of men were infected at one time or another in their lives or that 60 to 75 percent of the marriageable male population in larger cities were infected at any given time. Infected men were not the doctors' only concern, however. Because a stringent double standard of sexual morality existed, most girls and women were completely uninformed about sexual matters. Many monogamous wives were unknowingly infected by their husbands, many of them members of the middle and upper classes. Damage from these infections, doctors believed, necessitated many serious gynecological surgeries and also caused much infertility. They knew in addition that serious birth defects and infant blindness were caused by some venereal diseases. All of these concerns were also very important to the women's groups that became involved in the antiprostitution campaign.[37]

THE ELECTION OF 1900

The presidential election campaign of 1900 began against the backdrop of continuing American military efforts to subdue insurgents in the Philippines and manage the crisis in China.

The Republicans met in Philadelphia in June and renominated President McKinley unanimously on the first ballot. With a campaign slogan "Let well enough alone," their only problem was selecting a new vice presidential candidate, since Vice President Garret A. Hobart had died in 1899. President McKinley announced that he had no preference and wanted the convention to decide. New York Republicans, however, had a very definite preference. They wanted to send their governor, Theodore Roosevelt, to Washington—that is, they wanted to get him out of their state, and better yet to defang him in an office that was considered a dead-end job. After Roosevelt returned from the Spanish-American War as a hero, he had quickly and easily been elected governor. As governor, he had proven to be an energetic reformer. Roosevelt was clearly independent, unorthodox, and ambitious—qualities highly disconcerting to New York political insiders. For the same reason, President McKinley's campaign manager, Senator Mark Hanna of Ohio, did not want him in Washington. Hanna and many other moderate Republicans were also uncomfortable with Roosevelt's enthusiastic jingoism. But no alternative candidate was available, and Roosevelt was also popular in the West, where he spent colorful vacations at his cowboy ranch in North Dakota. On the first vice presidential roll call, the 41-year-old Roosevelt was unanimously selected. "Your duty to the country," the unhappy Hanna wrote to President McKinley after the convention, "is to live for four years from next March."[38]

The Democrats gathered in Kansas City on July 4. William Jennings Bryan was chosen the candidate, unanimously and without opposition. Adlai E. Stevenson of Illinois (father of the mid-20th-century presidential candidate of the same name) was nominated for vice president.

Within both the Republican and Democratic Parties, many of the breaches of 1896 had been healed by the return of prosperity. Among Populists, however, the breaches had widened, while their numbers and their influence had declined. The party split into two factions, which nominated different tickets. Seven other third parties also met in convention.

President McKinley again conducted a front porch campaign, while both his running mate Roosevelt and his opponent William Jennings Bryan traveled and campaigned widely. Bryan hoped to make the campaign a referendum on imperialism, but he also roundly condemned the trusts and once again argued in favor of free silver. The trust and silver issues confused the debate on imperialism, however, and drove away the many anti-imperialists who were conservative on economic issues. McKinley and Roosevelt, on the other hand, kept foreign policy separate from other issues and made it seem less partisan. They used only the term *expansionism,* never *imperialism,* and appealed to patriotism and duty.

President McKinley handily won reelection, becoming the first president in 28 years to win a consecutive term. He had a margin of nearly 900,000 popular votes, and 271 electoral votes to Bryan's 155. In the West, he even carried many former Populist strongholds. Overall, some 377,000 fewer votes were cast than in 1896. Some of the decline was a result of the successful disenfranchisement of black voters and some poor white voters in the South.

THE BEGINNINGS OF RADIO COMMUNICATIONS

At the beginning of the 20th century many scientists and inventors in Europe and North America were conducting experiments with radio. (Radio is a means of communication that uses electromagnetic waves sent through space at the speed of light.) Like both the automobile and the airplane in their early stages of development, radio was called by many different names at the time: aerography, electric waves, ether waves, spark telegraphy, space telegraphy, and perhaps most commonly, wireless.

In 1898, Guglielmo Marconi, a 24-year-old of Italian and Irish parentage, founded the Wireless Telegraph and Signal Company in England. Marconi worked with the form of radio transmission called wireless telegraphy, which uses Morse code messages. His original focus was ship-to-land communications. (At the time, ships could not communicate with shore from the time they left port until they reached their destination, sometimes weeks later.) Marconi soon demonstrated that radio communication could defeat bad weather and many geographical impediments across long distances, and his work attracted great interest worldwide. His next goal was transatlantic radio transmission between England and North America. In preparation Marconi had a station constructed in Massachusetts, but the huge antenna was destroyed by high winds. To avoid further delay he did not wait to rebuild. Instead he personally boarded a ship for St. John's, Newfoundland. There, on December 12, 1901, Marconi heard the three-dot Morse code signal for the letter S—received via a makeshift antenna of wire held aloft by a high-altitude kite. It was the first radio message sent some 2,000 miles across the Atlantic Ocean. The event was widely publicized and generated great excitement.

At the same time Marconi was perfecting wireless telegraphy, Canadian Reginald Fessenden was developing the form of radio transmission called radiotelephony, which transmits the human voice or other sounds. Fessenden, born in Quebec, had worked for both Thomas Edison and George Westinghouse (for whom he perfected the electric lighting system for the Chicago World's Fair). In December 1900, while working for the U.S. Weather Bureau, Fessenden became the first person to demonstrate the possibility of radiotelephony, making a one-mile voice transmission from his experimental station in the Potomac River. He left the bureau to work independently shortly after, when his superior ordered that all his patents be given to the U.S. government.

SPINDLETOP CHANGES TEXAS—AND AMERICAN—HISTORY

Prior to 1900, the primary source of American crude oil was in northern Pennsylvania. John D. Rockefeller's Standard Oil operations centered in Cleveland to be near the source. Since the late 1880s, a small amount of oil had also been extracted from East Texas fields. Near Beaumont, Texas, a self-taught geologist named Patillo Higgins was convinced that a large deposit lay beneath the Spindletop salt dome. Locally, Higgins was regarded as an eccentric. But Captain Anthony F. Lucas, an engineer and adventurer, and John Galey, a Pennsylvania oilman, were attracted by his story and began drilling at Spindletop in October 1900. On January 10, 1901, as the crew set to work lowering their equipment down their 1,000-foot hole, mud shot out. In seconds, oil followed. The gusher rose more than 150 feet—a height never before seen in American oil fields. At first the well produced nearly 100,000 barrels per day—more than all of the other wells in the United States combined.

By the end of 1901, 200 wells owned by more than 100 companies had produced more than 17 million barrels of oil at Spindletop. Among those companies were the beginnings of Gulf, Mobil, and Humble oil. Beaumont's population had grown from 10,000 to 50,000, and the oil industry had begun to reshape agricultural Texas. Prior to 1901, oil products were used primarily for lighting and lubrication of machinery. After the vast increase in supply from Spindletop, the modern petroleum industry was born. Oil products would soon make possible a revolution in industry and transportation, replacing coal in ships and trains, enabling great growth in the fledgling automobile industry, and even fueling flight.

A New Wave of Trusts—and Antitrust Sentiment

During the depression years of the mid 1890s, the merger of businesses into gigantic new combinations had slowed, and the public had been distracted by the baleful economy. As prosperity returned after 1897, however, a fierce new round of business mergers began. Both in pace and in the size of the combinations that resulted, it dwarfed what had come before. Between 1898 and 1902 alone, the 100 largest firms grew four times larger. The public, in turn, quickly moved the trusts back to the top of its list of pressing public problems.

New consolidations involving three giants of finance and industry—John D. Rockefeller, Andrew Carnegie, and J. Pierpont Morgan, an investment banker—especially roused the public. In 1892, the Ohio Supreme Court had forced the break up of Rockefeller's Standard Oil Trust. But by 1899 Rockefeller found a way to evade both the state court order and threat of the Sherman Anti-Trust Act. He reorganized in New Jersey, where recent laws permitted a corporation to own and control other corporations in other states. Technically, Standard Oil of New Jersey was a holding company. A holding company does not purchase other companies outright; instead, it purchases a controlling interest in their stock, enabling it to replace board members and exercise control. At its birth, Standard Oil of New Jersey refined more than 80 percent of the nation's oil.

Since the beginning of the depression in 1893, J. Pierpont Morgan had been quietly participating in the consolidation of distressed railroads with other investment banking firms like Kuhn, Loeb, and Company. Railroads were still the largest business in America—and as a result of the bankers' activity, six consolidated companies controlled more than 90 percent of the track by the turn of the century. The bankers, after combining small companies, reducing their staffs, and stabilizing their finances, would continue to control operations through a new board of directors. The public called reorganization of small competitors into larger but leaner companies "Morganization." Morgan and other powerful financiers they called the money trust.

Morgan had a personal passion for order. "Like the most ardent socialist," Joseph Frazier Wall writes, "he hated the waste, duplication, and clutter of unrestrained competition."[39] Morgan next turned to the steel industry. In 1898 he helped form the Federal Steel Company, making it the second-largest steel corporation in America. The largest was Carnegie Steel. Andrew Carnegie had been considering retiring to devote himself full time to his libraries and other philanthropies. Now, however, his competitive instincts aroused, he hinted that he might take on Morgan's Federal Steel—and enter railroading for good measure. Morgan delicately inquired if Carnegie would consider selling instead. Carnegie scribbled some figures on a slip of paper. When Morgan looked at it, he said simply, "I accept." The price was some $400 million, making Carnegie the richest man in America. Next, Morgan obtained the Mesabi Range ore fields in Minnesota from Rockefeller. He used them all to create the United States Steel Corporation. The new corporation was announced to an astonished public in March 1901. Capitalized at nearly a billion and a half dollars, it was the largest corporation in the world to date. At its birth it controlled about two-thirds of the iron and steel market. By engineering the merger, Morgan reportedly made $7 million.

Political Radicalism at the Turn of the Century

In July 1901, Eugene V. Debs and other socialist-leaning people met in Indianapolis and formed the Socialist Party of America. The group included Debs's Social Democratic Party, orthodox Marxists from Daniel De Leon's Socialist Labor Party, cooperative commonwealthers, Bellamyites, workers, farmers, intellectuals, even some anarchists. Although the party used Marxist terms like *class struggle,* Debs was not doctrinaire. He contradicted the public's stereotype of socialists and radicals, historian Albert Fried has written, because he was "neither a foreigner, an intellectual, nor a fanatic. He was a humble, sweet-tempered midwestern American who . . . spoke the plain language of his countrymen."[40] The platform the group agreed on in 1901 called for support of all unions, no matter how conservative. It urged many reforms formerly identified with the Populists: public ownership of utilities, transportation, and communication, for example, and democratic political reforms like initiative, referendum, and recall. It also called for government assistance to the unemployed and the elderly; universal education to age 18; and rights for minorities. Although these reforms are taken for granted today, in 1901 neither the Republican nor Democratic Party could have conceived of supporting them.

Most Americans at the turn of the century spurned socialism and it outraged conservatives. Nonetheless, prior to 1917 when the Russian Revolution violently installed the first actual socialist state, much socialist sentiment in America can be thought of as the far left wing of progressive reform. Some very prominent social reformers accepted socialist theories and many more agreed that the socialist criticism of living and working conditions in America was just. Few reformers imagined an actual socialist state, however; their goal was to correct the excesses and abuses of democratic capitalism.

The movement Americans most feared as radical and revolutionary at the turn of the century was not socialism, but anarchism. Anarchists advocated the abolition of all government because they believed that humans were meant to be free and that all forms of government and authority were coercive. After government was abolished, anarchists believed, a just and noncoercive society would appear. In 1900 one of the best-known advocates of anarchism was Emma Goldman, who later became a controversial advocate for radical personal freedom, labor rights, and pacifism. Goldman, an immigrant from Lithuania, had already served a year in prison for her role in planning the attempted assassination of Henry Clay Frick during the 1893 Homestead strike. During 1900–01, she traveled throughout the country, organizing rallies and delivering compelling speeches for the anarchist cause.

In the late 19th century, the most radical branch of the movement, called revolutionary anarchism, had begun to advocate violence, or violent acts, to hasten their ends. They were, in fact, terrorists. Their goal was to spread fear by murdering heads of state, prominent capitalists, and even religious leaders. These acts, they believed, would lead to reforms or even the end of the state. Between 1881 and 1900, anarchists assassinated the czar of Russia, the president of France, the empress of Austria, and the king of Italy—and in 1901, the president of the United States.

PRESIDENT MCKINLEY IS ASSASSINATED

More than 11 million people attended the Pan American Exposition in Buffalo, New York, in 1901, awed by the Electric Tower and the extensive use of electrical lighting on the grounds. On September 5 alone, more than 116,000 visitors arrived. Many were drawn by the prospect of hearing President McKinley speak at the fair that day. In his speech, he praised trade reciprocity—agreements between nations for low or no tariffs. Six months into his second term, the president seemed to be marking out a new path for Republican leadership, whose most important policy had long been extremely high tariffs to protect American manufacturers. He also seemed to be in tune with America's new role in the world. "We must not repose in fancied security that we can forever sell everything and buy little or nothing," he said. "The period of exclusiveness is past. . . . Reciprocity treaties are in harmony with the spirit of the times."[41]

The following afternoon, September 6, the president and first lady, Ida Saxton McKinley, returned to the fair to greet well-wishers. At 4 P.M. doors to the lavish Temple of Music, an auditorium, opened to admit the waiting crowds. Within 10 minutes, a slight, 28-year-old man named Leon Franz Czolgosz (pronounced "cholgush") had reached the front of the line. As he did he pulled out a handkerchief-wrapped revolver—purchased the day before in downtown Buffalo. He shot the president at point blank range.

The next man in line, James "Big Ben" Parker, an African-American waiter from Atlanta, leaped on the shooter. Secret service and police guards joined in, subdued Czolgosz, and, amid pandemonium and angry mobs, removed him. McKinley was rushed to the small emergency hospital on the Exposition grounds. The bullet had passed through his stomach. Although the doctors were unable to locate the bullet, they repaired the wounds. Sadly, they made fatal medical errors. At first it appeared that the President would recover. Vice President Roosevelt, who had rushed to Buffalo, confidently left for a vacation in the Adirondack Mountains. Unknown to the doctors, however, gangrene was spreading through the president's body. On September 14, he died—the third American president in less than 40 years to be felled by an assassin.

Nine days after McKinley's death, the assassin was brought to trial. Czolgosz had been born in Detroit to a Polish immigrant couple and grew up outside Cleveland. He originally told police his name was Nieman, or "nobody." Czolgosz was a convert to anarchism who imagined that his act would bring social change and greater justice for the workingman. He claimed to have been inspired by Emma Goldman, whom he had heard speak and met briefly twice in the preceding months. "She set me on fire!" he later reported.[42] Some Americans were convinced that an organized conspiracy lay behind the crime. Goldman and other anarchists were arrested on suspicion, but no evidence of a conspiracy was uncovered. At his one-day trial, Czolgosz refused to take the stand, so no additional information was gained. He was pronounced guilty and died in the electric chair on October 29, 1901.

President William McKinley, the 25th president of the United States, died in September 1901 from wounds inflicted by an anarchist assassin. *(Library of Congress, Prints and Photographs Division, LC-USZ62-120900)*

President McKinley's funeral train traveled from Buffalo to Washington, then to Canton, Ohio, his home, for burial. All along the way Americans gathered at train stations draped in black crepe to pay respects as the train passed by.

Meanwhile, Theodore Roosevelt, who had been summoned back to Buffalo immediately after the president's death, had been sworn in as the 26th president, and at 42 the youngest to hold the office. "I told William McKinley it was a mistake to nominate that wild man at Philadelphia," said the late president's anguished campaign manager, Mark Hanna. "Now look, that damned cowboy is President of the United States."[43]

A NEW PRESIDENT

Theodore Roosevelt's first words as president were both statesmanlike and politically astute. "I wish to say that it shall be my aim to continue absolutely unbroken the policy of President McKinley for the peace and prosperity and the honor of our beloved country," he said.[44] He announced that the entire cabinet would remain unchanged, and for a period it did. These acts reassured politicians, the stock market, and the nation.

In October 1901, a month after he became president, Theodore Roosevelt asked African-American leader Booker T. Washington to stay to dinner at the White House after a meeting. It was the first time an African American had dined with the president. The event caused a public furor. The president was criticized by white people throughout the nation but especially in the South, where whites held the social separation of the races to be unbreachable. The president refused to acknowledge his critics—but stunned by the uproar his act had caused he would never again ask an African American to dinner at the White House.

By the end of 1901, when the president sent his first Annual Message to Congress, he had begun to establish new directions in policy. (The Annual Message was the forerunner of the State of the Union Address. Prior to Woodrow Wilson's administration, presidents did not personally deliver the speech; the document was sent to Congress and read out by others.) In his message Roosevelt cautiously took up the problem of trusts. He announced that "combination and concentration should be, not prohibited, but supervised and within reasonable limits, controlled." He also spoke at length about the environment and conservation, the first American president to do so.[45]

CHRONICLE OF EVENTS

1898

William McKinley is president; Garret A. Hobart is vice president.

The gold rush of 1898–1902 to the Canadian Yukon and Alaska begins. As many as 200,000 men and women stampeders will head to the Far North. By the end of the year Congress extends the Homestead Act to Alaska, which is officially a district of the United States overseen by appointed officials.

Lynchings continue and begin to escalate into mob attacks on African-American citizens and race riots.

As the mid-1890s depression ends, immigration begins to increase again.

A fast-paced new round of business mergers begins, resulting in combinations of unprecedented size. The trusts again become an important public concern.

The commissioner of labor issues *The Economic Aspects of the Liquor Problem.* It confirms that the industry is becoming concentrated.

In Toledo reform mayor Samuel "Golden Rule" Jones takes office; in San Francisco reform mayor James D. Phelan succeeds in passing a new city charter that enacts many reforms.

In New York in 1898, the Outdoor Recreation League is founded by settlement house workers and prominent citizens to promote public playgrounds in crowded urban neighborhoods.

Charlotte Perkins Gilman publishes *Women and Economics,* a critical analysis of women's economic dependence, which is widely read and reprinted.

The influence of both socialism and anarchism is increasing in the United States.

South Dakota adopts initiative and referendum.

In Oklahoma, the Seminole Indians reach agreement with the Dawes Commission.

Representatives from the United Mine Workers (UMW) and many mining companies meet in Chicago and agree to collective bargaining in the bituminous coal region stretching from Pennsylvania to Kansas.

The Supreme Court upholds the Utah law limiting miners' working hours because it is such a dangerous occupation (*Holden v. Hardy,* 169 US 366).

January: In Havana, Cuba, riots occur.

January 25: The warship *Maine* arrives in Havana in the event that Americans must be evacuated from Cuba.

February: In Lake City, South Carolina, a white mob murders the black postmaster and several family members.

February 9: The *New York Journal* publishes a photographic reproduction of Spanish minister De Lôme's letter critical of President McKinley; many other newspapers publish a translation. De Lôme resigns instantly but the letter inflames American public opinion against the Spanish in Cuba.

February 15: The *Maine* explodes and sinks in the Havana harbor, killing more than 260 men.

March 9: Congress passes a $50 million appropriation bill to prepare the military for war.

March 28: The Court of Inquiry appointed to investigate the explosion of the *Maine* reports that it was probably caused by an external source, such as mine.

In *U.S. v. Wong Kim Ark,* the U.S. Supreme Court rules that a person born in the United States to resident alien parents is a citizen of the United States by right of birth—despite the fact that Chinese immigrants themselves are denied the right of citizenship.

April 11: President McKinley asks Congress for a war resolution against Spain.

April 19: Congress approves a war resolution that also recognizes Cuban independence, which the president signs the following day. The Teller amendment guarantees that the United States will not attempt to exercise control over Cuba after the war ends.

April 22: McKinley orders a naval blockade of Cuba, beginning the war.

April 24: Spain formally declares war on the United States.

April 25: Congress passes a resolution recognizing that a state of war has existed since April 21.

May 1: Commodore George Dewey sails into Manila Bay, Philippine Islands, and attacks and defeats the Spanish fleet there in the opening battle of the Spanish-American War. Dewey becomes an instant and widely celebrated popular hero.

May 12: Louisiana adopts the grandfather clause, which allows men to register to vote if their fathers or grandfathers were eligible to vote in 1867. Since no blacks could vote at that time, it effectively exempts whites from voting restrictions that now will apply only to blacks. The grandfather clause, the Mississippi Plan restrictions, the white primary, and other strategies continue to spread, disenfranchising blacks throughout the South.

May 19: A small Spanish fleet eludes the American blockade and enters the harbor of Santiago. Ill-prepared American troops soon leave Florida and put ashore near Santiago.

June: Convinced that a new radical movement is necessary, Eugene V. Debs has become a convert to socialism and forms the Social Democratic Party.

June 28: The Curtis Act becomes law. It provides for the survey and incorporation of towns in Indian Territory, establishes public schools, and abolishes tribal courts, making all residents subject to federal and state law.

July 1: American forces capture El Caney and San Juan Hill, fortified hills surrounding Santiago. The victory at San Juan Hill is made possible by the capture of Kettle Hill, taken after Theodore Roosevelt leads his Rough Riders and the African-American Ninth and Tenth Cavalry directly into Spanish fire. In the American press, Roosevelt emerges as the hero of the battle.

July 3: Naval forces destroy the Spanish fleet as it attempts to leave Santiago.

July 7: President McKinley signs a joint resolution of Congress annexing Hawaii.

July 15: The American Anti-imperialist League is organized.

July 17: The Spanish garrison at Santiago surrenders.

July 25: American forces arrive in the Spanish colony of Puerto Rico and take it with little resistance. Ground forces also arrive in the Philippines. Insurgents, who have been struggling for independence from Spain under Emilio Aguinaldo will organize to aid the United States, but tensions with them will soon increase.

August: Elihu Root, a lawyer with no military experience, becomes secretary of war. The reforms he achieves will launch the modern American military system.

August 12: Spain and the United States agree to an armistice; Spain ends control of Cuba, cedes Puerto Rico and Guam, and permits temporary U.S. occupation of Manila. As negotiations for a final treaty begin, the United States demands full control of the Philippines as well. In the United States a spirited anti-imperialist movement begins.

The United States formally transfers authority over Hawaii.

September: President McKinley declares the United States wants no special rights in China, only an Open Door for trading.

Gold is discovered at the future site of Nome, Alaska.

November: Theodore Roosevelt is elected governor of New York on the Republican ticket.

November 29: Filipino insurgents hold a constitutional convention and approve a constitution for a Philippine Republic.

December 10: Spain and the United States sign the Treaty of Paris. Spain renounces rights to Cuba, cedes Puerto Rico and Guam, and sells the Philippine Islands to the United States for $20 million. In America the debate over imperialism intensifies as Senate approval nears.

December 21: President McKinley issues a statement announcing U.S. sovereignty over the Philippines, although the Senate has not yet ratified the treaty with Spain.

1899

Congress establishes the third major national park, Mount Rainier, in the Cascade Mountains of Washington State.

John D. Rockefeller reorganizes Standard Oil as a holding company in New Jersey to evade antitrust rulings. The company controls more than 80 percent of the industry.

Thorstein Veblen, an economist, publishes *The Theory of the Leisure Class,* which introduces the concept of conspicuous consumption.

Minnesota passes the first law requiring government-regulated direct primary elections.

African-American pianist and composer Scott Joplin publishes the sheet music for *Maple Leaf Rag.* It reportedly sells more than a million copies and turns ragtime music into a national sensation.

January 1: In the Philippines Aguinaldo is declared president of the insurgents' republic. The United States does not recognize the government. In Congress the debate over the Treaty of Paris continues.

January 4: President McKinley's proclamation of American sovereignty is published in the Philippines; the Senate still has not approved the treaty with Spain and the debate continues.

January 20: President McKinley appoints the First Philippine Commission to investigate conditions in the islands and make recommendations.

February: British writer Rudyard Kipling publishes a poem entitled "The White Man's Burden." Although many anti-imperialists disagree with its sentiments, the phrase quickly enters the language.

February 4: American-Filipino tensions erupt into war. The brutal, bloody conflict will last until July 1902 and will be very costly in both lives and dollars.

February 6: The Senate approves the Treaty of Paris by one vote. Anti-imperialists introduce an act to grant the islands independence, but it is soon defeated.

March 3: Congress passes the Rivers and Harbors Act, containing the first federal law against pollution.

Summer: The Harriman Alaska Expedition of conservationists, scientists, and others explores and studies the coastline, eventually publishing 15 volumes of their results.

June 3: In New York, the Outdoor Recreation League opens a playground at Seward Park on the Lower East Side. It is an immediate success but the league will battle until 1902 to get the city to take it over and maintain it.

September: Canada holds a national referendum on prohibition. The drys win in all provinces except Quebec and overall have a majority of the total vote. No government action is taken, however.

September 6: Secretary of State John Hay sends his first Open Door notes asking foreign powers who have declared spheres of influence in China to refrain from preventing free trade there and to respect China's right to collect tariffs.

October 12: In South Africa the Boer War begins between the British and the Afrikaners. Canadian soldiers will fight overseas in an imperial war for the first time.

November 21: Vice President Garret A. Hobart dies.

1900

The population of the United States is 76 million; 40 percent of the population lives in urban areas.

In the Philippines, the war continues.

Six railroad companies, consolidated during the 1890s by J. P. Morgan and others, control more than 90 percent of the track in America.

The National Municipal League publishes a model program for city government. To end state political control it calls for Home Rule for cities; increasing the power of the mayor; electing councilmen at large rather than on a ward basis; and other reforms.

In the Yukon and Alaska, large corporations have begun to buy up individual claims. Large-scale, technological, corporate mining will soon end the gold rush frontier for individuals.

In Alaska, Congress allows for the incorporation of towns, permitting residents local self-government.

In the early months, gangs of Boxers in China begin destroying Christian missions and killing Chinese Christians.

Congress permits the incorporation of towns in Alaska and orders the capital moved from Sitka to Juneau. The non-Native population is more than 30,000 and is now larger than the Native population.

Utah adopts initiative and referendum.

January 10: The National Civic Federation (NCF) is founded in Chicago to help end the contentious relations between labor and management. Its members are to represent the public as well as labor and capital.

February: The New York Tenement House Exhibition draws more than 10,000 people and graphically demonstrates crowded and unsanitary conditions in poor neighborhoods. It travels to other cities where it also has a great impact.

February 5: Congressman George H. White of North Carolina, the only remaining African American in Congress, proposes a federal antilynching law; it does not come to a vote.

March 14: Congress passes the Gold Standard Act.

March 16: The Second Philippine Commission headed by William Howard Taft begins work to establish a legal code, government, and other reforms in the Philippines.

March 20: Hay's second Open Door note declares the policies of the first note in effect, although other foreign powers in China have given only equivocal agreement.

April 12: Congress passes the Foraker Act, terminating military rule in Puerto Rico and establishing a formal colonial government.

Susan B. Anthony led the women's suffrage movement from the mid-19th century to 1900, the year she retired from the presidency of the National American Women's Suffrage Association. This photograph was taken by Frances Benjamin Johnston. *(Library of Congress, Prints and Photographs Division, LC-USZ62-83146)*

April 30: Congress passes the Hawaii Organic Act, making the islands a territory of the United States. Sanford Dole is appointed the first governor. Whites and native Hawaiians have full U.S. citizenship; Chinese and Japanese residents of the islands do not.

May 9: Populists, who have divided into two factions, meet in separate conventions in Cincinnati and Sioux Falls.

Summer: In South Africa the formal Boer armies are defeated.

June: The Players' Protective Association is formed by major league baseball players. It does not affiliate with any major labor union and dies out in 1902.

June 1: Carry Nation accomplishes her first saloon smashing in Kiowa, Kansas, to protest the lax enforcement of liquor laws in Kansas, a supposedly dry state.

June 3: The International Ladies Garment Workers Union (ILGWU) is founded in New York and affiliated with the AFL.

June 13: In China the Boxers enter Peking (Beijing), looting and killing Chinese Christians.

June 14: The Boxers attack foreign legations in Tianjin (Tientsin).

June 19–21: The Republican convention meets in Philadelphia. It unanimously renominates President McKinley; for vice president it nominates 41-year-old Theodore Roosevelt, in part because New York power brokers want him removed from the governor's office, where he has been very independent and has supported many reforms.

June 20: The Boxers begin the siege of foreign legations in Peking.

June 21: The Dowager Empress Cixi (Tz'u Hsi), who sympathizes with the Boxers, declares war on the foreign powers although it is ignored in some regions.

July 3: Hay's third Open Door note declares that the United States intends to respect Chinese territorial and administrative integrity.

July 4–6: The Democratic convention meets in Kansas City. It again nominates William Jennings Bryan for president. The platform contains strong statements of opposition to imperialism and to trusts; Bryan also insists on a plank supporting free silver, although the issue has lost its importance to many people.

July 25: General Leonard Wood, military governor of Cuba, calls for election of delegates to a constitutional convention.

August 4: An international force of 20,000 sets out for Peking from *Tientsin.*

August 14: International forces in China relieve the siege and rescue foreigners.

September 8: Galveston is hit by a hurricane and tidal wave, devastating the city. To rebuild it the Texas governor appoints a five-man commission with both executive and legislative powers. It is a great success and the commission system of city government is soon adopted as a reform in small and medium-size towns throughout the nation.

September 12: UMW president John Mitchell calls a strike in northeastern Pennsylvania coal fields; nearly 150,000 miners participate. The strike is settled in October; the union wins a 10 percent wage increase but does not win recognition.

November: Britain declares the annexation of the Boer Republics to South Africa. Immediately Afrikaners begin guerrilla warfare. The brutal war will not end until May 1902.

Robert M. LaFollette, a Republican, is elected governor of Wisconsin on a reform platform.

November 5: The Cuban Constitutional Convention begins deliberations in Havana.

November 6: President McKinley easily wins reelection, with Theodore Roosevelt as vice president.

December: Reginald Fessenden, a Canadian-born scientist and engineer working for the U.S. Weather Bureau, demonstrates the possibility of actual voice transmission by radio, making a one-mile transmission from his experiment station in the Potomac River.

December 17: The rebuilt immigration processing center on Ellis Island opens. The impressive main building is fireproof.

December 28: Carry Nation takes her saloon-smashing campaign to the Kansas capital at Wichita.

1901

The war in the Philippines continues.

Florida and Oregon pass direct primary legislation; Minnesota extends its law.

In Oklahoma, the Cherokee and the Creek reach agreement with the Dawes Commission, the last of the Five Civilized Tribes to do so.

January 10: Drillers at Spindletop, near Beaumont, Texas, hit oil. Until capped the well produces nearly 100,000 barrels per day—more than all of the other wells

Andrew Carnegie became the richest man in America in 1900 when he sold Carnegie Steel to J. P. Morgan. Carnegie believed that wealth was a public trust and gave most of his fortune to found libraries and to other philanthropies. *(Library of Congress, Prints and Photographs Division, LC-USZ62-101767)*

in the United States combined. By the end of 1901, 200 wells owned by more than 100 companies have produced more than 17 million barrels and the oil industry has begun to reshape Texas. Prior to 1901 the oil industry centered in Cleveland and northern Pennsylvania.

January 22: In England, Queen Victoria dies, bringing the Victorian Age to an end. She is succeeded by King Edward VII; in England, the years prior to 1913 will be called the Edwardian Era.

February 2: The Army Reorganization Act is passed. It increases the size of the standing army to 90,000, reorganizes all branches, and clarifies command; it also establishes a permanent Army Nurse Corps. Also passed is an Anti-Canteen Law, forbidding the sale of alcoholic beverages on army bases.

March: The formation of the U.S. Steel Corporation is announced to an astonished public. J. P. Morgan has bought out Carnegie and formed a new company capitalized at 1.5 billion. It is the largest corporation in the world and controls about two-thirds of the iron and steel industry.

March 2: President McKinley signs the army appropriations bill; the Platt amendment attached to it demands numerous conditions of Cuba before American troops will be withdrawn.

March 4: President McKinley begins his second term.

March 23: General Frederick Funston and U.S. forces finally capture Aguinaldo. He will soon declare allegiance to the United States and ask insurgents to cease fighting, but some hostilities will continue until July 1902.

May 27: The Supreme Court hands down decisions in the Insular Cases. They declare that the "Constitution does not automatically follow the flag"; Congress can decide on a case-by-case basis how to deal with acquired territories. Fundamental rights, however, cannot be denied to residents of dependencies.

June 12: By a majority of one vote, the Cuban Constitutional Convention accepts American demands in the Platt amendment, although many Cubans have opposed it.

July: Eugene Debs and other socialist-leaning people and groups meet in Indianapolis, forming the Socialist Party of America.

August 29: Carry Nation and her Home Defenders carry the saloon-smashing campaign to New York. It has spread nationwide; traditional temperance advocates welcome the attention to lax law enforcement but are conflicted over her tactics.

September: Minor league baseball organizes, forming the National Association of Professional Base Ball Leagues.

September 6: At the Pan American Exhibition in Buffalo, New York, President McKinley is shot by anarchist Leon Czolgosz. Emergency doctors believe they have repaired the wounds to the president's stomach but do not locate the bullet to remove it. Unknown to them, gangrene will soon spread throughout his body.

September 7: China and the powers sign the Boxer Protocol, an agreement with harsh penalties for the Chinese.

September 14: President McKinley dies from his wounds. Vice President Theodore Roosevelt is sworn in as the 26th and youngest president.

October 16: Booker T. Washington dines at the White House, the first time an African American has done so, with President Roosevelt. The event touches off a furor, especially in the South.

October 29: Leon Czolgosz, speedily tried and convicted for the assassination of President McKinley, is put to death in the electric chair.

November 27: Secretary of War Root announces a new system of army education, capped by a War College to train high-level officers.

December 3: President Roosevelt makes his first Annual Message to Congress; he advocates conservation, becoming the first president to do so, and calls for regulation of business trusts.

December 12: Guglielmo Marconi, a young inventor in the field of radio transmission called wireless telegraphy, which uses Morse code messages, receives the first transatlantic radio transmission at St. John's, Newfoundland. It has been sent some 2,000 miles across the Atlantic ocean from a coworker in his company, based in England.

December 16: The Hay-Pauncefote Treaty is ratified by the Senate.

EYEWITNESS TESTIMONY

There are certain lesser figures characteristic of ward politics known as "heelers." They do the dirty work. As a rule, they prefer to serve the well-established boss, as he can best protect them if they are found out and prosecuted in the execution of their villainy. As a rule, a "heeler" is a broken-down "bum," afraid of work, fond of his cups, in touch with loafers and the semi-criminal class, more of a fox than they, energetic enough in a campaign, possessed of a strong dramatic sense, loving the excitement of ward politics with its dark plots and wire pulling, glad to be lifted into temporary importance by having money to spend on the "boys." . . .

Repeaters are important actors in ward politics. It is a curious fact that there are many men belonging to the loafing and semi-criminal class who, because of their nerve, can repeat at a caucus so deftly that they are regarded as "expert repeaters." They are known to the boss or his heelers, and are often employed in close elections. They of course feel fairly secure under the protection of the boss. One fellow whom I know boasted to me that in a certain election he was driven from ward to ward, changing his disguise occasionally, and voting eight times in the course of the day. On inquiry, I found it was in all probability true.

City politics, as explained by settlement workers at South End House in Boston, Woods, ed., The City Wilderness *(1898), pp. 129, 132.*

Nearly every step brought him into contact with the old regime. For example, the gas company in lighting the streets charged excessive rates, and the more lights there were the more money flowed in. Naturally it had put in as many gas lamps as it could possibly plant. Phelan in one stroke eliminated 600 of them, cutting the gas company's revenue in proportion. For this he was ostracized by the Pacific Union Club, which could not tolerate as a member a man who had torn up 600 gas lamps to save money for the people at the expense of the gas company. . . .

Then Phelan began his fight for a new city charter. He had found that the old charter was inadequate for the reforms he contemplated, and he proposed the election of a Board of Freeholders who would draft a new one. His administration was popular with the people, and their support was behind the plan for a new charter.

The [Southern Pacific] railroad immediately came into the fight with a nominated Board of Freeholders, known as the Martin Kelly Board. . . . *The Bulletin* supported the board nominated by Phelan and it was elected.

The Phelan board drafted the charter, and then came its election. By this time the railroad was really fighting in earnest. The new charter, as drafted, spread political power too much for the Southern Pacific's purposes. It provided for

many commissions—the police commission, election commission, and others—which would be difficult to control.

Fremont Older, editor of the San Francisco Bulletin, *describes Mayor Phelan's battles with the bosses, 1898,* My Own Story, *available online at "California as I Saw It." URL: http://lcweb2.loc.gov/ammem/cbhtml/cbhome.html.*

He had been such a practical businessman that he was worth half a million, a fairly good fortune for our town; but he had not been in office very long before all the business men were down on him, and saying that what the town needed was a business man for mayor, a statement that was destined to ring in my ears for a good many years. They disliked him of course because he would not do just what they told him to—that being the meaning and purpose of a business man for mayor—but insisted that there were certain other people in the city who were entitled to some of his service and consideration—namely, the working people and the poor. The politicians and the preachers objected to him on the same grounds: the unpardonable sin being to express in any but a purely ideal and sentimental form sympathy for the workers or the poor. It seemed to be particularly exasperating that he was doing all this in the name of the Golden Rule, which was for the Sunday-school; and they even went so far as to bring to town another Sam Jones, the Reverend Sam Jones, to conduct a "revival" and to defeat the Honorable Sam Jones. The Reverend Sam Jones had big meetings, and said many clever things, and many true ones, the truest among them being his epigram, "I am for the Golden Rule myself, up to a certain point, and then I want to take the shotgun and the club."

Brand Whitlock, lawyer, novelist, and future mayor of Toledo, describes his mentor Mayor Samuel Jones, ca. 1898, Forty Years of It *(1914), pp. 113–14.*

. . . attention is now called to a certain marked and peculiar economic condition affecting the human race, and unparalleled in the organic world. We are the only animal species in which the female depends on the male for food, the only animal species in which the sex-relation is also an economic relation. With us an entire sex lives in a relation of economic dependence upon the other sex, and the economic relation is combined with the sex-relation. The economic status of the human female is relative to the sex-relation. . . .

In the human species the condition is permanent and general, though there are exceptions, and though the present century is witnessing the beginnings of a great change in this respect. We have not been accustomed to face this fact beyond our loose generalization that it was "natural" . . .

Charlotte Perkins Gilman's widely read, unconventional analysis of women's economic dependence, Women and Economics *(1898), pp. 5–6.*

At Chilcoot Pass, Alaska, a continual stream of stampeders, or gold rushers, head for the Klondike in 1898. Some carried tons of equipment and supplies over the steep pass. *(Library of Congress, Prints and Photographs Division, LC-USZ62-96039)*

On the fourth afternoon when they had traversed something over 100 miles of Arctic wastes, Jim Daugherty left his sled at the entrance to a deep glen . . . [and] broke a path through the heavy snow drifts. . . . After a couple of miles he came suddenly to a small tree, which had been trimmed where it stood down to 4 feet from the ground. The sides near the top had been squared, and on them appeared some words written in pencil.

"This is my south-west stake," said Jim to his companions. "Now, Skiff, go back 500 feet and stake. You, Charley, go up 500 feet and stake; and you can go, Billy, north or south and stake adjoining to Skiff or Charley, as you think best."

The stampeders had all gathered in a group, and watched the proceedings in silence. It was the etiquette of the Klondike that the immediate friends of the discoverer, those who accompanied the sled, had the first privileges next to Discovery on either side. . . . Afterwards, for the rest, it was everyone for himself. . . .

Jim forced his way to the middle of the snowy glen. After looking about a bit, he pushed the snow aside and disclosed a shaft about 5 feet in diameter, filled with snow.

"Boys," he said, "this shaft is 15 feet to bedrock, and from the bottom we ran a little drift about 10 feet as a cross-cut. . . . if it holds out, and runs up and down the creek, we have a Bonanza here."

> *Jeremiah Lynch, a businessman who joined the gold rush in 1898,* Three Years in the Klondike, *pp. 106–07.*

In the first place, my fellow-citizens, we are all aware that this convention has been called by the people of the State of Louisiana principally to deal with one question, and we know that but for the existence of that one question this assemblage would not be sitting here to-day. We know that this convention has been called together by the people of the State to eliminate from the electorate the mass of corrupt and illiterate voters who have during the last quarter of a century degraded our politics. . . .

My fellow-delegates, let us not be misunderstood! Let us say to the large class of the people of Louisiana who will be disfranchised under any of the proposed limitations of the suffrage, that what we seek to do is undertaken in a spirit, not of hostility to any particular men or set of men, but in the belief that the State should see to the protection of the weaker classes; should guard them against the machinations of those who would use them only to further their own base ends; should see to it that they be not allowed to harm themselves. We owe it to the ignorant, we owe it to the weak, to protect them just as we would protect a little child and prevent it from injuring itself with sharp-edged tools placed in its hands.

> *Speaker at the Louisiana Constitutional Convention, convened to find ways to disenfranchise African-American men,* Official Journal of the Proceedings of the Constitutional Convention of the State of Louisiana, 1898, *reprinted in Osofsky,* Burden of Race *(1967), pp. 171–72.*

Steerage No. 1 is virtually in the eyes of the vessel, and runs clear across from one side to the other, without a partition. It is lighted entirely by portholes, under which, fixed to the stringers, are narrow tables with benches before them. The remaining space is filled with iron bunks, row after row, tier upon tier, all running fore and aft in double banks. A thin rod is all that separates one sleeper from another. In each bunk are placed "a donkey's breakfast" (a straw mattress), a blanket of the horse variety, a battered tin plate and pannikin, a knife, a fork, and a spoon. . . .

This steerage, with a capacity of 118, was kept solely for English-speaking males. Directly below it was steerage No. 2, of similar size, intended for foreign males. A little farther aft was steerage No. 3, with accommodations for 172 sleepers. Abaft on the port side, two flights take one down to the "married quarters." The single females are stowed in pockets on both sides of the ship. These, in distinction from the men's quarters, are divided into rooms holding from four to sixteen persons, and have a common room for meals. . . .

I set about to see what deck-room was bestowed upon us. With the exception of the square about the after hatch, we were under cover, and our perambulations were confined to the narrow space on each side of the deck-house, along which ran a narrow, comfortless seat. Limited enough in all conscience, then; but more so when, on the following day, half of it was roped off to keep us from going too near the [first class] passengers' windows. The whole upper and hurricane decks were reserved for our more fortunate shipmates. . . . The steerage is a little world in itself, revolving in an orbit far apart from these more important planets. Occasionally our singing would attract a few of the nabobs above, so that they looked over the rails, and threw down money and oranges and nuts. . . .

Journalist H. Phelps Whitmarsh, a journalist who traveled to the United States in steerage with immigrants from the British Isles and Scandinavia, "The Steerage of To-Day," Century, *vol. 55 (February 1898), pp. 531–32.*

No matter how diverting the evening's entertainment might be, however, it was [the newspaper correspondents'] habit to saunter into the telegraph office before bedtime in order to make certain that their stuff had been forwarded without delay. One of them was chatting with the operators a little before midnight, on February 15th, when this brief bulletin was picked off the wire:

Battleship Maine blown up in Havana harbor. Most of her crew killed. Probably a Spanish plot.

The startled correspondent loped up the street and burst into the Press Club, where he wrecked a poker game. It was like tossing a cannon cracker into the room. The tragic news meant war with Spain. The opinion was unanimous. War was a novelty almost incredible to an American generation which had grown up in happy ignorance of it. In the clamorous discussion the correspondents forgot the sheriff and his panicky deputies who had riddled the marching miners with sawed-off shotguns. Every man was hoping for the summons to proceed posthaste to Havana. The big story was there.

Journalist Ralph D. Paine describes newspaper correspondents covering the trial of peace officers who shot down 70 striking miners in Wilkes-Barre, Pennsylvania, February 15, 1898, in his Roads of Adventure *(1922), p. 187.*

BATTLE SHIP MAINE BLOWN UP IN THE HARBOR OF HAVANA
Terrific Explosion Rends the Magnificent Machine of War and Brings Death to Hundreds of the Brave Fellows Upon Her
Havana, February 15—At 9:45 o'clock this evening a terrible explosion took place on board the United States cruiser Maine in the Havana harbor.

Many sailors were killed or wounded.

The explosion shook the whole city. The windows were broken in many houses.

The wounded sailors of the Maine are unable to explain it. It is believe that the cruiser is totally destroyed.

A correspondent says he has conversed with several of the wounded sailors and understands from them that the explosion took place while they were asleep, so that they can give no particulars as to the cause. . . .
Havana, February 16—The wildest consternation prevails in Havana. The wharves are crowded with thousands of people. It is believed the explosion occurred in a small powder magazine.

The first theory was that there had been a preliminary explosion in the Santa Barbara (magazine) of powder or dynamite below the water.

Admiral Manterola [of Spain] believes that the first explosion was of a grenade that was hurled over the navy yard.

Captain Sigsbee and the other officers have been saved. It is estimated that over 100 of the crew were killed, but it is impossible as yet to give exact details.

Admiral Manterola has ordered that boats of all kinds should go to the assistance of the Maine and her wounded.

The Havana firemen are giving aid, tending carefully to the wounded as they are brought on shore. It is a terrible sight. . . .

At 1:15 the Maine continues burning.

San Francisco Chronicle, *February 16, 1896, p. 1.*

Outside Havana all is changed. It is not peace, nor is it war. It is desolation and distress, misery and starvation. . . .

Torn from their homes, with foul earth, foul air, foul water and foul food, or none, what wonder that one-half have died and that one-quarter of the living are so diseased that they cannot be saved. . . . Little children are still walking about with arms and chests terribly emaciated, eyes swollen, and abdomen bloated to three times the natural size. . . .

Deaths in the streets have not been uncommon. I was told by one of our consuls that people have been found dead about the markets in the morning where they had crawled hoping to get some stray bits of food from the early hucksters, and that there had been cases where they had dropped dead inside the market, surrounded by food. . . .

What I saw I cannot tell so that others can see it. It must be seen with one's own eyes to be realized.

Senator Redfield Proctor, Republican of Vermont, Senate speech on conditions in Cuba, March 17, 1898, Congressional Record, *55th Congress, vol. 37, p. 2917.*

. . . Nowhere in the civilized world save the United States of America do men, possessing all civil and political power, go out in bands of 50 to 5,000 to hunt down, shoot, hang or burn to death a single individual, unarmed and absolutely powerless. . . . To our appeals for justice the stereotyped reply has been that the government could not interfere in a state matter. Postmaster Baker's case was a federal matter, pure and simple. He died at his post of duty in defense of his country's honor, as truly as did ever a soldier on the field of battle. We refuse to believe this country, so powerful to defend its citizens abroad, is unable to protect its citizens at home. Italy and China have been indemnified by this government for the lynching of their citizens. We ask that the government do as much for its own.

> *Ida Wells Barnett, speech to President McKinley,*
> *March 21, 1898, as reported in the* Cleveland Gazette,
> *April 9, 1898, page 1.*

There were two explosions of a distinctly different character, with a very short but distinct interval between them, and the forward part of the ship was lifted to a marked degree at the time of the first explosion. The first explosion was more in the nature of a report, like that of a gun, while the second explosion was more open, prolonged and of greater volume. The second explosion was, in the opinion of the court, caused by the partial explosion of two or more of the forward magazines of the MAINE. . . .

In the opinion of the court, the MAINE was destroyed by the explosion of a submarine mine, which caused the partial explosion of two or more of her forward magazines. . . .

The court has been unable to obtain evidence fixing the responsibility for the destruction of the Maine upon any person or persons.

> *Official Report of the Naval Court of Inquiry into the loss of*
> *the Battleship* Maine, *March 28, 1898, available online at*
> Spanish American War. *URL: http://*
> *www.spanamwar.com/mainerpt.htm.*

I was delighted when we pitched camp on the main street, for I had been afraid C. J. [Berry, her brother-in-law] would pick a place 'way back and I should miss seeing things. Everything was new to me and most exciting. We had one tent for cooking and one for sleeping. . . . I liked Main Street as we were almost opposite a dance hall run by two women, and I'll say that they could take care of themselves. They could dance, sing, swear, play roulette, shake dice and play poker; in fact, they could do almost anything, and as I had never seen anybody like that before, I kept my eyes on their dance hall every minute. Of course, C. J. wouldn't let me go inside the place.

> *Alice Edna Bush Berry, who as a teenager accompanied family*
> *members to Sheep Camp, Alaska, on the Chilkoot Trail, spring*
> *1898, in Berry,* Bushes and the Berrys, *pp. 83–84.*

One of the best fruits of the mission was the handing in of over 2,500 signed promises of total abstinence; eight hundred of these were made by the young men alone. The sermon on intemperance was preached . . . each week, and a card given to each person present . . . and was to be signed and kept at home. . . . In this way a blow direct is delivered against the dominant vice of all city parishes, and it is effected without undue pressure, the signing being done after giving time to think and pray and advise with the "home authorities." The following is the card:

Total Abstinence Promise
Made
At the Mission given by the Paulist Fathers
in Church of St. Paul the Apostle
New York, January, 1898
For the love of God and for the good of my soul, I promise to
abstain from intoxicating drinks.

Name _____

For _____ years.

This card was used . . . to antagonize one of the deadliest foes of the church in our country, the saloon. . . .

> *Rev. Walter Elliott, C. S. P., in his "Story of a Mission,"*
> Catholic World, *vol. 67 (April 1898), pp. 106–07.*

. . . Mr. H. W. Bray sought out Aguinaldo . . . and . . . arranged for an interview between the insurgent leader and Mr. E. Spencer Pratt, consul-general of the United States in Singapore. Two (Aguinaldo says three) interviews were held with great secrecy and formality between these parties. . . . Just exactly what passed between the two principals to the interviews perhaps only the interpreter could tell, as the stories of the principals conflict. Consul-General Pratt reported officially at the time, and has always maintained, that he limited himself to endeavoring to secure the cooperation of Aguinaldo as a leader of insurgents with the American fleet; that this cooperation was, so far as his negotiations went, to be unconditional; and that he declined to discuss the future policy of the United States with regard to the Philippines. Aguinaldo claims that he was promised in these interviews that the United States "would at least recognize the independence of the Philippines under a naval protectorate," and that there was no need for putting the agreement in writing, as he asked, since "the words of Admiral Dewey and the American consul were sacred." The definite outcome of the conferences was that, in response to a cablegram of Mr. Pratt on April 24 that Aguinaldo was ready to come to Hongkong and arrange for "insurgent cooperation," Dewey at once replied: "Tell Aguinaldo come as soon as possible."

> *James A. LeRoy, American diplomat attached to the U.S.*
> *Philippine Commission, describing events of April 1898,*
> Americans in the Philippines, *vol. 1, pp. 180–81.*

The grounds for such intervention may be briefly summarized as follows:

First. In the cause of humanity and to put an end to the barbarities, bloodshed, starvation, and horrible miseries now existing there, and which the parties to the conflict are either unable or unwilling to stop or mitigate. It is no answer to say this is all in another country, belonging to another nation, and is therefore none of our business. It is specially our duty, for it is right at our door.

Second. We owe it to our citizens in Cuba to afford them that protection and indemnity for life and property which no government there can or will afford. . . .

Third. The right to intervene may be justified by the very serious injury to the commerce, trade, and business of our people and by the wanton destruction of property and devastation of the island.

Fourth, and which is of the utmost importance. The present condition of affairs in Cuba is a constant menace to our peace and entails upon this Government an enormous expense. With such a conflict waged for years in an island so near us and with which our people have such trade and business relations; when the lives and liberty of our citizens are in constant danger and their property destroyed and themselves ruined; where our trading vessels are liable to seizure and are seized at our very door by war ships of a foreign nation . . . with the resulting strained relations, are a constant menace to our peace and compel us to keep on a semi-war footing with a nation with which we are at peace.

President William McKinley, war request to Congress, April 11, 1898, in Richardson, ed., Messages and Papers, *vol. 10, pp. 147–48.*

Whereas the abhorrent conditions which have existed for more than three years in the Island of Cuba, so near our own borders, have shocked the moral sense of the people of the United States, have been a disgrace to Christian civilization, culminating, as they have, in the destruction of a United States battleship with two hundred and sixty-six of its officers and crew, while on a friendly visit in the harbor of Havana, and can not longer be endured. . . .

Resolved, First. That the people of the Island of Cuba are, and of right ought to be, free and independent.

Second. That it is the duty of the United States to demand, and the Government of the United States does hereby demand, that the Government of Spain at once relinquish its authority and government in the Island of Cuba and withdraw its land and naval forces from Cuba and Cuban waters.

Third. That the President of the United States be, and he hereby is, directed and empowered to use the entire land and naval forces of the United States, and to call into the actual service of the United States the militia of the several States, to such extent as may be necessary to carry these resolutions into effect.

Fourth. That the United States hereby disclaims any disposition or intention to exercise sovereignty, jurisdiction, or control over said Island except for the pacification thereof, and asserts its determination, when that is accomplished, to leave the government and control of the Island to its people.

Joint Congressional Resolution of War, April 19, 1898 (the fourth resolution is known as the Teller Amendment), U.S. Statutes at Large, *55th Congress, vol. 30, p. 738.*

. . . I doubt whether in the midst of any battle the nervous tension of officers and men was greater than on this night, as we entered the harbor of Manila. Not a light could be seen as the Olympia steamed slowly into the broad channel between the islands of Corregidor and El Fraile. Dark and grim the Spanish fortifications loomed on either side, and it seemed well-nigh hopeless that we should escape observation. . . . [S]uddenly from the summit of Corregidor, six hundred feet above us, leaped a rocket, and its blazing course lighted up the heavens. Instantly an answering signal came from the opposite fort, and a moment later the boom of great guns from the south shore showed that the Spaniards were aroused and knew that the enemy was at their gates.

Magical was the change in the bearing of the men on the Olympia. They sprang to the guns, eager to reply to the Spanish challenge, but Commodore Dewey forbade any firing. . . .

. . . We made a wide circle and came round opposite the city of Manila and down toward Cavite fortress, from which the red-and-yellow colors of Spain were proudly flying. At first we could not make out the Spanish fleet, and feared that it had really escaped; but a few minutes later we descried the flags fluttering from the vessels as they lay in a half-circle in Bakor Bay, just back of Cavite. On the Olympia the men stood at their guns with set teeth and the smile that one sees so often on the faces of men in the prize-ring.

When seven miles away puffs of smoke and roar of guns showed that the forts had begun their fire on us. But the shells did not reach, and the fleet sailed on without reply. Still silent, the Olympia drew near until she was only forty-four hundred yards away from fort and fleet. Then the roar of one of her forward eight-inch guns was the signal that the fight had opened.

Dr. Charles P. Kindleberger, junior surgeon aboard the Olympia, *describes May 1, 1898, in "The Battle of Manila,"* Century Magazine, *vol. 56 (August 1898), pp. 621–22.*

Sec. 3. He [the voter] shall be able to read and write, and shall demonstrate his ability to do so when he applies for registration, by making, under oath administered by the registration officer or his deputy, written application therefor. . . .

Sec. 4. If he be not able to read and write, . . . then he shall be entitled to register and vote if he shall, at the time he offers to register, be the bona fide owner of property assessed to him in this State at a valuation of not less than three hundred dollars. . . .

Sec. 5. No male person who was on January 1st, 1867, or at any date prior thereto, entitled to vote under the Constitution or statutes of any State of the United States, wherein he then resided, and no son or grandson of any such person not less than twenty–one years of age at the date of the adoption of this Constitution, and no male person of foreign birth, who was naturalized prior to the first day of January, 1898, shall be denied the right to register and vote in this State by reason of his failure to possess the educational or property qualifications prescribed by this Constitution. . . .

Article 197, constitution of the State of Louisiana, adopted May 12, 1898; Sec. 5 is known as the grandfather clause, in Fleming, ed., Documentary History of Reconstruction, *pp. 451–52.*

Captain Lee and I went out to the volunteer camps today . . . and it has depressed me very much. . . . nothing our men wear is right. The shoes, the hats, the coats, all are dangerous to health and comfort; one-third of the men can-not wear the regulation shoe because it cuts the instep, and buy their own, and the volunteers are like the Cuban army in appearance . . . One colonel of the Florida regiment told us that one-third of his men had never fired a gun. They live on the ground; there are no rain trenches around the tents, or gutters along the company streets; the latrines are dug to *windward* of the camp, and all the refuse is burned to windward.

Half of the men have no uniforms nor shoes. I pointed out some of the unnecessary discomforts the men were undergoing through ignorance, and one colonel, a Michigan politician, said, "Oh, well, they'll learn. It will be a good lesson for them." . . .

. . . I have written nothing for the paper, because, if I started to tell the truth at all, it would do no good, and it would open up a hell of an outcry from all the families of the boys who have volunteered. . . . It is the sacrifice of the innocents. . . . It seems almost providential that we had this false-alarm call with Spain to show the people how utterly helpless they are.

Journalist Richard Harding Davis, on assignment for the New York Journal, *with soldiers in Tampa awaiting shipment to Cuba, letter to his brother Charles, May 29, 1898,* Adventures and Letters, *pp. 241–44.*

A great rush of water came up the gangway, seething and gurgling out of the deck. The mass was whirling from right to left "against the sun:" it seized us and threw us against the bulwarks, then over the rail. Two were swept forward as if by a momentary recession, and one was carried down into a coal-bunker—luckless Kelly. In a moment, however, with increased force, the water shot him out of the same hole and swept him among us. The bulwarks disappeared. A sweeping vortex whirled above. We charged about with casks, cans, and spars, the incomplete stripping having left quantities on the deck. The life preservers stood us in good stead, preventing chests from being crushed, as well as buoying us on the surface; for spars came end on like battering rams, and the sharp corners of the tin cans struck us heavily.

Naval Constructor (architect) Richmond Pearson Hobson describes the deliberate sinking of a U.S. ship to block Santiago Harbor, June 3, 1898, which made him a national hero, in The Sinking of the "Merrimac," *pp. 74–75.*

The first column, the Rough Riders, was the first to strike the enemy in ambush . . . receiving a volley that would have routed anybody but an American. The first regulars, hearing the music as they called it, hurried forward to join in the dance, and awoke a hornet's nest of Spaniards on the left, north of the party engaging the Rough Riders, and had more music than they could furnish dancers for. But, to the credit of the uniform and the flag, there is no account of either column giving an inch. They advanced sufficiently to come into line, and holding their ground until the much abused and poorly appreciated sons of Ham [African-American soldiers] burst through the underbrush, delivered several volleys and yelling . . . advanced on a run. . . . [T]he Spaniards . . . could not stand it any longer, but broke and ran. . . .

Corporal John R. Conn, 24th Infantry, describes the battle at Siboney, Cuba, June 23, 1898, letter in the Evening Star, Washington D.C., *in Gatewood,* "Smoked Yankees" (1971), *pp. 66–67.*

The nurses quartered in an old Spanish house in Coamo, located in a banana grove. We drove to camp in mule ambulances. Put in long hours. . . . Sick men from 3rd Wisconsin, 16th Pennsylvania, and 3rd Kentucky Regiments cared for by Army Nurses. All water for any purpose hauled in barrels from a spring more than a mile away. Tents crowded, typhoid fever, dysentery and diarrhea, conditions bad, no ice, no diet kitchen.

Journal of army nurse, field hospital in Coamo, Puerto Rico, July 1898, available online at Army Nurse Corps History. URL: http://history.amedd.army.mil/ ANCWebsite/chrono.htm.

April 24, 1898: The 24th Infantry, an African-American unit, marches down the broad streets of Salt Lake City, Utah, to the railroad station. They were leaving their usual posting in the American West en route to Cuba and the Spanish-American War. *(Library of Congress, Prints and Photographs Division, LC-USZ62-119984)*

. . . the trail became steeper, the air warmer, and footholds without support impossible. I shed my sealskin jacket. I cursed my hot, high buckram collar, my tight heavily boned corsets, my long corduroy skirt, my full bloomers, which I had to hitch up with every step. We clung to stunted pines, spruce roots, jutting rocks. In some places the path was so narrow that, to move at all, we had to use our feet tandem fashion. Above, only the granite walls. Below, death leering at us . . .

Then my foot slips! I lose my balance. I fall only a few feet into a crevice in the rocks. The sharp edge of one cuts through my boot and I feel the flesh of my leg throbbing with pain. . . . George [her brother] becomes impatient. "For God's sake, Polly, buck up and be a man! Have some style and move on!" . . .

Then the descent! Down ever downward. Weight of body on shaky legs, weight growing heavier, and legs shakier. Sharp rocks to scratch our clutching hands. Snake-like roots to trip our stumbling feet. . . .

I had felt that I could make no greater effort in my life than the last part of the upward climb, but the last two miles into Lindeman was the most excruciating struggle of the whole trip. . . . The trail led through a scrub pine forest where we tripped over bare roots of trees that curled over and around rocks and boulders like great devilfishes. Rocks! Rocks! Rocks! Tearing boots to pieces. Hands bleeding with scratches. . . .

Martha Black, a Chicago woman who crossed the Chilkoot Pass, July 1898, in her My Ninety Years, *pp. 28–30.*

I started in the rear of the regiment, the position in which the colonel should theoretically stay. . . .

I soon found that I could get that line, behind which I personally was, faster forward than the one immediately in front of it, with the result that the two rearmost lines of the regiment began to crowd together; so I rode through them both, the better to move on the one in front. This happened with every line in succession, until I found myself at the head of the regiment. . . .

The Ninth Regiment was immediately in front of me, and the First on my left, and these went up Kettle Hill with my regiment. The Third, Sixth, and Tenth went partly up Kettle Hill (following the Rough Riders and the Ninth and First), and partly between that and the block-house hill, which the infantry were assailing. General Sumner in person gave the Tenth the order to charge the hills; and it went forward at a rapid gait. The three regiments went forward more or less intermingled, advancing steadily and keeping up a heavy fire. Up Kettle Hill Sergeant George Berry, of the Tenth, bore not only his own regimental colors but those of the Third, the color-sergeant of the Third having been shot down; he kept shouting, "Dress on the colors, boys, dress on the colors!" as he followed Captain Ayres, who was running in advance of his men, shouting and waving his hat. . . .

I spoke to the captain in command of the rear platoons, saying that I had been ordered to support the regulars in the attack upon the hills, and that in my judgment we could not take these hills by firing at them, and that we must rush them. He answered that his orders were to keep his men lying where they were, and that he could not charge without orders. I asked where the Colonel was, and as he was not in sight, said, "Then I am the ranking officer here and I give the order to charge"—for I did not want to keep the men longer in the open suffering under a fire which they could not effectively return. Naturally the Captain hesitated to obey this order when no word had been received from his own Colonel. So I said, "Then let my men through, sir," and rode on through the lines, followed by the grinning Rough Riders. . . .

Theodore Roosevelt describes the charge up Kettle Hill, July 1, 1898, in his Rough Riders, *pp. 126–30.*

Late in the afternoon [a mule-drawn] ambulance arrived. The surgeon in charge of it picked out the more serious cases, including me among them. My old friend Ducat, of the Twenty-fourth, with a wound in the abdomen, was laid on his back in the bottom of the vehicle. Another officer was stretched out on one of the seats, his head resting in the lap of the surgeon. On the same seat with me sat Captain Fornance, of the Thirteenth Infantry, with a mortal wound through the body. As we were slowly drawn over

This famous photo shows Colonel Theodore Roosevelt and his Rough Riders atop San Juan Hill, Cuba. The Rough Riders were a mixture of eastern Ivy League graduates, western cowboys, and Native Americans. *(Library of Congress, Prints and Photographs Division, LC-USZ62-7626)*

the rough road to the Division Hospital, about two miles distant, I was moved with sympathy and admiration for the wounded men I saw trudging along. There was nothing on wheels to carry them, not even an army wagon . . .

We reached the hospital after dark. I was the first to get out of the ambulance. As I hobbled up to one of the operating-tents the table, covered with white oil-cloth, was being sponged off. The sponge was thrown into a bucket of bloody water, the surgeon called "Next," and I stepped in. . . . The ground about the tent was strewn with wounded men lying on it, among whom other men, mostly wounded, were moving or standing. I lay down on the grass, and tried to go to sleep. . . . most of the wounded soldiers spent the night under the open sky, without blankets, and with nothing to eat.

Capt. John Bigelow, Jr., a white officer of the 10th Cavalry wounded at San Juan Hill, July 1, 1898, Reminiscences of the Santiago Campaign, *pp. 142–44.*

Whereas the Government of the Republic of Hawaii having, in due form, signified its consent . . . to cede absolutely and without reserve to the United States of America all rights of sovereignty of whatsoever kind . . ., and also to cede and transfer to the United States the absolute fee and ownership of all public, Government, or Crown lands, public buildings or edifices, ports, harbors, military equipment, and all other public property of every kind and description belonging to the Government of the Hawaiian Islands . . . Therefore

Resolved by the Senate and House of Representatives of the United States of America in Congress Assembled, That said cession is accepted, ratified, and confirmed, and that the said Hawaiian Islands and their dependencies be, and they are hereby, annexed as a part of the territory of the United States and are subject to the sovereign dominion thereof. . . .

Joint Resolution to Provide for Annexing the Hawaiian Islands to the United States, July 7, 1898, U.S. Statutes at Large, 55th Congress, vol. 30, pp. 750–51.

. . . neither I nor any other Puerto Rican patriot and republican would like to see the American people violate their mission as a great democratic nation by forcing our native island to become a dependency of the United States, instead of assisting it to shake off the yoke of its Spanish oppressors and then leave it to build up its own independent government and work out its own destiny. . . .

Let them establish over all their conquered territory not a protectorate, that is too much on the order of sovereignty, but rather a mentorate, backed by a show of actual interest. . . .

Eugenio María de Hostos, famous Puerto Rican writer, educator, and patriot, in America to request his island be permitted to vote on its destiny, quoted in "Señor E. M. Hostos Talks," New York Times, *July 22, 1898, p. 2.*

Upon arrival, was told by the Commanding Officer— "There is nothing for women to do on a military base, no quarters, no mess; in plain words, 'you are not wanted.'" . . . A tent hospital was set up consisting of four tents placed together—this housed 100 men ill with typhoid. Equipment consisted of twenty cots, one hand basin, one water pail and dipper, one bed pan, a stand by each cot, a corps man, no training. Many of these men had lain in the mud before sailing from Puerto Rica, rolled in a blanket; mud and filth had hardened on the men until separating man and blanket was almost impossible. They were soaked on rubber sheets, and a scrubbing brush was used for lack of adequate equipment.

The hard and conscientious work of the nurses and the recovery of the men proved there was definitely a place in the Army for nurses. Major DeWitt apologized for his curt reception and became most cooperative and interested in the nursing work.

Diary of Anna Turner, army nurse who arrived at Fortress Monroe, Virginia, September 1898, quoted in Sarnecky, History of the Army Nurse Corps, *p. 39.*

The attempt to divert the thoughts and interest of the American people from the wrongs that need attention at home, by occupying them with foreign complications of any kind, is criminal folly. The idea that we shall escape the duties which we owe to the people by becoming a nation of conquerors, is clearly in the minds of prominent advocates of "expansion" and "imperialism." They have indicated that they hope to see changes in our boundaries, talk of alliances and wars, and perhaps war and conquests, all to keep the workers and the lovers of reforms and simple justice diverted and powerless to dig out abuses and cure existing injustice. . . . Imperialism points to large armaments and more frequent wars. It means greater demands upon the workers in taxes, blood, and life. It tends to the more frequent and unblushing use of force against the weak and lowly. It subordinates right and justice to an unwise or blind greed of gain, and the exploitation of islands whose millions are to be made the tools, willing or unwilling, of the few thousand. And this is what some men call a cure for social unrest!

Samuel Gompers, head of the American Federation of Labor (AFL), "Address to the Chicago Civic Federation's National Conference on Foreign Policy," published in American Federationist, *Sept. 1898, Samuel Gompers Papers, vol. 5, p. 140.*

Tuesday, November 8: Started hole, dug a foot. All the other boys started too.
Wednesday, November 9: Working at hole; sunk 2 feet.
Wednesday, November 16: Working at hole, picking the muck. . . .
Wednesday, November 23: Working in hole, down about 20 feet. 42 below zero.
Thursday, November 24: THANKSGIVING: I worked in hole part of day. Had moose roast, plum pudding, cranberry sauce, potatoes etc., for dinner. . . .

Diary of New York native Charles Mosier, age 17, mining in the Klondike, 1898, available online at Center for the Study of the Pacific Northwest. URL: http:// www.washington.edu/uwired/outreach/cspn/ curklon/klondoc060.html.

The common ownership of natural resources follows a clear line of Christian teaching from the beginning of that teaching with Jesus Christ. Nearly all His statements of religious principles are in terms of human relations; and His idea was altogether more communistic than we care to discover. Reduced to economic terms, the realization of His ideal of the kingdom of Heaven could mean nothing less than an all-inclusive, non-exclusive communism of opportunity, use, and service. It may be a debatable matter whether any form of communism is practicable; but it is not open to question that Jesus never contemplated anything else than an organization of human life in which all men should work together for the common good. . . .

George D. Herron, Christian socialist, lecture to the Christian Citizenship League of Chicago, November 14, 1898, Between Caesar and Jesus, *p. 105.*

At a banquet in Paris American citizens celebrated and offered toasts, the first one, "Here's to the United States, bounded on the north by Canada, on the south by Mexico, on the east by the Atlantic Ocean, on the west by the Pacific." The second speaker: "In view of what President McKinley has termed manifest destiny and in consideration of the vast new responsibilities that loom before our country, I offer the toast: To the United States, bounded on the north by the North Pole, on the south by the South Pole, on the east by the rising sun, on the west by the setting sun." The third speaker: "With all due humility in view of the staggering tasks our country faces across the future, I would offer the toast: To the United States, bounded on the north by the Aurora Borealis, on the south by the Precession of the Equinoxes, on the east by Primeval Chaos, on the west by the Day of Judgment." It was a small war edging toward immense consequences.

Poet Carl Sandburg, who saw service in Puerto Rico, describes reaction to the Treaty of Paris, December 1898, in his autobiography, Always the Young Strangers, *p. 419.*

. . . the military commander of the United States is enjoined to make known to the inhabitants of the Philippine Islands that in succeeding to the sovereignty of Spain, in severing the former political relations of the inhabitants and in establishing a new political power, the authority of the United States is to be exerted for the security of the persons and property of the people of the islands and for the confirmation of all their private rights and relations. It will be the duty of the commander of the forces of occupation to announce and proclaim in the most public manner that we come not as invaders or conquerors, but as friends, to protect the natives in their homes, in their employments, and in their personal and religious rights. All persons who, either by active aid or by honest submission, co-operate with the government of the United States to give effect to these beneficial purposes, will receive the reward of its support and protection. All others will be brought within the lawful rule we have assumed, with firmness if need be, but without severity so far as may be possible.

President William McKinley to the secretary of war, Sovereignty Proclamation for the Philippines, December 21, 1898, published in the Philippines, January 4, 1899, in Welsh, The Other Man's Country (1900), *pp. 243–44.*

When I first became familiar with the principles of the initiative and referendum I was impressed with a sense of their value. The more I study these principles the more I am convinced that they will furnish us the missing link—the means needed—to make popular self-government do its best. Programs and reforms will then come as fast as the people need them, as fast as these changes are safe—only when a majority of the people are behind them. I would rather have the complete initiative and referendum adopted in state and nation than the most ideal political party that could be made, put into power, if one or the other could be secured.

Lars A. Ueland, Populist member of the North Dakota state legislature that passed initiative and referendum in 1899, quoted in Cronin, Direct Democracy (1989), *p. 46.*

Blacksmithing is my trade. And it has always given colour to my view of things. For example, when I was very young, I saw some of the evils in the conditions of life and I wanted to fix them. I couldn't. There were no tools. We had tools to do almost anything within the shop, beautiful tools, wonderful. And so in other trades, arts and professions; in everything but government. In government, the common trade of all men and the basis of all social life, men worked still with old tools, with old laws, with constitutions and charters which hindered more than they helped. Men suffered from this. There were lawyers enough; many of our ablest men were lawyers. Why didn't some of them invent legislative implements to help the people govern themselves? Why had we no tool makers for democracy?

William S. U'ren, reformer in the Oregon campaign for initiative and recall, adopted 1899–1902, quoted in Cronin, Direct Democracy (1989), *p. 49.*

Before 1899 the coal fields of Pennsylvania were not organized. Immigrants poured into the country and they worked cheap. There was always a surplus immigrant labor, solicited in Europe by the coal companies, so as to keep wages down to the barest living. Hours of work down under ground were cruelly long. Fourteen hours a day was not uncommon, thirteen, twelve. The life or limb of the miner was unprotected by any laws. Families lived in company owned shacks that were not fit for their pigs. Children died by the hundreds due to the ignorance and poverty of their parents. . . .

The United Mine Workers decided to organize these fields and work for human conditions for human beings. Organizers were put to work. Whenever the spirit of the men in the mines grew strong enough, a strike was called.

Mary "Mother" Jones, a labor organizer, describes conditions among coal miners in eastern Pennsylvania, 1899, Autobiography of Mother Jones, *p. 30.*

It shall be the special object of the National Consumers' League to secure adequate investigation of the conditions under which goods are made, in order to enable purchasers to distinguish in favor of goods made in the well-ordered factory. The majority of employers are virtually helpless to maintain a high standard as to hours, wages and working conditions under the stress of competition, unless sustained by the co-operation of consumers. . . . The National Consumers' League further recognizes and declares the following:

That the interests of the community demand that all workers shall receive fair living wages, and that goods shall be produced under sanitary conditions.

That the responsibility for some of the worst evils from which producers suffer rests with the consumers who seek the cheapest markets, regardless how cheapness is brought about.

That it is, therefore, the duty of consumers to find out under what conditions the articles they purchase are produced and distributed, and insist that these conditions shall be wholesome and consistent with a respectable existence on the part of the workers.

Constitution of the National Consumers' League, organized 1899, The Consumer's Control of Production, *p. 5.*

. . . [T]wo propositions are really amazing: First, that we have turned over to those men who work with their hands the fulfillment of certain obligations which we must acknowledge belong to all of us, such as protecting little children from premature labor, and obtaining shorter hours for the overworked; and, second, that while the trades unions, more than any other body, have secured orderly legislation for the defense of the feeblest, they are persistently misunderstood and harshly criticised by many people who are themselves working for the same ends. . . .

That all its citizens may be responsible is, then, perhaps the final reason why it should be the mission of the state to regulate the conditions of industry. . . . It may certainly be regarded as the duty of the whole to readjust the social machinery in such a way that . . . there shall be a moral continuity to society answering to its industrial development. This is the attempt of factory legislation.

Jane Addams, "Trade Unions and Public Duty," American Journal of Sociology, *vol. 4 (January 1899), pp. 448, 460.*

From the foregoing survey of the growth of conspicuous leisure and consumption, it appears that the utility of both alike for the purposes of reputability lies in the element of waste that is common to both. In the one case it is a waste of time and effort, in the other it is a waste of goods. Both are methods of demonstrating the possession of wealth. . . .

It is also noticeable that the serviceability of consumption as a means of repute . . ., as well as the insistence on it as an element of decency, is at its best in those portions of the community where the human contact of the individual is the widest and the mobility of the population is the greatest. . . . The exigencies of the modern industrial system frequently place individuals and households in juxtaposition between whom there is little contact in any other sense than that of juxtaposition. One's neighbors, mechani-

cally speaking, often are socially not one's neighbors, or even acquaintances; and still their transient good opinion has a high degree of utility. The only practicable means of impressing one's pecuniary ability on these unsympathetic observers of one's everyday life is an unremitting demonstration of ability to pay. . . . In order to impress these transient observers, and to retain one's self-complacency under their observation, the signature of one's pecuniary strength should be written in characters which he who runs may read. It is evident, therefore, that the present trend . . . is in the direction of heightening the utility of conspicuous consumption. . . .

Economist Thorstein Veblen invents the term conspicuous consumption, *in his* Theory of the Leisure Class *(1899), pp. 85–87.*

I watched the crowds at their play where Seward Park is to be. The Outdoor Recreation League had put up gymnastic apparatus, and the dusty square was jammed with a mighty multitude. It was not an ideal spot, for it had not rained in weeks, and powdered sand and cinders had taken wing and floated like a pall over the perspiring crowd. But it was heaven to them. A hundred men and boys stood in line, waiting their turn upon the bridge ladder and the travelling rings, that hung full of struggling and squirming humanity, groping madly for the next grip. No failure, no rebuff, discouraged them. Seven boys and girls rode with looks of deep concern—it is their way—upon each end of the seesaw, and two squeezed into each of the forty swings that had room for one, while a hundred counted time and saw that none had too much. It is an article of faith with these children that nothing that is "going" for their benefit is to be missed. . . . The sight of these little ones swarming over a sand heap until scarcely an inch of it was in sight, and gazing in rapt admiration at the poor show of a dozen geraniums and English ivy plants on the windowsill of the overseer's cottage, was pathetic in the extreme. They stood for ten minutes at a time, resting their eyes upon them. In the crowd were aged women and bearded men with the inevitable Sabbath silk hat, who it seemed could never get enough of it. They moved slowly, when crowded out, looking back many times at the enchanted spot, as long as it was in sight.

Playground advocate Jacob Riis describes the 1899 opening of Seward Park on New York's Lower East Side, The Battle with the Slum, *pp. 302–04.*

It is too late to argue about advantages of industrial combinations. They are a necessity. . . .

Their chief advantages are: (1) command of necessary capital; (2) extension of limits of business; (3) increase of number of persons interested in the business; (4) economy in the business; (5) improvements and economies which are derived from knowledge of many interested persons of wide experience; (6) power to give the public improved products at less prices and still make a profit for stockholders; (7) permanent work and good wages for laborers. . . .

I speak from my experience in the business with which I have been intimately connected for about forty years.

John D. Rockefeller, testimony before the U.S. Industrial Commission assigned to investigate trusts, 1899, Preliminary Report on Trusts and Industrial Combinations, *p. 795.*

The great foe of democracy now and in the near future is plutocracy. Every year that passes brings out this antagonism more distinctly. It is to be the social war of the twentieth century. In that war militarism, expansion and imperialism will all favor plutocracy. In the first place, war and expansion will favor jobbery, both in the dependencies and at home. In the second place, they will take away the attention of the people from what the plutocrats are doing. In the third place, they will cause large expenditures of the people's money, the return for which will not go into the treasury, but into the hands of a few schemers. In the fourth place, they will call for a large public debt and taxes, and these things especially tend to make men unequal, because any social burdens bear more heavily on the weak than on the strong, and so make the weak weaker and the strong stronger. Therefore expansion and imperialism are a grand onslaught on democracy.

Professor William Graham Sumner's lecture at Yale University, "Conquest of the U.S. By Spain," January 16, 1899, and published in the Yale Law Review, War and Other Essays, *pp. 325–26.*

There is not a civilized nation which does not talk about its civilizing mission just as grandly as we do. The English, who really have more to boast of in this respect than anybody else, talk least about it, but the Phariseeism with which they correct and instruct other people has made them hated all over the globe. The French believe themselves the guardians of the highest and purest culture, and that the eyes of all mankind are fixed on Paris, whence they expect oracles of thought and taste. The Germans regard themselves as charged with a mission, especially to us Americans, to save us from egoism and materialism. The Russians, in their books and newspapers, talk about the civilizing mission of Russia in language that might be translated from some of the finest paragraphs in our imperialistic newspapers. The first principle of Mohammedanism is that we Christians are dogs and infidels, fit only to be enslaved or butchered by Moslems. It is a corollary that wherever Mohammedanism extends it carries, in the belief of its votaries, the highest blessings, and that the whole human race would be enormously elevated if Mohammedanism should supplant Christianity everywhere.

To come, last, to Spain, the Spaniards have, for centuries, considered themselves the most zealous and self-sacrificing Christians, especially charged by the Almighty, on this account, to spread true religion and civilization over the globe. . . .

We assume that what we like and practice, and what we think better, must come as a welcome blessing to [Cubans, Puerto Ricans,] and Filipinos. This is grossly and obviously untrue. They hate our ways. They are hostile to our ideas. Our religion, language, institutions, and manners offend them. They like their own ways, and if we appear amongst them as rulers, there will be social discord in all the great departments of social interest.

The most important thing which we shall inherit from the Spaniards will be the task of suppressing rebellions. . . .

William Graham Sumner, "Conquest of the U.S. By Spain," January 16, 1899, War and Other Essays, *pp. 297, 303–05.*

Take up the White Man's burden—
    Send forth the best ye breed—
Go, bind your sons to exile
    To serve your captives' need;
To wait, in heavy harness,
    On fluttered folk and wild—
Your new-caught sullen peoples,
    Half devil and half child. . . .

Take up the White Man's burden,
    And reap his old reward—
The blame of those ye better
    The hate of those ye guard. . . .

Rudyard Kipling, "The White Man's Burden," McClure's Magazine, *vol. 12 (February 1899), pp. 290–91.*

The Nebraska regiment, posted on the high ground at Santa Mesa, was about one mile in advance of the lines held by the rest of our troops. And it now appears this point was beyond the limits assigned the United States under the terms of the protocol, which only gave us the right to occupy the bay, harbor, and city of Manila. At eight o'clock in the evening [Private William] Grayson was again on guard, when near him the same [insurgent] Filipino officer, who had disputed with him in the morning, endeavored to cross the American lines. Grayson stated to A. L. Mumper [of the Idaho regiment] that he challenged the Filipino twice, calling, "Halt! Halt!" The man answered, "Alto, alto," presumably in contempt. Grayson then fired, killing him. He then retired to Block-House No. 7, and reported to the sergeant on duty there what he had done. He was sent back to the line with a squad of men. Two or three more Filipinos were found crossing the line. Our soldiers fired upon them, either killing or wounding some.

This occurred, according to Grayson's statement, about fifteen minutes after the first shot had been fired. This encounter was followed by general firing from the Filipino lines. But it is evident that no attack had been anticipated by them, and that their assault on us was naturally provoked by the shooting of their men. Private Grayson was, of course, simply acting under orders.

Description of the event that touched off the Philippine War, February 4, 1899, Welsh, The Other Man's Country *(1900), p. 115.*

Take up the White Man's burden.
Send forth your sturdy kin,
And load them down with Bibles
And cannon-balls and gin. . . .

They need our labor question, too,
And politics and fraud,
We've made a pretty mess at home;
Let's make a mess abroad.

Anti-imperialist Ernest Crosby, "The Real 'White Man's Burden,'" the best-known parody of Kipling, first published in the New York Times, *February 15, 1899, in his* Swords and Ploughshares, *pp. 32–35.*

. . . it shall not be lawful to throw, discharge, or deposit, or cause, suffer, or procure to be thrown, discharged, or deposited either from or out of any ship, barge, or other floating craft of any kind, or from the shore, wharf, manufacturing establishment, or mill of any kind, any refuse matter of any kind or description whatever other than that flowing from streets and sewers and passing therefrom in a liquid state, into any navigable water of the United States, or into any tributary of any navigable water from which the same shall float or be washed into such navigable water. . . .

Section 13, Rivers and Harbors Act, U.S. Statutes at Large, 55th Congress, Vol. 30, Part 2, March 3, 1899, p. 1152.

I preach to you, then, my countrymen, that our country calls not for the life of ease but for the life of strenuous endeavor. The twentieth century looms before us big with the fate of many nations. If we stand idly by, if we seek merely swollen, slothful ease and ignoble peace, if we shrink from the hard contests where men must win at hazard of their lives and at the risk of all they hold dear, then the bolder and stronger peoples will pass us by, and will win for themselves the domination of the world. Let us therefore boldly face the life of strife, resolute to do our duty well and manfully; resolute to uphold righteousness by deed and by word; resolute to be both honest and brave, to serve high ideals, yet to use practical methods. Above all, let us shrink from no strife, moral or physical, within or without the nation, provided we are certain that the strife is justified, for it is only through strife, through hard and dangerous endeavor, that we shall ultimately win the goal of true national greatness.

Theodore Roosevelt, "The Strenuous Life," famous speech to the Hamilton Club of Chicago, April 10, 1899, Theodore Roosevelt, An American Mind, *p. 189.*

Sam Hose, the Negro murderer . . . was burned at the stake one mile and a quarter from this place this afternoon at 2:30 o'clock. Fully 2,000 people surrounded the small sapling to which he was fastened and watched the flames eat away his flesh, saw his body mutilated by knives and witnessed the contortions of his body in his extreme agony.

Such suffering has seldom been witnessed, and through it all the Negro uttered hardly a cry. During the contortions of his body several blood vessels bursted. The spot selected was an ideal one for such an affair, and the stake was in full view of those who stood about and with unfeigned satisfaction saw the Negro meet his death and saw him tortured before the flames killed him.

A few smoldering ashes scattered about the place, a blackened stake, are all that is left to tell the story. Not even the bones of the Negro were left in the place, but were eagerly snatched by a crowd of people drawn here from all directions, who almost fought over the burning body of the man, carving it with knives and seeking souvenirs of the occurrence.

Lynching, Newman, Georgia, described in the Atlanta Constitution, *April 24, 1899, reprinted in Wells-Barnett,* Lynch Law in Georgia, *available online at African American Perspectives. URL: http://memory.loc.gov/ammem/aap/aaphome.html.*

A study of nationalities likewise shows a great diversity, but it is a diversity in which the different nationalities almost invariably keep the same rank. Thus, whether we study the paupers in almshouses or the applicants for aid from the charity organization societies, the Irish yield the largest percentage of cases due to liquor; the Italians, Russians, Austrians, and Poles, the smallest. Between these two extremes the native-born Americans fall midway, being, as a rule, more addicted to liquor than the Germans and Scandinavians, but less so than the English, Canadians, and Scotch. The colored race, however, as compared with the white, shows a good record. Uniformly, the Negroes return fewer cases of poverty and pauperism due to liquor than the whites. . . .

. . . The saloon naturally varies with the character and nationality of the population which surrounds it . . . but that it supplies many wants besides the craving for intoxicants is seen in the fact that saloons flourish even among such races as the Jews, who are exceptionally temperate in the use of stimulants.

Henry Farman reporting for the Committee of Fifty, "Some Economic Aspects of the Liquor Problem." Atlantic Monthly, *vol. 83 (May 1899), pp. 649–50.*

To all this was added a new trouble,—the Fear of the North. This Fear was the joint child of the Great Cold and the Great Silence, and was born in the darkness of December, when the sun dipped below the southern horizon for good. It affected them according to their natures. Weatherbee fell prey to the grosser superstitions, and did his best to resurrect the spirits which slept in the forgotten graves. It was a fascinating thing, and in his dreams they came to him from out of the cold, and snuggled into his blankets, and told him of their toils and troubles ere they died. He shrank away from the clammy contact as they drew closer and twined their frozen limbs about him, and when they whispered in his ear of things to come, the cabin rang with his frightened shrieks. . . .

His own malady assumed a less concrete form. The mysterious artisan who had laid the cabin, log by log, had pegged a wind-vane to the ridge-pole. Cuthfert noticed it always pointed south, and one day, irritated by its steadfastness of purpose, he turned it toward the east. He watched eagerly, but never a breath came by to disturb it. Then he turned the vane to the north, swearing never again to touch it till the wind did blow. But the air frightened him with its unearthly calm, and he often rose in the middle of the night to see if the vane had veered,—ten degrees would have satisfied him. But no, it poised above him as unchangeable as fate.

"In a Far Country," short story by novelist Jack London, who spent 1897–98 in the Yukon and gained fame for his fiction of the Far North, Overland Monthly 33 *(June 1899): 544.*

. . . every house was entered, and if anything had been left by the former occupants it was thoroughly overhauled. Clothing was snatched out of bureaus and scattered over the floor in search of valuables. Boxes were broken open. Suspicious mounds in back yards were dug into. Cisterns were probed and bamboo thickets were inspected. Often caches of clothing, crockery, books, etc., were discovered, and their contents scattered in the search for valuables. . . . In one house I waded knee-deep in elegant gowns of silk, satin, and piña cloth. The condition of affairs in Malabon was much the same, and in every town entered by our troops until the past month, when the appointment of a provost-marshal and guard has been the first act of the commanding general. I have seen fine libraries scattered about and trampled under foot, many valuable books being carried away. I have

seen books nearly two centuries old in the possession of soldiers.

War correspondent H. L. Wells describes American looting in the Philippines, New York Evening Post, *July 20, 1899, quoted in Welsh,* The Other Man's Country *(1900), pp. 135–37.*

The whole population of the islands sympathize with the insurgents; only those natives whose immediate self-interest requires it are friendly to us. . . . and most of these, especially those formerly connected with the insurgent government, I believe to be spies of the enemy. It is a standing joke with the officers along the line that when the authorities send out word that there is going to be an attack on their forces at any one point, they may be sure that no attack will take place at the time specified. The most important moves of the insurgents have not reached the secret service department until after they have occurred. . . .

John Bass, war correspondent for the New York Herald *and* Harper's Weekly, *describes guerrilla warfare in the Philippines, August 1899, quoted in Welsh,* The Other Man's Country *(1900), p. 153.*

. . . the vital consideration connected with this problem of the trust is its effect upon our middle class—the independent, individual business man and the skilled artisan and mechanic.

How does the trust affect them? . . . It tends to concentrate the ownership and management of all lines of business activity into the hands of a very few. . . . This being so, it follows that the independent, individual business man, must enter the employment of the trust. . . . He becomes an employee instead of an employer. His trusted foremen and his employees must follow him.

They are both to become a part of a vast industrial army with no hopes and no aspirations—a daily task to perform and no personal interest and perhaps no pride in the success of their work.

Their personal identity is lost. They become cogs and little wheels in a great complicated machine. There is no real advance for them.

They may perhaps become larger cogs or larger wheels, but they can never look forward to a life of business freedom. . . .

The middle class of which I speak will lose their sense of independence. They are already being deprived of that equality of opportunity which has made this nation what it is. . . . The trust is therefore the forerunner, or rather the creator of industrial slavery.

Hazen S. Pingree, governor of Michigan and former reform mayor of Detroit, speech, in Chicago Conference on Trusts *(1990), pp. 265–67.*

. . . in my judgment, a government of the people, by the people, and for the people, will be impossible when a few men control all the sources of production and dole out daily bread to all the rest on such terms as the few may proscribe. I believe that this nation is the hope of the world. I believe that the Declaration of Independence was the grandest document, ever penned by human hands. The truths of that declaration are condensed into four great propositions: That all men are created equal; that they are endowed with inalienable rights; that governments are instituted among men to preserve those rights, and that governments derive their just powers from the consent of the governed. Such a government is impossible under an industrial aristocracy. Place the food and clothing, all that we eat and wear and use, in the hands of a few people, and instead of it being a government of the people, it will be a government of the syndicates, by the syndicates, and for the syndicates. Establish such a government, and the people will soon be powerless to secure a legislative remedy for any abuse.

William Jennings Bryan, speech,
in Chicago Conference on Trusts *(1900), p. 512.*

. . . The organization of trusts is admirable; it knocks into the heads of all with sledge-hammer blows the patent truth that system is better than planlessness. The machinery of the trust is all ready to give to the hands of democracy—to public control. No one would think of socializing an industry that was divided into a hundred thousand businesses. . . . That is why the trust movement is an irreversible step along the path to universal cooperation.

This we say, is the first answer to the question, what to do with the trusts: Look forward to the public ownership and management of their enterprises . . . prepare for it, make it the ideal of the coming century. . . .

Laurence Gronlund argues that trusts are a step
toward a cooperative commonwealth, speech,
in Chicago Conference on Trusts *(1900), p. 571.*

Earnestly desirous to remove any cause of irritation and to insure at the same time to the commerce of all nations in China the undoubted benefits which should accrue from a formal recognition by the various powers claiming "spheres of interest" that they shall enjoy perfect equality of treatment for their commerce and navigation within such "spheres," the Government of the United States would be pleased to see . . . assurances . . . that each, within its respective sphere of whatever influence—

First. Will in no way interfere with any treaty port or any vested interest within any so-called "sphere of interest" or leased territory it may have in China.

Second. That the Chinese treaty tariff of the time being shall apply to all merchandise landed or shipped to

all such ports as are within said "sphere of interest" (unless they be "free ports"), no matter to what nationality it may belong, and that duties so leviable shall be collected by the Chinese Government.

Third. That it will levy no higher harbor dues on vessels of another nationality frequenting any port in such "sphere" than shall be levied on vessels of its own nationality, and no higher railroad charges over lines built, controlled, or operated within its "sphere." . . .

Secretary of State John Hay's first Open Door note, sent to
ambassadors in Germany, England, Russia, Japan, France, and
Italy, September 6, 1899, Foreign Relations of
the United States, 1899, *pp. 129–30.*

When I realized that the Philippines had dropped into our laps I confess I did not know what to do with them. . . . I walked the floor of the White House night after night until midnight; and I am not ashamed to tell you, gentlemen, that I went down on my knees and prayed to Almighty God for light and guidance more than one night. And one night late it came to me this way—I don't know how it was, but it came: (1) That we could not give them back to Spain—that would be cowardly and dishonorable; (2) that we could not turn them over to France or Germany—our commercial rivals in the Orient—that would be bad business and discreditable; (3) that we could not leave them to themselves—they were unfit for self-government—and they would soon have anarchy and misrule over there worse than Spain's was; and (4) there was nothing left for us to do but to take them all, and to educate the Filipinos, and uplift and civilize and Christianize them, and by God's grace do the very best we could by them, as our fellowmen for whom Christ also died. And then I went to bed, and went to sleep, and slept soundly, and the next morning I sent for the chief engineer of the War Department (our mapmaker), and I told him to put the Philippines on the map of the United States, and there are, and there they will stay while I am President!

President McKinley's famous speech to a Methodist group
visiting the White House, November 21, 1899, quoted in
Olcott, The Life of William McKinley, *vol. 2,*
pp. 109–11.

"I'm not much iv an expansionist mesilf. F'r th' las' tin years I've been thryin' to decide whether 'twud be good policy an' thrue to me thraditions to make this here bar two or three feet longer, an manny's th' night I've laid awake tryin' to puzzle it out. But I don't know what to do with th' Ph'lippeens anny more thin I did las' summer, befure I heerd tell iv thim. We can't give thim to anny wan without makin' th' wan that gets thim feel th' way Doherty felt to Clancy whin Clancy med a frindly call an' give Doherty's childher th' measles. We can't sell thim, we can't ate thim, an' we can't throw thim into th' alley whin no wan is lookin'. An' 'twud be a disgrace f'r to lave befure we've pounded these frindless an' ongrateful people into insensibility. So I suppose, Hinnissy, we'll have to stay an' do th' best we can, an' lave Andhrew Carnegie secede fr'm th' Union. They'se wan consolation; an' that is, if th' American people can govern thimsilves, they can govern annything that walks."

The fictional Irish-American saloon keeper Mr. Dooley, popular creation of newspaper humor writer Finley Peter Dunne, satirizes President McKinley's reasoning in his speech to the Methodists, Mr. Dooley Now and Forever, *pp. 68–69.*

It kept leaking down from sources above that the Filipinos were "niggers;" no better than Indians, and were to be treated as such. Whether this policy came from Washington or was born in the minds of the ambitious officers who had not yet gained enough glory, I cannot say. But I can say that on more than one battle-field they were treated like Indians. At Caloocan I saw natives shot down that could have been taken prisoners, and the whole country around Manila set ablaze with apparently no other object than to teach the natives submission by showing them that with the Americans war was hell.

Abram L. Mumper, First Idaho Regiment, ca. 1900, quoted in Welsh, The Other Man's Country (1900), *p. 134.*

There was a saloon on every corner in Springfield in the old days. I was only a kid. They'd let kids buy beer. They had pitchers and pails. So they'd send me over—for $10 you'd get a big pail of beer. And the policemen would come in there too to watch my father working there. He had a few men working for him too. And they'd drink beer. Like you're drinking out of this glass, they'd pass the pail around and they'd all drink. They didn't think about sanitary conditions.

Michael Steinberg, a Jewish immigrant from Russia as an infant in 1890, describes his father's blacksmith shop in Springfield, Massachusetts, ca. 1900, Stave et al., eds., From the Old Country, *p. 74.*

No member of the Council shall hold any other public office or hold any office or employment the compensation for which is paid out of public moneys; or be elected or appointed to any office created or the compensation of which is increased by the Council while he was a member thereof, until one year after the expiration of the term for which he was elected; or be interested directly or indirectly in any contract with the city; or be in the employ of any person having any contract with the city, or of any grantee of a franchise granted by the city.

Proposed Municipal Corporations Act, 1900, in National Municipal League, A Municipal Program, *p. 349.*

The Secretary.—Have you any recommendation to make with reference to baths on the East Side in tenement houses?
Mr. Moscowitz.—Yes, sir; I think that baths are very essential. Because there are no baths in the tenement houses many of the tenants do not bathe as often as they otherwise would. I can say from experience that many tenants do not bathe more than six times a year, and often not because they would not take advantage of the opportunity, there are no opportunities.
The Secretary.—Cannot they take a bath in the rooms?
Mr. Moscowitz.—No, they cannot. There are no baths there. . . .
The Secretary.—Have you ever seen a bath-tub in a tenement house, Mr. Moscowitz?
Mr. Moscowitz.—Never.
The Secretary.—Never in seventeen years?
Mr. Moscowitz.—Never in seventeen years.

East Side tenement dweller and settlement worker Henry Moskowitz testifies before the New York Tenement House Commission of 1900, De Forest and Veiller, eds., The Tenement House Problem, *vol. 1, pp. 412–13.*

This was the beginning of my work years—jobs after school and during summer vacation to help the family and in order to be able to continue in school. Next I worked for several summers in a baking powder factory downtown on Barclay Street, passing the bakery delivery job to my younger brother Ralph. The hours at the factory were from seven-thirty in the morning until six at night and from eight until three on Saturdays. The wages were three dollars, out of which came sixty cents a week for carfare and sixty cents a week for lunch. This left me with only one dollar and twenty cents to take home to my mother. But every penny counted and helped to keep us going. . . .

"Nardo," my father repeated again and again. "In me you see a dog's life. Go to school. Even if it kills you. With the pen and with books you have the chance to live like a man and not like a beast of burden."

Leonard Covello, whose family immigrated to New York in 1896 and who later became a high school principal, ca. 1900, in his The Heart Is the Teacher, *pp. 39, 41.*

The Philippines are ours forever, "territory belonging to the United States," as the Constitution calls them. And just beyond the Philippines are China's illimitable markets. . . . We will not retreat from either. . . .

God has . . . made us the master organizers of the world to establish system where chaos reigns. He has given us the spirit of progress to overwhelm the forces of reaction throughout the earth. He has made us adepts in government that we may administer government among savage and senile peoples. Were it not for such a force as this the world would relapse into barbarism and night. And of all our race He has marked the American people as His chosen nation to finally lead in the regeneration of the world. This is the divine mission of America. . . . We are trustees of the world's progress, guardians of its righteous peace.

What shall history say of us? Shall it say that we renounced that holy trust, left the savage to his base condition, the wilderness to the reign of waste, deserted duty, abandoned glory? . . . Our fathers . . . unfurled no retreating flag. That flag has never paused in its onward march. Who dares halt it now—now, when history's largest events are carrying it forward?

Senator Albert J. Beveridge, Senate speech, January 9, 1900,
Congressional Record, *56th Congress, vol. 33, part 1,*
pp. 704, 711.

The housing question is the most fundamental of social problems relating to environment. The dictum of the late Cardinal Manning, "Domestic life creates a nation," is absolutely sound. The corollary is also true: the lack of domestic life will unmake a nation. The home is the character unit of society; and, where there is little or no opportunity for the free play of influences which make for health, happiness, and virtue, we must expect social degeneration and decay. Inspect the charts of the whole tenement region of New York City as they were displayed at the Tenement House Exhibition, and note the formidable part played by bad housing in the generation of social ills. Great cities are the danger points of modern civilization, and any community which leaves to a large part of its inhabitants inadequate facilities for the true development of domestic life must fight deteriorating forces at tremendous cost.

E. R. L. Gould, author of the Department of Labor's 1895
report on housing conditions, comments on the Veiller exhibit of
February 1900, "The Housing Problem in Great Cities,"
Quarterly Review of Economics, *vol. 14 (1899–1900),*
p. 378.

Believing that the tenement-house problem is at the root of most of our social evils, the committee has given attention to those subordinate problems which are affected by the housing problem, and which in turn deeply affect it. The need of playgrounds, parks, public baths, and libraries is shown in many ways. Probably the most interesting feature of this exhibit is a series of diagrams illustrating sixteen "city wildernesses" in New York. These are proposed as sites of needed parks, play-grounds, and public baths. The actual shape of the buildings on these blocks is shown, the number of people living in them, the character of the soil, whether near an underground stream or not, is stated; and the nearness to public schools, the character of the neighborhood, whether strictly a business neighborhood or one

where business is crowding out tenements, is most carefully considered. The parks proposed indicate the minimum needs of the city at the present time. . . . There is no way in which the city can neglect its own welfare more than by neglecting its children. . . . It would be economical for the city to spend many millions of dollars in providing play places of this kind, thus cutting down its future appropriations for jails, almhouses, hospitals, and dispensaries.

Lawrence Veiller, "The Tenement-House Exhibition,"
Charities Review, *vol. 10 (March 1900), pp. 21–22.*

. . . all persons born or naturalized in the United States . . . are entitled to and shall receive protection in their lives from being murdered, tortured, burned to death by any and all organized mobs commonly known as "lynching bees," whether said mob be spontaneously assembled or organized by premeditation for the purpose of taking the life or lives of any citizen . . .; and that whenever any citizen . . . shall be murdered by mob violence in the manner hereinabove described, all parties participating, aiding, and abetting in such murder and lynching shall be guilty of treason against the Government of the United States, and shall be tried for that offense in the United States courts. . . .

Proposed federal antilynching law (not passed), introduced in
the House of Representatives by Congressman George H.
White of North Carolina, February 5, 1900, available online
at African American Perspectives. URL: http://
memory.loc.gov/ammem/aap/aaphome.html.

Lift every voice and sing
Till earth and heaven ring,
Ring with the harmonies of Liberty;
Let our rejoicing rise
High as the listening skies,
Let it resound loud as the rolling sea.
Sing a song full of the faith that the dark past has taught us,
Sing a song full of the hope that the present has brought us,
Facing the rising sun of our new day begun
Let us march on till victory is won.

Poet James Weldon Johnson, "Lift Every Voice and Sing,"
called the "Negro National Anthem," first performed by
schoolchildren in Jacksonville, Florida, February 12, 1900,
available online at AfricanAmericans.com URL: http://
www.africanamericans.com/NegroNationalAnthem.htm.

As recognized by the Government of the United States of America, according to your excellency's note referred to above, the Imperial Government has, from the beginning, not only asserted, but also practically carried out to the fullest extent, in its Chinese possessions, absolute equality of treatment of all nations with regard to trade, navigation, and commerce. The Imperial Government entertains no thought of departing in the future from this principle, which at once excludes prejudicial or disadvantageous commercial treatment of the citizens of the United States of America, so long as it is not forced to do so, on account of considerations of reciprocity, by a divergence from it by other governments. If, therefore, the other powers interested in the industrial development of the Chinese Empire are willing to recognize the same principles, this can only be desired by the Imperial Government, which in this case upon being requested will gladly be ready to participate with the United States of America and the other powers in an agreement made upon these lines, by which the same rights are reciprocally secured.

February 19, 1900: Germany's equivocal response to Secretary of State John Jay's first Open Door note of September 1899, Foreign Relations of the United States, 1899, *pp. 141–42.*

The United States has not been fair to those who gave their hand to their redeemer . . . who turned their backs upon the old conditions and accepted the new, only to discover themselves cut off from all the world—a people without a country, a flag, almost without a name, orphans without a father. . . . In one voice these children by late adoption cry out to the mother country who redeemed them, "Who are we? What are we? Have we been invited to come under the sheltering roof, only to starve at the doorstep? Are we citizens or are we subjects? Are we brothers and our property territory, or are we bondmen of a war and our islands a crown colony?"

Memorial of Protest and Petition from the People of Puerto Rico, Feb 26, 1900, Congressional Record, *56th Congress, vol. 33, part 3, p. 2231.*

SIR: The _____ Government having accepted the declaration suggested by the United States concerning foreign trade in China, the terms of which I transmitted to you in my instruction No. _____ of _____, and like action having been taken by all the various powers having leased territory or so-called "spheres of interest" in the Chinese Empire, as shown by the notes which I herewith transmit to you, you will please inform the government to which you are accredited, that the condition originally attached to its acceptance that all other powers concerned should likewise accept the proposals of the United States—having been complied with, this Government will therefore consider the assent given to it by _____ as final and definitive.

You will also transmit to the minister of foreign affairs copies of the present enclosures, and by the same occasion convey to him the expression of the sincere gratification which the President feels at the successful termination of these negotiations. . . .

Hay's second Open Door note sent to American ambassadors, March 20, 1900, in Malloy, ed., Treaties, *vol. 1, p. 260.*

Since the insurgents have adopted their guerrilla methods of attacking weak parties of Americans, and boloing men who get outside our lines, a feeling of intense bitterness has sprung up among our soldiers. It is the old cry—"The only good Indian is a dead one"—repeated, with a deep thirst for revenge behind it to strengthen it. . . . Some of the most atrocious butcheries have been committed by the Filipinos, cases where a dozen or more natives have killed a single American, and hacked the body frightfully. The news reached the nearest post, and a scouting party goes out to the scene of the killing. It can be imagined that the comrades of the murdered man do not feel in a merciful mood, and they proceed to burn the village and kill every native who looks as if he had a bolo or a rifle.

Newspaper correspondent John T. McCutcheon, April 20, 1900, the Chicago Record's Stories of Filipino Warfare, *quoted in LeRoy,* Americans in the Philippines, *vol. 2, p. 226.*

The first thing which we discovered practically was that the wind flowing up a hillside is not a steadily flowing current like that of a river. It comes as a rolling mass, full of tumultuous whirls and eddies, like those issuing from a chimney; and they strike the apparatus with constantly varying force and direction, sometimes withdrawing support when most needed. It has long been known, through instrumental observations, that the wind is constantly changing in force and direction; but it needed the experience of an operator afloat on a gliding machine to realize that this all proceeded from cyclonic action; so that more was learned in this respect in a week than had previously been acquired by several years of experiments with models.

Octave Chanute, an early flight pioneer, "Experiments in Flying," McClure's Magazine, *vol. 15 (June, 1900), p. 128.*

I put the smashers on my right arm and went in. . . . These rocks and bottles being wrapped in paper looked like packages bought from a store. . . . Be wise as devils and harmless as doves. . . .

I said: "Mr. Dobson, I told you last spring, when I held my county convention here, (I was W. C. T. U. president of Barber County,) to close this place, and you didn't do it. Now I have come with another remonstrance. Get out of the way. I don't want to strike you, but I am going to break [up] this den of vice."

I began to throw at the mirror and the bottles below the mirror. Mr. Dobson and his companion jumped into a corner, seemed very much terrified. From that I went to another saloon, until I had destroyed three, breaking some of the windows in the front of the building. In the last place, kept by Lewis, there was quite a young man behind the bar. I said to him: "Young man, come from behind that bar, your mother did not raise you for such a place." I threw a brick at the mirror, which was a very heavy one, and it did not break, but the brick fell and broke everything in its way. I began to look around for something that would break it. I was standing by a billiard table on which there was one ball. I said: "Thank God," and picked it up, threw it, and it made a hole in the mirror. . . .

Carry Nation describes her first smashing, Kiowa, Kansas, June 1, 1900, in her autobiography, The Use and Need of the Life of Carry A. Nation, *Chapter 8, available online at Electronic Text Center, University of Virginia. URL: http://etext.lib.virginia.edu/toc/ modeng/public/NatUsea.html.*

No other course was possible than to destroy Spain's sovereignty throughout the West Indies and in the Philippine Islands. That course created our responsibility before the world, and with the unorganized population whom our intervention had freed from Spain, to provide for the maintenance of law and order, and for the establishment of good government and for the performance of international obligations. Our authority could not be less than our responsibility; and wherever sovereign rights were extended it became the high duty of the Government to maintain its authority, to put down armed insurrection and to confer the blessings of liberty and civilization upon all the rescued peoples.

The largest measure of self-government consistent with their welfare and our duties shall be secured to them by law.

Republican Party platform, on sovereignty in new possessions, adopted June 18–21, 1900, in Platforms of the Two Great Parties, *p. 121.*

We recognize the necessity and propriety of the honest co-operation of capital to meet new business conditions and especially to extend our rapidly increasing foreign trade, but we condemn all conspiracies and combinations intended to restrict business, to create monopolies, to limit production, or to control prices. . . .

Republican Party platform, statement on trusts, in Platforms, *p. 117.*

So far all safe and well but living in a suspense that cannot be imagined. . . . We are shut in this province with no communication with the coast for weeks. We have no way of knowing what the situation there is. We do not know whether there is war, what nations are implicated if there is war. But we can only live moment by moment, longing for something definite. It gives one the feeling of being caught in a trap with wicked people all about us desiring our extermination, and the feeling will come, in spite of trying to be brave and hopeful, that the Shansi missionaries may

need to give their lives for the growth of the Kingdom of God in China.

Journal of Eva Jane Price, American missionary in China later murdered by the Boxers, June 28, 1900, in her China Journal, *pp. 224–25.*

We adhere to the policy initiated by us in 1857, of peace with the Chinese nation, of furtherance of lawful commerce, and of protection of lives and property of our citizens by all means guaranteed under extraterritorial treaty rights and by the law of nations. . . . The purpose of the President is, as it has been heretofore, to act concurrently with the other powers, first, in opening up communication with Pekin and rescuing the American officials, missionaries, and other Americans who are in danger; secondly, in affording all possible protection everywhere in China to American life and property; thirdly, in guarding and protecting all legitimate American interests; and fourthly, in aiding to prevent a spread of the disorders to the other provinces of the Empire and a recurrence of such disasters. . . . [T]he policy of the government of the United States is to seek a solution which may bring about permanent safety and peace to China, preserve Chinese territorial and administrative entity, protect all rights guaranteed to friendly powers by treaty and international law, and safeguard for the world the principle of equal and impartial trade with all parts of the Chinese Empire.

Hay's third Open Door note, a circular telegram to many American ambassadors, July 3, 1900, Foreign Relations of the United States, 1900, *p. 299.*

We hold that the Constitution follows the flag. . . . We assert that no nation can long endure half republic and half empire, and we warn the American people that imperialism abroad will lead quickly and inevitably to despotism at home. . . .

We condemn and denounce the Philippine policy of the present administration. It has involved the Republic in an unnecessary war, sacrificed the lives of many of our noblest sons, and placed the United States, previously known and applauded throughout the world as the champion of freedom, in the false and un-American position of crushing with military force the efforts of our former allies to achieve liberty and self-government. . . .

The greedy commercialism which dictated the Philippine policy of the Republican administration attempts to justify it with the plea that it will pay; but . . . when trade is extended at the expense of liberty, the price is always too high.

We are not opposed to territorial expansion when it takes in desirable territory which can be erected into States in the Union, and whose people are willing and fit to become American citizens . . . But we are unalterably opposed to seizing or purchasing distant islands to be governed outside the Constitution, and whose people can never become citizens.

... [T]he burning issue of imperialism growing out of the Spanish war involves the very existence of the Republic and the destruction of our free institutions. We regard it as the paramount issue of the campaign. ...

Democratic Party platform adopted July 4–6, 1900, statement on imperialism, in Platforms of the Two Great Parties, *pp. 104–07.*

Private monopolies are indefensible and intolerable. They destroy competition, control the price of all material, and of the finished product, thus robbing both producer and consumer. They lessen the employment of labor, and arbitrarily fix the terms and conditions thereof, and deprive individual energy and small capital of their opportunity of betterment. They are the most efficient means yet devised for appropriating the fruits of industry to the benefit of the few at the expense of the many, and unless their insatiate greed is checked, all wealth will be aggregated in a few hands and the Republic destroyed. ...

We pledge the Democratic party to an unceasing warfare in nation, State and city against private monopoly in every form.

Democratic Party platform of 1900, statement on trusts, Platforms, *p. 109.*

It is argued by some that the Filipinos are incapable of self-government and that therefore we owe it to the world to take control of them. ... There are degrees of proficiency in the art of self-government, but it is a reflection upon the Creator to say that he denied to any people the capacity for self-government. Once admit that some people are capable of self-government, and that others are not, and that the capable people have a right to seize upon and govern the incapable, and you make force—brute force—the only foundation of government and invite the reign of the despot. I am not willing to believe that an all-wise and all-loving God created the Filipinos and then left them thousands of years helpless until the islands attracted the attention of European nations.

William Jennings Bryan, speech delivered in Indianapolis, August 8, 1900, reprinted in Schlesinger et al, eds., History of American Presidential Elections, *vol. 5, pp. 1950–51.*

Soon there were outspread acres and acres of ruins, leveled by shell-fire, by the torch, streets crowded with every army uniform under the sun, soldiers burdened with armfuls of plunder, gorgeous furs, priceless brocades and embroideries, sacks of jade or silver bullion—halting to quarrel while the stronger snatched the spoils from the weaker.

Then we came to the area of the defenses which had been so magnificently held by those few hundred allied marines, bluejackets, legation clerks, secretaries, and missionaries—gaunt, ragged walls, countless barricades of brick, and breast-works of sand-bags.

These ramparts of sand-bags were gorgeous to behold, thousands of sacks made of silk fabrics snatched from Chinese shops, crimson and yellow and blue and white. They had been cut and stitched together by the women gathered within the beleaguered walls, the wives of diplomats, the white-faced fugitives from distant mission stations, the native Christian girls—all these women mobilized in one building and stitching for their lives. They had glorified the prosaic sewing machine, purring its song by night and day while an inferno raged outside and the men fell dying at the loopholes or were fetched back bleeding from the desperate sortie.

Journalist Ralph Paine, arriving in Peking (Beijing) in late August 1900, Roads of Adventure, *pp. 304–05.*

As a rule, large capitalists are Republicans and small capitalists are Democrats, but workingmen must remember that they are all capitalists, and that the many small ones, like

Eugene V. Debs led the American Socialist Party and ran for president as its candidate many times. The genial Debs inspired much loyalty and affection among his followers and friends. *(Library of Congress, Prints and Photographs Division, LC-USZ62-106026)*

the fewer large ones, are all politically supporting their class interests, and this is always and everywhere the capitalist class.

Whether the means of production—that is to say, the land, mines, factories, machinery, etc.—are owned by a few large Republican capitalists, who organize a trust, or whether they be owned by a lot of small Democratic capitalists, who are opposed to the trust, is all the same to the working class. Let the capitalists, large and small, fight this out among themselves. . . .

The working class must get rid of the whole brood of masters and exploiters, and put themselves in possession and control of the means of production, that they may have steady employment without consulting a capitalist employer, large or small, and that they may get the wealth their labor produces, all of it. . . .

Eugene V. Debs, "Outlook for Socialism in the United States," International Socialist Review, *September, 1900, available online at Eugene V. Debs Internet Archive. URL: http://www.marxists.org/archive/debs/works/1900/outlook.htm.*

I reached home and found the water waist deep around my residence. I at once went to work assisting people who were not securely located into my residence until 40 or 50 people were housed therein. About 6:30 p.m. Mr. J. L. Cline . . . reached my residence with water around his neck. He informed me that . . . no further message could be gotten off on account of all wires being down and he had advised everyone he could see to go to the center of the city and he thought we had better make an attempt in that direction. At this time, however, the roofs of the houses and timbers were flying through the streets as though they were paper and it appeared suicidal to attempt a journey through the flying timbers. Many people were killed by flying timbers about this time while endeavoring to escape to town.

The water rose at a steady rate from 3:00 p.m. until about 7:30 p.m. when there was a sudden rise of about four feet in as many seconds. I was standing at my front door which was partly open watching the water which was flowing with great rapidity from east to west. The water at this time was about eight inches deep in my residence and the sudden rise of four feet brought it above my waist before I could change my position.

Meteorologist Isaac M. Cline, report to the National Weather Bureau Office following the September 8, 1900, disaster in Galveston, available online at 1900 Storm. URL: http://www.rosenberg-library.org/gthc/clinereport.html.

The Anglo-Saxon is pretty much the same wherever you find him, and he walks on the necks of every colored race he comes into contact with. Resistance to his will or interests means destruction to the weaker race. Confronted, as we are, within our own borders with this perplexing problem, why do we seek to incorporate nine millions more of brown men under the flag? . . .

We of the South have never acknowledged that the negroes were our equals, or that they were fitted for or entitled to participate in government; therefore, we are not inconsistent or hypocritical when we protest against the subjugation of the Filipinos, and the establishment of a military government over them by force. Conscious of the wrongs which exist in the South, and seeking anxiously for a just and fair solution of the Race Question, we strenuously oppose incorporation of any more colored men into the body politic.

Senator Ben Tillman, Democrat of South Carolina, "Causes of Southern Opposition to Imperialism," North American Review, *vol. 171 (October 1900), pp. 443–45.*

Yes, we are becoming Americanized; . . . but not by the Constitution that is so wise, nor through freedom that is so great, nor through the law that is so magnificent; we are becoming Americanized through privilege, through monopoly, through injustice, through despotism. We are being Americanized the wrong way, and from this wrong Americanization the dealers who put on sale the honor of the country are to blame; not the American people, who have not yet come to know us, but the adventurers who fall upon the fields of Puerto Rico like swarms of ravenous locusts.

Editorial, Puerto Rican newspaper La Democracia, *Oct 29, 1900, in Wagenheim, ed.,* The Puerto Ricans, *p. 111.*

I. That the government of Cuba shall never enter into any treaty or other compact with any foreign power or powers which will impair or tend to impair the independence of Cuba, nor in any manner authorize or permit any foreign power or powers to obtain by colonization or for military or naval purposes or otherwise, lodgement in or control over any portion of said island.

II. That said government shall not assume or contract any public debt, to pay the interest upon which . . . the ordinary revenues of the island, after defraying the current expenses of government, shall be inadequate.

III. That the government of Cuba consents that the United States may exercise the right to intervene for the preservation of Cuban independence, the maintenance of a government adequate for the protection of life, property, and individual liberty, and for discharging the obligations with respect to Cuba imposed by the treaty of Paris on the United States, now to be assumed and undertaken by the government of Cuba.

IV. That all Acts of the United States in Cuba during its military occupancy thereof are ratified and validated, and all lawful rights acquired thereunder shall be maintained and protected.

V. That the government of Cuba will execute, and as far as necessary extend, the plans already devised or other plans to be mutually agreed upon, for the sanitation of the cities of the island, to the end that a recurrence of epidemic and infectious diseases may be prevented, thereby assuring protection to the people and commerce of Cuba, as well as to the commerce of the southern ports of the United States and the people residing therein. . . .

VII. That to enable the United States to maintain the independence of Cuba, and to protect the people thereof, as well as for its own defense, the government of Cuba will sell or lease to the United States lands necessary for coaling or naval stations. . . .

The Platt Amendment, March 2, 1901, Treaties and Other International Agreements, *pp. 1116–17.*

I was prepared to find child-labor, for wherever easily manipulated machinery takes the place of human muscles the child is inevitably drawn into the labor market, unless there are laws to protect it. But one could hardly be prepared to find in America today white children, six and seven years of age, working for twelve hours a day—aroused before daybreak and toiling, till long after sundown in winter, with only half an hour for rest and refreshment. When the mills are tempted by pressure of work they make the same old mistakes of their industrial ancestry.

Child labor was an increasingly important reform issue. This photo, taken by Lewis Hine, shows young Hattie Hunter, a spinner, at work in the mills of Lancaster, South Carolina. *(Library of Congress, Prints and Photographs Division, LC-USZ6-1220)*

Some of them run the machinery at night, and little children are called on to endure the strain of all-night work—and are sometimes kept awake by the vigilant superintendent with cold water dashed into their faces. I should hardly have believed it had I not seen these things myself. . . .

"What do you do when you are very tired?" I asked a little girl, putting my mouth close to her ear to make myself heard. "I cry," she said, shyly. She would make no reply when I asked her what happened then, but another child, who had literally poked her head into the conversation, put in tersely, "The boss tells her to go on with her work."

Irene Ashby, sent by the AFL to investigate child labor in Alabama in December 1900, "Child Labor in Southern Cotton Mills," World's Work, *vol. 2 (October 1901), pp. 1290, 1293.*

. . . it has been permitted to me & my assistants to lift the impenetrable veil that has surrounded the causation of this [most] dreadful pest of humanity and to put it on a rational & scientific basis—I thank God that this has been accomplished during the latter days of the old century—May its cure be wrought out in the early days of the new century! The prayer that has been mine for twenty or more years, that I might be permitted in some way or sometime to do something to alleviate human suffering, has been answered!

Major Walter Reed, M.D., in Quemados, Cuba, letter to his wife, Emilie, on the eve of the new century, December 31, 1900, available online at Philip S. Hench Walter Reed Yellow Fever Collection. URL: http://yellowfever.lib.virginia.edu/reed/

A Salutation Speech from the Nineteenth Century to the Twentieth Taken down in shorthand by Mark Twain

I bring you the stately matron called CHRISTENDOM—returning bedraggled, besmirched and dishonored from pirate raids in Kiaochow [China, seized by Germany], Manchuria [occupied by Russia], South Africa and the Philippines; with her soul full of meanness, her pocket full of boodle and her mouth full of pious hypocrisies. Give her soap and a towel, but hide the looking-glass.

Mark Twain's anti-imperialist statement, December 31, 1900, published in the New York Herald, *widely reprinted, and distributed on cards by the Anti-Imperialist League,* Mark Twain's Weapons of Satire, *pp. 12–13.*

. . . in order not to seem eccentric I have swung around, now, and joined the nation in the conviction that nothing can sully a flag. I was not properly reared, and had the illusion that a flag was a thing which must be sacredly guarded against shameful uses and unclean contacts, lest it suffer pollution; and so when it was sent out to the Philippines to float over a wanton war and a robbing expedition I supposed it was polluted, and in an ignorant moment I said so. But I stand corrected. I concede and acknowledge that it was only the government that sent it on such an errand that was polluted. Let us compromise on that. I am glad to have it that way. For our flag could not well stand pollution, never having been used to it, but it is different with the administration.

Mark Twain responds to criticism for saying, in a widely reprinted speech, that the American flag was polluted, 1901, Mark Twain's Weapons of Satire, *pp. 16–17.*

But Filipino inhumanity to Filipino was far worse, and was exhibited on a far greater scale, than in the atrocities committed against American soldiers, the latter being, by comparison, very insignificant in number. Excluding the cases of sheer outlawry in a disordered time, and the instances where private vengeance was executed, the brutal outrages perpetrated upon natives by their fellow-countrymen, sometimes their own neighbors, because of failure to support the guerrilla forces . . ., or because of being charged with more overt demonstrations of friendship for the Americans, form a record of which the written evidence, in military trials, etc., is, though very incomplete, sufficiently horrible. . . . Murder was perpetrated on a wholesale plan in various towns from the northwest corner of Luzon down through Unión province, a band which operated at night burying alive in the sandy beach near one generally peaceful town some thirty people. . . .

James A. LeRoy describes Filipino brutality, ca. 1901, Americans in the Philippines, *vol. 2, pp. 228–33 passim.*

Playgrounds, well equipped and directed, we very early recognized to be a prime necessity for the children swarming the streets. They had no other place to play than where they ran the gauntlet of the dust-laden streets and their dangerous traffic. We could begin to supply this need only by cleaning up the tiny backyard of the Union Street house for the first playground of the vicinity. Neither of the two public schools in the neighborhood had any outdoor space for the children's play. . . . Later we rented two vacant lots on the crowded thoroughfare opposite the new Commons building for our first real playground. Immediately it was so overcrowded that the swings and the teeterboards had scarcely space to operate without hitting a child. The way was thus opened for the establishment of a city playground adjoining the new Washington School building, which covered the two vacant lots that our playground temporarily had occupied.

. . . Finding that few of the children living beyond a half mile from the larger parks and playgrounds ventured to go to them, our residents began playing games summer evenings on several less frequented streets. The children of those neighborhoods joyously rallied to these games, which proved to be popular neighborhood occasions enjoyed by family groups assembled on their front doorsteps. . . .

Graham Taylor, founder of the settlement house Chicago Commons, describes how the first playground of 1895 grew by 1901, in his Chicago Commons, *pp. 57–58.*

It was a commissioner's official railway map of the State of California. . . . Upon it the different railways of the State were accurately plotted in various colours, blue, green, yellow. However, the blue, the yellow, and the green were but brief traceries, very short, isolated, unimportant. At a little distance these could hardly be seen. The whole map was gridironed by a vast, complicated network of red lines marked P. and S. W. R. R. These centralised at San Francisco and thence ramified and spread north, east, and south, to every quarter of the State. From Coles, in the topmost corner of the map, to Yuma in the lowest, from Reno on one side to San Francisco on the other, ran the plexus of red, a veritable system of blood circulation, complicated, dividing, and reuniting, branching, splitting, extending, throwing out feelers, off-shoots, tap roots, feeders—diminutive little blood suckers that shot out from the main jugular and went twisting up into some remote county, laying hold upon some forgotten village or town, involving it in one of a myriad branching coils, one of a hundred tentacles, drawing it, as it were, toward that centre from which all this system sprang.

The map was white, and it seemed as if all the colour which should have gone to vivify the various counties, towns, and cities marked upon it had been absorbed by that huge, sprawling organism, with its ruddy arteries converging to a central point. It was as though the State had been sucked white and colourless, and against this pallid background the red arteries of the monster stood out, swollen with life-blood, reaching out to infinity, gorged to bursting; an excrescence, a gigantic parasite fattening upon the life-blood of an entire commonwealth.

Frank Norris's novel about the California railroad trust, The Octopus, *1901, pp. 204–05.*

The devilfish crushing a man in his long winding arms, and sucking his blood from his mangled body, is not so frightful an assailant as this deadly but insidious enemy [beer], which fastens itself upon its victim, and daily becomes more and more the wretched man's master, clogging his liver, rotting his kidneys, decaying his heart and arteries, stupefying and starving his brain, choking his lungs and bronchia, loading his body with dropsical fluids and unwholesome fat, fastening upon him rheumatism, erysipelas, and all manner of painful and disgusting diseases, and finally dragging him to his grave at a time when other men are in their prime of mental and bodily vigor. . . .

Dr. S. H. Burgen, a practitioner 35 years, 28 in Toledo, says: "I think beer kills quicker than any other liquor. . . . The first organ to be attacked is the kidneys; the liver soon sympathizes, and then comes, most frequently, dropsy or Bright's disease, both certain to end fatally. Any physician, who cares to take the time, will tell you that among the dreadful results of beer drinking are lockjaw and erysipelas, and that the beer drinker seems incapable of recovering from mild disorders and injuries not usually regarded of a grave character. Pneumonia, pleurisy, fevers, etc., seem to have a first mortgage on him, which they foreclose remorselessly at an early opportunity."

"Scientific Testimony on Beer," speech of Senator J. H. Gallinger of New Hampshire, January 9, 1901, available online at American Time Capsule. URL: http://memory.loc.gov/ammem/rbpehtml/pehome.html

And what is it that we do want to do? Why, it is, within the limits imposed by the Federal Constitution, to establish white supremacy in this State. . . .

. . . If we would have white supremacy, we must establish it by law—not by force or fraud. If you teach your boy that it is right to buy a vote, it is an easy step for him to learn to use money to bribe or corrupt officials or trustees of any class. If you teach your boy that it is right to steal votes, it is an easy step for him to believe that it is right to steal whatever he may need or greatly desire. The results of such an influence will enter every branch of society; it will reach your bank cashiers, and affect positions of trust in every department; it will ultimately enter your courts, and affect the administration of justice.

I submit it to the intelligent judgment of this Convention that there is no higher duty resting upon us, as citizens and as delegates, than that which requires us to embody in the fundamental law such provisions as will enable us to protect the sanctity of the ballot in every portion of the State.

Speaker at the Alabama constitutional convention, convened to find ways to disenfranchise blacks, Journal of the Proceedings of the Constitutional Convention of the State of Alabama, 1901, reprinted in Osofsky, Burden of Race, pp. 172–73.

We are also of opinion that the power to acquire territory by treaty implies, not only the power to govern such territory, but to prescribe upon what terms the United States will receive its inhabitants, and what their status shall be, . . .

. . . [N]o construction of the Constitution should be adopted which would prevent Congress from considering each case upon its merits. . . . If those possessions are inhabited by alien races, differing from us in religion, customs, laws, methods of taxation, and modes of thought, the

administration of government and justice, according to Anglo-Saxon principles, may for a time be impossible; and the question at once arises whether large concessions ought not to be made for a time, that ultimately our own theories may be carried out, and the blessings of a free government under the Constitution extended to them. We decline to hold that there is anything in the Constitution to forbid such action.

We are therefore of opinion that the island of Porto Rico is a territory appurtenant and belonging to the United States, but not a part of the United States. . . .

U.S. Supreme Court Justice Henry Billings Brown, writing the majority opinion in Downes v. Bidwell, one of the Insular Cases, decided May 27, 1901, 182 US 244.

This nation is under the control of a written constitution, the supreme law of the land and the only source of the powers which our government, or any branch or officer of it, may exert at any time or at any place. Monarchical and despotic governments, unrestrained by written constitutions, may do with newly acquired territories what this government may not do consistently with our fundamental law. . . . The idea that this country may acquire territories anywhere upon the earth, by conquest or treaty, and hold them as mere colonies or provinces,—the people inhabiting them to enjoy only such rights as Congress chooses to accord to them,—is wholly inconsistent with the spirit and genius, as well as with the words, of the Constitution.

Dissenting opinion of Supreme Court Justice John Harlan in Downes v. Bidwell, May 27, 1901, 182 US 244.

There are certain principles of natural justice inherent in the Anglo-Saxon character, which need no expression in constitutions or statutes to give them effect or to secure dependencies against legislation manifestly hostile to their real interests. . . .

We suggest, without intending to decide, that there may be a distinction between certain natural rights enforced in the Constitution by prohibitions against interference with them, and what may be termed artificial or remedial rights which are peculiar to our own system of jurisprudence. Of the former class are the rights to one's own religious opinions . . ., the right to personal liberty and individual property; to freedom of speech and of the press; to free access to courts of justice, to due process of law, and to an equal protection of the laws; to immunities from unreasonable searches and seizures, as well as cruel and unusual punishments. . . . Of the latter class are the rights to citizenship, to suffrage and to the particular methods of procedure pointed out in the Constitution. . . .

Whatever may be finally decided by the American people as to the status of these islands and their inhabitants . . . it does not follow that in the meantime, awaiting that decision, the people are in the matter of personal rights unprotected by the provisions of our Constitution and subject to the merely arbitrary control of Congress.

Justice Brown, majority opinion in Downes v. Bidwell,
May 27, 1901, 182 US 244.

The wise men who framed the Constitution, and the patriotic people who adopted it, were unwilling to depend for their safety upon . . . . "certain principles of natural justice inherent in Anglo-Saxon character. . . ." They proceeded upon the theory—the wisdom of which experience has vindicated—that the only safe guaranty against governmental oppression was to withhold or restrict the power to oppress. They well remembered that Anglo-Saxons across the ocean had attempted, in defiance of law and justice, to trample upon the rights of Anglo-Saxons on this continent, and had sought, by military force, to establish a government that could at will destroy the privileges that inhere in liberty.

Dissenting opinion of Justice Harlan in Downes v. Bidwell,
May 27, 1901, 182 US 244.

The entirely sufficient answer to [anti-imperialists] is a simple statement of the facts: Cuba, Porto Rico, and the Philippines have been delivered from the despotism of Spain, which has always treated her colonies as ancient Rome treated hers . . .; Cuba has been set free and is preparing herself for a trial of independent life, Porto Rico has been admitted to substantially all the privileges of the States and Territories of the Union . . .; the Philippines, freed from despotism long endured and anarchy seriously threatened, is already given a government in spirit, . . . and Cuba, Porto Rico, and the Philippines are being provided by us with the beginnings of that common-school system which universal experience has demonstrated to be absolutely essential to the permanent maintenance of a free republican government.

Pro-imperialism editorial, "The Anti-Imperialistic Address,"
Outlook, *vol. 68 (July 13, 1901), p. 616.*

It sizzles in the neighborhood of Hester Street on a sultry day. The pale-faced, stern-eyed push-cart men cry their wares, but competition dulls in the mugginess. On the shady side of the street the little mothers and fathers of the poor tend the babies; hot, sweat-splashed little things that get jounced up and down when they get too fretful, on the knees of their elders, who are often as many as ten years old. Sometimes they sleep in odd corners, while the caretakers play jacks, covered only with prickly heat and dirty shifts.

Wherever they can find room, on the pavement, in the street or hallways, the boys play their games, dodging, instinctively it seems, the pedestrian's foot or the horse's hoof. . . .

The crowd is warm. Blindness would not conceal the fact. The tenements crowd close; windows and fire escapes bulge with bedding; one bumps against people in the street, on the stairs, in the hallways, and the life of each man, woman, and child is so close, physically, to another like the inside of an uptown [street] car in the evening, that one wonders why the whole East Side does not get snappy as the conductors do.

It doesn't. It sweats and gasps and gets what relief it can. . . .

When it gets out and out painful—too much for Nature even—and thunder, a whirl of dust and papers, come over the high buildings out of the west, and slanting rain splashes into the street, there is a great scatterment of the elders. The children whoop. It is as good as an unguarded ice-wagon. They do not think of their clothes—they haven't many to think of—and jump their hot, dirty little bodies up and down in the puddles, sail chip ships in the torrents, dam the gutters, and get as close to alleviating Nature as they can. . . .

Robert Alston Stevenson describes New York's Lower East Side, in "The Poor in Summer," Scribner's,
vol. 30 (September 1901), pp. 259–60.

No builder of air castles for the amusement and benefit of humanity could have failed to include a flying machine among the productions of his imagination. The desire to fly like a bird is inborn in our race, and we can no more be expected to abandon the idea than the ancient mathematician could have been expected to give up the problem of squaring the circle. . . . [W]e cannot conclude that because the genius of the nineteenth century has opened up such wonders as it has, therefore the twentieth is to give us the airship. But even granting the abstract possibility of the flying machine or the airship, we are still met with the question of its usefulness as a means of international communication. It would, of course, be very pleasant for a Bostonian who wished to visit New York to take out his wings from the corner of his vestibule, mount them, and fly to the Metropolis. But it is hardly conceivable that he would get there any more quickly or cheaply than he now does by rail.

Professor Simon Newcomb, "Is the Airship Coming?"
McClure's Magazine, *vol. 17 (September 1901),*
p. 434.

A deafening medley of voices merged into a terrific "Hurrah for Carrie Nation!" A mob of thousands, beating this way and that, tearing, trampling each other for a sight of that determined squat little figure, marching on with the exaltation of a conquering hero, and the Kansas smasher was steered straight into the arms of three burly New York policemen and promptly "pinched".

It happened at Devery's corner, Twenty-eighth street and Eighth avenue, at 5:30 yesterday afternoon. The dauntless Carrie unmolested had:

Precipitated a riot in three saloons.

Invaded two Sunday concert halls.

Paraded the highways and byways with a tumultuous rabble at her heels. . . .

At Twenty-fourth street, satisfied by Mrs. Nation's friends that she was about to return to her hotel, the policeman released her and put her on a car amid a volley of "Hurrahs".

The Smasher's progress down Broadway was a veritable triumphal procession. . . .

New York World reports Carry Nation's second visit to New York, "Mrs. Nation Arrested," September 2, 1901, p. 12.

God and man have linked the nations together. No nation can longer be indifferent to any other. And as we are brought more and more in touch with each other, the less occasion is there for misunderstandings and the stronger the disposition, when we have differences, to adjust them in the court of arbitration, which is the noblest forum for the settlement of international disputes. . . .

Gentlemen, let us ever remember that our interest is in concord, not conflict, and that our real eminence rests in the victories of peace, not those of war. We hope that all who are represented here may be moved to higher and nobler effort for their own and the world's good, and that out of this city may come not only greater commerce and trade for us all, but, more essential than these, relations of mutual respect, confidence and friendship which will deepen and endure.

President McKinley's last speech, delivered at the Pan-American Exposition, September 5, 1901, as recorded in Our Martyred President, *by Rt. Rev. Samuel Fallows, 1901, available online at Bar Association of Erie County. URL: http://www.eriebar.org/about/pb.html.*

Nieman [Czolgosz] turned his eyes squarely upon the President's face and extended his left hand. . . . The touch of McKinley's hand seemed to rouse the assassin to action. He leaned suddenly forward, at the same time gripping the President's hand in a vice-like hold. He drew Mr. McKinley's breast a trifle toward him and the hidden right hand flashed from beneath his coat lapel. The hand and fingers were hidden by the folds of the handkerchief. Nieman thrust his hand fair against the President's breast and pulled the trigger of the weapon that the white bit of cloth was concealing. Then he fired again, the second shot following the first so quickly that the report was scarcely noticeable. President McKinley dropped the hand of the assassin and staggered back a pace toward his secretary, Mr. Cortelyou and President [of

the Exhibition] Milburn, who had been standing at his side. They caught him as he was falling. . . .

The shooting of President McKinley, September 6, 1901, as described in the San Francisco Chronicle, *September 7, p. 1.*

I heard the shots. I did what every citizen of this country should have done. I am told that I broke his nose—I wish it had been his neck. I am sorry I did not see him four seconds before. . . . I tried to do my duty. That's all any man can do. . . .

. . . I was startled by the shots. My fist shot out and I hit the man on the nose and fell upon him, grasping him about the throat. I believe that if he had not been suffering pain he would have shot again. I know that his revolver was close to my head. I did not think about that then though. . . . I struck the man, threw up his arm and then went for his throat. It all happened so quickly I can hardly say what happen[ed], except that the secret service man came right up. Czolgosz is very strong. I am glad that I am a strong man also or perhaps the result might not have been what it was.

"Big Ben" Parker describes his role subduing the president's assassin, September 6, 1901, interview in the Buffalo Times, *available online at African American History of Western New York State. URL: http://www.math.buffalo.edu/sww/0history/parker-mckinley-reports.html.*

He gave his name as Fred Nieman, said that he was . . . an anarchist, had killed the President and believed that he had done his duty and was glad of it. . . . The prisoner was at all times cool and collected, showing no indications of feelings of remorse or sorrow for the crime he had committed, repeatedly stating that he had done his duty and was not sorry for it and realizing fully the penalty of the crime upon conviction.

In the statement made by the prisoner he said his name was not Fred Nieman, but Leon Czolgosz. . . . Naturally the people were greatly excited; the streets were crowded with people threatening to assault police headquarters, take the prisoner from custody, and lynch him. As soon as word was received that the President had been shot the Superintendent ordered a heavy detail of patrolmen to report to Police Headquarters and all streets within two blocks of Police Headquarters were patrolled and carefully guarded. One or two demonstrations were made to break the police lines, and although within the breast of every patrolman was the same feeling that existed with the excited citizens that the assassin should be summarily dealt with, they felt that the majesty of the law must be upheld and that the prisoner and property of the city would be defended at all hazards.

Buffalo police report on the arrest of Czolgosz, September 6, 1901, available online at Bar Association of Erie County. URL: http://www.eriebar.org/about/mckinley.html.

All along through the great black lane of people that stretched from the McKinley home to the cemetery—quite two miles long—were men and women weeping as though it were their own dearest friend that was being borne to the grave. . . .

At either side of the hearse marched the guard of the military and naval honor, the Generals on the right led by General Miles, and the Admirals on the left led by Admiral Farquhar. Then came the long line of carriages for the relatives and friends, and after them, the innumerable military and civic organizations that had assembled to pay this last honor of the fallen chief. The shrill notes of the bugle had given the first sign to the waiting multitude outside the station that the coffin was approaching. Instantly the long lines of soldiers became rigid, standing at present arms. The black horses of the Cleveland Troop immediately facing the station stood motionless, their riders with sabers lowered. Slowly through the entrance came the stalwart soldiers and the carriage of President Roosevelt, who rode with brother-in-law Captain Cowles of the navy, the latter in full uniform, and Secretary Gage. The carriages of the other members of the Cabinet and those who had been near to the late President in public life were lined out for a half a mile.

"McKinley Borne to Tomb; Whole World Grieves," Daily Inter-Ocean, *Chicago, Friday, Sept 20, 1901, p. 1.*

The new Chinese Telephone Exchange is open and ready for business, after months of preparation. . . .

The front room, in which is placed the switchboard, is the most attractive feature of the place. It is gayly decorated with dragons and serpents of brilliant hue; there are rare lanterns hanging from the ceiling, in which electric lights have been placed, making a contrast of modernity and antiquity.

The walls are hung with banners in red and yellow and gold. Along one side of the room is a row of teakwood chairs with cushions of silk, while near the switchboard are the small black stools which are to be seen all over the Chinese quarter. The switchboard itself is exactly like those in the other exchanges of the city, except that the operatives are men and Chinese. . . .

The work of the exchange would drive an American operator insane. For, in addition to the 255 numbers on the exchange, there are at least 125 telephones which are either in Chinese lodging-houses or in clubs. The operatives have nearly 1500 names to remember, together with their owner's place of residence. For example, Woo Kee rings his telephone and says he wants to talk to Chung Hi Kin. He gives no number, for Chung lives in some big tenement and has no telephone number. It is the duty of the operative [the telephone operator] to remember all these names, and it is claimed he does so without effort.

"The New Chinese Telephone Company,"
San Francisco Examiner, *November 17, 1901 available online at Museum of the City of San Francisco. URL: http://www.sfmuseum.org/hist1/telco.html.*

4

Roosevelt Takes Command
1902–1904

A Reformer at the Helm

Theodore Roosevelt entered the White House with a public reputation as a reformer. He had gained it as a civil service commissioner, police commissioner, and reform governor of the state of New York. The youngest president to enter the office, to many people he represented not only a rising generation but also the rising tide of reform. Reform journalist Lincoln Steffens remembered in his autobiography, "I went to Washington to see him; many reformers went there to see the first reformer president take charge. . . . And he understood, he shared, our joy."[1] With the arrival of a president who supported reform at the nation's seat of power, progressivism began to open into full flower.

Progressivism was not one organized, national campaign, but an accumulation of many independent, occasionally interlocking, but sometimes unrelated and even contradictory reform movements. Reformers aimed variously to reform politics and government, business and the economy, and the conditions of labor and life in communities throughout America. Some wanted to better the quality of life for the entire public community, some fought altruistically to better the lives of the poor and the vulnerable, and others sought primarily to better their own group's interests. Some wanted to give ordinary people a greater political voice, while others sought to bypass politics altogether by relying on scientific knowledge and concentrating authority in the hands of nonpartisan experts. Few progressives adhered to every cause, but all progressives believed they were engaged in restoring democracy and widely shared American values, as they understood them. They agreed that life had grown more interdependent and less amenable to individual control. They recognized that collective public action was necessary to end corruption in politics, solve the social problems left in the wake of industrialism's surge, and counterbalance the power of the new corporate economy. And most of all, they shared a faith that the government itself could be used as the instrument of reform, if it could be freed from special interests to act as the expression of the public's collective will. Progressives not only supported but demanded an expansion of America's traditionally limited government. At first, they focused on the city and state, because America's tradition of state and local authority was strong. But slowly, many reformers were coming to believe that action at the national level was justified to accomplish their goals effectively and quickly.

Nonetheless, President Roosevelt moved with restraint in domestic policy during his first years in office—often balancing, for example, a decision in favor of labor with a decision in favor of employers. In part, he did so to stay in the good graces of powerful Republicans and win the nomination for a second term, although it is also true that he was not a radical by temperament. He could never decide, he said, whether he was a conservative Progressive or a progressive Conservative. Sometime in 1903, President Roosevelt introduced a famous slogan to describe his domestic policies: the Square Deal. According to Lincoln Steffens, it was he who suggested the term to Roosevelt. Half in jest, Steffens had scornfully admonished Roosevelt for supporting nothing more than a square deal, while reformers wanted him to champion thoroughgoing reform.[2] Roosevelt recognized the political attractiveness of the slogan immediately. It perfectly captured many widely shared progressive impulses. It declared his willingness, as chief executive, to be the "steward of the whole people," to mediate the alarming conflicts in the American community in an active but fair and even-handed way. It spoke to the idea of a nonpartisan public interest and even implied that there was a traditional American standard of right and wrong behind it. Roosevelt used the term often, and it became his campaign slogan in 1904.

In other ways, however, Roosevelt had gone beyond both tradition and restraint by the end of his terms in office. Decisive and active by temperament, he chose to exercise presidential power whenever the Constitution did not seem explicitly to forbid it. "I declined to adopt the view that what was imperatively necessary for the Nation could not be done by the President unless he could find some specific authorization to do it," he later wrote in his autobiography.[3] In the late 19th century, Congress had been more powerful than the chief executive. Roosevelt changed that equation, greatly contributing to the development of the powerful modern presidency.

THE ROOSEVELTS IN THE WHITE HOUSE

"The gift of the gods to Theodore Roosevelt was joy, joy in life," wrote Lincoln Steffens. "He took joy in everything he did, in hunting, camping, and ranching, in politics, in reforming the police or the civil service, in organizing and commanding the Rough Riders. . . . But the greatest joy in T. R.'s life was at his succession to the presidency."[4] The new president's joy communicated well to the press and from the press to the American public.

From the moment Theodore Roosevelt, his wife Edith Carow Roosevelt, and their six children arrived in Washington, the nation was intrigued with them. The press obliged by writing about the daily doings and activities not only of the president but of the entire first family—a precedent for the press and for America. The president and first lady had six energetic children who ranged in age from four to 17 in 1901—and the fun-loving president, it was often remarked, at times seemed merely the largest of them. The eldest child, daughter Alice, quickly became a celebrity in her own right and before her father left office had treated the nation to a White House wedding. Mrs. Roosevelt greatly expanded the social role and the public profile of the first lady, appointing the first paid White House social secretary to coordinate activities. The nation embraced the Roosevelts as a typical but model family, and, as historian Lewis Gould points out, the president "employed his family as a means of placing his personal social values before his fellow citizens."[5] Roosevelt had a firm appreciation of the value of good press. He was accessible to reporters and even enjoyed their company. He

This photo of President Theodore Roosevelt, First Lady Edith Carow Roosevelt, and their children was taken in 1903. Popular First Daughter Alice Roosevelt is standing in the center. *(Library of Congress, Prints and Photographs Division, LC-USZ62-113665)*

designated the first official press room at the White House. But he was also adroit at putting out the news as he wished it to appear.

The Roosevelt family moved into the White House, which was badly in need of expansion for both official office space and for family living quarters. In early 1902, famous New York architect Charles McKim undertook the remodeling, with an eye to stripping away a century's worth of Victorian updating and restoring the house to its original state in the era of the Founding Fathers. Mrs. Roosevelt, who oversaw the project, insisted on retaining some of the accumulated Victorian furnishings despite the architect's objections—one of them the Lincoln bed. As part of the remodeling, the present West Wing and East Wing were added to the White House, the first for staff offices and the second for social events. These additions made it possible to use the first floor of the White House for state occasions and the second floor for family quarters. The remodeling was many times more costly than the original appropriation, but both Congress and the public were pleased with the results. When the White House reopened in December 1902, President Roosevelt described it as "a simple and dignified dwelling for the head of a great Republic." He had also, shortly after taking office, officially changed its name from the Executive Mansion to the White House.[6]

THE TEDDY BEAR GETS ITS NAME

In November 1902, Theodore Roosevelt went on a hunting trip in Mississippi. Although his companions were successful, he was not. His hosts arranged to have a bear tied and left in his path—but upon finding it, the president refused to shoot it. A skilled hunter, he considered such behavior unsportsmanlike. The incident was exactly the kind of good copy the press loved from the president, and they reported it widely. Political cartoonist Clifford Berryman drew a cartoon called "Drawing the Line in Mississippi," which appeared on the front page of Washington newspapers the following day. It showed a small, restrained bear and the president firmly holding up his hand to show he would not shoot. It was also a play on words, because the political purpose of the president's trip had been to negotiate a boundary dispute between Louisiana and Mississippi. After that date, neither Berryman nor other political cartoonists across the nation ever tired of depicting Roosevelt with bears.

The story delighted the public. In Brooklyn, New York, small shopkeepers Morris and Rose Michtom asked for permission to put the president's popular nickname, Teddy, on a jointed bear that Mrs. Michtom made. (No one ever dared call the president Teddy to his face, however; he despised the nickname.) The toy, displayed as Teddy's Bear, was a great success. The famous Steiff toy company of Germany had also exhibited a jointed toy bear the previous year, and a buyer for New York toy merchant F. A. O. Schwartz hurried to place a huge order. Within a very short time the idea swept the nation and won the hearts of American children.

This New York workroom is manufacturing Teddy's Bear, a toy that swept the nation after President Roosevelt refused to shoot a small bear while on a hunt in Mississippi in 1902. *(Library of Congress, Prints and Photographs Division, LC-USZ62-108039)*

THE PRESIDENT TAKES ON THE TRUSTS

Theodore Roosevelt rose to the presidency in the midst of an unprecedented wave of business consolidations and increasing public concern about their growing economic and political power. Between 1898 and 1904, more than 5,000 independent companies vanished into some 300 huge corporations or trusts. U.S. Steel had a famously large capitalization of $1.4 billion at its founding in 1901, but other combinations were increasing their resources as well. The

American Tobacco Company, for example, was capitalized at $500 million in 1904. But money was not the only measure of power. Six railroad combinations controlled 95 percent of all the track in the nation. Several had more than 100,000 employees each, and each decision they made affected an astonishing number of workers.[7]

President Roosevelt was not an enemy of either big business or of wealth. He believed that large combinations were inevitable and a permanent feature of America's industrial economy. But he also believed that they sometimes abused their power. "We draw the line against misconduct, not against wealth," he said. "When I became President," Roosevelt later wrote in his autobiography, "the question as to the *method* by which the United States Government was to control the corporations was not yet important. The absolutely vital question was whether the Government had power to control them at all."[8]

During Roosevelt's first months as president, a battle occurred among three financial giants for control of railroads in the Northwest. J. P. Morgan, who owned the Northern Pacific, James J. Hill, owner of the Great Northern, and Edward H. Harriman, owner of Union Pacific, finally agreed to call a truce and join together as the Northern Securities Company—but not before their closed-door manipulations had caused a panic on Wall Street. Northern Securities Company was capitalized at $400 million in November 1901. Because it merged the three largest railroads north and west of Chicago, it could monopolize business there.

After the Northern Securities merger, the president decided to revive the Sherman Anti-Trust Act for its original purpose: protecting the public from monopolies. He believed that the new trust violated the act, and he was determined to show that the government and its president had the power to enforce it. He ordered Attorney General Philander Knox to file suit, which Knox did in March 1902. The action came as a surprise to the business community. It especially surprised Morgan, who tried to settle it by calling at the White House to tell the president, "If we have done anything wrong, send your man to my man and they can fix it up." President Roosevelt refused. Wall Street was up in arms, but elsewhere railroads were the most hated monopolies in America and the public applauded the act. In April, the federal district court in St. Paul (where the suit was filed) upheld the government's case against the trust. Two years later the Supreme Court agreed and ordered the trust dissolved.[9]

The Northern Securities case demonstrated that the president could and would use the law to dissolve trusts and monopolies. His willingness to take action was very popular, and the public approvingly identified him as a trustbuster. His success encouraged Congress to pass other measures that he requested for business regulation. In early 1903, Congress quickly passed the Expedition Act, which required courts to move antitrust suits to the head of the schedule. But in the long run, the president believed, an impartial administrative agency would be far more effective and efficient than the courts at regulating business. At his request, Congress created the Department of Commerce and Labor, with a cabinet-level secretary. Within the new department an investigatory agency, the Bureau of Corporations, was also established. The president believed that investigation and publicity alone would end much business misconduct. And in fact, several large corporations did choose to work with the new agency. Those who did not often found themselves the subject of antitrust suits.

The president also encouraged Congress to pass the Elkins Act in 1903 to further increase the regulation of railroads, which overall remained the largest and most powerful business in America. The battle to regulate the railroads, which was destined to continue for the remainder of the Progressive Era, focused primarily on rates for business and farm shipping. But it resonated deeply with the public as a whole. One reason was the political corruption to which railroads contributed by the purchase of influence, and another was the stock fleecing with which they were occasionally associated. But in addition, the public felt it had a stake in the railroads because trains were overwhelming important as a means of transportation—a fact that is easy to overlook today because there is no single contemporary equivalent. Trains filled the role of modern air travel, but also the role of modern motor vehicles for regional and interstate transportation. Every American who traveled even short distances from one town to the next was dependent on the railroads, and every hamlet lived or died according to its access to a rail line.

The 1903 act, named for West Virginia Republican Stephen Elkins, strengthened the Interstate Commerce Commission (ICC). It established penalties for railroad rebates—the custom of giving extremely large price breaks to large corporations, while small, independent shippers like farmers and small businessmen paid much higher rates. The railroads themselves had grown resentful of rebate demands and generally supported the Elkins legislation. The act made recipients as well as grantors of rebates guilty of violating the law.

THE COAL STRIKE OF 1902

In May 1902, John Mitchell, president of the United Mine Workers (UMW), called a strike in the anthracite (hard) coal fields of eastern Pennsylvania. In the anthracite region, the coal mining companies functioned almost like a trust because most were controlled by the large railroad corporations. Two years earlier, the mine company owners had agreed to raise miners' wages, but they were determined to grant no further concessions. They refused to negotiate with the workers and closed the mines.

Mitchell suggested arbitration by the National Civic Federation (NCF), founded in 1900 to lessen the antagonism between labor and capital. Throughout the strike he continued to appear reasonable and conciliatory. Public opinion was generally sympathetic to the miners. Sympathy increased when a letter from George F. Baer, president of the Reading Railroad and spokesman for the mining company owners, was widely published in newspapers. "The rights and interests of the laboring man will be protected and cared for not by the labor agitators," Baer wrote, "but by the Christian men and women to whom God in his infinite wisdom has given control of the property interests of the country." Editorialists and the public referred to it as Baer's "divine right" letter, a mocking phrase that recalled the old absolutist beliefs of European monarchs.[10]

As the strike dragged on into the autumn, the price of coal soared. Winter was approaching, coal was needed to heat homes and schools, and the public was clamoring for a solution. President Roosevelt summoned union and company officials to the White House on October 3. Mitchell readily agreed to arbitration by a commission of the president's choice. The coal operators refused even to speak to the union officials. The president was enraged. Privately, he reputedly admitted he thought of tossing Baer out a White House window. The president moved 10,000 troops to the anthracite fields and threatened to use them to mine coal, if necessary to prevent a disastrous public shortage of heating fuel. He also sent Secretary of War Elihu Root to talk to J. P. Morgan, who had financial ties to the mining companies. Root and Morgan quickly agreed to use an arbitration commission. Company officials acquiesced—on the condition that no labor union official be a member. With typical determination, the president named E. E. Clark, head of a railway union, to the commission—but retitled him an eminent sociologist. By October's end the companies had reopened the mines and the miners had returned to work. The commission eventually awarded miners a 10 percent pay increase and a workday of nine hours but no recognition for the union.

President Roosevelt's intervention and his stand in favor of arbitration were milestones in American labor history. For the first time, national officials did not automatically treat a strike as an uprising against property and public order. Instead, the president sought to mediate between workers and owners. The coal strike enhanced the public's perception of Roosevelt as a president who was willing to give the working-man a fair deal, but perhaps more important, one who was willing to take a firm stand for the public interest.

THE CONSERVATION PRESIDENT

When Theodore Roosevelt rose to the presidency, the young conservation movement gained one of its own in the White House. Roosevelt loved the outdoors and what he called the strenuous life. He was a passionate naturalist and bird-watcher as well as a hunter. He had been active in conservation organizations for many years. As president he immediately made conservation part of his domestic policy. In his first message to Congress in December 1901, three months after taking office, he outlined the goals of forest preservation, wildlife preserves, and irrigation projects for the arid west. Roosevelt was the first president to make the exploitation of natural resources a national issue. Many historians believe that his establishment of a conservation policy for America is the most significant legacy of his administration.

Today, it is easy to underestimate the change in viewpoint represented by President Roosevelt's stand for a national conservation policy. Since the first colonists arrived on the continent, Americans had always thought of land as plentiful, if not unlimited. They considered public lands and their natural resources to be a source of democratic opportunity. They expected that any unclaimed land in the public domain should and would be transferred to private ownership, if citizens were ready to develop it or its resources—transfers that took place routinely through homestead grants, land grants to railroads, mining claims, and purchases. Americans also traditionally assumed that few restrictions would hamper those who obtained property or those who simply wanted to use land that was in the public domain.

During the second half of the 19th century, however, traditional policies and assumptions collided with national growth and the vastly increased pace of economic development. Ruthless competition and the rush to development often encouraged reckless waste. Lumber companies cut without replanting and jammed waterways with logs, causing floods as well as impeding river traffic. Cattlemen and sheep ranchers grazed their herds until public lands were bare. Mining companies denuded the land, leaving it eroded. Corporations accumulated gigantic landholdings. But with the closing of the frontier some Americans became increasingly concerned about the fate of remaining land and resources. They believed that the nation and the public had legitimate interests in need of protection. Some, like Roosevelt, also had a genuinely altruistic interest in the fate of future generations.

A national conservation policy meant that the national government would henceforth protect or reserve some of the land and resources in the public domain instead of selling or granting them to private owners and would regulate and restrict their use. But the change did not occur without bitter political battles, especially in the West where most of the still-unclaimed land and resources were located. The West was well stocked with up-and-coming individuals who were determined to amass a fortune from its natural resources. In the West and elsewhere, many other Americans also disliked the idea of increased federal control that a national conservation policy implied. Because of this opposition, many historians believe, President Roosevelt's conservation initiatives probably would have been less successful if they had depended on Congressional approval. But instead, the president usually achieved his ends by using executive power or by expanding administrative authority. Twenty-six different agencies eventually made rules, regulations, and programs for aspects of forests, minerals, water issues, flood control, stock grazing, and wild or recreational facilities. The president also liberally used what he called a bully pulpit (the ability of the president to effect change by exhorting his fellow citizens) to convince Americans of conservation's value.

ROOSEVELT'S CONSERVATION AGENDA

One legacy of the Roosevelt years was a great increase in preservation of wilderness and wildlife. The president oversaw the establishment of five national parks during his presidency, beginning with Crater Lake National Park, Oregon, in 1902. The following year he established a federal wild bird refuge by executive order on Pelican Island, Indian River, Florida, the first of 51 bird and four large game wildlife sanctuaries he created before leaving office. After a 1903 visit to Yosemite with John Muir, he obtained the transfer of the entire Yosemite Valley from the state of California to the federal government. He set aside 18 areas as national monuments, including the Grand Canyon. He began the preservation of remaining buffalo herds. He multiplied the forest reserves.

Nonetheless, the overall federal policy which Roosevelt established was not one of preservation or protection of natural areas and resources for their own sake. It was a policy of managed (or regulated) use of resources. While the two camps of the conservation movement, managed use and preservationist, continued to join forces against common enemies throughout the Progressive Era, by the end of Roosevelt's presidency, the contrast and sometime conflict between them had become sharp.

Shortly after becoming president, Roosevelt met with Gifford Pinchot, a personal friend and chief of the Bureau of Forestry, to help him set the agenda for conservation. Pinchot, the first professional forester in the United States, became the president's chief adviser on the proper management of natural resources. At the time, forestry issues were the vanguard of conservation efforts worldwide. Traditionally, wood was an extremely important resource in human society, and deforestation and wood shortages had already become pressing issues in Europe. But the wood issue was pressing in on America too; by 1900, only one-quarter of the original virgin forest of the continental nation remained. "The Conservation movement was a direct outgrowth of the forest movement," Roosevelt later wrote in his autobiography. "It was nothing more than the application to our other natural resources of the principles which had been worked out in connection with the forests."[11]

Both the president and Pinchot believed that the proper policy was to regulate use of the nation's resources to benefit the public as a whole. They both took the progressive view that resource management could best be accomplished by nonpartisan scientists and other experts—not in the political arena, where competing claims and entrenched power always threatened to override the public interest. Instead, the president interpreted the federally managed use of resources as a policy that provided a square deal to both present and future generations. Both Roosevelt and Pinchot made special efforts to see that young people were educated about conservation questions.

Almost immediately upon becoming president, Roosevelt supported legislation to reclaim the arid lands of the West; that is, to use large-scale irrigation to open unusable areas to farming and settlement. The campaign for reclamation had been initiated many years before by naturalist and chief of the U.S. Geological Survey John Wesley Powell. Roosevelt, who had lived in the West, lent the authority of his personal experience to the cause, although many in his own party opposed it. In June of 1902 Congress passed the National Reclamation Act, also called the Newlands Act after its sponsor, Senator Francis Newlands, Democrat of Nevada. The act established the Bureau of Reclamation in the Department of the Interior. It also provided for the sale of public lands in 16 western and southwestern states. The proceeds would form a revolving Reclamation Fund to pay for dams, canals, reservoirs, and other federal water projects. In other words, reclamation was to be self-supporting. By 1915, 25 separate projects had been undertaken at a cost of some $80 million. The largest, completed in 1911, was the Roosevelt Dam in Arizona.

The Newlands Act established a new federal responsibility for water policy that would continue to grow in the 20th century. However, reclamation was destined to profoundly transform the landscape and ecology of areas with little rainfall—at direct odds with the policy of preserving the scenic landscape of the West.

ROOSEVELT AND RACIAL ISSUES

Inevitably, the issues of segregation and disenfranchisement of African Americans reached President Roosevelt, raising political as well as moral dilemmas. In general, he took the public stance that it was his responsibility to respond "cautiously, temperately, and sanely" to what he and almost every other white American called the Negro problem.[12] Roosevelt was not free of the racial prejudices of his day, but he nonetheless made a principled effort to include black Americans in his square deal on a number of occasions during his first term.

In the late 19th century, the Republican Party had maintained a policy of appointing some black Republicans to minor government posts in the South. By the time Roosevelt took office, however, even the few white Republicans in the South had joined the movement to exclude blacks from political party activities in general and government service in particular—even from those service jobs that whites had formerly considered appropriate for black citizens. In the fall of 1902, for example, whites in Indianola, Mississippi, began a campaign of petitions, public meetings, and outright personal harassment to remove the black postmistress. Under duress, Minnie M. Cox, who had served since President Harrison's administration, resigned. President Roosevelt refused to accept the resignation. He closed the Indianola post office rather than give in to what he called "a brutal and lawless element" and its "wrong and outrage of such flagrant character."[13] He also ordered that Cox continue to receive her salary until her appointed term ended in 1904.

Also during fall 1902, Roosevelt nominated Dr. William Crum, an African-American physician, to replace a white incumbent as collector of customs in Charleston. It was a prominent position in the town, and whites were outraged. Southern Democrats in Congress, aided by some Republicans, mounted a long campaign to block his confirmation. The president released an open letter to newspapers stating that he believed it to be "fundamentally wrong" that "the door of hope, the door of opportunity—is to be shut upon any man, no matter how worthy, purely upon the grounds of race or color."[14] The president refused to back down, and in 1905, Dr. Crum was finally confirmed.

THE FLOOD TIDE OF IMMIGRATION BEGINS

The heaviest decade of immigration that America has ever known began in 1901. During President Roosevelt's first term, the number of new arrivals rose from less than 500,000 in 1901 to more than 800,000 in 1904.

In the wake of President McKinley's assassination by an anarchist of immigrant parentage, Congress passed a new immigration act in 1903 that barred anarchists from entering the country. The law affected very few people seeking entry at the time. It did, however, mark the first time that immigrants could be examined and excluded for their political beliefs, a practice that would become more important in the future. The legislation also elaborated on the classes of people who had been excluded at least since 1891, such as contract laborers, persons with certain diseases, polygamists, prostitutes, criminals, and "paupers or persons likely to become public charges."[15]

REFORM COMES TO ELLIS ISLAND

Throughout summer 1901, reports about corruption and maltreatment of immigrants at Ellis Island engaged the New York press. Within a month after taking office, President Roosevelt began housecleaning. "I am more anxious to get this office straight than almost any other," he wrote to a friend. The major immigration officials—the commissioner general in Washington and the commissioner and assistant commissioner for the Port of New York—were all political appointees with highly placed supporters. But with greater or lesser degrees of force, Roosevelt replaced them all. He wanted an efficient, principled administration that would apply the laws strictly but fairly and equally to all immigrants seeking to enter the country.[16]

The president dismissed former Knights of Labor head Terrence Powderly as commissioner general and appointed Frank P. Sargent, an official in the Brotherhood of Locomotive Firemen. For political reasons, men with ties to labor usually held high office in the immigration service. Organized labor favored a close watch on immigration because they objected strongly to contract labor—immigrant workers whose transportation was paid by American manufacturers if they agreed to work at wages far below the national average.

More important, however, was the president's selection of William Williams, a young Wall Street lawyer, for New York commissioner of immigration and head of Ellis Island. Williams was noted for his high personal ethics and interest in reform. He took office in April 1902. Within days he posted signs throughout Ellis Island announcing to workers and newcomers alike, "Immigrants must be treated with kindness and consideration." Within months he had made sweeping changes. He awarded new contracts for food, concessions, and money changing, regardless of how many political friends the former suppliers had. The existing food service, for example, not only charged outrageous prices—it also served the food without offering utensils and without washing the dishes between uses. "The influence exerted here by the former holder of the feeding privilege in the face of such facts," wrote Williams, "is incomprehensible." It wasn't really incomprehensible, of course, as Williams probably knew. The profits actually went straight to a Republican political boss.[17]

Williams quickly corrected abuses by inspectors and boards of inquiry, the groups of immigration officers who determined admission in questionable cases. Often, he found, they extorted money from immigrants. He backed up all his new policies with reprimands and dismissals for employees who resisted. "There is no doubt of the almost revolutionary character of the changes that Williams brought about with the vigorous support of the president," writes historian Thomas Pitkin. The improvements that he instituted vastly improved the experience of most immigrants who passed through Ellis Island.[18]

Nonetheless, the job of managing Ellis Island at the flood tide of immigration was not an easy one. The commissioner's office and Williams personally became lightning rods for the growing national debate over immigration and its restriction. Williams favored more restriction, and he chose to enforce the existing laws stringently and to the letter, refusing admittance to those who did not meet the legal criteria. For doing so, he was attacked bitterly and often unconscionably by most of the foreign language press in America. Organized ethnic societies or immigration leagues were especially unhappy about his interpretation of the ban on those "likely to become a public charge," as the immigration law put it. Ethnic societies believed that some poor people were being unfairly denied the opportunity to improve their lot in America. Jewish groups in particular were very concerned by the situation of impoverished eastern European Jews, especially those in Romania and Russia, as pogroms (violent attacks on Jewish communities) continued to sweep their homelands. In 1904 the Hebrew Immigrant Aid Society (HIAS) was founded, joining other ethnic aid societies who stationed representatives at Ellis Island. All such societies helped immigrants through the process of admission, especially when questions about eligibility were raised and they faced a board of inquiry. In fact, fewer than 2 percent of all arrivals to America were denied admission during the Progressive Era. But each case was, of course, a personal tragedy.

Many problems remained entrenched at Ellis Island, and periodic investigations continued to occur, but Williams delivered the death blow to wholesale corruption. He left office in 1905 but returned for a second term in 1909.

THE ALASKA–CANADA BOUNDARY DISPUTE

When the United States purchased Alaska from Russia in 1867, it bought an unclear boundary line. The line between the Alaskan panhandle and the Canadian Yukon had been badly described in an 1825 treaty between Russia and Great Britain. No one was concerned until gold was discovered in the Yukon. Then the line quickly took on importance. The most accessible route to the gold fields in Canada was via the Alaskan panhandle coastline. Canada began to press a claim to ownership of several major water inlets there, including the Alaskan ports of Dyea and Skagway. The inlets would have provided Canada with direct sea access to and from the landlocked Yukon, without traveling through U.S. territory.

President Roosevelt was disinclined to compromise. He believed that the Canadian claims "did not have a leg to stand on," were "dangerously near blackmail," and were advanced as a ploy to extract some concessions as the price of settlement. In 1902 he renewed an offer for an arbitration panel of "six impartial jurists of repute"— three American, two Canadian, and one British.[19] Canada and Britain sent distinguished jurists. The United States sent Secretary of War Elihu Root, staunch nationalist Senator Henry Cabot Lodge, and Senator George Turner of Washington, the state closest to the area—none of whom were particularly impartial or even judges. The president instructed the Americans to concede nothing, and he let his orders be known to British diplomats in Washington. In the end, the British judge sided with the Americans. By a vote of 4–2, in 1903 the panel rejected the Canadian claims to a water inlet, although the boundary line was adjusted slightly.

The dispute had important repercussions among the three nations. Canadians were angered by what they viewed as British disloyalty. They were also embittered toward the United States for many years. Between the United States and Great Britain, however, the decision increased the new sense of cooperation that had begun in the

The U.S. cabinet in 1903 included (*left to right*) George Cortelyou, secretary to the president; Philander Knox, attorney general; Henry Payne, postmaster general; William H. Moody, secretary of the navy; John Hay, secretary of state; President Roosevelt; Ethan Allen Hitchcock, secretary of the interior; Elihu Root, secretary of war; Leslie Shaw, secretary of the treasury; James Wilson, secretary of agriculture. (*Library of Congress, Prints and Photographs Division, LC-USZ62-96155*)

1890s—partly due to a recognition of their similar traditions and partly because they both feared the growing power of Germany. Although today the two nations customarily think of one another as close allies, prior to the 1890s they did not. Early in the 19th century, Britain was in fact an enemy of the United States, and later a rival for trade. Prior to the 1890s, popular sentiment in America was often anti-British.

AN ISTHMIAN CANAL PROJECT TAKES SHAPE

Europeans, and later Americans, had dreamed of building a canal across the narrow Isthmus of Panama ever since the Spanish explorer Balboa crossed it in 1513. A canal would permit ships to pass between the Atlantic and Pacific Oceans, bypassing the arduous sea voyage around the continent of South America. In the 1880s, a private French company decided to attempt the project. Its head was Ferdinand de Lesseps, designer of the Suez Canal. Digging was unexpectedly difficult and the toll of tropical diseases on European workers was astonishingly high—by 1890 some 20,000 had died. The project proved beyond the financial capabilities of the private investors and was abandoned.

Meanwhile Americans were becoming more interested in an isthmian canal. Alfred Thayer Mahan argued in his influential writings that a canal would greatly increase American naval power. His point was well illustrated during the Spanish-American War. It took the battleship *Oregon*, stationed on the West Coast, more than two months to reach Cuba via the South American route—by which time the brief war was almost over. After the war, U.S. officials pursued the canal project in earnest.

The first obstacle was the 1850 Clayton-Bulwer Treaty with Britain, in which the two nations had agreed that they would share control over any future canal. In 1900 and 1901, diplomats negotiated the Hay-Pauncefote Treaty, in which Britain gave the United States the sole right to build, operate, and fortify a canal. Meanwhile, an American canal commission identified two possible sites. One was the abandoned French site in Panama and the other was in Nicaragua. Most commissioners believed the Nicaraguan site to be preferable. Then, in 1902 as Congress was in the process of choosing a site, a volcano erupted in Nicaragua. On the day of the Senate vote, Philippe Bunau-Varilla—head engineer of the former French project, a major stockholder in the French company, and a determined lobbyist for Panama—sent each senator a Nicaraguan stamp depicting another huge volcano a mere 20 miles from the canal site. Congress chose Panama, and on June 28 President Roosevelt signed the Isthmian Canal or Spooner Act into law.

At the time, Panama was a province of the nation Colombia, not an independent country. Secretary of State John Hay and the Colombian ambassador Thomas Herrán reached an agreement. The United States agreed to pay $10 million outright and a yearly rental of $250,000 for a canal zone. The U.S. Senate ratified the Hay-Herrán Treaty in 1903, but the Colombian Senate rejected it, believing the price to be too low. President Roosevelt was outraged, calling the rejection "pure bandit morality."[20]

The Panamanians themselves favored the canal. They had long been unhappy with the distant Colombian government and had attempted numerous revolts throughout the 19th century. With little difficulty, Bunau-Varilla helped organize another revolt. President Roosevelt, informed of the possibility, sent battleships to the area. Colombian troops could not reach Panama by land—nor could they risk arrival by sea. The bloodless Panamanian revolt succeeded on November 4, 1903, and America immediately recognized the new nation. Bunau-Varilla was appointed Panamanian ambassador to the United States. Within two weeks he had negotiated the Hay–Bunau-Varilla Treaty between the new nation and the United States. It permitted the construction of a canal under the same financial terms rejected by Colombia, and the canal zone was even enlarged from six to 10 miles wide. To the end of his life, Roosevelt denied wrongdoing in the Panamanian coup, defending his actions at some length in his autobiography. "I did not lift my finger to incite the revolutionists," he wrote. "I simply ceased to stamp out the different revolutionary fuses that were already burning." But U.S. actions offended many South American governments. In 1922, "to remove all misunderstandings growing out of the events of November 1903," the United States paid $25 million to Colombia.[21]

In early 1904, President Roosevelt created an Isthmian Canal Commission. The assets of the French company were bought out, and work began in May on what would be a 10-year-long project. A Canal Zone government was soon established for America's newest protectorate, with a governor, a legal code, a judicial system, and a school system. But the most pressing problem was sanitation. It was assigned to Dr. William C. Gorgas, who had been a member of Dr. Walter Reed's yellow fever team in Havana during the Spanish-American War. At first, Dr. Gorgas's methods met much opposition from other American officials, who believed them to be unproven. After a severe outbreak of yellow fever in late 1904, however, he won President Roosevelt's confidence and aid in obtaining the policies and supplies he needed. Within 18 months, he brought yellow fever and malaria under control in the Canal Zone. Dr. Gorgas gained worldwide acclaim for his work in ending the scourge of tropical diseases.

THE ROOT REFORMS CONTINUE

Under President Roosevelt, Secretary of War Elihu Root continued his efforts to reform the American military system. Aided by reform-minded military officers whom historian Peter Karsten calls "armed progressives," Root wanted to reorganize the army so that it could plan, coordinate, and supervise military activity like an efficient business corporation.[22]

Since beginning his efforts, Root's most important goal had been to clarify the command of America's armed forces. He believed that overall authority for the army should clearly proceed from the president to the secretary of war and from the secretary to a chief of staff. The chief of staff would be the head military adviser to the president as well as the executive who would supervise all operations of the army, through a general staff that reported to him. Along with these changes, Root wanted to limit terms of service in War Department bureaus to lessen the entrenched alliances with congressmen and other interests.

Root achieved some of his goals when Congress passed "An Act to Increase the Efficiency of the Army," known as the General Staff Act of 1903. Root successfully shepherded the bill past the opposition of both the current commanding general (head of the fighting forces) and many bureau chiefs (heads of decentralized administration and supply operations). The act authorized a chief of staff and a General Staff Corps of 44 officers, all on four-year rotations. The transition to the new organization was destined to be neither short nor smooth. Disputes over the command structure were still occurring when World War I began. Nonetheless, the General Staff Act was the beginning of modern American military organization.

In 1903, the navy still remained an entirely separate department with its own cabinet-level secretary. Later that year Root announced that he and the secretary of the navy, William H. Moody, had agreed to establish a joint board of four officers from each branch, to reach "common conclusions regarding all matters calling for the cooperation of the two services."[23]

Another part of Root's program was reform of what is now the National Guard. State guard units, usually called militias, had been established by the Militia Law of 1792. They still operated on a state-by-state basis without federal oversight and had no organizational connection to the U.S. Army. Of course, one purpose of state militias was to act as backup units in case of war. Nonetheless, service as a guardsman was entirely voluntary, even if the president issued a call to the state governor in wartime.

Many Americans continued to support this traditional, voluntary, and decentralized system of citizen soldiers. Some supported independent state militias because they believed in states' rights and opposed strong federal government. Others opposed a strong professional army. Traditionally, many Americans associated professional armies with the wars and oppressions of Europe and held them to be incompatible with democracy. The U.S. Army, for its part, would have preferred complete control of the state units but was especially unhappy with the lack of training and discipline and with the selection of officers, which usually reflected state politics.

Secretary Root worked skillfully with the various factions. He also had the support of President Roosevelt, whose Rough Riders had been organized as a militia unit. In 1903, Congress passed the "Act to Promote the Efficiency of the Militia," usually called the National Guard Act. It established an organized militia under joint state and federal control to be called the National Guard. The act gave the states federal money to maintain and equip their organized militia in exchange for increased coordination with the army. It also required members to serve for at least nine months if a state unit was called by the president.

THE MUCKRAKERS

In the first decade of the 20th century, a new kind of investigative, crusading journalism swept the nation. The writers came to be called *muckrakers,* a name given to them in a 1906 speech by President Roosevelt. The president did not mean the name to be flattering. The Man with the Muckrake, a character in *Pilgrim's Progress* by John Bunyan, raked up manure. But journalists embraced the name with pride, and to many people they were heroes and heroines.

In the 1890s, at the same time mass-circulation newspapers and yellow journalism appeared, magazine publishing also changed. Previously most magazines, like *North American Review, Harper's, Atlantic, Scribner's,* and *Century,* were published for small, stable, highly literate audiences. In the 1890s, mass-circulation magazines began to compete for readers. They carried more advertising, had slicker formats, and cost less. In October 1902, one of them, *McClure's,* published "Tweed Days in St. Louis," the first installment of journalist Lincoln Steffens's investigation into corruption in city government. Other journals had published exposés of corruption before, but Steffens's article created a sensation with the increasingly reform-minded public. The January 1903 issue of *McClure's* opened the floodgates of reform journalism. It contained Steffens's exposé of Minneapolis, Ray Stannard Baker on corruption in labor unions, and the second installment of Ida Tarbell's exposé of the Standard Oil trust. Soon many other popular magazines, such as *Cosmopolitan, Colliers, American,* and *Everybody's,* were specializing in the new muckraking journalism. Established magazines like *Forum* and the *Independent,* which had long roots in 19th-century reform and social justice issues, inquired into corruption for more intellectual audiences. Newspapers carried exposés. Many investigations were republished in book format, both Lincoln Steffens's *The Shame of the Cities* and Ida Tarbell's *The History of Standard*

McClure's Magazine was the first to emphasize the new, investigative journalism that President Roosevelt dubbed muckraking. This November 1903 cover lists articles by well-known muckrakers on typical subjects: labor and trusts, municipal corruption, and a threat to the public's health. *(Library of Congress, Prints and Photographs Division, LC-USZ62-75558)*

Oil, for example. One of the most famous muckraking works, Upton Sinclair's *The Jungle,* was a novel. Sinclair intended it to be a socialist exposé of worker exploitation in the meat-packing industry—but he did hard research and described astonishingly unsanitary practices in nauseating detail. "I aimed at the public's heart," Sinclair later commented, "and by accident I hit it in the stomach." The fictional Mr. Dooley advised, "If you want to reduce your butcher's bills, buy *The Jungle.*"[24]

REFORMING CITY GOVERNMENT

Periodically, a new scandal of corruption in city government would occur. As Tammany boss George Washington Plunkitt told reporter William Riorden in 1904, municipal reform committees were often "mornin' glories—looked lovely in the mornin' and withered up in a short time, while the regular machines went on flourishin' forever, like fine old oaks."[25] Nonetheless, both structural reform (which changes the way decision-making and city management occurs) and social-justice reform (which increases public services and amenities for all citizens) were working changes in American cities. Slowly, city government was becoming more effective and less corrupt. These changes did not end boss and machine rule in most cities. But in some, the bosses themselves began to support certain reform efforts. In Cincinnati, for example, boss George Cox undertook street paving, sewer building, and waterworks projects.

In 1901, one of the best known of all progressive mayors took office in Cleveland. Tom Johnson had made a fortune in steel and street railways by the age of 40, then began a second career as a Democratic politician and crusader for social justice. He claimed to have been converted by reading the works of single-tax reformer Henry George. "It is privilege that causes evil in the world," Johnson said, "not wickedness; and not men."[26]

During Johnson's eight years in office, Cleveland came to be called "the best governed city in America" (a phrase coined by muckraker Lincoln Steffens.)[27] The mayor attracted a talented group of reform-minded aides, who compiled a long list of accomplishments. Together they weeded out corruption and adopted a businesslike approach to management. They adopted strict housing and sanitary standards, built new water and sewage systems, paved and lighted the streets, and began garbage collection. They cleaned up the police department, which in turn cleaned up vice. They reformed the treatment of prisoners and the dependent. They improved river and lake shores and expanded parks, playgrounds, and public spaces. They even supported a City Beautiful plan to develop an attractive urban center with public buildings around a mall.

What Johnson was best known for, however, was his controversial campaign for municipal ownership of utilities, often called municipal socialism at the time. "I believe in municipal ownership of all public service monopolies for the same reason that I believe in the municipal ownership of waterworks, of parks, of schools," Johnson wrote in his autobiography. "I believe in the municipal ownership of these monopolies because if you do not own them they will in time own you. They will rule your politics, corrupt your institutions and finally destroy your liberties."[28] Johnson successfully established a municipal electrical plant and required streetcar companies to lower their fares, but he lost his battle for municipal ownership of the streetcar lines. Johnson enjoyed much support among ordinary people. But he was constantly under attack by powerful interests, including Senator Mark Hanna, who owned some of the streetcar lines the mayor wanted to take over. He was defeated for reelection in 1908 after four terms in office. In 1910, however, his aide Newton Baker won the mayor's office and continued his programs.

REFORMING THE PHYSICAL CITY: CITY PLANNING

Since the Chicago World's Fair of 1893, the City Beautiful movement had promoted the redesign of jumbled, ugly industrial cities to make them more attractive and more orderly. In 1902, the movement received a boost. The McMillan Commission, established by the U.S. Senate, issued an impressive new plan for Washington, D.C., with new elements like the Capitol Mall. It was the largest and most complete city plan to date and received national and overwhelmingly positive press coverage. For the remainder of the first decade of the 20th century, the City Beautiful movement was at its height. Major plans were commissioned for nearly 40 cities.

While the City Beautiful movement was commanding the publicity, a more utilitarian, functional city planning movement was also developing. The first attempts at functional city planning were made in the 1890s, when the first municipal boards of survey were established. Their modest goal was to unite public and private plans so that roads, railways, and utilities would be built where needed. But even that was not introduced without great opposition, usually from the courts.

Although functional city planning may seem like common sense today, it marked an important change in the way Americans thought about private property and the individual economic decisions its owners made. Land speculation and development was a time-honored way to make money in America. Throughout the 19th century, private speculators and developers subdivided their land as they chose and platted the streets where they wished. Many citizens "bitterly resented any limitation on private initiative and displayed militant impatience with government restriction," writes historian Mel Scott.[29] For example, in the 1890s when Boston's board of survey drew plans for future highways in outlying areas, the city was promptly sued. The state supreme court ruled it was unconstitutional even to lay out street lines in advance of development because it interfered with the rights of property owners. Even in 1902, the high-powered McMillan commission could not legally enforce its plans for highways radiating from Washington, D.C.—even though it included two cabinet-level secretaries and the chief engineers of the army. Instead, like a number of other cities, Washington accomplished its highway plan by refusing to extend utilities to private property owners who ignored it.

The publicity given to the elaborate City Beautiful plans during the first decade of the 20th century greatly raised the profile of functional city planning as well. Municipal reformers, civic leaders, and even businessmen were increasingly receptive to the idea that it was a legitimate activity, even a necessity, and that it worked in the public interest.

PROGRESSIVISM IN THE STATEHOUSE

As the 20th century got under way, progressive reformers began to extend their sights from city hall to the state capitol. It had become clear that municipal corruption was intertwined with corruption at the state level. Political machines in the cities and county courthouse gangs in rural areas were branches of state political machines. State machines, in turn, were in league with powerful business and economic interests. Some state legislatures were outright corrupt. One way reformers attempted to corral the state machines and legislatures was the direct-democracy campaign. The referendum was a way to veto the legislature's actions, and the initiative was a way to bypass it altogether. The direct primary and recall were ways to bypass or veto the state party bosses. Reform at the state level was particularly important, reformers believed, because the state legislature had the power to elect U.S. senators and thus extend the reach of corruption all the way to Washington. Muckraker Lincoln Steffens called his series of articles on municipal government "The Shame of the Cities," but he called his series on state corruption "Enemies of the Republic."

In 1900, Wisconsin elected the most famous reform governor of the era, Republican Robert M. La Follette. Born literally in a log cabin in rural Wisconsin, he had worked his way through the state university and law school before entering politics.

La Follette won the governorship, after two unsuccessful attempts, by defeating his own party machine—a pattern that would soon repeat itself in other states. He then found that conservative Republicans in the state legislature continued to block his reform efforts. Possessing a fervent personal commitment to reform, "Fighting Bob" criss-crossed the state speaking to small groups of farmers and other citizens. He explained his ideas and exhorted his listeners to take personal responsibility for reform when casting their votes. He successfully built a strong following that elected a reform legislature, returned him to the governor's office through 1906, then sent him on to the U.S. Senate. "La Follette never compromised," remembered William Allen White, famous editor of the Kansas *Emporia Gazette*. "In all my life I have never seen a braver man in politics. And he made his bravery count."[30]

Among reformers, Wisconsin became known as a "laboratory of democracy." La Follette's program included three major progressive interests: curtailing the power of political parties, bringing railroads and other corporations under public control, and increasing the opportunities, health, and welfare of the average citizen. Direct-democracy reforms and civil service merit systems for state employees were adopted. The power of lobbyists was reduced. A railroad commission was established to regulate railroads and other utilities. Taxes on railroads were increased by valuing their property according to the same standards used for farms and other properties. Graduated inheritance and income taxes were established. Laws to regulate the workplace and provide workers' compensation were passed.

At the heart of the Wisconsin idea, as it came to be called, was the union of expert knowledge and political action. It was accomplished by using experts drawn from Wisconsin's own state university. La Follette's method was to appoint researchers to study a problem, then use the facts they discovered to design reform legislation and popularize it with the public. The university also supported an extension program, with offices, agents, and programs throughout the state to provide up-to-date knowledge to farmers, homemakers, and small business owners. The Wisconsin idea was widely publicized by reform journalists and studied and imitated by reformers in other states.

A New View of Poverty Emerges

After 1900, a new view of poverty became more frequently and publicly advocated by reform-minded people in America. Prior to 1890, historian Robert Bremner explains, when either the public or charity workers referred to the poor, they meant paupers, the dependent, those who did not work, those who needed and received alms. They vaguely recognized any lesser degree of inadequate resources as honest poverty. But except to imagine that honest poverty was character building, an incentive to work harder, and probably normal and inevitable, neither the public nor charity workers paid it much heed. Throughout the 1890s, however, settlement workers, professional social workers, and many other socially concerned people became more and more aware that poverty in the new industrial economy did not fit the old definitions. They compiled information, surveys, studies, and personal knowledge showing that many employed, self-supporting laboring families lived in misery. In many cases father, mother, and children all worked long hours for tiny wages simply to eke out the most meager of livings. Especially in the teeming slums of larger cities, their lives were marked by overwork, exhaustion, ill health, disease, and "congestion" (overcrowded living conditions). Increasingly, reform-minded people came to view poverty not as a condition of complete dependency, but as what Bremner calls a state of "insufficiency and insecurity." The working poor lived in a constant state of insufficient food, clothing, shelter, and sanitary conditions. They lived in constant financial precariousness as well, with no social welfare programs, unemployment insurance, pensions, or even workmen's compensation for injuries.[31]

Settlement worker Robert Hunter's 1904 book, *Poverty,* illustrated the new view. It was one of the very first studies that attempted to estimate the overall causes and occurrence of poverty in American society. Hunter described the poor as people in any industrial nation who had "too little of the common necessities to keep themselves at their best." Hunter wrote, "To live miserably we know not why, to have the dread of hunger, to work sore and yet gain nothing—this is the essence of poverty." No central agencies yet collected statistics on poverty, nor had there yet been any national studies. But Hunter estimated that even in times of prosperity and good employment, at least 10 million Americans—about one out of every seven people at the time—lived in poverty.[32] Hunter's estimate was very controversial. All people were shocked by the figure and conservative Americans refused to give it credence.

The conservative were even less inclined to accept Hunter's insistence that society itself was unquestionably responsible for these conditions. The new view of poverty laid responsibility for social and economic conditions at the door of the public and challenged the public to modify them. But traditionally, Americans held an individualistic view of poverty. They considered the inability to support oneself with honest employment to result from character flaws that made one lazy, improvident, or vicious. They also believed that in America any ordinary self-reliant individual had an opportunity to achieve a decent, self-supporting life by hard work and honest labor. Furthermore, they viewed self-reliance and opportunity as mainstays of American democracy. But reformers like Hunter maintained that an economy dominated by mammoth industrial corporations had changed these conditions dramatically. Now, reformers argued, poverty had little relationship to individual effort and stemmed instead from conditions over which the individual had little control. They pointed to the indisputable fact that many people could not earn enough to live a decent life despite full-time employment, not to mention the problem of periodic unemployment when the economy soured. To be sure, even reformers did not completely reject the belief that poverty was related to individual character. But increasingly, progressive-minded people believed that poverty was at least equally dependent on miserable wages and inhumane working conditions. The new view of poverty raised a troubling political question as well. If opportunity had dwindled and self-reliance could no longer prevent poverty, was the foundation of democracy itself in danger of crumbling?

For these reasons, one of the most important areas of progressive reform was a group of initiatives to improve the conditions of labor. The new view of poverty and the optimistic belief that it could be substantially reduced was the thread that ran through campaigns to regulate working conditions and hours, end child labor, provide compensation for accidents or injuries on the job, establish pensions, as well as offer support for union efforts to organize workers and to obtain higher wages.

THE CAMPAIGN AGAINST CHILD LABOR BECOMES NATIONAL

Shortly after the turn of the century, public concern about child labor blossomed into a national crusade. Muckrakers publicized facts and statistics about the dreadful conditions of child labor and its effects on the health and moral development of America's children. Prominent people took up the cause. In 1902, the first child labor reform organizations were independently established in Alabama and New York.

Conditions in Alabama were considered the worst in the South. About 30 percent of cotton mill workers were children 15 and younger who worked 12-hour days, six days a week for 15 to 30 cents per day. In 1901, a child labor bill was defeated in the state legislature. Afterward, Episcopal clergyman Edgar Gardner Murphy formed the Alabama Child Labor Committee. It was the first organization of the type in America.

The committee included local judges, school officials, newspaper editors, and a former governor. Together they used photos and other documentation to rouse local public opinion. In 1903, Alabama passed the strictest child labor law in the southern states. It limited industrial work to children 12 and older (exceptions were orphans and those with dependent parents) and to 60 hours per week.

In New York, Florence Kelley of the National Consumers' League and Lillian Wald of Henry Street Settlement took the lead in establishing the New York Child Labor Committee. It was composed of social workers, reformers, philanthropists, and businessmen and headed by Robert Hunter of University Settlement. The New York committee quickly built ties with other civic and religious reform groups. Within a year it had inspired five child labor bills.

Soon, Edgar Gardner Murphy made the acquaintance of Felix Adler, a member of the New York committee and founder of the Ethical Culture Society (a spiritual congregation that stresses ethics rather than theism). Together they began to organize a national child labor group. In April 1904, the National Child Labor Committee (NCLC) had its first general meeting in Carnegie Hall. Dr. Samuel McCune Lindsay, a professor of sociology at the University of Pennsylvania, became its secretary or head. Two assistant secretaries were also appointed: Alexander McKelway, a Presbyterian minister and reformer from North Carolina, for the South and Owen R. Lovejoy, a Congregational minister in New York for the North. The NCLC board drew together more than 50 prominent figures such as Jane Addams; Robert de Forest, president of the Charity Organization Society; Ben B. Lindsey, a Denver judge who had founded the first juvenile court in America; former president Grover Cleveland; the president of the General Federation of Women's Clubs; representatives of the Kuhn, Loeb investment banking firm; and many other prominent corporate leaders and philanthropists, church and labor leaders, academics, and journalists. In some ways, writes historian Walter Trattner, the committee "represented a new approach to social reform, for by obtaining so prominent and influential a national membership it would command a respectful hearing despite its attack upon so controversial an issue."[33]

The crusade against child labor was controversial nonetheless, and the supporters of child labor so entrenched that it would take reformers the better part of two decades to achieve significant changes. Employers of children strongly defended the practice. They claimed that they could not stay in business without it, or that some jobs were particularly suited to children, or that working allowed children to learn the industry and move up as adults. They argued that giving jobs to children should be viewed almost as a philanthropic effort: it not only aided poor families, it also kept children occupied who might otherwise become delinquent. Many conservative Americans supported the employers' point of view. They argued, as they did with any labor reform, that restrictions violated the traditional freedom of contract between individual workers and employers. They also held that the state had no standing to interfere in family decisions if parents sent their own child to work. And in fact, some parents did want their children to work.

Reformers understood the plight of poor or dependent parents who could not make ends meet without their children's meager wages and wrote frequently about the subject. But there were, in addition, parents who believed it was a child's role to work, just as they did on a family farm, or who insisted that children help the family establish economic security, or who simply did not value schooling. These parental values were most common among southern white mill workers and some (but not all) immigrant groups in the urban North. Reformers viewed these parents as greedy, ignorant, lazy, or at the least shockingly unconcerned with their children's future. But even reformers, it should be noted, did not oppose all child labor. They primarily attacked labor for very young children, work done under unhealthful conditions or for unreasonable hours, and jobs that interfered with basic schooling.

As with other reform issues, the founding of a national organization gave a clear focus to the movement, although many other groups remained active in the cause. Lindsay, McKelway, and Lovejoy set up 17 state and local bodies throughout the nation within a year. The NCLC began researching and collecting information, "since a knowledge of the facts will be the most useful of all means of accomplishing results," as Adler put it.[34] They also drew up model legislation, based on recent child labor laws in Massachusetts, New York, and Illinois. The model law called for a minimum age of 16 in mining and 14 in manufacturing, a workday no longer than eight hours, no labor after 7 P.M., and documentary proof of age—a great stumbling block in the enforcement of existing legislation. In 1904 not one state in the nation required all those things.

PROHIBITION SENTIMENT GROWS

During the first decade of the 20th century, dry, or prohibition, sentiment began to increase noticeably in America—in part because alcohol consumption was clearly rising too. By 1900, there were 300,000 saloons in the nation—double the number in 1880 and a figure that represented one saloon for every 250 people. By 1910, the amount of alcohol Americans drank had increased 25 percent since 1900, reaching the highest rate since the 1840s. Liquor interests lobbied vigorously, openly, and sometimes at significant cost to defeat any proposed regulation, as well as proposed women's suffrage laws. Many people believed (incorrectly) there was an organized liquor trust manipulating the entire industry at the expense of the public interest.[35]

Not all saloons were unsavory, lower class, or even urban, nor were all liquor licenses in the hands of public saloons. Liquor was also sold in drugstores and groceries and many private clubs. Nonetheless, as alcohol consumption rose and saloons multiplied, reform-minded people were increasingly convinced that regulating both was the key to solving a host of other social and political problems. The saloon continued to figure in the exchange of money and favors that kept political machines in business. A clear link between saloons and vice was established by numerous investigations into prostitution and other problems. Many reformers believed there was a link between saloons and poverty. Child labor reformers saw liquor eating up wages, forcing children to work, and breeding domestic violence. Some saw a relationship between intemperance and the high rate of injuries in factories and in railroading. In the South the liquor problem took on an additional dimension, connected to the region's racial issues. Many middle-class whites, as well as blacks who supported temperance, believed that liquor played a role in the racial violence that infected the region.

Shortly after the turn of the century, the Anti-Saloon League (ASL) began to grow vigorously. The circulation of the ASL journal, *American Issue,* rose from 20,000 in 1903 to 60,000 by the end of 1904. The ASL was an independent, nonpartisan political action organization, but it had been founded by religiously affiliated men, and it called itself "the church in action against the saloon." After 1900 it began to include representatives of large national Protestant denominations on its state and national boards. It also welcomed any support or cooperation from Catholics and Jews. The ASL widely publicized the sentiments of prominent Catholic Archbishop John Ireland, for example, who was a strong temperance advocate. "Although the purely religious motive was a powerful stimulus to temperance reform," writes historian James Timberlake, "it alone would not have sufficed to jolt most middle-class Americans into

Saloons were a male institution that respectable women did not enter. They were concentrated in large cities, but they were situated in communities of all sizes. The saloon pictured here is in a small farming town in Minnesota. *(Courtesy Minnesota Historical Society, HF5.3/p51, neg. 40254)*

action." It was, he continues, "prudential reasons" that spurred rising interest among both churchgoers and nonchurchgoers.[36]

Political, economic, social, and moral issues were all important in the growing movement for more regulation of liquor. But another prominent influence was the advance of scientific and medical knowledge. Doctors and groups like the American Medical Association were gaining increasing knowledge about the injurious effects of alcohol on the body. The ASL and other temperance groups helped them publicize it, identifying the temperance movement with the authority of modern science.

AFRICAN AMERICANS CRITICIZE ACCOMMODATION

When Roosevelt took office, Booker T. Washington was the best known and most influential African-American leader in America. Many black Americans continued to support his economic gospel of self-help, hard work, and thrift. But Washington also counseled patience with political and social discrimination, believing that the first task for African Americans was to establish a firm economic foundation. Increasingly, the voices of black intellectuals who disagreed with this policy of accommodation were growing louder. Washington's critics also resented his enormous power. He enjoyed President Roosevelt's support, which in turn increased his authority as spokesman for all blacks. Washington had great influence over African-American political appointments and was always consulted by white philanthropists considering gifts to black groups and institutions. His critics compared his influence, which extended through a network of organizations like the National Negro Business League, to that of an urban boss. They call it the Tuskegee machine.

In 1903, black scholar W. E. B. DuBois, then a professor at Atlanta University, criticized Washington directly and openly in one chapter of his now-classic book of essays, *The Souls of Black Folk*. "Is it possible and probable that nine millions of men can make effective progress in economic lines," he asked, "if they are deprived of political rights . . .? If history and reason give any distinct answer to these questions, it is an emphatic No." DuBois argued that blacks should insist on full rights and equality immediately and should fight to obtain them. In another essay that same year, he also opposed Washington's theory of education. DuBois argued that the education of exceptional African Americans, for whom he coined the phrase the Talented Tenth, was of more importance than training ordinary people for economic success. Another critic of accommodation was William Monroe Trotter—like DuBois, a Harvard graduate—who founded the militant newspaper *Boston Guardian*. In 1903 Trotter was arrested and jailed in Boston for his part in organizing a group that disrupted a speech by Washington. "The most surprising thing about this disturbance, I confess," Washington later wrote, "is the fact that it was organized by the very people who have been loudest in condemning the Southern white people because they had suppressed the expression of opinion on public questions and denied the Negro the right of free speech."[37]

Historians often present the public disagreement between Washington and DuBois as a schism in the black community, destined to grow larger, over how to respond to the loss of rights during the progressive decades. Most African Americans, however, did not see the choice between accommodation and activism as an either-or situation at the time. Many did in fact use their exclusion from white society as an opportunity for economic self-help. They built successful, if segregated, small businesses and community institutions, such as banks, fraternal organizations, hospitals, and schools. But many of these same businesspeople and professionals also protested specific injustices and worked for an end to exclusion from broader American political, economic, and social life. Maggie Lena Walker, for example, who founded the St. Luke's Penny Savings Bank in 1903 (becoming the first women in America to head a bank), led a boycott against Jim Crow streetcars in Richmond in 1904. Most black newspaper editors who supported Washington also criticized injustice. Prominent clubwomen like Mary Church Terrell not only engaged in uplift activities but spoke out against lynching.

THE CHANGING FORTUNES OF ORGANIZED LABOR

Overall, organized labor made notable gains in the opening years of the 20th century. Union membership rose from 870,000 in 1900 to more than 2 million by 1904, nearly 1,700,000 of whom were affiliated with Samuel Gompers' American Federation of Labor (AFL).[38] The public's acceptance and good-will toward unions increased as well. But labor's growing strength caused many employers to draw back from the brief industrial peace touted by the National Civic Federation (NCF). Instead, employers began to join together to block further gains by labor.

One example was the Danbury Hatters case. In 1902, the United Hatters of North America, an AFL union, called a strike against Loewe Company hatmakers in Danbury, Connecticut. They also organized a very successful boycott against the company by other unions whose members handled their materials or products in any way. In response, Loewe Company spearheaded the organization of the American Anti-Boycott Association. It also sued the union in court under the Sherman Anti-Trust Act. The court ruled that the union boycott was in restraint of trade—and that union members were individually liable for financial damages resulting to the company. The decision, upheld by the Supreme Court in 1908, made it illegal for different unions to cooperate in boycotts, a traditional labor strategy that had always been very successful.

Other employers joined an aggressive open-shop campaign. An open shop guaranteed the right of any individual worker not to join a union—but in practice it often enabled employers to refuse to bargain with union representatives. In 1903, the Citizen's Industrial Association was founded under the auspices of the National Association of Manufacturers to coordinate the open-shop campaign nationwide. In practice, coordination often meant spying and blacklisting union advocates. The association also waged a general publicity campaign against unions, appealing to Americans' traditional beliefs in individualism and freedom of contract and to their fear of radical agitation.

In the summer of 1903, President Roosevelt issued an executive order establishing the open shop in government departments. He acted after a Government Printing Office employee was fired when he ceased to belong to the union. It was the type of situation in which the president often relished taking a public stand. "My business is to see fair play among all men, capitalists or wage workers," he wrote, "whether they conduct their private business as individuals or as members of organizations."[39] Even the NCF began to support the idea of an open shop, damaging its effectiveness as a conciliator. By 1904, strikes and labor violence had begun to increase once again.

Most labor unions still did not make efforts to organize women who worked for wages. Middle-class reformers often took a more active role than unions in helping women wage earners improve their lot. In 1903, middle-class reformers and philanthropists joined with working women in New York City to form the National Women's Trade Union League (WTUL), a kind of organization pioneered by reformers in Boston. Its purpose was to help women workers to unionize by providing financial support, publicity, and other assistance, especially during strikes. Branches soon developed in many cities and played an important role in coming years.

THE MOVEMENT TO LIMIT WORKING HOURS

Since the 19th century, labor unions had pressured states to limit the number of hours for workers on public works projects (that is, those funded by the government). They believed that public works laws would be acceptable to the public and the courts and that once established they could be used as an example for private industry. By 1902, eight states and many cities had established an eight-hour day for men on public works projects, and the federal government had established it for all federal projects. Observers debated the constitutionality of such laws, however, because they limited the freedom of contract between worker and employer. In 1903 that question was settled when the Supreme Court ruled in *Atkin v. Kansas* that a state could, in effect, make such hour limitations part of its contract with contractors or workers.

With the increasing support of reformers, unions also made additional progress in obtaining legislation to limit working hours in private industry. The earliest laws limiting men's hours applied to railroads, where it was easily proven that extremely long shifts increased accident rates. The first law had been passed in Ohio in 1890, and by 1904, 12 states had laws limiting consecutive hours on duty. In some places, similar laws were enacted for street railway (electric trolley) workers. Mining, a very dangerous occupation, also came under regulation in some states. The first law limiting the workday in mines to eight hours had been passed in Utah in 1896 and upheld by the Supreme Court in 1898. By 1904 four other states passed miners' hour laws. In scattered states, laws were also enacted in miscellaneous industries held to pose exceptional dangers.[40]

FLIGHT!

In the late 19th century, inventors throughout the western world—especially in France, Germany, and Britain—tackled the technological barriers to human flight. After 1890, flying machines like gliders, airships, dirigibles or zeppelins, and steam-powered planes were constantly tested, some with more and some with less success. In America, Samuel Langley tested unmanned aerodromes from atop houseboats in the Potomac River to audiences of prominent observers. Langley, a former professor of astronomy, was head of the Smithsonian Institution. He received a $50,000 appropriation from Congress in 1898, at the urging of the War Department, to develop a machine that a pilot could fly. On December 8, 1903, however, his manned flying machine crashed into the Potomac. The ill and aging Langley abandoned his work.

Less than two weeks later, two obscure, self-taught bicycle makers from Dayton, Ohio, working entirely independently and without institutional support, made the first successful manned, powered flight. Wilbur and Orville Wright were imaginative and determined. They were the only members of their family who did not attend college—or even receive high school diplomas. Instead, they trained themselves as engineers. They began their professional lives by establishing a printing business—and built the printing machinery for it. In 1892, as the craze for bicycling swept the nation, they also opened a shop to custom-build and repair bicycles. The brothers developed a research strategy as they worked together, carefully identifying, separating, and solving each mechanical problem before moving on to the next.

In the late 1890s, the Wright brothers began a progressive series of experimental flying machines: first a kite (1899), then three gliders (1900, 1901, 1902). With each step they came closer to enabling the pilot to control and balance the flying machine. The importance of this issue eluded other inventors, but the Wright brothers correctly understood that it was crucial. They even built their own wind tunnel, where they tested and refined their aeronautical calculations. Finally, they neared the goal. They engineered a propeller. With the help of a mechanic, they also engineered and built a lightweight engine because no engine manufacturer in the nation was willing to do it for them.

They returned to their testing camp at Kill Devil Hills, near Kitty Hawk, North Carolina, a wind-swept sand dune on the Outer Banks. There they assembled and tested the parts. Their flying machine was a biplane with double wings of 40-foot span. In the morning of December 17, 1903, with Orville in the plane, the Wright brothers succeeded in making the first manned, powered flight—12 seconds and 120 feet. They tested the machine three more times that day. The last test, with Wilbur at the controls, stayed aloft 59 seconds and covered 852 feet. As the brothers prepared for a fifth attempt, however, the plane was caught in the wind and broken apart. The first flying machine was not repairable and never flew again.

The events of December 17 attracted little attention. Happily for posterity, the Wright brothers were avid photographers who had attendants photograph many of their trials, including the first successful flight. The brothers themselves were somewhat skittish about publicity because they were denied a patent for their machine—the U.S. Patent Office received so many applications for fanciful flying machines that it routinely denied them all. The Wrights continued to describe their work in scientific publications, the main audience for flying experiments.

The brothers continued their experiments near Dayton, occasionally inviting a few reporters. In 1905 they demonstrated a clearly successful flying machine to a small crowd—it remained in the air more than half an hour and flew 24 miles. Finally, in 1906 the Wright brothers received a U.S. patent, having already received patents from France and Britain. Throughout the western world, many inventors also continued their work, but the Wright brothers retained the lead. By the end of 1908 their plane had stayed aloft a record two hours at the Coupe Michelin, an exhibition and race in France, and the brothers were internationally famous. At home, the U.S. Army awarded the brothers a contract for further development.

The invention of the airplane was a significant turning point in history. It would soon transform travel and commerce, stimulate international exchange and technological growth, and even change the way wars were fought.[41]

AMERICA'S NATIONAL GAME

The popularity of baseball, played by organized amateur clubs since the mid-1800s, exploded after the Civil War. By the turn of the century, more than 30 professional or semiprofessional leagues and 250 teams had made agreements on rules of the game and other matters. They were collectively called organized baseball. Baseball was on its way to becoming the first national, investor-owned, and profit-oriented team sport in America. At the time, football was almost exclusive a college sport, and basketball had only recently been invented by a YMCA leader.

During the 1890s, the 12 best professional baseball teams in America belonged to the National League. But in 1899 the league dropped four teams. Soon, a rival American League began forming, taking up the teams dropped by the Nationals. It was spearheaded by Byron Bancroft "Ban" Johnson, president of the Western (actually midwestern) League. During 1901–1902, a baseball war occurred between the leagues. The upstart American League added clubs and lured away some National League stars. In January 1903, officials of the two major leagues met in Cincinnati and called a truce. Just as captains of industry sought to do in other fields by creating trusts, baseball owners wanted to reduce free-for-all competition. They agreed not to compete for each other's players and to respect each other's territorial rights. They also formed a permanent three-man National Commission to oversee the game. The 1903 agreement recognized National League clubs in Brooklyn, Pittsburgh, and Cincinnati; American League clubs in Cleveland, Detroit, and Washington; and one club from each league in New York City, Boston, Philadelphia, Chicago, and St. Louis. (All of these teams remained in place for half a century.) The baseball magnates received much public criticism for letting financial interests dominate America's national game.

As the 1903 season ended, the owners of the champion teams in each league arranged to play a nine-game, post-season series to determine a world champion. On October 1, 1903, the first World Series began between the American League Boston Patriots (later called the Red Sox) and the National League Pittsburgh Pirates. In the eighth game, Boston won its fifth victory and the World Series. The Series was not held in 1904, but in 1905 the National Commission decided it should be an annual event and established permanent rules.

Baseball's growth went hand in hand with the growth of cities, which provided the necessary concentration of people to support the games. Major league teams, however, were only part of the baseball story. Spirited minor leagues were located throughout the country, including the South and West where no major league teams played. By 1913, more than 300 teams played in more than 40 minor leagues. Occasionally, a popular minor league team in a good-sized city drew more fans than big league clubs elsewhere. By the end of the first decade of the 20th century, the attendance at major and minor league games combined was some 24 million.

The popularity of baseball was reflected in popular newspapers and magazines, where sportswriters began to dedicate pages to all aspects of the game and its heroes. To sportswriters, baseball was clearly identified with America and American values. They liked the fact that it encouraged judgment and quick thinking in individuals while still requiring sacrifice for the team. They liked the fact it was wholesome and played in the healthful out-of-doors. They also liked the democratic aspects of the game. Players were judged solely on their ability. People from many walks of life attended and cheered together. The home team encouraged community pride and civic identity, important benefits in the diverse and conflict-ridden cities.

Another fact of American life that baseball reflected, unfortunately, was increasing racial division. In the 19th century, a few black ballplayers played for white organizations, although both minor and amateur African-American leagues also existed. As segregation tightened its grip after 1890, however, blacks quickly became unwelcome in white baseball. Some white players began to refuse to play if blacks were on the field. Major league owners soon developed agreements to hire no more blacks—a policy that would remain in place until 1945—and the minor league teams segregated as well. Although early major league baseball excluded blacks, a few well-known players were Native American. Even some all-female exhibition teams existed, and the occasional woman joined a men's semi-pro team.

PHOTOGRAPHY GAINS ACCEPTANCE AS AN ART FORM

At the turn of the century, photography was not yet recognized as a fine art in America. In 1902, prominent photographer Alfred Stieglitz, who had exhibited widely in Europe, organized a show in New York. Titled "An Exhibition of American Pictorial Photography Arranged by the Photo-Secession," it received an enthusiastic reception among most critics and viewers when it opened.

The Photo-Secession was a group of photographers and critics Stieglitz brought together to prepare the exhibit and to advance the cause of their art. (They took their name from similar groups in Europe, who "seceded" from conventional ideas of art and official art bodies.) Among the group was Edward Steichen and Gertrude Käsebier, the latter a pioneering art photographer and one of the most successful women artists of the era. One important result of their association was the publication of the quarterly journal *Camera Work* beginning in 1903. It reproduced the work of members and also served as a journal of ideas about modern art in general, of which the Photo-Secessionists considered photography a branch. Soon Stieglitz opened the Little Galleries of the Photo-Secession, usually called 291 after its address on New York's Fifth Avenue. The gallery exhibited photography, but also some works of modern European painters, and it became a center for artists and critics interested in the growing artistic ferment in Europe. In 1910, the Photo-Secessionists organized an extremely popular photography exhibit at Albright Art Gallery (now the Albright-Knox Art Gallery) in Buffalo, New York. Afterward, the gallery purchased some of the prints—the first public collection of photographs in the United States. The Photo-Secessionists had succeeded so well in establishing photography as an art form that many no longer saw the need to continue their work in an organized way, and the group declined. At the outbreak of World War I *Camera Work* ceased publication and 291 closed its doors.

ROOSEVELT, WORLD POWER, AND NATIONAL RESPONSIBILITY

While Theodore Roosevelt was president, Americans continued to differ over what America's role in the world should be, just as they had under President McKinley. Some, who deplored militarism or imperialism, continued to favor little international involvement or a stance of isolationism. Many were assertive nationalists. They believed that America had a duty to spread order, justice, and uplift—or, as the idea was expressed at the time, to take "civilization" to less-developed peoples. The president, too, believed there was a basic distinction between "civilized" and "uncivilized" nations. Civilized nations, he believed, were stable and economically developed. They usually behaved responsibly, sought a balance of power, and tried to reach objectives peacefully through negotiation. Together, these qualities gave them a right to police the "uncivilized." Most of the nations Roosevelt believed to be civilized were European and white, but the distinction was not entirely racial. He also counted highly industrialized Japan and the large, stable South American nations of Chile, Brazil, and Argentina in the civilized column. About European but czarist Russia, he had serious doubts.

The president never shrank from belief in America's role as a civilizing influence, but his overall viewpoint on foreign policy was more penetrating. He believed that order and peace in the world was fragile, due to great differences in power among nations created by 19th-century industrialization and development. He believed that powerful nations could not and should not avoid the obligation to assist in preserving world order. He believed, furthermore, that world order could be preserved only by the assertion of power and sometimes unavoidably by the use of force. The president was fond of describing these ideas by what he called a West African proverb, "Speak softly and carry a big stick." The phrase came to be closely associated with him during his presidency. By the end of his two terms in office he was well known for his willingness to "carry a big stick," but he was also known for his wide personal understanding of world affairs. Almost always, the president conducted foreign policy personally, face-to-face or by letter, instead of relying on emissaries and foreign ministers.

The foreign policy President Roosevelt defined and pursued— the active assertion of power in the interests of maintaining world order—was a new course for America. It lay behind his vigorous support for the enlargement of the navy and the reform of the army. It even lay behind his concern for the character of the American people. He believed that the strenuous life, or physical fitness and vigor, as well as high morals and the willingness to act on clear principles, were important personal qualities. Collectively, he believed, they maintained the strength of the nation, and he never shrank from using the bully pulpit to encourage them.[42]

THE ROOSEVELT COROLLARY IN THE CARIBBEAN

The United States was particularly concerned with stability and order in the Caribbean and Latin America. When Roosevelt became president in 1901, the nation already had interests there, a result of the protectorates established after the Spanish-American War. In 1902, a new crisis developed in Venezuela, on the northern or Caribbean coast of South America. The Venezuelan government was unable to pay debts owed to European bankers and governments. Britain, Italy, and Germany sent ships to the Caribbean to blockade the Venezuelan coast. The Germans threatened occupation, giving weight to rumors that they intended to establish a permanent base. Roosevelt in turn threatened to send the U.S. Navy to intervene, forcing the Germans and other Europeans to withdraw. Only two years later, a similar crisis began in the Dominican Republic. A revolution had occurred there in 1903, forcing out a corrupt regime, but the new government was soon in default of large debts to Europeans.

Since 1823, U.S. policy in the Americas had been guided by the Monroe Doctrine. The doctrine warned European powers not to establish new colonies in the Americas and not to exercise aggression against independent nations there "for the purpose of oppressing them, or controlling in any other manner their destiny." After the Venezuelan and Dominican incidents, President Roosevelt was persuaded that enforcing the Monroe Doctrine would require more than just vigilance against European aggression. It now appeared that an equally important problem was the existence of ineffective governments in the other nations of the Americas themselves. Their instability, disorder, and economic problems, the President believed, would be a constant threat to the interests of the United States and world peace. As a result, he concluded, the United States was justified in intervening in the domestic affairs of its southern neighbors to maintain order and thus forestall the aggression of other nations.

In his annual message to Congress of 1904, President Roosevelt formally announced this new policy. It came to be called the Roosevelt Corollary to the Monroe Doctrine. America, he said, wanted "stable, orderly, and prosperous neighbors." He continued:

> If a nation shows that it knows how to act with reasonable efficiency and decency in social and political matters, if it keeps order and pays its obligations, it need fear no interference from the United States. Chronic wrongdoing, or an impotence which results in a general loosening of the ties of civilized society, may in America, as elsewhere, ultimately require intervention by some civilized nation, and in the Western Hemisphere the adherence of the United States to the Monroe Doctrine may force the United States, however reluctantly, in flagrant cases of such wrongdoing or impotence, to the exercise of an international police power.[43]

The following year, by mutual agreement with the Dominican Republic, he put the Roosevelt Corollary into effect by establishing an American receivership in the island nation. The United States installed a customs officer who collected all duties, then distributed 55 percent to the Dominicans and 45 percent to the European creditors. Although the U.S. Senate refused to approve this arrangement until 1907, the president used his executive power to assign collection tasks to the navy.

The Roosevelt Corollary and its exercise of international police power was called into play again and again in the next two decades. Before the end of the Roosevelt administration in early 1909, the United States had intervened in Nicaragua (for the first of many times), Guatemala, and Honduras. The Roosevelt Corollary continues to influence U.S. policy in Latin America today.

AFFAIRS IN AMERICA'S DEPENDENCIES

In 1902, Congress passed an organic act for the Philippines. (An organic act establishes the fundamental law or governmental structure of a state.) The office of military governor was abolished, and a general amnesty was granted to Filipinos who participated in the Philippine-American War. The first legislature was not to be elected for five years, but when it finally was, it became the first popularly elected body in Southeast Asia. Filipino self-government was limited, however, by power of the Commission, whose U.S.-appointed members could approve or veto all legislative acts. William Howard Taft served as an able and popular proconsul, or civilian governor. In 1904, Taft returned to Washington to be secretary of war. Before leaving, he negotiated an agreement with the Vatican to purchase the large landholdings of Catholic religious orders and transfer ownership to individual Filipino farmers who worked the land as tenants. Philippine nationalists remained impatient for Philippine independence, as did American anti-imperialists at home.

Puerto Rico

Under terms of the Foraker Act of 1900, which established the institutions of government for Puerto Rico, the elected legislature of Puerto Rico had far less power than the U.S.-appointed governor and executive council. American officials aggravated the situation by their often arrogant attitudes. They embarked on a vigorous program of Americanization, with the intention of eliminating local institutions and the Spanish language.

As the limitations of this course became clearer to Puerto Ricans, sentiment in favor of more self-government grew. The two major Puerto Rican political parties, the Federal and Republican, which had not previously seen eye to eye on the issue, called a truce to their lengthy and sometimes violent feud. In February 1904 they united to form the Unión de Puerto Rico, or Union Party. They immediately attracted many former factions and groups. In 1904, the Union Party did not demand independence, but it stood firmly for increased self-government in some form. It also wanted to clarify the island's relationship to the United States and the citizenship status of its residents. The Union Party won a large majority in the Puerto Rican legislature.

Another provision of the Foraker Act allowed Puerto Rican sugar to enter the U.S. market without tariffs. Almost immediately a few large American sugar corporations invested on the island and became very powerful. Many small Puerto Rican farmers ceased farming their own land or growing their own food and became paid laborers on American-owned plantations. In bad years for sugar, they suffered unemployment and a rapid increase in poverty. The new economic situation further complicated political issues.

Hawaii

In the Territory of Hawaii, political disputes between Republicans, Democrats, and the Native Hawaiian Home Rule party had marred the first legislature of 1901. As the elections of 1902 approached, the Republicans formed an alliance with Johan Kuhio Kalanianaole, usually called Prince Kuhio, since he and his brothers were the designated heirs to Queen Lilioukalani. Prince Kuhio became the Republican nominee for Hawaii's representative to Congress. He defeated the incumbent Robert Wilcox, also a Native Hawaiian and leader of the Home Rule Party. Soon, the Home Rule Party ceased to exist. Prince Kuhio remained popular and continued to be reelected to Congress until his death in 1922, although his position was not always easy. Powerful Hawaii business interests, who continued to exercise great influence in Washington, often had different goals than the people of the islands.

THE ELECTION OF 1904

Since his elevation to office in September 1901, six months into President McKinley's second term, Theodore Roosevelt had become very popular with the American public. Little love was lost, however, between the president and many conservative Republican politicians, or between him and powerful businessmen who were traditionally the party's financial backbone. "The criminal rich and the fool rich," he was fond of saying, "will do all they can to beat me."[44]

As president, Roosevelt had confirmed the worst fears of national party insiders. He was independent, reform-oriented, and unpredictable. In addition, he had proven politically adept. He had secured passage of legislation or reforms he wanted—like tariff reduction, conservation programs, or trust-busting—by use of skillful persuasion, command of public opinion, and fearless assertion of presidential power, as well as by old-fashioned political maneuvering and even alliances with powerful state bosses. And most of all, the president had unprecedented personal appeal. In 1903, he traversed much of the country by train, en route to a Rough Riders reunion at the Grand Canyon. At every whistle stop, he greeted enthusiastic crowds. Throughout the nation people were pleased with one or another of his actions: prosecuting trusts, regulating the railroads, standing up for the working man, or pursuing an aggressive foreign policy.

Before Roosevelt served as McKinley's vice president, the office had come to be considered a dead-end job. The four previous vice presidents who had served out a deceased president's term had not won their party's nomination in their own right. Since McKinley's death, many powerful Republicans had been pushing Mark Hanna to run in place of Roosevelt in 1904. By the beginning of 1904, however, even President Roosevelt's confirmed opponents knew it would be political suicide not to nominate him; in any case, Hanna unexpectedly died in February.

Despite a distinct lack of enthusiasm among many party insiders, when the Republican convention met in Chicago in June, it was controlled by the president's supporters. (At the time, sitting presidents and candidates who expected to receive their party's nomination did not attend conventions in person.) The platform they adopted was bland rather than reform-oriented because the president worried that "the man of pronounced views and active life" was often at a disadvantage in an election. One exception was a plank suggesting that the southern representation in Congress should be reduced to reflect the disenfranchisement of its African-American citizens. Historian William Harbaugh writes that some prominent Republicans like Henry Cabot Lodge believed "for reasons both righteous and self-righteous that the party should keep racial issues in the public eye." Others hoped to make political capital among black voters. Roosevelt called it "the only insincere plank in the platform," but it was accepted by the convention with no dissent.[45] President Roosevelt received the nomination unanimously on the first ballot. Senator Charles W. Fairbanks of Indiana was nominated for vice president by acclamation.

On July 6, more than 14,000 Democrats met in St. Louis. Once again they were disorganized and feuding among themselves. The eastern, conservative wing of the

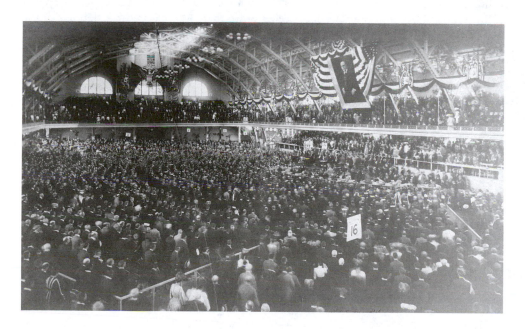

This photo was taken during the opening prayer at the 1904 Republican National Convention in Chicago. The large picture at the front is not of the president. It is of the recently deceased Senator Marcus Hanna, whom many party insiders had hoped to nominate instead of Theodore Roosevelt. *(Library of Congress, Prints and Photographs Division, LC-USZ62-53426)*

party worked hard to regain control of the party from Bryanites, silverites, and agrarians of all kinds. They even tried to convince former president Cleveland to run again. In the liberal wing, William Jennings Bryan also declined to be a candidate for a third time but pushed for a progressive platform. The final document, however, was quite moderate and said nothing at all about the money issue.

On the first ballot, eight different candidates were nominated for president. Among them was William Randolph Hearst, the newspaper publisher, now a New York congressman. Hearst was the only nominee with national name recognition, but his reputation as an extreme progressive and his unconventional personal life doomed his candidacy. On the second ballot the convention approved Alton B. Parker, chief justice of the New York Court of Appeals. Parker was known for his personal decency, skill as a reconciler, and judicial cautiousness. For vice president the convention nominated 80-year-old, former senator Henry G. Davis of West Virginia. The vote for Davis was interrupted, however, by a near-riot among silverites and agricultural interests—after the convention received a cable from Parker that he intended to support the gold standard. After midnight, the convention finally voted to reaffirm their nominee.

The Populist Party was much reduced by 1904, but it also fielded a nominee for president, Tom Watson of Georgia. The Socialist Party nominated Eugene V. Debs.

The most dramatic event of the campaign was a charge by the Democrats that George B. Cortelyou, secretary of commerce and chair of the Republican Party, had twisted the arms of certain industrialists for large campaign contributions. In return, accusers claimed, he had offered an unspoken promise that their known violations of antitrust laws would remain unprosecuted. Few responsible public commentators actually believed that outright blackmail had occurred. And if industrialists themselves thought they heard an unspoken promise from Cortelyou, they turned out to be badly deceived. Henry Clay Frick would later comment irately, "We bought [Roosevelt] and then he did not stay bought."[46] In the midst of the campaign finance scandal, however, some people began to argue that the time had come for political parties to be required to open their financial records to the public.

Despite the flurry of campaign excitement, President Roosevelt swept the election in every state outside the South. He won 336 electoral votes to Parker's 140, and the popular vote was 7.6 million to 5.1 million. It was clear that the outcome was a personal triumph for Roosevelt, because he won by far larger margins than Republican candidates in state races. "I am no longer a political accident," said the elated president to his wife.[47] Debs and the Socialists polled more than 400,000 votes, 3 percent of the total. The Prohibition Party polled nearly 2 percent.

Having served three and a half years of President's McKinley's term, on election night President Roosevelt issued a statement. "The wise custom which limits the President to two terms regards the substance and not the form. Under no circumstances will I be a candidate for or accept another nomination." It was a decision that many people, and probably Roosevelt himself, would regret by 1908.[48]

CHRONICLE OF EVENTS

1902

Theodore Roosevelt is president.

President Roosevelt and his influential head of the Forestry Department, Gifford Pinchot, begin to advance a conservation management policy of practical but regulated use of natural resources. Preservationists, who prefer to preserve wild places unchanged, increasingly disagree with this approach.

The city of San Francisco applies to dam Hetch Hetchy Valley in Yosemite National Park, for use as a reservoir. Before finally being approved in 1913, the proposal will cause a heated, decadelong battle that splits the conservation movement.

The last great strike of the Alaska-Yukon gold rush occurs in the Tanana Valley. It gives birth to the town of Fairbanks.

All-movie storefronts open in Chicago and Los Angeles; a few are known to have existed previously in New York and New Orleans.

The Photo-Secession, a group of photographers and critics newly brought together by Alfred Stieglitz to advance the recognition of photography as an art form, organize a well received show in New York.

In Alabama, Edgar Gardner Murphy forms the Alabama Child Labor Committee to fight child labor; it is the first organization of the type in America. By the end of the year Florence Kelley, Lillian Wald, Robert Hunter, and others take the lead in establishing the New York Child Labor Committee.

The New York Committee of Fifteen, formed to study the growing problem of prostitution, publishes *The Social Evil,* the first major report on urban vice. Vice reports, which detail the economic and political connections of prostitution in a city, will now become an increasingly popular tool of anti-prostitution groups.

In Oregon initiative and referendum become effective.

Australia gives women the right to vote.

January 1: The first Rose Bowl is played; Michigan defeats Stanford. Football is almost exclusively a college and school sport at this time.

January 24: The United States approves a treaty to extend its interests in the Caribbean by purchasing the Virgin Islands from Denmark, which owns them. The U.S. Senate will approve the treaty but the Danish Rigsday, or legislature, will not.

February 14: Congress enacts legislation prohibiting Americans from selling intoxicants, opium, and firearms to indigenous residents of the Philippines and other Pacific islands.

March 10: At the instruction of the president, Attorney General Philander Knox files an antitrust suit against Northern Securities Company, a holding company of western railroads formed by J. P. Morgan, James J. Hill, and Edward H. Harriman. It is Roosevelt's first major act of trust-busting. It comes as a surprise to the business community but is very popular with the public.

April 28: William Williams, an upright lawyer and Roosevelt appointee, takes office as New York commissioner of immigration. He will quickly institute many reforms in the immigration reception process on Ellis Island.

April 29: The Chinese Exclusion Act is modified to prevent Chinese people from entering the United States from the Philippines.

May 14: The United Mine Workers (UMW) begin a strike in the anthracite coalfields of eastern Pennsylvania. Mine owners refuse to negotiate and close the mines.

May 20: Tomás Estrada Palma is inaugurated as Cuba's first president and U.S. military forces withdraw from the island.

May 23: Crater Lake National Park, Oregon, is established; it is the first of five national parks established during Roosevelt's terms of office.

June: Maryland establishes the first worker's compensation program in America to provide payments to railway and mine workers who are injured or killed, without proof of liability, but the law is soon declared unconstitutional by state courts.

June 17: Congress passes the National Reclamation or Newlands Act. It establishes the Bureau of Reclamation and a policy of federal responsibility for water policy in the arid West and Southwest. By 1915 25 projects will be undertaken, the largest being Roosevelt Dam in Arizona.

June 25: Congress passes the Isthmian Canal (Spooner) Act, authorizing negotiations for a canal across Panama. It is signed by Roosevelt three days later.

July 4: President Roosevelt signs the Philippine Government Act, authorizing an appointed commission to govern the islands and declaring Filipinos to be citizens of the Philippines but not of the United States. The president also grants amnesty to Filipino insurgents, officially ending the war.

Fall: Roosevelt nominates an African American, Dr. William Crum, for collector of customs in Charleston, sparking white protests. Roosevelt refuses to back down; Congress finally confirms Crum in 1905. Whites in Indianola, Mississippi, force the African-American postmistress from her job. Roosevelt closes the Post Office. Both events indicate the increasing unwillingness of southern whites to accept any black person in political jobs or party activities.

September 3: The president narrowly escapes death when a trolley car crashes into his horse-drawn carriage in Pittsfield, Massachusetts. One Secret Service man dies in the accident. The president's injuries are more serious than he realizes at first and require an operation on his leg in a few weeks.

October: McClure's, one of the new mass-circulation magazines that appeared in the 1890s, publishes journalist Lincoln Steffens's investigation into corruption in city government, "Tweed Days in St. Louis." It creates a sensation with the reform-minded public.

October 3: President Roosevelt summons striking UMW officials and mine owners to the White House. After some resistance from the owners, the president threatens to reopen the mines with soldiers to prevent a coal shortage during the winter. Eventually all parties agree to an arbitration commission, and the mines reopen. Miners eventually win a 10 percent pay increase.

November 15: On a hunting trip in Mississippi, Roosevelt refuses to shoot a small, restrained bear. Reporters publicize the event. Soon toy makers will develop a new toy, a jointed stuffed animal called Teddy's Bear, which quickly becomes (and remains) a popular phenomenon.

December: The White House reopens after an intensive restoration and expansion overseen by architect Charles McKim. As part of the project, the modern East and West Wings are added. Roosevelt had previously changed its official name from the Executive Mansion.

Los Angeles becomes the first major city to adopt the direct-democracy device of recall, by a 4-1 margin. Many other California cities will quickly followed its lead.

1903

Roosevelt establishes a federal wild-bird refuge on Pelican Island, Florida, the first of 51 bird and four large-game wildlife refuges he creates before leaving office.

Wind Cave National Park, South Dakota, is established.

President Roosevelt introduces a famous phrase, the Square Deal. It signifies his willingness to act as a mediator between conflicting groups (such as labor, business, and the public) and insist that all receive fair treatment.

Congress passes a new immigration act, barring anarchists. For the first time immigrants will be examined for their political beliefs.

The National Women's Trade Union League is founded by women workers and middle-class supporters.

Edwin S. Porter's movie *The Great Train Robbery* is the first film to use editing to alternate between two separate but concurrent lines of action. It is also the first western. Films that tell fictional stories will quickly increase in number after this date.

The influential journal *Camera Work,* edited by photographer Alfred Stieglitz, begins publication. Until it ceases publication in 1917 it will advance photography as an art form and also serves as a journal of ideas about modern art in general.

Wisconsin passes the first comprehensive, complete, and compulsory statewide direct primary law. Delaware also enacts direct primary legislation.

In Vermont and New Hampshire, statewide prohibition is repealed and replaced by statewide local option; North Carolina passes a local option law for municipalities.

In Detroit Henry Ford forms the Ford Motor Company and introduces the first Model A. Most autos at the time are hand-crafted and expensive, but Ford's car is reasonably priced and sells very well. The first Cadillac appears.

The Alabama Child Labor Committee succeeds in getting the state legislature to pass the strictest law in the southern states. It limits industrial work to children 12 and older and limits hours to 60 per week.

W. E. B. DuBois's now classic book, *The Souls of Black Folk,* appears; it marks a public break with Booker T. Washington and his policies.

The Supreme Court rules that states can limit working hours on public works projects; to date eight states and many cities have declared an eight-hour day for public works (*Atkin v. Kansas,* 191 U.S. 207).

January: McClure's Magazine publishes three important exposés in one issue. The sensation it creates opens the floodgates of reform journalism, soon to be called muckraking.

January 9–10: Representatives of the National and American baseball leagues meet in Cincinnati to settle disputes and form the National Commission to oversee organized baseball. Baseball clubs placed in the two leagues will remain in the same locations until 1953. The leagues agree to a post-season series of games to determine the champion club.

January 21: Congress passes the National Guard Act establishing partial federal control over the previously decentralized state militias.

January 22: U.S. and Colombian diplomats sign the Hay-Herrán Treaty, granting the United States rights to build a canal in the Colombian province of Panama.

February 11: Congress passes the Expedition Act, giving antitrust cases scheduling preference in the courts.

February 14: Congress passes the Army General Staff Act, establishing a chief of staff and a general staff. Although the new organization will take some time to establish and perfect, it is the beginning of the modern American military system.

At the president's request Congress passes legislation creating the cabinet level Department of Commerce and Labor, and within it the Bureau of Corporations to investigate business misconduct.

February 19: Congress passes the Elkins Act, increasing federal regulation of railroads. It strengthens the Interstate Commerce Commission and outlaws rebates, the policy of giving major price breaks to large corporations.

February 25: Congress passes the Immunity Protection Act, intended to provide protection for employees who agree to testify in antitrust cases.

In Oregon, a law is passed limiting women's industrial workday to 10 hours.

April 9: The federal courts in St. Paul rule in favor of the government in the Northern Securities case; it will now be appealed to the Supreme Court.

May 20: The United States and Cuba formally sign a treaty restating the conditions of the Platt Amendment.

July: Roosevelt puts open-shop policies into effect in the federal civil service, meaning that an employee does not have to belong to a union.

August 8: In Cripple Creek, Colorado, a miner's strike begins. It will last until December 1904 and be marked by exceptional violence.

August 12: The Colombian Senate rejects the Hay-Herrán Treaty; they believe the price for Panama province is too low.

August 15: Lt. Gen. Samuel B. M. Young is appointed the first army chief of staff.

September: The Wright brothers demonstrate their plane to a few reporters near Dayton, Ohio.

September 3–October 20: The Alaska-Canada boundary commission meets to settle a longstanding dispute. The commission denies Canada's claims to a water inlet along the Alaskan panhandle coastline, which would have given them direct access to the Yukon gold fields without crossing U.S. territory. The decision causes hard feelings between the two nations.

October 1–13: The first World Series is played between the National League Pittsburgh Pirates and the American League Boston Patriots (later the Red Sox.) It is a nine-game series; in the eighth game Boston wins its fifth victory and the Series.

October 20: The Alaskan Boundary Commission issues its decision, primarily in favor of U.S. claims.

November 2: U.S. warships are ordered to sea-lanes around Panama.

November 3: The Panamanian revolution occurs with no bloodshed. Colombian ships cannot reach Panama from the South American mainland due to the presence of U.S. warships.

November 6: The United States recognizes the Republic of Panama.

November 8: The Chicago teachers' federation affiliates with the AFL, becoming the first official teachers' union.

November 18: U.S. and Panamanian diplomats sign the Hay–Bunau-Varilla Treaty. For $10 million and a yearly rental of $250,000 the United States receives permanent rights to a canal zone 10 miles wide.

December 8: Samuel Langley, head of the Smithsonian and the best-known U.S. experimenter with manned

This historic photograph is of the Wright Brothers' first successful powered flight, December 17, 1903, 10:35 A.M. Orville is in the plane, and Wilbur is running alongside. The starting rail is visible on the ground. *(Library of Congress, Prints and Photographs Division, LC-USZ62-6166A)*

flight, crashes his flying machine into the Potomac. He abandons his work.

December 10: The U.S. military base opens at Guantánamo Bay, Cuba.

December 17: Two obscure self-taught men from Dayton, Ohio, Wilbur and Orville Wright, make the first manned, powered flight near Kitty Hawk, North Carolina, with Orville at the controls. The flight is 12 seconds long and travels 120 feet. The Wright brothers test the machine three more times that day. The last test, with Wilbur at the controls, stays aloft 59 seconds and travels 852 feet. No reporters are present to witness the event; fortunately, the Wright brothers themselves take photographs.

1904

Underwater cables are laid from Seattle to Sitka and from Sitka to Valdez, linking Alaska to the lower states. The underwater cable across the Pacific is completed, and it is now possible to send a message by cable around the entire globe, which President Roosevelt will do ceremoniously on July 4.

Sullys Hill National Park, North Dakota, is established.

Twelve states have passed laws limiting consecutive hours on duty for railroad workers.

Oregon revises its direct-primary law to make it comprehensive; the law has been proposed by initiative. Alabama also enacts primary legislation.

Nevada adopts the referendum.

Oregon adopts local option law for liquor sales.

In San Francisco, ousted reform mayor James Phelan forms the Association for the Adornment and Improvement of San Francisco; the group hires City Beautiful architect Daniel Burnham to draw a plan for the city.

New Jersey becomes the second state to pass a housing regulations law; it is based largely on New York's law of 1901.

January 4: The Supreme Court rules in *Gonzalez v. Williams* that Puerto Ricans are not aliens and can freely enter the United States, although the decision does grant them U.S. citizenship.

February 4: Japan attacks the Russian fleet at Port Arthur, China, beginning the Russo-Japanese War.

March 14: In *Northern Securities Co. v. U.S.,* the Supreme Court orders a large railroad holding company dissolved on the basis of the Sherman Anti-Trust Act. It is President Roosevelt's first victory over the trusts and is very popular with the public.

April 15: The National Child Labor Committee (NCLC), organized by Edgar Gardner Murphy, Felix Adler, and others, holds its first general meeting in Carnegie Hall, New York City. Dr. Samuel McCune Lindsay, a professor of sociology at the University of Pennsylvania, becomes its secretary, or administrator.

May: Work begins on the Panama Canal. It will not be completed until 1914. Oversight of sanitation is assigned to Dr. William C. Gorgas. After a severe outbreak of yellow fever in the fall, he will bring the disease under control, receiving worldwide acclaim for his work.

May 5: The Socialist Party meets in Chicago, nominating Eugene V. Debs for president.

May 17: The Canal Zone government is established for America's newest protectorate in Panama.

June 19: The Prohibition Party meets in Indianapolis, and nominates Silas Swallow for president.

June 21–23: The Republican Party meets in convention in Chicago. Despite the lack of enthusiasm for President Roosevelt among many party insiders, his popularity with the public assures his nomination, with Charles W. Fairbanks of Indiana for vice president.

July 6–9: The Democratic Party meets in St. Louis, with many internal divisions. Eastern conservatives attempt to assert control; William Jennings Bryan, who has declined to be a candidate, attempts to counteract them. The party nominates the competent but colorless Judge Alton Parker of New York for president, and Henry G. Davis of West Virginia as vice president. Before the end of the convention, Parker confounds many delegates by announcing he supports the gold standard.

August: In Statesboro, Georgia, two black men convicted of a multiple murder are dragged from the courtroom and lynched; a race riot follows.

September: The Democratic campaign stirs up a hornet's nest by accusing the Republicans of "blackmailing" wealthy industrialists for campaign contributions, in exchange for freedom from prosecution for antitrust violations. Few commentators believe the charges; some suggest that the finances of political parties and campaigns should be opened to the public.

October 27: The first segment of the New York subway opens. It runs from the Brooklyn Bridge uptown. It is the nation's first rapid transit system.

November 8: Theodore Roosevelt sweeps the election, 336 electoral votes to 140. On election night, he announces that he considers the three and half years he has served of President McKinley's term to be his first term, and this to be his second; therefore he will not run again in 1908.

December 6: In his annual message to Congress, President Roosevelt announces the Roosevelt Corollary to the Monroe Doctrine. He states that it may be necessary for the United States to exercise international police power to stabilize nations in the Americas in order to forestall European aggression.

EYEWITNESS TESTIMONY

Reform was in the air. In forging new weapons of democracy in the state legislatures and in the Congress, the people were setting out on a crusade. . . .

. . . Some way, into the hearts of the dominant middle class of this country, had come a sense that their civilization needed re-casting, that their government had fallen into the hands of self-seekers, that a new relation should be established between the haves and the have-nots, not primarily because the have-nots were loyal, humble, worthy and oppressed—Heaven knows we knew that the under dog had fleas, mange and a bad disposition—but rather because we felt that to bathe and feed the under dog would release the burden of injustice on our own conscience. . . . We were joyous, eager, happily determined to make life more fair and lovely for ourselves by doing such approximate justice as we could to those who obviously were living in the swamps, morasses, deserts, and wildernesses of this world. It was not religious—at least not pious—this progressive movement. It was profoundly spiritual. And the insurgents, who were later called progressives, had the crusaders' ardor, and felt for one another the crusaders' fellow-ship. They sang songs, carried banners, marched in parades, created heroes out of their own ideals.

William Allen White, famous editor of the Kansas Emporia Gazette, *recalls the opening years of the 20th century, in his* Autobiography *(1946), pp. 428–30.*

The achievements of Wisconsin came through freedom, through freedom in thought as well as in action. There was an end of fear. Men dared stand for ideas. Freedom of speech and of research were preserved in the university. The by-products of political freedom were greater than the direct political gains which followed.

Political freedom made other reforms possible. No constructive programme can be developed in the midst of a class conflict. . . . There is no place for state building in the midst of a struggle between privilege and democracy. Men's minds are absorbed in warfare, not in state building. And in Wisconsin so long as men feared that new ideas would imperil their place or advancement, progressive legislation was out of the question. The press was influenced by its owners. It reflected the will of the ruling class. The University was subject to the same fear. Academic freedom was under espionage. . . . The extension of university teaching carried with it the germs of danger to the old system. It promoted discussion. It awakened the interest of the people.

Reformer Frederic Howe explains progressive reform in Wisconsin after 1901, in his Wisconsin, An Experiment in Democracy *(1912), pp. 187–88.*

The board of education of our city had one nongraded school for foreign children who couldn't talk any language but their own. . . . And my teacher, Miss Ford—I'm sure she is in heaven, because people like her can't be anywhere else—dealt with about 40 kids, boys mostly. There were some girls. Some of the foreigners, other than we—we still had our European clothes—but some of them from other nations, Italians, came in flour sacks and any way at all. . . .

Maxwell Lear, a Jewish immigrant from Russia as a child in 1900, recalls his school in New Haven, Connecticut, in the early 1900s, in Stave et al., eds., From the Old Country *(1994), p. 46.*

Suddenly we have found that there is no longer any Frontier. Until the day when the first United States marine landed in China we had always imagined that out yonder somewhere in the West was the border land where civilization disintegrated and merged into the untamed. Our skirmish line was there, our posts that scouted and scrimmaged with the wilderness, a thousand miles in advance of the steady march of civilization.

And the Frontier has become so much an integral part of our conception of things that it will be long before we understand that it is gone. We liked the Frontier; it was romance, the place of the poetry of the Great March, the firing line where there was action and fighting, and where men held each other's lives in the crook of the forefinger. Those who had gone out came back with tremendous tales, and those that stayed behind made up other and even more tremendous tales. . . .

. . . We may keep alive for many years yet the idea of a Wild West, but the hired cowboys and paid rough riders of Mr. William Cody are more like "the real thing" than can be found today in Arizona, New Mexico or Idaho. Only the imitation cowboys, the college-bred fellows who "go out on a ranch" carry the revolver or wear the poncho. The Frontier has become conscious of itself, acts the part for the Eastern visitor; and this self-consciousness is a sign, surer than all others, of the decadence of a type, the passing of an epoch. . . .

Novelist Frank Norris, "The Frontier Gone at Last," a non-fiction article in World's Work, *vol. 3 (1902), pp. 1728–29.*

Lounging there at ease against the wall was a slim young giant, more beautiful than pictures. His broad, soft hat was pushed back; a loose-knotted, dull-scarlet handkerchief sagged from his throat; and one casual thumb was hooked in the cartridge-belt that slanted across his hips. He had plainly come many miles from somewhere across the vast horizon, as the dust upon him showed. His boots were white with it. His overalls were gray with it. The weather-beaten bloom of his face shone through it duskily, as the ripe peaches look upon their trees in a dry season. But no dinginess of travel or shabbiness of attire could tarnish the splendor that radiated from his youth and strength. . . .

Five or six players sat over in the corner at a round table where counters were piled. Their eyes were close upon their cards, and one seemed to be dealing a card at a time to each, with pauses and betting between. Steve was there, and the Virginian; the others were new faces.

"No place for amatures," repeated the voice; and now I saw that it was the dealer's. There was in his countenance the same ugliness that his words conveyed.

"Who's that talkin'?" said one of the men near me, in a low voice.

"Trampas.". . .

"Who's he talkin' at?"

"Think it's the black-headed guy he's talking at."

"That ain't supposed to be safe, is it?"

"Guess we're all going to find out in a few minutes.". . .

It was now the Virginian's turn to bet, or leave the game, and he did not speak at once.

Therefore Trampas spoke. "Your bet, you son-of-a-bitch."

The Virginian's pistol came out, and his hand lay on the table holding it unaimed. And with a voice as gentle as ever, the voice that sounded almost like a caress, but drawl-ing a very little more than usual, so that there was almost a space between each word, he issued his orders to the man Trampas:—

"When you call me that, smile!"

Owen Wister's best-selling novel, The Virginian, *1902, dedicated to his friend Theodore Roosevelt, made the western cowboy a staple hero of American popular fiction, pp. 4–5, 26–29.*

Summer anywhere in New York is pretty bad. In my district, the heart of old Hell's Kitchen on the west side, the heat, the smells, the squalor made it something not to be believed. . . . My job was to start in this district every morning at seven o'clock, work until eleven, then return for two hours more—from four to six. I climbed stair after stair, knocked on door after door, met drunk after drunk, filthy mother after filthy mother and dying baby after dying baby. It was the hardest physical labor I ever did in my life: just backache and perspiration and disgust and dis-couragement and aching feet day in and day out.

I worked out one minor way to save myself by going up the long flights of stairs to the roof of one tenement and then climbing the dividing wall to go down the stairs of the next. Trailing street-sweeping skirts were not much of a help. There was no dodging the hopelessness of it all. It was an appalling summer too, with an average of fifteen hundred babies dying each week in the city; lean, miser-able, wailing little souls carried off wholesale by

dysentery. . . . The babies' mothers could not afford doctors and seemed too lackadaisical to carry their babies to the nearby clinics. . . . I do not mean that they were callous when their babies died. . . . They were just horribly fatalis-tic about it while it was going on. Babies always died in summer and there was no point in trying to do anything about it.

Dr. Josephine Baker, appointed a medical inspector for New York City Department of Health in 1902, Fighting for Life *(1939), pp. 57–58.*

The general strenuous impulse of the great civilized states of the world, to find and to establish markets and commer-cial relations outside their own borders and their own peo-ple, has led to multifold annexations, and to commercial and naval aggressions. In these the United States has had no part, but they have constituted a political situation that immensely increases her political and commercial anxieties, and consequently her naval responsibilities; for, as interests of this kind are outside the North American continent, it is upon the navy that their support rests.

Alfred Thayer Mahan, 1902, "Conditions Determining the Naval Expansion of the United States," Retrospect and Prospect, *p. 54.*

The situation about 1902 may be briefly indicated: The New York Central (controlled by the Vanderbilt interests, which had large holdings in the Lackawanna), and the Pennsylvania, jointly controlled the Reading Company, which owned the Reading Railway and the Central Rail-road of New Jersey. The output of the Delaware and Hud-son, a road usually credited with Vanderbilt affiliation, was largely handled by the Erie Railroad, controlled by Mr. Morgan, who was working in harmony with the other interests to make the anthracite coal trade profitable. The Reading, the Central of New Jersey, the Lackawanna, the Erie, and the New York Central (through the Lake Shore) exercised a considerable influence on the policies of the Lehigh Valley. The result of this close inter-relationship of interests was to secure an unusual degree of harmony in the anthracite coal trade. . . .

Closely connected with the community of interest among the railroads through the interweaving of stock ownership was an increasing representation of the railroads upon the directorates of other systems. Some examples of changes in this respect may be noted. During the years 1898 to 1900 none of the directors of the Reading Com-pany were on the board of the Central of New Jersey, but from 1900 to 1903 four of the Reading Company direc-tors were so represented. Two of the directors of the Read-ing Company in 1898 and one from 1899 to 1900 were directors of the Lehigh Valley, but in 1903 there were three of the directors of the Reading Company on the directorate of the Lehigh Valley. From 1898 to 1900 none of the directors of the Central of New Jersey were on the Lehigh Valley board, but from 1901 to 1902 two directors and in 1903 three directors were represented in the councils of the Lehigh Valley Railroad. The changes during these years naturally brought about a greater unity of action in the policies of these railroads.

Eliot Jones, professor at Iowa State University, describes the relationship among railroads in the coal regions of eastern Pennsylvania, ca. 1902, in Anthracite Coal Combination in the United States, *pp. 70–71.*

I do not believe in universal suffrage. I believe that negro suffrage has been a curse, a curse to the white people and an imminent threat to the negro. I believe that the Fifteenth Amendment was the crime of this age. I believe that the greatest evil flowing from negro suffrage has been that it has polluted the sources of governmental power, that the poison began where the evil was most accentuated and has spread into every limb of our body politic until, if allowed to go on, it would have made a mass of reeking corruption of the social and political order of this State. I believe that if the work we are now engaged on will accomplish what its advocates have claimed for it, a reformation of the electorate and the leaving of a minimum of dangerous element in that electorate, it is our bounden duty as citizens and as Democrats to lay down here the foundation rules which, so far as possible, will insure in the future a removal from Virginia of the suspicion that our people are wedded to those practices which would leave a stain and bring disaster upon any people who tolerate them. . . .

. . . I say I am going to show my faith in the work of this Convention . . . by voting to make our election process as clean as the cleanest and pure as constitutional language can enforce.

William E. Cameron, a white representative to the 1902 Virginia Constitutional Convention called to disenfranchise blacks, in Report of the Proceedings and Debates of the Constitutional Convention, *pp. 3031–3032.*

When the boundary work began there was no time to lose. An army of timber cruisers was scouting the forests of the West for the choicest bodies of Government timber. Once discovered and reported, these prizes would be claimed, fairly or fraudulently. . . . and then their forests would be lost to Forestry and the people. . . .

The boundary work was not easy. On horseback or on foot, their grub and blankets on pack horses or on their own backs, the boundary men went where their work led them, trail or no trail. And they moved fast. They had to, for they were working against as competent a body of land thieves as ere the sun shone on. The field men covered an average of about a township a day. Some of them even

declared that during one field season they could do 3,000,000 acres to the man.

In those early days, moreover, Forest Reserves were not popular, and there was much opposition. Settlers held indignation meetings, and the timberland grabbers neglected none of the tricks of their trade. As one man reported, "It was a mighty unpleasant corner to be in. We had balked several schemes on the part of the 'gang' to obtain valuable timberland, and they were in a mood to give us as much trouble and as many kinds of trouble as they could at every turn."

Sometimes it was a question of locating boundaries in hot haste and beating the grabbers with a wire to Washington recommending withdrawal; at other times of rejecting bribes or refusing to be bluffed. The boundary men needed courage, and they had it.

Gifford Pinchot describes the battle to map national forest reserves, 1902–1903, in Breaking New Ground, *pp. 251–52.*

In the spring of 1902 the Referendum League succeeded in having the general question of city ownership of street railways submitted to a popular vote. The result was nearly 143,000 for to 28,000 against. . . .

Unfortunately for the cause of municipal ownership, the local sentiment in Chicago did not extend to the state legislature. Although there was strong suspicion that the failure of the House committee to report the local transportation committee's bill in 1901 was occasioned by "undue influence" on the part of the traction interests, it was known that the brand "socialistic" had not been without influence upon some of the country [rural] members. In 1903, therefore, a somewhat simpler measure was advanced. . . . support finally centered on a measure mainly drafted by the secretary of the Municipal Voters' League and introduced by Senator Müller. The course of this measure, as had been expected, proved that traction influence was still strong at the state capitol.

The political situation at Springfield in the beginning of 1903 seemed to lend little hope for any measure opposed by the street railway companies of Chicago. The organization dominated by the Governor, Mr. William C. Lorimer, party boss of Chicago, and Mr. George W. Hinman, editor of the *InterOcean,* which had been purchased by Mr. Yerkes, controlled the organization of the House by a bare majority, and elected a weak and pliable speaker. . . .

[T]he bill passed the Senate just after the election, but was scheduled by the [party] organization for defeat in the House. . . . The final outcome was a union of all the forces opposed to the Lorimer organization. . . . This success, however, was achieved only after the speaker had attempted to jam the [party] organization measure through by refusing a roll call demanded by two-thirds of the membership of the House. Fear of personal violence was the only thing which induced the speaker to recede. The effect on the majority of the speaker's refusal to permit a roll call caused the somewhat precipitate retirement of that gentleman to his private room, from which he returned to the chair only upon assenting to a formal capitulation.

Professor Willard E. Hotchkiss of Northwestern University describes the politics of Chicago street railways, 1902–1903, in "Chicago Traction: A Study in Evolution," Annals of the American Academy of Political and Social Sciences, *vol. 28 (November 1906), pp. 35–36.*

Afognak village was actually two villages, two and a half miles apart, each on a shallow bay with a wooded cape jutting between them that concealed each settlement from the other. . . . One was Aleut, the other was thought of as Russian. . . .

Wherever people were home [in the Aleut village] I was greeted and entertained courteously. Parents and each child shook hands with me and offered the best chair or box in the room. The Aleut houses were all furnished scantily and crudely but they had plentiful bedding, all piled on one bed during the day. In some houses the pile almost reached the ceiling. . . .

. . . Homes [in the Russian village] were a marked contrast to the Aleuts'. Some boasted plush-covered chairs and tête-à-têtes in peacock blue or scarlet. . . . I was impressed by a sense of whiteness whenever we entered a best room: floors were sanded and scoured white; rugs were strips of pure white canvas; curtains were white lace brightened with pinned-on paper flowers. I never saw so much crochet work in my life; it adorned every available piece of furniture, and the white bedspreads were crocheted or knitted. A typical best room contained a bed, a table, some chairs (including a rocker), a sewing machine, some sort of music box and at least one accordion. In the center of the building, so it kept all the rooms warm, was a wood-burning Russian heater with thick clay walls. Once it was fired up, the heat it stored kept the place warm all night, which is why the indoor plants the Russian villagers loved did not freeze. . . .

. . . it seemed to me that the value of the boats, seines and hunting equipment I had noticed in the Aleut village represented at least as much investment as the Russians' houses and furnishings.

Hannah Breece, a teacher sent to the Aleutian Islands, Alaska, by the federal government in 1904 to operate a school, A Schoolteacher in Old Alaska, *pp. 13–17.*

Mr. Johnson called his ten years' fight against privilege a war for "A City on a Hill." To the young men in the movement, and to tens of thousands of the poor who gave it

their support, it was a moral crusade rarely paralleled in American politics. The struggle involved the banks, the press, the Chamber of Commerce, the clubs, and the social life of the city. It divided families and destroyed friendships. You were either for Tom Johnson or against him. If for him, you were a disturber of business, a Socialist, to some an anarchist. Had the term Red been in vogue, you would have been called a communist in the pay of Soviet Russia. Every other political issue and almost every topic of conversation was subordinated to the struggle.

. . . Before the expiration of the first two years of Mr. Johnson's term of mayoralty the city was divided into two camps along clearly defined economic lines. . . . On the one side were men of property and influence; on the other the politicians, immigrants, workers, and persons of small means. This line of cleavage continued to the end.

Reformer Frederic Howe, who worked for Cleveland mayor Tom Johnson, recalls his work, 1902–1909, Confessions of a Reformer *(1925), pp. 113–15, 119.*

Immigrants must be treated with kindness and consideration. Any government official violating the terms of this notice will be recommended for dismissal from the Service. Any other person so doing will forthwith be required to leave Ellis Island. It is earnestly requested that any violation hereof, or any instance of any kind of improper treatment of immigrants at Ellis Island, or before they leave the Barge Office, be promptly brought to the attention of the Commissioner.

Sign posted throughout Ellis Island by Commissioner William Williams after April 1902, in Tifft, Ellis Island, *p. 69.*

The place in which to attack anarchism is where the offenses grow which alone make anarchism possible. Let us secure the just, speedy, and impartial administration of law; let us elect legislators who seek honestly to conform human legislation to the divine laws of the social order, without fear or favor; let us teach in our churches and our schools and through the press the divine origin, the divine sanctity, and the divine authority of law; and let us, from this vantage ground, meet with fair-minded reason the wild cries of men who have been taught by the monstrous misuse of law to hate all law, both human and divine, and our question will be solved for us; because both anarchy and anarchists will disappear from American society. The way to counteract hostility to law is to make laws which deserve to be respected.

Protestant minister, editor, and reformer Lyman Abbott, "Anarchism: Its Cause and Cure," Outlook, *vol. 70 (February 22, 1902), pp. 470–71.*

Yes, General; there is a Quartermaster's Department, and the Quartermaster-General has charge of transportation. . . . The Paymaster-General pays the troops.

The Commissary-General pays for the food and the supplies which he has. Each one has his own machinery, and each one has his own business; and when it comes to the accomplishment of any single purpose there is no one to bring them together and see that they move step by step. . . .

In the successful business world work is not done in that way. What would happen if a railroad company, or a steel corporation, or any great business concern, should divide its business up in that way? What would become of that business?

Secretary of War Elihu Root, testimony before the Senate Committee on Military Affairs, March 12, 1902, reprinted in Military and Colonial Policy, *p. 412.*

On the 14th of May a cablegram from New Orleans announced that a part of the Isthmus of Nicaragua had been shaken by a violent earthquake on the shores of Lake Managua, an annex of the lake of Nicaragua. It was due, said the despatch, to an eruption of Momotombo. . . .

Naturally the gigantic sensation created by the thrilling and spectacular drama of . . . the Nicaraguan earthquakes, dominated the senatorial debate. . . .

Toward the end of the debate, the President of Nicaragua, Zelaya, sent a cablegram addressed to Señor Corea, Minister of Nicaragua at Washington, at the latter's request. Speaking of the earthquake reported by the telegram of May 15, the one resulting from the Momotombo eruption, he said:

News published about recent eruptions of volcanoes in Nicaragua entirely false.

Senator Morgan presented to the Senate the presidential telegram with a statement of Señor Corea to the effect that Nicaragua had had no volcanic eruption since 1835.

The vote was going to be taken under that falsified impression!

To overcome an official document—to demonstrate that what it said was a deliberate and wilful fabrication—another official document was necessary; more than that, absolutely indispensable. . . .

Suddenly a flash revealed to me the needed official document. I had it under my thumb. It was a postage stamp representing a magnificent volcano belching forth smoke across the country. At the foot of the volcano was the shore of the lake where the recent earthquakes had taken place. The smoking volcano was precisely: "Momotombo.". . .

I immediately began to collect the precious stamps in Washington and in New York, and on the 16th of June I sent one of them, pasted on a sheet of paper, to every senator.

Philippe Bunau-Varilla, lobbyist for Panama, describes his actions, May 14–June 16, 1902, in his Great Adventure of Panama *(1920), pp. 107–110.*

Be it enacted . . . , That all moneys received from the sale and disposal of public lands in Arizona, California, Colorado, Idaho, Kansas, Montana, Nebraska, Nevada, New Mexico, North Dakota, Oklahoma, Oregon, Utah, Washington, and Wyoming, beginning with the fiscal year ending June thirtieth, nineteen hundred and one, including the surplus of fees and commissions in excess of allowances to registers and receivers, and excepting the five per centum of the proceeds of the sales of public lands in the above States set aside by law for educational and other purposes, shall be, and the same are hereby, reserved, set aside, and appropriated as a special fund in the Treasury to be known as the "reclamation fund," to be used in the examination and survey for and the construction and maintenance of irrigation works for the storage, diversion, and development of waters for the reclamation of arid and semiarid lands in the said States and Territories, and for the payment of all other expenditures provided for in this Act.

Newlands Act, June 17, 1902, U.S. Statutes at Large, *57th Congress, vol. 32, part 1, p. 388.*

The insurrection against the sovereign authority of the United States in the Philippine Archipelago having ended, and provincial civil governments having been established throughout the entire territory of the archipelago not inhabited by Moro [Muslim] tribes, under the instructions of the President . . . the office of military governor in said archipelago is terminated. . . . [T]he military forces in the Division of the Philippines shall be at all times subject, under the orders of the military commander, to the call of the civil authorities for the maintenance of law and order and the enforcement of their authority.

Secretary of War Elihu Root's order acknowledging the end of war in the Philippines, July 4, 1902, Military and Colonial Policy *(1916), pp. 317–18.*

I do not know who you are. I see that you are a religious man, but you are evidently biased in favor of the right of the working-man to control a business in which he has no other interest than to obtain fair wages for the work he does.

I beg of you not to be discouraged. The interests of the laboring man will be protected and cared for, not by the labor agitators but by the Christian men to whom God in His infinite wisdom has given the control of the property interests of the country, and upon the successful management of which so much depends.

Do not be discouraged. Pray earnestly that right may triumph, always remembering that the Lord God Omnipo-

Coal mining was hard, dirty work—but even young boys did it. These miners were photographed at a West Virginia coal mine by famous muckraking photographer Lewis Hine. *(Library of Congress, Prints and Photographs Division, LC-USZ62-74043)*

tent still reigns, and that His reign is one of law and order and not of violence and crime.

> *George Baer, spokesman for the eastern Pennsylvania coal company owners during the 1902 miners' strike, responding to a letter from a concerned citizen, July 17, quoted in Lloyd,*
> Henry Demarest Lloyd *(1912), p. 190.*

. . . If there is a disagreement I wish it distinctly understood, not only that there will be no arbitration of the matter, but that in my message to Congress I shall take a position which will prevent any possibility of arbitration hereafter; a position I am inclined to believe, which will render it necessary for Congress to give me the authority to run the line as we claim it, by our own people, without any further regard to the attitude of England and Canada.

> *President Theodore Roosevelt, letter about the Alaskan boundary dispute to Supreme Court Justice Oliver Wendell Holmes in England, July 25, 1902, quoted in Bailey,*
> *"Shaking the Big Stick," p. 199.*

The [sewing] machines are all run by foot power and at the end of the day one feels so weak that there is a great temptation to lie right down and sleep. But you must go out and get air, and have some pleasure. So instead of lying down I go out, generally with Henry. Sometimes we go to Coney Island, where there are good dancing places, and sometimes we go to Ulmer Park to picnics. . . . I go to the theater quite often, and like those plays that make you cry a great deal. . . .

For the last two winters I have been going to night school at Public School 84 on Glenmore Avenue. I have learned reading, writing and arithmetic. . . . Plenty of my friends go there. Some of the women in my class are more than forty years of age. Like me, they did not have a chance to learn anything in the old country. . . .

Some of the women blame me very much because I spend so much money on clothes. They say that instead of a dollar a week I ought not to spend more than twenty-five cents a week on clothes, and that I should save the rest. But a girl must have clothes. . . . Those who blame me are the old country people who have old-fashioned notions, but the people who have been here a long time know better. . . .

I have many friends and we often have jolly parties. . . . Lately [Henry] has been urging me more and more to get married—but I think I'll wait.

> *Sixteen-year-old sweatshop worker Sadie Frowne of Brooklyn, a Jewish immigrant from Poland, describes her leisure-time activities, "The Story of a Sweatshop Girl," part of a series of working people's autobiographies in the* Independent, *vol. 54 (September 25, 1902), pp. 2281–82.*

"McClure's has courage." How often that remark was made after our undertaking was under way! But courage implies a suspicion of danger. Nobody thought of such a thing in our office. We were undertaking what we regarded as a legitimate piece of historical work. We were neither apologists nor critics, only journalists intent on discovering what had gone into the making of this most perfect of all monopolies. What had we to be afraid of?

I soon discovered, however, that, if we were not afraid, I must work in a field where numbers of men and women were afraid, believed in the all-seeing eye and the all-powerful reach of the ruler of the oil industry. They believed that anybody going ahead openly with a project in any way objectionable to the Standard Oil Company would meet with direct or indirect attack. Examination of their methods had always been objectionable to them. "Go ahead, and they will get you in the end," I was told by more than one who had come to that conclusion either from long observation or from long suffering.

Even my father said, "Don't do it, Ida—they will ruin the magazine."

> *Ida Tarbell recalls beginning research for her muckraking study of Standard Oil, which began appearing in* McClure's *in December 1902, in her* All in the Day's Work *(1939), pp. 206–07.*

When my employer had left me I observed the woman at my side: an untidy, degraded-looking creature, long past youth. Her hands beggared description; their covering resembled skin not at all, but a dark-blue substance, leatherlike, bruised, ingrained, indigo-hued. Her nails looked as though they had been beaten severely. One of her thumbs was bandaged.

Ida Tarbell, one of the best-known muckrakers, spent more than a decade researching the machinations of John D. Rockfeller's Standard Oil before publishing her exposé. She was photographed by Frances Benjamin Johnston. *(Library of Congress, Prints and Photographs Division, LC-USZ62-53912)*

"I lost one nail; rotted off."

"Horrible! How, pray?"

"That there water: it's poison from the shoe-dye."

Swiftly my hands were changing to a faint likeness of my companion's. "Don't tell him," she said, "that I told you that. He'll be mad; he'll think I am discouraging you. But you'll lose your forefinger nail, all right!". . .

"Once I tried to clean my hands up. Lord! it's no good! I scrub 'em with a scrubbin' brush on Sundays."

"How long have you been at this job?"

"Ten months."

Marie Van Vorst, a reformer who went undercover to investigate the life of working women, describes work in a shoe factory,
The Woman Who Toils *(1903), pp. 208–09.*

One of the best effects of the playground movement has been the cultivating in the children a sense of justice. In the street might makes right. When the playgrounds opened, the large children did not expect to wait their turns with the small children at the swings or apparatus. They went to the head of the line, or even pulled the small child out of the swing. This has changed, but whether it indicates any considerable reformation or only respect for authority it is hard to tell, but the influence on the child is sure to be good. This respect for the rights of others is one of the most needful lessons for a child to learn. . . .

The playgrounds of most cities were troubled at first by gangs of boys who came in for mischief. In the first week or so they often caused great annoyance, so that a police man was stationed in every playground in New York. The gang problem is becoming much less acute as the system becomes better organized and the workers learn better how to deal with them. The gang can often be conquered by turning them into a gymnasium or basketball team. In this they have the advantage over other teams in having a strong spirit of loyalty to each other. They will usually respect a gymnast who is capable and tries to help them, and they will expend their superfluous energy in work instead of mischief.

Henry S. Curtis, a leading playground activist, in the report of the U.S. Bureau of Education for 1903, in Mero,
American Playgrounds *(1908), pp. 254–55.*

East away from the Sierras, south from Panamint and Amargosa, east and south many an uncounted mile, is the Country of Lost Borders.

Ute, Paiute, Mojave, and Shoshone inhabit its frontiers, and as far into the heart of it as a man dare go. Not the law, but the land sets the limit. Desert is the name it wears upon the maps, but the Indian's is the better word. Desert is a loose term to indicate land that supports no man; whether the land can be bitted and broken to that purpose is not proven. Void of life it never is, however dry the air and villainous the soil.

This is the nature of that country. There are hills, rounded, blunt, burned, squeezed up out of chaos, chrome and vermilion painted, aspiring to the snow-line. Between the hills lie high level-looking plains full of intolerable sun glare, or narrow valleys drowned in a blue haze. The hill surface is streaked with ash drift and black, unweathered lava flows. After rains water accumulates in the hollows of small closed valleys, and, evaporating, leaves hard dry levels of pure desertness that get the local name of dry lakes. Where the mountains are steep and the rains heavy, the pool is never quite dry, but dark and bitter, rimmed about with the efflorescence of alkaline deposits. A thin crust of it lies along the marsh over the vegetating area, which has neither beauty nor freshness. In the broad wastes open to the wind the sand drifts in hummocks about the stubby shrubs, and between them the soil shows saline traces. The sculpture of the hills here is more wind than water work, though the quick storms do sometimes scar them past many a year's redeeming. In all the Western desert edges there are essays in miniature at the famed, terrible Grand Cañon, to which, if you keep on long enough in this country, you will come at last.

Writer Mary Austin's essay on the beauty of the West's arid lands before large-scale irrigation began, in her Land of Little Rain *(1903), pp. 3–5.*

The Negro race, like all races, is going to be saved by its exceptional men. The problem of education, then, among Negroes must first of all deal with the Talented Tenth; it is the problem of developing the Best of this race that they may guide the Mass away from the contamination and death of the Worst, in their own and other races. Now the training of men is a difficult and intricate task. Its technique is a matter for educational experts, but its object is for the vision of seers. If we make money the object of man-training, we shall develop money-makers but not necessarily men; if we make technical skill the object of education, we may possess artisans but not, in nature, men. Men we shall have only as we make manhood the object of the work of the schools—intelligence, broad sympathy, knowledge of the world that was and is, and of the relation of men to it—this is the curriculum of that Higher Education which must underlie true life. On this foundation we may build bread winning, skill of hand and quickness of brain, with never a fear lest the child and man mistake the means of living for the object of life.

W. E. B. DuBois, "The Talented Tenth," The Negro Problem *(1903), pp. 33–34.*

Section 1. That in the State penitentiary and in all county jails, stockades, convict camps, and all other places where State or county prisoners may at any time be kept confined, separate apartments shall be provided and maintained for white and negro prisoners.
Section 2. That separate bunks, beds, bedding, separate dining tables and all other furnishings, shall be provided and kept by the State and counties, respectively, for the use of white and negro prisoners, [and such items] after having been assigned to the use of, or after having been used by white or negro prisoners [shall never] be changed the one for the use of the other.
Section 3. That it shall be unlawful for any white prisoner to be handcuffed or otherwise chained or tied to a negro prisoner.

Arkansas Jim Crow legislation, Acts of Arkansas, *1903, no. 96, 161, reprinted in Bardolph,* Civil Rights Record *(1970), p. 137.*

There was nothing spectacular about these many trials, but the good humor of Wilbur, after a spill out of the machine, or a break somewhere, or a stubborn motor; was always reassuring; their patient perseverance, their calm faith in ultimate success, their mutual consideration of each other, might have been considered phenomenal in any but men who were well born and well reared. These flights, or spurts at flying, they always made in turn; and after every trial the two inventors, quite apart, held long and confidential consultation, with always some new gain; they were getting nearer and nearer the moment when a sustained flight would be made, for a machine that could maintain itself aloft two minutes might just as well stay there an hour, if everything were as was intended.

Professor William Werthner, a childhood friend of the Wright brothers, recalls their method of working, 1903 and after, "Personal Recollections of the Wrights," Aero Club of America News, *June 1912, available online at Wright Brothers Aeroplane Company. URL: http://www. first-to-fly.com/History/Wright%20Story/recollections.htm.*

As long as his writings exposed only the low and the vulgar politicians, ward heelers and bosses, and the like, he was quite popular; I believe he was even asked to deliver addresses before clubs of the *dilettante,* and even in churches, for the righteous were terrible in their wrath. But when he went more deeply, when he exposed the respectable connections of the machine politicians, some of his admirers fell away, and stood afar off, like certain disciples of old. The citizen was delighted when some city other than his own was under the scrutiny of the sharp eyes that gleamed behind those round glasses, but when he drew near for a local study, there was an uplifting of the hands in pious horror. Cincinnati applauded the exposure of Minneapolis, and St. Louis was pleased to have Philadelphia reformed. Reform is popular so long as some one else is to be reformed.

Brand Whitlock, later a reform mayor of Toledo, comments on the work of muckraker Lincoln Steffens in 1903, Forty Years of It *(1914), pp. 163–64.*

We did not plan it so; it is a coincidence that the January *McClure's* is such an arraignment of American character that should make every one of us stop and think. . . .

Capitalists, workingmen, politicians, citizens—all breaking the law, or letting it be broken. Who is left to uphold it? . . .

We are all doing our worst and making the public pay. The public is the people. We forget that we all are the people; that while each of us in his group can shove off on the rest the bill of today, the debt is only postponed; the rest are passing it on back to us. We have to pay in the end, every one of us. And in the end the sum total of the debt will be our liberty.

S. S. McClure, "Concerning Three Articles," editorial in the famous January 1903 edition of his magazine, McClure's, vol. 20, p. 336.

[T]he militia shall consist of every able-bodied male citizen of the respective States, Territories, and the District of Columbia, and every able-bodied male of foreign birth who has declared his intention to become a citizen, who is more than eighteen and less than forty-five years of age, and shall be divided into two classes—the organized militia, to be known as the National Guard of the State, Territory, or District of Columbia . . . and the remainder to be known as the Reserve Militia.

Sec. 2. . . . [N]othing in this Act shall be construed to require or compel any member of any well-recognized religious sect or organization at present organized and existing whose creed forbids its members to participate in war in any form. . . .

Sec. 5. [W]henever the President calls forth the militia of any State or Territory or of the District of Columbia to be employed in the service of the United States, he may specify in his call the period for which such service is required, not exceeding nine months, and the militia so called shall continue to serve during the term so specified, unless sooner discharged by order of the President. . . .

Sec. 7. That every officer and enlisted man of the militia who shall be called forth in the manner hereinbefore prescribed and shall be found fit for military service shall be mustered. . . . [A]ny officer or enlisted man of the militia who shall refuse or neglect to present himself to such mustering officer upon being called forth as herein prescribed shall be subject to trial by court-martial and shall be punished as such court-martial may direct.

An Act to Promote the Efficiency of the Militia (also called the Dick Act), creating a nationally supervised National Guard, January 21, 1903, U.S. Statutes at Large, 57th Congress, vol. 32, part 1, pp. 775–76.

Sect. 2. [T]he duties of the General Staff Corps shall be to prepare plans for the national defense and for the mobilization of the military forces in time of war; to investigate and report upon all questions affecting the efficiency of the Army and its state of preparation for military operations; to render professional aid and assistance to the Secretary of War and to general officers and other superior commanders, and to act as their agents in informing and coordinating the action of all the different officers who are subject under the terms of this Act to the supervision of the Chief of Staff; and to perform such other military duties not otherwise assigned by law as may be from time to time prescribed by the President. . . .

Sect. 4. [T]he Chief of Staff, under the direction of the President or of the Secretary of War, under the direction of the President, shall have supervision of all troops of the line and of the Adjutant-General's, Inspector-General's, Judge-Advocate's, Quartermaster's, Subsistence, Medical, Pay, and Ordnance Departments, the Corps of Engineers, and the Signal Corps, and shall perform such other military duties not otherwise assigned by law as may be assigned to him by the President.

An Act to increase the Efficiency of the Army (also called the General Staff Act, February 14, 1903, U.S. Statutes at Large, 57th Congress, vol. 32, part 1, p. 831.

The Chinese laundryman does not learn his trade in China; there are no laundries in China. The women there do the washing in tubs and have no washboards or flat irons. All the Chinese laundrymen here were taught in the first place by American women just as I was taught.

When I went to work for that American family I could not speak a word of English, and I did not know anything about housework. . . .

I did not know how to do anything, and I did not understand what the lady said to me, but she showed me how to cook, wash, iron, sweep, dust, make beds, wash dishes, clean windows, paint and brass, polish the knives and forks, etc., by doing the things herself and then overseeing my efforts to imitate her. . . . In six months I had learned how to do the work of our house quite well, and was getting $5 a week and board, and putting away about $4.25 a week. I had also learned some English, and by going to a Sunday school I learned more English. . . .

The ordinary laundry shop is generally divided into three rooms. In front is the room where the customers are received, behind that a bedroom and in the back the work shop, which is also the dining room and kitchen. The stove and cooking utensils are the same as those of the Americans. . . .

The reason why so many Chinese go into the laundry business in this country is because it requires little capital, and is one of the few opportunities that is open. . . .

Lew Chew, who emigrated from Canton, China, in the early 1880s and established successful laundries in numerous cities including New York, describes the Chinese laundry business, in "The Biography of a Chinaman," Independent, vol. 55 (February 19, 1903), pp. 420–22.

. . . I saw [Commissioner Williams] himself "soak" a Flemish peasant twice his size for beating and abusing a child. The man turned and towered above the commissioner with angry looks, but the ordinarily quiet little man presented so suddenly a fierce and warlike aspect that, though neither understood a word of what the other said, the case was made clear to the brute on the instant, and he slunk away. Commissioner Williams's law of kindness is all right. It is based upon the correct observation that not one in a thousand of those who land at Ellis Island needs harsh treatment, but advice and help—which does not prevent the thousandth case from receiving its full due.

Jacob Riis comments on immigration commissioner William Williams, "In the Gateway of Nations," Century, vol. 65 (March 1903), p. 681.

It was in the days before motor cars, and he and I drove about every night from one meeting to another in a little buggy he had, drawn by an old white mare named Molly. . . . I can see him now—climbing down out of the buggy, carefully blanketing old Molly against the raw blasts, then brushing the white hairs from his front with his enormous hands, and running like a boy up the stairway to the dim little hall in the Polish quarter where the crowd had gathered. The men set up a shout when they saw him, and he leaped on the stage and, without waiting for the chairman to introduce him—he scorned every convention that obtruded itself—he leaned over the front of the platform and said:

"What is the Polish word for liberty?"

The crowd of Poles, huddling about a stove in the middle of the hall, their caps on, their pipes going furiously, their bodies covered with the strange garments they had brought with them across the sea, shouted in reply.

"Wolność!"

And Jones paused and listened, cocked his head, wrinkled his brows, and said:

"What was that? Say it again!" Again they shouted it.

"Say it again—once more!" he demanded. And again they shouted it in a splendid chorus. And then—

"Well," said Golden Rule Jones, "I can't pronounce it, but it sounds good, and that is what we are after in this campaign."

Now that I have written it down, I have a feeling that I have utterly failed to give an adequate sense of the entire spontaneity and simplicity with which this was done. It was, of course, tremendously effective as a bit of campaigning, but only because it was so wholly sincere. Five minutes later he was hotly debating with a working man who had interrupted him to accuse him of being unfair to union labor in his shops. . . .

Brand Whitlock describes the last campaign of famous reform mayor Samuel Jones of Toledo, Spring 1903, Forty Years of It (1914), pp. 126–27.

All public expense means, by so much, personal deprivation. Income to the Government means outgo to the citizen. We have frequently remarked on the swollen and swelling naval appropriations of Great Britain, France and Germany. . . . But how stands our own account? We are pushing up our annual expenditure on the navy at a portentous rate. Twenty years ago the naval appropriation bill carried less than $15,000,000. . . . But the bill for the current year appropriated no less than $80,000,000. . . . New ships require new men; 3,000 more seamen are to be enlisted. . . . All told, we are at the present time clearly on a road which will speedily lead us to a naval establishment that will demand an outlay of $150,000,000 annually.

Thus rapidly are we wiping out, of our own motion, the advantage which we have always boasted that we had over European nations. Our isolation, with our expanding population, freed us from the necessity of going armed to the teeth. . . . Do not forget that the dread of vast military establishments which Americans have proverbially expressed has had to do primarily with their costliness.

Editorial opposing increases in the size and expense of the American military, "The Naval Folly," Nation, vol. 76 (April 23, 1903), p. 324.

For many years Cleveland had owned its waterworks, and though the municipal ownership of street railways was not nor is yet permitted, there was no legal obstacle to a municipal lighting plant and our administration took steps to establish one. On the night of May 4, 1903, when the new city government went into effect, an ordinance was introduced into council providing for a bond issue of two hundred thousand dollars. This passed by unanimous vote May 11. . . . At once the Cleveland Electric Illuminating Company got very busy. It didn't want to be obliged to compete in the lighting business with its own best customer—the city. It went to council. . . . The Illuminating Company succeeded in winning over three Democratic members. These men voting with the nine Republicans defeated the ordinance when it was again introduced. Another instance of what outside influence does to councils!

We decided then to call a special election on the bond issue and named September 8 as the date. On September 1 [Ohio] Attorney-General Sheets, at the instance of Thomas Hogsett, acting in the interests of the Cleveland Electric Illuminating Company, brought suit to prevent the special election. . . . The hearing was set for September 22, nearly two weeks after the date fixed for the election. . . .

Our campaign for the bond issue election had been planned and the first meeting was scheduled for that night, September 1, so a few hours after the restraining order had been served, Mr. Baker, Mr. Cooley, Mr. Springborn and I presented ourselves at the tent and found our audience waiting for us. . . .

We had another meeting the next night and another the next. . . . In the meantime City Solicitor Baker hastened to Columbus and managed to have the hearing set for Saturday, September 5, three days before the proposed election. . . . The supreme court refused to dissolve the injunction, our special election couldn't be held and our municipal lighting proposition was retired to temporary oblivion.

Reform mayor Tom Johnson of Cleveland explains how powerful interests defeated his first attempt to obtain municipally owned electricity, May–September 1903, My Story *(1913), pp. 192–94.*

After a long and weary march, with more miles to travel, we are on our way to see President Roosevelt at Oyster Bay. We will ask him to recommend the passage of a bill by Congress to protect children against the greed of the manufacturer. We want him to hear the wail of the children, who never have a chance to go to school, but work from ten to eleven hours a day in the textile mills of Philadelphia, weaving the carpets that he and you walk on, and the curtains and clothes of the people.

Fifty years ago there was a cry against slavery, and the men of the North gave up their lives to stop the selling of black children on the block. To-day the white child is sold for $2 a week, and even by his parents, to the manufacturer.

Fifty years ago the black babies were sold C.O.D. To-day the white baby is sold to the manufacturer on the installment plan. He might die at his tasks and the manufacturer with the automobile and the yacht and the daughter who talks French to a poodle dog, as you can see any day at Twenty-third Street and Broadway when they roll by, could not afford to pay $2 a week for the child that might die. . . .

The trouble is that the fellers in Washington don't care. I saw them last Winter pass three railroad bills in one hour, and when labor cries for aid for the little ones they turn their backs and will not listen to her. I asked a man in prison once how he happened to get there. He had stolen a pair of shoes. I told him that if he had stolen a railroad he could be a United States Senator.

Labor organizer "Mother" Mary Jones, during a march of textile mill children from Philadelphia to New York, "Mother Jones Speaks to Coney Island Crowd," New York Times, July 27, 1903, p. 10.

The spirit of lawlessness grows with what it feeds on. . . . In the recent cases of lynching over three-fourths were not for rape at all, but for murder, attempted murder, and even less heinous offences . . . the history of these recent cases shows the awful fact that when the minds of men are habituated to the use of torture by lawless bodies to avenge crimes of a peculiarly revolting description, other lawless bodies will use torture in order to punish crimes of an ordinary type. Surely no patriot can fail to see the fearful brutalization and debasement which the indulgence of such a spirit and such practices inevitably portends.

Theodore Roosevelt, public letter congratulating Indiana Governor Winfield Durbin for using troops to dispel a lynch mob, August 9, 1903, Letters, *vol. 3, p. 542.*

Simultaneously with the killing of the treaty by the Colombian Senate, a revolutionary Junta of wealthy Panamanians and resident Americans were in New York and Washington broaching their plan of a revolution and separation from Colombia as a way for the United States to get a Canal Zone. They authorized one of their number, Mr. J. Gabriel Duque, owner of the Panama Lottery, and a daily newspaper, to visit Secretary of State John Hay to ascertain the part the United States would play in the scheme. . . .

Mr. Duque was convinced by his conference with Secretary Hay that the United States was in a mood to try any plan that promised an early solution of the problem of securing a Canal Zone. Secretary Hay, of course, committed nothing to paper. . . .

Canal Zone commissioner William R. Scott describes events between August and November 1903, in The Americans in Panama *(1912), Chapter 8, available online at Panama and Canal Zone. URL: http://www.czbrats.com/AmPan/.*

That was probably the wildest World Series ever played. Arguing all the time between the teams, between the players and the umpires, and especially between the players and the fans. That's the truth. The fans were part of the game in those days. They'd pour right out onto the field and argue with the players and the umpires. . . .

I think those Boston fans actually won that Series for the Red Sox. We beat them three out of the first four games, and then they started singing. . . . *Tessie* for no particular reason at all, and the Red Sox won. They must have figured it was a good-luck charm, because from then on you could hardly play ball they were singing *Tessie* so damn loud. . . .

Tessie, you make me feel so badly,
Why don't you turn around.
Tessie, you know I love you madly,
Babe, my heart weighs about a pound. . . .

Only instead of singing "Tessie, you know I love you madly," they'd sing special lyrics to each of the Red Sox players: like "Jimmy, you know I love you madly." And for us Pirates they'd change it a little. Like when Honus Wagner came up to bat they'd sing:

Honus, why do you hit so badly,
Take a back seat and sit down.
Honus, at bat you look so sadly,
Hey, why don't you get out of town.

Spectators rush the field during a game of the first World Series, played in October 1903 between the Pittsburgh Pirates and the Boston Patriots (Red Sox). The game was played at the old Huntington Avenue Baseball Grounds in Boston. *(Courtesy Baseball Hall of Fame Library, Cooperstown, New York)*

Sort of got on your nerves after a while. And before we knew what happened, we'd lost the World Series.

> *Tommy Leach, third baseman for the Pittsburgh Pirates,*
> *remembers the first World Series, October 1903, in Ritter,*
> Glory of Their Times, *pp. 26–27.*

With Cy Young in the box and more than 16,000 persons looking on, the Pittsburg [sic] club won from Boston by a score of 7 to 3 in the first game in the series for the world's championship, at the Huntington [Avenue] grounds yesterday.

The crowd, which encircled the field, was held well back by ropes and a small army of policemen, and the best of order prevailed. Both teams received liberal applause for good work.

The Boston players evidently were a little nervous, as is usually the case with teams on the home grounds in an important series. As the game progressed, however, Collins'

boys got into their stride, and played grand ball when it was too late to overtake the Pirates.

Cy Young was hit hard. He fell considerably short of his best work, lacking speed, his winning ingredient. With Young off edge, the home players were carrying a big handicap.

> *Report of the first game of the first World Series, "Pittsburg a*
> *Winner in the First Clash,"* Boston Daily Globe,
> *October 2, 1903, p. 1.*

Another cause of pauperism is illness. A potent cause of disease is due to the breaking down of the organs which were subjected to abnormal uses before they were ready to bear it. I recall a tailor for whom the residents of Hull-House tried to get medical assistance. He died at the age of 33, and his death certificate bore the record, of "premature senility" due to the fact that he had run a sewing machine since he was 6 years old. It is no figment of the imagination to say that the human system breaks down when it is put to monotonous work before it is ready to stand up to that work, and that general debility and many diseases may be traced to premature labor. No horse trainer would permit his colts to be so broken down. . . .

The pauperization of society itself is another serious charge. When an industry depends upon the labor of boys and girls it takes them at a time when they ought to be at school. The wages paid to them are wages of mere subsistence. In almost all factories the work at which the children are employed leads to no trade. By the time they are old enough to receive adult wages they are often sick of the whole business. Such an industry is parasitic on the future of the community.

> *Jane Addams, "Evils of Child Labor," a letter printed in*
> *newspapers throughout the country, October 25, 1903,*
> *reprinted in Bremner, ed.,* Children and Youth in America
> *(1971), p. 655.*

You speak of your regret that the Commission was not composed exclusively of judges. I asked two judges of the Supreme Court, whom I thought most fit for the position, to serve. They both declined; and as I now think, wisely. On this Commission we needed to have jurists who were statesmen. . . . But my belief is that if you had had two of our Supreme Court judges on the American Commission, they would have stood out steadily for a decision on every point in favor of the American view—a determination which I think would have been technically proper, but in its results most unfortunate.

> *President Theodore Roosevelt defends his Alaska boundary*
> *dispute commissioners, letter to Arthur Hamilton Lee,*
> *December 7, 1903,* Letters, *vol. 3, pp. 665–66.*

Article I. The United States guarantees and will maintain the independence of the Republic of Panama.
Article II. The Republic of Panama grants to the United States in perpetuity, the use, occupation and control of a zone of land and land under water for the construction, maintenance, operation, sanitation and protection of said Canal of the width of ten miles extending to the distance of five miles on each side of the center line of the route of the Canal to be constructed. . . .
Article VII: . . . The Republic of Panama agrees that the cities of Panama and Colon shall comply in perpetuity, with the sanitary ordinances whether of a preventive or curative character prescribed by the United States and in case the Government of Panama is unable or fails in its duty to enforce this compliance by the cities of Panama and Colon with the sanitary ordinances of the United States the Republic of Panama grants to the United States the right and authority to enforce the same.

> *Hay–Bunau-Varilla Treaty, signed November 18, 1903,*
> *Malloy, ed.,* Treaties, Conventions, *vol. 2., pp. 1349–51.*

When we got up a wind of between 20 and 25 miles was blowing from the north. We got the machine out early and put out the signal for the men at the station. Before we were quite ready, John T. Daniels, W. S. Dough, A. D. Etheridge, W. C. Brinkley of Manteo, and Johnny Ward of Nags Head arrived. After running the engine and propellers a few minutes to get them in working order, I got on the machine at 10:35 for the first trial. The wind, according to our anemometers at this time, was blowing a little over 20 miles (corrected) 27 miles according to the Government anemometer at Kitty Hawk. On slipping the rope the machine started off increasing in speed to probably 7 or 8 miles. The machine lifted from the truck just as it was entering on the fourth rail. Mr. Daniels took a picture just as it left the tracks. I found the control of the front rudder quite difficult on account of its being balanced too

Dr. William C. Gorgas, born in Mobile, Alabama, gained worldwide fame for eradicating yellow fever and other tropical diseases in the Panama Canal Zone. Under his watch, the canal zone had a lower incidence of disease than some major American cities. *(Library of Congress, Prints and Photographs Division, LC-USZ62-28645)*

near the center and thus had a tendency to turn itself when started so that the rudder was turned too far on one side and then too far on the other. As a result the machine would rise suddenly to about 10 ft. and then as suddenly, on turning the rudder, dart for the ground. A sudden dart when out about 100 feet from the end of the tracks ended the flight. Time about 12 seconds (not known exactly as watch was not promptly stopped). The lever for throwing off the engine was broken, and the skid under the rudder cracked. After repairs, at 20 min.

Orville Wright describes the first flight in his diary, December 17, 1903, available online at Wright Brothers Aeroplane Company. URL: http://www.first-to-fly.com/History/Wright%20Story/OW121703.htm.

After the last flight, the machine was carried back to camp and set down in what was thought to be a safe place. But a few minutes later, while we were engaged in conversation about the flights, a sudden gust of wind struck the machine, and started to turn it over. All made a rush to stop it, but we were too late. Mr. Daniels, a giant in stature and strength, was lifted off his feet, and falling inside, between the surfaces, was shaken about like a rattle in a box as the machine rolled over and over. He finally fell out upon the sand with nothing worse than painful bruises, but the damage to the machine caused a discontinuance of experiments.

Orville and Wilbur Wright describe the fate of the first successful airplane on December 17, 1903 in their first account for a popular mass-market magazine, "The Wright Brothers Aëroplane," Century, vol. 76 (September 1908) p. 649.

I discussed chiefly freight rates. I would tell them how much it cost them to ship a carload of hogs from that town to Chicago, and how much it would cost an Iowa farmer to ship a carload of hogs from his town the same distance to market. And then I would tell them that we were trying to create in Wisconsin a railroad commission to which appeal could be made, instead of to a railroad official, for fair freight rates and adequate service. Then I would take the record of the last legislature on that question. I would say: "Now, I think you are entitled to know how your representative voted on this question. I am going to make no personal attack upon any individual, but he is your servant, and the servant of the people of this state. . . . I am here to-day to lay before you his record, and let you then decide whether that is the sort of service you want. There is no politics in this thing; it does not matter whether you get this legislation upon the vote of a Republican or a Democrat." Then I would tell them that I had interviewed the candidate on the Democratic side, and found him to be a man of integrity, that I had received from him assurance

that he would support the important legislation pledged in the Republican platform, and submitted to them whether the promise of this man was not better than the performance of the man who had betrayed them in the preceding session.

And I cleaned up the legislature.

Wisconsin governor Robert La Follette describes his campaign of 1904 to elect reformers of either party to the state legislature, Autobiography, pp. 341–42.

We welcome you . . . as warriors. The whole world loves a man that fights when he has justification for it. The timid good may have virtues, but the man who fights, the man who enters the arena and risks his future, his fortune and his life for others, such a one is dear to the hearts of his countrymen. To overthrow the liquor traffic means a terrific struggle, it means fighting, constantly, persistently and relentlessly, and you are sacrificing your time, your means, and it may be your very life blood to further this great cause. You are fighting at the point where the battle is on. . . . at the primary, at the caucus, the polls, in the courts, in short contesting every inch of ground and favoring everything that opposes the saloon.

Wayne Wheeler, ASL official, welcome to delegates at the 1904 convention, quoted in Blocker, Retreat from Reform, pp. 208–209.

It is hardly too much to say . . . that certain influences in society cast each year a large number of people into the most distressing poverty; and then, by an injudicious system of relief, miscalled charity, the poor are pauperized. . . . This seems at first glance an intemperate criticism of both society and philanthropy. It has been made, however, after many years of work in this field of social effort and not without careful consideration. In the first place it is obvious to inquiring persons that society, as a result of its industries, its tenements, its policy of almost unrestricted immigration and its system of education, ill-adapted in so many ways to the needs of the people, causes a large part of the poverty which exists amongst us. For instance, the aged, after years of honest and exacting toil, may find themselves at last thrown out of work, propertyless, and sometimes penniless. Dangerous trades cripple the bodies and undermine the health, of large numbers of workmen, and almost unrestricted immigration helps to increase an already too intense competition for wages in the underpaid, unskilled trades, with the result that the whole mass is more or less in poverty all of the time, and a certain percentage finds it necessary actually to apply periodically for charitable relief. The greed for profits on the part of owners of tenement-house property has so interfered with the enactment and enforcement of laws establishing certain minimum sanitary standards that a considerable number of working people have their labor power diminished or destroyed by tuberculosis and other diseases. It would be impossible to question the responsibility of society for such common and widespread causes of poverty.

Settlement worker and reformer Robert Hunter argues that society creates poverty, an idea still not completely accepted in 1904, in his influential book Poverty *(1906), pp. 66–68.*

Adolescence is a new birth, for the higher and more completely human traits are now born. The qualities of body and soul that now emerge are far newer. The child comes from and harks back to a remoter past; the adolescent is neo-atavistic, and in him the later acquisitions of the race slowly become prepotent. Development is less gradual and more saltatory, suggestive of some ancient period of storm and stress when old moorings were broken and a higher level attained. . . .

The social instincts undergo sudden unfoldment and the new life of love awakens. It is the age of sentiment and of religion, of rapid fluctuation of mood, and the world seems strange and new. Interest in adult life and in vocations develops. Youth awakes to a new world and understands neither it nor himself. The whole future of life depends on how the new powers now given suddenly and in profusion are husbanded and directed. Character and personality are taking form, but everything is plastic. Self-feeling and ambition are increased, and every trait and faculty is liable to exaggeration and excess. It is all a marvelous new birth, and those who believe that nothing is so worthy of love, reverence, and service as the body and soul of youth, and who hold that the best test of every human institution is how much it contributes to bring youth to the ever fullest possible development may well review themselves and the civilization in which we live to see how far it satisfies this supreme test.

Psychologist G. Stanley Hall's groundbreaking work defining adolescence as a separate and special developmental stage of life, Adolescence *(1904), pp. xiii–xv.*

The more important factories are now seldom found without the factory school, where—in spite of the many calls to the mill, to meet the exigencies of "rush orders"—the children, or a fraction of them, are given an elementary training in "the three R's." When the more ambitious boy or the more capable girl is advanced to "piece-work," the result of an active day is often a gratifying wage. But the period of satisfactory earning power reaches its maximum at about the eighteenth or nineteenth year, and the operative is held by the rewards of the industry at the only time when another career might seem possible and practicable. When it is clearly perceived that the strain of the long factory hours does not bring a really satisfactory adult wage, it is too late to change; and the few who pass upward in the

Lewis Hine photographed six-year-old Elsie Shaw in front of worker housing at the Seacoast Canning Company in Maine, where she was employed as a cartoner. Hine's documentary photos helped increase support for child labor reform. *(Library of Congress, Prints and Photographs Division, LC-USZ62-91562)*

Mill are but a small proportion of the mass. These, under the pressure of the economic situation just suggested, yield to that class tendency which is just as active among the poor as among the rich. The forces of a common origin, of neighborhood life, of a social experience shut in by the factory enclosure, with no opportunity for the home,—that best basis of social differentiation,—all conspire to emphasize the distinctions and the barriers of caste, and we find in process of creation a "factory people". . . .

Edgar Gardner Murphy, founder of the Alabama Child Labor Committee, Problems of the Present South *(1904), p. 106.*

The strike of 125 employees of the Cohen paper box factory, at 84 Bowery, has aroused the interest of the East Side as no other strike since the great conflict in the garment trades last summer. A large majority of the strikers are girls and of these most are very young, many being mere children of fourteen and fifteen years. . . .

The strike was caused by a proposed reduction of wages amounting to ten per cent. Before the cut the girls were getting three dollars a thousand boxes. There was no union at the time, but one was formed for the purpose of resisting the reduction. . . .

An extraordinary and deplorable feature of the strike has been the arrest of a number of the small girls on charges of assault. The youth and gentleness of these girls seem to make it most unlikely that they are guilty of the disorderly conduct with which they are charged. In each case the girls have been dismissed, but the small sums of money the strikers have been able to get together have been almost instantly disbursed by the arrests and fines levied against the men of the union who have been endeavoring to put their case before the new employees hired by Mr. Cohen. The strikers charge that the arrests are illegal and absolutely without cause.

The Woman's Trade Union League intends to get to the bottom of these arrests and to watch closely those that are made in the future. It has also directed the attention of the daily press to the strike and hopes that the pressure of public opinion will have some influence on the employer. . . .

Reformer and socialist William English Walling describes child strikers in 1904, "A Children's Strike on the East Side," Charities, vol. 13 (1904–1905), p. 305.

In the spring of 1904, through the kindness of Mr. Torrence Huffman of Dayton, Ohio, we were permitted to erect a shed, and to continue experiments, on what is known as the Huffman Prairie, at Simms Station, eight miles east of Dayton. The new machine was heavier and stronger, but similar to the one flown at Kill Devil Hill. When it was ready for its first trial, every newspaper in Dayton was notified, and about a dozen representatives of the press were present. Our only request was that no pictures be taken, and that the reports be unsensational, so as not to attract crowds to our experiment grounds. There were probably fifty persons altogether on the ground. When preparations had been completed, a wind of only three or four miles was blowing,—insufficient for starting on so short a track,—but since many had come a long way to see the machine in action, an attempt was made. To add to the other difficulty, the engine refused to work properly. The machine, after running the length of the track, slid off the end without rising into the air at all. Several of the newspaper men returned the next day, but were again disappointed. . . . Later, when they heard that we were making flights of several minutes' duration, knowing that longer flights had been made with air-ships, and not knowing any essential difference between airships and flying machines, they were but little interested.

Orville and Wilbur Wright describe flight trials in 1904, in their "Wright Brothers Aëroplane," Century, vol. 76 (September 1908), p. 650.

Not long afterward the Senator had a long, low shanty built on his place. A great big chimney, with a wide, open fireplace, was built at one end of it, and on each side of the house, running lengthwise, there was a row of frames or stalls just large enough to hold a mattress. The places for these mattresses were fixed one above the other, so that there was a double row of these stalls or pens on each side. They looked for all the world like stalls for horses. . . . Nobody seemed to know what the Senator was fixing for. All doubts were put aside one bright day in April when

about forty able-bodied negroes, bound in iron chains, and some of them handcuffed, were brought out to the Senator's farm in three big wagons. . . . This was the beginnings of the Senator's convict camp. . . . When I saw these men in shackles, I felt like running away, but I didn't know where to go. We free laborers held a meeting. We all wanted to quit. We sent a man to tell the Senator about it. Word came back that we were all under contract for ten years and that the Senator would hold us to the letter of the contract, or put us in chains and lock us up—the same as the other prisoners. It was made plain to us by some white people we talked to that in the contracts we had signed we had all agreed to be locked up in a stockade at night or at any other time that our employer saw fit. . . . In other words, we had sold ourselves into slavery. . . .

But this first batch of convicts was only the beginning. Within six months another stockade was built, and twenty or thirty other convicts were brought to the plantation, among them six or eight women! . . . Within two years the Senator had in all nearly 200 negroes working on his plantation—about half of them free laborers, so-called, and about half of them convicts. The only difference between the free laborers and the others was that the free laborers . . . were not locked up at night, and were not, as a general thing, whipped for slight offenses. The troubles of the free laborers began at the close of the ten-year period. . . . To a man, they all refused to sign new contracts. . . . And just when we thought that our bondage was at an end we found that it had really just begun. . . . [The Senator] had established a large store, which was called the commissary. All of us free laborers were compelled to buy our supplies—food, clothing, etc.—from that store. We never used any money in our dealings with the commissary, only tickets or orders. . . . Well, at the close of the tenth year, when we . . . meant to leave the Senator, he said to some of us with a smile (and I never will forget that smile—I can see it now):

"Boys, I'm sorry you're going to leave me. I hope you will do well in your new places—so well that you will be able to pay me the little balances which most of you owe me."

An African-American worker describes convict labor and peonage, "The New Slavery in the South—The Life Story of a Georgia Peon," Independent, vol. 56 (February 25, 1904), pp. 410–12.

First, every intelligence office [employment office] in New York City was visited in the capacity of employer and employee, so that we know the tone of every office. From this we selected about fifty which seemed questionable. There were others, but we could not take them up. To these fifty, men were sent in the guise of representatives of disreputable houses. In this way they became acquainted with the office men, talked to them, spent money freely, and were treated as any other such patrons, Thirty of these offices in this way admitted that they furnished girls for such purposes, said they had regular contracts and gave their "usual fee." Money was actually paid these offices to ascertain their good faith in the matter. Among these offices, these men found some that were disorderly houses, others that were Raines Law hotels [hotels used for prostitution], and still others that had their own places in the country or elsewhere. Not only this, but we had men in the guise of "runners" and visitors at Ellis Island to fathom the methods of the importation, and from every immigrant home we gathered experience and facts of people who for many years have been fighting these conditions single-handed. Through our own advertising and special agents, we learned of the extent to which negro girls are imported from the South and green country girls brought into the city. . . . So absolute is the negligence in New York City that in only *three* of the many offices where we asked for girls for men's club-houses were we asked any questions. When there is such utter indifference and girls are daily sent out of the city with absolute strangers to the office, both men and women, no one can estimate the extent of this practice.

Frances Kellor describes the methods College Settlement used to investigate the link between employment offices and prostitution, in "The Intelligence Office as a Feeder for Vice," Charities, *vol. 12 (March 5, 1904), p. 255.*

Every corporation created by a state is necessarily subject to the supreme law of the land. And yet the suggestion is made that to restrain a state corporation from interfering with the free course of trade and commerce among the states, in violation of an act of Congress, is hostile to the reserved rights of the states. . . . The affirmance of the judgment below will only mean that no combination, however powerful, is stronger than the law, or will be permitted to avail itself of the pretext that to prevent it doing that which, if done, would defeat a legal enactment of Congress, is to attack the reserved rights of the states. It would mean that the government which represents all, can, when acting within the limits of its powers, compel obedience to its authority. It would mean that no device in evasion of its provisions, however skilfully such device may have been contrived, and no combination, by whomsoever formed, is beyond the reach of the supreme law of the land, if such device or combination, by its operation, directly restrains commerce among the states or with foreign nations in violation of the act of Congress.

Supreme Court Justice John Harlan, writing for the majority of five in Northern Securities Co. v. U.S., *March 14, 1904, 193 US 197.*

Great cases, like hard cases, make bad law. For great cases are called great, not by reason of their real importance in shaping the law of the future, but because of some accident of immediate overwhelming interest which appeals to the feelings and distorts the judgment. These immediate interests exercise a kind of hydraulic pressure which makes what previously was clear seem doubtful, and before which even well-settled principles of law will bend. . . .

Supreme Court Justice Oliver Wendell Holmes, writing for the four dissenting justices in Northern Securities Co. v. U.S., *March 14, 1904, 193 U.S. 197.*

Of business interests the decision is conservative, not destructive, not obstructive. Because of it no wheel need cease to turn, no property is destroyed, no right of wealth invaded, no legitimate ambition assailed. The sun will rise and set as before, the rain will fall, the grain will grow as bravely in all that vast region which the merger sought to make subject in the important matter of transportation to one corporate will. . . .

Already there is talk of a campaign of education to secure the repeal of the Sherman Act. Against the folly of this attitude of an arrogant plutocracy cheated of its prey we enter protest. . . . No man of sense desires the destruction of all forms of capitalistic combination which the larger scale of modern industrial development demands. But the limit of safety is passed when the rights of the people are encroached upon. . . . The will of the people, as embodied in the law, is that this shall not be made possible. A "campaign of education," by all means; but let the school be opened in Wall Street, not on the farm!

New York World *on the Northern Securities decision, "The Merger Decision," March 15, 1904, p. 6.*

Not long since I visited a Southern city where the "Jim Crow" car law is enforced. I did not know of this law, and on boarding an electric car took the most convenient seat. The conductor yelled, "What do you mean? Niggers don't sit with white folks down here. You must have come from 'way up yonder. I'm not Roosevelt. We don't sit with niggers, much less eat with them."

I was astonished and said, "I am a stranger and did not know of your law." His answer was: "Well, no back talk now; that's what I'm here for—to tell niggers their places when they don't know them."

Every white man, woman and child was in a titter of laughter by this time at what they considered the conductor's wit.

These Southern men and women, who pride themselves on their fine sense of feeling, had no feeling for my embarrassment and unmerited insult. . . .

No one of them thought that I was embarrassed, wounded and outraged by the loud, brutal talk of the

Despite hardships in the Progressive Era, some African Americans established successful businesses and joined the vanguard of black leadership. This photo shows C. C. Dodson, a successful jeweler, in his store in Knoxville, Tennessee. It was included in a collection on "American Negro Life" compiled by W. E. B. DuBois for the Paris Exposition of 1900. *(Library of Congress, Prints and Photographs Division, LC-USZ62-53508)*

conductor and the sneering, contemptuous expressions on their own faces.

A middle-class African-American woman, wife of a doctor, in "The Race Problem—An Autobiography by a Southern Colored Woman," Independent, *vol. 56 (March 17, 1904), p. 588.*

The True Reformers' Hall was packed last Tuesday night with colored people who even lined the aisles and stair ways to attend the mass-meeting of citizens held for the purpose of making a dignified and conservative protest against the action of the Virginia Passenger and Power Company in making racial discrimination upon its [streetcar] lines in Richmond, Manchester and Petersburg.

A sensation was caused when Chairman Mitchell announced that the Presidents and Cashiers of the four colored Banks, and representing an aggregate capital of $180,000 had met Friday, April 15th, 1904 and pledged

their personal and financial support to any movement having for its purpose the transit of the colored people who must ride from one section of the city to the other. . . .

Mrs. Patsie K. Anderson's advice given in terse, explicit language was to do no talking but walk, walk, walk. She carried the house by storm and sat down amidst great applause. . . .

The African-American newspaper Richmond Planet *reports the streetcar boycott, April 4, 1904, p. 1.*

Our American institutions came into the world in the name of freedom. They have been seized upon by the capitalist class as the means of rooting out the idea of freedom from among the people. Our state and national legislatures have become the mere agencies of great propertied interest. . . .

Our political institutions are also being used as the destroyers of that individual property upon which all liberty and opportunity depend. The promise of economic independence to each man was one of the faiths upon which our institutions were founded. But, under the guise of defending private property, capitalism is using our political institutions to make it impossible for the vast majority of human beings ever to become possessors of private property as the means of life.

Socialist Party platform, adopted May 5, 1904, Proceedings of the National Convention of the Socialist Party, *p. 306, reprinted in Porter and Johnson, eds.,* National Party Platforms, *pp. 265–66.*

The Society for the Protection of Italian Immigrants . . . is constantly enlarging its activities. It has had the hearty cooperation of Commissioner Williams and of the police department. Its officials are stationed at Ellis Island and act as interpreters for the newcomers. With such immigrants as have friends either on Ellis Island or on the New York side, awaiting them, the society does not concern itself. Its attention is fully occupied in attending to those who have no friends and who have not the remotest ideas as to the place for which they are bound. These are taken directly to its office at 17 Pearl Street, and later turned over to its guards or runners. For this service the immigrant is charged a nominal fee. During the first two years and a half, 7,293 friendless immigrants were conducted to their destinations, in or about New York city, at an average cost of thirty-two cents apiece, as against an average expenditure of from $3.00 to $4.00, which immigrants formerly were forced to pay by sharpers.

Closely associated with the work of the Society for the Protection of Italian Immigrants is the Italian Benevolent Institute. . . . The institute has its headquarters in a double house, 165-7 West Houston street, which is intended as a place of refuge for the destitute.

Antonio Mangano describes the operation of an immigrant aid society, "The Associated Life of the Italians in New York City," Charities, *vol. 12 (May 7, 1904), pp. 478–79.*

What, then, is the cause of lynching? At the last analysis, it will be discovered that there are just two causes of lynching. In the first place, it is due to race hatred, the hatred of a stronger people toward a weaker who were once held as slaves. In the second place, it is due to the lawlessness so prevalent in the section where nine-tenths of the lynchings occur. . . .

Lynching is the aftermath of slavery. The white men who shoot negroes to death and flay them alive, and the white women who apply flaming torches to their oil-soaked bodies today, are the sons and daughters of women who had but little, if any, compassion on the race when it was enslaved. . . . It is impossible to comprehend the cause of the ferocity and barbarity which attend the average lynching-bee without taking into account the brutalizing effect of slavery upon the people of the section where most of the lynchings occur. . . .

For there can be no doubt that the greatest obstacle in the way of extirpating lynching is the general attitude of the public mind toward this unspeakable crime. The whole country seems tired of hearing about the black man's woes. The wrongs of the Irish, of the Armenians, of the Roumanian and Russian Jews, of the exiles of Russia and of every other oppressed people upon the face of the globe, can arouse the sympathy and fire the indignation of the American public, while they seem to be all but indifferent to the murderous assaults upon the negroes in the South.

Mary Church Terrell, "Lynching from a Negro's Point of View," North American Review, *vol. 178 (June 1904), pp. 860–61, 868.*

We favor such Congressional action as shall determine whether by special discrimination the elective franchise in any State has been unconstitutionally limited, and, if such is the case, we demand that representation in Congress and in the electoral college shall be proportionately reduced as directed by the Constitution of the United States. . . .

Combinations of capital and labor are the results of the economic movement of the age, but neither must be permitted to infringe upon the rights and interests of the people. Such combinations, when lawfully formed for lawful purposes, are alike entitled to the protection of the laws, but both are subject to the laws and neither can be permitted to break them.

Republican Party platform, June 21, 1904, Platforms of the Two Great Parties, *pp. 137–38.*

. . . communication by space telegraphy is maintained between the mainland of Southern California and the island of Santa Catalina, across some 30 miles of the Pacific Ocean. A "wireless" newspaper is published in Avalon, on the island, by the Los Angeles Times, Los Angeles being the nearest large city, and the work of transmission is done by the Western Union Telegraph Company over the land stretches and the Pacific Wireless Telegraph Company through the ether over the sea. . . .

Up to the time of the installation of this space-telegraph station there had been no telegraphic communication between the mainland and Santa Catalina, which is quite a summer resort, and having an almost perfect climate during the entire year, is becoming very popular as a winter resort as well. . . . The "wireless" station . . . is located on a high bluff on the north side of Avalon Bay. The space-telegraph instruments are of the Swenson type, and the service has been satisfactory to the present time, several thousand messages having been sent with accuracy and dispatch. . . . The instruments record the messages with accuracy, even during the most severe storms, which are of frequent occurrence about the island. These storms are terrific and the wind and waves are so high between the island and the mainland that the steamer communication is often stopped, and the space-telegraphic system is the only means of conveying messages to and from the mainland.

Frank C. Perkins, "Wireless Communication Between Santa Catalina Island and the Mainland," Western Electrician *(June 27, 1903), p. 503.*

We favor the enactment and administration of laws giving labor and capital impartially their just rights. Capital and labor ought not to be enemies. Each is necessary to the other. Each has its rights, but the rights of labor are certainly no less "vested," no less "sacred" and no less "inalienable" than the rights of capital. . . .

To revive the dead and hateful race and sectional animosities in any part of our common country means confusion, distraction of business, and the reopening of wounds now happily healed. . . .

We therefore deprecate and condemn the . . . selfish and narrow spirit of the Republican Convention at Chicago which sought to kindle anew the embers of racial and sectional strife. . . .

"Capital and Labor" and "Sectional and Race Agitation" planks, Democratic Party platform adopted July 6–9, 1904, Platforms of the Two Great Parties, *pp. 123, 131.*

I regard the gold standard as firmly and irrevocably established, and shall act accordingly if the action of the Convention to-day shall be ratified by the people.

As the platform is silent on the subject, my view should be made known to the Convention, and if it is proved to be unsatisfactory to the majority, I request you to decline the nomination for me at once, so that another may be nominated before adjournment.

Judge Alton Parker, telegram to the Democratic convention, July 9, 1904, as printed in the New York Times, *July 10, p. 1.*

The platform adopted by this Convention is silent upon the question of the monetary standard, because it is not regarded by us as a possible issue in this campaign, and only campaign issues are mentioned in the platform. Therefore there is nothing in the views expressed by you in the telegram just received which would preclude a man entertaining them from accepting a nomination on said platform.

Democratic convention replies to Parker, telegram reprinted in the New York Times, *July 10, p. 1.*

"Billy" Sunday, who was known in Base Ball circles years ago as the renowned outfielder of the Chicago Cubs, is doing missionary work in the Indiana gas belt towns and is talking to crowds of laboring people every night. He has become as widely known as an evangelist as he once was as a Base Ball player. . . .

He is telling the story of his conversion . . . to Indiana audiences every night and, incidentally, he has woven into his addresses the story of how prayer, as he verily believes, saved a game of Base Ball. As he tells the story, the fight for the pennant . . . with Detroit came. The score was close. Everybody was excited and the players were nerved to the highest pitch. . . .

"The last half of the ninth inning was being played," says the ex-ball player. "Two men were out and Detroit . . . had one man on second and another on third. He had two strikes on him and three balls called, when he fell on a ball with terrific force. It started for the clubhouse. Benches had been placed in the field for spectators and as I saw the ball sailing through my section of the air . . . I called 'Get out of the way.' The crowd opened and as I ran and leaped those benches I said one of the swiftest prayers that was ever offered. It was: 'Lord, if you ever helped a mortal man, help me get that ball.'

"I went over the benches as though wings were carrying me up. I threw out my hand while in the air and the ball struck and stuck. The game was ours. Though the deduction is hardly orthodox, I am sure the Lord helped me catch that ball, and it was my first great lesson in prayer."

Evangelist Billy Sunday described in an Indianapolis newspaper, July 12, 1904, reprinted in Spalding, America's National Game, *p. 284.*

I was beginning to learn English and at night in the boarding house the men who did not play cards used to read the paper to us. The biggest word was "Graft" in red letters on the front page. Another word was "Trust." This paper kept putting

these two words together. Then I began to see how every American man was trying to get money for himself. . . .

. . . At last I had a chance to help myself. Summer was over and Election Day was coming. The Republican in our district, Jonidas, was a saloonkeeper. A friend took me there. Jonidas shook hands and treated me fine. He taught me to sign my name, and the next week I went with him to an office and signed some paper, and then I could vote. I voted as I was told, and then they got me back into the [stock] yards to work, because one big politician owns stock in one of those houses. Then I felt that I was getting in beside the game. I was in a combine like other sharp men. Even when work was slack I was all right, because they got me a job in the street cleaning department. I felt proud, and I went to the back room in Jonidas's saloon and got him to write a letter to Alexandria to tell her she must come soon and be my wife.

Antanas Kaztauskis, a Lithuanian immigrant to Chicago, "From Lithuania to the Chicago Stockyards," Independent, *vol. 57 (August 4, 1904), pp. 246–47.*

It is worse than useless for any of us to rail at or regret the great growth of our industrial civilization during the last half century. . . . The practical thing to do is to face the conditions as they are and see if we can not get the best there is in them out of them. . . .

. . . The first thing we want is publicity; and I do not mean publicity as a favor by some corporations—I mean it as a right from all corporations affected by the law. I want publicity as to the essential facts in which the public has an interest. I want the knowledge given to the accredited representatives of the people of facts upon which those representatives can, if they see fit, base their actions later. The publicity itself would cure many evils. The light of day is a great deterrer of wrongdoing. The mere fact of being able to put out nakedly, and with the certainty that the statements were true, a given condition of things that was wrong, would go a long distance toward curing that wrong; and, even where it did not cure it, would make the path evident by which to cure it.

President Theodore Roosevelt describes his position on trusts and publicity, speech in Boston, August 25, 1902, in Addresses, *pp. 21, 25–26.*

Each great World's Exposition has been characterized by the presentation of some prominent invention. At the Centennial Exposition [1876] the telephone was first presented as a scientific curiosity; Chicago [1893] saw the incandescent lamp applied for the first time on an adequate scale for general and ornamental illumination; and the St. Louis Exposition may be similarly characterized as the first to present in an adequate and comprehensive way the new art of wireless telegraphy. . . .

This latest invention is well shown in the exhibit of the De Forest Wireless Telegraph Company, who have on the fair grounds ten operative sets of instruments representing seven separate stations. The De Forest observation tower stands prominently at the entrance to Orleans Plaza, 300 feet in height, and is equipped with two electric elevators. These are in constant operation, and the many visitors to the top of the tower evidence the popular interest in this new art of wireless telegraphy. . . .

Visitors to the Electricity Building have their attention drawn to the southwest corner by the sharp and penetrating crackle of the high-frequency, wireless-telegraph spark in the De Forest booth. . . . All day long the operators at this booth are busy transmitting and receiving messages. . . . A very popular test by the public is to write out messages at the station in the Fort Wayne exhibit and, strolling over to the main De Forest booth, find them already written out by the operator there.

"Wireless Telegraphy at the St. Louis Exposition," Electrical Age, *September, 1904, pp. 161–62.*

When it turned that circle, and came near the starting-point, I was right in front of it; and I said then, and I believe still, it was . . . the grandest sight of my life. Imagine a locomotive that had left its track, and is climbing up in the air right toward you—a locomotive without any wheels . . . but with white wings instead . . . spread 20 feet each way, coming right toward you with a tremendous flap of its propellers, and you have something like what I saw . . . I tell you, friends, the sensation that one feels is something hard to describe.

Amos Root, the owner of a beekeeping supply house in Medina, Ohio, who observed the Wright brothers flying on September 20, 1904, and published the account in his journal Gleanings in Bee Culture, *available online at Wright Brothers Aeroplane Company. URL: http://www. first-to-fly.com/History/Wright%20Story/oomph.htm.*

If you wished to keep your Administration free from suspicion, why did you select your corporation investigator [Mr. Cortelyou] to collect cash for your campaign fund? Do you not see the indelicacy of it, the impropriety of it? . . . What can you expect when people see the corporations and trusts that ought to be cowering in fear before your Department of Commerce contributing so generously to a campaign fund collected by a former Cabinet officer who knows their secrets? . . .

I sincerely believe that the reform measure most urgently needed in the United States is a corrupt practices act to forbid the receiving of national campaign contributions from corporations having business relations with the Federal Government or from corporations liable to punishment for violations of the Federal statutes regulating trade and commerce.

Joseph Pulitzer's eight-column open letter to President Roosevelt about campaign finance, "Mr. Roosevelt's Strange Policy," New York World, *October 1, 1904, pp. 6–7.*

After a triumphal progress through the streets of Brooklyn, and in the presence of all the leading Democrats of the borough at the Kings County Democratic Club, Judge Parker last night made answer to the attack made upon him in President Roosevelt's statement of the night before.

The part of his reply that evoked the wildest cheers was his answer to the President's insinuation that corporations had contributed to the Democratic [campaign] fund as well as the Republican fund. He said that this insinuation had forced him to make a revelation that he had not intended to make. . . . The judge impatiently stilled the cheering with his hand, and in a sharp, clear voice made his revelation.

It was that he had personally requested the National Committee to accept no contributions whatever from any trust and that they had complied with his request.

The Kings County Democrats simply went wild at this announcement. Hats went into the air, and instead of cheering, they yelled like men beside themselves. . . .

"Parker Barred the Trusts From Democratic Fund," New York Times, *November 6, 1904, p. 1.*

. . . let us cleave to the essential truth, which is that regardless of candidates and personalities, regardless of Mr. Roosevelt and Judge Parker, both honorable men, money is a mighty power in our politics.

Whichever way our sympathies may incline as between parties and candidates, let us not forget that the secret collection and secret use of enormous campaign funds, for whose control no one is responsible under the law, and about which, when once scattered, no one pretends to have the slightest knowledge—let us not forget that all this has become a national scandal, and confronts you and all of us as a deadly peril to the form of government and the institutions which we hold dear.

Editorial on the campaign finance scandal, Massachusetts Springfield Republican, *a politically independent paper, November 11, 1904, reprinted in Nevins, ed.,* American Press Opinion, *pp 488–89.*

5

A Reformer in the White House
1905–1908

NEW RELATIONS WITH EUROPEAN POWERS

As the United States assumed the role of a world power, it redefined its relations with Europe. Until the end of the 19th century, American statesmen had observed neutrality in European disputes, honoring George Washington's famous warning in his Farewell Address to avoid entangling alliances with the Old World.[1] But during the Roosevelt years, America's relationship with Europe began to change.

President Roosevelt believed that disputes among the nations of Europe were capable of posing great threats to world peace. He believed America should offer arbitration assistance to prevent the outbreak of general warfare. His first prominent opportunity came in early 1905 when a crisis occurred in Morocco on the northern coast of Africa. The European nations claimed spheres of influence in Africa, just as they did in Asia. Britain had agreed to respect France's growing influence in Morocco, and France to respect Britain's influence in Egypt. Germany, however, which was growing markedly stronger, begged to differ. Kaiser Wilhelm II publicly and noisily declared his support for Moroccan independence. Roosevelt persuaded the European powers to attend an international conference in Algeciras, Spain. There, American representatives oversaw the negotiation and signing of an agreement to leave an open door for trade in Morocco, while permitting France and Spain some control over policing the area. The Convention of Algeciras was even ratified by the U.S. Senate. The Senate, however, added a formal statement that its action was not to be regarded as a new departure from "the traditional American foreign policy which forbids participation by the United States in the settlement of political questions which are entirely European in their scope." Of course, it clearly was.[2]

Meanwhile, war was once again threatening in Asia. After the Boxer Rebellion of 1900, many Russian troops had remained in Manchuria, China's northernmost province. Russia continued to expand its authority there and appeared to have designs on neighboring Korea. Japan exercised great influence over Korea, and the United States originally hoped the two nations would check each other's power in the region. But in early 1904, the Japanese attacked and destroyed the Russian fleet at Port Arthur on the coast of Manchuria, then occupied Korea, beginning the Russo-Japanese War.

The president was more favorably inclined toward Japan than czarist Russia, which he considered brutal and backward. But as the Japanese scored impressive victories, he grew concerned about U.S. interests in Asia. Meanwhile, in Russia, portentous domestic events were occurring. The cost of the Russo-Japanese War was weighing heavily on the peasantry and other citizens, deepening the economic hardship that already existed. Many opposition groups were uniting to protest the czar's autocracy and repression. In January 1905, armed revolts, strikes, and terrorism began.

At the request of the Japanese, who could not afford a lengthy war either, President Roosevelt hosted a peace conference. It took place at Portsmouth, New Hampshire, in the fall of 1905. In the Treaty of Portsmouth, Japan won many concessions, including dominance in southern Manchuria and in Korea (which it formally annexed in 1910). Back in Russia, a month after the Treaty of Portsmouth was signed, the czar was forced to grant some concessions to his subjects, giving them Russia's first rudimentary constitution. Opposition to the czar quieted—but it did not disappear.

In 1906, President Roosevelt was awarded the Nobel Peace Prize for his work at Algeciras and Portsmouth. The two treaties doubtless postponed the start of a major war—but did not, unfortunately, prevent it.

CHANGING RELATIONS WITH JAPAN

Russia's loss to Japan in the Russo-Japanese War changed world perceptions of Japan's growing strength. While the Portsmouth Conference was underway, Philippine governor William Taft met with the Japanese minister in Tokyo at President Roosevelt's behest. He secured the Taft-Katsura agreement, in which Japan agreed to honor United States control of the Philippines and America accepted Japanese control of Korea. Three years later the Root-Takihira agreement, negotiated by Secretary of State Elihu Root with the Japanese ambassador, reaffirmed respect for the Open Door in China, as well as for China's national integrity. Despite these agreements, however, beneath the surface relations with Japan were tense and mistrustful. Japan had ambitions for expanding its power in Asia, while the United States was invested in maintaining the status quo there. Tensions were not eased by the discriminatory treatment of Japanese immigrants to the United States whose numbers rose markedly in the first decade of the 20th century, especially on the West Coast.

TRUSTBUSTING CONTINUES

During President Roosevelt's second term, the tide of public anger at trusts and corporate misconduct—the "malefactors of great wealth," as he memorably called them—rose even higher. President Roosevelt delighted in his reputation as a trustbuster, and throughout his second term, he continued to sound the theme that control over large corporations was necessary to address "the total change in industrial conditions on this continent during the last half century."[3] Nonetheless, Roosevelt used his trustbusting power selectively. He prosecuted companies that, in his judgment, either blatantly violated the public interest or defied the power of the government to uphold it. Before he left office, the government filed more than 40 antitrust suits, although not all succeeded. They included suits against Standard Oil of New Jersey, the American Tobacco Company, and the so-called Beef Trust, which controlled about 60 percent of "trade and commerce in fresh meats" in the nation. In the Beef Trust case (*Swift and Co. v. United States,* 1905) the Supreme Court found a way to circumvent its own 1895 ruling in the Sugar Trust (or *E.C. Knight*) case. The Sugar Trust decision held that manufacturing could not be regulated by the federal government, because manufacturing a product at one site was not interstate commerce. In the Beef Trust case the Court developed the so-called stream of commerce doctrine. It held that when manufacturers moved raw materials and finished products from state to state—livestock and processed meat in the case of the Beef Trust—they were engaging in interstate commerce, and subject to federal regulation.[4]

This political cartoon, which appeared in the humor magazine *Puck* in January 1904, is entitled "Jack and the Wall Street Giants." It shows President Roosevelt facing giants of business and finance J. P. Morgan, James J. Hill, John D. Rockefeller, and Jay Gould. Roosevelt is holding a typical progressive sword: public service. *(Library of Congress, Prints and Photographs Division, LC-USZ62-93557)*

Encouraged by his resounding endorsement in the election of 1904, President Roosevelt also pressed for further regulation of railroads, which remained a popular issue with the public. Despite great opposition from railroad interests, Congress passed the Hepburn Act in 1906. The act declared "every unjust and unreasonable charge" for rail transportation of people or property to be illegal. It required that schedules of rates and fares be available for public inspection and gave the Interstate Commerce Commission (ICC) power to approve maximum rates. It forbade the issuing of free passes, a practice long criticized by reformers because it was used to buy the influence of officials and politicians. It also extended the ICC's jurisdiction to other common carriers (businesses that transport goods for a fee) such as terminals, oil pipelines, and ferries. The Hepburn Act was less stringent than reform-minded supporters had hoped, however.[5]

PROTECTING THE CONSUMING PUBLIC

While the Hepburn Act fought its way through Congress, the public became even more concerned about another issue: the quality, wholesomeness, and outright safety of food and drugs in America. The campaign for consumer safeguards had begun in the 1890s. At that time, the food, meat, liquor, and drug industries successfully blocked efforts toward regulatory legislation. By 1905, the political environment had changed. Muckrakers had taken up the issue, as had professional medical journals.

One fact the journalists exposed was that many common patent medicines were primarily alcohol—and even contained drugs like opium. Since the Civil War, the use of opium, cocaine, morphine, and finally heroin had been known and generally quite legal in the United States. The exception was opium, the most commonly used drug at the time; some attempts had been made to regulate its importation and recreational use. (The public associate opium use with Chinese immigrants, who brought with them a greater cultural acceptance of the drug, but it was by no means restricted to them.) Narcotic drugs were also used by physicians as anesthetics and were widely prescribed for many illnesses. But by the 1890s, their most common use was as additives. Cocaine, for example, was a common additive to tonics and patent drugs for respiratory problems. It was also common in soft drinks—like Coca Cola.[6]

By the turn of the century, the medical profession had gained new insight into the addictive and dangerous potential of opiates and other narcotic substances, and scientific knowledge about them was increasing yearly. To be sure, the drugs were not yet viewed as the social problem they would be considered by the end of the 20th century—in fact, impure foods were considered a far greater threat at the time. But reformers increasingly viewed patent medicines with narcotic and alcohol additives just as they viewed impure foods—a form of adulteration and a threat to the health of unsuspecting consumers.

The National Consumers League (NCL) and the American Medical Association (AMA) lobbied for the president to address the food and drug issue. In his annual message to Congress in December 1905, he did. He recommended legislation to "regulate interstate commerce in misbranded and adulterated foods, drinks and drugs," in the interests of what he called the consuming public.[7] Before two weeks had passed a regulatory pure-food-and-drug bill was introduced into the Senate, but it did not advance. Some responsible food companies favored it, but many food, drug, and liquor manufacturers lobbied against it. Some congressmen also disliked extending federal jurisdiction into new regulatory territory.

A short while later in January 1906, Upton Sinclair published his novel *The Jungle,* which incorporated his research on grossly unsanitary conditions in the meat-packing industry. After reading it, the president instructed the secretary of agriculture to conduct an immediate probe of the Chicago stockyards. The secretary's report confirmed shocking conditions. By late May, Senator Albert Beveridge of Indiana had introduced a meat-inspection bill into the Senate. The president offered Congress a deal: he would not release the results of the federal investigation to the public—providing the legislation was quickly passed. But Congress balked and on June 4, the report was released. The public was outraged—and by June 19, the meat-inspection bill was passed. The furor the report created also pried loose the pure-food-and-drug bill introduced earlier, and it was passed as well. Both laws were signed by the president on June 30, 1906.

The Pure Food and Drug Act made the Department of Agriculture responsible for testing all foods and drugs destined for human consumption. It also required that patent medicines reveal on their labels any drugs and alcohol they contained. The act was based on the assumption that an informed public would cease to use them, but it did not make their sale illegal. The Meat Inspection Act required United States inspection of animals before slaughter and allowed inspection of carcasses afterward. It also established standards of cleanliness for slaughterhouses and meat processors.

THE HEYDAY OF MUCKRAKING

Muckraking journalism hit new heights of popularity during Roosevelt's second term. Reform-minded journalists expanded their investigations of corruption into all areas of life. They investigated insurance, railroads, Wall Street, government and the courts, the powerful, the wealthy, the poor, city tenements, labor unions, prostitution, crime, child labor, and even on occasion churches, race relations, and the press itself.

At first, President Roosevelt applauded. But when David Graham Phillips began exposing corruption in the U.S. Senate, he decided the muckrakers had gone too far. Phillips's "The Treason of the Senate" began appearing in *Cosmopolitan* in February 1906. It named many well-known senators, some the president's close colleagues. Two months later, Roosevelt delivered his famous speech equating the new journalists with the Man with the Muckrake, a character in John Bunyan's *Pilgrim's Progress* (the 1675 work, a Christian allegory, was still familiar to many people at the turn of the century). The Man with the Muckrake—who cleaned up manure—was so focused on looking down at something unpleasant that he never looked up to the heavens.[8]

Muckrakers, like most progressives, were very optimistic. They had great faith in democracy and in the American people. They wrote because they believed that exposing evils to the public view would lead to corrective actions. They almost always spoke with a tone of moral outrage and were occasionally intemperate in their attacks, but the best of their work was exhaustively researched and vividly written. After 1910, magazines would devote themselves less exclusively to exposés and return to a more varied format, but muckraking remained a permanent feature of journalism for the remainder of the Progressive Era. There is little doubt that the muckrakers, and the public dialogue they inspired, helped bring about many reforms.

ALASKAN DEVELOPMENT CONTINUES

In 1905, a Supreme Court decision was handed down that was crucial for Alaska's future. Like many such cases, its specifics seemed far afield of important political principles. *Rassmussen v. United States* was an appeal by an Alaska resident who had been convicted of "keeping a disreputable house" (that is, a house of prostitution), without benefit of judicial procedures guaranteed by the U.S. Constitution. In deciding in Rassmussen's favor, the Court called on the principle of incorporation, established in the Insular Cases of 1901. In the Court's eyes, if land controlled by the United States had been incorporated into the nation by a vote of Congress, it was entitled to full constitutional rights. The Court declared that Alaska had indeed been incorporated when Congress approved the Alaskan purchase treaty in 1867.[9]

The *Rassmussen* decision cleared the way for Alaska to become a U.S. territory and later a state. Congress soon changed its official designation from *district* to *territory,* although Alaska continued to be governed by a few official appointees with no elected legislative body. In 1906, the Delegate Act gave Alaska a nonvoting representative in Congress. Federal judge James Wickersham was elected to the post. He held it for many years, consistently advocating the establishment of self-government in Alaska.

The U.S. government continued to promote development in the Far North. It expanded a system of agricultural experiment stations begun in 1898 to develop sustainable crops and encouraged the development of schools, roads, and railways. In 1906, a private development combination called the Alaska Syndicate was organized by the Guggenheim Corporation, the largest mining trust in the United States, and J.P. Morgan Company bankers. The syndicate began in copper mining and soon expanded to steamship companies, salmon canneries, and railways. It had plans to expand into coal and oil, a scheme that would have given it control over the development of Alaska and that many antimonopolists found unacceptable.

Continuing development in Alaska inevitably affected Native Alaskans. Most belonged to one of four cultural groups: the coastal Indians (Tlingit, Haida, and Tsimshian), who traditionally occupied the panhandle coast; the Aleut, who occupied the western Seward Peninsula and Aleutian Islands; the Inuit and Alaska Natives, who occupied the western and northern coast of Alaska; and the Athabascans, who occupied the Arctic and subarctic interior. Because the history of white settlement in Alaska was very different from that of the lower states, no treaties, formal tribal recognition, or reservations existed for Native Alaskan peoples. In 1906, after a succession of reports, Congress passed the Alaska Native Allotment Act. Like the Dawes Act, it provided 160-acre homesteads for heads of families. Unlike the Dawes Act, it was less concerned with forcing Native people to end tribal relations than with permitting them to obtain formal title to some amount of their ancestral lands. Few accepted allotments, however—only 80 were ever issued. Between 1900 and 1950, the Native and non-Native populations in Alaska remained very close at roughly 30,000 each.

THE UNITED STATES REOCCUPIES CUBA

The United States occupied Cuba for four years after the Spanish-American War of 1898 but withdrew in 1902 upon the inauguration of Tómas Estrada Palma as president. The economy recovered well; sugar production, for example, grew nearly 400 percent between 1900 and 1905. But Cuba continued to be torn by political conflicts, and the nationalist government remained unsteady. Industry and land ownership was dominated by Americans, not Cubans. The Cuban upper class retained many ties and loyalties to Spain. In 1906, Estrada Palma was reelected, but many Cubans regarded the election as fraudulent. When civil war threatened, Estrada Palma requested United

States aid. Roosevelt sent two warships, troops, commissioners, and soon, a provisional governor. They reoccupied the island for three years.

PUERTO RICANS SEEK MORE SELF-DETERMINATION

In 1904, many Puerto Ricans had united in the new Union Party, which stood firmly for increased self-government in some form. In 1906, the Union Party won every seat in the legislature. The legislature continued to send memorials to Congress, passionately protesting government under the Foraker Act, but received no response.

Shortly after the 1906 legislative election, President Roosevelt visited the island while on a trip to inspect the canal construction in Panama—the first trip abroad ever made by a sitting president. Wherever he went in Puerto Rico, he met a warm reception but also pleas for more self-determination. Upon returning to Washington, however, the president announced that he fully supported the Foraker Act. He did recommend that the people of Puerto Rico be given American citizenship. (It took Congress another decade to agree, however.) The following year, José de Diego, Speaker of the Puerto Rican legislature, personally delivered another memorial to the president requesting more self-government, but received no response.

PROGRESSIVES IN THE GOVERNOR'S OFFICE

In the first decade of the 20th century, and gaining steam after 1905, reform interests in many states began to defeat state political machines and capture the governor's office. Often the battles occurred within rather than between political parties. In the Midwest, where the Republican Party was dominant, state after state saw revolts against the conservative party leadership and its ties to the interests. The Republican insurgency, as its supporters came to be called, built on long-standing complaints in farming regions that dated from the heyday of populism—against the trusts, railroad policies, and high tariffs that protected industrialists but made consumer goods more expensive. Robert La Follette in Wisconsin was the earliest and best known of these reform governors, but many other midwestern states also became progressive strongholds. Albert B. Cummins of Iowa (1902–08), for example, fought railroad interests to establish direct-democracy reforms and the direct primary. Cummins also introduced the popular Iowa Idea, an argument that tariffs should be removed from all imported items that were also manufactured by American trusts to force the trusts to compete. In Missouri, Joseph W. Folk was elected in 1905 after prosecuting a corrupt political ring in St. Louis. Reform governors also rose to office in the East. Charles Evans Hughes of New York (1906–10), for example, was elected after uncovering extensive fraud in the insurance industry.

The South remained very rural and continued to lag behind the rest of the nation in prosperity. This hardscrabble dairy farm was photographed in southwestern Louisiana at the end of the first decade of the 20th century. *(Library of Congress, Prints and Photographs Division, LC-USZ62-52804)*

In the South, the insurgent reform movement occurred within the dominant Democratic Party. Progressive Democrats in the South, however, were also strong supporters of formal black disenfranchisement and segregation legislation. They argued that progressive reform in the South would not otherwise be possible because whites would not accept it. In 1900 whites were actually a minority (less than 50 percent) of the population in two of the six deep-south states, Mississippi and South Carolina, and only a small majority of the population in the others, Alabama, Georgia, Louisiana, and Florida.[10] As long as blacks could vote, progressive southern Democrats believed, the fear of black political power would hold whites together under the established conservative leadership.

After the turn of the century, when it was clear that black disenfranchisement had succeeded, white progressives in the South began to challenge conservatives for control of the Democratic Party. A series of Southern Democratic governors took office who resembled their midwestern Republican counterparts on issues other than race. To win office, they built on the old agrarian grievances. They worked to end corruption and improve effectiveness in municipal and state government; regulate railroads, utilities, and other corporations; pass direct-democracy reforms; and institute social reforms to improve the health and welfare of citizens. In North Carolina, Charles B. Aycock (1901–05) stimulated the construction of some 1,100 schools—"a school a day" during his term of office. Governors Hoke Smith of Georgia (1907–09, 1911) and Braxton Bragg Comer of Alabama (1907–11) increased appropriations for the public schools and supported regulation of child labor. Napoleon Bonaparte Broward of Florida (1904–08) began the Everglades drainage project. Even James K. Vardaman of Mississippi (1904–08), remembered by historians as a particularly notorious racist, began a substantial list of progressive reforms in the state.[11]

Vardaman fought hard and successfully to abolish convict leasing in Mississippi, a practice which in fact affected more blacks than whites. After the Civil War, many southern states had begun renting convicts to private plantations, or such other businesses as railroads, to do hard labor. The system of granting convict leases was subject to much political corruption, but that was far from the worst problem. The lessee had complete control over the rented convicts, their food, and their housing. Convicts were brutally mistreated. One out of 10 died, creating a long-term scandal in the South. Worst of all, from the point of view of African Americans, convict leasing was closely interwoven with discriminatory law enforcement. Since renting convicts was profitable for states, some states declared small offenses such as loitering subject to long prison terms and arrested blacks disproportionately for them. In 1906, Vardaman succeeded in limiting convict work to prison farms and other public projects.

OKLAHOMA BECOMES A STATE

The question of statehood remained unsettled for what were commonly called the Twin Territories—Indian Territory and Oklahoma Territory (modern eastern and western Oklahoma, respectively). The territories were independent of each other. By 1906, 31 different proposals, some proposing one unified state and some proposing two separate states, had been introduced into Congress.

In Indian Territory, where Native Americans now numbered only about 10 percent of the total population, the Five Civilized Tribes resisted the idea of one unified state. Tribal leaders helped organize a convention to draft a constitution for a separate state. In 1905, 182 delegates elected by both Indian and non-Indian men in the territory met in Muskogee. They called their proposed state Sequoyah in honor of the Cherokee leader and inventor of the Cherokee alphabet. The delegates wrote many progressive reforms into the Sequoyah constitution. In a referendum it received overwhelming approval from the men of Indian Territory.[12]

In Washington, however, the issue of Oklahoma statehood was turning on national party politics. The Sequoyah constitution did not receive a warm welcome from President Roosevelt or from the Republican majorities in the House of Representatives and the Senate. In Washington, Indian Territory was correctly believed to be solidly Democratic, and Republicans had no wish to create a new, solidly Democratic state. In Oklahoma Territory to the west, on the other hand, Republicans were numerous enough to win state offices consistently. In 1906, when Congress approved an Oklahoma Enabling Act, it was for one new state combining both the Twin Territories— with the provision that its constitution meet the approval of President Roosevelt.

Calculations among Republican congressmen went for naught. As it happened, while Congress wrote an enabling act in Washington, reform sentiment surged into full gear in the Twin Territories, and the Democratic Party there successfully identified itself as the party of progressive reform. Unexpectedly, 100 of 112 state constitutional convention delegates were elected on the progressive Democratic ticket.

The Oklahoma constitutional convention produced a document of more than 50,000 words—"easily the world's longest constitution at that time," in the words of historians James Scales and Danney Goble.[13] It left few particulars of reform unspecified. The constitution declared monopolies "contrary to the genius of a free government" and all corporate books and records "liable and subject to the full visitorial and inquisitorial powers of the State."[14] It gave the state power to establish many kinds of taxes, including a graduated income tax and inheritance tax. It established a department of conservation and made the state responsible for social security, or support of the aged and infirm. It included provisions for direct democracy, established the eight-hour workday, abolished child labor, and required corporations to arbitrate disputes with employees. It offered statewide prohibition, which required a separate vote for ratification. While the convention rejected full women's suffrage, for which the territorial branch of the National American Women's Suffrage Association (NAWSA) had worked since the 1890s, the constitution did permit women to vote in school board elections.

Journalists from across the nation descended on the convention and publicized the constitution as a model progressive document. The *Arena* titled its article about the constitution "Monument to Progressive and Conscientious Citizenship." Oklahomans had "struggled against the combined terrors of the wilderness and the exactions of the grasping, merciless, tyrannical corporations," wrote the *Saturday Evening Post*'s correspondent. "It was not merely the birth of a new state, it was the birth of a new kind of state."[15] Although the constitution was deemed radically progressive by most observers pro and con, it also instituted the principle of racial segregation, establishing separate schools for black and white children. Other segregation laws were proposed at the convention, but blocked when President Roosevelt made it clear he would not approve the constitution if it contained them. (The laws were, however, later passed in the first state legislative session.)

President Roosevelt retained serious reservations about the constitution, especially its lengthy list of regulations for corporations. As the ratification vote approached, Democrats campaigned as its champions. Roosevelt sent Secretary of State William Taft to Oklahoma to help local Republicans campaign against it. Taft called the document a combination of "Bourbonism [southern conservatism] and despotism, flavored with Socialism." The national Democratic Party sent William Jennings Bryan, who had acted as an adviser to Oklahoma Democrats throughout the process. Bryan followed Taft around the state to assure listeners that the constitution was one of "the great documents of modern times."[16] Oklahoma citizens overwhelmingly ratified the constitution and elected Democrat Charles Haskell governor. They also elected Democrats to a huge majority in the state legislature and to four of their five new congressional seats. They voted a preference for two Democratic senators after which the new state legislature elected them officially. President Roosevelt declared his opinion on the outcome "not fit for publication." But on November 16, 1907, he reluctantly proclaimed Oklahoma the 46th state.[17]

NEW MEXICO AND ARIZONA DECLINE JOINT STATEHOOD

Residents of the territories of New Mexico and Arizona also were anxious for statehood and had made several unsuccessful attempts to obtain it. New Mexico had been a territory since 1850. It was created from land acquired in the Treaty of Guadalupe Hidalgo, which ended war between Mexico and the United States. Arizona had been a territory since 1863, when it was carved out of New Mexico territory and separated from it. Although the population in both territories was far larger than the threshold of 60,000 that Congress required for statehood, officials in Washington and much of the American public objected to their admission to the union.

Some objected for political reasons. The mining industry was strong in the territories, and eastern conservatives feared to augment the strength of silver mining interests, who opposed the gold standard. Republicans feared the states would send Democrats to the Senate, upsetting their majority. Reformers objected because muckrakers had revealed that certain sitting senators had financial interests in the territories and stood to gain from statehood. Others objected for ethnic and religious reasons. Both territories had large Hispanic and Native American populations and distinct Spanish, Indian, and Catholic heritages. In Arizona, Anglo, or English-speaking, settlers were now predominant, but in New Mexico the old Hispano oligarchy still wielded significant power. Some Americans feared they would not support U.S. institutions. And finally, many Americans feared the territories were too uncivilized for statehood. Misled by information sources like newspapers, magazines, and even novels and the movies, they continued to view the territories as the last outpost of the Wild West.

In the territories themselves, the clamor for statehood continued to grow. In 1906, the chair of the Senate Committee on Territories, Senator Albert Beveridge of Indiana, shepherded what he thought was a good political compromise through Congress. When Congress passed the enabling act to permit Indian and Oklahoma Territories to enter the union as one combined state, it also passed enabling legislation to admit New Mexico and Arizona as one combined state. The new state would have a capital at Santa Fe and the name Arizona the Great. Joint statehood, politicians believed, would balance Republican-leaning, Hispanic New Mexico with Democratic-leaning, English-speaking Arizona; it would also hold the number of new senators to two instead of four. "The only reason I want them in as one state now," President Roosevelt said, "is that I fear the alternative is having them as two states three or four years hence."[18]

The enabling act, however, required that each of the territories separately approve the arrangement. Most New Mexicans were willing to accept jointure to obtain statehood, although territorial governor Miguel Otero opposed it. They voted yes by nearly 2-1. Arizonans, however, feared they would be politically overwhelmed by New Mexico, which had a significantly larger population. They voted more than 5-1 against joint statehood, and the measure died. President Roosevelt, bowing to the inevitable, announced his support for separate statehood the following year.

DIRECT-DEMOCRACY REFORM CONTINUES

Direct-democracy reformers in many states continued to work for the initiative, referendum and recall, the direct primary election, and the direct election of senators. The leader in direct-democracy legislation was the state of Oregon. After initiative and referendum became effective there in 1902, a coalition of reformers used them vigorously to propose and achieve additional reforms of many kinds—a procedure that received national publicity and became known as the Oregon System. In 1908, Oregon became the first state to amend its constitution to allow for recall, which enables voters to remove government officials.

By the end of 1908, a total of eight states had adopted some form of initiative and referendum. A group of more than 100 members of the House of Representative even proposed national initiative and referendum to permit voters to propose, accept, or reject legislation passed by Congress, but the idea never awoke strong popular interest.

In 1903, Wisconsin passed the first comprehensive, complete, and compulsory statewide primary election law, requiring political parties to allow voters instead of party officials to select all candidates for office. By 1906, 13 states had passed direct primary laws although some required primaries only in large cities or for certain offices. In 1907 and 1908, 10 more states adopted the direct primary. After that the movement ignited. By 1917, 32 states had passed comprehensive direct-primary laws, and 12 more had passed limited or optional direct primaries. Only four states—Connecticut, New Mexico, Rhode Island, and Utah—remained without some form of primary election legislation at the close of the Progressive Era.[19]

Reformers also continued to push for the direct election of senators. Because the U.S. Constitution gives state legislatures the power to elect the state's U.S. senators, however, the reform could only be achieved by a constitutional amendment. By 1905, the House of Representatives had passed an amendment bill five times—two times unanimously. Each time the Senate killed it. By the same date, 31 of the 45 states had either petitioned Congress to pass the amendment or had endorsed the idea of a national constitutional convention to consider the issue. In the meantime, Oregon and a number of other states passed legislation to accomplish the same end without violating the Constitution. They established a preferential election for senator to take place at the same time as their new primary elections, then required or recommended that the state legislature officially elect the candidate preferred by the people.[20]

STATE LABOR LAWS AND THE COURTS

As states came under the increasing influence of progressivism, they made increasing efforts to improve the conditions of labor for working people, especially in dangerous occupations. Common areas of reform were factory safety laws and limits on working hours. One popular area of regulation was special protection for the health and welfare of women workers. Reform-minded people of many different political and economic persuasions found common ground with each other and with unions on the issue, due to widely shared beliefs that women workers also had an important role as mothers and future mothers. On the whole, however, the courts took a dim view of all state attempts to regulate working conditions. Courts usually upheld the traditional view that employers and workers had the liberty to make a contract of employment with any terms they agreed upon, without state interference.

Before the turn of the century, New York had passed a law limiting bakery workers to 60 work hours per week because flour dust was known to contribute to lung diseases. Eventually, Joseph Lochner, a bakery owner in Utica, New York, was arrested and fined for violating the law. He appealed to the Supreme Court. In 1905, the Supreme Court declared New York's law unconstitutional (*Lochner v. New York*) because it was "an illegal interference with the rights of individuals, both employers and employees, to make contracts regarding labor upon such terms as they may think best." The Court did acknowledge, however, that the state had an interest in protecting its citizens from clear and excessive threats to health and safety, even if doing so did violate an employment contract. But baking did not appear to be extremely hazardous to employees, nor did long working hours for bakers threaten public safety.

The Lochner decision called forth a famous dissent from Oliver Wendell Holmes, a justice whom President Roosevelt had appointed to the Court in 1902. Holmes argued that the other justices had not ruled on the basis of constitutional law, but on the basis of a particular economic theory—the 19th-century idea of laissez-faire, or no governmental interference in business at all. It was a theory, Holmes added, that "a large part of the country does not entertain." "A constitution is not intended to embody a particular economic theory," he continued. "It is made for people of fundamentally differing views." The Supreme Court should judge laws solely on whether or not they conflicted with the Constitution itself, he continued. And the Constitution, he argued, gave state legislatures the right to enact laws to protect their citizens from dangerous working conditions if they chose, without having their action overturned by a Supreme Court that held different economic views.[21]

In 1903, before the Lochner case had made its way through the courts, Oregon passed a law that limited women's working hours in laundries or factories to 10 hours a day. Twenty other states had also passed similar laws restricting women's working hours. Soon an Oregon laundry owner, Curt Muller, was fined for violating the law and requiring his women employees to work longer hours. After the Supreme Court handed down the Lochner decision, he decided to appeal. The National Consumers League (NCL), which was actively involved in efforts to reform the conditions of women's labor, wanted to help Oregon win the case. Florence Kelley, the head of the NCL, and Josephine Goldmark, an NCL researcher and publicist, had been convinced for some time that facts about the actual conditions under which wage-earning women worked were not widely understood and might be persuasive in court. The NCL engaged Louis Brandeis, a socially conscious and reform-minded attorney in Boston, to assist the Oregon attorney general.

Brandeis chose a novel approach in the legal brief he prepared for the court with Goldmark's help. Ordinarily, a Supreme Court brief is a reasoned argument based on the Constitution and legal precedents, or former court decisions. Brandeis, however, quickly stated the legal precedents in only two pages. Then he presented 100 pages of data, primarily from medical and social sciences. His starting point was the Court's point of view in the Lochner case. The Court had acknowledged that the state had an interest in protecting citizens from very serious threats to health or safety. Brandeis attempted to prove that a working day of more than 10 hours was exactly that. "Unless we know the facts on which the legislators may have acted, we cannot properly decide whether they were . . . unreasonable," Brandeis once said. "Knowledge is essential to understanding, and understanding should precede judging."[22] He marshaled much expert opinion to show that long hours for women caused health problems and even high infant mortality, that (quoting President Roosevelt himself) long hours affected "the home-life of the nation," that overwork drove "respectable women" into saloons. The Supreme Court was convinced, and upheld the constitutionality of the Oregon law limiting women's hours in February 1908.[23]

The Brandeis brief was an innovation in law because it attempted to show the effect of a legal issue on people's everyday lives. It became a model for reformers when other progressive laws were challenged in the courts. Even today, legal briefs that use medical, sociological, and psychological data are called Brandeis briefs.

The decision in *Muller v. Oregon* was widely praised by progressives. Over time, however, it presented women's rights advocates with a dilemma. All of the expert testimony in the Brandeis brief was based on the assumption that women were very different from men and required special laws to protect them. *Muller v. Oregon* established the right of the state to regulate working conditions, but it also acknowledged the legality of treating male and female employees differently.

THE WORKING DAY FOR MEN

During the first decade of the 20th century, unions were more influential than reformers in efforts to obtain legislation that reduced the working day for men. As the influence of progressivism grew, however, the public increasingly supported their efforts, especially in areas that affected public and worker safety. In railroading, where it was easily proven that long shifts increased accident rates, 12 states had passed laws limiting consecutive hours on duty by 1904. Between 1905 and 1907, the number almost doubled as 10 more states joined them. Many states also limited the shifts of train dispatchers (a job parallel to today's air traffic controllers). In 1907, Congress passed a national hours law that applied to all interstate trains. It required 10 hours' rest after a maximum of 16 hours at work for railroad men and a maximum shift of nine hours for dispatchers. Because the interstate provision covered almost all railway workers, few other states passed their own legislation after that.

Between 1905 and 1908, four more states passed laws to limit workers' hours in mining, a very dangerous occupation, bringing the total to nine. Miners' hours laws did not exist in the six most important mining states, however—in some because miners' unions were strong and negotiated reduced hours on their own and in others because they were weak and mine owners could block proposed laws.

CHILD LABOR REFORMERS TACKLE STATE LAWS

Within a year after its organization in 1904, the National Child Labor Committee (NCLC) had begun its work in earnest. The NCLC began state campaigns in both the North and South. In the North, it targeted Pennsylvania, where coal mines, glass factories, and other businesses employed as many children as all the southern states combined. Some 14,000 children worked legally in the coal mines alone. One NCLC investigation found another 10,000 working illegally, since no proof of age was required. In 1905, reformers saw a bill through the Pennsylvania legislature that required proof of age and educational standards. It was soon declared unconstitutional by the state courts. A law that passed Pennsylvania court tests was finally enacted in 1909—but it exempted glass factories, which continued to fight reform successfully for the next 10 years. NCLC-sponsored bills to raise the age for night-shift glass workers to 16, introduced in New Jersey, West Virginia, Indiana, and Pennsylvania, were all defeated—five times in New Jersey.

Child labor reformers expected their work to be even more difficult in the South. Of the four largest mill states, Georgia had no age or hour regulations at all, and Alabama, North Carolina, and South Carolina had only minimal restrictions. None of the four had any compulsory school attendance. Independent cotton mill owners often dominated the small towns in which they were located and pulled great weight in local politics. They never missed a chance to paint reformers as northern agitators attempting to interfere in southern affairs—despite the fact that the first child labor committee in the United States was organized in Alabama.

In the South, the NCLC campaign began in North Carolina in 1905. Reformers wanted to raise the working age to 14 for all girls and for boys who worked at night. A delegation of more than 70 manufacturers appeared to oppose the bill at legislative hearings and it was defeated. In Georgia, the child labor cause was taken up by Hoke Smith, a former secretary of the interior under Cleveland and a founding member of the NCLC. After he was elected as a reform governor in 1906, the first child labor legislation in Georgia was finally passed, setting a minimum age of 12. Throughout the South public concern about child labor was increasing and increasingly related to racial concerns. Child labor had helped to create an extremely high rate of illiteracy among white factory workers, not to mention a greatly reduced life expectancy.

These boys are working the night shift at an Indiana glass factory. Lewis Hine took this photo for the National Child Labor Committee, which campaigned to restrict the age and hours of young workers in dangerous glass factories. *(Library of Congress, Prints and Photographs Division, LC-USZ62-105650)*

Meanwhile, black children (who, like their parents, were not hired in southern factories) were much more likely to do farm labor, considered to be far more healthful, and to attend school.

In 1908, the NCLC gained an asset of incalculable importance: it hired Lewis Hine, a teacher and amateur photographer of New York's poor, as the official NCLC photographer. For the next two decades Hine compiled a photographic record of working conditions in factories, mines, canneries, fields, and on the streets. Claims of child labor investigators could always be disputed, but Hine's photos spoke for themselves. As historian Walter Trattner writes, Hine's photos of "the human and inhumane element in industry—the pathetic faces of the working children and the conditions under which they toiled—aroused public sentiment against child labor in a way that no printed page or public lecture could." The NCLC circulated them widely in many different forms.[24]

CONCERN ABOUT CHILD LABOR IN WASHINGTON

Among prominent reformers and social workers, the idea of a federal children's bureau had circulated since the turn of the century. As Florence Kelley wrote, it should accomplish for children what the U.S. Department of Agriculture had accomplished for the farm—that is, "make available and interpret facts concerning the mental, physical, and moral conditions and prospects of the children of the United States." Added Lillian Wald, who journeyed to Washington to convince President Roosevelt to support the idea, only a federal bureau could "tell us of the children with as much care as it tells us of the trees or the cotton crop."[25] With the president's full support, the National Child Labor Committee (NCLC) drafted a bill for a children's bureau. It was introduced into Congress in early 1906 but was not enacted into law.

Although the NCLC supported a federal children's bureau, on all other matters it worked exclusively for regulation at the state level during its early years. Nonetheless, concern about child labor reached the halls of Congress. In late 1906, Indiana senator Albert Beveridge introduced a bill to prohibit interstate transportation of articles made in any factory or mine that employed children younger than 14. NCLC trustees initially favored the bill. As a result, Edgar Gardner Murphy, the pioneer organizer of child labor reformers and an Alabamian, resigned from the organization. He believed the endorsement would make NCLC work impossible in the South, where most people strongly opposed federal intrusions on states' rights. The dispute continued and in subsequent meetings the NCLC officially voted not to endorse the Beveridge bill.

President Roosevelt himself believed that federal child labor legislation would be found unconstitutional by the Supreme Court. As always, he believed investigation and publicity were the best ways to obtain results. In 1904 and 1905, he asked Congress to authorize an investigation by the Bureau of Labor into conditions of working women and children but was turned down both times. In 1906, he sent the request again. He also suggested a child labor law for the District of Columbia (which Congress governed at the time) to serve as a model—although Washington had none of the industries in which abuses were prevalent. Faced with Beveridge's bill and a federal bureau on one hand and Roosevelt's more modest requests on the other, Congress chose to authorize the Labor Department study and pass the model law. Beveridge took the floor and spoke continually for three days, reading description after description of horrible child labor conditions. But the 59th Congress adjourned without taking action on his bill.

REFORMERS AND PLAYGROUNDS

In 1905, there were only 87 public playgrounds in America, spread among 24 different cities. Throughout urban America, city officials were reluctant to consider the needs of children a public responsibility. In spring 1906 a group of reformers well acquainted with the plight of children in overcrowded tenement neighborhoods met in Washington, D.C., and organized the national Playground Association of America (PAA). Leaders such as Jane Addams, Lillian Wald, and Jacob Riis believed the issues of urban playgrounds and supervised recreation for city children were extremely important. So did President Roosevelt, who agreed to be honorary president of the PAA. He recognized the importance of the group's founding in a well-publicized ceremony at the White House.

Reformers saw safe, supervised play areas as a key to lessening a host of social problems associated with poverty, vice, and crime in urban slums. Playground leaders, it was believed, could counteract the influence of street culture on children and provide moral direction. Supervised playground activities could also teach children proper behavior and such democratic social values as ethnic harmony, cooperation, and fair play to Americanize the children of immigrants. The PAA, a typical progressive organization, encouraged its affiliates across the country to do citywide surveys of needs, draw up plans, open a privately supported playground, then lobby for the municipal government to take responsibility. By 1908 the number of cities with supervised playgrounds had grown to more than 200 and a solid majority were supported with public funds rather than private philanthropy.[26]

CITY GOVERNMENT BY COMMISSION SPREADS

City government by a nonpartisan commission with both law-making and executive powers was a great success in Galveston, Texas, where it was first used after the hurricane disaster of 1900. Soon it began to be adopted in cities throughout the nation. In 1907, under Iowa's reform governor Albert B. Cummins, for example, the state legislature passed an act to enable all Iowa cities with more than 25,000 people to use commission government. Supporters of the system liked its clearly assigned lines of authority, which helped counteract the power of unelected bosses. Supporters compared it to a business corporation. They saw the commissioners as a board of directors who worked in a nonpartisan manner for the interest of all the stockholders, not for special interests. In 1908, Staunton, Virginia, launched an additional reform modeled on the business corporation, known as the city manager plan. It called for the city to hire a professional city manager with day-to-day authority to carry out the policies set by the council or commission. In other words, the council, functioning like a board of directors, would appoint a chief executive officer (CEO) responsible to them to run the business.

More than 500 cities adopted the commission system by the end of the Progressive Era but all were of medium or small size. Commissions did not spread to the very largest cities, where strong political interests and diverse populations were less receptive to a nonpartisan system.

MUNICIPAL ACCOUNTING

One seemingly humdrum issue that engaged municipal reformers in the first decade of the 20th century was city budgeting and accounting. Although it seems hard to fathom today, at the turn of the century city officials did not use overall budgets or even keep orderly financial records. They did not keep track of total revenues and did not know how city funds were divided among departments. Many city expenditures were funded by special taxes or funds—a school tax, for example, or an assessment to build sewers—and each department took care of its own accounts. In 1898, for example, San Francisco had published financial records that consisted of nothing but page after page of itemized, unsorted payments for labor and materials. But even that was enough to earn praise from the Department of Labor because other cities at the time did not publish even that much collective information. Lack of orderly records, of course, also made it easier for corruption to flourish.

The National Municipal League began promoting the idea of standardized municipal record-keeping in the 1890s. Finally, in 1903, the newly established federal Bureau of the Census helped develop and publicize a system. It divided city financial information into five areas: city administration; charities and corrections; public safety; highways and sanitation; education and recreation; and commercial (municipally owned utilities, docks, markets, etc.) Although these divisions seem commonsensical today, they permitted many a city to see for the first time how much it spent on education, for example, in relation to road building. In addition, when expenditures were divided by the number of people in the city, the resulting per capita, or per person, figures could be compared from city to city for the first time. In 1908, Simeon N. D. North, director of the Census Bureau, reported to the American Statistical Association, "To each of the 157 cities of the United States having a population of 30,000 and over, a representative of the census goes every year, and so classifies the receipts and expenditures for every purpose. . . . This is magnificent work, furnishing a most effective weapon in the crusade for municipal reform and rehabilitation now sweeping over the United States." By that year four states (Ohio, New York, Iowa, and Massachusetts) and 19 cities elsewhere passed laws requiring uniform municipal accounting. Many other cities voluntarily adopted the recommendations of the Census Bureau and the Municipal League.[27]

SAN FRANCISCO: CORRUPTION, DISASTER, AND REFORM

At the opening of the 20th century, San Francisco had a reform mayor, James Phelan. In the election of 1901, however, the business community backed another candidate, convinced that Phelan had mishandled a long and violent strike by dockworkers. Labor unions, equally convinced that the mayor had favored business interests, formed a new third party. Unexpectedly, the new Union Labor Party's candidate Eugene E. Schmitz—an orchestra conductor—captured the mayor's office by a substantial margin. Unfortunately, the new party instantly gave rise to a new, powerful, and corrupt behind-the-scenes boss, Abraham Ruef. Although labor prospered during the next four years in San Francisco, Ruef, the mayor, and the Board of Supervisors (city council) prospered more. Their machine wove a web of graft, bribes, payoffs, and vice throughout the city.

In 1905, a crusading newspaper editor, Fremont Older, began publishing exposés of the Ruef machine. Older, ex-mayor Phelan, sugar heir Rudolph Spreckels, and other reformers began a campaign to unseat the Union Labor Party and its unelected boss. By the following winter Older had enough evidence to visit Washington. He made contact with a special prosecutor in the Roosevelt administration, Francis J. Heney, a native of San Francisco.

Then the unforeseen occurred.

At 5:13 A.M. on April 18, 1906, the city of San Francisco was hit by a powerful earthquake. Buildings and walls crashed down, while others were so askew that people could not open doors to escape. Tall brick chimneys toppled through roofs, killing many in their beds. The poorly constructed tenements that housed the poor south of Market Street collapsed wholesale. Streets undulated. All the church bells in the city began to sway and clang. Cattle from a battered stockyard at the wharves began to rampage through the streets. Fires ignited from toppled lanterns and cooking and heating fires. Water mains ruptured as did gas mains, soon fueling the fires. An aftershock occurred at 8:15, collapsing more buildings and increasing the public panic. For the next four days fires continued to erupt and burn, destroying most of San Francisco. As many as 200,000 people out of the total population of 450,000 were left homeless and without food. For several months to follow, many lived in tent cities established by the American Red Cross. Today, historians believe that the total death toll in the city was more than 3,000 and the cost of the damage $500 million in 1906 dollars. Overall, the quake's damage stretched 400 miles along a 25-mile-wide swath, through towns and forests from Eureka to southern Fresno County. Shocks were felt from Los Angeles to Oregon and as far east as Nevada.[28]

By April 23, California governor George C. Pardee told a newspaper reporter, "The work of rebuilding San Francisco has commenced, and I expect to see the great metropolis replaced on a much grander scale than ever before."[29] As it happened, six months earlier architect Daniel Burnham, commissioned by a civic association, had presented an impressive City Beautiful plan to San Francisco. The printed bound copies were still at City Hall awaiting distribution. They were dug from the rubble. By summer, however, it was clear that Burnham's visionary city with community gardens, temples, fountains, and circular boulevards was beyond reach, and the plan was scrapped. Nonetheless, within three years, 20,000 buildings were rebuilt.

Mayor Schmitz rose to the occasion during the disaster, but reformers in San Francisco were neither placated nor deterred. They resumed their campaign forthwith. Shortly after the quake, Special Prosecutor Heney and well-known detective William J. Burns were in the city and on the job. While San Franciscans dug out, they read daily newspaper reports of the mounting evidence against the Ruef machine. The machine was not deterred either. Within a month of the earthquake, the Board of Supervisors took a $200,000 bribe in return for a new trolley franchise. Trolley company officials obtained small bills by exchanging gold for money donated to a disaster relief fund.

In November 1906, the first indictments against Ruef and his associates were issued—but only after reformers foiled an attempt by the machine to fix grand jury selection. Eventually the mayor, all 18 members of the Board of Supervisors, the chief of police, and others received indictments. More unusually, the bribe-givers from several corporations and utility companies were also indicted. The celebrated trials for extortion and bribery opened in March of 1907 in a local synagogue because the courthouse had not yet been rebuilt. The trials lasted for two years. Before they ended Heney had been shot in open court (he recovered), Older had been kidnaped, and the home of a key witness had been dynamited. Some related trials and appeals dragged on until 1912. Of all those indicted or convicted, only Ruef ever spent time in jail.

THE PROHIBITION MOVEMENT BECOMES A NATIONAL FORCE

Between 1905 and 1908, the movement for the prohibition of liquor developed into a national and very effective lobby. There were a multitude of different temperance organizations, such as the National Temperance Society, the Interchurch Temperance Association, and the Good Templars. But the two largest remained the Women's Christian Temperance Union (WCTU) and the Anti-Saloon League (ASL). They often cooperated with each other as well as with the smaller organizations to lobby for liquor-related legislation.

In 1905, the Ohio ASL scored an important political victory, successfully organizing a campaign to defeat incumbent Republican governor Myron T. Herrick and elect the dry Democratic challenger. Although Ohio was a solidly Republican state, Herrick had consistently opposed a statewide local option law. (Under local option, local communities are permitted to vote themselves dry or wet.) After the Ohio victory, which attracted attention nationwide, the national ASL increasingly functioned like the "central office of a diversified corporation," in the words of historian K. Austin Kerr,[30] giving the temperance movement a national profile and new cohesiveness. Its paid, professional staff kept watch for political opportunities nationwide. Only in the South—which was the most pro-temperance region in the nation—did other temperance organizations remain more influential.

Each year brought an increase in the number of localities that were dry. By 1906, 30 states had local option laws and six more had complete or partial prohibition. More than half the towns, villages, and townships in the nation were dry. In 1907 the citizens of Oklahoma voted to enter the union as a dry state. By the end of 1908, Georgia, Mississippi, Alabama, and North Carolina had approved statewide prohibition. When statewide prohibition went into effect in Mississippi (on January 1, 1909), it affected only nine counties—because the other 69 counties had already voted themselves dry under local option. Previously, ASL strategists had primarily worked for local option laws. Viewing the events of 1907 and 1908, however, they began to think the time had come to reorient their efforts to achieve statewide prohibition laws.[31]

By 1908, liquor manufacturers had also come to realize that the temperance movement, and the reputation of urban saloons in particular, posed a threat to their well-being. Ironically enough, although the public saw the manufacturers as a highly organized trust, the industry was competitive, and both manufacturers and retailers had a difficult time cooperating. Although they made some attempts at self-regulation, their efforts were never very successful.

A DRY SPELL FOR WOMEN'S SUFFRAGE LEGISLATION

After 1896, when Idaho became the fourth state to give women full voting rights, the women's suffrage movement met almost no visible success prior to 1910. No new states granted statewide suffrage to women during the intervening years. In fact, the issue was brought to a state vote in only four places—Washington, South Dakota, New Hampshire, and Oregon. In each case—and three separate times in Oregon—the states refused to extend suffrage to women. Even campaigns for limited voting rights on school, municipal, or tax issues were stagnant until 1908, when New York permitted women to vote on tax issues and in town meetings.

During these years, nonetheless, members of the National American Woman Suffrage Association (NAWSA) continued their educational crusade. Dedicated suffragists presented resolutions to state legislatures, gave testimony at the hearings of different investigative and reform groups, distributed literature and press releases, and delivered speeches to women's groups of all kinds, even those which were not actively involved in suffrage issues. Each year, more reform and labor groups passed resolutions endorsing their work. During the same years, the older generation of NAWSA leaders, who had led the suffrage movement since the mid-19th century, was replaced by new leadership. In 1900, Carrie Chapman Catt, a young activist who had led the Idaho campaign, replaced Susan B. Anthony as NAWSA's president. In 1904, Dr. Anna Howard Shaw, a minister and a physician, rose to the office.

A new generation of suffrage activists also appeared on the scene. In 1900, about 5,000 women won college degrees, and their achievements gave them a heightened sense of possibility. Some formed the College Equal Suffrage League. Others reached out to enlist wage-earning women in the cause of voting rights. In early 1907, a group of women led by Harriot Stanton Blatch, daughter of Elizabeth Cady Stanton, organized the Equality League of Self-Supporting Women (later renamed the Women's Political Union). It immediately drew a large membership among wage-earning women in New York. "There is only one way to redress their wrongs and that is by the ballot," Blatch told the 1908 NAWSA convention. "Of all the people who block the progress of woman suffrage the worst are the women of wealth and leisure who never knew a day's work and never felt a day's want, but who selfishly stand in the way of those women who know what it means to earn the bread they eat by the sternest toil and who, with a voice in the Government, could better themselves in every way."[32]

The new generation of suffrage activists was frustrated with the slow pace of change and increasingly willing to try new tactics. In England suffrage activity was becoming visibly militant. In 1903, a new English suffrage organization, the Women's Social and Political Union, had been founded by Emmeline Pankhurst. Within the year, some members were roughly handled by police and thrown in jail for heckling a politician at a public meeting. The incident caused a public uproar. Pankhurst's organization decided to continue deliberately provoking publicity by marches, mass meetings, and heckling—all astonishingly shocking activities for middle-class women at the time. Their new militancy generated much publicity and inevitably affected American activists. "We all believed that suffrage propaganda must be made dramatic, that suffrage workers must be politically minded," Blatch stated in her memoirs. "A vital idea had been smothered by uninspired methods of work."[33]

MUNICIPAL HOUSEKEEPERS BROADEN THE SUPPORT FOR WOMEN'S SUFFRAGE

Despite the lack of visible gains in voting rights for women in the first decade of the 20th century, a change was slowly occurring in public sentiment. In the words of historians Dorothy and Carl Schneider, "American society was warming into an environment favorable to woman suffrage."[34]

Via clubs and reform organizations, a growing number of women were moving into the public world to act on behalf of community welfare. Membership in women's clubs increased throughout the 1890s, and after the turn of the century it began to explode. Even in a rural state like Wisconsin, for example, 70 women's clubs formed a state federation in 1896; by 1910, the federation had 172 member clubs representing 7,350 active women.[35] Women's clubs represented a staggering array of social welfare interests and members put in many volunteer hours. They were beginning to effect important changes in American society by insisting on collective responsibility for many public problems. They began to see how much more they could accomplish if they had the political power of the vote.

Around 1905, the term *municipal housekeeping* became popular among reformers and clubwomen to describe women's community welfare responsibilities. Women, the traditional housekeepers (they argued), were needed in public life to keep their communities clean, orderly, and conducive to a healthy and moral life—just as they kept their homes. The term *municipal housekeeping* was unthreatening, but under its cover the 19th-century idea of women's sphere changed fundamentally. The term covered a hardheaded political agenda. For example, women led a popular campaign to purify the milk supply because contaminated milk was contributing to the era's high rate of infant mortality—but called for the regulation of private enterprise and tough laws that broke new legislative ground. Under the umbrella of municipal housekeeping, women tackled food inspection, factory safety, clear air, inspection of tenements, the conditions of working women, child labor, public health issues, public school and education issues, and even municipal government reform, among others. Like many progressive reformers, women's groups often set up pilot programs, then lobbied for the government to assume them and fund them.

The accomplishments of municipal housekeeping, comments historian Anne Firor Scott, are greatly underestimated in standard histories of the Progressive Era. Women's activities throughout the nation, she points out, "often transformed the health and appearance of whole towns."[36] For example, after the 1901 hurricane in Galveston,

Clubwoman multiplied their activities on behalf of community welfare in the early 20th century. This day nursery, or day care facility, was established by the African American Women's League of Newport, Rhode Island, to aid working mothers. *(Library of Congress, Prints and Photographs Division, LC-USZ62-51556)*

Texas, clubwomen formed the Women's Health Protective Association. In the following years they established a cemetery for victims who had been hastily buried in makeshift graves, replanted trees and other vegetation in the town, and worked for a wide variety of health and sanitation measures in cooperation with the new commission government. The Women's Health Protective Association of Philadelphia hired an engineer to design a safer water-supply delivery system, then saw to the passage of a bond issue to fund it. The anti-tuberculosis movement led by Kentucky clubwoman Madeline McDowell Breckinridge eventually succeeded in establishing a state system of sanatoria and other forms of treatment for the disease. The remarkable Chicago Women's Club carried out an astonishing array of activities. For one, the club organized and for a while financially supported the first formal juvenile court in America.

The conviction that women had a responsibility for public and community welfare issues gained wide acceptance in the early 20th century. As it did, support for women's suffrage moved into the mainstream of middle-class respectability and progressive thought. Broadly based reform groups like Frances Willard's WCTU had long argued that the vote was an extension of women's traditional roles as the moral guardians and charitable workers of society. The leading theorists of women's suffrage, however, had based their demand for the vote primarily on fundamental American political beliefs—natural rights and equal justice. Increasingly after 1900, however, NAWSA activists also began to make the argument that women's suffrage was necessary as a tool of reform. "They tell us that women can bring better things to pass by indirect influence. Try to persuade any man that he will have more weight, more influence, if he gives up his vote, allies himself with no party and relies on influence to achieve his ends!" a speaker told the 1908 NAWSA convention. "We want to get hold of the little device that moves the machinery," said another, Sophonisba Breckinridge, reformer and pioneer sociologist at the University of Chicago.[37]

As the arguments for women's suffrage broadened and moved away from the idea of fundamental rights, they also became increasingly entangled with other contemporary concerns about the franchise. Especially in the North, some people argued that one cause of political corruption was permitting illiterate men and immigrants who did not even speak English to vote, while denying suffrage to educated or literate middle-class women. In the South, some people justified women's suffrage as a way of cementing white supremacy. White southern women finally began to embrace the suffrage movement in the first decade of the 20th century but objected to including black women in suffrage organizations. African-American clubwomen themselves were usually staunch supporters of women's suffrage.

In 1908, there were still many people, including many women, who opposed the idea of women's suffrage. Some, like the General Federation of Women's Clubs (who did not sanction women's suffrage until 1914), continued to believe that women could actually exercise more influence on elected officials if they remained free from partisan allegiances. This belief flew in the face of political reality, but it was not completely illogical in an age when reformers of all stripes were working to lessen the power of political parties and partisanship. Some conservative women simply opposed the whole idea, believing women would be corrupted or overburdened by political participation. Conservative activists, called antis, even formed anti-suffrage organizations. Nonetheless, the idea of women's suffrage had permanently left the fringes of social thought and was closing in on its center.

RACIAL VIOLENCE CONTINUES

During the first decade of the 20th century, the white preoccupation with racial separation and other racial issues "reached its apex," in the phrase of historian James Grossman.[38] Particularly in the South, racially charged rhetoric was open, strident, and continual. Additional southern states formally disenfranchised blacks and passed segregation laws. Lynchings continued in the South but increased in the Midwest as well. Race riots became more frequent and more savage. The most serious riot of the decade erupted in Atlanta in 1906 after months of white political agitation for formal disenfranchisement. Whites rampaged for four days, destroying much of the city's prosperous black neighborhood. More than 20 people were killed. The riot that most shocked the nation, however, occurred in 1908 in Springfield, Illinois—hometown of Abraham Lincoln. It took 5,000 state militia to quell it.[39]

Racial issues were not a primary concern of most white progressive reformers and muckrakers. An exception was muckraker Ray Stannard Baker, whose *Following the Color Line* (1906) was a study of conditions and race relations in both the North and South. But for African Americans, of course, racial injustice was the most compelling issue of the Progressive Era.

THE NIAGARA MOVEMENT

Black intellectual W. E. B. DuBois and newspaper editor William Monroe Trotter increasingly opposed Booker T. Washington's policy of accommodation and his monopoly (as they saw it) on the black press and white public opinion. They were increasingly convinced that a new, uncompromising organization was needed to pursue African-American rights. In 1905, DuBois, Trotter, and 27 other men met in Canada near Niagara Falls, forming what became known as the Niagara Movement. DuBois drafted the Declaration of Principles, which insisted on full citizenship, equality in education and job opportunities, and an end to segregation. "We claim for ourselves every single right that belongs to a freeborn American, political, civil and social, and until we get these rights we will never cease to protest and assail the ears of America!" he said.[40] The Niagara Movement held four annual meetings and gained more members, most of whom were northern and college-educated. But it faced many obstacles. The black press saw the movement as elitist and radical. Most black editors ignored it, as did white philanthropists. Today, historians often consider it the forerunner of the National Association for the Advancement of Colored People (NAACP).

THE BROWNSVILLE INCIDENT

In August 1906, a few members of the First Battalion, Twenty-fifth Regiment, an African-American army unit stationed at Fort Brown, Texas, were involved in a riot in the nearby town. It left one white man dead and a police officer injured. President Roosevelt ordered an investigation. All the soldiers denied involvement or knowledge of what had happened or who had committed the crimes. Eyewitness testimony and physical evidence were contradictory. Nonetheless, the army report recommended that every one of the battalion's soldiers be discharged. "The secretive nature of the race, where crimes charged to members of their color is made, is well known," said the army report. Since all the soldiers "stand together in a determination to resist the detection of guilt . . . they should stand together when the penalty falls."[41] None of the soldiers were charged with crimes; none had legal representation; none were permitted to face their accusers or refute any evidence presented against them.

Two days before leaving on his inspection tour of Panama in November, President Roosevelt issued an order that all 170 soldiers be dishonorably discharged. Among their number were six who held the Medal of Honor.

African Americans were of course very angry with the action. Some white Americans agreed that the soldiers had been subjected to a discriminatory standard of justice. By the time Roosevelt returned from his trip some powerful congressmen led by Senator Joseph Foraker were questioning his action. The Senate held hearings on the incident. The matter was not finally concluded until several days before Roosevelt left office in March 1909. At that time he signed a compromise bill that allowed the soldiers to reenlist if they were individually cleared by a panel of army officers. Fourteen eventually did. But the issue remained alive for more than half a century, and in 1972 Congress rescinded the dishonorable discharges.

During his second term, President Roosevelt often sounded the theme (especially when speaking to black audiences) that "The colored man who fails to condemn crime in another colored man, who fails to co-operate in all lawful ways in bringing colored criminals to justice, is the worst enemy of his own people, as well as an enemy to all people."[42] Roosevelt's statement was very controversial among African Americans, but he apparently saw the Brownsville incident in those terms. He continued to insist that he had acted correctly—although he chose to leave the incident out of his autobiography. Many historians see Brownsville as the largest blot on the Roosevelt presidency.

IMMIGRATION AT FLOOD TIDE

Between 1901 and 1910, America experienced the heaviest decade of immigration that it has ever known, even to this day. In 1905 and 1906, the total number of newcomers jumped to more than 1 million per year; in 1907, it reached 1,285,349, the highest yearly total ever. In 1908, it dropped back to some 750,000, in response to the economic downturn of 1907. But all told, during the decade nearly 8.8 million immigrants arrived in America.[43] Not surprisingly, the national immigration service also grew tremendously. First established in 1891 with a staff of less than 30, it had more than 1,200 employees by 1907—although even that number was not adequate to deal with the 3,600 people processed *each day* of that year.

Despite heavy immigration, the percentage of foreign-born people in the American population actually remained steady overall. The native-born American population was growing rapidly at the same time, and, in addition, some immigrants returned to their homelands after working a few years. The foreign-born were a little over 13 percent of the American population in 1880 and little over 13 percent in 1920. In the years between, they never exceeded about 14.5 percent. These percentages, of course, do not count the American-born children of immigrants.

Most immigrants continued to concentrate in large cities, where their ethnic communities were very visible. The huge influx of newcomers, often poor and from cultures with no democratic traditions, led more and more Americans to look favorably on restricting immigration. Nonetheless, between the turn of the century and the beginning of World War I, no legislation to limit immigration overall was ever passed. Congress did tighten loopholes and support the enforcement of exclusions that already existed. In 1907, for example, new immigration legislation raised the head tax (the entry fee charged all immigrants) to four dollars to keep out "persons likely to become a public charge." But the act did not include the literacy test that some congressmen favored. Partly as a compromise with restrictionists, the 1907 act created a United States Immigration Commission and assigned it to investigate the impact of immigration on the nation. It also created an information division whose purpose was to encourage new arrivals to spread out "among the several States and Territories."[44]

Other changes affected immigrants from Asia. Almost all of them arrived on the West Coast. In 1905, the United States began construction of a western Ellis Island—an immigrant receiving station on Angel Island, a former U.S. Army base in San Francisco Bay (completed 1910). Part of its purpose was to facilitate the lengthy examinations to which Chinese and other Asian immigrants were subjected under the terms of Chinese exclusion acts.

Unlike the Chinese, the Japanese were not excluded and immigration from Japan continued to grow, reaching nearly 130,000 during the decade. Like Chinese immigrants, however, Japanese immigrants remained ineligible for American citizenship. In 1906, as San Francisco dug out from the earthquake and fire, the city school board ordered students of Japanese descent to attend the separate, segregated schools maintained for Chinese children. Japan considered the act an insult and protested. President Roosevelt obtained what is known as the Gentleman's Agreement of 1907 with Japan. Japan agreed to prevent additional poor, unskilled laborers from immigrating to the United States, and the United States agreed to permit the families of laborers already here to join them. The agreement was bound only by the word of the parties and was not set down in an official treaty. The president also convinced San Francisco to rescind its school order.

AMERICANIZING THE IMMIGRANTS

Since the 1890s, settlement and social workers, philanthropists, and other concerned individuals had been actively working to assimilate immigrants, especially those from southern and eastern Europe, to American civic and political culture and ways of life. The assimilation effort—or as it would soon be called, the Americanization crusade—was destined to become strident and controversial by the end of the Progressive Era. It began, however, partly as a humanitarian response to the neglect, exploitation, and struggle faced by newcomers; partly as an alternative to the immigration restriction movement that first appeared in the mid-1890s; and wholly as a typical progressive reform movement. Few Americans during the Progressive Era, to be sure, shared today's toleration for cultural pluralism. But at the same time, when the era opened the nation offered very little organized aid to help immigrants learn American ways—for example, the special school language programs, counseling on legal rights, and easily available information on naturalization that are taken for granted today. Prior to World War I Americanization efforts were generally supported and sometimes even initiated by immigrant leaders themselves.

One especially popular effort was the organization of night classes to teach English and civics, which early activists believed would solve many of the problems faced by both the immigrants and the nation that had received them. In many cases immigrant leaders themselves requested adult education to be undertaken by the public school system. (Special educational initiatives for immigrant children, however, were not usually a subject of great concern to either the community or to professional educators during this period—the children and their teachers made do as best they could.) New York City public schools had adult education classes for immigrants as early as 1900, Detroit had special classes for Jewish, Italian, and Greek adults by 1906, and school systems in other cities like Boston, Philadelphia, Cleveland, and Cincinnati also began programs in the first decade of the 20th century. In 1907, New Jersey became the first state in the nation to pass enabling legislation for school boards to establish evening schools for foreign-born residents.

Even more extensive efforts to help immigrants adjust to life in America were made by private and philanthropic groups. By 1893, the Educational Alliance had opened on the Lower East Side of New York City, funded largely by Jewish philanthropist Baron Maurice de Hirsch and offering a wide range of programs primarily for eastern European Jewish immigrants. The Society for Italian Immigrants initiated a program of labor camp schools in 1905 for construction gangs in western Pennsylvania and Upstate New York. The YMCA began English and other classes in 1907 and within five years operated them in some 300 branches throughout the nation. In New England, the American International College was founded by Congregationalists in 1908, specifically to educate leaders from the various immigrant communities. The Colonial Dames of America, the Sons of the American Revolution, and similar organizations also undertook activities to educate newcomers, often with the goal of steering them through the process by which they could obtain citizenship. A popular informational pamphlet on the naturalization process published by the Sons in 1908, for example, was printed in some 15 languages and published in full by many foreign-language newspapers within a few years.

Destined to play an even more prominent role was the North American Civic League for Immigrants (NACL). The nonsectarian league was founded in 1907, after a YMCA-sponsored conference of social, industrial, philanthropic, and other leaders from major ports of entry. The league quickly established a prominent presence in major eastern cities, where it began cooperating with the government and with other immigrant aid and religious groups in a wide range of activities, including lobbying for education and protective legislation.

In the Midwest, the Immigrant Protective League (League for Protection of Immigrants until 1910), was founded in 1908. It was organized by members of the Chicago Women's Trade Union League under the direction of Grace Abbott. (The WTUL was a nationwide organization which brought wage-earning women together with middle- and upper-class women who helped them unionize.) Founded at the height of the anti-prostitution campaign, the Immigrant Protective League grew from efforts to help women safely navigate the journey to their new home and obtain employment. It worked closely with the North American Civic League for the remainder of the Progressive Era.

UNIONS BEGIN TO LOOK TO POLITICS

After making gains in the opening years of the 20th century, labor saw its fortunes decline during President Roosevelt's second term—as did union membership. Employers' organizations waged publicity and court battles that stymied labor advances. The courts continued to issue injunction after injunction against striking unions under the Sherman Anti-Trust Act. (Injunctions are court orders issued without trial.) In a case that began in 1907, for example, the owner of Buck's Stove and Range Company—who was also president of the National Association of Manufacturers—obtained a sweeping injunction from the Court of Appeals in Washington, D.C. As usual, the injunction outlawed a boycott by other unions whose members handled the materials or products of the struck company. But in addition, it also forbade public discussion of the issue by union members—leading to the arrest of Samuel Gompers, head of the American Federation of Labor (AFL) and other officials. Their convictions, which were eventually reversed by the Supreme Court in 1911, caused great consternation for a time.

The AFL, the largest and strongest union in America, had always avoided partisan politics. But in 1906, Gompers decided the time had come to pursue labor's interests through the political system. For the first time, the AFL actively campaigned against congressmen hostile to labor issues. After the election Gompers reported to the AFL convention, "It is true we did not defeat as many men as we should like to have done, but I want to tell you what we did. We put the fear of God into them. We cut down their majorities, we cut down their pluralities. . . . Our opponents will not be so arrogant toward the representatives of labor as they have been in the past."[45] The union began lobbying to exempt unions from the Sherman Anti-Trust Act and to end the use of injunctions in labor disputes. In 1908, a presidential year, they took their campaign to both parties. Labor issues received a lukewarm endorsement from the Democrats, but none at all from the Republicans.

A DISASTROUS MONTH FOR COAL MINERS

Midmorning on December 6, 1907, explosions ripped through two connected mines of the Fairmont Coal company in Monongah, West Virginia. The blast was so intense that it was felt eight miles away. It brought down buildings, upended pavement, and even knocked a streetcar off its rails. All of the men in the mines perished. The official death toll determined from company pay rolls was 362, leaving some 250 widows and 1,000 orphans. Miners, however, worked on a kind of individual subcontracting or buddy system, taking their sons or other men into the mines with them and sharing the pay. These workers did not appear on the company rolls. The actual death toll, researchers believe, was more than 500. The cause of the explosion remained disputed. It was officially listed as human error.

Even the official death toll made Monongah the worst mining disaster in United States history. It was also the first to receive extensive national publicity. "Think of hell as a hollow hill and imagine that its power plant has exploded and blown a hole in the hillside. Then imagine a handful of reckless, begrimed men going into the cavern with lanterns, with sulfurous fumes in their faces, and dragging out the charred bodies of men. . . . That is what Monongah looked like," said writer Edgar Allen Forbes, who traveled to Monongah after the disaster.[46] Overwhelmed, the local relief committee made a nationwide appeal carried by some 2,000 newspapers. Then, two weeks later on December 19, another deadly explosion occurred at Darr Mines in Jacobs Creek, Pennsylvania. It took 239 lives. Adding in a smaller disaster in Fayette City, Pennsylvania, which took 34 lives on December 1, it was the deadliest three weeks in American mining history. It aroused public pressure for government action.

Soon after the explosion, the federal government issued a report on mining accidents. It documented a steady increase in accidents, the lack of safety regulations, and the lack of scientific knowledge about explosives used in mining. It also pointed out that mining accidents in Europe had declined under closer government supervision. Finally forced to act, in May 1908 Congress established a Geological Survey station for the investigation of mine explosions and two months later appropriated funds to establish a mine rescue operation. By year's end the station opened in Pittsburgh.

THE MINERS' WARS AND THE FOUNDING OF THE IWW

In the hard-rock mining regions of the West, miners were represented by the Western Federation of Miners (WFM), an independent union not affiliated with the United Mine Workers or the AFL. The WFM had been formed after a violent and unsuccessful strike in Coeur d'Alene, Idaho, in 1892. Since then, a continuing series of unprecedented conflicts between owners and miners had occurred. The violence was so serious that the years between 1892 and 1907 are often called the years of "miners' wars."

By the early 20th century, western mine owners were determined to rid themselves of the WFM. In 1903–1904, an exceptionally violent strike occurred at Cripple Creek, Colorado. In one of several bombing incidents, 13 nonunion workers were killed. The incident appeared to be the work of the WFM, although the union maintained the mine owners themselves were behind it. Eventually, with the help of military troops and private police, the owners drove all union miners out of town. Afterward, no miner was hired unless he disavowed the union.

Frustrated and angered by events in Cripple Creek and a decade of violent conflict in other western mining regions, some 200 radical labor figures met in Chicago in early 1905. They formed a new organization, the Industrial Workers of the World (IWW), often called the Wobblies. Organizers included former WFM leaders, socialists of many kinds, anarchists who supported direct political action, and more moderate proponents of unions. The Wobblies were openly militant. Their preamble began with the line, "The working class and the employing class have nothing in common." They looked forward to the overthrow of both capitalism and the state in what they called "one big strike," to establish a commonwealth led by workers' organizations. The IWW rejected the select, skilled craft unionism represented by the AFL. IWW leaders intended, in fact, to concentrate on organizing the least skilled workers at the bottom of the socioeconomic ladder. "This is the Continental Congress of the working class," said the union's leader William "Big Bill" Haywood, referring to the group of Founding Fathers who organized the American Revolution. "The aims and objects of this organization shall be to put the working-class in possession of the economic power, the means of life, in control of the machinery of production and distribution, without regard to capitalist masters."[47]

Six months after the Wobblies organized, former Idaho governor Frank Steunenberg was murdered by a bomb at his home. A suspect, Harry Orchard, was arrested and confessed. He claimed to be a terrorist working for WFM and IWW officials. On Orchard's testimony Big Bill Haywood and others were arrested. Many labor organizations, even those that looked askance at the IWW, drew together in support of the accused, who they believed were being framed.

In 1907, Haywood came to trial. In sensational testimony Orchard confessed to many violent acts during the 15-year miners' wars, including incidents at Cripple Creek, and received a life sentence. Haywood was ably defended by lawyer Clarence Darrow; both he and two other union defendants were acquitted on the charge of hiring Orchard to kill Steunenberg. As historian Anthony Lukas demonstrates in his exhaustive study of the trial, "Operative for operative, hired gun for hired gun, bought juror for bought juror, perjured witness for perjured witness," the crimes committed by the mine owners and the crimes committed by the miners during the miners' wars had "just about canceled each other out."[48]

SOCIAL PROBLEMS AND THE SOCIAL GOSPEL

The Social Gospel, a theology that supported social and economic reform as an expression of Christian doctrines, continued to expand its influence. In 1906 John A. Ryan, a Catholic priest and later professor at Catholic University, published his doctoral dissertation, *A Living Wage*. Ryan argued that "wages should be sufficiently high to enable the laborer to live in a manner consistent with the dignity of a human being."[49] Wages should allow a healthy and self-respecting life, he said, and allow some savings, insurance, and modest recreation. In addition, he contended that it should not be necessary for either a wife or children younger than 16 to work outside the home. At the time, fewer than half of adult male workers earned the yearly wages Ryan estimated to be necessary for such a life, about $600. Ryan became the leading Catholic theologian of the social gospel movement. His work popularized the phrase *a living wage* among progressives and became an intellectual foundation of the minimum-wage movement.

In 1907, Rev. Walter Rauschenbusch published *Christianity and the Social Crisis,* considered the foremost explanation and defense of the Protestant social gospel. The following year representatives of 33 Protestant groups met in Philadelphia and formed the Federal Council of Churches to act as a united voice for religiously motivated reform. The group developed a Social Creed that gave strong support to improving the conditions of laboring people. Of course, nationwide many Protestant as well as Catholic congregations and clerics continued to hold a more conservative viewpoint.

THE AUTOMOBILE AGE BEGINS

No one person invented the automobile. For many years in both Europe and America, many inventors had experimented with self-propelled vehicles. Like early flying machine inventors, they tested and exhibited their machines in races. At first, the vehicles were most often called horseless carriages, but they were known by many different names as well, such as gasoline buggies, locomobiles, and motorrigs. In 1900, when the first U.S. National Automobile Show was held and the first advertisement for an automobile appeared, there were 8,000 automobiles in the United States. By the end of 1908, there were 200,000, about one-third produced that year.

The earliest automobiles were heavy, handcrafted, distinctly luxury items. Early automobile makers did not agree on the best source of power. Some favored steam, some electricity, and some gasoline. The fastest cars, the Stanley Steamer and the White Touring Car, were powered by steam—just like trains and farm machinery. But they were complicated to keep in fuel, or water heated to a steaming temperature. The cleanest, quietest, and easiest-to-operate autos were electric-powered (that is, by battery). Even by 1908, however, they could run only 80 miles without recharging at a special facility. Even so, it was not obvious to people living at the time that the gasoline engine was the wave of the future. The first presidential automobile, not purchased until William Howard Taft took office in 1909, was a steam-powered White.

A few innovators saw the potential for an automobile that was moderately priced and could be widely marketed, chief among them Henry Ford. "I want to build a car for the great multitude," he famously said. "It will be so low in price that no man making a good salary will be unable to own one—and enjoy with his family the blessings of hours of pleasure in God's greatest open spaces." Ford, the inventive son of a disapproving Dearborn, Michigan, farmer, established his first auto company in 1899. It failed. His second company was sold by feuding investors to Henry Leland in 1902, who renamed it the Cadillac Motor Company. In 1903, Ford tried again, forming the Ford Motor Company. He intended to compete with Ransom E. Olds, who manufactured the popular but small and not particularly sturdy Runabout. Olds had introduced an important manufacturing innovation into auto making—the subcontracting of components, made to specifications by other manufacturers. It enabled him to produce 3,000 Merry Oldsmobiles at $450 each the year before Ford opened for business. Other autos at the time sold for $3,000 to $4,000 and up.

In June 1903, Ford's first wooden-bodied, buggy-like Model A appeared. It had a two-cylinder engine built by the Dodge Brothers machine shop. At the Ford plant, small groups of workers built one car at a time, hand-fitting the parts together. By the end of 1904 more than 1,700 Model As had been sold, at the price $750. By 1905 models B, C, and F appeared, and the company moved to larger quarters. In 1906, the model N appeared. It had a lighter, steel-alloy body and a four-cylinder engine.

Ford was aiming for a vehicle that was not only moderately priced but also practical, sturdy, and suited to the actual condition of America's rough, unpaved roads. In 1908, when the Model T appeared, he succeeded. It was built from a tough steel alloy and had four cylinders cast together in a single block. America took the Model T to its heart. Some 10,000 Tin Lizzies, priced at $850, were sold within a year. The Model T was so successful that Ford would sell it exclusively until 1927, by which time more than 15 million had been produced.[50]

Meanwhile, Henry Leland was at work refining the idea of parts manufactured to such precision that they could be used interchangeably rather than hand-fitted in an individual vehicle. In a 1908 demonstration in England, three of Leland's Cadillacs were taken apart, then reassembled with the parts scrambled. The reassembled cars operated perfectly—a major technical achievement. In the same year, Leland, Olds, and David D. Buick merged to form General Motors.

RADIO COMMUNICATIONS CONTINUE TO DEVELOP

The scientists and inventors Guglielmo Marconi (who sent the first transatlantic wireless telegraph communications in 1901, called wireless telegraphy) and Reginald Fessenden (who demonstrated the first radio voice communications in 1900, called radiotelephony) continued their work, as did many others interested in the wireless communications field. In 1907, Marconi's company established the first regular commercial transatlantic wireless telegraph service, transmitting between stations in Nova Scotia and Ireland.

On Christmas Eve, December 24, 1906, Fessenden made what is regarded as the first radio broadcast. Startled wireless operators within a 15-mile radius of his station at Brant Rock on the coast of Massachusetts picked up clearly transmitted voice messages and music, including a violin solo by Fessenden himself. During the following year, he accomplished another first: transmitting the first two-way radio voice conversation across the Atlantic between his stations in Massachusetts and Scotland. He also made similar transmissions within the United States. Unlike Marconi, the Canadian-born Fessenden was neither a good promoter not a good businessman, but historians point out he deserves to share the title father of radio. Eventually he discovered amplitude modulation (AM) radio.

Despite Fessenden's pioneering efforts, the potential of voice radio remained unappreciated during the first decade of the 20th century. Wireless telegraph communications, however, quickly spread worldwide. So many start-up companies and investment schemes were spawned to develop equipment, in fact, that by 1907 they were already the subject of a muckraking exposé.

THE BIRTH OF THE MOTION PICTURE INDUSTRY

Movie storefronts are known to have opened before the turn of the century in New York and New Orleans, and in Chicago and Los Angeles in 1902. The first actual movie theater, however, is attributed to McKeesport, Pennsylvania. In 1905, entrepreneurs John P. Harris and Harry Davis reused the furnishings of a former opera house to create a theater solely for showing motion pictures. After that date movie houses exploded exponentially throughout the United States. At first they were heavily concentrated in working-class neighborhoods or low-rent commercial streets. They were called nickelodeons, a term coined by Harris and Davis, because the show cost a nickel. Vaudeville theaters, on the other hand, usually charged a quarter to see a variety show with a movie included.

Working people and their families flocked to the affordable nickelodeon. Those who were recent immigrants did not even need to understand English because all movies were silent. (Movies did not talk until the 1920s). Shows were about half an hour in length and ran continually from morning to night, including Sundays. The program often changed daily. "Motion pictures have never had such a devoted and enthusiastic audience since these early years," writes film historian Eileen Bowser. "People went night after night, or from one show to another."[51]

The middle and upper classes did not attend the first nickelodeons. They certainly viewed films occasionally. But they saw them primarily in respectable settings like vaudeville houses, lecture or music halls, town halls, or church auditoriums. In these settings, films like documentaries and travelogues were popular and were considered wholesome, educational entertainment.

For a while, the explosion of movie storefronts, nick-elodeons, and movie production itself was overlooked by mainstream commentators and flourished under the radar of public oversight. Around 1907, news reporters finally discovered the "nickel madness" in working people's neighborhoods. The news reports generated public alarm. Middle- and upper-class people associated nickelodeons with other forms of unwholesome activity, if not outright vice, prevalent in poorer areas of the city. Settlement and charity workers, reformers, and reform-minded clergymen were dismayed at the physical and moral dangers posed when unwashed crowds, including unaccompanied young women and children, jammed into dark, unventilated rooms till late at night. All were concerned about the content of movies and their potential to be a debasing influence. All producers made the kind of films their largest audience preferred: highly wrought, blood-and-guts melo-dramas and uncouth comedies. But some had also begun making suggestive or bawdy films and films that showed unsavory lifestyles (*Scenes of a Convict Life,* for example).

As public alarm about nickelodeons multiplied, the police began closing theaters or seizing films in some towns. In New York, the police department requested the mayor to take action. After investigating, Mayor George B. McClellan ordered every one of the city's 550 nickelodeons closed, which they were without notice on Christmas Day, 1908. Some theater managers immediately and successfully sought court injunctions to permit them to reopen. But New York was the center of movie production and equipment manu-facturing in America at the time and Mayor McClellan's act naturally alarmed the young industry. (There were also three companies in Chicago, one in Philadelphia, and a few small enterprises scattered elsewhere in 1908—but none yet in California.) Major companies immediately began to consider how best to meet the threat.

Earlier the same year, another important change had occurred in the growing motion picture industry. Thomas Edison succeeded in a goal he had pursued for some time: the formation of a motion picture trust, called the Motion Picture Patents Com-pany. The major companies had become increasingly alarmed by patent wars and law-suits among themselves, as well as by competition from European and upstart American producers. Eleven of them agreed to pool their important patents for film, cameras, and projectors. Like all other business combinations of the era, the Trust (as it was openly called in the movie business) was an attempt to bring order to a disorderly, highly competitive industry and to monopolize it. The group quickly made an agree-ment with Eastman Kodak, so that only the producers the Trust licensed could obtain filmstock. They soon created the General Film Company to oversee distribution of completed movies. Distributors could obtain them only by signing an exclusive agree-ment, and theaters had to do the same with distributors in order to rent the films—in addition to paying a weekly royalty to the Edison company.

The popularity of moving pictures was sweeping the country. At first, middle-class people saw them at traveling movie exhibitions, like the one advertised in this poster, in town halls, or vaudeville houses. Working people patronized neighborhood nickelodeons. *(Library of Congress, Prints and Photographs Division, LC-USZ62-89709)*

A MILESTONE IN AMERICAN ART: THE EXHIBIT OF THE EIGHT

In the early 20th century, the most important American organization of artists, the National Academy of Design, was conservative, academic, and very exclusive in membership. Academy members, like most wealthy patrons of art at the time, insisted upon idealistic, classical, and refined subjects, carefully rendered according to established rules in a polished style. They were beholden to the aesthetic tastes and trends of Europe, although American artists were considered far inferior to their counterparts there.

In New York, a group of artists led by Robert Henri increasingly believed that American art was out of touch with modern life and with the great social questions that were in the air. In 1907, when the National Academy rejected their work for its annual exhibition—even Henri's, although he himself was a member—eight of them determined to exhibit together. The exhibit opened at Macbeth's Gallery in New York in February 1908. The Eight, as reporters came to call them, included Everett Shinn, John Sloan, Arthur B. Davies, Ernest Lawson, Maurice Prendergast, George Luks, and William J. Glackens in addition to Henri. They worked in a variety of styles but were united in their insistence that American artists should reject European models and Academy authority. Instead, they believed, American artists should strive for vitality and immediacy and portray contemporary life in a democratic fashion. Although the paintings of the Eight depicted many different subjects, including landscapes, some showed the era's uglier aspects—life on the urban streets, sweaty athletes, city views.

The exhibit of the Eight attracted dismissive comment from some observers, who called them "apostles of ugliness" and a "revolutionary gang." But it also drew favorable comment and noticeable interest from the gallery-going public—enough so that the group sent their work on tour to nine other cities. Much later, an art historian dubbed the Eight and a few additional artists the Ash Can School. They are often compared to muckrakers or the naturalistic novelists, and in their battle with the National Academy to the reformers who faced entrenched power in other areas of life. Several, in fact, did work as newspaper illustrators (photography was still not widely used to illustrate news stories) and two, Henri and Sloan, were socialists.

The 1908 exhibit of the Eight is considered a milestone in American painting. It marked out a new and independent direction for American artists and also demonstrated that viewers were interested in more than idealistic, genteel subjects.

NEW CONSERVATION INITIATIVES

During President Roosevelt's second term, conservation initiatives were almost continual. All told, during his two terms in office, President Roosevelt used executive orders to put almost 230 million acres under federal protection for various reasons, quadrupling protected acreage. Most was set aside under terms of the Forest Reserve Act of 1891, although the land was not necessarily heavily timbered; the act permitted reserves "wholly or in part covered with timber or undergrowth."[52]

In early 1905, Gifford Pinchot, with the president's assistance, achieved a long-time goal: transferring oversight of all forest reserves under federal protection from the General Land Office in the Department of the Interior to the Bureau of Forestry in the Department of Agriculture. The bureau, which Pinchot headed, was officially renamed the Forest Service and greatly expanded its authority as a regulating agency. Almost immediately, for example, it began charging fees to western sheep and cattle raisers who grazed their herds on government lands, over their strenuous objections. "That meant stepping on the toes of the biggest interests in the West," Pinchot wrote in his autobiography. "From that time on it was fight, fight, fight."[53]

President Roosevelt was also concerned about misappropriation of the nation's mineral deposits, especially coal. Often, speculators and large corporate combinations gained land by fraudulently accumulating homestead claims. By executive order in late 1906, he withdrew remaining public land with known or suspected coal deposits from claim, sale, or entry (use). The purpose of the withdrawals was to enable the government to collect better information about mineral deposits, which in turn would permit a plan for orderly, nonfraudulent development and a fair price for use. In February 1907, the president sent a message to Congress saying, "The nation should retain its title to its fuel resources, and its right to supervise their development in the interests of the public as a whole."[54] Soon after, all possible oil, gas, and phosphate deposits were withdrawn as well. As surveys were completed of withdrawn lands, those with little mineral value were returned to public availability. But Congress could not agree on an overall plan to manage the valuable deposits that did exist, and the deposits remained closed during the remainder of Roosevelt's term. Congress did not agree on a final policy until the Mineral Leasing Act of 1920.

By 1907, some congressmen were disenchanted, especially those from the West where almost all withdrawn lands were located. The president's set-asides had stepped on the toes of many of their powerful constituents. When Congress passed the agricultural appropriations bill that year, they attached a rider requiring that any additional set-asides in the six northwestern states be subject to congressional approval. But the president was not deterred. As he recalled in his autobiography, "For four years the Forest Service had been gathering field notes as to what forests ought to be set aside in these States, and so was prepared to act." Roosevelt offered no public opposition as the bill made its way through Congress. But before he signed it into law, Pinchot's staff had managed to survey and set aside a great deal more land in the Northwest. "When the friends of the special interests in the Senate got their amendment through and woke up," Roosevelt wrote, "they discovered that sixteen million acres of timberland had been saved for the people by putting them in the National Forests before the land grabbers could get at them. The opponents of the Forest Service turned handsprings in their wrath; and dire were their threats against the Executive; but the threats could not be carried out, and were really only a tribute to the efficiency of our action."[55]

Water power and waterways were another concern. President Roosevelt set aside many water power sites appropriate for the generation of hydroelectric power to prevent private monopoly. One was Muscle Shoals, Alabama, future site of the Tennessee Valley Authority project. In 1907, he appointed an Inland Waterways Commission to suggest a national plan for oversight of U.S. waterways and to address issues like water purity, flood control, and power development at the national level. The following year the National Waterways Commission was created.

In addition to his actions to enable the managed use of national resources, the president also acted to preserve many important sites. In 1906, Congress passed the Act for the Preservation of American Antiquities. Roosevelt interpreted the act broadly and applied it to the protection of natural as well as human-made sites. For example, he not only protected Native American cliff dwellings in Arizona but also declared sites like the Petrified Forest and some 800,000 acres surrounding the Grand Canyon to be national monuments. Congress itself passed an act to protect Niagara Falls, specifically referring to the importance of preserving its scenic grandeur.

One of Roosevelt's most important conservation initiatives was the first White House Conference on Conservation, called the Governors' Conference, held in May 1908. "It seems to me time for the country to take account of its natural resources," he wrote in his letter of invitations to state and territorial governors, "and to enquire how long they are likely to last."[56] The conference was also attended by Supreme Court justices, the Cabinet, congressmen, and other officials and influential Americans. The high-powered gathering clearly demonstrated the importance of the issue to the nation. As a result of the conference, state-level conservation commissions were established in 36 states and local conservation work began throughout the nation. Many states began copying the federal model, setting aside state-owned lands for preservation or managed use and establishing conservation departments to oversee them.

THE HETCH HETCHY CONTROVERSY BEGINS

The city of San Francisco had long wanted to build a large dam across the Tuolumne River, at the end of Hetch Hetchy Valley within Yosemite National Park. The idea had been the brainchild of reform mayor James Phelan in 1901. At the time, water (and electric) supply in the city was under the control of private and often corrupt franchises. Phelan wanted to use the dam to create a water supply that was under municipal, public ownership. But the dam and reservoir would, of course, flood the valley, and Hetch Hetchy was a spectacular gorge which preservationists had long celebrated. Secretary of the Interior Ethan Hitchcock denied the city's request in 1903 and again in 1905.

Gifford Pinchot was more favorable to the project. He believed there was a public interest in preventing private domination of the water supply, primarily because of the growing importance of hydroelectricity. While San Francisco had alternative sites that could supply its water, Hetch Hetchy Valley was ideally suited for generating electric power as well. When Secretary Hitchcock left office, Pinchot suggested to the city that it renew the application. Opponents within the conservation movement, led by John Muir, tried to block the action. But in May 1908, the new secretary of the interior James Garfield granted a permit to dam Hetch Hetchy. The next hurdle was winning Congressional consent. Almost all San Franciscans approved of the dam project (85 percent voted in favor of it in a referendum). But by the end of 1908, conservation-minded people nationwide had begun a campaign against it.

THE GREAT WHITE FLEET

While the U.S. Army was undergoing reorganization in the decade following the Spanish-American War, the U.S. Navy was modernizing and rebuilding. President Roosevelt, who believed that a strong navy was crucial to world power, was its strongest advocate. During his presidency, the size and effectiveness of the navy doubled, becoming second only to that of Great Britain. Expenditures for the navy multiplied as well, to the displeasure of some Congressmen and other Americans.

In 1907, the president decided to send the naval fleet on an unprecedented goodwill voyage around the world. The president had several reasons for sending the fleet on its journey. One was to show it to the American people to stimulate their pride and support. Another was to provide a training exercise for the newly enlarged navy. But the most important was to impress other nations—especially Japan—with America's new naval power. "In my own judgment the most important service that I rendered to peace," he later wrote in his autobiography, "was the voyage of the battle fleet around the world."[57] Because the battleships were painted gleaming white—a practice the navy abandoned soon after in favor of "battleship gray"—the ships that made the 1907 journey became known to history as the Great White Fleet.

On December 16, 16 new battleships, manned by 14,000 sailors and accompanied by many smaller support ships, steamed out of Hampton Roads, Virginia. The president reviewed them from his yacht *Mayflower*, anchored nearby, receiving a 21-gun salute from each battleship as it passed. The fleet proceeded around South America to California, then crossed the Pacific to Hawaii and proceeded to New Zealand, Australia, and the Philippines before reaching Japan and China. The ships passed through the Suez Canal, then crossed the Atlantic, arriving back in Hampton Roads on Washington's birthday, February 22, 1909. President Roosevelt and 60,000 Americans greeted them. All told, the fleet had traveled 43,000 miles and made 20 stops on six continents. They met cordial and often wildly enthusiastic welcomes in all ports.

THE PANIC OF 1907

In March 1907, the stock market suddenly dropped, calling a sharp halt to the prosperity that had reigned since the turn of the century. Unemployment rose and prices soared. President Roosevelt blamed business, and businessmen in turn blamed the president's economic policies. The immediate causes of the problem were bad corporate planning and irresponsible overspeculation in copper. But the underlying cause was the lack of an adequate national system of banking and money supply.

In late October, a large New York bank failed. The city's third-largest bank followed, and two days later the second-largest was also in trouble. America had no federal bank or monetary agency to assist shaky institutions, but J. P. Morgan, the most powerful banker in America, stepped in. He publicly urged depositors to remain calm and leave their funds in the banks (which were not insured as they are today). Morgan also persuaded the stock exchange not to close its doors. He then organized other bankers and trust officials into assembling a pool of assets to help weak institutions through the crisis—reportedly locking them in his library until they finished and signed the deal as the dawn broke November 4. Part of the solution, he informed President Roosevelt, was to permit a shaky New York bank to sell Tennessee Coal and Iron Company, whose stock it owned, to the behemoth trust U.S. Steel. Normally, U.S. Steel would have come under antitrust scrutiny for such a purchase. But for the deal to succeed, Roosevelt agreed to exempt it.

Within a year, the recession had ended. In the spring of 1908, Congress passed the Aldrich-Vreeland Act, a temporary measure to permit national banks to issue additional currency. The act also established the National Monetary Commission, chaired by Senator Nelson Aldrich of Rhode Island. The commission was assigned to study banking and currency systems and recommend thoroughgoing reforms.

THE ELECTION OF 1908

On the eve of his election victory in 1904, President Roosevelt had announced to the nation that he would not run for another term. Although he was only 50 years old in 1908 and probably regretted his words, he did not back down from them. Roosevelt remained extremely popular and many prominent Republicans tried to change his mind, but to no avail.

By early 1907, Roosevelt had decided to tap his secretary of war, William Howard Taft, as his successor. Taft, born in Cincinnati, had been a distinguished federal judge and the successful civil governor of the Philippines. His cherished wish in life was not the presidency but a seat on the Supreme Court, though he twice turned down an appointment by Roosevelt in order to fulfill responsibilities he already had undertaken. On many occasions he told friends, "I am not a politician and I dislike politics."[58] Thanks to Roosevelt's support and his own geniality, however, Taft commanded a solid majority of delegates well before the Republican convention. When it met in Chicago in June 1908, both Taft and a platform written under the president's direction were inevitable. In fact, an advance copy of the platform was released from the White House to the *New York Times,* which published it even before the convention met. Taft was nominated on the first ballot. For vice president the delegates chose James Schoolcraft Sherman of New York. Neither Taft nor Roosevelt was especially enthusiastic about the very conservative Sherman, but his selection was popular with business interests.

Among Democrats, the liberal William Jennings Bryan once again had assumed leadership of the party. Bryan insisted that the progressive viewpoint belonged to the Democratic Party, not to Republicans. On some reform issues, he had been one of Roosevelt's strongest supporters, often encouraging Democrats in Congress to support the president's reform initiatives. In fact, Bryan often pointed out that the program

Roosevelt was putting into effect had been outlined in the Democratic (Chicago) platform of 1896—which Republicans and even many Democrats at the time had assailed as the work of a lunatic fringe.

Bryan had declined to be the Democratic candidate in 1904. By the time the 1908 convention met at Denver in July, however, Bryan had a large majority of Democratic delegates committed to his support. Although the financially conservative wing did not like him any more than they ever did, he was elected on the first ballot. The convention chose John Kern of Indiana as the vice presidential candidate.

Bryan exercised great control over the Democratic platform. It supported reforms such as antitrust legislation, the direct election of senators, conservation, and control of communications by the ICC. (The silver issue was, however, finally dead.) The platform also attacked the Republicans for failing to support a campaign-contributions plank. Bryan himself promised to reject all corporate contributions, to publish all contributions over $100, and to raise as much money as possible in one-dollar donations from ordinary people, a program at which he met some success.[59]

Five third parties also met in convention. One, the new Independence Party, was founded and financially supported by William Randolph Hearst. Hearst had unsuccessfully attempted to play a role in the Democratic Party and had even thought of himself as presidential timber. The Independence Party approved a reform platform to the left of the Democrats and attracted some of that party's most liberal wing. The Socialist Party met in Chicago in May, more than 3,000 delegates in attendance. It again nominated Eugene V. Debs for president. Socialists had polled the third-highest number of votes in 1904 and now had formal organizations in 39 states. During the campaign, Debs traveled through much of the nation on a train called the Red Special. It generated publicity (much of it, of course, hostile) and enthusiasm among some farmers, miners, and other labor supporters. The Socialist Party had also begun to attract a number of dissatisfied, intellectually minded, and sometimes prominent reformers within the clergy, journalism, social work, and other professions. Also meeting in convention were the Prohibition Party, a small remnant of Populists, and Daniel De Leon's small and radical Socialist Labor Party.

Taft, who was easygoing and very overweight, lacked the oratorical skills of Bryan, not to mention the energy and charisma of Roosevelt. But he made no serious mistakes during the campaign and promised to continue Roosevelt's popular policies. He won the election by a popular vote of 51 to 43 percent, and an electoral majority of 321 to 162—less than Roosevelt's majority of 1904 but still impressive. Congress also remained in Republican control, although both the Democrats and the insurgent or reform wing of the Republicans made gains. The Socialist Party tallied close to 3 percent of the popular vote, a small decline in percentage although a small gain in total votes from 1904.

CHRONICLE OF EVENTS

1905

Theodore Roosevelt is president; Charles W. Fairbanks is vice president.

The population of the United States is nearly 84 million.

The federal government reacquires Yosemite Valley from the State of California. For the second time the city of San Francisco applies to the Department of the Interior to dam Hetch Hetchy Valley in Yosemite; again permission is denied.

The National Child Labor Committee (NCLC) begins its work in the North by supporting a Pennsylvania bill to require proof of age and educational standards for working children, later declared unconstitutional by the state courts. In the South the NCLC works for a North Carolina bill raising the working age to 14. A delegation of more than 70 manufacturers opposes it and it is defeated.

Direct primary legislation is enacted in Texas, Illinois, Michigan, Montana, and South Dakota.

Connecticut adopts a housing code modeled on the New York law of 1901.

The first known movie theater (in contrast to a storefront nickelodeon) opens in McKeesport, Pennsylvania.

By agreement with the Dominican Republic, the United States establishes a receivership to forestall European intervention in the island. It is the first action based on the Roosevelt Corollary.

Football was primarily a college sport in the Progressive Era. It caused many injuries because it was played without protective gear, as this photo of the Yale team at practice shows. In 1905, President Roosevelt summoned Ivy League officials to the White House to discuss the problem. By the end of the year, the Intercollegiate Athletic Association was founded to establish rules for college sports. *(Library of Congress, Prints and Photographs Division, LC-USZ62-128537)*

The United States ratifies the International Agreement for the Suppression of the Trade in White Women, which European nations have drafted to combat international prostitution rings.

January 9: In Russia, Bloody Sunday begins; it is a wave of armed uprisings by discontented peasants and many other groups opposed to the czar's policies.

January 27: Congress passes the Nelson Act supporting the development of roads in Alaska.

January 30: In *Swift and Co. v. United States,* the Supreme Court finds a way around the 1895 decision in *E.C. Knight* that the Sherman Anti-Trust Act can not be applied to manufacturers, by looking at interstate sales.

February 1: Congress moves administration of federal forest reserves from the Department of the Interior to Gifford Pinchot's bureau in the Department of Agriculture.

March 4: Theodore Roosevelt is inaugurated for his second (first elected) term.

April 10: In *Rassmussen v. U.S.,* the Supreme Court declares that Alaska was incorporated into the United States by the purchase treaty of 1867; therefore its residents are entitled to full constitutional rights.

April 17: In *Lochner v. New York,* the Supreme Court holds that it is unconstitutional to limit the number of hours a bakery employee can work because there is no clear danger to public health and safety.

May 23: Wilbur and Orville Wright are finally granted a U.S. patent for their flying machine.

June: Under the leadership of W. E. B. DuBois and William Monroe Trotter, the Niagara Movement is formed near Niagara Falls, Canada, to demand full political and social rights for African Americans.

June 27: Socialists, anarchists, and leaders of some radical unions meet in Chicago to form the Industrial Workers of the World (IWW). This radical and militant union will organize workers at the bottom of the socioeconomic ladder and soon earn a reputation for violence.

July 29: The Taft-Katsura agreement accepts Japanese control of Korea in return for recognition of U.S. control in the Philippines.

August 21: In Indian Territory (eastern Oklahoma) delegates propose a state named Sequoyah to be admitted separately from Oklahoma Territory. It is overwhelmingly approved by residents but declined in Washington.

September 5: Russia and Japan sign the Treaty of Portsmouth, which President Roosevelt has helped negotiate at a peace conference in New Hampshire.

September 27: City Beautiful architect Daniel Burnham presents his plan for San Francisco to the city council.

October: In Russia, the czar grants a constitution to quiet the unrest that has roiled the country for nine months.

October 3: The National Baseball Commission establishes the rules for an annual World Series.

October 5: The Wright brothers demonstrate their flying machine to a small group; it remains in the air more than half an hour and flies 24 miles.

December 5: Former Colorado governor Frank Steunenberg is murdered by a bomb in Idaho. Prominent WFM officials, including Big Bill Haywood, are accused of conspiracy to hire the confessed murderer.

1906

Congress authorizes a voteless delegate to Congress for Alaska and passes the Alaska Native Allotment Act providing 160-acre homesteads for heads of families of Native Alaskans.

In Alaska, a private development combination called the Alaska Syndicate is organized by J.P. Morgan Company bankers and the Guggenheim Corporation, the largest mining trust in the United States.

In Georgia, the first child labor legislation in the state is passed; it has the support of Hoke Smith, newly elected governor and a founding member of the NCLC.

Pennsylvania and Louisiana enact direct-primary legislation.

Montana adopts initiative and referendum.

President Roosevelt receives the Nobel Peace Prize for his work in arbitrating the Treaties of Portsmouth and Algeciras.

The United States intervenes in Guatemala and Nicaragua.

The AFL decides to actively enter politics for the first time, hoping to end the use of injunctions and the Sherman Anti-Trust Act against unions.

The National Liberal Immigration League is founded in New York to oppose further immigration restrictions and to help immigrants get settled in America.

Oscar S. Straus is appointed secretary of commerce and labor, becoming the first Jewish American to serve in the Cabinet.

Upton Sinclair's muckraking novel *The Jungle* is published. It exposes astonishingly unsanitary practices in the meat packing industry, causing great public outrage and influencing passage of the Pure Food and Drug Act and the Meat Inspection Act.

Senator Albert Beveridge introduces a bill to restrict child labor, but Congress does not act on it.

The Wasserman test for syphilis is developed. Reformers concerned about prostitution and venereal disease begin to work for state requirements that men be tested before obtaining a marriage license. By 1921, 20 states will adopt the requirement.

Finland gives women the right to vote.

January 10: At the behest of the NCLC, a proposal is introduced into Congress for the establishment of a federal children's bureau. It will not be passed until 1912.

April 7: European powers sign the Convention of Algeciras, which has been arbitrated by the United States, ending a dispute over Morocco. The Senate ratifies it but notes that it does not intend to change America's traditional policy of nonintervention in European conflicts.

April 12: Reformers Jane Addams, Lillian Wald, and Jacob Riis organize the National Playground Association of America (NPAA). President Roosevelt agrees to be the honorary president.

April 14: In a speech, President Roosevelt compares the crusading investigative journalists of the Progressive Era to the Man with the Muckrake in John Bunyan's Christian allegory *Pilgrim's Progress,* giving them the name by which they have been known ever since.

April 18: The city of San Francisco is hit by a powerful earthquake at 5:13 A.M. The fires that it ignites burn for four days and destroy much of the city. More than 3,000 people are killed; damage is $500 million.

June: In San Francisco, reformers have resumed investigations, interrupted by the earthquake, into rampant corruption under Mayor George Schmitz and boss Abe Ruef, with the help of a special prosecutor and Secret Service investigator from Washington.

June 8: Congress passes the Act for the Preservation of American Antiquities. Under its provisions Roosevelt will declare many natural sites national monuments.

June 16: The Oklahoma Act, also called the Hamilton Statehood Act, is signed into law. Residents of both Oklahoma and Indian Territories are to call a constitutional convention in preparation for becoming one state.

June 19: At the urging of President Roosevelt, Congress passes the Hepburn Act, giving more power to the ICC to regulate railroads and other transportation industries.

June 21: Congress passes a law requiring lists of those who pay liquor taxes in any given district to be available for public inspection.

June 29: Congress passes the Burton Act to prevent water diversion from Niagara Falls and instructs the president to negotiate with Canada to protect the falls. The act is in response to a popular campaign by environmental preservationists.

June 30: President Roosevelt signs the Meat Inspection Act, requiring federal inspection of meat, and the Pure Food and Drugs Act, requiring labeling.

August 2: Cuban president Thomas Estrada Palma requests U.S. aid to stabilize the government. President Roosevelt will send Secretary of War Taft to assess the situation, followed by warships, military forces, and a governor, who will remain in control until January 1909.

August 13: In Brownsville, Texas, a few members of the First Battalion, Twenty-fifth Regiment, an African-American army unit, are involved in a riot in the nearby town that leaves one white man dead and a police officer injured. President Roosevelt orders an investigation; all soldiers deny involvement or knowledge of who committed the crimes.

September 22: Race rioting begins in Atlanta, as whites attack black neighborhoods after rumors spread that black men are attacking white women. Three whites and 18 blacks will die in the rioting, and much property will be destroyed.

October 11: The San Francisco school board, which maintains segregated schools for students of Chinese descent, decrees that Japanese and Korean children must also attend them. Japan is highly insulted and protests sharply. President Roosevelt sends Secretary of Commerce and Labor Victor Metcalf to San Francisco to discuss how the rights of Japanese Americans can be protected.

November: Voters in New Mexico and Arizona Territories vote on admission to the union as one joint state. New Mexico approves; Arizona votes it down by more than 5 to 1 and the bill for joint statehood dies.

November 7: President Roosevelt orders the dishonorable discharge of 170 black soldiers at Brownsville, Texas.

November 9–26: President Roosevelt becomes the first sitting president to travel abroad when he visits the canal project in Panama.

November 15: San Francisco Mayor Eugene E. Schmitz, political boss Abe Ruef, and the chief of police are indicted for bribery and extortion.

November 20: Oklahoma delegates assemble in Guthrie, where they will write a highly detailed constitution providing for a long list of progressive reforms.

December: President Roosevelt asks Congress for the third time to authorize an investigation by the Bureau of Labor into conditions of working women and children. He also suggests a model child labor law for the District of Columbia. Congress will authorize the Labor Department study in January 1907.

December 24: Reginald Fessenden, a Canadian-born scientist and engineer working in the United States, makes the first radio (or radiotelephony) broadcast from his station at Brant Rock on the coast of Massachusetts. Wireless operators within a 15-mile radius clearly pick up the music and voice messages.

1907

Japan and the United States make a Gentleman's Agreement. Japan agrees to prevent Japanese laborers from immigrating to the United States.

The city of San Francisco again initiates efforts for federal approval to dam Hetch Hetchy Valley. Conservationists are waging a campaign to prevent the dam.

Publicity about the phenomenon of nickelodeons begins to appear in mainstream news media. The middle and upper classes react with alarm in the belief that nickelodeons are corrupting to health and morals.

Iowa, Nebraska, Missouri, North Dakota, and Washington enact comprehensive and complete direct primary legislation; South Dakota extends its law.

Colorado passes a local option law for liquor sales; Illinois passes local option for townships, villages, and cities. In a Delaware referendum, every place in the state except Wilmington and Newcastle County vote to abolish saloons. Tennessee passes state legislation banning saloons in all but four counties. Alabama and Georgia adopt statewide prohibition.

In Chicago, the Commissioner of Police is given power to censor motion pictures; it is challenged but upheld by the Illinois Supreme Court.

Prominent settlement house leaders and other reformers in New York found the Committee on Congestion of Population (CCP). It will give impetus to the city planning movement.

Congress passes a law limiting the consecutive hours of railway workers on interstate trains. Most railway workers are covered by the law.

Anti-liquor publicity appealed to the new authority of science and experts. This flier by the Scientific Temperance Federation and the Anti-Saloon League quotes a Massachusetts Institute of Technology professor, who calls alcohol "one of the enemies to be combatted in the battle for health." *(Courtesy Westerville, Ohio, Public Library, Anti-Saloon League Collection)*

Reginald Fessenden conducts the first two-way transatlantic voice or radiotelephony conversation between his stations in Massachusetts and Scotland.

Norway gives women the right to vote.

January 26: Congress passes an act forbidding corporations from contributing to the campaign funds of candidates for national office.

January 29: Congress authorizes an investigation of women's and child labor.

February: Congress passes a new immigration act and establishes a commission to do an in-depth study of immigration's effect on America.

February 25: Displeased with Roosevelt's land protection policies, Congress passes an Agricultural Appropriations Act that forbids additional forest set-asides in Washington, Oregon, Idaho, Montana, Colorado, and Wyoming, except by act of Congress. This bill also officially renames the Forest Reserves as National Forests.

March: U.S. military forces are sent to Honduras to help quell a political uprising.

March 4: The president signs the Agricultural Appropriations Bill passed February 25—but has the Forest Service set aside an additional 16 million acres first.

March 5: In San Francisco trials begin in the Schmitz-Ruef corruption cases.

March 13: The stock market drops and a financial panic and year-long recession begin. It is the first break in general prosperity since 1900.

In San Francisco the school board rescinds the school segregation order against Japanese students.

March 18: Sixteen of the 18 San Francisco city councilmen confess to the grand jury that they took bribes from several utilities and other companies.

June 13: Mayor Schmitz of San Francisco is convicted of bribery and extortion.

July: Big Bill Haywood, ably defended by lawyer Clarence Darrow, is found not guilty of conspiracy to murder Idaho governor Steunenberg.

July 10: The Oklahoma Constitutional Convention meets again to consider President Roosevelt's objections to their constitution; they make only a few minor changes.

September 17: The citizens of Oklahoma overwhelmingly ratify their proposed constitution as well as statewide prohibition, voted on separately.

October 21: The large Knickerbocker Trust Company in New York fails. In the coming weeks J. P. Morgan will personally organize private bankers to stabilize the nation's banks and ease the financial panic; no central U.S. banking system yet exists to help in financial crises.

November 16: With some reluctance, the president proclaims Oklahoma the 46th state.

December 6: The worst mining disaster in U.S. history occurs when an explosion rips through two connected mines in Monongah, West Virginia. The official death toll is 362 but more than 500 unofficially. Mining accidents have taken more than 3,000 lives in 1907 alone, but Monongah is the first to receive wide national publicity. It arouses public pressure for reform.

December 10: In San Francisco, corrupt boss Abe Ruef is found guilty.

December 16: The Great White Fleet, 16 new gleaming white battleships sent around the world by President Roosevelt, leaves Hampton Roads, Virginia, for a 14-month voyage to demonstrate American naval power and spread goodwill.

December 30: The Spalding Commission, after studying the issue, reports that baseball was invented by Abner Doubleday in Cooperstown, New York, in 1839, and is therefore an American invention. In fact, the game was described in English books well before that date.

1908

A second National Guard act is passed in response to Guard supporters. The act guarantees that state guardsmen will serve as units and will not be individually substituted into regular army divisions. It also establishes a National Guard Bureau in the War Department directly responsible to the secretary of war, not to the army chief of staff.

Famous muckraking photographer Lewis Hine becomes the official NCLC photographer.

Illinois, Kansas, Oklahoma, and Ohio enact direct primary legislation. Maine and Missouri adopt initiative and referendum. Oregon adopts recall.

Mississippi and North Carolina pass statewide prohibition of liquor sales; Indiana and Ohio pass local option law.

At the president's urging, Congress establishes a modest worker's compensation program for some federal employees.

January 10: Staunton, Virginia, becomes the first city in America to adopt the city manager plan of municipal government.

February: In New York, a group of artists called the Eight (later called the Ash Can School) exhibit their work, which includes pictures of formerly unacceptable subjects like urban streets and the city's poor. The show will come to be considered a milestone, marking out a new and independent direction for American art.

February 3: In a unanimous decision in *Loewe v. Lawler* (the Danbury Hatters Case), the Supreme Court declares that union boycotts are a restraint of trade under the Sherman Anti-Trust Act.

February 12: The New York-to-Paris automobile race begins. Racers travel cross-country, then by boat to Tokyo, through Russia, and on to Europe. An American auto, the Thomas Flyer, wins.

February 24: In a unanimous decision the Supreme Court rules in *Muller v. Oregon* that it is constitutional to limit the number of hours women employees can work. The case is the first use of a so-called Brandeis brief by attorney Louis Brandeis, which calls on social and psychological evidence and issues instead of relying solely on an argument about legal precedent.

April 2: The remnants of the Populist Party meet in St. Louis and nominate Thomas Watson for president.

May: The Department of the Interior approves San Francisco's request to construct a dam across Hetch Hetchy Valley in Yosemite National Park; city voters will authorize the project by a majority of 86 percent. The request must have congressional approval; conservationists begin a nationwide campaign to prevent it.

Congress establishes a station within the Geological Survey to investigate mining accidents; it will also appropriate funds to establish a mine rescue operation.

May 10: The Socialist Party meets in Chicago and again nominates Eugene V. Debs for president.

May 13–15: The Governors' Conference on Conservation, called by President Roosevelt, meets in Washington. The conference publicizes conservation to the public and stimulates many state and local initiatives. Many states begin to set aside state-owned lands and establish conservation departments.

May 28: Congress passes a model child labor law for the District of Columbia.

May 30: Congress passes the Aldrich-Vreeland Act, which temporarily modifies the American banking system, and names Senator Nelson W. Aldrich head of a National Monetary Commission to review the entire banking and monetary system of the nation.

June 16–19: The Republican Party meets in Chicago and nominates William Howard Taft for president and James S. Sherman of New York for vice president.

July 7–10: The Democratic Party meets in Denver and nominates William Jennings Bryan for president for the third time.

July 15: The Prohibition Party meets in Columbus and nominates a presidential candidate.

July 27: The Independence Party, funded and organized by renegade Democrat William Randolph Hearst, nominates a presidential candidate.

August 12: Henry Ford introduces the Model T, a car of moderate price designed to run on the rough roadways of America. Within a year, Americans will buy 10,000; the second best-selling car, the Buick, sells 8,800.

August 14: A serious race riot begins in Springfield, Illinois, Lincoln's hometown.

September 9: Thomas Edison and the heads of 10 other companies formally incorporate the Motion Picture Patents Company, which has been operating since 1907. They will share their important patents to eliminate other competitors and will soon establish interlocking agreements with Eastman Kodak, film distributors, and theater owners in an attempt to monopolize the movie industry.

November 3: William Howard Taft wins the presidential election, although by a closer margin than Roosevelt in 1904. The Republicans also retain control of both houses of Congress.

November 30: In the Root-Takahira agreement, America and Japan reaffirm the integrity of China and the Open Door policy there.

December 2–8: Meeting in Philadelphia, 33 Protestant groups form the Federal Council of Churches to act as a united voice for expressing the doctrines of the Social Gospel.

December 24: New York mayor George B. McClellan, who has investigated nickelodeons at the request of the police department, suddenly orders all 600 in the city closed.

December 31: Wilbur Wright wins the Coupe Michelin in France, setting a new world record for flight of two hours 20 minutes, covering nearly 125 kilometers.

Eyewitness Testimony

The social worker thus serves to unite the now scattered industrial, racial, and religious elements that are thrown together to make up the population particularly of our great city communities. He establishes bits of neutral territory where the descendant of the Puritans may meet the chosen leaders among the immigrants from Italy, Russia, and the Levant; where the capitalist may meet the trade-unionist; where the scholar may meet the ingenious, practical mechanic, or perhaps the philosopher or poet of the people; where the Protestant may meet the Catholic; where the Christian may meet the Jew; and where all can, by establishing friendly relations, aside from and in advance of the conflicts of social sectionalism, come to consider their common interests with regard to particular steps in political development, industrial progress, or the betterment of family life and neighborly intercourse.

Robert Woods explains "Social Work: A New Profession,"
paper read before the Harvard Ethical Society,
published in 1905, The Neighborhood in
Nation-Building *(1923),*
pp. 92–95.

The man who is so fortunate as to be married can take boarders and lodgers from among his own countrymen, and thus perhaps double the family income, besides gaining in social importance as a "boarding boss." It is, however, not only the desire to make money which leads the Slav, who loves privacy in his family life, thus to open his house. He feels that the young relative or the neighbor's son has a personal claim, and it is often more as a matter of kindness than of business that he makes room for him. Where else should the poor lad go? he thinks. . . .

This situation has both its good and its bad sides. Americans see the overcrowding and the occasional rows, and are perhaps scandalized at the presence of one woman in a house full of men. They do not realize that for a young fellow to camp with a number of others in one room in the house of some relative or acquaintance may be not demoralizing but a safeguard. It is indeed fair to construe much of the poorest, most crowded living as a temporary "roughing it" on the part of men who have gone out to seek their fortunes; as something intended only as a transition arrangement, just as our own eastern college boys are content for a time with rough living in the far West. It does not represent their standard of living in the sense of what would content them permanently.

Emily Greene Balch, Wellesley professor and scholar who
conducted an extensive study of Slavic immigration in
1905–06, Our Slavic Fellow Citizens *(1920),*
pp. 349–50.

Universal economic evils afflicting the working class can be eradicated only by a universal working-class movement. Such a movement of the working class is impossible while separate craft and wage agreements are made favoring the employer against other crafts in the same industry and while energies are wasted in fruitless jurisdiction struggles which serve only to further the personal aggrandizement of union officials.

A movement to fulfill these conditions must consist of one great industrial union embracing all industries, providing for craft autonomy locally, industrial autonomy internationally, and working-class unity generally. It must be founded on the class struggle, and its general administration must be conducted in harmony with the recognition of the irrepressible conflict between the capitalist class and the working class. It should be established as the economic organization of the working class, without affiliation with any political party.

Manifesto of the IWW, a call to meet in convention put out
by leaders in January 1905, reprinted in Bolshevik
Propaganda *(1919), p. 1040.*

The nation . . . cannot prescribe a dietary course for each individual; it cannot even enforce rules as to what each shall consume. But what it can do and what it morally should do is this: It should protect a man against all fraud and imposition, so that acting upon his own intelligence, supplemented, if need be, by the advice of a specialist, he may procure those articles of food, beverage, and drug necessary for his own physical condition; and what is more important, that he may avoid those which are deleterious. . . .

. . . I have before me a portion of a paper . . . by Prof. E. F. Ladd, Food Commissioner of North Dakota. The condition which he finds in that State is probably true of every state in the Union. I cull a few extracts from this paper:

"One might suppose that the meats offered for sale in the State would be generally pure and true to name, but while potted chicken and potted turkey are among common products, I have never yet found a can in the State which really contained in a determinable quantity either chicken or turkey."

"More than 90 per cent of the local meat markets in the State were using chemical preservatives, and in nearly every butcher shop could be found a bottle of Freezem, preservaline or iceine, as well as Bull Meat Flour. The amount of borax or boracic acid employed in these meats varied to a considerable extent, and expressed in terms of boracic acid in sausages and hamburger steak would probably range from 20 grains to 45 grains per pound, while the medical dose is from 5 to 9 grains per day. The use of these chemicals is not confined to local butchers; scarcely a ham could be found that did not contain borax. In the dried beef, in the smoked meats, in the canned bacon, in the canned chipped beef, boracic acid or borates is a common ingredient."

Porter J. M'Cumber, senator from North Dakota,
"The Alarming Adulteration of Food and Drugs,"
The Independent, *vol. 58 (January 5, 1905),*
pp. 28–29.

Any bright morning in the latter part of May I am out of bed at four o'clock; next, after I have dressed and combed my hair, I start a fire in the kitchen stove . . . and sweep the floors and then cook breakfast.

While the other members of the family are eating breakfast I strain away the morning's milk (for my husband milks the cows while I get breakfast) and fill my husband's dinner pail . . .

By this time it is half-past five o'clock, my husband is gone to his work. . . . I now drive the two cows a half-quarter mile and turn them in with the others, come back, and then there is a horse in the barn . . . which I take to a spring . . .; bring it back and turn it into a field with the sheep. . . .

The young calves are then turned out into the warm sunshine, and the stock hogs which are kept in a pen, are clamoring for feed, and I carry a pailful of swill to them, and hasten to the house and turn out the chickens and put out feed and water for them, and it is, perhaps, 6.30 a.m.

I have not eaten breakfast yet, but that can wait; I make the beds next and straighten things up in the living room. . . . When this is done I go to the kitchen . . . and uncover the table, and take a mouthful of food occasionally as I pass to and fro at the work. . . .

By the time the work is done in the kitchen it is about 7.15 a.m., and the cool morning hours have flown, and no hoeing done in the garden yet. . . . Finally children are washed and the churning done, and it is eight o'clock. . . . I use a hoe to good advantage until the dinner hour, which is 11.30 a.m.

An Illinois farm wife describes her morning chores,
"One Farmer's Wife," part of a series of working people's
autobiographies in the Independent, *vol. 58*
(February 9, 1905), pp. 295–96.

. . . we must never forget that beyond the individual interest there is a vast social interest at stake, the interest of American civilization, of human civilization, of all those generations that are to succeed us. The reason why child labor must be abolished, apart from the sufferings of individuals, is one which biology and ethics combine to enforce upon us. The higher the type of living being the finer the organism, the longer the period of time required for its maturing. The young of birds and of the lower animals are full grown after a few days or a few weeks. They acquire with incredible rapidity the use of inherited instincts, and after the shortest infancy are ready to take up the struggle for existence after the fashion of their species. The human being requires a period of preparation extending over years before he is ready to take up the struggle for existence after the human fashion. First infancy, then childhood, then early youth; and during all that period he must remain dependent on the protection and the nurture of adult kinsfolk. If that period is curtailed the end of Nature in this highest type of living being—man—is thwarted. It is for this reason that premature toil is such a curse. The child must develop physically, and to do so it must play; the child must develop mentally, and to do so it must be sent to school; the child must develop morally, and to do so it must be kept within the guarded precincts of the home.

Felix Adler, Columbia professor and chair of the National
Child Labor Committee, "Child Labor in the United States,"
address at the first annual meeting, February 14–16, 1905,
NCLC, *Addresses, pp. 14–15.*

The tap-root of the remarkable popularity of Mr. Roosevelt, we feel sure, is the absolute conviction that there is nothing about him that is mean or sordid. All his feats of physical prowess, his Rough Rider exploits, his youthful ardor and effervescence, would have proved quite unequal to captivating the American people were there not behind these qualities, attractive as they are to the multitude, something that appeals more strongly to the national heart and conscience. . . .

. . . Mr. Roosevelt's special strength lies largely in that part of him in which he is in marked opposition to the dominant tendency of his own party. The people are not so delighted with the prospect of a millionaire millennium as the Republican magnates have often seemed to imagine. Mere wallowing in prosperity—especially when that prosperity is so peculiarly distributed—does not meet all the aspirations of the American nature. Whether wisely and ably, or only vigorously and emphatically, Mr. Roosevelt has certainly entered an energetic protest against a complacent acceptance of things as they are. . . .

The Baltimore News *sums up Roosevelt's appeal as he is*
inaugurated for a second term, March 4, 1905, reprinted in
Nevins, ed., American Press Opinion, *pp. 491–92.*

The treaty concerning Alaska [of 1867], instead of exhibiting, as did the treaty respecting the Philippine Islands, the determination to reserve the question of the status of the acquired territory for ulterior action by Congress, manifested a contrary intention, since it is therein expressly declared, in article 3, that:

> The inhabitants of the ceded territory . . . shall be admitted to the enjoyment of all the rights, advantages, and immunities of citizens of the United States; and shall be maintained and protected in the free enjoyment of their liberty, property and religion.

In this Native Alaskan village at Howkan, each family has a totem pole, which shows family and clan crests and symbolizes other important issues. *(Library of Congress, Prints and Photographs Division, LC-USZ62-107271)*

This declaration, although somewhat changed in phraseology, is the equivalent . . . of the formula employed from the beginning to express the purpose to incorporate acquired territory into the United States, especially in the absence of other provisions showing an intention to the contrary.

Justice White, writing for the majority of the Supreme Court in Rassmussen v. U.S., *declares Alaska incorporated into the United States, April 10, 1905, 197 US 516.*

It is funny—how we all have found the octopus [that is, the railroad trust]; an animal whose very existence we denied ten or a dozen years ago. The question that naturally comes up for discussion is this: has the octopus just hatched out, or were . . . the old line Populists who put sand-burrs in his tail, and tied cans to it, smarter and further seeing and more frank and honest than we were?

The other day a pamphlet came to the *Gazette* which seemed about the right thing. It was going after railroad discrimination. It seemed sane and calm and well poised. The man who wrote it seemed to have his head full of facts ground through the wheels of logic. When, lo and behold, the pamphlet was written and printed in 1890, and was written by Percy Daniels [Populist lieutenant governor of Kansas]! The sun do move. This is a funny world!

Editor William Allen White on his fellow Republicans' change of opinion since the heyday of populism, "Soaking The Octopus," Kansas *Emporia Gazette, April 15, 1905, reprinted in* The Editor and His People, *p. 275.*

Any one may say that the organizations of labor invade or deny liberty to the workmen. But go to the men who worked in the bituminous coal mines twelve, fourteen, sixteen hours a day, for a dollar or a dollar and twenty five cents, and who now work eight hours a day and whose wages have increased 70 per cent. in the past seven years—go tell those men that they have lost their liberty and they will laugh at you.

Samuel Gompers to the National Civic Federation, April 25, 1905, available online at Samuel Gompers Papers. URL: http://www.history.umd.edu/Gompers/quotes.html.

The members of the conference . . . congratulate the Negro-Americans on certain undoubted evidences of progress in the last decade. . . .

At the same time, we believe that this class of American citizens should protest emphatically and continually against the curtailment of their political rights. We believe in manhood suffrage; we believe that no man is so good, intelligent or wealthy as to be entrusted wholly with the welfare of his neighbor.

We believe also in protest against the curtailment of our civil rights. All American citizens have the right to equal treatment. . . .

We especially complain against the denial of equal opportunities to us in economic life; . . . everywhere American prejudice, helped often by iniquitous laws, is making it more difficult for Negro-Americans to earn a decent living. . . .

We refuse to allow the impression to remain that the Negro-American assents to inferiority, is submissive under oppression and apologetic before insults. Through helplessness we may submit, but the voice of protest of ten million

Americans must never cease to assail the ears of their fellows, so long as America is unjust. . . .

The Niagara Movement Declaration of Principles, from the first conference of July 11–13, 1905, reprinted in Osofsky, ed., Burden of Race *(1967), pp. 215–17.*

The truth which is gradually forcing itself upon thoughtful students of our national life is that no scheme of education or religion can solve the race problem, and that Mr. Booker T. Washington's plan, however high and noble, can only intensify its difficulties.

This conviction is based on a few big fundamental facts, which no pooh-poohing, ostrich-dodging, weak-minded philanthropy or political rant can obscure.

The first one is that no amount of education of any kind, industrial, classical or religious, can make a Negro a white man or bridge the chasm of the centuries which separate him from the white man in the evolution of human civilization. . . .

The second big fact which confronts the thoughtful, patriotic American is that the greatest calamity which could possibly befall this Republic would be the corruption of our national character by the assimilation of the Negro race. . . .

Thomas Dixon of New York, a well-known novelist and propagandist for white supremacy, "Booker T. Washington and the Negro," Saturday Evening Post, *vol. 178 (August 19, 1905), pp. 2–3.*

I first satisfied myself that each side wished me to act, but that, naturally and properly, each side was exceedingly anxious that the other should not believe that the action was taken on its initiative. I then sent an identical note to the two powers proposing that they should meet, through their representatives, to see if peace could not be made directly between them, and offered to act as an intermediary in bringing about such a meeting, but not for any other purpose. Each assented to my proposal in principle. There was difficulty in getting them to agree on a common meeting place. . . .

As is customary—but both unwise and undesirable—in such cases, each side advanced claims which the other could not grant. The chief difficulty came because of Japan's demand for a money indemnity. I felt that it would be better for Russia to pay some indemnity than to go on with the war, for there was little chance, in my judgment, of the war turning out favorably for Russia, and the revolutionary movement already under way bade fair to overthrow the negotiations entirely. I advised the Russian Government to this effect, at the same time urging them to abandon their pretensions on certain other points. . . . I also, however, and equally strongly, advised the Japanese

This postcard commemorates the Portsmouth, New Hampshire, conference of 1905, which ended a war between Russia and Japan. It pictures the Russian czar, the Japanese mikado, President Roosevelt, and other negotiators. The president won the Nobel Peace Prize for his role in arranging the conference. *(Library of Congress, Prints and Photographs Division, LC-USZ62-78462)*

that in my judgment it would be the gravest mistake on their part to insist on continuing the war for the sake of a money indemnity. . . .

Theodore Roosevelt describes negotiations leading to the Treaty of Portsmouth, September 1905, Autobiography *(1913), pp. 555–57.*

As to what you say about disarmament—which I suppose is the rough equivalent of "the gradual diminution of the oppressive burdens imposed upon the world by armed peace"—I am not clear either as to what can be done or what ought to be done. . . . If this country had not fought the Spanish War . . . all mankind would have been the loser. While the Turks were butchering the Armenians the European powers kept the peace and thereby added a burden of infamy to the Nineteenth Century, for in keeping that peace a greater number of lives were lost than in any European war since the days of Napoleon, and these lives were those of women and children as well as of men; while the moral degradation, the brutality inflicted and endured, the aggregate of hideous wrong done, surpassed that of any war of which we have record in modern times. Until people get it firmly fixed in their minds that peace is valuable chiefly as a means to righteousness, and that it can only be considered as an end when it also coincides with righteousness, we can do only a limited amount to advance its coming on this earth.

President Theodore Roosevelt, letter to statesman Carl Schurz, September 8, 1905, reprinted in Autobiography *(1913), pp. 560–561.*

When speaking of "gradual disarmament," I did not mean to say that all the armies and navies of the world should be dismissed. . . . I meant only that the movement to be set on foot should have as its object to put a limit to the excessive and constantly growing armaments which are becoming so oppressive to the nations of the world. . . .

Neither do I deny that there have been wars which were useful to humanity in promoting progress, or in establishing justice, while at the same time I believe that there have also been many wars which were not only unnecessary in every sense, and therefore criminal, but which distinctly made for injustice, tyranny and demoralization. . . .

Admitting all you say of the Armenian atrocities, have we not to face the fact that the Powers stood by, without lifting a hand, although they were armed to the teeth? And does not this fact go far to show that they raised and maintained their vast and burdensome armaments not against the hosts of unrighteousness, but against one another—or at least because of fear, suspicion or jealousy of one another?

Carl Schurz, letter of September 14, 1905, in response to President Roosevelt's letter of September 8, in Schurz's Speeches, Correspondence and Political Papers *(1913), pp. 437–38.*

Gullible America will spend this year some seventy-five millions of dollars in the purchase of patent medicines. In consideration of this sum it will swallow huge quantities of alcohol, an appalling amount of opiates and narcotics, a wide assortment of varied drugs ranging from powerful and dangerous heart depressants to insidious liver stimulants; and far in excess of all other ingredients, undiluted fraud. For fraud, exploited by the skilfulest of advertising bunco men, is the basis of the trade. Should the newspapers, the magazines, and the medical journals refuse their pages to this class of advertisements, the patent medicine business in five years would be as scandalously historic as the South Sea Bubble. . . .

When one comes to the internal remedies, the proprietary medicines proper, they all belong to the tribe of Capricorn, under one of two heads, harmless frauds or deleterious drugs. For instance, the laxatives perform what they promise; but taken regularly, as thousands of people take them (and indeed, as advertisements urge), they become an increasingly baneful necessity. Acetanilid will undoubtedly relieve headache of certain kinds; but acetanilid, as the basis of headache powders, is prone to

remove the cause of the symptom permanently by putting a complete stop to the heart action. Invariably, when taken steadily it produces constitutional disturbances of insidious development which result fatally if the drug be not discontinued, and often it enslaves the devotee to its use. Cocaine and opium stop pain; but the narcotics are not the safest drugs to put in the hands of the ignorant, particularly when their presence is concealed in the "cough remedies," "soothing syrups," and "catarrhal powders" of which they are the basis. Few outside of the rabid temperance advocates will deny a place in medical practice to alcohol. But alcohol, fed daily and in increasing doses to women and children, makes not for health, but for drunkenness.

Muckraker Samuel Hopkins Adams, "The Great American Fraud," part of his series on patent medicines in Collier's, *vol. 36 (October 7, 1905), pp. 14–15.*

The Department of Justice has for the last four years devoted more attention to the enforcement of the antitrust legislation than to anything else. Much has been accomplished, particularly marked has been the moral effect of the prosecutions; but it is increasingly evident that there will be a very insufficient beneficial result in the way of economic change. The successful prosecution of one device to evade the law immediately develops another device to accomplish the same purpose. What is needed is not sweeping prohibition of every arrangement, good or bad, which may tend to restrict competition, but such adequate supervision and regulation as will prevent any restriction of competition from being to the detriment of the public—as well as such supervision and regulation as will prevent other abuses in no way connected with restriction of competition. Of these abuses, perhaps the chief, although by no means the only one, is overcapitalization—generally itself the result of dishonest promotion—because of the myriad evils it brings in its train; for such overcapitalization often means an inflation that invites business panic; it always conceals the true relation of the profit earned to the capital actually invested, and it creates a burden of interest payments which is a fertile cause of improper reduction in or limitation of wages; it damages the small investor, discourages thrift, and encourages gambling and speculation; while perhaps worst of all is the trickiness and dishonesty which it implies—for harm to morals is worse than any possible harm to material interests, and the debauchery of politics and business by great dishonest corporations is far worse than any actual material evil they do the public. Until the National Government obtains . . . proper control over the big corporations engaged in interstate commerce—that is, over the great majority of the big corporations—it will be impossible to deal adequately with these evils.

Theodore Roosevelt on governmental control of business corporations, Fifth Annual Message to Congress, December 5, 1905, Works, *vol. 15, pp. 273–74.*

The treason of the Senate! Treason is a strong word, but not too strong, rather too weak, to characterize the situation in which the Senate is the eager, resourceful, indefatigable agent of interests as hostile to the American people as any invading army could be, and vastly more dangerous; interests that manipulate the prosperity produced by all, so that it heaps up riches for the few; interests whose growth and power can only mean the degeneration of the people, of the educated into sycophants, of the masses toward serfdom.

A man cannot serve two masters. The senators are not elected by the people; they are elected by the "interests." A servant obeys him who can punish and dismiss. Except in extreme and rare and negligible instances, can the people either elect or dismiss a senator?

Muckraker David Graham Phillips, The Treason of the Senate, *(1906), p. 59.*

Resolved further, That the Senate, as a part of this act of ratification, understands that the participation of the United States in the Algeciras conference was with the sole purpose of preserving and increasing its commerce in Morocco, the protection as to life, liberty, and property of its citizens residing or traveling therein, and of aiding by its friendly offices and efforts, in removing friction and controversy which seemed to menace the peace between powers signatory with the United States to the treaty of 1880, all of which are on terms of amity with this Government; and without purpose to depart from the traditional American foreign policy which forbids participation by the United States in the settlement of political questions which are entirely European in their scope.

Reservations added to the Convention of Algeciras by the U.S. Senate, 1906, in Malloy, ed., Treaties, Conventions, *vol. 2, pp. 2182–83.*

I can't stand and live and breathe if I take this allotment. Under the allotment rules I would see all around me . . . people who are ready to grab from us my living and my home. If I would accept such a plan I would be going into starvation. To take and put the Indians on the land in severalty would be just the same as burying them, for they could not live.

Redbird Smith, a Cherokee, to the Congressional Select Committee to Investigate Matters Connected with Affairs in the Indian Territory, 1906, quoted in Baird and Goble, The Story of Oklahoma, *p. 319.*

Then I discovered East Broadway. I know of no street in the world which at that time teemed so tempestuously with movements, ideals, ideologies as did this broad and humble thorough-fare in the heart of New York's East Side. Here were Anarchists, Social Revolutionaries, Social Democrats, Social Populists, Zionists, Zangwillites, Assimilationists, Internationalists, Single Taxers, Republicans, Democrats, each group with its own gods, dead and alive, its own demons too, dead and alive, its own headquarters, its own press, its own lectures and debates and its own impassioned resolve to save something or somebody, the working peoples of America, the working peoples of the world, the Russian muzhiks, the Russian proletariat, all the Russian people, the Jews of America, the Jews of the world, the American farmer, the American proletariat, all the American people, all the immigrant peoples. I never had realized that there were so many different ways of achieving salvation or that there were so many people, indeed 101 masses of them, passionately engrossed in bringing it to somebody except to themselves. And lurking in quiet places, in basements, on stoops of houses was another set of crusaders, well-dressed, well-groomed, soft-spoken, always affable and smiling, and they were seeking to save everybody, but especially the immigrant Jews, for Jesus!

Maurice Hindus, a Russian who immigrated to New York at age 14 in 1905, describes New York's Lower East Side, ca. 1906, Green Worlds *(1938), pp. 100–01.*

At early dawn I was out on the street again to gaze at the buildings, one of which was large enough to house the people of my home town, and at Brooklyn Bridge, which was thrice as broad as the King's Highway running through Denmark, and at the trains above my head and under my feet that were ten times speedier than the narrow-gauge train of the dunes.

Frantic streams of sweatshop workers climbed the subway stairs, leaped out of street cars, poured forth from ferries, rushed down from elevated stations. Children carried box wood home from wholesale stores and market places. Bent old men carted bulky sacks of rags to their junk shops. Sailor tramps told doleful stories of shipwrecks in which they had lost their belongings, from the gold they had dug in Alaska to their mother's Bible. . . .

On West Street tangled teams and trucks and peddlers' carts blocked the horse cars that clanged their bells with yowling petulance, while teamsters cursed, peddlers sang, ferries tooted. On one side of the street rows on rows of immigrant liners lay moored. . . .

Labor bureaus shipped away immigrants to mines and mills and factories. The labor market was flooded. Weeping with gratitude they went. Every day brought fresh hordes ashore. For every man who found work a hundred others stepped ashore from the Ellis Island ferry.

Carl Christian Jensen, who immigrated from Denmark in 1906 at age 18, describes his first impressions of Manhattan, An American Saga *(1927), pp. 66–67.*

We had reached Riverside [California] without any plans and with very little money, not knowing what we could do for a living. After much discussion with friends, it was decided that Mother should cook for about thirty single men who worked in the citrus groves. Father did not like her to work, but it seemed to be the only way we could make a living for ourselves. She would make their breakfast at 5 A.M., pack their lunches, and cook them supper at 7 P.M. But my parents did not have the cooking utensils we needed, so Father went to the Chinese settlement and told them of our situation. He could not speak Chinese but he wrote *hanmun*, the character writing that is the same in Korean and Chinese. He asked for credit, promising to make regular payments from time to time. They trusted him and agreed to give us everything we needed to get started: big iron pots and pans, dishes, tin lunch pails, chopsticks, and so forth. They also gave us rice and groceries.

The Korean men went to the dumpyard nearby and found the wood to build a shack large enough for our dining area. They made one long table and two long benches to seat thirty men. Father made a large stove and oven with mud and straw, and he found several large wine barrels to hold the water for drinking and cooking. That was the start of our business. . . .

Mary Paik Lee, who arrived in the United States at age six from Korea via Hawaii in 1906, in her Quiet Odyssey *(1990), pp. 14–15.*

In 1905, 1906, and 1907, more than 1 million immigrants arrived in America each year. This photo shows the crowded deck of the SS *Patricia* in 1906. *(Library of Congress, Prints and Photographs Division, LC-USZ62-11202)*

As an abstract proposition, the state has the right and the duty to compel all employers to pay a Living Wage. The function of the state is to promote the social welfare. The social welfare means in practice the welfare of all individuals over whom the state has authority; and the welfare of the individual includes all those conditions that assist in the pursuit of his earthly end, namely, the reasonable development of his personality. The primary business of the state, then, is to protect men in the enjoyment of those opportunities that are essential to right and reasonable life. They may be summed up in the phrase "natural rights." . . . Now, a law requiring employers to pay a Living Wage . . . would be an attempt to protect natural rights and to provide one of the essential conditions of reasonable human life. Even those who hold that the sole function of the state is to safeguard individuals against violence and injustice, in other words, to protect life and property, could logically admit that the enactment of such a law would not be an undue exercise of power. To compel a man to work for less than a Living Wage is as truly an act of injustice as to pick his pocket. In a wide sense it is also an attack upon his life.

Father John Ryan, Catholic proponent of the social gospel, A Living Wage *(1906), pp. 301–02, 313–14.*

I hear that "States rights" is to be used as the excuse for killing this bill. I say there are no "States rights" involved in this bill. . . . [N]either in this nor in any other important question have the States ever succeeded in having uniform laws; and it is clear that this evil can not be remedied unless there are uniform laws upon it. . . .

A child that grows up in New York and becomes a citizen is not alone a citizen of New York. He is a citizen of the Republic as well. He does not vote exclusively if he is in North Carolina for North Carolina candidates. He votes for the President of the Republic; he votes for members of the legislature that elect a United States Senator; he votes for a Congressman. He is as much a citizen of the Nation as he is a citizen of the State, and when any system of labor or of lack of education ruins him for citizenship in the State he is ruined for citizenship in the Nation.

Senator Albert Beveridge, Republican of Indiana, speaks in favor of his bill to restrict child labor, January 29, 1909, Congressional Record, *59th Congress, vol. 41, part 2, p. 1808.*

One can not but wish that with his expressed desire for "fair play" and his policy of "a square deal" it had occurred to the President that, if five million American women are employed in gainful occupations, every principle of justice would demand that they should be enfranchised to enable them to secure legislation for their own protection. In all governments a subject class is always at a disadvantage and at the mercy of the ruling class. It matters not whether its name be

Empire, Kingdom or Republic, whether the rulers are one or many,—and in a democracy there is no way known for any class to protect its interests or to be secure in its most sacred rights except through the power of the ballot. . . .

Anna Howard Shaw, president of NAWSA, comments on President Roosevelt's policies, at the national convention in Baltimore, February 1906, in Harper, ed., History of Woman Suffrage, *vol. 5, p. 157.*

We Americans do not rank among the enlightened nations when we are graded according to our care of our children. We have, according to the last census, 580,000 who cannot read or write, between the ages of ten and fourteen years, not immigrant but native-born children, and 570,000 of them are in States where the women do not even use their right of petition. We do not rank with England, Germany, France, Switzerland, Holland or the Scandinavian countries when we are measured by our care of our children, we rank with Russia. The same thing is true of our children at work. We have two millions of them earning their living under the age of sixteen years. Legislation of the States south of Maryland for the children is like the legislation of England in 1844. . . . Surely it behooves us to do something at once or what sort of citizens shall we have?

Child labor activist Florence Kelley addresses NAWSA at its national convention in Baltimore, February 1906, in Harper, ed., History of Woman Suffrage, *vol. 5, pp. 164–65.*

Unsanitary housing, poisonous sewage, contaminated water, infant mortality, the spread of contagion, adulterated food, impure milk, smoke-laden air, ill-ventilated factories, dangerous occupations, juvenile crime, unwholesome crowding, prostitution and drunkenness are the enemies which the modern cities must face and overcome, would they survive. Logically their electorate should be made up of those who can bear a valiant part in this arduous contest, those who in the past have at least attempted to care for children, to clean houses, to prepare foods, to isolate the family from moral dangers; those who have traditionally taken care of that side of life which inevitably becomes the subject of municipal consideration and control as soon as the population is congested. To test the elector's fitness to deal with this situation by his ability to bear arms is absurd. These problems must be solved, if they are solved at all, not from the military point of view, not even from the industrial point of view, but from a third, which is rapidly developing in all the great cities of the world—the human-welfare point of view. . . .

City housekeeping has failed partly because women, the traditional housekeepers, have not been consulted as to its multiform activities. The men have been carelessly indifferent to much of this civic housekeeping, as they have always been indifferent to the details of the household. . . . The very multifariousness and complexity of a city government demand the help of minds accustomed to detail

and variety of work, to a sense of obligation for the health and welfare of young children and to a responsibility for the cleanliness and comfort of other people.

Jane Addams's classic municipal housekeeping address to NAWSA, at the national convention in Baltimore, February 1906, in Harper, ed., History of Woman Suffrage, *vol. 5, pp. 178–79*

Mr. Chairman, this is a great question. . . . One-twelfth of all the wealth in the United States is involved in greater or less degree in this bill. The earnings of the railways are so colossal that $2,100,000,000 mark the amount of this great interest in one year. Our whole wealth production is but ten times more than that. Think how colossal this is. But the aggregate of investments, the aggregate of annual earnings does not mark fairly the importance of this subject to the American people. Think how dependent we are for our prosperity, for the comforts of life even, upon the common carriers of the land. Think of the infinitude of the transactions between the carrier and those they serve millions and millions of transactions.

And yet, Mr. Chairman, the gentleman from Massachusetts announced the astonishing doctrine that . . . in all of these multiplied transactions there shall be no practical arbiter, no one to settle disputes except one of the parties in interest. . . .

William P. Hepburn, Republican representative from Iowa and sponsor of the railroad regulation bill named for him, speech in the House, February 7, 1906, Congressional Record, *59th Congress, 1 Session, p. 2253.*

As you know the enemies of our international trade unions, the so-called I.W.W. which is another name for the Socialists Labor Party, is doing all it can to get our fellow workmen into trouble wherever it can. The policy they now pursue is to insinuate all sorts of ulterior motives to the officers of international trade unions, and to have the men make demands which they know in advance will be unsuccessful to alienate the loyalty of these men from their international unions. This has been attempted in Schenectady, but which by timely action of some of our international union officers and this office has been checked. They are now engaged in such a movement in Youngstown, Ohio, and the Mahoning Valley. . . .

I am confident that the trade union movement is founded upon a basis of philosophy so strong, that it will overcome all of its enemies either individually or combined, but we can not remain indifferent to the assaults. . . .

Samuel Gompers, president of the AFL, to Lew Morton, secretary of the affiliated Actors' National Protective Union of America in New York, May 31, 1906, available online at Samuel Gompers Papers. URL:http://www.history. umd.edu/Gompers/iww1906.html.

Sec. 2. . . . That every Common carrier subject to the provisions of this Act shall file . . . and print and keep open to public inspection schedules showing all the rates, fares, and charges for transportation between different points on its own route and between points on its own route and points on the route of any other carrier by railroad, by pipe line, or by water when a through route and joint route have been established. . . . The schedules printed as aforesaid by any such common carrier shall plainly state . . . any rules or regulations which in any wise change, affect, or determine any part or the aggregate of such aforesaid rates, fares, and charges. . . .

No change shall be made in the rates, fares, and charges which have been filed and published by any common carrier in compliance with the requirements of this section, except after thirty days' notice to the [Interstate Commerce] Commission and to the public published as aforesaid, which shall plainly state the changes . . . in the schedule then in force and the time when the changed rates, fares, or charges will go into effect. . . .

Sec. 20. The Commission is hereby authorized to require annual reports from all common carriers subject to the provisions of this act . . . and to require from such carriers specific answers to all questions upon which the Commission may need information. . . .

The Hepburn Act, June 19, 1906, U.S. Statutes at Large,
59th Congress, vol. 34, part 1, pp. 586, 593.

Meantime it became known to [Abe] Ruef that [Golden M.] Roy had come over to our side, and in order to frighten him into silence Ruef had introduced into the Board of Supervisors an ordinance making it illegal for any girl under eighteen years of age to visit a skating rink without her mother. If this became a law, Roy and Maestretti's business, Dreamland [Rollerskating] Rink, was doomed.

Roy, far from being intimidated, responded to this threat with a brilliant idea. He suggested to us that by means of this proposed ordinance we could trap the supervisors. His plan was to bribe them to kill the ordinance, have them caught taking the money, and terrorize them into confessing the overhead trolley briberies.

We rehearsed for the plan in Roy's office at Pavilion Rink. There was another room next to his office, in which we planned to hide and watch the bribery. Burns borrowed a gimlet from a nearby grocery store, and we bored three holes through the door, so that three people could look into Roy's office. When this was done, Burns and I stood on the other side of the door and looked through the holes, while Roy rehearsed the coming scene.

Roy sat at his table with imaginary bills in his hand, and the chairs placed in such a position that we could see him. Then, leaning toward the empty chair in which the unsuspecting supervisor was to be placed, Roy began, pretending that Supervisor Tom Lonergan was present.

"Tom, I want that skating rink bill killed. If it goes through—"

We would interrupt. "A little louder, Roy—" "Move over to the right. Now go ahead."

"Tom, I want that skating rink bill killed. I'm willing to pay $500 for it, and here's the money. The bill's coming up tonight, and I want you to go against it."

The rehearsal was perfect. It was beyond my imagination to conceive of anything like that being fulfilled, and I said to Roy, "It's too much of a melodrama for me. I can't believe it's possible that anything like this will ever happen." Roy replied, "Don't worry. It will happen exactly as we have planned it."

And it did.

Newspaper editor Fremont Older describes the investigation of
corruption in San Francisco, fall of 1906, My Own Story,
Chapter 19, available online at "California As I Saw It."
URL: http://lcweb2.loc.gov/ammem/cbhtml/cbhome.html.

Another reason for my opposition to the liquor traffic was the evil effect it had in politics, and the administration of government. The liquor interests had no political convictions. The forces behind it gathered around them the worst elements in society and used them as the balance of power to defeat any party that would not favor the liquor traffic. This condition had a tendency to put men in office who were influenced and even corrupted by the liquor interests. Especially was this so in a new country where the standards of society had not become fixed and law enforcement was lax. . . .

Charles Haskell, first governor of Oklahoma state, November
1906, "Governor Haskell Tells of Two Conventions,"
Chronicles of Oklahoma, vol. 14 (June 1936),
pp. 212–13.

Affiant [the person giving an affidavit] . . . was garrisoned at Fort Browne, Tex., on the 13th day of August, 1906, and a member of Company B, Twenty-Fifth United States Infantry. That on August 13, 1906, near 4 o'clock, Lieut. George C. Lawson, and company commander, said to him, "Sergeant, are there any men in town on pass?" to which he replied "No, sir; no men on pass." Lieutenant Lawson said, "Send me two responsible men." Affiant obeyed said order, and sent Sergt. Walker McCurcy and Corporal Waddington. Said Officer Lawson told the men to go all over town and if they saw any of Company B's men to tell them to report at quarters once.

Said officer asked affiant to publish on retreat that no man of the company would be allowed in town after 8 o'clock.

Affiant further says that on the evening of the 13th of August, 1906, he retired to his quarters; that he was aroused about 12:30 by his wife, and that he heard firing, which, from his long army experience, he knew that there were mixed arms being fired. He at once rushed to his company's quarters, gave the order to fall in, and proceeded to call the roll. The time when he was first aroused and the calling of the roll consumed about ten minutes. That on roll call only 4 men were absent out of 57, and that the men absent were Elmer Brown, detailed at Major Penrose's stables as help; John Brown, assistant baker at post bake house; William Smith, who was upstairs in quarters asleep; Alfred N. Williams, on duty quartermaster corral; that as he called the roll the firing was still going on downtown. . . .

Affiant further says, according to his best knowledge and belief, every gun was intact and locked the previous evening. . . .

Affidavit of Sergeant Mingo Sanders concerning the Brownsville incident, November 24, 1906, United States War Department, Discharge of Enlisted Men, *p. 228.*

We turned out the lights early, as did all our neighbors. No one removed his clothes or thought of sleep. Apprehension was tangible. We could almost touch its cold and clammy surface. Toward midnight the unnatural quiet was broken by a roar that grew steadily in volume. . . .

Father told Mother to take my sisters, the youngest of them only six, to the rear of the house, which offered more protection from stones and bullets. My brother George was away, so Father and I, the only males in the house, took our places at the front windows of the parlor. The windows opened on a porch along the front side of the house, which in turn gave onto a narrow lawn that sloped down to the street and a picket fence. There was a crash as Negroes smashed the street lamp at the corner of Houston and Piedmont Avenue down the street. In a very few minutes the vanguard of the mob, some of them bearing torches, appeared. A voice which we recognized as that of the son of the grocer with whom we had traded for many years yelled, "That's where that nigger mail carrier lives! Let's burn it down! It's too nice for a nigger to live in!" In the eerie light Father turned his drawn face toward me. In a voice as quiet as though he were asking me to pass him the sugar at the breakfast table, he said, "Son, don't shoot until the first man puts his foot on the lawn and then— don't you miss!"

Walter White, later national secretary of the NAACP, remembers the Atlanta race riot, September 1906, when he was 13, in his autobiography, A Man Called White, *p. 10.*

I would especially urge the colored people in Atlanta and elsewhere to exercise self-control and not make the fatal mistake of attempting to retaliate, but to rely upon the efforts of the proper authorities to bring order and security out of confusion. If they do this they will have the sympathy of good people the world over. . . .

The Atlanta outbreak should not discourage our people, but should teach a lesson from which all can profit. And we should bear in mind also that while there is disorder in one community there is peace and harmony in thousands of others. As a colored man I cannot refrain from expressing a feeling of very deep grief on account of the death of so many innocent men of both races because of the deeds of a few despicable criminals.

Booker T. Washington, statement about the Atlanta riot quoted in "Atlanta Slays Black Citizens Scores Killed," New York Age, *September 27, 1906, p. 1.*

Uniform accounting plays much the same part in all business combinations that the high speed elevator plays in our twenty-story buildings; without it the whole structure would be useless and impossible. How is it with cities, with towns and other municipal divisions? Have they uniform and comparative accounting to-day? Most assuredly not. . . . Have, indeed, our municipalities as a whole anything in the nature of a scientific, comprehensive and yet concise and simple system for keeping their accounts and making their reports? My experience proves to me that as a whole they most certainly have not, and that on the contrary the accounting and reporting of the great majority of the municipalities throughout this country is crude, unsystematic, inaccurate and away behind the times. Could any of our great businesses be carried on to-day if their accounting was the same or no better than that of our cities and towns? The answer is self-evident; not one of them could live a year under such conditions.

Harvey S. Chase, public accountant and auditor in Boston, in his "Municipal Accounting," Annals of the American Academy of Political and Social Science, *vol. 28 (November 1906), p. 457.*

There is a matter to which I wish to call your special attention, and that is the desirability of conferring full American citizenship upon the people of Porto Rico. They are loyal, they are glad to be under our flag, they are making rapid progress along the path of orderly liberty. Surely, we should show our appreciation of them, our pride in what they have done, and our pleasure in extending recognition for what has thus been done, by granting them full American citizenship.

Under the wise administration of the present Governor and the Council, marked progress has been made in the difficult matter of granting to the people of the island the largest measure of self-government that can *with safety* be given at the present time. . . . It has not been easy to instill into the minds of people unaccustomed to the exercise of freedom the two basic principles of our American system—the principle that the majority must rule, and the principle that the minority has rights which must not be disregarded or trampled upon. Yet real progress has been made....

President Roosevelt's report to Congress after his visit to Puerto Rico, December 11, 1906, as printed in the New York Times, December 12, p. 7.

The program on Christmas Eve was as follows: first a short speech by me saying what we were going to do, then some phonograph music.—The music on the phonograph being Handel's 'Largo'. Then came a violin solo by me, being a composition of Gounod called 'O, Holy Night', and ending up with the words 'Adore and be still' of which I sang one verse, in addition to playing on the violin, though the singing of course was not very good. Then came the Bible text, 'Glory to God in the highest and on earth peace to men of good will', and finally we wound up by wishing them a Merry Christmas and then saying that we proposed to broadcast again New Year's Eve.

The broadcast on New Year's Eve was the same as before, except that the music was changed and I got someone else to sing. I had not picked myself to do the singing, but on Christmas Eve I could not get any of the others to either talk, sing or play and consequently had to do it myself.

On New Year's Eve one man, I think it was Stein, agreed to sing and did sing, but none of the others either sang or talked.

We got word of reception of the Christmas Eve program as far down as Norfolk, Va., and on the New Year's Eve program we got word from some places down in the West Indies.

Reginald Fessenden describes the first radio voice broadcasts, December 24 and December 31, 1906, in Fessenden, Fessenden, Builder of Tomorrows (1940), pp. 153–54.

Approximate equality is the only enduring foundation of political democracy. The sense of equality is the only basis for Christian morality....

That fundamental democracy of social intercourse, which is one of the richest endowments of our American life, is slipping from us. Actual inequality endangers the sense of equality.... It may be denied that the poor in our country are getting poorer, but it cannot well be denied that the rich are getting richer. The extremes of wealth and poverty are much farther apart than formerly, and thus the poor are at least relatively poorer. There is a rich class and a poor class, whose manner of life is wedged farther and farther apart, and whose boundary lines are becoming ever more distinct....

We hear passionate protests against the use of the hateful word "class" in America. There are no classes in our country, we are told. But the hateful part is not the word, but the thing. If class distinctions are growing up here, he

serves his country ill who would hush up the fact or blind the people to it by fine phrases....

Individual sympathy and understanding has been our chief reliance in the past for overcoming the differences between the social classes. The feelings and principles implanted by Christianity have been a powerful aid in that direction. But if this sympathy diminishes by the widening of the social chasm, what hope have we? It is true that we have an increasing number who, by study and by personal contact in settlement work and otherwise, are trying to increase that sympathetic intelligence. But it is a question if this conscious effort of individuals is enough to offset the unconscious alienation created by the dominant facts of life which are wedging entire classes apart.

Rev. Walter Rauschenbusch, Christianity and the Social Crisis *(1907), pp. 45–50.*

The Standard [Standard Oil] has repeatedly asserted that combination, as illustrated by its own history, is a great benefit to the public, in reducing costs and consequently prices. It may readily be observed that in some industries combination has had these beneficial results. It is probable that the Standard, by reason of its undoubtedly great efficiency, could, had it been content with reasonable profits, have made prices to consumers lower than would have been possible for smaller concerns, and thus have maintained its great proportion of the business by wholly fair and legitimate means.

The Standard is, however, a most conspicuous example of precisely the opposite—of a combination which maintains a substantial monopoly, not by superiority of service and by charging reasonable prices, but by unfair methods of destroying competition; a combination which then uses the power thus unfairly gained to oppress the public through highly extortionate prices. It has raised prices instead of lowering them. It has pocketed all the advantages of its economies instead of sharing them with the public, and has added still further monopoly profits by charging more than smaller and less economical concerns could sell for if the Standard allowed them the chance....

U.S. Bureau of Corporations, Report of the Commissioner of Corporations *on the petroleum industry and Standard Oil, 1907, pp. xliv–xlv.*

In order that the best results might follow from an enforcement of the regulations, an understanding was reached with Japan that the existing policy of discouraging emigration of its subjects of the laboring classes to continental United States should be continued, and should, by co-operation with the governments, be made as effective as possible. This understanding contemplates that the Japanese government shall issue passports to continental United States only to such of its subjects as are non-laborers or are laborers who, in coming to the continent, seek to resume a formerly acquired domicile, to join a parent, wife, or children residing there, or to assume active control of an already possessed interest in a farming enterprise in this country, so that the three classes of laborers entitled to receive passports have come to be designated "former residents," "parents, wives, or children of residents," and "settled agriculturists."

With respect to Hawaii, the Japanese government of its own volition stated that, experimentally at least, the issuance of passports to members of the laboring classes proceeding thence would be limited to "former residents" and "parents, wives, or children of residents." The said government has also been exercising a careful supervision over the subject of emigration of its laboring class to foreign contiguous territory.

Description of the Gentleman's Agreement with Japan in 1907, in Report of the Commissioner General of Immigration, *1908, reprinted in Commager, ed.,* Documents of American History, *vol. 2, p. 45.*

Three years ago I owned a little mountain farm of two hundred acres. I had two good horses, two good cows, plenty of hogs, sheep and several calves. I had three girls and two boys; ages run from 11 to 21. On my little farm I raised about four hundred bushels of corn, thirty to forty bushels of wheat, two hundred to three hundred dozen oats, and cut from four to eight stacks of hay during the summer. After I clothed my family, fed all my stock during the winter, I had only enough provisions and feed to carry me through making another crop, and no profit left. I sold my farm and stock, paid up all my debts and moved my family to a cotton mill. At that time green hands had to work for nothing til they learned their job, about one month, but now my youngest daughter, only 14 years old, is making $6 per week, my other two are making $7.50 each per week and my two boys are making $8 per week and I am making $4.50 per week; a total of $166 per month. My provisions average $30, house rent $2, coal and wood, $4, total $36; leaving a balance of $130, to buy clothes and deposit in the bank.

A flier circulated by a cotton mill in North Carolina to attract working families, Kohn, Cotton Mills of South Carolina *(1907), pp. 30–31.*

In Bunyan's Pilgrim's Progress you may recall the description of the Man with the Muckrake, the man who could look no way but down . . . but continued to rake to himself the filth of the floor.

. . . [H]e also typifies the man who in this life consistently refuses to see aught that is lofty, and fixes his eyes with solemn intentness only on that which is vile and debasing. Now, it is very necessary that we should not flinch from seeing what is vile and debasing. There is filth on the floor, and it must be scraped up with the muckrake; and there are times and places where this service is the most needed of all services that can be performed. But the man who never does anything else, who never thinks or speaks or writes save of his feats with the muck-rake, speedily becomes, not a help to society, not an incitement to good, but one of the most potent forces of evil.

. . . There should be relentless exposure of and attack upon every evil man, whether politician or businessman, every evil practice, whether in politics, in business, or in social life. I hail as a benefactor every writer or speaker, every man who, on the platform or in a book, magazine or newspaper, with merciless severity makes such an attack, provided always that he in his turn remembers that the attack is of use only if it is absolutely truthful. . . . It puts a premium upon knavery untruthfully to attack an honest man, or even with hysterical exaggeration to assail a bad man with untruth.

President Roosevelt gives the Muckrakers a name, "The Man With the Muck-Rake," speech at the cornerstone ceremony for the House Office Building, April 14, 1906, reprinted in Phillips, Treason of the Senate, *pp. 217–18.*

To the School Children of the United States:

. . . It is well that you should celebrate your Arbor Day thoughtfully, for within your lifetime the Nation's need of trees will become serious. We of an elder generation can get along with what we have, though with growing hardship; but in your full manhood and womanhood you will want what nature once so bountifully supplied and man so thoughtlessly destroyed; and because of that want you will reproach us, not for what we have used, but for what we have wasted.

For the Nation as for the man or woman and the boy or girl, the road to success is the right use of what we have and the improvement of present opportunity. . . .

A people without children would face a hopeless future; a country without trees is almost as hopeless; forests which are so used that they cannot renew themselves will soon vanish, and with them all their benefits. A true forest is not merely a storehouse full of wood, but, as it were, a factory of wood, and at the same time a reservoir of water. When you help to preserve our forests or to plant new ones you are acting the part of good citizens. . . .

Letter of President Roosevelt, April 15, 1907, distributed to the schools of the nation, available online at American Time Capsule. URL: http://memory.loc.gov/ ammem/rbpehtml/pehome.html.

EARTHQUAKE AND FIRE: SAN FRANCISCO IN RUINS

Death and destruction have been the fate of San Francisco. Shaken by a temblor at 5:13 o'clock yesterday morning,

San Francisco burning: On April 18, 1906, the city was hit by a powerful earthquake. Over the next four days much of the city was destroyed by fires that ignited in its wake. Historians call the event the Great Earthquake, but for many years San Franciscans called it the Great Fire. *(Library of Congress, Prints and Photographs Division, LC-USZ62-123115)*

the shock lasting 48 seconds, and scourged by flames that raged diametrically in all directions, the city is a mass of smouldering ruins. At six o'clock last evening the flames seemingly playing with increased vigor, threatened to destroy such sections as their fury had spared during the earlier portion of the day. Building their path in a triangular circuit from the start in the early morning, they jockeyed as the day waned, left the business section, which they had entirely devastated, and skipped in a dozen directions to the residence portions. As night fell they had made their way over into the North Beach section and springing anew to the south they reached out along the shipping section down the bay shore, over the hills and across toward Third and Townsend streets. Warehouses, wholesale houses and manufacturing concerns fell in their path. This completed the destruction of the entire district known as the "South of Market Street." How far they are reaching to the south across the channel cannot be told as this part of the city is shut off from San Francisco papers.

Front page of newspaper published jointly by three San Francisco newspapers on the presses of the Oakland Herald, *the* Call-Chronicle-Examiner, *April 19, 1906, p. 1.*

I was within a stone's throw of that city hall when the hand of an avenging God fell upon San Francisco. The ground rose and fell like an ocean at ebb tide. Then came the crash. Tons upon tons of that mighty pile slid away from the steel framework and destructiveness of that effort was terrific.

I had just reached Golden Gate avenue and Larkin street and had tarried a moment to converse with a couple of policemen. With me were two local newspapermen. We had just bid good-bye to the officers, who proceeded down Larkin street to the City Hall Station. They had gotten midway in the block when the crash came.

I saw those policemen enveloped in a shower of falling stone. Their lives must have been blotted out in an instant. [They survived, but one officer was slightly injured.—G.H.]

"Keep in the middle of the street, Mac," I shouted to one of my friends.

"That is the only avenue of escape," returned he.

We staggered over the bitumen.

It is impossible to judge the length of that shock. To me it seemed an eternity. I was thrown prone on my back and the pavement pulsated like a living thing. Around me the huge buildings, looming up more terrible because of the queer dance they were performing wobbled and veered. Crash followed crash and resounded on all sides. Screeches rent the air as terrified humanity streamed out into the open in agony of despair.

Fred J. Hewitt, "Wreck of City's Buildings Awful," San Francisco Examiner, *April 20, 1906, available online at Museum of the City of San Francisco. URL: http://www.sfmuseum.org/1906/ew4.html.*

We took a few bricks and built a fire between them in the middle of the street, like every one else, and ate our breakfast on the steps of our home.

Frequent "tremblers" sent us scurrying to the road, and as night came on, we gathered some bedding together and went into [Golden Gate] Park, the Mecca of all the city. All day I had been feeding homeless ones who had drifted out from the Mission district, where great clouds of angry smoke were rising and large areas had already been devastated....

I ... hastened to the Park through the gathering twilight, My husband and son had spread a mattress under the protecting branches of some bushes, with a great eucalyptus-tree towering over us. We crawled in, sleeping crosswise of the mattress, and my long coat kept me snug and warm.

The immense fires started by the earthquake now made such a ruddy glow that it was easy to see everything, although the flames were two miles away. No lights were allowed in the Park, and all was soon quiet except the wail of a baby, the clang of an ambulance, and the incessant roll of wheels and tramp of feet.... People were all about us in huddled groups, sleeping the sleep of exhaustion on the lawns and under the shrubbery.

Late in the night I heard a cry, "Bakers wanted! Bakers wanted!" over and over—the first cry of a stricken people for bread. Later came another through the silent night—"Union telegraphers wanted"—to tell the world our awful plight.

Emma M. Burke, wife of a San Francisco attorney, describes the aftermath of April 18, 1906, "Woman's Experience of Earthquake and Fire," Outlook 83 *(June 2, 1906), pp. 274–75.*

All night these tens of thousands fled before the flames. Many of them, the poor people from the labor ghetto, had fled all day as well. They had left their homes burdened with possessions. Now and again they lightened up, flinging out upon the street clothing and treasures they had dragged for miles.

They held on longest to their trunks. . . . The hills of San Francisco are steep, and up these hills, mile after mile, were the trunks dragged. Everywhere were trunks with across them lying their exhausted owners, men and women. Before the march of the flames were flung picket lines of soldiers. And a block at a time, as the flames advanced, these pickets retreated. One of their tasks was to keep the trunk—pullers moving. The exhausted creatures, stirred on by the menace of bayonets, would arise and struggle up the steep pavements, pausing from weakness every five or ten feet.

Often, after surmounting a heart-breaking hill, they would find another wall of flame advancing upon them at right angles and be compelled to change anew the line of their retreat. In the end, completely played out, after toiling for a dozen hours like giants, thousands of them were compelled to abandon their trunks. Here the shopkeepers and soft members of the middle class were at a disadvantage. But the working-men dug holes in vacant lots and backyards and buried their trunks.

Novelist Jack London describes events of April 18, "The Story of an Eyewitness," Collier's, *vol. 37 (May 5, 1906), available online at Museum of the City of San Francisco. URL: http://www.sfmuseum.net/hist5/jlondon.html.*

Yes, I am my brother's keeper. . . . there will be no material change in the condition of the people until we have a new social system based upon the mutual economic interests of the whole people; until you and I and all of us collectively own those things that we collectively need and use.

That is a basic economic proposition. As long as a relatively few men own the railroads, the telegraph, the telephone, own the oilfields and the gasfields and the steel mills, and the sugar refineries and the leather tanneries—own, in short, the sources and means of life—they will corrupt our politics, they will enslave the working class, they will impoverish and debase society, they will do all things that are needful to perpetuate their power as the economic masters and the political rulers of the people. Not until these great agencies are owned and operated by the people can the people hope for any material improvement in their social condition. . . .

Now, we Socialists propose that society in its collective capacity shall produce, not for profit but in abundance to satisfy human wants; that every man shall have the inalienable right to work and receive the full equivalent of all he produces. . . . Every man and every woman will then be economically free. . . .

We are not going to destroy private property. We are going to establish private property—all the private property necessary to house man, keep him in comfort, and satisfy his wants. Eighty percent of the people of the United States have no property today. A few have got it all. They have possessed the people, and when we get into power we will dispossess them.

Eugene V. Debs, "The Issue," speech at Girard, Kansas, after his nomination as Socialist Party candidate for president, May 23, 1908, Debs: His Life, Writings and Speeches, *pp. 475–89 passim.*

Shadyside, lying at the foot of the Palisades, furnished the background for practically every picture we made that first summer. It was a crude ugly little settlement with miserable shacks clinging to the side of the hill, but we had discovered it and had tested its possibilities, so we guarded it jealously from other picture companies.

We carried our suitcases and props up and down the steep road on each trip, and we made our headquarters in a boarding house run for laborers. . . .

It was [director Sidney] Olcott's ambition to finish each one-reel picture in a single day, so he held a stop watch on the final rehearsal. If during the actual training he heard the cameraman say quietly, "Speed up, Sid; film's running out," he would dance up and down shouting, "Hurry up, folks; film's going. Grab her, Jim; kiss her; not too long; quick! Don't wait to put her coat on—out of the scene—hurry now! Out, Max? Good lord! Why didn't you hurry? You should have cut across the side-lines."

For the first picture technique did not permit of the action's being stopped midway. . . .

. . . There were no close-ups, no subtle pauses. There could be no action directly across the foreground because this meant a blurred picture. . . . A stare had to be held, a start had to be violent. If the director wished certain spoken words to register, they were enunciated with exaggerated slowness, leaving no doubt in the mind of the spectator.

Gene Gauntier, early movie actress, writer, and producer, moviemaking in the summer of 1908, "Blazing the Trail," Woman's Home Companion, *vol. 55 (October 1928), pp. 181–82.*

For three hours and a half today Harry Orchard sat in the witness chair at the Haywood trial and recited a history of crimes and bloodshed, the like of which no person in the crowded courtroom had ever imagined. Not in the whole range of "Bloody Gulch" literature will there be found anything that approaches a parallel to the horrible story so calmly and smoothly told by this self-possessed, imperturbable murderer witness. . . .

In 1906 he with another man placed a bomb in the Vindicator Mine at Cripple Creek, Colorado, that exploded and killed two men. Later he informed the officials of the Florence and Cripple Creek Railroad of a plot of the Western Federation to blow up one of their trains, because he had not received money for work done for the federation. He watched the residence of Gov. Peabody of Colorado and planned his assassination by shooting. This was postponed for reasons of policy. He shot and killed a deputy, Lyle Gregory, in Denver. He planned and with another man executed the blowing up of the railway station at the Independence Mine at Independence, Col., which killed fourteen men. He tried to poison Fred Bradley, manager of the Sullivan and Bunk Hill mine, then living in San Francisco, by putting strychnine into his milk when it was left at his door in the morning. This failed, and in November, 1904, he arranged a bomb which blew Bradley into the street when he opened his door in the morning.

Oscar King Davis reports the confessions of Harry Orchard at the Haywood trial, "Orchard Tells About Murders,"
New York Times, *June 6, 1907, p. 1.*

All that nature has done for this state it has done for us, and we are entitled—if we want to use all of the water of the state we are entitled to use it. If we want to use all the mineral wealth and we can get it out we are entitled to use it. It is said that we have depleted the forests and that we have done various other things. That may be true to some extent. I can remember, myself, when there were great pine forests in the states of Pennsylvania and New York, and they have disappeared. What became of them? The great, lofty pines were cut down and put into lumber and went to build houses, to build cities and to build towns. Did they cut any more of that timber than was demanded by the needs and wants of the people? And in place of the unbroken forest which the Pilgrim Fathers found when they landed on the New England coast, in place of that you have smiling farms and thriving towns and cities. Which is the better? Which would you rather have today? Take central New York, with its unbroken farms from New York City to Buffalo, with houses such as no other portion of the United States has ever built for the farmer, and with all the conveniences of civilization possessed by any country in the world. Is it not better than an unbroken forest? Are not men better than trees, valuable as they are? (Great

applause.) I thank God that the trees are gone and that in their place have come men and women, Christian men and Christian women, liberty-loving men and liberty-loving women. . . .

Senator Henry Teller of Colorado defends the anticonservationist viewpoint of many westerners, at a Public Land Convention held in Denver, June 18–20, 1907, available online at Evolution of the Conservation Movement. URL: http://memory.loc.gov/ammem/amrvhtml/conshome.html.

SCHMITZ SENTENCED TO SAN QUENTIN FOR FIVE YEARS

Convicted Mayor Creates a Scene
He Brazenly Affronts Judge Dunne When the Court Pronounces Judgment

Eugene E. Schmitz, for five years Mayor of San Francisco, was yesterday sentenced by Judge Dunne to serve a term of five years—the extreme penalty for his crime—in the penitentiary at San Quentin.

Turbid with the outbursts of unrestrained passion, the scene in the courtroom when sentence was pronounced on the convict Mayor was marred by ugly retort and clamor, and justice strove with riot for a voice. Five times the defendent broke in upon the judge and interrupted him with vehement demands that he be sentenced and not lectured, and when the Court's last words were spoken that pronounced the sentence . . .upon the arrogant Schmitz a cheer broke from the crowd.

Jerry Dinan rose from his seat, but one in the back of the crowd cried out, "Send Dinan with him!" and the Chief of Police, who was himself in court as a defendant, slunk back into his chair beside his attorney.

"This is rather an abnormal proceeding," Attorney Fairall said to the Court, but the noise was such that only the stenographer and the Judge heard him. The bailiffs stood by as though they had been petrified.

Headline and lead story of the San Francisco Chronicle,
July 9, 1907, p. 1.

Mr. Abner Graves, at present a mining engineer of Denver, Colo., . . . claims that the present game of Base Ball was designed and named by Abner Doubleday, of Cooperstown, N.Y., during the Harrison Presidential campaign of 1839 . . .

In this connection it is of interest to know that this Abner Doubleday was a graduate of West Point in 1842, and afterward became famous in the Civil War as the man who sighted the first gun fired from Fort Sumter, April 12, 1861, which opened the War of the Rebellion between the North and South. He afterward became a Major General in the United States Army. . . .

Mr. Abner Graves was a boy playmate and fellow pupil of Abner Doubleday at Green's Select School in Cooperstown, N.Y., in 1839. Mr. Graves, who is still living, says that he was present when Doubleday first outlined with a stick in the dirt the present diamond-shaped Base Ball field, indicating the location of the players in the field on paper, with a crude pencil memorandum of the rules for his new game, which he named *"Base Ball."*

. . . It certainly appeals to an American's pride to have had the great national game of Base Ball created and named by a Major General in the United States Army, and to have that same game played as a camp diversion by the soldiers of the Civil War, who, at the conclusion of the war, disseminated Base Ball throughout the length and breadth of the United States, and thus gave to the game its national character.

Albert Spalding, letter to the Special Baseball Commission he called to determine if baseball was American in origin, July 28, 1907, reprinted in Sullivan, ed., Early Innings, p. 291.

The chief argument against [nickelodeons] was that they corrupted the young. Children of any size who could transport a nickel to the cashier's booth were welcomed. Furthermore, undesirables of many kinds haunted them. Pickpockets found them splendidly convenient, for the lights were always cut off when the picture machine was focused on the canvas. There is no doubt about the fact that many rogues and miscreants obtained licenses and set up these little show-places merely as snares and traps. There were many who thought they had sufficient pull to defy decency in the choice of their slides. Proprietors were said to work hand in glove with lawbreakers. Some were accused of wanton designs to corrupt young girls. Police-Commissioner Bingham denounced the nickel madness as pernicious, demoralizing, and a direct menace to the young. . . .

In of the crowded quarters of the city the nickelet is cropping up almost as thickly as the saloons, and if the nickel delirium continues to maintain its hold there will be, in a few years, more of these cheap amusement-places than saloons. Even now some of the saloon-keepers are complaining that they injure their trade. On one street in Harlem, there are as many as five to a block, each one capable of showing to one thousand people an hour. That is, they have a seating capacity for about two hundred and fifty, and give four shows an hour. Others are so tiny that only fifty can be jammed into the narrow area. They run from early morning until midnight, and their megaphones are barking their lure before the milkman has made his rounds.

Barton W. Currie, "The Nickel Madness," Harper's Weekly, vol. 51 (August 24, 1907), pp. 1246–7.

As Friday the 15th of November will be the last day of the Indian Territory and after that we will no longer be a nation, some of us feel that it is a very solemn and important crisis in the history of the Indians. And we want you to join with other women of your neighborhood and spend this last day in fasting and prayer to Almighty God.

I can remember as a little girl hearing my people tell of the trip from Alabama. I can remember them telling of their wrongs and how the white people induced them to come West and made such great promises. I can remember how some of the wiser ones used to predict that in the end all of our power would be taken from us.

Since I've grown up I've witnessed the sly encroachments, step by step, until now I've lived to see the last step taken and the Indian does not count any more even in his own territory. I tell you, our People would not have come out here if they had not been given great promises. They did not want to come. And we had a good government. Our chiefs governed well, I tell you.

One of the two senators elected for the new state of Oklahoma was Robert Owen, who had Cherokee Indian ancestry. Senator Owen later sponsored important progressive legislation, including the Federal Reserve Act and the Child Labor Act. *(Library of Congress, Prints and Photographs Division, LC-USZ62-115124)*

Our laws were enforced. We had order. We had none of this battling until the white people came among us. We had honesty in our dealings. Our chiefs and our judges were good men nearly all.

Mary Herrod, Creek Indian, letter to the Okmulgee Democrat, *November 1907, quoted in Okmulgee Historical Society,* History *(1985), p. 163.*

Article 9. Corporations.

Sect. 15. A Corporation Commission is hereby created, to be composed of three persons, who shall be elected by the people at a general election for State officers. . . .

Sect. 18. The Commission shall have the power and authority and be charged with the duty of supervising, regulating and controlling all transportation and transmission companies doing business in this State, in all matters relating to the performance of their public duties and their charges therefor, and of correcting abuses and preventing unjust discrimination and extortion by such companies; and to that end . . . prescribe and enforce against such companies . . . rates, charges, classifications of traffic, and rules and regulations. . . .

Sect. 40. No corporation organized or doing business in this State shall be permitted to influence elections or official duty by contributions of money or anything of value . . .

Sect. 42. Every license issued or charter granted to a mining or public service corporation, foreign or domestic, shall contain a stipulation that such corporation will submit any difference it may have with employees in reference to labor, to arbitration, as shall be provided by law.

First Oklahoma State Constitution, in effect November 16, 1907, available online at Oklahoma State Court Network. URL: http://www.lsb.state.ok.us/ok_const.html.

One of the two senators for the new state of Oklahoma was Thomas Gore. Senator Gore, who had lost his sight in a childhood accident, was known as the Blind Orator because he was such a powerful speaker. *(Library of Congress, Prints and Photographs Division, LC-USZ62-113073)*

Those who are "interested in the poor" are wondering whether the five-cent theatre is a good influence, and asking themselves gravely whether it should be encouraged or checked (with the help of the police).

Is the theatre a "good" or a "bad" influence? The adjectives don't fit the case. Neither do they fit the case of the nickelodeon, which is merely the theatre democratized. . . .

In this eternal struggle for more self-consciousness, the moving-picture machine, uncouth instrument though it be, has enlisted itself on especial behalf of the least enlightened, those who are below the reach even of the yellow journals. For although in the prosperous vaudeville houses the machine is but a toy, a "chaser," in the nickelodeons it is the central, absorbing fact, which strengthens, widens, vivifies subjective life; which teaches living other than living through the senses alone. Already, perhaps, touching him at the psychological moment, it has awakened to his first, groping, necessary discontent the spirit of an artist of the future, who otherwise would have remained mute and motionless.

Joseph Medill Patterson, "The Nickelodeons," Saturday Evening Post, vol. 180 (November 23, 1907), pp. 11, 38.

Prohibition is now an acute question in this State, and it can not be silenced by anything short of an act of the Legislature, which shall give it a fair trial, and it is likely to become still more acute until such an act is passed. If the selection of candidates shall take place in the disturbed and unsettled state of feeling on the whiskey question, it will be impossible to keep the prohibition question out of the politics of the State in the coming campaign, candidates will be compelled to declare themselves, and no matter which side they take, the other side will be angered, and thus you have the question in politics whether you want it or not.

There is another reason why it is better to have this question settled at once if it can be done. These whiskey elections tend to bring the negro back into politics. When we have one of these elections, my observation is that both sides, with rare exception, get on a brisk hunt for votes. I heard that in more than one of these elections negroes have been registered under the "Grandfather Clause."

Former Governor Jarvis of North Carolina, in Recent Utterances on State Prohibition Compiled by the North Carolina Anti-Saloon League, *1908, available online at Documenting the American South. URL: http://docsouth.unc.edu/nc/utterance/utterance.html*

The testimony of the country people given to me has been nearly uniform, that men coming to town have been largely spared the allurement to drink, and many women have expressed to me their gratification that the head of the family may now come home sober to his family, and without annoyance to them as formerly. . . .

But the strongest indication of the beneficent results of the abolition of the drink traffic appear in the constant prosperity of the retail stores, and their larger gross sales, as I am informed is the case; if this information be correct, then the families of our working population must be better nourished, fed and clothed than under the old order of things, when the earnings, the time, and the strength of our workers was dissipated. I have no reason to regret the change.

—*George B. Hanna, President of the Y. M. C. A., in* Anti-Saloon League of Charlotte, N.C., It Helps Business and Is a Blessing: What Leading Business Men, Bankers, Farmers, Laborers and Others Say about Prohibition in Charlotte, N.C., *1908, available online at Documenting the American South. URL: http://docsouth.unc.edu/ nc/antisaloon/antisaloon.html.*

We favor the passage and the enforcement of laws for the regulation of the drink traffic and for keeping such traffic free from unlawful and improper accessories, and we earnestly desire such improvement in the drinking habits of the people as will still further advance temperance, together with the spread of enlightenment as to the proper functions of drink, whereby the individual may be able to regulate his habits according to the requirements of wholesome living. . . .

The brewers are ready and anxious to do their share, to co-operate to the extent of their power in the work of eliminating abuses connected with the retail trade. While repudiating the charge that theirs is the chief responsibility for the existence of such abuses, they ask the co-operation of the public and of the proper authorities in the work of making the saloon what it ought to be—a place for wholesome refreshment and recreation. . . .

Declaration adopted at Convention of United States Brewers' Association, 1908, reprinted in Monahan, ed., Text-Book of True Temperance, *pp. 237–38.*

German and Italian, Slav and Hebrew played side by side. The day was a prophetic glimpse of the social spirit which will one day permeate the commingled nationalities which in the modern industrial city now crowd and jostle each other. Field Day and playgrounds are weighty units in the mass into which a solid republic is being welded, hammered into one rich alloy from many diverse races and nationalities. The first annual Field Day of the Playground Association, with its five thousand six hundred participants, is only a beginning.

Otto Mallery, head of the Philadelphia branch, National Playground Association of America, in his "Field Day," Playground, *vol. 2 (July 1908), p. 12.*

And yet in spite of the fact that the public school is the great savior of the immigrant district, and the one agency which inducts the children into the changed conditions of American life, there is a certain indictment which may justly be brought, in that the public school too often separates the child from his parents and widens that old gulf between fathers and sons which is never so cruel and so wide as it is between the immigrants who come to this country and their children who have gone to the public school and feel that they have there learned it all. The parents are thereafter subjected to certain judgment, the judgment of the young which is always harsh and in this instance founded upon the most superficial standard of Americanism. And yet there is a notion of culture which we would define as a knowledge of those things which have been long cherished by men, the things which men have loved because thru generations they have softened and interpreted life, and have endowed it with value and meaning. Could this standard have been given rather than the things which they see about them as the test of so-called success, then we might feel that the public school has given at least the beginning of culture which the child ought to have. At present the Italian child goes back to its Italian home more or less disturbed and distracted by the contrast between the school and the home.

Jane Addams speaks to the National Education Association on the perils of vigorous Americanization in the public schools, 1908, published in the NEA's Proceedings and Addresses, *pp. 99–100.*

Take me out to the ball game
Take me out with the crowd.
Buy me some peanuts and Cracker Jack
I don't care if I never get back,
Let me root, root, root for the home team,
For it's one, two, three strikes you're out
At the old ball game.

"Take Me Out To the Ball Game," written by vaudeville entertainer Jack Norworth, with music by Albert von Tilzer, introduced at the Amphion Theatre in Brooklyn, 1908, in Ward and Burns, Baseball, *pp. 96–97.*

Cardinal Gibbons, who was here today, when asked if he believed the people of America were growing better or worse, from a religious standpoint, said:

"The people of America are showing less respect for religion than fifty or sixty years ago. For instance, the statesmen of America of those days showed in their public addresses a familiarity with and regard for the Holy Scriptures and the word of God which I am sorry does not present itself today."

Cardinal James Gibbons of Baltimore decries the decline of public religion, "Public Men Irreligious," New York Times, January 29, 1908, p. 1.

With flags flying, amid the cheers of a dense throng that blocked all traffic on the boulevard in front of the offices of Le Matin, four of the contestants in the New York to Paris auto race left this city this morning on their way to New York to start in the historic contest. There were three French machines and one Italian, each carrying its full heavy equipment that will take it through the United States and Alaska. . . .

The four autos were followed by a large escort of automobiles and made a circuit of the principal boulevards of the city. . . . Crowds gathered everywhere along the route and cheered the brave drivers heartily.

At Rouen the men were met by a delegation of automobile enthusiasts and escorted into the city, where they were entertained at a banquet and toasted by the city officials. The houses were decorated and the streets crowded as on a holiday. . . .

"Cars Leave Paris for New York Race," New York Times, January 29, 1908, p. 1.

Williams Jennings Bryan is convinced that he is the proper legatee of the Roosevelt Administration, the most efficient executor of the Roosevelt policies, and the one most acceptable to the voters of the country, and that in effect is what he told the Democratic Senators who dined with Senator Newlands in his honor last night. . . .

Then he proceeded to tell the Senators how the Democrats ought to work in Congress to make more certain and easy his election by bringing forward measures in accordance with the recommendations of President Roosevelt in his messages. The strategy in this is to put the Republicans in a bad hole, either by forcing them to kill Roosevelt legislation or to adopt it on the Democratic initiative. . . .

After that the Senators listened with a solemn hush while Mr. Bryan lectured them on what they ought to do. He told them that the so-called "Roosevelt policies," which are, in fact "Bryan policies," were without doubt the most popular ones likely to come before the country in the approaching campaign. . . .

"Bryan Plans To Be Roosevelt's Heir," New York Times, January 29, 1908, p. 1.

There is war in Kentucky. In a score of towns what is virtually a state of martial law exists. In the farming districts cellars have been fortified and loaded arms stacked within easy reach. The "Night Riders" are abroad.

. . . By day the planters [that is, farmers] of tobacco, riding in companies, are doggedly proselytizing in protest against what they characterize as the oppressive methods of the American Tobacco Company. Their greeting is characteristic of whole-hearted Kentucky; generally their word of farewell is a warning, perhaps veiled, but menacing. By night bands of masked men are roving with flaming torches and ready revolvers, leaving behind them a trail of devastation and bloodshed. . . .

That the bread and butter of 75 percent of the farmers of the state is endangered, anarchy takes as an excuse for its sway. The so-called tobacco trust, the American Tobacco Company, has been defied by the planters. They are withholding their 1906, 1907, and, in some cases, their 1905 crops from the company's markets. . . .

On the night of the 2nd of March, 1906, they appeared suddenly in the streets of Princeton. They were on horseback, masked, armed, determined. With a preliminary scattering of shots, they applied the torch to several freight cars containing tobacco, some of which had been bought by the American Tobacco Company, and the rest owned by independents. Not until these fires had completely destroyed the tobacco did they leave the city and disappear into the darkness as mysteriously as they had come. . . .

Journalist Charles Tevis describes Kentucky tobacco farmers' method of opposing the tobacco trust, "A Ku-Klux Klan of To-day," Harper's Weekly, vol. 52 (February 8, 1908), p. 14.

That woman's physical structure and the performance of maternal functions place her at a disadvantage in the struggle for subsistence is obvious. This is especially true when the burdens of motherhood are upon her. Even when they are not, by abundant testimony of the medical fraternity continuance for a long time on her feet at work, repeating this from day to day, tends to injurious effects upon the body, and, as healthy mothers are essential to vigorous offspring, the physical well-being of woman becomes an object of public interest and care in order to preserve the strength and vigor of the race.

Still again, history discloses the fact that woman has always been dependent upon man. . . . [I]t is still true that in the struggle for subsistence she is not an equal competitor with her brother. Though limitations upon personal and contractual rights may be removed by legislation, there is that in her disposition and habits of life which will operate against a full assertion of those rights. She will still be where some legislation to protect her seems necessary to secure a real equality of right. . . . Differentiated by these matters from the other sex, she is properly placed in a class by herself, and legislation designed for her protection may be sustained, even when like legislation is not necessary for men, and could not be sustained. . . . The limitations which this statute places upon her contractual powers, upon her right to agree with her employer as to the time she shall labor, are not imposed solely for her benefit, but also largely for the benefit of all. Many words cannot make this plainer. The two sexes differ in structure of body, in the functions to be performed by each, in the amount of physical strength, in the capacity for long continued labor, particularly when done standing, the influence of vigorous health upon the future well-being of the race, the self-reliance which enables one to assert full rights, and in the capacity to maintain the struggle for subsistence. This difference justifies a difference in legislation, and upholds that which is designed to compensate for some of the burdens which rest upon her.

Justice Brewer, writing for the Court in Mueller v. Oregon, *upholds special legislation for women, February 24, 1908, 208 US 412.*

With flags and pennants flying from every building of importance along the beach and animated groups of men, women and children waiting expectantly, the faint smoke of the first squadron was descryed on the horizon, approaching in battle array in conformation with the shore line of the bay.

This was the signal that caused every whistle and siren in the city and the salutation of the field gun of the Naval Reserve located on the point beyond the San Lorenzo River to proclaim the approach of the men who are to be our guests for the next few days . . .

. . . as these immense fighting machines moved in line to their anchorage, a number of sky rockets, to which were attached parachutes, were sent skyward and from these immense American flags that were pendant, floated off over the vessels and disappeared in the distance.

Santa Cruz Morning Sentinel *describes the city's welcome of the Great White Fleet, May 3, 1908, p. 1, available online at Santa Cruz Public Libraries. URL: http://www.santacruzpl.org/history/20thc/whitefl.shtml.*

We the Governors of the States and Territories of the United States of America, in Conference assembled, do hereby declare the conviction that the great prosperity of our country rests upon the abundant resources of the land chosen by our forefathers for their homes and where they laid the foundation of this great Nation. . . .

We agree that our country's future is involved in this; that the great natural resources supply the material basis on

President Roosevelt and his chief adviser on conservation, Gifford Pinchot, toured America's rivers with the Inland Waterways Commission in 1907. As Roosevelt passed down the Mississippi, people lined the banks and lighted bonfires at night. One of Roosevelt's notable accomplishments was establishing a conservation policy for the United States. *(Library of Congress, Prints and Photographs Division, LC-USZ62-55630)*

which our civilization must continue to depend, and on which the perpetuity of the Nation itself rests.

We agree, in the light of facts brought to our knowledge and from information received from sources which we can not doubt, that this material basis is threatened with exhaustion. . . .

We declare our firm conviction that this conservation of our natural resources is a subject of transcendent importance, which should engage unremittingly the attention of the Nation, the States, and the People in earnest cooperation. These natural resources include the land on which we live and which yields our food; the living waters which fertilize the soil, supply power, and form great avenues of commerce; the forest which yield the materials for our homes, prevent erosion of the soil, and conserve the navigation and other uses of our streams; and the minerals which form the basis of our industrial life, and supply us with heat, light, and power.

Declaration of White House Conference on Conservation of Natural Resources, May 15, 1908, in Proceedings of a Conference of Governors, *p. 192.*

Nature has given to us the most valuable possession ever committed to man. It can never be duplicated, because there is none like it upon the face of the earth. And we are racking and impoverishing it exactly as we are felling the forests and rifling the mines. . . .

Every nation finds its hour of peril when there is no longer free access to the land or when the land will no longer support the people. Disturbances within are more to be feared than attacks from without. Our government is built upon the assumption of a fairly contented, happy, and prosperous people, ruling their passions, with power to change their institutions when such change is generally desired. It would not be strange if they should in their desire for change attempt to pull down the pillars of their national temple. Far may this day be from us! But since the unnecessary destruction of our land will bring new conditions of danger, its conservation, its improvement to the highest point of productivity promised by scientific intelligence and practical experiment appears to be a first command of any political economy worthy of the name.

Railroad baron James J. Hill, who was also an impassioned conservationist, address to the governors' conference on conservation, May 13–15, 1908, in his Natural Wealth of the Land, *13, 21–22.*

Chicago, June 18—William Howard Taft of Ohio was nominated for the presidency of the United States on the first ballot by the Republican Party assembled in convention here today. The roll was called in the midst of a deafening uproar and an attempt to stampede the convention for Roosevelt. . . .

For more than seven hours the delegates and 10,000 visitors had sweltered in the almost overpowering heat of the packed Coliseum. For many hours the task of nominating various candidates had been going on. Then at the close came the attempt at a stampede, and the ovation accorded President Roosevelt yesterday was repeated. Weary and warm though every one in the hall was, the tremendous outburst swept every one but the delegates and the Chairman from their feet, metaphorically, and had it not been for the fact that the delegates were not to be stampeded under any circumstances the result of the convention might have been very different.

As it was . . . there was never an instant when Taft's nomination was in doubt. From first to last the machine worked to perfection. . . .

"Taft Named; First Ballot," New York Times, *June 19, 1908, p. 1.*

A petition 46 feet long has been presented to President Schurman and the Board of Trustees of Cornell University by Ithaca Women's Christian Temperance Union asking that the trustees stop drunkenness among students at class banquets, and that the senior banquet be held in the armory hereafter. The petitioners say that the conduct of the students "is most disgraceful," and that the alumni are as bad as the undergraduates.

Complaints about college-age drinking, "Say Cornell Men Drink Too Much," New York Times, *June 20, 1908, p. 1.*

In the rear, reached by a narrow passage, is another tenement-house, a four-story brick building, occupied, when I was there, by seven families. If the front tenement is bad, what shall we say of the tenement in the rear? Whatever is abominable in the one is more abominable in the other. The gloom is worse, the ventilation is worse, the aspect of dreary decay and neglect is worse. Some, of the dwellers in the front house can get air and light; most of the dwellers in the rear house can get very little of either. When the building was new and clean, it might have been a tolerable place in which to house horses—temporarily; say for a day. It was never, at any time, a tolerable place in which to house human beings. For fifty or sixty years it has been unfit for anything except burning. How would you like to draw an income from the maintaining of such a place? . . .

Come, then, into the filthy little back yards at the rear. . . . On the wooden walls the clapboards sag and sway and are falling off, the ancient laths and plaster are exposed beneath. Window panes are broken out. On one of the days when I was there, a bitter day in December, an icy wind blew through these apertures. I went into some of the living-rooms. There were women and children around the fire in the one stove that cooked for them and gave them heat. . . .

Muckraker Charles Edward Russell shocks New York by describing slum housing owned by historic Trinity Church, "The Tenements of Trinity Church," Everybody's Magazine, *vol. 19 (July–December 1908), p. 50.*

There is a mixture of ingenuousness and deceit in the complaints of the defects in the direct primary brought out in the recent elections in Kansas, Oregon, Missouri, and Illinois. There are those who really believed that the new institution would be a panacea for all our political ills; that it would, like a magnet, draw every recalcitrant voter to the polls, where he would promptly put the rascals to flight and inaugurate an era of political purity. These innocents are now voicing their disappointment that the primary does not prevent fraud, and that in many cases, the voter being as indifferent to his new opportunity as he was to his old, the noxious machines, party and personal, are not yet completely smashed. On the other hand, the politicians are only too happy to have their doubts about the new law; they can see a hundred objections to it, and are suddenly displaying an altogether amusing solicitude for the sanctity of the ballot. . . . [T]the primary is no cure-all; it is but another means of maintaining government by the people. The voter may neglect it, if he is as indifferent to his trust as heretofore; but if he is roused and in earnest, he can destroy the politicians who attempt to undo him.

"The Primary No Cure-All," Nation, *vol. 87*
(August 13, 1908), p. 131.

. . . we have closed our eyes to the whole awful and menacing truth—that a large part of the white population of Lincoln's home, supported largely by the farmers and miners of the neighboring towns, have initiated a permanent warfare with the negro race.

We do not need to be informed at great length of the character of this warfare. It is in all respects like that of the South, on which it is modeled. Its significance is threefold. First, that it has occurred in an important and historical Northern town; then, that the negroes, constituting scarcely more than a tenth of the population, in this case could not possibly endanger the "supremacy" of the whites, and, finally, that the public opinion of the North, notwithstanding the fanatical, blind and almost insane hatred of the negro so clearly shown by the mob, is satisfied that there were "mitigating circumstances," not for the mob violence, which, it is agreed, should be punished to the full extent of the law, but for the race hatred, which is really the cause of it all. . . .

For the underlying motive of the mob . . . was confessedly to teach the negroes their place and to warn them that too many could not obtain shelter under the favorable tradition of Lincoln's home town. I talked to many of them the day of the massacre and found no difference of opinion on the question. "Why, the niggers came to think they were as good as we are!" was the final justification offered, not once, but a dozen times.

William English Walling, white socialist reformer and
journalist who traveled to Springfield, Illinois, in the wake of
the race riot of August 1908, "The Race War in the North,"
The Independent, *vol. 65 (September 3, 1908),*
pp. 529–30.

As poverty, in its various aspects, has for many years been the chief subject of my observation, it was with deep inter-est and concern that . . . I had decided to establish myself in our nearby and tiny group of the Catskills. . . .

As it had been my previous fortune to spend some years of work among the people of the poor districts of Chicago, it was but natural, with this life in the mountains, that comparisons would keep coming to me, and it was not long before I found myself saying that, if those were slums, these are slums also. That it is not crowded tenements and bad air that create the slum type. It is not ignorance, which is, I think, a result rather than a cause. . . .

Poverty being the cause of the slum condition, it is easy to find its results back in the mountains. The soil is sterile, yielding but a precarious livelihood. Houses must be small. Families must be large. Ventilation in winter is of the worst. Drainage, even in a mountain country, is but questionable. Food is scanty and ill-prepared. Indigestion and bad teeth are the consequent. The orchards yield hard cider for those men who must take to alcoholism as a relief. Overworked and overburdened wives take to scolding and hysteria. Parents scream to each other and to their children. The children can but answer with screaming. Slums—oh, yes, we have them in our mountains. We have them on the wide breadth of our prairies. The "renters," the day laborers in agriculture, may be slum-bred as well as urban neighbors.

Journalist Hervey White, "Our Rural Slums," Independent,
vol. 65 (October 8, 1908), pp. 819–20.

Another defect in the primary system is the great expense to which candidates are put. The lavish expenditure of money in campaigns is an evil, for it involves practical blackmail of candidates and corporations and the creation of political obligations that cannot honorably be paid without sacrificing the interests of the people. But if the expense is merely to be shifted from machines and organizations to individuals the wealthy candidates will have an undue advantage and the poor men will be discriminated against in the operation of the whole system. The individual candidate must circulate petitions, do a little advertising, pay hall rent and incur other legitimate expenses; and he must do this twice in many instances, before the primary and before the election.

Argument against the direct primary, The Chatauquan,
November 1908, reprinted in Fanning, ed., Selected Articles
on Direct Primaries *(1918), p. 21.*

The exchange of views between us, which has taken place at the several interviews which I have recently had the honor of holding with you, has shown that Japan and the United States, holding important outlying insular possessions in the region of the Pacific Ocean, the governments of the two countries are animated by a common aim, policy and intention in that region. . . .

1. It is the wish of the two governments to encourage the free and peaceful development of their commerce on the Pacific Ocean.

2. The policy of both governments, uninfluenced by any aggressive tendencies, is directed to the maintenance of the existing status quo in the region above mentioned and to the defense of the principle of equal opportunity for commerce and industry in China.

3. They are accordingly firmly resolved reciprocally to respect the territorial possessions belonging to each other in said region.

4. They are also determined to preserve the common interests of all powers in China by supporting by all pacific means at their disposal the independence and integrity of China and the principles of equal opportunity for commerce and industry of all nations in that Empire.

Note from Japanese ambassador Baron Takahira to Secretary of State Elihu Root, November 30, 1908, and confirmed by Root; the two notes are known as the Root-Takahira Agreement, Papers Relating to the Foreign Relations of the United States, 1908, *pp. 510–11.*

We deem it the duty of all Christian people to concern themselves directly with certain practical industrial problems. To us it seems that the churches must stand—

For equal rights and complete justice for all men in all stations of life.

For the right of all men to the opportunity for self-maintenance, a right ever to be wisely and strongly safeguarded against encroachments of every kind.

For the right of workers to some protection against the hardships often resulting from the swift crises of industrial change.

For the principle of conciliation and arbitration in industrial dissensions.

For the protection of the worker from dangerous machinery, occupational disease, injuries, and mortality.

For the abolition of child labor.

For such regulation of the conditions of toil for women as shall safeguard the physical and moral health of the community.

For the suppression of the "sweating system."

For the gradual and reasonable reduction of the hours of labor to the lowest practicable point, and for that degree of leisure for all which is a condition of the highest human life.

For a release from employment one day in seven.

For a living wage as a minimum in every industry and for the highest wage that each industry can afford.

For the most equitable division of the products of industry that can ultimately be devised.

For suitable provision for the old age of the workers and for those incapacitated by injury.

For the abatement of poverty.

"The Church and Modern Industry," a social gospel statement adopted by the first convention of the Federal Council of Churches, December 2–8, 1908, "The Social Conscience of the Churches," Outlook, *vol. 90 (December 19, 1908), p. 850.*

There are the familiar roadside signs: "Town Limit. Motor vehicles limited to twelve miles an hour." Has any motor party ever taken such a warning seriously?. . . .

. . . Only recently six men were arrested in New York after pursuit by a motorcycle policeman over the greater part of the island of Manhattan. The time was late night, a speed of forty miles an hour through the city streets was attained (according to the papers), the offenders united in urging the pursuing officer to "come on," and they were stopped at last only by the runaway gates on an East River bridge. The court, when they were arraigned, allowed all but the man who had been driving to go with fines of $2 each! . . .

The trouble seems to be that the legislators cling fondly to the idea that motor cars are still nothing but carriages without horses, to be dealt with in the same manner as the older vehicles. . . .

High-powered cars might with greater logic be regarded as morphine and cocaine are. Possession and ability to use, when combined with an inborn passion, create a temptation that many are unable to resist. . . . [C]ars capable of a harmful speed should not be allowed except under special conditions—as, for example, upon highways devoted to them exclusively as are railway tracks to trains. . . .

Frederick Dwight complains about a new problem, "Automobiles: The Other Side of the Shield," Independent, *vol. 65 (December 3, 1908), p. 1301.*

While no additional bodies were brought to the morgue here today, the general belief prevails here that the remains of at least 15 to 18 victims are still in the workings.

It is rumored, however, that five bodies were brought out of the mine before daylight this morning, though no trace of the men can be found around the workings.

An air of mystery seems to pervade the region round about the ill-fated Rachel and Agnes shafts. No longer is information volunteered as to conditions in the mine on the part of the workmen in charge. Coroner W.H. Sipe is no longer communicative and it is really difficult to learn anything about what is being done.

Some days ago officials of the company gave out the death list as 138.

It has gradually grown since that time until now it is practically certain that the list will overreach 150 and perhaps greatly exceed that number. Undertaker Barr, who has been on the scene since the day of the explosion stated today that he had not the least doubt that there were 15 to 18 bodies still in the shaft.

Since the body of James Roule was taken out and was permitted to be removed before it was viewed by the coroner's jury the suspicion has arisen that possibly other bodies have been thus quietly taken away.

"A Curtain of Mystery Is Drawn Over Affairs at the Stricken Marianna Mine," Washington [Pennsylvania] Observer, December 7, 1908, available online at Pennsylvania Bureau of Deep Mine Safety. URL: http://www.dep.state.pa.us/ dep/deputate/minres/dms/records/marianna.htm.

Let there be no illusion about the fate of Hetch Hetchy; it can not be submerged and retained; it can not be submerged and restored. The forests not only of the valley but of the neighboring region will be destroyed in the course of the construction of the proposed dam. Even the lake can not be seen from the precipitous walls of the canyon, and if could it would be a thing of unsightly border and artificial aspect. Satan himself would never have dared play such tricks with the Garden of Eden.

I protest in the name of all lovers of beauty—and in the case of rare, of phenomenal beauty—against the materialistic idea that there must be something wrong about a man who finds one of the highest uses of nature in the fact that it is made to be looked at. Such so-called practical men would have their days full correcting the mistakes of the Almighty in this respect. I call your attention to the fact that the great public—those who visit the park, and those who may visit it—have now nobody to look to but the Congress in defense of their rights in a wonderful reservation set apart for the use of all the people—indeed, of the whole world.

Conservationist Robert Underwood Johnston, statement to a congressional hearing on efforts of San Francisco to dam Hetch Hetchy Valley, December 16, 1908, available online at Evolution of the Conservation Movement. URL: http://memory.loc.gov/ammem/amrvhtml/conshome.html.

6

The Progressive Wave Rolls In
1909–1912

A NEW PRESIDENT

When William Howard Taft took office as the 26th president of the United States in March 1909, it was the fourth consecutive inauguration of a Republican president. But there were clouds on the horizon for his party. For one thing, there was a growing split in Congress between the Old Guard Republicans (conservative, business–oriented congressmen) and the progressive Republicans, who were called Insurgents. The last

On June 9, 1910, President Taft tossed out the first ball at a Washington baseball game, thus beginning a presidential tradition. *(Library of Congress, Prints and Photographs Division, LC-USZ62-10309)*

congressional elections had sent more reform-minded Republicans to Washington and the split was becoming more volatile. At the same time, the Democrats were gaining strength. The party still controlled the South and was also making gains among working people in the northern cities.

Taft was elected as the hand-picked successor of his popular predecessor, Theodore Roosevelt. Unfortunately, he was a far less vivid, vital, and activist personality. President Taft was a genial, ponderous, and reflective man who weighed some 300 pounds. He had a long history of distinguished government service, but he had never before held an elective office. He had little instinct for the give and take of politics and none of his predecessor's relish for political battles. He believed on principle that the president should not try to manipulate congressional decision making. When Taft later served as chief justice of the Supreme Court (1921–30), he held an office that was a far better match for his judicial temperament.

President Taft did, however, personally support the reforms of the Roosevelt administration. In his campaign he promised to continue them. "I have had the honor to be one of the advisers of my distinguished predecessor," he said in his inaugural address. "I should be untrue to myself, to my promises, and to the declarations . . . upon which I was elected to office, if I did not make the maintenance and enforcement of those reforms a most important feature of my administration."[1] Many times in the four years to follow he did just that—for example, he prosecuted more than twice as many antitrust cases in four years as Roosevelt had in eight. Unfortunately, the public did not give him credit for many of his progressive accomplishments.

THE PAYNE-ALDRICH TARIFF

President Taft made a promising start. Less than two weeks after taking office he called a special session of Congress to lower the tariff, or tax on materials and manufactured items imported from other countries. The tariff was a very important issue to both politicians and citizens. For one thing, it was the primary source of funds used to operate the federal government, much as the income tax (which did not exist in 1909) is today. But at the same time it was also a means of protecting American industries from foreign competition. In 1909 the tariff was at an all-time high. The public was increasingly angry at such considerable protection for American manufacturers. Since about 1898, consumer prices had been slowly but steadily increasing. The public referred to rising prices as the high cost of living, and they blamed it primarily on the tariff. They believed that high tariffs permitted American manufacturers to set the prices of consumer goods artificially high and abetted the formation of trusts. Taft had made lower tariffs a campaign promise.

Even before the president's special session got under way, insurgent Republicans in the House of Representatives flexed their muscles. They attempted to limit the power of archconservative Speaker of the House Joseph "Uncle Joe" Cannon of Illinois. Cannon had held the office since 1902. He used his considerable power to block any reform measures, even those desired by his fellow Republicans. Faced with growing insurgency in Republican ranks, Cannon made a deal with the president. Cannon offered to aid Taft's legislative program in return for a show of support against the Insurgents. He got it. The Insurgents failed to unseat him.

When the special session began, Representative Sereno Payne of New York proposed a bill to lower tariff rates moderately, as Taft wished. Because the federal government needed money to operate, however, the bill also established a modest inheritance tax to make up the lost revenue. Cannon would normally have blocked an inheritance tax, but he honored his deal with Taft and saw that the bill passed quickly and easily. When the bill reached the Senate, however, conservative Republican Senator Nelson Aldrich's finance committee first eliminated the inheritance tax, then attached 847 amendments to avoid lowering the tariff on various items. They even increased existing tariff rates on important goods like lumber, iron and steel, and textiles.

Nationwide, even many Republicans thought Aldrich had played fast and loose with public sentiment, not to mention the party's own campaign promises. The insurgent Republican senators were galvanized. The Insurgents, primarily from the midwestern farm belt, were led by Robert La Follette of Wisconsin and included others like Albert B. Cummins of Iowa, George Norris of Nebraska, Joseph Bristow of Kansas, Albert Beveridge of Indiana, and William Borah of Idaho. They decided to confront the Old Guard. They divided the 847 amendments among their supporters, studied them, and for three months commanded the floor of the Senate in continual debate on each and every one. The Insurgents made a progressive argument, speaking for the interests of the consuming public.

In the end, the Insurgents were unable to defeat the Payne-Aldrich tariff. Despite the fact that President Taft had called the special session to request a lower tariff, he did not intervene. In a similar situation Roosevelt would have taken his case to the public, but Taft did not do that either. As passed the tariff was a victory for manufacturing interests, not for reform or for consumers.

Public reaction to the new Payne-Aldrich tariff was highly unfavorable, particularly in the Midwest and West. President Taft left for a speaking tour to minimize the damage, traveling 13,000 miles by train from Boston to the West Coast. But unwisely, as he traveled through restive farming regions, he insisted that the new tariff was the best the Republicans had ever enacted. For good measure he sometimes chided its opponents for trying to split the party. In this, the opening salvo of his administration, he infuriated the midwestern Insurgents and alarmed progressives everywhere.

A Tax on Income: The Sixteenth Amendment Is Proposed

Amid the acrimony and politicking over the Payne-Aldrich tariff, a major reform was set in motion in the way America was to finance the national government: a constitutional amendment was passed to permit the establishment of the income tax. Today, it is difficult to think of income tax as a reform measure, but that is exactly how progressives regarded it. It was envisioned as a tax on ample incomes only, not as a universal tax, and was considered a kind of tax relief for people of modest means.

When President Taft took office, neither personal income nor corporate income was taxed. Both the lowliest unskilled workers and the wealthiest captains of industry took home all of their earnings tax free, while the government ran on the proceeds of the tariff. Income tax was not a new idea, however. A temporary income tax had been levied during the Civil War, but it expired in 1872. After that date, congressional Democrats periodically tried to reestablish it. Their ultimate goal was to make a large reduction in the tariff, which hurt the farm interests they represented. By the 1890s, when the Populists embraced the idea wholeheartedly, several western European nations, including Great Britain, had successfully established an income tax. Finally in 1894, Congress passed a small income tax as part of the Wilson-Gorman tariff—but the Supreme Court quickly declared it unconstitutional. By 1909, 33 constitutional amendments to permit it had been proposed and defeated in Congress. Some conservatives opposed the idea because they considered it an attack on private property. But many Republicans opposed income tax primarily because they wanted to keep the tariff high and protect American business.

According to economic historians, the actual effect of the tariff on American economic development, wages, and prices is a very complex topic. Many people who lived during the Progressive Era, however, believed that the effect was simple and clear. They thought the tariff worked much like a modern sales tax—adding an extra cost onto the real cost of consumer goods (both goods made more cheaply abroad but taxed, and those made in America but deliberately overpriced because they were protected from competition with the less costly imported goods). That added sales tax was quite significant to the average consumer, since by 1909 the average tariff rates were between 30 and 40 percent. According to Senator La Follette, for example, the Payne-Aldrich tariff actually increased the average tax on consumer goods from 40.21 percent to 41.77 percent.[2] If a farm couple with an income of $400 a year bought a kitchen table for $10, for example, they believed they had paid $6 for the value of the table and $4 due to the tariff. The lower a family's income, of course, the higher percentage of its income the $4 represented (a situation called a regressive tax). That is, the $4 tax on the kitchen table was a much higher percentage of the farmer's $400 a year than of the $4,000 earned by a prosperous businessman or the $400,000 earned by a wealthy manufacturer.

As most reform-minded Americans saw it, farmers and ordinary working people were actually paying a much higher rate of tax than the wealthy. A few radical reformers, it is true, saw an income tax as a tool to diminish the vast inequality in the distribution of wealth at the time. But most supporters of the tax saw it primarily as a way to lower the tariff, reduce the price of consumer goods, and remove an inequitable tax burden from people of modest income.

In the midst of the congressional battle over the Payne-Aldrich tariff, Democrats in the House of Representatives once again renewed their efforts to pass an income tax. They were not successful. But when the tariff bill reached the floor of the Senate with its 847 amendments, Democrats and insurgent Republicans joined forces. Senators Joseph Bailey of Texas (a Democrat) and Albert Cummins of Iowa (a Republican) jointly proposed to attach an income tax—a small, flat percent tax on both corporate and individual incomes over $5,000. In addition, Senator George Norris of Nebraska proposed a resolution supporting an income tax amendment to the Constitution to make sure the proposed tax could not be overturned.

Faced with insurgent revolt, Old Guard Republican leader Nelson Aldrich proposed a compromise—attaching a small tax on corporate (but not personal) incomes to the tariff bill now and writing a separate bill to propose a constitutional amendment that, when ratified, would permit a tax on personal income in the future. When the whole Senate voted, however, the corporate income tax attachment was defeated—as Aldrich probably knew it would be—and the Payne-Aldrich tariff passed without it. On the other hand, the bill proposing to amend the Constitution to allow income tax passed unanimously in the Senate and 318-14 in the House.

Conservatives joined in support for the proposed amendment, many historians believe, because they did not think it would ever become law. A constitutional amendment must not only pass Congress but must also be ratified by the legislatures of at least three-quarters of the states. But the Old Guard had miscalculated. Throughout the nation, sentiment in favor of reforming the tax burden by means of an income tax was growing—and it was given a final boost by popular indignation over the Payne-Aldrich tariff itself. One by one states ratified the income tax amendment, beginning with Alabama before the end of 1909. In 1913, the Sixteenth Amendment to the Constitution became law.

THE BALLINGER–PINCHOT AFFAIR

While the Payne-Aldrich tariff and the income tax made their way through Congress, a controversy related to conservation began brewing. It soon boiled over into a political catastrophe for the president. Taft had retained Roosevelt's trusted conservation adviser, Chief of Forestry Gifford Pinchot. But he had chosen a new secretary of the interior, Richard A. Ballinger, a Seattle attorney with ties to northwestern lumber and mining interests. Ballinger was sympathetic to westerners who disliked conservation set-asides. One of his first acts was to reopen more than a million acres of water-power sites that Roosevelt and Pinchot had withdrawn. Next, the secretary reopened coal lands and arranged to honor some old claims belonging to a group of Seattle businessmen who were his former legal clients. The claimants—possibly without his knowledge—had made a prior agreement with the Alaska syndicate of J. P. Morgan and the Guggenheim mining interests to resell the coal lands to them.

A young whistleblower in the interior department, Louis R. Glavis, alerted Pinchot to the events. Pinchot went to Taft—who took Ballinger's side and fired Glavis. Undeterred, Pinchot went public during the summer of 1909. Controversy raged, especially after Glavis published his side of the story in the November issue of *Collier's,* a muckraking magazine. Pinchot forced a showdown and in January 1910, Taft fired him for insubordination. A full-blown public brouhaha ensued. Nationwide, conservatives sided with Ballinger and progressives sided with Pinchot. For four months a joint congressional committee investigated. At the hearing, Glavis was represented by prominent reform lawyer Louis Brandeis. Ballinger did not admit wrongdoing. But under skillful questioning by Brandeis he did reveal a very limited commitment to conservation. Voting on party lines, the committee absolved Ballinger, although he resigned not long after.

Historians agree that the Ballinger-Pinchot affair had far more impact on politics than on conservation. For one thing, it convinced the reform-minded public that President Taft was in league with the interests. It also convinced them the president had abandoned Roosevelt's most important legacy. In fact, Taft compiled a very respectable record on conservation during his term of office. He replaced Ballinger and Pinchot with well-qualified conservationists. (Ballinger's replacement as secretary of the interior, Walter Fisher, invalidated the claims of the Seattle businessmen that had caused the controversy.) Taft withdrew more land reserves in one term than Roosevelt had in two, obtained the Appalachian Forest Reserve Act to permit him to purchase and protect private forest land in the East, and won the broad power to reserve lands for "any public purpose" in the Withdrawal Act. He also successfully negotiated the North Pacific Sealing Convention with Canada and Great Britain, Russia, and Japan to end the hunting of rapidly declining pelagic (seagoing) seals in the Bering Sea. But his firing of Pinchot almost guaranteed a break with Roosevelt. It was a giant step down the road to a formal split in the Republican Party.

The goals of conservationists and lumber interests often collided, especially in the Northwest. These loggers in Washington State must use a steam locomotive to move the huge trees they have cut. *(Library of Congress, Prints and Photographs Division, LC-USZ62-97669)*

SOME PROGRESSIVE VICTORIES IN CONGRESS

During 1909–1910, Congress did succeed in passing some progressive legislation, often at the behest of President Taft. In 1910, the Mann-Elkins Act, a further attempt to regulate the railroads, passed after much wheeling and dealing and another battle between insurgent and conservative Republicans. The act greatly increased the Interstate Commerce Commission's power to influence or control railroad rates. The ICC also received jurisdiction over communications for the first time—telephone, telegraph, cable, and wireless or radio, at the time considered primarily a communications medium. Another reform act was the Postal Deposit Savings Act. It enabled small depositors to establish savings accounts at their local post office at 2 percent interest. Postal Savings was partly intended to reassure people of modest means that their savings would not be lost in a bank collapse like that of 1907. It was the kind of trustworthy banking service long desired by rural and populist interests—although in practice, it proved far more popular among urban immigrants and workers.[3]

To pass progressive legislation like these acts, insurgent Republicans in the House of Representatives had begun to join with the Democrats on occasion. The coalition soon launched a new effort to limit the power of Joseph Cannon, Speaker of the House. They were not successful at unseating him, but they did end his stranglehold over appointment of all committee chairs and members. Eventually they succeeded in making all committee positions elective by the whole House. These changes were important because they increased the probability that reform-minded congressmen would have opportunities to hold influential committee positions, and in turn that committees would release (or "report") proposed reform legislation to the floor of the House for a debate and vote.

The actions of Republican insurgents increasingly irritated President Taft. Openly allying himself with the Old Guard, he joined Cannon and Aldrich in a campaign to stem the tide of progressive insurgency in Congress. Their plan was to unseat as many insurgent Republicans as possible in the upcoming midterm elections of 1910 by engineering the nomination process to substitute conservative Republican candidates. The effort failed spectacularly. The Insurgents fought hard, and in every case, their constituents chose to renominate them to stand for reelection in November.

ROOSEVELT ANNOUNCES THE NEW NATIONALISM

When President Taft took office in 1909, Theodore Roosevelt set sail for a yearlong big-game hunting safari in Africa—preceded and followed by triumphal tours of Europe, where he was also very popular. Roosevelt returned from his travels in June 1910, in the midst of the Republican intra-party skulduggery to defeat the Insurgents. Roosevelt's supporters trooped to his home at Oyster Bay, Long Island, to fill him in on doings in Washington—and to drop hints that his reentry into politics would be welcomed. Despite it all, Roosevelt did not openly break with President Taft, and in fact worked hard to heal the breach between progressive and conservative Republicans. He and President Taft exchanged polite but cool correspondence. "I shall keep my mind open as I keep my mouth shut," Roosevelt wrote to Taft.[4]

Roosevelt set out for a western speaking tour. His goal was to kindle enthusiasm for progressive positions and candidates, but he carefully endorsed the Taft administration and party unity as he did so. The tour soon turned into another triumphal procession for Roosevelt. At every train stop, crowds clamored for him.

In his speeches, Roosevelt laid out the principles of a program he called the New Nationalism. He endorsed a long list of reforms that included strong federal regulation of business and industry; direct-democracy reforms including recall of all elected officials and judges; many social welfare reforms; and tax reform. He proclaimed that traditional American values of democracy and equal opportunity could now be achieved only through untraditional means, specifically a much stronger national government to protect the individual from powerful interests. The New Nationalism implied a distinct reduction in traditional local and states' rights. "It left the great mass of Republican conservatives, including President Taft, in a state of shock," writes historian George Mowry.[5]

Roosevelt borrowed the term New Nationalism from an influential book by journalist and intellectual Herbert Croly, *The Promise of American Life*. Published in 1909, Croly's book drew progressive political principles together into a systematic statement. It also related them to different theories of government associated with two of American's Founding Fathers. One, the tradition of democracy and individual economic opportunity associated with Thomas Jefferson, was held to require small-scale competition and very limited, primarily local government. The other tradition, associated with Alexander Hamilton, held that a democratic republic demanded a strong central government to oversee and aid economic development of national scope. Croly, like Roosevelt, believed that America's new, large corporate economy was permanent. Therefore, he argued, Jeffersonian democracy and individual opportunity were no longer well served by limited government; instead, they required Hamilton's strong, active, and intervening government (Croly used the term *positive government*). As Croly put it, true reform united "the Hamiltonian principle of national political responsibility and efficiency with a frank democratic purpose."[6] Historians often refer to Croly's formula as using Hamiltonian means to achieve Jeffersonian ends.

Croly also argued for the importance of the public interest, even when it required individual sacrifice. "The Promise of American Life," he wrote, "is to be fulfilled not merely by a maximum amount of economic freedom, but by a certain amount of discipline; not merely by the abundant satisfaction of individual desires, but by a large measure of individual subordination and denial."[7] Croly's book did not really contain new ideas and it was not widely read by average Americans. But it was the first in which progressivism's main ideas were clearly laid out and clearly contrasted to the conservative idea of laissez-faire, which held that the government should never attempt to restrain the free economic behavior of individuals. It served to crystallize the thinking of many influential progressives.

THE MIDTERM ELECTION OF 1910

After the midterm election of November 1910, it was clear that the Taft-Aldrich plan to replace the Insurgents had not only failed but backfired. All the insurgent Republicans were reelected, with the one exception of Senator Albert Beveridge of Indiana. Meanwhile the Democrats had taken advantage of the split in Republican ranks. They campaigned as the true party of conservatism in some places and the true party of progressivism in others and gained many congressional seats. In the House, Democrats won a majority for the first time since 1892—and thus the archconservative Cannon's reign as Speaker of the House finally came to an end. (The Speaker is elected from the majority party). In the Senate, the Republican majority had been reduced so much that the insurgents had actually been handed the balance of power in contests between conservative Republicans and the Democrats. There were other signs of a shifting political climate as well. New England elected its first Democratic senator since the Civil War. The Democrats also won some important governorships such as that of New Jersey, where Woodrow Wilson, president of Princeton University and a newcomer to politics, was elected.

THE NATIONAL REPUBLICAN PROGRESSIVE LEAGUE

Soon after the midterm election, leading Republican insurgents announced plans to form a National Progressive Republican League. The league was clearly understood by political observers as an attempt to take the reins of the party and challenge President Taft's renomination for a second term. Senator Robert La Follette, the league's guiding spirit, was widely believed to be opening a run for president in 1912.

In early 1911, progressive Republican senators, representatives, midwestern governors, and other reformers gathered in Chicago for the league's first meeting. Soon six state organizations had been put in place, five in the Midwest and one in Washington State. Some eastern progressives also joined the league and members made many overtures to Roosevelt, although he did not join them.

In Congress, the group increased its efforts to push reform legislation. President Taft called them the "new Salvation Army."[8]

THE SEVENTEENTH AMENDMENT: DIRECT ELECTION OF SENATORS

The U.S. Constitution, as originally written, provided for U.S. senators to be elected by state legislatures. Since the 1890s, reformers had argued that voters themselves should elect their senators and that the Constitution should be amended to permit them to do so. Nonetheless, an amendment permitting direct election of senators would significantly alter the system of representative government designed by the Founding Fathers. In fact, it would effect the most pronounced change in American federalism (the relationship of the states to the national government) since the Constitution was written. Some people objected to it for that reason. Reformers, however, believed the change would greatly reduce corruption in state legislatures and the halls of the Senate itself. They held that it would actually restore the dignity to the Senate that the Founding Fathers intended it to have.

The House of Representatives had passed a direct election amendment bill many times since 1890, and in late 1910, it did so again. In prior years, when the House bill was sent to the Senate, a committee had always killed it, and it never came to a full vote. But this time, partly due to the changes in committee membership that the Insurgents had won, the bill was sent on to the floor of the Senate for consideration. Even conservative senators knew they could not avoid the issue forever, because direct election had a groundswell of popular support. Many states already held preferential elections for senator and required the state legislature to elect the candidate preferred by the people.

As the amendment was first proposed in 1910, however, it actually would have made two different changes in the Constitution. Of course, it changed the section which describes how senators are to be elected—Section 3 of Article 1. But it also proposed to change Section 4 of Article 1, which gives Congress itself the right to "make or alter" regulations for congressional elections in the various states. The bill proposed to take control of congressional elections away from Congress and give it instead to each state legislature. Southern senators, who supported the change, justified it as compensation to state legislatures for the loss of their power to elect senators. Many senators from outside the South, however, saw it as a bald attempt to eliminate federal oversight of elections—removing one more roadblock to the disenfranchisement of African-American voters. They dubbed that part of the bill the race rider. "This resolution virtually repeals the fourteenth and fifteenth amendments to the Constitution," said Republican Senator Chaucey DePew of New York. "It validates by constitutional amendment laws under which citizens of the United States, constituting in the aggregate more than one-tenth of the electorate, are to be permanently deprived of the right of suffrage."[9] The Senate voted down the race rider—then also voted down the direct election of senators itself. The 61st Congress adjourned without further action on the issue.

On April 11, 1911, the direct-election amendment was again introduced in the House—with the race rider intact. Another year's wrangling within and between the two houses of Congress followed. The issue of who should control congressional elections consumed as much debate as the direct election of senators itself. But the rider was finally eliminated, and the bill was passed to amend the Constitution to allow the direct election of senators with no change in the right of Congress to oversee congressional elections. On April 13, 1912, Congress sent the Seventeenth Amendment to the states for ratification.

Some historians believe that the tortuous history of the amendment in Congress was little more than a delaying tactic. In any case, its time had come. Within a year after the proposed amendment was submitted to the states, it was ratified by the necessary 36 of the 48 states. Two states, Vermont and Utah, rejected it, but elsewhere it, passed by significant margins—unanimously in 15 states. The Seventeenth Amendment was proclaimed in effect on May 31, 1913.

INTERNATIONAL RELATIONS UNDER TAFT: DOLLAR DIPLOMACY

During the Taft administration, Theodore Roosevelt's vision of international activism in the name of world stability fell by the wayside. President Taft did not actively pursue either arbitration of European disputes or improved relations with Japan. Instead, the president and his secretary of state, Philander C. Knox, engaged in a strategy that Taft described as "substituting dollars for bullets." Its opponents tagged it "dollar diplomacy." Dollar diplomacy was the policy of encouraging private American banking interests to invest in less-developed nations, especially those in which Europeans were already heavily invested. The goal of dollar diplomacy was to strengthen economic and political stability in weak nations while also increasing American influence there.

The policy was initiated in China in 1909. The president himself intervened with the Chinese government on behalf of American financial interests, who wanted to join a group of European investors in railroad development. According to Secretary Knox, American investment would help maintain the Open Door and the strength of Chinese nationhood by balancing the colonial aims of European nations. Americans did make significant investments in China but also aroused the enmity of both Japan and Russia there. The situation was further complicated by the revolution in China which began in October 1911. It was touched off, in fact, by a revolt related to foreign investment in railroads, although nationalist and republican sentiment against the Qing (Ch'ing) dynasty had been growing since 1900. In early 1912, the young emperor abdicated and Yuan Shikai (Yüan Shih-k'ai) was installed as the first president of the Republic of China.

American investment in China did not outlast the Taft administration. In the Caribbean, however, dollar diplomacy had greater staying power. The first large American investment was in Haiti in 1910. In 1911, Knox negotiated treaties with both Nicaragua and Honduras to provide private American refinancing for debts. The treaties also provided for collectors of customs to make payments to European creditors, as Roosevelt had done in Venezuela and the Dominican Republic. The Senate refused to approve the Knox treaties, however. Despite congressional disapproval, the Taft administration encouraged American bankers to continue private refinancing and investment initiative in nations with shaky national finances and unstable governments.

In Nicaragua government stability continued to deteriorate. In 1909, U.S. troops supported a successful revolt against dictator José Santos Zelaya, who was offering land to Germany and Japan to build a second canal to rival Panama's. In 1912, the new president Adolfo Díaz again requested American assistance in the face of growing disorder. Troops were sent and a customs collector was installed. U.S. military forces remained in Nicaragua until 1925, left for nine months, then returned to remain until 1933.

America's continuing intervention in the Caribbean and South America was based on the Monroe Doctrine (which warned foreign governments away from establishing new colonies in the Americas) and its Roosevelt Corollary (which stated America's interest in maintaining economic and political stability in the regions). During the Taft years the Monroe Doctrine received another extension. A Japanese syndicate tried to buy 400,000 acres of Baja California, Mexico, including Magdalena Bay. Senator Henry Cabot Lodge of Massachusetts sponsored a Senate resolution that extended the Monroe Doctrine to actions by foreign corporations. The Lodge Corollary, as it came to be known, was also the first application of the Monroe Doctrine to an Asian, rather than European, power.

THE HETCH HETCHY CONTROVERSY CONTINUES

As 1909 opened, some conservationists were waging a nationwide campaign to block construction of a dam across the Tuolumne River in Yosemite National Park, which would destroy scenic Hetch Hetchy Valley. The City of San Francisco wanted to build the dam to create a publicly owned water supply for the city. Conservationists thought that the whole nation, not just San Franciscans, had an interest at stake in a dam that would destroy part of a national park.

In early 1909, Congress held hearings on the controversial dam, but did not approve it. After President Taft took office, he and his new secretary of the interior, Richard Ballinger, toured Yosemite and Hetch Hetchy. They were escorted by America's most prominent conservationist, John Muir. After his visit, the president leaned toward preserving the valley. He was not an especially enthusiastic lover of nature, but he believed preservation was the intent of the law that created Yosemite National Park. Within a few months, Hetch Hechy was also entangled in the politics of the Ballinger-Pinchot affair. Neither President Taft, nor Ballinger, nor Ballinger's replacement as secretary of the interior, Walter Fisher, was inclined to champion a controversial project originally approved by Pinchot.

The City of San Francisco recognized that the political issues were insurmountable under the Taft administration and adopted the wait-and-see approach. In the meantime both proponents and opponents of the dam continued their public campaigns. Former San Francisco mayor James Phelan said that Muir "would sacrifice his own family for the preservation of beauty." John Muir characterized the politicians, engineers, and other technical experts who wanted to build the dam as "silly thieves and robbers."[10] All conservationists were not completely united on the issue, however. Most professionally employed conservationists did accept Pinchot's policy of managed use of natural resources rather than the policy of pure esthetic preservation championed by Muir—although some objected to damming Hetch Hetchy nonetheless because they did not like the precedent of dismantling national parks. Amateur conservationists, however—those who volunteered their time on behalf of the cause—lined up solidly for preserving Hetch Hetchy as a scenic wonder. They also had the support of much public opinion and many magazines and newspapers nationwide.

THE DILLINGHAM REPORT AND CONTROVERSY OVER IMMIGRATION RESTRICTION

Immigrants continued to pour into America. Between 1909 and 1912, newcomers averaged more than 875,000 each year. In 1910—when the total again reached more than 1 million in a single year—70 percent arrived from southern and eastern Europe, 19 percent from northwestern Europe including Germany, and 11 percent from Canada, Mexico, Asia, and elsewhere.[11]

In 1911, the United States Immigration Commission, also called the Dillingham Commission after its chair, Vermont senator William Dillingham, finally published its complete report. The commission had been established in 1907 to study the impact of immigration at the behest of congressmen who favored more restriction. The report, 41 volumes long, collected immense amounts of social and economic data on such subjects as literacy, education, and employment of immigrants. (Even today it remains the most extensive study of immigration ever conducted.) The Dillingham commission report introduced the terms *new immigration* to describe those from southern and eastern Europe, and *old immigration* to describe those from northern and western Europe, terms still in use by historians.

Much of the data appeared to paint an unflattering picture of southern and eastern Europeans. It suggested they were greatly responsible for overcrowded cities and other social and political problems. It also suggested they were less interested in being conscientious, contributing citizens than previous immigrants. "The old immigration movement was essentially one of permanent settlers," the report said. "The new immigration is very largely one of individuals a considerable proportion of whom apparently have no intention of permanently changing their residence, their only purpose in coming to America being to temporarily take advantage of the greater wages paid for industrial labor in this country."[12] The report asserted that nearly 40 percent intended to return to their native lands after a few years and therefore were unlikely to respect American standards. Like all social-scientific writing of the day, the report drew on the idea that each "race" (that is, ethnic group) had fundamental characteristics that affected its members' ability to adapt to American democracy. It also, however, contained a study by Columbia anthropologist Franz Boas, asserting that "fundamental traits of the mind, which are closely correlated with the physical condition of the body," could change on American soil. "The importance of this entirely unanticipated result," the commissioners acknowledged, "lies in the fact that even those characteristics which modern science has led us to consider as the most stable seem to be subject to thorough changes under the new environment."[13]

The report defined immigration as an economic problem, not as a desire for freedom or an escape from oppression. "While social conditions affect the situation in some countries," it concluded, ". . . as a rule those who emigrate to the United States are impelled by a desire for betterment rather than by the necessity of escaping intolerable conditions. This fact should largely modify the natural incentive to treat the immigration movement from the standpoint of sentiment and permit its consideration primarily as an economic problem. In other words, the economic and social welfare of the United States should now ordinarily be the determining factor in the immigration policy of the government."[14] On that basis, the report recommended some changes and some restrictions. It recommended encouraging families (rather than single men) to immigrate, encouraging settlement in rural areas rather than cities, reducing the number of unskilled workers permitted to enter the country, and discouraging the widespread practice among immigrants of sending money abroad. It also recommended continuing to ban Asian immigrants. But its two most important recommendations were the old idea of a literacy test and the new idea of quotas, or restricting "the number of each race [ethnic group] arriving each year to a certain percentage."[15]

In general, public opinion had come to favor some kind of restriction on immigration. Sentiment was strongest in the West, where objections to Asian immigration continued, and in the South, where residents increasingly resented the active recruitment of immigrants by business interests. But coast to coast many Americans, including reformers and social workers, believed that newcomers were arriving more quickly than they could be absorbed and that their sheer numbers needed to be curtailed. Nonetheless, "a substantial part of the American population seemed to regard the question as one of secondary importance," writes historian John Higham in his classic work on American responses to immigration, *Strangers in the Land*. The possibility of immigration restriction, however, remained an extremely important topic to the well-organized, active interest groups who opposed it. Anti-restrictionists included business interests, who wanted cheap and plentiful labor. "Why should I have to pay . . . six dollars a day for work that a Chinaman would do for fifty cents?" asked James J. Hill, head of the Northern Pacific Railroad. "Let down the bars!" Others who opposed restriction were immigrant and ethnic societies and the National Liberal Immigration League, as well as the immigrant or foreign language press, which was organized into a politically astute national association. These interest groups continued to lobby and press politicians to vote against restrictive policies.[16]

Neither Republicans nor Democrats wanted to alienate business or ethnic voters before the election of 1912. After the election, however, Congress quickly wrote a new immigration bill which included a literacy test. President Taft vetoed the bill before he left office in March 1913, just as President Cleveland had vetoed a similar bill in 1897. In the intervening years, however, congressional sentiment for restriction had grown. The Senate overrode Taft's veto. But the House failed to override it—by five votes— and the measure died.

Although restrictionists did not immediately achieve their goals, the Dillingham commission report was accepted as social-scientific backing for those who favored more rigorous restriction. Its influence was increasingly important during the next two decades, which would see the establishment of both the literacy test (1917) and national quotas (1924) it recommended.

THE MEXICAN REVOLUTION BRINGS IMMIGRANTS TO THE SOUTHWEST

By 1910, the long regime of Mexican president Porfirio Díaz was wobbling. Under Díaz the Mexican economy had prospered and the population had boomed. But at the same time a very small number of Mexicans had accumulated most of the property, while foreign investment and foreign economic control had soared. The vast majority of Mexicans were landless, maltreated, and increasingly rebellious. After a disputed presidential election in 1910, the loser, Francesco Madero, organized supporters and attacked Díaz's federal troops. In May 1911, Díaz was forced to resign. The following November Madero was declared president after an election, but dissatisfaction and turmoil continued on both the Left and the Right.

The decadelong Mexican Revolution would eventually involve the United States in hostilities. Even during the Taft administration troops were dispatched to the border. But at first the main effect of the revolution was to increase the flow of emigrants northward from Mexico into the American Southwest. Immigration from Mexico rarely figured into the restrictionist debates during these years, however. In the American Southwest, landowners were eager to employ Mexican farm laborers because new irrigation projects were opening more land to farming, and labor was in short supply. Mexican laborers often met poor treatment nonetheless.

REFORMING THE PHYSICAL CITY: CITY PLANNING

The year 1909 was a watershed for American city planning and the new profession it was creating. Wisconsin passed the first state law authorizing cities to create permanent planning commissions, Harvard introduced the first university course on Principles of City Planning, and prominent Bostonians organized a movement called Boston 1915 to provide a comprehensive plan for city growth. In Los Angeles, the city council passed the first zoning ordinance in America. The zoning plan created seven industrial districts, then declared the rest of the city a residential district. At first, zoning was considered a radical innovation because it limited the rights of property owners to use their land as they wished, and some business owners filed lawsuits to block it. It would soon become one of the most popular tools of city planning, however, supported by businessmen and homeowners alike.

In 1909, the City Beautiful movement also reached its zenith, when World's Fair architect Daniel Burnham unveiled his comprehensive and influential design for Chicago. In keeping with Burnham's motto, "Make no little plans. They have no magic to stir men's blood and probably will not be realized," the plan reached from Kenosha, Wisconsin, to Michigan City, Indiana.[17] It included a new town center, improved transportation routes, parks and beaches, and forest preserves. Over the next 15 years large parts of it were built, at a cost of some $300 million. In most other cities that commissioned City Beautiful plans, however, actual results were limited to a few buildings in a new town center or a system of parks.

The City Beautiful movement had a limited impact because it ignored the underlying economic causes of ugliness and disorder in industrial cities, as well as crucial issues like adequate housing for working people. Meanwhile, social reformers were at work on these very questions. In New York a group of prominent settlement house leaders and other reformers founded the Committee on Congestion of Population (CCP) in 1907, with representatives from 37 civic, philanthropic, and reform groups. (At the time the word *congestion* almost always referred to excessive density of population, not to traffic as today.) The committee's executive secretary Benjamin Marsh was an indefatigable crusader and activist. In 1909, he organized the first national conference on city planning, held in Washington, D.C. It was the first significant meeting at which social reformers and city planners were brought together. The National Conference on City Planning continued to meet yearly.

Unfortunately, city planning and zoning also began to develop a negative side. Some southern and border states began to write Jim Crow laws prescribing residential segregation. The laws, first put into effect in Baltimore, Richmond, Louisville, and Atlanta in 1912 and 1913, allotted certain blocks of the city to black people's residences and others to white people's residences. Both races were forbidden to live in the blocks allotted to the other.

REFORMING THE PHYSICAL CITY: HOUSING REFORM

In 1910, reformers whose primary interest was the housing of the poor also organized nationally. Lawrence Veiller and Robert de Forest, long prominent figures in New York tenement-house reform, founded the National Housing Association (NHA) with the financial assistance of the Russell Sage Foundation. The NHA promoted the idea that housing reform could be accomplished by private initiative, providing that good regulatory legislation was passed by cities and states. By 1910, according to de Forest, fewer than 10 cities outside the states of New York and New Jersey had passed any housing regulations at all. The NHA had a nationwide impact almost immediately. The organization published many pamphlets and other informational material. It sponsored meetings and seminars throughout the nation to help localities establish requirements for density of population, sanitation, and other issues. At the same time Veiller, who remained director of the NHA for the rest of the Progressive Era, wrote model laws and handbooks, which were widely consulted. In the decade following the establishment of the NHA the number of states with housing codes rose to 12, seven directly influenced by Veiller's work, and 40 cities wrote new or revised regulations.

THE FOUNDING OF THE NAACP AND THE URBAN LEAGUE

The violent race riot that shook Springfield, Illinois, in 1908, alarmed and aroused white reformers who were concerned about racial justice. It was now clear that the deteriorating social and political situation of African Americans was not confined to the South. In early 1909, newspaper editor Oswald Garrison Villard (descendant of a prominent abolitionist) and reformers Mary White Ovington and William English Walling, among others, decided to organize a national biracial conference to discuss the problem and its solutions. They invited African Americans in the ailing Niagara movement to join them. W. E. B. DuBois and most other Niagara members agreed, as did Ida B. Wells and Mary Church Terrell. The call to a meeting was issued on Lincoln's birthday, February 12. It was signed by more than 60 prominent people, including Jane Addams, Ray Stannard Baker, Harriot Stanton Blatch, John Dewey, William Dean Howells, Florence Kelley, Henry Moskowitz, Lincoln Steffens, Lillian Wald, Mayor Brand Whitlock of Toledo, Rev. Charles H. Parkhurst, and other Christian and Jewish clergymen. In May, when some 300 people met in New York, they decided to establish a permanent organization. In 1910, it took the name National Association for the Advancement of Colored People, or NAACP.

The NAACP brought together white philanthropists and reformers, black intellectuals, and middle-class black leaders. Together they decided to focus on equal protection of the law, the right to vote for all men (women's suffrage was not mentioned), an end to legal segregation, and equal educational opportunities for black children. They chose Moorfield Storey, a white constitutional lawyer and former head of the American Bar Association, as the first president. Almost immediately the organization began to challenge injustice through the legal system, and before the end of 1910, it had filed its first lawsuit. The organization also quickly launched an antilynching campaign. NAACP representatives researched each lynching to determine the facts surrounding it and photodocumented many as well.

The NAACP opened a national headquarters in New York and soon after, its first branch office in Chicago. By 1912 10 branches were open and by 1920 more than 400. Among the first national officers, the only African American was W. E. B. DuBois. Membership was predominantly African American from the start, however, and within a few years, blacks began to move into official leadership positions.

DuBois founded and devoted himself to the organization's journal, *The Crisis*. "The span of my life from 1910 to 1934 is chiefly the story of *The Crisis* under my editorship," he wrote in his autobiography.[18] He called it an "organ of propaganda and defense," and the viewpoints he expressed sometimes put him at loggerheads with other board members. In his hands, however, it grew into a very influential publication. By the end of the Progressive Era its circulation hit more than 100,000 a month.

In 1911, the National Urban League was founded in New York to work for the improvement of economic and social conditions for African Americans in large cities. (Prior to 1920 its official name was the National League on Urban Conditions among Negroes.) African Americans usually endured even worse housing and employment conditions than immigrants but met with far less assistance. The biracial organization was formed by George Edmond Haynes, founder of the department of sociology at Fisk and the first African American to receive a doctorate from Columbia; Ruth Standish Baldwin, a white philanthropist; and Edwin R. A. Seligman, a Columbia professor, among others. Booker T. Washington was a prominent sponsor.

By 1920, the Urban League had branches in more than 30 cities. Smaller than the NAACP, it brought together leading citizens and professionals. The league sponsored research on problems blacks faced in health, sanitation, recreation, housing, and employment and also sponsored social-work training for African-American students. It also functioned as a service agency for blacks, comparable to the settlement house for immigrants. One important focus was providing assistance to black urban migrants from the rural South, whose numbers were steadily increasing.

THE MOVEMENT FOR WOMEN'S SUFFRAGE REIGNITES

As the decade of the 1910s dawned, the movement for women's suffrage came to life again. At the time, the National American Woman Suffrage Association (NAWSA), headed by Dr. Anna Howard Shaw, was hobbled by internal dissension. But in the breach, local suffrage organizations took on new life throughout the nation, while new organizations tried out more militant and more political approaches.

In October 1909, more than 1,000 women met in Carnegie Hall in New York City to found the Woman Suffrage Party under the leadership of former NAWSA president Carrie Chapman Catt. Adopting the political methods of other interest groups, they organized the city by precinct and ward. The group members put pressure on politicians, made alliances, worked to defeat candidates who opposed women's suffrage, and stood as poll watchers. Another group, the Women's Political Union founded by Harriot Stanton Blatch, organized wage-earning women for the cause of suffrage while also introducing suffragists to women's labor issues. The union arranged for women factory workers to testify at hearings in the New York state legislature, for example. Their descriptions of working conditions gave lawmakers a new perspective on why women needed greater political influence.

Blatch and the Women's Political Union also helped introduce more militant tactics, pioneered by English suffragists, to the American scene. In 1910, the Union launched the first successful women's suffrage parade in New York. Parades quickly became popular and multiplied in size and frequency each year. In 1912, more than 10,000 women marched in New York. Throughout the nation, suffragists adopted new public activities, such as holding large outdoor meetings or speaking from streetcorner soapboxes. Such public displays—traditionally considered an affront to respectability among the middle and upper classes—broke new ground for women. Suffragists also organized statewide automobile tours, suffrage trains to the state capital, voiceless speeches (standing in store windows holding placards), and group attempts to register to vote. These new activities attracted considerable publicity and drew women of many backgrounds together in a common cause. Many wealthy women became more active in the women's suffrage cause and contributed their influence and resources. With the financial assistance of Alva Smith Vanderbilt Belmont, for example, NAWSA was able to open an official headquarters in New York in 1910.

STATE CAMPAIGNS FOR WOMEN'S SUFFRAGE

In 1910, Washington State gave women's suffrage its first victory since 1896. During the Washington campaign, suffragists spoke at grange halls, labor unions, churches, civic organizations, and even lumber camps. They sold cookbooks, held essay contests, gave prizes for suffrage floats at county and state fairs, and employed male workers to converse with men in places like hotels and trains. They made an agreement with the WCTU, which normally campaigned for both women's suffrage and prohibition, to avoid openly antagonizing the liquor interests. They arranged for a banner reading *Votes for Women* to fly from a dirigible over a 1909 exposition in Seattle. Dr. Cora Smith King, a member of the local Mountaineers' Club, carried a similar banner to the summit of Mt. Rainier. As election day drew near, many clergymen agreed to preach a suffrage sermon. Suffrage won by nearly a 2-1 margin, carrying every county and every city.

The victory in Washington inspired suffragists to renew their efforts nationwide. The next campaign, California, drew financial and moral support from across the nation. It set a new standard for size and activity—out of necessity because liquor interests were spending large sums to defeat the measure, especially in the cities. Suffrage organizations nationwide sent their best speakers. They blanketed rural areas and small towns to persuade the male voters to their cause. The morning after the vote, newspapers actually reported a defeat for women's suffrage, based on voting returns in the largest cities. Suffrage workers immediately dispatched poll watchers to oversee the vote counting elsewhere. In the cities, they hired detectives to guard the already-counted ballots, to make sure that the margin of defeat did not mysteriously grow larger. Four days later, when all the votes had been counted, suffrage won—by the small margin of 3,587 votes. Put another way, the victory represented a margin of one vote for each precinct in the state.[19]

Suffragists were not so lucky in Michigan in 1912, where the governor himself publicly accused liquor interests of complicity in voting fraud after suffrage was defeated. Suffrage also was defeated in Ohio and Wisconsin. But momentum was building. Between 1910 and 1912, five more states joined the suffrage column: Washington State in 1910, California in 1911, and in 1912, Kansas, Oregon, and Arizona, bringing the total to nine. The newly established legislature of Alaska territory also approved women's suffrage in 1912. NAWSA's convention in Philadelphia in late November drew so many attendees and onlookers, reported the *Woman's Journal*, "It looked more like an inauguration than like an old-fashioned suffrage meeting." "What had been only one more social reform current," writes suffrage historian Eleanor Flexner, "was becoming a political force to be reckoned with."[20]

PROHIBITION ADVOCATES AND FOES

Throughout America sentiment in favor of temperance, regulation of saloons, and oversight of the liquor industry was widespread. The most nationally prominent anti-liquor group, the Anti-Saloon League, increasingly attempted to funnel this sentiment into support for the statewide prohibition of manufacture and sale of alcohol beverages. Between 1905 and 1909, state campaigns met notable success, especially in the South, but success decelerated between 1910 and 1912. In six campaigns, five states defeated statewide prohibition and only one, West Virginia, approved it. In part, the change was due to increased anti-prohibition publicity and lobbying efforts by liquor industry associations, who also funded private anti-prohibition groups called personal liberty leagues. It was also true, however, that many Americans who heartily approved voluntary temperance movements, the control of saloons and the liquor industry, and even local option laws did not embrace total legal prohibition as enthusiastically.

Nonetheless, dry territory continued to expand overall under local option laws. As dry territory increased, however, so did the problems of enforcement where liquor was banned. According to an Interstate Commerce Commission estimate, for example, more than 20 million gallons of alcohol were shipped into dry localities in 1911.[21] Because interstate commerce was under the jurisdiction of the federal government, a dry state could not easily ban shipments of liquor from wet states if the liquor was sent to individuals for personal use. And in fact, only a few state prohibition laws outlawed the individual's possession, use, or even home manufacture of alcohol. But large personal

American Patriot was a monthly magazine published by the Anti-Saloon League between 1912 and 1916. This cover from May 1912 shows a saloon keeper telling a brewer that his best recruits are dying. The brewer replies, "You must fill the ranks with young boys." The prohibition campaign stressed that liquor interests tried to hook youngsters on their product—much as today's anti-smoking campaign stresses that the tobacco industry tries to encourage young people to smoke. *(Courtesy Westerville, Ohio, Public Library, Anti-Saloon League Collection)*

RUM'S RECRUITS.

shipments, of course, were often destined to supply illegal retail sale or illegal saloons. In response, officials of the Anti-Saloon League began to think that the next step was to find a way to control interstate commerce. They greatly increased their lobbying efforts at the national level.

THE CAMPAIGN AGAINST PROSTITUTION EXPANDS

Between 1910 and 1915, the Progressive Era campaign against prostitution was at its most intense. In one city after another vice commission reports appeared—35 in those five years alone. The most influential was *The Social Evil in Chicago,* published by the Chicago Vice Commission in 1911. Of all the sordid information it contained, the reform-minded public was probably most horrified to learn that prostitution had become highly organized and was now another form of big business. "The first truth that the Commission desires to impress upon the citizens of Chicago," the report said, "is the fact that prostitution in this city is a *Commercialized Business* of large proportions with tremendous profits of more than Fifteen Million Dollars per year, controlled largely by men, not women. . . . In juxtaposition with this group of professional male exploiters stand ostensibly respectable citizens, both men and women, who are openly renting and leasing property for exorbitant sums, and thus sharing, through immorality of investments, the profits from this *Business*. . . ."[22] No longer run by independent madams as it once was, prostitution reaped profits for a web of landlords, corrupt politicians and police, liquor interests, even beauticians and clothing makers, druggists and doctors. Of course, most people continued to consider prostitution a moral evil, but the vice commission reports clearly established that it was a social and economic issue as well. Furthermore, it was an issue that mirrored larger progressive concerns like the greed of big business, the exploitation of workers, and the corruption of politics.

Anti-prostitution reformers formed a typical progressive coalition, although not all reform-minded people agreed on the causes of prostitution or had the same goals. Many groups—clubwomen, suffragists, settlement house workers, immigrant protective societies, temperance advocates, doctors, religious groups, municipal civic leagues tackled distinct aspects of the problem. Even Socialists took up the cause. Civic and municipal reformers concentrated on efforts to close red-light districts by means of red-light abatement laws. The first statewide law, passed in Iowa in 1909, penalized landlords who rented their property for use in prostitution. It was often regarded as a model act, and by 1917, 31 states and a long list of major cities had adopted a similar law. Oregon's variation was called the tin plate law. It required every building to have a tin plate affixed to it, engraved with the name of the owner. Abatement laws were not passed without controversy, however. Well-funded opponents argued they were attacks on private property. And of course, the madams and their "girls" were often tipped off in advance of closings and simply moved elsewhere.

Women's groups took a variety of approaches to reform. Some reformers worked to raise the age of consent (at which a girl can legally consent to sexual relations, still set at 14 in many states in 1900), to make it possible to prosecute men who procured, seduced, or raped young girls. Some organized travelers' aid to assist young female newcomers to large cities or worked to provide safe housing options, such as YWCAs. Some attempted to rehabilitate the prostitute herself. These efforts usually involved training for domestic service plus personal moral guidance. Unfortunately, rehabilitation efforts often ran afoul of differences in values between middle-class reformers and many prostitutes. As historian Ruth Rosen points out, some poor women knowingly chose to work as prostitutes because they saw it as the least onerous alternative among their limited and unpleasant choices for economic survival. These women almost always saw prostitution as preferable to domestic service, an opinion that middle-class reformers found incomprehensible.[23]

Reformers concerned about venereal disease also continued their work. In many cities sanitary groups, as they were called, had formed among medical personnel to tackle the issue. In 1910, they organized into a national association, the American Federation for Sex Hygiene (American Social Hygiene Association after 1913). Social hygienists sought to educate the public, and many urged men to avoid prostitutes as a health measure. One of their goals was to require men to take the Wasserman test for syphilis, developed in 1906, before they could obtain a marriage license. By 1921, 20 states had adopted the requirement. Some sanitary reformers argued in favor of licensing and regulating prostitution, but they continued to meet much opposition. "In the first place, there is always a conflict between sanitary and moral ends," said anti-regulationist Edward Seligman in a speech to the Society of Sanitary and Moral Prophylaxis. "The sanitary point of view does not look at all to the chances of reformation. . . . The chief objection to regulation is that the state cannot regulate anything without recognising it; and that the state in modem times has no business to lend its active support to prostitution through recognition."[24]

Many reformers were beginning to agree that prostitution would not be reduced until low wages and poor working conditions for women were improved. Study after study showed that independent young working women, found it nearly impossible to exist on the wages they could earn. Vice report after vice report held that they were particularly susceptible to recruitment as prostitutes for the simple reason of their financial need. Of special concern were the young employees of department stores because they were poorly paid yet also expected to dress well. Of course, as many historians caution, standards of sexual behavior were beginning to change during the Progressive Era, and reformers sometimes saw prostitution in behavior later called promiscuity. But in any case, the anti-prostitution movement lent important support to the efforts of labor reformers to improve women's wages and working conditions.

Public Alarm Over White Slavery

In 1909, muckraker George Kibbe Turner dropped a bombshell with his influential article about New York's organized prostitution rings, titled "The Daughters of the Poor." Exposés like Turner's helped infuse the campaign against prostitution with public alarm over white slavery. "White slavery" was forced prostitution from which a woman was prevented leaving or escaping. Its victims were presumed to be unsuspecting young women who were lured or kidnapped by procurers, usually male, and delivered to brothel owners for a fee. Many Americans incorrectly came to believe that the majority of prostitution was forced prostitution.

The term *white slavery*, which originated in early 19th-century England to describe the condition of early industrial workers, referred to slave-like conditions that exist in fact but not in law. Although public concern focused on women who were in fact racially white, the term white slavery was also used at times to refer to Asian and (less often) African-American women forced into prostitution. In fact, the forced prostitution about which historians have the most information is the plight of some Chinese women, primarily in West Coast cities. They had been knowingly or unknowingly sold to procurers by their poverty-stricken families in China or had unknowingly agreed to let a procurer advance their passage money to America.

Without doubt, the white slavery scare was greatly sensationalized. Under cover of moral outrage, novelists, movie producers, and some journalists titillated audiences with material that otherwise might well have been censored. For a few years Americans were led to believe that villainous procurers were lurking everywhere with chloroformed handkerchiefs or hypodermic needles full of drugs. They were also prone to blame forced prostitution on foreigners, especially the French, or on the new immigrants, especially East European Jews and Italians. Some of the men involved in prostitution rings (but certainly not all of them) did belong to these groups. Their activities were a great concern to ethnic leaders and immigrant societies in many cities, who organized programs first to protect their own daughters and second to protect their own good names. Because of the ethnic stereotypes and sensationalism surrounding forced prostitution, some historians have been disposed to discount its existence almost entirely. Unfortunately, the facts "all lead to the conclusion that the sale of some women into sexual slavery is an inescapable fact of the American past," concludes historian Ruth Rosen, although she adds it probably never accounted for more than 10 percent of all prostitutes during the era.[25]

The traffic in forced prostitution, it should be noted, was an international concern in the Progressive Era. European nations organized to fight the problem at the turn of the century, then invited the United States to participate in a treaty called the International Agreement for the Suppression of the Trade in White Women. The treaty was ratified by the Senate in 1905 and proclaimed by Roosevelt in 1908. The following year a report by the Immigration Commission substantiated cases of young women imported to work in brothels in American cities. Congress responded in two ways. It significantly strengthened anti-prostitution exclusions in the Immigration Act of 1910. It also passed the Mann Act, officially named the Act to Further Regulate Interstate and Foreign Commerce by Prohibiting the Transportation Therein for Immoral Purposes of Women and Girls. The Mann Act, based on Congress's constitutional power to regulate interstate commerce, made it a felony to transport women across state lines for "immoral purposes."

THE PITTSBURGH SURVEY

Paul Kellogg, a committed progressive, was editor of *Charities and the Commons,* the journal of the New York–based Charity Organization Society (COS) and the Chicago Commons settlement. In 1907, he consented to oversee a new project. The COS, in cooperation with reformers in Pittsburgh, wanted to organize an encyclopedic study of conditions there. Pittsburgh appeared to be the perfect place to study the problems that engaged Progressive Era reformers. It was heavily industrial, environmentally degraded, and politically corrupt; it had a history of labor troubles and was home to both mighty industrialists and many new immigrants. The city raised "a great, grimed question mark as to whether this is the type of community which the leading industrial center of the country is to set," wrote Kellogg. "What are American standards anyway?"[26] The newly established Russell Sage Foundation, whose purpose was to support the improvement of social and living conditions, agreed to provide financial assistance for the study as its first major undertaking.

Soon several dozen social workers, sociologists, economists, and other experts descended on the city, accompanied by Lewis Hine and other photographers. Their goal was to document every aspect of life in an urban industrial center. The findings of the project, called the Pittsburgh Survey, were published during 1909 in *Charities and the Commons,* then elaborated in six books between 1910 and 1914. The survey amassed information on the steel industry, industrial accidents, women workers, and family living conditions in Homestead, where the bitter 1892 steel strike had occurred. All were accompanied by extensive photodocumentation.

The Pittsburgh Survey was the first large-scale, systematic study of social conditions that had been created by the nation's dizzying social and economic change. It emphasized sociological analysis, but it was colored by a muckraking spirit and a stated goal of promoting social reform. Its findings as well as its method were extremely influential among social experts and reformers for the remainder of the Progressive Era. The term survey became very popular for a large, comprehensive social investigation, some 2,500 more of which would be undertaken over the next two decades. Kellogg changed the name of *Charities and the Commons* to *The Survey* as well, and it became recognized as a leading source of information on social conditions.

THE CAMPAIGN AGAINST CHILD LABOR CONTINUES

The campaign against child labor did not proceed swiftly. During the Taft years the National Child Labor Committee (NCLC) concentrated its efforts on canneries and the street trades, both of which were almost completely unregulated in 1909. It had little immediate success achieving regulation of fruit, vegetable, and coastal seafood canneries, which employed the youngest of all child workers. It did make a few gains in the street trades—uniformed messenger, telegraph, and delivery services, independent newsboys and -girls, peddlers, and bootblacks. According to child labor researchers, street trades exposed children to unsavory influences. The NCLC investigated the night messenger service in 1909 and 1910 at the flood tide of the anti-prostitution campaign and concluded it was used almost exclusively in the operation of prostitution and other vices. By 1913, 17 states had passed legislation limiting work as night messengers to those older than 18 or (as reformers preferred) 21.

The census of 1910 actually showed a slight increase over 1900 in the percentage of children, ages 10 to 15, who were employed for wages. The same year, the *Report on Women and Child Wage-Earners in the United States* authorized by Congress in 1907 began to appear, eventually reaching 19 volumes. The report verified the dreadful conditions that reformers and social workers had reported for some time. Although many business interests denounced the report as reform propaganda, it received much publicity in popular sources. Still, by 1912, only nine states met all of the recommendations that the NCLC had set back in 1904: minimum ages of 14 in manufacturing and 16 in mining; an eight-hour day and no night labor for workers under 16; and documentary proof of age. Twenty-two of the 48 states still permitted children under 14 to work in factories; 30 allowed children under 16 to work in mines; 31 allowed children under 16 to labor more than eight hours a day; 28 allowed them to work at night; 23 did not require documentation of age. Child labor in home sweatshops, agriculture, canneries, and street trades other than night messenger services remained almost completely unregulated.

Nonetheless, the strength of child labor reformers was growing. The NCLC, founded by 50 people in 1904, had 6,400 contributing members by 1912. An increasing number of them were beginning to believe that only federal child-labor legislation could accomplish serious reform.[27]

THE CHILDREN'S BUREAU IS ESTABLISHED

The establishment of a federal children's bureau was a longtime goal of the National Child Labor Committee (NCLC). A proposal for the bureau had first been introduced into Congress in early 1906, but no action was taken. The NCLC continued its quest, each year mounting an extensive letter-writing campaign to Congress and producing a barrage of publicity materials.

In January 1909, shortly before he was to leave office, President Roosevelt convened the first White House

Julia Lathrop, a close associate of Jane Addams and Florence Kelley, was appointed head of the newly established U.S. Children's Bureau in 1912. She was the first woman to head a major federal agency. Child labor reformers had waged a long battle for the bureau. *(Library of Congress, Prints and Photographs Division, LC-USZ62-10274)*

Conference on the Care of Dependent Children at the urging of social workers and NCLC officials. After the widely publicized conference, the president sent a special message to Congress and again urged the establishment of a federal children's bureau, as the conference recommended. Congress finally began hearings on the bill. Not surprisingly, it met opposition from those with vested interests in child labor as well as from advocates of states' rights who opposed the extension of federal authority in general. Three years later, in April 1912, Congress finally passed an act establishing a federal Children's Bureau within the Department of Commence and Labor. The bureau was a research agency, charged to "investigate and report upon all matters pertaining to the welfare of children and child life among all our classes of people."[28] Although it did not have administrative power, it marked the first acknowledgment of federal responsibility for the welfare of American children.

The first head of the bureau was Julia Lathrop, an attorney, former Hull-House resident, and well-known reformer. Lathrop was the first woman to head a federal agency. She served successfully for the remainder of the Progressive Era.

MOTHERS' PENSIONS: THE BEGINNINGS OF MODERN PUBLIC WELFARE

Somewhat unexpectedly, the White House Conference on the Care of Dependent Children also jump-started another reform movement: the establishment of publicly funded mother's pensions. Less controversial than child labor issues at the time, mother's pensions marked the start of modern public welfare in America.

While child labor reformers were waging their campaign, charity organizations like Children's Aid Societies and Child Rescue Leagues had been grappling with the less visible but growing problem of dependent children. According to one estimate, the number of children in child asylums more than tripled between 1890 and 1920.[29] Some dependent children were orphans, some were delinquent, some were victims of neglect—but many were half orphans in the language of the day, usually due to the death of their breadwinning father. In an era with meager wages, high rates of disease, no unemployment insurance or compensation for injuries on the job, restricted opportunities for working women, and no state aid, such families often had no choice but to put the children in an institution. Opposition was growing, however, to filling institutions with children who had one competent, living parent. White House conferees came out solidly in favor of maintaining them in their families by aiding mothers.

The recommendations the conference presented to President Roosevelt opened by asserting, "Home life is the highest and finest product of civilization. It is the great molding force of mind and of character. Children should not be deprived of it except for urgent and compelling reasons." When misfortune intervened, the document continued, aid should be given to maintain the family for the children's sake. "The home should not be broken up for reasons of poverty," it stated, "but only for considerations of inefficiency or immorality."[30] Esteem for the home was a widely shared value and one of Roosevelt's favorite moral themes. He quoted the recommendation in its entirety to Congress. It also received favorable press attention.

White House conferees shared the progressive view that most poverty was a result of impersonal social and economic forces, not of individual character flaws. Nonetheless, many conferees disapproved of public funding for mother's pensions. The most vocal opponents were established, voluntary charity organizations, who preferred selective and personal social work. After debating the issue, the conference recommended that aid should be determined "by the general relief policy of each community" but "preferably in the form of private charity rather than of public relief."[31]

Despite the recommendation, the idea of publicly funded mother's pensions to safeguard children and the home struck a popular chord in an increasingly progressive nation. More and more Americans thought that traditional charity was outpaced by the conditions of modern industrial society and that government could and should step into the breach. Within two years of the conference, states began to pass legislation that authorized the use of public funds for assistance to widowed and sometimes to married but abandoned mothers of young children. (Unwed mothers were not covered.) Missouri passed the first law in 1911, although it applied only to Kansas City; Illinois passed the first statewide law the same year. The idea spread with remarkable speed. By 1913, 18 states had passed similar enabling acts, and by 1919, 39 had done so.

The first mother's pensions were small; usually mothers were expected to work to supplement them. Most early state laws did not even require aid to be given but merely permitted local communities to do so if they chose—and many did not. In no state were the pensions originally established as a right, nor automatically awarded; as historian Linda Gordon has titled her study of mothers' aid, the intended recipients were "pitied but not entitled." Social workers, as representatives of the state, had the authority to examine both the need and the moral worthiness of the mother before granting aid—and they did so. Nonetheless, the first mother's pensions enabled many families to remain together. They also marked an important milestone in public social policy. Mother's pensions eventually developed into Aid to Dependent Children programs, nationally instituted in the Social Security Act of 1935, and today often referred to by the abbreviated term *welfare*.

HOOKWORM AND OTHER PUBLIC HEALTH ISSUES

During the progressive decades, public health issues became increasingly urgent, due to tremendous urban growth, population congestion, inadequate sanitary facilities, contaminated water supplies, impure milk and food, and the spread of epidemics under these conditions. Luckily, late 19th-century discoveries in bacteriology and immunology had created a foundation for diagnostic and preventive medicine. Cities began to establish health departments, inspectors, and even diagnostic laboratories. Many voluntary reform groups organized crusades and educational campaigns on health-related issues. Increasingly, public health reformers created a typical progressive coalition. State boards of health were organized or greatly expanded, drawing together public, private, and voluntary groups. In 1912, Congress officially created the United States Public Health Service on the foundation of the existing Public Health and Marine Hospital Service.[32] The new federal Public Health Service was authorized to conduct investigations and research, aid state and local health departments, and oversee interstate control of communicable diseases.

Not all Progressive Era public health problems were confined to overcrowded cities, however. In the rural American South, the disease of hookworm was very common because the soil, warm temperatures, and people's habits were suitable to its growth. Hookworm, a parasitic worm that lives in the intestinal tract, is spread through soil contaminated by unsanitary disposal of human waste. The larvae hatch in the soil, then easily and quickly penetrate bare feet or the hands of agricultural workers to enter the body. Hookworm eventually causes anemia and sometimes death. Symptoms include protruding shoulder blades and bellies, eye problems, impaired mental development in the young, and great lack of energy. So widespread was the disease in the rural South that its symptoms had created a disparaging stereotype of "poor whites": thin, stooped, slovenly, dull-witted, and very lazy.

The man almost singlehandedly responsible for the progressive campaign to eradicate hookworm was Dr. Charles Wardell Stiles, born in South Carolina. In 1902, Dr. Stiles, a research zoologist with the Public Health and Marine Hospital Service,

identified hookworm as the "germ of laziness" that infected the South. His professional colleagues accepted his work, but at first public reaction was unbelieving in the
South and rollicking with mockery in the North. Stiles persevered and eventually
helped convinced John D. Rockefeller to donate $1 million to the cause. On October
26, 1909, the Rockefeller Sanitary Commission for the Eradication of Hookworm
Disease was organized to conduct a five-year campaign of cure and prevention in the
South. States that chose to participate appointed a director of sanitation to work with
the national experts. In 1910, Alabama, Arkansas, Georgia, Louisiana, Mississippi, North
Carolina, South Carolina, Tennessee, and Virginia began their work; Kentucky and
Texas joined later. Doctors and scientists identified and treated the victims and mounted extensive education campaigns. The campaign had rapid and dramatic results, greatly improving the health and vitality of rural southerners. In Mississippi, for example,
more than one out of every three adults and children had been infected with the disease. The national commission ended in 1914, but states continued the program and by
the 1920s had virtually eradicated the disease.

The most prominent nationwide public health campaign during the progressive
decades was against tuberculosis. In 1900, 11 percent, or more than one out of every
10 deaths in America, was due to the disease. Tuberculosis is exceedingly contagious.
Infection knew no class or neighborhood boundaries, but the disease particularly
ravaged the urban poor whose overcrowded living conditions made preventive
hygiene almost impossible. In 1904, the National Association for the Study and Prevention of Tuberculosis (later the American Lung Association) was organized, primarily by medical personnel. Anti-tuberculosis organizations soon arose throughout
the nation, while reform groups and women's clubs also took up the campaign to
educate the public. Reformers formed coalitions to demand the establishment of
state sanatoriums where patients could be isolated and treated. The campaign helped
contain the disease, although the cure for tuberculosis was not discovered during the
Progressive Era. In 1920, it remained the most deadly of all contagious diseases in
America.[33]

EXPLORERS REACH THE ARCTIC POLES

On April 6, 1909, two American explorers attained a long-sought goal: they reached
the North Pole. Robert Peary, the leader of the expedition, and Matthew Henson
were also accompanied by four Inuit men, Oatah, Egingwah, Seegloo, and Ookeah.
The event was surrounded by controversy, however. Peary telegraphed his news upon
his return to Labrador on September 6, 1909. But just a week earlier another explorer,
Dr. Frederick A. Cook, had telegraphed from the Shetland Islands that he had reached
the North Pole a full year sooner than Peary—on April 21, 1908.

For several decades Arctic explorers from a number of different nations had
attempted to reach the pole. Peary himself had made eight trips to the Arctic circle
beginning in 1883. In 1897, a group of wealthy men with interest in geographic
exploration formed the Peary Arctic Club to support his continuing efforts. Peary was
accompanied on most of his trips by Henson, an African-American explorer. On one
trip Peary's wife, Josephine, was a member of the expedition, and Dr. Cook himself
had been in Peary's party several times.

On the 1909, expedition Peary's party of 24 men set out from Ellesmere Island in
the Canadian Arctic to cross some 400 miles of ice floes. But the last 140 miles were
traversed only by Peary, Henson, the four Eskimo men, 40 dogs, and five sleds.

Dr. Cook had set out on his own expedition the previous year. When his wire
claiming success reached the States first, most people accepted it. But Peary, upon
learning of Cook's claim, immediately disputed it. Investigations ensued. Cook's truth-
fulness was disputed by Inuit witnesses. Peary's records were examined and accepted by

the scientific community. In 1911, Congress, after an investigation of its own, officially concluded Peary was first to reach the pole. Nonetheless some continued to believe that Peary's wealthy and influential backers had colluded to discredit Cook, and the controversy persisted. (Today, many scientists and historians believe that neither reached the pole.) Henson's role in the expedition received almost no attention at the time, and Peary himself was disinclined to share the credit.

Meanwhile, another explorer, Norwegian Roald Amundsen, successfully reached the South Pole in December 1911. News of the feat did not reach the world until March 1912.

CENSORSHIP OF THE MOVIES BEGINS

In late December 1908, all nickelodeons in New York City had been closed without warning, by order of the mayor. As the act powerfully demonstrated, reformers and civic leaders were increasingly apprehensive about the young motion picture industry, whose primary audience at the time was poor and working people. The Motion Picture Patents Company (a trust recently organized by Thomas Edison to manufacture movie equipment and make films for it) responded quickly. The Patents Company agreed to a form of self-regulation, setting a pattern the movie industry would follow throughout the 20th century.

In early 1909, the first motion picture regulatory group was created. It was organized by the People's Institute, a reform-minded, continuing education enterprise for working people, affiliated with Cooper Union in Lower Manhattan and directed by a board of distinguished philanthropists and reformers.[34] The Institute assembled representatives of 10 different New York civic and reform organizations, naming them the National Board of Motion Picture Censorship (called the National Board of Review of Motion Pictures after 1915). Each day, volunteers viewed films. They rejected or required cuts in those they believed to show too much crime or lawlessness (their most frequent objection), violence, or sexual suggestiveness. Edison's trust agreed not to release films that did not meet the board's approval.

Because New York was the center of movie production in 1909, the trust and the board both hoped that their seal of approval would be accepted nationwide. It was not. Local censors continued to apply local standards in communities throughout the nation. In Chicago, which was the second-largest center of movie production, for example, the police had had the power to censor films since 1907 and sometimes rejected those approved in New York. In some states, movie distributors and theater owners allied with reformers to support state-level regulations hoping to limit inconsistent local censorship of nationally distributed films. In 1912, Pennsylvania became the first state to pass movie censorship laws; Kansas and Ohio followed in 1913.

Although the influence of the Board of Review was limited, the ready cooperation of the Patents trust did improve the reputation of the movie industry overall. Civic leaders were reassured that entrepreneurs were respectable members of the business community with some concern for public well-being. Thomas Edison's studio even agreed to make films for reform or welfare organizations like the National Child Labor Committee and the American Red Cross. In return, some charitable, educational, religious, and reform interests began to promote motion pictures as a potential force for the good. Because movies were so popular and affordable for working people, some reformers believed they could be used for uplift—that is, to give ordinary people access to cultural landmarks, like Shakespeare's plays, that they could not afford or did not enjoy in other formats. Others thought movies could reinforce shared American values, helping to heal class divisions and acculturate new immigrants.

THE MOVIE INDUSTRY EXPANDS

While the movie industry wrestled with censorship, movies themselves began moving uptown. Films were becoming longer and more expensively produced, often adapting well-known plays or popular novels. At the same time, in both small towns and large cities entrepreneurs converted vaudeville houses and opera houses into permanent, more comfortable movie theaters, located in more respectable entertainment districts or commercial areas. By 1912, new "movie palaces" were also in the works. They were elaborately designed and spectacularly decorated theaters, with features like lavish restrooms, orchestra pits, and uniformed attendants to provide service and guarantee decorum. As these changes occurred, movie attendance by middle- and even upper-class people boomed, but working people also eagerly patronized the new movie houses. The new theaters charged a little more for admission than neighborhood nickeleons but still far less than performing arts events like plays, operas, or even vaudeville shows. Unlike almost any other kind of entertainment event, one price bought any seat in the house in most movie theaters—with the exception of segregated seating for African Americans in most places, usually in the balcony.

Although social reformers were becoming less concerned about the movie industry, those who disliked trusts were becoming more concerned. In 1909 the first major independent production company was founded. (Called the Independent Motion Picture Company or IMP, it was the forerunner of Universal Studios.) Independent producers and distributors soon began to sprout everywhere. Edison's Patents company trust made ruthless efforts to drive the independents out of business by filing lawsuits continually. The independents in turn lobbied Washington for relief. In the summer of 1912 as the presidential campaign heated up, the Taft administration filed an antitrust suit against the Patents company. Three years later the government won its case against the company. But by then, trustbusting in the movie industry was almost a moot point. In 1908, when the trust was organized, it had controlled almost 100 percent of movie production; as early as 1912, however, independent growth had been so vigorous that it controlled little more than half.[35]

Two other changes in the movie industry began to occur between 1909 and 1912. One was development of the star system. Previously, actors in movies were not identified by name. As independent companies sprang up, however, they discovered that certain actors could attract audiences and help them compete with the trust. Soon trust companies were billing their actors as well. Another change was the beginning of the industry's move from New York to Southern California. According to movie industry legend, independent producers first went west to escape harassment by the trust. Historian Eileen Bowser points out, however, that both independent and trust producers arrived more or less permanently in California in 1909. They were attracted by the climate and the varied scenery because almost all filming was done out-of-doors. By 1911, several trust members had established studios near Los Angeles; by 1912 an independent producer had built the first studio in the suburb called Hollywood.[36]

DISASTER AT SEA: THE *TITANIC*

On April 10, 1912, the White Star Line liner *Titanic* left Southampton, England, on its maiden voyage to New York. It was the largest and most luxurious ship yet built and, according to naval architects and engineers, its splendid design made it unsinkable. Many prominent people had booked passage for the much-publicized vessel's first voyage. The *Titanic* carried middle-class travelers as well and a steerage full of immigrants heading for the United States and Canada. Also on board was Bruce Ismay, the head of the White Star Line. Ismay hoped the ship would further impress the world by arriving in New York ahead of schedule.

As the voyage progressed, Captain Edward Smith steadily fired new boilers and increased the speed. He continued to do so, possibly at the behest of Ismay, as the ship sailed into an ice field near Newfoundland and received warnings to proceed cautiously. Shortly before midnight on April 14—a remarkably clear, calm night—the *Titanic* collided with an iceberg off the Banks of Newfoundland and began taking on water. Two hours and 40 minutes after the impact, the huge ship sank. Far too few lifeboats had been put on board. Of more than 2,200 passengers and crew, some 700 were saved, pulled from lifeboats around 4 A.M. by the steamship *Carpathia*. By April 16, the scope of the disaster was clear. More than 1,500 had died. Most survivors were women and children—although Ismay survived as well.

The disaster immediately took on the dimensions of myth. Survivors' accounts, songs, fiction, and drama quickly appeared. Part of the fascination was certainly the terrible human tragedy and the instances of bravery, cowardice, and endurance it inspired. But the event also seemed to epitomize many experiences and concerns of the Progressive Era: the blind glorification of technology, machines, speed, and size; the callous disregard of safety for the many by the powerful few; the voracious desire for sumptuousness among the wealthy. Perhaps most telling of all, the disaster highlighted the modern class privileges and divisions that worried so many progressives. Sixty percent of the first-class passengers survived, but only 42 percent of second class, 25 percent of third class or steerage, and 24 percent of the crew. Yet all, many a clergyman pointed out, were brought to grief by a power no human could control.[37]

By April 18, Michigan senator William Alden Smith had begun a congressional investigation, dispatching a cadre of senators to New York to subpoena Ismay before he could leave the country. The British also ordered an inquiry and heard testimony for over a month. Both commissions recommended changes in certain maritime safety procedures. But many questions remained unsatisfactorily answered and the British report in particular was widely regarded as a whitewash. Was there a ship within sight at the time of the collision that refused to aid the *Titanic*? Were lifeboats deliberately under-filled (the ship carried enough for some 1,700 people) because the crew or other passengers refused to load steerage passengers? Had Ismay ordered the captain to maintain a foolhardy speed? Interest in the 1912 disaster has only increased since the ship's remains were located on the ocean's floor, mostly intact, in 1985.

THE CONTOURS OF THE LABOR MOVEMENT

The years between 1909 and 1912 saw increasing strife between capital and labor, much of it violent. Employers' organizations kept up a barrage of antiunion publicity and continued the open-shop campaign to reduce or defeat union influence. Nonetheless, unions recovered from a slump in membership during Roosevelt's second term and began to grow again. By 1910, union membership again approached its 1904 high. Unions still represented only a small minority of American wage earners, mostly skilled craft workers. What historian James Green calls "the uprising of the unskilled," however, was about to begin. The diverse, unskilled or semiskilled industrial workers who did not belong to unions were showing a new militancy, holding mass and sometimes spontaneous strikes. Officials of the existing craft union movement did not digest this development overnight. But faced with hostility from employers on one side and challenges from radical labor advocates on the other, they began to rethink industrial (industrywide) unions to incorporate more workers.[38]

The labor movement "coalesced around three organizational centers," as historians Priscilla Murolo and A. B. Chitty put it—the AFL (American Federation of Labor), the IWW (Industrial Workers of the World), and the Socialist Party of America.[39] The AFL was by far the largest union but also the most exclusive and politically conservative. It was led by Samuel Gompers, who consistently denounced both radicalism and violence. It relied on collective bargaining, or the negotiation of contracts for workers by professional union representatives, and strikes only when necessary. The AFL had recently begun to take a role in politics, primarily to work for an end to injunctions against strikers under the Sherman Anti-Trust Act. It primarily represented skilled workers, although it included the large, industrywide United Mine Workers (UMW).

The IWW, often called the Wobblies, was a radical union aimed at the mass of unskilled workers. Many IWW members were migratory mining, timber, and agricultural workers. After 1908, IWW leaders gave almost no emphasis to political participation—because many members did not even have permanent homes and thus, could not vote. Instead leaders increasingly advocated militant direct action, such as strikes, and some advocated violence as well. They were avowedly revolutionary. Their ultimate goal was one big strike, enabling workers to take over industry and even government. Wobblies were masterful agitators, and they always drew quick responses from authorities who hoped to suppress them. They became known for free-speech campaigns. When IWW organizers were arrested in a town, the union would begin flooding it with new detachments of soapbox speakers until the jails could hold no more people. The first campaigns to gain national attention were in Missoula, Montana, and Spokane, Washington, both in 1909.

The same year, the IWW began to attract public attention by entering spontaneous strikes and organizing the workers. The first was against United States Steel at McKees Rocks, Pennsylvania. IWW organizers united the largely immigrant and multilingual unskilled workforce and also gained some cooperation from craft unions, an alliance which the AFL had never achieved. After a six-week strike that cost 13 deaths and hundreds of injuries, the Wobblies won some improvements for the workers. Similar strikes followed in other steel plants in Pennsylvania and Indiana.

Wobblies prided themselves on practicing no discrimination on any basis—race, color, gender, or national origin. During the southern lumber wars of 1911 to 1913 in Louisiana and East Texas, they even succeeded in forming an integrated union of both whites and blacks, although company and governmental opposition eventually defeated it. Although strikes and free-speech campaigns brought publicity and new recruits, the Wobblies were not successful at day-to-day maintenance of union locals.

THE SOCIALIST PARTY OF AMERICA

The growing Socialist Party of America also attracted many workers, including some labor union members. Socialist labor leaders opposed the AFL's lack of interest in broad programs of social and political change. Socialists believed that negotiated agreements on limited, concrete objectives could not end the class struggle between those who owned factories and those who worked in them. They supported the right of workers to strike at any time. They also looked forward to the ultimate goal of replacing private capitalism with collectively owned and worker-directed industry. In Europe, where socialism was more influential among workers, socialists and labor union officials usually worked together and supported a labor party in politics. In America, however, they did not. Instead, the unions themselves were the battleground, and the adherents and opponents of socialism wrangled constantly to dominate them. Socialists were strongest in the industrywide unions like those in mining and in the garment industry. Opponents of socialism, however—chief among them Samuel Gompers—succeeded in maintaining overall control of the union movement.

The Socialist Party of America was also home to a great variety of people and factions other than union members. Some were thoroughgoing Marxists who opposed capitalism and private property in all forms. At the other end of the spectrum were reformers not far to the left of mainstream progressivism, like Florence Kelley and William English Walling, or intellectuals and writers like Jack London, Upton Sinclair, and muckraker

Charles Edward Russell. The party also included many farmers. Under the inclusive leadership of Eugene V. Debs, the Socialist Party did not advocate violent revolution. Instead, it advocated using the electoral system to reach its twin goals: a thoroughly democratic cooperative commonwealth and public ownership of resources and industry. It also supported many immediate reform issues, such as clean, efficient government and even the campaign against prostitution. Socialist Party members, like other Americans, differed on such important public issues as immigration, racial segregation, and women's rights.

The Socialist Party reached its peak of influence in America during the Taft years. In 1912, its official membership was 118,000. The party published more than 300 periodicals in a number of different languages. The most important, *Appeal to Reason,* was 1913 reached a paid circulation of more than 760,000. In the same year, about 1,200 officials throughout the nation were in office on the Socialist Party ticket. Among them were a U.S. representative from Wisconsin, Victor Berger, and more than 70 mayors in medium-sized cities such as Milwaukee; Berkeley; Reading, Pennsylvania; and Butte, Montana. The public usually associated socialism with large cities like New York and Chicago. But, in fact, the party's greatest voting strength was in small towns and rural villages west of the Mississippi among miners, railroad workers, lumbermen, and farmers or agricultural workers. The largest state organization was in Oklahoma.[40]

THE UPRISING OF THE 20,000

The garment industry in New York employed thousands of workers—at least 30,000 in the ladies' shirtwaist (blouse) and dress trade alone. More and more, they worked in factories located in new loft buildings in lower Manhattan, rather than in smaller sweatshops. Although the work site had changed, however, conditions had improved but little. Workspaces were overcrowded, poorly maintained, unsanitary, and built with little thought to safety. Most shirtwaist workers were young women between 16 and 25; most were Italian or East European Jewish immigrants or the children of immigrants. They toiled 10-to-12-hour days, six or seven days a week, for six dollars a week in wages. They were closely overseen and sometimes sexually harassed.

In the fall of 1909, some workers at one of the largest shirtwaist factories, the Triangle Shirtwaist Company, tried to form a local chapter of the nine-year-old AFL-affiliated International Ladies' Garment Workers Union (ILGWU). The company fired them. The workers called a strike. The company hired strikebreakers and ruffians to harass and even beat the picketing workers and the police arrested the strikers. Soon the Women's Trade Union League (WTUL) came to their aid with financial and political support. The WTUL was a coalition of reformers, philanthropists, and working women founded to help women workers unionize to better their conditions. Socially prominent women such as Anne Morgan, daughter of banker J. P. Morgan, and Alva Vanderbilt Belmont were among those who took an active role.

On November 22, workers from many garment companies held a mass meeting in Cooper Union Hall. Samuel Gompers and other union officials spoke. Then a young worker named Clara Lemlich, who had been beaten on the picket line, took the stage. "I am tired of listening to speakers who talk in general terms," she cried. "What we are here for is to decide whether we shall or shall not strike. I offer a resolution that a general strike be declared—now." The audience rose to its feet, cheering, then took an old Jewish oath to support the cause.[41]

Beginning the next day more than 20,000 shirtwaist workers walked off the job, giving the strike its name, the uprising of the twenty thousand. New York was astonished. Rabbis, priests, and ministers supported the effort. Prominent WTUL women joined the picket lines, hoping to reduce the violence. The strike spread to Philadelphia. In December, the Waist and Dressmakers Manufacturers' Association offered a settlement. It reduced the workweek to 52 hours, increased wages, and improved sanitary conditions—but did not recognize the union. At the urging of union officials, the strikers rejected this offer. The strike continued until February 1910, by which time most companies had made separate agreements with their workers.

The "startling revolt" of the women garment workers, writes historian James Green, "signaled the beginning of the unskilled workers' movement toward industrial unionism and the opening of doors to women's renewed participation in the labor movement." It gave rise to a group of young, militant, and often socialist-affiliated women union leaders like Clara Lemlich and Rose Schneiderman, who also worked closely with WTUL reformers.[42] The strike also galvanized unionization throughout the garment industry. Membership of the ILGWU skyrocketed. In June 1910, the ILGWU called a strike of more than 50,000 cloak-and-suit makers in New York, most of whom were immigrant men. Reform lawyer Louis Brandeis mediated the settlement, called the protocol of peace. The protocol created a progressive arbitration board with labor, employer, and public representatives to settle future disputes and to eliminate both strikes and the employers' lockout. It also established a preferential union shop (union members were given preference in hiring but union membership could neither be required as in a closed shop nor ignored as in an open shop). In September, some 40,000 garment workers walked out in Chicago. The United Garment Workers of America, an older AFL craft union, took charge of the strike; the Chicago WTUL and Hull-House associates provided aid. The settlement, negotiated for labor by lawyer Clarence Darrow, also resulted in an arbitration board and other gains. These accords were the first major successes in improving wages and working conditions for unskilled and semi-skilled workers in the formerly "sweated" garment industry.

THE TRIANGLE SHIRTWAIST FACTORY FIRE

On March 25, 1911, a terrible fire took the lives of nearly 150 young workers trapped on the upper floors of the Triangle Shirtwaist Factory in New York. On the following day the entire front page of the *New York World,* shown here, was devoted to the tragedy, which horrified the nation. *(Library of Congress, Prints and Photographs Division, LC-USZ62-122315)*

Unsafe and onerous working conditions in the garment industry did not change overnight. On March 25, 1911, that fact was horrifically demonstrated to the entire nation. At about 4:30 on a Saturday afternoon, some 500 employees were still at work in the Triangle Shirtwaist factory, whose workers' efforts to unionize had spurred the uprising of the 20 thousand. The factory was located in a relatively new loft building a block off Washington Square, on floors eight through 10. A fire broke out in a large pile of scrap material on the eighth floor and spread rapidly upward. There were no adequate fire escapes and many exits were locked or blocked. Some of the terrified workers managed to escape. But while a gathering crowd watched in horror, nearly 50 trapped young women, some of them on fire, leaped or fell to their deaths on the streets below. Another 100 were trapped and died inside. Most of the dead were young Jewish or Italian women, several only 14 years old.[43]

Sadly, the Triangle fire was not the worst workplace calamity of the era measured by number of casualties—several mining disasters claimed more lives. But the youth and gender of the victims and the graphic reports of the way they died in the middle of the nation's largest city shocked the public into action. Union members, reformers, and ordinary New Yorkers organized memorial services and relief efforts for the injured and the families of the dead. The State of New York quickly appointed a Factory Investigating Commission. It included Frances Perkins of the National Consumers' League, who had gone to the site and watched the building burn. (In later years, Perkins became U.S. secretary of labor and the first woman cabinet member.) As a result of the commission's work, the most thorough to date on industrial safety, New York State passed legislation that improved fire and other safety regulations and limited women's workweek to 50 hours.

The owners of the factory, Isaac Harris and Max Blanck, were charged with manslaughter but found not guilty. Most Americans were shocked at the verdict: "147 Dead, Nobody Guilty," the *Literary Digest* titled its report. In 1913, as a result of civil suits by the families of some victims, Harris and Blanck agreed to pay $75 compensation per victim.

THE LAWRENCE TEXTILE STRIKE

Unskilled workers in New England textile mills like those of Lawrence, Massachusetts, also endured hard working conditions and low pay. At the urging of reformers, the Massachusetts state legislature passed a law limiting women's and children's workweek in the mills to 54 hours. In response to the law, the American Woolen Company of Lawrence announced on January 11, 1912, that all wages would be reduced proportionately Many workers made only six dollars per week and the average was nine. The next day workers began walking out. Soon more than 20,000 men and women throughout the city were on strike.[44]

The vast majority of textile mill workers in Lawrence were not union members, although a few of the highly skilled belonged to the AFL-affiliated United Textile Workers. Soon IWW organizers Joseph Ettor and Arturo Giovannitti arrived to organize the unskilled strikers. The American Woolen Company attempted to reopen the mills with strikebreakers and police assistance. In a picket line scuffle a young woman striker was shot and killed, and Ettor and Giovannitti were arrested as accessories to her death. IWW leader William "Big Bill" Haywood and fiery young IWW speaker Elizabeth Gurley Flynn arrived. The National Guard moved in.

As the strike continued, the strike committee contrived a plan to help striking families and publicize their plight. They arranged with people in nearby cities to take in the strikers' children temporarily. Several hundred children departed Lawrence by train for New York, where they were met at Grand Central Station by a cheering crowd. As the strikers had hoped, the children generated publicity and public sympathy. Soon Lawrence police issued orders to prevent any more from leaving the city. When the next group attempted to board a train, mothers and children were forcibly dragged off and arrested. Of course, the incident only magnified sympathy for the strikers. In Congress Victor Berger, elected as a Socialist, insisted upon a congressional hearing.

In the meantime, dynamite was discovered planted throughout Lawrence. It was immediately blamed on the IWW. The strikers protested that they were being framed. And indeed, the real culprits were soon identified as local businessmen.

In mid-March, with no sign of wavering among the strikers, the American Woolen Company settled. The strikers received higher wages and other improvements. Eventually, Ettor and Giovannitti were acquitted on the charge of murder. After the remarkable victory, some 18,000 mill workers joined the IWW. Its success in the textile mills was to be shortlived but significant nonetheless. Many Lawrence workers were recent immigrants, and the strikers hailed from as many as 40 different national and ethnic groups, speaking many different languages. Traditional craft-union officials had long insisted that unskilled immigrant workers, divided by culture and language, could not be organized. Lawrence conclusively proved that belief to be wrong.

The *Los Angeles Times* Bombing and Aftermath

Harrison Gray Otis, long-time owner of the *Los Angeles Times,* was an unrelenting opponent of labor unions. After he eliminated the union at the *Times* in 1890, he added a masthead to the paper reading "True Industrial Freedom" and kept up the attack on labor causes editorially. On October 1, 1910, while Los Angeles metal trades workers were in the midst of a unionizing drive, a bomb exploded outside the *Times* building. It collapsed and many workers were trapped inside. Twenty-one died and others were injured, some very seriously. Another bomb was found at Otis's home.

Otis saw to the hiring of a private investigator of national repute, William J. Burns. Burns soon implicated James McNamara and his brother John, secretary-treasurer of the International Union of Bridge and Structural Iron Workers. (Since 1905 the iron-building trades had been involved in some 80 dynamite explosions against open-shop employers.) The brothers were arrested—John in a raid on an Indiana union headquarters—and secretly returned to California with the aid of highly unorthodox legal maneuvering. Union members of all political persuasions united in their defense. Supporters were resolute in the belief that their arrest was a vicious attempt to frame and discredit the whole union movement. Samuel Gompers and the AFL hired famous trial lawyer Clarence Darrow to defend the brothers.

Darrow was known for his support of labor causes. But after he had examined all the evidence, he concluded that they were in fact guilty and would doubtless be executed. At his urging the brothers confessed and pleaded guilty in a deal to avoid the death penalty, as the trial was about to begin in early December 1911. James McNamara received a life sentence and John McNamara was sentenced to 15 years.

The McNamara confessions stunned Gompers, union members, and the reform-minded public. Some people, both in and out of the labor movement, continued to believe that the brothers had confessed falsely in order to avoid execution. Darrow himself was indicted for jury tampering (he was acquitted) but also castigated by many union members for his handling of the case.

Alarmed by the McNamara confessions and the escalating war between labor and capital, a group of prominent reformers prepared a memorial to Congress, requesting an extensive investigation of industrial conditions nationwide. It was signed by figures such as Henry Morganthau, Lillian Wald, Samuel McCune Lindsay, Louis Brandeis, and Jane Addams. In February 1912, President Taft asked Congress to create a commission to study the causes of disagreement between capital and labor. He continued, "The magnitude and complexity of modern industrial disputes have put upon some of our statutes and our present mechanism for adjusting such differences—where we can be said to have any mechanism at all—a strain they were never intended to bear."[45] The Commission on Industrial Relations was established in August, to be composed of three representatives each from labor, management, and the public. President Taft's appointees were not confirmed before he left office, however, and action awaited the next administration.

Government Acts to Protect Workers

Events like the Lawrence strike, the Triangle fire, and the Los Angeles *Times* bombing attracted a lion's share of attention from progressive journalists and reformers. During the Taft years, however, labor turmoil was occurring North to South and coast to coast. The militancy of the IWW and the growing threat of socialism had been added to the traditional threat of union-sponsored strikes, and the public was more and more concerned. Reformers continued to publicize the terrible conditions and wages that many American workers endured and increasingly sought government action to alleviate them. Increasingly some business leaders themselves were persuaded of the need to conciliate labor—primarily, as James Weinstein and other historians argue, to deflect the possibility of more radical change.[46] Under pressure from business leaders, reformers, and the public, a wave of labor legislation swept over America between 1910 and 1913.

The Federal Government Responds to Mining Disasters

On November 13, 1909, a fire broke out in the coal mine near Cherry, Illinois. Nearly 500 men and boys were at work, some in shafts 500 feet beneath the earth's surface. The fire quickly spread. Some workers were rescued and a week later 21 were found alive, having survived in total darkness behind a wall of mud and timbers they had built to shut out the smoke and poisonous fumes. But 259 men and boys perished, including 12 members of the last team to attempt rescue efforts on the day of the fire. Cherry was the second-worst mining disaster in American history. It was the fourth within two years to claim victims numbering in the hundreds; all told, more than 1,500 coal miners lost their lives in that 24-month period.

In all, more than 4,000 miners died in accidents in the decade from 1901 to 1910, and the year 1909 saw the largest number of individual coal mine disasters in American history.[47] Congress faced mounting pressure from progressives to act. In May 1910 Congress established a Bureau of Mines in the Department of the Interior, originally recommended by Roosevelt in 1907. The Bureau of Mines was established as a scientific and technological research agency only and during the Progressive Era did not have inspection authority.[48] Under Dr. Joseph Holmes, a geologist, the bureau concentrated on increasing safety and reducing the death rate. Holmes coined the quickly popular slogan "Safety First." He developed rescue teams, which traveled in railroad cars specially built for mining emergency response and were outfitted with equipment like breathing or oxygen helmets. When not in action the teams and cars traveled about to provide training to companies and communities.

Worker's Compensation

The accident rate for American workers was very, very high not only in mines but in railroading and manufacturing enterprises. Every year between 1888 and 1908, one study revealed, an estimated 35,000 workers were killed and 536,000 injured.[49] America's accident rate was far higher than that of industrialized nations in Europe. It was a growing concern of reformers and a frequent target of muckraking journalists.

Britain and other industrialized European nations had established programs of automatic payments for workers injured or killed on the job, known as workmen's compensation. In America such programs did not exist. The only recourse for American workers or their heirs was the courts. Lawsuits were expensive and often very long. On top of that, the state laws used to decide such cases were based on common law doctrines established in preindustrial days, which provided many defenses for employers against charges of negligence. These laws made it very difficult for workers to collect damages. Since the late 19th century, trade unions had urged passing new employers' liability laws to reduce the defenses an employer could use if workers were injured or killed. They had the most success securing laws to cover railroad workers. By 1908, 26 states had increased employer liability in railroading and a few had done so in mining.

Under employers' liability laws, of course, it was still necessary for the worker to file a lawsuit to collect. European workmen's compensation laws, on the other hand, did not require either side to go to court or to prove negligence. Nonetheless, in the opening years of the 20th century union officials opposed workers' compensation. They feared it would reduce their strength and their independence at the bargaining table. Samuel Gompers argued that any benefits set by the government would be very low but would be labeled sufficient and nonnegotiable by employers. For the same reasons, unions rarely supported laws setting maximum hours or minimum wages, except for women and children.

Among reformers, however, the idea of workmen's compensation became increasingly popular, as study after study showed the dire effects on families when the breadwinner was killed or injured. The drive to promote it was led by the American Association for Labor Legislation (AALL), an organization of progressive economists, sociologists, and political scientists founded in 1906. In 1908 at Roosevelt's urging, Congress established a very modest workmen's compensation program for a few federal employees. The idea also won support from some prominent leaders of big business. International Harvester, United States Steel, and a few other very large corporations even established their own modest, voluntary programs.

The National Civic Federation (NCF), an organization of business, labor, and civic representatives, also began to promote workmen's compensation. The NCF published model legislation in 1909 and began lobbying state legislatures to adopt the idea. Many states responded by appointing commissions—three in 1909, eight in 1910, 12 in 1911, seven in 1913, and four more by 1919. All these commissions gathered evidence on the high social costs of workplace accidents and all recommended in favor of worker's compensation. The first systematic study of accidents in a limited time and place, Crystal Eastman's *Work Accidents and the Law,* was published in 1910 as part of the Pittsburgh Survey. "Considered in the light of social economy, she concluded, . . . "continuing recurrence of preventable work-accidents is not only an injustice to the victims but clearly a tremendous social waste. . . . It is not necessary to point out that such individual hardships as we have described are a tax upon a community's real prosperity." That same year the conservative National Association of Manufacturers, which represented small and medium-size businesses, polled 25,000 employers and found 95 percent favored some form of automatic, no-fault compensation. Even labor unions began to give the idea grudging approval.[50]

Montana enacted a workmen's compensation law in 1909, but like a 1902 attempt in Maryland, it was quickly declared unconstitutional by the state supreme court. The first prototype law as recommended by the NCF was passed in New York in 1910. It too was quickly declared unconstitutional by state courts. (Courts objected to worker's compensation because it denied the right to trial by jury and the right of equal protection for the employer, since the award to the employee was automatic regardless of fault.) But the tide of reform could not be stemmed. Ten states passed workmen's compensation laws in 1911; in 1912 and 1913, 11 more states passed them and New York reenacted its legislation. These early laws were not comprehensive—most made the programs voluntary or were limited to hazardous occupations—but they were the beginnings of modern worker's compensation.[51]

Other State Reforms for Working People

In 1908, the Supreme Court, in *Muller v. Oregon,* upheld the constitutionality of laws limiting the number of hours some wage-earning women could be required to work. In response, nine states passed new hour laws for women and nine of the 21 states that already had such laws strengthened them between 1909 and 1912. The Muller decision did not have a great effect on men's hours during the same years, however.

A more challenging effort to better the condition of wage-earning people was the campaign to set a minimum wage, first undertaken by reformers on behalf of adult and minor female workers. The campaign gained its legs in the flurry of vice commission reports and other studies that showed the great difficulty women had living independently on the wages they could earn. The first minimum wage law in America was passed in Massachusetts in 1912. It applied only to women and girls, was not compulsory, and did not prescribe an across-the-board figure. It nonetheless broke important new ground in the expansion of state responsibility. In 1909 wage laws had been enacted in all of Great Britain; in America, however, they were destined to be far more controversial than hours, safety, or worker's compensation legislation.

SCIENTIFIC MANAGEMENT COMES OF AGE

Since the 1890s, the ideas of scientific industrial management had been slowly gaining ground in some industries, and as the 1910s opened they captured the attention of the nation. Scientific management was sometimes called Taylorism after its most prominent developer, Frederick W. Taylor. Taylor had dropped out of Harvard as a young man, learned to be a machinist, then took an engineering degree. Since the 1880s he had been researching ways to increase industrial productivity.

Scientific was a favorite word of progressive thinkers. To Taylor, it meant conclusions based on experiment, careful observation, and measurement. He would, for example, conduct time and motion studies, carefully measuring which of several small body movements would enable a worker to shovel the largest amount of coal with the least physical stress or tiredness. Taylor thought he could not only increase the productivity of workers but their wages as well by introducing a piecework bonus system, which paid workers more if they produced more than the experimentally determined average output. At the time, many employers and most workers still held the traditional view that increased output per worker meant harder labor, fewer jobs, and lower wages. Taylor understood, however, that better-paid workers could also fuel continuing economic growth by purchasing more goods. In fact, to him scientific management was also a social reform because he believed it could produce harmony between capital and labor. "The majority of these men believe that the fundamental interests of employés and employers are necessarily antagonistic," he wrote in his influential book, *Principles of Scientific Management*. "Scientific management, on the contrary, has for its very foundation the firm conviction that the true interests of the two are one and the same; that prosperity for the employer cannot exist through a long term of years unless it is accompanied by prosperity for the employé and vice versa; and that it is possible to give the workman what he most wants—high wages—and the employer what he wants—a low labor cost."[52] Taylor summed up his ideas, "Science, not rule of thumb. Harmony, not discord. Cooperation, not individualism. Maximum output, in place of restricted output. The development of each man [worker] to his greatest efficiency and prosperity."[53]

Taylor's ideas had a natural appeal to many progressives seeking to reduce both social conflict on one hand and the exploitation of workers on the other. In 1910 they became front page news. Reform attorney Louis Brandeis called Taylor to testify in the Eastern Rate Case, a railroad rate dispute being heard by the Interstate Commerce Commission. Brandeis used the testimony of Taylor and other scientific management experts to argue that railroads did not need to increase their rates; instead, they could cut their costs "a million dollars a day" (a phrase that got wide publicity) and raise wages to boot if they adopted scientific management. The following year Taylor's ideas were in the news again, for a different reason. The ironworkers at the federal arsenal in Watertown, Massachusetts, called a strike in part because they objected to aspects of Taylorism that had been introduced there—such as preassigned, measured times allowed for each small task. Congress quickly called hearings where Taylor testified. For the next several years scientific management was on everyone's tongue.

Taylorism had another important aspect as well. Taylor believed that trained managers understood the science or theory of efficient production in a way that workers could not, and should plan and closely supervise all workers' tasks. Put another way, scientific management replaced the worker's independent judgment with the authority of the expert or professional manager. It justified the growth of middle management already underway in business and manufacturing. But it also deprived ordinary workers of control over their work and further reduced the need for highly skilled craftsmen. "In the past the man has been first," wrote Taylor, "in the future the system must be first."[54]

The use of scientific management progressed rapidly in some areas of manufacturing, although not all businessmen accepted it. It also became a mania among a wide variety of government officials and reformers, who attempted to apply its principles to administration and to many social services. Labor leaders and workers, however, almost universally opposed it.

NEW MEXICO AND ARIZONA COMPLETE THE CONTINENTAL UNITED STATES

By the end of the first decade of the 20th century, the population of New Mexico had reached more than 327,000 and the population of Arizona more than 204,000. Some Americans remained wary of the two territories' partly Hispanic heritage, while others still thought of them as the Wild West. But it was clear that statehood could no longer be postponed. President Taft reiterated his support during a tour of the West in the fall of 1909. In June 1910, Congress passed an enabling act, permitting the two territories to call constitutional conventions. For New Mexico, the enabling act required that "schools shall always be conducted in English" and that "ability to read, write, speak, and understand the English language sufficiently well to conduct the duties of the office without the aid of an interpreter shall be a necessary qualification for all state officers and members of the state legislature."[55]

In New Mexico, Republicans dominated the constitutional convention. The Republican majority was about equally divided between Anglo and Hispano representatives. The latter used their political leverage to protect their interests, and the convention agreed to write safeguards for Spanish-speaking citizens into the constitution. The convention adopted provisions prohibiting disenfranchisement of Hispanic citizens who did not speak English and prohibiting discrimination in schooling; Spanish-speaking children could not be confined to separate schools, for example, as were African-American children in the South. In other ways the New Mexico constitution was not notably progressive. It did not give women full suffrage, although they were permitted to vote in school elections. It did, however, instruct the legislature to consider such reform issues as child labor and anti-monopoly laws.

President Taft approved the New Mexico constitution but the Senate did not, holding that it contained requirements for passing future amendments that were much too stringent. The constitutional convention had written the strict requirements deliberately. They were designed to ensure that the guarantees for the Spanish-speaking minority could not easily be changed, even if the non-Hispanic majority became much larger. Congress nonetheless pressed the principle and required New Mexicans to change their amendment process. In return, Congress eliminated the requirement (specified in the enabling act) that all state officials be proficient in English. On January 6, 1912, New Mexico became the 47th state.

In Arizona, progressive Democrats dominated the constitutional convention. Only one representative was Hispanic—partly because many Hispanics had been effectively

When New Mexico became the 47th state in 1912, it was home to many Pueblo Indians who still maintained traditional ways. This photo shows a Tewa woman winnowing wheat at San Juan Pueblo. It was taken by Edward S. Curtis, who compiled an invaluable 20-volume photographic record of North American Indian groups during the Progressive Era. *(Library of Congress, Prints and Photographs Division, LC-USZ62-112217)*

disenfranchised by a 1909 act of the territorial legislature, which established an English literacy requirement for voting. The convention approved many progressive measures and direct-democracy reforms, even the controversial recall of any elected or appointed official. It declined to adopt either prohibition or women's suffrage, however. Voters approved the constitution. But as conservatives had warned, President Taft objected to the idea of recalling judges and vetoed the statehood bill. Congress required Arizonans to remove the recall provision, amid much debate over the issue.

Finally, on February 14, 1912, Arizona was admitted as the 48th state, completing the political union of the continental United States. The following November, by use of the referendum, Arizonans restored the recall provision which Congress had forced them to omit, by a margin of more than 5-1. They also approved full state suffrage for women.

ALASKA BECOMES A SELF-GOVERNING TERRITORY

In Alaska, the Ballinger-Pinchot affair of 1909–10 increased the influence of home-rulers, who disliked the inability of Alaskans to control issues that affected them. Alaska had a governor appointed by Washington, no legislature, and only a nonvoting delegate to Congress. Alaska's delegate, James Wickersham, led the battle for full territorial status.

President Taft opposed making Alaska a self-governing territory. He preferred a governing commission, like the one he himself had headed in the Philippines. Other interests also wanted Alaska to remain under federal control. Business interests, especially the Alaska Syndicate, feared that a territorial legislature would impose closer oversight and regulation. Conservationists feared that a territorial government would be dominated by local entrepreneurs out to get rich by rampant development. (In several Alaskan towns, such entrepreneurs had burned Pinchot in effigy during the Ballinger affair.) Prohibitionists and other reformers feared that good civic order would not be maintained because Alaska had a large transient population.

In 1912, Wickersham introduced a bill for full territorial status—the third time he had done so. In June, the Democrats adopted a plank in favor of Alaskan self-government at their national convention. The new Progressive Party supported it as well. Wickersham himself joined the Progressive Party, and in early August when Alaskans held their elections he won reelection on its ticket. Republican Party leaders quickly decided to eliminate the Alaska issue (and any possible reminder of the Ballinger affair) from the ongoing presidential campaign. Alaska's Second Organic Act passed speedily through Congress and was signed by President Taft on August 24, Wickersham's birthday. The act created an eight-member Senate and a 16-member House of Representatives. To pacify various interests, however, the act did put many limitations on home rule. The federal government retained control over resources like land, coal, and oil, and over matters relating to liquor, divorce, gambling, and the formation of towns and counties. The legislature's powers to levy taxes and to regulate the important mining and fishing industries were very limited. The governor remained a presidential appointee. Many Alaskan home-rulers were angered and dissatisfied with the bill.

DIRECT-DEMOCRACY REFORM: THE DEBATE OVER RECALL

Recall, the removal of a public official from office upon petition and a special election, was the most controversial of the direct-democracy devices sought by progressives. In 1908 Oregon became the first state to adopt recall statewide, and during the Taft years it became a matter of great public controversy. In late 1911, the debate reached the halls of Congress when President Taft vetoed statehood for Arizona territory until the proposed state constitution was amended to eliminate the recall of judges.

Recall had been advocated by populists in the 1890s, and by 1900 a few communities in the West had adopted it. In December 1902, Los Angeles became the first major city to adopt recall—by a 4-1 margin—and many other California cities followed suit. In 1909, the voters of Los Angeles put it to use, initiating a recall of their mayor for collusion in several kinds of vice and corruption—although the mayor (having meanwhile been indicted along with several police officials) left town before the recall could be held. "This campaign and its outcome," wrote contemporary observers in 1912, "were hailed by the sponsors of the new device as a perfect demonstration of its righteousness." Well satisfied, Californians adopted it statewide in 1911.[56] In 1912, Colorado, Nevada, Washington State, and the new state of Arizona followed. In Washington, Seattle soon recalled its mayor, Herman Gill. Gill had not only established a legal vice district but was also involved in utilities franchise corruption. Based on evidence gathered by a citizens' league the courts issued an injunction, but the city council refused to impeach him. "In this situation Seattle was confronted by the emergency which the recall was designed to meet," wrote a Seattle official.[57]

Recall, writes political scientist Thomas Cronin, "is plainly an attempt to make government more representative in a dramatic way—by increasing the responsiveness of elected officials to the will of the majority."[58] It sparked a sharp division of opinion, even among progressives. Advocates of recall argued that it would give voters greater control over their officials, prod the officials to be honest and attentive, reduce the influence of special interests, and provide an alternative to impeachment, which requires a much higher standard of deliberate malfeasance. Opponents of recall argued that it would weaken representative government as the Founding Fathers conceived it; compel officials to avoid unpopular but necessary decisions to satisfy the mass will, right or wrong; and introduce turmoil and divisiveness into civic life by encouraging abuses by rival political groups. "Fifteen or even 10 percent of the number of voters at a preceding election—gathered in all probability from the defeated party, may vote for the recall and bring on the turmoil of a new electoral campaign," wrote opponent Archbishop John Ireland.[59]

Conservatives, moderates, and even some progressives especially objected to the recall of judges or, as Roosevelt proposed during the 1912 presidential campaign, the recall of unpopular judicial decisions. Advocates of judicial recall argued that it was justified because judges have the power to void acts passed by elected legislatures. Opponents held that the independence of the judiciary, responsible only to the law, was the final bulwark of democracy. "The judiciary is the only branch to which the minority can turn for preservation at all times," said Representative George Legaré of South Carolina. "Destroy this branch of the government, and you destroy the only hope of the minority, and at the same time you remove all restraint from the majority and leave them to be glutted with an unholy and uncontrollable power." By the end of the Progressive Era a total of six states permitted recall of all elected officials and four more of all officials except judges.[60]

THE REPUBLICANS LOOK TOWARD THE ELECTION OF 1912

By 1911, the Republican party was seriously divided between its conservative and progressive wings—and the progressives were organizing to unseat their own party's president. President Taft had become thoroughly identified with the conservatives. As the year unfolded, he further alienated the Insurgents and at the same time managed to reduce the enthusiasm of the Old Guard for his administration.

Early in 1911, Taft negotiated a reciprocal trade agreement with Canada. Like the United States, Canada had used protective tariffs since the late 19th century to encourage its own economic development. The reciprocity treaty lowered some tariff rates on both sides. It also permitted free entry to the United States of many Canadian agricultural products and natural resources. "By giving our people access to Canadian forests," President Taft told Congress, "we shall reduce the consumption of our own."[61] But to American farmers in the Midwest, forests were not the issue. In Canada, agriculture was flourishing. The western prairie provinces were experiencing a spectacular wheat boom, second only to the United States in volume produced. Free trade would end protection for American crops and farmers were furious.

Congress approved the treaty. But in Canada, a 1911 election brought a change of government. The Liberal Party that had negotiated the treaty lost to the Conservative Party, which preferred high tariffs. Many Canadians also took offense at a speech by U.S. Speaker of the House Champ Clark announcing he supported the treaty because he hoped "to see the day when the American flag will float over every square foot of the British North American possessions clear to the North Pole."[62] The Canadian parliament did not approve the treaty and Canadian reciprocity did not take effect. It did, however, hand insurgent Republicans from the midwestern farm belt another reason to oppose President Taft.

Conservative Republicans, on the other hand, disliked the president's antitrust campaign. Antitrust suits against Standard Oil and the American Tobacco Company, which had been initiated by Roosevelt but vigorously prosecuted by Taft, were both handed down in favor of the government in May 1911. To extensive publicity and comment, both trusts were ordered dissolved. Even more important to future politics, however, was the antitrust suit that Taft initiated against United States Steel Corporation (USS) the following October. The suit complained about USS's acquisition of its competitor Tennessee Valley Iron and Coal Company—which had been approved by Roosevelt to make it possible for J. P. Morgan to rescue a failing bank and abate the Panic of 1907. Before the suit was filed, relations between Roosevelt and Taft were strained. But after, Roosevelt was afire with righteous indignation.

To date, Roosevelt had declared that he would not be a candidate for president in 1912. In private, he even maintained that the Republican Party was bound to lose the election—a view shared by much of Washington by late 1911. After Taft filed the USS antitrust suit, however, Roosevelt let friends know he would run "in response to popular demand." In February 1912 eight Republican governors obliged, formally requesting his candidacy. Soon after, Roosevelt told reporters in characteristically quotable fashion, "My hat is in the ring! The fight is on and I'm stripped to the buff." Roosevelt made the statement while on a speaking tour of Ohio, Taft's home state, and it was front page news nationwide.[63]

One consequence of Roosevelt's announcement was the collapse of the candidacy of Robert La Follette, leader of the Insurgents. La Follette appeared to seal his own fate with a confused and impolitic speech at a press club banquet in Philadelphia, probably occasioned by nervous exhaustion. But behind the scenes, many of La Follette's supporters had already privately agreed to support Roosevelt. La Follette and his close friends remained bitter and intransigent for the duration of the campaign.

Another consequence of Roosevelt's announcement was that Republican Party professionals tightened their grip on the party's state organizations. Their goal was to make sure that delegates to the 1912 nominating convention were Taft supporters. Meanwhile, Roosevelt himself frightened moderates into the Taft camp by taking positions that were far more radically progressive than those he supported while in office. Roosevelt believed that the nation's sentiment was increasingly progressive. His strategy was to gain convention delegates by sweeping primary elections. Many delegates were still chosen in conventions by party regulars, but enough states had adopted primary elections that they would be an important factor for the first time. In the states that held presidential primaries, Roosevelt won nine (including Ohio, Taft's home state), La Follette won two, and Taft won one (narrowly).[64]

As the June convention in Chicago approached, delegates stood at 432 for Roosevelt, 326 for Taft, 41 for La Follette, and 254 contested. The battle between Taft and Roosevelt for the contested delegates was, in the words of historian George Mowry, "rough and riotous."[65] Roosevelt arrived in Chicago to a tumultuous public welcome. He let it be known he would feel no duty to abide by party decisions that did not respect the public will. But Taft and party leaders kept a tight grip. The credentials committee allotted 235 of the 254 contested delegates to the president, assuring his renomination on the first ballot—and foreclosing a long battle which, some historians speculate, might well have resulted in the nomination of Roosevelt. Party leaders also arranged for 1,000 uniformed policemen to be in attendance at the convention in case protests grew violent.

Taft was nominated, but 344 of the Roosevelt delegates refused to participate in the vote. Instead, by prearrangement they marched out of the hall together. They reassembled in Orchestra Hall and agreed to form the Progressive Party, to meet in convention in August.

In their absence, the Republican convention proceeded. The party renominated the ailing vice president, James Sherman. They adopted a platform that was moderately conservative but supported some progressive reforms, such as limitations on labor by women and children; the establishment of workmen's compensation; and monetary and banking reform that included easier credit for farmers. The platform firmly rejected the idea of judicial recall.

THE DEMOCRATS MEET

A week after the Republican convention, elated Democrats met in Baltimore. With the Republicans split, they knew they had a good chance to elect their first president since 1892. William Jennings Bryan, their western, populist, three-time nominee and party leader, was not seeking the nomination again. With no obvious front-runner, many candidates appeared. When the convention opened, James Beauchamp "Champ" Clark of Missouri, Speaker of the House, had the largest number of delegates. But there were other major contenders as well, one of them New Jersey governor Woodrow Wilson. None was close to commanding the two-thirds "super majority" that the Democratic Party required for nomination.

Historians often apply the adjective *meteoric* to the rise of Woodrow Wilson in politics. The former president of Princeton, he had gained a national reputation as an educational reformer by building it into a first-rate university—over the objections of wealthy alumni who preferred social exclusiveness. In 1910, he entered politics as a candidate for governor at the behest of machine Democrats in New Jersey. At the time, Wilson, who was born in Virginia and raised in the South, was considered a political conservative. But within two years as governor of New Jersey, he had taken on both the machine and powerful corporate interests—and won. He pressed the legislature to pass strict controls on corporations and to pass other progressive reforms, such as the regulation of railroads and utilities, a workmen's compensation law, a corrupt practices act, and the establishment of primary elections. He quickly became known throughout the nation as a rising star among progressives.

The Democratic convention deadlocked through five straight days of balloting. Clark slowly gained strength and appeared to be winning. Ups and downs and deals and bargains continued. Finally, on the ninth day of the convention and the 46th ballot, Woodrow Wilson gained the nomination. The swing to Wilson was due partly to Bryan, who considered Clark too friendly with urban machines, and partly to skillful behind-the-scenes deal making by Wilson's campaign managers. It was, in the words of Wilson scholar Arthur Link, "one of the miracles of modern politics."[66]

For vice president the Democrats nominated Thomas R. Marshall of Indiana. They adopted a platform that condemned monopoly, called for a lower tariff and a decentralized banking system, and reaffirmed states' rights. It also repeated the moderate support for labor issues that had been adopted in 1908.

THE NEW PROGRESSIVE PARTY MEETS

While attending the Republican convention Roosevelt told reporters, "I feel fit as a bull moose."[67] The quote, widely publicized, gave the new Progressive Party its symbol and its nickname—the Bull Moose Party. They met in Chicago in early August—15,000 strong counting spectators as well as delegates. By that date it was clear that few Bull Moosers would be professional politicians. Many Republican officials supported Roosevelt, but most (including most congressional insurgents and most of the governors who originally endorsed him) chose not to change their party affiliation. Instead, the convention gathered together a distinguished array of social, political, and economic reformers. Social workers flocked to the party and Jane Addams herself delivered one of the nominating speeches for Roosevelt. Journalists, writers, and intellectuals like Herbert Croly and Kansas newspaper editor William Allen White attended, as did some muckrakers and many young enthusiasts whose names would become famous in the future, such as Walter Lippmann. Direct-democracy and municipal reformers came. Women delegates—doctors, professors, settlement workers, suffragists, and leaders of civic reform and women's clubs—even helped to write the party platform. The crowd was not totally lacking political regulars; it also included a western governor and political boss or two, former officials like Gifford Pinchot and Oscar Strauss, and such wealthy power brokers as newspaper magnate Frank Munsey and International Harvester industrialist George Perkins.

"We stand for a nobler America," said Albert Beveridge in his keynote address. "We stand for an undivided nation. . . . We stand for social brotherhood against savage individualism. We stand for intelligent co-operation instead of a reckless competition. . . . We stand for a representative government that represents the people. We battle for the actual rights of man." The Progressive platform drew together many strands of social, political, and economic reform. "It is time to set the public welfare in first place," it announced. It outlined the most comprehensive program for reform since the Populist platform of 1892—and one that would, in most particulars, gradually be realized in the course of the 20th century. About the party's nominee for president there was no debate. For vice president, the Progressives nominated Hiram Johnson, the prominent reform governor of California.[68]

Many African Americans were interested in the new party. The arrival of black delegates from the South presented the Progressives with a dilemma, however, since white southerners would not accept integrated political organizations. Roosevelt agreed not to seat the southern blacks and to accept a whites-only party in the South. (To be seated at a political convention means to be accepted as a voting member of a delegation.) Black delegates from northern and border states were seated, however. The decision angered African Americans while failing to satisfy white southerners.

On the last day, Roosevelt arrived to a standing ovation that continued for 52 minutes. The first presidential nominee to deliver an acceptance speech in person to a convention, he titled his speech "A Confession of Faith." It summed up many of the themes of progressivism. He labeled the old parties "husks, with no soul within either. . . . boss ridden and privilege controlled." He called progressivism "a movement which proposes to put at the service of all our people the collective power of the people, through their Governmental agencies." He pointed out that reform was "a corrective to Socialism and an antidote to anarchy." He ended by repeating the words he used in a public address the night before the Republican convention opened. "To you who gird yourselves for this great new fight in the neverending warfare for the good of mankind," he said, "we stand at Armageddon, and we battle for the Lord." (Armageddon, in Christian scripture, is the place where the final battle between the forces of good and evil is to be fought.) Delegates responded in kind to the call for a righteous crusade, singing "Battle Hymn of the Republic," "Onward Christian Soldiers," and other hymns.[69]

THE SOCIALIST PARTY MEETS

The Socialists, who met at Indianapolis in May, were at the peak of their electoral power in the United States. They were, however, as bitterly divided as the Republicans. The party included gradualists who hoped to conquer through the ballot box, a position strongest among intellectuals and midwestern labor unionists; direct action labor radicals, led by Big Bill Haywood and the Wobblies; radical farmers from the Southwest; doctrinaire Marxists and anarchists. At the convention, however, the gradualist majority succeeded in voting to oust those "who oppose political action or advocate sabotage or other methods of violence as a weapon of the working class."[70] They also removed Haywood himself from the National Committee. Eugene Debs was again nominated for president; Emil Seidel, the socialist mayor of Milwaukee, was nominated for vice president. They ran on a platform that called for the gradual nationalization of industry through use of the vote.

THE CAMPAIGN OF 1912

From the perspective of historians, the election of 1912 is one of the most significant in American history. An unusual race between three candidates of comparable stature, it pitted two former presidents and one future president against each other. It presented voters with a unusual debate on basic principles and important questions about the nature of American democracy and its future direction. How much responsibility for social welfare was the government to assume? To what extent should it control business and labor? How far should popular democracy extend and should female citizens have the right to vote? The candidates offered voters a comprehensive range of answers to these questions, extending from the Socialists and Eugene Debs on the left to conservative Republicans and Taft on the right. In the middle were the two most popular contenders for the office, Wilson and Roosevelt, each representing a different approach to progressivism.

Both Roosevelt and Wilson wanted to use government to promote public welfare. Roosevelt's New Nationalism looked forward to a powerful, centralized social-service government in Washington. Wilson's program, dubbed the New Freedom, supported many social reforms but held that most were properly accomplished at the state level. Much of the campaign focused on the issue of big business, trusts, and monopoly. Roosevelt maintained, as always, that big business was a permanent feature of the modern era. He argued that the national government should not worry about the size of a business as long as it behaved properly. He wanted to oversee the behavior of big business by means of a national commission modeled on the Interstate Commerce Commission. Wilson, on the advice of his close adviser, reform lawyer Louis Brandeis, developed the opposite argument. He held that size and monopoly themselves were the problem. He maintained that the proper role of national government was to restore individual opportunity by breaking up large monopolies, reforming the banking and monetary system to eliminate Wall Street influence, and reducing the tariff protection that permitted monopolies to grow. Other issues could be left to states and individuals. "I do not want to be taken care of by the government, either directly, or by any instruments through which the government is acting," he said in his speeches. "Give me right and justice and I will undertake to take care of myself."[71]

None of the four parties gave much attention to foreign affairs in 1912 although war clouds were clearly gathering in Europe. Republicans, Democrats, and Progressives did condemn Russia's recent decision to cease honoring the passports of American Jews, however. On the question of women's suffrage, both the Democrats and Republicans were silent; the Progressive and Socialist parties both gave it support.

Compared with the conventions, the campaign itself was low key. President Taft, who did not expect to win reelection, made a few dignified speeches but did little other campaigning. Wilson maintained a courteous stance toward both Taft and Roosevelt. There were no direct debates. The most dramatic moment of the campaign had little to do with the issues. In mid-October Roosevelt, about to deliver a speech in Milwaukee, was shot at point-blank range. The bullet was deflected by Roosevelt's eyeglass case and the thick manuscript of his speech, folded in his breast pocket. Roosevelt was wounded, although he insisted on delivering his speech before seeking medical attention. He was sidelined for the remaining weeks of the campaign. The would-be assassin, John Schrank, was immediately apprehended. He believed President McKinley had come to him in a dream and told him to kill Roosevelt. Schrank was found insane and institutionalized for life.

Less than a week before the election, the ailing vice president, Sherman, died. Nicholas Murray Butler, president of Columbia, agreed to fill in on the Republican ticket.

To the surprise of few people, Taft and Roosevelt split the Republican vote and Wilson won. In electoral votes, the Democratic victory was sweeping: 435 for Wilson to 88 for Roosevelt and only eight for President Taft (he won only Utah and Vermont.) In terms of popular vote, however, the outcome looked very different. Wilson won less than a majority of the popular vote—only 42 percent. Roosevelt won 27 percent, Taft 23 percent, and Debs 6 percent, the highest percentage ever polled by the Socialist Party. Nonetheless, the Democratic victory extended to Congress, where the party won solid majorities in both the House and Senate. The party looked forward to its strongest position since the Civil War.

Although historians believe that the election offered fundamental choices about America's future, only 58 percent of all eligible voters chose to cast a ballot in 1912. It was the lowest turnout to date in a presidential election. Wilson actually won with fewer total votes than William Jennings Bryan had received in any of his three losses as the Democratic candidate.

CHRONICLE OF EVENTS

1909

Theodore Roosevelt is president; Charles Fairbanks is vice president. A new administration headed by William Taft has been elected and will be inaugurated in March.

Seven states—Arizona, Arkansas, California, Idaho, Nevada, New Hampshire, and Tennessee—enact their first direct primary legislation; Michigan extends its law.

Montana passes a compulsory worker's compensation program for miners, but it is declared unconstitutional by the state supreme court.

Minnesota and Missouri enact laws limiting women's working hours; 23 states now have these laws.

Women have full suffrage in four states (Wyoming, Colorado, Idaho, and Utah). Twenty-two states and territories permit them to vote in school elections (Arizona territory and the states of Connecticut, Delaware, Illinois, Iowa, Kansas, Kentucky, Massachusetts, Michigan, Minnesota, Mississippi, Montana, Nebraska, New Hampshire, New Jersey, New York, North Dakota, Ohio, Oklahoma, Oregon, Vermont, Wisconsin). Six states give women municipal or tax-related voting rights (Iowa, Louisiana, Kansas, Michigan, Montana, and New York). In 18 of the 46 states and New Mexico and Hawaii territories women have no voting rights.

South Carolina, Idaho, Arizona, Utah, and Washington pass statewide local option, giving local communities power to prohibit or allow liquor sales. In Utah, the governor vetoes the law, but more than half the state's counties nonetheless vote to abolish saloons. In Arkansas, both the state house and senate pass liquor restriction measures but cannot come to agreement on one bill. Louisiana prohibits the sale of liquor to blacks and whites in the same building.

The campaign against prostitution is widespread. The first statewide red-light abatement law is passed in Iowa; it penalizes landlords whose property is used for prostitution. By 1917, 31 states will adopt similar laws.

Wisconsin passes a housing code for first-class (large) cities to replace a code passed in 1907 and declared unconstitutional. Indiana passes a code with provisions similar to the 1901 New York law.

Wisconsin passes the first state law authorizing cities to create permanent planning commissions. Harvard introduces the first university course on principles of city planning. Los Angeles adopts the first zoning ordinance in America.

The first movie production companies settle in Southern California. The first major production company independent of the Patents Company trust is founded; independents begin to multiply quickly.

There are now more than 900,000 automobiles in the United States.

January 25–26: The White House Conference on the Care of Dependent Children meets. It has been called by President Roosevelt at the urging of social workers and child labor reformers. It recommends mothers' pensions, the forunner of what will later be called welfare.

January 28: The provisional American governor of Cuba turns the nation back to its newly elected Cuban president, José Miguel Gómez, ending the occupation of 1906–1909. American troops remain through March.

February: The Great White Fleet returns to Hampton Roads to a triumphant public welcome. It has visited 20 ports on six continents.

February 12, Lincoln's birthday: A call for a biracial national meeting to discuss the growing social and economic discrimination against African Americans, is issued by white reformers in cooperation with black leaders such as W. E. B. DuBois. The end result will be the formation of the National Association for the Advancement of Colored People (NAACP).

March 4: William Howard Taft is inaugurated as the 27th president of the United States; James Sherman is vice president. Taft and Secretary of State Philander Knox inaugurate dollar diplomacy, the policy of encouraging private American investment in less-developed nations to strengthen stability and reduce European influence.

March 15: In Alaska, Judge James Wickersham is elected territorial delegate. He will serve for many years as a vigorous supporter of home rule.

March 23: Former president Roosevelt leaves for an extended safari in Africa; he will also tour Europe twice to tumultuous welcomes.

March 25: The National Board of Motion Picture Censorship, a volunteer group formed by 10 New York civic organizations, meets for the first time to view films.

March 26: The voters of Los Angeles recall their mayor for collusion in vice and corruption; the mayor leaves town before the election can be held. It garners favorable national attention for the direct-democracy device of recall, an important issue for the remainder of the Taft years.

April 6: Two Americans, Robert Peary and Matthew Henson, reach the North Pole.

April 9: Despite a split between insurgent and Old Guard Republicans, Congress passes the Payne-Aldrich tariff. Although public sentiment strongly supports lowered tariffs and President Taft promised them during his campaign, the tariff raises average rates.

May 21: The first national conference on city planning meets in Washington, organized by Benjamin Marsh of the New York Committee on Congestion of Population (CCP). It brings together prominent social reformers, city planning advocates, philanthropists, and other reformers.

May 31: The meeting of the National Negro Conference, called in February, is held by a distinguished group of white reformers, scholars, and philanthropists, and African-American leaders.

July 12: A proposed amendment to the Constitution permitting income tax is approved by Congress. Conservative Republicans have sponsored it in order to pass the Payne-Aldrich tariff, incorrectly assuming that it will never be ratified by the required number of states.

August 22: The Ballinger-Pinchot affair begins when President Taft exonerates his secretary of state Richard Ballinger and fires whistleblower Louis Glavis, who has alerted Chief of Forestry Gifford Pinchot that Ballinger is reopening coal lands to former business associates who have agreed to sell them to the Alaska Syndicate.

September 2: Newspapers coast to coast headline news that the North Pole was reached on April 21, 1908, by Dr. Frederick Cook, an American who accompanied prominent explorer Captain Robert Peary on several previous expeditions. The news was cabled to the Danish government from a ship on which Cook was returning to civilization. Peary himself is in search of the pole and from the outset many experts question Cook's claim.

September 6: The world learns that Peary reached the North Pole on April 6, 1909, when he cables from Canada. An immediate controversy ensues over Cook's claims.

September 27: President Taft sets aside 3 million acres of oil-bearing lands.

October: In New York more than 1,000 women meet in Carnegie Hall and found the Woman Suffrage Party. It introduces the explicitly political methods of other interest groups to the women's suffrage movement.

In New York workers at a large shirtwaist factory, the Triangle Company, are fired after trying to form a local chapter of the International Ladies' Garment Workers Union. The workers go on strike.

October 15: Dr. Cook, the arctic explorer, arrives in New York and is given a hero's welcome. The same day his claims to have climbed Mt. McKinley are exposed as fraudulent, giving weight to Peary's claims to have been the first to reach the North Pole.

October 26: The Rockefeller Sanitary Commission for the Eradication of Hookworm Disease is organized, thanks to the untiring efforts of Dr. Charles Wardell Stiles and a gift from John D. Rockefeller. Over the next five years it will achieve dramatic improvement in the health of rural southerners, who are widely infected with the disease. The symptoms of the disease have created the disparaging stereotype of poor whites as thin, stooped, slovenly, dull witted, and very lazy.

November 13: Collier's publishes an article by L. R. Glavis, telling his side of the Ballinger-Pinchot controversy. A public uproar ensues.

A fire in the coal mines at Cherry, Illinois, kills 259 men and boys. It is the second-worst mining disaster in American history. It is the fourth coal mine disaster within two years to claim victims numbering in the hundreds and brings the total fatalities in that period to more than 1,500.

November 18: U.S. warships leave for Nicaragua to intervene in an impending revolution.

November 23: In New York more than 20,000 shirtwaist workers, many of them young immigrant women, walk off the job.

December 7: President Taft proposes a commission government for Alaska in his annual message, but the Ballinger-Pinchot affair has increased the influence of home-rulers in Alaska.

1910

Colorado and Maryland enact direct-primary legislation.

Arkansas and Colorado adopt initiative and referendum.

Florida, Oregon, and Missouri defeat statewide prohibition.

Kentucky passes a housing code law.

Washington State gives women full suffrage, becoming the fifth state to do so. The territory of New Mexico gives women the right to vote in school elections.

NAWSA opens an official headquarters in New York.

New York State passes the first law influenced by the business-supported campaign for worker's compensation. It is quickly declared unconstitutional by New York state courts, but the decision does not stem the tide of reform.

The campaign against prostitution is at its peak for the next five years; 35 cities will publish vice-commission reports. The nation is also gripped by an exaggerated panic over white slavery, or forced prostitution, which attributes the problem to kidnappings and forcible confinement of women in brothels.

The American Federation for Sex Hygiene (American Social Hygiene Association after 1913) is organized on a national level to alleviate the problem of venereal disease.

Social reformers Robert de Forest and Lawrence Veiller found the National Housing Association to promote housing reform.

New York City creates a permanent city-planning commission.

Under public pressure to respond to the high number of fatalities in mining, Congress establishes the Bureau of Mines. It is to conduct research toward reducing and responding to accidents; it does not have inspection authority.

Glacier National Park is established.

Angel Island Immigration Station opens on the West Coast, primarily to serve as a facility to enforce immigration regulations for people from China, Japan, and other Asian countries.

The Photo-Secessionists led by Alfred Stieglitz organize an extremely popular photography exhibit at Albright Art Gallery in Buffalo, New York. Afterward, the gallery purchases some of the prints—the first photographs added to the collection of a public gallery in the United States.

January: Taft fires Pinchot for insubordination.

January 26: A joint congressional committee begins hearings on the Ballinger-Pinchot affair. Glavis is defended by well-known reform attorney Louis Brandeis.

February: The shirtwaist makers' strike in New York ends. Most workers have made agreements with their companies for improved wages and conditions. After the strike the membership of the union increases vastly, and the corner is turned for unionization in the garment industry.

March 26: In a new immigration act, Congress strengthens antiprostitution provisions in response to evidence in the 1909 report of the Immigration Commission that women are imported to serve in brothels.

May 12: The second meeting of the National Negro Conference convenes. They adopt the name National Association for the Advancement of Colored People (NAACP) and open an office in New York. The organization will focus on enforcement of the Fourteenth and Fifteenth Amendments, an end to legal segregation, equal educational opportunities, and an antilynching campaign.

May 20: After four months of testimony on the Ballinger-Pinchot affair, lawyers begin their closing arguments. The congressional investigating committee votes 7-5 to exonerate Ballinger. The public dislikes the way Taft handled the issue and Roosevelt is angered.

In New York, the first successful women's suffrage parade is held. It marks a change of tactics in the women's movement to more public and militant demonstrations.

June 18: Congress passes the Mann-Elkins Act, which extends the control of the ICC over railroad rates and also extends its jurisdiction to telephone, telegraph, wireless (radio), and cable.

June 20: Congress passes an enabling act for New Mexico and Arizona, permitting them to call constitutional conventions in preparation for statehood.

June 25: Congress passes the Mann Act, making it a felony to transport women across state lines for immoral purposes. It is passed in response to the international treaty to suppress prostitution rings, ratified in 1905, and in response to the general white-slavery panic in the nation.

Congress passes the Withdrawal Act, authorizing the president to reserve land for any reason.

The Postal Deposit Savings Act is passed, establishing Postal Savings Banks through local post offices, primarily intended as secure depositories for farmers and workers.

June 28: In New York, 50,000 garment workers vote on strike.

August 10: In a speech at Ossawatomie, Kansas, Theodore Roosevelt announces his New Nationalism.

September 22: In Chicago, a large clothing company cuts garment workers' wages, starting a walkout which eventually numbers 40,000 workers.

October 1: The *Los Angeles Times* printing plant is bombed, resulting in the deaths of 21 employees. Owner Harrison Gray Otis, a prominent foe of unions, immediately blames labor. A crack private investigator is hired.

October 3: In New Mexico, the state constitutional convention opens. The constitution it writes is conservative although it seeks to guarantee the rights of Spanish-speaking citizens.

October 10: In Arizona, the state constitutional convention opens. The constitution it writes is extremely progressive and spells out many reforms.

November: In the midterm elections, Republican insurgents increase their power. Democrats make large gains in Congress. In the House, the Democrats hold the majority for the first time since 1892. In New Jersey Democratic newcomer Woodrow Wilson, the president of Princeton University, is elected governor.

W. E. B. DuBois publishes the first issue of the NAACP's journal, *The Crisis,* which he will edit until 1934. It is immediately successful and circulation will increase with each month.

December 31: The New York garment workers' strike is settled by a "protocol of peace" negotiated by Louis Brandeis, establishing an arbitration board with employer, labor, and public representatives.

1911

Four states—Maine, Massachusetts, New Jersey, and Wyoming—enact direct-primary legislation Two states, Arizona and California, adopt initiative and referendum; New Mexico adopts referendum only. California becomes the second state to adopt recall.

California passes full suffrage for women, becoming the sixth state to do so.

Ten new states pass worker's compensation laws: California, Illinois, Kansas, Massachusetts, Nevada, New Hampshire, New Jersey, Ohio, Washington, Wisconsin. Twelve other states appoint commissions to study the issue, and 11 more will pass laws by the end of 1913.

Four states—California, Ohio, South Carolina, and Utah—enact laws limiting women's working hours.

Illinois passes the first law enabling publicly funded mothers' pensions, the forerunner of modern welfare or Aid to Families with Dependent Children. By 1919, 39 states will have similar laws.

Wisconsin passes the first state income tax.

Three existing organizations join to found the National League on Urban Conditions among Negroes, known after 1920 as the National Urban League. It will work for the improvement of economic and social conditions in large cities.

The Chicago Vice Commission issues *The Social Evil in Chicago,* the most influential of all vice reports. It stresses the fact that prostitution has become another form of big business.

Secretary of State Philander Knox negotiates treaties with Nicaragua and Honduras to refinance debts and install collectors of customs to make payments to European creditors. The Senate refuses to approve the treaties, but the Taft administration encourages private American bankers to continue the refinancing and investment initiative, an example of dollar diplomacy.

Efficiency expert Frederick Taylor publishes his influential *Principles of Scientific Management.* For the next few years scientific management, which rearranges work processes and measures discrete tasks in order to reduce the time they consume, becomes a mania not only among manufacturers but also reformers of all kinds.

Congress makes Robert Peary a rear admiral, confirming his claim to have been the first to reach the North Pole.

January 12: New Mexico voters overwhelming approve the proposed state constitution.

January 13: A bill to amend the U.S. Constitution to allow for direct election of senators, already passed by the House, is finally brought to the floor of the Senate. Much controversy will focus on the attempt, primarily by southern senators, to end Congress's control over state congressional elections at the same time. Wrangling continues for more than a year.

January 21: Under the leadership of Robert LaFollette, leading Republican insurgents form the National Progressive Republican League for "the promotion of popular government and progressive legislation."

February: Seattle recalls its corrupt mayor, giving more publicity to the recall movement.

February 3: In Chicago, the garment workers' strike finally ends; it has resulted in the establishment of arbitration boards and a large increase in union membership for the United Garment Workers of America.

February 9: In Arizona, voters overwhelmingly approve the proposed state constitution, although they have been warned that President Taft opposes the provision for recall of judges.

March: Secretary of the Interior Ballinger resigns, pleading poor health.

March 7: U.S. troops are dispatched to the U.S.-Mexican border, where a long period of turmoil called the Mexican Revolution has begun. They will remain until June.

March 25: Fire sweeps through the Triangle Shirtwaist Factory in Manhattan. Due to locked doors, inadequate fire escapes, and other safety problems, 100 of the 500 workers are trapped and burned; another 50 fall or jump to their deaths on the streets below in front of horrified onlookers.

As a result, New York State launches a major investigation of factory safety conditions and will pass many new regulations; public support for unionization in the garment industry also increases.

April 17: Ellis Island processes 11,745 immigrants, its all-time record.

April 22: Union official John McNamara is arrested in Indiana in connection with the *Los Angles Times* bombing of October 1910; his brother James and some others have also been arrested. Organized labor rushes to the brothers' defense, and Clarence Darrow is hired to defend them.

May: In Mexico, the forces of Francisco I. Madero force President Porfirio Díaz to resign and flee. In the November elections Madero will be elected president, but turmoil continues.

The Supreme Court hands down its decisions in antitrust suits against Standard Oil and American Tobacco Company, which Roosevelt originally filed but Taft prosecuted vigorously. Both trusts are ordered dissolved.

The Supreme Court reverses the 1908 federal court decision in *Gompers v. Bucks Stove & Range Co.,* which prohibited union officials from speaking publicly about a boycott.

July 26: President Taft signs a negotiated trade reciprocity treaty with Canada. It does not take effect because the Canadian parliament refuses to approve it; but it still angers American farm interests and their insurgent representatives in Congress.

August 8: Congress approves statehood for Arizona and New Mexico. President Taft announces he will veto the bill because he objects to the recall of judges in the Arizona constitution. Although the veto is not officially received until August 22, Congress meanwhile adopts a second statehood bill, deleting the recall provision in the Arizona constitution.

October 26: The Taft administration announces an antitrust suit against United States Steel Corporation, partly due to its acquisition of Tennessee Valley Iron and Coal which Roosevelt approved during the Panic of 1907. The suit infuriates Roosevelt and seals his willingness to run against his old friend Taft in the 1912 presidential election.

November: Isaac Harris and Max Blanck, owners of the Triangle Shirtwaist Factory, are found not guilty on manslaughter charges resulting from the March fire.

December 1: Shortly before their trial is to begin for bombing the *Los Angeles Times* building, brothers John and James McNamara plead guilty on the advice of Clarence Darrow, who believes they will be executed if the case goes to trial. James receives life and John 15 years.

1912

Three states, Kentucky, Montana, and Virginia, enact direct-primary legislation; Pennsylvania extends its law.

Four states—Idaho, Nebraska, Ohio, and Washington—adopt initiative and referendum; Nevada adopts initiative.

Four states—Arizona, Colorado, Nevada, and Washington—adopt recall.

Massachusetts passes a housing code law.

Kansas and Oregon become the seventh and eighth states to give women full suffrage; after its admission to statehood Arizona joins them.

West Virginia adopts a state constitutional amendment prohibiting liquor.

Kentucky, Maryland, and Vermont enact laws limiting women's working hours; 30 states now have these laws.

Massachusetts passes the first minimum wage law in America. It has limited applicability but breaks important new ground in the expansion of state responsibility.

Congress creates the United States Public Health Service.

The first movie studio is built in the suburb of Hollywood; several others already exist in and around Los Angeles. Pennsylvania passes the first statewide movie censorship law.

Alabama-born African-American musician W. C. Handy publishes *Memphis Blues;* it is the first blues to appear in sheet music form, the primary means by which new popular music circulates at the time. Handy will become known as the "father of the blues" for his role in publishing orchestrated versions of this traditional black musical form, one of the antecedents of jazz.

U.S. forces return briefly to Cuba at the request of President José Miguel Gómez to help quell a civil revolt. They also intervene in Honduras and Nicaragua.

January 6: President Taft proclaims New Mexico the 47th state.

The National Monetary Commission, appointed in 1908 to study the banking system and chaired by Senator Aldrich, issues its report.

January 11: In Lawrence, Massachusetts, the American Woolen Company announces that it will cut all textile mill workers' wages. Workers begin to walk out spontaneously, and within weeks more than 20,000 are on strike. IWW officials soon arrive.

February 2: In Philadelphia, Republican insurgent Robert La Follette delivers a rambling speech, probably due to nervous exhaustion. His hopes for the presidential nomination are effectively ended. Many of his supporters have already privately agreed to support Roosevelt.

February 10: The *New York Times* reports that some Republican governors have arrived in the city to formally request Roosevelt's candidacy.

February 11: IWW strike organizers in Lawrence, Massachusetts, begin sending strikers' children to temporary

When Arizona became the 48th state in 1912, many Americans still thought of it as the Wild West. As this photo of Tucson shows, however, the new state had towns like those throughout America. An electric trolley, cars, and bicycles are all in evidence on its main street. *(Courtesy Arizona Historical Society-Tucson, AHS #B89551c)*

homes in other cities, hoping to relieve striking families and generate publicity.

February 14: President Taft signs the bill making Arizona the 48th state and completing the political union of the continental United States.

February 24: Dismayed by the national attention the evacuated children of Lawrence have received, the city orders police to prevent any more departures. As children attempt to board a train, a melee breaks out, and many mothers and children are dragged to prison. The incident generates extensive sympathy for the strikers.

In Ohio, Roosevelt announces that his hat is in the ring for the presidential nomination.

April: A House subcommittee known as the Pujo Committee after Representative Arsène Pujo begins its investigations; it will hold well-publicized hearings on the money trust and report in 1913.

April 9: President Taft signs into law an act creating the U.S. Children's Bureau. Reformer, attorney, and social worker Julia Lathrop is named head of the bureau, becoming the first women to head a major federal department.

April 10: The White Star Line steamship *Titanic* leaves Southampton, England, on its maiden voyage to New York. The largest and most luxurious ship ever built, it is considered unsinkable.

April 13: Congress submits the Seventeenth Amendment permitting direct election of senators to the states for ratification.

April 14: Shortly before midnight, the *Titanic* hits an iceberg off the Banks of Newfoundland and begins to sink. It is soon discovered that there are not nearly enough lifeboats for those aboard.

April 15: At about 2:40 A.M. the *Titanic* goes under. Around 4 A.M. the ship *Carpathia* arrives to rescue the survivors.

April 16: The scope of the *Titanic* disaster has become clear. Some 1,500 people have perished in the disaster.

Harriet Quimby, born on a Michigan farm, becomes the first woman aviator to fly across the English Channel; Quimby will lose her life in an aircraft accident on July 1.

May 4: More than 10,000 women march in the New York suffrage parade.

May 12–19: The Socialist Party meets in Indianapolis and nominates Eugene Debs for president.

June 14: Roosevelt arrives in Chicago in preparation for the Republican convention. He tells reporters he feels fit as a bull moose and the name Bull Moose Party will stick to the party he forms.

June 18–22: The Republican convention meets in Chicago, renominating President Taft and Vice President James Sherman.

June 22: Roosevelt's supporters walk out of the Republican convention and reconvene at Orchestra Hall, where they agree to form the Progressive Party and to meet in convention in August.

June 25–July 2: The Democratic convention meets in Baltimore. On the 46th ballot on July 2, they nominate Woodrow Wilson for president.

August 2: In response to an attempt by a Japanese corporation to buy land in Baja California, Senator Henry Cabot Lodge introduces a resolution to extend the Monroe Doctrine to private foreign companies. After it passes it is called the Lodge Corollary.

August 5: The new Progressive Party meets in Chicago, nominating Theodore Roosevelt for president and reform governor Hiram Johnson of California for vice president.

August 16: The United States files suit under the Sherman Anti-Trust Act against the Patents Company, the motion picture trust organized by Thomas Edison in 1908.

August 24: President Taft signs Alaska's Second Organic Act, giving Alaska a bicameral legislature and limited home rule.

October 14: Theodore Roosevelt is shot and wounded by an assassin in Milwaukee, but delivers his speech before going to the hospital for treatment. He will be sidelined for the rest of the campaign.

October 30: Vice President James Sherman dies; Republicans substitute Nicholas Murray Butler, president of Columbia, as the vice presidential candidate for the upcoming election.

November: In the new state of Arizona, citizens use initiative and referendum to restore the recall of judges, which Congress deleted from their constitution; they also give women full suffrage, becoming the ninth state to do so.

November 5: With the Republicans split, Democrat Woodrow Wilson wins the presidential election, carrying 40 of 48 states. Roosevelt carries six states and Taft only two. Democrats also win their largest majorities since the Civil War in the House and Senate.

EYEWITNESS TESTIMONY

. . . our American past, compared to that of any European country, has a character all its own. Its peculiarity consists, not merely in its brevity, but in the fact that from the beginning it has been informed by an idea. From the beginning Americans have been anticipating and projecting a better future. From the beginning the Land of Democracy has been figured as the Land of Promise. Thus the American's loyalty to the national tradition rather affirms than denies the imaginative projection of a better future. An America which was not the Land of Promise, which was not informed by a prophetic outlook and a more or less constructive ideal, would not be the America bequeathed to us by our forefathers. In cherishing the Promise of a better national future the American is fulfilling rather than imperiling the substance of the national tradition.

. . . From the point of view of an immigrant this Promise may consist of the anticipation of a better future, which he can share merely by taking up his residence on American soil; but once he has become an American, the Promise can no longer remain merely an anticipation. It becomes in that case a responsibility, which requires for its fulfillment a certain kind of behavior on the part of himself and his fellow-Americans.

Herbert Croly, The Promise of American Life *(1909), pp. 3–4.*

City Planning is the adaptation of a city to its proper function. This conception can be indefinitely expanded but its significance will be appreciated if we admit that no city is more healthy than the highest death rate in any ward or block and that no city is more beautiful than its most unsightly tenement. The back yard of a city and not its front lawn is the real criterion for its standards and its efficiency.

This involves a radical change in the attitude of citizens toward government and the functions of government, but one to which the exigencies and the complexity of city life in nearly all great American cities is resistlessly impelling us. It compels a departure from the doctrine that government should not assume any functions aside from its primitive and restrictive activities and boldly demands the interest and effort of the government to preserve the health, morals and efficiency of the citizens equal to the effort and the zeal which is now expended in the futile task of trying to make amends for the exploitations by private citizens and the wanton disregard of the rights of the many.

Benjamin Marsh, executive secretary of the New York Committee on Congestion of Population, in his An Introduction to City Planning *(1909), p. 27.*

Do you know that the labor organizations of this country . . . have taken their earnings and sent men to the capitals of every State and the capital of the nation to plead for legislation that would make safety appliances for railroads and cars; that would make mines safe; that would protect life. They have been there year after year, pleading to take little children out of the mines; to take them away from the spindles and put them into the schools; to prevent women from taking the jobs from their husbands and fathers. Have you ever been to a legislative body and found a committee of prohibitionists there to help you plead your cause? Have they ever raised their voices in behalf of your lives, of your limbs, of your wives, of your children? Have they ever done anything except to shout Rum? While you have been there pleading for your homes and your families and your lives, over here in the corner is raised a hoarse cry of the prohibitionists saying: "For God's sake, don't take that! Don't give us the Employers' Liability Act! Don't give us the Safety Appliance Act! Don't do anything about mills and mines; just wait. Don't take up that. Let's first destroy Rum. Join with us on a moral issue. Let us get rid of Rum and then we will help you."

Lawyer Clarence Darrow, antiprohibition speech, 1909, reprinted in Monahan, ed., Text-Book of True Temperance, *pp. 90–91.*

AGENT: How do you know they are whore houses?

MESSENGER: Don't I get called to them with messages?

AGENT: How can they call?

MESSENGER: Well, they all have call boxes. We go in all of 'em. We see some great sights there. Last week I got a call in the ———— Hotel on 13th Street, and when I answered the woman let me in her room where she was all naked, except for a little shirt she had on, and that could cover very little of her. . . . She sent me to get her something to eat and when I came back she was laying flat on the bed. . . . I get mine alright.

AGENT: What do you mean?

MESSENGER: Well, a lot of girls like to stay with us messengers. We have whores come to our office too. We have a table there and do the trick on it. We get a lot of coats and lay them over the table and in that way make a soft spot. . . .

AGENT: Does your manager know what goes on?

MESSENGER: I should say he does. He sends us out after the whores, and then he takes his whack first.

An NCLC agent interviews a 17-year-old messenger boy, ca. 1909, quoted in Trattner, Crusade for the Children *(1970), p. 113.*

At present, however, most improbable tales [that is, movies] hold the attention of the youth of the city night after night, and feed his starved imagination as nothing else succeeds in doing. In addition to these fascinations, the five-cent theater is also fast becoming the general social center and club house in many crowded neighborhoods. It is easy of access from the street, the entire family of parents and children can attend for a comparatively small sum of money, and the performance lasts for at least an hour; and, in some of the humbler theaters, the spectators are not disturbed for a second hour. . . .

Hundreds of young people attend these five-cent theaters every evening in the week, including Sunday, and what is seen and heard there becomes the sole topic of conversation, forming the ground pattern of their social life. That mutual understanding which in another social circle is provided by books, travel and all the arts, is here compressed into the topics suggested by the play.

Jane Addams, The Spirit of Youth and the City Streets *(1909), pp. 85–87.*

. . . [T]he minimum below which a working girl cannot live decently and be self-supporting in Pittsburg is $7.00 a week. . . .

From the introductory table . . . it will be seen that they are 20 per cent of the whole number. Seventeen per cent more are earning slightly larger pay. The wages paid 60 per cent of the working women of Pittsburg do not afford them even this meagre subsistence. It may be said that if . . . a girl's wages are supplemented by her family, her condition is really far from desperate. . . . In many cases, this is true. . . . Clearly, however, the tradition that a girl's father and brothers always help toward her support has become, in the Pittsburg district at least, in many cases illusory.

That a girl is one of a family group is quite as likely to indicate that she is the chief breadwinner, as that her family is her chief bulwark against the world. . . .

Few will hesitate to condemn the degradation that attends the woman who chooses unsocial means of self-support. Yet one form of subsidizing a wage-worker leads to another form of subsidizing, and so long as custom or fact render the payment of a full living wage non-essential, economic needs impel many a girl toward a personally degrading life. . . .

For social strength, it would seem that the question ought to be: What wage must a girl have in order to live decently, maintain sound health, and have reasonable recreation?

Elizabeth Beardsley Butler, in her Women and the Trades, *volume 1 of the Pittsburgh Survey (1909), pp. 346–49.*

The Children's Bureau would not merely collect and classify information, but it would be prepared to furnish to every community in the land information that was needed, diffuse knowledge that had come through experts' study of

facts valuable to the child and to the community. . . . Evils that are unknown or underestimated have the best chance for undisturbed existence and extension, and where light is most needed there is still darkness. Ours is, for instance, the only great nation which does not know how many children are born and how many die in each year within its borders; still less do we know how many die in infancy of preventable diseases; how many blind children might have seen the light, for one-fourth of the totally blind need not have been so had the science that has proved this been made known in even the remotest sections of the country.

Lillian Wald, "A Plea for the Creation of the Children's Bureau," speech at the White House, January 25, 1909, in Proceedings of the Conference on the Care of Dependent Children, *p. 6.*

The secretary read as follows: Should children of parents of worthy character, but suffering from temporary misfortune, and the children of widows of worthy character and reasonable efficiency, be kept with their parents—aid being given the parents to enable them to maintain suitable homes for the rearing of the children? Should the breaking of a home be permitted for reasons of poverty, or only for reasons of inefficiency or immorality? . . .

Mr. [Michael Scanlan, president, New York Catholic Home Bureau for Dependent Children]: . . .For us Catholics there can be no question where we stand. The teaching of our church has always been in favor of the preservation of family ties, and the wisdom of this teaching has been commended by those separated from her. . . . The special object of our society, its fundamental work, is the visiting of the poor at their homes. . . . It is only a very last resort and for very grave reasons and after many trials that a family group is broken up. . . . It should be the cardinal aim of charity workers to keep intact the family circle of the poor. Children should be reared in the family where God Almighty has placed them. . . .

Mr. [James Jackson, superintendent of Cleveland Associated Charities]: . . .When anything happens to the breadwinner, if the mother is capable, it seems to be perfectly clear that it is our business, either as a state or as individuals, to see that she has material support. . . . Either the state or the individual, or the two in cooperation, should see that the mother has the necessities of existence. . . . Should she lack the capacity, if she is inefficient or below the community standard of morality, the mother is thereby unable to rear good men and women. Then we must help substitute capacity for her incapacity, or if that is impossible the children must be rescued from her. . . .

Mr. [Mornay Williams, chair of the New York Child Labor Committee]: . . . I suppose that I am in a minority here to-day, because I am not entirely convinced that even in the case of dependent children it is always best to leave them in their own homes. . . . I believe that for the child always the best thing should be done, and my own belief is that for the normal boy—not the abnormal boy, but the normal boy—at a certain age the discipline of the school [that is, a reform or boarding institution] is absolutely essential. . . . I speak of that out of the experience I have had with street boys. To my mind . . . the street boy is the great problem of to-day. . . .

Judge [Julian Mack, Chicago, Judge of Cook County Circuit Court]: . . . But the question before us now is, shall a parent, merely because of poverty . . . be deprived of the care and custody of the child? To that I can see but one answer. That answer of course is in the negative. I can not understand why poverty alone should give anybody the right to deprive that child of that which it needs most in life—its own parents' love and care and sympathy [applause]. . . .

In my personal experience I know of nothing sadder than the case of children that were taken away, or the case of the mother who came into the juvenile court ready to give up her child, ready to give it up merely because of poverty. I saw the twofold danger, the danger to the child in losing that mother's love and companionship, no matter how good a substitute we might find in any institution or in any foster home; and I saw again, time after time, the terrible danger that confronted the young mother without proper stay in the world except that child's love, forced to go out and fight the battle alone in the big cities. [Applause.]

Debate over supporting dependent mothers and children,
Proceedings of the Conference on the Care of
Dependent Children, *January 25 and 26, 1909,*
pp. 41–53 passim.

Home life is the highest and finest product of civilization. It is the great molding force of mind and of character. Children should not be deprived of it except for urgent and compelling reasons. Children of parents of worthy character, suffering from temporary misfortune and children of reasonably efficient and deserving mothers who are without the support of the normal breadwinner, should, as a rule, be kept with their parents, such aid being given as may be necessary to maintain suitable homes for the rearing of the children. This aid should be given by such methods and from such sources as may be determined by the general relief policy of each community, preferably in the form of private charity, rather than of public relief. Except in unusual circumstances, the home should not be broken up for reasons of poverty, but only for considerations of inefficiency or immorality.

Letter to the president, relating the conclusions of the first
White House Conference on the Care of Dependent Children,
January 25 and 26, 1909, Proceedings, pp. 192–97.

Far be it from *The Outlook* to say that San Francisco should not be given the opportunity to wash and dress itself properly and drink a moderate amount of pure water. The point we wish to make here is that if its drinking water is to be kept pure, it means that the Hetch-Hetchy Water Company must eventually be given practical supervision of at least half of the Yosemite National Park. We have neither the knowledge nor the time to go into details of rainfall, watershed topography, or bacteriological chemistry, but we do know that if a municipal water-works is permitted to erect its plant in the Hetch-Hetchy Valley, it means that the Yosemite Park will become the back yard of a great municipal utility instead of a recreation ground for all the people of the country. . . .

If this country were in danger of habitually ignoring utilitarian practice for the sake of running after sentimental dreams and aesthetic visions, we should advise it to cut down the California big trees to shelter its citizens from the weather, and to dam the Tuolumne River in order to instruct its citizens in the use of the bathtub. But the danger is all the other way. The National habit is to waste the beauty of nature and save the dollars of business.

Lyman Abbott, "Saving the Yosemite Park," Outlook, *vol. 91*
(January 30, 1909), pp. 234, 236.

The celebration of the centennial of the birth of Abraham Lincoln widespread and grateful as it may be, will fail to justify itself if it takes no note and makes no recognition of the colored men and women to whom the great emancipator labored to assure freedom. Besides a day of rejoicing, Lincoln's birthday in 1909 should be one of taking stock of the nation's progress since 1865. How far has it lived up to the obligations imposed upon it by the Emancipation Proclamation? How far has it gone in assuring to each and every citizen, irrespective of color, the equality of opportunity and equality before the law, which underlie our American institutions and are guaranteed by the Constitution?

If Mr. Lincoln could revisit this country he would be disheartened by the nation's failure in this respect. . . .

Silence under these conditions means tacit approval. The indifference of the North is already responsible for more than one assault upon democracy, and every such attack reacts as unfavorably upon whites as upon blacks. Discrimination once permitted cannot be bridled. . . . Hence we call upon all the believers in democracy to join in a national conference for the discussion of present evils, the voicing of protests, and the renewal of the struggle for civil and political liberty.

The call that led to the founding of the NAACP; written by
Oswald Garrison Villard and signed by 60 others, issued
February 12, 1909, from a manuscript copy in the Library of
Congress, available online at African American Odyssey.
URL: http://memory.loc.gov/ammem/
aaohtml/exhibit/aolist.html.

Mary Church Terrell, the first president of the National Association of Colored Women in the 1890s, was also a founding member of the NAACP in 1909. *(Library of Congress, Prints and Photographs Division, LC-USZ62-84496)*

The Hetch-Hetchy is one of a dozen mountain gorges, and, while beautiful, it is not unique. It is accessible over difficult trails about three months during the year, and few ever visit it. The Yosemite Valley satisfies every craving for large numbers of tourists. . . . California would not countenance the desecration of any of her scenery, and yet the State Legislature, now in session, has unanimously petitioned Congress to pass this bill. President Roosevelt, Secretary Garfield, Forester Pinchot, will yield to none in their love of nature; yet they strongly favor this bill. . . . The only question is, after all, the conversion of the Hetch-Hetchy Meadow into a crystal clear Lake—a natural object of indeed rare beauty. . . . It will be made accessible by good roads . . . and it will be a delight to visitors, while at the same time it serves a great and useful purpose. . . . There are eight hundred miles of wild mountain scenery in the Sierras, and, according to John Muir, "There are a dozen

Yosemites;" then why deplore the loss of a mosquito meadow? . . .

By yielding their opposition, sincere lovers of nature will turn the prayers of a million people to praise for the gifts bestowed upon them by the God of Nature, whom they cannot worship in his temple, but must perforce live in the sweltering cities. A reduced death rate is a more vital consideration than the discussion of the relative beauties of a meadow or a lake.

Former San Francisco mayor James Phelan, "Why Congress Should Pass the Hetch Hetchy Bill," letter to Outlook, *vol. 91 (February 13, 1909), pp. 340–41.*

With the weather worse that it has been at any time since the great March blizzard of twenty-one years ago, the ceremony of inaugurating Mr. Taft was carried through today. . . .

The going of Mr. Roosevelt was in sharp contrast to his own inauguration four years ago. Then the sun shone brightly, and although there were traces of snow underfoot, the sky was as benignant as could be. . . .

Following the ceremonies in the Senate President Roosevelt, again a private citizen, bade an affectionate adieu to his successor, and then hurried away through a side door to take a train to New York. As he passed out he got an ovation.

Outside the Capitol he was met by 800 members of the New York County Committee and under their escort was driven to the Union Station. . . . He was compelled time and time again to acknowledge the cheers from the throng which lined his way. . . . As he made his way to the train shortly after 3 o'clock he was cheered by thousands.

To all with whom he spoke, Mr. Roosevelt declared that while he had "a bully time" as President, he was glad to lay down the duties of the office.

"Taft Is Sworn In Senate Hall," New York Times, *March 5, 1909, page 1.*

From the minute we left Washington I began to miss the excitement, which always attended President Roosevelt on these trips. Even before we left Washington, President Taft took no notice of the crowd—it was not a large one— which had assembled at the depot. He entered his car and never came out to wave a good-bye, and I think even the depot employees missed the "Good-bye, good-luck" of the ex-President. There was a large crowd at Baltimore, and the President never went even to the platform to wave his hand—and so it was all the way to New York. Of course, I am committed to the Roosevelt school of policy and think that the people have a right to expect some return attention from the President when it assembles anywhere to see him pass. But I do not think Mr. Taft will ever care a hang about this form of popularity. . . .

At the depot in Jersey City and on the New York side there was a great lot of people gathered, but we were so surrounded by police and secret service men that we had little trouble in reaching our motor. . . . The President did not even look out of the window to respond to the *banzai* of the people of the street. Jimmie Sloan, the secret service man, whispered to me:

"What an opportunity he is missing! For God's sake, captain, get him to lift his hat when the people yell, for if he don't they will stop yelling when he will want them most."

Captain Archie Butt, military aide to Presidents Roosevelt and Taft who later perished on the Titanic, *comments on the differences between the two, letter to his sister-in-law, Clara Butt, March 21, 1909, in his* Taft and Roosevelt, *vol. 1, pp. 18–19.*

. . . under the guise of protecting some of our people against foreign competition, [the tariff] robs the many to enrich the few. The purpose of protection is, as its firmest supporters assert, to give the American producer an advantage over his foreign competition, but the effect of it is to tax the American consumer for the benefit of the American manufacturer; for to the dullest mind it must be self-evident that any law which enables one man to obtain more for his goods when he sells them must compel another man to pay for those goods when he buys them. . . .

. . . Such legislation is so outrageously unjust that I marvel at the patience with which it has been endured by an intelligent and justice-loving people. To mitigate this injustice in some slight degree, and to the end that Congress may emancipate consumption from some part of the great burden which it has borne for so many years, I have prepared . . . an income-tax amendment to the pending bill. . . .

I hope in this way to lift $80,000,000 annually from the stooping shoulders of those whose toil nets them only a modest return at best and to lay it upon those who can pay this tax without sacrificing a single comfort. This relief will mean much to men of moderate circumstances, and yet it will not be felt by those from whose abundant incomes we will supply the loss of revenue. . . . The apologists of special privilege may continue to cry aloud against the dangerous and leveling doctrines of Socialism, but I tell them here and now that the best way to eradicate Socialism is to renew the people's faith in the justice of their Government. The best way to make the poor respect the rights of the rich is to make the poor understand that the rich respect their rights.

Senator Joseph Bailey, Democrat of Texas, introducing an income tax amendment to the Payne-Aldrich tariff, April 26, 1909, Congressional Record, 61st Congress, 1st session, vol. 44, p. 1534.

. . . I read an interview the other day by that distinguished American, Mr. Carnegie. He said that [an income tax] was not Republican, that its only result was to incite men to perjury. Well, Mr. Carnegie did not make the Republican party. . . . Mr. Carnegie told us time out of mind that he could not run his mills or manufacturing plants without the protection which he demanded. In view of the fact that he did run his mills after the protection was given, and accumulated wealth which he will not live long enough to distribute, it seems to me that the Republican party did make Mr. Carnegie. . . .

I favor [an income tax] not for the purpose of putting all the burdens of government upon property or all the burdens of government upon wealth, but that it may bear its just and fair proportion. . . .

Senator William Borah of Idaho, progressive Republican, in debate over the income tax, May 3, 1909, Congressional Record, 61st Congress, 1st session, vol. 44, p. 1682.

It is not a fact that in this Republic property does not now bear a very great proportion of the burden of taxation. I find in looking at the precise figures . . . that in 1902 . . . the property in the United States upon which the [real estate] taxes for the support of the Government, county, municipal, and other local governments, were levied amounted at a true value to $97,810,000,000; that taxes were levied upon that property at the rate . . . in round numbers, three-fourths of 1 percent; and that would amount in round numbers to the equivalent of an income tax of 15 percent, assuming an income of 5 percent, which is a high figure to place upon the income from property. . . . But that is not all the tax that is imposed upon property. There are also . . . taxes upon corporations, taxes in the nature of licenses, taxes for the right to carry on business of various kinds, . . ., inheritance taxes. . . .

So, . . . while I am not now arguing against the imposition of an income tax, I beg the Senators to remember in their arguments that property in the United States does bear a tax for the support of government in the United States equal to nearly eight times the income tax that they are proposing to assess upon it.

Senator Elihu Root of New York, in debate over an income tax, May 4, 1909, Congressional Record, 61st Congress, 1st session, vol. 44, p. 1701.

"We denounce the ever growing oppression of our 10,000,000 colored fellow citizens as the greatest menace that threatens the country. Often plundered of their just share of the public funds, robbed of nearly all part in the government, some murdered with impunity and all treated with open contempt by officials, they are held in some states in practical slavery to the white community. The systematic persecution of law-abiding citizens and their disfranchisement on account of their race alone is a crime that will ultimately drag down to an infamous end any nation that allows it to be practiced. . . .

"As first and immediate steps . . . we demand of Congress and the executive:

(1) That the Constitution be strictly enforced and the civil rights guaranteed under the Fourteenth Amendment be secured impartially to all.

(2) That there be equal educational opportunities for all and in all the states, and that public school expenditure be the same for the Negro and white child.

(3) That in accordance with the Fifteenth Amendment the right of the Negro to the ballot on the same terms as other citizens be recognized in every part of the country."

With these resolutions all seemed satisfied but the further question of practical work brought out the diversity of radical, disagreeing elements seeking unity but undecided and unsettled among themselves. The debate was warm and even passionate. . . .

Resolutions of the May 31, 1909 conference which led to the founding of the NAACP, reported in W. E. B. DuBois, "National Committee on the Negro," The Survey, vol. 22 (June 12, 1909), pp. 408–09.

. . . if a manufacturer comes before one of the committees of the American Congress and says the wages in a foreign country are lower than the wages here and we must have a tariff of 75 per cent or 125 percent to protect us, his testimony is at once accepted. . . . because . . . he is seeking to maintain industries in America and furnish employment to American labor. There is no other place in our whole system of government, in the courts or elsewhere, where the rights of men are determined upon any such one-sided testimony as that. . . .

I undertake to say . . . that the great mass of people of this country have an interest here. I do not believe that the American consuming public wants these [tariff] rates so reduced as no longer to protect American labor. But everybody knows that with no foreign competition conditions suppress domestic competition and put prices up and extort from the consumer what they please. The consumer has a right to demand that this shall not be done with the aid of his government. Is he unreasonable? Why has he not a day here?

Senator Robert La Follette of Wisconsin, Republican insurgent, in debate over the Payne-Aldrich tariff, June 3, 1909, Congressional Record, 61st Congress, 1st session, vol. 44, p. 2696.

Mr. President [that is, of the Senate], there [exhibiting] is colored cotton cloth. It comes in the class of 100 to 130 threads to the square inch. The actual count of threads in that is 148 threads to the square inch. It is 26 inches wide, and it costs 5 3/8 pence a square yard. The value is 15.1 cents per square yard, and the present duty under paragragh 306 in the Dingley Act at 35 per cent ad valorem amounts to 5.29 cents. The proposed duty under paragraph 814 of the Senate bill [the Payne-Aldrich tariff], specific, based on value is 7 cents per square yard. For mercerization another cent is added, which makes the specific duty on this piece of cloth the yard value of which is 15.1 cents, 8 cents per square yard, or an increase of 27 cents per square yard over the existing rate, a duty increase of 51 1/4 percent. This is cheap dress goods, a substitute for silk, which the masses can afford to buy. It retails at 19 cents a yard and is sold all over the United States. . . .

Mr. President, permit me to say I shall be able to furnish Senators with a small piece of each of these samples, mounted upon a sheet of paper, with the data which I have given printed upon it, and they can examine them at their convenience.

Senator La Follette, in an example of the detailed speeches Insurgents presented hoping to defeat the Payne-Aldrich tariff, June 4, 1909, Congressional Record, 61st Congress, 1st session, vol. 44, p. 2739.

Four miles from Grand Island the rear axle broke again. A farm family took us in while a mechanic from Denver brought another. Nettie was happy to give her place to the mechanic and ride the train ahead to Cheyenne. Near Ogallala, Nebraska, we were halted by a nondescript sheriff's posse on horseback. They were looking for two murderers and at first didn't believe us when we explained that we were only trying to drive from New York to San Francisco. It was not until the lawmen were convinced that no firearms or suspects were concealed in the Maxwell that they allowed us to go on.

At Fort Steele, Wyoming, we pulled up short at a dead-end in the road where the bridge over the swollen North Platte had been washed out. I sent my passengers ahead on foot across a paralleling Union Pacific railroad trestle and then bumped the Maxwell for three-quarters of a mile on the ties to the opposite side. Across Wyoming the roads threaded through privately owned cattle ranches. My companions were obliged to take turns opening and closing the gates of the fences which surrounded them as we drove through. If we got lost we'd take to the high ground and search the horizon for the nearest telephone poles with the most wires. It was a sure way of locating the transcontinental railroad which we knew would lead us back to civilization.

Alice Huyler Ramsey of New Jersey, the first woman to drive coast to coast, Manhattan to San Francisco, June 9 to August 7, 1909, available online at Early Adventures with the Automobile. URL:http:// www.ibiscom.com/auto.htm.

August 17, 1909, Etah, North Greenland . . . I learn that Dr. Cook came over from Ellesmere Land with his two boys, Etookahshoo and Ahpellah, and in a confidential conversation with Mr. Whitney made the statement that he had reached the North Pole. Professor MacMillan and I have talked to his two boys and have learned that there is no foundation in fact for such a statement, and the Captain and others of the expedition have questioned them, and if they were out on the ice of the Arctic Ocean it was only for a very short distance, not more than twenty or twenty-five miles. The boys are positive in this statement, and my own boys, Ootah and Ooqueah, have talked to them also, and get the same replies. It is a fact that they had a very hard time and were reduced to low limits, but they have not been any distance north, and the Commander and the rest of us are in the humor to regard Mr. Whitney as a person who has been hoodwinked. We know Dr. Cook very well and also his reputation, and we know that he was never good for a hard day's work; in fact he was not up to the average, and he is no hand at all in making the most of his resources. He probably has spun this yarn to Mr. Whitney and the boatswain to make himself look big to them.

Matthew Henson, diary entry while accompanying Peary to the North Pole, August 17, 1909, included in his autobiography, A Black Explorer at the North Pole, pp. 177–78.

Commander Robert E. Peary, U.S.N., has discovered the north pole. Following the report of Dr. F. A. Cook that he had reached the top of the world comes the certain announcement from Mr. Peary, the hero of eight polar expeditions, covering a period of twenty-three years, that at last his ambition has been realized, and from all over the world comes full acknowledgment of Peary's feat and congratulations on his success.

The first announcement of Peary's exploit was received in the following message to The New York Times:

Indian Harbor, Labrador, via Cape Ray, N. F., Sept. 6. . . .

I have the pole, April sixth. Expect arrive Chateau Bay, September seventh. Secure control wire for me there and arrange expedite transmission big story. PEARY

Following the receipt of Commander Peary's message to The New York Times several other messages were received in this city from the explorer to the same effect.

Soon afterward The Associated Press received the following: . . .

Stars and Stripes nailed to the pole. PEARY. . . .

The New York Times reports Peary's telegrams announcing he reached the North Pole on April 6, 1909; the telegrams were sent September 6, "Peary Discovers the North Pole After Eight Trials in 23 Years," September 7, 1909, p. 1.

Now, the promise of the Republican platform was not to revise everything downward, and in the speeches which have been taken interpreting that platform, which I made in the campaign, I did not promise that everything should go downward. What I promised was, that there should be many decreases, and that in some few things increases would be found to be necessary. . . .

On the whole, however, I am bound to say that I think the Payne tariff bill is the best tariff bill that the Republican party ever passed; that in it the party has conceded the necessity for following the changed conditions and reducing tariff rates accordingly. This is a substantial achievement in the direction of lower tariffs and downward revision, and it ought to be accepted as such.

President Taft defends the Payne-Aldrich tariff, speech at Winona, Minnesota, September 17, 1909, Supplement to the Messages and Papers of the Presidents, p. 7773.

Every one who lives in the South or who has traveled there knows the "crackers," "sandhillers," "barrenites" . . . Feeble, slow-moving creatures, most of them, some emaciated, some bloated with dropsy, you recognize them at once by their lusterless eye and a peculiar pallor—"the Florida complexion"; their skin is like tallow, and you seem to be looking through a semi-transparent upper layer into an ashy or saffron layer beneath it. If you speak to one of these saffron-hued natives, especially to one of the children, you are generally met by a very curious, fish-eyed stare without a gleam of intelligence back of it, and you wait long before you get a reply. . . .

These people, the "poor whites," shiftless, ignorant, poverty-pinched, and wretched, are of pure Anglo-Saxon stock—as purely Anglo-Saxon as any left in the country; and if this arouses your interest to ask more about them, you will doubtless be told that they are "utterly wuthless; they've got 'the big lazy,' and wouldn't do a day's work to save their lives" . . .

It is estimated that scattered over the Atlantic seaboard, from the Potomac, round the Gulf, to the Mississippi River, there are to-day two millions of these poor whites—our native-born whites—suffering with anemia, and hardly one of those two million knows, or even suspects, that he is really suffering from an internal parasite—that his disease is caused by the hookworm. . . .

. . . From fifteen to seventy-five cents' worth of two cheap drugs, thymol and Epsom salts, the dose varying according to the severity of the infection, will cure any ordinary case. Two million dollars will pay the whole bill for the cure of the South, for many doctors are giving their services for nothing; and when the cure is complete, the South will take her place with the North and West in agricultural and industrial prosperity, for her two million sick whites will be two million able workers. . . .

Marion Hamilton Carter, "The Vampire of the South,"
McClure's, vol. 34 (October 1909), pp. 617–18.

It is interesting to see how the picking up of girls for the trade in and outside of New York is carried on by these youths on the East Side of New York, which has now grown, under this development, to be the chief recruiting ground for the so-called white slave trade in the United States, and probably in the world. It can be exploited, of course, because in it lies the newest body of immigrants and the greatest supply of unprotected young girls in the city. These now happen to be Jews—as, a quarter and a half century ago, they happened to be German and Irish.

. . . [T]he girls must go to work at the earliest possible date, and from the population of 350,000 Jews east of the Bowery tens of thousands of young girls go out into the shops. There is no more striking sight in the city than the mass of women that flood east through the narrow streets in a winter's twilight, returning to their homes in the East Side tenements. The exploitation of young women as money-earning machines has reached a development on the East Side of New York probably not equaled anywhere in the world. . . .

But the largest and most profitable field for exploitation of the girls of the East Side is in procuring them for the white slave traffic. This line of swindling is in itself specialized. Formerly its chief recruiting grounds were the public amusement parks of the tenement districts; now for several years they have been the dance halls. . . .

Muckraker George Kibbe Turner, "The Daughters of the
Poor," McClure's, vol. 34 (November 1909), pp. 55–56.

On the day of the fire I was at work in the second vein, about a mile from the main shaft in a southerly direction. . . . We were, I think, about the farthest away from the shaft of any of the men working in the mine. . . . we stopped working as usual shortly before half-past three o'clock, and set out for the shaft, to be hoisted out. With us went an old man named Alexander Kroll and his fifteen-year-old son, who worked near us.

After we had proceeded about half a mile towards the shaft we detected a faint odour of smoke, which became more marked as we advanced, until it was almost unendurable. Then we knew that the mine was on fire and that there was danger ahead. . . . Mr. Kroll, who was not as strong as the rest of us, was almost overcome by the smoke, and would have fallen had we not helped him along. It was pitiful to hear the boy exhorting us to save his father.

After what seemed an interminable time we finally reached the bottom of the main shaft. Everything combustible in the large open space about the shaft was enveloped in flames. . . . The heat was intolerable, and the smoke so dense that one could see only a few feet before him. It made our eyes smart so that tears ran from them. Staggering and choking, we groped our way to the shaft and looked for the cage, but it was not there.

Thomas White, a survivor of the Cherry mining disaster,
November 13, 1909, as told to Louis Murphy, "Eight Days
In A Burning Mine," World Magazine, October 1911,
available online at Mine Safety and Health Administration.
URL: http://www.msha.gov/CENTURY/
MAG/MAGCVR.asp.

On November 12, 1906, President Roosevelt withdrew all coal lands in Alaska from public entry; but previous to that time there were about 900 claims filed, covering about 100,000 acres (nearly the whole of the coal fields.) The law attempts to prevent monopoly of such claims by limiting the amount of each claim and providing that each claimant must take up the land in his own interest and for his own use. This law has been interpreted by the Supreme Court of the United States to forbid speculating in coal lands before entry—either by dummy entrymen or by previous agreements to consolidate claims after entry. Of these 900 claims to Alaska coal lands—among them the so-called Cunningham group—the majority are fraudulent.

As to the action of the Land Office on these claims, I assert that Land Office ordered the Cunningham claims to patent without due investigation when Commissioner Ballinger knew that they were under suspicion; that while in office Commissioner Ballinger urged Congress to pass a law which would validate fraudulent Alaska claims; that shortly after resigning from office he became attorney for the Cunningham group and other Alaska claims; that soon after he became Secretary of the Interior his office rendered a decision which would have validated all fraudulent Alaska claims. . . .

L. R. Glavis, "The Whitewashing of Ballinger—Are The
Guggenheims in Charge of the Deparment of the Interior?"
Collier's, November 13, 1909, reprinted in Investigation
of the Department of the Interior and
the Bureau of Forestry,
vol. 7, p. 4383.

The decision to strike was reached yesterday at the Cooper Union meeting which was addressed by Samuel Gompers, president of the AFL. . . .

Clara Lemlich, who was badly beaten up by thugs during the strike in the shop of Louis Leiserson, interrupted Jacob Panken just as he started to speak, saying: "I wanted to say a few words." Cries came from all parts of the hall, "Get up on the platform!" Willing hands lifted the frail little girl with flashing black eyes to the stage, and she said simply: "I have listened to all the speakers. I would not have further patience for talk, as I am one of those who feels and suffers from the things pictured. I move that we go on a general strike!"

As the tremulous voice of the girl died away, the audience rose en masse and cheered her to the echo. A grim sea of faces, with high purpose and resolve, they shouted and cheered the declaration of war for living conditions hoarsely.

"The Cooper Union Meeting," The Call, a socialist newspaper in New York, November 23, 1909, p. 1.

. . . 150 well-to-do women gathered in the Colony Club, Madison Avenue and Thirteenth Street, at the invitation of Miss Anne Morgan, Miss Elizabeth Marbury, and Mrs. Egerton L. Winthrop, Jr., to hear representatives of the striking shirtwaist makers tell their side of the fight, now in its fourth week. . . .

More of the strikers spoke, as well as several women and men sympathizers, and then Mrs. Philip M. Lydig and Elsie De Wolf passed around two hats, which brought back over $1,300. It was announced, also, that the Shuberts would give 50 per cent of the receipts of one of their New York theatres all next week to the strikers. . . .

Mrs. J. Borden Harriman. . . . introduced Miss Mary Dreier of the Woman's Trade Union League, as Chairman of the meeting. This league, which many women of wealth and social position are joining, is heartily in favor of the strikers. . . .

"Girl Strikers Tell the Rich Their Woes," New York Times, December 16, 1909, p. 3.

. . . When peaceably practiced, picketing has for years been upheld by the New York courts as legal. The girls, however, have been arrested literally by the dozen, taken to court and fined sometimes as high as $10 each, without even a hearing.

There has been considerable difference in the way various members of the bench have handled the cases. Detective and neighborhood thugs have threatened the pickets steadily, by profanity and even by blows which the police have somehow failed to see while no smallest gesticulation of a picket has escaped their notice or failed to be construed as an assault. For weeks the girls have endured what they believed to be injustice at the hands of the officers of law and order, and if at times recently they have become aggressive, it is hardly to be wondered at. One member of the Women's Trade Union League who with three other witnesses saw a scab assault a picket, applied to a magistrate for a warrant for the girl's arrest. She reports receiving this astonishing response from the bench: "You have no right to picket; you have no right to be on Washington Place. Every time you go down there you will get what is coming to you and I shall not interfere. No, I'll give you no warrant."

Constance D. Leupp, "The Shirtwaist Makers' Strike," The Survey, vol. 23 (December 18, 1909), pp. 384–85.

Thomas J. Barton, employee of Jones and Laughlin, working at night with a wrecking train, was run down and killed. This man was fifty-one, and earned $9.50 a week. He had two sons working, one an electrician and one a machinist, besides five younger children in school. They owned their own house of six rooms and had but $1,000 more to pay on it, but they carried no insurance. Mrs. Barton did not try to get money from the company,—even for funeral expenses, which were $195,—and they did not offer her anything. The oldest son soon married. This left the family dependent on an eighteen-year-old machinist making $12 a week. So the next boy, aged sixteen, left school and became an apprentice, adding $4.50 to the weekly income; and finally the fourteen-year-old boy left school and brought in $3.60 a week as a special messenger. . . .

William Evans, miner for the Pittsburgh Coal Company, was a widower. When he was killed, there was left a family of six, his oldest daughter with a baby, a boy of sixteen who had been Evans' helper in the mine, a girl of thirteen, and two boys eleven and eight. There was nothing for this family to do but scatter. The sixteen-year-old boy went off and took care of himself by working in a glass factory. The grown daughter took her baby and youngest brother and went to live with a sister. This left the two children of thirteen and eleven, for the grandparents, Evans' father and mother-in-law, to take care of. They lived in a small house, and were supported by an unmarried son of twenty-three, a miner earning $15 a week. The old man is crippled with rheumatism, and his wife who is sixty-two, after a long hard life, had given up going out to work, and settled down to look after her husband and son. When the two children came back upon her, she began again going out by the day to do washing for her neighbors. . . .

Reformer Crystal Eastman's investigation of fatal industrial accidents in Allegheny County, Pennsylvania, Work Accidents and the Law, 1910, volume 2 of the Pittsburgh Survey, pp. 139–42.

Unionism is not entirely dead in the mill towns; at least the spirit of it is to be found among the men, though the form is absent. Some of them expect to see again an organization in the mills. Others have given up hope of gaining

Progressive Era workers lived close to the factories in which they labored. This photo shows the neighborhood around the Homestead steel works, site of a bitter strike in 1892 and part of a large study by social scientists in 1909 called the Pittsburgh Survey. *(Library of Congress, Prints and Photographs Division, LC-USZC2-5119)*

ular times for eating, snatch a bite between tasks, though some, whose work permits, stop for a leisurely meal. I even heard of men who took steaks to cook on the hot plates about the machines. But they usually rely on the cold meal, and the women take great pains to make it appetizing, especially by adding preserves in a little cup in a corner of the bucket. They try to give the man what he likes the most, apparently half from pity at the cold food and hard work that fall to his lot. . . .

The men are inclined to trust all financial matters to their wives. It is the custom in Homestead for the workman to turn over his wages to his wife on pay day and to ask no questions as to what it goes for. He reserves a share for spending money; otherwise his part of the family problem is to earn and hers to spend. When the man was at home and I suggested they keep accounts for this investigation he usually referred the matter genially to the wife, saying, "Oh, she's the one who knows where the money goes. If she wants to help you out she can."

Margaret Byington, Homestead: The Households of a Mill Town, *1910, volume 4 of the Pittsburgh Survey, pp. 64, 108.*

shorter hours or higher wages through collective bargaining, and are looking for government interference and a legal eight-hour day. There is considerable variety of opinion as to how this is to be brought about. Pittsburgh steel workers are traditionally republican in politics; Speaker Cannon himself does not fear "tinkering" with the tariff more than they. The majority of them have been hoping that their representatives would after a while consider and pass the labor legislation that the workingmen desire. However, there has been much loss of faith in the last few years.

In telling about . . . fellows who are numbered today among the rank and file, I have tried to introduce the leading types—the twelve-hour man, the eight-hour man, the church member, the man who is at outs with the church, the union man and the socialist. . . . It is highly significant that there are such men as these in the Pittsburgh mills. In a discussion of the labor problem in the steel industry, it must be borne in mind that these men are more than workers; they are thinkers, and must be reckoned with.

John Fitch, The Steel Workers, *1910, volume 3 of the Pittsburgh Survey, pp. 17, 21.*

In mill-town economics, the dinner pail must be reckoned with as part of the table, and a bill of fare must be read with that in mind. I was struck with the pains often taken with the "mister's" bucket. The women used to carry lunches to the mill, but they are not now allowed inside without a pass. Most of the men, as they are not given reg-

The work I did with Miss Cameron was called rescue work. We would find the Chinese girls who were sold to work in the dives, or as domestic servants, and bring them to Cameron House so they could be free. Sometimes people reported to us or sometimes the slave girls themselves would slip a note under our front door and we would find it, and go to the place where the girl wanted to be rescued. Usually we had to go to the dives. When we went on the raid we always took several of our own girls with us to help. Generally I would follow Miss Cameron as interpreter and she and I would go into the house through a door or a window. Sometimes the slave girls got scared and ran out, so the other girls from the home had to wait outside and grab them when they tried to run away. Then when they caught the girl they would blow the police whistle, so we knew. After we got the girl, sometimes we had to go to court over thirty times to free her from her owner. . . .

Lilac Chen, who was sold into domestic servitude by her family at age six in 1893 and brought to America by a madam, describes her later work with Presbyterian Mission House in San Francisco, which rescued Chinese women forced into prostitution, ca. 1910, Nee, ed., Longtime Californ', *pp. 86, 88.*

What is really the cause of the trade in women? Not merely white women, but yellow and black women as well. Exploitation, of course; the merciless Moloch of capitalism that fattens on underpaid labor, thus driving thousands of women and girls into prostitution. . . .

It would be one-sided and extremely superficial to maintain that the economic factor is the only cause of prostitution. There are others no less important and vital. . . .

It is a conceded fact that woman is being reared as a sex commodity, and yet she is kept in absolute ignorance of the meaning and importance of sex. . . . Yet it is nevertheless true that so long as a girl is not to know how to take care of herself . . . we need not be surprised if she becomes an easy prey to prostitution, or to any form of a relationship which degrades her to the position of an object for mere sex gratification.

Emma Goldman's view of prostitution, "The Traffic in Women," Anarchism and Other Essays, *1910, pp. 178–79, 184.*

The history of women in industry in the United States is the story of a great industrial readjustment, which has not only carried woman's work from the home to the factory, but has changed its economic character from unpaid production for home consumption to gainful employment in the manufacture of articles for sale. Women have always worked, and their work has probably always been quite as important a factor in the total economy of society as it is to-day. But during the nineteenth century a transformation occurred in their economic position and in the character and conditions of their work. Their unpaid services have been transformed into paid services, their work has been removed from the home to the factory and workshop, their range of possible employment has been increased and at the same time their monopoly of their traditional occupations has been destroyed. The individuality of their work has been lost in a standardized product.

Helen Sumner, History of Women in Industry in the United States, *volume 9 of the* Congressional Report on Women and Child Wage-Earners in the United States, *1910, p. 7.*

The mother ought not to be compelled to engage in work that will call her away from her own home, nor be forced, in her own home, to perform so large a quantity of work as to cause her to neglect her children. . . . Above all, the keeping of lodgers, other than those related by blood ties to the family, should be prohibited absolutely. The family should not be allowed to remain in the poorer overcrowded neighborhoods of the city, but . . . they should be required to move out into suburban or less closely settled neighborhoods, where the opportunities for fresh air and healthful play are unrestricted. . . . But, for the proper working out of this class of cases, a much greater degree of supervision must be provided than is furnished by any of the existing New York agencies. . . . Too often the mother is not competent to spend wisely the amount of money that may be necessary to give her

adequate relief. The friendly visitor, sympathetic, tactful, with a knowledge of good house-keeping, can be of invaluable service to her. In addition to assisting in the expenditure of funds and the management of the family budget, she may find work to do in advice concerning the preparation of foods and the foods to be used; the cleanliness of the children, their schooling and amusement. With proper supervision, I believe this kind of work can become extremely valuable; without it, I am convinced that it can result only in failure.

Solomon Lowenstein, superintendent of the Hebrew Orphan Asylum, New York City, "A Study of the Problem of Boarding Out Jewish Children and of Pensioning Widowed Mothers," speech to the National Conference of Jewish Charities in the United States, 1910, Proceedings, *pp. 218–19.*

Conservation is the most democratic movement this country has known for a generation. It holds that the people have not only the right, but the duty to control the use of the natural resources, which are the great sources of prosperity. And it regards the absorption of these resources by the special interests, unless their operations are under effective public control, as a moral wrong. . . .

The danger to the Conservation policies is that the privileges of the few may continue to obstruct the rights of the many, especially in the matter of water power and coal. . . .

It is of the first importance to prevent our water powers from passing into private ownership as they have been doing, because the greatest source of power we know is falling water. Furthermore, it is the only great unfailing source of power. Our coal, the experts say, is likely to be exhausted during the next century, our natural gas and oil in this. Our rivers, if the forests on the watersheds are properly handled, will never cease to deliver power. Under our form of civilization, if a few men ever succeed in controlling the sources of power, they will eventually control all industry as well. If they succeed in controlling all industry, they will necessarily control the country. This country has achieved political freedom; what our people are fighting for now is industrial freedom. And unless we win our industrial liberty, we can not keep our political liberty.

Gifford Pinchot, summarizing his beliefs in The Fight for Conservation, *1910, pp. 81–86.*

We are only beginning to learn what freedom means. It is not the privilege of doing, irrespective of everybody else, what one wants to do. That would make the tramp the ideally free man. Freedom lies in the recognition and joyful acceptance of relationships. In organized play, where every child is a unit on a larger, mutually responsible whole, all reach a higher and more significant state of individual freedom than is possible on the unorganized, free-for-all playground.

Dr. Luther Gulick, physical educator and
founder of the Playground Association of America,
The Healthful Art of Dancing, *1910, p. 16.*

I remember a gray day in 1910. I was six years old. My grandfather was ill, and usually, he would be on a small cot in the dining room of our apartment on Indiana Avenue. I was dreamily playing with my baseball pictures. In those days pictures of ball players were inserted in packages of cigarettes. . . . My brother Earl had a large collection of these pictures and I, following his example, had managed to get a sizeable one. . . . I was not able to read, but I knew the name of every player on my pictures. . . .

Suddenly, I heard that Father Dondaville had come to see my grandfather. . . . He was a big, jolly, rather plump, and understanding priest. I liked the friendliness of his voice. I believed that he liked me. He paid attention to me, and flattered me in the way he asked questions about baseball and my pictures. He also asked me to show him how the various players batted, and talked to me about the game. I had not then, of course, learned to imitate the stances of the players accurately, but I did it nonetheless. He held the cards in his hands and asked me who each player was, and I identified the players correctly, and according to the teams on which they played. I told him what players batted and threw right or left-handed. All of this was knowledge that I had absorbed and heard, mainly from my older brother. The priest was amazed. . . . He gave me the nickname of "Young Ty Cobb."

American novelist James Farrell remembers his childhood in
Chicago, 1910, My Baseball Diary, *pp. 1–2.*

If work was action the *barrio* was where the action was. . . . Horse drawn drays with low platforms rumbled up and down our street carrying the goods the city traded in, from kegs of beer to sacks of grain. Within a few blocks of our house there were smithies, hand laundries, a macaroni factory, and all manner of places where wagons and buggies were repaired, horses stabled, bicycles fixed, chickens dressed, clothes washed and ironed, furniture repaired, candy mixed, tents sewed, wine grapes pressed, bottles washed, lumber sawed, suits fitted and tailored, watches and clocks taken apart and put together again, vegetables sorted, railroad cars unloaded, boxcars iced, barges freighted, ice cream cones molded, soda pop bottled, fish scaled, salami stuffed, corn ground for masa, and bread ovened. To those who knew where these were located in the alleys, as I did, the whole *barrio* was an open workshop. . . .

We found the Americans as strange in their customs as they probably found us. Immediately we discovered that

Baseball cards were included in cigarette packages. This card is the New York Giants' Christy Mathewson, one of the most popular players. The back reads, "Piedmont, The Cigarette of Quality." It was issued by the American Tobacco Company from 1909 to 1911. *(Library of Congress, Prints and Photographs Division, LC-USZc2-5119)*

there were no *mercados* and that when shopping you did not put the groceries in a *chiquihuite* [basket]. Instead everything was in cans or in cardboard boxes or each item was put in a brown paper bag. . . . The grocers did not give children a *pilón*. They did not stand at the door and coax you to come in. . . . The fruits and vegetables were displayed on counters instead of being piled up on the floor. The stores smelled of fly spray and oiled floors, not of fresh pineapple and limes.

Ernesto Galarza, later an economist, whose family fled the Mexican Revolution to California, ca. 1910,
Barrio Boy, *pp. 202–04.*

In a composite people like the American, it is inevitable that the color of the whole should appear different to those who view it from different points. The Englishman is apt to think of the United States as literally a new England, a country inhabited in the main by two classes; on the one hand descendants of seventeenth century English colonists, and on the other newly arrived foreigners.

The continental European, on the contrary, is apt to suffer from the complementary illusion, and to believe that practically all Americans are recent European emigrants, mainly, or at least largely, from his own country. Frenchmen have insisted to me that a large proportion of the United States is French, and Germans often believe that it is mainly German. . . . "I visited for two weeks in Cedar Rapids and never spoke anything but Bohemian," said a Prague friend to me. An Italian lady in Boston said, speaking in Italian, "You know in Boston one naturally gets so little chance to hear any English. . . ." On each side such exaggerated impressions are very hard to shake off. . . .

In spite of [some immigrants'] belief that America is not a nation, it has in truth the deepest right to consider itself such. It is an organic whole, inter-sensitive through all its parts, colored by one tradition and bound together not only by love of one material motherland but by one conception of the country's mission and of the means—liberty, enlightenment, prosperity—by which that mission is to be accomplished.

Emily Greene Balch, scholar of immigration,
Our Slavic Fellow Citizens, *1910, pp. 399–402.*

The theory that Hottentots or any other uneducated, altogether unintelligent class is fitted for self-government at once or to take part in government is a theory that I wholly dissent from—but this qualification is not applicable here. The other qualification to which I call your attention is that the class should as a whole care enough to look after its interests, to take part as a whole in the exercise of political power if it is conferred. Now if it does not care enough for this, then it seems to me that the danger is, if the power is conferred, that it may be exercised by that part of the class least desirable as political constituents and be neglected by many of those who are intelligent and patriotic and would be most desirable as members of the electorate. [Hissing from the crowd.] Now, my dear ladies, you must show yourselves equal to self-government by exercising, in listening to opposing arguments, that degree of restraint without which self-government is

impossible. If I could be sure that women as a class in the community, including all the intelligent women most desirable as political constituents, would exercise the franchise, I should be in favor of it.

President Taft addresses the NAWSA convention in Washington, D.C., April 14–19, 1910, eliciting the shocking reaction of hissing from some attendees, in Harper, ed.,
History of Woman Suffrage, *vol. 5, pp. 271–72.*

This experience in the outside world is educating her [the working woman], for she is studying conditions. She sees that she is forced to compete with those who have full political rights while she herself is a political nonentity. She finds that she must contend with and protect her-self against conditions which are more often political than economic, thus forcing upon her the conviction that she too is entitled to be a voter. She sees that politics, business and industrial life generally are so united that one affects the other and that since she is a factor in two she should be granted the rights and privileges of the third. Think of the number of women wage-earners in this country who are without political representation, there being no men in the family, and at present laws all made without a woman's point of view! . . . The working woman does not ask for the ballot as a panacea for all her ills. She knows that it carries with it responsibilities but all that it is to man it will be and even more to woman. Let her remain man's inferior politically and unjust discriminations against her as a wage-earner will continue, but let her become his equal politically and she will then be in a position to demand equal pay for equal work.

Laura J. Graddick, a Washington, D.C., labor union representative, speech to the NAWSA convention, April 1910, in Harper, ed., History of Woman Suffrage, *vol. 5, pp. 304–05.*

The automobile branch of the Woman Suffrage procession moved down Fifth Avenue yesterday to the meeting of protest in Union Square, well guarded by the mounted police.

The protest was against the action, or lack of it, taken by the legislators at Albany in regard to the Woman Suffrage bill which they cannot be persuaded to vote out of committee and was read yesterday to an assemblage of people in the square. The women say they have worked quietly and ineffectually for sixty years asking for consideration, and now they believe that the legislators should be made to feel that they are in earnest.

There were 10,000 persons in Union Square who listened to the speeches the women made. It was the biggest suffrage demonstration ever held in the United States.

The women taking part in the demonstration went in procession, some in automobiles and others on foot. Many of them had never taken part in anything of the kind before, and were resolute, but a good deal scared. The automobile branch of the procession started from the Fifth Avenue entrance of Central Park at Fifty-ninth Street. That was where the first auto stood, but the line ran up to Sixty-fifth Street. There were ninety of them all told, and the public ones as far as it was possible were yellow taxicabs, the suffrage color.

"Suffrage Parade Has Police Guard," describing the first suffrage parade on May 20, 1910, New York Times, *May 21, 1910, p. 1.*

Ought he not to be a subject of the greatest admiration that he should have had the courage to stand up against all the slaves who surrounded him, and come out like a man, and showed that, high or low, in America a man is a man who makes himself so, regardless of his position, and that the Secretary of the Treasury or the President of the United States himself is no better than the humblest citizen, if that humblest citizen has the courage and other qualities of manhood.

This idea of insubordination, gentlemen, and the horror with which some men view insubordination, involves an absolute misconception of what we ought to do and what we ought to strive for in American government. The danger in America is not of insubordination, but it is of too complacent obedience to the will of superiors. With this great Government building up, ever creating new functions, getting an ever increasing number of employees who are attending to the people's business, the one thing we need is men in subordinate places who will think for themselves and who will think and act in full recognition of their obligations as a part of the governing body. . . .

Louis Brandeis, closing argument in defense of Louis Glavis, May 27, 1910, Investigation of the Department of the Interior and the Bureau of Forestry, *vol. 9, pp. 4922–23.*

That the importation into the United States of any alien for the purpose of prostitution or for any other immoral purpose is hereby forbidden; and whoever shall, directly or indirectly, import, or attempt to import, into the United States, any alien for the purpose of prostitution or for any other immoral purpose, or whoever shall hold or attempt to hold any alien for any such purpose in pursuance of such illegal importation, or whoever shall keep, maintain, control, support, employ, or harbor in any house or other place, for the purpose of prostitution or for any other immoral purpose, in pursuance of such illegal importation, any alien, shall, in every such case be deemed guilty of a felony. . . . Any alien who shall be found an inmate of or connected with the management of a house of prostitution or practicing prostitution after such alien shall have entered the United States, or who shall receive, share in, or derive benefit from any part of the earnings of any prostitute; or who is employed by, in, or in connection with any house of prostitution or music or dance hall or other place of amusement or resort habitually frequented by prostitutes, or where prostitutes gather, or who in any way assists, protects, or promises to protect from arrest any prostitute, shall be deemed to be unlawfully within the United States and shall be deported. . . . Any alien who shall be convicted under any of the provisions of this section shall, at the expiration of his sentence, be taken into custody and returned to the country whence he came, or of which he is a subject or a citizen. . . . In all prosecutions under this section the testimony of a husband or wife shall be admissible and competent evidence against a wife or a husband.

Greatly enlarged anti-prostitution provisions of the Immigration Act, March 26, 1910, U.S. Statutes at Large, 61st Congress, vol. 36, part 1, pp. 264–65.

SEC. 2. That any person who shall knowingly transport or cause to be transported, or aid or assist in obtaining transportation for, or in transporting, in interstate or foreign commerce . . . any woman or girl for the purpose of prostitution or debauchery, or for any other immoral purpose, or with the intent and purpose to induce, entice, or compel such women or girl to become a prostitute or to give herself up to debauchery or to engage in any other immoral practice; or who shall knowingly procure or obtain, or cause to be procured or obtained, or aid or assist in procuring or obtaining, any ticket or tickets, or any form of transportation or evidence of the right thereto, to be used by any woman or girl . . . in going to any place for the purpose of prostitution or debauchery, or for any other immoral purpose, or with the intent or purpose on the part of such person to induce, entice, or compel her to give herself up to the practice of prostitution . . . shall be deemed guilty of a felony. . . .

The Mann Act, June 25, 1910, U.S. Statutes at Large, 61st Congress, vol. 36, part 1, p. 825.

Be it enacted . . . That the President may, at any time in his discretion, temporarily withdraw from settlement, location, sale, or entry any of the public lands of the United States including the District of Alaska and reserve the same for water-power sites, irrigation, classification of lands, or other public purposes to be specified in the order of withdrawals, and such withdrawals or reservations shall remain in force until revoked by him or by an Act of Congress. . . .

SEC. 3. . . . *And Provided further,* That hereafter no forest reserve shall be created, nor shall any additions be made to one heretofore created within the limits of the States of

Oregon, Washington, Idaho, Montana, Colorado, or Wyoming, except by Act of Congress.

Withdrawal Act, authorizing land reserves for any reason, June 25, 1910, U.S. Statutes at Large, 61st Congress, vol. 36, part 1, pp. 847–48.

. . . We made San Jose. . . . Our transmission brake was in need of repairs and oil pump was not working satisfactorily. We spent a few hours next morning having them repaired. Left San Jose at 11:45 a.m., for San Francisco, by way of Oakland. . . .

Beyond Modyville . . . an old bridge tumbled down with us. We blocked up the rear wheels, worked a bridge timber, upon which the fly-wheel of our machine rested, out of the way, and the machine pulled herself out on her own power. Some people, who had assembled on hearing the crash when the bridge fell, warned us of three other bridges. We passed them safely by getting out of the auto and pulling it over with a rope.

The number of automobiles in America was multiplying every year. Adventuresome owners delighted in road trips and races, despite the lack of paved roads. These autos are descending a mountain near Colorado Springs, Colorado. *(Library of Congress, Prints and Photographs Division, LC-USZ62-100875)*

Near Garberville we ran out of gasoline. A dwelling was near by. We found a lady there from whom we got two gallons of coal oil (the Franklin will run on coal oil). . . .

On June 13th . . . the spring which was injured when the bridge broke down, succumbed. We took off the upper half of the spring, reversed it, set the broken end under a bolt passed through the eye of the lower half, held same in place with a clip, securely bolted in place with a flat monkey wrench also held in place by the same clip, over the broken spring, so that the end could not fly up or get sideways. Thus mended, this spring carried us safely six hundred and thirty miles, until we got to San Francisco and had it repaired. . . .

Lawyer and banker Jackson Graves describes his 2,275-mile automobile trip through northern California, July 1910, California Memories, pp. 167–183 passim.

I do not ask for overcentralization; but I do ask that we work in a spirit of broad and far-reaching nationalism when we work for what concerns our people as a whole. We are all Americans. Our common interests are as broad as the continent. I speak to you here in Kansas exactly as I would speak in New York or Georgia, for the most vital problems are those which affect us all alike. The national government belongs to the whole American people, and where the whole American people are interested, that interest can be guarded effectively only by the national government. The betterment which we seek must be accomplished, I believe, mainly through the national government.

The American people are right in demanding that New Nationalism, without which we cannot hope to deal with new problems. The New Nationalism puts the national need before sectional or personal advantage. It is impatient of the utter confusion that results from local legislatures attempting to treat national issues as local issues. It is still more impatient of the impotence which springs from overdivision of governmental powers, the impotence which makes it possible for local selfishness or for legal cunning, hired by wealthy special interests, to bring national activities to a deadlock. This New Nationalism regards the executive power as the steward of the public welfare. It demands of the judiciary that it shall be interested primarily in human welfare rather than in property, just as it demands that the representative body shall represent all the people rather than any one class or section of the people.

Theodore Roosevelt's famous speech at Ossawatomie, Kansas, announcing his program of New Nationalism, August 10, 1910, Works, vol. 17, pp. 18–20.

The devils in human form, who murdered and maimed the men employed in its news and mechanical departments, will not escape. Ropes are dangling for them and prison doors are yawning for them. The eyes of a sleepless vigilance are upon each and all of them. With all their cunning, traces of the work are picked up every hour. There is no quarter of the earth to which they can flee, where they will not be followed and from which they will not be returned. . . .

Tho the dynamiters escape human justice, yet the righteous wrath of God will overtake them. When they drink the blood of their victims will be in their cup. When they would sleep the shrieks of the murdered ones will be in their ears.

Los Angeles Times reports the bombing of its own building the previous night, October 2, 1910, p. 1.

The object of this publication is to set forth those facts and arguments which show the danger of race prejudice, particularly as manifested today toward colored people. It takes its name from the fact that the editors believe that this is a critical time in the history of the advancement of men. Catholicity and tolerance, reason and forbearance can today make the world-old dream of human brotherhood approach realization: while bigotry and prejudice, emphasized race consciousness and force can repeat the awful history of the contact of nations and groups in the past. We strive for this higher and broader vision of Peace and Good Will.

The policy of The Crisis will be simple and well defined: It will first and foremost be a newspaper: it will record important happenings and movements in the world which bear on the great problem of inter-racial relations, and especially those which affect the Negro-American. . . .

Finally, its editorial page will stand for the right of men, irrespective of color or race, for the highest ideals of American democracy, and for reasonable but earnest and persistent attempt to gain these rights and realize these ideals. The Magazine will be the organ of no clique or party and will avoid personal rancor of all sorts.

W. E. B. DuBois, editorial in the first issue of the NAACP's journal, The Crisis, *vol. 1 (November 1910), pp. 10–11.*

The game is in the open, too. Twenty thousand people can cluster round a diamond and see every move the Base Ball players on it make. There is no chance for secret cheating, therefore there is no tendency in that direction. It is not alone the umpire who can see what happens on the field, but every newsboy, every millionaire, among the spectators.

Interview with Albert Spalding, New York Times, November 13, 1910, reprinted in Spalding, America's National Game, *p. 342.*

Ten horribly mutilated bodies—the victims of the explosion of mine No. 3, of the Providence Coal Co., were removed from the bottom of the shaft today. All the bodies have been identified, although three were so fearfully mangled that identification could be made only from the clothing and articles found in the pockets of the victims. . . .

The Government rescue corps under J. Y. Williams and A. A. Samms reached Providence at 6 o'clock this morning on a special mine rescue demonstration car. . . . .

At 7 o'clock three members of the rescue party were lowered into the mine by a windlass erected during the night by the coal company. The experts, wearing helmets and other apparatus used in the perilous work, were lowered without difficulty. . . . Several miners were lowered in the mine to assist the experts but owing to the foul gases that filled the shaft they had to be hoisted to the surface. . . .

The dead miners are:
—Wesley Fugate, white, 50; married, wife and seven children.
—Edward Vaughn, 22, unmarried.
—Cissel Shackleford, colored, 40, unmarried.
—John Woolfork, colored, 27, wife and one child.
—Willis Roscoe, colored, 32, wife and five children.
—George Johnson, colored, 45, wife and five children.
—Coley Johnson, colored, ten years of age.
—Coleman Northfleet, colored, 30, married.
—Louis Ligon, 40, wife and four children.
—Hope Shelton, 42, wife and three children.

Mining disaster at Providence, Kentucky, November 26, 1910, "Mangled Bodies of Miners Recovered at Providence," Crittenden [Kentucky] Record-Press, *December 1, 1910, available online at RootsWeb. URL: http://www.rootsweb.com/~kywebste/mines/1910prov/1910prov.htm.*

I am not working at anything, and I am ashamed to admit it, for I always felt that if a person sincerely wanted to work they could readily find work, even though it was not exactly the sort of work they prefer, and I still believe that, so the plain truth must be that I do not sincerely want work. In my mind, I explain my inability to get work this way. I am not fitted for any work that is a trade, as stenography, etc.; and as for the sort of work that a general education and some "horse sense" fits you for, I cannot work at [that], for that is almost always clerking in the public stores, and where they see me they will not employ me because of the appearance I present with this patch on my eye. I am invariably told that they will be glad to take me on when I—or rather my eye—"get well." Of course, there is scrubbing of floors and dishwashing to be considered—and since I wouldn't do that, it is plain to be seen I do not *sincerely* want to go to work. I could not need money any worse than I do, and yet I would not do work of that sort,

NOTICE
TO YOUNG WOMEN AND GIRLS

Do not go to the large cities for work unless you are compelled to. If you must go, write at least two weeks in advance to the Woman's Department, Bureau of Labor, St. Paul, or to the Young Women's Christian Association in the city where you want to work.

They will obtain for you such a position as you ask; tell you about wages, boarding places and whatever you want to know.

Two days before you leave home, write again and tell the day and hour when your train will arrive and a responsible woman will meet you at the station and take you safely to your destination.

Do not ask questions of strangers nor take advice from them.

Ask a uniformed railway official or a policeman.

This advice is issued by the State Bureau of Labor and posted through the courtesy of the Railway Officials of this road.

Mrs. Perry Starkweather,
Assistant Commissioner
Woman's Dept.

W. E. McEWEN,
Commissioner of Labor.
STATE CAPITOL, ST. PAUL.

Antiprostitution reformers feared that unsuspecting women from rural backgrounds were being lured into prostitution. Many localities and volunteer groups provided aid to women traveling to cities, like the service advertised in this ca. 1910 poster from Minnesota. *(Courtesy Minnesota Historical Society, MHS LOC H63.19/a1, Neg. 32677)*

so I must admit that I am not serious when I say I would do any sort of work.... I just cannot be moral enough to see where drudgery is better than a life of lazy vice....

Maimie Pinzer, a reformed prostitute, to Boston reformer Fanny Quincy Howe, December 9, 1910, in a long, unique series of letters between the two, in Rosen and Davidson, eds., The Maimie Papers, *pp. 3–4.*

One of the most important facts established by the investigation concerns the American-born children of immigrants—the "second generation."...

From these records it appears that a clear tendency exists on the part of the second generation to differ from the first or immigrant generation in the character of its criminality. It also appears that this difference is much more frequently in the direction of the criminality of the American-born of non-immigrant parentage than it is in the opposite direction. This means that the movement of second-generation crime is away from the crimes peculiar to immigrants and toward those of the American of native parentage....

The races or nationalities which stand out prominently in these records of crime as exhibiting clearly defined criminal characteristics are these:

American (including all native-born persons, both white and colored).—In three of the five sets of data the aggregate gainful offences form a higher percentage of the crimes of Americans than of those of any other groups of offenders. The highest percentage of the specific crime of burglary ... also belong to the American-born.

French.—In the data from the New York city magistrates' courts and the police department of Chicago natives of France have a higher percentage than any other persons of the aggregate offenses against chastity and of the specific "crimes connected with prostitution ..."

Greek.—The records of the city magistrates' courts ... in New York, and of the Chicago police department show the highest percentage of violations of city ordinances to be that of persons born in Greece.

Italian.—The Italians have the highest percentages of the aggregate offenses of personal violence shown by the data from New York.... Of blackmail and extortion the Italians also have the highest percentage.... In all five sets of data the Italians have the highest percentage of homicide....

Russian.—The Russian percentage of the specific crimes of larceny and receiving stolen property is also striking....

Analysis of immigration and crime, United States Immigration Commission, Abstracts of Reports, *1911, vol. 2, pp. 173–75.*

From 1820 to 1883 more than 95 percent of the total immigration from Europe originated in the United Kingdom, Germany, Scandinavia, the Netherlands, Belgium, France, and Switzerland. In what follows the movement from these countries will be referred to as the "old immigration." Following 1883 there was a rapid change in the ethnical character of European immigration, and in recent years more than 70 percent of the movement has originated in southern and eastern Europe. The change geographically, however, has been somewhat greater than the change in the racial character of the immigration, this being due very largely to the number of Germans who have come from Austria-Hungary and Russia. The movement from southern and eastern Europe will be referred to as the "new immigration."....

The United States Immigration Commission introduces a term, Abstracts of Reports, *1911, vol. 1, p. 23.*

FINNISH. Best defined for the purposes of this work from a linguistic point of view in a narrow sense as the race or people of Finno-Tataric stock which now constitutes the chief population of Finland and embraces also the related peoples of northwestern Russia, exclusive of the Lapps. This group may be also called the "Finns Proper" or "Western Finns".... The Karelians extend nearly to the center of Russia and are called by some "Eastern Finns." ... Although speaking languages similar to the Western Finns or Suomi, they are widely different from the latter in blood, and to a great extent in civilization. The Western and Eastern Finns are more unlike than the North and South Italians, who are, for a similar reason, counted separately by the Bureau of Immigration.

Finnish immigration . . . is practically confined to the Western Finns or Finns proper. These are Caucasian rather than Mongolian in appearance, while the Eastern or Volga Finns, who are not known to come as yet to America, show distinctly their Asiatic origin. . . .

. . . Until 1809 Finland was a part of Sweden, and before the dawn of history the Finns and Swedes were no doubt intermingling. This will account in part for the prevailing blondness and European cast of countenance amongst the Finns, which had led the Bureau of Immigration to put them into the "Teutonic" division of races. But the entire Urgo-Finnic stock seems to have been in origin, lighter in color than most other Mongolians, perhaps as a result of their northern residence. . . . Whatever their original stock the Finns of Finland are to-day the most truly European of any race possessing a Mongolic speech, and in some respects their institutions are abreast of any in Europe. . . .

Example of Progressive Era "racial" [ethnic] classification,
United States Immigration Commission,
Dictionary of Races or Peoples, *1911, pp. 58–59.*

My determination to stand by the program which I had worked out during the years that I had been at Tuskegee and which I had expressed in my Atlanta speech, soon brought me into conflict with a small group of colored people who sometimes styled themselves "The Intellectuals," at other times "The Talented Tenth." As most of these men were graduates of Northern colleges and made their homes for the most part in the North, it was natural enough, I suppose, that they should feel that leadership in race matters, should remain, as heretofore, in the North. . . .

In college they gave little thought or attention to preparing for any definite task in the world, but started out with the idea of preparing themselves to solve the race problem. They learned in college a great deal about the history of New England freedom; their minds were filled with the traditions of the anti-slavery struggle; and they came out of college with the idea that the only thing necessary to solve at once every problem in the South was to apply the principles of the Declaration of Independence and the Bill of Rights. They had learned in their studies little of the actual present-day conditions in the South and had not considered the profound difference between the political problem and the educational problem, between the work of destruction and construction as it applies to the task of race-building.

Booker T. Washington responds to DuBois and
other critics in the second volume of his autobiography,
My Larger Education, *1911, p. 112.*

Sept. 10. (X746b) hall, North Clark street. Investigator counted 51 girls. Some appeared to be 18 or 19 years of age. Investigator met one girl who gave the name of Marcella (X746c) and said that she worked in the basement of department store. Marcella said her salary was $6 per week, out of this she pays $3 for meals and $2 room rent, besides 60 cents carfare. She "hustles" three nights a week for extra money to pay for washing, clothes and other things. She told investigator that she can be found in rear room of saloon on North Clark street. She is about 20 years old. . . .

Sept. 21. (X746f) hall on North Clark street. Counted 185 girls and women from 17 to 30 years of age. Dance hall is on third floor, with two stairways leading down to second floor, where there is a bar. On this floor are tables, which are crowded with girls drinking with fellows, between the dances. Dances are conducted here every night and on Sundays. The hall has a bad reputation and a man can "pick up" a girl any time. Investigator talked with the following girls who were all drinking:

Violet works in department store, salary $5 per week. Was seduced and left home. Baby died and she "solicits" on the side' to support herself. Is 19 years of age, born and raised in (X748). Rooms on North Clark street, but would not give number.

Mag, 18 years old. Works in department store. Salary $5.50 per week. Tells parents she receives more. Helps support parents and "solicits" at dances for spending money. Father is sickly.

Details on lives of prostitutes found in a dance hall by an
investigator for the Chicago Vice Commission; numbers are
codes to protect anonymity, in The Social Evil in Chicago,
pp. 186–87.

If the city would preserve for its inhabitants the greatest gift in its possession . . . —the opportunity for varied and humanizing social relationships, it must undertake . . . to provide centers in which social life may be organized and carried on steadily and normally. A fair argument may be made . . . that this provision is a public function. It may even be charged that it is a solemn obligation of the modern heterodox city. . . . The patriotism of the modern state must be based not upon a consciousness of homogeneity but upon a respect for variation, not upon inherited memory but upon trained imagination. . . .

. . . As immigrants to America work together in factories, every effort is made that they should conform to a common standard; . . . only on the playground or in the recreation center do they find that variety is prized, that distinctive folklore and national customs as well as individual initiative are at a premium. They meet together and enjoy each other's national dances and games, and as the sense of comradeship and pleasure grows, they are able to express, as nowhere else, that sense of being unlike one's fellows which is at the basis of all progress. . . . In the play festivals of Chicago sustained in the various small parks, the Italians, Poles,

Lithuanians, and Norwegians meet each other with a dignity and freedom, with a sense of comradeship, which they are unable to command at any other time.

Jane Addams, "Recreation as a Public Function in Urban Communities," American Sociological Society, Proceedings, vol. 6 (1911), pp. 35–36.

If the court shall find any male child under the age of seventeen years or any female child under the age of eighteen years to be dependent or neglected within the meaning of the Act, the court may allow such child to remain at its own home subject to the friendly visitation of a probation officer, and if the parent, parents, guardian or custodian, consent thereto. . . .

If the parent or parents of such dependent or neglected child are poor and unable to properly care for the said child, but are otherwise proper guardians and it is for the welfare of such child to remain at home, the court may enter an order: finding such facts and fixing the amount of money necessary to enable the parent or parents, to properly care for such child, and thereupon it shall be the duty of the county board, through its county agent or otherwise, to pay to such parent or parents, at such times as said order may designate the amount so specified for the care of such dependent or neglected child until the further order of the court.

The first mother's pension law, Illinois, 1911, Laws of Illinois, p. 127, reprinted in Bremner, ed. Children and Youth in America, vol. 2, pp. 369–70.

The snow on the high mountains is melting fast, and the streams are singing bankfull, swaying softly through the level meadows and bogs, quivering with sun-spangles, swirling in pot-holes, resting in deep pools, leaping, shouting in wild, exulting energy over rough boulder dams, joyful, beautiful in all their forms. No Sierra landscape that I have seen holds anything truly dead or dull, or any trace of what in manufactories is called rubbish or waste; everything is perfectly clean and pure and full of divine lessons. This quick, inevitable interest attaching to everything seems marvelous until the hand of God becomes visible; then it seems reasonable that what interests Him may well interest us. When we try to pick out anything by itself, we find it hitched to everything else in the universe. One fancies a heart like our own must be beating in every crystal and cell, and we feel like stopping to speak to the plants and animals as friendly fellow-mountaineers. Nature as a poet, an enthusiastic workingman, becomes more and more visible the farther and higher we go; for the mountains are fountains—beginning places, however related to sources beyond mortal ken.

John Muir describes the divine properties preservationists found in nature in a memoir, My First Summer in the Sierra, 1911, pp. 211–12.

The people came in throngs; they came by boat, by train, by private conveyance for 20 and 30 miles. Our records contain stories of men, women, and children walking in over country roads 10 and 12 miles, the more anemic at times falling by the way, to be picked up and brought in by neighbors passing with wagons. As many as 455 people have been treated at one place in one day. Such a dispensary group will contain men, women, and children from town and country, representing all degrees of infection and all stations in life. A friend who had just visited some of the dispensaries said to me recently: "It looks like the days of Galilee."

Wycliffe Rose, administrative secretary of the Rockefeller Sanitary Commission to Eradicate Hookworm, Second Annual Report, 1911, quoted in Ettling, The Germ of Laziness, p. 160.

By the time of our arrival the men had moved the benches from the schoolroom and arranged them under the large oak trees in the yard. Tables had been placed for the dispensary exhibit and for the microscopist, and more than a hundred specimens had already been brought in. On another table were bottles containing worms which had been recovered from patients following treatment.

Covington was a master at handling a crowd of this kind. First he got the microscopists started at their task. Then he called up people who had received treatment . . . and interviewed them. All declared they had received great improvement; and the doctor listened to each one's chest with his stethoscope, presumably to determine if his heart was improved. This procedure was called "sounding" by the people.

Treated patients having been seen, the doctor next gave a lecture. He stood on a box and held a set of charts to which he pointed as he talked. . . . By the time the lecture was over the microscopists had examined a number of specimens. Persons found positive were called up to receive their treatment.

The exhibit was next explained to the crowd and, again, it was told how hookworm disease is spread. . . .

The demonstration over, Dr. Covington asked if a Sunday School singing leader was present. There was; and a lean tall man came forward with a tuning fork . . . and the singing continued for perhaps half an hour. By this time the microscopists had more specimens to report on. . . .

Dr. Benjamin Washburn, a member of the Rockefeller Sanitary Commission to Eradicate Hookworm, describes Dr. Platt Covington at work in Mills Spring, North Carolina, ca. 1911, As I Recall, pp. 12–14.

Legally, over half of the United States is "dry" territory. Prohibition literature states that five-eighths of the incorporated towns, cities and villages of the United States forbid the sale of liquor. . . .

... I have traveled over the United States in all sections, stopping in hundreds of towns. I never have found a city, town, or cross-roads village in the last five years in which, within two hours, I failed to get a drink. This is regardless of laws, their enforcement, or the feeling of the community as expressed at the polls. This is a broad statement, but anyone possessing the price of a drink can get it *anywhere.* ...

It is the same everywhere. I have purchased drinks in at least fifty "dry" towns and never have encountered serious difficulty anywhere. ...

One of the favorite arguments of prohibitionists is that even if they cannot prevent drinking men from getting drinks the next generation will not be tempted and therefore will not know the curse of liquor. ... Observation in dry places does not bear out the theory. In almost every hidden den and "blind pig" I visited I found that a great proportion of those drinking were minors. I found that the boys were drinking whiskey, and not beer. ...

Anonymous muckraking article, "Drinking in Dry Places,"
American Magazine, vol. 71 (January 1911),
pp. 371, 377.

Without imputing any actual motive to oppress, we must consider the natural operation of the statute here in question ... and it is apparent that it furnishes a convenient instrument for the coercion which the Constitution and the Act of Congress forbid; an instrument of compulsion peculiarly effective as against the poor and the ignorant, its most likely victims. There is no more important concern than to safeguard the freedom of labor upon which alone can enduring prosperity be based. The provision designed to secure it would soon become a barren form if it were possible to establish a statutory presumption of this sort, and to hold over the heads of laborers the threat of punishment for crime, under the name of fraud, but merely upon evidence of failure to work out their debts.

The Supreme Court holds against debt peonage, a form of
forced labor that affected many southern blacks, Justice Charles
Evans Hughes writing for the majority, Bailey v. State of
Alabama, *January 3, 1911, 219 US 219.*

Article 7, Sec. 3. The right of any citizen of the state to vote, hold office, or sit upon juries, shall never be restricted, abridged or impaired on account of religion, race, language or color, or inability to speak, read or write the English or Spanish languages as may be otherwise provided in this Constitution; and the provisions of this section and of section one of this article shall never be amended except upon the vote of the people of this state in an election at which at least three-fourths of the electors in the whole state, and at least two-thirds of those voting in each county of the state, shall vote for such amendment. ...

Article 12, Sec. 8. The legislature shall provide for the training of teachers in the normal schools or otherwise so that they may become proficient in both the English and Spanish languages, to qualify them to teach Spanish-speaking pupils and students in the public schools and educational institutions of the State, and shall provide proper means and methods to facilitate the teaching of the English language and other branches of learning to such pupils and students. ...

Sec. 10. Children of Spanish descent in the State of New Mexico shall never be denied the right and privilege of admission and attendance in the public schools or other public educational institutions of the State, and they shall never be classed in separate schools, but shall forever enjoy perfect equality with other children in all public schools and educational institutions of the State, and the legislature shall provide penalties for the violation of this section. This section shall never be amended except upon a vote of the people of this State, in an election at which at least three-fourths of the electors voting in the whole state and at least two-thirds of those voting in each county in the State shall vote for such amendment. ...

Article 20, Sec. 12. For the first twenty years after this constitution goes into effect all laws passed by the legislature shall be published in both the English and Spanish languages and thereafter such publication shall be made as the legislature may provide. ...

Provisions of the New Mexico state constitution protecting
Spanish-speaking residents, adopted by voters January 12,
1911, reprinted in Ellis, ed., New Mexico Historic
Documents, *pp. 114, 127–28, 133, 138.*

It seems to me the proposed change instead of destroying the object and purpose of the [founding] fathers will serve those purposes. ...

... Our fathers understood the science of government as no other single group of men has ever understood it. It is altogether probable that if the plan upon which they built fails, with it will pass the hope of a democratic-republican form of government. But it will not fail if, studying closely the changed conditions brought about by our marvelous industrial progress and great economic changes, we make only such changes and modification in government as will prevent those industrial conditions and economic changes from themselves working in subtle and silent ways modifications and changes in our institutions. We do not want to find ourselves in the attitude of a people who are satisfied with the shell of a government from which all real power has departed. We want the substance at all time, not the shadow. We want the real power and the real responsibility to remain precisely where the fathers placed it, with the people.

Senator William Borah of Idaho, progressive Republican,
debate over a constitutional amendment to permit direct election
of senators, January 13, 1911, Congressional Record,
61st Congress, 3rd session, vol. 46, p. 1103.

. . . the further objection . . . that the adoption of this amendment would give to the Southern States the power and the opportunity to disenfranchise the Negro voters of those States, is but a makeshift . . . to divert the argument and furnish some excuse for the former advocates of the force bill [of 1890] to vote against this amendment so universally demanded by the people. It is not desired . . . by the people in my state, and I think I can safely speak for the entire South, to disenfranchise the Negro, notwithstanding the fact that we believe the greatest crime that was ever committed against a helpless, defenseless people was the giving to the then ignorant, vicious, half barbaric Negroes of the South the right to vote and the right to hold office, and for the time, sir, the clouds were dark and threatening.

. . . I for one rejoice that that dark period has passed and that the Negro of the South to-day realizes more thoroughly than ever before that his former master and his children are his truest and best friends. Few of them care to vote and none ask to hold office, except when stirred by this same disturbing element of the Republican party usually imported from the North or East. . . .

What is the government . . . that it cannot be altered and changed, even in its fundamentals, by the people, who are in fact the source of all power under the Constitution . . . ?

Senator Jeff Davis, Democrat of Arkansas, speaking in favor of the race rider to the direct-election amendment, January 30, 1911, Congressional Record, 61st Congress, 3rd session, vol. 46, p. 1635.

Stripped of every subterfuge, the burden of all the speeches that have been made against this proposition [direct election] is that American people as a whole are not capable of wisely selecting the men who shall represent them in the upper branch of the National Legislature. Various pretexts are resorted to in an effort to produce argument against this amendment without definitely making such a statement, but the ultimate analysis of every speech that has been made against this proposition is that people as a whole have not that calm temperament and intelligent judgement necessary to enable them wisely to select their Senators. . . .

Now on a given day, quietly and without excitement, millions of American citizens choose their executive ruler for a period of four years, by what is in fact a direct vote, and the decision of the majority is accepted without protest by the entire population. The quiet and orderly way by which the people of this mighty Nation, with its widely extended territory exalt one of their number into, and depose another from, the most powerful political position among men, is the greatest tribute that could be offered to the patriotism and stability of character of the American

citizen. If the people are capable of electing their Presidents by direct vote, as in fact they do, are they not capable of electing their Senators? Is that task more perplexing?

Senator Joseph Bristow, insurgent Republican from Kansas and supporter of direct election, February 9, 1911, Congressional Record, 61st Congress, 3rd session, vol. 46, pp. 2178–79.

It [direct election] is an expression of distrust for representative government. It does not stand alone. It is a part of the great movement which has been going on now in these recent years throughout the country and in which our people have been drifting away from their trust in representative government. These modern [state] constitutions which are filled with specific provisions, limiting and directing the legislature in every direction, furnishing such startling contrasts to the simplicity of the Constitution of the United States, are an expression of distrust in representative government. The initiative is an expression of distrust in representative government. The referendum is an expression of distrust in representative government.

This resolution is an expression of the same sentiment. And strangely, sir, this movement comes at the very time when the development of our country in its business and social and political life makes it all the more necessary that we should depend upon representative government. We have gone far, far away from the days of the old New England town meeting. I doubt if some of the Senators coming from States of small population realize how far we have gone in the great industrial communities of the East and Middle West from that condition in which direct democratic government is possible.

Senator Elihu Root of New York, a conservative Republican and opponent of direct election, February 10, 1911, Congressional Record, 61st Congress, 3rd session, vol. 46, pp. 2243.

"So the police commenced arresting men on the charge of vagrancy and disturbing the peace. They would come up to a bunch of men talking industrial unionism on the street and order them to 'move on.' They would see a number of I.W.W. men on the street as early as nine o'clock and order them to go home. . . .

". . . our local decided that as long as they were to be harrassed by the police, they might just as well obtain the use of the streets while they were about it. But first they again asked the chief of police for a permit to speak on the streets. It was refused. Then they went to the mayor . . .; this also was refused. Then one night eight boys, one after another, got on the soap box on the street. The first one got to talk a few minutes, after that all the men could say would be 'fellow worker' and the police would grab him and take him to jail. . . .

"There are about one hundred I.W.W. men in jail now with different charges, but all are arrested for the same offense. . . . Some of the best speakers were tried and convicted of vagrancy, by juries of business men. Four of them got six months apiece, although they proved that they were not vagrants. Many of the boys have been imprisoned fifty-one days today, without trial. . . .

". . . Frank is one of the 94 I.W.W. men confined in a bull pen, 4.7 x 28 feet. . . ."

> Mrs. Frank Little, whose husband was in jail, describes an IWW free-speech fight in Fresno, California, "Court Crookedness in Fresno," Appeal to Reason, February 11, 1911, reprinted in Graham, ed., "Yours for the Revolution," pp. 117–18.

So it seems that every piece of good-will that neighbor countries show each other is to be regarded as a thin end of a wedge of enmity. According to this the only kindness the United States is free to show us without being denounced as a sly and scheming enemy is to freeze up her whole boundary against us. . . . We have never had the least doubt that the United States wanted to annex Canada. She has wanted it ever since Benjamin Franklin started *The Gazette* in Montreal a hundred and forty years ago to convert us to that way of thinking. As it has not yet occurred, and indeed has never been advocated since then, except for a brief time in that later forties of the last century, when the Montreal Conservatives in rebellious mood made an attempt at it, there will not, we think, be any need . . . to put down any uprising on its behalf or to meet Mr. Champ Clark's war balloon.

> Montreal Daily Witness *editorial in favor of reciprocity, quoted in "Annexation Agitation in Canada,"* Literary Digest, *vol. 42 (March 4, 1911), p. 309.*

Every elective public officer of the State of California may be removed from office at any time by the electors entitled to vote for a successor of such incumbent, through the procedure and in the manner herein provided for, which procedure shall be known as the recall . . .

The procedure hereunder to effect the removal of an incumbent of an elective public office shall be as follows: A petition signed by electors entitled to vote for a successor of the incumbent sought to be removed, equal in number to at least twelve per cent of the entire vote cast at the last preceding election for all candidates for the office which the incumbent sought to be removed occupies; provided, that if the officer sought to be removed is a state officer who is elected in any political subdivision of the state, said petition shall be signed by electors entitled to vote for a successor to the incumbent sought to be removed, equal in number to at least twenty per cent of the entire vote cast at the last preceding election for all candidates, for the office

which the incumbent sought to be removed occupies, demanding an election of a successor to the officer named in said petition, shall be addressed to the secretary of state and filed with the clerk, or registrar of voters, of the county or city and county in which the petition was circulated; provided, that if the officer sought to be removed was elected in the state at large such petition shall be circulated in not less than five counties of the state, and shall be signed in each of such counties by electors equal in number to not less than one per cent of the entire vote cast, in each of said counties, at said election, as above estimated. Such petition shall contain a general statement of the ground on which the removal is sought. . . .

> Section 1, Article 23, of the California state constitution, establishing recall, approved by the Assembly March 7, 1911, and the voters October 10, 1911, reprinted in Beard and Schultz, eds. Documents on the State-Wide Initiative, Referendum, and Recall, *pp. 265–67.*

A certain motion picture director, one of the best, by the way, declares that the letters written to The Spectator regarding identities of players and the replies thereto are causing the very deuce to pay with some of the actors and actresses to whom publicity is thus given. According to this complaining director the players immediately swell up and want fabulous salaries. Mirror in hand, one of them will assail the powers that be and, pointing to his or her name in agate type, will declare: "See what a great player I am. Why, here's a person out in Punxsutawney, Pa., who wants to know my name. Gimme more pay or I quit."

> Frank Woods, "The Spectator" for the New York Dramatic Mirror, *March 8, 1911, p. 39, quoted in Bowser,* Transformation of Cinema, *pp. 109–10.*

It can now safely be said that there are no obscene pictures publicly exhibited in New York. Occasionally an indecent film, unauthorized by the Board of Censorship, is surreptitiously introduced by a manufacturer. Such a film is, however, immediately run down and eliminated.

It is not claimed, of course, that the pictures exhibited in New York are of the highest class. The members of the Board of Censorship are necessarily influenced by the practical necessities of the moving picture art which call for a policy of steady but gradual improvement rather than uncompromising severity. Many pictures exhibited today may be classified as silly. Others, in the course of unrolling a dramatic theme depict the commission of some crime. It is against this latter class that criticism is frequently directed. Pictures of this sort are approved by the Board of Censorship on the theory that the motion picture is a form of dramatic art and, together with the theatre, must be allowed a certain liberty in depicting moral problems. The Board of Censorship, however, condemns any sensational representation of crime, or "crime for crime's sake." Some crimes, needless to say, are always debarred, as for instance, pictures of arson, poisoning, etc., together with certain socially forbidden themes.

Raymond B. Fosdick "Report on Motion Picture Theatres of Greater New York," prepared for Mayor William J. Gaynor, printed in Film Index, *March 22, 1911, available online at CinemaWeb. URL: http://www.cinemaweb.com/ silentfilm/bookshelf/17_fi_3.htm*

Samuel Levine, a machine operator on the ninth floor. . . . told this story . . .: "I was at work when I heard the shout of 'Fire!' The girls on the floor dropped everything and rushed wildly around, some in the direction of windows and others toward the elevator door. I saw the elevator go down past our floor once. It was crowded to the limit and no one could have got on. It did not stop. Not another trip was made.

"There were flames all around in no time. Three girls, I think from the floor below, came rushing past me. Their clothes were on fire. I grabbed the fire pails and tried to pour the water on them, but they did not stop. They ran screaming toward the windows. I knew there was no hope there, so I stayed where I was, hoping that the elevator would come up again.

"I finally smashed open the doors to the elevator. I guess I must have done it with my hands. I reached out and grabbed the cables, wrapped my legs around them, and started to slide down. I can remember getting to the sixth floor. While on my way down, as slow as I could let myself drop, the bodies of six girls went falling past me. One of them struck me and I fell to the top of the elevator. I fell on the dead body of a girl. My back hit the beam that runs across the top of the car. . . ."

The Triangle fire, "Stories of Survivors and Witnesses and Rescuers Outside Tell What They Saw," New York Times, *March 26, 1911, p. 4.*

Up in the top floor girls were burning to death before our very eyes. They were jammed in the windows. No one was lucky enough to be able to jump, it seemed. But, one by one, the jams broke. Down came the bodies in a shower, burning, smoking—flaming bodies, with disheveled hair trailing upward. . . .

. . . these fire torches, suffering ones, fell inertly, only intent that death should come to them on the sidewalk instead of in the furnace behind them.

On the sidewalk lay heaps of broken bodies. A policeman later went about with tags, which he fastened with wires to the wrists of the dead girls, numbering each with a lead pencil, and I saw him fasten tag no. 54 to the wrist of a girl who wore an engagement ring. A fireman who came downstairs from the building told me that there were at least fifty bodies in the big room on the seventh floor. Another fireman told me that more girls had jumped down an air shaft in the rear of the building. I went back there, into the narrow court, and saw a heap of dead girls. . . .

The floods of water from the firemen's hose that ran into the gutter were actually stained red with blood. I looked upon the heap of dead bodies and I remembered these girls were the shirtwaist makers. I remembered their great strike of last year in which these same girls had demanded more sanitary conditions and more safety precautions in the shops. These dead bodies were the answer.

William G. Shepherd, an Associated Press reporter, "Eyewitness at the Triangle," Milwaukee Journal, *March 27, 1911, p. 1.*

While upon the face of this measure it merely provides for the taking of statistics, the accumulation of knowledge, yet we know from other measures which have been introduced, some from the same source, that it contemplates the establishment of a control, through the agencies of government, over the rearing of children. There are other measures now pending in committees of this body going much further, going to the extent of interference with the control of a parent over the child. I believe I read on Saturday a bill which has been introduced that prevents the employment of any child under 16 years of age. . . .

. . . We have sometimes an oversupply of sympathy, or that which is supposed to be based upon sympathy for our fellow kind, sympathy for the children whose condition in life is not as favorable as that of some other children. Our sympathies are human; you can not avoid them; but those clothed with the responsibility of government must be on guard against being swept away on unsafe seas in legislation.

Senator Welburn Heyburn, Republican of Idaho, objects to the bill to establish a children's bureau during Senate debate, April 1911, Congressional Record, *62nd Congress, 2nd session, vol. 48, part 1, p. 189.*

I believe in the right of the people to rule. I believe that the majority of the plain people of the United States will, day in and day out, make fewer mistakes in governing themselves than any smaller class or body of men, no matter what their training, will make in trying to govern them. . . .

My opponents charge that two things in my program are wrong because they intrude into the sanctuary of the judiciary. The first is the recall of judges, and the second, the review by the people of judicial decisions on certain constitutional questions. . . . But—I say it soberly—democracy has a right to approach the sanctuary of the courts when a special interest has corruptly found sanctuary there; and this is exactly what has happened in some of the States where the recall of judges is a living issues . . .

. . . Mr. Taft says that the judiciary ought not to be "representative" of the people in the sense that the legislature and the executive are. This is perfectly true of the judge when he is performing merely the ordinary functions of a judge in suits between man and man. It is not true of the judge engaged in interpreting. . . . When he exercises that function he has no right to let his political philosophy reverse and thwart the will of the majority.

Theodore Roosevelt, The Right of the People to Rule, *address at Carnegie Hall, March 20, 1912, pp. 3–9 passim.*

A House which is divided against itself can not stand, but people are beginning to suspect that a trust which has been divided up into as many as thirty-four separate parts can not only stand, but may be actually worth more than before its disintegration. We are reminded on every hand that when the Supreme Court issued that more or less fatal decree last May, the Standard Oil properties were worth $633,793,525, while on the 8th of this month they had a stock-market valuation of $885,044,700. . . . Back in 1901 . . . Standard Oil stock reached the record mark of $845 a share. During the present month this record has been exceeded, and on one day the shares sold at 900. . . .

This "very remarkable situation" demonstrates to the Washington *Herald* that "the so-called dissolution of the trusts is to their pecuniary advantage." It even raises the question in the mind of the New York *Herald* "whether the dissolution decision has restored competition or whether it has merely forced the controlling factors in the organization to go a roundabout way to attain the same old results." . . . "This startling advance following the dissolution of the trust," simply means, according to the New York *American*'s interpretation, . . . that the oil monopoly is now "secure from governmental prosecution, which immunity makes its securities more valuable . . ."

"How a Dissolved Trust Prospers," Literary Digest, *vol. 44 (March 23, 1912), p. 576.*

I have been told that the city is hopeless. I do not believe that this is true. Rather I should say the city is the most hopeful of our institutions. The change in the past ten years is like a revolution. . . . A few years ago we talked only of "turning the rascals out," of "good government," of a "business man's administration by business men." We thought we could reform the city by putting some bad men in jail and some good men in the city hall. We were looking for a Man, a Man to save us from ourselves. . . .

We are fast leaving that behind. . . . Municipal reform is becoming industrial, economic, social. For the first time we are beginning to think of the city as an entity, to plan it, mold it, fashion it so that it will serve humanity rather than destroy it. . . .

A new profession has come into existence. . . . A city . . . planned from center to circumference far in advance of its needs and with provision for every social want, that is the meaning of city planning. It is the newest of the sciences and possibly the greatest of them all.

Reformer Frederic Howe, "The American City of To-Morrow," Hampton's Magazine, *vol. 26 (May 1911), pp. 573–75.*

The arrests of J. J. McNamara, his brother, J. B. McNamara, and Ortie McManigal culminate, in my opinion, the most atrocious and far-reaching criminal conspiracy of modern times. These men are responsible for all the dynamiting outrages which have been perpetrated on structural iron, such as the North Randall, Ohio, explosion; Milwaukee West Fuel Company explosion; McClintock, Marshall, Construction explosion at Peoria, Ill.,; wreck of the Lucas Iron Works at Peoria, Ill., wreck of the tower of the municipal building at Springfield, Mass., wreck of the Llewellyn Iron Works at Los Angeles; the Los Angeles *Times* explosion, Vonsprechelson Construction Company explosion in Indianapolis, and many others. . . .

At the time of the arrest of the three prisoners we found in their possession twelve clock attachments with fuse, batteries, and fulminating caps all ready to be applied. At the time of the arrest of J. J. McNamara we found in his possession large quantities of dynamite and nitroglycerin. . . .

Detective William J. Burns, telegraph to the New York Times, *quoted in "Unionism, Capitalism, and Dynamite,"* Literary Digest, *vol. 42 (May 6, 1911), pp. 867–68.*

The whole affair smacks of well laid prearrangement . . .

The stage was all set, the properties arranged carefully, and then up goes the curtain with a blare of trumpets upon the first act of a tragedy contemplating the assassination of organized labor. . . .

Ever since the Los Angeles *Times* tragedy the interests have been trying to fasten guilt upon organized labor. It might just as well be McNamara as another. . . . The interests of corporate wealth are always trying to crush the organized labor movement, and they use the best way—to strike at the man having the confidence of the people.

Samuel Gompers, quoted in "Unionism, Capitalism, and Dynamite," Literary Digest, *vol. 42 (May 6, 1911), p. 868.*

On the Governor's side, the fight for progressive legislation in redemption of platform promises was perhaps the most scientific political battle ever waged in New Jersey. Wilson was the man the skulkers and reactionaries were afraid of. His methods were open and sincere, and his insistence that party promises be kept literally and fully overcame the wavering and drove opposition to the wall. The victory Governor Wilson won is a revelation of the man's character and leadership and a marvel to the country. No governor has ever achieved so much in so short a time.

It has been a history-making session. The good that has come of it not only vastly exceeds the bad, but is sufficient to make Jerseymen rub their eyes in wonderment. . . .

The Jersey City Journal, *a Republican paper, on Democrat Woodrow Wilson's accomplishments, quoted in "The New Order in New Jersey,"* Literary Digest, *vol. 42 (May 6, 1911), p. 870.*

A popular government is not a government of a majority, by a majority, for a majority of the people. It is a government of the whole people by a majority of the whole people under such rules and checks as will secure a wise, just, and beneficent government for all the people. . . .

By the recall in the Arizona constitution it is proposed to give to the majority the power to remove arbitrarily, and without delay, any judge who may have the courage to render an unpopular decision. . . . We cannot be blind to the fact that often an intelligent and respectable electorate may be so roused upon an issue that it will visit with condemnation the decision of a just judge, though exactly in accord with the law governing the case. . . . The recall is devised to encourage quick action and to lead the people to strike while the iron is hot. . . . On the instant of an unpopular ruling . . . he is to be hailed before the electorate as a tribunal, with no judicial hearing, evidence or defense, and thrown out of office and disgraced for life because he has failed, in a single decision, it may be, to satisfy the popular demand. Think of the opportunity such a system would give to unscrupulous political bosses. . . . Think of the enormous power for evil given to the sensational, muckraking charges and insinuations. . . . Supporters of such a system seem to think that it will work only in the interest of the poor, the humble, the weak and the oppressed; that it will strike down only the judge who is supposed to favor corporations and be affected by the corrupting influence of the rich. Nothing could be further from the ultimate result.

President Taft's veto of the Arizona statehood bill, announced August 15 and delivered to Congress August 22, 1911, reprinted in Chronology and Documentary Handbook of . . . Arizona, *pp. 107, 109–110.*

It is not difficult to turn back to the supreme crises in American history when its greatest figures were heroically struggling for what they saw to be for the interests of their country, and, if the policy of the Recall had been in force, to see how the whole course of history might have been changed, and how ambition and envy might have utilized a temporary opportunity to terminate some splendid career.

As an illustration take Lincoln in the earlier days of his administration. The disastrous defeats that the Union armies had suffered had been relieved only by slight successes. Lincoln scarcely had a friend even in his own Cabinet. . . . the abolitionists were unsparing in their criticism, the great organs of public opinion were hostile to him; and there can be little doubt that if a proceeding for Recall could have been had against him at the moment when he was enveloped in the clouds of unpopularity, the career of the greatest of Americans would have been brought to a disgraceful ending, with results to civilization it is melancholy to contemplate.

Samuel W. McCall, "Representative as Against Direct Government," Atlantic Monthly, *vol. 108 (October 1911), p. 555.*

Q. Now, Chief, about the occupation of these buildings. In your experience in fighting fires, what have you found to be the condition of these buildings. . . .

A. Some buildings you go into are kept nicely, but the majority of others you go in are unkept; they are dirty; they are unclean; their stock is strewed all over the floor. Where they use machinery there are no passageways whatsoever.

Q. Tell the Commission about the difficulties in fighting a fire of that kind.

A. In a great many cases there is only about one door on that loft you can get in. Goods are piled up in front of the windows, in front of the doors, and you have got to use a battering ram to get into any of them.

Q. How about the passageways being blocked?

A. Piled right to the ceiling. Many a time the firemen get into places in the night time and there is no room for a man to go through the passages.

Q. How about the passageway to a fire-escape? Do you find those blocked or open?

A. Find them blocked.

Q. How about locked doors to the staircases? Have you found that?

A. Oh, yes, plenty of them. The doors going to the roof are locked. They pay absolutely no attention to the fire hazard or to the protection of the employees in these buildings. That is their last consideration.

Edward F. Croker, New York fire chief, testimony before the state commission investigating the Triangle Fire, October 10, 1911, New York Factory Investigating Commission, Preliminary Report, *vol. 2, pp. 17–19.*

Wherever we left a booth unprotected, I am sure we lost votes—we may perhaps have lost thousands that way in all the large cities of the state. In my own booth I had to exercise the utmost vigilance to see that the announcer called off "yes" against our amendment, and not "no," which he could easily do . . . and to check the entries of the two tally clerks, and that they put a vote for us in the "yes" column and not in the "no" column . . . the entire election board in the booth was hostile to a marked degree. We were on duty from 5:30 A.M. to 11:30 P.M., when we saw our votes entered on the tally sheet.

California suffrage worker Clara Schlinghyde, letter to Carrie Chapman Catt, November 11, 1911, original at the Library of Congress, quoted in Flexner, Century of Struggle, p. 265.

"Please say to the papers that I am guilty, but I did what I did for principle, and that I did not intend to murder a man. We put that bomb in Ink Alley, just as the papers have said. and we set it to go off after all the men in the building had gone home, in the early morning, but the clock went back on us, and you know what followed.

"Think what all this means to us, who have been fighting, fighting always for a right to live. When I set that bomb I meant only to throw a scare into those fellows who owned The *Times.* The paper had been fighting us for years. The situation throughout the country was critical, and so we decided that something must be done, and we were sent to do it. I was horribly shocked when I learned of the deaths that followed, but I am prepared to pay the price for my crime, if it can be called that, when it was done for principle."

James B. McNamara, as quoted from his cell by a Los Angeles reporter, "The McNamara Confessions," Literary Digest, vol. 43 (December 9, 1911), p. 1084.

. . . every evening in every city the downtown street corners were all occupied by soapboxes, literally sometimes, and sometimes we just called them that when they were little platforms with a flag. There was usually somebody from headquarters who would get up and make an opening talk. Then whoever it was would introduce the speaker.

You would know you were going to speak that night and you'd have some kind of subject to talk about besides the general one. You'd talk for maybe fifteen or twenty minutes and then you'd ask for questions and try to answer them. Mostly we spoke about suffrage but we also talked about the right of a woman to have control of her own earnings. . . . we thought primarily that the way to help women was to give them the vote so they could be citizens, too.

We never had any physical violence. . . . We got jeers and catcalls. . . . we'd be interrupted, of course, and heckled. That was all part of it. You expected that and learned how to handle it.

Miriam Allen DeFord describes her suffrage activities in Boston, ca. 1912, in Gluck, ed., From Prison to Parlor, p. 147.

The movement for women's suffrage gained new vitality as the 1910s opened. The headquarters pictured here is in Cleveland, Ohio, in 1912. The woman holding the flag is Florence Allen, a lawyer, suffragist, and reformer who later became the first woman in the nation to serve as a state supreme court justice. At the far right is Belle Sherwin, who later became national president of the League of Women Voters. *(Library of Congress, Prints and Photographs Division, LC-USZ62-30776 DLC)*

. . . [T]he average male opponent of woman suffrage to-day, is constantly assuming that his right to vote rests on natural, if not divine, sanctions. He knows nothing about the origin of it. He is ignorant of the fact that not many generations ago kings, priests and nobles regarded the common man of his class and intelligence just exactly as he regards woman to-day. James I's motto was, "Let the cobbler stick to his last"—which meant to him, "Let the merchant, the banker, the trader, the artisan and laborer in the fields stick to their jobs and not interfere with the affairs of state, which are such high mysteries as to be beyond the reach of common intellects." So the anti-suffragist has for his motto, "Let women stick to their jobs, and leave the affairs of state to my supreme wisdom—so celebrated through the ages ever since the apple episode in the Garden." He does not know that his ancestors won political power by agitation and violence, and were ridiculed with the very same "arguments" which he now addresses to the women . . .

Progressive historian Charles Beard, "The Common Man and the Franchise," published by the Men's League for Women's Suffrage, 1912, reprinted in Kimmel, ed., Against the Tide, pp. 263–64.

That anyone would try to destroy [Hetch Hetchy Valley] seems incredible; but sad experience shows that there are people good enough and bad enough for anything. The proponents of the dam scheme bring forward a lot of bad arguments to prove that the only righteous thing to do with the people's parks is to destroy them bit by bit as they are able. Their arguments are curiously like those of the devil, devised for the destruction of the first garden. . . .

These temple destroyers, devotees of ravaging commercialism, seem to have a perfect contempt for Nature, and, instead of lifting their eyes to the God of the mountains, lift them to the Almighty Dollar.

Dam Hetch Hetchy! As well dam for water-tanks the people's cathedrals and churches, for no holier temple has ever been consecrated by the heart of man.

> *John Muir,* The Yosemite, *1912, pp. 261–62.*

Whereas, the preservation of the public morals, public health and public order, in the cities and towns of this commonwealth, is endangered by the residence of white and colored people in close proximity to one another; therefore,

1. Be it enacted by the general assembly of Virginia, That in the cities and towns of this commonwealth where this act shall be adopted . . . the entire area within the respective corporate limits thereof shall . . . be divided into districts, the boundaries whereof shall be plainly designated in such ordinance and which shall be known as "segregation districts." . . .

3. That the council of each such city or town shall provide for . . . a map showing the boundaries of all such segregation districts, . . .

4. That after twelve months . . . it shall be unlawful for any colored person, not then residing in a district so defined and designated as a white district, or who is not a member of a family then therein residing to move into and occupy as a residence any building or portion thereof in such white district, and it shall be unlawful . . . for any white person not then residing in a district so defined and designated as a colored district, or who is not a member of a family then therein residing, to move into and occupy as a residence any building, or portion thereof, in such colored district. . . .

> *Residential segregation act passed by the Virginia legislature, 1912,* Acts of Virginia, *chapter 157, pp. 330–32, reprinted in Bardolph,* Civil Rights Record, *pp. 197–98.*

From the days of slavery Negroes have tried the fortunes of the market place and under freedom their enterprises have increased. . . . At the present time Southern-born and West Indian Negroes form the bulk of the business men, the latter far in excess of their proportion in the Negro population. This success of West Indians is partly a result of training and initiative developed in a more favorable environment. . . .

Although they gained the meagre capital chiefly from domestic and personal service occupations, Negroes have entered and maintained a foothold in a number of lines of business unrelated to these previous occupations. One of the most important findings is that Negroes form few partnerships and that those formed are rarely of more than two persons. Co-operative or corporate business enterprises are the exceptions. This fact has its most telling effect in preventing accumulations of capital for large undertakings. But co-operation in business is largely a matter of ability born of experience and where can Negroes get this experience in well-organized firms, under experienced supervision? For it is more than a matter of school instruction in book-keeping, and the like. In practically the entire metropolis, they rarely get beyond the position of porter, or some similar job.

> *George E. Haynes, a founder of the Urban League,* The Negro at Work in New York City, *his Columbia doctoral dissertation, 1912, pp. 146–47.*

You cannot view the class struggle through the stained-glass windows of a cathedral, or through the eyes of capitalist-made laws. . . . Few know what the class struggle means. These men who were locked in the jail in Los Angeles and later went to San Quentin know what it means. They know, and for that reason my heart is with the McNamara boys so long as they are fighting against the capitalist. Let the capitalists count their own dead. There are twenty-one dead in Los Angeles and we have 207 dead in Briceville, Tenn., due to the capitalists. Those deaths in that mine in Briceville were just as much murder as any premeditated crimes could be. The mine-owners knew that if the mine had been properly ventilated there would be no accumulation of fire-damp or gas. But that would cost money and those capitalists spent no money for the protection of the workers. Again, I repeat that I am with the McNamaras and always will be.

> *"Big Bill" Haywood, head of the Wobblies, addressing a socialist meeting at Cooper Union, in New York City, quoted in "Kind Words for the McNamaras,"* Literary Digest, *vol. 44 (January 6, 1912), p. 3.*

It is "one of the disheartening failures of justice which are all too common in this country," declares the *New York Tribune,* which goes on to say:

> . . . The monstrous conclusion of the law is that the slaughter was no one's fault, that it couldn't be helped, or perhaps even that, in the fine legal phrase which is big enough to cover a multitude of defects of justice, it was 'an act of God!' This conclusion is revolting to the moral sense of the community. . . ."

The point of view of those who must day after day submit themselves to risks similar to those which obtained in the Triangle factory in thus voiced by the *New York Call* (Socialist):

> "There are no guilty. There are only the dead. . . .
> Capital can commit no crime when it is in pursuit of profits." . . .

The juror whose conscience now troubles him is Victor Steinman. To a reporter from the *New York Evening Mail* he said:

> "I believed that the Washington Place door, on which the district-attorney said the whole case hinged, was locked at the time of the fire. But I could not make myself feel certain that Harris and Blanck knew. . . . the judge had charged us that we could not find them guilty unless we believed that they knew the door was locked then. . . .
>
> It would have been much easier for me if the State factory inspectors instead of Harris and Blanck had been on trial. For there would have been no doubt in my mind then as to how to vote."

The Literary Digest *summarizes New York press opinion on the not guilty verdict in the Triangle Shirtwaist criminal trial against owners Harris and Blanck, "147 Dead, Nobody Guilty," vol. 44 (January 6, 1912), pp. 6–7.*

I remember very well the first and last place from which I was dismissed. I lost my place because I refused to let the madam's husband kiss me. He must have been accustomed to undue familiarity with his servants, or else he took it as a matter of course, because without any love-making at all, soon after I was installed as cook, he walked up to me, threw his arms around me, and was in the act of kissing me, when I demanded to know what he meant and shoved him away. I was young then, and newly married, and didn't know then what has been a burden to my mind and heart ever since: that a colored woman's virtue in this part of the country has no protection. I at once went home, and told my husband about it. When my husband went to the man who had insulted me, the man cursed him, and slapped him, and had him arrested. The police judge fined my husband $25. I was present at the hearing, and testified on oath to the insult offered me. The white man, of course, denied the charge. The old judge looked up and said, "This court will never take the word of a nigger against the word of a white man."

Unidentified African-American nursemaid in Georgia, "More Slavery at the South," part of a series of working people's autobiographies in the Independent, *vol. 72 (January 25, 1912), pp. 197–98.*

Now, gentlemen, shoveling is a great science. . . . [W]e selected two first-class shovelers. . . . These men were then talked to in about this way, "See here, Pat and Mike, you fellows understand your job all right; both of you fellows are first-class men. . . . We are going to ask you to do a lot of damn fool things, and when you are doing them there is going to be some one out alongside of you all the time, a young chap with a piece of paper and a stop watch and pencil. . . ."

The number of shovel loads which each man handled in the course of the day was counted and written down. At the end of the day the total tonnage of the material handled by each man was weighed and this weight was divided by the number of shovel loads handled. . . . [O]ur first experiment showed that the average shovel load handled was 38 pounds, and that with this load on the shovel the man handled, say, about 25 tons per day. We then cut the shovel off, making it somewhat shorter, so that instead of shoveling a load of 38 pounds it held a load of approximately 34 pounds. The average, then, with the 34 pound load, of each man went up and instead of handling 25 he had handled 30 tons per day. . . . [A]t about 21 or 22 pounds per shovel we found that these men were doing their largest day's work. If you cut the shovel off still more, say until it averages 18 pounds . . . the tonnage handled per day will begin to fall off. . . .

Frederick Taylor explains his technique to Congress, January 25, 1912, Hearings Before Special Committee of the House of Representatives to Investigate the Taylor and Other Methods of Shop Management, 62nd Congress, 2nd session, reprinted in Taylor, Scientific Management, pp. 52–55.

To greet the children a crowd of 5,000 men, women, and children packed the Grand Central Station concourse, singing the "Marseillaise" in many tongues. They waved red flags, some with black borders, and all bearing Socialistic mottoes. It was noticed that not one in that crowd waved aloft the Stars and Stripes.

. . . The black borders, it was said, were marks of mourning for those of the strikers who have lost their lives in Lawrence. Besides the flags, there were banners, also red. . . . One painted in gold letters on a long, red streamer, read:

> Ye exploiters, kneel down before the sons of your victims.

Another banner announced that the "libertarians of New York affirm their solidarity to the strikers of Lawrence." . . . There was also another flaming piece of bunting on which was painted the information that certain Harvard students favored "a free country." . . .

. . . When the children were escorted from the cars they were in charge of fourteen men and women from Lawrence, one of whom was a trained nurse. The children were formed in columns of twos, and at a signal from a young man who was one of those in charge they announced their arrival with a yell.

This is the way the yell goes, and the children shouted it all the way out of the station:

Who are we, who are we, who are we! Yes we are, yes we are, yes we are. Strikers, strikers, strikers.

"150 Strike Waifs Find Homes Here," New York Times,
February 11, 1912, pp. 1–2.

On February 24, 1912, a group of 40 strikers' children were to go from Lawrence to Philadelphia. . . . At the railroad station in Lawrence, where the children were assembled accompanied by their fathers and mothers, just as they were ready to board the train they were surrounded by police. Troopers surrounded the station outside to keep others out. Children were clubbed and torn away from their parents and a wild scene of brutal disorder took place. Thirty-five frantic women and children were arrested, thrown screaming and fighting into patrol wagons. They were beaten into submission and taken to the police station. There the women were charged with "neglect" and improper guardianship and ten frightened children were taken to the Lawrence Poor Farm. The police station was besieged by enraged strikers. Members of the Philadelphia committee were arrested and fined. . . . Famous newspaper reporters and writers flocked to Lawrence. . . .

IWW speaker Elizabeth Gurley Flynn, an eyewitness
to events at Lawrence, February 24, 1912,
I Speak My Piece,
pp. 128–29.

Some of the most telling service which is being rendered by the settlements to-day consists in the calculated influence that comes through whole-hearted participation by the residents in the amusements of the young people of their neighborhoods. By entering fully into the game, on the existing terms . . . with neighborhood young people, one comes often to have a marvelous authority as to the whole management and spirit of recreation. Often in this way one can from within make points in character . . . which otherwise would fall on listless ears. . . .

There is, indeed, a certain spiritual kinship between the movement for play and the revival of the neighborhood. The great tradition of spontaneous play goes with the village green. It is the outcropping of a simple common life. Play on the one hand, and this simple nascent form of collective life on the other, are each a means of grace; that is, through them as from above comes into our lives a blessing greater than we can understand.

Robert Woods, "The Neighborhood as a Recreation Unit,"
speech to Y.M.C.A Training School, Springfield,
Massachusetts, March 1912, Neighborhood in
Nation-Building, *pp. 121–22.*

I was in a Northern city recently. . . .

I was traveling. I got off at a station almost starved. I begged the keeper of a restaurant to sell me a lunch in a paper and hand it out of the window. He refused, and I was compelled to ride a hundred miles farther before I could get a sandwich.

I was in a white church on official business. It was a cold, blowing day, raining, sleeting, freezing. Warm lunch was served in the basement to my white brothers. I could not sit in the corner of that church and eat a sandwich. I had to go nearly two miles in the howling winds and sleet to get a lunch.

I have seen in the South white and black workingmen elbowing each other, eating their lunches at noon and smoking the pipe of peace. Worldly men give me a welcome in their stores. The Government post office serves me without discrimination. But not so in that church run in the name of Jesus.

I could not help but feel that Jesus, too, like me, an unwelcome visitor, was shivering in the cold, and could not find a place in that inn, and was saying: "I was hungered and ye gave me no meat. I was thirsty and you gave me no drink." . . .

Dr. R. S. Lovingood, president of Samuel Houston College in
Austin, widely reprinted comments on discrimination
in the North, "A Black Man's Appeal to
His White Brothers," The Crisis, *vol. 3*
(March 1912), p. 196.

A large majority of these strikers were Italians, Poles, Greeks, Syrians or other untutored people. These poor people . . . did not even understand English and were an easy prey to the agitation. About this time Joseph J. Ettor appeared upon the scene. Ettor is only twenty-six years of age but has been a leader in frightful outbreaks in Brooklyn and Patterson and prominent in the bloody riots of Schoenville, Pa. . . . In a few days he had become the idol of the workers of all the races, who believed every word of his incendiary speeches. He even fooled the general public and until he advocated the use of violence, which resulted in bloodshed he had the majority of the people with him. . . . And it was generally taken for granted that the mill operatives were a much trodden, badly treated and under paid lot of people. This is not a fact. Instead of receiving five dollars a week as has been stated, the average wage . . . is between nine and ten dollars and it is largely a man's own fault if he receives only the average wage. Any intelligent person may become a skilled weaver and receive twenty to twenty-five dollars. . . . The un-Americanized foreign element, however, are not educated up to things of this kind and if their pay was many times what it is they unquestionably would prefer to live as they do. Half a dozen families in one small tenement, eight or ten in a room wallowed in dirt.

Walter M. Pratt, an officer in the militia that served at Lawrence, Massachusetts, during the textile strike, "The Lawrence Revolution," New England Magazine, *vol. 41 (March 1912), pp. 7–8.*

Mr. [Edward] POU, [Democrat, North Carolina] You have been in the homes of these factory people, of course, frequently?

Miss LISS. Yes, sir; I am a factory girl myself.

Mr. POU. I want you to describe to the committee what sort of food these people live on.

Miss LISS. Well, bread and sirup and molasses and beans.

Mr. POU. As a rule, how often do the factory people have meat?

Miss LISS. Well, they do not have meat very often. They buy a soup bone and make soup.

Mr. POU. Do they have it as often as once a week?

Miss LISS. Yes; perhaps once a week. . . .

Mr. POU. . . . It is because, you say, they have not the money to buy the meat with?

Miss LISS. Yes.

Mr. POU. You say very few of them have that much money?

Miss LISS. Yes, sir; on five and six dollars a week you can not have everything. You have to pay rent.

Testimony of Josephine Liss, 21, a Polish-American weaver at Lawrence, at the Congressional hearings, March 2–7, 1912, The Strike at Lawrence, Massachusetts, *pp. 244–45.*

The spread of radical, not to say revolutionary doctrines, was never more conspicuously or surprisingly illustrated than by the participation of two Wellesley College professors in the mass meeting of Lawrence strikers last night. The question of personal motive was less to be criticized than the propriety of the conditions that were chosen for its expression. The feminine instinct of pity for distress is something that we hope will never grow weaker than it is. . . .

But the affiliation is a strange one—the educated and refined instructors of Wellesley College, lending their aid and influence to Haywood and Ettor and the other professional organizers of misrule and social chaos. . . .

One of these professors is reported as stating the doctrine that "there is no just wage as long as there is one dollar in dividends, as long as there is a surplus to be paid to people who do not do the work." We hesitate to believe that she was correctly quoted. In what way could wages be earned if there was no incentive for capital to furnish the opportunity? Were that our economic condition there would be no Wellesley College or any other. Such a doc-

trine lacks not merely common sense but even sanity. . . . If such doctrines are the teachings of Wellesley College how many of its present patrons would care to have their daughters under such influences, and how many new ones would care to place their children in an institution where the rankest Socialism, to call it by no worse name, is proclaimed or permitted. . . .

"A Strange Alliance," editorial condemning professors Vida Scudder and Ellen Hayes, Boston Evening Transcript, *March 5, 1912, p. 12.*

Mrs. Taft, wife of the President, seated . . . beside Victor Berger, the Socialist member of Congress, listened attentively to-day to testimony relating to the strike of mill workers at Lawrence, Mass. This was the second day that Mrs. Taft has appeared at the hearing. Mrs. Taft was attired in a dark blue street dress and brown-plumed hat. . . .

It was learned to-day that another visitor at the hearing yesterday was Miss Anne Morgan of New York, daughter of J. P. Morgan. . . .

Capt. John J. Sullivan, Acting Chief Marshal of Lawrence. . . . recounted to the committee several incidents in which he said children were sent out of Lawrence by the strikers without the consent or even the knowledge of their parents. . . .

. . . "I notified the Strike Committee and had it published that no children would be permitted to leave Lawrence without the written consent of their parents."

Capt. Sullivan said the Strike Committee had published broadcast that the "children were going despite Capt. Sullivan's order." Just before the time of the trouble at the depot, he said, a system of picketing by women had been inaugurated by the strikers, the women being chiefly Poles, Russians, &c. These pickets would not obey the police.

"They felt that they were martyrs, heroines, and wanted to go to jail," said the Captain. "When they were fined for assaults, they appealed their cases.". . .

The Captain denied that there was any violence used, and said he was on the spot all the time, and that no soldiers were there with guns and bayonets.

The New York Times *reports the Congressional hearings on Lawrence, "Police Say Women Led Lawrence Mobs," March 7, 1912, p. 6.*

Be it enacted. . . . The said bureau shall investigate and report to said department upon all matters pertaining to the welfare of children and child life among all classes of our people, and shall especially investigate the questions of infant mortality, the birth rate, orphanage, juvenile courts, desertion, dangerous occupations, accidents and diseases of children, employment, legislation affecting children in the several States and Territories. But no official, or agent, or representative of said bureau shall, over the objection of the head of the family, enter any house used exclusively as a family residence. The chief of said bureau may from time to time publish the results of these investigations in such manner and to such extent as may be prescribed by the Secretary of Commerce and Labor.

Act establishing the Children's Bureau, signed into law April 9, 1912, U.S. Statutes at Large, 62nd Congress, vol. 37, part 1, pp. 79–80.

Suddenly a queer quivering ran under me, apparently the whole length of the ship. Startled by the very strangeness of the shivering motion, I sprang to the floor. . . . Some one knocked at my door, and the voice of a friend said: "Come quickly to my cabin; an iceberg has just passed our window; I know we have just struck one."

No confusion, no noise of any kind, one could believe no danger imminent. Our stewardess came and said she could learn nothing. Looking out into the companionway I saw heads appearing asking questions from half-closed doors. All sepulchrally still, no excitement. I sat down again. My friend was by this time dressed. . . . Then I saw she was frightened, and for the first time I was too, but why get dressed, as no one had given the slightest hint of any possible danger? An officer's cap passed the door. I asked: "Is there an accident or danger of any kind?" "None, so far as I know," was his courteous answer, spoken quietly and most kindly. This same officer then entered a cabin a little distance down the companionway and, by this time distrustful of everything, I listened intently, and distinctly heard, 'We can keep the water out for a while.' Then, and not until then, did I realize the horror of an accident at sea. Now it was too late to dress; no time for a waist, but a coat and skirt were soon on; slippers were quicker than shoes; the stewardess put on our life-preservers. . . .

Elizabeth Shutes, a governess traveling with a family on the Titanic, *describes the collision shortly before midnight, April 14, 1912, "When the* Titanic *Went Down," in* Gracie, The Truth About the Titanic, *pp. 125–26.*

Then, above the clamor of people asking questions of each other, there came the terrible cry: "Lower the boats. Women and children first!" Some one was shouting those last four words over and over again: "Women and children first! Women and children first!". . . .

The third boat was about half full when a sailor caught Marjorie [her eight-year-old daughter] in his arms, and tore her away from me and threw her into the boat. . . .

"You too!" a man yelled close to my ear. "You're a woman. Take a seat in that boat, or it will be too late."

The deck seemed to be slipping under my feet. It was leaning at a sharp angle; for the ship was then sinking fast, bows down. I clung desperately to my husband. I do not know what I said; but I shall always be glad to think that I did not want to leave him.

A man seized me by the arm. Then, another threw both his arms about my waist and dragged me away by main strength. I heard my husband say: "Go, Lotty! For God's sake, be brave, and go! I'll get a seat in another boat." The men who held me rushed me across the deck, and hurled me bodily into the lifeboat. I landed on one shoulder and bruised it badly. . . .

The bottom of our boat slapped the ocean, as we came down, with a force that I thought must shock us all overboard. We were drenched with ice-cold spray; but we hung on, and the men at the oars rowed us rapidly away from the wreck. . . .

Charlotte Collyer, an English grocer's wife traveling in second class, around 1 A.M. April 15, 1912, "How I Was Saved from the Titanic," *Semi-Monthly Magazine, May 26, 1912, reprinted in Forsyth et al., eds.,* Titanic Voices, *135–36.*

The Captain-stoker told us that he had been at sea twenty-six years and had never yet seen such a calm night on the Atlantic. As we rowed away from the Titanic we looked from time to time back to watch her, and a more striking spectacle it was not possible for any one to see. . . . In the distance she looked an enormous length, her great hulk outlined in black against the starry sky, every porthole and saloon blazing with light.

It was impossible to think anything could be wrong with such a leviathan were it not for that ominous tilt downward in the bow, where the water was by now up to the lowest row of portholes. . . .

Presently, about 2 a.m., as near as I can remember, we observed her settling very rapidly, with the bows and the bridge completely under water. . . . She slowly tilted straight on end, with the stern vertically upward, and as she did the lights in the cabins and saloons, which had not flickered for a moment since we left, died out, came on again for a single flash, and finally went altogether.

At the same time the machinery reared down through the vessel with a rattle and a groaning that could be heard for miles. . . . But this was not quite the end.

To our amazement she remained in that upright position for a time . . . the Titanic above the sea and looming black against the sky.

Then with a quiet slanting dive she disappeared beneath the waters. . . .

Lawrence Beesley, an English science teacher traveling second class, describes the sinking of the Titanic, 2:20 A.M., *April 15, 1912, "Colonel Astor Went Down Waving Farewells,"* New York Times, *April 19, 1912, p. 2.*

BOSTON, April 15—A wireless message picked up late last night relayed from the Olympic says that the Carpathia is on her way to New York with 866 passengers from the steamer Titanic aboard. They are mostly women and children, the message said, and it concluded:

"Grave fears are felt for the safety of the balance of the passengers and crew."

NEW YORK, April 15—Latest reports indicate that 1800 persons probably perished when the Titanic went down.

The text of the message from the steamer Olympic, reporting the sinking of the Titanic and the rescue of 675 survivors, which reached here late last night, expressed the opinion that 1800 lives were lost. . . .

It is hoped and believed here that this is an error, unless the Titanic had more passengers on board than was reported. The list as given out showed 1310 passengers and crew of 860, or 2170 in all. Deducting 675, the known saved, would indicate a loss of 1495 persons.

The Olympic's dispatch follows:

"Carpathia reached Titanic position at day break. Found boats and wreckage only. Titanic sank about 2:20 A.M. in 41:16 N, 50:14 W. All her [life] boats accounted for containing about 675 souls saved, crew and passengers included. Nearly all saved women and children. Leyland liner Californian remained and searching exact position of disaster. Loss likely total 1800 souls."

LONDON, April 15—At the White Star office here it was said that the total number of persons aboard the Titanic was 2358. . . .

> *Conflicting dispatches to the* San Francisco Chronicle, *"Gigantic Liner Titanic Sinks," April 16, 1912, p. 1.*

The picture which presents itself before my eyes is that of the glassy, glaring eyes of the victims, staring meaninglessly at the gilded furnishings of this sunken palace of the sea; dead helplessness wrapt in priceless luxury; jewels valued in seven figures becoming the strange playthings of the queer creatures that sport in the dark depths. Everything for existence, nothing for life. Grand men, charming women, beautiful babies, all becoming horrible in the midst of the glittering splendour of a $10,000,000 casket!

And there was no need of it. It is just so much sacrifice laid upon the accurst altar of the dollar. . . . They knew that the ice was there. They dared it. They would dare it now were it not for the public. It is cheaper to run by the short route. There is more money in it for the stockholders. The multimillionaires want more money. They want as much as they can get of it. . . .

It is a lesson all around to the effect that commercialism, when pushed beyond a certain pace, breaks down and results in stringency and poverty, and that action, when crowded, produces reaction that wipes out the results of action. . . .

The two sore spots which really run into one another and which constitute the disease that is gnawing into our civilization are love of money and passion for luxury. Those two combined are what sunk the Titanic and sent 1,500 souls prematurely to their final account.

> *Rev. Charles H. Parkhurst, sermon on the Titanic disaster, "Religious Views of the Titanic,"* Literary Digest, *vol. 44 (May 4, 1912), p. 939.*

SUFFRAGE ARMY OUT ON PARADE
Perhaps 10,000 Women and Men Sympathizers March for the Cause.
Cheers for the Women and Some Good-Natured Jesting at the Men.
Aged Leaders Applauded
They Rode in Flower-Bedecked Carriages—Women on Horseback and "Joan of Arc" Win Plaudits.

Part IX. of this morning's Times consists of four pages of pictures of yesterday's suffrage parade.

Ten thousand strong, the army of those who believe in the cause of woman's suffrage marched up Fifth Avenue at sundown yesterday in a parade the like of which New York never knew before. Dusty and weary, the marchers went to their homes last night satisfied that their year of hard work in preparing for the demonstration had borne good fruit.

It was an immense crowd that came out to stand upon the side-walks to cheer or jeer. It was a crowd far larger than that which greeted the homecoming of Theodore Roosevelt and the homecoming of Cardinal Farley. It was a crowd that stood through the two hours of the parade without a thought of weariness. Women, young and old, rich and poor, were all handed into a great sisterhood by the cause they hold dear.

> *The suffrage parade in New York, May 4, 1912, reported in the* New York Times *May 5, p. 1.*

Men generally view the woman suffrage movement calmly, seeming not to care much whether or not the women get the right to vote, and heeding little the consequences of the social revolution which would result from the triumph of the present agitation. A few men believe that the right of suffrage should be extended forthwith to the women. Our observation does not justify the inference that they are wise and thoughtful men, but they are certainly more admirable and entitled to more respect than the men who, believing the contrary, possessed of the knowledge that the vote will secure to woman no new privilege that she either deserves or requires, that the enfranchisement of women must inevitably result in the weakening of family ties, yet look upon the woman suffrage movement complacently and dismiss it. . . .

The situation is dangerous. We often hear the remark nowadays that women will get the vote if they try hard enough and persistently, and it is true that they will get, and play havoc with it for themselves and society, if the men are not firm and wise enough and, it may as well be said, masculine enough to prevent them. . . . There are numberless explanations of the conduct of otherwise nice and womanly women in this matter. There are few that can fairly be called "reasons." . . .

Anti-suffrage editorial, "The Uprising of the Women,"
New York Times, *May 5, 1912, p. 14.*

In a moment I was in the air, climbing steadily in a long circle. I was up fifteen hundred feet within thirty seconds. From this high point of vantage my eyes lit at once on Dover Castle. It was half hidden in a fog bank. . . . but I made directly for the flagstaff of the castle, as I had promised the waiting Mirror [*London Daily Mirror,* a newspaper] photographers and the moving-picture men I should do.

In an instant I was beyond the cliffs and over the channel. Far beneath I saw the Mirror's tug, with its stream of black smoke. . . . Then the quickening fog obscured my view. Calais was out of sight. I could not see ahead of me or at all below. There was only one thing for me to do and that was to keep my eyes fixed on my compass.

My hands were covered with long Scotch woolen gloves which gave me good protection from the cold and fog; but the machine was wet and my face was so covered with dampness that I had to push my goggles up on my forehead. I could not see through them. I was traveling at over a mile a minute. . . . and I knew that land must be in sight if I could only get below the fog and see it. So I dropped from an altitude of about two thousand feet until I was half that height. The sunlight struck upon my face and my eyes lit upon the white and sandy shores of France. . . .

Harriet Quimby, the first woman aviator to fly across the
English Channel, *on April 16, 1912, "An American Girl's*
Daring Exploits," Leslie's Weekly, *vol. 114 (May 16,*
1912), reprinted in Harris, The First to Fly, *pp. 185–86.*

For sixteen years I have been a fighting man. Performing what I regard as a public duty, I have not hesitated to speak out on any public question . . . and I have not hesitated to raise the hostility and the enmity of individuals where I felt it my duty to do so in behalf of my country. . . .

I recognize that a man who fights must carry scars, and I decided long before this campaign commenced that I had been in so many battles and had alienated so many that my party ought to have the leadership of some one who had not thus offended and who thus might lead with greater hope of victory.

And to-night I come with joy to surrender into the hands of the one chosen by this convention a standard which I have carried in three campaigns, and I challenge my enemies to declare that it has ever been lowered in the face of the enemy. . . .

It is not because the Vice Presidency is lower in importance than the presidency that I decline. There is no office in this nation so low that I would not take it if I could serve my country by accepting it.

I believe that I can render more service to my country . . . than I could as a candidate, and your candidate will not be more active in this campaign than I shall be. My services are at the command of the party, and I feel a relief now that the burden of leadership is transferred to other shoulders. . . .

William Jennings Bryan, valedictory speech to the Democratic
convention declining a nomination to run as Wilson's vice
president, quoted in "Indiana Governor Is Named for Vice
President at 1:56 A.M.," New York Times,
July 3, 1912, page 1.

[The Republicans] are so indoctrinated with the idea that only the big business interest of this country understand the United States and can make it prosperous that they cannot divorce their thoughts from that obsession. They have put the government into the hands of trustees, and Mr. Taft and Mr. Roosevelt were the rival candidates to preside over the board of trustees. . . .

. . . We have restricted credit, we have restricted opportunity, we have controlled development, and we have come to be one of the worst ruled, one of the most completely controlled and dominated, governments in the civilized world—no longer a government by free opinion, no longer a government by conviction and the vote of the majority, but a government by the opinion and the duress of small groups of dominant men. . . .

The Roosevelt plan is that there shall be an industrial commission charged with the supervision of the great monopolistic combinations which have been formed under the protection of the tariff, and that the government of the United States shall see to it that these gentlemen who have conquered labor shall be kind to labor. I find, then, the proposition to be this: that there shall be two masters, the great corporation, and over it the government of the United States; and I ask who is going to be master of the government of the United States? It has a master now,—those who in combination control these monopolies. And if the government controlled by the monopolies in its turn controls the monopolies, the partnership is finally consummated. . . .

Woodrow Wilson, The New Freedom, *an edited collection of*
speeches made during the July 3–November 5, 1912
presidential campaign, pp. 198–201, 206–07.

Resolved, that when any harbor or other place in the American continents is so situated that the occupation thereof for naval or military purposes might threaten the communications or the safety of the United States, the government of the United States could not see without grave concern the possession of such harbor or other place by any corporation or association which has such a relation to another government, not American, as to give that government practical power of control for national purposes....

This resolution rests on a generally accepted principle of the law of nations, older than the Monroe Doctrine. It rests on the principle that every nation has a right to protect its own safety, and that if it feels that the possession by a foreign power, for military or naval purposes, of any given harbor or place is prejudicial to its safety, it is its duty as well as its right to interfere.

Senator Henry Cabot Lodge, the Lodge Corollary, August 2, 1912, Congressional Record, 62 Congress, 2nd Session, vol. 48, p. 10045.

Now, friends, this is my confession of faith.... I believe in a larger use of the governmental power to help remedy industrial wrongs, because it has been borne in on me by actual experience that without the exercise of such power many of the wrongs will go unremedied. I believe in a larger opportunity for the people themselves directly to participate in government and to control their governmental agents, because long experience has taught me that without such control many of their agents will represent them badly. By actual experience in office I have found that, as a rule, I could secure the triumph of the causes in which I most believed, not from the politicians and the men who claim an exceptional right to speak in business and government, but by going over their heads and appealing directly to the people themselves. . . . Whatever of power I at any time had, I obtained from the people....

Theodore Roosevelt, "Confession of Faith," delivered August 6, 1912, to the Progressive Party convention, Chicago, Works, vol. 17, p. 297.

. . . I stopped all along the way east and I heard some politics talked. It looks like Wilson out here. All the interests are determined to beat T. R. at any rate. They have given up Taft, and they don't care for Wilson, but the man they hate is the Bull Moose and they are bound to beat him if they can. It's personal, you see. There's no bigger view taken here than in California. The President is the point. I think, as you know, that Congress is important and that the Progressive movement is the most important. But no one talks that. Heroes and Devils still rule our minds....

Lincoln Steffens, letter to his brother-in-law after traveling from Los Angeles to New York, September 12, 1912, Letters, vol. 1, p. 308.

October . . .

Tues. 8 . . . I went to my Bible Class at Y.W.C.A. and at 3:30 to the Auditorium to meet some of Good Gov. Club ladies and distribute our Suffrage Campaign Literature to the crowds of men gathered to see and hear Gov. Woodrow Wilson of New Jersey, the Democratic nominee for President. We found the majority of men for us, and almost every one courteous: occasionally there was a "smart aleck.". . .

Fri. 18 A grand day and I so wanted to be out doors but it was my day to stay in the Good Government Club Booth, at the Cooking School held this week in the Auditorium, so I was there all afternoon and until 11 o'clock at night. . . .

Sat. 26 . . . This evening met Good Gov. Club at Mills and went in the Suffragist Parade at 7:45 . . . Gov. Stubbs car headed the parade and we were lead by the Knights and Ladies Band . . . sat on the platform during the address of Rev. Anna Shaw [head of NAWSA], on Suffrage. And she made a fine address. Big crowd. . . .

November . . .

Mon. 4 . . . hurried away at 1 o'clock to the Y.W.C.A. to "stand in line" for the Good Government Club "Tea Party". A Suffrage affair of course and we had an immense crowd; about two thousand called between 2 and 6 o'clock. . . .

Wed. 6 *"This is the day after."* And so bright and sunny—a glorious day . . . for while I went to bed last night a *slave*, I awoke this morning a *free* woman. . . .

Diary of Martha Farnsworth, a teacher and housewife, during the successful campaign for woman's suffrage in Kansas, October 8–November 6, 1912, Plains Woman, pp. 215–17.

The shooting took place in the street in front of the Hotel Gilpatrick. Col. Roosevelt reached Milwaukee shortly after 5 o'clock and making his way through the crowd which had gathered at the station, entered an automobile and was driven to a private dining room on the main floor with the members of the party on his private car.

After dinner Col. Roosevelt stood up, waving his hat in answer to the cheers of the crowd. The assassin was standing in the crowd a few feet from the automobile. He pushed his way to the side of the car and, raising his gun, fired.

Henry F. Cochems, former athlete and Chairman of the Progressive Party speaker's bureau, and Albert Martin, Roosevelt's stenographer, seized the man and held him until policemen came up. John Schrank, who is small of stature, admitted firing the shot and said that "any man looking for a third term ought to be shot."

Col. Roosevelt barely moved as the shot was fired. Before the crowd knew what had happened, Martin, who is six feet tall and a former football player, had landed squarely on the assassin's shoulders and borne him to the ground. He threw his right arm about the man's neck with a death-like grip and with his left arm seized the hand that held the revolver. In another second he had disarmed him.

All this happened within a few seconds . . . before the stunned crowd realized what was going on.

The Detroit Free Press *reports the attempt against Roosevelt's life on October 14, 1912, available online at History Buff. URL: http://www.historybuff.com/ library/refteddy.html.*

Friends, I shall ask you to be as quiet as possible. I don't know whether you fully understand that I have just been shot; but it takes more than that to kill a Bull Moose. But fortunately I had my manuscript, so you see I was going to make a long speech, and there is a bullet—there is where the bullet went through—and it probably saved me from it going into my heart. The bullet is in me now, so that I cannot make a very long speech, but I will try my best.

. . . First of all, I want to say this about myself: I have altogether too many important things to think of to feel any concern over my own death. . . . It was just as when I was colonel of my regiment. I always felt that a private was to be excused for feeling at times some pangs of anxiety about his personal safety, but I cannot understand a man fit to be a colonel who can pay any heed to his personal safety when he is occupied as he ought to be with the absorbing desire to do his duty.

I am in this cause with my whole heart and soul. I believe that the Progressive movement is making life a little easier for all our people; a movement to try to take the burdens off the men and especially the women and children of this country. I am absorbed in the success of that movement.

Roosevelt's speech, delivered October 14, 1912, after the attempt on his life, from a stenographic record that differs from the prepared manuscript, available online at Theodore Roosevelt Association. URL: http:// www.theodoreroosevelt.org/research/ speech%20kill%20moose.htm.

The winning of California last year wrought so complete a change in the work of the national press bureau that it was like taking up an entirely new branch. Before that victory our time was employed in furnishing suffrage arguments, replying to adverse editorials and letters published in the newspapers and writing syndicate articles. Now this department has resolved itself into a bureau of information, news being the one thing required. Each week we send to our mailing list 3,000 copies of the press bulletin. . . . These go into every non-suffrage State in the Union, to Canada, Cuba and England. . . . Almost every mail brings letters from newspapers asking to be placed on the regular mailing list. . . . Since the winning of the four States on November 5, newspapers and press associations from all over the United States have written us asking for help to establish woman suffrage departments. The time has come when our question is a paying one from a publicity point of view. . . .

Caroline I. Reilly, chair of NAWSA's Press Bureau, report to the 1912 convention, Philadelphia, November 21–26, in Harper, ed., History of Woman Suffrage, *vol. 5, pp. 336–37.*

7

Progressivism and Preparedness
1913–1916

THE WILSON ADMINISTRATION

Woodrow Wilson, a former professor who held a Ph.D. in political history, had thought deeply and written widely about government and power before arriving at the White House. He had concluded that the political party in power should be the engine of American government, and that it should have a clearly defined program to keep executive, administrative, and legislative responsibility moving on the same track. He had also concluded that the president should lead his party and take an active role in policy making. He preferred to obtain his policy goals by passing legislation rather than issuing administrative orders, and he preferred to pass legislation by resolving disagreements with fellow Democrats rather than by building coalitions with Republicans. Even in his inaugural address, he took the unusual approach of laying out the agenda of legislation he hoped to pass. After he took office he began actively guiding legislation through Congress.

Most historians have concluded that Woodrow Wilson had impressive skills as a party politician and exercised exceptional leadership for much of his presidency. But he was also fortunate to become president when conditions were receptive to a strong president and party leader. When he took office in March 1913, he was supported by a large Democratic majority in Congress. Perhaps more important, the Democrats had their first opportunity since the Civil War to have a significant impact on national policy. Congressional Democrats, naturally determined to make a success of the opportunity, were particularly cooperative with their president.[1]

Woodrow Wilson had a high level of personal intelligence, a highly principled and even idealistic character, the gift of expressing moral principles very clearly, and exceptional eloquence as a speaker. He was destined to bring progressivism to a peak in national legislation, while further strengthening the modern presidency. Wilson's first administration, although soon laboring under the distractions of war in Europe, passed an astonishing amount of domestic legislation. In fact, by 1916, Wilson and the Democrats had put into effect important parts of the 1892 Populist platform, much of the social reform that had emerged primarily under the aegis of urban Republicans, and much of the 1912 Progressive Party platform authored by the man he defeated, Theodore Roosevelt.

A LOWER TARIFF AND THE FIRST MODERN INCOME TAX

Shortly after taking office, President Wilson called Congress into a special session to act on a Democratic campaign promise: a lower tariff. Tariff cuts were a very important issue to the American public, just as income tax cuts are today, because the tariff was the primary source of federal income in 1913 just as income tax is today. The high tariff, many Americans believed, taxed the average person too heavily because it raised the prices of consumer goods, while at the same time creating artificially large profits for powerful manufacturers and making it possible for trusts to flourish.

The president astounded Washington by announcing he would appear in person before the special session to support tariff reform. No president had spoken before Congress since John Adams in 1800. Ever since, the text of presidential messages had been read aloud by others, and not even the voluble Theodore Roosevelt had thought of breaking the tradition. On April 8, one day after the special congressional session opened, Woodrow Wilson delivered his speech. It was a highly anticipated event that attracted great public attention.

President Wilson made it clear that he expected the new Democratic majority to avoid repeating the debacle of his predecessor Taft's Payne-Aldrich tariff. "While the whole face and method of our industrial and commercial life were being changed beyond recognition the tariff schedules have remained what they were," he said. "We are to deal with the facts of our own day, with the facts of no other and to make laws which square with those facts."[2] In the House a tariff reduction bill sponsored by Representative Oscar Underwood of Alabama passed quickly. When the bill reached the Senate, however, lobbyists for business and manufacturers invaded Washington. They pressured senators to exempt this or that special interest. Even some Democratic senators, whose states were directly affected by cuts on certain products, like sugar, wanted changes and exceptions.

Unlike Taft before him, Wilson quickly seized the reins. While leaning on backsliding Democrats in private, he took his case to the public. He issued a statement to the press that denounced lobbyists. It was a serious concern, he said, "that the people at large should have no lobby and be voiceless in these matters, while great bodies of astute men seek to create an artificial opinion and to overcome the interests of the public for their private profit."[3] Angry citizens wrote their congressmen, and public opinion makers demanded reform. A group of progressive senators led by Robert La Follette launched an inquiry into lobbying and compelled their fellow senators to divulge any financial holdings that were affected by the tariff. Democratic senators not only lined back up in favor of cutting the tariff, they also made additional reductions. The Underwood-Simmons bill, the first major cut in tariffs since the Civil War, was signed into law on October 3. It reduced duties on more than 950 items and added some 100 to the free list, including important consumer items such as woolens, sugar, cement, coal, farm machinery, steel, and wood. Overall, it had the effect of lowering average tariff rates from nearly 40 percent to less than 30 percent.[4]

A lower tariff, however, would reduce federal income—and federal spending had been increasing yearly for the last decade. Congress knew that a new source of tax monies was necessary.

As part of the Underwood tariff legislation, therefore, Congress also passed the first national personal income tax, as permitted by the newly ratified Sixteenth Amendment. During congressional debates, the opponents of income tax continued to argue that it was an attack on the wealthy; its proponents held that it was simply a fairer way of raising

Many reformers considered the establishment of a national income tax in 1913 to be an important accomplishment. As this political cartoon illustrates, they believed it would relieve the tax burden on ordinary working people. It was drawn by John Scott Clubb, a newspaper cartoonist in Rochester, New York. *(Library of Congress, Prints and Photographs Division, LC-USZ62-84130)*

revenue and discouraging trusts, not a way of redistributing wealth. But the real battle had occurred when the amendment passed Congress in 1912, and in 1913 the debate was neither long nor fierce. The tax rates were set at 1 percent on incomes greater than $3,000 for single people and more than $4,000 for married couples. There was also an additional graduated tax that rose from 1 percent on incomes of $20,000 to 6 percent on incomes greater than $500,000. Although those bottom brackets seem tiny to today's ears, Congress did not intend that nearly everyone would pay the tax, as is the case today, or even that a majority of Americans would. In 1913, the average annual income of wage earners was $621—making the $4,000 floor more than six times that amount.[5] In fact, Congress estimated that less than 4 percent of the U.S. population would pay the tax. Although that estimate turned out to be low, the tax still affected only a small minority of Americans in its first few years.

REFORMING MONEY AND BANKING: THE FEDERAL RESERVE ACT

President Wilson insisted that Congress remain in session during the summer to tackle reform of the money and banking system. The system, established at the time of the Civil War, had been vastly outpaced by the growth of industry and commerce. It had no central oversight and no way to pool reserves when necessary to prevent panics and bank closings. Since the Panic of 1907, officials, authorities, and the informed public had all agreed that changes were long overdue.

Nonetheless, blocs in Congress as well as various interests nationwide were furiously divided over how to reform the system. Conservative Republicans and the private banking community approved of the plan recommended by Senator Nelson Aldrich's National Monetary Commission. It called for a powerful central bank under control of private bankers. Democrats and many Republican progressives, on the other hand, were more impressed by the conclusions of the House Banking and Currency Committee, chaired by Democratic representative Arsène Pujo of Louisiana. The Pujo Committee released its final report in early 1913, having held well-publicized hearings at which it scrutinized the nation's most prominent bankers. The report substantiated an extreme concentration of both wealth and control in the hands of a very few East Coast financiers. (The public, which had long imagined a money trust, was nonetheless shocked at such detailed evidence of its existence.) Conservative Democrats called for an end to Wall Street domination and introduced a bill written by Carter Glass of Virginia, head of the House Banking Committee, proposing a decentralized but private system. Progressive Democrats and Republicans, on the other hand, maintained that control of the system should be public and rest with the government. Facing so many factions the president wrote to a friend, "To form a single plan and a single intention about it seems at times a task so various and so elusive that it is hard to keep one's heart from failing."[6]

The money and banking reform finally constructed under Wilson's direction, many historians believe, is his administration's most important legislative legacy and one of his most politically adroit accomplishments. Wilson, after pondering the issue, came to an important conclusion. On June 22, 1913, he went before Congress for the second time in his presidency. He urged Congress to recognize that ultimate control of money and banking "must be public, not private, must be vested in the Government itself, so that the banks may be the instruments, not the masters, of business and of individual enterprise and initiative."[7] Representative Glass of Virginia revised his bill accordingly. It created 12 regional, Federal Reserve banker's banks, owned by the private member banks in the area (not by the government). Each regional bank was overseen by a board of nine members, six chosen by the privately owned member banks and three federally appointed. The regional reserve banks were capped by a national

Federal Reserve Board to exert general supervision and national coordination. The Federal Reserve Board governors, as its members were called, were all publicly appointed; private bankers exercised no direct control over their selection.

The bill succeeded in a very divided House. In the Senate, it faced additional wrangling between conservatives who denounced it as near socialism and progressives who viewed it as a near sellout to the money trust. But finally, on December 19, the Glass-Owen Federal Reserve Act was signed into law.

The blended regional and national, private and public system corrected the major problems that had developed over time in the American system of money and banking. In each region, the national banks were required to deposit a certain amount of their reserves in the regional Federal Reserve bank. These reserves provided greater security in times of crisis, but they also reduced the amount of the nation's money concentrated in New York and controlled by powerful bankers there. The regional reserves made credit more readily available throughout the nation and thus reinforced private local control. In addition, the regional banks purchased (the technical term is *rediscounted*) loans made by their member banks and gave them Federal Reserve notes (that is, currency or paper money) in return. The money could be used to make additional loans locally, but it was ultimately backed up by the federal government, not a private bank or banker. At the top of the system, the central Federal Reserve Board exercised review over the rediscount or interest rates that all the regional banks charged their member banks. The rates could be raised or lowered to stimulate business or tighten credit, to fight recession or inflation. Although important changes were made in the Federal Reserve System in the 1930s, the basic system constructed during the Wilson administration remains the conduit through which America's money and banking system is conducted even today.

ATTACKING THE TRUSTS: THE FTC AND THE CLAYTON ANTI-TRUST ACT

The third item on Wilson's legislative agenda was reining in the trusts to restore competition to the American economy. This point was at the heart of his New Freedom program and remained an important issue with the American public. With his tariff and banking reforms in place by the end of 1913, the president appeared before Congress in January 1914 to call for a dual attack on trusts: a new central regulatory agency and a new and stronger antitrust law. Earlier, during the campaign of 1912, he had rejected the idea of a regulatory agency, proposed by Roosevelt. But on the advice of progressive lawyer Louis Brandeis (who had helped him formulate the New Freedom economic program during the 1912 campaign), Wilson had concluded it was a necessary part of antitrust reform because a regulatory agency could respond to changes in business conditions and technology more quickly than the law and the courts. The regulatory agency, the Federal Trade Commission (FTC), was enacted in September 1914 and replaced the Bureau of Corporations. The five-member FTC was given the power to define "unfair trade practices." It could also hear and decide complaints about unfair competition, launch investigations, issue cease and desist orders without going to court, and file lawsuits against corporations. On the insistence of congressional conservatives, businesses retained the right to appeal FTC orders to courts of law for review.

A month later, Congress also enacted the second part of Wilson's antitrust program, the Clayton Anti-Trust Act. Unlike the Sherman Anti-Trust Act of 1890, it was lengthy and detailed. It spelled out exactly what practices were prohibited in many cases, such as charging different customers different prices or setting up interlocking directorates (seating the same people on the boards of different large corporations). It also prescribed penalties or remedies for violations—and made individual corporate officials responsible for them. The provisions of the Clayton Act which caused the most debate in Congress concerned unions. Since 1894, when the Sherman Act was first used to issue injunctions against striking workers, union interests had worked to secure an exemption from antitrust laws. At Wilson's urging the Clayton Act declared that unions were not by definition "illegal combinations or conspiracies in restraint of trade." Furthermore, the bill banned court injunctions against striking unions "unless necessary to prevent irreparable injury to property." Perhaps equally important, the bill declared "the labor of a human being is not a commodity or article of commerce."[8] In practice, the Clayton Act did not prove to be complete protection for strikers, but it was famously hailed by American Federation of Labor (AFL) head Samuel Gompers as "labor's Magna Carta." (The Magna Carta, a milestone 13th-century English document, limited the formerly absolute rights of the king.) Since 1914, amendments have been attached to the Clayton Act, but it nonetheless remains the basis of American antitrust law even today.

SEGREGATION REACHES THE FEDERAL GOVERNMENT

Given racial politics and party allegiances in the Progressive Era, there was little expectation that a Democratic president would make new appointments of African Americans to government jobs. But much to the surprise and dismay of blacks and of many white progressives outside the South, soon after Wilson took office he apparently approved a plan to formally segregate black and white workers in federal offices and workplaces. It was Postmaster General Albert S. Burleson who first suggested setting up separate restrooms, dining rooms, and even working space. But if there were "any foes of segregation in the Cabinet," writes historian Arthur Link, "they did not then or afterward raise their voice." Soon the post office, the census bureau, and the Bureau of Printing and Engraving began to introduce segregation nationwide. In the South, many black federal employees were even demoted or discharged. "I have recently spent several days in Washington," wrote Booker T. Washington to Oswald Garrison Villard in August 1913, "and I have never seen the colored people so discouraged and bitter as they are at the present time."[9] They were particularly distressed because Wilson had reached out to blacks during the 1912 campaign and some had abandoned their traditional allegiance to the Republicans to support him.

Although some informal and customary segregation had always existed in federal workplaces, outside the South many white Americans disliked setting a federal seal of approval on formal Jim Crow policies. The president was both surprised and distressed by the outcry the action provoked. The NAACP led a protest campaign that received support from many religious leaders, civic leaders, newspapers, and reformers. "It is small, mean, petty discrimination, and Mr. Wilson ought to have set his heel upon [it] the moment it was established," editorialized Villard's *New York World,* a Democratic paper. "It is a reproach to his Administration and to the great political principles which he represents." The Treasury Department quietly reversed its policy and formal segregation was not extended to any additional departments, but many historians consider Wilson's public silence on the issue a failure of leadership.[10]

THE HETCH HETCHY CONTROVERSY IS DECIDED

Since 1902, the city of San Francisco had been unsuccessfully seeking federal permission to dam the Tuolumne River and flood Hetch Hetchy Valley in Yosemite National Park to create a municipal water supply. Nationwide, the preservationist wing of the conservation movement had blocked the project for a decade.

The election of 1912 sealed the fate of Hetch Hetchy Valley. During the campaign Democratic promises of local control received much support from San Franciscans, who overwhelmingly approved the dam and identified conservationists with the Republican and Progressive parties. Upon taking office President Wilson appointed Franklin K. Lane—a close associate of former San Francisco mayor and longtime dam advocate James Phelan—as the new secretary of the interior. The Wilson administration soon underwrote a bill to permit the damming of Hetch Hetchy, and it was passed by Congress before the end of 1913. The long controversy had, however, permanently raised the public profile of the conservation movement.

LEARNING ABOUT FOREIGN RELATIONS

When Woodrow Wilson assumed the presidency he had little background in foreign relations and diplomacy. As he remarked before taking office, "It would be an irony of fate if my administration had to deal chiefly with foreign affairs."[11] Fate was indeed waiting in the wings. The first year and a half of Wilson's administration was a crash course in international relations. Fortunately, many historians have commented, it gave him the experience that made it possible to deal successfully with war in Europe in the subsequent years of his administration.

President Wilson shared with his first secretary of state, William Jennings Bryan, a religiously based devotion to moral principle and idealism about America's mission as a democratic beacon for the world. Almost immediately under the new Wilson administration, for example, the United States became the first nation in the world to extend recognition to the new Republic of China, which had recently overthrown the Qing (Ch'ing) dynasty. The administration also quickly repudiated Taft's policy of dollar diplomacy there, fearing it would compromise China's independence. But there were differences between Wilson's view of the world and Bryan's. Bryan had been a lifelong anti-imperialist (Wilson had not) and had long led the Democratic opposition to Republican expansionism in foreign affairs. As historian John Milton Cooper puts it, Bryan's approach to international relations, drawn from his Christian beliefs, "bordered on pacifism." Bryan believed wholeheartedly that political leaders had a duty to seek peaceful solutions to disputes among nations.[12] During 1913, Bryan devoted most of his time and energy to negotiating innovative "cooling off" treaties with 30 nations. Nations that signed the treaties agreed to delay any declaration of war for a year after disagreements arose, while an international arbitration panel attempted to resolve the problems.

Wilson and Bryan also attempted—unsuccessfully—to form a Pan-American Alliance. It would have bound North and South American nations to respect each other's independence and territory and to submit disputes to peaceful arbitration. Despite this initiative, the Wilson administration actually extended U.S. intervention in Latin America. Under Roosevelt and Taft, intervention in debt-ridden and unstable nations had been undertaken to protect American security interests and specifically to protect the Panama Canal. Wilson and Bryan, however, justified intervention in far different terms. They hoped to encourage freedom and democratic institutions, not only in struggling nations but also in unenlightened nations dominated by tyrants. Historian Arthur Link tagged this approach "missionary diplomacy"—not because it involved religious work, but because it was justified by their ideals and concept of what was right, instead of by national self-interest or expediency, and because they were confident that their ideals should be extended to other nations. "I am going to teach the Latin American nations to elect good men," Wilson told a British diplomat.[13] Between 1912 and 1916, American forces entered and remained in Nicaragua, Haiti, and the Dominican Republic.

WAR IN MEXICO

The first and most immediate international challenge for the Wilson administration, however, was close at hand in Mexico. In 1911, Francisco Madero had overthrown longtime Mexican president Porfirio Díaz. Under Díaz, land ownership had been concentrated in the hands of fewer and fewer *haciendados,* or owners of great estates, while the great mass of peasants, called peons, had become landless, impoverished, and powerless. Díaz had encouraged foreign investment, especially in mining and oil—and the British, Germans, and Americans in particular had obliged. By 1911, Mexico's oil fields, the third most productive in the world, supplied Britain's Royal Navy. By 1912, powerful American corporate interests alone owned more than 75 percent of the silver, lead, and copper mines as well as 60 percent of the oil. Throughout the long, complicated Mexican Revolution (it was also a civil war), all sides claimed to stand for two policies: land reform and "Mexico for Mexicans," or national control of Mexico's natural resources.[14]

In February 1913, a month before Wilson's inauguration, Francesco Madero was himself ousted and murdered in a military coup by General Victoriano Huerta. Other nations routinely recognized governments once they had successfully installed themselves in power and many acknowledged Huerta, including Great Britain. But faced with a military dictator on the nation's southwestern border a week after taking office, President Wilson announced, as Ray Stannard Baker put it, "that his evangel of democracy was to be applicable to the world as well as to America." In a statement that startled foreign diplomats and even surprised many Americans, Wilson said, "We hold, as I am sure all thoughtful leaders of republican government everywhere hold, that just government rests upon the consent of the governed," and he refused to recognize the regime.[15] And, in fact, an anti-Huerta countermovement in favor of elected, constitutional government soon appeared in Mexico. It was led by Venustiano Carranza, the governor of the northern province of Coahuila. Carranza, a *haciendado,* was joined by two military leaders of peon origins, Emiliano Zapata in the south and Francisco "Pancho" Villa in the north. Prior to 1916, Villa enjoyed considerable popularity in the United States, with many viewing him as a Mexican Robin Hood who robbed the rich to give to the poor.

Wilson and Bryan hoped to influence an outcome of reform and self-determination in Mexico. They continued to resist strong pressure from American corporate interests and others to support Huerta or at least to intervene in the turmoil, especially when it destroyed American-owned property and even took some American lives. They did offer to mediate in favor of constitutional elections, but the offer was rebuffed by all sides, including the Carrancistas, or constitutionalists, because it was seen as interference in the affairs of the Mexican people. In August 1913, Wilson announced a policy of "watchful waiting" in a speech to Congress.

THE SHOCK OF THE NEW: THE ARMORY SHOW

In the history of art, it is usually hard to single out one specific date or event as an important turning point. But in February 1913, just such an event occurred. The International Exhibition of Modern Art opened in exhibition space at the Sixty-ninth Regiment Armory in New York City. It exhibited 1,250 paintings, drawings, and sculptures by some 300 artists, about two-thirds of whom were Americans. Known ever after as the Armory Show, it was "the most important event in the history of American modernism," in the words of art historian Barbara Rose.[16] The Armory Show introduced America to new, nonrepresentational styles of art. It astonished and fascinated the public—and outraged not a few. It drew more than 100,000 people in New York, another 150,000 when it traveled to Boston and Chicago, and generated much comment coast to coast.

The Armory show was planned and assembled by a group of practicing American artists, not by a museum or gallery. The artists were led by painter Arthur B. Davies and other members of the Association of American Painters and Sculptors, founded in

1911. At the time, American artists were considered inferior to European artists. But in addition, modern movements in European art were almost unknown in America, except among practicing artists themselves. "We want this old show of ours to mark the starting point of a new spirit in art, at least as far as America is concerned," wrote painter Walt Kuhn to Walter Pach, who acted as publicist.[17] To emphasize the revolutionary aspects of their actions, they adopted the pine tree symbol that had been used on the flag of Massachusetts during America's Revolutionary War.

The works on exhibit ranged from the mid-19th century through 1913. But it was the moderns, and especially those from Europe, who made the Armory show a *succès de scandale.* It was the first major showing in America of such post-impressionist artists as Cézanne, Van Gogh, Gauguin, and Matisse. Art students in Chicago burned Matisse in effigy, but overall it was cubists like Pablo Picasso who aroused the most hostility. Marcel Duchamp's *Nude Descending a Staircase,* a cubist work in which no human figure was discernable, was famously labeled "an explosion in a shingle factory." It provided political cartoonists with a subject of caricature for months to come. Wrote Theodore Roosevelt, "There is in my bath-room a really good Navajo rug which, on any proper interpretation of the Cubist theory, is a far more satisfactory and decorative picture."[18]

Prior to 1913, American museum-goers had never before seen a work of art that did not look like everyday reality. To the public, the Armory show presented an unsettling visual confirmation that the modern world of the 20th century was indeed profoundly different from the traditional world of the 19th. Most were perplexed, and not a few were unfavorably reminded of political radicalism. Among practitioners of the arts, however—not just painters and sculptors but writers, poets, dramatists, musicians, dancers—the Armory show was widely credited for opening their vision to the ferment of modernism.

During the progressive decades, wealthy and philanthropic Americans had been voraciously purchasing European Old Masters for themselves and for the American museums they were endowing. They rarely purchased the work of American artists, nor did they purchase European modernists. As a result of the Armory show, however, nearly 300 works were sold. New York's Metropolitan Museum of Art purchased Paul Cézanne's *Poorhouse on the Hill,* its first modern work. Few museums followed the Met's lead and plunged into modern art in 1913. But a number of wealthy Americans began collections, which eventually became important parts of the Philadelphia Museum of Art, the Chicago Museum of Art, and the Museum of Modern Art (MOMA), among others.

A Literary Flowering

During the decade of the 1910s, American literature was affected by the same ferment that marked painting and other fine arts. Many writers believed it was important to find realistic and specifically American subject matter, and many were willing to push beyond the boundaries of established practices, subjects, and authorities. Some writers pursued American subjects in regionally specific writing; others migrated to European centers of modernism.

The mid-1910s were an especially important period for American poetry. It not only flourished but became an important front in the general artistic rebellion of modernism. Poets refused to be bound by traditional subjects, and many experimented with form, abandoning traditional meter, rhyme, and verse forms in favor of free verse. Although all serious periodicals gave some space to poems, numerous important "little magazines" appeared that were devoted exclusively to the genre. (A little magazine is an often short-lived periodical focused on avant-garde ideas and intended for a small, specific audience, with little thought to commercial success.) Leading the way was

Poetry, founded in Chicago October 1912 by Harriet Monroe with expatriate poet Ezra Pound as assistant editor. It became an influential home for literary insurgents and helped make Chicago the center of the American literary world for a few years. T. S. Eliot's first important work, "The Love Song of J. Alfred Prufrock" was first published in *Poetry* in 1915; Eliot himself soon became an expatriate modernist. *Poetry* also helped establish the reputation of Carl Sandburg, whose book *Chicago Poems* was published in 1916, and Vachel Lindsay, whose "Abraham Lincoln Walks at Midnight," set in his home town of Springfield, Illinois, was published in the *Independent* in 1914. Other important poets at work in the mid-1910s included New Englander Robert Frost, whose first book, *A Boy's Will,* was published in 1913, and Edgar Lee Masters, whose *Spoon River Anthology* (1915) created the entire citizenry of a fictional midwestern town. Poet Amy Lowell led the imagist movement in America, also compiling three anthologies between 1915 and 1917 that helped popularize it. The imagists, who faded as a separate group after 1917, championed poems centered on images that were direct, precise, and concise.

Fiction writers also insisted on portraying what they saw to be the realities of American life—the ruthlessness of American business, the costs of pursuing material success, materialism in general, sexual mores, and, especially among women writers, the role of women in a changing society. Established naturalist Theodore Dreiser, whose scandalous *Sister Carrie* had been suppressed in 1900 but reissued in 1911, published *The Titan* in 1914, part of a trilogy based on the career of discredited street railway titan Charles Yerkes. Edith Wharton satirized the social climbing of the same midwestern entrepreneurs in *The Custom of the Country* (1913), whose soulless antiheroine Undine was named by her parents for the women's hair curling product that made them rich. Other writers explored American regions. Willa Cather, who had spent the years 1906 to 1911 as the managing editor of *McClure's,* began portraying the hard life of immigrant farmers on the Nebraska prairie where she grew up, in short stories and in *O Pioneers!* (1913). Ellen Glasgow used Virginia as the setting for novels about the South.

New Prohibition Campaigns

In late 1912, the Anti-Saloon League (ASL), the Women's Christian Temperance Union (WCTU), and many other temperance organizations began a joint campaign for national legislation to ban interstate shipments of liquor to dry states. Because interstate commerce was under the jurisdiction of the federal government, dry localities could not easily control shipments of liquor to their residents. Liquor wholesalers in wet states advertised heavily in dry states and even sent traveling salesmen to take orders. In fact, only a few dry states were actually "bone-dry" (as it was called), completely banning the possession and use as well as the manufacture and sale of alcohol. The majority of dry states did not criminalize the personal use of liquor; most even allowed home manufacture or periodic purchases from suppliers in non-prohibition states, providing it was for personal use. But many such personal purchases in fact supplied illegal saloons or retail sale.

Prohibition activists drafted a proposed bill written to uphold states' rights—it banned only shipments "to be received, possessed, sold, or in any manner used in violation of any law of such state."[19] They hoped this approach would quell the objections of conservatives who disliked the growing power of federal government and in particular reassure southerners who were strong supporters of prohibition but equally strong supporters of states' rights. Somewhat to the surprise of activists themselves, Congress did not prove difficult to convince. In February 1913, the last month of William Taft's presidency, both houses of Congress passed the bill banning interstate shipments by large margins. President Taft promptly vetoed the Webb–Kenyon bill, as it was named, arguing it overstepped constitutional authority. On March 1, three days before Woodrow Wilson was to be inaugurated, Congress easily overrode the veto. "Party lines were cut to pieces," ASL strategist Ernest Cherrington telegraphed to editors of the league's publication, *American Issue*.[20]

ASL strategists concluded that the time was right to begin a campaign for a constitutional amendment to completely prohibit the manufacture and sale of alcohol nationwide. Two-thirds of U.S. territory, home to half of the American population, was already dry. Congress had recently established a federal income tax—which meant that the need for liquor excise taxes, traditionally the second-largest source of federal income after tariffs, was a less important consideration. ASL strategists nonetheless expected that the campaign would require many years of temperance education, especially in large urban centers where working people and new immigrants generally joined upper-class society in voting against liquor control measures. In fact, in 1913 they estimated the amendment would take 20 years to accomplish.[21]

In December 1913, the ASL, the WCTU, and anti-liquor advocates from nearly 100 other organizations descended on Washington, with a parade down Pennsylvania Avenue 4,000 strong. At the Capitol, marchers presented a resolution to Senator Morris Shepherd of Texas and Congressman Richard Pearson Hobson of Alabama, who had agreed to introduce a bill. The Shepherd-Hobson bill proposed to prohibit the manufacture and sale of alcoholic beverages nationwide but did not ban or criminalize personal possession or use of alcohol. It did not succeed, but it allowed prohibition activists to identify their strongest opponents and supporters.[22]

A RISING TIDE OF PROHIBITION SENTIMENT

Prohibition activists were not acting in a public vacuum. During Woodrow Wilson's first term, a rising tide of prohibition sentiment began to inundate the United States. Fifteen more states voted themselves dry: Washington, Colorado, Arizona, Oregon, and Virginia in 1914; Idaho, North Dakota, Iowa, Alabama, Arkansas, and South Carolina in 1915; Montana, South Dakota, Nebraska, and Michigan in 1916. By 1915, the superintendent of legislation of the Women's Christian Temperance Union—which had grown by 61,000 members since 1913—announced that she could contact a WCTU member in every county in the nation. In part, Americans were responding to the "personal and social damage they saw around them," as historian Jack Blocker puts it, due to a rise in consumption that had reached the highest levels since the 1840s. Some Americans were inspired by the religious revivalism that swept the nation in the early 20th century.[23] As always, religious interests remained vitally committed to the cause because they believed that liquor interfered with spiritual health, family life, and social morality; evangelical Protestant clergy in particular viewed intemperance as an impediment to the personal conversion and battle with sin central to their beliefs. But those facts alone do not completely explain the development.

Liquor control had always been one strand in the warp and woof of reform initiatives that define the progressive decades. Between 1913 and 1916, however, it emerged on the public stage as the most mainstream of progressive reforms in its own right. Perhaps most crucially, the weight of anti-liquor opinion reached a tipping point among social workers, employers, and, most important, doctors and scientists. Opinion was firmly based in rapidly accumulating new scientific knowledge and sociological studies. Only a few years earlier doctors had regarded alcohol as a stimulant and warming agent (it is actually a depressant and causes the body to lose heat), as well as the drug of choice for many diseases. Some had even classified it as a food. In 1899, for example, Massachusetts General Hospital had expended $3,002 for therapeutic alcohol; in 1906, the figure was $738. By 1914 a convention of psychiatrists and neurologists adopted a resolution declaring alcohol "a definite poison to the brain and other tissue." By 1915, whiskey and brandy were dropped from the authoritative U.S. Pharmacopeia (an encyclopedia of drugs used by medical personnel) by vote of the committee in charge of its revision.

Popular and muckraking magazines publicized the new scientific evidence as well as accumulated statistical evidence about the effects of alcohol. They did not lack for sources. Insurance companies had compiled actuarial studies about alcohol and longevity. Social workers and medical personnel had statistically related alcohol to mental degeneracy and suspected a connection between parental drinking and problems of infants and children (although they did not yet have today's more precise scientific understanding of these issues). Labor reformers and employers had related alcohol to accidents on railroads and in machinery-laden workplaces where, by long tradition predating industrialization, many workingmen drank alcoholic beverages during the day as a matter of course. Scientific agriculturalists had observed that the equally traditional workday imbibing of small farmers, especially in the South, interfered with the use of scientific farming techniques to increase productivity. To top it off, social workers had observed that charity or relief cases had declined in some areas where liquor was banned.[24] Other studies related alcohol consumption to crime.

The weight of science and scientific studies carried much authority among up-to-date people in the Progressive Era. It became a fashionable social trend for businessmen and professionals to decline or reduce the use of alcohol at social events. College fraternities joined in, and even professional baseball coaches encouraged their athletes to stay dry. To be sure, many dry advocates were in fact "drinking drys," moderate consumers of alcohol who viewed the scientific evidence as personally compelling and liquor control as a linchpin for many other important reforms. In retrospect, it appears obvious that drinking drys would find their position untenable if all alcohol were banned nationwide. But at the time, national prohibition had begun to speak directly to a widely shared progressive belief: changes in the social environment were crucial to improvements in the wellbeing of individual lives.

Liquor manufacturers, for their part, remained almost unbelievably obtuse. "For the first time in American business history," writes historian K. Austin Kerr, "two sizeable industries faced extinction, without any financial compensation, as a result of the deliberate efforts of a reform movement." Yet brewers (beer makers) and distillers

Anti-prohibition forces tried to counter the barrage of publicity from reformers who wanted to outlaw alcohol. This billboard claims that President Wilson and former presidents Taft and Roosevelt all oppose prohibition. *(Library of Congress, Prints and Photographs Division, LC-USZ62-95933)*

(liquor manufacturers) refused to abandon their long-standing mutual hostility and rivalry to cooperate effectively. Brewers clung to their belief that beer would be exempted from any national prohibition, while distillers mounted a half-hearted campaign to substitute a governmental regulating agency.[25]

IMPORTANT CHANGES IN THE WOMEN'S SUFFRAGE MOVEMENT

As 1913 opened, women had full suffrage in nine states. All were western states, none were of crucial political importance on the national scene, and together they represented only 45 of the 531 electoral votes cast in the 1912 presidential election. Many long-time suffragists were beginning to turn a critical eye on state-by-state campaigns. The National American Woman Suffrage Association (NAWSA) seemed increasingly disorganized and lacking in a clear, overall strategy nationwide.

By the time Woodrow Wilson took office in March, however, the suffrage movement was in the throes of a transformation. Alice Paul, a young activist who had recently returned from several years' work with militant suffragists in England, wanted to renew the drive for a women's suffrage amendment to the U.S. Constitution. Although NAWSA had worked primarily for state-level suffrage since 1890, some support for a constitutional amendment had long existed. The Susan B. Anthony amendment (as it came to be called after the great suffrage leader) was first introduced into Congress in 1878 and had even been brought to an unsuccessful vote in 1887. Although the amendment was reintroduced in Congress every year, since 1896 it had not been reported out of committee for full congressional debate.

NAWSA agreed to appoint Paul as head of its nearly inactive Congressional Committee. In January 1913, she set up shop in Washington. Along with associates like reformer and lawyer Crystal Eastman and historian Mary Beard, Paul began organizing a suffrage parade for March 3—the day before Woodrow Wilson was to be inaugurated. Wilson arrived in the city on the day of the parade to almost no popular reception at the railroad station because half a million people were watching more than 5,000 women, three heralds, nine bands, four mounted brigades, and some 20 floats attempt to make their way down Pennsylvania Avenue. (One of the heralds was Nellie Bly, the pioneering stunt reporter who had gone around the world in 1890. Black activist Ida B. Wells Barnett also marched—and refused to be sent to the back of the line to satisfy the wishes of some white delegations.) Unfortunately, the parade route was not adequately policed. A hostile crowd impeded progress from the beginning—spitting, catcalling, striking marchers, and hurling lighted cigar butts, for example—and at times degenerated into near-riot. The secretary of war finally called in a cavalry unit from a nearby fort to restore order. The women determinedly finished the march, although there were many injuries. The nationwide publicity galvanized many suffrage supporters. Said the *Women's Journal,* "Washington has been disgraced. Equal suffrage has scored a great victory. Thousands of indifferent women have been aroused. Influential men are incensed and the United States Senate demands an investigation."[26] The congressional investigation resulted in the dismissal of the police chief.

The following month, Paul and her associates formed a separate lobbying organization called the Congressional Union to work aggressively for quick passage of a women's suffrage amendment. It quickly attracted much support. Although Paul originally intended the Union to function as an arm of NAWSA, serious differences quickly became obvious. Following English precedent, Paul's group intended to work actively against the party in power—that is, against all Democrats regardless of any individual candidate's position on suffrage. NAWSA, on the other hand, had always treated suffrage as a nonpartisan issue. NAWSA leaders had observed that suffrage legislation always required cross-party coalitions—and a constitutional amendment would require a two-thirds majority in each house of Congress as well as approval by legislatures in three-quarters of the states. After February 1914 the two organizations split, not entirely on cordial terms. The flourishing union began to move increasingly in the direction of dramatic action and pressure politics; NASWA continued to insist upon "gentility, persuasion, and tact."[27]

Meanwhile, state suffrage organizations continued to work actively. In 1913, Illinois women won a new kind of partial suffrage. The governor had refused to call a referendum, necessary for amending the state constitution to allow women to vote. Instead, the Illinois Equal Suffrage Association and the Illinois Progressive Party successfully lobbied the state legislature to grant voting rights in presidential elections—based on an article in the U.S. Constitution that gives state legislatures oversight of the presidential electoral vote.[28] Although the Illinois law was not full suffrage, the populous state controlled 29 electoral votes and activists were gratified by the outcome.

Each state victory, however, awakened stronger antisuffrage forces elsewhere. In 1914, women waged arduous, expensive, and unsuccessful campaigns in North and South Dakota, Nebraska, Missouri, and Ohio (where a campaign had also failed in 1910). Campaigns in Montana and Nevada did succeed, making them the 10th and 11th states to give women full suffrage. But both were small states with little national clout.

Meanwhile, Alice Paul's single-minded ability to inspire women to accomplish the impossible was becoming legendary. The Congressional Union kept a national suffrage amendment constantly before the eyes of the president and Washington. In early 1914, the union succeeded in its goal to bring the suffrage amendment to the floor of the Senate for the first time since 1896, and a year later to the floor of the House, although it was defeated in both.

REFORMERS AND IMMIGRANTS

Interest was growing in programs to aid immigrants, and especially to Americanize them, or help them adapt to American civic and political culture and ways of life. Originally, the Americanization movement grew from the same soil as many other progressive social reform movements. The first reference to immigrant aid in a national political platform, that of the Progressive Party in 1912, for example, decried the "fatal policy of indifference and neglect which has left our enormous immigrant population to become the prey of chance and cupidity."[29] Most of the early Americanizers not only sought to provide aid and protect the immigrant from exploitation but also to foster tolerance and reduce bigotry on the part of the native born.

Two large organizations had been founded to promote immigrant welfare, the North American Civic League for Immigrants (NACL) in the East and the Immigrant Protective League in Chicago. Between 1910 and 1915, they helped convince states with large immigrant populations to investigate the immigrants' situation and establish bureaus to aid them. New York established the first state bureau in 1910; New Jersey, Massachusetts, California, and Pennsylvania followed. In Chicago, a federal bureau was established to coordinate the activities of various immigrant agencies and provide inspectors and matrons at railroad stations. These commissions and bureaus generally focused on four similar concerns: oversight of transportation to protect newly arriving immigrants from various kinds of swindles and crime; reform and regulation of housing, sanitation, and similar issues in immigrant neighborhoods, generally referred to as "establishing American standards of living;" distribution, or efforts to encourage immigrants to leave congested cities and spread out to areas with labor needs and job opportunities; and educational services, especially evening schools for adults in English, literacy, and civics. It was, asserted the New York bureau in its first annual report, "no longer an individual matter, but a community matter. . . . to assure the alien a fair start and a safe road to travel."[30]

Reformers who championed programs for immigrants were, like all progressives, also concerned with the democratic health of the nation. Many recent immigrants had little experience with democracy. Some, because of unhappy encounters in the Old World, brought with them a distrust of government officials, institutions, courts, and legal systems. On top of that, many met poor treatment at the hands of American employers. NACL founders believed that democracy could not survive if established Americans—especially industrialists and other businessmen awash in a sea of profit maximizing—remained apathetic to the immigrants' plight. The national NACL targeted eastern industrialists and philanthropists and was successful at convincing them to contribute large sums to immigrant aid programs. They appealed to industrialists' fear of labor turmoil and radicalism, which many accredited to their employees' ignorance of American values rather than to working conditions and wages.

In 1914, the New York–New Jersey Committee (or affiliate) of the NACL changed its name to the Committee for Immigrants in America and reinvented itself as a national lobbying organization. Headed by Frances Kellor, a lawyer, former settlement worker, and head of the New York immigrant bureau, it was soon regarded as the headquarters for the Americanization movement throughout the nation. The committee immediately set about to convince Secretary of the Interior Franklin K. Lane that the federal government should assume some responsibility for the education of immigrants. He agreed to establish a Division of Immigrant Education in the Federal Bureau of Education (an agency within the interior department). For the five years the division operated, providing information and sponsoring programs throughout the nation, it was actually funded and staffed by the NACL.

HENRY FORD, THE ASSEMBLY LINE, AND THE FIVE-DOLLAR DAY

When Henry Ford introduced his sturdy, reasonably priced Model T in 1908, the Tin Lizzie's immediate success with the American public created a demand that outstripped Ford's ability to produce it. To solve the problem, he hired managers to apply the techniques of scientific management to auto production. Based on their advice, Ford opened a large new factory at Highland Park, Michigan. It was designed to speed up production by rearranging the workflow and creating a minute division of labor, in part by use of a moving assembly line. Ford did not invent the assembly line—he claimed to have been inspired by observing its use in a meat packing plant—but over the next three years at Highland Park he perfected it. In doing so he revolutionized modern mass production.

Previously, Ford workers assembled one car at a time, retrieving each part from its storage place as need. Ford first installed gravity slides to move parts of cars from one work group to the next. Soon he was using an increasingly complete system of chain-driven, constantly moving conveyor belts. Along different belts workers stood in place and did small, discrete tasks to assemble ever larger parts of autos; eventually the parts met up through exact timing at a larger line where they were attached to a chassis. In 1908, it had taken 728 minutes, or more than 12 hours, to assemble a Model T. By January 1914, when Ford announced the completion of the assembly line, it took 93 minutes, or an hour and a half, from start to finish. By the end of 1914, 600 Model Ts a day were rolling off the assembly line. By the end of 1916, the price of the car, which in 1908 had cost $850, had fallen to $360. Other automobile manufacturers soon began to adopt Ford's methods as well. In 1910, a total of 187,000 automobiles and trucks were manufactured and sold in America, in 1915, 970,000, and in 1920, 2,227,000. In 1900, there were 8,000 registered autos in the United States, in 1910, there were 458,000, by 1915, there were 2.3 million, and by 1920, more than 8 million, plus another 1 million trucks and busses.[31]

This miracle in production technology had a price, however. Workers hated the monotonous, small repetitive tasks that the assembly line and scientific management had introduced. A worker might, for example, spend all of each and every workday tightening bolt number 10 on part number 32. Assembly line work demoted many skilled workers, ended their authority over how to accomplish their work, and robbed them of their traditional pride of craftsmanship. "They have cheapened products," wrote a social gospel minister, "but they have also cheapened the producers."[32]

The new methods created so much resistance among workers that by 1913 Ford's turnover rate was 380 percent. To solve the problem he made an astounding decision. In January 1914, when he announced the completion of the assembly line, he also announced that he was more than doubling the wages at his factory, from an average $2.34 to five dollars a day. At the same time, Ford also cut the workday from nine to eight hours and created three successive eight-hour shifts to keep the factory operating constantly round-the-clock. Ford's announcement made front-page headlines coast to coast. So many workers flocked to his factory and lined up at the doors to apply for jobs—10,000 the first day alone—that riots sometimes broke out. The news was also stunning to reform-minded people deeply concerned about workers' inadequate wages and long hours. Overnight, Ford became an international celebrity and a folk hero. The business world, however, was considerably less pleased. The Five-Dollar Day outraged Ford's fellow manufacturers and scandalized conservatives, who feared it would lead to increased demands from labor and turmoil throughout the nation. At the time, steel workers earned an average of $1.75 a day and coal miners $2.50.[33]

Ford had sound business reasons for what he did. The cost reductions created by the assembly line made the five-dollar day possible, while the pay increase immediately solved the turnover problem and inspired workers to boost their output. "The five dollar day was the greatest cost-cutting move I ever made," Ford later wrote. But Ford had a larger goal as well. Other manufacturers traditionally paid their workers as small a wage as possible to keep their costs low and (as they thought) their profits high. Ford, however, believed that if workers received more of the profits they helped to create, the market for his cars would expand even further. Put simply, he wanted workers to become prosperous consumers and to buy Ford cars. Time would prove his approach to be sound, and by 1916, the profits of the Ford Motor Company were double the 1914 figure. Ford, already "considered 'the best friend the working man ever had' for developing the Model T," writes historian Douglas Brinkley, "suddenly became more than a captain of industry; he was elevated into a social philosopher."[34]

Ford also saw the Five-Dollar Day as a kind of force for social reform, which he believed could be achieved by a paternalistic employer-worker relationship. One-half of the five-dollar wage could be withheld if the worker's lifestyle and behavior did not meet the expectations of the company. Ford established a Sociological Department to investigate and aid workers whose families fell short of what he believed to be the American standard of living. By 1916, the qualities that Ford believed led to a responsible life and good work habits were set down in a written set of instructions. The Sociological Department also oversaw English language and Americanization classes for workers who were immigrants, operated what today would be called a credit union to help families purchase homes, and provided marriage counseling. Some workers doubtless found Fordism intrusive in the extreme. "It was kind of a funny idea in a free state," one worker commented later.[35]

In 1913, Henry Ford began to use the moving assembly line in automobile manufacture—and doubled his workers' wages at the same time. Soon more and more reasonably priced Model Ts were rolling off the line, and automobiles began to multiply in America. *(Library of Congress, Prints and Photographs Division, LC-USZ62-63968)*

But others took advantage of the programs and even embraced the opportunity to achieve some upward mobility. In any case, Ford's Sociological Department did not outlast the Progressive Era and was dismantled in 1920.

THE COMMISSION ON INDUSTRIAL RELATIONS

In 1913, the Commission on Industrial Relations, authorized under Taft, began its study to determine the causes of labor unrest and violence between workers and employers. The commission had members from labor, industry, and the public and was chaired by Frank P. Walsh, a lawyer from Missouri with good standing in the Democratic Party and the national reform community. For two years, the commission held hearings across the country. Walsh took testimony from 740 witnesses, representing a remarkable variety of people with equally divergent social and economic points of view. His examination of powerful industrial and financial figures like John D. Rockefeller, Jr., J. P. Morgan, and Andrew Carnegie riveted the public. But the affable chairman permitted all witnesses, from Rockefeller to "Big Bill" Haywood to immigrant workers, to speak openly.

The report of the commission, published in 1915, ran to 11 volumes. It demonstrated once again that a few powerful men controlled the largest corporations, and that furthermore they had a startling lack of knowledge or even interest in the conditions of labor. It revealed, with abundant documentation, employers' determination to prevent workers from organizing unions, the almost feudal control some employers exercised over their workers, the brutal treatment of strikers at the hands of hired police and colluding local officials, and the resulting growth of class consciousness among workers—all of which dismayed the reform-minded American public. The enormous gap in power between concentrated wealth and workers, the commission concluded, lay behind continuing worker-employer violence. The commission made specific recommendations, such as government protection for workers' freedom of speech. But it also urged such fundamental economic reforms as inheritance tax, new land policies, and federal chartering of philanthropic foundations which it concluded were extending the reach of wealthy industrialists. None of these recommendations was taken up by the Wilson administration or enacted by Congress. Nonetheless, in a more general sense, the searchlight the Commission on Industrial Relations turned on industrial conditions helped created a more favorable environment for labor reform.

VIOLENCE CONTINUES BETWEEN LABOR AND EMPLOYERS

While the commission was at work, violence between employers and wage earners did not cease. The industrial commission unexpectedly found itself hearing testimony on the most infamous confrontation between labor and capital during the Progressive Era, the so-called Ludlow massacre, which took place in April 1914. In September 1913, Colorado coal miners struck the Rockefeller-owned Colorado Fuel and Iron Company (CF&I) and other companies, all of whom refused to deal with unions. The United Mine Workers (UMW) established tent colonies for the miners evicted from company housing and the companies hired a large force of private detectives, guards who were deputized by the local government, and strikebreakers. CF&I head Lamont Bowers wrote to John D. Rockefeller, Jr., "Our net earnings would have been the largest in the history of the company by $200,000 but for the increase in wages paid the employees during the last few months. With everything running so smoothly and with an excellent outlook for 1914, it is mighty discouraging to have this vicious gang [the UMW] come into our state and not only destroy our profit but eat into that which has heretofore been saved."[36]

The ensuing strike lasted for months and spawned continuing sporadic violence. It climaxed on April 20. During a 14-hour battle with the miners, the state militia burned the tent colony at Ludlow to the ground. Among those killed were two women and 11 children who suffocated in a pit underneath one of the tents, where they had taken cover. Fighting raged for 10 days until the arrival of federal troops, who disarmed all sides and reestablished peace. Events at Ludlow were widely laid at the feet of John D. Rockefeller, Jr., and tarnished his philanthropic family's reputation in the eyes of the public. Rockefeller belatedly struggled to find a way to address the situation. Determined to avoid the settlement that President Wilson and Secretary of Labor William Wilson proposed, he engaged Canadian labor minster MacKenzie King (later prime minister) to develop a workable, nonunion solution. King designed a system of elected representatives among the miners to act on their behalf on wages, working conditions, and any other grievances or issues. It came to be called the Colorado Industrial Plan.

THE TAMPICO INCIDENT

Although President Wilson continued to resist pressure to intervene in Mexico's political turmoil, he had stationed American warships to patrol the Gulf of Mexico to prevent foreign arms shipments from reaching military dictator General Victoriano Huerta. In early 1914, Huertistas arrested some American sailors who had gone ashore in the city of Tampico, a center of oil production. Although the Americans were quickly released with an apology, the incident hatched a dispute between American and Mexican military officers over the exchange of salutes to their national flags. Wilson took the opportunity, or pretext, to authorize landing American forces in the nearby port of Veracruz, presumably to prevent the arrival of an ammunition ship from Germany, whose nationals had significant investments in Mexico. Perhaps naively, Wilson did not anticipate hostilities, but fighting broke out immediately. U.S. forces soon occupied Veracruz with the loss of 19 Americans and more than a hundred Mexicans.

In America, Wilson was criticized both by noninterventionists and by interventionists who believed America should apply the Roosevelt Corollary to the Monroe Doctrine and invade full force. In Mexico Huerta's foes united—not against him but in strong opposition to the American occupation. The Constitutionalists threatened to resist further American aggression and the dictator Huerta momentarily appeared as the defender of Mexican nationhood.

To contain the fiasco, Wilson accepted an offer of arbitration from Argentina, Brazil, and Chile, called the ABC powers. They recommended that American troops withdraw and that Huerta resign. In the face of growing pressure Huerta finally abdicated in July 1914. Carranza then set up a provisional capital in Veracruz, where American military forces (who did not withdraw immediately) were at work cleaning and introducing sanitation, as they had done in Panama.

SARAJEVO: THE LAMPS GO OUT IN EUROPE

On June 28, 1914, a Serbian terrorist and nationalist named Gavrilo Princip assassinated Archduke Franz Ferdinand, heir to the throne of Austria-Hungary, and his wife, Sophie. The event occurred in Sarajevo, capital of Bosnia, which the Austrians had recently occupied and annexed. Austria, in consultation with its ally Germany, made great retaliatory demands on Serbia. Serbia requested aid from Russia. Russia was allied with France. France, like Germany, was involved in layers of alliances that had long marked European diplomacy. By August 3, when Germany declared war on France, most of Europe was plunging into war.

Since the turn of the 20th century, the United States had played a newly powerful role in world affairs, even accumulating a small empire of dependencies. But the nation still followed its tradition of avoiding, as George Washington put it, "entangling alliances" in Europe. It had not joined in any of the diplomatic understandings that connected European nations into two competing but relatively balanced coalitions. On August 4, President Wilson firmly declared the United States a neutral nation. Two days later the president suffered a personal tragedy when First Lady Ellen Axson Wilson died. But within two weeks he returned to public life to address Congress and the American people. He urged Americans to be "neutral in fact as well as in name in these days that are to try men's souls, . . . impartial in thought as well as action." Both the president and Secretary of State William Jennings Bryan hoped not only to maintain neutrality but to serve as peacemakers for the nations at war. Both saw a special role for America as a mediating nation. "We must face the situation," Wilson wrote in a private letter to his adviser Edward House, "in the confidence that Providence has deeper plans than we could possibly have laid ourselves."[37]

For two decades, European nations had conducted what today is called an arms race, while also competing for markets and territory and encouraging nationalistic fervor. Perhaps, Bryan suggested hopefully, when war broke out, the world simply needed "one more awful object lesson to prove conclusively the fallacy of the doctrine that preparedness for war can give assurance for peace."[38] Meanwhile, in the ethnically and linguistically diverse empires of Austria-Hungary, Russia, and Turkey (the Ottoman Empire), ethnic antagonisms and oppressions had created a nationalistic fervor of their own—movements among small ethnic groups for rights or their own nation-states. In the Balkan Peninsula (a region in southeastern Europe surrounded by the Adriatic, Aegean, and Black Seas), these movements were so numerous and so powerful that the region was called "the powderkeg of Europe."

Britain (which had the strongest navy in the world and was the most powerful commercial and colonial nation at the time) joined France, Italy, Russia, Rumania, and Japan to form the Allied Powers or Allies. Germany (which had the strongest army and ambitions to equal Britain in other ways), Austria-Hungary, Bulgaria, and Turkey formed the Central Powers. Germany intended to take the offensive by quickly moving west through Belgium to France, capturing Paris, then turning its attention east to Russia. But the Belgians resisted, and soon the Allied and Central armies had fallen into two lines along the western front, a 475-mile-long line through France extending from the coast of the English Channel in the Netherlands to the Alps in Switzerland. Each dug networks of trenches and faced each other to a stalemate across a field of battle strewn with coils of barbed wire—even as war spread to Asia, Africa, and the South Seas.

"WAGING NEUTRALITY"

On the eve of the Great War, as it was usually called—people also used the term *World War* but were, of course, unaware that it was only the first—most Americans believed such a conflagration was impossible. Many held the popular progressive belief that "civilized" nations could solve international disputes peacefully through negotiation. Many progressive thinkers even considered war to be "unscientific" and obsolete. But war spread with lightning quickness, and in the first month of fighting more than half a million men died. Americans' first reaction was shock. Their second was a conviction that the United States did not have truly vital interests at stake, and their third, that the oceans protected them from involvement they did not desire and foreclosed any need for extensive military build-up.

Yet for both the nation's leaders and its people, it did not prove easy to "wage neutrality."[39] Some Americans, including prominent progressive reformers, joined peace movements almost immediately. By August 19, Lillian Wald led a peace parade in New York of 1,200 social workers and soon became president of the newly founded

American Union Against Militarism. By January 1915, Carrie Chapman Catt helped organize the Women's Peace Party to speak for "the mother half of Humanity" and "to substitute Law for War." Jane Addams accepted the presidency and the organization soon had 25,000 members.[40] Just as quickly, other Americans volunteered to take part in the war effort. Some 10,000 young men, many of them from prominent families, attended volunteer summer officer training camps (called the Plattsburg movement) established by Chief of Staff Leonard Wood.[41] Others, including the future novelists Ernest Hemingway and John Dos Passos, volunteered for ambulance units where they drove sturdy Ford Model Ts donated by wealthy Americans. Some recent immigrants returned to their homelands to join the struggle. Women trained as nurses joined the Red Cross or other medical services in Europe. Celebrated novelist Edith Wharton, living in Paris at the time, founded the Children of Flanders Rescue Committee to care for children found in devastated Belgium and later France. In 1916 France made her Chevalier of the Legion of Honor for her work, its highest civilian honor.

President Wilson and Secretary of State Bryan also faced increasing difficulties in waging neutrality. The outbreak of war was quickly reflected in the American stock exchange, which Wilson closed on July 31, 1914—it remained closed until December 12—to prevent panicked disposal of European securities. The war immediately interrupted trade, an economic downturn quickly followed, and unemployment rose. The price of cotton and other agricultural products dropped, and tariff revenues to the U.S. Treasury declined. Traditionally, neutral nations loaned freely to combatant nations during wartime, but at first the Wilson administration banned loans to any nations at war. Bryan believed that "Money is the worst of all contrabands because it commands everything else," and Wilson agreed that a ban on loans would help end the war quickly.[42] But because the Allied nations had previously conducted far more trade with the United States than did the Central Powers, the policy did not in fact operate in a neutral way. It clearly hurt the Allies more, and by October 1914 the administration had begun to modify the no-loan policy.

From the beginning, the majority of Americans probably favored the Allies. The nation was tied to Britain by language and by political tradition. Belgium's valiant but costly resistance had earned great admiration and the atrocities inflicted by the Germans generated public outrage. As for Allied France, every American schoolchild knew that the French had aided the Patriots during the American Revolution and more recently had presented America with its increasingly beloved symbol, the Statue of Liberty. However, there were exceptions and limitations to Americans' support for the Allies. Many Irish Americans vowed to work against Britain's cause, and Jewish Americans had little sympathy for Allied Russia, the seat of state-approved anti-Semitic violence in recent years. In addition, many Americans had a far more favorable view of Germany in 1914 than might be assumed today in the light of later 20th-century history. Many immigrants had arrived from Germany since 1870, when it officially became a unified nation, and were sympathetic to their homeland. Many other Americans considered Germany the center of European intellectual culture. German universities were the most advanced in the world, and many American scholars and physicians had been trained there. Reformers also admired Germany for its pioneering social reforms and social planning.

IMMIGRATION SLOWS AS THE WAR BEGINS

Largely under pressure from a deteriorating political situation in Europe, more than a million immigrants arrived in America in both 1913 and 1914. As war began to spread throughout Europe after August 1914, however, immigration declined drastically. In both 1915 and 1916 only about 300,000 people arrived. In addition, many recent male immigrants returned to Europe to see to their families or to support the war effort in

More than a million immigrants entered the United States in both 1913 and 1914, but not all of them came from Europe. Many emigrated from Mexico to escape the turmoil of the Mexican Revolution. This man is crossing from Nuevo Laredo, Mexico, into Laredo, Texas. *(Library of Congress, Prints and Photographs Division, LC-USZ62-97491)*

their country of origin, so net immigration (arrivals minus returnees) was considerably lower. One group that made continuing efforts to seek asylum in America and Canada were Armenians. In 1915, the small subject nation was subjected to the third and worst wave of genocidal massacres inflicted by the Ottoman Empire Turks since the 1890s. In addition, in the American Southwest arrivals from Mexico also increased as the Mexican Revolution continued.

In early 1913, with immigration apparently on the rise and restrictionist sentiment growing, Congress again passed a literacy test bill. Before leaving office in March, President Taft vetoed it. In early 1914, the House resurrected the literacy test bill. The Senate delayed acting on the divisive issue until after the November 1914 midterm elections. By that time the war had interrupted trade and unemployment was rising. The Senate quickly passed the bill. In January 1915, it was sent to President Wilson.

President Wilson had already indicated to congressional leaders that he could not support a literacy test. For one thing, he had courted immigrant groups with promises of liberal immigration policies during the 1912 presidential campaign. But he also objected on the basis of democratic and humanitarian principles because the bill made no exemption for refugees from political oppression. The issue was a special concern for Jewish groups and others concerned about the worsening persecution of Jews in Russia, and they had lobbied hard but unsuccessfully for an exemption for refugees. Wilson followed the example of Presidents Cleveland and Taft and vetoed the literacy test bill. Although his predecessors had primarily stressed economic issues like the need for labor, however, President Wilson's veto message stressed American ideals. The bill, he wrote, closed the "gates of asylum" and excluded those who had been denied opportunity, "without regard to their character, their purposes, or their natural capacity." Congress attempted to override his veto but failed by four votes.[43]

A LANDMARK MOVIE, BLACK PROTEST, AND MOVIE CENSORSHIP

On February 8, 1915, director D. W. Griffith's highly anticipated epic film spectacle *The Birth of a Nation* premiered in Los Angeles.[44] Its subject was the Civil War and the war's aftermath in the South. The silent movie was an unprecedented three hours long, had the largest cast and budget to date, and cost an astonishing $2.00 admission in some places. It contained scenes of exceptional artistry and introduced the moviegoing audience to pathbreaking camera and editing methods such as cross-cutting and long-distance panoramic shots. *The Birth of a Nation* remains a landmark in cinematic technique. It quickly became the most financially successful film to date, attracting record-breaking crowds coast to coast. Unfortunately it also remains a landmark of demeaning portrayals of African Americans.

The film was based on novels by Thomas Dixon, *The Leopard's Spots* and *The Clansman* (the latter was also a Broadway play in 1906). The white southern families at its center suffer continuing indignities at the hands both of evil, cunning northern whites and of southern blacks, most of whom are depicted as ignorant, vicious, lazy, and sexually predatory. Against this backdrop, the Ku Klux Klan rises heroically and, at the end, in one of the most cinematically successful scenes of the movie, literally rides to the rescue of threatened whites. When the film opened in New York, it was accompanied by actors dressed in Klan regalia riding through city streets, as a publicity stunt. But during the summer of 1915, a group in Georgia, inspired by the film, reorganized the real Ku Klux Klan, which had originally flourished during the Reconstruction Era (and which as it gained strength over the following decade would oppose aliens, Jews, and Catholics as well as blacks). When *The Birth of a Nation* opened in Atlanta the following November, thousands of real Klansmen paraded through the streets.

Even before the film opened nationwide, the NAACP and prominent white reformers began protests. "Singing marchers, well-dressed pickets, drums of printers' ink, and court injunctions accompanied the film in its circuit of openings," writes David Levering Lewis.[45] Protesters objected to the degrading caricatures but also feared that the film would inflame further racial violence. In New York, the National Board of Review of Motion Pictures, the voluntary censorship body whose decisions many film producers agreed to honor, required deletion of a few scenes deemed particularly offensive. In Boston and Chicago, vigorous campaigns led to temporary bans and cuts in the movie and a few cities elsewhere blocked its opening.

Many progressives and even some officials of the NAACP, however, were divided over the important question of censorship. On one hand, prominent progressive Frederic Howe resigned as chair of the National Board of Review because he thought the majority had been too lenient in the cuts they required. Booker T. Washington, on the other hand, came down on the side of freedom of speech. W. E. B. DuBois wrote in *The Crisis,* the NAACP-sponsored journal that he edited, "We are aware now and then that it is dangerous to limit expression, and yet without some limitations civilization could not endure."[46] The NAACP campaign against *The Birth of a Nation* had mixed results. It failed to convince the general public that the movie was pernicious and in fact generated much free publicity for it. But the campaign was the most publicly visible effort to date by the six-year-old civil rights organization and it mobilized many new supporters. It also spurred production of the first films by black filmmakers, some funded by philanthropists, although their work remained little known outside the black community.

The firestorm over *The Birth of a Nation* brought the question of movie censorship into the national spotlight. By 1913 three states, Ohio, Kansas, and Pennsylvania, had established boards of censorship to preview and license acceptable films before they could be opened in the state. Many cities and towns elsewhere licensed locally because they considered the standards of New York's National Board of Review too liberal. But immediately after Griffith's movie opened in February, a bill was introduced into Congress to set up a Federal Motion Picture Commission in the Department of the Interior to license all films transmitted by interstate commerce—and intercept any film that was "obscene, indecent, immoral, inhuman, or depicts a bull fight or a prize fight, or is of such a character that its exhibition would tend to impair the health or corrupt the morals of children or adults or incite to crime."[47] The bill was defeated although it was reintroduced many times in subsequent years.

By the end of February, however, an important Supreme Court decision upheld the legality of state movie censorship and officially denied First Amendment or free speech protection to movies. *Mutual Film Corporation v. Industrial Commission of Ohio* had been brought by a Detroit distributing company to challenge Ohio's state censorship law. In a unanimous decision, the court held that the movies were entertainment, not vehicles of ideas, and therefore not protected speech. Wrote Justice Joseph McKenna, "the exhibition of moving pictures is a business, pure and simple, originated and conducted for profit, like other spectacles, not to be regarded. . . . as part of the press of the country, or as organs of public opinion."[48] The *Mutual Film* decision stood for 37 years. The court did not specifically include entertainment materials of any kind under protected speech until 1946 and did not overturn its 1915 decision on movie censorship (or even hear another movie censorship case) until 1952.[49]

NEUTRAL RIGHTS ON THE HIGH SEAS

Traditionally, according to international law and to conventions of warfare dating from the 19th century, during wartime the rights of a neutral nation such as the United States also included freedom of the seas; that is, neutral ships could travel to and trade with all warring nations. Wilson insisted upon that right for the United States, but by 1915 it had begun to cause conflict with both the Allied and the Central Powers. As the Great War intensified, European strategists discovered the 19th century conventions were mismatched to 20th-century technology and international trade. Britain mined the North Sea, forced neutral ships to go through the Straits of Dover for inspection, and instituted a blockade of Central-Power ports. On February 2, 1915, Germany declared a submarine blockade of the British Isles and warned that even enemy merchant ships were vulnerable to attack. Traditional rules of naval engagement required warning before striking. But German submarines, called U-boats (from the German *Unterseeboot*), could be easily destroyed if they surfaced. Therefore, U-boats relied on the advantage of surprise and began to attack from below without notice.

President Wilson protested against Britain's naval strategies but condemned Germany's submarine warfare much more strongly. On February 10, 1915, the president issued a warning that the United States would hold Germany to "strict accountability." The nation would, he continued, "safeguard American lives and property and secure to American citizens the full enjoyment of their acknowledged rights on the high seas."[50]

On May 7, 1915, a German U-boat torpedoed and sank the unarmed British luxury liner *Lusitania* off the coast of Ireland. Among the 1,198 passengers who lost their lives were many women and children and 128 Americans. Newspapers coast to coast denounced the act, some calling for a declaration of war. Germany correctly claimed that the ship was also carrying munitions, and Secretary of State Bryan urged President Wilson to consider that fact in his response. He also urged the president to forbid Americans from further travel on ships of any of the nations at war. The president refused to issue a prohibition on travel and prepared a strong protest demanding that Germany end unrestricted submarine warfare. When Germany did not make a satisfactory response, he wrote an even stronger message dated June 9. The United States, he said, was "contending for nothing less high and sacred than the rights of humanity."[51] Bryan, who feared the note was close to a declaration of war, resigned as secretary of state rather than sign it. His replacement, Robert Lansing, was far less invested in restraint, neutrality, and negotiation.

FROM NEUTRALITY TO PREPAREDNESS

By the time the *Lusitania* incident occurred, prominent spokesmen like Theodore Roosevelt, Elihu Root, and Senator Henry Cabot Lodge had been lobbying for military build-up for half a year. In December 1914, they joined other prominent easterners to form the National Security League, which undertook an energetic publicity campaign for preparedness. The league was strictly nonpartisan, however, and in August 1915 a group of Republicans followed Roosevelt to form the American Defense Society, aimed at pointedly attacking the neutral policies of the Democratic Wilson administration. In fact, Wilson had already instructed the naval department and the war department (which oversaw the army) to draft proposals for preparedness during the summer of 1915. In his annual message that December, he told Congress that budget requests would be forthcoming.

Although the *Lusitania* incident increased the support for military preparedness among many Americans, there remained significant antiwar sentiment in America. Many Americans strongly disapproved of a large military establishment when the nation was not at war, just as they had since the colonial era. Many congressional representatives of the rural South and West remained adamant that eastern industrialists saw easy profits in warmongering. Congressional progressives like Robert La Follette opposed preparedness. Many prominent reformers were pacifists. In New York, the League to Limit Armaments formed. Henry Ford set sail for Norway on his Peace Ship to attempt to find a solution.

But neutrality was becoming harder and harder to maintain. The British blockade was successful in reducing America's trade with the Central Powers, which had declined to little more than $1 million by 1916 while exports to Allied powers grew to $3.2 billion.[52] In October 1915, the U.S. ban on loans to warring powers was quietly abandoned to the benefit of the Allies. By the end of the year, Britain and France had obtained a loan of $500 million. Meanwhile, Germany continued submarine warfare and in March 1916, sank an unarmed French steamer, the *Sussex*. Several Americans were injured. Wilson warned Germany that continued unrestricted submarine warfare would lead to the severing of diplomatic relations (an act usually considered a prelude to war). In response Germany offered the *Sussex* Pledge, an agreement to cease striking merchant vessels without warning if the United States would also intervene with the Allies to obey international law on the high seas. Wilson accepted the pledge but little change occurred in British activities.

PREPARING THE MILITARY FOR WAR—AND PAYING FOR IT WITH MORE INCOME TAX

When plans for enlarging the military reached Congress in the spring of 1916, they included a proposal for a large, voluntary, army reserve force to be called the Continental Army. Unlike the state National Guard units, it was to be wholly under control of the professional, national military establishment. The plan met considerable opposition, and Secretary of War Lindley Garrison resigned in the face of it. He was replaced by the prominent progressive mayor of Cleveland, Newton Baker.

Under the compromise reached in the National Defense Act of June 3, the regular army was expanded from 90,000 to 175,000, with an increase to 223,000 permitted in case of war. The act enlarged the state units of the National Guard to 40,000 and provided funds for their training. It also established a reserve corps for officers and enlisted men and the Reserve Officers Training Corps, or ROTC.[53] Expansion of the navy proved less controversial in Congress. A Naval Construction Act authorized a three-year program to build 76 battleships, cruisers, or destroyers and 72 submarines. Congress also created a National Shipping Board to built or retrofit merchant ships to be used as backups. In August, the Army Appropriations Act established a Council of National Defense, composed of the secretaries of war, the navy, interior, agriculture, commerce, and labor, with a separate civilian advisory board to oversee the economic planning for a possible war effort. The Council of National Defense soon established a multiplicity of boards and bureaus while the advisory board established more than 150 subcommittees for different industries.

Progressive congressmen and Democrats representing agricultural interests in the South and West agreed to compromise on military preparedness—but they had an important condition. They wanted the bills to be paid by affluent Americans rather than farmers and working people. In the Revenue Act of 1916 they doubled the basic income tax rate from 1 to 2 percent, raised the marginal tax to an additional 13 percent on incomes exceeding $2 million, added a 12.5 percent tax on the gross income of munitions makers, a graduated estate tax, and various corporate income taxes. The personal income tax still applied only to a tiny minority of Americans, those with incomes of more than $4,000, a figure many times the average income of U.S. wage earners.

AMERICANIZATION INITIATIVES BECOME A PUBLIC CRUSADE

Had the world remained at peace, the history of the Americanization movement might well have been very different. As late as 1914 it was of interest primarily to professional social workers, educators, philanthropists, and private organizations offering practical aid to immigrants—but it was not a public crusade. But by 1915, it began to attract public enthusiasm—and also underwent a quick change in emphasis to become more coercive. As "civilized" nations and peoples continued to slaughter each other throughout Europe, established Americans began to fear that such animosities might have counterparts among large groups of recent immigrants. Were they willing to give up their Old World hatreds? In case of war, would their first loyalty be to America or to their country of origin? Many Americans began to think that it was imperative to insist that immigrants abandon their separate languages and customs, leave their ethnic enclaves, integrate into the larger society, and most of all declare their intentions by becoming citizens.

By 1915, there was a noticeable increase in public efforts to encourage immigrants to become U.S. citizens. The Federal Bureau of Naturalization sponsored a standard nationwide course of classes to be offered by the public schools. To help publicize the issue, the bureau persuaded the mayor of Philadelphia to hold a public ceremony for new citizens on May 10. President Wilson himself agreed to speak. "You have dreamed dreams of what America was to be, and I hope you have brought the dreams with you," he told the large crowd. "No man who does not see high visions will ever realize any high hope. . . . You are enriching us if you came expecting us to be better than we are." The event was very successful. The Committee for Immigrants in America decided to organize Americanization Day on July 4, when similar celebrations could be held throughout the nation. A National Americanization Committee of civic, religious, and philanthropic leaders was formed to oversee the event, and some 150 cities participated. Indianapolis, for example, featured speeches in 11 different languages, all given by new citizens on the responsibilities of citizenship. Reported *The Survey,* "Emphasis in almost every city celebration was laid on the fact that while European nations were locked in deadly combat, the sons of these same nations in America through common interests and loyalties could live in peaceful neighborliness."[54]

The National Americanization Committee (which continued to function until 1919) soon launched English First and America First campaigns to encourage immigrants to attend night school, learn English, and become citizens. They especially encouraged employers to join the effort. Some, like Henry Ford, established classes and compelled employees to attend. The National Chamber of Commerce and the National Association of Manufacturers (NAM) also took up what came to be called the industrial Americanization movement, promoting the job benefits of learning English. Even many labor union leaders, including Samuel Gompers, came to support the movement.

THE PUBLIC DEBATE OVER HYPHENATES

The Americanization movement was accompanied by active public interest in the long-standing (and still continuing) debate over national unity and its relationship to the historic diversity of the American people. Many leaders, including both Theodore Roosevelt and Woodrow Wilson, publicly chided immigrants who thought of themselves as hyphenated Americans, that is, as Irish Americans or Italian Americans, especially in terms of political loyalties. They doubtless spoke for many citizens. At least to some extent, many Americans accepted the idea that the United States was a melting pot (a term popularized by a 1908 play of the same name). They were optimistic that most people were capable of change and that most newcomers eventually blended into one large new culture in most significant matters.

Some people, however, did not embrace the metaphor of the melting pot, nor did everyone value giving up historic group identities. On the left of public opinion, some progressives and public intellectuals such as educational theorist John Dewey and philosopher Horace Kallen argued that American political unity did not require a single way of life and even that it was undemocratic to expect it. Kallen, who was himself a Jewish immigrant from Silesia, believed very different ethnic groups could live together in peace without abandoning their distinctive cultures, an idea for which he later coined the term *cultural pluralism*. On the right of public opinion were eugenicists (scientists who believed that desirable physical and mental qualities were not distributed evenly in human populations) and racialists (the term for a more popular belief that mental qualities were inborn and unchangeable and that some groups had far less desirable qualities than others). Eugenicists and racialists usually believed that people they variously called Anglo-Saxon, Teutonic, or Nordic were superior to other groups. In 1916 amateur anthropologist Madison Grant argued, in his popular and influential *The Passing of the Great Race,* that mixing America's nothern European peoples with the new immigrants from eastern and southern Europe would inevitably dilute American culture and spell ruin for its institutions.[55]

Most white Americans at the time (including recent immigrants themselves) viewed black Americans and Asian Americans through a racialist lens, regardless of how they thought about "hyphens" from European nations. Even advocates of pluralism rarely included African Americans or Asian Americans in their thinking during the Progressive Era. Native Americans were often in a special category. Many Americans romanticized Indian cultures of the past, although they believed their day had come and gone and modern Indians should be incorporated into mainstream ways of life.

THE CAMPAIGN FOR WOMEN'S SUFFRAGE AT A CROSSROADS

In the spring of 1915, Alice Paul's Congressional Union, having extended its campaign for a woman's suffrage amendment to all 48 states, sponsored a well-publicized San Francisco-to-Washington automobile pilgrimage. (Autos were still enough of a novelty to guarantee publicity, especially when driven by women.) Meanwhile, NAWSA activists mounted extensive and well-run campaigns in Pennsylvania, New York, New Jersey, and Massachusetts hoping to break the suffrage barrier in the populous, industrialized East. President Wilson, who declined to endorse national suffrage legislation, publicly announced his plans to travel to his home state of New Jersey to vote in favor of the state referendum on the issue. But liquor interests, political machines, antis (anti-suffrage women), and other opponents of votes for women also came out in full force. Suffrage lost in all four states.

The November 1915 defeats brought discontent to a head in NAWSA. Anna Howard Shaw, president since 1904, announced her retirement. An immediate movement began to draft Carrie Chapman Catt. She had successfully held the office from 1900 to 1904, organized the International Suffrage Alliance and the Women's Suffrage Party, and once again proven her organizational talents in the recent New York campaign. In 1914, she had also been the surprised recipient of a $2 million bequest from the recently deceased publisher Miriam Florence Follin Leslie, who had resuscitated and managed the bankrupt publishing empire of her late husband Frank Leslie after his death in 1880. Leslie's will instructed Catt to use the bequest "to the furtherance of the cause of woman suffrage."[56]

Catt resumed the presidency at the end of 1915 and almost overnight brought organizational coherence to NAWSA, extending from the local to the state to the

Wage-earning women increasingly supported the movement for women's suffrage. This photo shows Margaret Hinchey, head of a New York laundry workers' union, leading a group in a 1914 suffrage parade. *(Library of Congress, Prints and Photographs Division, LC-USZ62-29287)*

national level. Her presidency marked a turning point. Catt hand-picked a board of financially independent women who agreed to devote full time and full attention to the campaign—just as Alice Paul had done in the Congressional Union. The full-time boards, historian Eleanor Flexner points out, had the effect of professionalizing the suffrage movement.[57] By the opening of the important election year 1916, both groups were tightly organized and enthusiastic. The more militant Congressional Union aimed at confrontational tactics and NAWSA at its traditional, careful organization of political districts.

WAR CONTINUES IN MEXICO

In October 1915, the United States recognized the constitutionalist government of Venustiano Carranza in Mexico, and in November American forces withdrew from Veracruz. By that time, however, the revolutionary armies of both Emiliano Zapata and Pancho Villa were at war with their former ally Carranza and with each other. Other factions as well as groups that were little more than bandits also promoted ongoing fighting and disorder. The United States continued to teeter on the brink of active intervention in Mexico.

By the opening of 1916, Villa, the best known anti-Carranza insurgent leader, had begun actions to provoke American intervention, probably hoping to destabilize Carranza and his government. In January, he seized a train in northern Mexico and murdered 16 American mining engineers. In March he raided and burned the American town of Columbus, New Mexico, where the U.S. Thirteenth Cavalry was stationed, killing 19.[58] Other attacks on border towns also occurred, especially in Texas and New Mexico. Wilson mobilized the National Guard to guard the U.S.-Mexican border. He also reluctantly, and with the equally reluctant approval of Carranza, dispatched some 6,000 troops under the command of General John J. Pershing to pursue and capture Villa. Although Pershing's troops pursued Villa as he drew them some 300 miles into Mexico, they never caught him. They did awaken Mexican suspicions that they were in effect an occupation force, as Villa had probably calculated they would do.

Wilson's refusal to withdraw the troops, Carranza's insistence that he do so, and a hostile incident at Carrizal in northern Mexico led to a tense situation in June 1916.

Beginning in September, American and Mexican commissioners began meeting to resolve the issues.

THE ESTABLISHMENT OF THE NATIONAL PARK SYSTEM

By 1916, the Department of the Interior supervised 14 national parks and 21 national monuments, but there was no central administration of these sites nor any official to advocate their interests. The appointees who supervised the sites varied in competence and performed their duties in the absence of policy. Some parks even relied on army troops and engineers for road and building construction, protection, enforcement of regulations, and visitor services.

The outcome of the Hetch Hetchy controversy in 1913 had made it clear to the preservation wing of the conservation movement that their voice was too weak in Washington to advocate effectively for the national parks. But among the public "scenic nationalism," as historian Alfred Ruente calls it—pride in America's scenic wonders and belief that they were part of America's national identity—was growing. Increasingly, a coalition of groups like the American Civic Association (a national organization supporting municipal reform, city parks, and city beautification), women's clubs, garden clubs, sportsman clubs, as well as such organizations as the Sierra Club and the Audubon Society all lent their energies to the park cause. They also had influential allies in the business world among railroads, hotel interests, and others who saw the economic benefits in the promotion of scenic tourism. As early as 1904 the Sante Fe Railroad had completed a majestic lodge at the Grand Canyon, for example, and the Great Northern Railway built two equally impressive lodges at Glacier National Park between 1911 and 1915. "See Europe if You Will, but See America First," urged a Soo Railroad brochure.[59]

Under increasing pressure from advocates of the national parks, in 1915, Secretary of the Interior Franklin K. Lane appointed Stephen T. Mather, a Chicago businessman and park advocate who had attended the University of California at Berkeley, as assistant to the secretary for park matters. Mather proved to be a skillful politician. Preservationists usually emphasized the spiritual value of nature, but he made peace with the managed-use wing of the conservation movement by emphasizing the usefulness of the parks instead. He stressed the potential economic benefits of national tourist attractions and the potential educational value of preserved wilderness. He conducted a vigorous public relations campaign in popular magazines and distributed the profusely illustrated *National Parks Portfolio*, its costs underwritten by western railroads, to congressmen and civic leaders. Wrote Secretary Lane in the *Portfolio's* introduction, "It is the destiny of the national parks, if wisely controlled, to become the public laboratories of nature study for the nation."[60]

The efforts soon bore fruit. On August 25, 1916, President Wilson signed a bill into law creating the National Park Service to oversee existing and future parks and monuments. The act directed the park service "to conserve the scenery and the natural and historic objects and the wild life therein and to provide for the enjoyment of the same in such manner and by such means as will leave them unimpaired for the enjoyment of future generations."[61] Mather became the Park Service's first director.

WILSON AND THE DEMOCRATS TURN TO SOCIAL REFORM

In 1912, Woodrow Wilson had gained the presidency with a minority of the popular vote, thanks to a fractured Republican Party and a three-way split in the vote between Republicans, Progressives, and Democrats. The midterm elections of November 1914 had put the Democrats on notice that such a situation was unlikely to occur again in

1916. There were clear signs that the Republican divisions of 1912 were healing and that the Republicans were regaining their long-held status as the nation's majority party. Meanwhile the third-way Progressive Party, headed by Theodore Roosevelt, was floundering. Roosevelt told journalist William Allen White that Progressive loyalists were "spurring a dead horse" and soon began signaling that he would return to the Republican fold in time for the 1916 election.[62] President Wilson and the Democrats, long the minority political party in America, wanted to continue as a viable, competitive party and wanted specifically to remain in power in 1916. It was clear to them that it was necessary to remake and enlarge the traditional Democratic coalition. They hoped to do so by consolidating progressive support and identifying themselves as the party of progressive reform.

Despite the demands of international events, by the end of 1914, President Wilson had accomplished the major economy and business-related reforms which he had laid out in his New Freedom program and which progressives almost universally applauded. Most progressives, however, saw social reform as equally necessary to an improved future for America.

During 1913 and 1914, Wilson had given scant attention to social justice issues. In general, he held to the traditional Democratic view that most social reforms and legislation to benefit specific groups should be carried out at the state and not the federal level. One of the few federal social initiatives he supported during the first two years of his presidency was the Smith-Lever Act of 1914. Proposed by Senator Hoke Smith of Georgia and Representative A. F. Lever of South Carolina, it aimed to improve agricultural productivity in poor farming regions by providing aid for farm demonstration agents to be administered by state land grant colleges.

After 1915, however, as Democrats began to seek a workable new coalition that incorporated progressives, they began to reconsider their traditional antipathy to federal social legislation. Both Wilson's New Freedom and the Progressive Party's New Nationalism of 1912 accepted an enlarged role for government in a modern industrial society with enormous corporate wealth and power. Wilson saw the federal government's expanded role primarily as that of moderator, maintaining equal opportunity by insuring the system operated fairly. But many progressives, especially those connected to the Progressive Party, believed it was necessary for the federal government to be more interventionist and to actively promote social justice by constructive legislation. By 1916, the Democratic Party and its president had agreed to compromise by supporting many kinds of social reform programs, some of which benefitted their traditional agrarian constituency. In fact, they were about to accomplish the farthest-reaching program of national social legislation prior to America's depression years of the 1930s.

Only one significant piece of social reform legislation was passed during 1915, the La Follette Seaman's Act, named after Wisconsin's progressive Republican senator. Seamen in the merchant marine (private commercial ships) worked under some of the most brutal labor conditions of the era, and union president Andrew Furuseth had worked long and hard for reform. The Seaman's Act set standards for food and safety, limited the power of captains over their men, and regulated the contracts that had previously amounted almost to indentured servitude.

By 1916, Wilson had an extensive program of farm, labor, and other social reform initiatives ready for Congress. He began by nominating Louis Brandeis to the Supreme Court. Brandeis had a high profile as the people's lawyer and a social-justice reformer, and his nomination greatly pleased progressives of all parties. Conservatives, especially on Wall Street, were correspondingly outraged. They waged a vigorous attempt in Congress to defeat his confirmation, aided by some covert antisemitism (Brandeis was Jewish). He was finally confirmed, however, becoming the first Jewish American to sit on the high court.

Next on the agenda were reforms for farmers. On July 17, the Federal Farm Loan Act became law and within two weeks was in operation. It was designed to solve the special credit needs of farmers, a subject of agitation since the early days of the populist movement. The act established a system of 12 Federal Land Banks parallel to the Federal Reserve system. The land banks, under control of a Federal Farm Loan Board, backed up low-interest, long-term loans on farm land offered by local banks. Congress also passed the Warehouse Act, which addressed the problems populists brought to attention in their sub-treasury plans of the 1890s. The act did not establish federal warehouses for agricultural produce, but it did provide licensing or bonding for private facilities. Farmers who stored their produce in these federally backed warehouses could use it as collateral for short-term loans, to finance seasonal needs, or wait out price fluctuations.

The Federal Highways (or Good Roads) Act, also passed in July, also had roots in populist demands. Farmers had long argued that the federal government should support public road construction and maintenance to help them haul their goods to market. By 1916, the good roads movement was equally popular with automobile enthusiasts and businessmen, especially those concerned with tourism. But although federal involvement in highway building is taken for granted today, traditionally it was not considered within the federal government's authority or responsibility. Even the Good Roads Act was limited to post roads, or those over which federal mail is carried. The act established a Bureau of Roads within the Department of Agriculture and allowed matching grants to states.

Next came three acts that fulfilled progressive labor reform movements of long standing. In August, the Kern-McGillicudy bill was passed, drafted by reformers of the American Association for Labor Legislation. It established a model worker's compensation program for federal employees. On September 1, President Wilson signed the Keating-Owen Child Labor Act, prohibiting interstate transportation of goods made by children under 14. On September 3, he signed the Adamson Act, which legislated an eight-hour day for railroad workers—and averted a nationwide railroad strike set for the following day. In these and the Seamen's Act, write historians Arthur Link and William Leary, Wilson "brought the power of the federal government to bear on labor-management relations in a way never before known in American history."[63]

PASSING THE NATIONAL CHILD LABOR ACT

The Democratic Party achieved political goals by moving successfully in the direction of national social reform in 1916. But they were able to do so because the reform-minded public itself, regardless of party affiliation, had become increasingly receptive to national legislation on a variety of long-standing interests, not least of which was child labor reform. The passing of the Child Labor Act is a good illustration.

The National Child Labor Committee (NCLC) had worked at the state level since its founding, but by 1913 activists had concluded that federal legislation was acceptable and even necessary. The NCLC appointed a special committee to write model legislation. The bill they drafted prohibited interstate commerce in goods produced by children whose employers did not meet the following standards: no employment of children younger than 14 in factories, workshops (sweatshops), and canneries; no children under 16 in mines; and no children under 16 who worked more than eight hours a day or at night. The bill was introduced in Congress in February 1915 by a large margin, but the Senate did not act on it before the 63rd Congress adjourned.

When the 64th Congress opened the following December, the bill was reintroduced, with Representative Edward Keating of Colorado and Senator Robert L. Owen of Oklahoma as sponsors. The Keating-Owen bill generated wide support from reform-minded professionals, officials, and journalists across the nation. Southern textile mill owners waged a publicity campaign against it, but in January 1916, it passed the House by 343 to 46. In the Senate, the battle promised to be more difficult, and no action had been taken by early June when Congress recessed for party conventions to nominate presidential candidates.[64]

Florence Kelley began her career at Hull-House, investigating sweatshops, factories, and child labor in Chicago. As head of the National Consumers' League after 1898, she continued fighting to end child labor and improve working conditions for women for the remainder of the Progressive Era. *(Library of Congress, Prints and Photographs Division, LC-USZ62-76842)*

So the situation stood as President Wilson and Democratic Party leaders planned their strategy for the convention and upcoming election. As they evaluated ways to attract former Progressive Party members, Senator Owen suggested that they adopt the social justice plank from the 1912 Progressive Party platform. The president rejected that idea but requested Owen to suggest specific, widely acceptable reform issues that might be embraced without violating states' rights. Naturally enough, Owen, twice the cosponsor of child labor legislation, included it on the list, and Wilson agreed to support it. When the Democratic platform was adopted on June 16, it included the statement, "We favor the speedy enactment of an effective Federal Child Labor Law." The Republican Party adopted a similar plank as well.[65]

Nonetheless, when Congress reconvened after the convention, Democratic senators from the South objected vociferously to the Keating-Owen bill, threatening a filibuster. Party leaders removed it from the list of legislation they deemed crucial to reelect Wilson. NCLC official Andrew McKelway hurried to the White House. He pointed out to the president that public demand for the bill was at an all-time high. With the bill, he argued, Democrats could seize the mantle of the party of reform; without it, they would likely lose crucial support in November, especially since the Republicans were sure to make the failure to pass it an issue.

President Wilson was convinced. He decided to postpone his speech accepting renomination until he rallied congressional support for child labor legislation. (At the time, candidates did not deliver acceptance speeches at the nominating conventions, which they did not attend, but at a later date.) On July 18, the president summoned unsuspecting party leaders. He wrote to McKelway the next day, "I went up to the Senate yesterday to urge the immediate passage of the Child Labor Bill and am encouraged to believe that the situation has changed considerably."[66] A week later the Democratic Caucus added child labor legislation to its list of priorities.

When the bill was placed in consideration in the Senate on August 3, Democratic opponents did not filibuster. A full 32 senators abstained from voting, but the Keating-Owens act passed, 52–12. Even the Republican *New York Tribune* conceded, "While [Wilson] was merely taking up near its end the campaign carried on by reformers for years, he gave aid when it was much needed and he took his stand regardless of offending wealthy Southerners whose political support he may need." President Wilson made his acceptance speech on September 2, the day after he signed the bill. "The test is contained in the record," he said and listed among his administration's accomplishments, "the emancipation of the children of the country . . . from hurtful labor."[67]

In fact, only about 150,000 of the nation's 2 million known working children were covered by the legislation. The vast majority of working children—those who labored on farms, in the street trades, and in their homes—were not.[68] Nonetheless the law, which was to go into effect on September 1, 1917, faced immediate court challenges. It would be in effect less than a year before being declared unconstitutional by the Supreme Court.

SELF-GOVERNMENT FOR THE PHILIPPINES

America's dependency in the Philippines also benefitted from the active legislative season of 1916. For well over a decade many Democrats and anti-imperialists (including

the still-active Anti-Imperialist League) had continued to lobby for Philippine independence, as had Filipinos themselves. Since taking office President Wilson had
appointed a majority of Filipinos (rather than Americans) to the Philippine Commission, and many Americans in the Philippine civil service had been replaced. The president gave his approval to a bill by Representative William Jones of Virginia to grant
independence to the island nation. The bill met extensive opposition, however, from
Republicans, army officials, and Catholic interests (the church hierarchy feared an
independent Filipino government would confiscate church property.)[69] As finally
passed in 1916, the Jones Act for Philippine Self-Government did not grant independence or even set a certain date for independence but stated an intention to grant
independence as soon as "a stable government" was established. In the meantime it
created an all-Filipino legislature with two houses, ended the appointed Philippine
Commission, and gave the island nation almost complete autonomy over its own legislative affairs. The Governor-General, who retained a veto power, remained an
appointed position.

THE CONVENTIONS OF 1916 AND THE END OF THE PROGRESSIVE PARTY

When the Democrats met in St. Louis in mid-June their platform, originally drafted
by Wilson himself, bore strong evidence of the remaking of the party. For the first time
in the party's history, it advocated a new commitment to international activism both to
protect America's interests and to "assist the world in securing settled peace and justice." It also advocated a full and strong program of federal actions to further social justice and economic progress—again for the first time in the party's history. But it was
keynote speaker Governor Martin Glynn of New York who, to his own surprise, discovered the true enthusiasm of the delegates. During his description of incidents in
which the United States refused to be provoked into war, delegates began chanting
after each example, "What did we do? What did we do?" and Glynn would respond,
"We didn't go to war!" At the end the hall erupted in cheers, William Jennings Bryan
wept, and Wilson's campaign had its slogan: "He kept us out of war." Later, Bryan
addressed the convention. "I have differed with our President on some of the methods
employed," he said, "but I join with the American people in thanking God that we
have a President who does not want this nation plunged into war." The slogan was
even inserted into the platform, and "Peace, Prosperity, and Preparedness" became the
campaign's rallying cry.[70]

The Republicans, for their part, had become increasingly sure of two things in the
months before the 1916 conventions. The first was that they had to heal the breach
between their conservative and progressive wings and find a candidate acceptable to
both. The second was that they did not want to renominate either of their former
presidents, Theodore Roosevelt or William Howard Taft. By July, when the convention
convened in Chicago, most insiders and delegates had settled on Charles Evans Hughes, a Supreme Court justice. Hughes had come to national attention in 1905 when he
had exposed the corruption in the insurance industry and had later served as the moderately progressive governor of New York. But he was acceptable to conservatives as
well and in fact was a Taft appointee to court.

The Republican convention reveled in harmony and decorum. "We did not
divide over fundamental principles [in 1912]," keynote speaker Senator Warren G.
Harding of Ohio implausibly told the gathered crowd. "We did not disagree over a
national policy. We split over methods of party procedure."[71] In 1916 rules, delegate
seatings, and the platform vote all proceeded without significant disputes. The platform
blandly supported peace, international rights, and military preparedness, as well as tariffs and mildly progressive social programs. Except for a half-hour-long demonstration

for Roosevelt—conducted mainly by onlookers, not delegates—the convention proceeded like clockwork. Hughes defeated various favorite sons and gained the nomination on the third ballot. Charles W. Fairbanks of Indiana was chosen as the vice presidential nominee, an office he had held under Roosevelt.

Meanwhile, reform minded members of the Progressive Party had also assembled in Chicago, although with little encouragement from their founder and leader Roosevelt, who for some time had been signaling his desire to abandon third-party politics and return to the Republican fold. Roosevelt sent Progressive representatives a letter insisting they meet behind the scenes with the Republicans to explore a possible accommodation, which they grudgingly obeyed. The outcome Roosevelt doubtless hoped for was his own nomination as joint candidate of the two parties. No accommodation was reached. The Progressives nominated Roosevelt on their own. He refused to accept. Two weeks later, the Progressive Party's national committee endorsed Hughes—then formally disbanded the party as a separate organization. A minority faction endorsed Wilson instead.

THE ELECTION OF 1916

In the campaign that followed, Wilson ran on his record. Hughes, a warm and genial man in private, proved a lackluster but long-winded speaker. He refused to engage a professional campaign manager, relying instead on close associates. Most seriously, he failed to lay out a distinct and arousing program. Nonetheless, America was a nation with a Republican majority in 1916. On election night in November, the early returns from the East Coast and near midwestern states appeared to be creating a landslide for Hughes. The president went to sleep on November 7 without conceding, but believing he had lost. Throughout the night returns began to come in from western states and during the next day a slow trend to Wilson became stronger. By midnight on the 8th he had 251 electoral votes to Hughes's 247. But it was nearly midnight on November 9 before it was finally certain that Wilson had triumphed in California and been reelected. The East and near Midwest had gone almost entirely for Hughes but the South and West had gone almost entirely for Wilson. He won by 277 electoral votes to Hughes's 254 and a popular vote of 9 million to 8.5 million, becoming the first Democrat to serve a second consecutive term in the White House since Andrew Jackson in 1832. Although the course of the new Democratic coalition would not run smoothly for many years to come, the election of 1916 foreshadowed the party's direction for the next half-century. The Socialist Party candidate, A. L. Benson (Eugene V. Debs had declined to run), polled some 3 percent of the vote, down from the party's 1912 high of 6 percent.

In Congress, the Democrats retained a small majority in the Senate, but the Republicans recaptured the House. The election was also notable because it sent suffragist and progressive Jeannette Rankin, born on a ranch near Missoula, Montana, to the U.S. House of Representatives. The first newspaper reports declared she lost—Democrats swept Montana and Rankin ran as a progressive Republican—but when all votes were in she was the victor. Four years before the majority of American women could vote, Rankin became the first woman to serve in Congress and one of the first to serve in a representative body in the entire world.

A NEW PLAN FOR SUFFRAGE

In early June, immediately before the Republican convention, the Congressional Union met in Chicago and organized the National Women's Party. Its explicit intention was to work for the defeat of Democrats in the 11 suffrage states in order to "teach Mr. Wilson and his party—and all on-looking parties—that the group which opposes national suffrage for women will lose women's support."[72] NAWSA chose a more conciliatory path. It organized a parade 10,000 strong in Chicago, which marched to the Republican convention through a blinding rainstorm. When the Democrats met in St. Louis, women lined the streets wearing yellow sashes, the suffrage color. Both national parties were hoping for support from women who had the vote and from progressives who favored suffrage. Both included a suffrage plank in their platforms, but both supported it at the state and not the federal level.

In light of both parties' silence on a national suffrage amendment, in September Carrie Chapman Catt called an emergency convention of NAWSA. Both presidential candidates were invited, but only President Wilson attended. After he had delivered a somewhat ambiguous address, Dr. Anna Howard Shaw rose to respond. "We have waited so long, Mr. President, for the vote—we had hoped it might come in your administration." Spontaneously, the entire audience rose and turned to him. Ever after, Catt believed that moment marked Wilson's conversion to the cause of a suffrage amendment, although he did not publically declare for it until 1917.[73]

During the NAWSA convention, Catt met in secret with national officers and all the state suffrage organization presidents. At the meeting she laid out and gained agreement for what was later called her Winning Plan. State organizations signed a pledge to work for the plan until it succeeded and to keep its existence private, which they did until years later. The plan pledged the women to a concerted national campaign for a national suffrage amendment, while also committing them to continue work at the state level—or as Catt put it, "to keep so much suffrage noise going all over the country that neither the enemy nor friends will discover where the real battle is."[74] States with suffrage were to seek state legislative memorials to Congress. Some states were to work for the Illinois approach of presidential suffrage, others to undertake campaigns for full state suffrage. Southern one-party states were to work through Democratic primaries. All, of course, would work with the sense that they possessed a strong organization, an overall plan, and clear goals. A million-dollar budget was authorized, and a number of NAWSA activists went home to pack up and establish a residence in Washington for the duration—which in 1916 Catt estimated would take another six years.

CHRONICLE OF EVENTS

1913

William Howard Taft is president; a new administration headed by Woodrow Wilson will be inaugurated in March.

Florida and New York enact direct primary legislation.

Michigan adopts initiative and referendum and recall.

By the end of 1913, Arizona, Connecticut, Iowa, Maryland, Michigan, Minnesota, Nebraska, Oregon, Rhode Island, Texas, and West Virginia have joined the list of states with workmen's compensation laws. New York has also reenacted its law, bringing the total to 22 states.

California, Colorado, Minnesota, Nebraska, Oregon, Utah, Washington, and Wisconsin enact minimum-wage laws for women workers, joining Massachusetts.

Eighteen states have passed enabling or other legislation for mothers' pensions.

Women have full suffrage in nine states (Wyoming, Colorado, Idaho, Utah, Washington, California, Kansas, Oregon, Arizona) and the territory of Alaska. Twenty-one other states permit them to vote in school elections, tax-related, municipal, or similar matters. In 18 of the 48 states (Maine, Rhode Island, Pennsylvania, Maryland, West Virginia, Virginia, Tennessee, North Carolina, South Carolina, Georgia, Florida, Alabama, Arkansas, Texas, Missouri, Indiana, South Dakota, Nevada) and in Hawaii territory women have no voting rights.

Ohio and Kansas pass state laws for movie censorship.

Massachusetts, California, and Pennsylvania create agencies to oversee immigrant issues.

The Commission on Industrial Relations begins two years of hearings throughout the nation to study the sources of labor unrest and industrial violence.

January: Suffragist Alice Paul, trained in militant British suffragist tactics, takes over the Congressional Committee of NAWSA and sets up shop in Washington to work for a constitutional amendment allowing women to vote.

February 3: Delaware, Wyoming, and New Mexico ratify the Sixteenth Amendment permitting tax on income, making it law. It is officially declared in effect on February 25.

February 14: President Taft vetoes the immigration bill passed in late 1912 requiring a literacy test for admission to the nation. Congress tries to override it but fails.

February 17: The International Exhibition of Modern Art, known as the Armory Show, opens in New York and later travels to Boston and Chicago. It is the first large exhibition of modern art in America.

February 18: In Mexico, President Francisco Madero is ousted and soon murdered in a military coup by General Victoriano Huerta.

February 28: The Pujo Committee (or House Banking and Currency Committee) releases its report. It reveals an extreme concentration of control as well as wealth in the hands of a very few banks and financiers.

March: In civil suits by the families of the 1910 Triangle Shirtwaist Fire victims, factory owners Isaac Harris and Max Blanck agree to pay $75 compensation per victim.

The Migratory Bird (or Weeks–McLean) Act becomes effective; it puts migratory birds under the protection of the federal government.

Alice Paul forms the Congressional Union to work exclusively for a constitutional amendment allowing women's suffrage. It quickly attracts many supporters.

March 1: Congress easily overrides outgoing president Taft's veto of the Webb–Kenyon Act, which prohibits interstate shipments of liquor into dry states for uses violating state law.

March 3: Some 5,000 women, organized by Alice Paul and her associates, march for suffrage in Washington. The parade route is not adequately policed and there is a near riot; soldiers must be called in to restore order.

March 4: Woodrow Wilson is sworn in as the 28th president of the United States; Thomas Marshall is vice president.

The Department of Commerce and Labor is officially separated into two departments, each with its own secretary, when Wilson's cabinet takes office.

March 12: To the surprise of foreign diplomats and many Americans, Wilson announces he will not recognize the Huerta regime in Mexico because it does not rest on "the consent of the governed."

April 8: President Wilson appears in person before Congress to urge revision of the tariff, the first major legislative goal of his administration. He is the first president to address Congress in person since John Adams in 1800; personal addresses will now become standard procedure.

Connecticut becomes the 36th state to ratify the Seventeenth Amendment, Direct Election of Senators, making it law. It is officially declared in effect on May 31.

May: The North American Civic League for Immigrants (NACL) sponsors the first national conference on the education of immigrants.

May 10: In New York, the annual women's suffrage parade draws 10,000 marchers.

June 22: President Wilson appears in person before Congress a second time to urge that some federal, public control be included in the new system of money and banking currently under consideration in Congress. Reform of the system is his second major legislative goal.

July 31: In Washington, suffrage women conduct an automobile procession to present a petition containing 200,000 signatures from around the United States.

October 3: The Underwood–Simmons Tariff Act becomes law. It reduces the tariff on many items and enacts the nation's first personal-income tax, as allowed by the

Sixteenth Amendment. It also contains a provision to prohibit the importation of wild bird feathers, a result of years of pressure by conservation groups.

October 11: In Mexico, President Victoriano Huerta declares himself dictator. An anti-Huerta countermovement in favor of constitutional government and elections is led by Venustiano Carranza.

November: Illinois gives women the right to vote in presidential elections..

December 13: Anti-liquor advocates from nearly 100 organizations open the campaign for a prohibition amendment, with a parade in Washington, D.C., 4,000 strong. Senator Morris Shepherd of Texas and Congressman Richard Hobson of Alabama introduce a bill, although it fails to obtain the necessary two-thirds majority.

December 19: The Federal Reserve Act is passed, reforming the American system of money and banking. It creates 12 regional Federal Reserve Banks owned by private member banks under the oversight of a publicly appointed national Federal Reserve Board.

The Raker Act is passed, permitting the damming and flooding of Hetch Hetchy Valley in Yosemite National Park, which preservationists have fought for a decade.

1914

North Dakota adopts initiative and referendum.

Kansas and Louisiana adopt recall.

Washington, Colorado, Arizona, Oregon, and Virginia adopt statewide prohibition.

Women win suffrage in Montana and Nevada, bringing the total number of suffrage states to 11.

The New York–New Jersey branch of the NACL changes its name to the Committee for Immigrants in America and becomes a national clearinghouse for information about aid to immigrants and a national lobbying organization. A Division of Immigrant Education is established in the Federal Bureau of Education with funds and staff provided by the NACL.

The American Association for Labor Legislation (AALL) holds the First National Conference on Unemployment in New York to consider the idea of unemployment insurance, which is available in many European nations and Britain. The idea makes little headway in America during the Progressive Era.

Four years after the founding of the National Housing Association, legislation to regulate housing is in effect in at least 87 cities in 23 states and Canada.

January 4: Henry Ford announces completion of the first moving automobile assembly line at his factory in Highland Park, Michigan. He also stuns the nation by announcing he is doubling his workers' wages to $5.00 a day and reducing the workday to eight hours. Overnight he becomes an international celebrity.

As leisure time slowly increased, amusement parks became popular attractions, especially for working people who wanted to escape the crowded city and relax. Coney Island was the largest and most famous, but amusement parks were built throughout the nation. Pictured here, with its roller coaster in the foreground, is Columbia Gardens in Butte, Montana, in the early 1910s. *(Library of Congress, Prints and Photographs Division, LC-D431-T01-600005-L-X)*

March 19: The Senate defeats a bill for a women's suffrage amendment, which the Congressional Union has successfully brought to the floor of Congress for the first time since 1896.

April 9: In Mexico, the Tampico Incident begins when U.S. sailors who have gone ashore are arrested. They are released with an apology, but the incident escalates when military commanders quarrel over a salute to the flag.

April 20: At Ludlow, Colorado, where miners have been on strike against the Rockefeller-owned Colorado Fuel and Iron Company (CF&I) since September, a 10-day armed battle begins. The state militia burns the tent colony in which the miners have been living, killing two women and 11 children. The Ludlow Massacre is most infamous confrontation between labor and capital during the Progressive Era.

April 21: In Mexico, U.S. forces occupy Veracruz, partly to prevent a German ship from landing with ammunition for military dictator Huerta. The occupation will continue until November and will be viewed unfavorably by all the warring sides in the Mexican conflict.

May 8: Congress passes the Smith-Lever Act, providing aid for agricultural extension work to be administered through land grant colleges.

May 20 to July 2: Delegates from the United States, Mexico, and the ABC powers (Argentina, Brazil, and Chile) meet in Canada to attempt to resolve the Mexican situation. Meanwhile, dictator Huerta's power is diminishing and that of the constitutionalists increasing.

May 25: The British Parliament passes a bill granting home rule to Ireland; it will not be put into effect due to the outbreak of World War I.

June 28: In Sarajevo, Bosnia, on the Balkan Peninsula, Archduke Franz Ferdinand of Austria-Hungary and his wife are assassinated by a Serbian terrorist and nationalist. The event will touch off World War I. In consultation with its ally Germany, Austria rejects a British offer of mediation and makes great retaliatory demands on Serbia.

July 15: In Mexico, military dictator Huerta resigns.

July 28: Austria-Hungary declares war on Serbia, and World War I begins.

July 30: Russia, an ally of Serbia, mobilizes its army.

August 1: Germany declares war on Russia. Switzerland and the Scandinavian nations Sweden, Norway, and Denmark declare neutrality.

August 2: Germany demands that Belgium allow troops to pass through; Belgium declares neutrality and refuses.

August 3: Germany declares war on France and prepares to launch its offensive through Belgium.

August 4: Great Britain declares war on Germany in defense of Belgium. The United States declares neutrality.

August 5: The United States offers to mediate in Europe; the offer is ignored. Montenegro declares war on Austria-Hungary.

First Lady Ellen Axson Wilson dies of kidney disease.

August 6: Austria-Hungary declares war on Russia.

August 8: France and Britain begin an offensive against Germany in the border province of Lorraine.

August 12: France and Great Britain declare war on Austria-Hungary.

August 15: The United States bans private loans to warring nations, believing it will help end the war quickly.

The Panama Canal is officially opened for use. Due to the war, festivities do no occur.

August 18: Russia invades Galicia (in modern Poland).

August 19: In a speech, President Wilson urges Americans to be neutral in "thought, as well as action."

August 20: In Mexico, followers of Carranza enter Mexico City. His two military leaders Emiliano Zapata in the south and Francisco "Pancho" Villa in the north will soon turn against him and each other.

In Europe, Brussels, the capital of Belgium, falls to the Germans. The fighting in Lorraine is deadlocked. Pope Pius X dies; he will be succeeded by Benedict XV.

August 23: In Asia, Japan declares war on Germany and attacks Qingdao (Tsingtao), a city in the German sphere of China.

August 26–29: On the eastern front Russian forces suffer a disastrous defeat at the hands of the German army; 30,000 Russians are killed and 92,000 taken prisoner.

August 28: The British navy sinks three German ships in the North Sea; the naval war begins.

August 29: In the South Seas, troops from New Zealand (part of the British Empire) capture German Samoa; soon they will also capture German New Guinea.

September 5: Russia, Great Britain, and France agree to a formal alliance against Germany and Austria-Hungary.

September 6–9: In northern France, the Allies are victorious in the first Battle of the Marne. Germany is prevented from advancing to Paris, but a stalemate makes it apparent that there will not be an easy victory for either side. The western front is established; it will eventually be a 475-mile-long line through France from the coast of the English Channel in the Netherlands to the Alps in Switzerland. Each side will have networks of trenches separated by a field of battle; the line will remain almost stationary for the duration of the war.

September 26: Congress passes the Federal Trade Commission act, half of Wilson's program to control trusts and restore competition in the American economy. The commission has the power to investigate and penalize unfair business practices.

October: The United States begins to modify its ban on loans to warring nations, which has hurt the Allies much more than the Central Powers.

October 1: Canadian troops sail to Europe to join the fighting for Great Britain.

October 10: The Belgian port city of Antwerp falls to the Germans; Britain begins to fear an invasion from across the English Channel.

October 15: Congress passes the Clayton Anti-Trust Act, the second half of Wilson's program to control trusts. It spells out many violations and penalties and holds individual corporate officers liable. It also states that unions are not by definition "illegal combinations in restraint of trade."

October 21: On the western front Allied and German forces battle at Ypres; the fighting goes on for a month, takes 250,000 lives, and ends in a stalemate.

October 30: The Ottoman Empire (Turkey), a German ally, declares war on Russia and Great Britain.

November: In New York, Meyer London becomes the second Socialist elected to Congress.

Britain declares the North Sea a war zone and plants mines there.

November: The midterm elections show that Republicans are healing their split of 1912 and regaining their position as the majority party. The Progressive Party has little success. Democrats are put on notice that their party must develop a larger coalition if they want to retain the presidency in 1916. Over the next two years, Wilson and the Democratic Party will increasingly support federal social reform measures to attract progressives.

November 3: Russia declares war on Turkey.

November 5: Great Britain declares war on Turkey.

November 12: In South Africa (part of the British Empire) the Boers are defeated; they have revolted in support of German troops, under attack in neighboring South–West Africa.

December 1: Prominent American advocates of military preparedness organize the National Security League to publicize their cause.

December 11: The British navy wins a victory over Germany near the Falkland Islands in the South Atlantic.

December 16: Great Britain makes Egypt a protectorate.

December 18: President Wilson remarries; the new first lady is Edith Bolling Galt.

1915

Indiana, North Carolina, South Carolina, Vermont, and West Virginia enact direct primary legislation.

Kentucky and Maryland adopt referendum.

Idaho, North Dakota, Iowa, Alabama, Arkansas, and South Carolina adopt statewide prohibition.

Arkansas and Kansas pass minimum-wage laws.

A total of 23 states have passed mothers' pensions since the first laws were enacted in 1911.

Florida gives women municipal voting rights.

Denmark approves women's suffrage.

Congress establishes Rocky Mountain National Park, Colorado.

John Muir dies; he has led the preservation wing of the conservation movement.

The Commission on Industrial Relations issues its report after two years of study. It places blame for industrial violence on the enormous gap in power between concentrated wealth and workers and on employers' determination to stamp out unionization at all costs.

January 12: A bill for a women's suffrage amendment is defeated in the House of Representatives.

February: After this date Alice Paul's Congressional Union and NAWSA will go their separate ways, not entirely on good terms.

On the eastern front, Central Powers battle Russian troops and will slowly push them back into Russia through Poland over the next nine months.

February 2: Germany announces a naval blockade of the British Isles and France of both military and merchant ships to be enforced by its U-boats or submarines.

February 8: Director D. W. Griffith's anticipated epic film spectacle *The Birth of a Nation* premieres in Los Angeles. A week later it is shown to President Wilson, the first film screened in the White House. Its pathbreaking cinematic technique makes it the most profitable movie to date, but it contains demeaning portrayals of African Americans and sparks nationwide protests by the NAACP.

February 23: In *Mutual Film Corp. v. Industrial Commission of Ohio,* the Supreme Court unanimously upholds prior censorship of movies by state agencies. The decision will not be overturned until 1952.

March 1: Britain announces a complete blockade of Germany including neutral ports. It also announces it will dock neutral ships to search them.

April 22–May 25: At the second Battle of Ypres in northern France poison gas is used for the first time; German troops fire mortar shells of chlorine into Allied lines. The battle ends without victory for either side, although Allies suffer double the casualties of Germany.

April 25: At Gallipoli, in Turkey, nine months of brutal fighting begins between Allied and Central Powers.

May 7: Without issuing a warning, a German U-boat sinks the British passenger liner *Lusitania* off the coast of Ireland. Nearly 1,200 people die, including 128 Americans. The Wilson administration protests; Germany claims the ship was carrying munitions. In the United States anti-German feeling is heightened.

May 10: The Bureau of Naturalization sponsors a ceremony at Philadelphia for new citizens at which President Wilson speaks, part of increasing Americanization efforts. Many Americans fear that Europe's ethnic and national animosities will be repeated in America.

May 13: The Wilson administration issues a strong protest to Germany on the Luisitania incident, demanding an end to unrestricted submarine warfare.

May 23: Italy joins the Allies and declares war on Austria.

Summer: The Ku Klux Klan, which originally flourished during the Reconstruction era, is reorganized in Georgia. The new Klan, which will reach its peak of power in the 1920s, will extend its opposition to aliens, Jews, and Catholics as well as blacks.

June 1: Germany attempts its first zeppelin, or airship, attack on eastern England but is not successful.

June 9: The Wilson administration issues a second and stronger protest to Germany on the *Lusitania* sinking, having not received a satisfactory response to the first. Secretary of State William Jennings Bryan resigns in protest, believing the issue is not sufficient to risk war.

July: Although it is not announced publicly, Wilson instructs the navy and war departments to propose plans for military preparedness.

July 4: The National Americanization Committee, a group of civic leaders, sponsors Americanization Day, celebrations for newly naturalized citizens.

July 28: American forces seize Port-au-Prince, Haiti; the nation is in a state of near anarchy due to civil disorder and foreign debt. Forces will remain until 1934.

September 1: The German ambassador delivers a pledge that passenger liners will not be sunk by U-boats without warning; it is known as the *Arabic* Pledge, after another British liner that has been sunk.

October: America lifts its ban on loans to warring nations.

Pioneering birth control advocate Margaret Sanger returns from England to face 1914 charges of violating obscenity laws by sending her magazine, *The Woman Rebel,* through the mails; but the government drops the charges. She embarks on a national tour to support her cause.

October 14: Bulgaria joins the Central Powers and declares war on Serbia.

October 19: New Jersey defeats a referendum for women's suffrage, although the president announces he is in favor of it and travels to the state to cast a vote.

In Mexico, the United States and several Latin American nations acknowledge the government of Venustiano Carranza, who establishes a capital in Veracruz; American troops will soon be withdrawn from the city. Revolutionary factions continue to fight Carranza and each other.

October 21: The first transatlantic radio voice communications (radiotelephony) is made between Arlington, Virginia, and Paris.

November 2: A referendum for women's suffrage is defeated in New York, Massachusetts, and Pennsylvania. The defeats bring discontent in NAWSA to a head, and long-time president Dr. Anna Howard Shaw resigns. Carrie Chapman Catt resumes the position and almost immediately brings a new spirit of organization to the campaign.

November 14: African-American leader Booker T. Washington dies.

November 25: Albert Einstein completes his General Theory of Relativity.

December: Wilson delivers his annual message to Congress, warning that budgetary proposals for military build-ups will be coming soon.

1916

Montana, South Dakota, Nebraska, and Michigan adopt statewide prohibition.

Congress establishes Hawaii National Park and Lassen Volcanic National Park, California.

In fall and winter 1916–17, the movement of African Americans from the South to cities in the North begins in earnest; it is often called the Great Migration.

January and February: Wilson's adviser Edward House visits London, Paris, and Berlin for a third time in a year, offering U.S. aid in mediation, but finds the nations unwilling to come to the table.

January 10: In northern Mexico, Pancho Villa seizes a train and murders nearly 20 American mining engineers; he hopes to provoke American intervention to destabilize Mexican president Venustiano Carranza.

January 28: Wilson nominates reform lawyer Louis Brandeis to the Supreme Court. The act pleases progressives but occasions much debate in the Senate.

February 21: In northern France the Battle of Verdun begins. It will be the longest battle of the war, continuing until December and claiming nearly a million lives.

March 9: Mexican rebel leader Pancho Villa attacks Columbus, New Mexico, killing 19 Americans.

Germany declares war on Portugal.

March 15: In Mexico General John J. Pershing leads troops in pursuit of Pancho Villa on Wilson's orders. They will be unable to locate him and will be withdrawn in early 1917 after penetrating 300 miles into Mexico.

March 24: The French vessel *Sussex* is sunk by a German U-boat. Germany again pledges to cease sinking merchant ships without warning.

April 25: In Dublin, the Easter Uprising against Great Britain begins. Within a week it is put down by the British, and Sinn Fein leaders are soon executed.

May 15: U.S. troops seize Santo Domingo, Dominican Republic, and take control of the government, which is in a state of near anarchy due to successive revolutions. In November they will establish a U.S. military government; troops will remain until 1924.

May 31: The naval battle of Jutland is fought off Denmark. The British lose seven ships and nearly 7,000 men; the Germans lose three ships and 2,300 men. Both sides claim to be the victor.

June 1: Louis Brandeis's appointment to the Supreme Court is confirmed; he becomes the first Jewish-American justice.

June 3: The National Defense Act authorizes enlargement of the regular army and National Guard.

June 5–7: The Congressional Union, a women's suffrage group working for a national amendment, meets in Chicago and founds the National Women's Party.

June 7–10: The Republican National Convention meets in Chicago, nominating Charles Evans Hughes for president.

The Progressive Party meets in Chicago. Representatives meet in private with Republicans at Theodore Roosevelt's request but fail to reach an accommodation. The Progressives nominate Roosevelt for president; he declines. The executive committee endorses Hughes and disbands the party.

June 14–16: The Democrats meet in St. Louis and renominate Wilson. Their platform approves international involvement and the use of federal power to achieve social justice reform at home, both new stances for the party. Delegates enthusiastically endorse the slogan, "He kept us out of war."

June 21: A hostile incident occurs at Carrizal in northern Mexico. First reports indicate an ambush of American troops and Wilson prepares a war request. Within a week it becomes clear that American troops were the aggressors and there is a widespread public and official demand to settle the Mexican problem peacefully.

July 1: Along the Somme in northeastern France, the Allies begin an offensive that lasts until November. They advance several miles but do not break through the German line. There will be more than 1 million casualties.

July 11: The Good Roads, or Federal Highway, Act is signed, authorizing funds to states for road construction.

July 17: Congress passes the Federal Farm Loan Act. It establishes a system of federal land banks parallel to the Federal Reserve System to provide long-term, low-interest loans to farmers.

August 4: The United States agrees to purchase what will become the Virgin Islands from Denmark; the treaty will be confirmed by the Senate in January 1917.

August 11: Congress passes the agricultural Warehouse Act. It establishes federal licensing for agricultural warehouses; receipts for produce deposited there can then be used as collateral for farm loans.

August 15: The Naval Construction Act allows a three-year ship-building program to cost up to $600 million.

August 25: President Wilson signs legislation creating the National Park Service to manage all existing and future national parks and monuments.

August 27: Italy declares war on Germany, Germany declares war on Romania, and Romania declares war on Austria.

August 29: The Army Appropriations Act establishes the Council of National Defense (six cabinet secretaries) and a civilian National Defense Advisory Commission to coordinate economic planning and preparedness.

Congress passes the Organic Act of the Philippine Islands (Jones Act), granting legislative self-rule and promising independence "as soon as a stable government can be established."

September: Allies use tanks in the Battle of the Somme, the first time such motorized vehicles are used in warfare.

September 1: The Keating-Owen Child Labor Act is passed; it bans interstate commerce in items made by children younger than 14; it will later be found unconstitutional.

September 3: President Wilson signs the Adamson Act, which orders an eight-hour working day for railroad employees and averts a national strike scheduled for the following day.

September 4–10: NAWSA meets in Atlantic City. President Carrie Chapman Catt, in a private meeting with the executive board and state presidents, pledges the women to work for what is later called her Winning Plan.

September 6: Mexican and American commissioners begin meeting to negotiate U.S-Mexican disputes.

September 7: Congress creates the United States Shipping Board to build or purchase merchant vessels for use as auxiliaries to the navy.

Congress passes the Workmen's Compensation Act, applicable to federal employees.

September 8: The Emergency Revenue Act doubles the rate of income tax to finance military preparedness. The tax still applies only to a small minority of Americans.

September 27: Greece declares war on Bulgaria and Bulgaria declares war on Romania.

October 15: Margaret Sanger opens the nation's first birth control clinic in Brownsville, Brooklyn, to serve poor and working women who do not have even the limited access to information available to some middle- and upper-class women. Nine days later the clinic is raided and Sanger arrested. Sanger will be convicted and spend 30 days in prison; the publicity surrounding the incident will provide her with wealthy supporters to build an organized movement for birth control reform.

October 16: In the Philippines, the new autonomous legislature meets for the first time.

November 7: The 1916 presidential election takes place. Although the result is not certain until November 9, President Wilson is reelected, 277 electoral votes to Hughes's 254 and a popular vote of 9 million to 8.5 million. The Democrats retain a small majority in the Senate, but the Republicans recapture the House. Jeannette Rankin is elected to the U.S. House of Representatives, the first woman to serve in Congress and one of the first to serve in a representative body in the entire world.

EYEWITNESS TESTIMONY

Sometimes bills come up that many Legislators do not favor but to preserve their good records they feel obliged to vote for, then afterwards these Legislators appeal to the Speaker of the House and ask him to save them by preventing it from ever coming to a final vote. If he is adroit, this can be done without the people as a whole knowing what has happened to some of their favorite measures. . . . The young Speaker of the House . . . told me . . . that hundreds of men from Chicago and from other parts of Illinois had come down and begged him to never let the suffrage bill come up for the final vote, and threatened him with political oblivion if he did. He implored me to let him know if there was any suffrage sentiment in Illinois.

I immediately telephoned to Chicago to Margaret Dobyne, our faithful Press Chairman, to send the call out for help all over the State, asking for telegrams and letters to be sent at once to Speaker McKinley asking him to bring up the suffrage measure and have it voted upon. . . . In the meantime I also phoned Mrs. Harriette Taylor Treadwell, President of the Chicago Political Equality League. . . . She organized the novel, and now famous, telephone brigade, by means of which Speaker McKinley was called up every 15 minutes by leading men as well as women, both at his home and at his office from early Saturday morning until Monday evening, the days he spent in Chicago. His mother, whom we entertained at a luncheon after the bill had passed, said that it was simply one continuous ring at their house and that someone had to sit right by the phone to answer the calls.

Grace Wilbur Trout, president of the Illinois suffrage association, describes work leading to the passage of the Illinois suffrage law in 1913, "Sidelights on Illinois Suffrage History," Journal of the Illinois State Historical Society, *vol. 12 (July 1920), reprinted in Scott and Scott,* One Half the People, *p. 118.*

It is a fair deduction from the testimony that the most active agents in forwarding and bringing about the concentration of control of money and credit . . . have been and are—

J. P. Morgan & Co.
First National Bank of New York
National City Bank of New York
Lee, Higginson & Co., of Boston and New York
Kidder, Peabody & Co., of Boston and New York
Kuhn, Loeb & Co. . . .

Summary of Directorships Held by These Members of the Group. . . . It appears there that firm members or directors of these institutions together hold:

One hundred and eighteen directorships in 34 banks and trust companies having total resources of $2,679,000,000 and total deposits of $1,983,000,000.

Thirty directorships in 10 insurance companies having total assets of $2,293,000,000. One hundred and five directorships in 32 transportation systems having a total capitalization of $11,784,000,000 and a total mileage (excluding express companies and steamship lines) of 150,200.

Sixty-three directorships in 24 producing and trading corporations having a total capitalization of $3,339,000,000.

Twenty-five directorships in 12 public utility corporations having a total capitalization of $2,150,000,000.

In all, 341 directorships in 112 corporations having aggregate resources or capitalization of $22,245,000,000.

The members of the firm of J. P. Morgan & Co. hold 72 directorships in 47 of the greater corporations. . . . making in all for these members of the group 150 directorships in 110 of the greater corporations.

The Pujo Committee reports on the Money Trust, 1913, 62nd Congress, 3rd session, House Report No. 1593, vol. 3, pp. 90–97.

Increased farm production and farm efficiency are the direct result of increased investments of capital for the improvement of soil fertility, for improved live stock, for improved farm machinery and for farm labor. There are very few farmers using all the capital that could be used profitably in the operation of their farms. The rate of interest paid by farmers is not as important a consideration as the terms of the loan and the convenience with which it may be secured. There is a widespread sentiment among farmers against going in debt due to the unfavorable terms on which they have been able to borrow and the disastrous results that have often followed. This opposition to borrowing credit is reflected in the popular grange song, entitled "Don't Mortgage the Farm."

The American farmer as yet has not learned to use credit for productive purposes as the European farmer uses it. Neither has American agriculture assumed the permanent form of the European systems. Increased rural credit facilities are fundamental in bringing about these results and the federal and state governments can do no better service for the American farmer and our national welfare than to interest themselves in establishing rural credit systems suitable to American conditions.

Homer C. Price, dean of the College of Agriculture, Ohio State University, "Effect of Farm Credits on Increasing Agricultural Production and Farm Efficiency," 1913, p. 190.

Our friends from other states refer to the fact that Ohio seems to have "the good-roads fever.". . . But, like other states, Ohio is far behind the needs in road improvement, and it is our purpose now to bring her to the front as rapidly as possible. This is to be done by paving with brick or concrete many of our more prominent roads, and by macadamizing and using gravel upon the remainder. We have provided a special levy for road improvement, which guarantees us ample funds for the present. . . .

. . . There has never been a period in our history when so many of our citizens were interested in the subject. This is in part due, of course, to the tremendous number of automobiles now in use. By the end of the year we shall have practically 100,000 motor driven vehicles upon our roads and highways. But all of this interest is in no sense due to the adoption of motor vehicles. It is due to a gradual awakening on the part of the people to the fact that bad roads cost more than good ones. Our farmers are coming to be business men in every sense of the word. They are capable of figuring upon the cost of transportation. They therefore readily see the financial advantage of having improved highways.

Ohio Governor James M. Cox, "Improved Public Highways,"
1913, pp. 35–36.

In 1913, architect Cass Gilbert's Woolworth Building opened to great acclaim at Park and Broadway in lower Manhattan. Its modern steel framing allowed it to rise to the record height of 60 stories, although its exterior was Gothic, complete with gargoyles. It remained the tallest building in the world until 1929. This photo dates from 1919. *(Library of Congress, Prints and Photographs Division, LC-USZ62-107486)*

The shipment or transportation, in any manner or by any means whatsoever, of any spirituous, vinous, malted, fermented, or other intoxicating liquor of any kind, from one State, Territory, or District of the United States, or place noncontiguous to but subject to the jurisdiction thereof, which said spirituous, vinous, malted, fermented, or other intoxicating liquor is intended, by any person interested therein, to be received, possessed, sold, or in any manner used, either in the original package or otherwise, in violation of any law of such State, Territory, or District of the United States, or place noncontiguous to but subject to the jurisdiction thereof, is hereby prohibited.

The Webb-Kenyon Act, March 1, 1913, U.S. Statutes at
Large, 62nd Congress, vol. 37, p. 699.

But the evil has come with the good, and much fine gold has been corroded. With riches has come inexcusable waste. We have squandered a great part of what we might have used, and have not stopped to conserve the exceeding bounty of nature, without which our genius for enterprise would have been worthless and impotent, scorning to be careful, shamefully prodigal as well as admirably efficient. We have been proud of our industrial achievements, but we have not hitherto stopped thoughtfully enough to count the human cost, the cost of lives snuffed out, of energies overtaxed and broken, the fearful physical and spiritual cost to the men and women and children upon whom the dead weight and burden of it all has fallen pitilessly the years through. The groans and agony of it all had not yet reached our ears, the solemn, moving undertone of our life, coming up out of the mines and factories, and out of every home where the struggle had its intimate and familiar seat. . . . The great Government we loved has too often been made use of for private and selfish purposes, and those who used it had forgotten the people.

We have come now to the sober second thought. The scales of heedlessness have fallen from our eyes. We have made up our minds to square every process of our national life again with the standards we so proudly set up at the beginning and have always carried at our hearts. Our work is a work of restoration.

Woodrow Wilson, inaugural address, March 4, 1913,
Inaugural Addresses of the Presidents, pp. 28–29.

"This is not a sudden disruption or eruption in the history of art. It is the inevitable result of a tendency . . . to abandon all discipline, all respect for tradition, and to insist that art shall be nothing but an expression of the individual. . . .

"With the Post-Impressionists, the personality of the artist became the only matter of moment. It ended in the deification of Whim.

"As I have said, the Cubists and the Futurists simply abolish the art of painting. They deny not only any representation of nature, but also any known or traditional form of decoration. . . .

". . . These men have seized upon the modern engine of publicity and are making insanity pay. . . .

"But, getting back to Matisse . . . many of his paintings are simply the exaltation to the walls of a gallery of the drawings of a nasty boy.

"I have always championed the nude. . . . but I feel that in the drawings of some of these men there is a professed indecency which is absolutely shocking.". . .

"These men who would make art merely expressive of their personal whim, make it speak in a special language only understood by themselves, are as truly anarchists as are those who would overthrow all social laws."

Artist and critic Kenyon Cox, interviewed by a reporter on the Armory show, "Cubists and Futurists Are Making Insanity Pay," New York Times, magazine section, March 16, 1913, p. 1.

Probably we err in treating most of these pictures seriously. It is likely that many of them represent in the painters the astute appreciation of the powers to make folly lucrative which the late P. T. Barnum showed with his faked mermaid. There are thousands of people who will pay small sums to look at a faked mermaid; and now and then one of this kind with enough money will buy a Cubist picture, or a picture of a misshapen nude woman, repellent from every standpoint. . . .

. . . But this does not in the least mean that the extremists whose paintings and pictures were represented are entitled to any praise, save, perhaps, that they have helped to break fetters. Probably in any reform movement, any progressive movement, in any field of life, the penalty for avoiding the commonplace is a liability to extravagance. It is vitally necessary to move forward and to shake off the dead hand, often the fossilized dead hand, of the reactionaries; and yet we have to face the fact that there is apt to be a lunatic fringe among the votaries of any forward movement. In this recent art exhibition the lunatic fringe was fully in evidence. . . .

Theodore Roosevelt, "A Layman's Views of an Art Exhibition," Outlook, vol. 103 (March 29, 1913), p. 718.

One of the distinctive features of the University of Wisconsin has been its relation to government. It is often supposed, and especially have I found the opinion in the East, that Wisconsin is a radical state, in favor of all sorts of strange and irrational things. However, if one considers the characteristics of the Wisconsin advances of government during recent years, it will be appreciated that the state is really conservative. The Wisconsin movement did not begin by putting upon the whole people the solution of various intricate problems; it began by the development of

government by experts; indeed this is the distinctive feature of the Wisconsin system. . . .

These new conditions of the new century confront our nation with a new crisis. We must pass from the period of individualism which was the characteristic of the nineteenth century, to the period of social responsibility which will be characteristic of the twentieth century. This will be as great a readjustment of ideals as have ever been demanded by seer or prophet of any people at any time. This is the reason why the wise, constructive leadership of men of thought is so necessary at this time. Therefore the universities, while confessedly the very centers of unrest, the sources of disturbances, contain the possible leaders who may point the way to the inevitable readjustment without disaster.

Charles R. Van Hise, president, University of Wisconsin, address to a group from Philadelphia who came to study the state's progressive innovations, May 13, 1913, DiNovo, ed., Selected Readings in American History, pp. 246–47.

I think that the public ought to know the extraordinary exertions being made by the lobby in Washington to gain recognition for certain alterations of the Tariff bill. Washington has seldom seen so numerous, so industrious or so insidious a lobby. The newspapers are being filled with paid advertisements calculated to mislead the judgement of public men not only, but also the public opinion of the country itself. There is every evidence that money without limit is being spent to sustain this lobby and to create an appearance of a pressure of opinion antagonistic to some of the chief items of the Tariff.

It is of serious interest to the country that the people at large should have no lobby and be voiceless in these matters, while great bodies of astute men seek to create an artificial opinion and to overcome the interests of the public for their private profit. It is thoroughly worth the while of the people of this country to take knowledge of this matter. Only public opinion can check and destroy it.

President Wilson's "Statement to the Press" denouncing lobbying, May 26, 1913, New York Times, May 27, p. 1.

As Californians, we rather resent gentlemen from different parts of the country outside of California telling us that we are invading the beautiful natural resources of the State or in any way marring or detracting from them. We have a greater pride than they in the beauties of California, in the valleys, in the big trees, in the rivers, and in the high mountains. We have the highest mountain in the United States in California, Mount Whitney, 15,000 feet above the sea, as we have the lowest land, in Death Valley, 300 feet below the sea. We have the highest tree known in the world, and the oldest tree. Its history goes back 2,000 years, I believe, judged by the internal evidences; as we have the youngest in the world, Luther Burbank's plumcot.

All of this is of tremendous pride, and even for a water supply we would not injure the great resources which have made our State the playground of the world. By constructing a dam at this very narrow gorge in the Hetch Hetchy Valley, about 700 feet across, we create, not a reservoir, but a lake . . .; so, coming upon it, it will look like an emerald gem in the mountains; and one of the few things in which California is deficient, especially in the Sierras, is lakes, and in this way we will contribute, in a large measure, to the scenic grandeur and beauty of California.

Testimony of former San Francisco mayor James Phelan, Congressional hearings on Hetch Hetchy, June 1913, House Committee on the Public Lands, Hetch Hetchy Dam Site, *63rd Congress, pp. 165–66.*

What is at stake is not merely the destruction of a single valley, one of the most wonderful works of the Creator, but the fundamental principle of conservation. Let it be established that these great parks and forests are to be held at the whim or advantage of local interests and sooner or later they must all be given up. One has only to look about to see the rampant materialism of the day. It can only be overcome by a constant regard for ideas and for the good of the whole country now and hereafter. The very sneers with which this type of argument is received are a proof of the need of altruism and imagination in dealing with the subject. . . .

The opponents of the bill invite your careful attention to the fact that whereas at first the scheme was put forward as one appealing to humane instincts—to provide a great city with potable water—it is now clearly seen to be aiming at quite another purpose—the production of power for use and for sale. This is commercialism pure and simple, and the far-reaching results of this disposition of the national parks when the destruction of their supreme features is involved, is something appalling to contemplate.

Conservationist Robert Underwood Johnson, letter to Representative Scott Ferris of California, June 25, 1913, read into the record during the hearings on Hetch Hetchy, House Committee on the Public Lands, Hetch Hetchy Dam Site, *63rd Congress, pp. 236–37.*

The National Association for the Advancement of Colored People, through its Board of Directors, respectfully protests the policy of your Administration in segregating the colored employees in the Departments at Washington. It realizes that this new and radical departure has been recommended, and is now being defended, on the ground that by giving certain bureaus or sections wholly to colored employees they are thereby rendered safer in possession of their offices and are less likely to be ousted or discriminated against. We believe this reasoning to be fallacious. It is based on a failure to appreciate the deeper significance of the new policy; to understand how far reaching the effects of such a drawing of caste lines by the Federal Government may be, and how humiliating it is to the men thus stigmatized.

Never before has the Federal Government discriminated against its civilian employees on the ground of color. Every such act heretofore has been that of an individual State. . . . The colored people themselves will tell you how soon sensitive and high-minded members of their race will refuse to enter the Government service which thus decrees what is to them the most hateful kind of discrimination. Indeed, there is a widespread belief among them that this is the very purpose of these unwarrantable orders. And wherever there are men who rob the Negroes of their votes, who exploit and degrade and insult and lynch those whom they call their inferiors, there this mistaken action of the Federal Government will be cited as the warrant for new racial outrages that cry out to high Heaven for redress. . . .

Letter of the biracial board of the NAACP to President Wilson, August 15, 1913, as printed in Cleveland Plain Dealer, *August 18, p. 1.*

We must prove ourselves [the Latin American nations'] friends, and champions upon terms of equality and honor. . . . We must show ourselves friends by comprehending their interest whether it squares with our own interest or not. It is a very perilous thing to determine the foreign policy of a nation in the terms of material interest. It not only is unfair to those with whom you are dealing, but it is degrading as regards your own actions.

Comprehension must be the soil in which shall grow all the fruits of friendship, and there is a reason and a compulsion lying behind all this which is dearer than anything else to the thoughtful men of America. I mean the development of constitutional liberty in the world. Human rights, national integrity, and opportunity as against material interests—that, ladies and gentlemen, is the issue which we now have to face. I want to take this occasion to say that the United States will never again seek one foot of territory by conquest. She will devote herself to showing that she knows how to make honorable and fruitful use of the territory she has, and she must regard it as one of the duties of friendship to see that from no quarter are material interests made superior to human liberty and national opportunity. I say this, not with the thought that anyone will gainsay it, but merely to fix in our consciousness what our real relationship with the rest of America is. It is the relationship of a family devoted to the development of constitutional liberty.

Woodrow Wilson, address at Mobile, Alabama, October 27, 1913, outlining his policy for Latin America, 63rd Congress, 1st session, Senate Document 226.

. . . the keystone of our [socialists'] principal difficulties is that large and decisive group of progressive voters which holds the balance of power in America today. These Progressives are hard to describe. They are more numerous than the Bull Moose; their national leaders include Roosevelt, Wilson, Bryan, La Follette; they are single-taxers and prohibitionists, anti-trust people, anti-Tammany, efficiency enthusiasts like John Purroy Mitchel, unclassifiable men like Brand Whitlock, Linsey or Steffens; they are Collier's Weekly and the Saturday Evening Post, they are the muckraking magazines, the social workers, the conservationists, white slave crusaders and woman suffragists; they are the most widely spread element in public life. They hold their party ties lightly; they are today in a liquid condition, and under certain circumstances they will flow towards us. They are not afraid of Socialism, not of the name anyway. They like Socialism a great deal better than they do the Socialists.

The temper of these Progressives is to use any political machine that will serve them.

Political commentator Walter Lippmann, briefly secretary to the socialist mayor of Schenectady, letter to a party official, October 29, 1913, "On Municipal Socialism, 1913," pp. 188–89.

The millions of adult men and women, of children older than the upper limit of the compulsory school attendance age, must be looked after; they must be prepared for American citizenship and for participation in our democratic, industrial, social, and religious life. For the enrichment of our national life as well as for the happiness and welfare of individuals we must respect their ideals and preserve and strengthen all of the best of their Old World life they bring with them. We must not attempt to destroy and remake— we can only transform. Racial and national virtues must not be thoughtlessly exchanged for American vices.

The proper education of these people is a duty which the nation owes to itself and to them. It can neglect this duty only to their hurt and to its peril. No systematic effort has ever been made to work out the best methods therefor. We have little definite usable knowledge of the varying characteristics of the several races [ethnic groups]. We are ignorant even of the surest and quickest way to teach them to speak and understand English.

Commissioner of Education P. P. Claxton, letter to Secretary of the Interior Franklin K. Lane, November 1, 1913, "Education of the Immigrant," U.S. Bureau of Education, Bulletin, 1913, No. 51, pp. 5–6.

The goose that lays golden eggs has been considered a most valuable possession. But even more profitable is the privilege of taking the golden eggs laid by somebody else's goose. The investment bankers and their associates now enjoy that privilege. They control the people through the people's own money. If the bankers' power were commensurate only with their wealth, they would have relatively little influence on American business. Vast fortunes like those of the Astors are no doubt regrettable. They are inconsistent with democracy. They are unsocial. And they seem peculiarly unjust when they represent largely unearned increment. But the wealth of the Astors does not endanger political or industrial liberty. It is insignificant in amount as compared with the aggregate wealth of America, or even of New York City. It lacks significance largely because its owners have only the income from their own wealth. The Astor wealth is static. The wealth of the Morgan associates is dynamic. The power and the growth of power of our financial oligarchs comes from wielding the savings and quick capital of others. In two of the three great life insurance companies the influence of J. P. Morgan & Co. and their associates is exerted without any individual investment by them whatsoever. . . . The fetters which bind the people are forged from the people's own gold.

Louis Brandeis, Other People's Money, which explained and popularized the findings of the Pujo Commission, 1914, pp. 18–19.

At the time of its [New York's housing law of 1901] enactment there were in the city of New York fruitful sources of disease in the shape of more than 9,000 "school sinks" or privy vaults, located in tenement house yards. These "school sinks" were practically open privies for the common use of all the inmates of the houses to which they were appurtenant, flushed occasionally into the sewers with water. The law required the abolition of these "school sinks" and the substitution for them of toilets in the houses, and prescribed that no toilet should furnish accommodation for more than two apartments. It also prescribed that these toilets should open to the outer air. At the present time only 375 "school sinks" exist in the city of New York. . . . At the time this law was enacted there were over 350,000 dark rooms in the city of New York; that is, rooms which had no opening to the outer air. The law made the ventilation of these rooms to the outer air obligatory. At the present time there remain . . . only about 76,324 such rooms. . . . The death rate in New York City for 1900, before this new cause began to operate, was 20.057 in the thousand. This has gradually decreased, until the death rate in 1912 was only 14.11 in the thousand. Translating this into human lives, based on a population of 5,000,000, it means an annual saving of nearly 30,000. Translating it into immunity from sickness would give much larger figures.

Robert DeForest, president of the National Housing Association, "A Brief History of the Housing Movement in America," 1914, pp. 15–16.

If you go to an elder of the Boston race and ask why new projects are so unexceptionally bad, he will tell you that without reverence for tradition life becomes unsettled, and a nation loses itself for lack of cohesion.

These essays are based upon that observation, but added to it is the observation, just as important, that tradition will not work in the complexity of modern life. For if you ask Americans to remain true to the traditions of all their Fathers, there would be a pretty confusion if they followed your advice. . . .

The only possible cohesion now is a loyalty that looks forward. . . .

To do this men have to substitute purpose for tradition: and that is, I believe, the profoundest change that has ever taken place in human history. We can no longer treat life as something that has trickled down to us. We have to deal with it deliberately, devise its social organization, alter its tools, formulate its method, educate and control it. In endless ways we put intention where custom has reigned. We break up routines, make decisions, choose our ends, select means. . . .

. . . This is what mastery means: the substitution of conscious intention for unconscious striving.

Political commentator Walter Lippmann, Drift and Mastery, *1914, pp. 265–69.*

Progressivism means a relation between political and social democracy which is both mutually dependent and mutually supplementary. Thoroughgoing political democracy is unnecessary and meaningless except for the purpose of realizing the ideal of social justice. The ideal of social justice is so exacting and so comprehensive that it cannot be progressively attained by any agency, save by the loyal and intelligent devotion of the popular will. . . .

. . . One of the great weaknesses of professional democrats in this country has been their tendency to conceive democracy as essentially a matter of popular political machinery. . . . They did not pretend that the people could not go wrong; but they conceived democracy as an air-ship with an automatic balancing and stabilizing mechanism. The free use of the ballot box was sufficient to render it proof against fools and knaves. This conception of democracy, precisely because it fails to associate democracy with the conscious realization of a social ideal, always assumes a negative emphasis. Its dominant object is not to give positive momentum and direction to popular rule. It seeks, above all, to prevent the people from being betrayed—from being imposed upon by unpopular policies and unrepresentative officials. But to indoctrinate and organize one's life chiefly for the purpose of avoiding betrayal is to invite sterility and disintegration.

Herbert Croly, Progressive Democracy, *1914, the year he founded the influential progressive journal* New Republic, *pp. 211–13.*

Frank Lloyd Wright, one of America's greatest architects, was also a progressive concerned about affordable housing. He designed partially prefabricated American System-Built Houses between 1915 and 1917, like the one pictured here in a catalog of a Wisconsin construction company. *(Library of Congress, Prints and Photographs Division, LC-USZ62-106445)*

The men were in no sense agitators or inclined to demand unreasonable concessions. Their grievance lay at the root of modern industrialism; they experienced the change from personal relationship to a "boss," who was once of their own class, to a Limited Liability Stock Company, with its divided ownership and its absentee landlordism. . . .

Then came the change, gradually, but not painlessly. The old men were dropped without ceremony. Their pay envelopes were handed them with the last week's wages inside, and "You need not report next week," outside. . . . Then came a sharp reduction of wages. Ordinarily the men would have faced courageously the problem of how to live on a smaller wage; but now they were sullen and resentful. . . .

So the workingmen struck. They hung about in groups, they yelled "scab," threw rocks, blocked switches and demolished trains. There were deputy sheriffs and constables and hired ruffians by the hundreds; but they did not compel the men to go back to work. It was the hunger of their children that did. . . .

I have been told frequently that we import Socialists and Anarchists. . . . Perhaps a few of them are imported; but we have quite a respectable home industry, what one might call an infant industry, in the manufacture of Anarchists. This one, like many infant industries, has grown colossal, having fed upon the result of special privileges to the few, and special wrongs to the many.

Edward A. Steiner, an Austrian immigrant who became a well-known social gospel minister, describes a railroad strike in his congregation in the Northwest, From Alien to Citizen, *1914, pp. 281–85.*

All circuses, shows and tent exhibitions, to which the attendance of the public of more than one race is invited or expected to attend shall provide for the convenience of its patrons not less than two ticket offices with individual ticket sellers, and not less than two entrances to the said perfor-

mance, with individual ticket takers and receivers, and in the case of outside or tent performances, the said ticket offices shall not be less than twenty-five feet apart; that one of the said entrances shall be exclusively for the white race, and another exclusively for persons of the colored race. . . .

Louisiana segregates its ticket booths, Acts of Louisiana, 1914 *(no. 235, sec. 1), 465, quoted in Bardolph,* Civil Rights Record, *p. 197.*

Something there is that doesn't love a wall,
That sends the frozen-ground-swell under it,
And spills the upper boulders in the sun;
And makes gaps even two can pass abreast.
Robert Frost, "Mending Wall," from North of Boston, *1914, p. 11.*

W. E. B. DuBois helped found the NAACP and edited its journal, *The Crisis,* from 1910 until the 1930s. After the death of Booker T. Washington in 1915, he was the leading spokesman for African Americans. *(Library of Congress, Prints and Photographs Division, LC-USZ62-36176)*

. . . to my mind, unaccustomed to such things, the whole room, with its interminable aisles, its whirling shafts and wheels, its forest of roof-supporting posts and flapping, flying, leather belting, its endless rows of writhing machinery, its shrieking, hammering, and clatter, its smell of oil, its autumn haze of smoke, its savage-looking foreign population—to my mind it expressed but one thing and that was delirium. . . .

Fancy a jungle of wheels and belts and weird iron forms—of men, machinery and movement—add to it every kind of sound you can imagine: the sound of a million squirrels chirking, a million monkeys quarreling, a million lions roaring, a million pigs dying, a million elephants smashing through a forest of sheet iron, a million boys whistling on their fingers, a million others coughing with the whooping cough, a million sinners groaning as they are dragged to hell—imagine all of this happening at the very edge of Niagara Falls, with the everlasting roar of the cataract as a perpetual background, and you may acquire a vague conception of that place.

Julian Street describes a visit to Ford's Highland Park automobile assembly line, 1914, Abroad at Home, *pp. 93–94.*

In our investigations here we use the following questions: Are you married? If married, how many dependent upon you? If single, how many dependent upon you and to what extent? Relationship of dependents? Residence of dependents? Married men: do you live with your wives [sic]? Have you ever had domestic troubles? Are your habits good or bad? Have you a bank account? What is the name of the bank and the number of the book? Last employment? Reasons for leaving? Would your home conditions be bettered were your income increased? Would you be willing to follow some systematic plan of saving suggested by the company?

Instructions for investigating employees, sent by Ford Motors to its operating offices, 1914, quoted in Brinkley, Wheels for the World, *p. 173.*

"The commonest laborer who sweeps the floor shall receive his $5 per day," said Henry Ford.

"It is our belief," said Mr. Couzens, "that social justice begins at home. We want those who have helped us to produce this great institution and are helping to maintain it to share our prosperity. We want them to have present profits and future prospects. Thrift and good service and sobriety all will be encouraged and recognized."...

"The public need have no fear that this action of ours will result in any increase in prices of our products. On the contrary we hope to keep up our past record of reducing prices each year."...

"The girl and women employees will not share in the profit distribution?" Mr. Couzens was asked.

"No," he replied. "They are not the same economic factors as the men are. They do not control the standard of living. There are 200 or 300 women employed in the electrical department. The rest that are here do office work. The average woman employee cannot be regarded as a fixture in a business as a man can be. A woman will leave at almost any time, for almost any reason, and when she stays long enough to be a dependable worker, she is apt to get married and have someone else support her. It is the man we aim to benefit. However, in connection with the profit sharing, the women employees will not lose, for there will be substantial raises of wages for them."...

"The sociological side of profit sharing is one of great importance . . ." added Mr. Couzens. . . .

"We want to see that our employees do not lose their efficiency because of prosperity. . . . Employees who cannot remain sober and industrious will be dismissed, but no one will be let out without being given every possible chance to make good. No one will be discharged until we find that he is of no use to us in any way whatever."

Interview with James Couzens, vice president of Ford Motors, January 4, 1914, Detroit Journal, *January 5, page 1.*

Every person in and in the vicinity of the colony reports the training of machine guns on women and children as targets in the open field. Mrs. Low, whose husband kept a pump-house for the railroad near the tent-colony, tells me that she had gone to Trinidad the day of the massacre. She came back at 12:45, alighted at a station a mile away, and started running across the prairie to save her little girl whom she had left alone in a tiny white house exactly in the line of fire. They trained a machine gun on her as she ran there.

"I had bought six new handkerchiefs in Trinidad," she said, "and I held them up and waved them for truce flags, but the bullets kep' coming. They come so thick my mind wasn't even on the bullets, but I remember they struck the dust and sent it up in my face. Finally some of the strikers saw I was going right on into the bullets—I was bound to save my little girl—and they risked their lives to run out

from the arroyo and drag me down after them. I didn't know where my baby was, or whether she was alive, til four-thirty that afternoon."

Her baby had run to her father in the pump-house at the first fire, and had been followed in there by a rain of .48-calibre bullets, one of which knocked a pipe out of her father's hand while she was trying to persuade him to be alarmed. He carried her down into the well and they stayed there until nightfall, when a freight train stopped in the line of fire and gave them a chance to run up the arroyo where the mother was hiding.

Editor Max Eastman, describing events at Ludlow, Colorado, April 1914, for his radical journal The Masses, *June 1914, available online at Ludlow Massacre Curriculum. URL:http://www.cobar.org/group/ index.cfm?category=673&EntityID=dpwfp.*

1. We find that the remote cause of this, as of all other battles, lies with the coal operators, who established in an American industrial community a numerous class of ignorant, lawless and savage South-European peasants. . . . The immediate cause of the battles was an attack upon the soldiers by the Greek inhabitants of the tent colony, who misinterpreted a movement of troops on a neighboring hill.

2. These Greeks and more violent element of the strikers had prepared for such an event by bringing back into the colony the arms secreted to escape the searches of the guardsmen. This was done in the latter part of March. They also secured a large amount of ammunition, and awaited a favorable moment for an engagement in which, they hoped to catch the soldiers unprepared. . . . Their plans miscarried and the battle precipitated suddenly on Monday morning was unexpected by all. . . .

7. The origin of the fire in the tent colony was accidental; that is to say, it was due either to an overturned stove, and explosion of some sort, or the concentrated fire directed at one time against some of the tents. . . . Afterwards it was deliberately spread by the combatants. . . . During the fire the soldiers, upon learning that women and children were still in the colony, went through the tents, calling upon all the persons in the colony to come forth, and with difficulty rescuing men, women and children. . . . Then the tents were fired. . . .

15. The soldiers were lawfully and dutifully bearing arms. It was lawful for them to possess the machine gun and to bring it to the hill. The strikers, on the other hand, were acting unlawfully in securing and using their arms and ammunition. . . .

Report of the Special Board of Officers appointed by the governor of Colorado to investigate the events at Ludlow, *April 20, 1914, available online at Colorado Bar Association Ludlow Massacre Curriculum. URL: http://www.cobar.org/group/ index.cfm?category=673&EntityID=dpwfp.*

The Grand Smash is come. Last night the German Ambassador at St. Petersburg handed the Russian Government a declaration of war. To-day the German Government asked the United States to take its diplomatic and consular business in Russia in hand. Herrick, our Ambassador in Paris, has already taken the German interests there.

It is reported in London to-day that the Germans have invaded Luxemburg and France. Troops were marching through London at one o'clock this morning. . . .

People came to the Embassy all day to-day (Sunday), to learn how they can get to the United States—a rather hard question to answer. . . .

Returned travellers from Paris report indescribable confusion—people unable to obtain beds and fighting for seats in railway carriages. . . .

The possible consequences stagger the imagination. Germany has staked everything on her ability to win primacy. . . .

I walked out in the night a while ago. The stars are bright, the night is silent, the country quiet—as quiet as peace itself. Millions of men are in camp and on warships. Will they all have to fight and many of them die—to untangle this network of treaties and alliances and to blow off huge debts with gunpowder so that the world may start again?

*U.S. ambassador to Great Britain Walter Hines Page,
memorandum August 2, 1914, Hendrick,
Life and Letters of Walter H. Page,
vol. 1, pp. 301–302.*

First: Money is the worst of all contrabands because it commands everything else. . . . I know of nothing that would do more to prevent war than an international agreement that neutral nations would not loan to belligerents. While such an agreement would be of great advantage, could we not by our example hasten the reaching of such an agreement? We are the one great nation which is not involved, and our refusal to loan to any belligerent would naturally tend to hasten a conclusion of the war. We are responsible for the use of our influence through example. . . .

Second: . . . a loan would be taken by those in sympathy with the country in whose behalf the loan was negotiated. If we approved of a loan to France we could not, of course, object to a loan to . . . any other country, and if loans were made to these countries, our citizens would be divided into groups, each group loaning money to the country which it favors. . . .

Third: The powerful financial interests which would be connected with these loans would be tempted to use their influence through the newspapers to support the interests of the Government to which they had loaned because the value of the security would be directly affected by the result of the war. We would thus find our newspapers vio-

lently arrayed on one side or the other, each paper supporting a financial group and pecuniary interest. All of this influence would make it all the more difficult for us to maintain neutrality. . . .

*Secretary of State William Jennings Bryan to President
Woodrow Wilson, August 10, 1914, in support of forbidding
American loans to warring nations, available online at World
War I Document Archive, URL:
http://www.lib.byu.edu/~rdh/wwi/
1914/bryanloan.html.*

The spirit of the Nation in this critical matter will be determined largely by what individuals and society and those gathered in public meetings do and say, upon what newspapers and magazines contain, upon what ministers utter in their pulpits and men proclaim as their opinions on the street.

The people of the United States are drawn from many nations, and chiefly from the nations now at war. It is natural and inevitable that there should be the utmost variety of sympathy and desire among them with regard to the issues and circumstances of the conflict. Some will wish one nation, others another, to succeed in the momentous struggle. It will be easy to excite passion and difficult to allay it. Those responsible for exciting it will assume a heavy responsibility for no less a thing than that the people of the United States, whose love of their country and whose loyalty to its government should unite them as Americans all, bound in honor and affection to think first of her and her interests, may be divided in camps of hostile opinion, not against each other, involved in the war itself in impulse and opinion if not in action. . . .

I venture, therefore, my fellow countrymen, to speak a solemn word of warning to you against that deepest, most subtle, most essential breach of neutrality which may spring out of partisanship, out of passionately taking sides. The United States must be neutral in fact, as well as in name, during these days that are to try men's souls. We must be impartial in thought, as well as action, must put a curb upon our sentiments, as well as upon every transaction that might be construed as a preference of one party to the struggle before another.

*President Wilson appeals for neutrality, Message to the Senate,
August 19, 1914, Supplement to the Messages and
Papers of the Presidents Covering the First Term of
Woodrow Wilson, pp. 7978–79.*

Be it enacted . . . ,
SEC. 5. That unfair methods of competition in commerce are hereby declared unlawful.

The commission is hereby empowered and directed to prevent persons, partnerships, or corporations, except banks, and common carriers subject to the Acts to regulate commerce, from using unfair methods of competition in commerce.

Whenever the commission shall have reason to believe that any such person, partnership, or corporation has been or is using any unfair method of competition in commerce . . . it shall issue and serve . . . a complaint stating its charges in that respect, and containing a notice of a hearing. . . . If upon such hearing the commission shall be of the opinion that the method of competition in question is prohibited by this Act, it shall . . . issue . . . an order requiring such person, partnership, or corporation to cease and desist. . . .

If such person, partnership, or corporation fails or neglects to obey such order . . . the commission may apply to the circuit court of appeals of the United States. . . . The findings of the commission as to the facts, if supported by testimony, shall be conclusive. . . . The judgment and decree of the court shall be final, except that the same shall be subject to review by the Supreme Court. . . .

SEC. 9. That for the purposes of this Act the commission . . . shall at all reasonable times have access to . . . and the right to copy any documentary evidence of any corporation being investigated or proceeded against; and the commission shall have power to require by subpoena the attendance and testimony of witnesses and the production of all such documentary evidence relating to any matter under investigation. . . .

No person shall be excused from attending and testifying or from producing documentary evidence . . . on the ground . . . that the testimony or evidence, documentary or otherwise, required of him may tend to criminate him or subject him to a penalty or forfeiture. . . .

Federal Trade Commission Act, September 26, 1914, U.S. Statutes at Large, 63rd Congress, vol. 38, pp. 717ff.

Be it enacted. . . .,

SEC. 2. That it shall be unlawful for any person engaged in commerce, in the course of such commerce, either directly or indirectly to discriminate in price between different purchasers of commodities, which commodities are sold for use, consumption, or resale within the United States or any Territory thereof or the District of Columbia or any insular possession or other place under the jurisdiction of the United States, where the effect of such discrimination may be to substantially lessen competition or tend to create a monopoly in any line of commerce. . . .

SEC. 6. That the labor of a human being is not a commodity or article of commerce. Nothing contained in the anti-trust laws shall be construed to forbid the existence and operation of labor, agricultural, or horticultural organizations, instituted for the purposes of mutual help, and not having capital stock or conducted for profit, or to forbid or restrain individual members of such organizations from

lawfully carrying out the legitimate objects thereof; nor shall such organizations, or the members thereof, be held or construed to be illegal combinations or conspiracies in restraint of trade, under the anti-trust laws.

SEC. 7. That no corporation engaged in commerce shall acquire, directly or indirectly, the whole or any part of the stock or other share capital of another corporation engaged also in commerce, where the effect of such acquisition may be to substantially lessen competition . . . or tend to create a monopoly of any line of commerce.

Clayton Anti-Trust Act, October 15, 1914, U.S. Statutes at Large, 63rd Congress, vol. 38, pp. 730ff.

Bryan spoke to me about peace as he always does. He sighs for the Nobel Prize, and besides that he is a really convinced peaceman. He has just given me a sword beaten into a ploughshare six inches long to serve as a paperweight. It is adorned with quotations from Isaiah and himself. No one doubts his sincerity, but that is rather embarrassing for us at the present moment, because he is always at us with peace propositions. This time, he said he could not understand why we could not say what we were fighting for. The nation which continued war had as much responsibility as the country which began it. The United States was the one great Power which was outside the struggle, and it was their duty to do what they could to put an end to it.—I felt rather cross and said that the United States were signatories to the Hague Convention, which had been grossly violated again and again without one word from the principal neutral nation. They were now out of court. They had done nothing to prevent the crime, and now they must not prevent the punishment. . . .

Letter from Sir Cecil Spring-Rice to Sir Arthur Nicolson about William Jennings Bryan, November 13, 1914, available online at World War I Document Archive. URL: http: www.lib.byu.edu/~rdh/wwi/1914/bryice.html.

Some are trying to defend alcohol by saying that its abuse only is bad and that its temperate use is all right. Science absolutely denies it, and proclaims that drunkenness does not produce one-tenth part of the harm to society that the widespread, temperate, moderate drinking does. Some say it is adulteration that harms. Some are trying to say that it is only distilled liquors that do harm. Science comes in now and says that all alcohol does harm; that the malt and fermented liquors produce vastly more harm than distilled liquors, and that it is the general public use of such drinks that has entailed the gradual decline and degeneracy of the nations of the past. . . .

The first finding of science that alcohol is a protoplasmic poison and the second finding that it is an insidious, habit-forming drug, though of great importance, are as unimportant when compared with the third finding, that alcohol degenerates the character of men and tears down their spiritual nature. . . .

Democratic Congressman Richmond P. Hobson of Alabama, speaking in favor of the prohibition amendment he introduced into the House of Representatives, December 22, 1914, Congressional Record, 63rd Congress, 3rd session, vol. 52, pp. 602–04.

The Nation is a web and woof of citizenship, and a single torn thread mars the whole fabric. The task of statesmanship today is to end the anarchy of selfish individualism and to discover the principles underlying great social movements and to direct their development along lines of human welfare. . . .

The entire trend of legislation for many years shows how increasingly great is the necessity for governmental action in realms formerly held to be purely matters of individual conduct. Providing for public schools, penalizing adulteration of food, regulating hours of labor for women, prohibiting child labor, stamping out contagious diseases, securing sanitary conditions, dealing with white slavery, establishing restrictions of all kinds upon the individual in order to promote the common welfare—all these are eloquent witnesses to the governmental activities which are to-day almost universally recognized and commended.

. . . The enlightened conscience of America is not demanding that Government keep its hands off everything except the preservation of peace. It demands that the Government put its hands on everything that will promote the common good more effectively than individual effort.

Republican congressman Melville C. Kelly of Pennsylvania, debate over the Hobson prohibition resolution, December 22, 1914, Congressional Record, 63rd Congress, 3rd session, vol. 52, p. 503.

First. Prohibition is a deathblow to the liberty of the individual because it prohibits what is not wrong in itself. . . . In other words, we are dealing in this case with what John Stuart Mill called "the tyranny of the majority," an evil against which the Nation must protect itself if it desires to remain free. . . .

Second. Prohibition runs counter to human nature because the taste and appetite of man can not be regulated by law. . . .

Third. Prohibition undermines manliness. Its premise is that men are children, who must be led in the leading strings of law. . . .

Fourth. Prohibition undermines respect for the law. A thousand ways will be found to evade the law, and the result will be a Nation of lawbreakers, a condition which must inevitably lead to lawlessness and anarchy.

Fifth. National prohibition by constitutional amendment is unworthy of a great people. A constitution should be a bill of rights for the protection of life, liberty, and property, and especially for the protection of the minority. By incorporating in it mere police regulations our National Constitution . . . will be perverted, defaced, and desecrated.

Sixth. National prohibition means the complete subversion of the fundamental theories upon which our system of government rests. By the wise foresight of the fathers of the Republic the police power was reserved to the separate States . . .

Seventh. Prohibition means the confiscation of property valued at a thousand million dollars, property which has been acquired strictly in accordance with State and Federal law. . . .

Eighth. Prohibition will take the bread from the mouths of hundreds of thousands of employees and workingmen. . . .

Ninth. Prohibition will cause a deficit in the National Treasury of at least $280,000,000 a year, for this is the amount which the Government now collects from beer, wine, and spirituous liquors, and which, by the way, far exceeds our total expenses for Army and Navy. . . .

Tenth. Prohibition does not prohibit. . . . you can vote a town dry, but you can not vote a man dry.

Republican Congressman Richard Bartholdt of Missouri offers 10 reasons to defeat prohibition, December 22, 1914, Congressional Record, 63rd Congress, 3rd session, vol. 52, pp. 549–50.

I am really not in France but Belgium. I cannot tell you just where, but it is within ten miles of the firing line. . . . It is a regular field hospital and is composed of a great many portable huts or sheds. . . . It is a little colony set down in the fields and the streets are wooden sidewalks.

The first night I arrived I did not sleep, for the guns roared all night long, and we could see the flashes from the shells quite plainly; the whole sky was aglow. The French and English guns sounded like a continuous roar of thunder; but when the shells from the German guns landed on this side we could feel a distinct shock, and everything in our little shanty rattled.

Yesterday I saw my first battle in the air between German and French aeroplanes. We could scarcely see the machines, they were so high up in the air, but we could see the flashes from their guns quite distinctly and hear the explosion of the shells. To-day a whole fleet of aeroplanes passed over our heads; it was a wonderful sight. . . .

We have a man in our ward who had a piece of shrapnel the size of an egg in his abdomen; they had to take out about half a yard of intestines, which had been torn to pieces. . . . The Germans are using a new kind of gas bomb that blinds the men.

Letter home by a Canadian nurse, 1915, "My Beloved Poilus," available online at The Medical Front. URL: http://www.ku.edu/carrie/specoll/medical/canadian/cnurse.htm

3. The concentration of ownership and control is greatest in the basic industries upon which the welfare of the country must finally rest.

4. With few exceptions each of the great basic industries is dominated by a single large corporation. . . .

5. In such corporations, in spite of the large number of stockholders, the control through actual stock ownership rests with a very small number of persons. . . .

6. Almost without exception the employees of the large corporations are unorganized as a result of the active and aggressive "nonunion" policy of the corporation management.

Furthermore, the labor policy of the large corporations almost inevitably determines the labor policy of the entire industry. . . .

8. The lives of millions of wage earners are therefore subject to the dictation of a relatively small number of men.

9. These industrial dictators for the most part are totally ignorant of every aspect of the industries which they control except the finances, and are totally unconcerned with regard to the working and living conditions of the employees in those industries. Even if they were deeply concerned, the position of the employees would be merely that of the subjects of benevolent industrial despots. . . .

12. The domination by the men in whose hands the final control of a large part of American industry rests is not limited to their employees, but is being rapidly extended to control the education and "social service" of the Nation. . . .

U.S. Commission on Industrial Relations,
Final Report and Testimony, vol. 1, pp. 80–81.

My observation leads me to believe that while there are many contributing causes to [labor] unrest there is one cause which is fundamental. That is . . . the contrast between our political liberty and our industrial absolutism. We are as free politically, perhaps, as free as it is possible for us to be. Every male has his voice and vote; and the law has endeavored to enable . . . him to exercise his political franchise without fear. He therefore . . . can secure an adequate part in the government of the country in all of its political relations; that is, in all relations which are determined directly by legislation or governmental administration.

On the other hand, in dealing with industrial problems, the position of the ordinary worker is exactly the reverse. The individual employee has no effective voice or vote. And the main objection, as I see it, to the very large corporation is that it makes possible—and in many cases makes inevitable—the exercise of industrial absolutism. . . . But we have the situation of an employer so potent, so well-organized, with such concentrated forces and with such extraordinary powers of reserve and the ability to endure against strikes and other efforts of a union, that the relatively loosely organized masses of even strong unions

Lawyer Louis Brandeis, born in Kentucky, was a fervent and effective advocate for many reform efforts during the Progressive Era. In 1916, he became the first Jewish American to sit on the Supreme Court. *(Library of Congress, Prints and Photographs Division, LC-USZ62-92924)*

are unable to cope with the situation. We are dealing here with a question, not of motive but of condition.

Louis Brandeis, testimony before the U.S. Commission on
Industrial Relations, Final Report and Testimony,
vol. 8, p. 7659.

The statute law of Colorado ordered a semimonthly payday, checkweighmen so that we might not be cheated, the right to form unions, the eight-hour day, and payment in cash—not scrip. We charged that the Colorado Fuel & Iron Co. had violated these and other laws, and in addition we told of evil housing conditions, high rents, company-store extortions, saloon environment, armed guards, and the denial of freedom in speech, education, religion, and politics. When 12,000 men back up such claims by taking their wives and children into windswept tents, surely they would seem to be deserving of consideration.

Yet upon the stand, throughout three whole days this week, John D. Rockefeller, Jr., insisted that he was absolutely ignorant of every detail of the strike. He stated that he had not received reports on labor conditions, he could not tell within several thousands how many men worked for him in Colorado, he did not know what wages they received or what rent they paid, he had never considered what the proper length of a working day should be, he did not know what constituted a living wage, and, most amazing of all, he had never even read the list of grievances that the strikers filed with the governor of Colorado and gave to the world through the press.

United Mine Workers official John Lawson, testimony before the U.S. Commission on Industrial Relations on the miners' strike in Colorado, Final Report and Testimony, *vol. 8, p. 8005.*

Whatever difference of opinion may exist concerning the meaning of the progressive movement, every thinking man and woman must be convinced that the nation to-day is passing through a severe political crisis. After a period of unprecedented industrial and commercial expansion, during which time little or no attention has been given to the problems of government, the people have suddenly realized that government is not functioning properly and that radical changes are needed. . . . Everywhere there are evidences that the nation has passed into a new political era.

In this widespread political agitation that at first sight seems so incoherent and chaotic, there may be distinguished . . . three tendencies. The first of these tendencies is found in the insistence by the best men in all political parties that special, minority, and corrupt influence in government—national, state, and city—be removed; the second tendency is found in the demand that the structure or machinery of government, which has hitherto been admirably adapted to control by the few, be so changed and modified that it will be more difficult for the few, and easier for the many, to control; and, finally, the third tendency is found in the rapidly growing conviction that the functions of government at present are too restricted and that they must be increased and extended to relieve social and economic distress. These three tendencies with varying emphasis are seen to-day in the platform and program of every political party; . . . and, because of their universality and definiteness, they may be said to constitute the real progressive movement.

Benjamin Parke DeWitt's pioneering analysis, The Progressive Movement, *1915, pp. 4–5.*

Films of a "moral, educational, or amusing and harmless character shall be passed and approved," are the words of the [Ohio] statute. No exhibition . . . will be prevented if its pictures have those qualities. . . . But they may be used for evil, and against that possibility the statute was enacted. Their power of amusement, and, it may be, education, the audiences they assemble, not of women alone nor of men alone, but together, not of adults only, but of children, make them the more insidious in corruption by a pretense of worthy purpose or if they should degenerate from worthy purpose. Indeed, we may go beyond that possibility.

They take their attraction from the general interest, eager and wholesome it may be, in their subjects, but a prurient interest may be excited and appealed to. Besides, there are some things which should not have pictorial representation in public places and to all audiences. . . . We would have to shut our eyes to the facts of the world to regard the precaution unreasonable or the legislation to effect it a mere wanton interference with personal liberty. . . .

Are moving pictures within the principle [of free speech], as it is contended they are? They, indeed, may be mediums of thought, but so are many things. So is the theater, the circus, and all other shows and spectacles, and their performances may be thus brought by the like reasoning under the same immunity from repression or supervision as the public press, made the same agencies of civil liberty. . . .

It cannot be put out of view that the exhibition of moving pictures is a business, pure and simple, originated and conducted for profit, like other spectacles, not to be regarded . . . as part of the press of the country, or as organs of public opinion.

Justice Joseph McKenna writing the unanimous decision of the Supreme Court, February 23, 1915, Mutual Film Corp. v. Industrial Commission of Ohio, *236 US 230.*

. . . . Thus "American civilization" may come to mean the perfection of the cooperative harmonies of "European civilization," the waste, the squalor, and the distress of Europe being eliminated—a multiplicity in a unity, an orchestration of mankind. As in an orchestra, every type of instrument has its specific timbre and tonality, founded in its substance and form; as every type has its appropriate theme and melody in the whole symphony, so in society each ethnic group is the natural instrument, its spirit and culture are its theme and melody, and the harmony and dissonances and discords of them all make the symphony of civilization, with this difference: a musical symphony is written before it is played; in the symphony of civilization the playing is the writing, so that there is nothing so fixed and inevitable about its progressions as in music, so that within the limits set by nature they may vary at will, and the range and variety of the harmonies may become wider and richer and more beautiful.

Horace Kallen, who later coined the term "cultural pluralism," "Democracy Versus the Melting Pot," Part 2, The Nation, *vol. 100 (February 25, 1915), p. 220.*

The man was forty-five and his wife, a tired-looking woman in a sunbonnet and a calico dress, a year or two younger. . . . Levi Stewart was one of eleven children—all but one "renters" like himself. He had married a neighbor's daughter when she was fifteen. They had eleven children, eight still living. They worked. "We got up early and stayed with it late," he said. They went into the fields "by sunup." He plowed and hoed. And his wife hoed. There were no amusements at all during "crop times," and crop time was from the middle of February to the middle of July. We asked who picked their cotton. "I and her picked it around them times." He had some railroad land for a year but cotton went down, and everything got balled up and he couldn't pay for it. He had cleared three acres of land and built a house with his own hands. One year he had "no wagon." His oldest boy never got more than one year's schooling. . . . Wearily it went on. Year after year they raised corn and cotton, cotton and corn. He'd been obliged to give chattel mortgages and had to pay ten per cent interest. He'd always had to pay extra credit prices for his goods at the store. His wife never went to town, except once when she had erysipelas, he'd carried her to town. . . . Chairman Walsh had me do the questioning of his wife. My own back seemed to ache as she went on with the story of their life.

Florence Harriman recounts hearing testimony from tenant farmers in Texas as a member of the U.S. Industrial Commission, March 1915, From Pinafores to Politics, *pp. 170–72.*

"The producer seems to have followed the principle of gathering the most vicious and grotesque individuals he could find among colored people, and showing them as representatives of the truth about the entire race," she said in describing her impressions of the play. "It is both unjust and untrue. The same method could be followed to smirch the reputation of any race. For instance, it would be easy enough to go about the slums of a city and bring together some of the criminals and degenerates and take pictures of them purporting to show the character of the white race. It would no more be the truth about the white race than this is about the black. . . .

"How far did you observe that this attitude of mind influenced the spectators?"

". . . Certainly I felt that they were made to feel a prejudice against negroes; some showed approval in applause when the hero refuses to shake hands with the mulatto politician, and they were roused to the point of clapping enthusiastically, before the end of the pictures, whenever the Ku Klux Klan appeared. That was the noticeable thing about the play—the success of the glorification of the activities of the Ku Klux Klan, contrasted with the base and elemental character of the negroes misrepresented in the ludicrously perverted scenes of plantation life. The production is the most subtle form of untruth—a half-truth."

"Jane Addams Condemns Race Prejudice Film" on The Birth of a Nation, New York Evening Post, *March 13, 1915, p. 4.*

We were scheduled for a mid-day meeting at Raleigh, that was Good Friday, and I was to speak that night at Chapel Hill. The Raleigh newspaper came out with an article announcing that they would meet me at the train with a brass band and parade through the streets. It was an April Fool joke, but it made the suffragists tear their hair. They are trying to get suffrage there in the most lady-like manner, without having anybody find out they want it. They just had me in the middle of the day like a Lenten Service. As I spoke under the portrait of my great-grandfather [Henry Clay], and as he had dedicated the capitol in the forties, that lent a little respectability to me and suffrage. I think it also comforted them when the Bishop of North Carolina called, because he is one of my mother's Hart relatives—I found them all through that part of North Carolina. I took pains to tell him that the Bishop of South Carolina and his wife had both come to the meeting and that they were both suffragists.

Madeline McDowell Breckinridge of Lexington, Kentucky, letter to a friend describing campaigning for suffrage in the South, April 15, 1915, Breckinridge, Madeline McDowell Breckinridge, *p. 210.*

Boulogne, April 25.—The gaseous vapor which the Germans used against the French divisions near Ypres last Thursday, contrary to the rules of The Hague Convention, introduces a new element into warfare. The attack of last Thursday evening was preceded by the rising of a cloud of vapor, greenish gray and iridescent. That vapor settled to the ground like a swamp mist and drifted toward the French trenches on a brisk wind. Its effect on the French was a violent nausea and faintness, followed by an utter collapse. It is believed that the Germans, who charged in behind the vapor, met no resistance at all, the French at their front being virtually paralyzed.

Everything indicates long and thorough preparation for this attack. The work of sending out the vapor was done from the advanced German trenches. Men garbed in a dress resembling the harness of a diver and armed with retorts or generators about three feet high and connected with ordinary hose pipe turned the vapor loose towards the French lines. Some witnesses maintain that the Germans sprayed the earth before the trenches with a fluid which, being ignited, sent up the fumes. The German troops, who followed up this advantage with a direct attack, held inspirators in their mouths, thus preventing them from being overcome by the fumes.

In addition to this, the Germans appear to have fired ordinary explosive shells loaded with some chemical which had a paralyzing effect on all the men in the region of the explosion. Some chemical in the composition of those shells produced violent watering of the eyes, so that the men overcome by them were practically blinded for some hours.

War Correspondent Will Irwin describes gas warfare, first used at Ypres, France, April 22, 1915, "Germans use Blinding Gas to Aid Poison Fumes," New York Tribune, April 27, p. 1.

I spent a month in Van while our school was the target of the Turks. I saw them kill, burn and persecute. . . . I saw our town become a part of a barren waste. I saw Turks bury Armenian victims with the dogs, divide the women among them as wives and throw babies into the lake. The school was burned, the missionaries fled, and 35,000 of the 75,000 inhabitants of the Van district were killed or starved to death. . . .

For miles around the Armenians congregated at Van, drove out the Turks and made trenches. Stones, earth and sand-bags were piled over the school buildings. The Turks attacked, and for more than a month in April and May kept up a steady fire.

Finally the Russians came. We were under their protection for a month. The Turks, fleeing before the Russians, killed all Armenian prisoners and wounded.

Russian treachery became evident when they evacuated the town. They pillaged every standing home. . . . the general said: 'If you don't want us to leave you, come along.'

Only old men and feeble women refused the invitation. Fifteen grandchildren of mine, three daughters and their husbands, my son and myself made up our forlorn party. We travelled towards Russia on foot. There was no other way to go. We walked for twelve days—like dead men and women. As far ahead as we could see, there were women carrying or dragging their babies and wounded men staggering along at their sides. Death was common.

First one and then another of the children died. Typhoid was doing its work everywhere. We buried the babies where we happened to be. Seven of them in all died on the journey. When we arrived at Tiflis my husband died.

Sylvia Gazarian, founder of a Christian School in Armenia, survivor of the Armenian massacres by the Turks, April–August 1915, and emigrant to America, as interviewed by the St. Paul Pioneer Press, reprinted in Toynbee, ed., The Treatment of Armenians in the Ottoman Empire, also available online at World War I Document Archive. URL: http://www.lib.byu.edu/~rdh/wwi/1915/bryce/a03.htm#20.

The truth is that this new means for public amusement and education [that is, movies] has brought with it grave perils which we are only just beginning to realize, for side by side with its educational possibilities are the dangers of unrestricted propaganda. As the Rev. Dr. Crothers has pointed out, we have lulled ourselves into a sense of security by repeating to ourselves that the "past at least is secure." But along comes this play, which is not only designed to make large sums for its promoters, but is admittedly a deliberate propaganda to degrade and injure ten millions of citizens, besides misrepresenting some of the noblest figures in our past, Stevens, Sumner, and Lincoln, and perverting history, if only by the one-sidedness of its portrayal. . . .

Yet so excellent a newspaper as the Boston *Advertiser* feels that the proposed censorship may be a most dangerous infringement of our freedom of speech and of expression, on a par with the efforts to suppress Garrison and Phillips in anti-slavery days. The Boston *Transcript and Herald* appear to believe that if one bill proposed should become a law any citizens who indulged in a fight over a play could stop it, and that any play with a lesson to teach or one which undertook to dwell on the weaknesses of a group of our citizens might easily be driven off the stage.

The Nation comments on censorship and The Birth of a Nation, "The Regulation of Films," Nation, vol. 100 (May 6, 1915), p. 487.

This is the only country in the world which experiences this constant and repeated rebirth. . . . by the gift of the free will of independent people it is constantly being renewed from generation to generation by the same process by which it was originally created. It is as if humanity had determined to see to it that this great nation, founded for the benefit of humanity, should not lack for the allegiance of the people of the world.

You have taken an oath of allegiance to a great ideal, to a great body of principles, to a great hope of the human race. You have said, "We are going to America," not only to earn a living . . . but to help forward the great enterprises of the human spirit—to let man know that everywhere in the world there are men who will cross strange oceans . . ., knowing that, whatever the speech, there is but one longing and utterance of the human heart, and that is for liberty and justice. . . .

And while you bring all countries with you, you come with a purpose of leaving all other countries behind you—bringing what is best of their spirit, but not looking over your shoulders and seeking to perpetuate what you intended to leave in them. I certainly would not be one even to suggest that a man ceases to love the home of his birth and the nation of his origin—these things are very sacred and ought not to be put out of our hearts—but it is one thing to love the place where you were born and it is another thing to dedicate yourself to the place to which you go. You cannot dedicate yourself to America unless you become in every respect and with every purpose of your will thorough Americans. You cannot become thorough Americans if you think of yourselves in groups. America does not consist of groups. A man who thinks of himself as belonging to a particular national group in America, has not yet become an American, and the man who goes among you to trade upon your nationality is no worthy son to live under the Stars and Stripes.

Woodrow Wilson, "Americanism and the Foreign-Born," address to the naturalization celebration, Philadelphia, May 10, 1915, Supplement to the Messages and Papers of the Presidents Covering the First Term of Woodrow Wilson, *pp. 8066–67.*

Turning suddenly to the left from the main road, I drove our little Ford three kilometres along the road . . . then turning left again we drove slowly to a village so full of soldiers that it seemed impossible so many could even find shelter—a quick turn to the right—up—up—up—first speed—along a very narrow road with just room for the car. On both sides were stuck up cut tree branches to make the Germans think there was no road. Up we went through another tiny hill village full of artillery, and on every side, underground dugouts where they all live . . . and at last we reached the top. The water in the radiator was boiling, so we stopped, walked a bit in the most beautiful woods, and picked flowers and wild strawberries to the tune of birds and distant cannon. In this wood are heavy naval guns, but from where and how they were ever taken there is a puzzle. . . .

The thick woods teemed with soldiers, and dotted through the forests were little huts, very low, where they live—thousands of them—pathways starting every twenty yards to some new wood village. We heard music, and on reaching our destination were invited to inspect these quaint habitations. We walked down a path past hut after hut, and then suddenly the wood opened out and we came to a kind of amphitheatre. . . . and we listened . . . to a band of three, banjo, violin, and dulcimer. . . .

. . . On my first arrival at this little mountain village I was horrified to see two people lying dead in the road in huge pools of blood. Six German "150's" had been suddenly launched into the village which is full of soldiers, and killed six soldiers and wounded some thirty. . . . Two of our ambulances were in the street at the time and only chance spared them.

Letter by Leslie Buswell, American volunteer ambulance driver in Alsace, June 1915, With The American Ambulance Field Service in France, *also available online at The Medical Front. URL: http://www.ku.edu/carrie/ specoll/medical/ambindex.htm.*

Whatever may be the contentions of the Imperial German Government regarding the carriage of contraband of war on board the Lusitania or regarding the explosion of that material by the torpedo, it need only be said that in the view of this Government these contentions are irrelevant to the question of the legality of the methods used by the German naval authorities in sinking the vessel.

But the sinking of passenger ships involves principles of humanity which throw into the background any special circumstances of detail that may be thought to affect the cases, principles which lift it, as the Imperial German Government will no doubt be quick to recognize and acknowledge, out of the class of ordinary subjects of diplomatic discussion or of international controversy. . . .

The Government of the United States is contending for something much greater than mere rights of property or privileges of commerce. It is contending for nothing less high and sacred than the rights of humanity, which every Government honours itself in respecting and which no Government is justified in resigning on behalf of those under its care and authority. . . .

The second Lusitania note, signed by Robert Lansing after William Jennings Bryan resigned, June 9, 1915, Foreign Relations of the United States, 1915, *Supplement, p. 436.*

It is with sincere regret that I have reached the conclusion I should return to you the commission of Secretary of State with which you honored me at the beginning of your administration.

Obedient to your sense of duty, and actuated by the highest motives, you have prepared for transmission to the German government a note in which I can not join without violating what I deem to be an obligation to my country, and the issue involved is of such moment that to remain a member of the cabinet would be as unfair to you as it would be to the cause which is nearest my heart, namely, the prevention of war.

I, therefore, respectfully tender my resignation, to take effect when the note is sent unless you prefer an earlier hour. Alike desirous of reaching a peaceful solution of the problems arising out of the use of submarines against merchantmen we find ourselves differing irreconcilably as to the methods which shall be employed.

It falls to your lot to speak officially for the nation: I consider it to be none the less my duty to endeavor as a private citizen to promote the end which you have in view by means which you do not feel at liberty to use.

William Jennings Bryan, letter of resignation to President Wilson, June 9, 1915, Papers of Woodrow Wilson, *vol. 33, p. 375.*

When the German bombardment began, the west front of Rheims was covered with scaffolding: the shells set it on fire, and the whole church was wrapped in flames. Now the scaffolding is gone, and in the dull provincial square there stands a structure so strange and beautiful that one must search the Inferno, or some tale of Eastern magic, for words to picture the luminous unearthly vision. The lower part of the front has been warmed to deep tints of umber and burnt sienna. This rich burnishing passes, higher up, through yellowish-pink and carmine, to a sulphur whitening to ivory; and the recesses of the portals and the hollows behind the statues are lined with a black denser and more velvety than any effect of shadow to be obtained by sculptured relief. The interweaving of colour over the whole blunted bruised surface recalls the metallic tints, the peacock-and-pigeon iridescences, the incredible mingling of red, blue, umber and yellow of the rocks along the Gulf of Ægina. And the wonder of the impression is increased by the sense of its evanescence; the knowledge that this is the beauty of disease and death, that every one of the transfigured statues must crumble under the autumn rains, that every one of the pink or golden stones is already eaten away to the core, that the Cathedral of Rheims is glowing and dying before us like a sunset . . .

American novelist Edith Wharton describes the famous cathedral at Rheims, France, August 13, 1915, Fighting France, *pp. 185–86.*

If the European countries cannot find means to pay for the excess of goods sold to them over those purchased from them, they will have to stop buying and our present export trade will shrink proportionately. The result would be restriction of outputs, industrial depression, idle capital and idle labor, numerous failures, financial demoralization, and general unrest and suffering among the laboring classes.

. . . [T]here is only one means of avoiding this situation which would so seriously affect economic conditions in the country, and that is the flotation of large bond issues by the belligerent governments. Our financial institutions have the money to loan and wish to do so. . . .

The difficulty is . . . that the Government early in the war announced that it considered "war loans" to be contrary to "the true spirit of neutrality." A declaration to this effect was given to the press about August 15, 1914, by Secretary Bryan. . . .

Now, on the other hand, we are face to face with what appears to be a critical economic situation, which can only be relieved apparently by the investment of American capital in foreign loans to be used in liquidating the enormous balance of trade in favor of the United States.

Can we afford to let a declaration as to our conception of "the true spirit of neutrality" made in the first days of the war stand in the way of our national interests which seem to be seriously threatened?

Secretary of State Robert Lansing to President Wilson, September 6, 1915, World War I Document Archive, *available online at URL: http://www.lib.byu.edu/~rdh/wwi/1915/us/oans.html.*

. . . There is no room in this country for hyphenated Americanism. When I refer to hyphenated Americans, I do not refer to naturalized Americans. Some of the very best Americans I have ever known were naturalized Americans, Americans born abroad. But a hyphenated American is not an American at all. This is just as true of the man who puts "native" before the hyphen as of the man who puts German or Irish or English or French before the hyphen. Americanism is a matter of the spirit and of the soul. Our allegiance must be purely to the United States. We must unsparingly condemn any man who holds any other allegiance. But if he is heartily and singly loyal to this Republic, then no matter where he was born, he is just as good an American as any one else.

The one absolutely certain way of bringing this nation to ruin, of preventing all possibility of its continuing to be a nation at all, would be to permit it to become a tangle of squabbling nationalities, an intricate knot of German-Americans, Irish-Americans, English-Americans, French-Americans, Scandinavian-Americans or Italian-Americans, each preserving its separate nationality, each at heart feeling more sympathy with Europeans of that nationality, than with the other citizens of the American Republic. . . .

We cannot afford to continue to use hundreds of thousands of immigrants merely as industrial assets while they remain social outcasts and menaces any more than fifty years ago we could afford to keep the black man merely as an industrial asset and not as a human being. . . .

Theodore Roosevelt, "Americanism," October 12, 1915, speech to the Knights of Columbus, New York, Davis, ed., Immigration and Americanization, *p. 77.*

It is reasonably certain, however, that the courts in no section of the country would uphold a case where Negroes sought to segregate white citizens. This is the most convincing argument that segregation is regarded as illegal, when viewed on its merits by the whole body of our white citizens. . . .

. . . Where attempts are being made to segregate the races legally, it should be noted that in the matter of business no attempt is made to keep the white man from placing his grocery store, his dry goods store, or other enterprise right in the heart of a Negro district. This is another searching test which challenges the good faith of segregationists. . . .

It is true that the Negro opposes these attempts to restrain him from residing in certain sections of a city or community. He does this not because he wants to mix with the white man socially, but because . . . it usually means that he will receive inferior accommodations in return for the taxes he pays. If the Negro is segregated, it will probably mean that the sewerage in his part of the city will be inferior; that the streets and sidewalks will be neglected, that the street lighting will be poor; that his section of the city will not be kept in order by the police and other authorities, and that the "undesirables" of other races will be placed near him, thereby making it difficult for him to rear his family in decency.

Booker T. Washington, "My View of Segregation Laws," New Republic, *vol. 5 (December 4, 1915), p. 113. [Washington died on November 14; this article was published posthumously.]*

I have guided many distinguished foreign guests who came here to study the strange ways of this country which they had called "the Dollar Land." If they were discerning, and some of them were, they discovered that this country is held together by a finer metal than gold and a nobler symbol than the eagle of our coinage.

They found that although there have come here in the last twenty years some thirteen millions of aliens, broken bits, torn patches of all nationalities and races, we are being knitted to one another as a nation. . . . These students of our national life were amazed and confounded as they observed the change in the expression, bearing and deportment of the peoples whom they knew in the Old World as sullen, rebellious, suspicious and incapable of cohesion.

Edward Steiner, Confession of a Hyphenated American, *1916, pp. 12–13.*

Failure to recognize the clear distinction between race and nationality and the still greater distinction between race and language, the easy assumption that the one is indicative of the other, has been in the past a serious impediment to an understanding of racial values. Historians and philologists have approached the subject from the view-point of linguistics, and as a result we have been burdened with a group of mythical races, such as the Latin, the Aryan, the Caucasian, and, perhaps, most inconsistent of all, the "Celtic" race. . . . . Religious teachers have also maintained the proposition not only that man is something fundamentally distinct from other living creatures, but that there are no inherited differences in humanity that cannot be obliterated by education and environment.

It is, therefore, necessary at the outset for the reader to thoroughly appreciate that race, language, and nationality are three separate and distinct things. . . .

. . . [I]n the beginning all differences of class, of caste, and of color, marked actual lines of race cleavage. . . . In the city of New York, and elsewhere in the United States, there is a native American aristocracy resting upon layer after layer of immigrants of lower races, and the native American . . . has, up to this time, supplied the leaders of thought and the control of capital, of education, and of the religious ideals and altruistic bias of the community.

In the democratic forms of government the operation of universal suffrage tends toward the selection of the average man for public office rather than the man qualified by birth, education, and integrity. How this scheme of administration will ultimately work out remains to be seen, but from a racial point of view, it will inevitably increase the preponderance of the lower types and cause a corresponding loss of efficiency in the community as a whole.

Madison Grant, The Passing of the Great Race, *1916, available online at URL: http://www.africa2000.com/ XNDX/madgrant01.html.*

Mr. Keating. You say that this legislation will put 25,000 boys and girls out of employment in the mills of the South.
Mr. Clark. Practically so. . . .
Mr. Keating. Now, in what particular would the mill owner be injured? Would he be compelled to pay higher wages?
Mr. Clark. The mill itself would not be so greatly injured. The operative is going to feel it more than the mill. The greatest opposition to this bill is from the operatives.
Mr. Keating. Then, as I understand you, you are not speaking in behalf of the owners of the mills, but on behalf of those who work in the mills.
Mr. Clark. I am speaking on behalf of both of them. . . .
Mr. Keating. The principal thought is to safeguard the interest of the children?
Mr. Clark. It is not a question of safeguarding interests. The mill people need employment, and what are you going to offer them? They have not money enough to seek education. What are you going to do for them when you turn them out of the mills?. . . .

We all know how kind your intentions are. If you drive these children out of the mills, they have to go on earning money, they must exist. You do not drive them into the schools. Some of them would probably loaf around. Some of them, of course, would go back to the farms, where they would eke out probably a scanty living, but without the same advantages. You do not get all your education from books, from going to school. So far as intelligence and getting information is concerned, one boy in an ordinary cotton-mill village will learn better how to take care of himself, acquit himself in company, to be a good man and a good citizen, in 12 months than out on some lonely mountain farm in two or three years.

You can not appreciate that. You gentlemen who live in great cities and in thickly populated communities, can not understand the lonesome life that many people in our agricultural communities endure.

Testimony of David Clark, editor of the Southern Textile Bulletin *and organizer of opposition to child labor legislation, at Senate hearings on the Keating-Owen bill, January 1916,* Hearings on H.R. 8234, *64th Congress, 1st session, pp. 11–13.*

One of the most astonishing sights in the traveling world is the annual flow and flux of tourists in Florida. It starts when the snow begins to bluster in Maine and Minnesota; and the tide turns back when the winds grow mild in Massachusetts. It is exactly like the passage of birds. . . .

By all means the tourist or the homeseeker, going to Florida for the winter, should hire a cottage. . . . somewhere in the central part of the state, but near enough a town to hire a motor, provided you do not own one yourself. . . .

Make sure that the cottage is free from infection, not already the property of mosquitoes, and that water supply is perfect. These are vital points. . . .

Be sure not to locate near a swamp, and listen not at all to land sharks. Look for yourself, and observe for yourself, even where the towns are of good size and the land fairly well settled. It will take at least half a century to make a large part of this state comfortably inhabitable. . . .

The Florida home builder must be content to be a pioneer, and build from the bottom up, with as much self-denial and persistence as characterized the New Englanders when they went westward. With such settlers Florida is destined to lead the states in agricultural industry.

E. P. Powell, "Call of Florida," Independent, vol. 85 (January 31, 1916), pp. 156–58 passim.

The last you heard of me I was waiting for wounded. Well, they came 300 in one night, the latest victims of Verdun, in such a condition as beggars description, and pales all my former experiences. We've never had such a rush as this. . . . Usually the rough filth of the trenches is removed in the dépouillage, but on that night there was no time for such daintiness, and they were dumped right into their beds with all manner of blood and mud caked to their shivering bodies. Imagine my despair over my clean sheets, so hard to come by! But such despair was too trivial, beside the horrors one was powerless to cope with. Both operating rooms worked all night and all the next day and most of the next night (the same équipe!) but in spite of that more than one life was lost that could have been saved had there been a third. . . . One poor fellow, an Arab, and as beautiful a son of Islam as ever ranged the desert, had lain two days with an undressed wound in the leg before he was picked up. As soon as I looked at his body I knew it was gangrène gazeuse. . . . He was conscious, talked disconnectedly of home and mother. . . . I gave him half an injection of morphine . . . and left toward dawn to get a few hours' sleep before the next day's engagement. "You are going, Mlle.," "Yes, but . . . I'll come back early, and then we'll write a nice long letter to your mother." He made a movement as if to detain me. Then changing to Arab "Alesh," he murmured, which is equivalent to our "God's will be done" and smiled faintly. A few hours later when I opened the door, the bed was empty and only a ghastly pool where he had lain. But I mustn't tell you any more of such tales.

Letter home from an American nurse serving in a French army hospital, March 13, 1916, "Mademoiselle Miss," available online at The Medical Front. URL:http://www.ku.edu/carrie/ specoll/medical/MMiss.htm.

Having formerly lulled ourselves to sleep with the word "melting-pot" we have now turned to the word "hyphenate" as denoting the last thing in scares with a thrill. . . .

A speech of Major General [Leonard] Wood as reported in a Philadelphia newspaper puts the matter more vividly. "It is a pretty dangerous situation to turn loose in this country all kinds of humanity seen on the docks at Ellis Island, to turn them loose with no sense of responsibility to their new land. They come in racial groups, drift through our schools in racial groups and are controlled by a dialect press. We are doing absolutely nothing to make these people understand that they are Americans, at least in the making." Then with swift intuition comes the remedy. "There is nothing like compulsory military service to accomplish this." . . .

. . . Until we have at least made a beginning in nationalizing our system of education, it is premature to appeal to the army . . . to remedy the evils of a lack of national mindedness. . . .

I can see a vision of a national government which takes an interest at once paternal and scientific in our alien visitors, which has a definite policy about their reception, and about their distribution, which guards them even more jealously than its own sons against industrial exploitation, and which offers them at every turn educational facilities under its own charge. . . . Until we have developed an independent and integral educational policy, the tendency to assume that military service will be an efficient tool of public education indicates a deplorable self-deception.

Progressive philosopher of education John Dewey, "Universal Service as Education," New Republic, vol. 6 (April 22, 1916), pp. 309–10.

Just as I had anticipated, certain Southern senators stalled for time. It was a presidential year—1916. Congress would adjourn early for the Primaries and conventions. One night the Democratic leaders of the Senate cruised down the Potomac and agreed on a program. The Southerners said they would go along if the Child Labor bill could be pushed aside.

The moment he got to Washington Senator John W. Kern, then Democratic floor leader in the Senate, told me what had happened. The next day I rushed to the White House. The President said he couldn't intervene. Congress must adjourn! Apparently my Child Labor bill was ditched.

Fortunately, the Republicans secured the details of the Democratic program, and Senator Gallinger of New Hampshire, then Republican floor leader, led an effective assault on the Democratic position.

He emphasized that, in their eagerness to start the hunt for votes, the Democrats were willing to sacrifice *even* child labor legislation; furthermore, that they were doing this at the command of Southern senators, who spoke for textile interests.

A day or two later my secretary burst into office exclaiming: "Do you know what's happened? President Wilson is on Capitol Hill, demanding the Senate pass your Child Labor bill!"

I couldn't believe it—I still remembered Wilson's statement that the legislation was unconstitutional—but the story was true.

Senator Edward Keating describes the battle over child labor legislation, June 1916, The Gentleman from Colorado, *p. 353.*

It is not reasonable to expect an intelligent understanding of American ideals or patriotism among those whose daily lives are filled with industrial injustice and who meet with nothing but abuse and exploitation. Any serious attempt to Americanize the foreign-workers who have been crowded into our industrial centers and our mining districts must concern itself also with the problem of Americanizing employers, trusts, and corporations. Before the employes of the United States Steel Corporation can have an opportunity to understand the ideal for which America stands, the United States Steel Corporation must first express that ideal in its dealings with its employes. So long as that corporation hires armed thugs to beat into submission workers who have the manhood to make a fight for their rights, that corporation will remain an institution destructive to the American spirit and an obstacle to the work of Americanizing aliens within our country. The United States Steel Corporation, as well as many other institutions with similar methods and standards, has taken away from aliens who have already been wronged through being lured to this country through false pretenses, opportunities to earn a decent living, to give their families decent homes, food, and clothing and the things necessary to make life worth while; and gravest of all it has robbed them of their ideals, their faith in mankind, and proper respect for their own personalities.

Samuel Gompers, "Americanizing Foreign Workers," American Federationist *23 (August 1916), pp. 689–90.*

Why should it be called revenge for women who desire the political freedom of others to vote against a party openly unfriendly to the only method by which Nation-wide suffrage for women can be gained? It is no more revenge to vote in the interests of the freedom of *other women* than to vote in the interests of peace and preparedness. . . . And why should suffrage as an all-absorbing issue be side-tracked by the women of the West for "Americanism"? There never was a greater opportunity to make "suffrage first" the paramount issue. Both great parties are vociferous in claiming the issues of peace and preparedness. . . .

In this connection, I must confess that I do not know just precisely what Americanism means. But if it means, as I believe it does, the dedication of all that is best in our beloved country to making this Nation, not only strong and peaceful, but also *just,* then surely there is no reason why Western women should not vote as women in woman's cause of freedom.

Abby Scott Baker, chair of the Woman's Party press committee, letter to the editor, Outlook, *vol. 113 (August 23, 1916), p. 1004.*

"I did not raise my girl to be a voter!" sings the Anti, or anti-suffrage, woman in this 1915 cartoon from the humor magazine *Puck.* Many antis were conservative society ladies, but, as this pro-suffrage cartoon points out, their allies were the political boss, procurer, saloon owner, child labor employer, grafter, cadet (pimp), and sweatshop owner.
(Library of Congress, Prints and Photographs Division, LC-USZC2-1196)

Whereas it was never the intention of the people of the United States in the incipiency of the War with Spain to make it a war of conquest or for territorial aggrandizement; and

Whereas it is, as it has always been, the purpose of the people of the United States to withdraw their sovereignty over the Philippine Islands and to recognize their independence as soon as a stable government can be established therein; and

Whereas for the speedy accomplishment of such purpose it is desirable to place in the hands of the people of the Philippines as large a control of their domestic affairs as can be given them without, in the meantime, impairing the exercise of the rights of sovereignty by the people of the United States, in order that, by the use and exercise of popular franchise and governmental powers, they may be the better prepared to fully assume the responsibilities and enjoy all the privileges of complete independence: Therefore

Be it enacted. . . .

Sec. 2. That all inhabitants of the Philippine Islands who were Spanish subjects on [April 11, 1899] and then resided in said islands, and their children born subsequent thereto, shall be deemed and held to be citizens of the Philippine Islands. . . .

Sec. 12. The general legislative powers in the Philippines . . . shall be vested in a legislature which shall consist of two houses. . . .

Organic Act of the Philippine Islands (Jones Act), August 29, 1916, U.S. Statutes at Large, 64th Congress, vol. 39, pp. 545ff.

Then she started to explain that no amount of work in Washington was likely to bring about the submission of the amendment unless new victories were won in the states. . . . On the contrary, as I soon learned, her plan was essentially a demand for legislative activity in every part of the country during the coming sessions of the state legislatures.

Pointer in hand, she stepped to the map and traced four divisions of states, to each of which she assigned a particular form of legislative work. . . .

When the fourfold plan had been made clear, she described the procedure necessary to put it into effect. An immediate start upon the work was imperative, she explained, in order to have everything ready at the beginning of the legislative sessions, most of which opened in January. If our campaigns were simultaneous, the opposition, taken by surprise and unprepared for a fight on so many fronts at once, would be forced to concentrate on a few states or else to spread itself too thin to be effective. Then, warning her listeners that the plan would fail if its scope leaked out, she requested from them a definite pledge that they would disclose no details. . . .

Last of all, she presented a compact to be signed by the representatives of suffrage associations in at least thirty-six states. She reminded us that, since thirty-six was the minimum number of states necessary for the ratification of a federal amendment, a failure on the part of a single state would mean ultimate defeat for all.

Suffragist Maud Park Wood describes Carrie Chapman Catt's presentation of her Winning Plan to the executive board of NAWSA, September 1916, Front Door Lobby, pp. 16–17.

AN ACT To prevent interstate commerce in the products of child labor . . .

Be it enacted . . . That no producer, manufacturer, or dealer shall ship or deliver for shipment in interstate or foreign commerce, any article or commodity the product of any mine or quarry situated in the United States, in which within thirty days prior to the time of the removal of such product therefrom children under the age of sixteen years have been employed or permitted to work, or any article or commodity the product of any mill, cannery, workshop, factory, or manufacturing establishment, situated in the

Carrie Chapman Catt, who began her career as an Iowa schoolteacher, reassumed the presidency of the National American Woman Suffrage Association in 1915. Her leadership was crucial in obtaining the Nineteenth Amendment, giving women the right to vote. *(Library of Congress, Prints and Photographs Division, LC-USZ62-109793)*

United States, in which within thirty days prior to the removal of such product therefrom children under the age of fourteen years have been employed or permitted to work, or children between the ages of fourteen years and sixteen years have been employed or permitted to work more than eight hours in any day, or more than six days in any week, or after the hour of seven o'clock postmeridian, or before the hour of six o'clock antemeridian: Provided, That a prosecution and conviction of a defendant for the shipment or delivery for shipment of any article or commodity under the conditions herein prohibited shall be a bar to any further prosecution against the same defendant for shipments or deliveries for shipment of any such article or commodity before the beginning of said prosecution. . . .

SEC. 3. That for the purpose of securing proper enforcement of this Act the Secretary of Labor, or any person duly authorized by him, shall have authority to enter and inspect at any time mines, quarries, mills, canneries, workshops, factories, manufacturing establishments, and other places in which goods are produced or held for interstate commerce. . . . .

> *Keating-Owen Child Labor Act, September 1, 1916,* U.S. Statutes at Large, *64th Congress, vol. 39, part 1, pp. 675–76.*

Although Charles Evans Hughes of New York had apparently been elected President . . . on returns received up to 5 A.M. today there were important shifts after that hour which leave the result undetermined, but indicating strongly the re-election of President Wilson. At this writing Mr. Wilson has 264 electoral votes and Mr. Hughes 251, with 16 still in doubt in two states.

The still doubtful states are California, with 13 votes and new Mexico with 3.

There were landslide majorities for Hughes in the bigger states, and he may prove to have a landslide in the popular vote, but he will have no landslide majority in the Electoral College. The States which went for Wilson by smaller but still safe majorities have prevented that.

> *"Election Close," headline story of the* New York Times, *November 8, 1916, p. 1.*

Woodrow Wilson . . . [has] again been elected President. . . . Soon after 11 o'clock all the doubtful States, except New Hampshire and Minnesota, had given such a steady lead that his election was no longer in doubt. When, at 11:25, the news came that Chester H. Rowell, the Republican State Chairman in California, had conceded the State to the Democrats, the disputed election of 1916 was not longer in dispute. . . .

California was the pivot on which the election of 1916 swung. The big vote for Wilson in San Francisco was what gave Wilson his first lead. But that was not decisive. It all depended on the northern and southern parts of the state and there the Progressive vote failed Hughes and gave the State to Wilson. But without the City of San Francisco Woodrow Wilson would have had to quit the White House. . . .

> *"With 272 [277] Electoral Votes, Wilson Wins," headline story of the* New York Times, *November 10, 1916, p. 1.*

8

War and the End of an Era
1917–1920

THE LAST EFFORTS FOR PEACE

During the 1916 presidential campaign, the Democratic Party promoted the reelection of Woodrow Wilson with the popular slogan, "He Kept Us Out of War." In private, however, President Wilson himself was never comfortable with the slogan. "I can't keep the country out of war," he commented to one of his advisers. "Any little German lieutenant can put us into war at any time by some calculated outrage."[1] In the closing months of 1916, however, Germany appeared to be refraining from submarine attacks on merchant vessels, although Britain less promisingly refused to reduce blockade pressure on neutral commerce. But in the muddy, polluted, trenches of the western front, soldiers of the Allied and Central powers remained deadlocked.

Immediately after being reelected in November 1916, the president began another effort to negotiate an end to the war. On December 12, Germany publicly announced it would discuss peace terms. Six days later President Wilson sent identical notes to both sets of warring nations asking them to state their war aims. In fact, he had drafted the notes before Germany's public announcement. The British were suspicious that he had consulted with Germany first, however, and were deeply affronted by his statement that the goals of both sides were "virtually the same."[2] But they did indicate they were willing to open negotiations. Germany replied that it would discuss peace terms only at a conference of warring nations—in other words, that America was not welcome at the peace table.

On January 22, 1917, the president reacted to the replies he had received by delivering a memorable address to the Senate. It was also meant for the people of the world and laid out Wilson's vision for constructing a new, postwar world order. It was "inconceivable," he first of all asserted, that the United States did not have a right and obligation "to add their authority and their power to the authority and force of other nations" to establish "the foundations of peace among the nations." That foundation, he continued, would have to be a "peace without victory," because only a "peace among equals" would be likely to endure. "There must be," he said, "not a balance of power but a community of power." He further recommended government by consent of the governed, freedom of the seas, disarmament, and most important of all a permanent, international league of nations to maintain world peace. "I would fain believe that I am speaking for the silent mass of mankind everywhere," he said, and concluded that his stipulations were "the principles of mankind and must prevail." Generally, Americans applauded Wilson's vision. La Follette, Bryan, and former president Taft expressed public approval; Senator Ben Tillman, Democrat of South Carolina, labeled it "the noblest utterance since the Declaration of Independence."[3]

The idea for a permanent league of nations found a providential advocate in Woodrow Wilson, although the idea did not originate with him. Cultivated by progressive optimism, it had been discussed by both American and European thinkers since the first international Hague Conference in 1899. Increasingly, some viewed it as the logical conclusion of progressive faith in conciliation of conflict through representative bodies or structures. To promote the idea, prominent Americans had organized a formal League to Enforce Peace in 1915, headed by former president William Taft; in England the League of Nations Society formed the same year. Nonetheless, a small but vociferous group of Americans opposed the idea as soon as Wilson publicly announced it. Some were traditional isolationists, some believed a strong neutral power with no "entangling alliances" could maintain world peace more effectively than a league, and some disliked the idea of surrendering American independence to a multinational body. But worldwide, as historian Thomas Bailey has written, the speech "further magnified Wilson's stature as the emerging moral leader of the world."[4]

The German response to Wilson's noble and progressive aims came on February 1. Germany announced the immediate resumption of unrestricted submarine warfare on all ships, including neutral passenger and merchant ships. German military strategists had decided to launch a major new assault on the western front while simultaneously attacking supply lines to Britain. They doubtless knew the policy might force America into the war but calculated that they could starve the Allies out far more quickly than America could prepare an army.

The announcement was a bitter disappointment to the president and caused a storm of debate throughout the nation. On February 3 he announced before a joint session of Congress that the United States had broken off diplomatic relations with Germany. Perhaps hoping that Germany was bluffing, he also announced that only "actual overt acts" on the part of Germany would convince him to take additional steps toward war.

On February 24, President Wilson was notified privately that British authorities had intercepted and decoded a note from Alfred Zimmermann, Germany's foreign secretary, to the German ambassador in Mexico. It instructed the ambassador to offer Venustiano Carranza, head of the Mexican government, an incredible scheme: "make war together, make peace together." It promised Mexico the return of their "lost provinces"—Texas and the American Southwest—for joining an alliance against the United States. The note also suggested that Mexico encourage Japan, an Allied power, to switch sides and join them. On March 1, American newspapers coast to coast headlined the Zimmermann note. It stunned the nation. It also converted many former advocates of nonintervention into hawks, especially in the West and Southwest where the threat of Mexican and Japanese hostilities hit closest to home. The president, now surer of Germany's intentions, immediately asked Congress for authority to arm merchant ships and "to employ any other instrumentalities or methods" he found necessary to protect American ships and citizens. But in the Senate a group of 11 anti-interventionist senators, some of them Republican insurgents like Robert La Follette and some Bryan Democrats, strongly objected to Wilson's opened-ended request for "instrumentalities" that could enable him to wage an undeclared war. They filibustered until the congressional session ended on March 4 and the bill to arm merchant ships died. The Senate floor came close to erupting in violence. Many other Americans also disliked the spectacle of "playing politics" with defense. Wilson famously commented, "A little group of willful men, representing no opinion but their own, have rendered the great Government of the United States helpless and contemptible." But the president was not so easily dismissed. The state department located an old law from 1792 that allowed the arming of merchant ships, and arming proceeded.[5]

In early March 1917, another important international event occurred. In Russia, an Allied power but also a repressive and feudal autocracy, the czarist government was overthrown in a spontaneous uprising, and a provisional republic was established. This new government was itself destined to be overthrown the following November by the Bolsheviks—but in the meantime Americans were reassured that all of the Allied powers were fighting for the principle of "consent of the governed."

AMERICA DECLARES WAR

The president had announced he would await actual overt acts from Germany, and unfortunately they soon occurred. German submarines attacked and sank five unarmed U.S. merchant ships, three of them on March 18. On March 20, the cabinet, after sharp debate, unanimously but privately agreed for war. The following day the president called for a special session of Congress. It met on April 2, with no advance publicity of what the president would say. President Wilson asked that Congress "formally accept the status of belligerent" which had "been thrust upon" the nation. "Our motive will not be revenge or the victorious assertion of the physical might of the nation, but only the vindication of right, of human right, of which we are only a single champion," he said and concluded, "The right is more precious than the peace." In what became the speech's most famous passage, he added, "The world must be made safe for democracy. Its peace must be planted upon the tested foundations of political liberty."[6]

Wilson agonized mightily over the decision, historians point out, and even at the end maintained a strong personal desire to remain out of the hostilities.[7] Why, then, did he decide to intervene? At the time, war hawks presumed he had finally conceded to majority opinion. Progressives in and out of Congress, as well as the radical Left, blamed the influence of big business and Wall Street. "Hyphenated Americans" who favored the Central Powers maintained that Wilson had never really embraced neutrality. Most of Congress and most of the American public—even those who had

In this historic photograph of April 2, 1917, President Woodrow Wilson stands before Congress, requesting a declaration of war against Germany. On April 6 America entered the Great War, later called World War I. *(Library of Congress, Prints and Photographs Division, LC-USZ62-17146)*

embraced the slogan "He Kept Us Out of War" less than a year earlier—probably inclined to the simpler explanation that Wilson himself offered: war had been "thrust upon" the nation by German attacks. The war resolution passed the Senate on April 4, 82 to 6, and the House on April 6, 373 to 50. One of the dissenting votes came from America's first congresswoman, Jeannette Rankin, Republican of Montana. Elected as a known pacificist, Rankin broke silent roll call protocol to rise and state, "I want to stand by my country, but I cannot vote for war. I vote no." In any case, as of Good Friday, April 6, 1917, the United States was at war.[8]

THE UNITED STATES MOBILIZES

When war was declared in April 1917, Americans did not know exactly what to expect, but few thought American troops would see extensive action. The army was small and unprepared. Most assumed America's primary contribution would be economic and material aid, with some naval support and token troop support. In fact, at Wilson's insistence America did not become an Allied Power but instead an "associate" of the Allied Powers (they were henceforth the Allied and Associated Powers.) Opposition to the war and to American intervention did not disappear from the public scene overnight, and in truth few Americans had a good understanding of the causes and rivalries that originally underlay the fighting. But many Americans, even those who had previously opposed entering the war, embraced the concept of national honor in the face of German attacks or the concept of duty in the cause of democracy that the president so ably pronounced. With dispatch, Congress took up legislation that the president requested, and most Americans took up the task of mobilization with remarkable vigor.

Once America declared for war, however, British and French delegations revealed shocking news to the Wilson administration: the Germans' all-out submarine warfare had indeed taken a tremendous financial toll in a short time. Food and materials were increasingly scarce, financial collapse loomed, and armies had almost reached the end of manpower reserves. Wilson administration officials quickly agreed that only conscription, or the draft, could raise the necessary American troops hurriedly and fairly. The Selective Service or draft bill occasioned harsh debate in Congress, especially in Wilson's own party. "In the estimation of Missouri there is precious little difference between a conscript and a convict," said the Democratic speaker of the House, Champ Clark.[9] But the bill passed by comfortable margins and was signed on May 18. It required men aged 21 to 30 (expanded to 18 to 45 in August) to register but put control of selection in the hands of local and civilian draft boards, not the military. The first day of registration on June 5 went smoothly and over 9.5 million men signed up. Secretary of War Newton later publicly drew draft numbers from a fishbowl, blindfolded. Eventually more than 24 million men registered for the draft, and 2,810,296 were called and inducted. Nearly 2 million more Americans voluntarily enlisted.[10]

America needed time to train its troops, but meanwhile the Allies strongly urged an immediate token show of military support to bolster morale. Wilson selected Major General John J. Pershing, back from Mexico, to head the American Expeditionary Force (AEF). Pershing arrived in France in June with 14,500 men and entered Paris to great celebration. Having insisted on his own bailiwick at the front, he was sent east of Verdun. Meanwhile naval forces and their commander, Rear Admiral William S. Sims, made an immediate and important contribution to the Allied effort. Sims convinced reluctant British naval officials to switch from patrolling wide sea lanes to adopting a convoy system of guarding merchant vessels. The convoys, enlarged by American destroyers, achieved a significant drop in shipping losses almost immediately. That in turn began to ease critical shortages in Europe and later made it possible for American troops and their supplies to cross the Atlantic.

Another immediate need of the Allies was for credit. Before the end of April, the first War Loan Act was passed, authorizing the first sale of Liberty Bonds to the amount of $5 billion. By October Congress enacted a new revenue bill. It imposed taxes on corporate profits that ran as high as 60 percent, increased the base income tax to 4 percent and raised the marginal surtax as high as 63 percent—as progressives in both parties insisted. It also increased excise taxes and levied consumption taxes on luxury items. By 1920, war costs would total $33.5 billion, $23 billion of it borrowed in the form of Liberty Bonds and other loans. (The Liberty Bonds, like modern savings bonds, were government debts and eventually paid back with interest to the citizens who bought them.) The remaining $10.5 billion came from tax money. Prior to 1915, the entire federal budget had not often topped $1 billion.[11]

THE WAR AT HOME: MOBILIZING INDUSTRY

To many progressives, government regulation and planning by experts were important keys to reforming American society. But as many historians have commented, the mobilization program put into effect in 1917 and 1918 brought more government control of industry, and more planning, than most progressive reformers could have dreamed. Most programs remained voluntary, not coercive, and most took some months to gain their sea legs. But by the war's end it was clear that many had accomplished spectacular results. Many politicians, many leaders of business, industry, and labor, and many ordinary Americans who had not been especially progressive before the war came out of the effort applauding enlarged government powers, or at least closer relations between the government and corporate world.

The Army Appropriation Act of 1916 had readied a basic mechanism for mobilization by establishing a Council of National Defense, composed of cabinet members, and a civilian advisory board to oversee economic planning. In July of 1917 Wilson formally replaced the advisory board and its industry subcommittees with the War Industries Board (WIB). The WIB had six members and a host of "dollar-a-year" men, successful businessmen on leave from their companies to oversee planning and negotiations for production, price, and labor in various sectors of industry. The WIB floundered at first. After March 1918, however, in the hands of Bernard Baruch, a prominent Wall Street broker (and like Wilson a former southerner), it became the most powerful mobilization agency. The WIB received information on war needs from both the United States and the Allies, then decided which factories should convert to war production to supply those needs first. The board also decided prices and who got which scarce resources, especially high-demand steel. When automakers resisted pressure to supply war orders instead of civilian demand, for example, Baruch told them, "You won't get your steel. That is all."[12]

Mobilization also included oversight of labor issues, as neither labor officials, progressives, nor the Wilson administration wanted to see the gains of recent decades swallowed by the need for fast production. Secretary of Labor William Wilson established the U.S. Employment Service, which registered and placed millions of job-seeking Americans in war industries that needed them. In April 1918 the National War Labor Board (NWLB) was formally set up under the bipartisan command of former president Taft and lawyer Frank P. Walsh. The NWLB was a court of last resort for labor disputes, and it heard well over 1,000 cases by the war's end. Occasionally, it coerced settlements on one side or the other. The NWLB took over a Smith and Wesson arms factory in Massachusetts when the company rejected its settlement, for example, and in other cases threatened striking workers with the loss of draft exemptions if they refused to return to work. A separate War Labor Policies board, headed by lawyer Felix Frankfurter (later a Supreme Court justice), was set up to oversee working conditions, hours, housing conditions, and other issues in industries related to the war effort.

An immediate need of the Allies was for increased shipments of food. The Lever Food and Fuel Control Act, passed in August 1917 after sharp disagreement in Congress, gave the president extensive control over the production, prices, and distribution of foodstuffs and farm equipment. Wilson immediately created the Food Administration, under the head of Herbert Hoover, former head of the Commission for Relief in Belgium (later a U.S. president). Hoover's efforts to increase agricultural production and reduce food consumption to help supply Europe were very successful. Hoover soon had American housewives observing Wheatless Mondays and Meatless Tuesdays, planting war gardens, and developing new recipes. The Fuel Administration was headed by Harry A. Garfield, son of former president James Garfield. One of Garfield's innovations was Daylight Savings Time, passed by Congress in early 1918 to conserve energy.

One area where voluntary cooperation did not happen immediately was the railroads. Industry recalcitrance was compounded by an exceptionally severe winter in 1917–1918 that left many tracks blocked and men, materials, and food for the war effort stranded. On January 1, 1918, President Wilson ordered government control of the railroads and appointed William Gibbs McAdoo, secretary of the treasury, as the head of the Railroad Administration. McAdoo molded the nation's lines into a single coordinated system and gave precedence to war over passenger traffic to get soldiers and supplies moving across the nation.

THE WAR AT HOME: MOBILIZING PUBLIC OPINION

President Wilson and other government leaders believed that uniting the American public behind the war effort was also an important part of mobilization. During the two and a half years that America remained neutral, many groups and individuals had spoken out against the war or American intervention: progressives and farmers, pacifists, church groups, women's groups, some German- and Irish-American groups, intellectuals and political groups on the Left such as the Socialists. When war was declared, many of them voluntarily and promptly began to back the war effort and even embraced ardent patriotism. Nonetheless, pockets of opposition still existed. A week after the declaration, President Wilson created the Committee on Public Information (CPI) to mobilize public opinion and increase unity. Composed of the secretaries of state, war, and the navy, it was headed by George Creel, a progressive journalist and former muckraker from Denver. Creel believed the correct approach was publicity, not censorship—"expression, not repression," as he put it. He did, however, institute "voluntary guidelines" for journalists, with which they had to comply as the price of maintaining access to information.

Borrowing from advertising techniques, Creel organized what was soon the largest campaign to disseminate propaganda yet undertaken by a government. He organized a cadre of 75,000 "Four Minute Men"—various public figures, including famous actors and baseball players, who delivered brief speeches to encourage Americans to conserve food, buy Liberty Bonds, or remain united. He also assembled an impressive roster of artists, writers, historians, and filmmakers to aid the effort in 19 subdivisions of work. Artist Montgomery Flagg, for example, designed the still-famous poster of a pointing Uncle Sam—"I want YOU for the U.S. Army"—for the Creel committee. In words and poster art, the CPI presented the Allies as civilized peoples fighting an honorable campaign for democracy and freedom and presented the Germans as brutal, autocratic "Prussians" or barbaric "Huns" bent on destroying all civilized values.[13] The Creel Committee's work was not limited to the United States. It also worked to influence foreign opinion in Allied nations and behind the lines of the Central powers. The CPI distributed tons of material to shape a favorable view of Wilson and America, often using Wilson's own words and peace goals. In some places it made the president a veritable icon.

Unfortunately, the pervasive agitation of the Creel committee to rouse public opinion also contributed to fears and hatreds that sometimes slipped into hysteria, persecution, and violence before the war ended. The slogan of the day became "100 percent Americanism." All things German seemed tainted with disloyalty. Schools dropped German-language courses, libraries removed Goethe and Kant from their shelves, churches ceased German-language services, symphonies stopped playing Bach and Beethoven, sauerkraut became "liberty cabbage" and dachshunds "liberty pups." Various self-appointed citizens' groups maintained a vigilant ear for rumors and subversives, harassed German Americans, kept a close eye on all immigrants, and persecuted anyone who expressed opinions against the war. The American Protective League, for example, established in 1917 by a Chicago advertising executive, enjoyed a semi-official relationship with the Justice Department. It had nearly 600 branches and 100,000 members by June 1917, reaching 250,000 by the war's end.[14] Senator La Follette was burned in effigy and censured at the University of Wisconsin for voting against the war, a pacificist minister in Cincinnati was mobbed and beaten, and even worse isolated incidents of violence occurred.

CIVIL LIBERTIES IN TIME OF WAR

It is a common and perhaps inevitable practice for nations at war to take measures to protect themselves from enemies within, and Creel's publicity campaign did not avert official suppression of dissent. In June 1917, the Espionage Act mandated fines up to $10,000 and 20-year jail sentences for spying on military material and information—but it also included brief sections that banned less clearly defined activities like obstructing the draft or circulating false information with the intent of aiding the enemy. The postmaster general was also given moderate powers of censorship to ban from the mails any materials "urging treason, insurrection, or forcible resistance to any law." Gradually, the government's power over dissent and the mails expanded. In October 1917, the Trading with the Enemy Act forbade all commerce with the Central Powers and subjected all foreign-language newspapers to Post Office review. In May 1918, the Sedition Act was passed. It made sabotage or willful destruction of war materials into federal crimes, a provision primarily aimed at suppressing strikes by the radical labor union IWW (International Workers of the World). Rounding out suppressive legislation was the Alien Act of October 1918, which gave the commissioner of immigration broad powers to deport aliens if they were suspected of promoting radical ideas or belonging to radical organizations. By definition, an alien was a person born outside the United States who had not become a naturalized citizen; aliens born in countries with whom the United States was at war were designated enemy aliens.

The Sedition Act revised a section of the earlier Espionage Act to permit prosecution of people who merely *said* anything "disloyal, profane, scurrilous, or abusive" about the government, the Constitution, the flag, the armed forces, or even Liberty Bonds. In the hands of some zealous local officials, the sweeping language proved quite successful tools to suppress any political dissent. Many isolated absurdities occurred—like the jail sentence of a movie director whose picture about the American Revolution was held to portray America's ally Britain in a bad light. More seriously, the act was used to undermine dissenting groups like the Socialist Party of America. In June 1918, longtime Socialist Party leader Eugene V. Debs was arrested and sentenced to 10 years in jail for a speech against the war in Canton, Ohio. The Sedition Act also denied mail delivery to any person suspected of harboring opinions deemed illegal under its terms. In the hands of the eager postmaster general, Albert S. Burleson, power over the mail came to reach far and wide, even on at least one occasion to the *New York Times,* the *Saturday Evening Post,* and the venerable *Nation.* But it became primarily a means of suppressing radical publications, including the *Appeal to Reason,* the *New York Call,* and *The Masses,* a left-intellectual "little magazine" edited by Max Eastman in New York, all of which depended on mail for distribution. Wisconsin's duly elected Socialist congressmen Victor Berger was charged and convicted as editor of the socialist paper *Milwaukee Leader* and later denied his seat in Congress.[15]

In fact, many Americans were calling for far more severe measures. Theodore Roosevelt, for example, proposed permitting military censorship of all publications, and some congressmen were demanding that those charged with sedition be tried in military courts. During the war years strikes by the radical IWW, especially in the copper mines of the West, called forth an extraordinarily violent response. The IWW, which reached its peak membership of about 100,000 the same year America entered the war, maintained that class loyalty came before national loyalty and refused to cooperate with the War Labor Board's activities. On September 5, 1917, Attorney General Gregory and the Department of Justice raided every IWW hall in the United States. Eventually more than 300 IWW leaders were tried for violating the various acts and others deported.

Neither censorship nor the repression of civil liberties in America ever reached the extent or severity they did in the warring European nations—where, for example, enemy aliens were often jailed without recourse and suspected traitors executed in secret and without trial. But the prosecutions nonetheless violated a tradition of civil liberties that many Americans valued and believed to be guaranteed by the Constitution. In 1917, a young social worker, Roger Baldwin, affiliated with the American Union Against Militarism, founded the National Civil Liberties Bureau (in 1920, it became the American Civil Liberties Union, or ACLU), to support the defense of free speech and opinion in America.

The president himself remained distanced from the movement to suppress dissent, and historians often fault his failure to rein in the more zealous members of his administration. All together, the federal government brought more than 2,000 cases under the espionage and sedition acts and won about half of them before the laws expired in 1921. No appeals reached the Supreme Court until the war ended, but in 1919 the Supreme Court upheld the Espionage Act in *Schenck v. United States.* In time of war, Justice Oliver Wendell Holmes's famous opinion maintained, it was reasonable to deny speech that was the equivalent of "falsely shouting fire in a theatre and causing a panic." The important question for the courts to consider, he continued, was whether the language under question created "a clear and present danger." Holmes, however, believed that war was an exceptional situation and became known as a great advocate of civil liberties in later decisions. In another sedition case in 1919, he wrote a dissent to the majority, reemphasizing the importance of immanent threat. "Congress certainly cannot forbid all effort to change the mind of the country," he wrote. He continued, "the best test of truth is the power of the thought to get itself accepted in the competition of the market."[16]

"OVER THERE"

During 1917, the war did not go well for the Allies. French and British campaigns on the western front in France resulted in many casualties but few gains. (The western front was a 475-mile-long, arc through northern France from the coast of the English Channel to the Alps in Switzerland.) On the Italian front, on the border of northeastern Italy and Austria-Hungary, the Italians suffered great losses at Caporetto, later memorialized in Ernest Hemingway's famous novel, *A Farewell to Arms.* The Russians suffered even greater losses on the eastern front, to the east of Germany and Austria-Hungary. After the Bolsheviks captured the fledgling Russian republic in early November 1917, Russia withdrew from the war. Germany, no longer fighting Russia to the east, began to move its eastern-front troops to join the trench warfare on the western front, where Allied and Central Powers soldiers lived in networks of muddy, polluted trenches, facing each other across the field of battle the trenches defined.

General Pershing had long since informed Washington that far more American troop support than first anticipated would be necessary, but by the end of 1917 little more than 100,000 American soldiers had yet reached Europe. Augmented by the eastern troops, Germany began to hit the western front in late 1917 and launched new all-out offensives in early 1918, desperate to break the Allied lines before large numbers of American reinforcements arrived. In March and April, German offensives on northern points along the western front resulted in heavy Allied losses. In a May offensive about midpoint along the western front, German troops pushed to the Marne River and reached Château-Thierry, only 50 miles from Paris.

In the face of an increasingly critical situation, the Allies appointed Marshal Ferdinand Foch of France as supreme commander of all Allied forces, including those of the United States. American troops, slowly increasing since the first of the year, finally begun to pour into Europe in April, and at last they began to make a difference. Foch

During World War I the airplane found a new use: warfare. Twenty-one-year-old Frank Luke, Jr., of Arizona compiled a legendary record in battle before becoming the first American combat pilot to die in war. *(Courtesy Arizona Historical Society-Tucson, AHS #61037)*

sent them first to Catigny (north of the western front's midpoint), where they were successful, then to Château-Thierry for their first major action of the war. There, they helped French troops push Germans back across the Marne, then further into retreat at Belleau Woods in June. In July, American troops joined Foch to defeat Germany's last great drive of the war, a second attempt to reach Paris by moving south toward Château-Thierry between Rheims and Soissons (the Second Battle of the Marne). In August American troops 500,000 strong began their first independent offensive at St. Mihiel, a point further south on the western front. Under Pershing's personal command, the offensive succeeded there as well.

By October 1918, American service personnel in Europe had reached almost 2 million and the tide of war was turning. More than a million American troops played the major role in the successful, month-long Allied offensive northward from St. Mihiel and Verdun near the Meuse River and the Argonne Forest (the Meuse-Argonne offensive). Austria sued for peace, the German lines began to crumble, and the German navy mutinied. Germany's civil population was in turmoil, and on November 8, the German kaiser, Wilhelm II, abdicated. The Allies had not in fact expected the war to end so quickly, but German leaders sued for peace on the basis of the aims laid out in Wilson's Fourteen Points. Early in the morning of November 11, 1918, an armistice was signed and at the 11th hour of the 11th day of the 11th month, the guns were silenced.

Clearly, in the last months of the war the American contribution of personnel and materials had tipped the balance for the Allies. But compared to the losses and suffering of both the soldiers and civilian population of European nations, the Americans had endured far less and for a far shorter time. All told, nearly 9 million uniformed soldiers died in the war. While 116,516 Americans lost their lives (53,402 battle deaths and 63,114 other deaths, primarily from the Spanish flu), the British Empire lost

908,000, the French 1.4 million, including half its men between 20 and 32, and the Russians 1.7 million. The Germans lost 1.8 million, Austria-Hungary 1.2 million. This difference created perspectives among the Allies that diverged markedly from Woodrow Wilson's, as to the proper terms of settlement at the peace table.[17]

AMERICAN SERVICE PERSONNEL IN WORLD WAR I

America's previous experience with the draft, Civil War conscription, had become the subject of harsh debate and resentments. Civil War policies had permitted men of means to purchase exemptions and had occasioned riots in New York. While the local draft boards first established in the World War I Selective Service legislation were certainly not immune to local politics, favoritism, and in some southern communities a marked tendency to draft blacks before whites, on the whole they functioned as intended, with reasonable fairness and no mass resistance. By the war's end, some 4.8 million draftees and enlistees served in the armed forces. About 2 million crossed the Atlantic and 1.4 million saw combat.[18]

The AEF included about 250,000 African-American soldiers. Trained at scattered camps to allay white fears and often assigned menial tasks even in Europe, they remained in segregated units led primarily by white officers, although before the war's end some 600 black officers had also been commissioned. Some of the units fought with great distinction, and a number received the French Croix de Guerre, including the entire 369th Regiment whom the French nicknamed the Hellfighters.[19]

World War I also saw increased participation of women in military efforts. Members of the Army Nurse Corps and the Naval Nurse Corps, established 1909 and 1908, respectively, served at the front in Europe, on transport ships, at bases in the Pacific and the Caribbean, and in hospitals in the United States. By the armistice, the Army had over 21,000 nurses, more than 5,000 of whom served overseas; the Navy had nearly 1,500.[20] Although the nurse corps were official branches of the military, however, the nurses did not have military rank or benefits.

Early in America's war effort, General Pershing faced an immediate labor shortage for vital noncombat army support jobs, as had his Allied counterparts in Europe, and requested women workers. The AEF command suggested forming a regular enlisted, uniformed women's service corps like the British Women's Auxiliary Army Corps (WAACs), which was performing with great success in England. The proposal even reached Congress, but Secretary of War Newton Baker (the cabinet level authority for the army) refused to be persuaded of "the desirability or feasibility of making this most radical departure in the conduct of our military affairs."[21] The army did begin to recruit women as civilian contract workers for jobs formerly filled by male army personnel, however, and some of them served overseas. At Pershing's insistence, for example, women telephone operators from America and Canada who were fluent in French were recruited to serve with the U.S. Army Signal Corps in France. The women, dubbed "Hello Girls," sometimes served close to the front transmitting information about troop movements and battle plans.

Secretary of the Navy Josephus Daniels, on the other hand, took a different view than Secretary Baker. He simply chose to interpret the navy's legislative authority to enlist qualified persons as gender-neutral. On his order and without debate or congressional involvement, the navy began inducting women for support service in March 1917. Daniels, a North Carolinian whose country manners and temperance advocacy amused some Washington sophisticates, caused further consternation by announcing that women were to receive the same rank and pay as men. (At the time, the modern idea of equal pay for equal work was unheard of. As a matter of course, women hired to replace draftees in factories and in other fields were paid far less than the men had been.) The navy women were enlisted as yeomen and assigned a uniform and insignia—the first American women granted full military status, rank, and benefits. By the time the nationwide draft for men began in June, some were already on duty to process the papers. Popularly known as yeomanettes, they eventually performed a variety of jobs such as recruiters, drivers, translators, and radio operators. Under the slogan "Free a Man to Fight," more than 11,000 women served in the navy by the armistice, and another 300 had joined the marines, who opened their ranks in August 1918.[22]

More than 5,000 American women also worked overseas as part of volunteer civilian groups such as the Red Cross, YMCA, and Salvation Army. Only a very few of the women who died overseas died as a result of battle, but a number succumbed to the influenza epidemic.

WILSON AND THE PEACE CONFERENCE

During the war, President Wilson had deliberately tried to keep the American contribution separate and in clear view of the other Allies. His goal was to increase America's influence at the peace table. He knew quite well that the aims of the Allies, as well as the causes of the war, were far from idealistic. The Allies wanted to break up the Austro-Hungarian Empire and destroy German military might, of course, but they also wanted to annex territory and colonies and punish Germany severely by demanding reparations. In fact, some of the Allies had entered into secret treaties before and during the war, laying out how they would divide the spoils after—as the world now knew, because in December 1917 the Russian Bolsheviks found the secret agreements in Russia and published them.

Wilson, on the other hand, was firmly committed to his vision of a new international order based on self-determination and collective security—and if necessary to imposing it on the Allies. He had sketched his objectives in his "peace without victory" speech of early 1917; on January 8, 1918, he had appeared before Congress and stated them precisely in his famous Fourteen Points. Points one to five outlined the conditions he believed were necessary for a just and lasting peace: open diplomacy rather than secret treaties, freedom of the seas, lower barriers to trade, disarmament, and an "impartial adjustment of all colonial claims" weighted toward self-determination of subject peoples. Points six to 13 dealt with specific territorial issues raised by the war and again insisted that self-determination be considered. The 14th point called for a "general association of nations" to afford "mutual guarantees of political independence and territorial integrity to great and small states alike"—the League of Nations.[23]

President Wilson insisted upon attending the peace conference and conducting the negotiations personally, causing consternation in Washington and among opinion makers nationwide. It was the first time an American president had met with other leaders for such negotiations, the first time a president was to spend such a long period of time out of the country, and even the first time a president had visited Europe while in office. Wilson's decision made it clear to the world that he was determined to pursue his stated goals.

At home, however, the progressive coalition that twice elected him to the White House was showing signs it had begun to unravel. When America entered the war Wilson had insisted, "Politics is adjourned," and in fact had received much Republican cooperation during wartime. Just before the November 1918 midterm elections, however, he took a partisan stance that backfired. He appealed to the American people to return a Democratic congress as a vote of confidence, hoping it would further his peace aims. Republicans were understandably angered, and a week before the armistice the electorate chose instead to elect Republican majorities to both the House and the Senate. While it is standard in American politics for the president's party to lose congressional seats at midterm elections, many opinion makers took the election on the terms that Wilson himself had set for it: they interpreted it as a rejection of his policies. Wilson did not help his cause in Congress when he failed to appoint a single prominent Republican—former president Taft would have been a logical choice—to the peace commission.

In December 1918, the president sailed for France, with an entourage of some 200 experts on matters such as history, geography, and ethnic groupings. If some Americans were beginning to have doubts about Wilson's policies, Europeans were not. He met huge and fervent welcomes from citizens in England, France, and Italy, who had come to view him as the world's moral leader and the spokesman for lasting peace. The peace conference opened in the palace at Versailles, France, on January 18, 1919, and continued until the treaty was signed on June 28. By the time World War I had ended, 32 Allied nations had declared war against one or more of the Central Powers, and representatives from all of them attended the conference. But it was a meeting of the victors; Germany was not invited.

The conference met in a world much changed since the summer of 1914. Many of those changes centered on the former Russian Empire and on newly awakened hopes for self-determination by formerly subject peoples. Hanging over all the peace negotiators was the new threat of revolutionary bolshevism or communism. In November 1917, a Bolshevik revolution led by Vladimir Ilyich Lenin had seized power in Russia. The Bolsheviks had negotiated a harsh separate peace with Germany. The Treaty of Brest-Litovsk surrendered huge chunks of Russia's former territory, industrial capacity, and population to Germany, including Finland and the Baltic provinces of Estonia, Latvia, and Lithuania. Now, in the wake of the Central Powers' defeat, those peoples as well as other European and Middle Eastern peoples formerly subject to Russia, Austria-Hungary, or the Ottoman (Turkish) Empire were also beginning to assert independence. Even among the colonial peoples of Britain and France, movements for self-determination were stirring.

The large diplomatic congress in Versailles soon became unwieldy and negotiations were assumed by the so-called Big Four: Woodrow Wilson from America and three tough-minded Europeans: David Lloyd George of Britain, Georges Clemenceau of France, and Vittorio Orlando of Italy. Conflict among them was inevitable. The European Allies cared far more about their own national interest and their citizens' demands for retribution than about a new world order. France wanted German military capability destroyed, having suffered several German invasions over the decades. Britain wanted extensive reparations. Italy wanted the territory it had been promised in a secret treaty. Italy and several other European nations wanted territory formerly controlled by the Austro-Hungarian and the Turkish empires, while Japan wanted spoils in Asia.

As negotiations progressed President Wilson made many reluctant compromises on the first 13 of his points. Harsh terms were imposed on Germany, freedom of the seas was blocked, and guarantees of open rather than secret diplomacy were scrapped. But Wilson did accomplish some important outcomes. He made progress on the issue of disarmament. He established that colonies of the defeated Central Powers should not become possessions of the victors but should instead be administered in trusteeships called *mandates* and prepared for future self-determination. (The fate of colonies belonging to the Allies, however, was not at issue in the conference.) Self-determination could not always be aligned with ethnic groupings, but the conference formed and

President Woodrow Wilson called for establishing a League of Nations in his peace plan called the Fourteen Points. Some Americans considered it a progressive idea but many opposed it. This cartoon portrays a league to maintain peace as too ambitious a project. It was published in *Punch*, a British humor magazine, in 1919. *(Library of Congress, Prints and Photographs Division, LC-USZ62-70331)*

OVERWEIGHTED.

PRESIDENT WILSON. "HERE'S YOUR OLIVE BRANCH. NOW GET BUSY."
DOVE OF PEACE. "OF COURSE I WANT TO PLEASE EVERYBODY; BUT ISN'T THIS A BIT THICK?"

recognized the new independent nations of Poland, Czechoslovakia, Yugoslavia, Austria, and Hungary. These nations were also intended to serve as a buffer, called a "quarantine zone," between communist Russia and western Europe.

Each compromise Wilson made, however, made him more determined to achieve his 14th point and most important goal, the League of Nations—not only to solve future international controversies and prevent future wars but also to assure continuing American leadership in fulfilling the terms of the treaty. Wilson chaired the commission to develop a plan for the league, and he worked into the nights drafting it after long days of other negotiations. The other Allies agreed to place the league agreement at the beginning of the treaty as the first and most important condition. The agreement provided for an assembly of all member nations to debate means of resolving disputes, where each had an equal voice; a nine-member council with authority to implement the decisions, with Britain, France, Italy, the United States, and Japan as permanent members; an administrative staff in Geneva; and a permanent Court of International Justice (World Court) to hear and determine certain disputes. Article 10 of the league agreement, which Wilson called its "heart," called for members to protect each other's territorial integrity and "existing political independence."

When the Germans were presented with the terms of the peace in May, they attempted to protest its many violations of the Fourteen Points, on which the armistice had been based. But threatened with military occupation, they signed it on June 28, 1919.

OPPOSITION TO THE LEAGUE AT HOME

Wilson's commission on the League of Nations had completed a draft of its covenant in mid-February 1919, after which the president returned briefly to Washington. Opposition to the league was already bubbling in the Republican-controlled Senate. Henry Cabot Lodge, chair of the Senate Foreign Relations Committee, presented a statement requesting changes, signed by enough senators to block ratification. When the president returned to Paris he accordingly renegotiated.

Wilson returned home for good with the final version of the treaty, including the league covenant, on July 8. He met an enthusiastic popular welcome. Among the public, support for the treaty and the League of Nations was high. To be sure, conservatives questioned the rein on America's freedom to act, progressives were disappointed by the compromises made in the treaty, and isolationists objected to the entire idea of postwar international commitments. On Capitol Hill, the opposition was increasingly organized. Congressional "reservationists" took their name from a list of 14 reservations about the treaty that Lodge developed. (Lodge, who personally despised the president, was making a snide reference to Wilson's Fourteen Points.) Of particular concern to reservationists, and even more to the out-and-out isolationists called irreconcilables, was Wilson's cherished Article 10. It was an international commitment to collective security, and some feared it could be used to send American troops to war without congressional approval. The president—perhaps due to deteriorating health (for one thing, he had suffered a bout of the Spanish influenza while in Paris)—was uncharacteristically intransigent and refused to negotiate with his opponents.

While Lodge engaged in delaying tactics, the president decided to take his case to the American people. He set out on an exhausting tour, traveling more than 9,000 miles to deliver speeches in 29 cities. Great crowds gathered to hear him speak eloquently of a new world community, maintained in peace and security with the help of American leadership. But sadly, the strains of the last year had taken their toll. On September 25, 1919, in Pueblo, Colorado, he collapsed and was forced to return to Washington. There, on October 2, he suffered a serious stroke with paralysis of his left side. For two weeks it was uncertain if he would live, and for six weeks more he was incapacitated. Although eventually he recovered partially, his leadership was debilitated at the moment his long-time goal was close at hand, and in retrospect his political judgment was probably altered for the remainder of his term.

Meanwhile, Lodge proposed that the Senate accept the treaty with 14 reservations. Wilson instructed Democrats to reject the treaty instead of accepting it in altered form, which the Senate did on November 19. The public clamored for action, however, and the treaty was eventually set for another vote with the Lodge reservations intact. Wilson again demanded no compromise. On March 19, 1920, the Senate again failed to reach the necessary two-thirds majority. Most historians believe that a significant majority of the Senate—more than the required two-thirds—in fact favored ratification in some form, as did the public. But the necessary leadership never appeared on either side, and the Treaty of Versailles with its League of Nations Covenant was never ratified by the United States. On May 20, Congress passed a joint resolution declaring that the war was over—and Wilson promptly vetoed it. The resolution was not passed nor peace officially concluded with Germany, Austria, and Hungary, until Warren G. Harding took office as president of the United States in 1921. Woodrow Wilson was awarded the Nobel Peace Prize for 1919, but his own nation never participated in the league he had designed and cherished.

THE GREAT INFLUENZA PANDEMIC OF 1918–1919

In the spring of 1918, a wave of influenza struck Fort Riley, a military training camp in Kansas. But flu, or the grippe, was not uncommon, and it received little notice, even when it popped up on additional military bases. By the end of August, it had arrived in the busy port of Boston and could no longer be ignored. America was in the grasp of the deadly Spanish influenza, so called because of its prevalence in Spain that spring, reportedly 8 million cases. Before the pandemic (worldwide epidemic) ended in 1919, one out of every four Americans had been infected, and an estimated 675,000 of them had died. But the flu also circled the globe. Worldwide during those two years it killed the astonishing figure of more than 20 million (some estimate as high as 40 million)—far more deadly than the Plague, or Black Death, of the 14th century and probably the most devastating epidemic in history. Its appearance during an extensive war helped spread it very quickly as soldiers and materials moved from place to place. Unfortunately, its wartime appearance also meant that information about it was neglected or even censored. At the time some feared that trench warfare was the source of the disease or that the Germans had unleashed a new plague. Germans themselves knew better because their troops suffered just as badly. In fact, the influenza may have helped bring the war to a quicker end, by ravaging troops and ship crews. Among American troops alone, one researcher has estimated that half the casualties were due to disease, primarily Spanish influenza.[24]

The Spanish influenza virus was a particularly deadly strain that caused pneumonic complications and quickly killed a larger than normal percentage of those who contracted it. Victims fell extremely ill within a matter of hours and often died within a few days. The pandemic was also unusual because so many young adults aged 20 to 40, normally the most resistant group, died of it. Although the new sciences of infectious agents and immunology had made great strides, physicians still lacked means to combat the infection.

COMPLETING THE REFORM AGENDA

The Antiprostitution Campaign Joins the War Effort

World War I revived and transformed the Progressive Era antiprostitution campaign. Previously, reformers had focused primarily on protecting women or on reforming urban corruption, although the antiprostitution coalition also included medical personnel concerned about venereal disease. After 1916, the coalition absorbed the idealistic warrants of the war effort and became a campaign to keep America's troops physically healthy, morally strong, and fit representatives of American democracy and values.

During 1916, Secretary of State Newton Baker received reports of rampant venereal disease, prostitution, and drunkenness in army camps in the Southwest, where troops had been stationed in the wake of raids from Mexico by Pancho Villa. To investigate, Baker sent Raymond Fosdick, a former settlement house worker and antiprostitution researcher for the Rockefeller Foundation. Fosdick recommended closing saloons near the camps and other measures that were successful in reducing prostitution and disease. Soon Fosdick and Baker began evolving a program based in part, as Baker put it, on "the fact which every social worker knows to be true, that opportunities for wholesome recreation are the best possible cure for irregularities in conduct which arise from idleness and the basic temptations." As a result, after America entered the war the federal Commission on Training Camp Activities (CTCA) was established to oversee programs at some 16 training camps with populations averaging 48,000. Chaired by Fosdick, the CTCA aimed to suppress prostitution and saloons near the camps, treat venereal infections, promote recreational programs, and exhort the troops about certain values and ideals under the slogan "Fit to Fight." "America is the land where women are partners, not chattels," as one CTCA spokesman put it, ". . . the Government is fostering one of the basic principles of a well ordered democracy—the sanctity of the home."[25]

The venereal-disease treatment program, under the authority of an American Social Hygiene Association official, was very successful both stateside and among American troops in Europe. Planned recreational facilities and programs, a well-established aspect of progressive reform by 1917, were successfully organized with the cooperation of the YMCA, the Knights of Columbus, and the Jewish Welfare League. In addition, the CTCA took up and completed the work begun by vice commissions and civic reformers. Using federal authority derived from the Selective Service Act, which prohibited houses of prostitution within a certain radius of army camps, the commission closed down segregated districts (red-light, or vice areas of cities) throughout the nation. Even in Europe, where many cities licensed brothels, army policy prohibited soldiers from red-light districts. (In France, General Pershing found it necessary to politely decline an offer by Premier Georges Clemenceau to set up special houses of prostitution for American troops.) While reality doubtless fell short of the CTCA's goals for sexual behavior, American troops experienced nothing of the disabling venereal epidemics that ravaged army divisions of both European Allies and the Central powers.

In July 1918, Congress passed the Chamberlain Kahn Act, expanding the antivenereal program in America. The act set up an Interdepartmental Hygiene Board of cabinet secretaries with power to "adopt measures for the purpose of assisting the various States in caring for civilian persons [that is, prostitutes] whose detention, isolation, quarantine, or commitment to institutions may be found to be necessary for the protection of the military and naval forces of the United States against venereal diseases."[26] With this broad federal authority and a generous appropriation, the board, the CTCA, the Department of Justice, and the Public Health Service worked together to detain, examine, impose medical treatment, and sometimes offer rehabilitation to prostitutes found near military camps. Soon many states had constructed detention and treatment centers. In some cases, the women detained were not professional prostitutes but simply camp followers who violated traditional standards of female morality. By the war's end some 30,000 women had been detained, usually without normal legal procedures or protections—one of the lesser-known curtailments of civil rights that occurred as part of the war effort.

In one sense, the wartime program wrote a typical progressive ending to antiprostitution reform. It gave the campaign national coherence and even institutionalized it in a federal agency. The antiprostitution program, however, could not be sustained after the war when it could no longer be justified as an emergency defense measure. In fact, public concern about prostitution dissipated quickly after World War I, partly because sexual mores changed and partly because other progressive issues to which it was originally related no longer compelled public attention.

War and Prohibition

Between 1912 and 1916, public support for temperance, liquor control, and even prohibition had reached a new high among progressive, forward-looking middle-class Americans. Encouraged by public sentiment, leaders of the Anti-Saloon League, the leading political pressure group of the prohibition movement, had begun what they expected to be a 20-year campaign for a prohibition amendment. As 1917 opened victories for prohibition continued. In January the Supreme Court upheld the Webb-Kenyon Act (1913), which permitted dry states to ban interstate shipments of liquor into their territory from elsewhere, if they wished. Congress also passed a prohibition law for Alaska and Washington, D.C., and permitted the people of Puerto Rico to vote on the issue, after which the island went dry.

Meanwhile, strategists for the Anti-Saloon League (ASL) were caught in an unanticipated quandary. In February 1917, Congress took up a bill to prohibit sending liquor advertisements through the mail. Wets led by Senator James Reed of Missouri, thinking to defeat the bill by extremism, introduced an attachment to ban the ordering, purchase, or sale of all liquor in all dry states. Most existing state prohibition laws banned only the manufacture and sale of liquor but permitted personal use of alcoholic beverages purchased by mail. To date, the ASL had deliberately avoided so-called bone-dry legislation because they believed it was still too far-reaching and would harm their long-term cause with the public. (Some individuals and some other prohibition groups did support it, however.) The league withheld official public comment—but to the astonishment and chagrin of wets, the bill passed Congress by a large margin.

In private, league officials were, momentarily, not entirely clear how to proceed. The league's strategists had always been political realists who knew they could not successfully achieve national prohibition until the majority of the American public supported them. League leaders such as Ernest Cherrington believed that many years of incremental changes would be necessary to modify people's behavior and successfully maintain a dry society. But at the same time, the ASL had proven remarkably successful in America's political arena through use of the nonpartisan pressure group tactics they pioneered. The league used its ardent supporters as balance of power voters, to help elect individual officials of either party who agreed to support its interests. After the 1916 elections, due to the ASL's successful political work, Congress itself had a two-thirds majority of members pledged to support dry causes. It was the necessary majority to pass a constitutional amendment—whether or not two-thirds of the American public were enthusiastic prohibitionists.

After the Reed bill victory, league officials who were more aggressive and more impatient to enter the corridors of power began to speak more loudly. The most important was Wayne Wheeler, a remarkably successful lobbyist destined to be the chief framer of national prohibition. The ASL chose to seize the main chance. On April 4, 1917, two days after the opening of the 65th Congress and two days before war was officially declared, a new prohibition amendment resolution was submitted to Congress. Soon recast as a war issue, prohibition achieved its final rush of victories entangled in the war effort.

The declaration of war against Germany encouraged support for prohibition in several ways. The war created an immediate need for increased efficiency among workers in the industrial plants of America and for order and military discipline among a large, untrained army of recruits, neither of which was aided by the use of alcohol. The anti-German furor encouraged by the war also had important consequences because many national brewers were of German descent. A 1918 congressional investigating commission revealed that the German-American Alliance, which had actively supported Germany prior to 1917, received financial support from the United States Brewers' Association. As one prohibitionist put it, "We have German enemies across the water. We have German enemies in this country too. And the worst of all our German enemies . . . are Pabst, Schlitz, Blatz, and Miller."[27]

The war also created an urgent need to conserve food, so that European distress could be adequately relieved. To conserve grain, several European nations had already enacted prohibition laws by the time America entered the war. The Lever Food and Fuel Control Act of August 1917 forbade the use of foodstuffs in the production of liquor. Beer and wine were temporarily exempted under threat of a filibuster by wets, but the law gave the president the power to regulate them in the future. In December, he issued orders reducing the alcoholic content of beer and lowering the amount of grain that could be used for its manufacture in the coming year. Many people applauded; as the *Independent* asked, "Shall the many have food, or the few have drink?"[28]

Finally, the war called forth public willingness to sacrifice nonnecessities on the home front and created a consensus that Congress and the president could legitimately exercise extraordinary powers in the national interest. The ASL's Washington lobbyists took every advantage of public sentiment to press their cause aggressively—often to the annoyance of President Wilson, who was not only standoffish to the prohibition cause but on several occasions found the ASL a distracting irritant as he sought to pass war-related legislation.

The proposed amendment did not explicitly criminalize the use or possession of alcohol, but it did prohibit all sale, transportation, importation, and exportation for beverage purposes. It did not make an exception for home manufacture. When Congress took up the bill there was some debate about destroying an established industry without compensation, about the loss of tax revenue, and about the perennial question of states' rights and federal oversight, which many believed would not really succeed in prohibiting consumption in any case. But with what in retrospect seems little discussion and great speed, the Senate passed the prohibition amendment resolution in July 1917 and the House in December. In its final form, the amendment gave state and federal governments joint powers of enforcement and was to become effective one year after the required three-quarters of state legislatures ratified it. Meanwhile, dry forces continued to press for more immediate victories. In November 1918, after the armistice had already been declared, Congress also passed the Wartime Prohibition Act. It prohibited the manufacture of wine and beer after May 1919 and the sale of all intoxicating beverages after June, under the justification of maintaining prohibition during demobilization. In effect, the law was the real beginning of Prohibition and lasted until the Eighteenth Amendment was ratified.

Less than a month after Congress submitted the Eighteenth Amendment to the states, Mississippi became the first state to ratify it and just two years later, in January 1919, Nebraska became the 36th. (Eventually 46 of the 48 state legislatures voted yes.) Both drys and wets were surprised by the speed of the ratification process. "It was not manufactured sentiment," Wayne Wheeler later told a *New York Times* reporter. "The sentiment was there all right; what we did was simply to direct it."[29]

All that was left was federal legislation to enforce the new amendment. That came in October 1919 when Congress passed the National Prohibition Act, usually known as the Volstead Act, after Minnesota Representative Andrew Volstead, who introduced it. To the great surprise of many Americans, the law set the definition for intoxicating beverages extremely low—0.5 percent—prohibiting virtually any beverage that contained alcohol. (Congress, having assigned enforcement to the Internal Revenue Service [IRS], had adopted the IRS's existing figure for beverages subject to excise tax.) The Volstead Act did reflect certain political compromises. It protected the use of alcohol in private homes by the owner, his family, and his "bona fide guests," and prohibited searches of private homes. It permitted the manufacture of nonintoxicating cider and fruit juices at home and exempted them from the 0.5 percent standard in favor of a case-by-case test of their power to intoxicate, which would fall to local courts. It also spelled out the intended exemption of alcohol for religious, medicinal, or industrial purposes. President Wilson, recovering from his debilitating stroke, issued a veto to the Volstead Act but it was quickly overridden. The Volstead Act took effect at midnight on January 16, 1920. There was little fanfare for the nation had been effectively dry for some time.

The speed with which the states ratified the amendment was, it would later appear, more an ill omen than a sign of thoroughgoing support. Intoxicating beverages had not been defined in the amendment itself, and some state legislatures obviously interpreted the intent too liberally. After the Volstead Act was passed, several states passed laws allowing low-alcohol beer and light wine—but state independence in the matter was disallowed by the Supreme Court in the National Prohibition Cases of 1920. Fourteen states refused to pass any state legislation at all to enforce the Volstead Act.

After the Eighteenth Amendment was passed, establishing Prohibition, the Anti-Saloon League continued to publicize the drawbacks of drinking alcohol. This flier from 1920 shows the effect of alcohol on brain cells. *(Courtesy Westerville, Ohio, Public Library, Anti-Saloon League Collection)*

Votes for Women

As 1917 opened, only 11 states granted full suffrage to women. The two national women's suffrage groups were organized and energized, although a standing rift between them remained. The smaller and more militant was the National Woman's Party (NWP), formerly the Congressional Union, with about 50,000 members. The larger group was NAWSA (National American Woman Suffrage Association), with 2 million members by 1917. NAWSA president Carrie Chapman Catt's Winning Plan called for suffrage campaigns at the state level combined with diplomatic lobbying in Washington for a constitutional amendment. As suffrage states increased in number, NAWSA anticipated, their senators and representatives would be more likely to vote for a national amendment, and the women's vote overall would become a more compelling issue to national party organizations.

In early 1917, NAWSA's executive council met in Washington. Two years earlier, Catt had helped organize the Women's Peace Party to oppose American participation in the war. Now, however, with the nation drawing close to a declaration, NAWSA publicly announced its loyalty and offered its services in the effort to the secretary of war. But NAWSA had no intentions of putting the suffrage cause aside. "Men were talking in that day and hour of democracy, of liberty and justice, as they had talked after the Civil War," Catt and Nettie Rogers Shuler related in their history of the women's suffrage movement. "Keenly alive to the fact that idealism was aroused by the crisis of war," NAWSA began an all-out appeal for immediate consideration of a women's suffrage amendment.[30]

Meanwhile, the NWP pursued a more dramatic route. In December 1916, when President Wilson delivered his annual message to Congress, members had silently if shockingly displayed a long banner from the balcony asking, "Mr. President, What Will You Do For Women's Suffrage?" It served notice of dramatic new tactics to come. On January 10, 1917, the first silent sentinels—pickets for suffrage—appeared outside the gates of the White House, bearing signs with similar slogans. Picketing the White House—let alone by women—was a new event in 1917. At first neither the Wilson administration nor police were sure how to deal with the situation and paid little official attention. When Woodrow Wilson exited the gates for his usual afternoon drive, he would tip his hat to the women. Passersby were often sympathetic to the pickets, who stood day after day and marched silently in a circle around the White House when inauguration ceremonies took place in March.

After war was declared, the NWP began to highlight "the inconsistency between a crusade for world democracy and the denial of democracy at home," as one member put it.[31] The pickets began waving Wilson's own writings on democracy at him as he passed. ("Governments derive all their just powers from the consent of the governed," he had said in his famous "peace without victory" speech of January 22.) By summer, their slogans had become more provocative and onlookers far less approving. Placards labeled the president "Kaiser Wilson," a comparison to the authoritarian ruler of Germany. When representatives of France and England arrived at the White House, the signs announced "Democracy Should Begin at Home." In June, when representatives of the new Russian republic arrived (having given Russian women the vote), a banner announced "We the Women of America Tell You That America Is Not a Democracy. . . . Tell Our Government it Must Liberate its People Before it Can Claim Free Russia as an Ally." Onlookers began to physically attack the picketing women, and on June 22 police began to arrest the pickets and remove them. Forewarned, that day they carried signs quoting the conclusion of the president's April 2 speech to Congress: "We Shall Fight . . . for Democracy . . . For the Right of Those Who Submit to Authority to Have a Voice in Their Own Government."

At first, the courts dismissed the charges, but as both picketing and skirmishes continued the women were sentenced to jail. Before the 65th Congress adjourned in October 1917, 218 women from 26 states had been arrested for "obstructing the sidewalk." Ninety-seven had been sent to prison.[32] Treated harshly and even brutally, they demanded to be considered political prisoners and soon went on a hunger strike. Prison officials began force-feeding them—heedless of the earlier public outrage created by the force-feeding of militant suffragists in England. It created outrage in America as well. Some of the women were well known, like Lavinia Dock, an internationally known nursing expert and associate at Lillian Wald's Henry Street Settlement; some were of mature age; and many were from well-connected families. Under the glare of constant and harsh publicity, the Wilson administration intervened to release all prisoners in late November.

In many ways, the dissimilar tactics of NAWSA and the NWP during 1917, historians have concluded, were complementary—although at the time neither group supported, approved, or even acknowledged the other's contribution to the suffrage cause.[33] In any case, by the end of 1917 there had been significant gains. Six new states granted women the right to vote for president, a procedure called the Illinois plan (in two the legislation was voided, however). The southern barrier was broken when Arkansas gave women the right to vote in primary elections, which almost universally determined the actual victor in the solidly Democratic South. The eastern industrial barrier was also broken, when New York became a full-suffrage state and brought the total to 12. In Congress, a suffrage amendment bill was introduced in both chambers, and the House finally established a suffrage committee to examine it. With great political astuteness America's first congresswoman, Republican Jeannette Rankin of Montana, declined an offer to chair the committee, pointing out the chair should be a Democrat, the majority party at the time.

The House finally set a vote for January 10, 1918. The week before, it was widely reported that Theodore Roosevelt had urged the Republican National Committee to favor the amendment and had even suggested that the committee add women members from each of the suffrage states. President Wilson, who had undergone a slow conversion to the suffrage viewpoint since taking office, announced to the press that he advised congressional Democrats that it was "an act of right and justice to the women of the country and of the world."[34] Much public and editorial sentiment was swaying toward the position that democratic ideals, so prominently publicized in the war effort, required the extension of suffrage to women. Women had willingly assumed many new roles and burdens since the outbreak of war—substituting for men in munitions factories and on the farms, for example—and that too resonated with the public's patriotic enthusiasm. During the House hearings on suffrage, Senator Joseph Bailey of Texas had argued that women were not entitled to vote because they were not "capable of performing all the duties of citizenship," that is, of serving in the army. Representative Rankin had replied, "We have men in the United States Senate who cannot serve in the Army, and yet they make splendid Senators." She asked Congress, "Is it not possible that the women of the country have something of value to give the nation at this time? . . . Shall our women, our home defense, be our only fighters in the struggle for democracy who shall be denied federal action?" Her speech received "prolonged applause."[35]

The vote of January 10 was expected to be close, and a number of congressional supporters made extraordinary efforts to be present. One congressman left his suffragist wife's deathbed, voted yes, then returned home for her funeral. The amendment passed the House by the necessary two-thirds majority, 274 to 136. Members of both NAWSA and the NWP, who had packed the galleries, poured out of the Capitol singing "Praise God From Whom All Blessings Flow," a well-known Christian hymn.

The battle had been joined, but it was far from won. The Senate vote remained, and the Senate as a body was traditionally far more conservative and (since senators stood for reelection every six years instead of every other year like representatives) less likely to respond quickly to shifts in public sentiment. Although NAWSA and the NWP lobbied hard, Senate opponents delayed the vote until October. By then many other western nations, mindful of their women citizen's crucial role under the stresses of war, had given them the right to vote—including Canada and Great Britain. President Wilson was increasingly attentive to the contradiction. The day before the vote he took the highly unusual step of appearing personally before the Senate with only momentary notice. "Democracy means that women shall play their part in affairs alongside of men and upon an equal footing with them," he said. Suffrage was not only necessary to winning the war, he continued, but also "vital to the right solution of the problems we must settle, and settle immediately, when the war is over."[36] But the suffrage amendment fell two votes short of a two-thirds majority and was defeated in the Senate, 62 in favor to 34 opposed.

The defeat was largely attributable to southern Democrats, and it helped decrease the party's support from progressives in the 1918 midterm elections. But in the November elections three more states joined the suffrage column—South Dakota, Michigan, and Oklahoma. During 1918, Texas had also given women the primary vote. Meanwhile, at the White House gates the NWP silent sentinels were still picketing. After the Senate voted the amendment down, they also began to publicly burn President Wilson's speeches on democracy.

By the time the 66th Congress (elected in November 1918) opened in May 1919, world powers were weeks away from signing the Treaty of Versailles. After the war ended, suffrage workers had redoubled their efforts, concerned that postwar readjustment might consign their cause to the sidelines. Early in 1919 six additional states passed the Illinois plan, permitting women to vote in presidential elections and bringing the total number of electoral votes women could influence to 339 out of 435. Twenty-four states sent memorials to Congress asking for a suffrage amendment to be passed, and some 500 resolutions and other petitions poured in from various civic, church, labor, and farm organizations. President Wilson, still in Europe, added his recommendation by cable. On the opening day, May 19, the House of Representative re-passed the amendment, this time by the increased margin of 304 to 89. In the Senate, opponents continued to make halfhearted objections but saw the handwriting on the wall. With little of the drama that had marked earlier votes, on June 3, 1919, the U.S. Senate passed the Nineteenth Amendment, which would give American women the right to vote upon ratification by 36 of the 48 states.

SUFFRAGE OPPONENTS AND THE CAMPAIGN FOR RATIFICATION

Seasoned suffrage workers in NAWSA and the National Women's Party knew that the battle was not yet over. Carrie Chapman Catt had set a high priority on maintaining state suffrage organizations even in full suffrage states in anticipation of the ratification battle. Now, they swung into action. Because 36 of 48 states had to ratify the amendment, suffrage opponents or antis had to block it in only 13 to defeat it. Opponents of women's suffrage knew it was their last chance and mounted their most intense campaign.

The original antis were primarily women of means and high social position. They believed that contact with politics would be an overwhelming burden for respectable women and at best betrayed a naïveté about the vast majority of American women's lives. They continued to testify at hearings and distribute materials through their organizations. But antis had come to serve mainly as a convenient public face for elected officials and other men who opposed suffrage. Some religious leaders, for example, found suffrage to be at odds with their beliefs about the proper role of women. The antis made extensive use of prominent Catholic clergymen who opposed suffrage, such as Cardinal James Gibbons, but in fact clergy of all faiths could be found on both sides of the argument.

Most historians credit the extensive, long-term opposition to enfranchising American women—26 other western nations acted before America did—to other sources. "Not so open but more politically potent than antisuffrage organizations," write historians Anne Firor Scott and Andrew Scott, "were the economic groups that organized to oppose suffrage."[37] Liquor interests were clearly an important opponent, underwriting much financial support of anti-suffrage activity, especially in the Midwest. In the East, big business objected to women's suffrage. Their objection was partly due to social conservatism but also rested on the calculation that women voters would support reform measures that business opposed. Political machines opposed women's suffrage in part because they were beholden to big business and often to liquor interests. But machine politicians were also disposed to oppose major political change on principle because it would require them to reorganize in new ways to maintain their power. And lastly, opposition to women's suffrage was very strong in the South, partly due to social conservatism and partly due to racial issues. While a few whites argued that women's suffrage would increase the number of white voters, the amendment clearly enfranchised black as well as white women. Many white southerners viewed any new federal and especially constitutional attention to voting as a Pandora's box, threatening the disenfranchisement of African-American men that they had successfully established.

By August 1920, 35 states had ratified the women's suffrage amendment—one short of the necessary number. Both pro- and anti-suffrage activists believed that only one state, Tennessee, had any chance of ratifying the amendment before the upcoming November elections. When a special session of the Tennessee legislature opened on August 9, they flocked to Nashville. For the next 10 days anti-suffrage interests poured the liquor, despite Prohibition, and offered deals to recalcitrant pro-suffrage legislators. According to Catt, "I was more maligned, more lied about, than in the thirty previous years I have worked for suffrage. I was flooded with anonymous letters, vulgar, ignorant, insane. Strange men and groups of men sprang up. . . . They appropriated our telegrams, tapped our telephones, listened outside our windows and transoms. They attacked our public and private lives."[38]

Despite anti-suffrage efforts the Tennessee legislature ratified the amendment, although in the statehouse it came down to the last vote—that of 24-year-old state representative Harry Burn, who had promised his suffragist mother he would vote yes only if his vote was needed. It was and he did. On August 26, 1920, the amendment was proclaimed in effect, women at long last had the right to vote, and the number of Americans with access to one of the most basic rights of democracy was doubled.

CONTINUING THE REFORM AGENDA: CHILD LABOR REFORMERS KEEP AT THE TASK

In September 1916, President Wilson had signed the Keating-Owen bill into law, placing federal restrictions on child labor in manufacturing and mining industries that used interstate commerce to distribute their products. The law was scheduled to go into effect in September 1917. It did not affect the majority of child workers—those working at home, at agricultural labor, or in street trades. But child labor reformers considered it a very important victory nonetheless, since it established a uniform standard throughout the nation and put federal authority on the side of regulation.

No sooner was the ink dry on the Keating-Owen Act, however, than child labor reformers faced new opposition in the name of the wartime labor shortage. Southern mill owners under the leadership of David Clark, editor of the *Southern Textile Bulletin,* quickly announced they intended to challenge the act in court. In August 1917, a month before the law was to become effective, they filed a case in the name of Roland Dagenhart. Dagenhart was the father of two children who stood to lose their jobs in a Charlotte, North Carolina, textile mill. Judge James E. Boyd, a conservative and known opponent of child labor laws, granted an injunction against the Keating-Owen Act in the state of North Carolina, on the grounds that the law was unconstitutional. His orders (issued orally, rather than in writing) indicated that he believed Congress did not have the right to regulate local labor conditions and that the law denied parents their legal right to a child's earnings.

In the rest of the nation the law went into operation as planned, while the Attorney General and the Justice Department appealed the North Carolina injunction to the Supreme Court. Legal scholars were generally critical of Judge Boyd's actions, and many people observed that other recent wartime legislation favored national authority. Yet to the surprise and dismay of child labor reformers, on June 3, 1918, the Supreme Court ruled 5-4 in *Hammer v. Dagenhart* that the Keating-Owen Act was indeed unconstitutional because it overstepped the legitimate uses of the interstate commerce clause. The ruling did not ban the regulation of child labor, but it denied the use of federal power over interstate commerce as the means of doing it. Justice Oliver Wendell Holmes filed a spirited dissent for the four justices who disagreed.

During the nine months the Keating-Owen law had been in effect, most factories had complied, reducing the hours of young workers and dismissing those under 16. Immediately after the ruling they quickly reinstated 10- or 11-hour days and rehired young workers. Said the president of the Cotton Manufacturers' Association, "the southern industry is due the thanks and gratitude of the nation because they fought alone in the face of blind prejudice aroused by paid agitators all over the country."[39]

But, in fact, the public as a whole still strongly supported the restriction of child labor. On the heels of the Supreme Court ruling came new demands for government action from a wide variety of reform-minded people. Felix Frankfurter, head of the War Labor Policies Board, agreed to add the standards of the Keating-Owen Act to all federal contracts, making them mandatory for any company engaged in supplying the government. Various congressmen immediately introduced bills and amendments for study. Experts for the National Child Labor Committee (NCLC) set to work exploring constitutionally acceptable legislation. In the Senate, Atlee Pomerene, an Ohio Democrat, introduced a plan to tax products made by child labor. The child labor tax (also called the Pomerene amendment because it was an attachment or amendment to the general revenue bill) levied 10 percent on the net profits of all mines that employed children under 16 and all manufacturers that employed children younger than 14, or on any concern that employed children under 16 for more than eight hours a day, six days a week, or at night. In other words, it reenacted the standards of the Keating-Owen Act—and even extended them to canneries and workshops—by making child labor expensive. With little debate the bill passed both houses of Congress, and President Wilson signed it into law on February 24, 1919.

Southern textile manufacturers again filed suit. In May, the litigants again met in Judge Boyd's North Carolina courtroom. This time the judge announced he had no need to hear the arguments—he had already made up his mind. He declared the tax unconstitutional.

Supporters of child labor reform were of course outraged. But many people—including state officials and employers of child workers—believed that this time the carefully drafted law would be upheld by the Supreme Court. The case was argued before the Court in December 1919, but the decision would not be issued until 1922. In the meantime many states strengthened their compulsory school attendance laws and enacted new child labor laws to meet the federal requirements, and many employers revised their policies for child workers. Because of these changes, the end of the Progressive Era saw a decline in child labor.

But about the Supreme Court, the prognosticators were wrong. In 1922, the child labor tax was declared unconstitutional, this time by an 8-1 decision—and the work of child labor reformers continued.[40]

A New Immigration Act

Although the beginning of the war in Europe had drastically reduced immigration, Congress remained concerned that it would resume even more heavily upon the war's end. Shortly before the United States entered the conflict, Congress passed a new comprehensive bill, which historian Roger Daniels describes as "the first significant general restriction of immigration."[41] The bill included a literacy test, the fourth time since 1897 that such a test had passed Congress. The three previous attempts to enact it in 1897, 1913, and 1915 had resulted in presidential vetoes, and once again in 1917 President Wilson vetoed the bill. This time, however, the veto was easily and quickly overridden, and on February 5, 1917, the bill became law. Strong congressional support reflected growing nationalism and even nativist fears. But it also reflected the reduced influence of ethnic group lobbyists, some of whom were tarred by their support of the Central Powers as America drew close to entering the war.

The literacy test itself was designed fairly. Adult immigrants could prove literacy in any recognized language or dialect. In the case of families, only the husband need be literate, not the wife, and other exceptions were made for parents, grandparents, and unmarried adult daughters. Ironically, after two decades of demand for the test, it was to have little observable effect. Immigration would again reach 800,000 by the 1921 reporting year (July 1, 1920 to June 30, 1921), but only 1,450 were denied admission because they did not pass the literacy test.[42]

Of more effect, the 1917 act also contained a so-called Asiatic barred zone, described in latitude and longitude. The zone was enacted primarily in response to restrictionist pressure on the West Coast. It barred immigration from Asian nations that to date had not been excluded, including India and all the nations or colonies of Southeast Asia. The act excepted the Philippines (an American dependency) and Japan, although it did not rescind international agreements like the Gentleman's Agreement of 1908 that barred unskilled Japanese workers. Other provisions of the act repeated or extended long-standing restrictions against criminals, prostitutes, polygamists, paupers, anarchists and other revolutionaries, and people with certain diseases.

IMMIGRANTS AND ALIENS

When America declared war against the Central Powers in 1917, the Census Bureau estimated that 4,662,000 residents of the United States had been born in nations with which America was now at war, primarily Germany and the Austro-Hungarian Empire. Many had not yet become naturalized citizens of the United States and were therefore officially called enemy aliens. Still on the books was the Alien Enemy Act of 1798, which gave the president power to imprison without trial those believed to be dangerous. On that basis, on April 6, 1917, the day war was declared, President Wilson published a proclamation regulating the behavior of enemy aliens, forbidding them to publish attacks on America or aid the Central powers, and subjecting them to summary arrest and confinement if they did. (Later they could also be charged under the espionage and sedition acts.) More than 2,000 were confined before the war's end in three army camps built in Georgia and Utah. The camps also housed German prisoners of war, primarily crews of ships seized in American ports when the war began. In Canada internment was far more widely practiced. Twenty-four camps there eventually housed more than 8,500.[43]

Without question, the hand of anti-foreign harassment fell most heavily on German Americans during the war. Despite heightened fears and suspicions of all foreign-born people, immigrants from other countries were not generally singled out if they appeared to support the war effort. Many of the national or ethnic groups from the Austro-Hungarian Empire were well known to despise their former rulers. The CPI, or Creel Committee, took great care to portray immigrants from the Central powers sympathetically, to discourage ethnic and religious animosities, and to stimulate unity under the slogan Americans All. And, in fact, as the American public increasingly focused on a common enemy, many focused less on the differences of immigrants. As a religious periodical, the *Missionary Review,* put it in 1918, "These handicapped races [ethnic groups] are showing such loyalty, such devotion to our country, that we are realizing our former undemocratic, unchristian attitude toward them."[44] The heightened cohesion during the war years, some historians have even suggested, gave some immigrants their first sense of welcome and participation in the national community. In many locales, immigrant and ethnic churches and other organizations were enlisted in Red Cross projects or Liberty Bond drives. For the Fourth of July in 1918, the Creel Committee organized great multiethnic pageants at which immigrants demonstrated both their cultures and their patriotism. And although noncitizens were exempted from the draft under the Selective Service Act, many aliens pleasantly surprised other Americans by enlisting. Eventually foreign-born soldiers (both citizen and alien) made up 18 percent of U.S. Army troops, higher than the percentage of foreign-born people in the population overall.[45]

During the war years, the public was otherwise distracted from the Americanization crusade of the preparedness years. In the postwar period, however, groups such as the American Legion began new and, to some, excessively zealous Americanization programs. Reformers, dismayed by what they saw as the continuing excesses of "100 percent Americanism," lost interest in the programs and some immigrant leaders became hostile. Aspects of the earlier reform campaign, such as English-language and citizenship instruction, moved into schools and teacher training colleges.

PUERTO RICANS GAIN MORE SELF-GOVERNMENT

Since early in Theodore Roosevelt's presidency, Puerto Rican leaders had protested the colonialist government established by the United States via the 1900 Foraker Act. Puerto Rico had an elected assembly, but it was headed by a governor and executive council appointed by the president. In Congress, it was represented by a resident commissioner who was elected but could not vote. Its people were not U.S. citizens, and the unincorporated territory was neither an independent country nor officially part of the United States. Some Puerto Rican leaders preferred statehood, some independence, and some territorial home rule, but all wanted increased self-government and a clearer definition of Puerto Rico's relationship to America.

Traditionally, the Democratic Party opposed the acquisition and rule of American dependencies. During his first term Woodrow Wilson appointed the first majority of Puerto Ricans, rather than mainland Americans, to the Executive Council. He also supported a new organic act for the island. Early in 1917, Congress passed the Jones-Shafroth Act; it made Puerto Ricans citizens of the United States, with all rights of citizenship, and abolished the council in favor of an elected legislature with two houses. The President, however, retained veto power over any law passed, and Congress maintained control of financial and economic matters as established in the Foraker Act. The island remained unincorporated, and its resident commissioner in Congress remained without a vote. Almost all Puerto Ricans were very pleased with the decision on citizenship and with the increased legislative power, but many remained unsatisfied with the failure to define the island as fully self-governing.

During World War I, Americans were suspicious of foreigners, especially German Americans. This cartoon, published in the *New York Herald* in 1918, depicts the popular opinion that the nation had too many enemy aliens threatening American beliefs and freedoms from within. The alien is drawn as a stereotypical German. *(Library of Congress, Prints and Photographs Division, LC-USZ62-105705)*

THE GREAT MIGRATION: AFRICAN AMERICANS MOVE NORTH

In 1865, at the end of the Civil War, about 91 percent of African Americans lived in the South—a number that had changed little since 1790 when the first census was taken. As late as 1910, 89 percent of African Americans remained there, and 80 percent of them lived in rural areas. But a slow trickle cityward and northward was beginning, and in the following decade it became a rush. Between 1910 and 1920, probably at least half a million blacks left the South, most of them after 1916. By 1920, the black population of the South was 450,000 less than it had been in 1910, despite an overall increase of 15 percent in U.S. population during the decade. Most of the migrants headed for northern cities although a few headed west, especially to Los Angeles. By 1920, New York had seen an increase of 55 percent in its African-American population, Chicago 148 percent, Detroit 611 percent, and Philadelphia 500 percent.

Within the South itself, blacks were also leaving the countryside and moving to cities. The Great Migration, as historians call this large population redistribution, became even larger in the decade of the 1920s and did not end until 1960, by which time 40 percent of African Americans would live in the North or West and three-quarters would live in urban rather than rural areas.[46]

Blacks who moved north in the 1910s had both social and economic reasons for doing so. In the South, blacks could not vote, they were restricted at every turn by Jim Crow legislation, and they lived constantly under the shadow of lynching and other kinds of racial violence and maltreatment. In most cases, however, the immediate motive for their move was a search for economic opportunity. In the South, marginal farmers and agricultural laborers were in especially dire straits. As World War I began, cotton prices in the South took a brief plunge, followed by a severe plague of boll weevils that lasted several years, compounded by floods in some places. Meanwhile, the industrial North had been hit by a labor shortage. The war had abruptly cut off the usual source of cheap labor, immigration. By 1916, when war orders began to underwrite an industrial boom, the need for workers in the North became pronounced, and after the draft began it became acute. Traditionally, blacks had not been hired for industrial labor. In 1916, however, labor agents began visiting the South to recruit blacks to come north and work on the railroads, in the packing houses, in the steel mills, and in many other factories, offering free passes and wages unheard of in rural areas. In the next few years, many followed friends and relatives who had gone ahead, encouraged by the constant drumbeat of publicity in the *Chicago Defender* and other widely circulated black newspapers and by information sources that included organizations like the National Urban League.

In the South, where the economy depended on black workers for domestic, agricultural, and other of labor, the exit of so many African-American workers alarmed white planters, employers, and opinion makers. Labor agents were run out of the region, and in some places, historians suggest, wages and conditions for blacks may even have improved a bit. Those who did move North found far from ideal conditions, especially in housing choices, and no lack of discrimination and prejudice—nor were established African-American middle-class leaders in the urban North entirely comfortable with the migrants' ways. Nonetheless, the migration continued, and many called it a second emancipation. A migrant to Philadelphia told a *Survey* investigator, "Miss, if I had the money I would go South and dig up my fathers' and my mothers' bones and bring them up . . . I am forty-nine years old and these six weeks I have spent here are the first weeks in my life of peace and comfort."[47]

JAZZ BECOMES A NATIONAL PHENOMENON

On February 26, 1917, the same day that President Wilson asked Congress to arm American merchant ships against German submarines, the Original Dixieland Jazz Band made a record in New York for the Victor Talking Machine Company (later RCA Victor). The band, a group of white musicians from New Orleans, were attracting attention by playing a new style of music in one of New York's night spots. The record was released on March 7—"Livery Stable Blues" on one side and "Dixieland Jass Band One-Step" on the other—and created an immediate sensation. Despite the fact that most Americans had never before heard anything quite like it, it sold a million copies. Almost overnight, the new music swept the nation.

The exact origins of jazz remain shrouded because it developed in performance without being recorded or published. Even the word *jazz,* or *jass* or *jasz* as it was first written, is of uncertain and disputed origin. But authorities do agree that jazz did not begin with white musicians like the Original Dixieland Jazz Band, although it probably did begin in New Orleans. Still in its infancy in 1917, jazz evolved from two kinds of popular music, both of African-American origin. One was the blues, a traditional musical form named for one of its distinctive characteristics, blue notes, or notes flattened by a half step. The other was ragtime, a lively syncopated music that swept the country after 1895. (In syncopated music, note divisions and accents play against the strong and weak beats of the meter or rhythm in which it is written.) Unlike the blues, ragtime had antecedents in European musical form.

Jazz incorporated musical features of both ragtime and blues. But its distinctive characteristic was improvisation on a given musical line by an individual or by a group of musicians in collaboration with each other. Jazz may have appeared first in the music-loving city of New Orleans because it was home to two interacting groups of African-American musicians: those from the Creole community, who were trained in European musical styles (New Orleans's distinctive Creole culture had both African and French roots), and those from the hardscrabble black community who improvised while playing spirituals, work songs, and blues. But music also permeated the wall that divided blacks and whites in other aspects of life. Although audiences and dances were segregated, whites often heard black and Creole bands, and blacks heard street performances of white bands as well. Ironically, one of the best early black New Orleans jazz bands, Freddie Keppard's Original Creole Orchestra, turned down Victor's offer to make the first jazz record in 1915. Keppard was afraid other musicians would steal his techniques.

It was not long before jazz left American shores. On January 1, 1918, the 369th Regiment, an African-American unit later known as the Hellfighters, landed in France accompanied by a large regimental band. It was led by Lieutenant James Reese Europe, the best known society bandleader in New York before he volunteered. Europe's band added ragtime, blues, and jazz elements to their marches and soon took Europe by storm. Prominent British, French, and Italian bandleaders asked to see the instruments, assuming some new design was the source of the new music. The Original Dixieland Jazz Band also toured. On the day the Versailles Treaty was signed, they headlined the victory celebration at the elegant Savoy Restaurant in London.

As jazz developed in the 20th century it would increasingly be considered an art form. It remains America's unique contribution to world music.

A GREAT AMERICAN COMPOSER: CHARLES IVES

The beginning of jazz was not the only musical milestone of the late 1910s. During the same years, an innovating composer of modern symphonic music, Charles Ives, was completing, revising, or assembling much of his work, written over a period of at least two decades. Almost none of his works would find appreciative listeners before the 1930s, although a few largely private performances were held beginning in the late 1910s—leaving most musicians bewildered by the musical complexity and most critics dumbfounded. By the time of Ives's death in 1954, however, his experiments in musical form were widely honored. Today he is not only regarded as the nation's greatest serious composer, but also one who is distinctly American.

For a composer, Ives led a singular life. Trained as a musician and church organist by his father and at Yale (he even contributed a song to McKinley's 1896 presidential campaign), he left professional performance shortly after college and became a highly successful insurance man, nationally known for his innovations in the industry. All the while, he continued to compose in the evenings and weekends, experimenting more and more with form and tonal dissonance. At the time, other symphonic composers trained in Europe and followed set musical rules, while European composers themselves were considered far superior to any American—a situation very similar to the one American painters faced during the progressive decades.

Ives's compositions usually have specifically American references and many evoke the sounds and moods of certain places and experiences. His most popular work, the

Concord Sonata (*Second Sonata for Piano: Concord, Mass., 1840–1860,* published in 1920 although not performed in full until 1938), for example, has movements entitled *Emerson, Hawthorne, The Alcotts,* and *Thoreau;* the *New England Holidays* symphony (assembled ca. 1917–1919, first performed in full 1954) has movements entitled *Washington's Birthday, Decoration Day, Fourth of July,* and *Thanksgiving.* But to music historians, it is Ives's innovation in structures, harmonies, and rhythms that notably capture the dissonance of the 20th-century world and especially the heterogeneity of American life. In Ives's music, classical European traditions are integrated with the forms and the melodies of many different kinds of America music: folk song, popular song, Civil War marches, gospel hymns, patriotic tunes, even ragtime and square dance. In any given work disparate and clashing elements are presented in many different layers at the same time, the layers often written in different meters or keys (or in no key at all, a characteristic called atonality) which might come together in new ways, then separate again.

In the writings Ives published to explain his music, he also exhibited ideas that were typical of progressives. Music, he believed, could express the spirit of what he called the Majority or the People, as opposed to the Minority or Non-People, vocal but small special interests.

POSTWAR TURMOIL AT HOME

Even before negotiators left the peace table in France, American society at home was experiencing abrupt and unsettling changes. The war had ended more quickly than predicted, and the Wilson administration had no overall plan for demobilization and reconstruction, or readjustment of society and the economy to peacetime. As soon as the armistice was declared, the military began to discharge troops. Within a year nearly the entire uniformed force of 4 million men and women had been returned to civilian life. Even more speedily, officials in Washington began canceling all war contracts—so fast, according to report, that they jammed long-distance telephone lines out of Washington. The various war boards, which had exercised unprecedented control over business, labor, and the economy, dismantled almost overnight and provided little transitional guidance.

Immediate economic disaster did not occur because the wartime boom continued for the short term. Both Americans and war-ravaged Europeans wanted consumer goods, and Congress continued high levels of spending for a time, partly to relieve distress in Europe. The bubble burst at the end of 1920, but, meanwhile, it brought raging inflation. In 1919, prices were 77 percent higher than their prewar level and by 1920 105 percent higher, wiping out the modest wage gains many workers had experienced during the war years.[48] In the nation as a whole, the heightened sense of purpose and unity during the war years evaporated. The optimistic Progressive Era drew to a close amid turbulent strikes, violent race riots, and widespread fears that Bolsheviks, communists, and other radicals were conspiring against the American way of life.

INFLATION AND AN UNPRECEDENTED WAVE OF STRIKES

As the war ended, workers worried about holding on to their jobs as the millions of veterans returned—but they were even more concerned about the inflation or high cost of living, as it was called, that ate up their paychecks. To make matters worse, with the abrupt end of wartime controls over industry and labor, many employers attempted to rescind the improved wages, working conditions, and union recognition they had been pressured to grant during the war emergency. Workers, for their part, had joined unions in record numbers during the war, and they were determined to hold on to wartime gains. During the war, they had been pressured not to strike, but that too ended abruptly. During 1919 more than 4 million workers took part in an unprecedented wave of over 3,600 strikes—the greatest labor unrest since the early 1890s.

A mere four days after the armistice, the Amalgamated Clothing Workers struck in New York and Chicago, winning a 40-hour week and a wage increase that was afterward adopted throughout the clothing industry. One after the other, New England textile workers, telephone and telegraph operators, longshoremen, railway switchmen, coal miners (now led by the rising John L. Lewis), and other groups of workers followed. Many strikes succeeded, and by 1920 union membership was at an all-time high of more than 5 million, nearly double what it had been in 1915.[49]

Several of the most dramatic strikes of the postwar era, however, not only failed but contributed more than their share to growing public disenchantment with unions and fears that workers were turning into Bolsheviks. In late January 1919 some 35,000 shipyard workers walked out in Seattle, Washington. The walkout soon became a general strike (that is, every other union in town also struck to support the shipyard workers) under leadership of the IWW-dominated Central Labor Council. For five days the city was brought to a standstill. General strikes, according to IWW belief, foreshadowed a workers' revolution; they were also widely used by European unions at the time. Apprised of that information, the otherwise progressive mayor of Seattle, Ole Hansen, inflamed public fears that the strike was a radical and possibly foreign plot, called for military assistance, and broke the strike, to the approbation of opinion makers nationwide. In September 1919, the public was alarmed for different reasons when Boston's police went on strike after the commissioner fired several for joining an AFL union. Newly returned veterans, Harvard students, and other Bostonians volunteered to patrol the streets but could not prevent widespread looting and disorder. The Massachusetts governor, Calvin Coolidge, called out the National Guard, personally took its command, restored order, broke the strike, fired all the policemen who had participated, and assembled a new police force. Coolidge, later to become U.S. president, first gained nationwide fame when he declared to AFL president Samuel Gompers, "There is no right to strike against the public safety by anybody, anywhere, anytime."[50]

Shortly before the Boston police struck, 343,000 employees of U.S. Steel walked out in several eastern and midwestern cities, beginning the most extensive and most important strike of the postwar era. Steel was a large and crucial basic industry. But steelworkers had not had effective union representation since the Homestead strike of 1892 and the unskilled still received bare subsistence wages. Workers responded eagerly to an AFL organizing drive in 1918 and 1919. Captains of the steel industry, especially Elbert H. Gary of U.S. Steel, hewed to longstanding policy and refused to treat with union representatives in any way. In September 1919, workers struck for union recognition, an end to 12-hour days, and higher wages. The strike was bitter from the start. To some extent skilled workers, who were better compensated and usually American-born, did not completely support the efforts of the unskilled, many of whom were immigrants. Owners blamed the strike on the Bolsheviks and the "Red" element. They hired strikebreakers and private police to prevent picketing and generally succeeded in keeping the mills open. But the strike soon turned violent. In Gary, Indiana, riots erupted and military troops were called in. By January 1920, 18 workers had been killed, hundreds beaten or injured, and many more subjected to violations of civil liberties. The American public, however, was increasingly focused on fears of radical subversion and turned almost universally hostile to the striking workers. In January 1920 the strike collapsed.

THE RED SUMMER

The summer of 1919 also saw an unprecedented outbreak of racial conflict. African-American poet James Weldon Johnson labeled it the Red Summer, referring to the blood that was shed.

Racial tensions had increased for several reasons. One factor was the migration of blacks to northern cities, which expanded the arena of conflict. In the North, the increasing black population raised hostility among white urban residents and became a special object of hatred to unskilled white workers, many of them immigrants, with whom they competed for jobs. As early as July 1917 in East St. Louis, Illinois, where northward-moving blacks took the places of striking white workers, riots had resulted in many deaths. A second factor was an increasing willingness among blacks to fight back when riots began and a new militancy among African-American leaders. After the East St. Louis riot, the NAACP organized a protest parade 8,000 strong in New York, where silent marchers accompanied by muffled drums carried signs with messages like, "Mr President, Why Not Make America Safe for Democracy?" Black expectations of more equitable treatment were further raised by participation of black troops in the war and by the experience of the troops themselves in the freer society of France. Conversely, the army training of so many black men had raised fears among whites, especially after some black soldiers at a Houston army base rioted in 1917, leaving several white civilians dead.

In July 1919, whites attacked the black neighborhood of Longview, Texas, beginning six months of violence in 25 different places. Longview was followed a week later by four days of rioting in the streets of Washington, D.C. Before the end of the month one of the most fearful race riots in American history occurred in Chicago. It began when a black teenager swam near a white beach on the shores of Lake Michigan and drowned, possibly after being hit with a rock. For 13 days both black and white mobs roamed areas of the city, destroying property, setting fires, looting, fighting, and killing. The city was almost at war, and even the National Guard was unable to restore order until a rainstorm helped drive people indoors. When the riot was finally subdued, 38 people had been killed (15 whites and 23 blacks), more than 500 people injured, and more than 1,000 families left homeless. The 1919 riots climaxed in November in rural Elaine, Arkansas, where black tenant farmers attempted to organize. Officially, five whites and 25 blacks were recorded as having lost their lives, but oral reports widely indicated that many more blacks had been killed.[51]

Riots were not the only kind of racial violence. Especially in the South, lynchings increased again. In 1919, the total included 10 black veterans, some in uniform, and 10 victims who were publicly burned. The year also saw the beginning of a large increase in the membership of the Ku Klux Klan, which had been revived in 1915. By year's end, Klan organizations existed in 27 states and numbered more than 100,000 active members. White-hooded night riders accosted and beat many victims, especially in the South and Southwest.[52]

In the face of these events, new responses arose. The NAACP increasingly counseled resistance and began a new campaign against lynching. In New York, Jamaican-born Marcus Garvey began attracting African Americans to his doctrine of black nationalism. Garvey's United Negro Improvement Association (UNIA) encouraged black pride and business cooperation and soon launched a scheme for blacks to return to Africa. At the same time, a few whites in the South began to work publicly for improved racial relations for the first time. In Atlanta the Commission on Interracial Cooperation was founded in 1919 and in coming years encouraged similar organizations elsewhere.

THE RED SCARE

Rapid demobilization, crushing inflation, labor turmoil, and racial violence all contributed to a sense of turbulence in the immediate postwar years. But important and well-publicized world events also encouraged many Americans to view unrest as a more threatening sign. In November 1917, the Bolshevik revolution in Russia had installed revolutionary Marxists in the seats of power. They opposed not only capitalism but also liberal and even socialist reform, accomplished by evolutionary or democratic means. In March 1919, Russia's revolutionary leaders held a meeting in Moscow attended by radical groups from many nations. Lenin, the Russian leader, declared that Bolsheviks should rename themselves communists. They organized the Third International, or Comintern, dedicated to spreading revolution worldwide by both aboveboard and subversive means. Indeed, in the same month the Comintern met, a communist uprising succeeded in Hungary. Radical beliefs were no longer just theories.

In the United States, the Socialist Party of America soon experienced a major split. Leaders of the party had always maintained that socialism was democratic in character and goals, and they supported reform, evolutionary change, and democratic methods. The party claimed 104,000 members at the beginning of 1919, however, and many wanted to declare allegiance to the Comintern and the immediate overthrow of capitalism. By August 1919, some 60,000 had either been expelled or had withdrawn. They formed two new groups. The smaller Communist Labor Party, organized in August and led by journalist John Reed, had between 10,000 and 30,000 members by the end of the year. The Communist Party of America, composed primarily of ethnic or immigrant associations, had between 30,000 and 60,000 members by the end of the year.[53]

Aided by constant newspaper publicity of revolutionary doings, America's wartime fears of radical and disloyal activity moved seamlessly into postwar fears of Bolshevism or communism in 1919 and 1920, a reaction known as the Red Scare. Public concern, not surprisingly, was magnified by a series of bombings in 1919. On April 28, a package bomb was sent to the mayor of Seattle. The next day, the African-American maid of a Georgia senator had her hands blown off when she received a package for him at his Atlanta home. The Post Office launched an immediate investigation and uncovered 16 bomb packages in New York alone. Some 20 were discovered elsewhere. They were addressed to such figures as J. P. Morgan and John D. Rockefeller but also to a long list of officials who had participated in various activities that had impacted radicals: the Postmaster General, Supreme Court Justice Oliver Wendell Holmes, former reformer Frederic Howe and former Representative Anthony Caminetti, both now immigration commissioners, as well as Chicago judge Kenesaw Mountain Landis, who had sentenced Eugene V. Debs to jail. In early June, numerous bombs exploded in eight cities on the same day, one on the doorstep of Attorney General A. Mitchell Palmer's house in Washington.

The perpetrators were never caught, and most historians assume they were anarchists and a radical fringe. But the bombings helped persuade many Americans that the nation faced a real and immanent threat from organized revolutionaries, likely of foreign birth. Every form of dissent and even justifiable protest began to hint at a nationwide conspiracy. Retaliation was quick and powerful and did not discriminate among its victims. California and New York launched investigations, and nearly 30 states passed new sedition laws aimed at organizations that advocated violence. In Centralia, Washington, members of the newly formed American Legion attacked IWW headquarters. Four of the attackers were killed; townspeople lynched an IWW member in retaliation, and seven others were convicted of murder. In New York, a mob of veterans destroyed the offices of the socialist newspaper *The Call*. Congress denied Socialist Party member Victor Berger his duly elected seat in 1919 and again in 1920, and the New York state legislature expelled five duly elected socialists. University administrations sought out and dismissed faculty members whose opinions were suspect; at Columbia, prominent progressive Charles Beard resigned in protest. Many cities forced teachers to sign loyalty oaths. Women's reform groups such as the National Consumer's League and beloved figures like Jane Addams, a Quaker who had remained a pacifist even during the war, were targeted by right-wing innuendo. In many communities, there were acts of violence against suspected radicals, and in Indiana a jury acquitted a naturalized citizen who murdered an immigrant for yelling "To Hell with the United States!"

The federal government itself began to lead the campaign against subversives. Attorney General Palmer, perhaps understandably convinced that the threat was real (but also holding presidential ambitions), organized a vigorous campaign against communists and other radicals. Palmer tried but could not convince Congress to pass a new and stricter sedition bill. Instead, in August 1919, he appointed a young assistant, J. Edgar Hoover, to head a new a bureau in the Justice Department dedicated to uncovering subversive activity, later named the Federal Bureau of Investigation or FBI.

In November, Palmer rounded up about 250 radicals in 12 cities, and the following day cooperating local police arrested another 500. In December 249 were deported, including Emma Goldman and some others previously convicted under wartime acts. Then, on January 2, 1920, thousands of federal agents and local law officers conducted simultaneous raids on every known communist headquarters across the nation. Some 4,000 people in 33 cities and 23 states were arrested in these Palmer Raids. In time about a third were released. Of the remaining two-thirds, the American citizens were turned over to local authorities. The aliens were subjected to deportation hearings. Eventually, 556, all of them members of the Communist Party, were deported.[54] President Wilson, who had never regained complete vigor after his stroke, probably was not fully involved in Palmer's decisions.

To many Americans, Palmer was a national hero for having conducted the raids. He continued to maintain that Red plots threatened the nation's welfare. No more raids occurred, however, although in April 1920 anarchists Nicola Sacco and Bartolomeo Vanzetti were jailed for the murder of a shoe factory paymaster in Massachusetts, a case destined to be a cause célèbre in the coming decade. Then, on September 20, the most devastating bombing of the Red Scare occurred in front of J. P. Morgan's bank on Wall Street. Forty-three people died as a result, and 200 were injured. But the Red Scare had played itself out. Fears of an organized revolutionary threat had declined, and Palmer's claims began to seem alarmist to much of the American public.[55]

THE BLACK SOX BASEBALL SCANDAL

Baseball became America's national game during the Progressive Era. Among the public, it also became an article of faith that the game represented the best of America's values and character. "A clean straight game," President Taft had said; "rugged honesty" said Roosevelt. The game's publicists encouraged the belief that the sport was distinguished by its integrity. "Baseball belongs to the American people. For baseball to be unclean would not only be, in American life, a sporting calamity but a moral calamity," said Chicago Cubs' owner William Veeck.[56] Sportswriters cooperated to maintain a good image for the public regardless of what went on behind the scenes. But behind the scenes, organized gambling was increasing.

In 1919, the postwar interest in America's game was very high as the World Series approached. The Chicago White Sox, making their second appearance in three years, were 5-1 favorites to defeat the Cincinnati Reds, who had made it to the series for the first time. Nonetheless, the Reds won the series in the eighth game of nine. Oddly, a few days before the series had opened, large amounts of betting money had moved to the Reds. Well-known sportswriter Hugh Fullerton, observing the gamblers pouring into Chicago, suspected a fix was afoot. He and former pitching great Christy Mathewson, a recently returned veteran, observed the series together and did not like what they saw. Immediately after the series, Fullerton hinted something was amiss, and in

Although African Americans were excluded from major league baseball in the early 20th century, they formed vibrant and popular minor leagues and barnstorming teams. This photo shows the Colored Gophers of St. Paul. *(Courtesy Baseball Hall of Fame Library, Cooperstown, New York)*

December he made open accusations and quoted sources. The sportswriting fraternity attacked him in outrage.

The rumors did not die. The following September, as a result of an investigation into a different fix in a Cubs-Phillies game, several White Sox confessed to throwing the 1919 series. Eventually, eight players were indicted and were ever after called the Black Sox.

When the news broke on September 27, 1920, a week after the bombing of Morgan's Wall Street bank, the public was shocked, outraged, and thoroughly disillusioned. One of the Black Sox was outfielder "Shoeless Joe" Jackson, an illiterate southern country boy but one of the best hitters in the game. On the 30th, reported the *Chicago Herald and Examiner,*

> As Jackson departed from the Grand Jury room, a small boy clutched at his sleeve and tagged along after him.
> "Say it ain't so, Joe," he pleaded. "Say it ain't so."
> "Yes kid, I'm afraid it is," Jackson replied.

The incident was, in fact, an invention of the *Herald's* writer, but it accurately captured the public's mood. There was talk in Congress of federal legislation. Baseball owners knew they had to take action to restore the game's public image. In November they dissolved the three-member, owner controlled National Commission and appointed a single, powerful baseball commissioner. Their choice was Judge Kenesaw Mountain Landis, who had settled a 1916 antitrust suit against the American and National Leagues. Landis soon announced, "If I catch any crook in baseball the rest of his life is going to be a hot one."[57] The Black Sox were charged with conspiracy (there was no law against fixing a baseball game at the time), but their confessions mysteriously disappeared from the court files, and in 1921 they were acquitted. Nonetheless Landis banned all of them from baseball for life.

Completing the Reform Agenda: Railroads and Conservation

Regulation of the large and politically powerful railroad industry had been one of the earliest goals of regional reformers during the progressive decades and one of the most tenaciously pursued in both state and federal legislation. The long legislative battle to regulate railroads, impelled by discriminatory shipping rates, stock frauds, and the purchase of influence, also continued to resonate deeply with the public because everyone was dependent on train travel. Even by the end of the Progressive Era regular air transportation did not yet exist, and transportation of both people and goods by motor vehicles was still extremely limited. Relatively few people yet owned autos or trucks but even if they had, there were no highway systems, and the vast majority of local roads that did exist were still unpaved.

During the war, the federal government had taken over managing the railway transportation system, although ownership remained private. Although federal oversight had been very successful, as the nation demobilized the owners sought to regain management control. President Wilson announced that he would end federal management on March 1, 1920, unless Congress enacted new legislation. A plan to nationalize the system permanently received little congressional support. Instead, Congress passed the Esch-Cummins Transportation Act in February 1920, drafted by midwestern Republican progressives John J. Esch of Wisconsin and Albert Cummins of Iowa. The act did nothing to change the private status or management of the railroad industry. But it did impose the thoroughgoing federal control that reformers had long sought. It gave the Interstate Commerce Commission (ICC) complete control over rates and supervision over sale of railroad stocks and the profits they generated. It permitted lines to pool traffic for economy and gave the ICC authority to regroup small railroads into a limited number of systems. It also established a Railway Labor Board to arbitrate labor disputes. Railroad owners and investors, who had come to see advantages in a close relationship with the federal government during the war, generally applauded the act. Labor was less enthusiastic because arbitration by the labor board was not compulsory.

Two other legislative acts of February 1920 completed aspects of the conservation agenda begun under Theodore Roosevelt to control and manage natural resources in the interests of the public. The Water Power Act established public supervision of hydroelectric development on all navigable waterways and within all public lands. It represented a compromise on the question of payment to the government for the privilege of development, over which conservatives (who wanted no payments) and progressives (who wanted high payments) had deadlocked for more than a decade. The act split the revenue from moderate development fees between the federal reclamation fund, the federal treasury, and the states in which the projects were located. It also established the Federal Power Commission, composed of the secretaries of war, interior, and agriculture, with authority to issue permits for dams and hydroelectric plants. Congress did not, however, establish Federal oversight of multipurpose development that Roosevelt-allied conservationists had long championed. *Multipurpose development* referred to comprehensive, regional public planning over entire large basins (including hydroelectricity, irrigation, erosion and flood control, water supply, and even recreation), regardless of private or local interests. Nonetheless, electricity was clearly increasingly important, and most conservation interests were pleased that federal regulation of power company development was finally established.

In the Mineral Leasing Act of 1920, Congress developed a system for opening and overseeing oil deposits on public lands. Oil reserve withdrawals had begun under Roosevelt and increased under Taft and Wilson, reaching nearly 5.6 million acres. Private prospectors pressed for development, but Congress proved unable to agree on a plan for managed use. The Mineral Leasing Act decreed that the oil lands remain in

FIRST ANNUAL PALM FÊTE...
...The Bathing Suit P

A different kind of women's parade: By the end of the Progressive Era, the freedoms as well as the rights of women had grown dramatically. At the first Palm Fete in Miami, Florida, in 1920, women modeled the changes in swimwear fashions over the decades. *(Library of Congress, Prints and Photographs Division, LC-USZ62-127282)*

federal ownership but established a system of leases for developers, with the revenue to be returned to the region for irrigation projects and other uses.[58]

THE ELECTION OF 1920

Wilson, ailing and increasingly unpopular with his party and the public, clung to his dream for a League of Nations as the election year opened. The election would be, he maintained, a "great and solemn referendum" on the issue. To some, he seemed to be signaling that he might run for an unprecedented third term. Democratic insiders were strongly against the idea. Both political leaders and Wilson's friends pressed him to deny he was a candidate, which he refused to do for some time.[59]

When the Republicans met in Chicago in June, they were in high spirits. The midterm election of 1918 had shown that the party was firmly reunited and had reclaimed its former position as the majority party of the nation. Party leaders suspected that all they had to do to recapture the White House was to put forward a reasonably acceptable candidate. Such minimal requirements brought forth an overabundance of contenders and the convention soon deadlocked. A group of powerful party insiders entered a legendary smoke-filled room at a Chicago hotel to find a compromise. They exited with a dark-horse candidate, Warren G. Harding, an undistinguished and, they hoped, malleable Ohio senator and former newspaper publisher. For vice president the convention nominated Massachusetts governor Calvin Coolidge, who had recently won popular approbation for his handling of the Boston police strike.

The Democrats met later in the month in San Francisco. Wilson's long refusal to announce he was not a candidate had complicated and finally ended the possibility of a campaign by his popular son-in-law, William McAdoo, former secretary of the treasury, who at one time had been the front-runner. Attorney General Mitchell Palmer and more than 10 other candidates wanted the job as well. Finally, on the 44th ballot the convention compromised on James M. Cox, former governor of Ohio. For vice president they nominated Franklin D. Roosevelt, assistant secretary of the navy (the same position his Republican cousin Theodore, who had died in 1919, had once held).

The Socialist Party, its ranks decimated, nonetheless met to nominate once again Eugene V. Debs, still in the Atlanta penitentiary for sedition. A new party, the Farmer-Labor, also appeared on the scene. It was a conglomeration of labor interests, certain progressive remnants, and fringe reform interests of very long standing, including some

1920. MIAMI, FLORIDA
Miami Beach...

populists and even single-taxers. The public had difficulty distinguishing them from Socialists in 1920, although the Farmer-Labor party did not advocate public ownership.

Cox campaigned actively, as did the two vicepresidential candidates. Harding stayed put to conduct a front-porch campaign like that of William McKinley two decades earlier—even redesigning his porch to resemble the late president's. Wilson's hope that the election would be a solemn referendum on his League of Nations was a vain one. The Democratic platform itself fell short of ringing endorsement. The Republican platform equivocated, and Harding more than matched it by his ability to wrap any issue he could not evade in obfuscation and vagueness. His speeches, said McAdoo, were "an army of pompous phrases moving over the landscape in search of an idea."[60]

American voters—who included, for the first time, newly enfranchised American women—nonetheless embraced Harding's promise of "not nostrums, but normalcy." He won with over 60 percent of the popular vote (the largest margin yet recorded) and 404 out of 531 electoral votes. Cox won only the states of the solid South, and even there he lost the border state of Tennessee. Signs of things to come, the returns traveled the radio airwaves for the first time from KDKA in Pittsburgh and WWJ in Detroit. But voters stayed away from the polls in record numbers, fewer than 50 percent of those eligible casting a ballot.

Many historians see the election of 1920 as a turning point. Wilson's hope for American leadership in a new world order based on collective security was not to be realized in the immediate future. His progressive coalition had dissolved in the disillusionment of a brutal war and the turmoil of readjustment. Some Americans were embracing the pleasures of mass consumption, some the calculus of business values, some the alienations of modernism, some the comforts of fundamentalism. But after 1920 fewer and fewer embraced progressivism and reform.

CHRONICLE OF EVENTS

1917

Woodrow Wilson is president; Thomas Marshall is vice president.

Utah, Indiana, and New Hampshire adopt statewide prohibition. By April 26, states prohibit liquor.

Women's suffrage makes significant gains. By the end of the year women have full suffrage in 12 states (Wyoming, Colorado, Idaho, Utah, Washington, California, Kansas, Montana, Nevada, Oregon, Arizona, and New York) and the territory of Alaska. Illinois, Michigan, Nebraska, North Dakota, and Rhode Island give them the right to vote in presidential elections. (Indiana and Ohio pass presidential suffrage as well, but it is nullified and does not take effect). Arkansas will grant the right to vote in primary elections, becoming the first southern suffrage state. Indiana, North Dakota, Nebraska, and Vermont pass municipal suffrage; a number of other states also allow women to vote in municipal, tax-related, or school elections. As the year closes women will remain without any voting rights at all in 12 of the 48 states (Pennsylvania, Maryland, West Virginia, Virginia, North Carolina, South Carolina, Georgia, Alabama, Mississippi, Texas, Missouri, and Tennessee), and the territory of Hawaii.

Mexico and Russia enfranchise women.

Arizona passes a minimum-wage law.

Congress establishes Mount McKinley National Park, Alaska.

In response to suppression of dissent about the war, the National Civil Liberties Bureau is founded; in 1920, it will become the American Civil Liberties Union. (ACLU).

January 10: The first suffrage pickets appeared outside the gates of the White House.

January 22: In an important speech to Congress, President Wilson asserts America's right to participate in a peace settlement and calls for "peace without victory" and a permanent league of nations to maintain world peace.

January 27: The withdrawal of Pershing's troops from Mexico, where they have unsuccessfully pursued Pancho Villa, begins.

January 31: Germany announces the resumption of unrestricted submarine warfare, to take effect the following day.

February 3: The United States breaks off diplomatic relations with Germany in response to the resumption of unrestricted submarine warfare. Boliva, Peru, and Brazil do so as as well.

February 5: Congress overrides President Wilson's veto of a literacy test for new immigrants.

In Mexico Venustiano Carranza's government officially adopts a constitution.

February 23: Congress passes the Smith-Hughes Act, funding agricultural and vocational education.

February 24: Britain gives the U.S. ambassador the Zimmerman note, an intercepted cable from Germany to its ambassador in Mexico. It offers Mexico aid to conduct hostilities against the United States and promises the return of Texas, New Mexico, and Arizona if they are successful. It also urges Mexico to try to convince Allied Japan to join their cause.

February 26: The president appears before Congress and requests authority to arm merchant ships and "to employ any other instrumentalities or methods" necessary. In the Senate, a small group of senators who object to vague "instrumentalities" filibuster the bill and it dies. The state department locates an old law from 1792 allowing the arming of merchant ships.

March 1: The Zimmermann note is headline news coast to coast. It pushes many Americans farther toward support for entering the war, especially those in the West, one of the former strongholds for neutrality.

March 2: Congress passes the Jones-Shafroth Act, giving Puerto Rico expanded self-government and making its residents U.S. citizens.

March 5: President Wilson is inaugurated for his second term.

March 8: The Russian Revolution begins when rioting and strikes in protest of wartime hardships erupt in St. Petersburg and troops are dispatched there.

March 12: The United States announces its merchant ships are armed and will fire on belligerent submarines.

In Russia the parliament or Duma establishes a provisional government.

March 13: The United States recognizes the constitutional regime headed by Carranza in Mexico.

March 16: In Russia, Czar Nicholas II abdicates.

April 2: The first session of the 65th Congress, known as the War Congress, opens and will run until October. In the House of Representatives is Jeannette Rankin, the first woman member of Congress. President Wilson addresses a joint session of Congress to request a declaration of war against Germany, to "make the world safe for democracy."

April 4: The Senate votes to declare war, 82-6.

April 6: The House of Representatives votes 373-50 to declare war; one of the no votes is Jeannette Rankin, a pacifist. President Wilson signs a declaration of war against Germany. America is now at war with the Central powers as an Associated Power of the Allies.

April 14: Wilson establishes the Committee on Public Information to propagandize for the war effort; its head is George Creel, a journalist.

April 17: In Russia, Bolshevik leader Vladmir Lenin arrives in a sealed train provided by the Germans, who hope he will foment revolution and force Russia to sue for peace.

April 24: Congress passes the War Loan Act, called the Liberty Loan Act. It authorizes up to $5 billion in war bonds.

May 18: Congress passes the Selective Service Act. It authorizes a draft to raise troops and requires all men ages 21 to 30 to register.

June 4: Brazil declares war on Germany.

June 12: In Greece, King Constantine abdicates; he has been allied with the Central Powers.

June 14: General John J. Pershing, commander of the American Expeditionary Force (AEF) arrives in Paris.

June 15: Congress passes the Espionage Act. It is now a crime to interfere with army recruitment and engage in disloyal acts.

June 17: In England, the royal family renounces its ties to German ancestors and changes its name from the House of Saxe-Coburg-Gotha to the House of Windsor.

June 20: At the White House, onlookers begin harassing the National Women's Party suffrage pickets, whose placards have become more pointed and inflammatory.

June 22: Arrest of the White House suffrage pickets begins. At first the courts will dismiss charges, but as picketing and skirmishes continue the suffragists will be sentenced to jail. By the end of October, 218 women from 26 states will have been arrested for "obstructing the sidewalk" and 97 sent to prison.

June 26: In France, the first 14,500 American troops land.

June 29: The Ukraine declares its independence from Russia.

July 2: In East St. Louis, Illinois, a race riot occurs.

July 14: In Germany, a new chancellor supported by the Germany military takes office.

Finland declares its independence from Russia.

July 16: In Russia, the provisional (Duma) government puts down the Bolsheviks, and Lenin flees to Finland. Soon Aleksandr Kerensky is named prime minister.

July 24: Congress appropriates $640 million to develop an army air force.

July 28: The War Industries Board (WIB) is established to coordinate America's industrial mobilization.

In New York, an NAACP Silent Protest Parade protests violence against blacks.

August 10: Congress passes the Lever Food and Fuel Control Act. Under its powers the Food Administration headed by Herbert Hoover and the Fuel Administration headed by Harry Garfield will successfully coordinate the production and conservation of food and energy, making it possible to supply the Allies.

August 20: French troops break through the German lines at Verdun.

August 31: In North Carolina, a federal judge issues an injunction against the Keating-Owen Child Labor Act, due to go into effect the next day, as a result of a suit brought at the behest of textile mill owners. The Justice Department will appeal to the Supreme Court.

September 1: The Keating-Owen Child Labor Law (passed September 1, 1916) goes into effect in every state except North Carolina; it will be in effect for 275 days before being declared unconstitutional.

September 15: Russia is proclaimed a republic.

October 3: Congress passes the War Revenue Act. It doubles the basic income tax rate of 1916, raises the marginal tax as high as 63 percent, and adds many new excise taxes and a tax on corporate profits as high as 60 percent.

October 6: Congress passes the Trading with the Enemy Act, which authorizes various controls on imports and exports and authorizes the Postmaster General to censor foreign-language newspapers.

October 24: In Italy, Italian troops suffer great losses at the Battle of Caporetto.

November 3: In France, U.S. troops see their first action and suffer their first casualties.

November 6: In New York state, women's suffrage passes by a margin of some 100,000 votes.

In Flanders, the third battle of Ypres is won by Canadian troops.

November 7: The October Revolution occurs in Russia. (Under the old Russian calendar, the date is October 26.) Lenin and the Bolsheviks oust the Kerensky government.

November 9: Arthur Balfour, the British foreign secretary, announces plans for a Jewish homeland in Palestine, to be established after the war.

November 26 and 27: In the glare of publicity about brutal treatment of jailed suffrage pickets, the Wilson administration releases all of them from prison.

December 5: Germany and Russia agree to an armistice.

December 6: In the Halifax, Nova Scotia, harbor a French munitions ship and a Belgian relief ship collide, killing more than 1,600 and destroying part of the city.

December 7: The United States declares war on Austria.

December 9: British troops capture Jerusalem.

December 18: The Eighteenth Amendment to the Constitution, prohibiting the sale, manufacture, and transportation of alcohol, is passed by Congress. It must now be ratified by the states.

1918

Massachusetts adopts initiative and referendum.

Texas grants women the right to vote in primary elections.

Canada, England, Ireland, Wales, Scotland, Germany, Poland, Austria, Czechoslovakia, and Hungary enfranchise women.

A minimum-wage law is enacted for the District of Columbia.

Spanish influenza begins to sweep the world; before it ends in 1919, it will kill more than 21 million people. It is the worst pandemic since the 14th-century plague.

January 1: Wilson orders government control of the railroads in light of overwhelming problems delivering men, food, and materials. He appoints William Gibbs McAdoo, secretary of the treasury, as the head of the Railroad Administration. McAdoo will mold the nation's lines into a single coordinated system.

January 8: In an address to a joint session of Congress, President Wilson describes his proposal for peace, known as the Fourteen Points.

January 10: In a close and dramatic vote, the House of Representatives passes the women's suffrage amendment by the necessary two-thirds majority for the first time, 274 to 136; it still must be passed by the Senate.

January 18: In Russia, Lenin proclaims a dictatorship of the proletariat.

February 6: In Great Britain, married women over 30 are granted the right to vote, and property ownership is ended as a qualification for suffrage.

February 24: Estonia declares independence from Russia.

March 3: Russia and the Central Powers sign a separate peace, the Treaty of Brest-Litovsk. It cedes much of eastern Europe to the Central powers but will later be annulled by the Treaty of Versailles.

Allied troops land in northwestern Russia; they will remain on Russian soil until 1920.

March 4: Wilson names Bernard Baruch, a prominent Wall Street broker, head of the War Industries Board. Although the WIB has floundered since being established, Baruch will quickly bring it to a high level of effectiveness.

March 19: Congress passes legislation establishing Daylight Savings Time to conserve energy for the war effort.

March 21: Congress passes the Railroad Control Act, authorizing federal control of the railroads.

In Europe the second Battle of the Somme begins; the Germans hope to make a major advance into France before a larger number of American troops arrive.

March 26: Ferdinand Foch is appointed supreme commander of the Allied Forces.

April 1: In Britain, the Royal Air Force is established as a separate branch of the military.

April 5: Congress creates the War Finance Corporation to support war industries.

April 8: The National War Labor Board (NWLB) is established to conciliate labor disputes.

May 7: Romania, defeated by German troops, signs a treaty with the Central Powers.

May 16: Congress passes the Sedition Act, which outlaws any speech or act that undermines the war effort and

further extends the power of the Postmaster General to censor the mail, applied primarily to socialist and other radical publications.

May 19: In Ireland, 500 Sinn Féin troops are imprisoned.

May 20: Congress passes the Overman Act, giving the president broad powers to coordinate the war effort.

May 27 through June: In France, Allied, Central, and American forces battle. American troops are successful at Cantigny on the north-central western front. By the end of June American forces have won the Battle of Belleau Wood and stopped a German advance; some 8,000 American soldiers are killed.

June 3: In *Hammer v. Dagenhart* the Supreme Court rules 5 to 4 that the Keating-Owen Act is unconstitutional because it oversteps the federal government's power over interstate commerce. Mill owners reinstate long hours and child labor again increases quickly. Child labor reformers seek a new way to outlaw it.

June 4: U.S. troops stop a German advance at Château-Thierry.

June 8: The War Labor Policies Board (WLPB) is created to maintain standard wages, hours, and working conditions in American war industries.

July 8: The Chamberlain Kahn Act expands the American military's venereal-disease control program; under its broad powers some 30,000 women suspected as prostitutes will be detained, usually without benefit of normal legal protections.

July 12: The WPLB under Felix Frankfurter orders that all federal contracts contain a clause regulating child labor.

July 15: In France, a German advance is repelled in the second Battle of the Marne.

July 16: In Russia, Czar Nicholas and his entire family are executed by the Bolsheviks.

July 18: The Ainse-Marne offensive begins, with some 250,000 American troops pushing the Germans back between the cities of Soissons and Rheims.

August: American troops join the Allies in northern Russia and Siberia.

August 8: In northern France, the Allies launch a new offensive.

August 15: The United States ends diplomatic relations with the Soviet Union.

August 12–13: At St-Mihiel U.S. troops capture about 15,000 German soldiers.

August 30: Bulgaria surrenders to the Allies.

September 14: Eugene V. Debs is found guilty of sedition and sentenced to 10 years in prison under the Espionage Act; in 1921 his sentence will be commuted by President Warren G. Harding.

September 18: Great Britain launches its last offensive of the war, against the Turks.

September 26-November 11: Over a million U.S. troops join the final major battle of the war, the Meuse-Argonne offensive.

October 1: Despite a personal appearance and plea by President Wilson, the Senate defeats the women's suffrage amendment, 62 in favor to 34 opposed, two votes short of the necessary two-thirds majority. The staunchest opponents are southern Democrats, damaging independent progressive support for the party.

October 3: In Germany, public unrest is growing over a string of military defeats. A new chancellor is named.

October 4: Austria-Hungary signals willingness to pursue peace under the terms of Woodrow Wilson's Fourteen Points.

October 6: Poland (formerly part of the Austro-Hungarian Empire) becomes an independent republic.

October 15: Czechoslovakia (formerly part of the Austro-Hungarian Empire) becomes an independent republic.

October 16: The Alien Act is passed, permitting the exclusion or deportation of aliens (noncitizens) who are suspected of promoting radical ideas or belonging to radical organizations.

October 17: Hungary declares itself independent of Austria.

October 24: The remaining Central Powers troops are driven from Italy.

October 31: The Ottoman Empire surrenders.

November: Michigan, Oklahoma, and South Dakota grant women suffrage, bringing the number of full suffrage states to 15.

November 3: The Allies sign an armistice with Austria-Hungary.

November 5: In the midterm elections Republicans gain control of both houses of Congress. The results are seen as a repudiation of President Wilson's policies because he has asked the nation to return a Democratic Congress.

November 9: In Germany, Kaiser Wilhelm II abdicates and the chancellor resigns.

November 11: At 11 A.M. an armistice goes into effect, ending the fighting in World War I. Germany agrees to surrender its weapons and withdraw east of the Rhine.

November 12: Emperor Charles II of the former Austro-Hungarian Empire renounces his throne.

November 18: President Wilson announces he will personally attend the peace conference in Europe.

Latvia becomes an independent republic.

December 13: President Wilson arrives in France for the peace conference to a wild welcome.

1919

North Dakota, Texas, and Puerto Rico pass minimum-wage laws.

Eight more states grant women the right to vote in presidential elections.

Holland, Belgium, Luxembourg, Sweden, Iceland, British East Africa, Rhodesia, and Uruguay enfranchise women.

A total of 39 states have passed enabling or other legislation for mothers' pensions since the first laws were enacted in 1911.

Congress establishes Grand Canyon National Park, Arizona; Zion National Park, Utah; and Lafayette (later renamed Acadia) National Park, Maine, the first national park east of the Mississippi; all three were previously national monuments.

By the end of the year the national debt will be $26 billion, up from $2 billion at the end of 1917.

During the year 4 million workers will take part in an unprecedented wave of strikes.

January 5: Soviet troops occupy Lithuania.

January 9: Former president Theodore Roosevelt dies at age 60.

January 18: The Paris Peace Conference begins at Versailles, France.

January 21: In Seattle, 35,000 shipyard workers walk out under leadership of the IWW. A general strike will begin February 6. The strike will be broken by the mayor with military assistance.

January 29: The Eighteenth Amendment, establishing Prohibition, is ratified; it will be repealed in 1933.

February: In Russia, White Russian troops (those who want to restore czarist government) fight the Red Army, led by Leon Trotsky.

February 14: President Wilson proposes the League of Nations in Paris and the following day sails for America to confer with Congress.

February 24: The Pomerene amendment or child labor tax is passed as an attachment to the Revenue Act; it assesses a 10 percent tax on net profits of mines or factories that use unregulated child labor, with the intention of forcing employers to abandon it. Southern textile manufacturers again file suit and the tax will eventually be declared unconstitutional in 1922. In the meantime, however, many states will extend compulsory schooling and pass new state child labor laws to conform to federal expectations, and many manufacturers will change their child labor policies, causing a drop in child labor.

March: In the Far East, Korean nationalists attempt to declare independence from Japan but are put down by Japanese troops.

March 3: The 65th Congress adjourns.

March 4: Senator Henry Cabot Lodge publicizes a list of senators who oppose the League of Nations in its present form. Wilson returns to Europe the following day.

Bolsheviks and communist representatives throughout Europe form the Third International (Comintern) to coordinate international revolutionary communist activity.

In 1901 major oil deposits had been discovered at Spindletop in agricultural Texas. By the end of the Progressive Era, the economy and the appearance of the state had been transformed. This photo of Burkburnett, Texas, was taken in 1919. *(Library of Congress, Prints and Photographs Division, LC-USZ62-109213)*

March 15: The American Legion is organized by units of the AEF.

March 21: In Hungary, the communists seize power.

March 23: In Italy, Benito Mussolini founds a new political party, the Fascists, to combat communism and liberalism.

March 30: In India, Mohandas Gandhi begins acts of civil disobedience to protest continued British rule.

April 10: In Mexico, insurgent leader Emiliano Zapata is killed by government troops.

April 28: Mayor Ole Hansen of Seattle receives a bomb in the mail.

April 29: A Georgia senator receives a bomb in the mail; it maims his maid.

April 30: Investigators discover more than 30 bombs in the mail. They have been sent to prominent figures and those connected to the prosecution of radicals.

May: In China, students protest some terms of the Paris Peace Conference ceding control of Shantung province to Japan; China will refuse to sign the Treaty of Versailles.

May 19: The 66th Congress opens. The House of Representatives passes the women's suffrage amendment, 304 to 89.

June 2: In eight cities, a number of bombs explode, one on the doorstep of Attorney General Mitchell Palmer's house in Washington, D.C.

June 3: With little of the drama that had marked earlier votes, the U.S. Senate passes the Nineteenth Amendment, which will give women the right to vote if it is ratified by 36 of the 48 states.

June 21: Germany sinks its remaining naval fleet.

June 28: Allied powers sign the Treaty of Versailles, creating a League of Nations to solve future international disputes. World War I officially ends.

July: A race riot occurs in Longview, Texas, setting off six months of violence known as the Red Summer because so much blood is shed.

July 10: President Wilson submits the Treaty of Versailles and the League of Nations proposal to the Senate.

July 20: In Washington, D.C., a race riot begins.

July 27: In Chicago, one of the worst race riots in American history begins. Before the National Guard restores order, 38 people will be killed and more than 500 injured.

August: Attorney General Mitchell Palmer appoints a young assistant, J. Edgar Hoover, to head a new bureau in the Justice Department dedicated to uncovering subversive activity; it will later become the Federal Bureau of Investigation, or FBI.

August 4: Romanian troops oust communist leadership from Hungary.

August 25: The first international daily air service begins between Paris and London.

September 3: President Wilson undertakes a nationwide tour to promote the Treaty of Versailles and the League of Nations.

September 9: In Boston, more than 1,000 policemen go on strike. The National Guard, under command of Governor Calvin Coolidge, will finally restore order. All the strikers are dismissed and the city hires a new force.

September 22: 365,000 steelworkers, who have not had union representation since 1892, go on strike. They still work very long hours, and the unskilled workers are paid little. Owners will paint the strike as the work of Bolsheviks, and the public will fail to support it. It will be broken within four months with little gain to the workers.

September 25: President Wilson collapses in Pueblo, Colorado, and returns to the White House, where he suffers a serious stroke from which he will not fully recover.

October 1–9: In the World Series the heavily favored Chicago White Sox lose to the Cincinnati Reds. Rumors of a fix begin to swirl.

October 28: Congress passes the Volstead Act to implement Prohibition. To the surprise of many it outlaws any beverage with more than 0.5 percent alcoholic content.

November: By the end of the month Attorney General Palmer has rounded up some 250 radicals; in December many will be deported.

November 6: Lodge announces his 14 reservations to the League of Nations.

November 19: The U.S. Senate fails to ratify the Treaty of Versailles.

December 15: Writing in the *New York Evening World,* sportswriter Hugh Fullerton openly claims that the October World Series was fixed.

1920

New York, the largest American city, has a population of more than 9,400,000; Chicago, the second-largest, has a population of nearly 3,900,000. The 1920 census reveals that 51 percent of Americans now live in urban areas and less than 30 percent of the population is engaged in farming.

As the year opens 22 states have ratified the women's suffrage amendment; 36 are needed. Two have voted not to ratify.

North Dakota adopts the direct democracy device of recall, the 10th state to do so. By this date 32 of 48 states have comprehensive, mandatory direct-primary laws; 12 states have limited or optional primaries; only four states have no direct-primary legislation. Nineteen states have adopted initiative and referendum; three other states have adopted referendum only.

January 2: Federal agents begin raids on suspected radicals; some 4,000 people are detained in 33 cities.

January 5: The Supreme Court upholds the constitutionality of the Volstead Act.

January 6: News hits the press that Boston Red Sox star Babe Ruth has been traded to the New York Yankees.

January 10: The Treaty of Versailles takes effect.

January 16: The Volstead Act goes into effect; America is officially dry.

February 23: Congress passes the Mineral Leasing Act, establishing a system of leases to private developers for oil reserves on public lands, withdrawn since Roosevelt's presidency.

February 28: Congress passes the Esch-Cummins Transportation Act, restoring railroads to private management but imposing the thoroughgoing system of regulation via the ICC that progressives have sought for many years. The act also establishes the Railroad Labor Board to arbitrate disputes.

March 10: Russia invades Poland.

In 1920, the U.S. Census reported for the first time that a majority of Americans lived in towns and cities and were classified as urban. The lives of rural people had changed dramatically too. Some farms, like this one in Owyhee County, Idaho, had electricity and telephone service. *(Library of Congress, Prints and Photographs Division, LC-USZ62-132347)*

March 19: The Senate again rejects the League of Nations and the Treaty of Versailles.

April 23–25: The Allies designate Palestine a Jewish state under British protection.

May 5: Two anarchists, Nicola Sacco and Bartolomeo Vanzetti are arrested for the murder of two men during a payroll robbery in Braintree, Massachusetts. Their case will become a cause célèbre among the Left before they are executed in 1927.

May 8–14: The Socialist Party meets in convention in New York, nominating Eugene V. Debs, who remains imprisoned, for president.

May 17: In Mexico, Venustiano Carranza is defeated and flees Mexico City.

May 21: Carranza is assassinated.

June 7: The Supreme Court abrogates all state laws that allow light wines and beer.

June 8–12: The Republican Party meets in convention in Chicago, nominating Warren G. Harding for president.

June 28–July 5: The Democratic Party meets in San Francisco, nominating James M. Cox of Ohio for president and former assistant secretary of the navy Franklin Delano Roosevelt as vice president.

July 1: Railroad workers go on strike.

August 1–2: In New York, 25,000 African Americans gather to hear Marcus Garvey speak at the national convention of the Universal Negro Improvement Association.

August 18: The Tennessee state legislature ratifies the women's suffrage amendment by a close vote, becoming the necessary 36th state.

August 26: The secretary of state proclaims the Nineteenth Amendment in effect, enfranchising all American women.

September 8: Transcontinental airmail service begins with a flight from New York to San Francisco.

September 27: The Philadelphia *North American* publishes a page-one story breaking news that the 1919 World Series was fixed; the information has surfaced in an investigation into another scandal. Soon several players will confess and eight will be indicted; in July 1921 all will be acquitted but banned from baseball for life.

November 2: Warren G. Harding is elected president in a solid victory, with 60 percent of the popular vote.

In Pittsburgh, station KDKA radio transmits the election returns for the first time.

November 11: To restore public trust in baseball, owners appoint Chicago judge Kenesaw Mountain Landis the sole baseball commissioner, replacing the three-member national commission.

EYEWITNESS TESTIMONY

STANDARDS OF INDUSTRY FOR GOVERNMENT CONTRACTS

1. Adult labor.
2. Wages
    a. The highest prevailing rate of wages in the industry which the contract affects.
    b. Equal pay for equal work.
    c. Those trades where there is no wage standard whatsoever shall be placed in the hands of an adjustment committee.
    d. That all wages be adjusted from time to time to meet the increased cost of living. . . .
3. The eight-hour day.
    4. One day rest in seven.
    5. Prohibition of night work for women.
    6. Standards of sanitation and fire protection.
    7. Protection against over-fatigue and industrial diseases.
    8. Prohibition of tenement house labor.
    9. Exemption from the call into industry of women having small children needing their care.
    10. Exemption from the call into industry of women two months before and after child birth. . . .

Recommendations of the National Women's Trade Union League (WTUL) for women war workers, 1917, Clarke, American Women and the World War, available online at URL: http://www.lib.byu.edu/~rdh/wwi/comment/Clarke/Clarke10.htm.

Whereas, this country is now engaged in the greatest war in history, and,

Whereas, the advocates of the Federal Amendment, though urging it as a war measure, announce, through their president, Mrs. Catt, that its passage "means a simultaneous campaign in all states; it demands organization in every precinct: activity, agitation, education in every corner. Nothing less than this nation-wide, vigilant, unceasing campaign will win the ratification," therefore be it

Resolved, that our country in this hour of peril should be spared the harassing of its public men and the distracting of its people from work for the war, and further

Resolved, that the United States Senate be respectfully urged to pass no measure involving such a radical change in our government while the attention of the patriotic portion of the American people is concentrated on the all-important task of winning the war and during the absence of over a million men abroad.

Petition of the Women Voters Anti-Suffrage Party of New York to the U.S. Senate, ca. 1917, available online at NARA Digital Classroom. URL: http://www.archives.gov/digital_classroom/lessons/woman_suffrage/ny_petition.html.

In Massachusetts the minimum wage has now been in operation for more than two years in the brush industry and for one year in retail stores. After the minimum wage had been in operation in the brush industry for a year the commission made a careful investigation for the purpose of determining its effects. This investigation showed: (1) that the establishment of the minimum wage in the brush industry had been followed by a remarkable increase in the number of women employed; (2) that the employment of women at ruinously low rates had been practically stopped; (3) that the proportion of women employed at more than the prescribed minimum rate had greatly increased, and (4) that this had been accomplished without putting an unreasonable financial burden upon the industry. . . .

The experience with the minimum wage in the states where it has received a fair trial seems to indicate that the good results anticipated by the original advocates of the legal minimum wage for women are being secured. It is deeply to be regretted that the enforcement of the various laws has been greatly hampered by litigation. . . .

A. N. Holcombe, member of the Massachusetts Minimum Wage Commission, "The Effects of the Legal Minimum Wage for Women," 1917, pp. 38, 41.

. . . it is an axiom in the business world that no sooner is an adequate system of insurance set up than it incites efforts for the reduction of the risk against which it offers protection. Fire underwriters not only insure against fire—they inspect buildings and raise the standards of safety against conflagration. Workmen's compensation not only secures indemnity to the injured workman or his orphaned children, but it provokes a movement for "Safety First!" Large industrial concerns such as the General Electric Company and the American Locomotive Company are now proudly preventing from 30 to 60 per cent of the accidents which before the coming of compensation they accepted as "inevitable." In the same way the proponents of health insurance confidently count on the adoption of the standard bill to launch a mighty movement for "Health First."

As has been said, employers, employes and the state are today jointly responsible for sickness. Persistent monthly levies upon their several pocketbooks to meet the expenses of the prescribed benefits should rouse a campaign for industrial and social sanitation such as no army of factory and housing inspectors could ever hope to.

John Andrews, secretary of the American Association for Labor Legislation, "Social Insurance," 1917, pp. 48–49.

R. S. Horton, wife and daughter. Proprietor Hattiesburg Barber Shop 35th St near Rhodes. Came to Chicago in January 1917. For 19 years he had been awaiting what he would regard the right time to move. . . . His particular interest and grievance was in politics. It was not so much that he couldn't vote there that made him "mad" but the fact that colored people not only could vote in the North, but in Chicago could elect whom they wished. Learned much of this thru the Defender. In his barber shop he did "some dangerous talking himself" when he saw that it was coming time for Negroes to learn. Would buy 40 and 50 copies of the Defender and sell them without profit just for the sake of distributing the news of a "fearless paper". Didn't need to move for money, because he was making as much there as he could make in Chicago. . . .

His friends leaving, he began to encourage the movement. He was a deacon in the Church. He and pastor in exciting argument in deacons meeting. The pastor discouraged the movement. . . . Finally he got up a club of about 40 and left. . . . Has heard from the pastor since establishing himself here. The Hattiesburg settlement has offered to bring him up to shepherd them. He has agreed to come. . . .

Firmly believes this an act of God. . . . God was stirring them up. Had been praying for that time to come.

Interview of Chicago migrant by Urban League representative Charles S. Johnson, "Chicago Study, Migration Interviews," 1917, Box 86, Series 6, Records of the National Urban League, Library of Congress, available online at HistoryMatters "Many Pasts." URL: http://historymatters.gmu.edu/d/5337/

In my neighborhood, there were probably more West Indian than American-born blacks. They wanted to succeed in America, and were very industrious, both husbands and wives—always trying to start small businesses. They were looking ahead, with the goal of attaining naturalization so they could vote. There was some antagonism between the American-born blacks and the West Indian immigrants. They all wanted to come to the United States because they could live better here. . . . In Harlem, all the buildings had running water and gas, and electricity was coming into a lot of places. . . .

. . . I think the only ones who considered him [Marcus Garvey] to be a leader were the West Indians.

I heard a lot about him, and then I started seeing him. They used to have parades along 7th Avenue frequently. Garvey would always be standing up in a big open-top car with his immediate aides riding with him. He dressed like an admiral. He wore one of those cockade hats that admirals wear, and a uniform. There were marchers in front and behind him, carrying banners. The women were in white dresses, and the men wore suits. . . .

Thomas C. Fleming describes his Harlem neighborhood where the Garvey movement began, "Marcus Garvey Comes to Harlem," ca. 1917, available online at URL: http://www.freepress.org/fleming/flemng05.html.

Don't use vile language in public places.

Don't act discourteously to other people in public places. Don't allow yourself to be drawn into street brawls. Don't use liberty as a license to do as you please.

Don't take the part of law breakers, be they men, women, or children. Don't make yourself a public nuisance.

Don't encourage gamblers, disreputable women or men to ply their business any time or place.

Don't congregate in crowds on the streets to the disadvantage of others passing along.

Don't live in unsanitary houses, or sleep in rooms without proper ventilation.

Don't violate city ordinances, relative to health conditions. . . .

Don't be a beer can rusher or permit children to do such service. . . .

Instructions and advice from established African Americans in Chicago to new black migrants from the South, ca. 1917, printed frequently in the Chicago Defender, *quoted in Grossman,* Land of Hope, *pp. 145–46.*

. . . we developed the idea of placing a carefully selected song leader in every army and navy camp in the country.

. . . As one of the song leaders reported, "singing seemed to spread through the camp like a fire." It was soon discovered that a single song leader was not enough, and regimental and company leaders were selected from their own outfits and given a course of training. What the doughboy sang troubled him little. . . . sturdy old hymns for his more solemn moments, national anthems for ceremonial needs, old favorites for sentiment's sake, and for relaxed periods, gloriously bawdy songs like the extemporized verses of *Mademoiselle from Armentières,* which he sang in France. . . .

. . . I remember another scene—in France, east of Chateau-Thierry—when an American regiment came swinging down the road to reinforce a dangerously sagging position at the front. As a kind of stunt they had fastened to their helmets bunches of the poppies that grow wild in French fields, and the song they sang with joyous abandon as they marched was:

Hail, hail, the gang's all here;

What the hell do we care now!

Raymond Fosdick describes the singing soldiers of World War I, part of the Commission on Training Camp Activities program, 1917, Chronicle of a Generation, *pp. 154–57.*

The policy of isolation that was urged upon the American people in Washington's Farewell Address was constructed upon thin hypothesis:

Europe has a set of primary interests which to us have none, or a very remote connection. Hence she must be engaged in frequent controversies the causes of which are essentially foreign to our concerns.

This was true in 1796 when the United States was a great experiment in self-government, when there was no steamship, no railroad no cable, no wireless, when the republic was geographically as well as politically isolated from the rest of the world; but is it true today? . . .

. . . [T]his murder in Sarajevo brought the United States to the verge of another civil war. It will cost the American people thousands of millions of dollars in taxation. It has set back for half a century the work of assimilating the immigrant population of this country. It has diverted the mind of the nation from its most vital domestic problems. It has all but embroiled us in the most ghastly war of human history. It has complicated our affairs with the whole world, disorganized all internal affairs, and in a way left us denationalized, divided into hostile camps of European tribesmen. . . .

This war marked the collapse of the system of entangling alliances intriguing for the balance of power. Civilization, in its own interest, is now compelled to take a step forward. Is American democracy to hold aloof?

"1796 or 1917?" editorial by Frank I. Cobb,
New York World, January 30, 1917, p. 8.

Be it enacted. . . . That the following classes of aliens shall be excluded from admission into the United States: . . .

. . . persons who are natives of islands not possessed by the United States adjacent to the Continent of Asia, situate south of the twentieth parallel latitude north, west of the one hundred and sixtieth meridian of longitude east from Greenwich and north of the tenth parallel of latitude south or who are natives of any country, province, or dependency situate on the Continent of Asia west of the one hundred and tenth meridian of longitude east from Greenwich and east of the fiftieth meridian of longitude east from Greenwich and south of the fiftieth parallel of latitude north, except that portion of said territory situate between the fiftieth and the sixty-fourth meridians of longitude east from Greenwich and the twenty-fourth and thirty-eighth parallels of latitude north, and no alien now in any way excluded from or prevented from entering, the United States shall be admitted to the United States. . . .

. . . All aliens over sixteen years of age, physically capable of reading, who can not read the English language, or some other language or dialect, including Hebrew or Yiddish: Provided, That any admissible alien, or any alien heretofore or hereafter legally admitted, or any citizen of the United States, may bring in or send for his father or grandfather over fifty-five years of age, his wife, his mother, his grandmother, or his unmarried or widowed daughter, if otherwise admissible, whether such relative can read or not; and such relative shall be permitted to enter. That for the purpose of ascertaining whether aliens can read the immigrant inspectors shall be furnished with slips of uniform size, prepared under the direction of the Secretary of Labor, each containing not less than thirty nor more than forty words in ordinary use, printed in plainly legible type in some one of the various languages or dialects of immigrants. . . .

The Asiatic "barred zone" and literacy test provisions
of the Immigration Act of February 5, 1917,
U.S. Statutes at Large, 64th Congress, vol. 39, p. 874.

We intend to begin on the first of February unrestricted submarine warfare. We shall endeavor in spite of this to keep the United States of America neutral. In the event of this not succeeding, we make Mexico a proposal or alliance on the following basis: make war together, make peace together, generous financial support and an understanding on our part that Mexico is to reconquer the lost territory in Texas, New Mexico, and Arizona. The settlement in detail is left to you. You will inform the President of the above most secretly as soon as the outbreak of war with the United States of America is certain and add the suggestion that he should, on his own initiative, invite Japan to immediate adherence and at the same time mediate between Japan and ourselves. Please call the President's attention to the fact that the ruthless employment of our submarines now offers the prospect of compelling England in a few months to make peace.

The Zimmerman telegram, released March 1, 1917 (dated
January 19), available online at Our Documents. URL:
http://www.ourdocuments.gov/content.php?doc=60.

I know what war means. I have been with the armies of all the belligerents except one, and I have seen men die, and go mad, and lie in hospitals suffering hell; but there is a worse thing than that. War means an ugly mob-madness, crucifying the truth-tellers, choking the artists, sidetracking reforms, revolutions, and the working of social forces. Already in America those citizens who oppose the entrance of their country into the European melee are called "traitors," and those who protest against the curtailing of our meagre rights of free speech are spoken of as "dangerous lunatics.". . . The press is howling for war. The church is howling for war. Lawyers, politicians, stockbrokers, social leaders are all howling for war. . . .

Whose war is this? Not mine. I know that hundreds of thousands of American workingmen employed by our great financial "patriots" are not paid a living wage. I have seen poor men sent to jail for long terms without trial, and even without any charge. Peaceful strikers, and their wives and children, have been shot to death, burned to death, by private detectives and militiamen. The rich have steadily become richer, and the cost of living higher, and the workers proportionally poorer. These toilers don't want war—not even civil war. But the speculators, the employers, the plutocracy—they want it, just as they did in Germany and in England; and with lies and sophistries they will whip up our blood until we are savage—and then we'll fight and die for them.

Radical journalist John Reed, "Whose War?," in the prominent left-leaning "little magazine" The Masses, April 1917, reprinted in John Reed for The Masses, *pp. 164–65.*

Not more than a year ago men would say . . . "Next thing you'll be wanting women in Congress," as if that was the reductio ad absurdum, and here she was coming in, escorted by an elderly colleague, looking like a mature bride rather than a strong minded female, and the men were clapping and cheering in the friendliest way. She wore a well-made dark blue silk and chiffon suit, with open neck, and wide white crepe collar and cuffs: skirt was a modest walking length, and she walked well and unselfconsciously. . . . She carried a bouquet of yellow and purple flowers. . . . She didn't look to right or left until she reached her seat, far back on the Republican side, but before she could sit down she was surrounded by men shaking hands with her. I rejoiced to see that she met each one with a big-mouthed frank smile and shook hands cordially and unaffectedly. . . . She was just a sensible young woman going about her business. When her name was called, the House cheered and rose, so that she had to rise and bow twice, which she did with entire self-possession. She was not pretty, but had an intellectual face and a nice manner.

Journal of Ellen Maury Sladen, wife of a Texas congressman who observed Jeannette Rankin of Montana take her seat as the first woman member of Congress, April 2, 1917, quoted in Smith, Jeannette Rankin, *p. 110.*

At eight o'clock, Monday evening, April second, the great auditorium of the House was crammed to overflowing. To the left of the Speaker sat the members of the Cabinet and immediately behind them the ambassadors of foreign powers; in front of the Speaker's desk were the members of the Supreme Court. . . . the public galleries were crowded to suffocation, while people sat on the steps and stood in the doorways which led into the corridors. Every possible space was occupied by those who had been fortunate enough to obtain tickets of admission to the building.

Shortly before eight-thirty it was announced that the Senate had arrived. . . . Vice-President Marshall, who led them proceeding to the raised dais and taking a chair beside the Speaker. A moment later the Clerk of the House announced "The President of the United States." Mr. Wilson came through the doorway to the left of the Speaker, followed by his bodyguard of Secret Service men, and with deliberation mounted to the reading desk in front of and a little below the high platform on which sat the Vice-President and the Speaker. The solemnity of the occasion

was evinced by the unbroken silence which prevailed. Not a whisper was to be heard in all the vast throng. Not a smile showed on the hundreds of faces turned toward the President as he stood with determination showing in the lines of his face, which seemed unusually pale and stern as he gazed over the white sea of faces awaiting to hear the message that he, as the spokesman of one hundred million people, was about to deliver.

In low measured tones and with that fine command of his emotions which Mr. Wilson always possessed, he began to speak. . . .

Secretary of State Robert Lansing describes Wilson's speech requesting a declaration of war, April 2, 1917, War Memories of Robert Lansing, *pp. 239–40.*

Our object now, as then, is to vindicate the principles of peace and justice in the life of the world as against selfish and autocratic power and to set up amongst the really free and selfgoverned peoples of the world such a concert of purpose and of action as will henceforth insure the observance of those principles Neutrality is no longer feasible or desirable where the peace of the world is involved and the freedom of its peoples, and the menace to that peace and freedom lies in the existence of autocratic governments backed by organized force which is controlled wholly by their will, not by the will of their people. . . .

But the right is more precious than peace, and we shall fight for the things which we have always carried nearest our hearts,—for democracy, for the right of those who submit to authority to have a voice in their own Governments, for the rights and liberties of small nations, for a universal dominion of right by such a concert of free peoples as shall bring peace and safety to all nations and make the world itself at last free. To such a task we can dedicate our lives and our fortunes . . . with the pride of those who know that the day has come when America is privileged to spend her blood and her might for the principles that gave her birth and happiness and the peace which she has treasured. God helping her, she can do no other.

Woodrow Wilson's address to Congress asking for a declaration of war, April 2, 1917, available online at Our Documents. URL: http://www.ourdocuments.gov/content.php?doc=61.

. . . The poor, sir, who are the ones called upon to rot in the trenches, have no organized power, have no press to voice their will upon this question of peace or war; but, oh, Mr. President, at some time they will be heard. . . . I think, sir, if we take this step, when the people to-day who are staggering under the burden of supporting families at the present prices of the necessaries of life find those prices multiplied, when they are raised a hundred per cent, or 200 per cent, as they will be quickly, aye, sir, when beyond that those who pay taxes come to have their taxes doubled and again doubled to pay the interest on the nontaxable bonds held by Morgan and his combinations, which have been issued to meet this war, there will come an awakening; they will have their day and they will be heard. . . .

. . . Are the people of this country being so well represented in this war movement that we need to go abroad to give other people control of their governments? Will the President and the supporters of this war bill submit it to a vote of the people before the declaration of war goes into effect? Until we are willing to do that, it hardly becomes us to offer as an excuse for our entry into the war the unsupported claim that this war was forced upon the German people by their Government "without their previous knowledge or approval."

Senator Robert La Follette, speech against the war resolution, April 4, 1917 Congressional Record, *65th Congress, 1st Session, vol. 53, p. 55.*

The majority report called upon the workers of all countries to refuse support to their Governments in war. The sacrifices in the European struggle were declared to be "wanton offerings upon the altar of private profit."

The report pledged the Socialists to opposition to the war by all means within their power, unyielding opposition to conscription, resistance to censorship of the press and mails, restriction of free speech, assemblage and organization, and to compulsory arbitration and limitation of the right to strike. It advocated propaganda against military training and militaristic training in the public schools, organization of workers to shorten the war and establish lasting peace, education in the relations between capitalism and war and organization for destruction of the causes of war.

"Socialists Denounce U.S. Entry Into War," St. Louis Post-Dispatch, *April 12, 1917, p. 1.*

The Woman Suffrage Party of New York City now has a signed up membership of 500,000. It has twenty city officers, fifty borough officers, sixty-three leaders of assembly districts and 2,127 captains of election districts. . . . It is a most democratic organization, which is considered remarkable in a woman's organization, which is usually conspicuous for carefully drawn social lines. . . .

"Big Boss" Mary Garrett Hay, the Greater New York leader, sees her borough officers whenever they have need of advice. On the walls of her office are five carefully detailed political maps of the five boroughs, where points of difficulty may be pointed out in consultations. In addition to this there is what Miss Hay calls her "Suffrage Bible.". . . Entered in this book are totals of votes cast in every district in the city from 1915 and 1916, the names of male political leaders and how they voted, the list of districts that are strong for suffrage, those that are lukewarm,

and those that are actively opposed to it. She can tell to a vote what is need to carry the city for the women this year.

"Suffragists' Machine Perfected in All States Under Mrs. Catt's Rule; Votes for Women Campaign Is Now Run with All the Method of Experienced Men Politicians," New York Times, *April 29, 1917, p. 8.*

Our deplorable situation as to munitions was fully discussed at a conference called by the Secretary of War in his office on the afternoon of May 10th. A general survey of our requirements for the immediate future was made as to rifles, machine guns, light and heavy artillery, ammunition and airplanes. It was brought out that we had for issue, not in the hands of troops, only about 285,000 Springfield rifles, 400 light field guns, and 150 heavy field guns. . . .

As it was impossible, because of manufacturing difficulties, for our factories to turn out enough Springfield rifles within a reasonable time, the Secretary, after hearing the facts, decided to adopt the Enfield rifle for our infantry. It was then being manufactured for the British in large quantities at private factories in our country. . . .

Although Congress had appropriated $12,000,000 for the procurement of machine guns in 1916, it was reported to the conference that we had less than 1,500 guns and that these were of four different types. This condition existed because the War Department had not decided definitely which type to adopt for our Army, although an order had been placed late in 1916 for a quantity of the heavy Vickers-Maxims. Tests of machine guns were held in May, 1917, and an entirely new type was pronounced acceptable and adopted by the Ordnance Department. Until these could be manufactured we had to purchase machine guns of the Hotchkiss type from the French.

General John J. Pershing describes America's munitions in May 1917, My Experiences in the World War, *vol. 1, pp. 26–27.*

I have counted myself happy in the companionship of the men and women who called themselves pacifists. There was not a State or national or international peace society of which I was not a member, and in many instances an officer. As a trade unionist, with its practices and its philosophies, I have been in happy accord with our movement for international peace. . . .

I was sent as a delegate from the American Federation to the International Congress of Labor in 1909, held at Paris, France . . . at which the representatives of the labor movement of each country declared that there would not be another international war.

And I went home, happy in the further proof that the time of universal peace had come. . . . and until 1914 I was in that Fool's Paradise. I doubt if there were many who

Samuel Gompers, head of the American Federation of Labor throughout the entire Progressive Era, led the movement to unionize American workers. *(Library of Congress, Prints and Photographs Division, LC-USZ62-83830)*

were so thoroughly shocked to the innermost depths of their being as I was with the breaking out of the European War. . . .

I am made ill when I see or bear any one suffering the slightest pain or anguish, and yet I hold that it is essential that the sacrifice must be made that humanity shall never again be cursed by a war such as the one which has been thrust upon us.

Samuel Gompers, response to the May 18, 1917, proclamation of the draft, Horne, ed., Source Records of the Great War, *vol. 5, pp. 189–90.*

The tops of the cars of every train in the station were crowded with workmen. As the tall, slender American commander stepped into view, the privileged observers on the car-tops began to cheer.

A minute later, there was a terrific roar from beyond the walls of the station. The crowds outside had heard the cheering within. They took it up with thousands of throats. They made their welcome a ringing one. Paris took Pershing by storm. . . .

General Pershing and M. Painlev, Minister of War, took seats in a large automobile. . . . The procession started to

the accompaniment of martial music by massed military bands in the courtyard of the station. . . .

The crowds overflowed the sidewalks. . . . From the crowded balconies and windows overlooking the route, women and children tossed down showers of flowers and bits of coloured paper.

The crowds were so dense that other street traffic became marooned in the dense sea of joyously excited and gesticulating French people. Vehicles thus marooned immediately became islands of vantage. They were soon covered with men and women and children, who climbed on top of them and clung to the sides to get a better look at the khaki-clad occupants of the autos.

Floyd Gibbons, war correspondent for the Chicago Tribune, *describes General Pershing's arrival in Paris, June 14, 1917, in "And They Thought We Wouldn't Fight," pp. 54–56.*

Title I, Sec. 3. Whoever, when the United States is at war, shall wilfully make or convey false reports or false statements with intent to interfere with the operation or success of the military or naval forces of the United States or to promote the success of its enemies and whoever when the United States is at war, shall wilfully cause or attempt to cause insubordination, disloyalty, mutiny, refusal of duty, in the military or naval forces of the United States, or shall wilfully obstruct the recruiting or enlistment service of the United States, to the injury of the service or of the United States, shall be punished by a fine of not more than $10,000 or imprisonment for not more than twenty years, or both. . . .

Title XII, Sec. 2. Every letter, writing, circular, postal card, picture, print, engraving, photograph, newspaper, pamphlet, book, or other publication, matter or thing, of any kind, containing any matter advocating or urging treason, insurrection, or forcible resistance to any law of the United States, is hereby declared to be nonmailable.

Espionage Act, June 15, 1917, U.S. Statutes at Large, *65th Congress, vol. 40, pp. 217ff.*

To uncertain natures, wild sound and meaningless noise have an exciting, almost intoxicating effect, like crude colors and strong perfume, the sight of flesh or the sadistic pleasure in blood. To such as these, the jass [jazz] is a delight. A dance to the unstable bray of the sackbut is a sensual delight more intense and quite different from the languor of a Viennese waltz or the refined sentiment and respectful emotion of the eighteenth century minuet.

New Orleans Times-Picayune, June 17, 1917, quoted in Meltzer, ed., Reading Jazz, *pp. 52–53.*

Do you remember Jane Addams statement that everyone in America jeered at, about the French soldiers—all the soldiers in fact, being doped with rum? Its absolutely true . . .

people couldn't stand the frightful strain of deathly—literally so—dullness without some stimulant—In fact strong tobacco very strong red wine, known to the poilus [soldiers] as Pinard, and a composition of rum & ether—in argot, agnol, are combined with the charming camaraderie you find everywhere. . . .

Having our headquarters in the much bombarded remnants of a village, we do our business in a fantastic wood, once part of the forests of Argonne—now a "ghoul haunted woodland"; smelling of poison gas, tangled with broken telephone wires, with ripped pieces of camouflage—(the green cheesecloth that everything is swathed in to hide it from aeroplanes), filled in every hollow with guns that crouch and spit like the poisonous toads of the fairytales. In the early dawn after a night's bombardment on both sides it is the weirdest thing imaginable to drive through the woodland roads, with the guns of the batteries tomtomming about you & the whistle of departing shell & the occasional rattling snort of an arriveé. A great labor it is to get through, too, through the smashed artillery trains, past piles of splintered camions and commissariat wagons. The wood before and since the attack . . . has been one vast battery—a constant succession of ranks of guns hidden in foliage, and dugouts, from which people crawl like gnomes when the firing ceases. . . .

Future novelist John Dos Passos, an ambulance driver in France near Verdun, letter to his college friend Rumsey Marvin, August 29, 1917, The Fourteenth Chronicle, *pp. 97–98.*

There were no certificates on file for 30.4 per cent of the children under 16 years of age employed about these mines in Pennsylvania, and of those on file 20 per cent had been so irregularly issued that they constituted a protection to employers in the violation of the law. For example, in one town visited, a superintendent of schools who had recently been removed had made a practice of selling certificates to under-age children, and certificates issued by him were found both inside and outside the district in which he had taught. Most of these children were two years younger, than the age given on the certificate. . . .

Eight of the nine coal mines inspected in West Virginia were violating the Federal standards. There were 15 children under 16 years of age working inside the mines as trapper boys (opening and closing doors), and in tending switches, coupling cars, and even as miners, picking out coal and loading cars. While the inspectors were at work in the State a boy was seriously crippled in one mine, and another a colored trapper boy—who was in fact 15 years old, but whose mother had made affidavit that he was 16 years of age—was run over by a car. . . . The boy did not live long, and one of the officials, taking advantage of the

"Fuel will win the war" slogan, said: "The boy has died for his country". . . .

Grace Abbott, director of the Child Labor Division, federal Children's Bureau, reports inspections under the Keating-Owen Act between September 1, 1917 and June 3, 1918, The Child and the State, *pp. 493–95.*

The task . . . was entered upon and discharged in such manner as to startle many at home and to amaze even foreigners who had become habituated to prodigious operations. I well remember some characteristic remarks of Lord Northcliffe during his visit to Washington. Suddenly stopping and turning to me, he said, "Am I dreaming?" I asserted that he did not look like a dreamer. He

Food was considered crucial to the war effort during World War I. This 1918 poster advertises the Women's Land Army Training School at the University of Virginia. The Land Army organized female volunteers to maintain and harvest crops while male agricultural workers were away at war. *(Library of Congress, Prints and Photographs Division, LC-USZ62-42546)*

continued: "I am told that Congress declared war on the sixth of April, authorized the Secretary of the Treasury to borrow approximately eleven and a half billion dollars, enacted a new tax law designed to raise two and a half billions in addition to ordinary revenues, appropriated or authorized nine billions for the army and navy, over a billion for ships, with a maximum authorization of nearly two billions, six hundred and forty millions for aeroplanes, credits to the Allies of seven billions, a total of actual appropriations and authorizations of twenty-one billions, gave power to commandeer plants, ships and materials, provided for conscription, which England had not fully resorted to and Canada had not then adopted, that there had been registered or enlisted nearly ten and a half million men, that Pershing was in France and naval vessels were in Europe, that the food-production and food-control measures had been passed, and that authority had been given for the control of exports and imports and of priorities." He repeated: "Am I dreaming or is it true?" I replied that unless I was dreaming it was true. He said: "I can't believe it." I told him I could believe it but that I could not comprehend it.

Secretary of Agriculture D. F. Houston describes mobilization efforts, ca. October 1917, Source Records of the Great War, *vol. 5, p. 419.*

Militants of the [National] Woman's Party serving time in the District of Columbia Workhouse for demonstrations before the White House were charged today with mutiny as a result of their rough-and- tumble fight yesterday with guards and negro women prisoners. The development furnishes a new phase for the investigation of conditions at the workhouse, undertaken by the Board of Charities on complaints of the militants.

. . . [T]he Superintendent is suspended pending outcome of the inquiry. A long story is told . . . of how the eighteen suffragists attacked the Acting Superintendent, the prison matron, and three male guards who had been called to the rescue when the officers sought to remove one of their number, Mrs. Margaret Johns, for medical treatment. . . .

It tells of negro women of the prison kitchen force rallying to the aid of their boss, the matron, when she was threatened with a blow on the head with a club, of a general wild scramble about the workhouse corridors and yard, and eventually of Mrs. Johns's departure for the hospital in a doctor's automobile after she and her guards had been much mauled and hauled about. The Acting Superintendent emphasizes the statement that extreme forbearance was shown the prisoners, the male guards obeying orders to handle them with every possible consideration in spite of all that happened.

"'Pickets' Mutiny in Workhouse," New York Times, *October 5, 1917, p. 1.*

Well Dr. with the aid of God I am making very good I make $75 per month. I am carrying enough insurance to pay me $20 per week if I am not able to be on duty. I don't have to work hard. dont have to mister every little white boy comes along I havent heard a white man call a colored a nigger you no now—since I been in the state of Pa. I can ride in the electric street and steam cars any where I get a seat. I dont care to mix with white what I mean I am not crazy about being with white folks, but if I have to pay the same fare I have learn to want the same acomidation. and if you are first in a place here shoping you dont have to wait until the white folks get thro tradeing yet amid all this I shall ever love the good old South and I am praying that God may give every well wisher a chance to be a man regardless of his color, and if my going to the front would bring about such conditions I am ready any day. . . .

African-American migrant to Philadelphia, letter home to Mississippi, October 7, 1917, Journal of Negro History, *vol. 4 (1919), p. 461.*

The convoy sailed at night. No white lights of any kind were lighted except in the engine and fire rooms, and below decks where it was sure lights could not be seen from outside. In other localities where it was necessary for some illumination . . . pale blue lights were used which gave a gruesome and none too cheerful aspect to the moist and hot berthing spaces below decks, crowded to the ceiling with men.

. . . It was imperative immediately upon leaving port to form the convoy. Big ships maneuvered at close distance to each other and at almost full speed. The captains and the principal officers were familiar with cruising in formation, but many of the watch officers engaged in this difficult maneuver for the first time. . . .

The convoy sailed in line-abreast formation and, at night, with no lights showing. When the moon was obscured the next ship abreast could be seen as a deeper shadow in the gloom unless by chance she edged in too close and then to the captain and officer of the deck she loomed like a mountain too near for comfort. . . .

Captain Yates Sterling, commander of the convoy taking the 42nd or Rainbow Division to Europe, mid-October 1917, Journal of the Naval Institute Proceedings, *September 1925, reprinted in Angle, ed.,* American Reader, *pp. 494–95.*

These boys are going to France; they are going to face conditions that we do not like to talk about, that we do not like to think about. They are going into an heroic enterprise, and heroic enterprises involve sacrifices. I want them armed; I want them adequately armed and clothed by their Government; but I want them to have invisible armor to take with them. I want them to have an armor made up of a set of social habits replacing those of their homes and communities, a set of social habits and a state of social mind born in the training camps, a new soldier state of mind, so that when they get overseas and are removed from the reach of our comforting and restraining and helpful hand, they will have gotten such a set of habits as will constitute a moral and intellectual armor for their protection.

Secretary of State Newton Baker, "Invisible Armor," speech to the National Conference on War Camp Community Recreation Service, October 23, 1917, Frontiers of Freedom, *94.*

Suddenly the door literally burst open and Whittaker [the prison warden] burst in like a tornado; some men followed him. We could see a crowd of them on the porch. They were not in uniform. Mrs. Lewis . . . had hardly begun to speak, saying we demanded to be treated as political prisoners, when Whittaker said, "You shut up. I have men here to handle you." Then he shouted, "Seize her!" I turned and saw men spring toward her, and then someone screamed, "They have taken Mrs. Lewis."

A man sprang at me and caught me by the shoulder. I remember saying, "I'll come with you; don't drag me; I have a lame foot." But I was jerked down the steps and away into the dark. I didn't have my feet on the ground. I guess that saved me.

. . . We were rushed into a large room that opened on a large hall with stone cells on each side. They were perfectly dark. Punishment cells is what they call them. . . .

I saw Dorothy Day [radical activist from New York] brought in. She is a frail girl. The two men handling her were twisting her arms above her head. Then suddenly they lifted her up and banged her down over the arm of an iron bench—twice. . . .

At the end of the corridor they pushed me through a door. Then I lost my balance and fell against the iron bed. Mrs. Cosu [chair of the Louisiana Women's Party] struck the wall. . . . Mrs. Lewis was literally thrown in. Her head struck the iron bed. We thought she was dead. . . . Mr. Whittaker came to the door and told us not to dare to speak, or he would "put the brace and bit in our mouths and the straitjacket on our bodies."

Mary Nolan, 73-year-old suffrage pioneer from Jacksonville, Florida, describes the treatment of suffrage pickets in Occoquan Workhouse prison, November 1917, quoted in Stevens, Jailed for Freedom, *pp. 122–23.*

Groups of women from colleges and seasonal trades have ploughed and harrowed, sowed and planted, weeded and cultivated, mowed and harvested, milked and churned, at Vassar, Bryn Mawr and Mount Holyoke, at Newburg and Milton, at Bedford Hills and Mahwah. It has been demonstrated that our girls from college and city trade can do farm work, and do it with a will. And still better, at the end of the season their health wins high approved from the doctors and their work golden opinions from the farmers. . . .

The Women's Agricultural Camp, known popularly as the "Bedford Unit," proved an experiment rich in practical suggestion. Barnard students, graduates of the Manhattan Trade School, and girls from seasonal trades formed the backbone of the group. They were housed in an old farmhouse, chaperoned by one of the Barnard professors, fed by student dietitians from the Household Arts Department of Teachers College, transported from farm to farm by seven chauffeurs, and coached in the arts of Ceres by an agricultural expert. The "day laborers" as well as the experts were all women.

. . . When the prejudice of the farmers was overcome, the demand for workers was greater than the camp could supply.

Harriot Stanton Blatch describes the women's land army movement, Mobilizing Woman-Power, *1918, pp. 166–68, 175.*

War is the health of the State. It automatically sets in motion throughout society those irresistible forces for uniformity, for passionate cooperation with the Government in coercing into obedience the minority groups and individuals which lack the larger herd sense. The machinery of government sets and enforces the drastic penalties; the minorities are either intimidated into silence, or brought slowly around by a subtle process of persuasion which may seem to them really to be converting them. Of course, the ideal of perfect loyalty, perfect uniformity is never really attained. . . . Minorities are rendered sullen, and some intellectual opinion bitter and satirical. But in general, the nation in wartime attains a uniformity of feeling, a hierarchy of values culminating at the undisputed apex of the State ideal, which could not possibly be produced through any other agency than war. Loyalty—or mystic devotion to the State—becomes the major imagined human value.

Intellectual Randolph Bourne, "The State," a work left unfinished at his death from influenza in 1918, The Radical Will, *pp. 360–61.*

Fall passed into winter and the terrible flu broke out all over Ft. Riley. . . . People were dying so fast. One day you would be working with a friend, the next day they didn't come to work, and the report said they were dead.

It went on and on. The soldiers were dying so fast that caskets wouldn't be found for them. We heard that the bodies were being kept in a warehouse until arrangement could be made to send them home for burial.

We were all so frightened, wondering who would be next. As luck would have it, none of our gang had it bad.

My sister got it. She was put in a room by herself, and Dr. Clarkson came and gave her medicine. A woman was hired to come and take care of her.

My brother and I were told to stay away. . . .

I followed all the health rules I could and still worried. . . .

At last the flu left, as fast as it had come.

Jessie Lee Brown Foveaux, a 19-year-old laundry worker at
Ft. Riley during the flu epidemic of 1918,
Any Given Day, *p. 145.*

It cannot be denied that the governmental mandate to communities, "Here comes a soldier. Clean up!" was in the beginning looked upon askance. . . . Some military men of the "old school" thought it not only unwise, but a menace to the liberty of the soldier to have the "red light" districts near camps closed. . . . In some cases the investigations of the commissions have brought to light the gross negligence of civil servants, and the appeal has been so strongly to the patriotism of political constituents that occasionally reform has been hastily substituted by the politicians themselves to save their own heads! . . . Even more drastic action was necessary with a city in the vicinity of a large national army camp in the West.

"Clear the street-walkers from your boulevards and stamp out those dancing-hall hells where the bootleggers lie thick," warned the commanding officer of the camp, "or not a man of my thirty thousand will enter your city."

The mayor and the police of this city thought that the general was bluffing; neither took positive action. But the general was not bluffing. . . . Not a soldier was permitted to enter the city. For a thousand miles around the papers laughed in loud headlines; editorially, they jeered. It did not take long for the indignant citizens to get together in mass-meetings and finally force the municipal authorities by sheer weight of public opinion to clean up the town.

Frank Edward Allen and Raymond Fosdick,
Keeping Our Fighters Fit, *1918, pp. 199–201.*

I. Open covenants of peace, openly arrived at, after which there shall be no private international understandings of any kind but diplomacy shall proceed always frankly and in the public view.

II. Absolute freedom of navigation upon the seas, outside territorial waters, alike in peace and in war, except as the seas may be closed in whole or in part by international action. . . .

III. The removal, so far as possible, of all economic barriers and the establishment of an equality of trade conditions among all the nations consenting to the peace. . . .

IV. Adequate guarantees given and taken that national armaments will be reduced to the lowest point consistent with domestic safety.

V. A free, open-minded, and absolutely impartial adjustment of all colonial claims, based upon a strict observance of the principle that in determining all such questions of sovereignty the interests of the populations concerned must have equal weight with the equitable claims of the government whose title is to be determined. . . .

X. The peoples of Austria-Hungary . . . should be accorded the freest opportunity to autonomous development. . . .

XII. The Turkish portion of the present Ottoman Empire should be assured a secure sovereignty, but the other nationalities which are now under Turkish rule should be assured an undoubted security of life and an absolutely unmolested opportunity of autonomous development. . . .

XIII. An independent Polish state should be erected. . . .

XIV. A general association of nations must be formed under specific covenants for the purpose of affording mutual guarantees of political independence and territorial integrity to great and small states alike.

Woodrow Wilson's Fourteen Points, address to Congress
January 8, 1918, available online at Our Documents. URL:
http://www.ourdocuments.gov/doc.php?flash-true&doc-62.

I wonder why I feel so sad this morning. I got up very early and went to breakfast, and every one of my sisters and brothers looked very sad and stared at me with eyes full of tears, which made me feel I would very much hate to part with them. When I kissed little Blanche, she said, "Are you going to war today?" . . .

My, such a crowd of people at the depot. I was amazed. I never realized the Rolla [North Dakota] people would take so much interest in me. . . . They loaded me down with boxes of chocolates, magazines, and other gifts: a watch, a petticoat, a $5 gold piece, two handkerchiefs and two corset cover drawstrings, and a statue of the Blessed Virgin Mary, a swell pendant, and the cutest and smallest watch I'd ever seen. My darling sister Zelda [gave me] a leather toilet case, and Papa paid my fare to Grand Forks. . . . The men started a collection and collected somewhere near $60 for me. . . .

Then we heard the train whistles and every body was giving me a tight handshake and a hurried kiss and some were crying and telling me to be sure and write, and if I saw any of their boys in France to let them know how they were getting along.

Cordelia Dupuis, who volunteered for the Army Signal Corps,
diary entry February 9, 1918, quoted in Gavin,
American Women in World War I, *p. 80.*

. . . Washington is no longer a city of set routine and fixed habit. It is at last the center of the nation. New York is no longer even the financial center. The newspapers are edited from here. Society centers here. All the industrial chiefs of the nation spend most of their time here. It is easier to find a great cattle king or automobile manufacturer or a railroad president or a banker at the Shoreham or the Willard Hotel than it is to find him in his own town. . . . The dinners are Hooverized,—three courses, little or no wheat, little or no meat, little or no sugar, a few serve wine. And round the table will always be found men in foreign uniforms, or some missionary from some great power who comes begging for boats or food. These dinners used to be places of great gossip, and chiefly anti–administration gossip, but the spirit of the people is one of unequaled loyalty. The Republicans are as glad to have Wilson as their President as are the Democrats, I think sometimes a little more glad, because many of the Democrats are disgruntled over patronage or something else. . . . Every woman carries her knitting, and it is seldom that you hear a croaker even among the most luxurious class. . . . The President keeps up his spirits by going to the theatre three or four times a week. There are no official functions at the White House, and everybody's teeth are set.

Secretary of the Interior Franklin Lane describes life in Washington, to ambassador to Britain Walter Hines Page, letter dated March 16, 1918, Letters, *pp. 274–76.*

I believe in the United States of America as a government of the people, by the people, for the people; whose just powers are derived from the consent of the governed; a democracy in a republic; a sovereign Nation of many sovereign States; a perfect union, one and inseparable; established upon the principles of freedom, equality, justice, and humanity for which American patriots sacrificed their lives and their fortunes.

I therefore believe it is my duty to my country to love it, to support its Constitution, to obey its laws, to respect its flag, and to defend it against all enemies.

William Tyler Page, "The American's Creed," winning entry in national contest, recognized by the House of Representatives April 13, 1918, available online at US Constitution Online, URL: http://www.usconstitution.net/creed.html.

SEC. 3. Whoever, when the United States is at war, shall wilfully make or convey false reports or false statements with intent to interfere with the operation or success of the military or naval forces of the United States, or to promote the success of its enemies, or shall wilfully make or convey false reports, or false statements, or say or do anything except by way of bona fide and not disloyal advice to an investor . . . with intent to obstruct the sale by the United States of bonds . . . or the making of loans by or to the United States, or whoever, when the United States is at war, shall wilfully cause . . . or incite . . . insubordination, disloyalty, mutiny, or refusal of duty, in the military or naval forces of the United States, or shall wilfully obstruct . . . the recruiting or enlistment service of the United States, and

whoever, when the United States is at war, shall wilfully utter, print, write, or publish any disloyal, profane, scurrilous, or abusive language about the form of government of the United States, or the Constitution of the United States, or the military or naval forces of the United States, or the flag . . . or the uniform of the Army or Navy of the United States, or any language intended to bring the form of government . . . or the Constitution . . . or the military or naval forces . . . or the flag . . . of the United States into contempt, scorn, contumely, or disrepute . . . or shall wilfully display the flag of any foreign enemy, or shall wilfully . . . urge, incite, or advocate any curtailment of production in this country of any thing or things . . . necessary or essential to the prosecution of the war . . . and whoever shall wilfully advocate, teach, defend, or suggest the doing of any of the acts or things in this section enumerated and whoever shall by word or act support or favour the cause of any country with which the United States is at war or by word or act oppose the cause of the United States therein, shall be punished by a fine of not more than $10,000 or imprisonment for not more than twenty years, or both. . . ."

Sedition Act, May 16, 1918, amending provisions of the Espionage Act of 1917, U.S. Statutes at Large, *66th Congress, vol. 40, p. 553.*

That there should be limitations upon the right to employ children in mines and factories in the interest of their own and the public welfare, all will admit. . . .

In interpreting the Constitution it must never be forgotten that the nation is made up of states to which are entrusted the powers of local government. . . . To sustain this statute would not be in our judgment a recognition of the lawful exertion of congressional authority over interstate commerce, but would sanction an invasion by the federal power of the control of a matter purely local in its character. . . .

We have neither authority nor disposition to question the motives of Congress in enacting this legislation. The purposes intended must be attained consistently with constitutional limitations and not by an invasion of the powers of the states. . . .

. . . The far reaching result of upholding the act cannot be more plainly indicated than by pointing out that if Congress can thus regulate matters entrusted to local authority by prohibition of the movement of commodities in interstate commerce, all freedom of commerce will be at an end, and the power of the states over local matters may be eliminated, and thus our system of government be practically destroyed.

Supreme Court Justice William R. Day, writing for a majority of five declaring the Keating-Owen child labor law unconstitutional, Hammer v. Dagenhart, *June 3, 1918, 247 US 251.*

. . . the purpose of the Allies is exactly the purpose of the Central Powers, and that is the conquest and spoliation of the weaker nations that has always been the purpose of war. . . .

The master class has always declared the wars; the subject class has always fought the battles. The master class has had all to gain and nothing to lose, while the subject class has had nothing to gain and all to lose—especially their lives. . . .

And here let me emphasize the fact—and it cannot be repeated too often—that the working class who fight all the battles, the working class who make the supreme sacrifices, the working class who freely shed their blood and furnish the corpses, have never yet had a voice in either declaring war or making peace. It is the ruling class that invariably does both. They alone declare war and they alone make peace. . . .

Eugene V. Debs, speech to the Ohio Socialist Party, June 16, 1918, for which he was sentenced to a 10-year jail term under the Espionage Act, available online at Eugene V. Debs Internet Archive. URL: http://www.marxists.org/archive/debs/works/1918/canton.htm.

Your Honor, years ago I recognized my kinship with all living beings, and I made up my mind that I was not one bit better than the meanest on earth. I said then, and I say now, that while there is a lower class, I am in it, and while there is a criminal element I am of it, and while there is a soul in prison, I am not free. . . .

Standing here this morning, I recall my boyhood. At fourteen I went to work in a railroad shop; at sixteen I was firing a freight engine on a railroad. I remember all the hardships and privations of that earlier day, and from that time until now my heart has been with the working class. I could have been in Congress long ago. I have preferred to go to prison. . . .

I am thinking this morning of the men in the mills and the factories; of the men in the mines and on the railroads. I am thinking of the women who for a paltry wage are compelled to work out their barren lives; of the little children who in this system are robbed of their childhood . . . to feed the monster machines while they themselves are being starved and stunted, body and soul. I see them dwarfed and diseased and their little lives broken and blasted because in this high noon of Christian civilization money is still so much more important than the flesh and blood of childhood. In very truth gold is god today and rules with pitiless sway in the affairs of men.

Eugene V. Debs, statement to the court upon being convicted of sedition, September 18, 1918, available online at Eugene V. Debs Internet Archive. URL: http://www.marxists.org/archive/debs/works/1918/court.htm.

This epidemic started about four weeks ago, and has developed so rapidly that the camp is demoralized. . . .

These men start with what appears to be an ordinary attack of LaGrippe or Influenza, and when brought to the Hosp. they very rapidly develop the most viscous type of Pneumonia that has ever been seen. Two hours after admission they have the Mahogany spots over the cheek bones, and a few hours later you can begin to see the Cyanosis extending from their ears and spreading all over the face, until it is hard to distinguish the coloured men from the white. It is only a matter of a few hours then until death comes, and it is simply a struggle for air until they suffocate. It is horrible. One can stand it to see one, two or twenty men die, but to see these poor devils dropping like flies sort of gets on your nerves. We have been averaging about 100 deaths per day, and still keeping it up. There is no doubt in my mind that there is a new mixed infection here, but what I don't know. . . .

. . . It takes special trains to carry away the dead. For several days there were no coffins and the bodies piled up something fierce, we used to go down to the morgue (which is just back of my ward) and look at the boys laid out in long rows. It beats any sight they ever had in France after a battle. . . .

Letter of an Army doctor stationed at Camp Devens near Boston, September 29, 1918, published in British Medical Journal, *December 22–29, 1979, available online at "Influenza." URL: http://web.uct.ac.za/depts/mmi/jmoodie/influen2.html#Pandemic%20influenza.*

Through many, many channels I have been made aware of what the plain, struggling, workaday folk are thinking upon whom the chief terror and suffering of this war falls. . . . They think in their logical simplicity, that democracy means that women shall play their part in affairs alongside men and upon an equal footing with them. . . .

We have made partners of the women in this war; shall we admit them only to a partnership of suffering and sacrifice and toil and not to a partnership of privilege and right? This war could not have been fought, either by the other nations engaged or by America, if it had not been for the services of the women—services rendered in every sphere—not merely in the fields of effort in which we have been accustomed to see them work, but wherever men have worked, and upon the very skirts and edges of the battle itself. . . .

I tell you plainly that this measure which I urge upon you is vital to the winning of the war and to the energies alike of preparation and of battle.

And not to the winning of the war only. It is vital to the right solution of the great problems which we must settle, and settle immediately, when the war is.

Woodrow Wilson addresses the U.S. Senate on women's suffrage, September 30, 1918, 65th Congress, 1st session, Senate document 284.

The congressional elections are at hand. They occur in the most critical period our country has ever faced or is likely to face in our time. If you have approved of my leadership and wish me to continue to be your unembarrassed spokesman in affairs at home and abroad, I earnestly beg that you will express yourselves unmistakably to that effect by returning a Democratic majority to both the Senate and the House of Representatives.

I am your servant and will accept your judgment without cavil. But my power to administer the great trust assigned me by the Constitution would be seriously impaired should your judgement be adverse....

The leaders of the minority in the present Congress have unquestionably been pro-war, but they have been anti-administration. At almost every turn since we entered the war they have sought to take the choice of policy and the conduct of the war out of my hands....

The return of a Republican majority to Congress would, moreover, certainly be interpreted on the other side of the water as a repudiation of my leadership ...

Woodrow Wilson's appeal for a Democratic Congress, October 25, 1918, Congressional Record, *65th Congress, 2nd session, vol 54, p. 11,494.*

From the very beginning of the great war, as the members of our group gradually became defined from the rest of the community, each one felt increasingly the sense of isolation which rapidly developed after the United States entered the war into that destroying effect of "aloneness," if I may so describe the opposite of mass consciousness. We never ceased to miss the unquestioning comradeship experienced by our fellow citizens during the war, nor to feel curiously outside the enchantment given to any human emotion when it is shared by millions of others. The force of the majority was so overwhelming that it seemed not only impossible to hold one's own against it, but at moments absolutely unnatural, and one secretly yearned to participate in "the folly of all mankind." Our modern democratic teaching has brought us to regard popular impulses as possessing in their general tendency a valuable capacity for evolutionary development. In the hours of doubt and self-distrust the question again and again arises, has the individual or a very small group, the right to stand out against millions of his fellow countrymen? ... The misunderstanding on the part of old friends and associates and the charge of lack of patriotism was far easier to bear than those dark periods of faint-heartedness....

Jane Addams on remaining a pacifist through the war's end in November 1918, Peace and Bread in Time of War, *chapter 7, available online at URL:http://www2.pfeiffer.edu/ ~lridener/DSS/Addams/pb7.html.*

Every person appearing on the public streets, in any public place, or in any assemblage of persons or in any place where two or more persons are congregated, except in homes where only two members of the family are present, and every person engaged in the sale, handling or distribution of foodstuffs or wearing apparel shall wear a mask or covering except when partaking of meals, over the nose and mouth, consisting of four-ply materials known as butter-cloth or fine mesh gauze.

San Francisco ordinance to prevent the spread of influenza, effective November 1 to 21, 1918, quoted in Crosby, Epidemic and Peace, 1918, *p. 102.*

The President is now just beginning to pay the price which he was always bound to pay at some time for the peculiar method adopted by him of running the country during the war. This method was in brief to promote a sound democratic purpose by means which were in certain respects autocratic and coercive. He used the intense patriotic feelings of one of the most patriotic peoples in the world in order to unite the nation during the war under his own leadership, but the unity which he obtained in this way was artificial and forced. . . . Now when the war is over the forced unity disappears, and he is left dangerously isolated at the moment when the success of his policy is being challenged by enemies no less stiff-necked and hostile than the Germans. His own party is disgruntled; the Republican party is aggrieved and embittered; nonpartisan liberals cannot get over his harsh and unnecessary suppression of freedom of utterance; Congress as a body resents the extent to which he has failed during the war to consult its leaders; the war bureaucracy does not inspire so much trust as it should; people find it hard to understand why he should surround himself with so many inferior men; and they find his frequent failure to take public opinion into his confidence equally a cause of suspicion. Finally, and most important, it is only too clear that his fellow-countrymen have not grasped the meaning of his international policy....

"America and the League of Nations," New Republic, *vol. 17 (November 30, 1918), p. 118.*

The general level of wages attained during the war should not be lowered. In a few industries, especially some directly and peculiarly connected with the carrying on of war, wages have reached a plane upon which they cannot possibly continue for this grade of occupations. But the number of workers in this situation is an extremely small proportion of the entire wage-earning population. The overwhelming majority should not be compelled or suffered to undergo any reduction in their rates of remuneration for two reasons: first, because the average rate of pay has not increased faster than the cost of living; second, because a considerable majority of the wage earners of the United States, both men and women, were not receiving living wages when prices began to rise in 1915....

The principal beneficiaries of a general reduction of wages would be the less efficient among the capitalists and the comfortable sections of the consumers. The wage earners would lose more in remuneration than they would gain from whatever fall in prices occurred as a direct result of the fall in wages. On grounds both of justice and sound economics, we should give our hearty support to all legitimate efforts made by labor to resist general wage reductions.

"Bishops' Program of Social Reconstruction," drafted by Father John Ryan for the National Catholic War Council, 1919, Annals of America, *vol. 14, p. 210.*

If the workers consider that sabotage is necessary, that in itself makes, sabotage moral. Its necessity is its excuse for existence. And for us to discuss the morality of sabotage would be as absurd as to discuss the morality of the strike or the morality of the class struggle itself. In order to understand . . . it is necessary to accept the concept of the class struggle. If you believe that between the workers on the one side and their employers on the other there is peace, there is harmony such as exists between brothers, and that consequently whatever strikes and lockouts occur are simply family squabbles; if you believe that a point can be reached whereby the employer can get enough and the worker can get enough, a point of amicable adjustment of Industrial warfare and economic distribution, then there is no justification and no explanation of sabotage intelligible to you....

Sabotage is to this class struggle what the guerrilla warfare is to the battle. The strike is the open battle of the class struggle, sabotage is the guerrilla warfare, the day-by-day warfare between two opposing classes.

IWW organizer Elizabeth Gurley Flynn, "Sabotage," a pamphlet reprinted in Bolshevik Propaganda, *1919, p. 1037.*

The rosy promise of "Freedom, for All, Forever," is dispelled before the reality of the bankruptcy of capitalism. The world may now be safe for democracy, of the soup-house variety, but that is small consolation to the people who have slaved and sacrificed for some vague thing they believed would guarantee happiness and prosperity to them.

When again the flabby-brained and looselipped orators of the capitalistic class come before the workers with their rosy promises they will hear the shout:
Ye are liars!
Your Democracy is a lie!
Your Freedom is a lie!

Your Prosperity is a lie!
Your Equality is a lie!
Your Humanity is a lie!
Your Liberty is a lie!
Your Religion is a lie!
Your Eternal Justice is a lie!
Your God is a lie!
Everything you praise, all that you eulogize and adore, is a lie!

International Weekly, Seattle, January 24, 1919, reprinted *in* Bolshevik Propaganda, *p. 1,051.*

We admit that in many places and in ordinary times the defendants in saying all that was said in the circular would have been within their constitutional rights. But the character of every act depends upon the circumstances in which it is done. . . . The most stringent protection of free speech would not protect a man in falsely shouting fire in a theatre and causing a panic. It does not even protect a man from an injunction against uttering words that may have all the effect of force. . . . The question in every case is whether the words used are used in such circumstances and are of such a nature as to create a clear and present danger that they will bring about the substantive evils that Congress has a right to prevent. It is a question of proximity and degree. When a nation is at war many things that might be said in time of peace are such a hindrance to its effort that their utterance will not be endured so long as men fight and that no Court could regard them as protected by any constitutional right.

Justice Oliver Wendell Holmes writing for the majority to uphold the Espionage Act, Schenck v. U.S., *March 3, 1919, 249 US 47.*

It has, of course, been everything but a peace *conference.* So far as the word is concerned, it is a palpable fraud upon the world. A small executive committee, first of ten men, then of five, then of four, has been parcelling out the globe in sessions so secret that their closest associates, the members of their own delegations, have not known what was going on. The very existence of this committee is the result of an arrogant, unauthorized assumption of power, for never and nowhere did the conference endow Messrs. Wilson, Orlando, Clemenceau, and Lloyd George with the authority to transact all business and come to all the decisions. The Germans need not complain if they are arbitrarily summoned to Versailles and told to take the treaty and sign it without discussion. They are only in the same category with all the various Allied delegates to the "Conference," except four. . . .

How is it possible to procure a democratic peace or a lasting one under such conditions? A democratic peace, frankly, it can never be; a lasting peace it can be only if heaven shows an unexampled favor. When the Conference assembled, eleven wars were going on in which heavy cannon were being used; at the beginning of 9 April, it was jestingly said at the Hotel Crillon (the American headquarters) that it was quite fitting that the wars had grown to fourteen, because there was thus one to each of the fourteen peace terms. But if the wars have multiplied, the fourteen peace terms. . . .

Oswald Garrison Villard, "The Truth About the Peace Conference," writing to The Nation *from Paris, vol. 108 (April 26, 1919), pp. 646–47.*

We return from the slavery of uniform which the world's madness demanded us to don to the freedom of civil garb. We stand again to look America squarely in the face and call a spade a spade. We sing: This country of ours, despite all its better souls have done and dreamed is yet a shameful land.

It *lynches. . . . It disfranchises* its own citizens. . . . It encourages ignorance. . . . It steals from us. . . . It insults us. . . .

We *return.* We *return from fighting.* We *return fighting.*

Make way for Democracy! We saved it in France, and by the Great Jehovah, we will save it in the U.S.A., or know the reason why.

W. E. B. DuBois, "Returning Soldiers," editorial in The Crisis, *vol. 18 (May 1919), pp. 13–14.*

There are more than 2,000 radical agitators in New York City who have been preaching Bolshevism and the overthrow of the United States Government, and every one of those persons is now under investigation by Federal and local authorities. That the conspirators sought the assassination of prominent men in all parts of the country, by mailing bombs to them, will be found among these agitators, is the theory. . . . These statement were made yesterday by one of the highest officials connected with Federal investigation activities in this part of the country. . . .

This same official said he was certain that several persons are concerned in the plot. Whether they are anarchists, I.W.W., or members of some other revolutionary group, he said he was not in position to say. The indexed file of alien and domestic agitators, which is in the possession of the Government, recites the activities of these trouble-makers in great detail and shows that they have been under almost continuous surveillance ever since the outbreak of war in Europe. . . .

. . . [I]t was said yesterday that more than 75 percent of these persons are citizens or subjects of foreign nations. . . .

It was said by an official of the Department of Justice that never before in the history of this country have so many anarchistic and otherwise incendiary publications. . . . been printed as since the signing of the armistice. . . . and

they are outspoken in agitating for the overthrow of American institutions and the substitution of a Government similar to that of Lenin and Trotsky in Russia. . . .

"Radicals Watched in Bomb Plot Hunt," New York Times, *May 4, 1919, p. 12.*

I warn every man here today that when the test comes, as it will come, when the clamor for Negro rights shall have come, that you Senators from the South voting for [women's suffrage] have started it here this day. . . . If it was a crime to enfranchise the male half of this race, why is it not a crime to enfranchise the other half? You have put yourselves in the category of standing for both amendments, and when the time comes, as it will, when you meet the results of this act, you cannot charge that it was a crime to pass the 15th amendment. . . . By thus adding the word "sex" to the 15th amendment you have just amended it to liberate them all, when it was perfectly competent for the legislatures of the several states to so frame their laws as to preserve our civilization without entangling legislation involving women of the black race.

Democratic Senator Ellison Smith, South Carolina, Senate debate over the women's suffrage amendment, June 3, 1919, Congressional Record, *66th Congress, 1st session, vol. 58, p. 619.*

The outrages of last night indicate nothing but the lawless attempt of an anarchistic element in the population to terrorize the country and thus stay the hand of Government. This they have utterly failed to do.

The purposes of the Department of Justice are the same today as yesterday. These attacks by bomb throwers

On September 20, 1920, anarchists set off bombs in front of J. P. Morgan's bank on Wall Street, killing over 40 people. *(Library of Congress, Prints and Photographs Division, LC-USZ62-67516)*

will only increase and extend the activities of our crime-detecting forces.

We are determined now, as heretofore, that organized crime directed against organized government in this country shall be stopped.

Statement of Attorney General Mitchell Palmer responding to bombings in eight cities, including his home, June 2, 1919, as printed in the New York Times, *June 4, p. 1.*

As heretofore publicly stated and repeated, our Corporation and subsidiaries, although they do not combat labor unions as such, decline to discuss business with them. The Corporation and subsidiaries are opposed to the "closed shop." They stand for the "open shop," which permits one to engage in any line of employment whether one does or does not belong to a labor union. This best promotes the welfare of both employees and employers. In view of the well-known attitude as above expressed, the officers of the Corporation respectfully decline to discuss with you, as representatives of a labor union, any matter relating to employees. In doing so no personal discourtesy is intended.

. . . In wage rates, living and working conditions, conservation of life and health, care and comfort in times of sickness or old age, and providing facilities for the general welfare and happiness of employees and their families, the Corporation and subsidiaries have endeavored to occupy a leading and advanced position among employers.

Letter of Elbert Gary to AFL committee organizing the steel strike, New York, August 27, 1919, available online at Chicago Metro History Education Center. URL: http://www.uic.edu/orgs/cmhec/3_steel.html.

I have already refused to remove the Police Commissioner of Boston. I did not appoint him. He can assume no position which the courts would uphold except what the people have by the authority of their law vested in him. He speaks only with their voice.

The right of the police of Boston to affiliate has always been questioned, never granted, is now prohibited. . . . Here the Policemen's Union left their duty, an action which President Wilson characterized as a crime against civilization.

Your assertion that the commissioner was wrong cannot justify the wrong of leaving the city unguarded. . . . There is no right to strike against the public safety by anybody, anywhere, any time. . . .

Calvin Coolidge, Governor of Massachusetts, "Gov. Coolidge's Reply to Samuel Gompers," Boston Globe, *September 15, 1919, p. 1.*

I spoke often to the strikers. Many of them were foreigners but they knew what I said. I told them, "We are to see whether Pennsylvania belongs to Kaiser Gary or Uncle Sam. . . . Your boys went over to Europe. They were told to clean up the Kaiser. Well, they did it. And now you and your boys are going to clean up the kaisers at home. Even if they have to do it with a leg off and an arm gone, and eyes out. . . .

I was speaking in Homestead. A group of organizers were with me in an automobile. As soon as a word was said, the speaker was immediately arrested by the steel bosses' sheriff. I rose to speak. An officer grabbed me.

"Under arrest!" he said. . . .

We were ordered to appear in the Pittsburgh court the next morning. A cranky old judge asked me if I had had a permit to speak on the streets.

"Yes, sir," said I. "I had a permit."

"Who issued it?" he growled.

"Patrick Henry; Thomas Jefferson; John Adams!" said I.

The mention of those patriots who gave us our charter of liberties made the old steel judge sore. He fined us all heavily.

Labor organizer Mother (Mary Harris) Jones, in her eighties, at the steel strike that began September 1919, Autobiography of Mother Jones, *chapter 24. URL: http://womenshistory.about.com/library/etext/mj/bl_mj24.htm.*

There is only one power to put behind the liberation of mankind, and that is the power of mankind. It is the power of the united moral forces of the world, and in the Covenant of the League of Nations the moral forces of the world are mobilized. For what purpose?

Reflect, my fellow citizens, that the membership of this great League is going to include all the great fighting nations of the world, as well as the weak ones. . . .

And what do they unite for? They enter into a solemn promise to one another that they will never use their power against one another for aggression; that they never will impair the territorial integrity of a neighbor; that they never will interfere with the political independence of a neighbor; that they will abide by the principle that great populations are entitled to determine their own destiny and that they will not interfere with that destiny; and that no matter what differences arise amongst them they will never resort to war without first having . . . either submitted the matter of controversy to arbitration, . . . or submitted it to the consideration of the council of the League of Nations, laying before that council all the documents, all the facts, agreeing that the council can publish the documents and the facts to the whole world. . . .

In other words, they consent, no matter what happens, to submit every matter of difference between them to the judgment of mankind, and just so certainly as they do that, my fellow citizens, war will be in the far background, war will be pushed out of that foreground of terror in which it has kept the world for generation after generation, and men will know that there will be a calm time of deliberate counsel.

Woodrow Wilson, last address in favor of the League of Nations, Pueblo, Colorado, September 25, 1919, available online at First World War. URL: http://www.firstworldwar.com/source/ wilsonspeech_league.htm.

. . . about four o'clock in the morning of September 20, 1919, Doctor Grayson Knocked at the door of my sleeping compartment and told me to dress quickly, that the President was seriously ill. As we walked toward the President's car, the Doctor told me in a few words of the President's trouble and said that he greatly feared it might end fatally if we should attempt to continue the trip, . . . When we arrived at the President's drawing room I found him fully dressed and seated in his chair. With great difficulty he was able to articulate. His face was pale and wan. One side of it had fallen, and his condition was indeed pitiful to behold. . . . Looking at me, with great tears running down his face, he said "My dear boy, this has never happened to me before. I felt it coming on yesterday. I do not know what to do." He then pleaded with us not to cut short the trip. Turning to both of us, he said: "Don't you see that if you cancel this trip, . . . the Treaty will be lost.". . .

Never was the President more gentle or tender than on that morning. Suffering the greatest pain, paralyzed on his left side, he was still fighting desperately for the thing that was so close to his heart—a vindication of the things for which he had so gallantly fought on the other side. Grim old warrior that he was, he was ready to fight to the death for the League of Nations.

Joseph Tumulty, the president's secretary, describes his stroke September 25, 1919, Woodrow Wilson as I Knew Him, *pp. 446–48.*

When Dr. Grayson was asked tonight if the President would be taken to some quiet retreat . . . he replied that no plans whatever had been made for the removal of the President to some other point.

The heat in Washington was very oppressive, and it affected the President somewhat for several hours this afternoon. . . . It is also learned that jazz music in a hotel roof garden within two blocks of the White House had also bothered the President several nights. This was brought to the attention of the management of the hotel, where it had not been realized that the sounds of the music were wafted as far as the President's sick room, and the hotel manager promptly ordered a cessation of the music. . . .

"President Gains Strength," New York Times, *October 6, 1919, p. 1.*

. . . Almost everything went backward, so that so an evil minded person might believe the stories that have been circulated during the series. . . . The Reds are not the better club . . . but they play ball together, fight together and hustle together, and remember that a flivver [that is, a Model T] that keeps running beats a Rolls Royce that is missing on several cylinders. The Sox were missing on several. . . .

Yesterday's game in all probability is the last that ever will be played in any world's series. If the club owners and those who have the interests of the game at heart have listened during this series they will call off the annual interleague contests. If they value the good name of the sport they will do so beyond doubt.

Yesterday's game also means the disruption of the Chicago White Sox as a ball club. There are seven men on the team who will not be there when the gong sounds next Spring and some of them will not be in either major league.

Sportswriter Hugh Fullerton hints at problems in the 1919 World Series, "Fullerton Says Seven Members of the White Sox Will Be Missing Next Spring," Chicago Herald and Examiner, *October 10, 1919, reprinted in Sullivan, ed.,* Middle Innings, *p. 90.*

1. . . . [I]n case of notice of withdrawal from the League of Nations . . . the United States shall be the sole judge as to whether all its international obligations and all its obligations under the aid Covenant have been fulfilled, and notice of withdrawal by the United States may be given by a concurrent resolution of the Congress of the United States.

2. The United States assumes no obligation to preserve the territorial integrity or political independence of any other country or to interfere in controversies between nations—whether members of the League or not—under the provisions of Article 10, or to employ the military or naval forces of the United States under any article of the Treaty for any purpose, unless in any particular case the Congress, which, under the Constitution, has the sole power to declare war or authorise the employment of the military or naval forces of the United States, shall by act or joint resolution so provide. . . .

4. The United States reserves to itself exclusively the right to decide what questions are within its domestic jurisdiction, and declares that all domestic and political questions relating wholly or in part to its internal affairs, including immigration, labour, coast-wise traffic, the tariff, commerce, the suppression of traffic of women and children and in opium and other dangerous drugs, and all other domestic questions are solely within the jurisdiction of the United States and are not under this Treaty to be submitted in any way either to arbitration or to the consid-

eration of the Council or of the Assembly of the League of Nations. . . .

Senator Henry Cabot Lodge's "reservations" to the League of Nations, November 6, 1919, Congressional Record, 66th Congress, 1st session, vol. 56, pp. 8777–78.

Persecution for the expression of opinions seems to me perfectly logical. If you have no doubt of your premises or your power and want a certain result with all your heart you naturally express your wishes in law and sweep away all opposition. . . . But when men have realized that time has upset many fighting faiths, they may come to believe even more than they believe the very foundations of their own conduct that the ultimate good desired is better reached by free trade in ideas—that the best test of truth is the power of the thought to get itself accepted in the competition of the market, and that truth is the only ground upon which their wishes safely can be carried out. That at any rate is the theory of our Constitution. It is an experiment, as all life is an experiment. Every year if not every day we have to wager our salvation upon some prophecy based upon imperfect knowledge. While that experiment is part of our system I think that we should be eternally vigilant against attempts to check the expression of opinions that we loathe and believe to be fraught with death, unless they so imminently threaten immediate interference with the lawful and pressing purposes of the law that an immediate check is required to save the country.

Justice Oliver Wendell Holmes's dissent in an espionage and sedition case, Justice Brandeis concurring, Abrams v. U.S., November 10, 1919, 250 US 616.

Why need you gentlemen across the aisle worry about a reservation here or there when we are sitting in the council and in the assembly [of the League of Nations] and bound by every obligation in morals, which the President said was supreme above that of law, to comply with the judgment which our representatives and the other representatives finally form? Shall we go there, Mr. President, to sit in judgment, and in case that judgment works for peace join with our allies, but in case it works for war withdraw our cooperation? . . .

What is the result of all this? We are in the midst of all of the affairs of Europe. We have entangled ourselves with all European concerns. We have joined in alliance with all the European nations which have thus far joined the league, and all nations which may be admitted to the league. We are sitting there dabbling in their affairs and intermeddling in their concerns. In other words, Mr. President—and this comes to the question which is fundamental with me—we have forfeited and surrendered, once and for all, the great policy of "no entangling alliances" upon which the strength of this Republic has been founded for 150 years.

Republican Senator William Borah of Idaho, an "irreconcilable" against the League of Nations, speech to the Senate, November 19, 1919, Congressional Record, 66th Congress, 1st session, vol. 56, p. 8782.

In almost every line of the reservations is implied antagonism of senators toward the President. Suspicion and mistrust of the nations associated with this government in the recent war are reflected by the reservations, sometimes poorly concealed, often clearly evinced.

The avowed purpose is to completely repudiate every obligation of this government to encourage and sustain the new and feeble states separated, by our assistance during the war, from their former sovereignties by withholding from them the moral and military power of the United States. . . .

Membership in the League of Nations is treated, in the reservations, with so little dignity and as of such slight importance as to authorize its termination by the passage of a mere concurrent resolution of Congress. This attempt to deny to the President participation in withdrawal by this government from the League and to vest that authority solely in the two houses of Congress in disregard of the plain provision of the Constitution displays a spirit of narrow opposition to the executive unworthy of the subject and unworthy of the Senate of the United States.

Democratic Senator Joseph Robinson of Arkansas, defending the League of Nations, speech to the Senate, November 19, 1919, Congressional Record, 66th Congress, 1st session, vol. 56, p. 8781.

The share-tenant system in vogue in the Mississippi Delta region, of which Phillips County, Ark., is a part, is one of the most iniquitous systems of peonage in the United States. Under President Roosevelt's Administration, the Brattons, white lawyers . . . assisted the District Attorney in convicting nearly a dozen white men of peonage in this part of Arkansas. Small wonder that the Brattons . . . have been blamed for the present disturbances, and one of them nearly lynched and imprisoned thirty-one days, without trial or charge.

As a matter of fact, the share system enables the landlords completely to control labor and wages. No itemized accounts are ever given. . . . The laborer is allowed to get certain supplies at the company store at exorbitant prices. A year or less later, after his crop has been harvested, he is given a slip telling him how much he owes for supplies, how much his crop was worth and what is the balance due. To dispute this statement is, in Arkansas custom, to dispute "white supremacy."

This is bad enough, but lately, with the high price of cotton and the great demand for labor, an additional injustice has been added. On the Fathauer and other plantations, cotton sold in the fall of 1918 and was not settled for until July, 1919; and then the statement was verbal, without items. This year the same method was attempted again. . . . The Negroes . . . objected. And they did exactly as any law-abiding American ought to have done—they went to the largest town in the county and hired lawyers.

W. E. B. DuBois describes conditions that led up to the Elaine race riot, "The Arkansas Riots," New York World, *November 28, 1919, p. 12.*

The greatest crime that has ever been taught the world and particularly the American portion of this sphere, is the theory of large families. Almost without exception large families occur only among the very poor. Generally those who have the most children are, for the benefit of humanity, those who should have the fewest.

When we are once truthful with ourselves and really love our fellow creatures and hope to better them, then we shall stop all this talk about encouraging large families. We shall without doubt not only teach birth control, but enact new laws which will prevent children being born in the world to those who shouldn't have them.

One needs only be familiar with the children's wards in hospitals and with public institutions and children's asylums, to be appalled and horrified at the sight of born misery.

Veteran journalist Nelly Bly defends birth control in her editorial/advice column for the New York Evening Journal, *December 23, 1919, pp. 1–2.*

. . . the war was not fought in France alone. Back of the firing-line, back of armies and navies, back of the great supply-depots, another struggle waged with the same intensity and with almost equal significance attaching to its victories and defeats. It was the fight for the minds of men, for the "conquest of their convictions," and the battle-line ran through every home in every country.

It was in this recognition of Public Opinion as a major force that the Great War differed most essentially from all previous conflicts. The trial of strength was not only between massed bodies of armed men, but between opposed ideals, and moral verdicts took on all the value of military decisions. Other wars went no deeper than the physical aspects, but German Kultur raised issues that had to be fought out in the hearts and minds of people as well as on the actual firing-line. . . .

The Committee on Public Information was called into existence to make this fight for the "verdict of mankind," the voice created to plead the justice of America's cause before the jury of Public Opinion. . . . In no degree was the Committee an agency of censorship, a machinery of concealment or repression. Its emphasis throughout was on the open and the positive. At no point did it seek or exercise authorities under those war laws that limited the freedom of speech and press. In all things, from first to last, without halt or change, it was a plain publicity proposition, a vast enterprise in salesmanship, the world's greatest adventure in advertising.

We did not call it propaganda, for that word, in German hands, had come to be associated with deceit and corruption.

George Creel, How We Advertised America, *1920, pp. 3–4.*

The excerpts . . . are typical of the letters which come to me by the thousands. They tell their own story, simply—sometimes ungrammatically and illiterately, but nevertheless irresistibly. It is the story of slow murder of the helpless by a society that shields itself behind ancient, inhuman moral creeds. . . . Can children carried through nine months of dread and unspeakable mental anguish and born into an atmosphere of fear and anger, to grow up uneducated and in want, be a benefit to the world? Here is what the mother says:

> I have read in the paper about you and am very interested in Birth Control. I am a mother of four living children and one dead the oldest 10 and baby 22 months old. I am very nervous and sickly after my children. I would like you to advise me what to do to prevent from having any more as I would rather die than have another. I am keeping away from my husband as much as I can, but it causes quarrels and almost separation. All my babies have had marasmus in the first year of their lives and I almost lost my baby last summer. I always worry about my children so much. My husband works in a brass foundry it is not a very good job and living is so high that we have to live as cheap as possible. I've only got 2 rooms and kitchen and I do all my work and sewing which is very hard for me.

Birth control advocate Margaret Sanger, Women and the New Race, *1920, pp. 74–75.*

No longer is the schooling of the immigrant to be an overtime task performed by teachers with only a casual training. . . . There is a distinct pedagogy in this work with adult immigrants and a very distinct methodology. The teacher of the immigrant must be acquainted with these. She must have a knowledge of the important aims in her work, namely: (1) what she is to teach; (2) how she is to teach; (3) what standard of achievement she may expect. She must know more specifically also what her aims should be in the task of teaching immigrants to talk English and how this can best be done. . . .

Finally, and of greatest importance, she must appreciate that her big task is Americanization—the making of Americans—and must understand just what that means and how it can best be brought about. All this means that the teacher must go to school to learn another lesson in her business of teaching. Colleges, normal schools, state departments of education, large city school systems, all should take it upon themselves to put the work of teacher training in this new field on an established basis. . . .

John J. Mahoney, state supervisor of Americanization for Massachusetts, Bureau of Education Bulletin no. 12, 1920.

Analysis of the wages . . . results in the following conclusions directly bearing on the causes of the strike: The annual earnings of over one-third of all productive iron and steel workers were, and had been for years, below the level set by government experts as the minimum of subsistence standard for families of five. The annual earnings of 72% of all workers were, and had been for years below the level set by government experts as the minimum of comfort level for families of five. This second standard being the lowest which scientists are willing to term an "American standard of living," it follows that nearly three-quarters of the steel workers could not earn enough for an American standard of living. The bulk of unskilled steel labor, with exceptions hereafter noted, earned less than enough for the average family's minimum subsistence. . . .

Maintenance of this non-unionism alternative entailed serious social consequences for steel communities and for the nation. The consequences were normal in the industry; they became pronounced and grave during the strike.

Maintaining the non-unionism alternative entailed, for the employers, (1) discharging workmen for unionism, (2) blacklists, (3) espionage and the hiring of "labor detective agencies' operatives," (4) strike breakers, principally negroes.

Maintaining the non-unionism alternative entailed, for communities, (1) the abrogation of the right of assembly, the suppression of free speech and the violation of personal rights (principally in Pennsylvania); (2) the use of state police, state troops and (in Indiana) of the U.S. Army; (3) such activities on the part of constituted authorities and of the press and the pulpit as to make the workers believe that these forces oppose labor. . . .

Report on the Steel Strike of 1919, published in 1920 by a commission of the Interchurch World Movement, an interdenominational Protestant organization founded after the war to pursue social betterment, pp. 85, 245.

The Socialist Committee of the Fifth Wisconsin congressional district, with a half hour of receiving the news that Victor L. Berger had been excluded from Congress a second time, re-nominated him.

"We will keep on nominating Berger until Hades freezes over if that un-American aggregation called Congress continues to exclude him," declared a statement issued by the committee.

"We want every person in this country to understand that the voters of the Fifth Wisconsin district know exactly whom they want as their representative in Congress, and we do not propose to let Gillette and his bunch of Wall Street fawners dictate to us on the subject. Berger is our congressman and the action of Congress in unseating him a second time only starts the real fight that will not end until every one of the reactionaries who voted in today's disgraceful proceedings has been retired by the ballot to the oblivion they so richly deserve."

"Vacant Seat Berger Renominated After Second Expulsion," headline story of the Minneapolis Sunday Tribune, *January 11, 1920, p. 1.*

The anxiety of that period in our responsibility when Congress, ignoring the seriousness of these vast organizations that were plotting to overthrow the Government, failed to act, has passed. The time came when it was obviously hopeless to expect the hearty co-operation of Congress in the only way to stamp out these seditious societies in their open defiance of law by various forms of propaganda.

Like a prairie-fire, the blaze of revolution was sweeping over every American institution of law and order a year ago. It was eating its way into the homes of the American workman, its sharp tongues of revolutionary heat were licking the altars of the churches, leaping into the belfry of the school bell, crawling into the sacred corners of American homes, seeking to replace marriage vows with libertine laws, burning up the foundations of society.

Robbery, not war, is the ideal of communism. This has been demonstrated in Russia, Germany, and in America. As a foe, the anarchist is fearless of his own life, for his creed is a fanaticism that admits no respect of any other creed. Obviously it is the creed of any criminal mind, which reasons always from motives impossible to clean thought. Crime is the degenerate factor in society.

Upon these two basic certainties, first that the "Reds" were criminal aliens, and secondly that the American Government must prevent crime, it was decided that there could be no nice distinctions drawn between the theoretical ideals of the radicals and their actual violations of our national laws.

Attorney General Mitchell Palmer, "The Case Against the Reds," Forum, vol. 63 (February 1920), pp. 173–74.

During the twenty-two and a half months it has been in operation the air mail has carried more than 25,000,000 letters between Chicago, Cleveland, New York and Washington, at better than twice the speed of the Congressional or the Twentieth Century Limited [high performance trains]. . . .

On the New York—San Francisco route night flying is to be attempted for the first time by postal planes. We are at present developing a gigantic lamp, throwing a white beam high in the air, to serve as a lighthouse for our ships of the air. Night flying will be undertaken only across the prairies where the country is one broad landing field. . . .

In seeking to make flying safe for its pilots and their cargoes, the Post Office Department has developed many wonderful devices of the greatest service in commercialization of aircraft. . . .

Our aviators, forced to fly in all kinds of weather, sometimes found difficulty in locating their fields when the earth was covered with fog. The Bureau of Standards at our request developed a set of sirens and a microphone that allowed the aviator to catch the sound waves above the roar of his engines miles away.

It was soon discovered, however, that flying fields not be located exactly by sound. Then there developed an amazing invention enabling an aviator to know, through a barrage of radio waves surrounding the field, just when he was above the center of the field. Reaching the neutral spot, he could spiral to the ground through clouds and fog without danger of a mishap.

Postmaster General Albert Burleson, "The Story of Our Airmail," Independent, vol. 102 (April 3, 1920), p. 8.

America's present need is not heroics, but healing; not nostrums but normalcy; not revolution, but restoration; not agitation, but adjustment; not surgery but serenity; not the dramatic, but the dispassionate; not experiment but equipoise; not submergence in internationality, but sustainment in triumphant nationality. . . .

The world called for peace, and has its precarious variety. America demands peace, formal as well as actual, and means to have it, regardless of political exigencies and campaign issues. If it must be a campaign issue, we shall have peace and discuss it afterwards, because the actuality is imperative, and the theory is only illusive. Then we may set our own house in order. We challenged the proposal that an armed autocrat should dominate the world; it ill becomes us to assume that a rhetorical autocrat shall direct all humanity. . . .

My best judgment of America's needs is to steady down, to get squarely on our feet, to make sure of the right path. Let's get out of the fevered delirium of war, with the hallucination that all the money in the world is to be made in the madness of war and the wildness of its aftermath. Let us stop to consider that tranquility at home is more precious than peace abroad, and that both our good fortune

and our eminence are dependent on the normal forward stride of all the American people.

Warren G. Harding, speech at Boston, May 14, 1920, available online at PBS Great Speeches. URL: http://www.pbs.org/greatspeeches/timeline/w harding s.html.

The Republican party stands for agreement among the nations to preserve the peace of the world. We believe that such an international association must be based upon international justice, and must provide methods which shall maintain the rule of public right by the development of law and the decision of impartial courts, and which shall secure instant and general international conference whenever peace shall be threatened by political action, so that the nations pledged to do and insist upon what is just and fair may exercise their influence and power for the prevention of war.

We believe that all this can be done without the compromise of national independence, without depriving the people of the United States in advance of the right to determine for themselves what is just and fair when the occasion arises, and without involving them as participants and not as peacemakers in a multitude of quarrels, the merits of which they are unable to judge.

League of Nations plank, Republican platform, adopted June 8–12, 1920, Porter and Johnson, eds., National Party Platforms, *p. 213.*

The Democratic Party favors the League of Nations as the surest, if not the only, practicable means of maintaining the permanent peace of the world and terminating the insufferable burden of great military and naval establishments. It was for this that America broke away from traditional isolation and spent her blood and treasure to crush a colossal scheme of conquest. . . .

We endorse the President's view of our international obligations and his firm stand against reservations designed to cut to pieces the vital provisions of the Versailles Treaty. . . .

We advocate the immediate ratification of the treaty without reservations which would impair its essential integrity; but do not oppose the acceptance of any reservations making clearer or more specific the obligations of the United States to the league associates. Only by doing this may we retrieve the reputation of this nation among the powers of the earth and recover the moral leadership which President Wilson won and which Republican politicians at Washington sacrificed.

League of Nations plank, Democratic platform, adopted June 28–July 5, 1920, Porter and Johnson, eds., National Party Platforms, *p. 231.*

The political fate of the women of the nation now rested in the hands of a minority of a single legislative chamber.

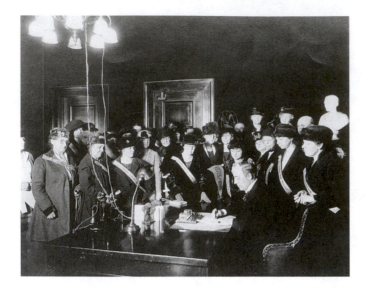

In many states that ratified the Nineteenth Amendment, giving women the right to vote, suffragists gathered to observe the signing ceremony. This photo shows Kentucky governor Edwin Morrow signing the amendment on January 6, 1920, surrounded by women wearing *Votes for Women* sashes. *(Library of Congress, Prints and Photographs Division, LC-USZ62-78691)*

hard on the alleged illegalities of ratification by the Tennessee Legislature. . . .

Carrie Chapman Catt and Nettie Rogers Shuler describe the political battle in Tennessee, the 36th and final state to ratify the suffrage amendment, August 1920, Woman Suffrage and Politics, *pp. 445–47.*

Just a slight hesitation on the player's part will let a man get to base or make a run. I did it by not putting a thing on the ball. You could have read the trade mark on it the way I lobbed it over the plate. A baby could have hit 'em. Schalk was wise the moment I started pitching. Then, in one of the games, the first I think, there was a man on first and the Reds' batter hit a slow grounder to me. I could have made a double play out of it without any trouble at all. But I was slow—slow enough to prevent the double play. It did not necessarily look crooked on my part. It is hard to tell when a game is on the square and when it is not. A player can make a crooked error that will look on the square as easy as he can make a square one. Sometimes the square ones look crooked.

Then, in the fourth game, which I also lost, on a tap to the box I deliberately threw badly to first, allowing a man to get on. At another time, I intercepted a throw from the outfield and deliberately bobbled it, allowing a run to score. All the runs scored against me were due to my own deliberate errors. In those two games, I did not try to win. . . .

Chicago White Sox star pitcher Eddie Cicotte, statement to the Grand Jury September 28, 1920, telling how he helped throw the 1919 World Series, available online at Black Sox Trial. URL: http://www.law.umkc.edu/faculty/projects/ftrials/blacksox/courtdox.html.

From day to day the House ominously postponed the date of the vote. . . . Meanwhile the male anti-suffrage lobby, from early morning of each day until the wee small hours of the next, threatened and cajoled the embattled sixty-two who had signed pledges. They were baited with whisky, tempted with offers of office, loans of money, and every other device which old hands at illicit politics could conceive or remember. . . .

Engaged in this nefarious intrigue was what old-timers recognized as the former "whisky lobby" in full force, the one-time railroad lobby which was alleged to have directed Tennessee politics for years, and a newer manufacturer's lobby. All pretense was thrown aside and all three worked openly as one man, although who paid the bills the public never knew. Every day men dropped from the poll. In some cases the actual consideration was noised about. One man who had written nine letters in which he declared that he would be on hand "to vote for woman suffrage until I am called up yonder" had fallen early. Before the end all men checked as bribable on the poll, taken before the Legislature met, fell from it.

The American Constitutional League . . . (formerly the Men's Anti-Suffrage League), formed a branch in Nashville, and its members, mainly politicians, joined in the bombardment of legislators friendly to suffrage. . . . Women antis pressed the sharp point of Negro woman suffrage into Southern traditions; the men antis bore

The campaign was extraordinarily unexciting. . . . The gods had gone, and, compared to them, those who took their places, the present presidential candidates, were hardly even half-gods, barely quarter-gods. For more than a generation, three great personalities—Wilson, Bryan, and Theodore Roosevelt—had dominated the American political scene. That all three were immense personalities everyone would concede; as to any one of them, a partisan might like or not like the kind of personality, but could hardly fail to concede quantity of it. In every presidential election for twenty-four years, since 1896, one of these had been a candidate, and sometimes two; and when any of them was not a candidate, he was active, sometimes overtowering the candidate. Now all three had passed to one kind or another of desuetude. Theodore Roosevelt lay in a hillside grave at Oyster Bay. Wilson was broken physically and politically—in the Democratic convention of 1920 his name had figured in one ballot of the forty-four, and he received the vote of two delegates out of a total of 1,094—he who less than two years before had truly bestrode the world.

Bryan, with his extraordinary vitality, . . . was still active, still had much prestige, still exercised some power. At the Democratic convention of 1920 he had been the most impressive figure, had made by far the most stirring speech, a plea for a "dry" plank in the platform. The convention listened respectfully, paid him complete deference—but did not adopt his plank. . . .

Journalist Mark Sullivan describes the presidential campaign, fall 1920, Our Times, *pp. 608–09.*

The population of Jacksonville at present is estimated at 90,000—Negroes numbering between 45,000 and 50,000. The enfranchisement of women caused this majority held by Negro voters to be of grave significance to the Democratic Party of Florida. Coupled with this was the fear which is in general throughout the South that the colored woman voter is more difficult "to handle" than colored men have been. The Jacksonville Metropolis of September 16th carried a scare head, "DEMOCRACY IN DUVAL COUNTY ENDANGERED BY VERY LARGE REGISTRATION OF NEGRO WOMEN". . . .

On Election Day each polling booth was provided by the election officials with four entrances—one each for white women, white men, colored women and colored men. Two each were to be taken simultaneously from the head of each line, according to the published instructions. This was not done. No white voter was delayed or hindered in voting while every possible handicap was put in the way of colored voters. More than 4,000 colored men and women stood in line from 8:00 A.M. to 5:40 P.M., the closing hour, determined to vote if possible. Colored women served sandwiches and coffee to the lines at all of the booths. Later the names, addresses and registration certificate numbers were taken of the more than 4,000 refused voters. . . .

NAACP official Walter White describes the election November 5, 1920, "Election by Terror in Florida," New Republic, *vol. 25 (January 12, 1921), p. 195.*

APPENDIX A
Documents

1. The Monroe Doctrine: excerpts from President James Monroe's seventh annual message to Congress, December 2, 1823
2. The Sherman Anti-Trust Act, July 2, 1890
3. National People's Party (Populist) platform, July 4, 1892
4. Booker T. Washington: the Atlanta Exposition address, September 6, 1895
5. Excerpts from *Plessy v. Ferguson,* May 18, 1896
6. Platform of the American Anti-Imperialist League, October 18, 1899
7. Excerpts from President Theodore Roosevelt's first annual message to Congress, December 3, 1901
8. Muckraking: Lincoln Steffens, "Tweed Days in St. Louis," 1902, 1904
9. Muckraking: excerpt from Ida M. Tarbell, "The Rise of the Standard Oil Company," 1902, 1904
10. Excerpt from W. E. B. DuBois, *The Souls of Black Folk,* Chapter 3, "Of Mr. Booker T. Washington and Others," 1903
11. Child labor exposed: excerpt from Francis H. Nichols, "Children of the Coal Shadow," February 1903
12. "Muscle Trust": excerpt from David M. Parry, president's address to the National Association of Manufacturers, April 1903
13. Excerpt from Ernest Poole, "Waifs of the Street," May 1903
14. Excerpt from President Theodore Roosevelt's fourth annual message to Congress, December 6, 1904
15. Excerpt from William L. Riordon, *Plunkitt of Tammany Hall,* Chapter 23, "Strenuous Life of the Tammany District Leader," 1905
16. Excerpt from Charles Edward Russell, *The Greatest Trust in the World,* 1905
17. Excerpt from Upton Sinclair, *The Jungle,* 1906
18. Excerpt from John Spargo, *The Bitter Cry of the Children,* 1906
19. Excerpt from the Pure Food and Drug Act, June 30, 1906
20. Excerpt from Louis D. Brandeis's brief in support of the state of Oregon in *Muller v. Oregon,* 1907
21. Excerpt from Ray Stannard Baker, *Following the Color Line,* 1908
22. Income tax—the Sixteenth Amendment, passed by Congress July 2, 1909, ratified February 3, 1913
23. Direct election of senators—the Seventeenth Amendment, passed by Congress May 13, 1912, ratified April 8, 1913
24. Declaration of principles of the Progressive Party, platform adopted August 7, 1912
25. "Peace Without Victory": President Woodrow Wilson's address to the Senate, January 22, 1917
26. Prohibition—the Eighteenth Amendment, passed by Congress December 18, 1917, ratified January 16, 1919
27. Women's suffrage—the Nineteenth Amendment, passed by Congress June 4, 1919, ratified August 18, 1920

1. The Monroe Doctrine: Excerpts from President James Monroe's Seventh Annual Message to Congress, December 2, 1823

. . . the occasion has been judged proper for asserting, as a principle in which the rights and interests of the United States are involved, that the American continents, by the free and independent condition which they have assumed and maintain, are henceforth not to be considered as subjects for future colonization by any European powers. . . .

. . . Of events in that quarter of the globe [Europe], with which we have so much intercourse and from which we derive our origin, we have always been anxious and interested spectators. . . . In the wars of the European powers in matters relating to themselves we have never taken any part, nor does it comport with our policy to do so. It is only when our rights are invaded or seriously menaced that we resent injuries or make preparation for our defense. With the movements in this hemisphere we are of necessity more immediately connected, and by causes which must be obvious to all enlightened and impartial observers. The political system of the allied powers is essentially different in this respect from that of America. This difference proceeds from that which exists in their respective Governments; and to the defense of our own which has been achieved by the loss of so much blood and treasure, and matured by the wisdom of their most enlightened citizens and under which we have enjoyed unexampled felicity, this whole nation is devoted. We owe it, therefore, to candor and to the amicable relations existing between the United States and those powers to declare that we should consider any attempt on their part to extend their system to any portion of this hemisphere as dangerous to our peace and safety. With the existing colonies or dependencies of any European power we have not interfered and shall not interfere. But with the Governments who have declared their independence and maintain it, and whose independence we have, on great consideration and on just principles, acknowledged, we could not view any interposition for the purpose of oppressing them, or controlling in any other manner their destiny, by any European power in any other light than as the manifestation of an unfriendly disposition toward the United States.

Source: Messages and Papers of the Presidents, 1789–1907, edited by J. Richardson, vol. 2 (New York: Bureau of National Literature and Art, 1908, ca. 1897), pp. 207 ff.

2. The Sherman Anti-Trust Act, July 2, 1890

An ACT to protect trade and commerce against unlawful restraints and monopolies. . . . Be it enacted

SEC. 1. Every contract, combination in the form of trust or otherwise, or conspiracy, in restraint of trade or commerce among the several States, or with foreign nations, is hereby declared to be illegal. Every person who shall make any such contract or engage in any such combination or conspiracy, shall be deemed guilty of a misdemeanor, and, on conviction thereof, shall be punished by fine not exceeding five thousand dollars, or by imprisonment not exceeding one year, or by both said punishments, in the discretion of the court.

SEC. 2. Every person who shall monopolize, or attempt to monopolize, or combine or conspire with any other person or persons? to monopolize any part of the trade or commerce among the several States, or with foreign nations, shall be deemed guilty of a misdemeanor, and, on conviction thereof, shall be punished by line not exceeding five thousand dollars, or by imprisonment not exceeding one year, or by both said punishments, in the discretion of the court.

SEC. 3. Every contract, combination in form of trust or otherwise, or conspiracy, in restraint of trade or commerce in any Territory of the United States or of the District of Columbia, or in restraint of trade or commerce between any such Territory and another, or between any such Territory or Territories and any State or States or the District of Columbia, or with foreign nations, or between the District of Columbia and any State or States or foreign nations, is hereby declared illegal. Every person who shall make any such contract or engage in any such combination or conspiracy, shall be deemed guilty of a misdemeanor, and, on conviction thereof, shall be punished by fine not exceeding five thousand dollars, or by imprisonment not exceeding one year, or by both said punishments, in the discretion of the court.

SEC. 4. The several circuit courts of the United States are hereby invested with jurisdiction to prevent and restrain violations of this act; and it shall be the duty of the several district attorneys of the United States, in their respective districts, under the direction of the Attorney-General, to institute proceedings in equity to prevent and restrain such violations. Such proceedings may be by way of petition setting forth the case and praying that such violation shall be enjoined or otherwise prohibited. When the parties complained of shall have been duly notified of such petition the courts shall proceed, as soon as may be, to the hearing and determination of the case; and pending such petitions and before final decrees, the court may at any time make such temporary restraining order or prohibition as shall be deemed just in the premises. . . .

SEC. 7. Any person who shall be injured in his business or property by any other person or corporation by reason of anything forbidden or declared to be unlawful by this act, may sue therefor in any circuit court of the United States in the district in which the defendant resides or is found, without respect to the amount in controversy, and shall recover three fold the damages by him sustained, and the costs of suit, including a reasonable attorney's fee.

SEC. 8. That the word "person," or "persons," wherever used in this act shall be deemed to include corporations and associations existing under or authorized by the laws of either the United States, the laws of any of the Territories, the laws of any State, or the laws of any foreign country.
Source: U.S. Statutes at Large, 51st Congress, vol. 26, p. 209.

3. NATIONAL PEOPLE'S PARTY (POPULIST) PLATFORM, JULY 4, 1892

Assembled upon the 116th anniversary of the Declaration of Independence, the People's Party of America, in their first national convention, invoking upon their action the blessing of Almighty God, puts forth in the name and on behalf of the people of this country, the following preamble and declaration of principles:—

Preamble

The conditions which surround us best justify our co-operation; we meet in the midst of a nation brought to the verge of moral, political, and material ruin. Corruption dominates the ballot-box, the Legislatures, the Congress, and touches even the ermine of the bench. The people are demoralized; most of the States have been compelled to isolate the voters at the polling places to prevent universal intimidation and bribery. The newspapers are largely subsidized or muzzled, public opinion silenced, business prostrated, homes covered with mortgages, labor impoverished, and the land concentrating in the hands of the capitalists. The urban workmen are denied the right to organize for self-protection, imported pauperized labor beats down their wages, a hireling standing army, unrecognized by our laws, is established to shoot them down, and they are rapidly degenerating into European conditions. The fruits of the toil of millions are boldly stolen to build up the fortunes for a few, unprecedented in the history of mankind; and the possessors of these, in turn, despise the Republic and endanger liberty. From the same prolific womb of governmental injustice we breed the two great classes—tramps and millionaires.

The national power to create money is appropriated to enrich bondholders; a vast public debt, payable in legal tender currency, has been funded into gold-bearing bonds, thereby adding millions to the burdens of the people. Silver, which has been accepted as coin since the dawn of history, has been demonetized to add to the purchasing power of gold by decreasing the value of all forms of property as well as human labor, and the supply of currency is purposely abridged to fatten usurers, bankrupt enterprise, and enslave industry. A vast conspiracy against mankind has been organized on two continents, and it is rapidly taking possession of the world. If not met and overthrown at once it forebodes terrible social convulsions, the destruction of civilization, or the establishment of an absolute despotism.

We have witnessed for more than a quarter of a century the struggles of the two great political parties for power and plunder, while grievous wrongs have been inflicted upon the suffering people. We charge that the controlling influences dominating both these parties have permitted the existing dreadful conditions to develop without serious effort to prevent or restrain them. Neither do they now promise us any substantial reform. They have agreed together to ignore in the coming campaign every issue but one. They propose to drown the outcries of a plundered people with the uproar of a sham battle over the tariff. so that capitalist, corporations, national banks, rings, trust, watered stock, the demonetization of silver, and the oppressions of the usurers may all be lost sight of. They propose to sacrifice our homes, lives, and children on the altar of mammon; to destroy the multitude in order to secure corruption funds from the millionaires.

Assembled on the anniversary of the birthday of the nation, and filled with the spirit of the grand general and chief who established our independence, we seek to restore the government of the Republic to the hands of "the plain people," with which class it originated. We assert our purposes to be identical with the purposes of the National Constitution, "to form a more perfect union and establish justice, insure domestic tranquility, provide for the common defense, promote the general welfare, and secure the blessings of liberty for ourselves and our posterity." We declare that this Republic can only endure as a free government while built upon the love of the whole people for each other and for the nation; that it cannot be pinned together by bayonets; that the civil war is over, and that every passion and resentment which grew out of it must die with it, and that we must be in fact, as we are in name, one united brotherhood of free men.

Our country finds itself confronted by conditions for which there is no precedent in the history of the world; our annual agricultural productions amount to billions of dollars in value, which must, within a few weeks or months, be exchanged for billions of dollars of commodities consumed in their production; the existing currency supply is wholly inadequate to make this exchange; the results are falling prices, the formation of combines and rings, the impoverishment of the producing class. We pledge ourselves, if given power, we will labor to correct these evils by wise and reasonable legislation, in accordance with the terms of our platform. We believe that the power of government—in other words, of the people—should be expanded (as in the case of the postal service) as rapidly and as far as the good sense of an intelligent people and the teaching of experience shall justify, to the end that oppression, injustice, and poverty shall eventually cease in the land.

While our sympathies as a party of reform are naturally upon the side of every proposition which will tend to make men intelligent, virtuous, and temperate, we nevertheless regard these questions—important as they are—as secondary to the great issues now pressing for solution? and upon which not only our individual prosperity but the very existence of free institutions depend; and we ask all men to first help us to determine whether we are to have a republic to administer before we differ as to the conditions upon which it is to be administered, believing that the forces of reform this day organized will never cease to move forward until every wrong is remedied, and equal rights and equal privileges securely established for all the men and women of this country.

Platform

We declare, therefore—

First—That the union of the labor forces of the United States this day consummated shall be permanent and perpetual; may its spirit enter into all hearts for the salvation of the Republic and the uplifting of mankind!

Second—Wealth belongs to him who creates it, and every dollar taken from industry without an equivalent is robbery. "If any will not work, neither shall he eat." The interests of rural and civic labor are the same; their enemies are identical.

Third—We believe that the time has come when the railroad corporations will either own the people or the people must own the railroads; and, should the government enter upon the world of owning and managing all railroads, we should favor an amendment to the Constitution by which all person engaged in the government service shall be placed under a civil-service regulation of the most rigid character, so as to prevent the increase of the power of the national administration by the use of such additional government employees.

FINANCE.—We demand a national currency, safe, sound, and flexible, issued by the general government only, a full legal tender for all debts, public and private, and that without the use of banking corporations, a just, equitable, and efficient means of distribution direct to the people, a tax not to exceed two per cent per annum, to be provided as set forth in the sub-treasury plan of the Farmers' Alliance, or a better system; also by payments in discharge of its obligations for public improvements.

1. We demand free and unlimited coinage of silver and gold at the present legal ratio of 16 to 1.

2. We demand that the amount of circulating medium be speedily increased to not less than $50 per capita.

3. We demand a graduated income tax.

4. We believe that the money of the country should be kept as much as possible in the hands of the people, and hence we demand that all State and national revenues shall be limited to the necessary expenses of the government, economically and honestly administered.

5. We demand that postal savings banks be established by the government for the safe deposit of the earnings of the people and to facilitate exchange.

TRANSPORTATION.—Transportation being a means of exchange and a public necessity. the government should own and operate the railroads in the interest of the people. The telegraph, and telephone, like the post-office system, being a necessity for the transmission of news, should be owned and operated by the government in the interest of the people.

LAND.—The land, including all the natural sources of wealth, is the heritage of the people, and should not be monopolized for speculative purposes, and alien ownership of land should be prohibited. All land now held by railroads and other corporations in excess of their actual needs, and all lands now owned by aliens should be reclaimed by the government and held for actual settlers only.

Source: Edward McPherson, ed., *A Handbook of Politics for 1892* (Washington: J. J. Chapman, 1892), 269ff.

4. BOOKER T. WASHINGTON: THE ATLANTA EXPOSITION ADDRESS, SEPTEMBER 6, 1895

One-third of the population of the South is of the Negro race. No enterprise seeking the material, civil, or moral welfare of this section can disregard this element of our population and reach the highest success....

Not only this, but the opportunity here afforded will awaken among us a new era of industrial progress. Ignorant and inexperienced, it is not strange that in the first years of our new life we began at the top instead of at the bottom; that a seat in Congress or the state legislature was more sought than real estate or industrial skill; that the political convention of stump speaking had more attraction than starting a dairy farm or truck garden.

A ship lost at sea for many days suddenly sighted a friendly vessel. From the mast of the unfortunate vessel was seen a signal, "Water, water; we die of thirst!" The answer from the friendly vessel at once came back, "Cast down your bucket where you are." A second time the signal, "Water, water; send us water!" ran up from the distressed vessel, and was answered, "Cast down your bucket where you are." And a third and fourth signal for water was answered, "Cast down your bucket where you are." The captain of the distressed vessel, at last heeding the injunction, cast down his bucket, and it came up full of fresh, sparkling water from the mouth of the Amazon River. To those of my race who depend on bettering their condition in a foreign land or who underestimate the importance of cultivating friendly relations with the Southern white man who is their next-door neighbour, I would say: "Cast down your bucket where you are"—cast it down in making friends in every manly way of the people of all races by whom we are surrounded.

Cast it down in agriculture, mechanics, in commerce, in domestic service, and in the professions. And in this connection it is well to bear in mind that whatever other sins the South may he called to bear, when it comes to business, pure and simple, it is in the South that the Negro is given a man's chance in the commercial world, and in nothing is this Exposition more eloquent than in emphasizing this chance. Our greatest danger is that in the great leap from slavery to freedom we may overlook the fact that the masses of us are to live by the productions of our hands, and fail to keep in mind that we shall prosper in proportion as we learn to dignify and glorify common labour and put brains and skill into the common occupations of life; shall prosper in proportion as we learn to draw the line between the superficial and the substantial, the ornamental gewgaws of life and the useful. No race can prosper till it learns that there is as much dignity in tilling a field as in writing a poem. It is at the bottom of life we must begin, and not at the top. Nor should we permit our grievances to overshadow our opportunities.

To those of the white race who look to the incoming of those of foreign birth and strange tongue and habits for the prosperity of the South, were I permitted I would repeat what I say to my own race, "Cast down your bucket where you are." Cast it down among the eight millions of Negroes whose habits you know, whose fidelity and love you have tested in days when to have proved treacherous meant the ruin of your firesides. Cast down your bucket among these people who have, without strikes and labour wars, tilled your fields, cleared your forests, builded your railroads and cities, and brought forth treasures from the bowels of the earth, and helped make possible this magnificent representation of the progress of the South. Casting down your bucket among my people, helping, and encouraging them as you are doing on these grounds, and to education of head, hand, and heart, you will find that they will buy your surplus land, make blossom the waste places in your fields, and run your factories. While doing this, you can be sure in the future, as in the past, that you and your families will be surrounded by the most patient, faithful, law-abiding, and unresentful people that the world has seen. As we have proved our loyalty to you in the past, nursing your children, watching by the sick-bed of your mothers and fathers, and often following them with tear-dimmed eyes to their graves, so in the future, in our humble way, we shall stand by you with a devotion that no foreigner can approach, ready to lay down our lives, if need

be, in defence of yours, interlacing our industrial, commercial, civil, and religious life with yours in a way that shall make the interests of both races one. In all things that are purely social we can be as separate as the fingers, yet one as the hand in all things essential to mutual progress.

There is no escape through law of man or God from the inevitable:—

The laws of changeless justice bind
Oppressor with oppressed;
And close as sin and suffering joined
We march to fate abreast.

Nearly sixteen millions of hands will aid you in pulling the load upward, or they will pull against you the load downward. We shall constitute one-third and more of the ignorance and crime of the South, or one-third its intelligence and progress; we shall contribute one-third to the business and industrial prosperity of the South, or we shall prove a veritable body of death stagnating, depressing, retarding every effort to advance the body politic.

Gentlemen of the Exposition, as we present to you our humble effort at an exhibition of our progress, you must not expect overmuch. Starting thirty years ago with ownership here and there in a few quilts and pumpkins and chickens (gathered from miscellaneous sources), remember the path that has led from these to the inventions and production of agricultural implements, buggies, steam-engines, newspapers, books, statuary, carving, paintings, the management of drug-stores and banks, has not been trodden without contact with thorns and thistles. While we take pride in what we exhibit as a result of our independent efforts, we do not for a moment forget that our part in this exhibition would fall far short of your expectations but for the constant help that has come to our educational life, not only from the Southern states, but especially from Northern philanthropists, who have made their gifts a constant stream of blessing and encouragement.

The wisest among my race understand that the agitation of questions of social equality is the extremest folly, and that progress in the enjoyment of all the privileges that will come to us must be the result of severe and constant struggle rather than of artificial forcing. No race that has anything to contribute to the markets of the world is long in any degree ostracized. It is important and right that all privileges of the law be ours, but it is vastly more important that we be prepared for the exercises of these privileges. The opportunity to earn a dollar in a factory just now is worth infinitely more than the opportunity to spend a dollar in an opera-house.

. . . I pledge that in your effort to work out the great and intricate problem which God has laid at the doors of the South, you shall have at all times the patient, sympathetic help of my race; only let this be constantly in mind, that . . . far above and beyond material benefits will be that higher good, that, let us pray God, will come, in a blotting out of sectional differences and racial animosities and suspicions, in a determination to administer absolute justice, in a willing obedience among all classes to the mandates of law. This, this, coupled with our material prosperity, will bring into our beloved South a new heaven and a new earth.

Source: Booker T. Washington, *Up from Slavery: An Autobiography* (New York: Doubleday, Page, 1901) pp. 218–225.

5. Excerpts from *Plessy v. Ferguson*, May 18, 1896

. . . Mr. Justice BROWN . . . delivered the opinion of the court.

This case turns upon the constitutionality of an act of the general assembly of the state of Louisiana, passed in 1890, providing for separate railway carriages for the white and colored races. . . .

The constitutionality of this act is attacked upon the ground that it conflicts both with the thirteenth amendment of the constitution, abolishing slavery, and the fourteenth amendment, which prohibits certain restrictive legislation on the part of the states.

1. That it does not conflict with the thirteenth amendment, which abolished slavery and involuntary servitude, except as punishment for crime, is too clear for argument. . . .

A statute which implies merely a legal distinction between the white and colored races—a distinction which is founded in the color of the two races, and which must always exist so long as white men are distinguished from the other race by color—has no tendency to destroy the legal equality of the two races, or re-establish a state of involuntary servitude. . . .

2. By the fourteenth amendment, all persons born or naturalized in the United States, and subject to the jurisdiction thereof, are made citizens of the United States and of the state wherein they reside; and the states are forbidden from making or enforcing any law which shall abridge the privileges or immunities of citizens of the United States, or shall deprive any person of life, liberty, or property without due process of law, or deny to any person within their jurisdiction the equal protection of the laws.

. . . The object of the amendment was undoubtedly to enforce the absolute equality of the two races before the law, but, in the nature of things, it could not have been intended to abolish distinctions based upon color, or to enforce social, as distinguished from political, equality, or a commingling of the two races upon terms unsatisfactory to either. Laws permitting, and even requiring, their separation, in places where they are liable to be brought into contact, do not necessarily imply the inferiority of either race to the other, and have been generally, if not universally, recognized as within the competency of the state legislatures in the exercise of their police power. The most common instance of this is connected with the establishment of separate schools for white and colored children, which have been held to be a valid exercise of the legislative power even by courts of states where the political rights of the colored race have been longest and most earnestly enforced. . . .

The distinction between laws interfering with the political equality of the negro and those requiring the separation of the two races in schools, theaters, and railway carriages has been frequently drawn by this court. Thus in Strauder v. West Virginia. 100 U.S. 303, it was held that a law of West Virginia limiting to white male persons 21 years of age, and citizens of the state, the right to sit upon juries, was a discrimination which implied a legal inferiority in civil society, which lessened the security of the right of the colored race, and was a step towards reducing them to a condition of servility. Indeed, the right of a colored man that, in the selection of jurors to pass upon his life, liberty, and property, there shall be no exclusion of his race, and no discrimination against them because of color, has been asserted in a number of cases. . . .

It is claimed by the plaintiff in error that, in a mixed community, the reputation of belonging to the dominant race, in this instance the white race, is "property," in the same sense that a right of action or of inheritance is property. Conceding this to be so, for the purposes of this case, we are unable to see how this statute deprives him of, or in any way affects his right to, such property. If he be a white man, and assigned to a colored coach, he may have his action for damages against the company for being deprived of his so-called "property." Upon the other hand, if he be a colored man, and be so assigned, he has been deprived of no property, since he is not lawfully entitled to the reputation of being a white man.

In this connection, it is also suggested by the learned counsel for the plaintiff in error that the same argument that will justify the state legislature in requiring railways to provide separate accommodations for the two races will also authorize them to require separate cars to be provided for people whose hair is of a certain color, or who are aliens, or who belong to certain nationalities, or to enact laws requiring colored people to walk upon one side of the street, and white people upon the other, or requiring white men's houses to be painted white, and colored men's black or their vehicles or business signs to be of different colors, upon the theory that one side of the street is as good as the other, or that a house or vehicle of one color is as good as one of another color. The reply to all this is that every exercise of the police power must be reasonable, and extend only to such laws as are enacted in good faith for the promotion of the public good, and not for the annoyance or oppression of a particular class. . . .

So far, then, as a conflict with the fourteenth amendment is concerned, the case reduces itself to the question whether the statute of Louisiana is a reasonable regulation, and with respect to this there must necessarily be a large discretion on the part of the legislature. In determining the question of reasonableness, it is at liberty to act with reference to the established usages, customs, and traditions of the people, and with a view to the promotion of their comfort, and the preservation of the public peace and good order. Gauged by this standard, we cannot say that a law which authorizes or even requires the separation of the two races in public conveyances is unreasonable, or more obnoxious to the fourteenth amendment than the acts of congress requiring separate schools for colored children in the District of Columbia, the constitutionality of which does not seem to have been questioned, or the corresponding acts of state legislatures.

We consider the underlying fallacy of the plaintiff's argument to consist in the assumption that the enforced separation of the two races stamps the colored race with a badge of inferiority. If this be so, it is not by reason of anything found in the act, but solely because the colored race chooses to put that construction upon it. The argument necessarily assumes that if, as has been more than once the case, and is not unlikely to be so again, the colored race should become the dominant power in the state legislature, and should enact a law in precisely similar terms, it would thereby relegate the white race to an inferior position. We imagine that the white race, at least, would not acquiesce in this assumption. The argument also assumes that social prejudices may be overcome by legislation, and that equal rights cannot be secured to the negro except by an enforced commingling of the two races. We cannot accept this proposition. If the two races are to meet upon terms of social equality, it must be the result of natural affinities, a mutual appreciation of each other's merits, and a voluntary consent of individuals. . . . Legislation is powerless to eradicate racial instincts, or to abolish distinctions based upon physical differences, and the attempt to do so can only result in accentuating the difficulties of the present situation. If the civil and political rights of both races be equal, one cannot be inferior to the other civilly or politically. If one race be inferior to the other socially, the constitution of the United States cannot put them upon the same plane. . . .

The judgment of the court below is therefore affirmed.

Mr. Justice BREWER did not hear the argument or participate in the decision of this case.
Mr. Justice HARLAN dissenting.

. . . In respect of civil rights, common to all citizens, the constitution of the United States does not, I think, permit any public authority to know the race of those entitled to be protected in the enjoyment of such rights. Every true man has pride of race, and under appropriate circumstances, when the rights of others, his equals before the law, are not to be affected, it is his privilege to express such pride and to take such action based upon it as to him seems proper. But I deny that any legislative body or judicial tribunal may have regard to the race of citizens when the civil rights of those citizens are involved. Indeed, such legislation as that here in question is inconsistent not only with that equality of rights which pertains to citizenship, national and state, but with the personal liberty enjoyed by every one within the United States.

The thirteenth amendment does not permit the withholding or the deprivation of any right necessarily inhering in freedom. It not only struck down the institution of slavery as previously existing in the United States, but it prevents the imposition of any burdens or disabilities that constitute badges of slavery or servitude. It decreed universal civil freedom in this country. This court has so adjudged. But, that amendment having been found inadequate to the protection of the rights of those who had been in slavery, it was followed by the fourteenth amendment, which added greatly to the dignity and glory of American citizenship, and to the security of personal liberty, by declaring that "all persons born or naturalized in the United States, and subject to the jurisdiction thereof, are citizens of the United States and of the state wherein they reside," and that "no state shall make or enforce any law which shall abridge the privileges or immunities of citizens of the United States; nor shall any state deprive any person of life, liberty or property without due process of law, nor deny to any person within its jurisdiction the equal protection of the laws." These two amendments, if enforced according to their true intent and meaning, will protect all the civil rights that pertain to freedom and citizenship. Finally, and to the end that no citizen should be denied, on account of his race, the privilege of participating in the political control of his country, it was declared by the fifteenth amendment that "the right of citizens of the United States to vote shall not be denied or abridged by the United States or by any state on account of race, color or previous condition of servitude."

These notable additions to the fundamental law were welcomed by the friends of liberty throughout the world. They removed the race line from our governmental systems. . . .

It was said in argument that the statute of Louisiana does not discriminate against either race, but prescribes a rule applicable alike to white and colored citizens. But this argument does not meet the difficulty. Every one knows that the statute in question had its origin in the purpose, not so much to exclude white persons from railroad cars occupied by blacks, as to exclude colored people from coaches occupied by or assigned to white persons. Railroad corporations of Louisiana did not make discrimination among whites in the matter of accommodation for travelers. The thing to accomplish was, under the guise of giving equal accommodation for whites and blacks, to compel the latter to keep to themselves while traveling in railroad passenger coaches. No one would be so wanting in candor as to assert the contrary. The fundamental objection, therefore, to the statute, is that it interferes with the personal freedom of citizens. "Personal liberty," it has been well said, "consists in the power of locomotion, of changing situation, or removing one's person to whatsoever places one's own inclination may direct, without imprisonment or restraint, unless by due course of law." If a white man and a black man choose to occupy the same public conveyance on a public highway, it is their right to do so; and no government, proceeding alone on grounds of race, can prevent it without infringing the personal liberty of each.

It is one thing for railroad carriers to furnish, or to be required by law to furnish, equal accommodations for all whom they are under a legal duty to carry. It is quite another thing for government to forbid citizens of the white and black races from traveling in the same public conveyance, and to punish officers of railroad companies for permitting persons of the two races to occupy the same passenger coach. If a state can prescribe, as a rule of civil conduct, that whites and blacks shall not travel as passengers in the same railroad coach, why may it not so regulate the use of the streets of its cities and towns as to compel white citizens to keep on one side of a street, and black citizens to keep on the other? Why may it not, upon like grounds, punish whites and blacks who ride together in street cars or in open vehicles on a public road or street? Why may it not require sheriffs to assign whites to one side of a court room, and blacks to the other? And why may it not also prohibit the commingling of the two races in the galleries of legislative halls or in public assemblages convened for the consideration of the political questions of the day? Further, if this statute of Louisiana is consistent with the personal liberty of citizens, why may not the state require the separation in railroad coaches of native and naturalized citizens of the United States, or of Protestants and Roman Catholics? . . .

The white race deems itself to be the dominant race in this country. And so it is, in prestige in achievements, in education, in wealth, and in power. So, I doubt not, it will continue to be for all time, if it remains true to its great heritage, and holds fast to the principles of constitutional liberty. But in view of the constitution, in the eye of the law, there is in this country no superior, dominant, ruling class of citizens. There is no caste here. Our constitution is color-blind, and neither knows nor tolerates classes among citizens. In respect of civil rights, all citizens are equal before the law. The humblest is the peer of the most powerful. The law regards man as man, and takes no account of his surroundings or of his color when his civil rights as guarantied by the supreme law of the land are involved. It is therefore to be regretted that this high tribunal, the final expositor of the fundamental law of the land, has reached the conclusion that it is competent for a state to regulate the enjoyment by citizens of their civil rights solely upon the basis of race. . . .

. . . It is scarcely just to say that a colored citizen should not object to occupying a public coach assigned to his own race. He does not object, nor, perhaps, would he object to separate coaches for his race if his rights under the law were recognized. But he does object, and he ought never to cease objecting, that citizens of the white and black races can be adjudged criminals because they sit, or claim the right to sit, in the same public coach on a public highway. The arbitrary separation of citizens, on the basis of race, while they are on a public highway, is a badge of servitude wholly inconsistent with the civil freedom and the equality before the law established by the constitution. It cannot be justified upon any legal grounds.

If evils will result from the commingling of the two races upon public highways established for the benefit of all, they will be infinitely less than those that will surely come from state legislation regulating the enjoyment of civil rights upon the basis of race. We boast of the freedom enjoyed by our people above all other peoples. But it is difficult to reconcile that boast with a state of the law which, practically, puts the brand of servitude and degradation upon a large class of our fellow citizens,—our equals before the law. The thin disguise of "equal" accommodations for passengers in railroad coaches will not mislead any one, nor atone for the wrong this day done. . . .

I am of opinion that the state of Louisiana is inconsistent with the personal liberty of citizens, white and black, in that state, and hostile to both the spirit and letter of the constitution of the United States. If laws of like character should be enacted in the several states of the Union, the effect would be in the highest degree mischievous. Slavery, as an institution tolerated by law, would, it is true, have disappeared from our country; but there would remain a power in the states, by sinister legislation, to interfere with the full enjoyment of the blessings of freedom, to regulate civil rights, common to all citizens, upon the basis of race, and to place in a condition of legal inferiority a large body of American citizens, now constituting a part of the political community, called the "People of the United States," for whom, and by whom through representatives, our government is administered. Such a system is inconsistent with the guaranty given by the constitution to each state of a republican form of government . . .

For the reason stated, I am constrained to withhold my assent from the opinion and judgment of the majority.
Source: 163 U.S. 537

6. PLATFORM OF THE AMERICAN ANTI-IMPERIALIST LEAGUE, OCTOBER 18, 1899

We hold that the policy known as imperialism is hostile to liberty and tends toward militarism, an evil from which it has been our glory to be free. We regret that it has become necessary in the land of Washington and Lincoln to reaffirm that all men, of whatever race or color, are entitled to life, liberty, and the pursuit of happiness. We maintain that governments derive their just powers from the consent of the governed. We insist that the subjugation of any people is "criminal aggression" and open disloyalty to the distinctive principles of our government.

We earnestly condemn the policy of the present national administration in the Philippines. . . . We deplore the sacrifice of our soldiers and sailors, whose bravery deserves admiration even in an unjust war. We denounce the slaughter of the Filipinos as a needless horror. We protest against the extension of American sovereignty by Spanish methods.

We demand the immediate cessation of the war against liberty. . . .

The United States have always protested against the doctrine of international law which permits the subjugation of the weak by the strong. A self-governing state cannot accept sovereignty over an unwilling people. The United States cannot act upon the ancient heresy that might makes right.

Imperialists assume that with the destruction of self-government in the Philippines by American hands, all opposition here will cease. This is a grievous error. Much as we abhor the war of "criminal aggression" in the Philippines, greatly as we regret that the blood of the Filipinos is on American hands, we more deeply resent the betrayal of American institutions at home. The real firing line is not in the suburbs of Manila. The foe is of our own household. The attempt of 1861 was to divide the country. That of 1899 is to destroy its fundamental principles and noblest ideals.

Whether the ruthless slaughter of the Filipinos shall end next month or next year is but an incident in a contest that must go on until the Declaration of Independence and the Constitution of the United States are rescued from the hands of their betrayers. Those who dispute about standards of value while the foundation of the republic is undermined will be listened to as little as those who would

wrangle about the small economies of the household while the house is on fire. The training of a great people for a century, the aspiration for liberty of a vast immigration are forces that will hurl aside those who in the delirium of conquest seek to destroy the character of our institutions.

We deny that the obligation of all citizens to support their government in times of grave national peril applies to the present situation. If an administration may with impunity ignore the issues upon which it was chosen, deliberately create a condition of war anywhere on the face of the globe, debauch the civil service for spoils to promote the adventure, organize a truth-suppressing censorship, and demand of all citizens a suspension of judgement and their unanimous support while it chooses to continue the fighting, representative government itself is imperiled. . . .

We hold with Abraham Lincoln, that "no man is good enough to govern another man without that other's consent. When the white man governs himself, that is self-government, but when he governs himself and also governs another man, that is more than self-government—that is despotism." "Our reliance is in the love of liberty which God has planted in us. Our defense is in the spirit which prizes liberty as the heritage of all men in all lands. Those who deny freedom to others deserve it not for themselves, and under a just God cannot long retain it." . . .
Source: Reprinted in Carl Schurz, *The Policy of Imperialism;* (Chicago: American Anti-Imperialist League, 1899; Liberty Tract No. 4).

7. EXCERPTS FROM PRESIDENT THEODORE ROOSEVELT'S FIRST ANNUAL MESSAGE TO CONGRESS, DECEMBER 3, 1901

The Congress assembles this year under the shadow of a great calamity. On the sixth of September, President McKinley was shot by an anarchist while attending the Pan-American Exposition at Buffalo, and died in that city on the fourteenth of that month.

Of the last seven elected presidents, he is the third who has been murdered, and the bare recital of this fact is sufficient to justify grave alarm among all loyal American citizens. Moreover, the circumstances of this, the third assassination of an American president, have a peculiarly sinister significance. . . . President McKinley was killed by an utterly depraved criminal belonging to that body of criminals who object to all governments, good and bad alike, who are against any form of popular liberty if it is guaranteed by even the most just and liberal laws, and who are as hostile to the upright exponent of a free people's sober will as to the tyrannical and irresponsible despot. . . .

[Anarchism] . . . The defenders of those murderous criminals who seek to excuse their criminality by asserting that it is exercised for political ends inveigh against wealth and irresponsible power. But for this assassination even this base apology cannot be urged. . . .

. . . [T]he harm done is so great as to excite our gravest apprehensions and to demand our wisest and most resolute action. This criminal was a professed anarchist, inflamed by the teachings of professed anarchists, and probably also by the reckless utterances of those who, on the stump and in the public press, appeal to the dark and evil spirits of malice and greed, envy and sullen hatred. The wind is sowed by the men who preach such doctrines, and they cannot escape their share of responsibility for the whirlwind that is reaped. This applies alike to the deliberate demagogue, to the exploiter of sensationalism, and to the crude and foolish visionary who, for whatever reason, apologizes for crime or excites aimless discontent.

The blow was aimed not at this president, but at all presidents; at every symbol of government. President McKinley was as emphatically the embodiment of the popular will of the nation expressed through the forms of law as a New England town meeting is in similar fashion the embodiment of the law abiding purpose and practice of the people of the town. On no conceivable theory could the murder of the president be accepted as due to protest against "inequalities in the social order," save as the murder of all the freemen engaged in a town meeting could be accepted as a protest against that social inequality which puts a malefactor in jail. Anarchy is no more an expression of "social discontent" than picking pockets or wife beating.

The anarchist, and especially the anarchist in the United States, is merely one type of criminal, more dangerous than any other because he represents the same depravity in a greater degree. The man who advocates anarchy directly or indirectly, in any shape or fashion, or the man who apologizes for anarchists and their deeds, makes himself morally accessory to murder before the fact. The anarchist is a criminal whose perverted instincts lead him to prefer confusion and chaos to the most beneficent form of social order. His protest of concern for workingmen is outrageous in its impudent falsity; for if the political institutions of this country do not afford opportunity to every honest and intelligent son of toil, then the door of hope is forever closed against him. The anarchist is everywhere not merely the enemy of system and of progress, but the deadly foe of liberty. If ever anarchy is triumphant, its triumph will last for but one red moment, to be succeeded for ages by the gloomy night of despotism. . . .

. . . No man or body of men preaching anarchistic doctrines should be allowed at large any more than if preaching the murder of some specified private individual. Anarchistic speeches, writings, and meetings are essentially seditious and treasonable.

I earnestly recommend to the Congress that in the exercise of its wise discretion it should take into consideration the coming to this country of anarchists or persons professing principles hostile to all government and justifying the murder of those placed in authority. . . . No matter calls more urgently for the wisest thought of the Congress.

The federal courts should be given jurisdiction over any man who kills or attempts to kill the president or any man who by the Constitution or by law is in line of succession for the presidency. . . .

. . . . This great country will not fall into anarchy, and if anarchists should ever become a serious menace to its institutions, they would not merely be stamped out, but would involve in their own ruin every active or passive sympathizer with their doctrines. The American people are slow to wrath, but when their wrath is once kindled it burns like a consuming flame. . . .

[New Industrial Conditions and Trusts] During the last five years business confidence has been restored, and the nation is to be congratulated because of its present abounding prosperity. Such prosperity can never be created by law alone, although it is easy enough to destroy it by mischievous laws. If the hand of the Lord is heavy upon any country, if flood or drought comes, human wisdom is powerless to avert the calamity. Moreover, no law can guard us against the consequences of our own folly. . . . Fundamentally the welfare of each citizen, and therefore the welfare of the aggregate of citizens which makes the nation, must rest upon individual thrift and energy, resolution, and intelligence. Nothing can take the place of this individual capacity; but wise legislation and honest and intelligent administration can give it the fullest scope, the largest opportunity to work to good effect.

The tremendous and highly complex industrial development which went on with ever accelerated rapidity during the latter half of the nineteenth century brings us face to face, at the beginning of the twentieth, with very serious social problems. The old laws, and the old customs which had almost the binding force of law, were once quite sufficient to regulate the accumulation and distribution of wealth. Since the industrial changes which have so enormously increased the productive power of mankind, they are no longer sufficient.

The growth of cities has gone on beyond comparison faster than the growth of the country, and the upbuilding of the great industrial centers has meant a startling increase, not merely in the aggregate of wealth, but in the number of very large individual, and especially of very large corporate, fortunes. The creation of these great corporate fortunes has not been due to the tariff nor to any other governmental action, but to natural causes in the business world, operating in other countries as they operate in our own.

The process has aroused much antagonism, a great part of which is wholly without warrant. It is not true that as the rich have grown richer the poor have grown poorer. On the contrary, never before has the average man, the wage-worker, the farmer, the small trader, been so well off as in this country and at the present time. There have been abuses connected with the accumulation of wealth; yet it remains true that a fortune accumulated in legitimate business can be accumulated by the person specially benefitted only on condition of conferring immense incidental benefits upon others. Successful enterprise, of the type which benefits all mankind, can only exist if the conditions are such as to offer great prizes as the rewards of success.

The captains of industry who have driven the railway systems across this continent, who have built up our commerce, who have developed our manufactures, have on the whole done great good to our people. Without them the material development of which we are so justly proud could never have taken place. Moreover, we should recognize the immense importance to this material development of leaving as unhampered as is compatible with the public good the strong and forceful men upon whom the success of business operations inevitably rests. . . .

An additional reason for caution in dealing with corporations is to be found in the international commercial conditions of today. The same business conditions which have produced the great aggregations of corporate and individual wealth have made them very potent factors in international commercial competition. Business concerns which have the largest means at their disposal and are managed by the ablest men are naturally those which take the lead in the strife for commercial supremacy among the nations of the world. America has only just begun to assume that commanding position in the international business world which we believe will more and more be hers. It is of the utmost importance that this position be not jeopardized, especially at a time when the overflowing abundance of our own natural resources and the skill, business energy, and mechanical aptitude of our people make foreign markets essential. Under such conditions it would be most unwise to cramp or to fetter the youthful strength of our nation. . . .

Moreover, it cannot too often be pointed out that to strike with ignorant violence at the interest of one set of men almost inevitably endangers the interests of all. The fundamental rule in our national life—the rule which underlies all others—is that, on the whole, and in the long run, we shall go up or down together. . . . Disaster to great business enterprises can never have its effects limited to the men at the top. It spreads throughout, and while it is bad for everybody, it is worst for those furthest down. The capitalist may be shorn of his luxuries but the wage-worker may be deprived of even bare necessities. . . .

All this is true; and yet it is also true that there are real and grave evils, one of the chief being overcapitalization because of its many baleful consequences; and a resolute and practical effort must be made to correct these evils.

There is widespread conviction in the minds of the American people that the great corporations known as trusts are in certain of their features and tendencies hurtful to the general welfare. This springs from no spirit of envy or uncharitableness, nor lack of pride in the great industrial achievements that have placed this country at the head of the nations struggling for commercial supremacy. . . . It is based upon sincere conviction that combination and concentration should be, not prohibited, but supervised and within reasonable limits controlled; and in my judgment this conviction is right.

It is no limitation upon property rights or freedom of contract to require that when men receive from government the privilege of doing business under corporate form, which frees them from individual responsibility, and enables them to call into their enterprises the capital of the public, they shall do so upon absolutely truthful representations as to the value of the property in which the capital is to be invested. Corporations engaged in interstate commerce should be regulated if they are found to exercise a license working to the public injury. It should be as much the aim of those who seek for social betterment to rid the business world of crimes of cunning as to rid the entire body politic of crimes of violence. Great corporations exist only because they are created and safeguarded by our institutions; and it is therefore our right and our duty to see that they work in harmony with these institutions.

The first essential in determining how to deal with the great industrial combinations is knowledge of the facts-publicity. In the interest of the public, the government should have the right to inspect and examine the workings of the great corporations engaged in interstate business. Publicity is the only sure remedy which we can now invoke. What further remedies are needed in the way of governmental regulation, or taxation, can only be determined after publicity has been obtained, by process of law, and in the course of administration. The first requisite is knowledge, full and complete-knowledge which may be made public to the world.

Artificial bodies, such as corporations and joint stock or other associations, depending upon any statutory law for their existence or privileges, should be subject to proper governmental supervision, and full and accurate information as to their operations should be made public regularly at reasonable intervals. The large corporations, commonly called trusts, though organized in one state, always do business in many states, often doing very little business in the state where they are incorporated. There is utter lack of uniformity in the state laws about them; and as no state has any exclusive interest in or power over their acts, it has in practice proved impossible to get adequate regulation through state action. Therefore, in the interest of the whole people, the nation should, without interfering with the power of the states in the matter itself, also assume power of supervision and regulation over all corporations doing an interstate business. This is especially true where the corporation derives a portion of its wealth from the existence of some monopolistic element or tendency in its business. . . .

When the Constitution was adopted, at the end of the eighteenth century, no human wisdom could foretell the sweeping changes, alike in industrial and political conditions, which were to take place by the beginning of the twentieth century. At that time it was accepted as a matter of course that the several states were the proper authorities to regulate, so far as was then necessary, the comparatively insignificant and strictly localized corporate bodies of the day. The conditions are now wholly different and wholly different action is called for. I believe that a law can be framed which will enable the national government to exercise control along the lines above indicated, profiting by the experience gained through the passage and administration of the Interstate Commerce Act. If, however, the judgment of the Congress is that it lacks the constitutional power to pass such an act, then a constitutional amendment should be submitted to confer the power.

There should be created a Cabinet officer, to be known as Secretary of Commerce and Industries, as provided in the bill introduced at the last session of the Congress. It should be his province to deal with commerce in its broadest sense; including among many other things whatever concerns labor and all matters affecting the great business corporations and our merchant marine. . . .

[Labor] . . . The National Government should demand the highest quality of service from its employees; and in return it should be a good employer. . . . So far as practicable under the conditions of Government work, provision should be made to render the enforcement of the eight-hour law easy and certain. In all industries carried on directly or indirectly for the United States Government women and children should be protected from excessive hours of labor, from night work, and from work under unsanitary conditions. The Government should provide in its contracts that all work should be done under "fair" conditions, and in addition to setting a high standard should uphold it by proper inspection, extending if necessary to the subcontractors. The Government should forbid all night work for women and children, as well as excessive overtime. For the District of Columbia a good factory law should be passed. . . .

The most vital problem with which this country, and for that matter the whole civilized world, has to deal is the problem which has for one side the betterment of social conditions, moral and physical, in large cities, and for another side the effort to deal with that tangle of far-reaching questions which we group together when we speak of "labor." The chief factor in the success of each man—wage-worker, farmer, and capitalist alike—must ever be the sum total of his own individual qualities and abilities. Second only to this comes the power of acting in combination or association with others. Very great good has been and will be accomplished by associations or unions of wage-workers, when managed with forethought, and when they combine insistence upon their own rights with law-abiding respect for the rights of others. The display of these qualities in such bodies is a duty to the nation no less than to the associations themselves. Finally, there must also in many cases be action by the government in order to safeguard the rights and interests of all. . . .

[Immigration] Our present immigration laws are unsatisfactory. We need every honest and efficient immigrant fitted to become an American citizen, every immigrant who comes here to stay, who brings here a strong body, a stout heart, a good head, and a resolute purpose to do his duty well in every way and to bring up his children as law-abiding and God-fearing members of the community. But there should be a comprehensive law enacted with the object of working a threefold improvement over our present system. First, we should aim to exclude absolutely not only all persons who are known to be believers in anarchistic principles or members of anarchistic societies, but also all persons who are of a low moral tendency or of unsavory reputation. . . .

The second object of a proper immigration law ought to be to secure by a careful and not merely perfunctory educational test some intelligent capacity to appreciate American institutions and act sanely as American citizens. This would not keep out all anarchists, for many of them belong to the intelligent criminal class. But it would do what is also in point, that is, tend to decrease the sum of ignorance, so potent in producing the envy, suspicion, malignant passion, and hatred of order, out of which anarchistic sentiment inevitably springs. Finally, all persons should be excluded who are below a certain standard of economic fitness to enter our industrial field as competitors with American labor. There should be proper proof of personal capacity to earn an American living and enough money to ensure a decent start under American conditions. This would stop the influx of cheap labor, and the resulting competition which gives rise to so much of bitterness in American industrial life; and it would dry up the springs of the pestilential social conditions in our great cities, where anarchistic organizations have their greatest possibility of growth.

Both the educational and economic tests in a wise immigration law should be designed to protect and elevate the general body politic and social. A very close supervision should be exercised over the steamship companies which mainly bring over the immigrants, and they should be held to a strict accountability for any infraction of the law.

[Sections on the Tariff and Reciprocity and on Monetary Issues omitted]

[Railroad Regulation] In 1887 a measure was enacted for the regulation of interstate railways, commonly known as the Interstate Commerce Act. . . . Experience has shown the wisdom of its purposes, but has also shown, possibly that some of its requirements are wrong, certainly that the means devised for the enforcement of its provisions are defective. . . .

The act should be amended. The railway is a public servant. Its rates should be just to and open to all shippers alike. The government should see to it that within its jurisdiction this is so and should provide a speedy, inexpensive, and effective remedy to that end. At the same time it must not be forgotten that our railways are the arteries through which the commercial lifeblood of this nation flows. Nothing could be more foolish than the enactment of legislation which would unnecessarily interfere with the development and operation of these commercial agencies. The subject is one of great importance and calls for the earnest attention of the Congress. . . .

[Conservation] Public opinion throughout the United States has moved steadily toward a just appreciation of the value of forests, whether planted or of natural growth. The great part played by them in the creation and maintenance of the national wealth is now more fully realized than ever before.

Wise forest protection does not mean the withdrawal of forest resources, whether of wood, water, or grass, from contributing their full share to the welfare of the people, but, on the contrary, gives the assurance of larger and more certain supplies. The fundamental idea of forestry is the perpetuation of forests by use. Forest protection is not an end of itself; it is a means to increase and sustain the resources of our country and the industries which depend upon them. The preservation of our forests is an imperative business necessity. We have come to see clearly that whatever destroys the forest, except to make way for agriculture, threatens our well-being. . . . The forest reserves will inevitably be of still greater use in the future than in the past. Additions should be made to them whenever practicable, and their usefulness should be increased by a thoroughly businesslike management.

At present the protection of the forest reserves rests with the General Land Office, the mapping and description of their timber with the United States Geological Survey, and the preparation of plans for their conservative use

with the Bureau of Forestry, which is also charged with the general advancement of practical forestry in the United States. These various functions should be united in the Bureau of Forestry, to which they properly belong. The present diffusion of responsibility is bad from every standpoint. It prevents that effective cooperation between the government and the men who utilize the resources of the reserves, without which the interests of both must suffer. The scientific bureaus generally should be put under the Department of Agriculture. The president should have by law the power of transferring lands for use as forest reserves to the Department of Agriculture. He already has such power in the case of lands needed by the departments of War and the Navy.

The wise administration of the forest reserves will be not less helpful to the interests which depend on water than to those which depend on wood and grass. The water supply itself depends upon the forest. In the arid region it is water, not land, which measures production. The western half of the United States would sustain a population greater than that of our whole country today if the waters that now run to waste were saved and used for irrigation. The forest and water problems are perhaps the most vital internal questions of the United States.

Certain of the forest reserves should also be made preserves for the wild forest creatures. All of the reserves should be better protected from fires. Many of them need special protection because of the great injury done by livestock, above all by sheep. The increase in deer, elk, and other animals in the Yellowstone Park shows what may be expected when other mountain forests are properly protected by law and properly guarded. Some of these areas have been so denuded of surface vegetation by overgrazing that the ground breeding birds, including grouse and quail, and many mammals, including deer, have been exterminated or driven away. At the same time the water-storing capacity of the surface has been decreased or destroyed, thus promoting floods in times of rain and diminishing the flow of streams between rains.

In cases where natural conditions have been restored for a few years, vegetation has again carpeted the ground, birds and deer are coming back, and hundreds of persons, especially from the immediate neighborhood, come each summer to enjoy the privilege of camping. Some at least of the forest reserves should afford perpetual protection to the native fauna and flora, safe havens of refuge to our rapidly diminishing wild animals of the larger kinds, and free camping grounds for the ever-increasing numbers of men and women who have learned to find rest, health, and recreation in the splendid forests and flower-clad meadows of our mountains. The forest reserves should be set apart forever for the use and benefit of our people as a whole and not sacrificed to the shortsighted greed of a few.

[Waterways and Reclamation of Arid Lands] The forests are natural reservoirs. By restraining the streams in flood and replenishing them in drought they make possible the use of waters otherwise wasted. They prevent the soil from washing, and so protect the storage reservoirs from filling up with silt. Forest conservation is therefore an essential condition of water conservation.

The forests alone cannot, however, fully regulate and conserve the waters of the arid region. Great storage works are necessary to equalize the flow of streams and to save the flood waters. Their construction has been conclusively shown to be an undertaking too vast for private effort. Nor can it be best accomplished by the individual states acting alone. Far-reaching interstate problems are involved; and the resources of single states would often be inadequate. It is properly a national function, at least in some of its features. It is as right for the national government to make the streams and rivers of the arid region useful by engineering works for water storage as to make useful the rivers and harbors of the humid region by engineering works of another kind. The storing of the floods in reservoirs at the headwaters of our rivers is but an enlargement of our present policy of river control, under which levees are built on the lower reaches of the same streams. The government should construct and maintain these reservoirs as it does other public works. Where their purpose is to regulate the flow of streams, the water should be turned freely into the channels in the dry season to take the same course under the same laws as the natural flow. The reclamation of the unsettled arid public lands presents a different problem. Here it is not enough to regulate the flow of streams. The object of the government is to dispose of the land to settlers who will build homes upon it. To accomplish this object water must be brought within their reach.

The pioneer settlers on the arid public domain chose their homes along streams from which they could themselves divert the water to reclaim their holdings. Such opportunities are practically gone. There remain, however, vast areas of public land which can be made available for homestead settlement, but only by reservoirs and main-line canals impracticable for private enterprise. These irrigation works should be built by the national government. The lands reclaimed by them should be reserved by the government for actual settlers, and the cost of construction should so far as possible be repaid by the land reclaimed. The distribution of the water, the division of the streams among irrigators, should be left to the settlers themselves in conformity with state laws and without interference with those laws or with vested rights. The policy of the national government should be to aid irrigation in the several states and territories in such manner as will enable the people in the local communities to help themselves, and as will stim-

ulate needed reforms in the state laws and regulations governing irrigation. . . .

[America's Dependencies; paragraphs on Hawaii, Cuba, Puerto Rico, and the Philippines omitted]

[The Isthmian Canal] No single great material work which remains to be undertaken on this continent is of such consequence to the American people as the building of a canal across the Isthmus connecting North and South America. Its importance to the nation is by no means limited merely to its material effects upon our business prosperity; and yet with view to these effects alone it would be to the last degree important for us immediately to begin it. . . .

[The Monroe Doctrine] . . . Peace can only be kept with certainty where both sides wish to keep it; but more and more the civilized peoples are realizing the wicked folly of war and are attaining that condition of just and intelligent regard for the rights of others which will in the end, as we hope and believe, make worldwide peace possible. The peace conference at The Hague gave definite expression to this hope and belief and marked a stride toward their attainment. This same peace conference acquiesced in our statement of the Monroe Doctrine as compatible with the purposes and aims of the conference. The Monroe Doctrine should be the cardinal feature of the foreign policy of all the nations of the two Americas, as it is of the United States. Just seventy-eight years have passed since President Monroe in his Annual Message announced that "the American continents are henceforth not to be considered as subjects for future colonization by any European power." In other words, the Monroe Doctrine is a declaration that there must be no territorial aggrandizement by any non-American power at the expense of any American power on American soil. . . . It is simply a step, and a long step, toward assuring the universal peace of the world by securing the possibility of permanent peace on this hemisphere. . . .

[The Navy] The work of upbuilding the navy must be steadily continued. No one point of our policy, foreign or domestic, is more important than this to the honor and material welfare, and above all to the peace, of our nation in the future. Whether we desire it or not, we must henceforth recognize that we have international duties no less than international rights. Even if our flag were hauled down in the Philippines and Puerto Rico, even if we decided not to build the Isthmian Canal, we should need a thoroughly trained navy of adequate size. . . . Unless our commerce is always to be carried in foreign bottoms, we must have war craft to protect it. . . .

[I]t is imperative that our navy should be put and kept in the highest state of efficiency, and should be made to answer to our growing needs. So far from being in any way a provocation to war, an adequate and highly trained navy is the best guarantee against war, the cheapest and most effective peace insurance. . . . The navy offers us the only means of making our insistence upon the Monroe Doctrine anything but a subject of derision to whatever nation chooses to disregard it. We desire the peace which comes as of right to the just man armed; not the peace granted on terms of ignominy to the craven and the weakling.

The American people must either build and maintain an adequate navy or else make up their minds definitely to accept a secondary position in international affairs, not merely in political, but in commercial, matters.

[The Army] It has been well said that there is no surer way of courting national disaster than to be "opulent, aggressive, and unarmed." It is not necessary to increase our army beyond its present size at this time. But it is necessary to keep it at the highest point of efficiency. . . .

A general staff should be created. As for the present staff and supply departments, they should be filled by details from the line, the men so detailed returning after a while to their line duties. It is very undesirable to have the senior grades of the army composed of men who have come to fill the positions by the mere fact of seniority. . . . Pressure for the promotion of civil officials for political reasons is bad enough, but it is tenfold worse where applied on behalf of officers of the army or navy. Every promotion and every detail under the War Department must be made solely with regard to the good of the service and to the capacity and merit of the man himself. . . .

[Section on Merit Civil Service omitted]

[Native Americans] In my judgment the time has arrived when we should definitely make up our minds to recognize the Indian as an individual and not as a member of a tribe. The General Allotment Act is a mighty pulverizing engine to break up the tribal mass. It acts directly upon the family and the individual. Under its provisions some sixty thousand Indians have already become citizens of the United States. We should now break up the tribal funds, doing for them what allotment does for the tribal lands; that is, they should be divided into individual holdings. . . . A stop should be put upon the discriminate permission to Indians to lease their allotments. The effort should be steadily to make the Indian work like any other man on his own ground. The marriage laws of the Indians should be made the same as those of the whites. In the schools the education should be elementary and largely industrial. The need of higher education among the Indians is very, very limited. . . . The Indian should be treated as an individual—like the white man. . . . In dealing with the aboriginal races few things are more important than to preserve them from the terrible physical and moral degradation resulting from the liquor traffic. . . .

[Comments on the National Zoo, the Library of Congress, the Postal Service, Relations with China and with Pan-American Nations omitted]

[Conclusion] The death of Queen Victoria caused the people of the United States deep and heartfelt sorrow, to which the government gave full expression. When President McKinley died, our nation in turn received from every quarter of the British Empire expressions of grief and sympathy no less sincere. . . . In the midst of our affliction we reverently thank the Almighty that we are at peace with the nations of mankind; and we firmly intend that our policy shall be such as to continue unbroken these international relations of mutual respect and goodwill.

Source: Messages and Papers of the Presidents, ed. J. Richardson, vol. 10 (New York: Bureau of National Literature and Art, 1917), 207ff.

8. MUCKRAKING: LINCOLN STEFFENS, "TWEED DAYS IN ST. LOUIS," 1902, 1904

St. Louis, the fourth city in size in the United States, is making two announcements to the world: one that it is the worst-governed city in the land; the other that it wishes all men to come there (for the World's Fair) and see it. It isn't our worst-governed city; Philadelphia is that. But St. Louis is worth examining while we have it inside out.

There is a man at work there, one man, working all alone, but he is the Circuit (district or State) Attorney, and he is "doing his duty." . . . The Circuit Attorney, finding that his "duty" was to catch and convict criminals, and that the biggest criminals were some of these same politicians and leading citizens, went after them. It is magnificent, but the politicians declare it isn't politics.

The corruption of St. Louis came from the top. The best citizens—the merchants and big financiers—used to rule the town, and they ruled it well. . . . gain business and population. And it was a close race. Chicago, having the start, always led, but St. Louis had pluck, intelligence, and tremendous energy. It pressed Chicago hard. It excelled in a sense of civic beauty and good government; and there are those who think yet it might have won. But a change occurred. Public spirit became private spirit, public enterprise became private greed.

Along about 1890, public franchises and privileges were sought, not only for legitimate profit and common convenience, but for loot. Taking but slight and always selfish interest in the public councils, the big men misused politics. The riffraff, catching the smell of corruption, rushed into the Municipal Assembly, drove out the remaining respectable men, and sold the city—its streets, its wharves, its markets, and all that it had—to the now greedy business men and bribers. In other words, when the leading men began to devour their own city, the herd rushed into the trough and fed also.

So gradually has this occurred that these same citizens hardly realize it. Go to St. Louis and you will find the habit of civic pride in them; they still boast. The visitor is told of the wealth of the residents, of the financial strength of the banks, and of the growing importance of the industries, yet he sees poorly paved, refuse-burdened streets, and dusty or mud-covered alleys; he passes a ramshackle fire-trap crowded with the sick, and learns that it is the City Hospital; he enters the "Four Courts," and his nostrils are greeted by the odor of formaldehyde used as a disinfectant, and insect powder spread to destroy vermin; he calls at the new City Hall, and finds half the entrance boarded with pine planks to cover up the unfinished interior. Finally, he turns a tap in the hotel, to see liquid mud flow into wash-basin or bath-tub.

The St. Louis charter vests legislative power of great scope in a Municipal Assembly, which is composed of a council and a House of Delegates. Here is a description of the latter by one of Mr. Folk's grand juries:

"We have had before us many of those who have been, and most of those who are now, members of the House of Delegates. We found a number of these utterly illiterate and lacking in ordinary intelligence, unable to give a better reason for favoring or opposing a measure than a desire to act with the majority. In some, no trace of mentality or morality could be found; in others, a low order of training appeared, united with base cunning, groveling instincts, and sordid desires. Unqualified to respond to the ordinary requirements of life, they are utterly incapable of comprehending the significance of an ordinance, and are incapacitated, both by nature and training, to be the makers of laws. The choosing of such men to be legislators makes a travesty of justice, sets a premium on incompetency, and deliberately poisons the very source of the law."

These creatures were well organized. They had a "combine"—a legislative institution—which the grand jury described as follows:

"Our investigation, covering more or less fully a period of ten years, shows that, with few exceptions, no ordinance has been passed wherein valuable privileges or franchises are granted until those interested have paid the legislators the money demanded for action in the particular case. Combines in both branches of the Municipal Assembly are formed by members sufficient in number to control legislation. To one member of this combine is delegated the authority to act for the combine, and to receive and to distribute to each member the money agreed upon as the price of his vote in support of, or opposition to, a pending measure. So long has this practice existed that such members have come to regard the receipt of money for action on pending measures as a legitimate perquisite of a legislator."

One legislator consulted a lawyer with the intention of suing a firm to recover an unpaid balance on a fee for the grant of a switch-way. Such difficulties rarely occurred, however. In order to insure a regular and indisputable rev-

enue, the combine of each house drew up a schedule of bribery prices for all possible sorts of grants, just such a list as a commercial traveler takes out on the road with him. There was a price for a grain elevator, a price for a short switch; side tracks were charged for by the linear foot, but at rates which varied according to the nature of the ground taken; a street improvement cost so much; wharf space was classified and precisely rated. As there was a scale for favorable legislation, so there was one for defeating bills. It made a difference in the price if there was opposition, and it made a difference whether the privilege asked was legitimate or not. But nothing was passed free of charge. Many of the legislators were saloon-keepers—it was in St. Louis that a practical joker nearly emptied the House of Delegates by tipping a boy to rush into a session and call out, "Mister, your saloon is on fire,"—but even the saloon-keepers of a neighborhood had to pay to keep in their inconvenient locality a market which public interest would have moved.

From the Assembly, bribery spread into other departments. Men empowered to issue peddlers' licenses and permits to citizens who wished to erect awnings or use a portion of the sidewalk for storage purposes charged an amount in excess of the prices stipulated by law, and pocketed the difference. The city's money was loaned at interest, and the interest was converted into private bank accounts. City carriages were used by the wives and children of city officials. Supplies for public institutions found their way to private tables; one itemized account of food furnished the poorhouse included California jellies, imported cheeses, and French wines! A member of the Assembly caused the incorporation of a grocery company, with his sons and daughters the ostensible stockholders, and succeeded in having his bid for city supplies accepted although the figures were in excess of his competitors'. In return for the favor thus shown, he endorsed a measure to award the contract for city printing to another member, and these two voted aye on a bill granting to a third the exclusive right to furnish city dispensaries with drugs. . . .

The blackest years were 1898, 1899, and 1900. Foreign corporations came into the city to share in its despoilation, and home industries were driven out by blackmail. Franchises worth millions were granted without one cent of cash to the city, and with provision for only the smallest future payment; several companies which refused to pay blackmail had to leave; citizens were robbed more and more boldly; pay-rolls were padded with the names of non-existent persons; work on public improvements was neglected, while money for them went to the boodlers.

Some of the newspapers protested, disinterested citizens were alarmed, and the shrewder men gave warnings, but none dared make an effective stand. Behind the corruptionists were men of wealth and social standing, who, because of special privileges granted them, felt bound to support and defend the looters. Independent victims of the far-reaching conspiracy submitted in silence, through fear of injury to their business. Men whose integrity was never questioned, who held high positions of trust, who were church members and teachers of Bible classes, contributed to the support of the dynasty,—became blackmailers, in fact,—and their excuse was that others did the same, and that if they proved the exception it would work their ruin. The system became loose through license and plenty till it was as wild and weak as that of Tweed in New York.

Then the unexpected happened—an accident. There was no uprising of the people, but they were restive; and the Democratic party leaders, thinking to gain some independent votes, decided to raise the cry "reform" and put up a ticket of candidates different enough from the usual offerings of political parties to give color to their platform. . . .

When somebody mentioned Joseph W. Folk for Circuit Attorney the leaders were ready to accept him . . . and Folk became Circuit Attorney for the Eighth Missouri District. . . .

One afternoon, late in January, 1903, a newspaper reporter, known as "Red" Galvin, called Mr. Folk's attention to a ten-line newspaper item to the effect that a large sum of money had been placed in a bank for the purpose of bribing certain Assemblymen to secure the passage of a street railroad ordinance. No names were mentioned, but Mr. Galvin surmised that the bill referred to was one introduced on behalf of the Suburban Railway Company. An hour later Mr. Folk sent the names of nearly one hundred persons to the sheriff, with instructions to subpoena them before the grand jury at once. The list included Councilmen, members of the House of Delegates, officers and directors of the Suburban Railway, bank presidents and cashiers. In three days the investigation was being pushed with vigor, but St. Louis was laughing at the "huge joke." Such things had been attempted before. The men who had been ordered to appear before the grand jury jested as they chatted in the ante-rooms, and newspaper accounts of these preliminary examinations were written in the spirit of burlesque.

It has developed since that Circuit Attorney Folk knew nothing, and was not able to learn much more during the first days; but he says he saw here and there puffs of smoke and he determined to find the fire. It was not an easy job. The first break into such a system is always difficult. Mr. Folk began with nothing but courage and a strong personal conviction. He caused peremptory summons to be issued, for the immediate attendance in the grand jury room of Charles H. Turner, president of the Suburban Railway, and Philip Stock, a representative of brewers interests, who, he had reason to believe, was the legislative agent in this deal.

"Gentlemen," said Mr. Folk, "I have secured sufficient evidence to warrant the return of indictments against you for bribery, and I shall prosecute you to the full extent of the law and send you to the penitentiary unless you tell to this grand jury the complete history of the corruptionist methods employed by you to secure the passage of Ordinance No. 44. I shall give you three days to consider the matter. At the end of that time, if you have not returned here and given us the information demanded, warrants will be issued for your arrest."

They looked at the audacious young prosecutor and left the Four Courts building without uttering a word. He waited. Two days later, ex-Lieutenant Governor Charles P. Johnson, the veteran criminal lawyer, called, and said that his client, Mr. Stock, was in such poor health that he would be unable to appear before the grand jury.

"I am truly sorry that Mr. Stock is ill," replied Mr. Folk, "for his presence here is imperative, and if he fails to appear he will be arrested before sundown." That evening a conference was held in Governor Johnson's office, and the next day this story was told in the grand jury room by Charles H. Turner, millionaire president of the Suburban Railway, and corroborated by Philip Stock, man-about-town and a good fellow: The Suburban, anxious to sell out at a large profit to its only competitor, the St. Louis Transit Co., caused to be drafted the measure known as House Bill No. 44. So sweeping were its grants that Mr. Turner, who planned and executed the document, told the directors in his confidence that its enactment into law would enhance the value of the property from three to six million dollars. The bill introduced, Mr. Turner visited Colonel Butler, who had long been known as a legislative agent, and asked his price for securing the passage of the measure. "One hundred and forty-five thousand dollars will be my fee," was the reply. The railway president demurred. He would think the matter over, he said, and he hired a cheaper man, Mr. Stock. Stock conferred with the representative of the combine in the House of Delegates and reported that $75,000 would be necessary in this branch of the Assembly. Mr. Turner presented a note indorsed by two of the directors whom he could trust, and secured a loan from the German American Savings Bank.

Bribe funds in pocket, the legislative agent telephoned John Murrell, at that time a representative of the House combine, to meet him in the office of the Lincoln Trust Company. There the two rented a safe-deposit box. Mr. Stock placed in the drawer the roll of $75,000, and each subscribed to an agreement that the box should not be opened unless both were present. Of course the conditions spread upon the bank's daybook made no reference to the purpose for which this fund had been deposited, but an agreement entered into by Messrs. Stock and Murrell was to the effect that the $75,000 should be given Mr. Murrell as soon as the bill became an ordinance, and by him distributed to the members of the combine. Stock turned to the Council, and upon his report a further sum of $60,000 was secured. These bills were placed in a safe-deposit box of the Mississippi Valley Trust Co., and the man who held the key as representative of the Council combine was Charles H. Kratz.

All seemed well, but a few weeks after placing these funds in escrow, Mr. Stock reported to his employer that there was an unexpected hitch due to the action of Emil Meysenburg, who, as a member of the Council Committee on Railroads, was holding up the report on the bill. Mr. Stock said that Mr. Meysenburg held some worthless shares in a defunct corporation and wanted Mr. Stock to purchase this paper at its par value of $9,000. Mr. Turner gave Mr. Stock the money with which to buy the shares.

Thus the passage of House Bill 44 promised to cost the Suburban Railway Co. $144,000, only one thousand dollars less than that originally named by the political boss to whom Mr. Turner had first applied. The bill, however, passed both houses of the Assembly. The sworn servants of the city had done their work and held out their hands for the bribe money.

Then came a court mandate which prevented the Suburban Railway Co. from reaping the benefit of the votebuying, and Charles H. Turner, angered at the check, issued orders that the money in safe-deposit boxes should not be touched. War was declared between bribe-givers and bribe-takers, and the latter resorted to tactics which they hoped would frighten the Suburban people into submission—such as making enough of the story public to cause rumors of impending prosecution. It was that first item which Mr. Folk saw and acted upon.

When Messrs. Turner and Stock unfolded in the grand jury room the details of their bribery plot, Circuit Attorney Folk found himself in possession of verbal evidence of a great crime; he needed as material exhibits the two large sums of money in safe-deposit vaults of two of the largest banking institutions of the West. Had this money been withdrawn? Could he get it if it was there? Lockboxes had always been considered sacred and beyond the power of the law to open. "I've always held," said Mr. Folk, "that the fact that a thing never had been done was no reason for thinking it couldn't be done." He decided in this case that the magnitude of the interests involved warranted unusual action, so he selected a committee of grand jurors and visited one of the banks. He told the president, a personal friend, the facts that had come into his possession, and asked permission to search for the fund.

"Impossible," was the reply. "Our rules deny anyone the right."

"Mr.—," said Mr. Folk, "a crime has been committed, and you hold concealed the principal evidence thereto. In the name of the State of Missouri I demand that you cause the box to be opened. If you refuse, I shall cause a warrant to be issued, charging you as an accessory."

For a minute not a word was spoken by anyone in the room; then the banker said in almost inaudible tones:

"Give me a little time, gentlemen. I must consult with our legal adviser before taking such a step."

"We will wait ten minutes," said the Circuit Attorney. "By that time we must have access to the vault or a warrant will be applied for."

At the expiration of that time a solemn procession wended its way from the president's office to the vaults in the subcellar—the president, the cashier, and the corporation's lawyer, the grand jurors, and the Circuit Attorney. All bent eagerly forward as the key was inserted in the lock. The iron drawer yielded, and a roll of something wrapped in brown paper was brought to light. The Circuit Attorney removed the rubber bands, and national bank notes of large denomination spread out flat before them. The money was counted, and the sum was $75,000!

The boodle fund was returned to its repository, officers of the bank were told they would be held responsible for it until the courts could act. The investigators visited the other financial institution. They met with more resistance there. The threat to procure a warrant had no effect until Mr. Folk left the building and set off in the direction of the Four Courts. Then a messenger called him back, and the second box was opened. In this was found $60,000. The chain of evidence was complete.

From that moment events moved rapidly. Charles Kratz and John K. Murrell, alleged representatives of Council and House combines, were arrested on bench warrants and placed under heavy bonds. Kratz was brought into court from a meeting at which plans were being formed for his election to the National Congress. Murrell was taken from his undertaking establishment. Emil Meysenburg, millionaire broker, was seated in his office when a sheriff's deputy entered and read a document that charged him with bribery. The summons reached Henry Nicolaus while he was seated at his desk, and the wealthy brewer was compelled to send for a bondsman to avoid passing a night in jail. The cable flashed the news to Cairo, Egypt, that Ellis Wainwright, many times a millionaire, proprietor of the St. Louis brewery that bears this name, had been indicted. Julius Lehmann, one of the members of the House of Delegates, who had joked while waiting in the grand jury's anteroom, had his laughter cut short by the hand of a deputy sheriff on his shoulder and the words, "You are charged with perjury." He was joined at the bar of the criminal court by Harry Faulkner, another jolly good fellow.

Consternation spread among the boodle gang. Some of the men took night trains for other States and foreign countries; the majority remained and counseled together. Within twenty-four hours after the first indictments were returned, a meeting of bribe-givers and bribe-takers was held in South St. Louis. The total wealth of those in attendance was $30,000,000, and their combined political influence sufficient to carry any municipal election under normal conditions.

This great power was aligned in opposition to one man, who still was alone. . . .

Mr. Folk at once felt the pressure, and it was of a character to startle one. Statesmen, lawyers, merchants, clubmen, churchmen—in fact, men prominent in all walks of life—visited him at his office and at his home, and urged that he cease such activity against his fellow-townspeople. Political preferment was promised if he would yield; a political grave if he persisted. Threatening letters came, warning him of plots to murder, to disfigure, and to blackguard. Word came from Tennessee that detectives were investigating every act of his life. Mr. Folk told the politicians that he was not seeking political favors, and not looking forward to another office; the others he defied. Meantime he probed the deeper into the municipal sore. With his first successes for prestige and aided by the panic among the boodlers, he soon had them suspicious of one another, exchanging charges of betrayal, and ready to "squeal" or run at the slightest sign of danger. One member of the House of Delegates became so frightened while under the inquisitorial cross-fire that he was seized with a nervous chill; his false teeth fell to the floor, and the rattle so increased his alarm that he rushed from the room without stopping to pick up his teeth, and boarded the next train. . . .

Source: Lincoln Steffens, chapter 1 of *The Shame of the Cities,* (New York: McClure, Phillips, 1904), 19–41; first published in *McClure's,* October 1902.

9. Muckraking: Excerpt from Ida M. Tarbell, "The Rise of the Standard Oil Company," 1902, 1904

In the fall of 1871, while Mr. Rockefeller and his friends were occupied with all these questions, certain Pennsylvania refiners, it is not too certain who, brought to them a remarkable scheme, the gist of which was to bring together secretly a large enough body of refiners and shippers to persuade all the railroads handling oil to give to the company formed special rebates on its oil, and drawbacks on that of other people. If they could get such rates it was evident that those outside of their combination could not compete with them long and that they would become eventually the only refiners. They could then limit their output to actual demand, and so keep up prices. This done, they could easily persuade the railroads to transport no crude for exportation, so that the foreigners would be forced to buy American refined. They believed that the price of oil thus exported could easily be advanced fifty per cent. The control of the refining interests would also enable them to fix their own price on crude. As they would be the only buyers and sellers, the speculative character of the business would be done away with. In short, the scheme they worked out put the entire oil business in their hands. It looked as simple to put into operation as it was dazzling in its results. Mr. Flagler has sworn that neither he nor Mr. Rockefeller believed in this scheme.★ But when they found that their friend Peter H. Watson, and various Philadelphia and Pittsburg parties who felt as they did about the oil business, believed in it, they went in and began at once to work up a company-secretly. It was evident that a scheme which aimed at concentrating in the hands of one company the business now operated by scores, and which proposed to effect this consolidation through a practice of the railroads which was contrary to the spirit of their charters, although freely indulged in, must be worked with fine discretion if it ever were to be effective.

The first thing was to get a charter-quietly. At a meeting held in Philadelphia late in the fall of 1871 a friend of one of the gentlemen interested mentioned to him that a certain estate then in liquidation had a charter for sale which gave its owners the right to carry on any kind of business in any country and in any way; that it could be bought for what it would cost to get a charter under the general laws of the state, and that it would be a favour to the heirs to buy it. The opportunity was promptly taken. The name of the charter bought was the "Southern (usually written South) Improvement Company." For a beginning it was as good a name as another, since it said nothing.

With this charter in hand Mr. Rockefeller and Mr. Watson and their associates began to seek converts. In order that their great scheme might not be injured by premature public discussion they asked of each person whom they approached a pledge of secrecy. Two forms of the pledges required before anything was revealed were published later. The first of these, which appeared in the New York Tribune, read as follows:

I, A. B., do faithfully promise upon my honour and faith as a gentleman that I will keep secret all transactions which I may have with the corporation known as the South Improvement Company; that, should I fail to complete any bargains with the said company, all the preliminary conversations shall be kept strictly private; and, finally, that I will not disclose the price for which I dispose of my product, or any other facts which may in any way bring to light the internal workings or organisation of the company. All this I do freely promise.

Signed ....
Witnessed by...................

A second, published in a history of the "Southern Improvement Company," ran:

The undersigned pledge their solemn words of honour that they will not communicate to any one without permission of Z (name of director of Southern Improvement Company) any information that he may convey to them, or any of them, in relation to the Southern Improvement Company

....

Witness..........................

That the promoters met with encouragement is evident from the fact that, when the corporators came together on January 2, 1872, in Philadelphia, for the first time under their charter, and transferred the company to the stockholders, they claimed to represent in one way or another a large part of the refining interest of the country. At this meeting 1,100 shares of the stock of the company, which was divided into 2,000 $100 shares, were subscribed for, and twenty per cent of their value was paid in. Just who took stock at this meeting the writer has not been able to discover. At the same time a discussion came up as to what refiners were to be allowed to go into the new company. Each of the men represented had friends whom he wanted taken care of, and after considerable discussion it was decided to take in every refinery they could get hold of. This decision was largely due to the railroad men. Mr. Watson had seen them as soon as the plans for the company were formed, and they had all agreed that if they gave the rebates and drawbacks all refineries then existing must be taken in upon the same level. That is, while the incorporators had intended to kill off all but themselves and their friends, the railroads refused to go into a scheme which was going to put anybody out of business—the plan if they went into it must cover the refining trade as it stood. It was enough that it could prevent any one in the future going into the business.

*See Appendix, Number 4. Testimony of Henry M. Flagler on the South Improvement Company.
Source: Ida Tarbell, *History of the Standard Oil Company,* vol. 1 (New York, McClure, Phillips, 1904), chapter 2, pp. 54–59; first published in McClure's, December 1902.

10. EXCERPT FROM W. E. B. DuBois, *THE SOULS OF BLACK FOLK,* CHAPTER 3, "OF MR. BOOKER T. WASHINGTON AND OTHERS," 1903

Easily the most striking thing in the history of the American Negro since 1876 is the ascendancy of Mr. Booker T. Washington. It began at the time when war memories and ideals were rapidly passing; a day of astonishing commercial development was dawning; a sense of doubt and hesitation overtook the freedmen's sons,—then it was that his leading began. Mr. Washington came, with a simple definite programme, at the psychological moment when the nation was a little ashamed of having bestowed so much sentiment on Negroes, and was concentrating its energies on Dollars. His programme of industrial education, conciliation of the South, and submission and silence as to civil and political rights, was not wholly original. . . . But Mr. Washington first indissolubly linked these things; he put enthusiasm, unlimited energy, and perfect faith into this programme, and changed it from a by-path into a veritable Way of Life. And the tale of the methods by which he did this is a fascinating study of human life.

It startled the nation to hear a Negro advocating such a programme after many decades of bitter complaint; it startled and won the applause of the South, it interested and won the admiration of the North; and after a confused murmur of protest, it silenced if it did not convert the Negroes themselves.

To gain the sympathy and cooperation of the various elements comprising the white South was Mr. Washington's first task; and this, at the time Tuskegee was founded, seemed, for a black man, well-nigh impossible. And yet ten years later it was done in the word spoken at Atlanta: "In all things purely social we can be as separate as the five fingers, and yet one as the hand in all things essential to mutual progress." This "Atlanta Compromise" is by all odds the most notable thing in Mr. Washington's career. The South interpreted it in different ways: the radicals received it as a complete surrender of the demand for civil and political equality; the conservatives, as a generously conceived working basis for mutual understanding. So both approved it, and to-day its author is certainly the most distinguished Southerner since Jefferson Davis, and the one with the largest personal following.

Next to this achievement comes Mr. Washington's work in gaining place and consideration in the North. Others less shrewd and tactful had formerly essayed to sit on these two stools and had fallen between them; but as Mr. Washington knew the heart of the South from birth and training, so by singular insight he intuitively grasped the spirit of the age which was dominating the North. And so thoroughly did he learn the speech and thought of triumphant commercialism, and the ideals of material prosperity, that the picture of a lone black boy poring over a French grammar amid the weeds and dirt of a neglected home soon seemed to him the acme of absurdities. One wonders what Socrates and St. Francis of Assisi would say to this.

And yet this very singleness of vision and thorough oneness with his age is a mark of the successful man. It is as though Nature must needs make men narrow in order to give them force. So Mr. Washington's cult has gained unquestioning followers, his work has wonderfully prospered, his friends are legion, and his enemies are confounded. To-day he stands as the one recognized spokesman of his ten million fellows, and one of the most notable figures in a nation of seventy millions. One hesitates, therefore, to criticise a life which, beginning with so little, has done so much. And yet the time is come when one may speak in all sincerity and utter courtesy of the mistakes and shortcomings of Mr. Washington's career, as well as of his triumphs, without being thought captious or envious, and without forgetting that it is easier to do ill than well in the world. . . .

Among his own people, however, Mr. Washington has encountered the strongest and most lasting opposition, amounting at times to bitterness. . . . Some of this opposition is, of course, mere envy; the disappointment of displaced demagogues and the spite of narrow minds. But aside from this, there is among educated and thoughtful colored men in all parts of the land a feeling of deep regret, sorrow, and apprehension at the wide currency and ascendancy which some of Mr. Washington's theories have gained. . . .

Mr. Washington represents in Negro thought the old attitude of adjustment and submission; but adjustment at such a peculiar time as to make his programme unique. This is an age of unusual economic development, and Mr. Washington's programme naturally takes an economic cast, becoming a gospel of Work and Money to such an extent as apparently almost completely to overshadow the higher aims of life. Moreover, this is an age when the more advanced races are coming in closer contact with the less developed races, and the race-feeling is therefore intensified; and Mr. Washington's programme practically accepts the alleged inferiority of the Negro races. . . .

In answer to this, it has been claimed that the Negro can survive only through submission. Mr. Washington distinctly asks that black people give up, at least for the present, three things,—

First, political power,

Second, insistence on civil rights,

Third, higher education of Negro youth,—

and concentrate all their energies on industrial education, the accumulation of wealth, and the conciliation of the South. This policy has been courageously and insistently advocated for over fifteen years, and has been triumphant for perhaps ten years. As a result of this tender of the palm-branch, what has been the return? In these years there have occurred:

1. The disfranchisement of the Negro.

2. The legal creation of a distinct status of civil inferiority for the Negro.

3. The steady withdrawal of aid from institutions for the higher training of the Negro.

These movements are not, to be sure, direct results of Mr. Washington's teachings; but his propaganda has, without a shadow of doubt, helped their speedier accomplishment. The question then comes: Is it possible, and probable, that nine millions of men can make effective progress in economic lines if they are deprived of political rights, made a servile caste, and allowed only the most meagre chance for developing their exceptional men? If history and reason give any distinct answer to these questions, it is an emphatic No. And Mr. Washington thus faces the triple paradox of his career:

1. He is striving nobly to make Negro artisans business men and property-owners; but it is utterly impossible, under modern competitive methods, for workingmen and property-owners to defend their rights and exist without the right of suffrage.

2. He insists on thrift and self-respect, but at the same time counsels a silent submission to civic inferiority such as is bound to sap the manhood of any race in the long run.

3. He advocates common-school and industrial training, and depreciates institutions of higher learning; but neither the Negro common-schools, nor Tuskegee itself, could remain open a day were it not for teachers trained in Negro colleges, or trained by their graduates. . . .

It would be unjust to Mr. Washington not to acknowledge that in several instances he has opposed movements in the South which were unjust to the Negro; he sent memorials to the Louisiana and Alabama constitutional conventions, he has spoken against lynching, and in other ways has openly or silently set his influence against sinister schemes and unfortunate happenings. Notwithstanding this, it is equally true to assert that on the whole the distinct impression left by Mr. Washington's propaganda is, first, that the South is justified in its present attitude toward the Negro because of the Negro's degradation; secondly, that the prime cause of the Negro's failure to rise more quickly is his wrong education in the past; and, thirdly, that his future rise depends primarily on his own efforts. Each of these propositions is a dangerous half-truth. The supplementary truths must never be lost sight of: first, slavery and race-prejudice are potent if not sufficient causes of the Negro's position; second, industrial and common-school training were necessarily slow in planting because they had to await the black teachers trained by higher institutions ..; and, third, while it is a great truth to say that the Negro must strive and strive mightily to help himself, it is equally true that unless his striving be not simply seconded, but rather aroused and encouraged, by the initiative of the richer and wiser environing group, he cannot hope for great success.

In his failure to realize and impress this last point, Mr. Washington is especially to be criticised. His doctrine has tended to make the whites, North and South, shift the burden of the Negro problem to the Negro's shoulders and stand aside as critical and rather pessimistic spectators; when in fact the burden belongs to the nation, and the hands of none of us are clean if we bend not our energies to righting these great wrongs....

Source: W. E. B. DuBois, *The Souls of Black Folk;* Essays and Sketches (Chicago: A. C. McClurg, 1903).

11. CHILD LABOR EXPOSED: EXCERPT FROM FRANCIS H. NICHOLS, "CHILDREN OF THE COAL SHADOW," FEBRUARY 1903

The School of the "Breaker"

The company's nurseries for boys of the coal shadow are the grim black buildings called breakers, where the lump coal from the blast is crushed into marketable sizes.

In speaking of the events of his childhood, the average man is far more apt to refer to the time "when I was working in the breaker" than to any occurrence of his school-days. After being ground in heavy machinery in the cupola of the breaker, the broken coal flows down a series of chutes to the ground floor, where it is loaded on freight cars waiting to receive it. The chutes zigzag through the building, about three feet apart. Between them, in tiers, are nailed a series of planks; these serve as seats for the "slate-pickers." Mixed with the coal are pieces of slate rock which it is the duty of the slate-picker to detect as they pass him, and to throw into another chute which passes to the refuse heap below. A few of the slate-pickers are white-haired old men, superannuated or crippled miners who are no longer able to blast coal below ground, and who for the sake of a dollar a day pass their last years in the breaker; but an overwhelming majority in all the breakers are boys. All day long their little fingers dip into the unending grimy stream that rolls past them.

Dangers and Hardships of the Work

The coal so closely resembles slate that it can be detected only by the closest scrutiny, and the childish faces are compelled to bend so low over the chutes that prematurely round shoulders and narrow chests are the inevitable result. In front of the chutes is an open space reserved for the "breaker boss," who watches the boys as intently as they watch the coal.

The boss is armed with a stick, with which he occasionally raps on the head and shoulders a boy who betrays lack of zeal. The breakers are supposed to be heated in winter, and a steam pipe winds up the wall; but in cold weather every pound of steam is needed in the mines, so that the amount of heat that radiates from the steam pipe is not sufficient to be taken seriously by any of the breakers' toilers. From November until May a breaker boy always wears a cap and tippet; and overcoat if he possesses one, but because he has to rely largely upon the sense of touch, he cannot cover his finger-tips with mittens or gloves, from the chafing of the coal his fingers sometimes bleed, and his nails are worn down to the quick. The hours of toil for slate-pickers are supposed to be from seven in the morning until noon, and from one to six in the afternoon; but when the colliery is running on "full capacity orders," the noon recess is reduced to half an hour, and the good-night whistle does not blow until half-past six. For his eleven hours' work the breaker boy gets no more pay than for ten.

The wages of breaker boys are about the same all over the coal regions. When he begins to work at slate picking a boy receives forty cents a day, and as he becomes more expert, the amount is increased until at the end of, say, his fourth year in the breaker, his daily wage may have reached ninety cents. This is the maximum for an especially industrious and skillful boy. The average is about seventy cents a day. From the ranks of the older breaker boys are chosen door-boys and runners, who work in the mines below ground.

The number of boys who work in hard coal mines is imperfectly realized in the rest of the United States. According to the report of the Bureau of Mines of Pennsylvania for 1901, 147,651 persons were employed "inside and outside the mines of the anthracite region." Of these, 19,564 were classified as slate-pickers, 3,148 as door-boys and helpers, and 10,894 as drivers and runners.

The report makes no classification of miners by their ages, but I am convinced that 90 percent of the slate-pickers, 30 per cent of the drivers and runners, and all of the door-boys and helpers are boys. In other words, a total of 24,023, or nearly one-sixth of all the employees of the anthracite coal mines, are children.

Age Certificates and What They Amount To

According to the mining laws of Pennsylvania, "no boy under the age of fourteen shall be employed in a mine, nor shall a boy under the age of twelve be employed in or about the outside structures or workings of a colliery" (*i.e.,* in a breaker). Yet no one who stands by the side of a breaker boss and looks up at the tiers of benches that rise from the floor to the coal-begrimed roof can believe for a minute that the law has been complied with in the case of one in ten of the tiny figures in blue jumpers and overalls bending over the chutes. The mine inspector and the breaker boss will explain that "these boys look younger than their ages is," and that a sworn certificate setting forth the age of every boy is on file in the office.

Children's age certificates are a criminal institution. When a father wishes to place his son in a breaker, he obtains an "age blank" from a mine inspector, and in its spaces he has inserted some age at which it is legal for a boy to work. He carries the certificate to a notary public or justice of the peace, who, in consideration, of a fee of twenty-five cents, administers oath to the parent and affixes a notarial seal to the certificate.

Justifiable and Unjustifiable Perjury

According to the ethics of the coal fields, it is not wrong for a minor or his family to lie or to practise any form of deceit in dealing with coal-mine operators or owners. A parent is justified in perjuring himself as to his son's age on a certificate that will be filed with the mine superintendent, but any statement made to a representative of the union must be absolutely truthful. For this reason, my inquiries of mine boys as to their work and ages were always conducted under the sacred auspices of the union.

Testimony "On the Level"

The interrogative colloquy was invariably something like this:

"How old are you?"

Boy: "Thirteen; going on fourteen."

Secretary of the Local: "On the level now, this is union business. You can speak free, understand."

Boy: "Oh, dat's a diffurnt t'ing altogether. I'm nine years old. I've been working since me fadder got hurted in th' explosion in No. 17 a year ago last October."

Source: Francis H. Nichols, "Children of the Coal Shadow," *McClure's*, vol. 20 (February 1903), pp. 435–44.

12. "Muscle Trust": Excerpt from David M. Parry, President's Address to the National Association of Manufacturers, April 1903

Note: This speech argues the conservative view of Labor as the "Muscle Trust."

The chief work that lies within the province of this Association is an educational one. Organized labor owes its present power mainly to the support of public opinion, and this it obtained through constant agitation. The thought and sentiment of thousands who lean toward the cause of labor are based upon *ex parte* consideration. Carried away by the insistent and specious pleas for the "poor working-man," they have lost sight of the grave issues that are at stake. The duty that lies before us is, therefore, a plain one. It is to arouse the great middle class to a realization of what trades unionism really means. . . .

Organized labor knows but one law, and that is the law of physical force—the law of the Huns and Vandals, the law of the savage. All its purposes are accomplished either by actual force or by the threat of force. It does not place its reliance in reason and justice, but in strikes, boycotts, and coercion. It is, in all essential features, a mob power, know-

ing no master except its own will, and is continually condemning or defying the constituted authorities. The stronger it grows the greater a menace it becomes to the continuance of free government, in which all the people have a voice. It is, in fact, a despotism springing into being in the midst of a liberty-loving people.

In setting itself up as a power independent of the power of the state, it does not regard itself as bound to observe the Fourteenth Amendment to the Constitution of the United States, which says:

> No state shall make or enforce any law which shall abridge the privileges or immunities of citizens of the United States, nor shall any state deprive any person of life, liberty, or property without due process of law, nor deny to any person within its jurisdiction equal protection of the laws.

It has not, in times past, hesitated to resort to violence and the destruction of property to compel the acceptance of its demands. Its history is stained with blood and ruin. Many a man whose only fault was that he stood upon his rights has been made to suffer outrage, and even death, and many an employer has been brought face to face with financial ruin. These wrongs cry unto heaven, and yet an unaroused public sentiment too often permits them to go unheeded and unpunished.

It now demands of the public and of Congress the privilege to violate the laws forbidding violence and property destruction that it may continue to maintain its power through terrorism. It extends its tactics of coercion and intimidation over all classes, dictating to the press and the politicians, and strangling independence of thought and American manhood.

It denies to those outside its ranks the individual right to dispose of their labor as they see fit, a right that is one of the most sacred and fundamental of American liberty. It holds a bludgeon over the head of the employer, laying down the terms upon which he shall be permitted to do business. It says to him that he must deal direct with the union; that, while he shall pay the men who work in his factory, they shall be beholden more to the union than to him for their positions; that he cannot employ or discharge men without the endorsement and consent of the union, and that he must pay them the wage fixed by the union, without regard to their individual worth or the economic ability of the employer to pay.

It denies to the individual the right of being his own judge as to the length of time he shall work and as to how much he shall do within the time prescribed. It takes no account of the varying degree of natural aptitude and powers of endurance displayed by individuals, and seeks to place all men in each particular trade on the same dead level, as respects his daily output and his daily wage. Thus a premium is placed on indolence and incompetence, and there is a restriction of human effort, reducing the aggregate production and increasing the cost of the things produced. . . . The eight-hour law, which it demands is merely the extension to a wider field of the principle it enforces in trades under its domination.

While it seeks to compel men already employed in the trades to enlist under its banner, it at the same time seeks to prevent outsiders from entering the trades. It foists upon employers rules limiting the number of apprentices, some unions going so far as to say there shall be no apprentices whatever. The boys from the farms now come to the cities and find the doors to the trades shut against them. While lawyers, doctors, and men in other unorganized vocations are glad to teach young men their knowledge the trades unionist refuses to do so, and employers are now forced to endow technical schools in the hope of obtaining that supply of new blood for their workshops which is essential to the prevention of dry rot.

Organized labor is an organization of manual labor, trained and untrained, of men who do as they are told and who depend upon the brains of others for guidance. That wide field of labor in which mental capacity is a greater or less requisite on the part of the workers is not represented by it, and cannot be for the obvious impossibility of organizing brains. . . .

Organized labor is particularly denunciatory of trusts, but what greater trust is there than itself? It is the grand trust of the times, it is the muscle trust, the trust of men who make their living by manual labor. . . .

Source: National Association of Manufacturers of the United States of America. *Proceedings of the Annual Convention,* No. 8, 1903.

13. EXCERPT FROM ERNEST POOLE, "WAIFS OF THE STREET," MAY 1903

We all glance in passing at the shrewd little newsboys, peddlers, messengers, and bootblacks that swarm by day and night through every crowded street of busy New York. We catch only a glimpse. The paper is sold in a twinkling, and like a flash the little urchin is off through the crowd. We admire his tense energy, his shrewd, bright self-reliance. We hear of newsboys who in later life have risen high; and we think of street work, if we think of it at all, as a capital school for industry and enterprise. Those who follow deeper are forced to a directly opposite conclusion. The homeless, the most illiterate, the most dishonest, the most impure—these are the finished products of child street work. They are the minority of its workers. But this is only because the greater number stay but a few years, and so leave before thoroughly trained to the service. It is of the finished products that I wish mainly to write. They poison the rest, for in the street morals spread, like a new slang word, with amazing rapidity. And what is true of hundreds applies in some degree to most of the recruits around them.

The main characteristic of street work is its unwholesome irregularity. The work is almost wholly dependent on the crowds in the street, and is shaped to meet their irregular tastes and habits. The crowd pays best, and pays most carelessly, at night. In cold or rainy weather business drops almost to the vanishing point. It comes up with a rush in every time of excitement, for excitement, good or bad, is what street work is built on. This is especially true of the messenger service. Messenger boys are the most irregular of all street workers. One of the large New York companies employs one thousand boys at a time, but employs six thousand during the year. The night shift seems generally the most popular. Night messengers do all-night work between all-night houses and all-night people—some every week, some alternate weeks, some in four-hour shifts, and some twelve hours at a stretch. In one office of nineteen boys the oldest was sixteen, the youngest looked barely twelve. They went on at eight o'clock at night, and I found them still there at ten the next morning. It is the business of their manager to employ just enough boys to keep them all on the street all through the night.

For many this nervous irregular life is sustained and poisoned by hastily bolted meals, with often double a man's portion of coffee, cigars, and cigarettes . . .

Smoking is almost universal, and coffee is used to an amazing excess. I know over a hundred boys who average at least three huge bowls each night, and some who often drink six at supper. In thousands of cases, too, the work makes the sleep irregular. Several hundred at least sleep all night on the streets, in stables, condemned buildings, and halls of tenements, waiting until after midnight when the lights are all out . . .

Irregular work brings irregular pay. Newsboys get their papers on credit, are not forced to save for the next day's business, and so keep in debt most of the time. Messenger boys do a large side business in tips. The peddlers and bootblacks are paid on the spot. All classes have ready money—some in copper, some in silver—and reckless spending is a most natural result. . . .

The street's improvidence is a natural result of its irregularity. Gambling and improvidence go together. Most street workers are inveterate players at the game of "craps." This whiles away the time between the irregular working periods, and often runs well up into the dollars. In one of the large messenger offices on Broadway it is common for boys to lose the entire week's earnings in the hall and stairway before reaching the street. . . .

Source: Ernest Poole, "Waifs of the Street," *McClure's,* vol. 21 (May 1903), pp. 40–44.

14. Excerpt from President Theodore Roosevelt's Fourth Annual Message to Congress, December 6, 1904

The steady aim of this Nation, as of all enlightened nations, should be to strive to bring ever nearer the day when there shall prevail throughout the world the peace of justice. There are kinds of peace which are highly undesirable, which are in the long run as destructive as any war. Tyrants and oppressors have many times made a wilderness and called it peace. Many times peoples who were slothful or timid or shortsighted, who had been enervated by ease or by luxury, or misled by false teachings, have shrunk in unmanly fashion from doing duty that was stern and that needed self-sacrifice, and have sought to hide from their own minds their shortcomings, their ignoble motives, by calling them love of peace. The peace of tyrannous terror, the peace of craven weakness, the peace of injustice, all these should be shunned as we shun unrighteous war.

The goal to set before us as a nation, the goal which should be set before all mankind, is the attainment of the peace of justice, of the peace which comes when each nation is not merely safe-guarded in its own rights, but scrupulously recognizes and performs its duty toward others. Generally peace for righteousness; but if there is conflict between the two, then our fealty is due first to the cause of righteousness. Unrighteous wars are common, and unrighteous peace is rare; but both should be shunned. The right of freedom and the responsibility for the exercise of that right can not be divorced. One of our great poets has well and finely said that freedom is not a gift that tarries long in the hands of cowards. Neither does it tarry long in the hands of those too slothful, too dishonest, or too unintelligent to exercise it. The eternal vigilance which is the price of liberty must be exercised, sometimes to guard against outside foes; although of course far more often to guard against our own selfish or thoughtless shortcomings.

If these self-evident truths are kept before us, and only if they are so kept before us, we shall have a clear idea of what our foreign policy in its larger aspects should be. It is our duty to remember that a nation has no more right to do injustice to another nation, strong or weak, than an individual has to do injustice to another individual; that the same moral law applies in one case as in the other. But we must also remember that it is as much the duty of the Nation to guard its own rights and its own interests as it is the duty of the individual so to do. Within the Nation the individual has now delegated this right to the State, that is, to the representative of all the individuals, and it is a maxim of the law that for every wrong there is a remedy.

But in international law we have not advanced by any means as far as we have advanced in municipal law. There is as yet no judicial way of enforcing a right in international law. When one nation wrongs another or wrongs many others, there is no tribunal before which the wrongdoer can be brought. Either it is necessary supinely to acquiesce in the wrong, and thus put a premium upon brutality and aggression, or else it is necessary for the aggrieved nation valiantly to stand up for its rights. Until some method is devised by which there shall be a degree of international control over offending nations, it would be a wicked thing for the most civilized powers, for those with most sense of international obligations and with keenest and most generous appreciation of the difference between right and wrong, to disarm. If the great civilized nations of the present day should completely disarm, the result would mean an immediate recrudescence of barbarism in one form or another. Under any circumstances a sufficient armament would have to be kept up to serve the purposes of international police; and until international cohesion and the sense of international duties and rights are far more advanced than at present, a nation desirous both of securing respect for itself and of doing good to others must have a force adequate for the work which it feels is allotted to it as its part of the general world duty. . . . A great free people owes it to itself and to all mankind not to sink into helplessness before the powers of evil. . . .

It is not true that the United States feels any land hunger or entertains any projects as regards the other nations of the Western Hemisphere save such as are for their welfare. All that this country desires is to see the neighboring countries stable, orderly, and prosperous. Any country whose people conduct themselves well can count upon our hearty friendship. If a nation shows that it knows how to act with reasonable efficiency and decency in social and political matters, if it keeps order and pays its obligations, it need fear no interference from the United States. Chronic wrongdoing, or an impotence which results in a general loosening of the ties of civilized society, may in America, as elsewhere, ultimately require intervention by some civilized nation, and in the Western Hemisphere the adherence of the United States to the Monroe Doctrine may force the United States, however reluctantly, in flagrant cases of such wrongdoing or impotence, to the exercise of an international police power.

If every country washed by the Caribbean Sea would show the progress in stable and just civilization which with the aid of the Platt Amendment Cuba has shown since our troops left the island, and which so many of the republics in both Americas are constantly and brilliantly showing, all question of interference by this Nation with their affairs would be at an end. Our interests and those of our southern neighbors are in reality identical. They have great natural riches, and if within their borders the reign of law and justice obtains, prosperity is sure to come to them. While they thus obey the primary laws of civilized society they may rest assured that they will be treated by us in a spirit of cordial and helpful sympathy. We would interfere with them only in the last resort, and then only if it became evident that their inability or unwillingness to do justice at home and abroad had violated the rights of the United States or had invited foreign aggression to the detriment of the entire body of American nations. . . .

Source: Messages and Papers of the Presidents, ed. J. Richardson, vol. 14 (New York: Bureau of National Literature and Art, 1917), 6920ff.

15. Excerpt from William L. Riordon, *Plunkitt of Tammany Hall,* Chapter 23, "Strenuous Life of the Tammany District Leader," 1905

Note. This chapter is based on extracts from Plunkitt's Diary and on my daily observation of the work of the district leader.— W.L.R.

The life of the Tammany district leader is strenuous. To his work is due the wonderful recuperative power of the organization. . . .

No other politician in New York or elsewhere is exactly like the Tammany district leader or works as he does. As a rule, he has no business or occupation other than politics. He plays politics every day and night in the year, and his headquarters bears the inscription, "Never closed."

Everybody in the district knows him. Everybody knows where to find him, and nearly everybody goes to him for assistance of one sort or another, especially the poor of the tenements. . . .

A philanthropist? Not at all. He is playing politics all the time. . . .

This is a record of a day's work by Plunkitt:

2 A.M.: Aroused from sleep by the ringing of his door bell; went to the door and found a bartender, who asked him to go to the police station and bail out a saloon-keeper who had been arrested for violating the excise law. Furnished bail and returned to bed at three o'clock.

6 A.M.: Awakened by fire engines passing his house. Hastened to the scene of the fire, according to the custom of the Tammany district leaders, to give-assistance to the fire sufferers, if needed. Met several of his election district captains who are always under orders to look out for fires, which are considered great vote-getters. Found several tenants who had been burned out, took them to a hotel, supplied them with clothes, fed them, and arranged temporary quarters for them until they could rent and furnish new apartments.

8:30 A.M.: Went to the police court to look after his constituents. Found six "drunks." Secured the discharge of four by a timely word with the judge, and paid the fines of two.

9 A.M.: Appeared in the Municipal District Court. Directed one of his district captains to act as counsel for a widow against whom dispossess proceedings had been instituted and obtained an extension of time. Paid the rent of a poor family about to be dispossessed and gave them a dollar for food.

11 A.M.: At home again. Found four men waiting for him. One had been discharged by the Metropolitan Railway Company for neglect of duty, and wanted the district leader to fix things. Another wanted a job on the road. The third sought a place on the Subway and the fourth, a plumber, was looking for work with the Consolidated Gas Company. The district leader spent nearly three hours fixing things for the four men, and succeeded in each case.

3 P.M.: Attended the funeral of an Italian as far as the ferry. Hurried back to make his appearance at the funeral of a Hebrew constituent. Went conspicuously to the front both in the Catholic church and the synagogue, and later attended the Hebrew confirmation ceremonies in the synagogue.

7 P.M.: Went to district headquarters and presided over a meeting of election district captains. Each captain submitted a list of all the voters in his district, reported on their attitude toward Tammany, suggested who might be won over and how they could be won, told who were in need, and who were in trouble of any kind and the best way to reach them. District leaders took notes and gave orders.

8 P.M.: Went to a church fair. Took chances on everything, bought ice-cream for the young girls and the children. Kissed the little ones, flattered their mothers and took their fathers out for something down at the corner.

9 P.M.: At the club-house again. Spent $10 on tickets for a church excursion and promised a subscription for a new church-bell. Bought tickets for a base-ball game to be played by two nines from his district. Listened to the complaints of a dozen pushcart peddlers who said they were persecuted by the police and assured them he would go to Police Headquarters in the morning and see about it.

10:30 P.M.: Attended a Hebrew wedding reception and dance. Had previously sent a handsome wedding present to the bride.

12 P.M.: In bed.

Source: William L. Riordon, Plunkitt of Tammany Hall (New York: McClure, Phillips, 1905), pp. 171–76.

16. Excerpt from Charles Edward Russell, *The Greatest Trust in the World,* 1905

The mainspring of the American Beef Trust, the centre and source of its existence, is the refrigerator car. You that live in cities and know of railroad operations only what the newspapers tell you, can have scant idea of the importance of this curious vehicle. . . .

Gustavus Swift [was] the chief founder and almost the creator of the refrigerator car as a factor in modern conditions. . . . He and his brothers had been butchers in Massachusetts; he had drifted westward with no particular aim except to find some road wealth. . . .

. . . A man named Tiffany had lately invented and was trying to introduce a refrigerator freight car—a car with tanks or bunkers for ice and with an intelligent arrangement of doors so as to exclude heat. Mt. Swift studied this scheme also and gradually unfolded in his mind a plan, having the prospect of enormous profits- or enormous disaster.

In the meantime he had become the proprietor of a small packing-plant at the Chicago Stock-Yards. When his plan was matured he offered it to certain railroad companies. It was merely that the railroads should operate the refrigerator cars summer and winter, and that he should furnish them with fresh dressed meats for the Eastern market. This proposal the railroads promptly rejected.

Thus thrown upon his own resources, Mr. Swift determined to make the desperate cast alone. Commercial history has few instances of a courage more genuine. The risk involved was great. The project was wholly new; not only demand and supply had to be created, but all the vast and intricate machinery of marketing. Failure meant utter ruin. Mr. Swift accepted the hazard. He built refrigerator cars under the Tiffany and other patents and began to ship out dressed meats, summer and winter.

The trade regarded the innovation as little less than insanity. Mr. Swift's immediate downfall was genially prophesied on all sides, and truly only a giant in will and resources could have triumphed, so beset. He must needs demonstrate that the refrigerator car would do its work, that the meat could be perfectly preserved, and then he must overcome the deep-seated prejudices of the people, combat the opposition of local butchers, establish and distribute products. All this he did. People in the East found that Chicago dressed beef was better and cheaper than their own, the business slowly spread, branch houses were established in every Eastern city, and the Swift establishment began to thrive. By 1880 the experiment was an indubitable success.

As soon as it was discovered that Mr. Swift was right, a great revolution swept over the meat and cattle industries, and eventually over the whole business of supplying the public with perishable food products. The other packing-houses at the Stock-Yards went into the dressed-meat trade, refrigerator cars ran in every direction, shipments of cattle on the hoof declined, the great economy of the new process brought saving to the consumer and profit to the producer, and the new order began to work vast and unforeseen changes in the life and customs of the nation.

Of these changes, one of the most important was that, before long, certain parts of the country were supplying all the rest with certain products. As soon as it was discovered that the refrigerator car would safely transport everything perishable, towns and cities began to seek their food supplies wherever on the continent such supplies could best be had. . . .

Source: Charles Edward Russell, *The Greatest Trust in the World* (New York: Ridgway-Thayer, 1905), pp. 21–25.

17. EXCERPT FROM UPTON SINCLAIR, *THE JUNGLE*, 1906

It was only when the whole ham was spoiled that it came into the department of Elzbieta [a worker]. Cut up by the two-thousand-revolutions-a-minute flyers, and mixed with half a ton of other meat, no odor that ever was in a ham could make any difference. There was never the least attention paid to what was cut up for sausage; there would come all the way back from Europe old sausage that had been rejected, and that was moldy and white—it would be dosed with borax and glycerine, and dumped into the hoppers, and made over again for home consumption. There would be meat that had tumbled out on the floor, in the dirt and sawdust, where the workers had tramped and spit uncounted billions of consumption germs. There would be meat stored in great piles in rooms; and the water from leaky roofs would drip over it, and thousands of rats would race about on it. It was too dark in these storage places to see well, but a man could run his hand over these piles of meat and sweep off handfuls of the dried dung of rats. These rats were nuisances, and the packers would put poisoned bread out for them; they would die, and then rats, bread, and meat would go into the hoppers together. This is no fairy story and no joke; the meat would be shoveled into carts, and the man who did the shoveling would not trouble to lift out a rat even when he saw one—there were things that went into the sausage in comparison with which a poisoned rat was a tidbit. There was no place for the men to wash their hands before they ate their dinner, and so they made a practice of washing them in the water that was to be ladled into the sausage. There were the butt-ends of smoked meat, and the scraps of corned beef, and all the odds and ends of the waste of the plants, that would be dumped into old barrels in the cellar and left there. Under the system of rigid economy which the packers enforced, there were some jobs that it only paid to do once in a long time, and among these was the cleaning out of the waste barrels. Every spring they did it; and in the barrels would be dirt and rust and old nails and stale water—and cartload after cartload of it would be taken up and dumped into the hoppers with fresh meat, and sent out to the public's breakfast. Some of it they would make into "smoked" sausage—but as the smoking took time, and was therefore expensive, they would call upon their chemistry department, and preserve it with borax and color it with gelatine to make it brown. All of their sausage came out of the same bowl, but when they came to wrap it they would stamp some of it "special," and for this they would charge two cents more a pound.

Source: Upton Sinclair, *The Jungle* (New York: Doubleday, 1906), pp. 168–69.

18. EXCERPT FROM JOHN SPARGO, *THE BITTER CRY OF THE CHILDREN*, 1906

I shall never forget my first visit to a glass factory at night. It was a big wooden structure, so loosely built that it afforded little protection from draughts, surrounded by a high fence with several rows of barbed wire stretched across the top. I went with the foreman of the factory and he explained to me the reason for the stockade-like fence. "It keeps the young imps inside once we've got 'em for the night shift," he said. The "young imps" were, of course, the boys employed, about forty in number, at least ten of whom were less than twelve years of age. It was a cheap bottle factory, and the proportion of boys to men was larger than is usual in the higher grades of manufacture. Cheapness and child labor go together,—the cheaper the grade of manufacture, as a rule, the cheaper the labor employed. The hours of labor for the "night shift" were from 5.30 P.M. to 3.30 A.M. I stayed and watched the boys at their work for several hours, and when their tasks were done saw them disappear into the darkness and storm of the night . . .

In the middle of the room was a large round furnace with a number of small doors, three or four feet from the ground, forming a sort of belt around the furnace. In front of these doors the glassblowers were working. With long wrought-iron blowpipes the blowers deftly took from the furnace little wads of waxlike molten "metal" which they blew into balls and then rolled on their rolling boards. These elongated rolls they dropped into moulds and then blew again, harder than before, to force the half-shaped mass into its proper form. With a sharp, clicking sound they broke their pipes away and repeated the whole process . . .

Then began the work of the boys. By the side of each mould sat a "take-out boy," who, with tongs, took the half-finished bottles—not yet provided with necks—out of the moulds. Then other boys, called "snapper-ups," took these bodies of bottles in their tongs and put the small ends into gas-heated moulds till they were red hot. Then the boys took them out with almost incredible quickness and passed them to other men, "finishers," who shaped the necks of the bottles into their final form. Then the "carrying-in

boys," sometimes called "carrier pigeons," took the red-hot bottles from the benches, three or four at a time, upon big asbestos shovels to the annealing oven, where they are gradually cooled off. . . . The Work of these "carrying-in boys," several of whom were less than twelve years old, was by far the hardest of all. They were kept on a slow run all the time from the benches to the annealing oven and back again. I can readily believe what many manufacturers assert, that it is difficult to get men to do this work, because men cannot stand the pace and get tired too quickly. . . . I did not measure the distance . . . but my friend, Mr. Owen R. Lovejoy, has done so in a typical factory. . . . The distance to the annealing oven in the factory in question was one hundred feet, and the boys made seventy-two trips per hour, making the distance travelled in eight hours nearly twenty-two miles. Over a half of this distance the boys were carrying their hot loads to the oven. The pay of these boys varies from sixty cents to a dollar for eight hours' work. About a year ago I gathered particulars of the pay of 257 boys in New Jersey and Pennsylvania; the lowest pay was forty cents per night and the highest a dollar and ten cents, while the average was seventy-two cents. . . .

The effects of the employment of young boys in glass factories, especially by night, are injurious from every possible point of view. The constant facing of the glare of the furnaces and the red-hot bottles causes serious injury to the sight; minor accidents from burning are common. "Severe burns and the loss of sight are regular risks of the trade in glass-bottle making," says Mrs. Florence Kelley. Even more serious than the accidents are the physical disorders induced by the conditions of employment. Boys who work at night do not as a rule get sufficient or satisfactory rest by day. . . . Indeed, most boys seem to prefer night work for the reason that it gives them the chance to play during the daytime. Even where the mothers are careful and solicitous, they find it practically impossible to control boys who are wage-earners and feel themselves to be independent. This lack of proper rest, added to the heat and strain of their work, produces nervous dyspepsia. From working in draughty sheds where they are often, as one boy said to me in Zanesville, O., "burning on the side against the furnace and pretty near freezing on the other," they are frequently subject to rheumatism. Going from the heated factories to their homes, often a mile or so distant, perspiring and improperly clad, with their vitality at its lowest ebb, they fall ready victims to pneumonia and to its heir, the Great White Plague. In almost every instant when I have asked local physicians for their experience, they have named these as the commonest physical results. Of the fearful moral consequences there can be no question. The glass-blowers themselves realize this and, even more than the physical deterioration, it prevents them from taking their own children into the glass houses. One practically never finds the son of a glass-blower employed as "snapper-up," or "carrying-in boy," unless the father is dead or incapacitated by reason of sickness. "I'd sooner see my boy dead than working here. You might as well give a boy to the devil at once as send him to a glass factory," said one blower to me in Glassborough, N.J.; and that is the spirit in which most of the men regard the matter....

In some districts, especially in New Jersey, it has long been the custom to import boys from certain orphan asylums and "reformatories" to supply the demand of the manufacturers. These boys are placed in laborers' families, and their board paid for by the employers, who deduct it from the boys' wages. Thus a veritable system of child slavery has developed, remarkably like the old English pauper-apprentice system." ... It is perhaps only indicative of the universal readiness of men to concern themselves with the mote in their brothers' eyes without considering the beam in their own, that I should have attended a meeting in New Jersey where the child labor of the South was bitterly condemned, but no word was said of the appalling nature of the problem in the state of New Jersey itself.

Source: John Spargo, *The Bitter Cry of the Children* (New York: Macmillan, 1906), chapter 4, pp. 155–162.

19. Excerpt from the Pure Food and Drug Act, June 30, 1906

Be it enacted . . . That is shall be unlawful for any person to manufacture within any State or Territory or the District of Columbia any article of food or drug which is adulterated or misbranded, within the meaning of this Act. . . .

SEC. 7. That for the purposes of this Act an article shall be deemed to be adulterated: In case of drugs:

First. If, when a drug is sold under or by a name recognized in the United States Pharmacopoeia or National Formulary, it differs from the standard of strength, quality, or purity, as determined by the test laid down in the United States Pharmacopoeia or National Formulary official at the time of investigation: Provided, that no drug defined in the United States Pharmacopoeia or National Formulary shall be deemed to be adulterated under this provision if the standard of strength, quality, or purity be plainly stated upon the bottle, box, or other container thereof although the standard may differ from that determined by the test laid down in the United States Pharmacopoeia or National Formulary.

Second. If its strength or purity fall below the professed standard or quality under which it is sold.
In the case of confectionery:

If it contain terra alba, barytes, talc, chrome yellow, or other mineral substance or poisonous color or flavor, or other ingredient deleterious or detrimental to health, or

any vinous, malt or spirituous liquor or compound or narcotic drug.
In the case of food:

First. If any substance has been mixed and packed with it so as to reduce or lower or injuriously affect its quality or strength.

Second. If any substance has been substituted wholly or in part for the article.

Third. If any valuable constituent of the article has been wholly or in part abstracted.

Fourth. If it be mixed, colored, powdered, coated, or stained in a manner whereby damage or inferiority is concealed.

Fifth. If it contain any added poisonous or other added deleterious ingredient which may render such article injurious to health: Provided, That when in the preparation of food products for shipment they are preserved by any external application applied in such manner that the preservative is necessarily removed mechanically, or by maceration in water, or otherwise, and directions for the removal of said preservative shall be printed on the covering or the package, the provisions of this Act shall be construed as applying only when said products are ready for consumption.

Sixth. If it consists in whole or in part of a filthy, decomposed, or putrid animal or vegetable substance, or any portion of an animal unfit for food, whether manufactured or not, or if it is the product of a diseased animal, or one that has died otherwise than by slaughter.

SEC. 8. That the term, "misbranded," as used herein, shall apply to all drugs, or articles of food, or articles which enter into the composition of food, the package or label of which shall bear any statement, design, or device regarding such article, or the ingredients or substances contained therein which shall be false or misleading in any particular, and to any food or drug product which is falsely branded as to the State, Territory, or country in which it is manufactured or produced.

That for the purposes of this Act an article shall also be deemed to be misbranded: In case of drugs:

First. If it be an imitation of or offered for sale under the name of another article.

Second. If the contents of the package as originally put up shall have been removed, in whole or in part, and other contents shall have been placed in such package, or if the package fail to bear a statement on the label of the quantity or proportion of any alcohol, morphine, opium, cocaine, heroin, alpha or beta eucaine, chloroform, cannabis indica, chloral hydrate, or acetanilide, or any derivative or preparation of any such substances contained therein.
In the case of food:

First. If it be an imitation of or offered for sale under the distinctive name of another article.

Second. If it be labeled or branded so as to deceive or mislead the purchaser, or purport to be a foreign product when not so, or if the contents of the package as originally put up shall have been removed in whole or in part and other contents shall have been placed in such package, or if it fail to bear a statement on the label of the quantity or proportion of any morphine, opium, cocaine, heroin, alpha or beta eucaine, chloroform, cannabis indica, chloral hydrate, or acetanilide, or any derivative or preparation of any such substances contained therein.

Third. If in package form, and the contents are stated in terms of weight or measure, they are not plainly and correctly stated on the outside of the package.

Fourth. If the package containing it or its label shall bear any statement, design, or device regarding the ingredients or the substances contained therein, which statement, design, or device shall be false or misleading in any particular. . . .

Source: U.S. Statutes at Large, 59th Congress, vol. 34, part 1, pp. 768ff.

20. Excerpt from Louis D. Brandeis's Brief in Support of the State of Oregon in *Muller v. Oregon,* 1907

This case presents the single question whether the Statute of Oregon. . . . which provides that "no female be employed in any mechanical establishment, or factory, or laundry" "more than ten hours during any one day," is unconstitutional and void as violating the Fourteenth Amendment of the Federal Constitution.

The decision in this case will, in effect, determine the constitutionality of nearly all the statutes in force in the United States, limiting the hours of labor of adult women. . . .

The facts of common knowledge of which the Court may take judicial notice . . . establish, we submit, conclusively that there is reasonable ground for holding that to permit women in Oregon to work in a "mechanical establishment, or factory, or laundry" more than ten hours in one day is dangerous to the public health, safety, morals, or welfare. . . .

The leading countries in Europe in which women are largely employed in factory or similar work have found it necessary to take action for the protection of their health and safety and the public welfare, and have enacted laws limiting the hours of labor of women. . . .

Twenty States of the Union . . . have enacted laws limiting the hours of labor for adult women. . . .

In the United States, as in foreign countries, there has been a general movement to strengthen and to extend the operation of these laws. In no State has any such law been held unconstitutional, except in Illinois. . . .

1. The Danger of Long Hours
A. Clauses
(1) Physical Differences between Men and Women
Report of Select Committee on Shops Early Closing Bill, British House of Commons, 1895.

Dr. Percy Kidd, physician in Brompton and London Hospitals:

The most common effect I have noticed of the long hours is general deterioration of health; very general symptoms which we medically attribute to over-action and debility of the nervous system; that includes a great deal more than what is called nervous disease, such as indigestion, constipation, a general slackness, and a great many other indefinite symptoms.

Are those symptoms more marked in women than in men?

I think they are much more marked in women. I should say one sees a great many more women of this class than men; but I have seen precisely the same symptoms in men, I should say not in the same proportion. . . . Another symptom especially among women is anemia, bloodlessness or pallor, that I have no doubt is connected with long hours indoors. . . .

Report of the Maine Bureau of Industrial and Labor Statistics, 1888.

Let me quote from Dr. Ely Von der Warker (1875):

Woman is badly constructed for the purposes of standing eight or ten hours upon her feet. I do not intend to bring into evidence the peculiar position and nature of the organs contained in the pelvis, but to call attention to the peculiar construction of the knee and the shallowness of the pelvis, and the delicate nature of the foot as part of a sustaining column. The knee joint of woman is a sexual characteristic. Viewed in front and extended, the joint in but a slight degree interrupts the gradual taper of the thigh into the leg. Viewed in a semiflexed position, the joint forms a smooth ovate spheroid. The reason of this lies in the smallness of the patella in front, and the narrowness of the articular surfaces of the tibia and femur, and which in man form the lateral prominences, and thus is much more perfect as a sustaining column than that of a woman. The muscles which keep the body fixed upon the thighs in the erect position labor under the disadvantage of shortness of purchase, owing to the short distance, compared to that of men, between the crest of the ilium and the great trochanter of the femur, thus giving to man a much larger purchase in the leverage existing between the trunk and the extremities. Comparatively the foot is less able to sustain weight than that of man, owing to its shortness and the more delicate formation of the tarsus and metatarsus . . .

Infant Mortality: A Social Problem. George Newrnan, M.D., London, 1906.

The results of fatigue become manifest in various ways, not the least being the occurrence of accidents or of physical breakdown. The former, as is now well recognized, occur most frequently in fatigued workers. For example, since 1900 there has been a steady increase in the number of accidents to women over eighteen years of age in laundries. In 1900 such accidents numbered 131; in 1904, 157. Now it has been shown that whilst the first half of the day yields about the same number of accidents as the second half, more accidents, amounting to nearly double the number, occur between the hours of 11 A.M. and 1 P.M., and between 4 P.M. and 7 P.M. than at any other time. . . .

Relations between Labor and Capital. United States Labor Committee, 1883.

. . . Testimony of Robert Howard . . . in Fall River Cotton Mills.

I have noticed that the hard, slavish overwork is driving those girls into the saloons, after they leave the mills evenings . . . good, respectable girls . . .

Drinking is most prevalent among working people where the hours of labor are long. . . .

President Roosevelt's Annual Message . . . to . . . Congress, December 4, 1906.

More and more . . . people are growing to recognize the fact that the questions which are not merely of industrial but of social importance outweigh all others; and these two questions (labor of women and children) most emphatically come in the category of those which affect in the most far-reaching way the home-life of the nation. . . .

Industrial Conference National Civic Federation, 1902.

The most striking fact about this question of hours of labor seems to be its universality. In virtually every country dominated by Western civilization the daily worktime in mechanical industries is being cut down by successive movements that appear to be as inevitable as the tide, and that have the appearance of steps in the path of human progress. . . .

That the time is now ripe for another general reduction in the daily working time is indicated by the testimony of physicians and the mortality statistics of occupations. . . .

Laundries

The special prohibition in the Oregon Act of more than ten hours' work in laundries is not an arbitrary discrimination against that trade. Laundries would probably not be included under the general term of "manufacturing" or "mechanical establishments"; and yet the special dangers of long hours in laundries, as the business is now conducted, present strong reasons for providing a legal limitation of the hours of work in that business. . . .

Conclusion

We submit that in view of the facts above set forth and of legislative action extending over a period of more than sixty years in the leading countries in Europe and in twenty of our States, it cannot be said that the Legislature of Oregon has no reasonable ground for believing that the public health, safety, or welfare did not require a legal limitation on women's work in manufacturing and mechanical establishments and laundries to ten hours in one day.

Source: Transcripts of Records and File Copies of Briefs, 1907, vol. 24 (Cases 102–107), Library of the Supreme Court, Washington, D.C.

21. EXCERPT FROM RAY STANNARD BAKER, *FOLLOWING THE COLOR LINE,* 1908

One of the questions I asked of Negroes whom I met both North and South was this:

"What is your chief cause of complaint?"

In the South the first answer nearly always referred to the Jim Crow cars or the Jim Crow railroad stations; after that, the complaint was of political disfranchisement, the difficulty of getting justice in the courts, the lack of good school facilities, and in some localities, of the danger of actual physical violence.

But in the North the first answer invariably referred to working conditions.

"The Negro isn't given a fair opportunity to get employment. He is discriminated against because he is colored."

Professor Kelly Miller, one of the acutest of Negro writers, has said:

"The Negro (in the North) is compelled to loiter around the edges of industry."

Southern white men are fond of meeting Northern criticism of Southern treatment of the Negro with the response:

"But the North closes the doors of industrial opportunity to the Negro."

And yet in spite of this complaint of conditions in the North, one who looks Southward can almost see the army of Negroes gathering from out of the cities, villages and farms, bringing nothing with them but a buoyant hope in a distant freedom, but tramping always Northward. . . .

And why do they come if their difficulties are so great? Is it true that there is no chance for them in industry? Are they better or worse off in the North than in the South?

In the first place, in most of the smaller Northern cities where the Negro population is not increasing rapidly, discrimination is hardly noticeable. Negroes enter the trades, find places in the shops, or even follow competitive business callings and still maintain friendly relationships with the white people.

But the small towns are not typical of the new race conditions in the North; the situation in the greater centers of population where Negro immigration is increasing largely, is decidedly different.

As I traveled in the North, I heard many stories of the difficulties which the colored man had to meet in getting employment. Of course, as a Negro said to me, "there are always places for the colored man at the bottom." He can always get work at unskilled manual labor, or personal or domestic service—in other words, at menial employment. He has had that in plenty in the South. But what he seeks as he becomes educated is an opportunity for better grades of employment. He wants to rise. . . .

In New York I had a talk with William L. Bulkley, the colored principal of Public School No. 80, attended chiefly by colored children, who told me of the great difficulties and discouragements which confronted the Negro boy who wanted to earn his living. He relates this story. . . .

"The saddest thing that faces me in my work is the small opportunity for a colored boy or girl to find proper employment. A boy comes to my office and asks for his working papers. He may be well up in the school, possibly with graduation only a few months off. I question him somewhat as follows: 'Well, my boy, you want to go to work, do you? What are you going to do?' 'I am going to be a door-boy, sir.' 'Well, you will get $2.50 or $3 a week, but after awhile that will not be enough; what then?' After a moment's pause he will reply: 'I should like to be an office boy.' 'Well, what next?' A moment's silence, and, 'I should try to get a position as bell-boy.' 'Well, then, what next?' A rather contemplative mood, and then, 'I should like to climb to the position of head bell-boy.' He has now arrived at the top; farther than this he sees no hope. He must face the bald fact that he must enter business as a boy and wind up as a boy.'" . . .

"Why do they come?" I asked a Negro minister in Philadelphia.

"Well, they're treated more like men up here in the North," he said, "that's the secret of it. There's prejudice here, too, but the color line isn't drawn in their faces at every turn as it is in the South. It all gets back to a question of manhood."

In the North prejudice is more purely economic than it is in the South—an incident of industrial competition.

In the South the Negro still has the field of manual labor largely to himself, he is unsharpened by competition; but when he reaches the Northern city, he not only finds the work different and more highly organized and specialized, but he finds that he must meet the fierce competition of half a dozen eager, struggling, ambitious groups of foreigners, who are willing and able to work long hours at low pay in order to get a foothold. He has to meet often for the first time the Italian, the Russian Jew, the Slav, to say nothing of the white American laborer. . . .

Source: Ray Stannard Baker, "The Negro's Struggle for Survival in the North," *Following the Color Line.* (New York: Doubleday Page, 1908) chapter 7; also published with slight variations in *American Magazine,* March 1908.

22. INCOME TAX— THE SIXTEENTH AMENDMENT, PASSED BY CONGRESS JULY 2, 1909, RATIFIED FEBRUARY 3, 1913

The Congress shall have power to lay and collect taxes on incomes, from whatever source derived, without apportionment among the several States, and without regard to any census or enumeration.

Note: This amendment modifies Article I, section 9, of the Constitution.

23. DIRECT ELECTION OF SENATORS— THE SEVENTEENTH AMENDMENT, PASSED BY CONGRESS MAY 13, 1912, RATIFIED APRIL 8, 1913

The Senate of the United States shall be composed of two Senators from each State, elected by the people thereof, for six years; and each Senator shall have one vote. The electors in each State shall have the qualifications requisite for electors of the most numerous branch of the State legislatures.

When vacancies happen in the representation of any State in the Senate, the executive authority of such State shall issue writs of election to fill such vacancies: Provided, That the legislature of any State may empower the executive thereof to make temporary appointments until the people fill the vacancies by election as the legislature may direct.

This amendment shall not be so construed as to affect the election or term of any Senator chosen before it becomes valid as part of the Constitution.

Note: This amendment modifies Article I, section 3, of the Constitution.

Source: The United States Constitution and Amendments are available online at Charters of Freedom, National Archives and Records Administration, URL: http://www.archives. gov/national_archives_experience/constitution.html

24. DECLARATION OF PRINCIPLES OF THE PROGRESSIVE PARTY, PLATFORM ADOPTED AUGUST 7, 1912

The conscience of the people, in a time of grave national problems, has called into being a new party, born of the Nation's awakened sense of justice. We of the Progressive Party here dedicate ourselves to the fulfillment of the duty laid upon us by our fathers to maintain that government of the people, by the people and for the people whose foundation they laid.

We hold with Thomas Jefferson and Abraham Lincoln that the people are the masters of their Constitution, to fulfill its purposes and to safeguard it from those who, by perversion of its intent, would convert it into an instrument of injustice. In accordance with the needs of each generation the people must use their sovereign powers to establish and maintain equal opportunity and industrial justice, to secure which this Government was founded and without which no republic can endure.

This country belongs to the people who inhabit it. Its resources, its business, its institutions and its laws should be utilized, maintained or altered in whatever manner will best promote the general interest.

It is time to set the public welfare in the first place.

The Old Parties

Political parties exist to secure responsible government and to execute the will of the people.

From these great tasks both of the old parties have turned aside. Instead of instruments to promote the general welfare, they have become the tools of corrupt interests which use them impartially to serve their selfish purposes. Behind the ostensible government sits enthroned an invisible government, owing no allegiance and acknowledging no responsibility to the people.

To destroy this invisible government, to dissolve the unholy alliance between corrupt business and corrupt politics is the first task of the statesmanship of the day.

The deliberate betrayal of its trust by the Republican Party, and the fatal incapacity of the Democratic Party to deal with the new issues of the new time, have compelled the people to forge a new instrument of government through which to give effect to their will in laws and institutions.

Unhampered by tradition, uncorrupted by power, undismayed by the magnitude of the task, the new party offers itself as the instrument of the people to sweep away old abuses, to build a new and nobler commonwealth.

A Covenant with the People

This declaration is our covenant with the people, and we hereby bind the party and its candidates in State and Nation to the pledges made herein.

The Rule of the People

The Progressive Party, committed to the principle of government by a self-controlled democracy expressing its will through representatives of the people, pledges itself to secure such alterations in the fundamental law of the several States and of the United States as shall insure the representative character of the Government.

In particular, the party declares for direct primaries for nomination of State and National officers, for Nation-wide preferential primaries for candidates for the Presidency, for the direct election of United States Senators by the people; and we urge on the States the policy of the short ballot, with responsibility to the people secured by the initiative, referendum and recall.

Amendment of Constitution

The Progressive Party, believing that a free people should have the power from time to time to amend their fundamental law so as to adapt it progressively to the changing needs of the people, pledges itself to provide a more easy and expeditious method of amending the Federal Constitution.

Nation and State

Up to the limit of the Constitution, and later by amendment of the Constitution, if found necessary, we advocate bringing under effective national jurisdiction those problems which have expanded beyond reach of the individual states.

It is as grotesque as it is intolerable that the several States should by unequal laws in matter of common concern become competing commercial agencies, barter the lives of their children, the health of their women and the safety and well-being of their working people for the profit of their financial interests.

The extreme insistence on States' rights by the Democratic Party in the Baltimore platform demonstrates anew its inability to understand the world into which it has survived or to administer the affairs of a Union of States which have in all essential respects become one people.

Social and Industrial Strength

The supreme duty of the Nation is the conservation of human resources through an enlightened measure of social and industrial justice. We pledge ourselves to work unceasingly in State and Nation for:—

Effective legislation looking to the prevention of industrial accidents, occupational diseases, overwork, involuntary unemployment, and other injurious effects incident to modern industry;

The fixing of minimum safety and health standards for the various occupations, and the exercise of the public authority of State and Nation, including the Federal control over inter-State commerce and the taxing power, to maintain such standards;

The prohibition of child labor;

Minimum wage standards for working women, to provide a living scale in all industrial occupations;

The prohibition of night work for women and the establishment of an eight hour day for women and young persons;

One day's rest in seven for all wage-workers;

The abolition of the convict contract labor system; substituting a system of prison production for governmental consumption only; and the application of prisoners' earnings to the support of their dependent families;

Publicity as to wages, hours and conditions and labor; full reports upon industrial accidents and diseases, and the opening to public inspection of all tallies, weights, measures and check systems on labor products;

Standards of compensation for death by industrial accident and injury and trade diseases which will transfer the burden of lost earnings from the families of working people to the industry, and thus to the community;

The protection of home life against the hazards of sickness, irregular employment and old age through the adoption of a system of social insurance adapted to American use;

The development of the creative labor power of America by lifting the last load of illiteracy from American youth and establishing continuation schools for industrial education under public control and encouraging agricultural education and demonstration in rural schools;

The establishment of industrial research laboratories to put the methods and discoveries of science at the service of American producers.

We favor the organization of the workers, men and women as a means of protecting their interests and of promoting their progress.

Business

We believe that true popular government, justice and prosperity go hand in hand, and so believing, it is our purpose to secure that large measure of general prosperity which is the fruit of legitimate and honest business, fostered by equal justice and by sound progressive laws.

We demand that the test of true prosperity shall be the benefits conferred thereby on all the citizens not confined to individuals or classes and that the test of corporate efficiency shall be the ability better to serve the public; that those who profit by control of business affairs shall justify that profit and that control by sharing with the public the fruits thereof.

We therefore demand a strong National regulation of inter-State corporations. The corporation is an essential part of modern business. The concentration of modern business, in some degree, is both inevitable and necessary for National and international business efficiency. but the existing concentration of vast wealth under a corporate system, unguarded and uncontrolled by the Nation, has placed in the hands of a few men enormous, secret, irresponsible power over the daily life of the citizen—a power insufferable in a free government and certain of abuse.

This power has been abused, in monopoly of National resources, in stock watering, in unfair competition and unfair privileges, and finally in sinister influences on the public agencies of State and Nation. We do not fear commercial power, but we insist that it shall be exercised openly, under publicity, supervision and regulation of the most efficient sort, which will preserver its good while eradicating and preventing its evils. . . .

Currency

We believe there exists imperative need for prompt legislation for the improvement of our National currency system. We believe the present method of issuing notes through private agencies is harmful and unscientific. . . .

The issue of currency is fundamentally a government function and the system should have as basic principles soundness and elasticity. The control should be lodged with the Government and should be protected from domination and manipulation by Wall Street or any special interests. . . .

Conservation

The natural resources of the Nation must be promptly developed and generously used to supply the people's needs, but we cannot safely allow them to be wasted, exploited, monopolized or controlled against the general good. We heartily favor the policy of conservation, and we pledge our party to protect the National forests without hindering their legitimate use for the benefit of all the people.

Agricultural lands in the National forests are, and should remain, open to the genuine settler. Conservation will not retard legitimate development. The honest settler must receive his patent promptly, without needless restrictions or delays.

We believe that the remaining forests, coal and oil lands, water powers and other natural resources still in State or National control (except agricultural lands) are more likely to be wisely conserved and utilized for the general welfare if held in the public hands.

In order that consumers and producers, managers and workmen, now and hereafter, need not pay toll to private monopolies of power and raw material, we demand that such resources shall be retained by the State or Nation and opened to immediate use under laws which will encourage development and make to the people a moderate return for benefits conferred.

In particular we pledge our party to require reasonable compensation to the public for water-power rights hereafter granted by the public.

We pledge legislation to lease the public grazing lands under equitable provisions now pending which will increase the production of food for the people and thoroughly safeguard the rights of the actual homemaker. Natural resources, whose conservation is necessary for the

National welfare, should be owned or controlled by the Nation.

Waterways

. . . It is a National obligation to develop our rivers, and especially the Mississippi and its tributaries, without delay, under a comprehensive general plan covering each river system from its source to its mouth, designed to secure its highest usefulness for navigation, irrigation, domestic supply, water power and the prevention of floods . . .

Panama Canal

The Panama Canal, built and paid for by the American people, must be used primarily for their benefit.

We demand that the canal shall be so operated as to break the transportation monopoly now held and misused by the transcontinental railroads by maintaining sea competition with them. . . .

Alaska

The coal and other natural resources of Alaska should be opened to development at once. They are owned by the people of the United States, and are safe from monopoly, waste or destruction only while so owned. . . .

We promise the people of the Territory of Alaska the same measure of local self-government that was given to other American territories. . . .

Equal Suffrage

The Progressive Party, believing that no people can justly claim to be a true democracy which denies political rights on account of sex, pledges itself to the task of securing equal suffrage to men and women alike.

Corrupt Practices

We pledge our party to legislation that will compel strict limitation on all campaign contributions and expenditures, and detailed publicity of both before as well as after primaries and elections.

Publicity and Public Service

We pledge our party to legislation compelling the registration of lobbyists; publicity of committee hearings except on foreign affairs, and recording of all votes in committee; and forbidding Federal appointees from holding office in State or National political organizations, or taking part as officers or delegates in political conventions for the nomination of elective State or National officials.

The Courts

The Progressive Party demands such restriction of the power of the courts as shall leave to the people the ultimate authority to determine fundamental questions of social welfare and public policy. To secure this end it pledges itself to provide:

1. That when an act, passed under the police power of the State, is held unconstitutional under the State Constitution, by the courts, the people, after an ample interval for deliberation, shall have opportunity to vote on the question whether they desire the act to become a law, notwithstanding such decision.

2. That every decision of the highest appellate court of a State declaring an act of the Legislature unconstitutional on the ground of its violation of the Federal Constitution shall be subject to the same review by the Supreme Court of the United States as is now accorded to decisions sustaining such legislation.

Administration of Justice

The Progressive Party, in order to secure to the people a better administration of justice and by that means to bring about a more general respect for the law and the courts, pledges itself to work unceasingly for the reform of legal procedure and judicial methods.

We believe that the issuance of injunctions in cases arising out of labor disputes should be prohibited when such injunctions would not apply when no labor disputes existed.

We also believe that a person cited for contempt in the disputes, except when such contempt was committed in the actual presence of the court or so near thereto as to interfere with the proper administration of justice, should have a right to trial by jury.

Department of Labor

We pledge our party to establish a Department of Labor with a seat in the cabinet, and with wide jurisdiction over matters affecting the conditions of labor and living.

Country Life

. . . We pledge our party to foster the development of agricultural credit and co-operation, the teaching of agriculture in schools, agricultural college extension, the use of mechanical power on the farm, and to re-establish the Country Life Commission, thus directly promoting the welfare of the farmers, and bringing the benefits of better farming, better business and better living within their reach.

Health

We favor the union of all the existing agencies of the Federal Government dealing with the public health into a single National health service without discrimination against or for any one set of therapeutic methods, school of medicine, or school of healing with such additional powers as may be necessary to enable it to perform efficiently such duties in the protection of the public from preventable diseases as may be properly undertaken by the Federal authorities....

[Sections on Patents, Interstate Commerce Commission, and Good Roads Omitted]

Inheritance and Income Tax

We believe in a graduated inheritance tax as a National means of equalizing the obligations of holders of property to government, and we hereby pledge our party to enact such a Federal law as will tax large inheritances returning to the States an equitable percentage of all amounts collected.

We favor the ratification of the pending amendment to the Constitution giving the Government power to levy an income tax.

Peace and National Defense

The Progressive Party deplores the survival in our civilization of the barbaric system of warfare among nations with its enormous waste of resources even in time of peace, and the consequent impoverishment of the life of the toiling masses. We pledge the party to use its best endeavors to substitute judicial and other peaceful means of settling international differences.

We favor an international agreement for the limitation of naval forces. Pending such an agreement, and as the best means of preserving peace, we pledge ourselves to maintain for the present the policy of building two battleships a year.

Treaty Rights

We pledge our party to protect the rights of American citizenship at home and abroad. No treaty should receive the sanction of our government which discriminates between American citizens because of birthplace, race or religion, or that does not recognize the absolute right of expatriation.

The Immigrant

Through the establishment of industrial standards we propose to secure to the able-bodied immigrant and to his native fellow workers a larger share of American opportunity.

We denounce the fatal policy of indifference and neglect which has left our enormous immigrant population to become the prey of chance and cupidity.

We favor governmental action to encourage the distribution of immigrants away from the congested cities, to rigidly supervise all private agencies dealing with them and to promote their assimilation, education and advancement.

[Sections on Pensions for American Soldiers, the Creation of Parcel Post, and Civil Service Omitted]

Government Business Organization

We pledge our party to readjustment of the business methods of the National Government and a proper co-ordina-

tion of the Federal bureaus, which will increase the economy and efficiency of the Government service, prevent duplications and secure better results to the taxpayers for every dollar expended.

Government Supervision Over Investment

The people of the United States are swindled out of many millions of dollars every year, through worthless investments. The plain people, the wage-earner and the men and women with small savings, have no way of knowing the merit of concerns sending out highly colored prospectuses offering stock for sale, prospectuses that make big returns seem certain and fortunes easily within grasp.

We hold it to be the duty of the Government to protect its people from this kind of piracy. We, therefore, demand wise carefully-thought-out legislation that will give us such Governmental supervision over this matter as will furnish to the people of the United States this much-needed protection, and we pledge ourselves thereto.

Conclusion

On these principles and on the recognized desirability of uniting the Progressive forces of the Nation into an organization which shall unequivocally represent the Progressive spirit and policy we appeal for the support of all American citizens without regard to previous political affiliations.

Source: Theodore Roosevelt, *Progressive Principles; Selections from Addresses Made During the Presidential Campaign of 1912, Including the Progressive National Platform,* ed. Elmer H. Youngman (New York: Progressive National Service, 1913).

25. "Peace Without Victory": President Woodrow Wilson's Address to the Senate, January 22, 1917

I have sought this opportunity . . . to disclose to you without reserve the thought and purpose that have been taking form in my mind in regard to the duty of our Government in the days to come when it will be necessary to lay afresh and upon a new plan the foundations of peace among the nations.

It is inconceivable that the people of the United States should play no part in that great enterprise. . . . They cannot in honor withhold the service to which they are now about to be challenged. They do not wish to withhold it. But they owe it to themselves and to the other nations of the world to state the conditions under which they will feel free to render it.

That service is nothing less than this, to add their authority and their power to the authority and force of other nations to guarantee peace and justice throughout the world. Such a settlement cannot now be long postponed. It is right that before it comes this Government should frankly formulate the conditions upon which it would feel justified in asking our people to approve its formal and solemn adherence to a League for Peace. I am here to attempt to state those conditions.

The present war must first be ended; but we owe it to candor and to a just regard for the opinion of mankind to say that, so far as our participation in guarantees of future peace is concerned, it makes a great deal of difference in what way and upon what terms it is ended. The treaties and agreements which bring it to an end must embody terms which will create a peace that is worth guaranteeing and preserving, a peace that will win the approval of mankind, not merely a peace that will serve the several interests and immediate aims of the nations engaged. . . .

No covenant of co-operative peace that does not include the peoples of the New World can suffice to keep the future safe against war; and yet there is only one sort of peace that the peoples of America could join in guaranteeing. The elements of that peace must be elements that engage the confidence and satisfy the principles of the American governments, elements consistent with their political faith and with the practical convictions which the peoples of America have once for all embraced and undertaken to defend. . . .

It will be absolutely necessary that a force be created as a guarantor of the permanency of the settlement so much greater than the force of any nation now engaged or any alliance hitherto formed or projected that no nation, no probable combination of nations could face or withstand it. If the peace presently to be made is to endure, it must be a peace made secure by the organized major force of mankind.

The terms of the immediate peace agreed upon will determine whether it is a peace for which such a guarantee can be secured. The question upon which the whole future peace and policy of the world depends is this: Is the present war a struggle for a just and secure peace, or only for a new balance of power? If it be only a struggle for a new balance of power, who will guarantee, who can guarantee the stable equilibrium of the new arrangement? Only a tranquil Europe can be a stable Europe. There must be, not a balance of power, but a community of power; not organized rivalries, but an organized common peace.

Fortunately we have received very explicit assurances on this point. . . . I think it will be serviceable if I attempt to set forth what we understand them to be.

They imply, first of all, that it must be a peace without victory. It is not pleasant to say this. . . . I am seeking only to face realities and to face them without soft concealments. Victory would mean peace forced upon the loser, a victor's terms imposed upon the vanquished. It would be accepted in humiliation, under duress, at an intolerable sacrifice, and would leave a sting, a resentment, a bitter memory upon which terms of peace would rest, not permanently, but only as upon quicksand. Only a peace between equals can last. . . .

The equality of nations upon which peace must be founded if it is to last must be an equality of rights; the guarantees exchanged must neither recognize nor imply a difference between big nations and small, between those that are powerful and those that are weak. Right must be based upon the common strength, not upon the individual strength, of the nations upon whose concert peace will depend. Equality of territory or of resources there of course cannot be; nor any sort of equality not gained in the ordinary peaceful and legitimate development of the peoples themselves. But no one asks or expects anything more than an equality of rights. Mankind is looking now for freedom of life, not for equipoises of power.

And there is a deeper thing involved than even equality of right among organized nations. No peace can last, or ought to last, which does not recognize and accept the principle that governments derive all their just powers from the consent of the governed, and that no right anywhere exists to hand peoples about from sovereignty to sovereignty as if they were property. . . . [H]enceforth inviolable security at life, of worship, and of industrial and social development should be guaranteed to all peoples who have lived hitherto under the power of governments devoted to a faith and purpose hostile to their own. . . .

So far as practicable, moreover, every great people now struggling towards a full development of its resources and of its powers should be assured a direct outlet to the great highways of the sea. . . . With right comity of arrangement no nation need be shut away from free access to the open paths of the world's commerce.

. . . The freedom of the seas the *sine qua non* of peace, equality, and co-operation. . . . The free, constant unthreatened intercourse of nations is an essential part of the process of peace and of development. . . .

It is a problem closely connected with the limitation of naval armaments and the cooperation of the navies of the world in keeping the seas at once free and safe. And the question of limiting naval armaments opens the wider and perhaps more difficult question of the limitation of armies and of all programs of military preparation. Difficult and delicate as these questions are, they must be faced with the utmost candor and decided in a spirit of real accommodation if peace is to come with healing in its wings, and come to stay. Peace cannot be had without concession and sacrifice. There can be no sense of safety and equality among the nations if great preponderating armaments are henceforth to continue here and there to be built up and maintained. The statesmen of the world must plan for peace and nations must adjust and accommodate their policy to it as they have planned for war and made ready for pitiless contest and rivalry. The question of armaments, whether on land or sea, is the most immediately and intensely practical question connected with the future fortunes of nations and of mankind.

I have spoken upon these great matters without reserve and with the utmost explicitness because it has seemed to me to be necessary if the world's yearning desire for peace was anywhere to find free voice and utterance. Perhaps I am the only person in high authority amongst all the peoples of the world who is at liberty to speak and hold nothing back. I am speaking as an individual, and yet I am speaking also, of course, as the responsible head of a great government....

I am proposing, as it were, that the nations should with one accord adopt the doctrine of President Monroe as the doctrine of the world: that no nation should seek to extend its polity over any other nation or people, but that every people should be left free to determine its own polity, its own way of development, unhindered, unthreatened, unafraid, the little along with the great and powerful.

I am proposing that all nations henceforth avoid entangling alliances which would draw them into competitions of power; catch them in a net of intrigue and selfish rivalry, and disturb their own affairs with influences intruded from without. There is no entangling alliance in a concert of power. When all unite to act in the same sense and with the same purpose all act in the common interest and are free to live their own lives under a common protection.

I am proposing government by the consent of the governed; that freedom of the seas which in international conference after conference representatives of the United States have urged with the eloquence of those who are the convinced disciples of liberty; and that moderation of armaments which makes of armies and navies a power for order merely, not an instrument of aggression or of selfish violence.

These are American principles, American policies. We could stand for no others. And they are also the principles and policies of forward looking men and women everywhere, of every modern nation, of every enlightened community. They are the principles of mankind and must prevail.
Source: Senate Document 685, 64th Congress, 2nd sess.

26. PROHIBITION— THE EIGHTEENTH AMENDMENT, PASSED BY CONGRESS DECEMBER 18, 1917, RATIFIED JANUARY 16, 1919

Section 1 . After one year from the ratification of this article the manufacture, sale, or transportation of intoxicating liquors within, the importation thereof into, or the exportation thereof from the United States and all territory subject to the jurisdiction thereof for beverage purposes is hereby prohibited.

Section 2. The Congress and the several States shall have concurrent power to enforce this article by appropriate legislation.

Section 3. This article shall be inoperative unless it shall have been ratified as an amendment to the Constitution by the legislatures of the several States, as provided in the Constitution, within seven years from the date of the submission hereof to the States by the Congress.

Note. This amendment was repealed by the Twenty-First Amendment to the Constitution, 1933

Source: The United States Constitution and Amendments are available online at Charters of Freedom, National Archives and Records Administration, URL: http://www.archives. gov/national_archives_experience/constitution.html

27. WOMEN'S SUFFRAGE— THE NINETEENTH AMENDMENT, PASSED BY CONGRESS JUNE 4, 1919, RATIFIED AUGUST 18, 1920

The right of citizens of the United States to vote shall not be denied or abridged by the United States or by any State on account of sex.

Congress shall have power to enforce this article by appropriate legislation.

Source: The United States Constitution and Amendments are available online at Charters of Freedom, National Archives and Records Administration, URL: http://www.archives. gov/national_archives_experience/constitution.html

Appendix B
Biographies of Major Personalities

Adams, Henry Brooks (1838–1918) *historian, editor*
Adams, a historian and man of letters, was born in Boston to a distinguished family; his grandfather was President John Quincy Adams and his great grandfather was President John Adams. He was a professor of history at Harvard, editor of the *North American Review* in the 1870s, and a pessimistic critic of turn-of-the-century America. His intellectual autobiography, *The Education of Henry Adams* (1907), is considered a classic of American literature.

Adams, Samuel Hopkins (1871–1958) *muckraking journalist*
Hopkins was born in New York State and attended Hamilton College. A journalist, he joined *McClure's* and became a muckraker, specializing in public health issues. His 1905 series for *Collier's,* "The Great American Fraud," was the classic exposé of patent medicines. The American Medical Association reprinted and distributed many copies, and it is credited with helping to pass the Pure Food and Drugs Act of 1906. Hopkins later became a novelist and screenwriter; his best known screenplay is *It Happened One Night.*

Addams, Jane (1860–1935) *settlement founder, reformer, social theorist*
Addams, born to Quaker parents in Cedarville, Illinois, was the best known and most beloved woman in America during the Progressive Era. After graduating from Rockford Female Seminary, she visited Toynbee Hall, the first settlement house, founded in the slums of London. Upon her return to America she and a friend, Ellen Gates Starr, founded Hull-House in Chicago in 1889. It became a model settlement and trained many of the activists who played a prominent role in reform in the decades to follow. Addams became widely known and respected as a social theorist who supported social justice as well as social reform. More than most other reformers, she was sympathetic to immigrants and defended the rich cultural heritage they brought with them. She wrote 12 books, most of which interpreted the experiences of the urban poor in terms that middle-class Americans could understand. Although she was called beloved lady and even Saint Jane, she lost some popular approval during World War I when she became a prominent international peace activist. In addition to her contributions to social justice for the poor, Addams also helped win acceptance for a new professional role for educated women. In 1931 she was one of two awardees of the Nobel Peace Prize. The other was Nicholas Murray Butler.

Adler, Felix (1851–1933) *ethicist, reformer*
Born in Germany, Adler immigrated to the United States as a child. In 1876, he founded the Society for Ethical Culture in New York. The Ethical Culture movement (which became international and is still active today) had for its motto "Deed, not creed." A non-theistic religious, or philosophical, congregation, it drew from Judaism, Christianity, American transcendentalism, and even socialism, and stressed the betterment of human life as the most important religious goal. Adler was active in the anti-imperialist movement, educational reform, child labor reform, and housing reform, among other movements. In 1902 he became a professor of ethics at Columbia, a position he held until his death.

Aguinaldo, Emilio (1869–1964) *Filipino insurgent leader*
Born to a family of wealthy Filipino landowners, Aguinaldo was in his twenties when he joined the insurgent movement against Spain. He soon became a successful military leader. After assisting the American military during the Spanish-American War, he then led a revolutionary movement for Filipino independence from the United States that became the Philippine-American War. Aguinaldo was elected president of the republic declared by the revolutionaries. After being captured in early 1901, he swore allegiance to the United States and retired to private life. In 1935 he ran unsuccessfully for the Philippine presidency against Manuel Quezon, threatening to lead a military revolt when he lost. During the Japanese occupation of the Philippines in World War II, when he was in his seventies, he was required to broadcast radio appeals to soldiers defending Corregidor, urging them to surrender. But he refused to join a Filipino movement to lead Japanese troops against the Americans.

Aldrich, Nelson W. (1841–1915) *conservative Republican politician*
Born on a farm in Rhode Island, Aldrich began his career as a wholesale grocer while still in his teens. Elected to the House in 1878 and the Senate in 1881, he served until 1913 and wielded great power. The Republican insurgency in Congress during the progressive decades was a response to the policies of Aldrich and a few other powerful, conservative senators. Aldrich played a large role in reforming the monetary system and developing the Federal Reserve Act (1913), although he retired from the Senate in 1911. The marriage of his daughter to John D. Rockefeller, Jr., symbolized the marriage of politics and big business to many Americans; Aldrich himself was a self-made multimillionaire.

Altgeld, John Peter (1847–1902) *early Democratic reform governor*
Born in Germany, Altgeld grew up in Ohio and later moved to Chicago to practice law. In 1892, he was elected governor of Illinois on the Democratic ticket. He earned the disapproval of many when in 1893 he pardoned the jailed anarchists convicted of the 1886 Haymarket bombing. The pardons and his stance during the Pullman strike of 1894, when he objected strongly to the use of federal troops and injunctions in Chicago, ended his political career before the heyday of state progressivism, but some historians call him the earliest progressive governor.

Anthony, Susan Brownell (1820–1906) *women's rights and suffrage leader*
Born in Massachusetts to a Quaker farm family, Anthony grew up in upstate New York. She taught school and worked in the anti-slavery movement before beginning her work for women's rights, which she would continue for the remainder of her life. In 1869, she joined Elizabeth Cady Stanton to found the National Woman Suffrage Association. She remained a tireless worker, writer, and international speaker for suffrage. She served the merged National-American Woman Suffrage Association (NAWSA) as its second president from 1892 to 1900.

Baer, George F. (1842–1914) *conservative businessman*
A close associate of J. P. Morgan, Baer was president of several eastern Pennsylvania railroads and their associated coal companies at the time of the coal miners strike of 1902. He gained infamy for a letter published in a newspaper during the strike that intimated that he and other wealthy industrialists had been chosen by God to manage the affairs of the working man. He was eventually forced to negotiate a settlement to the strike. He died a multimillionaire.

Baker, Newton D. (1871–1936) *Democratic reform politician*
Born in West Virginia, Baker first met Woodrow Wilson as a student at Johns Hopkins, where Wilson was an instructor. Baker became a lawyer, took a postition in Cleveland, and became the legal adviser and city attorney under Cleveland's reform mayor, Tom Johnson. In the election of 1911, he was voted in as mayor in his own right. He successfully continued Johnson's reforms and secured a progressive home rule charter for the city. In 1916, he became secretary of war under President Wilson, eventually overseeing the mobilization of troops for World War I. After Wilson left office, he returned to Ohio and later served on the Permanent Court of Arbitration at The Hague.

Baker, Ray Stannard (1870–1946) *muckraking journalist*
Baker, born in Michigan, began his career as a journalist on a Chicago newspaper after graduating from Michigan State University. After working at *McClure's* from 1898 to 1906, he and fellow muckrakers Ida Tarbell and Lincoln Steffens joined *American Magazine*. As a serious journalist he is best remembered for his path-breaking study of race relations, *Following the Color Line* (1908), a subject few muckrakers undertook, and for his multivolume documentary biography of Woodrow Wilson. Baker also wrote best-selling popular romantic novels under the pseudonym David Grayson.

Balch, Emily Greene (1867–1961) *scholar of immigration, pacifist*
Balch graduated from Bryn Mawr College in its first class, then helped found Denison House settlement in Boston. After graduate study she joined the faculty of Wellesley, specializing in economics and immigration. She was also one of the founders of the Women's Trade Union League. With Jane Addams she formed the pacifist group Women's International League for Peace and Freedom and was dismissed from Wellesley in 1918 for her activism and outspoken opposition to World War I. Balch became a well-known pacifist leader and in 1946 shared the Nobel Peace Prize with John R. Mott.

Baruch, Bernard Mannes (1871–1965) *federal official during World War I*
Born in South Carolina, Baruch grew up in New York and graduated from City College. He quickly gained exceptional success as a Wall Street stockbroker. In 1918, Wilson appointed him chair of the War Industries Board where he successfully coordinated war production. He continued to advise presidents until his death during Lyndon Johnson's administration, often holding forth on a park bench near the White House.

Bates, Katharine Lee (1859–1929) *professor, author of "America the Beautiful"*
Born in Falmouth, Bates received bachelor's and master's degrees from Wellesley, becoming an instructor there and eventually head of the English department. A prolific poet

and writer, she was also a Shakespearean scholar. She is remembered for her poem "America the Beautiful," which she wrote after climbing Pikes Peak in 1893. She revised the words in 1904, publishing them in the *Boston Evening Transcript.* In the late 1920s, advocates promoted it for the national anthem set to the tune of an old hymn, but in 1931 the "Star Spangled Banner" was officially adopted instead. The only payment Bates ever received for the poem was a small amount for its first publication in 1895 in a Congregational magazine.

Beard, Charles Austin (1874–1948) *progressive historian*
After receiving a doctorate in history from Columbia, Beard became a professor of history there. He helped advance the New History, which used the social sciences, especially economics, to explain political events of the past. In 1913, he became nationally prominent when *An Economic Interpretation of the Constitution* was published. He later resigned from Columbia to protest dismissals of faculty who opposed World War I and began a second career as head of the Training School for Public Service of the New York Bureau of Municipal Research. He also helped found the New School for Social Research in 1919.

Belmont, Alva Ertskin Smith Vanderbilt
(1853–1933) *philanthropist of suffrage movement*
Born in Mobile, Alabama, Alva Smith married William K. Vanderbilt and became known in the late 19th century for her successful effort to force New York's social elite, the Four Hundred, to accept newly rich families like hers. In 1895 she divorced her husband and married Oliver Hazard Perry Belmont. By the 1910s, she had begun to devote herself and her financial resources to reform causes, especially women's suffrage, founding the Political Equality League. Gifted as an architectural designer, she was the first woman elected to the American Institute of Architects.

Berger, Victor Louis (1860–1929) *socialist, congressman*
Born in Austria-Hungary to a prosperous family, Berger immigrated to the United States as a teenager. A teacher, then journalist and newspaper editor in Milwaukee, Berger was a socialist who helped found the Socialist Party of America, remaining on its national board throughout his life. He was a leader of the conservative socialists who wanted to use electoral politics to achieve change. Prominent in Milwaukee politics for many years, in 1910, he became the first socialist elected to the U.S. Congress. During World War I he was indicted and convicted under the Espionage Act for his dissent, after which Congress twice voted to exclude him. But his constituents re-elected him and in 1921 the Supreme Court overturned his conviction. He served three more terms in Congress before dying of injuries in a streetcar accident.

Beveridge, Albert Jeremiah (1862–1927) *progressive Republican senator*
Born in Ohio to an unsuccessful farmer, Beveridge began working as a railroad hand at age 14 but eventually was able to attend DePauw University. He quickly became known for his oratorical skills and while still in college lent his talents to the Republican party in every election. In 1899, when he was 36, the Indiana state legislature sent him to the Senate. He served until 1911, a strong supporter of imperialism abroad and reform at home, and was identified with the Insurgents. He joined the Progressive Party and was nominated for various offices on its ticket but never regained public office. He had a second successful career as a historian and biographer.

Bly, Nelly (Nellie Bly) (1867–1922) *pioneering journalist*
Born Elizabeth Cochrane in Cochrane Mills, Pennsylvania, Bly took her pen name from a Stephen Foster song. As a pioneering journalist for Pulitzer's *New York World,* she gained fame for sensational exposés that often involved dangerous undercover work to obtain inside information. She became internationally famous for her 72-day trip around the world in 1889–90 and was still a practicing journalist in New York at the time of her death.

Brandeis, Louis Dembitz (1856–1941) *reform lawyer, Supreme Court Justice*
Born in Louisville to prosperous parents who were Jewish immigrants from Prague, Brandeis compiled a legendary academic record at Harvard Law School and soon established a law firm in Boston with a classmate. By the turn of the century, he was financially independent and increasingly devoted himself to wide-ranging reform interests. His noted contribution in law is the Brandeis brief, which uses social and economic research in the service of a legal argument. He also enunciated some of the earliest arguments against invasion of privacy in modern society, which he called "the right to be let alone." During the 1912, presidential campaign he became an influential adviser to Woodrow Wilson. In 1916, Wilson appointed him to the Supreme Court, where he was the first Jewish-American justice. He came to be viewed as the Court's most liberal justice, supporting legislative regulation in the public interest but opposing all government efforts to limit civil liberties. Brandeis refused outside writing and speaking engagements, employed few law clerks and no secretarial help, and refused to move into the new Supreme Court Building in 1935, believing it unnecessary. Brandeis was also active in the Zionist cause, or the movement to establish a Jewish homeland.

Breckinridge, Madeline McDowell (1872–1920) *reformer, suffragist*
Breckinridge was an active reformer in Kentucky, writing frequently for the Lexington *Herald,* which her husband

edited. She helped found a settlement house and the Lexington Civic League and led the state campaign for women's suffrage. She was also active in many educational reforms and was a moving force in the campaign to improve treatment of tuberculosis and establish a system of state sanitoria; she herself suffered from the disease and eventually died from it. Her sister-in-law was Sophonisba Breckenridge.

Breckinridge, Sophonisba (1866–1948) *sociologist, reformer*
Breckinridge earned a Ph.D. from the University of Chicago in economics and political science and became dean of the School of Civics and Philanthropy in Chicago, later part of the University of Chicago. One of the most influential scholar-activists in the development of professional social work, she played a large role in the Mother's Pension movement and the development of juvenile courts. She was affiliated with Hull-House for many years, as well as the National Women's Trade Union League, the Immigrant Protective League, NAWSA, and the NAACP. Her sister-in-law was Madeline McDowell Breckinridge.

Bryan, William Jennings (1860–1925) *politician, three-time Democratic candidate for president*
Born in Illinois, Bryan received a law degree from what is now Northwestern University, then moved to Nebraska. He was elected to Congress in 1890, where he became known as an effective orator for tariff reform and the free-silver movement. Nominated for president by the Democratic Party after his stunning Cross of Gold speech at the 1896 convention, he ran on a ticket of agrarian reform, inspired much conservative opposition, and was soundly defeated. He ran and was defeated again in 1900 and 1908, but he continued to lead the liberal wing of the Democratic Party for a generation. In that role, he exerted much influence on the passage of the four Progressive Era amendments to the Constitution as well as much of Wilson's reform legislation. In 1912, he became secretary of state under Wilson. Always a religious conservative, he became a strong supporter of biblical literalism and a foe of teaching evolutionary theory in public schools in the last years of his life, facing Clarence Darrow in the famous Scopes monkey trial of 1925.

Burleson, Albert Sidney (1863–1937) *Democratic politician, influential postmaster-general*
Burleson received a law degree from the University of Texas, the state in which he was born. Elected to congress, he served from 1899 until 1913, when he resigned to become postmaster-general in the Wilson administration. Burleson was an adroit party politician who helped Wilson successfully maintain control of the Democratic Party, pri-
marily through patronage. As postmaster-general Burleson increased rural services, established motorized delivery, and pioneered air mail service. But he also supported segregation in federal workplaces, was unsympathetic to labor, and exercised great power during the war years when federal legislation gave him extensive powers to censor the mail. After Wilson left office he returned to business interests in Texas and took little part in national politics.

Burnham, Daniel Hudson (1846–1912) *architect, City Beautiful movement leader*
An architect, Burnham was chief of construction for the 1893 Columbian World Exposition and largely responsible for its unified plan and style. He led the City Beautiful movement, taking a role in the early 20th-century revitalization of Washington, D.C., and creating a monumental plan for Chicago that laid out its future development.

Burns, William John (1861–1932) *famous detective*
Burns was born in Maryland and grew up in Ohio, entering detective work when his father became police commissioner of Columbus. In 1889, he joined the United States Secret Service, where his reputation grew by leaps and bounds until he became the most famous detective in America. He pursued perpetrators regardless of their social or political status. In 1897, he identified the perpetrators of a multiple lynching in Indiana; in 1903, he linked a U.S. senator to huge land frauds in the West; and after 1906, spent three years investigating corruption in San Francisco. In 1909, he founded the William J. Burns National Detective Agency with branches in many cities. The following year he found evidence that the McNamara brothers were responsible for the bombing of the *Los Angeles Times* building. In 1912, he successfully linked a New York City police lieutenant to a murder. In 1914, he found evidence that Leo Frank, charged with a murder in Georgia and later lynched, was not guilty; Burns narrowly escaped a lynch mob himself. In 1921, Burns became head of the Federal Bureau of Investigation but returned to private work in 1924. At times, Burns was criticized for using techniques of questionable legality and was twice charged with a misdemeanor for his activities.

Butler, Nicholas Murray (1862–1947) *president of Columbia, reformer*
A prominent educator, Butler founded Teacher's College at Columbia University and, in 1901, became Columbia's president. He also took an active role in civic and other reform movements and was an adviser to Roosevelt, Wilson, and later Harding. In 1912, he filled in as Taft's vice presidential candidate when James Sherman died shortly before the election. In 1900, Butler helped found the College Entrance Examination Board.

Butt, Archibald (Archie Butt) (1865–1912) *military aide to presidents*
Born in Georgia, Butt attended the University of the South before entering the military. He served as personal military aide to Presidents Roosevelt and Taft, developing a great loyalty to both men. In the spring of 1912, as the conflict between the two was growing, he took a leave to vacation in Europe. Unfortunately he booked return passage on the *Titanic*. Before going down with the ship he helped direct the loading of the lifeboats; President Taft delivered a eulogy at the memorial service.

Cannon, Joseph G. (1836–1926) *arch-conservative Republican politician*
Born in North Carolina to a Quaker family that later moved to Indiana, "Uncle Joe" Cannon became a powerful and very conservative Republican congressman from Illinois, serving from 1872 to 1923, with the exception of two terms. From 1901 to 1911, he was Speaker of the House. During that time a coalition of progressive Republicans and Democrats joined together to oppose his constant use of his power to block reform legislation. Despite the insurgent revolt (and his reputation for exceptionally profane language), "Uncle Joe" remained popular with his constituents and retained general regard among members of Congress.

Carnegie, Andrew (1835–1919) *captain of industry, philanthropist*
Born in Scotland, Carnegie arrived in Allegheny, Pennsylvania, with his impoverished family in 1848. He began working as a twelve-year-old bobbin boy, quickly moving up to telegraph operator, private secretary, executive, and investor. After 1873, he began to multiply his steel interests primarily by strict control of costs and reinvestment of profits into the business itself. While accruing phenomenal financial and business success he became a writer and lecturer. In 1887, he published the "Gospel of Wealth," which argued that the very wealthy had a responsibility to fund philanthropic activities that aided others to climb the ladder of success. In 1901, he became the richest man in America by selling his steel holdings to United States Steel Corporation. He devoted the rest of his life to philanthropic activities such as the Carnegie Endowment for Peace, educational programs, and Carnegie libraries which he funded throughout the nation.

Carver, George Washington (ca. 1864–1943) *scientist*
Carver was born to a slave mother who was purchased by an anti-slavery Missouri family, the Carvers, and set free. She was, however, apparently kidnapped by Confederate raiders, effectively orphaning her infant son, who was raised to age 13 by the Carvers. Carver then moved to Kansas, supporting himself in various ways and gaining a local reputation for his skill with plants. After receiving a bachelor's and master's degree at what is now Iowa State University, he headed the agricultural department and experiment station at Tuskegee Institute for almost 50 years until his death. He had only modest financial resources for his agricultural research but was nonetheless very successful. He became best known for his development of the peanut as a high protein substitute for meat. Carver also worked hard to disseminate practical information to the poor farmers of the South. By the time of his death, he and his work were nationally known.

Catt, Carrie Chapman (1859–1947) *suffrage leader*
Born in Wisconsin, Catt grew up in Iowa and attended what is now Iowa State University. She entered the temperance and suffrage movements in the 1880s and moved into leadership roles in the National American Woman Suffrage Association after its founding in 1890, serving as president from 1900 to 1904. Widowed for the second time in 1905, she worked with the International Woman Suffrage Alliance until 1915. She returned to the NAWSA presidency and played a crucial role in the achievement of the Nineteenth Amendment.

Cherrington, Ernest Hurst (1877–1950) *prohibition movement leader*
Born in Ohio, Cherrington taught school and edited a newspaper before becoming a full-time temperance worker for the Anti-Saloon League in 1902. An effective organizer and administrator, he soon rose in the organization, eventually he became editor of the league's newspaper, *American Issue*. Under his management, the league's publishing enterprises flourished, producing vast quantities of effective material in favor of prohibition. As secretary of the national executive committee, he made a large contribution to many other aspects of the Anti-Saloon League as well, organizing its speakers' bureau and bringing businesslike management to its finances. Never a publicity hound like some other figures in the prohibition movement, Cherrington was at least equally responsible for obtaining the Eighteenth Amendment. After 1919, he devoted his energies to the World League against Alcoholism, which he helped found. Throughout his life Cherrington was also an active layperson in the national Methodist Church.

Cleveland, Grover (Stephen Grover Cleveland) (1837–1908) *24th president of the United States*
The only president to serve two nonconsecutive terms, Cleveland was born in New Jersey. Unable to afford college because of his father's death, he taught school then read for the law and was admitted to the bar in Upstate New York. He entered Democratic politics and became mayor of Buffalo, then governor of New York, and in 1884, was

nominated for president. During the campaign, it was revealed that the unmarried Cleveland had an illegitimate child, but despite the scandal, he was elected. In the second year of his term, the 49-year-old Cleveland married 21-year-old Frances Folsom, who became a popular hostess. Eventually the couple had five children, three of whom survived childhood. Cleveland lost his bid for re-election in 1888 to Benjamin Harrison in the Electoral College, although he won the popular vote. He ran again and recaptured the presidency in 1892.

Cooper, Anna Julia Hayward (1858–1964) *theorist of African-American and women's rights*
Born in slavery in North Carolina, Anna Hayward obtained a bachelor's and master's degree in mathematics from Oberlin, after which she spent most of her professional life at M Street High School (called Paul Laurence Dunbar High School after 1916), a famed preparatory school for African Americans in Washington, D.C. She became an internationally known speaker and writer on both African-American rights and women's rights and, at age 66, earned a doctorate, from the Sorbonne, in France.

Cortelyou, George B. (1862–1940) *cabinet official*
Born in New York, Cortelyou took what was then a common path for young men entering business management or public service, becoming a private secretary and stenographer. He first served President Cleveland and was officially appointed secretary to the president under McKinley and Roosevelt. In this role, he organized and administered many functions of the growing national government. In 1903, he became the first secretary of the new Department of Commerce and Labor. He was Roosevelt's campaign manager in 1904, then became postmaster general, and in 1907, secretary of the treasury. In 1909, he left public service to become head of the New York Gas Company.

Crane, Stephen (1871–1900) *writer*
Born to a Methodist minister and his wife in New Jersey, as a young, struggling novelist and poet in New York City, Crane was forced to publish *Maggie, a Girl of the Streets* privately because publishers found his open treatment of slum life and prostitution scandalous. His next novel, *The Red Badge of Courage* (1895), established him as a major talent and eventually came to be considered a classic American novel. After its publication he became a war correspondent in Greece and Cuba. He contracted tuberculosis and died from the disease at the age of 28.

Creel, George (1876–1953) *federal official during World War I*
Born in Missouri to an unreconciled Confederate officer and his wife, Creel became a reform newspaper journalist and editor first in Kansas City, where he campaigned against corrupt politics, and then Denver, where he campaigned against child labor. He became the head of the U.S. Committee on Public Information in 1917, which became known as the Creel Committee. Its war propaganda efforts were so successful that it unintentionally played a role in arousing intolerance and the suppression of civil liberties. After the war Creel turned to writing popular history.

Croly, Herbert (1869–1930) *progressive journalist*
Croly first entered Harvard in 1886, finally leaving for good in 1899, still not having taken a degree. He edited an architectural journal until 1906. In 1909, he published *The Promise of American Life,* a work of political analysis and philosophy that advocated a vigorous program of social reform on the national level. It was one of the most influential books of the Progressive Era. Croly founded the *New Republic* in 1914 and edited it until his death; it quickly became the leading progressive journal of opinion.

Croly, Jane Cunningham (1829–1901) *pioneering woman journalist and woman's club founder*
Born in England, Jane Cunningham immigrated to New York as an adolescent with her father, a Unitarian minister, and the rest of her family. In 1855, she began writing for newspapers under the pseudonym Jennie June. She continued her career after marrying a fellow journalist, an act almost unheard of at the time, while also raising four children. In 1868, Croly founded Sorosis, a significant woman's club, after women journalists were denied admittance to a dinner given by the New York Press Club for visiting British author Charles Dickens. In 1889, she founded the New York Women's Press Club and in 1892 the nationwide General Federation of Women's Clubs.

Crosby, Ernest (1856–1907) *anti-imperialist writer*
A lawyer who gave up his practice when he came to believe the law supported violence, Crosby was a disciple of the pacifist Russian writer Tolstoy and of the single tax reform movement. He was cofounder and president of the Anti-Imperialist League of New York (1900–1905) and vice president until his death. He wrote widely and edited several small journals.

Cummins, Albert Baird (1850–1926) *progressive Republican politician*
Born in Pennsylvania to a family of modest means, Cummins eventually studied law in Chicago, after which he moved to Iowa and founded what later became the state's best-known law firm. He gained fame by defending a suit brought by a farmers' organization against the barbed wire monopoly, eventually winning at the Supreme Court. His

election as governor in 1902, despite the opposition of the Republican Old Guard in the state, inaugurated the progressive moment in Iowa. In 1909, he moved on to the U.S. Senate, becoming one of the leading Republican Insurgents there. He served as president pro tempore of the Senate from 1919 to 1925.

Curtis, Edward Sheriff (1868–1952) *photographer*
Born on a Wisconsin farm, Curtis attended elementary school but soon left school to help support his family. After moving to Washington State he began photographing local Native Americans as a hobby while doing farm labor. By chance, while on a photography expedition, Curtis rescued conservationist and editor George Bird Grinnell, who had become lost on a climb of Mount Rainier. Grinnell arranged for Curtis to photograph the 1899 Harriman expedition to Alaska. Curtis soon began to study and record Indian life and culture seriously and systematically. Roosevelt made him the official photographer for his daughter Alice's wedding and suggested he contact J. P. Morgan to fund his Indian project, which Morgan did enthusiastically. The 20-volume work *The North American Indian* was published from 1907 to 1930.

Curtis, Namahyoke Sockum (unknown–1935) *nurse*
Curtis organized black nurses who, like her, had recovered from yellow fever and were immune, to work during the Spanish-American War. She also worked with Clara Barton and the Red Cross after the Galveston disaster in Texas in 1900. Curtis was married to Dr. Austin M. Curtis, Sr., a path-breaking black surgeon who served as chief of surgery at Freedman's Hospital, Washington, D.C.

Daniels, Josephus (1862–1948) *federal official during World War I*
Born in modest circumstances in North Carolina, Daniels became a very influential progressive southern journalist and newspaper publisher. Active in Democratic politics, he became secretary of the navy under Wilson, and later ambassador to Mexico.

Darrow, Clarence S. (1857–1938) *famous trial lawyer*
Born in Ohio, Darrow attended Allegheny College and one year of law school before beginning his legal practice in the Chicago firm of John Peter Altgeld. Darrow became the most famous defense trial lawyer of his age, often representing clients considered labor radicals. He failed to save only one of his 50 clients accused of first-degree murder from execution. Darrow is also remembered for his defense of evolutionary theory in the Scopes monkey trial of 1925 in Tennessee, which pitted him against William Jennings Bryan and religious fundamentalism.

Davis, Richard Harding (1864–1916) *journalist*
Born in Philadelphia to novelist Rebecca Harding Davis, Davis attended Lehigh and Johns Hopkins Universities before becoming a successful journalist and popular fiction writer. He gained fame as a war correspondent, covering six wars, and as a travel writer. He was handsome and something of a dandy, and some believe that he was the model for the man who appears as the Gibson girl's escort in illustrator Charles Dana Gibson's drawings.

Debs, Eugene Victor (1855–1926) *labor leader, Socialist party founder, socialist candidate for president*
Born in Indiana, Debs left school at 15 and began working for the railroad, where he soon became active in the Brotherhood of Locomotive Firemen. He served one term in the Indiana legislature and became a well known labor leader. He founded the American Railway Union and helped found the International Workers of the World and the Socialist Party of America. Debs was charismatic, non-doctrinaire, and almost universally loved by his associates. He ran for president five times, even winning a million votes in 1922 while imprisoned for his dissent during World War I. He continued to lead a socialist movement until his death.

De Leon, Daniel (1852–1914) *socialist leader*
Born in Curaçao and educated in Europe, De Leon immigrated to America in 1874. An uncompromising Marxist, he became leader of the small Socialist Labor Party. Although he participated in founding both the Socialist Party and the IWW, he split from both.

Dewey, George (1837–1917) *naval hero*
Dewey was born in Vermont and attended the U.S. Naval Academy. He served in the Civil War and later in various positions in the U.S. Navy. As commander of the Asiatic Squadron in the Pacific, he launched the successful attack on Manila Bay at the start of the Spanish-American War that earned him a promotion to admiral. His immense popularity with the public caused some to urge him to run for president, but the death of McKinley and the rising popularity of Roosevelt effectively ended the idea.

Dewey, John (1859–1952) *progressive educational philosopher*
Born in Vermont, Dewey earned a Ph.D. at Johns Hopkins and became an influential scholar-philosopher of progressivism, particularly well known for his philosophy of education. He had a distinguished academic career at Chicago and Columbia universities, published very widely, was associated with Jane Addams and Lillian Wald at their settlements, and also took a role in founding the NAACP, the American Federation of Teachers, the American

Association of University Professors, and the American Civil Liberties Movement. Dewey promoted instrumentalism, often thought of as an effort to adapt the scientific method of verifiable experiments and experience to the problems of society.

Dewitt, Benjamin Parke (1889–1965) *early historian of progressivism*
Born in New York and a graduate of NYU, Dewitt was an attorney. In 1914 he published the earliest history of progressivism, *The Progressive Movement*. It revealed that similar themes appeared in many reform initiatives supported people with different political allegiances.

Dixon, Thomas (1864–1946) *segregationist writer*
Born in North Carolina, Dixon attended Wake Forest University and law school before becoming a Baptist minister, in which profession his powerful speaking ability brought him fame and success. But in 1899, he left the ministry for a career as a writer, eventually publishing over 20 novels as well as plays and screenplays. Believing that *Uncle Tom's Cabin* was far too sympathetic to blacks, he wrote *The Leopard's Spots* in 1903 and *The Clansman* in 1905, the novel from which D. W. Griffith made his famous movie *The Birth of a Nation*.

Donnelly, Ignatius (1831–1901) *Populist party founder*
Born in Pennsylvania, Donnelly moved to Minnesota after becoming a lawyer and served in state political offices as a Republican, rising to lieutenant governor. He took an active role in the Farmer's Alliance and helped found the Populist party in 1892, writing its famous preamble. From the 1880s Donnelly also wrote science fiction novels, some of them widely read in their day.

Dreiser, Theodore (1871–1945) *writer*
Born into a large impoverished family of German immigrants in Terre Haute, Indiana, Dreiser left home at 15 to work in Chicago. He began a journalistic career, working his way slowly from St. Louis to New York. He began to write fiction; his first novel, *Sister Carrie,* was acclaimed but controversial, and Dreiser continued to run afoul of those who objected to the naturalistic portrayal in literature of grim realities. His unconventional romantic entanglements also caused difficulty at various times. Sympathetic to communism during the 1930s, he also published political writings that had little merit or influence. Today, *An American Tragedy* (1925) is considered his most important novel.

DuBois, William Edward Burghardt (W. E. B. DuBois) (1868–1963) *African-American leader*
Born in Massachusetts, DuBois attended Fisk University and in 1895 became the first African American to receive a

Ph.D. from Harvard. Until 1910, he taught at Atlanta University. A founder of the Niagara Movement in 1905, he took a leading role in founding the biracial NAACP in 1909. He founded and edited its journal, *The Crisis,* making it into an influential publication especially among its black readership. DuBois challenged Booker T. Washington's compromise on political and social rights and supported full integration, but he was also an unabashed elitist who upheld the idea of a "talented tenth" among blacks. He assumed the role of spokesman for African Americans after Washington's death in 1915. He eventually joined the Communist Party and emigrated to Ghana, where he died.

Dunne, Finley Peter (1867–1936) *humor writer*
Dunne was born in Chicago and after a public school education became a newspaper reporter there. In 1893, he began a humorous series of Irish-American dialect columns for the *Chicago Evening Post* featuring the saloon keeper Mr. Dooley, who commented on political and other issues of the day with homespun shrewdness. "Mr. Dooley" became widely popular and collections of the columns appeared regularly in book form. Dunne moved to New York in 1900, where he continued to write Dooley columns and also wrote for *Collier's*. In 1906, he was one of the founders of the muckraking *American Magazine*.

Eastman, Crystal (1881–1928) *reformer, pacifist*
Born in Massachusetts to two ministers, Eastman graduated from Vassar College and also received a master's in sociology from Columbia University and a law degree from New York University in 1907. She joined the Pittsburgh Survey, for which she investigated industrial accidents, later drafting New York's workmen's compensation law and working for the U.S. Industrial Commission. A socialist and suffragist, she took an active role in the World War I peace movement and the founding of the National Civil Liberties Union.

Eastman, Max (1883–1969) *reformer, editor of* The Masses
After receiving degrees from Williams College and Columbia University, Eastman joined the cultural rebellion centered in Greenwich Village. In 1912, he became editor of *The Masses,* a journal of political and cultural radicalism. He opposed World War I and was twice tried, but not convicted, under the Espionage Act. At first he strongly supported Lenin, Trotsky, and their Russian regime but by the 1950s had become a prominent critic of Soviet communism and even a supporter of Senator Joe McCarthy. He was the brother of Crystal Eastman.

Edison, Thomas Alva (1847–1931) *inventor, American folk hero*
Born in Ohio, Edison grew up in Michigan. Even as a child he showed an interest in experimentation; unhappy at

school, what education he received was largely at home from his mother, a former teacher. From the age of 12 he worked as a newspaper salesman on a train, setting up a laboratory in the baggage car, and after 16 he worked as a telegraph operator. He received his first patent in 1869 for a voting machine, and while still in his 20s received enough money for improvements to a stock ticker and in telegraph technology to establish a workshop at Menlo Park, New Jersey. Dedicated to research and invention, the establishment was itself an innovation and a prototype of the modern industrial research laboratory. In 1877, he invented the phonograph while in pursuit of a way to improve the telephone. He then turned to inventing a usable household light bulb, and in the process revolutionized the way in which electrical generating and delivery systems were designed, making possible their vast expansion and eventual displacement of the gaslight. Edison himself opened the first central generating station in New York City, with about 85 customers, in 1882, the beginning of the electric lighting industry in America. In the 1890s, he turned to motion pictures, marketing the kinetoscope viewer in 1893. In the early 20th century, he developed a reliable car battery and also experimented with construction materials to lower the cost of housing. Throughout his life Edison also started numerous businesses to manufacture his inventions, including a company to produce films. The last consuming interest of his life was to find an indigenous American plant to produce less expensive rubber for automobile tires, but he did not succeed. A folk hero during his own lifetime, Edison received over 1,000 patents, achieving most of his discoveries through trial and error.

Eliot, Charles W. (1834–1926) *president of Harvard University*
Born in Boston, Eliot graduated from Harvard, joined its faculty, and in 1896 became its influential president. He is especially known for introducing the idea of electives into Harvard's prescribed curriculum, but in general he oversaw the emergence of the elite undergraduate college into a major university.

Elkins, Stephen B. (1841–1911) *Republican senator*
Elkins was born in Ohio, grew up in Missouri, and became the territorial representative from New Mexico after moving there to practice law. He became a wealthy mine and railroad owner, founding the company town of Elkins, West Virginia. He eventually served as that state's senator and sponsored two railroad regulation bills which bear his name.

Ely, Richard (1854–1943) *progressive economist*
Born in New York, Ely became an influential academic economist and founder of the American Economic Associ-

ation (1885), as well as an influential voice for the Social Gospel movement. As head of the department of economics and political science at the University of Wisconsin, he became closely identified with the Wisconsin idea of using the state university to aid state government and reform.

Fairbanks, Charles (1852–1918) *vice president under Roosevelt*
Born in Ohio, Fairbanks became a wealthy railroad lawyer and conservative senator from Indiana before serving as Theodore Roosevelt's vice president from 1904 to 1908. In 1916, he was again nominated as Charles Evans Hughes's running mate, but the ticket was defeated.

Folk, Joseph W. (1869–1923) *reformer, Missouri governor*
Born in Tennessee, Folk became an attorney in St. Louis. In 1904, he won the Missouri governorship on a Democratic reform ticket after his prosecution of a corrupt boss and city council gained national fame in Steffens's *Shame of the Cities.* He later served as prosecutor for the Interstate Commerce Commission in the Wilson administration.

Foraker, Joseph Benson (1846–1917) *Republican senator*
Born in Ohio, Foraker graduated from Cornell before becoming Ohio governor. He served as a conservative Republican senator from 1896 to 1908, frequently opposing Roosevelt's reforms. He hoped to run for president in 1908, but his political career ended when it was revealed in the Hearst newspapers that he had been on the payroll of Standard Oil throughout his career in Washington.

Ford, Henry (1863–1947) *inventor, innovator in the automotive industry*
Ford was born near Dearborn, Michigan, and grew up on a farm. He had little formal education but great natural skill as a mechanic. In 1903, he formed Ford Motor Company, where he was a pioneer of the moving, mass production assembly line. In 1914, he decreed an eight-hour day and doubled wages for all his employees. Other automakers formed a trust to oppose his policies, but he became a popular hero in the Progressive Era. After 1920, he suffered a slow decline in both popularity and business success, as he began to fight labor unions, promote anti-Semitism, and fall behind in auto innovations.

Fosdick, Raymond Blaine (1883–1972) *reformer*
Born in Buffalo, New York, to progressive parents, Fosdick received degrees from Princeton where he made the acquaintance of Woodrow Wilson, then took a law degree in New York while working at Henry Street Settlement with Lillian Wald. As counsel for the City of New York, he

investigated many issues, including prostitution, and gained a reputation as a reformer. During World War I, he oversaw the organization of military training camps for the army and navy. Fosdick was a devoted internationalist and in 1919, Wilson appointed him representative to the League of Nations. When Congress did not approve the League covenant he resigned to found the League of Nations Association to continue American support for the idea. He opened a law firm in New York, eventually becoming an official of many Rockefeller family philanthropies.

Frick, Henry Clay (1849–1919) *industrialist*
Frick was the son of a poor Pennsylvania farmer, although his mother's family was wealthy. He had little formal education and went to work at an early age. During the 1870s, he became a millionaire, primarily by investing in coke ovens, whose product was used as fuel in the growing steel industry. By the 1880s, he was associated with Andew Carnegie and eventually became chair of Carnegie Steel. He gained notoriety for his fierce defense of the interests of capital during the Homestead strike, during which an anarchist attempted to murder him. After the formation of U.S. Steel, he became a director of the new corporation.

Garland, Hannibal Hamlin (1860–1940) *novelist*
Garland was born in Wisconsin and grew up in Iowa, and as a young adult farmed a claim in North Dakota. He moved to Boston in his twenties and soon gained fame for his regional fiction portraying the difficult lives of homesteaders on what he called the Middle Border as they struggled in a hostile environment. He eventually moved to New York and won the Pulitzer Prize in 1922 for *A Daughter of the Middle Border,* one of his memoirs that are considered superior to his later fiction.

Gary, Elbert H. (1846–1927) *industrialist*
Born in Illinois, Gary became a corporate lawyer before joining J. P. Morgan in the formation of Federal Steel and U.S. Steel, which he led. He strongly supported the open shop movement and his refusal to come to terms with union demands led to the bitter steel strike of 1919.

George, Henry (1839–1897) *author of the single tax idea*
Born in Philadelphia, George eventually became a journalist in California. In 1879, he published his best known work, *Progress and Poverty,* which argued that the growth of poverty that accompanied the growth of wealth in America was due to the monopoly of land and could be solved by a panacea called the single tax. Professional economists did not accept the theory, but many reform minded Americans in the Progressive Era were very impressed with it. In the 1880s, George twice ran for mayor of New York, but was defeated by the Tammany machine candidate.

Gibbons, James Cardinal (1834–1921) *Roman Catholic leader*
Gibbons was the second American to be appointed cardinal in the Roman Catholic Church and was archbishop of Baltimore, his birthplace, from the 1870s to 1921. The leader of American Catholicism during the Progressive Era, he was generally conservative but did strongly support the rights of workingmen and influenced the American Catholic clergy to uphold the rights of unionization.

Gilman, Charlotte Perkins Stetson (1860–1935) *feminist writer*
Born in Connecticut, Gilman spent most of her life as a resident of California. She established a career as a writer and lecturer after divorcing her first husband (Stetson). Her *Women and Economics* (1898) and several works to follow, which examine the economic bases of relations between the sexes, became foundational intellectual works of the feminist movement. She also published a magazine, *The Forerunner,* from 1909 to 1917.

Glass, Carter (1858–1946) *Democratic politician*
A lifelong Virginian, Glass entered Democratic politics after a career as a newspaper editor. He served as a congressman from 1901 to 1918, secretary of the treasury until 1920, and a senator after that date. He consistently supported the states' rights philosophy. In 1913, he drafted the Federal Reserve Act and, later, in 1933, the legislation that created the Federal Deposit Insurance Corporation (FDIC).

Goldman, Emma (1869–1940) *radical activist and writer*
Born in Russia (modern Lithuania), Goldman immigrated in 1885. By the end of the decade, she had become associated with the anarchist cause. During the following decades, she supported various causes, published the magazine *Mother Earth,* and wrote and lectured on a wide range of topics. Goldman consistently supported limiting the power of government over the lives of individuals. She was imprisoned for opposing the draft during World War I, then deported. She remained active as writer and lecturer in Europe and in Canada, where she lived after being denied reentry to the United States.

Goldmark, Josephine Clara (1877–1950) *reformer*
Goldmark was born in Brooklyn to a prominent Jewish family and became a lifelong social reformer. She graduated from Bryn Mawr and became the collaborator of Florence Kelley, holding the position of research and publications director for the National Consumers' League. She did most of the research for her brother-in-law Louis

Brandeis's famous brief in the *Muller v. Oregon* case of 1908. She did numerous investigations of factory conditions and served on the commission appointed to investigate the Triangle Shirtwaist Fire.

Gompers, Samuel (1850–1924) *labor leader*
Gompers was born in England to a Dutch Jewish family. He became a cigar maker at age 10 and soon after immigrated to New York with his family. He took an active role in founding a craft union federation, which became the American Federation of Labor in 1886. Gompers served as its president until his death and for four decades was the most prominent labor leader in America. Unlike earlier leaders, he accepted the new industrial economy. He concentrated on achieving higher wages and benefits for workers and did not propose sweeping programs to remake society.

Goodnow, Frank J. (1859–1939) *political scientist, president of Johns Hopkins University*
Born in Brooklyn, Goodnow graduated from Amherst College and Columbia University, becoming a professor of political science there. He served as the first president of the newly formed American Political Science Association in 1903. He gained fame as an expert on municipal reform and maintained that separating policymaking from administration was the best approach. After 1914 he was president of Johns Hopkins.

Gore, Thomas P. (1870–1949) *Democratic senator*
Gore was born in Mississippi and attended law school in Tennessee. By the age of 20 he had lost his sight as the result of childhood accidents. He moved to Texas, then Oklahoma, entering politics as a Populist but soon becoming allied with the Democrats. He gained a reputation as a powerful speaker and debater and became one of Oklahoma's first senators in 1907, serving until 1920.

Gorgas, William Crawford (1854–1920) *international public health expert*
Born in Alabama, Gorgas attended the University of the South, then trained as a physician in New York before obtaining an appointment to the U.S. Army Medical Corps in 1880. Gorgas contracted and recovered from yellow fever, thus becoming immune, and after the Spanish-American War gained his reputation working to control the disease in Cuba. In 1904, he was appointed to head sanitation work on the Panama Canal project. Despite opposition from officials who scorned his mosquito control measures, he eventually succeeded in conquering yellow fever there, without which the project might have been impossible. His work gained an international reputation and he served numerous governments and organizations as consultant. From 1914 to 1918, he served as surgeon general.

Grant, Madison (1865–1937) *defender of Anglo-Saxon superiority*
Born to a distinguished upper-class family in New York City, Grant took an active role in many organizations relating to natural history and conservation. He is best remembered, however, as a defender of Anglo-Saxon or Nordic superiority and the need for immigration restriction in America, points elaborated in his influential 1916 work, *The Passing of the Great Race.*

Griffith, D. W. (1875–1948) *pioneering movie director*
Griffith, born in Kentucky, became a writer, actor, and finally director for movie companies after moving to New York. He made many popular movies for the company Biograph, developing many cinematic techniques for the new movie medium, such as the close-up. *The Birth of a Nation* (1915), based on Thomas Dixon's novel *The Clansman,* is regarded as Griffith's masterpiece, but unfortunately glorified the Ku Klux Klan.

Gulick, Luther H., Jr. (1865–1918) *playground movement activist*
Born in Honolulu to missionary parents of the American Bible Association, Gulick attended Oberlin College and became an expert in and college instructor of physical education. Long associated with the YMCA, he served as head of the New York City public school physical education program and was a founder of the Playground Association of America.

Hall, G. Stanley (1844–1924) *psychologist of adolescence*
Hall was born in Massachusetts and received the first Ph.D. in psychology in the United States in 1878 from Harvard. He taught at Johns Hopkins and served as president of Clark. He is best known for his pioneering and influential work in child and adolescent psychology and education, and is credited with inventing the idea of adolescence as it is now understood.

Hanna, Marcus Alonzo (1837–1904) *Republican politician*
Born in Ohio, Hanna entered the family grocery business and later his wife's family's coal and iron business, before moving into banking and street railways. He became involved in Ohio politics and managed both of William McKinley's Presidential campaigns. He was elected to the Senate in 1897 and until his death he maintained a high profile, advocating a pro-business agenda. Conservative Republicans hoped he would mount his own campaign for President in 1904, but he died unexpectedly, clearing the way for Roosevelt.

Harding, Warren Gamaliel (1865–1923) *29th president of the United States*

Born in Ohio, Harding was a journalist before entering politics at the state level, where he held several offices. Harding was an effective orator and in 1912, gave the nominating speech for Taft at the Republican convention. From 1914 to 1920, he served in the Senate, compiling an undistinguished, relatively conservative record. A favorite of a small group of Republican senators, he became the party's nominee for president in 1920 after the convention deadlocked. Using the slogan "a return to normalcy," in the November election, he won by a large margin, largely because of voter unhappiness with Wilson and his party—and despite accusations that he had some African-American ancestry. Having accomplished little, he died in office in 1923, just as serious corruption charges against several members of his administration began to surface.

Harlan, John Marshall (1833–1911) *Supreme Court justice*

Born in slave-owning Kentucky, Harlan became a Republican politician who consistently defended the principles of civil rights and equality before the law. In 1877, he was appointed to the Supreme Court, serving until his death. His judicial philosophy was often in conflict with his colleagues' usual support for the rights of property. He is most remembered for his powerful dissent to *Plessy v. Ferguson* (1896).

Harper, Ida Husted (1851–1931) *suffrage publicist*

Born in Indiana, Harper was a high school principal before becoming a writer/publicist for NAWSA, a position she held during its successful campaign to pass the Nineteenth Amendment. A collaborator with Susan B. Anthony on the fourth volume of *History of Women's Suffrage,* she compiled and wrote the final two volumes.

Harrison, Benjamin (1833–1901) *23rd president of the United States*

The grandson of President William Henry Harrison, he was born in Ohio and settled with his family in Indianapolis after he was admitted to the bar. He became active in Republican politics. He served in the Civil War, was a U.S. senator for one term, campaigned for civil service reform, and gained the nomination for president in 1888, although he was not especially well known nationally. His Democratic opponent, Grover Cleveland, won the popular vote, but Harrison won the presidency in the Electoral College. In the election of 1892, however, he lost to Cleveland.

Harrison, Caroline Lavinia Scott (Carrie Harrison) (1832–1892) *first lady of the United States*

Born in Ohio, Caroline Scott married Benjamin Harrison, a future president, in 1853. The couple had three children, one of whom died shortly after birth. While serving as first lady (1889–1892), she refurbished the White House and conducted a comprehensive inventory of each room, the first such catalogue ever of its historic furniture and objects. A talented amateur artist, she also personally designed new White House china and established the mansion's china collection. Harrison successfully led a fund raising drive for the new Johns Hopkins Medical School after the school agreed to her condition that they admit women on the same basis as men. She also served as the first president of the Daughters of the American Revolution. She died of tuberculosis during the campaign of 1892.

Harrison, Carter Henry II (1860–1953) *reform mayor of Chicago*

Harrison followed his father into politics, and between the two of them they served a total of ten terms as mayor of Chicago. A successful politician, Harrison was allied with famous Chicago bosses, but was also a supporter of reform who cooperated with the Municipal Voters League and attempted to rein in utility magnates. He was defeated for a sixth term primarily because his efforts to regulate vice were not popular. He served as mayor from 1897 to 1905 and again from 1911 to 1915.

Harvey, William Hope (1851–1936) *writer and proponent of free silver*

Born in West Virginia to a farm family, Harvey became a lawyer, eventually moving to Ohio and Chicago before taking up real estate promotion and mining interests in Colorado and other western states. In 1893, Harvey returned to Chicago and devoted himself to promoting the cause of free silver. He established the Coin Publishing Company and Coin's Financial Series of small, paperbound books on the subject. The third, *Coin's Financial School* (1894), a fictional series of lectures with easily understood arguments and cartoons, sold as many as 1 million copies and became a powerful tool for the free-silver movement. In the following decades, he took up other causes such as trusts, imperialism, rent, interest rates, profit, and taxes. In 1900, he moved to Arkansas to construct a resort area; he also began work on an obelisk intended to inform future eras about the causes of his own civilization's downfall. In the 1930s, he was nominated twice for president by small splinter groups.

Haywood, William Dudley (Big Bill Haywood) (1869–1928) *radical labor leader*

Born in Salt Lake City, Haywood began his career as a labor leader as an official of the Western Federation of Miners. In 1905 he helped found the Industrial Workers of the World. The following year he was charged with murder of the Idaho governor but won an acquittal with the assistance of Clarence Darrow. He continued his labor leadership but during World War I was prosecuted (along with other IWW leaders) for conspiracy to sabotage the war effort. He was deported to Russia, where he eventually died. The communist leadership there received him warmly at first, but as time went on he was consigned to oblivion.

Hearst, William Randolph (1863–1951) *newspaper publisher, yellow journalist*

Born into a wealthy San Francisco family, Hearst took control of the family's paper, *The Examiner,* in 1886. In 1895, he purchased the *New York Journal* and began to compete with Pulitzer's *World.* He played a large role in encouraging public opinion to support a war with Spain in 1898. After the war, Hearst supported reform efforts. An active Democrat, he entered politics, serving in Congress from 1902 to 1906 and making a bid for President in 1904. He also lost close races for mayor and governor of New York. He eventually owned twenty newspapers and thirteen magazines.

Heney, Francis Joseph (1858–1937) *prosecutor in San Francisco corruption cases*

Born in New York, Heney grew up in San Francisco and became a lawyer, although he had little formal education. In the early 1900s, he established a reputation as a reformer by his investigation and prosecution of land grant frauds. In 1906, he undertook the prosecution of municipal graft. He won more than 300 indictments, but only four convictions, having alienated many business interests by exposing their corruption along with that of bosses and officials. He remained active in reform and Democratic politics and in 1931 was appointed superior court judge in Los Angeles, serving until his death.

Herron, George D. (1862–1925) *social gospel minister*

Born in Indiana, Herron became a Congregational minister in the 1880s. In the 1890s, he became extremely well known as a reformer and was appointed to a chair in applied Christianity, or social gospel, at Iowa (Grinnell) College. By 1899, he had resigned and shortly thereafter left the ministry aligning for a time with the Socialist Party. He supported World War I, and while living in Italy performed diplomatic services for the Wilson administration during the peace process.

Hillquit, Morris (1869–1933) *socialist, labor activist*

Hillquit was born in Latvia and after immigrating received a law degree at New York University. Long active in organizing and representing garment workers, in 1901, he became one of the founders of the Socialist party. Less doctrinaire than DeLeon, but also less conservative than Debs, he led the party during its opposition to World War I but also broke with Russian Communists over the issue of violent revolution. He ran as the party's candidate for Congress and for mayor of New York in numerous elections.

Hindus, Maurice Gerschon (1891–1969) *journalist*

Hindus immigrated from Russia with his widowed mother and siblings. He attended Colgate University and Harvard, becoming a writer and journalist who specialized in Russian affairs.

Hine, Lewis Wickes (1874–1940) *muckraking photographer*

Born in Wisconsin, Hine received a degree from New York University and first used a camera to record activities at the Ethical Culture School in New York, where he worked as a teacher. He then began to photograph immigrants arriving at Ellis Island and soon to document their tenement neighborhoods as well. Some of his most famous images, published between 1907 and 1914, were taken of child laborers for the National Child Labor Committee, often by means of stealth to avoid the wrath of their employers. In 1909 he joined *Charities and the Commons* (later *Survey*) as a photographer. He photographed relief efforts in Europe after World War I, the daily work on the Empire State Building in New York City, and other groups of working people.

Hobart, Garret Augustus (1844–1899) *vice president under McKinley*

Hobart was born in Long Branch, New Jersey, and attended Rutgers University before entering the practice of law. Marked by geniality, he rose quickly in Republican state politics, becoming speaker of the assembly at the age of 30. Meanwhile he also accumulated a fortune in various business investments, and in 1896 the New Jersey delegation to the Republican convention succeeded in securing his nomination as McKinley's vice president. He died in office in November 1899 after a brief illness.

Holmes, Joseph Austin (1859–1915) *mine safety activist*

Born in Laurens, South Carolina, Holmes attended Cornell before becoming professor of geology and natural history at the University of North Carolina. After serving as state geologist, he became head of the technological branch of the United States Geological Survey, expanded into the United States Bureau of Mines in 1910. He worked tirelessly to improve mine safety, coining the slogan Safety First. He died from tuberculosis.

Holmes, Oliver Wendell, Jr. (1841–1935) *Supreme Court justice*

Holmes was born in Boston, son of American author Oliver Wendall Holmes, Sr. After serving in the Civil War, he became a law professor at Harvard, his alma mater. Appointed to the Massachusetts Supreme Court in 1882, he was elevated to the U.S. Supreme Court in 1902. During his tenure he established a reputation as the court's most articulate liberal, especially for his opinions (often expressed in dissents to the majority) upholding the government's right of reasonable regulation of business and the citizen's right to free expression.

Hoover, Herbert Clark (1874–1964) *federal official during World War I, 31st President of the United States*

Hoover was born in Iowa and attended Stanford University, becoming a mining engineer and soon earning a reputation as an administrator. During World War I, he was head of the American Commission for Relief in Belgium, which had a budget of over a billion dollars. After America's entry into the war, he served as Wilson's successful head of food administration and later oversaw relief of the Soviet Union. He served as secretary of commerce for Harding and Coolidge and was elected president in 1928, in time to preside over the worst stock market crash in American history and the onset of severe economic depression. Defeated for re-election in 1932, he remained active in politics and pubic service until his death.

Hostos y Bonilla, Eugenio María de (1839–1903) *advocate of Cuban independence*

Born in Puerto Rico, Hostos attended law school in Spain before undertaking lifelong work as a reformer in politics and education in Cuba (he was a member of the revolutionary junta), the Dominican Republic, and South American nations, as well as his native land. He was a prolific writer.

Howe, Frederic C. (1867–1940) *reformer*

Howe, born in Pennsylvania, attended Allegheny College and earned a Ph.D. at Johns Hopkins University. In 1892 he went to Cleveland to practice law and live in a settlement house. After Mayor Tom Johnson took office, Howe became part of his inner circle and was also elected to the Ohio senate in 1903, earning a reputation as a progressive reformer. In 1910, he moved to New York to head the People's Institute and also wrote widely on cities and reform. In the period 1914–19, he served as commissioner of immigration, but resigned in disagreement with restrictions instituted by the Wilson administration. He remained active in liberal politics through the 1930s.

Howells, William Dean (1837–1920) *novelist, editor*

Born in Ohio, Howells first came to attention for writing a campaign biography of Abraham Lincoln. After the Civil War, he joined E. L. Godkin's *Nation* and later moved to *The Atlantic* and *Harper's*. During the 1880s and 1890s, he wrote several very successful novels that turned a critical eye on America's newly materialistic society. But he was equally well known for his promotion of realism in literature and his encouragement of other, younger writers through his editorial positions.

Hughes, Charles Evans (1862–1948) *Republican politician, Chief Justice of the Supreme Court*

Hughes was born in New York, attending Colgate (then called Madison) University and Columbia Law School. While practicing law in New York he became counsel for two investigative committees of the New York legislature in 1905–1906, the first on corruption in gas utilities and the second on the insurance industry, positions that earned him immediate fame among reformers. He served two terms as governor, doing battle with both Tammany Hall and conservatives in his own Republican Party to institute many reforms. In 1910, he became a Supreme Court justice but resigned in 1916 to accept the Republican presidential nomination. He lost a close election to Wilson. During the 1920s, he served as secretary of state, was reappointed to the Supreme Court, and in 1930 became chief justice, serving until 1941.

Hunter, Robert (1874–1943) *writer on poverty*

Born in Indiana, Hunter became a social worker and resident at Hull-House, moving to New York in 1902 and affiliating with University Settlement there. In 1904, he published *Poverty*, asserting that society bore some responsibility for the poverty of individuals. In 1905, he joined the Socialist Party and stood as their candidate frequently in elections. Hunter inherited wealth and also married a very wealthy woman; they were known as the millionaire Socialists. In 1914, he broke with the party and moved to California. Hunter was not one of the most prominent reformers of the era, but *Poverty* remains one of its most prominent works.

Ireland, John (1838–1918) *Roman Catholic leader*

Born in Ireland, Ireland immigrated to America with his family in 1849 and soon moved to St. Paul. Educated for the priesthood in France, he returned to America, was ordained, then served in the Civil War before returning to St. Paul. He was a social and political activist at the center of the late 19th-century movement to Americanize the Catholic Church in America and a participant in many reform movements, including temperance. The first archbishop of St. Paul, he helped found Catholic University in Washington, D.C.

Ives, Charles Edward (1874–1954) *pioneering composer of modern classical music*

Born in Danbury, Connecticut, Ives was trained as a musician by his father, a bandleader in the Civil War, and later at Yale University. After college, he left professional music and became a great success in the insurance industry. During his evenings and weekends, he continued to write experimental and pioneering symphonic music. Most of Ives's music was composed between 1896 and 1916, although he continued to revise most of it for many years. Very little of it was performed prior to the 1920s, and many works were not performed in full until several decades later. At the end of the 1910s, having suffered a heart attack, Ives began to organize and publish his work, distributing it to musicians and organizations without charge. His experiments in musical form not only covered almost all innovations that would eventually mark modern classical music, such as atonality or the use of many meters at once, but predated their use by most other composers by several decades. In addition, Ives's work is notable for interweaving many kinds of American popular and folk music, which sometimes seem to clash and at other times sound quite beautiful. Unlike many prophets in the arts, Ives did live to see his work recognized and honored by other composers, and in 1947 won the Pulitzer Prize for his *Third Symphony*. His influence continued to grow after his death.

James, Henry (1843–1916) *novelist*

Born in New York, James attended Harvard before becoming a novelist. He is often regarded as the most important serious fiction writer at the turn of the century, known for his psychological subtlety. In 1875, he moved to London, eventually becoming a British citizen, and his novels often treat the contrast between American and European society. He is the brother of William James.

James, William (1842–1910) *philosopher*

A psychologist and philosopher who taught at Harvard throughout his life, James is known as one of the founders of pragmatism, a philosophical movement that judges the truth of an idea by its practical consequences and is often said to be distinctly American. Henry James is his brother.

Johnson, Hiram Warren (1866–1945) *progressive Republican politician*

Johnson was born in Sacramento. A lawyer, he became well known as a prosecutor in the San Francisco graft trials of 1906. In 1910, he became governor of California on a Republican reform ticket. A forceful advocate of reform, he took a leading role in the Progressive Party in 1912 and ran on its ticket as Roosevelt's vice president. In 1916, he was elected to the Senate, where he served until his death.

Johnson, Tom L. (1854–1911) *reform mayor*

Born in Kentucky, Johnson had two years of schooling. He quickly rose in the business world, becoming wealthy through street railways and, later, steel. Attracted to the reform ideas of Henry George, he served two terms as a congressman before being elected the reform mayor of Cleveland in 1901, serving until his defeat for a fifth term in 1909. Known for the tent meetings at which he attempted to educate ordinary citizens on various issues, at his death he left a large group of committed progressives who continued reform in Cleveland.

Johnston, Frances Benjamin (1864–1952) *photographer*

Born in West Virginia, Johnston grew up in Washington. After art training in Paris and Washington, she opened a photography studio in 1890. A relative of Grover Cleveland's wife, she photographed the White House and did several historically important projects during the 1890s, photographing Pennsylvania coal fields and Massachusetts shoe factories, Hampton Institute, and the return of Admiral Dewey from Manila. After the turn of the century she became increasingly interested in photographing architecture. In 1929, a Library of Congress exhibition of her photos from Virginia led Congress to appropriate funds to document historic early American architecture, the foundation of the Historic American Buildings Survey (HABS).

Jones, Mary Harris (Mother Jones) (ca. 1830–1930) *itinerant labor organizer*

Having emigrated from Ireland as a child, Jones trained as a teacher in Toronto and taught in Canada and the United States, including Memphis, where she married George E. Jones, an iron worker, in 1861. Six years later, her husband and four children died in a yellow fever epidemic. She moved to Chicago, became a dressmaker, and affiliated with the Knights of Labor, where she became committed to improving the lot of working people. For the rest of her life she was an itinerant labor agitator, organizer, and effective orator, moving from town to town and strike to strike. In 1903, she led a group of child textile workers from Philadelphia to President Theodore Roosevelt's home at Oyster Bay, New York, to publicize the evils of child labor. She was most often at work among coal miners of West Virginia and Colorado, where her own courage in the face of violence, arrest, and jail was a powerful inspiration. Workers almost universally loved her although she did not always see eye to eye with labor organization officials. Mother Jones also organized miners' wives to demonstrate but did not believe it should be necessary for women themselves to work outside the home and publicly opposed women's suffrage. She spent her last years living with the family of Terrence Powderly.

Jones, Samuel M. (Golden Rule Jones) (1846–1904)
reform mayor
Jones was born in Wales and grew up in New York State after immigrating with his parents. He had little education but became very wealthy after inventing improved drilling equipment, and his manufacturing company was a model of enlightened labor policies. He was elected reform mayor of Toledo on the Republican ticket in 1897, and after the party denounced him won three more terms as an independent. He died in office. Jones was known for his social reform initiatives and gained a high profile in the Christian socialist movement.

Kallen, Horace Meyer (1882–1974) *theorist of cultural pluralism*
Born in Silesia, Kallen immigrated to the United States as a child. He attended Harvard and taught at several universities before helping to found, in 1919, the New School for Social Research, where he remained until his death. An active reformer, he wrote widely and was best known as a voice for his theory of cultural pluralism, first expressed in 1915, although the term itself did not appear until 1924.

Kelley, Florence (1859–1932) *labor reformer*
Kelley was born in Philadelphia to a wealthy industrialist who was a Quaker and former abolitionist who also served as a Republican congressman. She attended Cornell University, then studied in Europe, where she completed highly regarded translations of Karl Marx and Friedrich Engels. She married and had three children, then divorced her abusive husband and became a resident at Hull-House. She became an active labor investigator and reformer and the first state factory inspector of Illinois, serving until 1897. Duing the same years, she received a law degree from Northwestern. She moved to New York, became a resident at Henry Street Settlement, then became the secretary (administrator) of the National Consumers' League. She worked tirelessly and aggressively for labor reform, especially for women and children.

Kellogg, Paul U. (1879–1958) *reform journalist*
Born in Michigan, Kellogg worked as a journalist before moving to New York and joining the staff of the Charity Organization Society's journal, *Charities.* In 1907, was selected to direct the Pittsburgh Survey and in 1912, became editor in chief of the renamed journal *The Survey,* which became widely respected. During World War I he served with the American Red Cross in Europe and helped found the American Civil Liberties Union.

Kellor, Frances A. (1873–1952) *reformer*
Born in Ohio and raised in Michigan by a single mother who worked as a housekeeper, Kellor earned a law degree

from Cornell before enrolling at the University of Chicago to study the new field of sociology. She became an authority on unemployment issues and worked actively for reforms to aid black migrants and white immigrants to New York, where she lived after 1904. In 1908, she became secretary of the New York State Immigration Commission and continued work in organizations devoted to Americanization and other immigrant issues into the 1920s. Kellor took an active role in the Progressive Party. In 1926, she helped found the American Arbitration Association, and for the remainder of her life worked as an expert in industrial and international arbitration.

Knox, Philander C. (1853–1921) *Cabinet member*
A resident of Pennsylvania, Knox served as attorney general under McKinley and Roosevelt, then one term as senator. Under Taft he became secretary of state and one of the most influential cabinet members, best known for his policy of dollar diplomacy.

La Follette, Robert Marion, Sr. (1855–1925) *leader of progressive Republicans*
Born on a Wisconsin farm, La Follette first achieved fame as an orator at the University of Wisconsin. After admission to the bar he served as a Republican U.S. congressman from 1884 to 1890, then returned to Wisconsin and entered state politics. He increasingly disagreed with the Republican establishment. He was elected governor in 1900 and immediately began instituting a comprehensive program of reform that included reliance on experts at the state university and eventually became known as the Wisconsin Idea. In 1905, he was elected to the U.S. Senate, where he quickly became the leader of progressive senators, called Insurgents, who advocated various reforms and opposed many policies of the Republican Old Guard. He founded *La Follette's Magazine* in 1909 to spread his ideas (now called the *Progressive,* it is still published today.) He sought the Republican presidential nomination in 1912, contributing to the split in the party. During the Wilson administration, he supported strict neutrality and opposed entry into World War I, a stance that cost him much support. In 1924, he ran for president on an independent ticket, polling almost 5 million votes.

Lansing, Robert (1864–1928) *secretary of state during World War I*
Born in Watertown, New York, Lansing attended Amherst and later joined his father's law firm, soon specializing in international law and serving as counsel in many important international negotiations, including the Alaskan Boundary Tribunal (1903). Wilson appointed him counsel in the State Department and as Secretary of State after the 1915 resignation of William Jennings Bryan. He did not entirely

support Wilson's League of Nations idea, and Wilson forced him to resign after he attempted to direct the Cabinet after the president's stroke. Lansing continued to practice law in Washington.

Lathrop, Julia Clifford (1858–1932) *reformer, first head of the Children's Bureau*
Born in Rockford, Illinois, she attended Rockford College and Vassar, then joined Jane Addams at Hull-House. She gained a national reputation for expertise in the care of the mentally ill, and participated in many other social service initiatives. In 1912, Taft appointed her head of the newly established Children's Bureau, making her the first woman to head a federal agency. Modest, low profile, but politically astute, she served for a decade and later served as child welfare assessor for the League of Nations.

Lawson, Thomas W. (1857–1925) *muckraking journalist*
Lawson, born in Massachusetts, had little formal education, but rose to prominence and made a fortune on Wall Street, handling financial deals for Standard Oil, among others. In 1905, however, he turned muckraker, exposing financial manipulations in a series for *Everybody's* magazine, "Frenzied Finance." The series led directly to the New York investigation of the insurance industry and the rise of Charles Evans Hughes. Lawson eventually lost much of his personal fortune.

Lease, Mary Elizabeth Clyens (1853–1933) *Populist orator*
Born in Pennsylvania, Mary Clyens moved with her family to New York, then Kansas, where she became a teacher and married a pharmacist. The mother of four children, she was admitted to the bar in that state. Known as a dramatic orator, she soon became active in the Farmer's Alliance and People's party, making hundreds of speeches during their campaigns in the early 1890s. When the Populists won Kansas in 1892, she became head of the State Board of Charities. After 1896, she turned to writing but continued to champion many reform causes, supporting the Progressive party in 1912. Late in life she moved to a farm in New York State.

Lindsey, Benjamin Barr (1869–1943) *judge, juvenile court reformer*
Born in Tennessee, Lindsey moved to Colorado and became a lawyer, judge, and crusader for reforming the treatment of juvenile offenders. Lindsey used a county court in Colorado as a juvenile court, gaining a national reputation. In 1901, he succeeded in establishing a formal juvenile court system, where young males were declared wards of the court, kept separate from the adult prison population, and offered rehabilitation. This model gained great popularity among juvenile reformers. He served as judge there until 1927, after which he also became known for advocacy of reform of marriage and divorce laws.

Lippmann, Walter (1889–1974) *journalist*
Lippmann was born in New York and attended Harvard, then began a career as a writer and political analyst, publishing *A Preface to Politics* and *Drift and Mastery* in 1913 and 1914, when he was still in his early 20s. He wrote more than 20 books during his lifetime and was on the staff of the *New Republic* and numerous national newspapers. His famous syndicated column, "Today and Tomorrow," ran in 250 newspapers in the mid-20th century, by which time he was considered the elder statesman of journalist-commentators on public issues.

Lloyd, Henry Demarest (1847–1903) *reform journalist*
Born in New York, Lloyd attended Columbia and Columbia Law School and began his career on the Chicago *Tribune*. After 1885 he became an early reformer and muckraker, writing 10 books, including *Wealth Against Commonwealth*. He was an advocate for farmers and workers and in the 1890s supported first Populism and then Debs's Socialist Party.

Lodge, Henry Cabot (1850–1924) *Republican senator*
Lodge was born in Boston to a prominent family. He attended Harvard and throughout his life published volumes of historical studies and his own essays. He served in the House of Representatives from 1887 to 1893 and after that in the Senate until his death. Lodge consistently supported voting and other rights for African Americans, immigration restriction, anti-monopoly measures, and a strong, imperialistic stance in international affairs. His opposition to the Versailles treaty at the end of World War I, at which time he was chair of the Senate Foreign Relations Committee, led to its defeat.

London, Jack (1876–1916) *novelist*
London grew up in an impoverished home in San Francisco. As a teenager, he worked as a sailor and began traveling across the United States as a hobo. During that time, he worked at many laboring jobs and converted to socialism. After joining the Klondike Gold Rush for a year, he returned to California and began to write fiction based on his adventures. In 1903, *The Call of the Wild,* a novel set in the Yukon, brought him international fame and success as a writer. London was a realist and naturalist, who stressed a dark vision of survival of the fittest in the natural world. Although he died at 40, he published more than 50 books and hundreds of short stories. He struggled for many years with alcoholism.

Lovejoy, Owen R. (1866–1961) *child labor reformer*
Born in Michigan, Lovejoy became a Methodist and later a Congregational minister. He served as the general secretary of the National Child Labor Committee but resigned after the failure of the Child Labor Amendment to be ratified. He continued his work with other child and social welfare agencies.

Mack, Julian W. (1866–1943) *judge, child labor reformer*
Born in San Francisco, he received a law degree from Harvard and settled in Chicago, where he was associated with various charities. In 1903, he became a judge of the Circuit Court of Cook County, becoming involved in the pioneering juvenile court there. Later a federal circuit court judge, he remained involved in child labor and other reform issues.

Mahan, Alfred Thayer (1840–1914) *naval advocate*
Born at West Point, Mahan graduated from Annapolis, served in the Civil War, and in 1886, became president of the newly founded Naval War College. His 1890 book, *The Influence of Sea Power upon History,* had enormous influence in Europe as well as America. It encouraged the rebuilding of the U.S. Navy as well as a new willingness to look outward in foreign affairs. One of a group of prominent Washington officials who formulated the justification for imperialism, he was later given the rank of admiral in recognition of his influence.

Mann, James R. (1856–1922) *Republican congressman*
Mann was born in Illinois and entered government as a good government reform councilman in Chicago from 1892 to1896. He moved on to the House of Representatives as a conservative Republican, gaining great influence and eventually replacing Joe Cannon as party leader. Mann gave his name to two important acts he sponsored in 1910: the Mann-Elkins act, which expanded the role of the ICC, and the Mann Act (or White Slave Traffic Act).

Marsh, Benjamin Clarke (1877–1952) *city planning reformer*
Marsh was born in Bulgaria to Congregational missionaries. After graduate study at the universities of Chicago and Pennsylvania, he entered social work and in 1907 became administrator of the Committee on Congestion of Population (CCP) in New York. He gained a high profile as an advocate of city planning, organizing the first national conference in 1909. He was also an advocate of Henry George–like radical tax reform, however, and eventually lost influence by continually advocating it, becoming a one-man lobby in Washington.

Marshall, Thomas R. (1854–1925) *vice president under Wilson*
Born in Indiana, Marshall attended Wabash College and became a lawyer before entering Democratic politics, winning the governorship by a narrow margin in 1908. He supported good government reform and also won increased child labor and employers' liability legislation, gaining national attention. In 1912, he became vice president under Wilson, and the pair was re-elected in 1916. When Wilson became incapacitated in 1919, he performed admirably, preventing a national crisis.

Martí y Pérez, José Julián (1853–1895) *Cuban poet and patriot*
Born in Havana to poor Spanish immigrants, Martí became committed to Cuban independence. He was arrested during the Ten Years' War, Cuba's first struggle for independence, and went in exile to Spain where he attended university. After 1881 he lived primarily in New York, working as a correspondent for many Latin American newspapers and also writing essays and poetry. In 1892, he founded the Cuban Revolutionary Party to actively plan another struggle for Cuban independence but was killed in battle shortly after the revolution began. In the 1920s Martí was rediscovered as a hero by Cuban and other Latin American nationalists.

McAdoo, William Gibbs (1863–1941) *Democratic senator, Cabinet member*
Born in Georgia and educated at the University of Tennessee, McAdoo practiced law in New York, where he took an active role in the Democratic Party. In 1912, he became secretary of the Treasury under Wilson, also serving as chair of the Federal Reserve Board and in other important federal positions. In 1918, he successfully oversaw the federal reorganization and direction of railways for the remainder of World War I. Popular within the Democratic Party, McAdoo was a strong early favorite to succeed Wilson in 1920. But he had married the president's daughter, Eleanor Wilson, and could not openly campaign for the office before Wilson belatedly denied he would seek a third term, by which time other candidates had gained ascendancy. He was a strong candidate for the nomination again in 1924, losing to a compromise candidate after over a hundred ballots. He moved to California, practiced law, and served there as a U.S. senator from 1932 to 1938.

McClure, Samuel Sidney (1857–1949) *editor*
Having emigrated from Protestant Ireland as a child, McClure graduated from Knox College and entered the editorial and publishing business, founding an organization to syndicate the work of authors. In 1893, he established *McClure's,* hoping to bring high quality journalism to a more

popular audience. It soon became the leading journal of muckraking in America, although ironically McClure himself was conservative. Many of his most prominent writers left in 1906 to found *American Magazine,* but *McClure's* continued with other writers of equal talent. McClure was never a good financial manager and lost control of the magazine in 1911; in 1914, he abandoned editing entirely. In later years, he wrote several books on political issues but none were widely read.

McGee, Anita Newcomb (1864–1940) *organizer of the Army Nurse Corps*
Born in Washington, D.C., to an astronomer father and an equally intellectual mother, Anita Newcomb attended Cambridge and the University of Geneva. After her marriage, she enrolled in medical school, receiving an M.D. degree from George Washington University and postgraduate training at Johns Hopkins. During the Spanish-American War she organized female nurses for the army and later drafted the legislation that created the Army Nurse Corps, while serving as assistant surgeon general. During the Russo-Japanese War, she and a group of nurses traveled to Japan to work with Japanese nurses, for which she was honored by the Japanese government.

McKelway, Alexander J. (1866–1918) *child labor reformer*
Born in Pennsylvania, McKelway was educated in Virginia and became a Presbyterian minister. From 1898 to 1905, he edited a North Carolina newspaper, after which he headed the southern campaigns for the new National Child Labor Committee. In 1909, he became a Washington lobbyist for the Committee and had great influence with Wilson and the Democratic party.

McKinley, William (1843–1901) *25th president of the United States*
McKinley was born in Ohio and attended one term at Allegheny College before enlisting in the Civil War. After studying law and being admitted to the bar, he served as a member of the House of Representatives from 1877 to 1891. He won two terms as Ohio governor and in 1896, became the Republican Party's successful candidate for president, winning re-election in 1900. When he took office, McKinley was best known for his domestic policy of high tariffs. Before he was cut down by an assassin's bullet in September 1901, however, he had established a new role for America on the international scene, gaining an empire for America as a result of the Spanish American War.

Merriam, Charles Edward (1874–1953) *political scientist*
Born in Iowa, Merriam became a well-known professor of political science at the University of Chicago who advocated using social science to help formulate national policy. He served as a reform Republican city councilman for two terms. In 1923, he founded the Social Science Research Council and later served on the National Resources Planning Board during the New Deal.

Mitchell, John (1870–1919) *labor leader*
Mitchell began working in the coal mines of Illinois at the age of 12. By 1899, he was president of the United Mine Workers of America, serving until 1908. Considered a conservative labor leader, he worked with the National Civic Federation and later served on the New York Workmen's Compensation Commission and the U.S. Industrial Commission.

Morgan, John Pierpont (J. P. Morgan) (1837–1913) *banker*
Morgan was born in Hartford to a banking family and in the late 19th and early 20th centuries, became the most powerful finance capitalist in America. Because he focused on merging companies into giant corporations and trusts, he came to symbolize the money trust. Powerful enough to organize the acquisition of gold for the U.S. Treasury in the 1890s and to coordinate a private financial response to the panic of 1907 in the absence of a central bank, he was nonetheless subjected to the Pujo investigations of 1912.

Moskowitz, Henry (1879–1936) *reformer*
Born in Romania, Moskowitz grew up on New York's Lower East Side and attended City College, later earning a Ph.D. in Europe. From the 1890s, he was involved in many reform movements, including settlement work, and took a role in the new Progressive Party after 1912. His wife, Belle Israels Moskowitz, was also active in reform causes.

Muir, John (1838–1914) *conservationist*
Born in Scotland, Muir grew up in frontier Wisconsin and attended the state university there. Before moving to California in 1868, he walked from Indiana to the Gulf of Mexico. After that date, he established himself as a writer on the natural environment in the West, becoming an increasingly prominent advocate of conservation and eventually the leader of the preservationist movement. A founder of the Sierra Club in 1892, he led an unsuccessful campaign to preserve Hetch Hetchy Valley in Yosemite National Park. Muir authored 12 books and countless articles for prominent national magazines.

Munsey, Frank (1854–1925) *publisher*
Munsey was born to a farming family in Maine and rose to be a millionaire through shrewd investments in several enterprises. One prominent area of investment was magazines and newspapers, where his influence was universally

regarded as detrimental by journalists. He joined the Progressive Party in 1912 and became one of its chief financial backers. In 1913, via a front page editorial in his *New York Press,* he abandoned the party and urged it to reunite with the Republicans.

Murphy, Edgar Gardner (1869–1913) *child labor reformer*

Murphy was born in Arkansas and ordained as an Episcopalian minister after attending the University of the South. He wrote widely on social, reform, and racial issues from 1901 to 1910 while serving in Montgomery, Alabama, and other southern parishes. He was administrator of the Southern Education Board, an organization of northern philanthropists and southern educators, which eventually grew into the General Education Board. Murphy was especially concerned about the conditions of labor, and under his promotion, the National Child Labor Committee was organized in 1904, although he later resigned because he did not support federal legislation on the issue.

Norris, Frank (Benjamin Franklin Norris)

(1870–1902) *novelist*

Born in Chicago, Norris moved with his family to San Francisco as a teenager. He attended Harvard before becoming a journalist and an editor at Doubleday, Page, where he discovered Theodore Dreiser. Norris was meanwhile writing fiction himself and is considered one of the pioneers of literary realism and naturalism. His novel *The Octopus* is a study of the railroad's stranglehold upon the West.

Norris, George William (1861–1944) *progressive Congressman*

Born in Ohio, Norris moved to Nebraska to practice law and entered Republican politics. He was elected to Congress in 1902 and in 1909, joined the Insurgents, taking a leading role in the movement to limit the power of House Speaker Joseph Cannon. In 1913, he moved to the Senate, serving until 1943.

Olmstead, Frederick Law, Jr. (1870–1957) *landscape architect*

Born in New York, Olmstead attended Harvard and trained under his father, the famous landscape architect who designed Central Park, before entering the same profession. He designed the grounds of the Chicago World's Fair and helped redesign Washington, D.C., in 1901. He was very active in city planning organizations and played a key role in its development as a profession, creating at Harvard the first landscape architecture and city planning program in the United States.

Otis, Harrison Gray (1837–1917) *publisher*

Born in Ohio, Otis had little formal education. After distinguished service in the Civil War (he later reenlisted during the Spanish American War) he moved to California. He bought an interest in the *Los Angeles Times,* serving as its editor, and eventually became its sole owner and the head of a newspaper chain. A conservative Republican, Otis was an active civic booster but a strident opponent of labor unions. He was eventually one of the city and state's most prominent power brokers.

Outcault, Richard Felton (1863–1928) *cartoonist*

Born in Ohio, where he studied art, Outcault moved to New York and became a cartoonist. He drew his Yellow Kid cartoon, considered the first American newspaper comic, for Pulitzer's *New York World,* then for William Randolph Hearst's *New York Journal.* The competition between the two newspapers the cartoon inspired gave yellow journalism its name. He later introduced the Buster Brown comic serial.

Ovington, Mary White (1865–1951) *advocate for African-American rights*

Born in Brooklyn to a comfortable family, Ovington became a social worker and reformer. She focused increasingly on the plight of African Americans and in 1909, was a founding member of the interracial NAACP. From then until her retirement in 1947 she took an active and courageous role in the organization, chairing the board from 1919 to 1932, and was central to its growth.

Paine, Ralph Delahaye (1871–1925) *journalist*

Born in Illinois, Paine grew up in Florida and as a teen worked as a reporter to gain the funds to enter Yale. An athlete at Yale, he was also employed as a sports writer for a newspaper syndicate. He worked as a war correspondent during the Cuban revolution, the Spanish-American War, the Boxer Rebellion in China, and World War I, then as a newspaper muckraker for the *New York Herald.* He ceased newspaper work to write history and fiction.

Palmer, A. Mitchell (1872–1936) *attorney general*

A Quaker born in Pennsylvania, Palmer attended Swarthmore College. A progressive Democrat, he served in Congress from 1909 to 1915, then as alien property custodian during World War I before becoming attorney general in 1919. In that office, he oversaw the arrest and deportation of alien radicals, in the so-called Palmer Raids, during the Red Scare at the end of the war. Many Democrats wanted him as the party's nominee for president in 1920, although labor did not, and he did not win the nomination. For the remainder of his life, he practiced law in Washington, remaining active in politics.

Paul, Alice (1885–1977) *suffragist and women's rights advocate*

A Quaker born in New Jersey, Paul attended Swarthmore College, then received a Ph.D. at the University of Pennsylvania, as well as law degrees elsewhere. She joined suffragists in England from 1909 to 1912, then returned to America, where she had a prominent role in introducing the militant tactics of British suffragists. In 1914, she formed the Congressional Union, known after 1917 as the National Woman's Party, to campaign aggressively for a federal amendment. Paul was arrested many times. In 1923, Paul introduced the idea of an equal rights amendment. She spent much of the 1920s and 1930s working in Europe for international women's rights.

Pershing, John Joseph (1860–1948) *military leader*

Pershing, born in Missouri, graduated from West Point, where he returned to teach in 1897. He served in the Spanish American and Philippine-American Wars and was promoted to general by Roosevelt in 1906 as a result of his reports on the Russo-Japanese War. He commanded American troops who attempted to capture Pancho Villa during the Mexican Revolution, and when World War I began, was made commander of the American Expeditionary Forces in France. His success as a general led to appointment as army chief of staff. He retired in 1924, although he continued to act as military adviser, and in 1931 won the Pulitzer prize for his memoirs of the war.

Phelan, James Duval (1861–1930) *reform mayor*

Phelan was born in San Francisco to a comfortable merchant family with extensive banking interests. From 1897 to 1902, he served as reform mayor of San Francisco, where he worked for many civic and governmental improvements, a city-owned water supply, and the exclusion of Asian immigrants. In 1906, he helped back the graft investigations and also served as administrator of relief after the earthquake. In 1914, he was elected to the Senate.

Phillips, David Graham (1867–1911) *muckraking journalist*

Born in Madison, Indiana, Phillips attended DePauw University, rooming with the future Senator Albert Beveridge, then graduated from Princeton in 1887. He worked as a newspaper journalist before quitting in 1902 to pursue a successful career as a popular novelist under the pseudonym John Graham. His fiction, which addressed various contemporary issues, sold well in its own day, but Phillips is best remembered for a nonfiction work, *The Treason of the Senate* (1906); it inspired Roosevelt's speech naming reform journalists muckrakers. He was shot and killed by a man who believed one of Phillips's novels was a disguised attack on his family.

Pinchot, Gifford (1865–1946) *federal official, conservationist*

Pinchot was born in Connecticut and graduated from Yale before studying forestry in France. He worked as a private forester on the Vanderbilt estates, then began a career in the U.S. Department of Agriculture in 1898. He oversaw a great expansion of the forestry service and became the chief architect of conservation policy under Theodore Roosevelt, developing the principle of managed use of resources. After being dismissed from the federal government during the Ballinger-Pinchot affair of 1909, he joined the new Progressive Party and ran unsuccessfully for senator on its ticket in 1914. He later served two terms as Republican governor of Pennsylvania.

Pingree, Hazen S. (1840–1901) *reform mayor*

Born in Maine, Pingree had little formal education. He began his working life as a cobbler and became the owner of a very successful shoe factory in Detroit. In 1889, he won the mayor's office as a Republican reformer, serving until 1897. He was well known nationwide as an advocate of municipal ownership of utilities and other social reforms. He continued his reforms as governor of Michigan, where he forced the first realistic appraisal of railroad and other corporate property as a basis for tax reform.

Poole, Ernest Cooke (1880–1950) *journalist, novelist*

Born in Chicago, Poole attended Princeton during Woodrow Wilson's tenure as university president, then spent two years at University Settlement in New York. He was aquainted with many social reformers, and he was the brother-in-law of Walter Weyl, a prominent progressive economist. Poole began publishing muckraking articles about the life of the poor. In 1905, he reported on the turmoil in Russia, the first of several trips abroad as a correspondent. Poole joined the Socialist Party but broke with it over American entry into World War I, even contributing his talents to the Creel Committee. He continued writing modestly successful fiction through the 1940s.

Powderly, Terence Vincent (1849–1924) *labor leader*

Employed on the railroad from the age of 13, Powderly was head of the early national labor union the Knights of Labor from 1879 to 1893 during its growth and decline. He also served as mayor of Scranton, Pennsylvania, for three terms and in other government posts.

Pujo, Arsène Paulin (1861–1939) *Democratic congressman*

Born in Calcasieu Parish, Louisiana, Pujo was admitted to the bar and in 1902, elected to Congress. As chair of the House Banking and Currency Committee, he headed the 1912 Pujo Committee, a subcommittee that held sensational hearings on the so-called money trust, after which he retired from politics to maintain a successful legal practice in Louisiana.

Pulitzer, Joseph (1847–1911) *journalist, philanthropist*
Pulitzer, son of a prosperous Hungarian Jewish family, emigrated to the United States. He began his career reporting for a German-language newspaper in St. Louis owned by Carl Schurz, served in the Missouri legislature, was admitted to the bar, then purchased a St. Louis newspaper and made it into a crusading journal to expose corruption. In 1883, he purchased the *New York World,* meeting great success with his pioneering sensationalist and humanitarian stories, dramatic headlines, self-promotion, but usually solid reporting. He retired in 1890, suffering from ill health for the remainder of his life. He endowed both the Columbia School of Journalism and the Pulitzer Prize.

Quimby, Harriet (1875–1912) *pioneering woman pilot*
Born on a struggling Michigan farm, Quimby headed for California seeking a life on the stage, then in 1903 moved to New York and became a theater critic for *Leslie's Illustrated Weekly.* Daring and independent, in 1911 she became the first American woman to take flying lessons. She was soon flying in popular air exhibitions, a sensation in her purple satin flying suit. In April 1912, three years after a French pilot had first flown across the English Channel, she became the first woman to do so. The following July, she lost her life when she was flung from her plane, for reasons that are not clear, into Boston Harbor during an exhibition.

Rankin, Jeannette (1880–1973) *first female member of Congress*
Rankin, born in Missoula, Montana, to a ranching family, became an active suffragist, helping to win votes for women in Washington and her own state. In 1916, before women nationwide had the right to vote, she became the first woman elected to the House of Representatives. Four days later she voted against entry into World War I. She was defeated for reelection in 1918 and worked through the 1920s and 1930s for various pacifist organizations and the National Consumers' League. In 1940, she was reelected to the House, where she cast the only vote against U.S. entry into World War II.

Rauschenbusch, Walter (1861–1918) *social gospel minister*
Rauschenbusch was born in Rochester, New York. After study in Germany he became pastor of an urban, immigrant congregation in New York. His experience led him to organize liberal, reform-minded clergymen to support social reform. His *Christianity and the Social Crisis* (1907) is considered the most important statement of the Protestant social gospel. Rauschenbusch himself was a Christian socialist. He spent most of his professional career affiliated with the Rochester theological seminary. His public influence waned when he opposed World War I.

Reed, John (1887–1920) *radical journalist*
Born in Portland, Oregon, and educated at Harvard, Reed became a well-known radical journalist. He first received national attention for his firsthand account of the Mexican revolution, but his presence in Russia at the time of the Bolshevik revolution of 1917, and his account of it in *Ten Days That Shook the World* (1919) made him famous. He returned to the United States and participated in the founding of the Communist party but returned to Russia in 1919, where he died and is buried.

Riis, Jacob August (1849–1914) *journalist, reformer*
Riis was born in Denmark and immigrated to the United States in 1870. While working as a newspaper police reporter, which exposed him to life in the slums of New York, he documented life there with both camera and pen. In 1890, he published the landmark *How the Other Half Live.* For the remainder of his life he wrote and engaged in various reform movements. In 1907, he introduced the United States to Denmark's idea of selling decorative stamps, later known as Easter Seals, to raise money for the public health campaign against tuberculosis.

Rockefeller, John Davidson (John D. Rockefeller)
(1839–1937) *captain of industry*
Born in Richford, New York, Rockefeller had become president of Standard Oil of Ohio by 1870, after which he began to seek ways to introduce order into the wildly competitive oil business. He was first to use the trust in 1882, which was declared illegal in 1892 in Ohio. He next developed the holding company in 1889; it, too, was ordered dissolved in 1911 by the Supreme Court, by which time Standard Oil had become the most successful international petroleum company. Rockefeller, a symbol to the public of both enormous wealth and nefarious business dealings, devoted his later life to philanthropy.

Roosevelt, Theodore (1858–1919) *26th president of the United States*
Roosevelt, the sickly child of a wealthy New York City family, overcame his limitations through physical activity and remained a fitness buff to the end of his life. After attending Harvard University and Columbia Law School, he entered New York state politics as a member of the legislature in 1881, an unusual choice for a young man from his background in the days of widespread political corruption. He was only 26 when his first wife died in 1884, shortly after the birth of their daughter Alice. To recover, he went west to a

North Dakota ranch and took up the life of a cowboy. In 1886, he returned to the city to run unsuccessfully for mayor, after which he was appointed civil service commissioner, police commissioner, and assistant secretary of the navy. He volunteered for service when the Spanish-American War broke out and gained great national fame for his role in the Battle of San Juan Hill. Soon after, he was elected governor of New York, undertaking reform initiatives. Less than a year after running as vice president in 1900, he ascended to the presidency when McKinley was assassinated. By then, Roosevelt, who had remarried, had a family of six children. As president, he became the symbol and national spokesman for progressive reform. He was known as a trust buster but actually preferred to regulate corporations instead. In foreign affairs, he believed powerful, developed nations should maintain world order through an assertion of power, either in arbitration or even warfare. Roosevelt believed that the president should represent the national or public interest. He helped create the powerful modern presidency and used publicity shrewdly to gain his ends. Having declined to run for a third term in 1908 (actually his second elected term), he founded and ran unsuccessfully as candidate of the new Progressive party in 1912. He declined to run again in 1916.

Root, Elihu (1845–1937) *cabinet member, senator*
A lawyer born in Clinton, New York, Root was a conservative but anti-machine Republican. He served as secretary of war from 1899 to 1903, where he was responsible for the creation of the modern army and for overseeing the organization of America's new dependencies in the Caribbean and the Pacific. In 1905, he became secretary of state and in 1912, was awarded the Nobel Prize for his various efforts to maintain peace in Latin America and with Japan. Root served as a senator from New York from 1909 to 1915 and despite his long alliance with Roosevelt, supported Taft in 1912. From 1910 to 1925, he was head of the Carnegie Endowment for International Peace.

Ross, Edward A. (1886–1951) *sociologist*
Born in a small town in Illinois, Ross took a Ph.D. at Johns Hopkins and became a pioneering sociologist. After leaving Stanford in a widely publicized academic freedom case, he came to the University of Wisconsin in 1906, joining the influential group of reform minded social scientists there. His most famous work was *Social Control* (1904), which advocated firm societal regulation as an antidote for social disintegration in America.

Russell, Charles Edward (1860–1941) *muckraking journalist*
Born in Iowa, Russell became a journalist and after the turn of the century a well respected muckraker. He joined the Socialist Party in 1908, ran many times for governor, mayor, and legislator for New York on its ticket, but was expelled in 1917 for supporting America's entry into World War I. He held various government-related appointments after that, including the Industrial Relations Commission. Russell was one of the founders of the NAACP.

Ryan, John A. (1869–1945) *social gospel priest and theorist of a minimum wage*
Ryan, a Catholic priest and professor at Catholic University after 1915, was born into a large Minnesota farm family. In 1906, his doctoral dissertation, *A Living Wage,* made him spokesman for a social gospel among Catholics and was the intellectual foundation of the minimum wage movement. In 1916, his work *Distributive Justice* popularized that term as well. After World War I, he served as head of the new Catholic Welfare Conference's Social Action Department. In the 1930s, he defended Franklin Roosevelt's New Deal against conservative Catholics who called it communistic.

Sanger, Margaret Higgins (1879–1966) *founder of the birth control movement*
Sanger, who was born into a socialist-leaning family of 11 children in Corning, New York, became the driving force and leader of the birth control movement in the United States after 1913. A trained nurse, Sanger was introduced to the desire of women to limit their families while working on a maternity ward. In 1910, she and her architect husband moved to New York City and joined the socialist movement. Sanger became an IWW organizer and wrote about sexual issues in socialist publications. She defied constant threats of suppression and in 1914, began to publish a magazine, *The Woman Rebel.* Soon arrested, she fled to Europe for a year; meanwhile, her cause became a national controversy. Charges against her were dropped, and in 1916, Sanger and associates opened the first birth control clinic in America in Brooklyn, New York. She was soon arrested and sentenced to prison for 30 days, and the clinic closed. Sanger founded the National Birth Control League in 1914 and in 1921, the Planned Parenthood Foundation of America. Later in the century, she was instrumental in the development of the birth control pill. Sanger lived to see the landmark Supreme Court decision of 1965 that guaranteed the legality of contraceptives in America.

Schneiderman, Rose (1882–1972) *labor reformer*
An immigrant from Poland in 1890, Schneiderman began working at the age of 13 and took a leading role in unionizing New York garment workers. In 1910, she became a full-time organizer for the WTUL, serving as the president from 1919 to 1949.

Schurz, Carl (1829–1906) *statesman*
Born in Germany, Schurz was a leader there in the failed democratic revolution of 1848 while still a student. He immigrated to the United States, eventually settling in Wisconsin, where he became very active in Republican politics and the antislavery movement. Schurz was admitted to the bar and also did much writing, returning to journalism in various capacities throughout his life. Lincoln made him ambassador to Spain, but he returned to the United States to take a role in the Union army. After the war, his investigations of the South became the basis of the Republican Reconstruction program. He served one term as a senator, was secretary of the interior under Rutherford B. Hayes, was a leader of national civil service reform organizations, and became prominent in the anti-imperialist movement during the Spanish American and Philippine Wars. He lived in New York at the time of his death.

Seligman, Edwin R. A. (1861–1939) *economist, reformer*
Educated at Columbia through the Ph.D., Seligman spent his entire academic career there as a professor of political economy (or economics). He took a prominent role in public affairs and reform movements; known for his work on taxation, he supported the income tax. He helped found both the American Economic Association and the American Association of University Professors.

Shaw, Anna Howard (1847–1919) *suffrage leader*
Born in England, Shaw grew up in frontier Michigan. She earned both an M.D. and doctor of divinity, becoming the first woman ordained by the Methodist Church. Shaw was widely known as a temperance orator when she became a full time suffrage lecturer and organizer for NAWSA, later serving as its president from 1905 to 1915. She continued to work for suffrage and also received the Distinguished Service Medal for her work with the Council of National Defense during World War I.

Sherman, James Schoolcraft (1855–1912) *vice president under Taft*
Born in New York State, Sherman graduated from Hamilton College before joining the bar and entering Republican politics. Sherman served many years in the House of Representatives, closely allied with Joseph Cannon and the conservatives. In 1908, Republicans selected him as the vice presidential candidate to balance the progressivism of Taft. He was renominated in 1912 but died shortly before the election.

Simkhovich, Mary Kingsbury (1867–1951) *settlement founder*
Born near Boston, Simkhovich became a settlement worker and together with her husband, a Russian émigré professor at Columbia, founded Greenwich House Settlement. Simkhovich, who did graduate work at Radcliffe College and Columbia University, also taught social economics at various New York institutions of higher education.

Sinclair, Upton Beall (1878–1968) *novelist*
Sinclair was born in Baltimore to the poor relations of a wealthy and patrician family. He wrote pulp fiction to support himself while attending the College of the City of New York and Columbia University. A struggling novelist and socialist sympathizer, in 1906 he became famous when his novel *The Jungle* exposed the Chicago meatpacking industry. He broke with the Socialist Party over U.S. entry into World War I.

Smith, Hoke (1855–1931) *progressive Southern Democratic politician*
Born in North Carolina, Smith became a lawyer and later owner of the *Atlanta Journal*. He served as secretary of the interior under Cleveland in 1892, governor of Georgia in 1906, and U.S. Senator in 1911, remaining in the Senate until 1921. A Southern progressive, he oversaw many reforms in Georgia, although he also led the movement to disenfranchise black voters there. As a congressman, he was instrumental in legislation to establish the agricultural extension service and the vocational-technical education in public schools.

Spargo, John (1876–1966) *muckraking writer*
Born in England, Spargo immigrated in 1902 and quickly became well known as a writer. His 1906 book, *The Bitter Cry of the Children,* had a great impact on various child-welfare reform movements; parts were even read in the Senate. Spargo was a Socialist Party member but left it to support World War I and became an increasingly conservative critic of communism.

Spencer, Herbert (1820–1903) *promoter of Social Darwinism*
Spencer, an English journalist, became identified with a radical laissez faire (non government intervention) position in economic life. He used analogies to Darwin's evolutionary theories to explain society, beliefs known generally as Social Darwinism. In particular, he argued that unfettered economic competition served the same purpose as natural biological selection, permitting the fittest to survive.

Stanton, Elizabeth Cady (1815–1902) *woman's rights leader*
Born in New York State, Elizabeth Cady Stanton from an early age devoted herself to securing equal rights for women, while also marrying and giving birth to nine children. Involved in temperance and antislavery reform

activities, she made the acquaintance of Lucretia Mott, a Quaker reformer, and in July 1848, they organized the first woman's rights convention at Seneca Falls. In 1851, she met and formed a historic alliance with Susan B. Anthony. Together they organized the National Woman Suffrage Association in 1869. Stanton served as president until 1890, when the organization merged with the American Woman Suffrage Association; Stanton headed the combined organization, the National American Woman Suffrage Association, for two more years. In 1898, she completed the Woman's Bible, which reinterpreted passages of scripture that were derogatory to women; it occasioned consternation even among her fellow suffragists.

Stead, William T. (1849–1912) *English journalist*
An English journalist, Stead visited the Chicago World's Fair in 1893 and stayed for a year, during which he published *If Christ Came to Chicago,* exposing corruption and vice in the city. Widely read and very influential, the book helped spur the formation of the Chicago Civic Federation, one of the earliest major municipal reform groups. Stead lost his life in the *Titanic* disaster.

Steffens, Lincoln (Joseph Lincoln Steffens, Jr.)
(1866–1936) *muckraking journalist*
Born to a prosperous San Francisco family, Steffens attended the University of California and European universities. He worked on New York newspapers then began his career as a muckraker when *McClure's* published his essays, collectively titled *The Shame of the Cities.* In 1906, he joined other muckrakers to found *American Magazine.* After 1911, he became an activist himself, helping to mediate the McNamara bombing case in Los Angeles, and under Wilson took a role as an emissary in the Mexican Revolution and the Russian revolution. He was increasingly acclaimed as a radical and mentored several prominent younger journalists, such as Walter Lippman and John Reed.

Stevenson, Adlai Ewing (1835–1914) *vice president under Cleveland*
Born in Kentucky, Stevenson grew up in Bloomington, Illinois, becoming a lawyer. A Democrat, he served two terms in Congress and became assistant postmaster-general under Cleveland in 1885 and in 1892, was elected as his vice president. He later ran, unsuccessfully, with William Jennings Bryan in 1900.

Stieglitz, Alfred (1864–1946) *pioneering photographer*
Stieglitz grew up in Manhattan and attended City College but accompanied his family to Germany before graduating and completed his studies in Berlin. While in Europe, he purchased his first camera and soon became an avid photographer, winning several awards in European shows. On the family's return to America in 1890, he became a partner in a photoengraving business at his father's insistence, but after its failure five years later devoted himself increasingly to photography and to his goal of making it a valid art form. He began to search for subjects in the streets of New York but increasingly emphasized composition, not subject, in his work. In 1902, he brought together a group of photographers as the Photo-Secession Movement to advance recognition of the art. The Photo-Secession Movement, *Camera Work* (the journal Stieglitz established in 1903), and the Little Galleries of the Photo-Secession (known as 291) all became important forces in the art world, promoting not only photography but modern artists and avant-garde aesthetics as well. The group declined after 1910, by which time art photography had been validated, and *Camera Work* and 291 closed at the beginning of World War I. At about the same time, Stieglitz met the young artist Georgia O'Keefe, whom he eventually married. In 1925, Stieglitz opened a new gallery in Greenwich Village, and in 1929, he opened An American Place, which exhibited the work of American artists exclusively.

Stiles, Charles Wardell (1867–1941) *leader of campaign to eradicate hookworm in the South*
Stiles, born in New York State, studied science in Europe, receiving the Ph.D. at the University of Leipzig, where he concentrated in zoology and parasitology. He returned to the United States in 1891 and worked as a zoologist in the Department of Agriculture and, after 1902, in the United States Public Health and Marine Hospital Service. Throughout his life he was prominent in the field of systematic zoology in the United States. But he is best remembered for leading the campaign to eradicate hookworm in the American South, after discovering an American variety of the parasite. Appointed to President Roosevelt's Country Life Commission in 1908, he made contacts which resulted in the formation of the Rockefeller Sanitary Commission in 1909. Stiles continued to work on other public health issues until his retirement in 1931.

Sullivan, Louis H. (1856–1924) *architect*
Born in Boston, Sullivan became a prominent architect in Chicago, where his firm built many of the early skyscrapers. Considered the first modern architect in America, he also promoted the idea of a distinctively American architecture in his writings. Ignored and in dire financial straits at the time of his death, today Sullivan is considered the father of the Prairie School architects, including Frank Lloyd Wright, who worked for him at the beginning of his career.

Sullivan, Mark (1876–1952) *progressive journalist*
Born in Pennsylvania, Sullivan graduated from Harvard and became a journalist, supporting many reform issues. He

wrote a six-volume informal history of the Progressive era, *Our Times,* published between 1926 and 1936.

Sumner, William Graham (1840–1910) *scholar, anti-imperialist*
An immigrant from England, Sumner attended Yale and became an Episcopal clergyman before joining the Yale faculty as a professor of political economy. Although he gained notoriety for his defense of conservative economics in the late 19th century, he increasingly supported civic reform and wrote widely read essays supporting the anti-imperialist position. His later writing was in the field of sociology, and in 1906, he introduced the term *folkways* in a book of that name.

Taft, William Howard (1843–1930) *27th president of the United States, Chief Justice of the Supreme Court*
Born in Cincinnati into a prosperous family, Taft attended Yale and the University of Cincinnati Law School before entering Republican politics. As judge on the state supreme court and U.S. Solicitor General after 1890, he distinguished himself for his legal knowledge. Historians often blame an ambitious wife for pushing Taft into elective office rather than the judicial career he always preferred. After 1900 Taft served with great success and respect as the first civil governor of the Philippines, then joined the cabinet of Theodore Roosevelt, who had been a friend since Taft's early days in the federal government. Roosevelt made him his successor to the presidency in 1908, but their relationship cooled almost immediately after Taft took office. In fact, Taft accomplished more progressive legislation in four years that Roosevelt in eight. But he did not assume the prominent leadership that distinguished the Roosevelt presidency, nor did he use the press effectively. After failing to win reelection in 1912, he taught at Yale Law School and later served as chief justice of the Supreme Court from 1921 until his death. In his lifetime Taft was considered an undistinguished president but a distinguished chief justice; today historians usually reverse those evaluations.

Tarbell, Ida Minerva (1857–1944) *muckraking journalist*
Tarbell was born in Erie, Pennsylvania, to a father whose small oil business was ruined when Rockefeller began consolidating the industry. She was the sole woman graduate of Allegheny College in 1880, after which she became a writer and journalist. She joined the staff of *McClure's* on its founding in 1893, where her biographies of such figures as Napoleon and Lincoln were highly successful. Her 1904 study of Standard Oil, although inspired by personal circumstances, was a model of in-depth investigation and objective writing. In 1906, she helped found *American Magazine.*

Taylor, Frederick W. (1856–1915) *scientific management expert*
Born in Philadelphia, Taylor took an engineering degree and entered the steel industry before establishing an independent career as a consultant and inventor in the field of managerial methods soon called scientific management. His work made him independently wealthy, and he devoted his later years to writing and publicizing his ideas.

Taylor, Graham (1851–1938) *settlement founder and reformer*
Born in New York State and a graduate of Rutgers University, Taylor was a social gospel minister before founding Chicago Commons settlement in 1894. In 1896, he founded *The Commons,* a settlement house magazine, which later merged with the Charity Organization Society's *Charities.* In 1908, he established the University of Chicago's School of Civics and Philanthropy, later the Graduate School of Social Service. He wrote widely and took a prominent role in many national social service groups.

Terrell, Mary Eliza Church (1863–1954) *clubwoman, activist for African-American rights*
Mary Church was born in Memphis to parents who had been born in slavery. Her father became very wealthy in business, probably the wealthiest African American in the South in the late 19th century and the first black millionaire. Her parents sent her to live with friends in Yellow Springs, Ohio, to provide her a better education. She received a bachelor's and a master's degree from Oberlin College, then insisted upon working as a teacher, although her father strongly disapproved. While teaching in Washington, D.C., she met and married Robert Terrell, eventually a judge of the District of Columbia Municipal Court. She began a role as an activist after the 1892 Memphis lynchings, even visiting the White House with Frederick Douglass to plead for federal leadership against racial violence. In 1894, she became the first president of the National Association of Colored Women and in 1895, the first black woman to serve on the Washington Board of Education. Terrell also entered the women's suffrage movement and became known internationally as a lecturer on both African-American and women's issues. Although Terrell remained a friend and supporter of Booker T. Washington, she also joined W. E. B. DuBois in founding the NAACP. She continued to work for civil rights for the remainder of her life. Near the age of 90, she lead anti-segregation demonstrators in Washington to desegrate all-white restaurants.

Tillman, Benjamin Ryan (Pitchfork Ben Tillman) (1847–1918) *Southern Democratic senator*
Tillman grew up on a South Carolina plantation but entered Democratic politics as a champion of poor farm-

ers. He served as governor from 1890 to 1894, instituting some reforms associated with populism, then entered the U.S. Senate in 1895, remaining there until his death. He was known as an outspoken advocate of racial separation. Like many other southern politicians during the Progressive era, he worked for reform while also working to suppress black civil rights. Tillman also was active in the anti-imperialist movement during the Spanish-American War.

Tumulty, Joseph Patrick (1879–1954) *Democratic politician*
Born in New Jersey to parents of modest means, Tumulty graduated from St. Peter's College and became a lawyer. He became active in politics, allied with the Democratic machine but supporting many reforms. After serving in the New Jersey assembly, he became an adviser to Woodrow Wilson and helped secure his nomination for president in 1912. Upon taking office, Wilson named Tumulty secretary to the president, a position that at the time was a combination of adviser and press secretary. Tumulty was the first Catholic to hold the White House post. In 1914, when President Wilson planned to remarry only months after the death of his first wife, Tumulty candidly urged him to wait, since his actions were occasioning much bad publicity in the nation. Wilson proceeded, however, and his second wife, Edith Bolling Galt, soon joined with other Tumulty political enemies in an attempt to oust him from his White House post. Tumulty remained, after offering to resign, but never again held the complete confidence of the president, to whom he was devoted. After Wilson left office, Tumulty practiced law in Washington, D.C., but was no longer at the center of Democratic politics.

Turner, Frederick Jackson (1861–1932) *historian, originator of the frontier thesis*
Born in Wisconsin, Turner attended the state university before receiving his Ph.D. from Johns Hopkins. He taught history at the University of Wisconsin and after 1910, at Harvard. He is remembered for his 1893 paper on "The Significance of the Frontier in American History." The frontier thesis that he presented argued that geographical and environmental factors—free land and socioeconomic opportunity on the frontier—were more important in creating American institutions than British political antecedents.

U'ren, William S. (1859–1949) *advocate of the Oregon System*
Born in Wisconsin, U'ren worked as a miner and blacksmith in Colorado before becoming a lawyer, newspaper editor, and politician in Oregon. Elected to the Oregon legislature as a Populist in 1896, he campaigned for the initiative and referendum, then used them to advance a series of direct-democracy and other reforms that were known as the Oregon System. He was also a lifelong advocate of Henry George's single tax but did not succeed in winning approval for various tax reforms he sponsored.

Van Hise, Charles R. (1857–1918) *president of the University of Wisconsin*
Born in Wisconsin, Van Hise attended the state university (he was a classmate of Robert La Follette) and in 1903 became its president. He believed that the ideal of the university was service to the state, and under his leadership it developed close ties to progressive reform movements. By training, Van Hise was a geologist, and he was personally a strong supporter of the conservation movement.

Vardaman, James Kimble (1861–1930) *Southern Democratic politician*
Vardaman was born in Texas and grew up in Mississippi, where he entered Democratic politics after working as a lawyer and newspaper editor. After three terms in the Mississippi legislature, he became governor. Like many southern progressive officials he combined strongly racist appeals for segregation and disenfranchisement (Vardaman even advocated ending education for African Americans) with equally strong reform programs in other areas, such as public school funding, corporate regulation, and penal reform. In 1917, he was one of six senators who voted against entry into World War I; the following year, he was voted out of office.

Veblen, Thorstein B. (1861–1930) *scholar, social critic*
Born in Wisconsin, Veblen received doctorates from both Yale in philosophy and Cornell University in political economy, or economics. He taught at both the University of Chicago and Stanford University but by 1909 had lost both jobs because of scandalous extramarital sexual liaisons. He later taught at the University of Missouri and the New School of Social Research. An economist, he became known for his social and cultural criticism, especially of America's business mentality and of what he was the first to call conspicuous consumption.

Veiller, Lawrence Turnure (1872–1959) *housing reformer*
Born in New Jersey, Veiller attended City College of New York and volunteered at University Settlement before persuading the Charity Organization Society to enter the field of tenement reform. He developed technical knowledge of construction as well as knowledge of social issues and was throughout the Progressive era the most prominent housing reformer in America. He helped create the New York State Tenement House Commission,

New York City's Tenement House Department, and in 1910 established the National Housing Association, serving as its director until it ceased existence in the 1930s. In these roles, he influenced much of the housing legislation passed nationwide during the Progressive era. Veiller did not support public subsidies for housing, however, and his influence began to decline in the 1920s as that issue became more important.

Villard, Oswald Garrison (1872–1949) *editor, reformer*
The grandson of abolitionist William Lloyd Garrison and the son of railroad magnate and publisher Henry Villard, Garrison graduated from Harvard and assumed editorship of his father's *New York Evening Post.* Throughout his life, he supported many reform issues, including equal rights for women, birth control, civil liberties, and civil rights for African Americans. Villard wrote the original call for the conference that organized the NAACP and took an active role in the organization. An anti-militarist, he sold his newspaper in 1918 after bitter disagreement with his staff over America's entry into World War I, which he opposed. He then revamped the venerable weekly journal of opinion, *The Nation,* which his family also owned.

Wald, Lillian D. (1867–1940) *settlement founder, reformer*
Born in Cincinnati to a prosperous Jewish family, Wald came of age in Rochester, New York. She completed the New York Hospital Training School for Nurses and sought advanced training at the Women's Medical College. While there she organized classes for immigrant women on the Lower East Side and soon became dedicated to the idea of nursing settlement work. In 1895, she and fellow nurse Mary Brewster opened the House on Henry Street and inaugurated public health nursing in the United States. Wald helped create the first school nurse programs in America and was active in the playground and child labor movements. She joined with other prominent reformers to oppose America's entry into World War I, but once war was declared, she worked for the Council of National Defense.

Walling, William English (1877–1936) *reformer*
Walling was born in Louisville, graduated from the University of Chicago, and inherited significant wealth, which enabled him to devote his life to social reform. He helped organize the Women's Trade Union League and the NAACP. Walling married a Russian socialist woman while visiting there and in 1910, joined the Socialist Party of America. He left it in 1917 because he supported America's entry into World War I and later helped promote the American Federation of Labor.

Walsh, Francis P. (Frank Walsh) (1864–1939) *federal official under Wilson*
Born in St. Louis, Walsh was admitted to the bar and took an active role in Kansas City reform movements. In 1913 President Wilson appointed him chair of the Commission on Industrial Relations, where he garnered much publicity for his questioning of prominent industrialists. In 1918, he cochaired the War Labor Board, consistently defending the rights of workers.

Washington, Booker T. (1856–1915) *African-American leader, founder of Tuskeegee Institute*
Born into slavery in Virginia, Washington graduated from Hampton Institute, a school founded to provide industrial (occupational) education for blacks. He arrived to head the black-controlled and -staffed Tuskegee Institute in 1881 when the physical school did not yet exist. By 1900, it was the best endowed of all the historically black colleges and continued to attract financial support from philanthropists. Washington's overriding belief was that blacks would not progress until they had established a strong economic base, and he geared his educational program to that belief. In 1895, he delivered a famous speech called the Atlanta Compromise; it seemed to offer black acquiescence to political and civic inequality in return for economic assistance and success. It was so well received that Washington was considered spokesman for African Americans by whites and most blacks after that date. For the remainder of his life he wielded considerable political power, consulted by politicians on appointments and philanthropists on grants to black institutions. In 1901, President Roosevelt invited him to dine at the White House, a groundbreaking event that raised a furor among many whites. His autobiography, *Up From Slavery,* published the same year, enhanced his stature. A few blacks, however, always disagreed with Washington's accommodationist approach, and criticism became increasingly vocal after 1900. Washington also founded the National Negro Business League.

Watson, Thomas E. (1856–1922) *Southern populist*
Born in Georgia, Watson became a lawyer and a vocal champion of farmers. He went to Congress as a Democrat in 1890 but joined the Populist party in 1892 and was never again elected to office, although he ran on the Populist ticket. He practiced law, published a reform magazine, and remained active in politics and reform. Although in the 1890s Watson was remarkable for defending the similar interests of black and white farmers, after 1900, he increasingly supported racial separation.

Wheeler, Wayne Bidwell (1869–1927) *prohibition movement leader*
Born on an Ohio farm, Wheeler worked his way through Oberlin College, a hotbed of the temperance movement at

the time. He accepted a position with the Anti-Saloon League after graduation, studying for the law at the same time in order to become the league's attorney. Especially talented at developing political strategies, in 1915 he went to Washington as the league's general counsel and soon became legislative superintendent or chief lobbyist as well. During his career, he prosecuted over 2,000 liquor law–related cases, including constitutional challenges to prohibition laws, and claimed (probably inaccurately) to have authored the Volstead Act. Wheeler was aggressive, persistent, tireless, thoroughly convinced of his own beliefs, and far more interested in obtaining prohibitionists' goals by laws and penalties than by temperance education. Some historians suggest that among the reasons prohibition was doomed was the heavy handed method Wheeler used.

White, Edward Douglass, Jr. (1845–1921) *chief justice of the Supreme Court*

Born in Thibodaux, Louisiana, and educated in Jesuit schools and at Georgetown, White studied law at Tulane after service as a Confederate soldier. Having served on the state supreme court and as a U.S. senator, he was appointed to the Supreme Court by Grover Cleveland in 1894 and elevated to chief justice by William Howard Taft in 1910. He headed the Supreme Court during the height of Progressive legislation but remained a conservative and was usually overshadowed and outvoted by more brilliant and more liberal justices. He wrote the famous rule of reason in the Standard Oil anti-trust case of 1911, which declared that only "unreasonable" combinations were outlawed under the Sherman Anti-Trust Act.

White, William Allen (1868–1944) *famous small town newspaper editor*

Born in Emporia, Kansas, White became a newspaperman and purchased the *Emporia Gazette* in 1895. His editorial "What's the Matter with Kansas?" captured national attention during the McKinley campaign of 1896, and he soon developed a nationwide reputation as the voice of the conservative, small town, anti-populist Midwest. Eventually, however, White became a reform-minded Roosevelt supporter and progressive, maintaining his national prominence throughout.

Whitlock, Brand (1869–1934) *reform mayor, ambassador*

Born in Urbana, Ohio, Whitlock was a journalist who became a reformer while working for the administration of Illinois governor John Peter Altgeld. He moved to Toledo to practice law, beginning a successful career as a novelist on the side. He soon developed a close relationship with reform mayor Samuel "Golden Rule" Jones and after Jones's death, succeeded him in office for four terms (1905–1913), compiling an extensive record of reform.

From 1914 to 1919, he served as ambassador to Belgium and remained in Europe at the end of the war.

Wickersham, James (1857–1939) *legislator for Alaska*

Born in Illinois, Wickersham was admitted to the bar there before moving to Washington state, where he served as a judge and Republican state legislator. In 1900, he moved to Alaska when he was appointed district judge there, resigning in 1908 to run for Congress as territorial representative. He served in that office until 1920 and again from 1931 to 1932. He practiced law in Juneau and wrote on Alaskan historical and literary subjects.

Willard, Frances Elizabeth Caroline (1839–1898) *leader of the WCTU*

Born in New York State, Willard grew up in Ohio and graduated from North Western Female College in Evanston, Illinois. She became its president in 1871 and two years later, when it was absorbed into Northwestern University, was named dean of women. Active in the WCTU, she became its national president in 1879, holding the position until her death. Under her leadership, the WCTU became a wide ranging reform organization which emphasized advancing suffrage and other women's causes as well as temperance.

Wilson, Woodrow (Thomas Woodrow Wilson) (1856–1924) *28th president of the United States*

Born in Staunton, Virginia, Wilson attended Davison College, Princeton, and the University of Virginia Law School before taking a Ph.D. at Johns Hopkins. A professor of law and politics at Princeton, he became its president in 1902, quickly gaining a reputation as an educational reformer. He resigned in 1910 in the face of opposition to those reforms by some faculty and alumni and was elected Democratic governor of New Jersey. He had considerable success in passing reform legislation, attracting national attention. In 1912 he won the Democratic nomination for President and was elected on a program he called the New Freedom. Wilson successfully lowered tariffs, strengthened antitrust laws, established the Federal Reserve system and continued to enact reform legislation in areas begun under Roosevelt. He was destined to be most remembered, however, not as a domestic reformer but as an international leader during World War I. At first determined to keep America neutral, in 1917 he led the country into the conflict under the idealistic phrase "make the world safe for democracy." His peace plan, called the Fourteen Points, was the basis for peace negotiations and convinced Europeans to found a League of Nations. At home, however, Congress refused to approve the plan. Wilson suffered a stroke in 1919 and was partially incapacitated for the remainder of his term.

Woodruff, Clinton Rogers (1868–1948) *municipal reformer*
Born in Philadelphia, Woodruff attended the University of Pennsylvania Law School and served in the state legislature before becoming secretary (administrator) of the National Municipal League from its organization in 1894 until 1920. He authored or edited many publications on the reform of city government.

Woods, Robert Archey (1865–1925) *settlement head*
Born in Pittsburgh, Woods attended Amherst and Andover Theological Seminary before becoming head of South End House, Boston's first settlement house. The settlement attracted many volunteers from nearby colleges, who published important early studies of urban dysfunction. Woods was especially active in organizing neighborhood residents to obtain community facilities. He was active in national organizations of social workers and became a Progressive Party member in 1912.

Wright, Carroll Davidson (1840–1909) *federal statistician*
Born in New Hampshire, Wright held state offices in Massachusetts before becoming the first chief of the U.S. Bureau of Labor in 1885. In that role he pioneered the collection and use of statistics, a practice that would become a hallmark of progressive reformers.

Wright, Frank Lloyd (1867–1912) *architect*
Born in Wisconsin, Wright attended the state university briefly before beginning his career as an apprentice with architects Louis Sullivan and Dankmar Adler in Chicago. Wright became world renouned, especially for his prairie-style houses, and is considered by some the greatest American architect to date. Many of his ideas were expressions of progressive thinking; he believed architecture and city planning were closely related to social reform.

Wright, Orville (1871–1948) and **Wright, Wilbur** (1867–1912) *inventors of powered flight*
The Wright brothers grew up in Dayton, Ohio, with a mechanically inclined mother and a father who was a bishop in the United Brethren Church. The only members of their family not to attend college, they were self-trained engineers who ran a print shop and a bicycle shop before experimenting with the dynamics of flight. Slowly refining their ideas, they finally achieved the first powered flight on December 17, 1903. During 1908–1909, with their inventions finally under patent protection, they began to demonstrate their accomplishments more publicly in America and Europe and soon became known worldwide.

Appendix C
Tables and Maps

POPULATION OF THE UNITED STATES, 1880–1920

Year	Population	Percent Increase	Percent Urban/Rural	Percent White/Nonwhite
1880	50,155,783	. . .	28/72	. . .
1890	62,947,714	26	35/65	88/12
1900	75,994,575	21	40/60	88/12
1910	91,972,266	21	46/54	89/11
1920	105,710,620	15	51/49	90/10

Source: Calculated from *Historical Statistics of the United States,* Series A 73-81.

POPULATION OF THE UNITED STATES BY CENSUS RACIAL CLASSIFICATION, 1890–1920

Year	Population	White	African American	Native American	Japanese	Chinese
1890	62,948,000	55,101,000	7,489,000	248,000	2,000	107,000
1900	75,995,000	66,809,000	8,834,000	237,000	24,000	90,000
1910	91,972,000	81,732,000	9,828,000	266,000	72,000	72,000
1920	105,711,000	94,821,000	10,463,000	244,000	111,000	62,000

Note: All numbers rounded to the nearest 1,000.
Source: Calculated from *Historical Statistics of the United States,* Series A 91-104.

EDUCATION OF THE AMERICAN POPULATION, 1890–1920

	HIGH SCHOOL GRADUATE		BACHELOR'S DEGREE OR EQUIVALENT		
Year of Degree	Number of Degrees	Percent of All 17-Year-Olds	Number of Degrees	Percent of All 23-Year-Olds	Percent Awarded to Females
1890	44,000	3.5	15,500	. . .	17
1900	95,000	6.3	27,400	0.19	19
1910	156,000	8.6	37,200	0.20	23
1920	311,000	16.3	48,600	0.26	34

Source: Historical Statistics of the United States, Series H 598-601 and Series H 751-765.

LITERACY OF THE AMERICAN POPULATION, 1890–1920

	PERCENT ILLITERATE IN THE POPULATION		
Year	Native-Born Whites	Foreign-Born Whites	African Americans and Other Nonwhites
1890	7.7	13.1	56.8
1900	6.2	12.9	44.5
1910	5.0	12.7	30.5
1920	4.0	13.1	23.0

Source: Historical Statistics of the United States, Series H 664-668.

URBAN GROWTH, 1880–1920

(Population of cities having 10,000 inhabitants or more)

POPULATION	NUMBER OF CITIES				
	1880	**1890**	**1900**	**1910**	**1920**
10,000–24,999	146	230	280	369	465
25,000–49,000	42	66	82	119	143
50,000–99,000	15	30	40	59	76
100,000–249,000	12	17	23	31	43
250,000–499,000	4	7	9	11	13
500,000–999,000	3	1	3	5	9
1 million or more*	1	3	3	3	3
Total with at least 25,000	77	124	160	228	287
Total with at least 50,000	35	58	78	109	144
Total with at least 100,000	20	28	38	50	68
Total with at least 250,000	8	11	15	19	25
Total with at least 500,000	4	4	6	8	12

*The three cities with over 1 million population from 1890 to 1920 were New York, Chicago, and Philadelphia.
Source: Calculated from *Historical Statistics of the United States,* Series A 43-56.

SOURCES OF IMMIGRATION, 1880–1920

Year	Total All Countries	Non-European[1]		Northwestern Europe[2]		Germany		Central Europe Other Than Germany; Southern Europe; Eastern Europe[3]	
		Number	Percent	Number	Percent*	Number	Percent*	Number	Percent*
1880	457,257	108,566	23	225,575	49	84,638	18	38,478	08
1890	455,302	9,622	02	193,697	42	92,427	20	159,556	35
1900	448,572	23,872	05	85,212	19	18,507	04	320,981	72
1910	1,041,570	115,279	11	170,915	16	31,283	03	724,093	70
1920	430,001	183,706	42	85,997	20	1,001	. . .	159,297	37

*Percent of total immigration from all countries, including non-European nations.
[1]Can include Canada, Mexico, Central and South America, the Caribbean, Africa, and Asia.
[2]Includes Great Britain, Ireland, Scandinavia (Norway, Sweden, Denmark, Iceland), Netherlands, Belgium, Luxembourg, Switzerland, and France.
[3]Central includes Poland and Austria-Hungary; Eastern includes Russia, Latvia, Estonia, Lithuania, Finland, Romania, Bulgaria, Turkey; Southern includes Italy, Spain, Portugal, Greece.
Source: Calculated from *Historical Statistics of the United States,* Series C 89-119.

IMMIGRATION BY YEAR AND DECADE, 1890–1920

Decade	Decade Total	Decade	Decade Total	Decade	Decade Total	Decade	Decade Total
1881–1890	5,246,613	1891–1900	3,687,564	1901–1910	8,795,386	1911–1920	5,735,811
Year	**Yearly Total**	**Year**	**Yearly Total**	**Year**	**Yearly Total**	**Year**	**Yearly Total**
1890	455,302	1891	560,319	1901	487,918	1911	878,587
		1892	579,663	1902	648,743	1912	838,172
		1893	439,730	1903	857,046	1913	1,197,892
		1894	285,631	1904	812,870	1914	1,218,480
		1895	258,536	1905	1,026,499	1915	326,700
		1896	343,267	1906	1,100,735	1916	298,826
		1897	230,832	1907	1,285,349	1917	295,403
		1898	229,299	1908	782,870	1918	110,618
		1899	311,715	1909	751,786	1919	141,132
		1900	448,572	1910	1,041,570	1920	430,001

Source: Calculated from *Historical Statistics of the United States,* Series C 89-119, Immigrants by Country, 1820–1970.

PRESIDENTS AND CABINET OFFICERS, 1889–1920

President Benjamin Harrison, 1889–1893

Vice President	Levi P. Morton	1889–1893
Secretary of State	James G. Blaine	1889–1892
	John W. Foster	1892–1893
Secretary of Treasury	William Windom	1889–1891
	Charles Foster	1891–1893
Secretary of War	Redfield Proctor	1889–1891
	Stephen B. Elkins	1891–1893
Attorney General	William Miller	1889–1893
Postmaster General	John Wannamaker	1889–1893
Secretary of Navy	Benjamin F. Tracy	1889–1893
Secretary of Interior	John W. Noble	1889–1893
Secretary of Agriculture	Jeremiah M. Rusk	1889–1893

President Grover Cleveland, 1893–1897

Vice President	Adlai E. Stevenson	1893–1897
Secretary of State	Walter Q. Gresham	1893–1895
	Richard Olney	1895–1897
Secretary of Treasury	John G. Carlisle	1893–1897
Secretary of War	Daniel S. Lamont	1893–1897
Attorney General	Richard Olney	1893–1895
	James Harmon	1895–1897
Postmaster General	Wilson S. Bissell	1893–1895
	William L. Wilson	1895–1897
Secretary of Navy	Hilary A. Herbert	1893–1897
Secretary of Interior	Hoke Smith	1893–1896
	David R. Francis	1896–1897
Secretary of Agriculture	Julius S. Morton	1893–1897

President William McKinley, 1897–1901

Vice President	Garret A. Hobart	1897–1899
	Vacant	1899–1901
	Theodore Roosevelt	1901
Secretary of State	John Sherman	1897–1898
	William R. Day	1898
	John Hay	1898–1901
Secretary of Treasury	Lyman J. Gage	1897–1901
Secretary of War	Russell A. Alger	1897–1899
	Elihu Root	1899–1901
Attorney General	Joseph McKenna	1897–1898
	John W. Griggs	1898–1901
	Philander C. Knox	1901
Postmaster General	James A. Gary	1897–1898
	Charles E. Smith	1898–1901
Secretary of Navy	John D. Long	1897–1901
Secretary of Interior	Cornelius N. Bliss	1897–1899
	Ethan A. Hitchcock	1899–1901
Secretary of Agriculture	James Wilson	1897–1901

President Theodore Roosevelt, 1901–1909

Vice President	Vacant	1901–1904
	Charles Fairbanks	1905–1909
Secretary of State	John Hay	1901–1905
	Elihu Root	1905–1909
	Robert Bacon	1909
Secretary of Treasury	Lyman Gage	1901–1902
	Leslie M. Shaw	1902–1907
	George B. Cortelyou	1907–1909
Secretary of War	Elihu Root	1901–1904
	William H. Taft	1904–1908
	Luke E. Wright	1908–1909
Attorney General	Philander C. Knox	1901–1904
	William H. Moody	1904–1906
	Charles J. Bonaparte	1906–1909
Postmaster General	Charles E. Smith	1901–1902
	Henry C. Payne	1902–1904
	Robert J. Wynne	1904–1905
	George B. Cortelyou	1905–1907
	George von L. Meyer	1907–1909
Secretary of Navy	John D. Long	1901–1902
	William H. Moody	1902–1904
	Paul Morton	1904–1905
	Charles J. Bonaparte	1905–1906
	Victor H. Metcalf	1906–1908
	Truman H. Newberry	1908–1909
Secretary of Interior	Ethan A. Hitchcock	1901–1907
	James R. Garfield	1907–1909
Secretary of Agriculture	James Wilson	1901–1909
Secretary of Labor and Commerce	George B. Cortelyou	1903–1904
	Victor H. Metcalf	1904–1906
	Oscar S. Straus	1906–1909
	Charles Nagel	1909

President William Howard Taft, 1909–1913

Vice President	James S. Sherman	1909–1913
Secretary of State	Philander C. Knox	1909–1913
Secretary of Treasury	Franklin MacVeagh	1909–1913
Secretary of War	Jacob M. Dickinson	1909–1911
	Henry L. Stimson	1911–1913
Attorney General	George W. Wickersham	1909–1913
Postmaster General	Frank H. Hitchcock	1909–1913
Secretary of Navy	George von L. Meyer	1909–1913
Secretary of Interior	Richard A. Ballinger	1909–1911
	Walter L. Fisher	1911–1913
Secretary of Agriculture	James Wilson	1909–1913
Secretary of Labor and Commerce	Charles Nagel	1909–1913

President Woodrow Wilson, 1913–1921

Vice President	Thomas R. Marshall	1913–1921
Secretary of State	William Jennings Bryan	1913–1915
	Robert Lansing	1915–1920
	Bainbridge Colby	1920–1921
Secretary of Treasury	William G. McAdoo	1913–1918
	Carter Glass	1918–1920
	David F. Houston	1920–1921
Secretary of War	Lindley M. Garrison	1913–1916
	Newton D. Baker	1916–1921
Attorney General	James C. McReynolds	1913–1914
	Thomas W. Gregory	1914–1919
	A. Mitchell Palmer	1919–1921
Postmaster General	Albert S. Burleson	1913–1921
Secretary of Navy	Josephus Daniels	1913–1921
Secretary of Interior	Franklin K. Lane	1913–1920
	John B. Payne	1920–1921
Secretary of Agriculture	David F. Houston	1913–1920
	Edwin T. Meredith	1920–1921
Secretary of Commerce	William C. Redfield	1913–1919
	Joshua W. Alexander	1919–1921
Secretary of Labor	William B. Wilson	1913–1921

PRESIDENTIAL ELECTIONS—POPULAR VOTE AND VOTER PARTICIPATION, 1888–1920

Year	Candidates	Party	Popular Vote	Percent Popular Vote	Percent Voter Participation
1888	**Benjamin Harrison**	**Republican**	5,433,892*	47.8	78.3
	Grover Cleveland	Democrat	5,534,488	48.6	
	Clinton Fisk	Prohibition	249,819	2.2	
	Alson Streeter	Union Labor	146,602	1.3	
	Minor Candidates		8,519	0.1	
1892	**Grover Cleveland**	**Democrat**	5,551,883	46.1	74.7
	Benjamin Harrison	Republican	5,179,244	43.0	
	James B. Weaver	Populist	1,024,280	8.5	
	John Bidwell	Prohibition	270,770	2.2	
	Minor Candidates		29,920	0.2	
1896	**William McKinley**	**Republican**	7,108,480	51.0	79.3
	William Jennings Bryan	Democrat/Populist	6,551,495	46.7	
	John M. Palmer	National Democrat	133,435	1.0	
	Joshua Levering	Prohibition	125,072	0.9	
	Minor Candidates		57,256	0.4	
1900	**William McKinley**	**Republican**	7,207,923	51.7	73.2
	William Jennings Bryan	Democrat/Populist	6,358,133	45.5	
	John G. Wooley	Prohibition	209,004	1.5	
	Eugene V. Debs	Socialist	86,935	0.6	
	Minor Candidates		98,147	0.7	
1904	**Theodore Roosevelt**	**Republican**	7,623,593	56.4	65.2
	Alton B. Parker	Democrat	5,082,898	37.6	
	Eugene V. Debs	Socialist	402,489	3.0	
	Silas Swallow	Prohibition	258,596	1.9	
	Minor Candidates		148,388	1.1	
1908	**William H. Taft**	**Republican**	7,678,258	51.6	65.4
	William Jennings Bryan	Democrat	6,406,801	43.0	
	Eugene V. Debs	Socialist	420,380	2.8	
	Eugene Chapin	Prohibition	252,821	1.7	
	Minor Candidates		126,474	0.8	
1912	**Woodrow Wilson**	**Democrat**	6,293,152	41.8	58.8
	Theodore Roosevelt	Progressive	4,119,207	27.4	
	William H. Taft	Republican	3,486,333	23.2	
	Eugene V. Debs	Socialist	900,389	6.0	
	Minor Candidates		241,902	1.6	
1916	**Woodrow Wilson**	**Democrat**	9,126,300	49.2	61.6
	Charles E. Hughes	Republican	8,546,789	46.1	
	A. L. Benson	Socialist	589,924	3.2	
	J. Frank Hanley	Prohibition	221,030	1.2	
	Minor Candidates		50,979	0.3	
1920	**Warren G. Harding**	**Republican**	16,153,115	60.3	49.2
	James M. Cox	Democrat	9,133,092	34.1	
	Eugene V. Debs	Socialist	915,490	3.4	
	Parley Christensen	Farmer-Labor	265,229	1.0	
	Minor Candidates		301,687	1.1	

*Harrison lost the popular vote but won in the Electoral College.

Source: Candidate vote totals from *Presidential Elections, 1789–1992* (Washington, D.C.: Congressional Quarterly, 1995), pp. 102–110.

CONGRESSIONAL SESSION DATES AND PARTY MEMBERSHIP, 1889–1921

Cong.	Opened	Adjourned	Year Elected*	HOUSE OF REPRESENTATIVES				SENATE				PRESIDENT
				Dem	Rep	Other	Total**	Dem	Rep	Other	Total	
51st	Dec 2, 1889	Mar 3, 1891	1888	152	179	1	332	37	51	0	88	Harrison-Rep
52nd	Dec 7, 1891	Mar 3, 1893	1890M	238	86	18	332	39	47	2	88	
53rd	Aug 7, 1893	Mar. 3, 1895	1892	218	124	14	356	44	40	4	88	Cleveland-Dem
54th	Dec 2, 1895	Mar 3, 1897	1894M	93	254	10	357	40	44	6	90	
55th	Mar 15, 1897	Mar 3, 1899	1896	124	206	27	357	34	44	12	90	McKinley-Rep
56th	Dec 4, 1899	Mar 3, 1901	1898M	161	187	9	357	26	53	10	89***	
57th	Dec 2, 1901	Mar 3, 1903	1900	151	200	6	357	32	56	2	90	McKinley-Rep Roosevelt-Rep
58th	Nov 9, 1903	Mar 3, 1905	1902M	176	207	3	386	33	57	0	90	
59th	Dec 4, 1905	Mar 3, 1907	1904	135	251	0	386	32	58	0	90	Roosevelt-Rep
60th	Dec 2, 1907	Mar 3, 1909	1906M	167	223	1	341	31	61	0	92	
61st	Mar 15, 1909	Mar 3, 1911	1908	172	219	0	391	32	60	0	92	Taft-Rep
62nd	Apr 4, 1911	Mar 3, 1913	1910M	230	162	2	394	44	52	0	96	
63rd	Apr 7, 1913	Mar 3, 1915	1912	291	134	10	435	51	44	1	96	Wilson-Dem
64th	Dec 6, 1915	Mar 3, 1917	1914M	230	196	9	435	56	40	0	96	
65th	Apr 2, 1917	Mar 3, 1919	1916	214	215	6	435	54	42	0	96	Wilson-Dem
66th	May 19, 1919	Mar 3, 1921	1918M	192	240	2	435	47	49	0	96	
67th	Apr 11, 1921	Mar 3, 1923	1920	131	302	2	435	37	59	0	96	Harding-Rep

*M indicates a midterm or nonpresidential-year election

**Total voting members; does not include nonvoting territorial delegates

***1 seat vacant

Sources: Office of the Clerk, U.S. House of Representatives, available online, URL: http://clerk.house.gove/histHigh/Congressional_History/Session_Dates/index.html; and http://clerk.house.gov/histHigh/Congressional_History/partyDiv.htm.

Senate statistics from Senate Historical Office, available online, URL: http://www.senate.gov/pagelayout/history/one_item_and_teasers/partydiv.htm.

PROGRESSIVE ERA PRESIDENTIAL ELECTION RESULTS, 1892

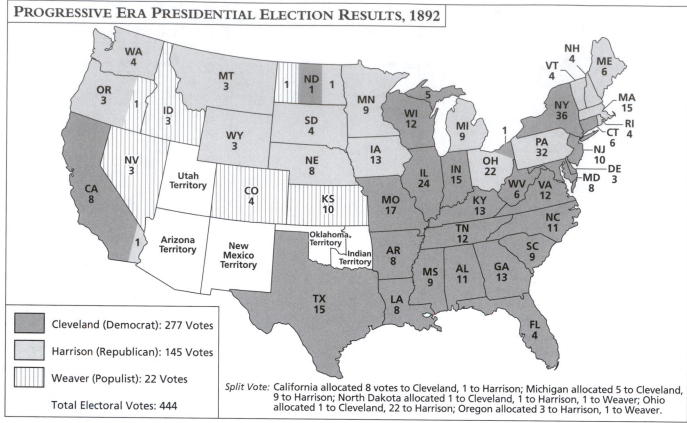

Cleveland (Democrat): 277 Votes

Harrison (Republican): 145 Votes

Weaver (Populist): 22 Votes

Total Electoral Votes: 444

Split Vote: California allocated 8 votes to Cleveland, 1 to Harrison; Michigan allocated 5 to Cleveland, 9 to Harrison; North Dakota allocated 1 to Cleveland, 1 to Harrison, 1 to Weaver; Ohio allocated 1 to Cleveland, 22 to Harrison; Oregon allocated 3 to Harrison, 1 to Weaver.

PROGRESSIVE ERA PRESIDENTIAL ELECTION RESULTS, 1896

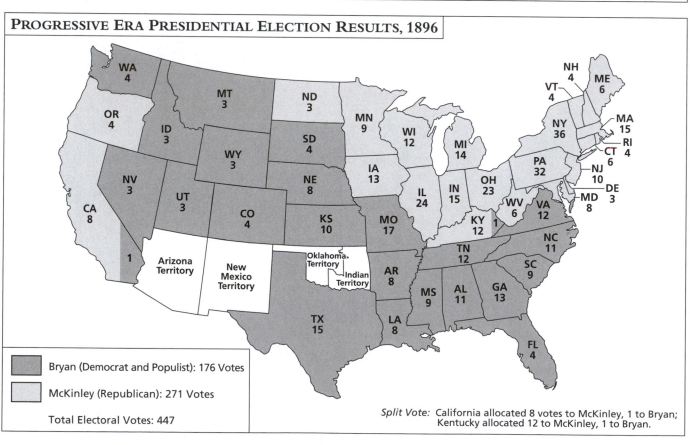

Bryan (Democrat and Populist): 176 Votes

McKinley (Republican): 271 Votes

Total Electoral Votes: 447

Split Vote: California allocated 8 votes to McKinley, 1 to Bryan; Kentucky allocated 12 to McKinley, 1 to Bryan.

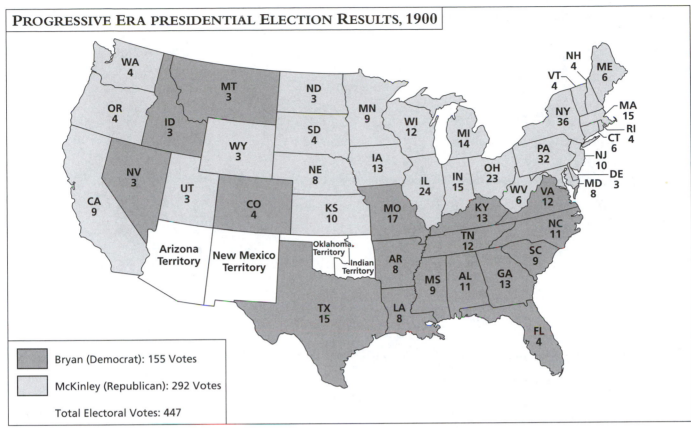

PROGRESSIVE ERA PRESIDENTIAL ELECTION RESULTS, 1900

Bryan (Democrat): 155 Votes

McKinley (Republican): 292 Votes

Total Electoral Votes: 447

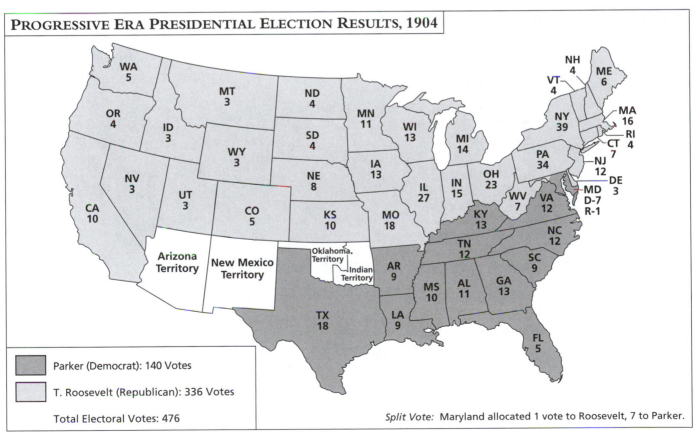

PROGRESSIVE ERA PRESIDENTIAL ELECTION RESULTS, 1904

Parker (Democrat): 140 Votes

T. Roosevelt (Republican): 336 Votes

Total Electoral Votes: 476

Split Vote: Maryland allocated 1 vote to Roosevelt, 7 to Parker.

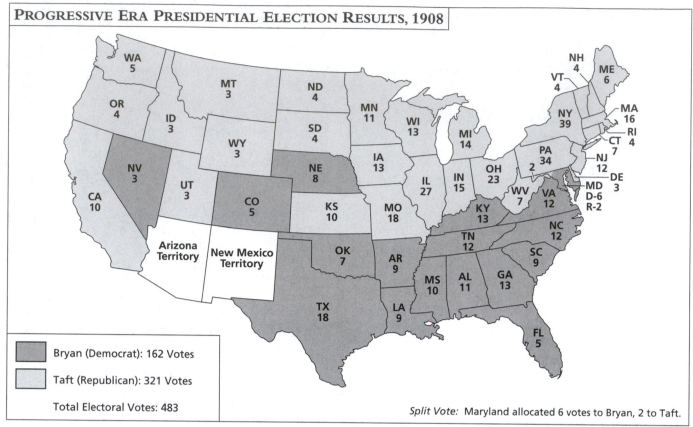

PROGRESSIVE ERA PRESIDENTIAL ELECTION RESULTS, 1908

Bryan (Democrat): 162 Votes

Taft (Republican): 321 Votes

Total Electoral Votes: 483

Split Vote: Maryland allocated 6 votes to Bryan, 2 to Taft.

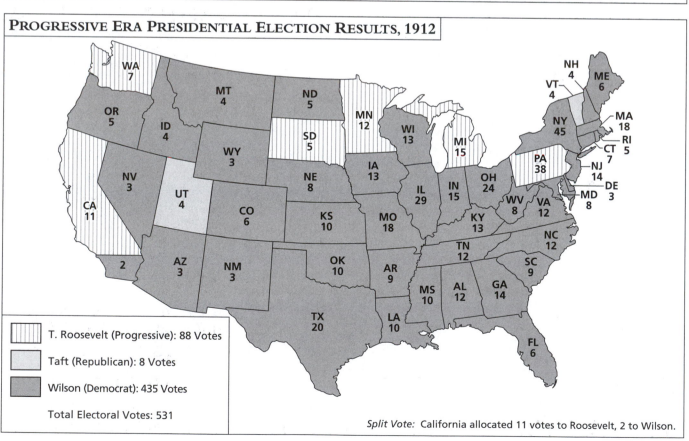

PROGRESSIVE ERA PRESIDENTIAL ELECTION RESULTS, 1912

T. Roosevelt (Progressive): 88 Votes

Taft (Republican): 8 Votes

Wilson (Democrat): 435 Votes

Total Electoral Votes: 531

Split Vote: California allocated 11 votes to Roosevelt, 2 to Wilson.

PROGRESSIVE ERA PRESIDENTIAL ELECTION RESULTS, 1916

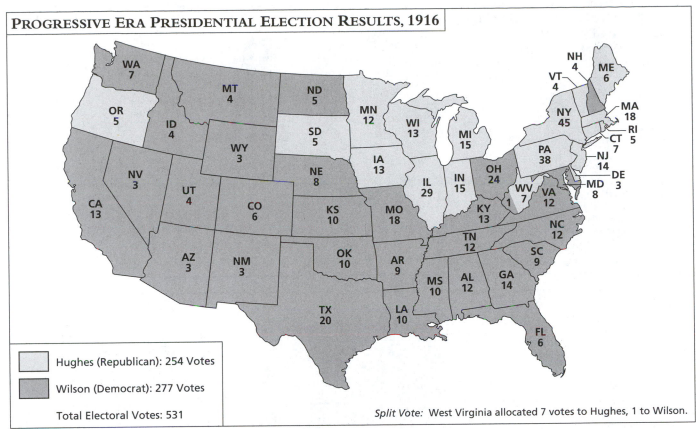

Hughes (Republican): 254 Votes

Wilson (Democrat): 277 Votes

Total Electoral Votes: 531

Split Vote: West Virginia allocated 7 votes to Hughes, 1 to Wilson.

PROGRESSIVE ERA PRESIDENTIAL ELECTION RESULTS, 1920

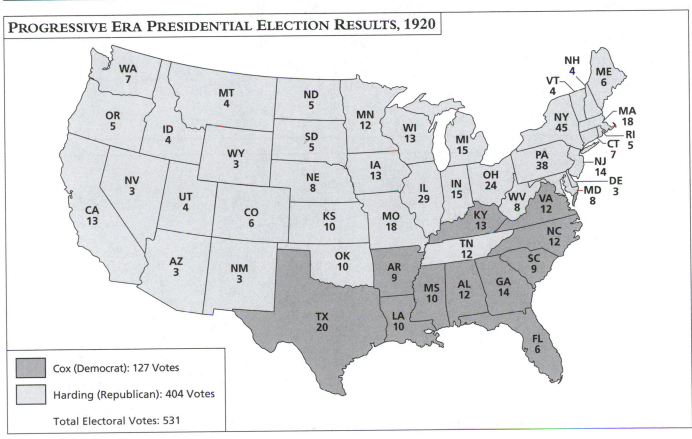

Cox (Democrat): 127 Votes

Harding (Republican): 404 Votes

Total Electoral Votes: 531

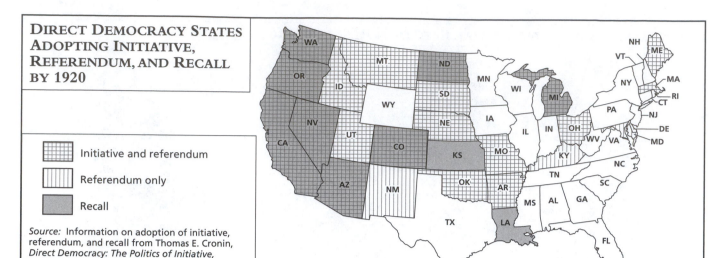

DIRECT DEMOCRACY STATES ADOPTING INITIATIVE, REFERENDUM, AND RECALL BY 1920

Initiative and referendum

Referendum only

Recall

Source: Information on adoption of initiative, referendum, and recall from Thomas E. Cronin, *Direct Democracy: The Politics of Initiative, Referendum, and Recall* (Cambridge, Mass.: Harvard University Press, 1989), Tables 3.1 and 6.1.

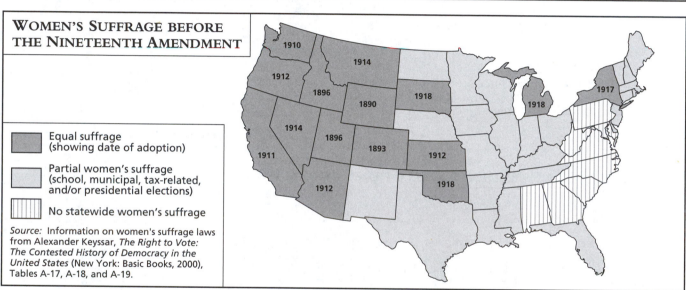

WOMEN'S SUFFRAGE BEFORE THE NINETEENTH AMENDMENT

Equal suffrage (showing date of adoption)

Partial women's suffrage (school, municipal, tax-related, and/or presidential elections)

No statewide women's suffrage

Source: Information on women's suffrage laws from Alexander Keyssar, *The Right to Vote: The Contested History of Democracy in the United States* (New York: Basic Books, 2000), Tables A-17, A-18, and A-19.

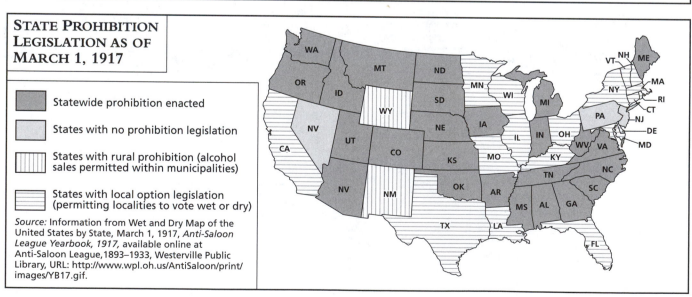

STATE PROHIBITION LEGISLATION AS OF MARCH 1, 1917

Statewide prohibition enacted

States with no prohibition legislation

States with rural prohibition (alcohol sales permitted within municipalities)

States with local option legislation (permitting localities to vote wet or dry)

Source: Information from Wet and Dry Map of the United States by State, March 1, 1917, *Anti-Saloon League Yearbook, 1917,* available online at Anti-Saloon League, 1893–1933, Westerville Public Library, URL: http://www.wpl.oh.us/AntiSaloon/print/images/YB17.gif.

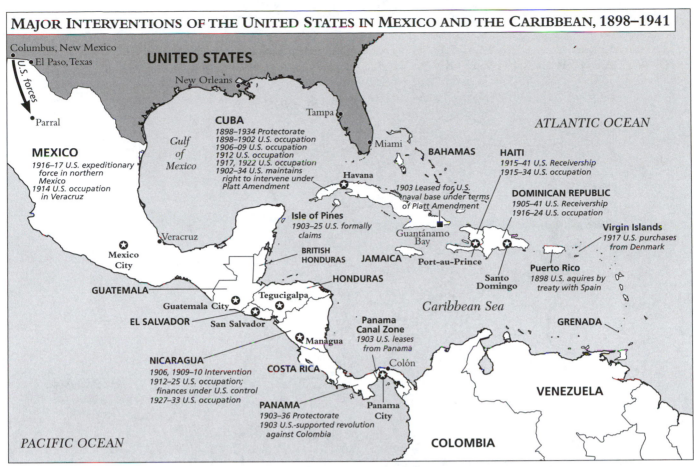

MAJOR INTERVENTIONS OF THE UNITED STATES IN MEXICO AND THE CARIBBEAN, 1898–1941

Columbus, New Mexico
El Paso, Texas
U.S. forces
Parral

UNITED STATES

New Orleans

Tampa

Miami

ATLANTIC OCEAN

Gulf of Mexico

CUBA
1898–1934 Protectorate
1898–1902 U.S. occupation
1906–09 U.S. occupation
1912 U.S. occupation
1917, 1922 U.S. occupation
1902–34 U.S. maintains right to intervene under Platt Amendment

BAHAMAS

HAITI
1915–41 U.S. Receivership
1915–34 U.S. occupation

MEXICO
1916–17 U.S. expeditionary force in northern Mexico
1914 U.S. occupation in Veracruz

Havana

1903 Leased for U.S. naval base under terms of Platt Amendment

DOMINICAN REPUBLIC
1905–41 U.S. Receivership
1916–24 U.S. occupation

Veracruz

Isle of Pines
1903–25 U.S. formally claims

Guantánamo Bay

Virgin Islands
1917 U.S. purchases from Denmark

Mexico City

BRITISH HONDURAS

JAMAICA

Port-au-Prince

Santo Domingo

Puerto Rico
1898 U.S. acquires by treaty with Spain

GUATEMALA

HONDURAS

Tegucigalpa

Caribbean Sea

GRENADA

Guatemala City

EL SALVADOR

San Salvador

Panama Canal Zone
1903 U.S. leases from Panama

Managua

Colón

NICARAGUA
1906, 1909–10 Intervention
1912–25 U.S. occupation; finances under U.S. control
1927–33 U.S. occupation

COSTA RICA

VENEZUELA

PANAMA
1903–36 Protectorate
1903 U.S.-supported revolution against Colombia

Panama City

PACIFIC OCEAN

COLOMBIA

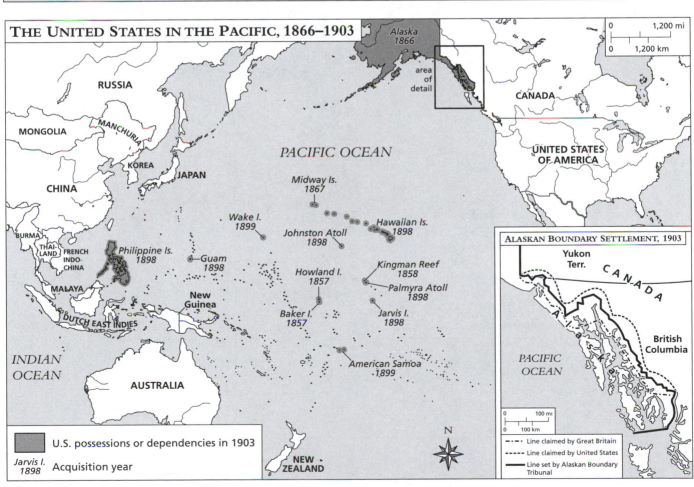

THE UNITED STATES IN THE PACIFIC, 1866–1903

Alaska 1866

area of detail

0   1,200 mi
0   1,200 km

RUSSIA

CANADA

MONGOLIA

MANCHURIA

KOREA

JAPAN

CHINA

PACIFIC OCEAN

UNITED STATES OF AMERICA

Midway Is. 1867

BURMA

Wake I. 1899

Johnston Atoll 1898

Hawaiian Is. 1898

THAILAND

FRENCH INDO-CHINA

Philippine Is. 1898

Guam 1898

Kingman Reef 1858

ALASKAN BOUNDARY SETTLEMENT, 1903

Yukon Terr.

CANADA

MALAYA

Howland I. 1857

Palmyra Atoll 1898

New Guinea

Baker I. 1857

Jarvis I. 1898

British Columbia

DUTCH EAST INDIES

INDIAN OCEAN

PACIFIC OCEAN

AUSTRALIA

American Samoa 1899

0   100 mi
0   100 km

N

NEW ZEALAND

U.S. possessions or dependencies in 1903

Jarvis I. 1898 Acquisition year

—·—·— Line claimed by Great Britain
—————— Line claimed by United States
————— Line set by Alaskan Boundary Tribunal

THE WESTERN FRONT, 1914–1918

NETHERLANDS

BELGIUM

Strait of Dover

Nieuport
Ostend
Dunkirk
Calais
Ypres
Lille

Somme R.

FRANCE

Soissons
Aisne R.
Château-
Thierry
Reims
Oise R.

Paris
Marne R.
Seine R.

Antwerp

Brussels

Schelde R.

Meuse R.

ARDENNES FOREST

ARGONNE FOREST

Verdun
St-Mihiel

Nancy

Rhine R.

LUXEM-
BOURG

GERMANY

Metz

Strasbourg

Meuse R.
Moselle R.

SWITZER-
LAND

N

0   50 mi
0   50 km

- - - - - Front line, August 22, 1914

────── Front line, July–August, 1918

············· German line at time of
           Armistice, November 11, 1918

NOTES

INTRODUCTION

1. Charles Beard and Mary Beard, *The Rise of American Civilization,* vol. 2, *The Industrial Era* (New York: Macmillan, 1927, 1930), 529.

CHAPTER 1

1. Events at Wounded Knee are described in the documentary collection, Colin G. Calloway, ed., *Our Hearts Fell to the Ground* (Boston: Bedford Books, St. Martin's Press, 1996), chaps. 13 and 14.
2. Census quoted in Frederick Jackson Turner, "The Significance of the Frontier in American History," in *The Frontier In American History* (New York: Henry Holt, 1920), 1. The ill-fated 1890 census records, damaged by an 1896 fire, were almost completely destroyed by fire in 1921, an event that led to the founding of the National Archives.
3. Turner, "The Significance of the Frontier in American History," 38.
4. Historians are not even certain who actually wrote the forest reserve provision, Section 24 of the act. See Homer Socolofsky and Allan Spetter, *The Presidency of Benjamin Harrison* (Lawrence: University Press of Kansas, 1987), 70ff.
5. On the founding of the Sierra Club and the first battles for Yosemite, see Holway Jones, *John Muir and the Sierra Club* (San Francisco: Sierra Club, 1965), chap. 1.
6. Hofstadter's frequently quoted comment is the opening sentence of *The Age of Reform* (New York: Random House, Vintage, 1955), 23.
7. Frank Lloyd Wright, "Louis H. Sullivan, His Work," *Architectural Record* 56 (July 1924): 29. Both Wright and Sullivan believed the Wainwright building had a central place in architectural history, although some critics hold that its reputation as a symbol of a new age rests more on their pronouncements than on its merits.
8. Beard and Beard, *Rise of American Civilization,* vol. 2, 176.
9. The phrase is from Alan Brinkley, *The Unfinished Nation* (New York: Alfred A. Knopf, Borzoi, 1997), 500.
10. Terrence Powderly, "The Homestead Strike," *North American Review* 155 (September 1892): 373.
11. Jacob Riis, introduction to *How the Other Half Lives* (London: Sampson Low, Marston, Searle, and Rivington, 1891), 3.
12. Walter Trattner, *From Poor Law to Welfare State,* 6th ed. (New York: Free Press, 1999), 171.
13. On Catholic settlements, see Deirdre Moloney, *American Catholic Lay Groups and Transatlantic Social Reform in the Progressive Era* (Chapel Hill: University of North Carolina Press, 2002), chap. 4.
14. Allen Davis, "Introduction to the 1984 Edition," *Spearheads for Reform* (New Brunswick, N.J.: Rutgers University Press, 1967, 1984), xxii.
15. Ingalls, *Congressional Record,* 51st Congress, vol. 20, 807, quoted in Davis Rich Dewey, *National Problems, 1885–1897* (New York: Harper and Brothers, 1907), 167. In using the term "Force Bill" Southern congressmen were alluding to the Reconstruction era Force Acts of 1870–71 (sometimes called the Ku Klux Klan acts), passed to end violence and intimidation of black voters by imposing federal penalties on anyone obstructing a citizen's right to vote. The original Force Bill of 1833 permitted the use of army troops to force South Carolina to obey national laws, specifically customs collections resulting from the tariff.

    In 1890 nearly half the population of the South was black and African Americans were counted as citizens for purposes of apportioning the number of congressional representatives each state was allowed. Therefore, when blacks were disenfranchised each white Southerner in effect had his representation in Congress doubled; in other words, each congressman from the South really represented only about half as many voters as a congressman from northern states. Because white Southerners always elected Democrats, this political fact sometimes influenced Republican efforts to enforce the 15th Amendment.
16. Reed cited in Dewey, *National Problems,* 186.
17. On land runs, see Arrell Morgan Gibson, *Oklahoma, a History of Five Centuries* (Norman: University of Oklahoma Press, 1981), chap. 14.

18. On Native Americans in Oklahoma, see Danney Goble, *Progressive Oklahoma* (Norman: University of Oklahoma Press, 1980), chaps. 2 and 3; and David Baird and Danney Goble, *The Story of Oklahoma* (Norman: University of Oklahoma Press, 1994), chap. 15, census statistics, 284.

19. Burritt quoted in T.A. Larson, *History of Wyoming,* 2nd ed. rev. (Lincoln: University of Nebraska Press, 1978), 249; water rights discussed 253–54.

20. The contrast in values between Mormons and non-Mormons in late 19th-century Utah is discussed in Dean May, *Utah, A People's History* (Salt Lake City: University of Utah Press, 1987), chap. 6.

21. May, *Utah,* 125. The influence of the polygamous lifestyle is, of course, greatly understated if the statistic measuring it reflects only the number of men who took more than one wife.

22. Woodruff quoted in Gustive Larson, "The Campaign and Manifesto," chap. 14 in *Utah's History,* ed. Richard Poll (Logan: Utah State University Press, 1989), 272.

23. Harrison proclamation available online at URL: http://www.polygamyinfo.com/Harrision-proclamation.htm.

24. Lewelling quoted in George Tindall, *America, A Narrative History,* vol. 2 (New York: W.W. Norton, 1984), 849.

25. The founding of the Populist party is discussed in Robert McMath, *American Populism* (New York: Hill and Wang, Farrar, Straus and Giroux, 1993), chap. 5.

26. C. Vann Woodward, *The Strange Career of Jim Crow,* 3rd rev. ed. (New York, Oxford University Press, 1974), 50; Charleston newspaper editor quoted, 49.

27. Calhoun quoted in Neil McMillan, *Dark Journey* (Urbana: University of Illinois Press, 1989), 43.

28. Kennell Jackson, *America Is Me* (New York: Harper-Collins Publishers, 1996), 215.

29. Barbara Bair, "Though Justice Sleeps: 1880–1900," chap. 6 in *To Make Our World Anew,* ed. R. Kelley and E. Lewis (New York: Oxford University Press, 2000), 320.

30. Solomon quoted online at "Hannah Greenebaum Solomon," Jewish Women's Archive, Women of Valor Exhibit, URL:http://www.jwa.org/exhibits/wov/solomon/hs1.html. Mrs. Harrison's speech excerpted in Ann Arnold Hunter, *A Century of Service* (Washington, D.C.: National Society Daughters of the American Revolution, 1991), 42. The DAR, founded in part because women were excluded from Sons of the American Revolution, was one of several new late 19th organizations that focused on early American history and ancestry. Although it later gained a reputation for being especially conservative, during the Progressive era it was comparable to many other progressive women's service clubs.

31. Maud Nathan describes the beginnings of the National Consumer's League in *The Story of an Epoch-Making Movement* (Garden City, N.Y.: Doubleday, Page, 1926), chaps. 2 and 3, 15–59.

32. Anthony quoted in Carl Abbott et al., *Colorado,* rev. ed. (Boulder: Colorado Associated University Press, 1982), 185. The Colorado campaign is described in Abbott *et al.,* 182–88, and in Ida Husted Harper *et al.,* eds., *History of Woman Suffrage,* vol. 4 (Rochester and New York: 1902), chap. 29.

33. The history of the WCTU to 1900 is discussed in Ruth Bordin, *Woman and Temperance* (Philadelphia: Temple University Press, 1981); information on publications, 90 ff., membership statistics 3–4.

34. Ida Wells Barnett's conflict with the WCTU is discussed in Bair, "Though Justice Sleeps," 342; one of Wells Barnett's denunciations of Willard is available in *A Red Record,* in *On Lynchings* (1892, 1895, 1900; reprint, Amherst, N.Y.: Humanity Books, 2002), 129–38.

35. The YWCA and the Salvation Army are discussed in detail in Daphne Spain, *How Women Saved the City* (Minneapolis: University of Minnesota Press, 2002).

36. Construction problems on Ellis Island are discussed in Robert Twombly, "Ellis Island: An Architectural History," in *Ellis Island,* ed. S. Jonas (New York: Aperture Foundation in association with the National Park Service and Montclair State College, n.d); architects' report and House committee quoted 127–28.

37. McLuckie quoted in Paul Krause, *The Battle for Homestead, 1880–1892* (Pittsburgh: University of Pittsburgh Press, 1992), 1. The mayor of Homestead was officially called a burgess.

38. Cable dated November 21, 1892, available online at Strike at Homestead Mill: The Homestead Letters, URL: http://www.pbs.org/wgbh/amex/carnegie/sfeature/mh_letters.html. Profit figures from Krause, *Battle for Homestead,* 361.

39. On the election of 1892 see H. Wayne Morgan, "Election of 1892," in *History of American Presidential Elections, 1789–2001,* Vol. 5: 1892–1908, ed. A. M. Schlesinger, Jr., and F. M. Israel (Philadelphia: Chelsea House Publishers, 2001), 1703–1732. The Populist convention is described in more detail in McMath, *American Populism,* chap. 5.

40. Henry Adams, *The Education of Henry Adams* (Boston, New York: Houghton, Mifflin, 1918), 339.

41. Hamlin Garland, *A Son of the Middle Border* (1917; reissue, New York: Grosset and Dunlap, 1927), 458.

42. Ray Stannard Baker, *American Chronicle* (New York: C. Scribner's Sons, 1945), 2.

43. "Comprehensiveness of Derangement in Business Affairs," *Commercial and Financial Advertiser* 57 (August 26, 1893): 321.

CHAPTER 2

1. Wilson speech from *Congressional Record,* 53rd Congress, vol. 26, 193, quoted in Dewey, *National Problems,* 280. The much quoted Cleveland comment was made in a letter to Democratic Representative Thomas Catchings of Mississippi, August 27, 1894, and published in *Public Opinion,* vol. 17 (August 30, 1894), 511; cited in Dewey, 285.

2. The proposed 1894 income tax, like the one finally instituted in 1913, was designed to apply only to the wealthiest Americans. For example, in 1896 the average yearly wage of salaried employees in business was $954 and of government employees in the executive branch $1084; both would have been well under the $4,000 floor. Unfortunately for historians, until the income tax was actually put into effect in 1913 the government did not collect income data; therefore historical statistics on income must usually be reconstructed. The average income figures cited in the text and above are from Paul Douglass, *Real Wages in the United States, 1890–1926* (Boston: Houghton Mifflin, 1930), Table 147, considered a standard source. According to the Inflation Calculator, created by S. Morgan Friedman and available online at URL: http://www.westegg.com/inflation. $4,000 in 1894 would translate to $83,024 in 2002 dollars.

3. *Congressional Record,* 53rd Congress, vol. 26; Bryan, speech to the House January 30, 1894, 1657; Sherman, speech to the Senate June 22, 1894, 6695.

4. On the breadline, see Edwin Burrows and Mike Wallace, *Gotham* (New York: Oxford University Press, 1999), 1189. On Tacoma see Carlos Schwantes, *Coxey's Army* (Lincoln: University of Nebraska Press, 1985), 16. Baker, letter to his father, December 15, 1893, quoted in Robert Bannister, *Ray Stannard Baker* (New Haven, Conn.: Yale University Press, 1966), 43. Baker, who accompanied Coxey for the *Chicago Tribune,* discusses the march in his *American Chronicle,* chap. 2.

5. The secretary of agriculture quoted in McMath, *American Populism,* 182.

6. Schwantes, *Coxey's Army,* 46.

7. David Papke, *The Pullman Case* (Lawrence: University Press of Kansas, 1999), 20.

8. Henry Demarest Lloyd, *Wealth Against Commonwealth* (1896; reprint, Westport, Conn.: Greenwood Press, 1963), 159.

9. William Hope Harvey, *Coin's Financial School* (Chicago: Coin, 1894), preface (not paginated).

10. Statistics from Richard Poll, ed., *Utah's History;* Table G, Ethnic Characteristics of Utah, 1850–1970 and Table H, Membership of Religious Denominations in Utah, 1870–1975, 691–92.

11. Butler, "A Plea for High Ground in Municipal Reform," speech to the 1894 Conference on Good City Government, quoted in Kenneth Fox, *Better City Government* (Philadelphia: Temple University Press, 1977), 52–53.

12. Addams, in *Hull-House Maps and Papers,* quoted in Davis, *Spearheads for Reform,* 148. Davis recounts the story of Addams and garbage collection on 151ff; Addams' own account is in *Twenty Years at Hull-House* (New York: Macmillan, 1910), chap. 13.

13. Riis, *How the Other Half Lives,* 185.

14. For a review of drinking behavior in the early 19th century, see Thomas Pegram, *Battling Demon Rum* (Chicago: Ivan R. Dee, 1998), chaps. 1 and 2; statistics 31. See also Pegram's source review, 390–91.

15. The 1894 study is cited in Ernest Cherrington, *The Evolution of Prohibition in the United States* (Westerville, Ohio: American Issue Press, 1920), 261; it was conducted by Rev. Parkhurst's City Vigilance League and reported in the league's publication, *The City Vigilant.* Riis quote from *How the Other Half Lives,* 215.

16. Jack Blocker, *American Temperance Movements* (Boston: Twayne, 1989), 99. Austin Kerr asserts that the league copied the centralized, bureaucratic model pioneered by late 19th-century business firms and more generally relied on the increasingly accepted idea of expertise and experts; see *Organized for Prohibition* (New Haven, Conn.: Yale University Press, 1985), especially chap. 3.

17. The "rum shop door" reference was made famous in Willard's first proposal for the "home protection ballot," submitted to the national WCTU in 1878: "*Resolved:* That as the responsibility of the training of the children and youth rests largely upon woman, she ought to be allowed to open or close the rum shop door over against her home." The proposal was defeated in 1878 but approved in 1883. Proposal quoted in Janet Giele, *Two Paths to Women's Equality* (New York: Twayne Publishers, 1995), 105.

18. Jay Dolan, *The American Catholic Experience* (Garden City, N.Y.: Doubleday, 1985), 326. Many historians from Richard Hofstadter onward have viewed liquor regulation as a weapon of rural and small-town Protestants engaged in a cultural struggle against cities and increasingly diverse lifestyles; some have even reduced it to a simplistic ethnocultural struggle against "new immigrants" (primarily Catholics and Jews, whose combined percentage of the American population increased roughly from 10 percent in 1890 to 20 percent in 1920.) Although this explanation perisists, recent historians in the field have shown that the full story is far more complicated. "Old stock" Protestant Americans themselves drank heavily at various times during America's colonial and pre–Civil War era, and continued to do so in the rural South and West after that date. In fact, support for temperance during the Progressive Era was

strongest in the South and West, not in the urban Northeast, where most "new immigrants" lived. Some historians point out that over time interest in temperance developed alongside the development of industrialism and machine production or of commercial agriculture. Historians of Catholicism find significant temperance support among the church hierarchy and some Catholic laypeople; several Catholic priests even served as officers of the ASL. The ASL and other anti-liquor organizations did utilize preexisting Protestant church organizations, and many anti-liquor crusaders of all religions understood themselves more generally to represent the organized power of religiously based moral stewardship (as did many reformers in other movements.) But it is also true that many progressives considered liquor regulation a liberal reform, not a repressive one, and did not see it as the isolated and perverse issue it would come to seem after the failure of prohibition. For a review of regional differences and other explanations for the support of prohibition in the Progressive era, see Blocker, *American Temperance Movements,* 106–119.

19. Ely in his *Social Aspects of Christianity,* 1889, quoted in Paul Minus, *Walter Rauschenbusch* (New York: Macmillan, 1988), 64. Rauschenbusch, *Christianity and the Social Crisis* (New York: Macmillan, 1907), 305.

20. Mel Piehl, *Breaking Bread* (Philadelphia: Temple University Press, 1982), 34, quoted in Dolan, *American Catholicism,* 335. The text of *Rerum Novarum* is available online at Catholic Social Teaching, URL: http://www.osjspm.org/cst/rn.htm.

21. Arthur Link and Richard McCormick, *Progressivism* (Wheeling, Ill.: Harlan Davidson, 1983), 23. Historians at one end of the spectrum ignore the religious influence in progressivism. At the other end, some consider it the most important influence of all; see for example Richard Crunden, *Ministers of Reform* (Urbana: University of Illinois Press, 1984).

22. "The Chicago Nomination," *New York World,* July 11, 1896, 6. Bryan's "Cross of Gold Speech," above, is included in his *The First Battle* (Chicago: B. Conkey Company, 1896), 201ff.

23. Gilbert Fite, "Election of 1896," *History of American Presidential Elections, 1789–2001,* vol. 5 (Philadelphia: Chelsea House Publishers, 2001), 1814.

24. McKinley quoted in Fite, "Election of 1896," 1824.

25. Historians conventionally set Republican funds at between 3 and 4 million, the figure reported by Hanna; see Louis Gould, *The Presidency of William McKinley* (Lawrence, Kans: Regents' Press of Kansas, 1980), 11. Some, however, believe the total was much higher, "perhaps three to five times as much," according to H. W. Brands, *Reckless Decade* (New York: St. Martin's Press,

1995), 273. The Democrats had only about half a million.

26. "Timely Counsel and Warning," November 18, 1896, reprinted in Allen Nevins, ed., *American Press Opinion, Washington to Coolidge* (Boston: D.C. Heath, 1928), 423–25.

27. The source of this often-quoted statement by Debs is his open letter to railway workers published in the *Railway Times* and elsewhere on January 1, 1897; quoted in Nick Salvatore, *Eugene V. Debs* (Urbana: University of Illinois Press, 1982), 161–62.

28. White quoted in Tindall, *America,* vol. 2, 903. Lease, speaking in 1915, quoted in Gene Clanton, *Kansas Populism* (Lawrence: University Press of Kansas, 1969), 238. Historians of populism, however, usually see progressives as far less interested in fundamental democratic reform than the populists who preceded them.

29. Ruffin, address to the first National Conference of Colored Women at Boston, July 29, 1895, *The Women's Era,* vol. 2, no. 5 (1895): 14; reprinted in Gerda Lerner, ed., *Black Women in White America* (New York: Vintage, 1972), 440–43.

30. Washington includes his speech in *Up from Slavery* (New York: Doubleday, Page, 1901), 218–225; he quotes the *Atlanta Constitution* editorial by editor Clark Howell on 226.

31. John Hope Franklin and Alfred Moss, Jr., *From Slavery to Freedom,* 8th ed. (New York: Alfred A. Knopf, 2000), 306.

32. Carver quote, dated January 16, 1929, in *George Washington Carver in His Own Words,* ed. G. Kremer (Columbia: University of Missouri Press, 1987), 102. Carver made many similar statements throughout his writings. The phrase "the man farthest down" was well known at Tuskegee; it was the title of a 1912 book by Booker T. Washington, *The Man Farthest Down: A Record of Observation and Study in Europe.* On the "Jesup Agricultural Wagon," named for the New York philanthropist who helped fund it, see Linda McMurray, *George Washington Carver* (New York: Oxford University Press), 125ff.

33. Circular advertising the Tuskegee Conference quoted in Bair, "Though Justice Sleeps," 326.

34. Tourgée quoted in Brands, *Reckless Decade,* 228.

35. The complete text of *Plessy v. Ferguson* and all other Supreme Court decisions after 1893 are available online at Findlaw, URL: http://www.findlaw.com/casecode/supreme.html.

36. Gerald Mast, *A Short History of the Movies,* 4th ed. (New York: Macmillan Publishing, 1986), 23. *New York Dramatic Mirror* quoted in David Shipman, *The Story of Cinema* (New York: St. Martin's, 1982), 18.

37. Remington reportedly telegrammed Hearst after two weeks in Cuba, "Everything is quiet. There is no trouble

here. There will be no war. I wish to return." Hearst's famous reply was, "Please remain. You furnish the pictures. I'll furnish the war." Quoted in Douglas Allen, *Frederic Remington and the Spanish American War* (New York: Crown, 1971), 11.

38. Gavan Daws, *Shoal of Time* (New York: Macmillan, 1968), 287.

CHAPTER 3

1. The term *jingo,* referring to aggressive patriots who support a belligerent foreign policy, was first applied to those who clamored for Britain's 1877 intervention in the Russo-Turkish War. It comes from a British music-hall song popular at the time: "We don't want to fight, but, by Jingo! If we do,/We've got the ships, we've got the men, we've got the money, too."

2. Roosevelt, "Washington's Forgotten Maxim," Address at the Naval War College, June 2, 1897, *The Works of Theodore Roosevelt,* vol. 8 (New York: Charles Scribner's Sons, 1926), 182–99. Beveridge, address at the Ulysses S. Grant anniversary banquet before the Middlesex Club of Massachusetts, April 27, 1898, *The Meaning of the Times,* 43.

3. Letter of De Lôme to Don José Canalejas, in Henry Steele Commager, ed., *Documents of American History,* 8th ed., vol. 1 (New York: Appleton-Century-Crofts, 1968), 632. Roosevelt quoted in James Rhodes, *The McKinley and Roosevelt Administrations, 1897–1909* (New York: Macmillan Company, 1922), 57.

4. Roosevelt, letter to Benjamin Diblee, February 6, 1898, *Letters of Theodore Roosevelt,* ed. E. Morison *et al.,* vol. 2 (Cambridge: Harvard University Press, 1951–54), 775.

5. The Spanish conducted their own investigation at the time and concluded the cause was internal. In 1911 the ship was raised and a second American investigation conducted, which generally agreed with the conclusions of the first. In 1976 another review was conducted under Admiral Hyman Rickover, based on the records that existed (the *Maine* itself had been towed out to sea and sunk after the 1911 enquiry.) The Rickover investigation concluded that "no technical evidence" indicated an external explosion, and the most probable cause was that heat from the coal bunkers had ignited ammunition stored in a nearby magazine. See Geoff Simons, *Cuba* (New York: St. Martin's Press, 1996), 188ff.; Rickover report quoted 191. Historians generally agree that even if the *Maine* was indeed sabotaged, the least likely suspect was the Spanish government, which certainly did not want war with America. On other possible suspects, such as the Spanish military, Cuban insurgents who wanted Americans to enter the war, or Americans themselves, see Philip Foner, *The Spanish-Cuban-American*

War, vol. 2 (New York: Monthly Review Press, 1972), chap. 12, especially 244ff.

6. The Teller Amendment is the fourth resolution of the Joint Congressional Resolution of War, April 20, 1898, *U.S. Statutes at Large,* vol. 30, 738.

7. Hay, letter from London where he was serving as an ambassador, to Theodore Roosevelt, July 27, 1898, quoted in Page Smith, *The Rise of Industrial America* (New York: McGraw-Hill, 1984), 881. Hoar quoted in Brands, *Reckless Decade,* 316.

8. Letter dated June 10, 1898, *Selected Letters of Theodore Roosevelt,* ed. H.W. Brands (New York: Cooper Square Press, 2001), 185.

9. All sources agree that far more Americans died of disease than battle wounds, but the number of casualties in the Spanish-American War is still a matter of disagreement. Totals depend partly on what inclusive dates are used. For the period from the declaration of war until the official peace treaty was signed in 1899, the Department of Defense gives 385 deaths in battle and 2,061 from disease (these figures do not including deaths in the *Maine* explosion, which occurred before war was declared); available online at Principal Wars in Which the United States Participated, Table 2–23, URL: http://web1.whs.osd.mil/mmid/m01/SMS223R.HTM. The problems arise when trying to count the deaths after 1899 from diseases contracted during the war, as well as deaths resulting from post-1899 fighting in the Philippines, which was not a declared war. The Philippine insurrection was officially declared over in 1902, but sporadic resistance continued until the last insurgent general was captured in 1907 and some guerrilla fighting continued as late as 1916. More than 125,000 troops saw service in the Philippines; a frequently cited figure for American battle deaths is some 4,200, but some historians give much higher numbers and it is assumed twice as many probably died of disease. Some estimate total Filipino deaths may have reached a million.

10. Carl Sandburg, *Always the Young Strangers* (New York: Harcourt, Brace, and World, 1952, 1953), 419.

11. Carnegie, "Distant Possessions: The Parting of the Ways," *The Andrew Carnegie Reader,* ed. J. F. Wall (Pittsburgh: University of Pittsburgh Press, 1992), 300; originally published in *North American Review,* August 1898.

12. McKinley's speech quoted in Charles Olcott, *The Life of William McKinley,* vol. 2 (Boston: Houghton Mifflin, 1916), 109–11.

13. Bradley Fiske, *War Time in Manila* (Boston: R. G. Badger, 1913), 67. Fiske, later an admiral, was navigator of the U.S.S. *Petrel* at the time.

14. Statistics, Allen Millett and Peter Maslowski, *For the Common Defense* (New York: Free Press, 1984), 296; see also note 9 above.

15. The insurgents established "invisible governments" to enact terrorism and atrocities against other Filipinos, which they called "exemplary punishment on traitors to prevent the people of the towns from unworthily selling themselves for the gold of the invader." The "kill everyone" comment was made by General Jacob Smith and was widely reported and commented on in the American press. See Millett and Maslowski, *For the Common Defense,* 293, 295. The summary of press opinion on Smith appearing in the *Literary Digest,* May 10, 1902, is available online at Anti-Imperialism in the United States, 1898–1935, ed. Jim Zwick, URL: http://www.boondocksnet.com/centennial/sctexts/atrocities020510.html. Smith faced a court martial in May 1902 but was retired by Roosevelt without further punishment. *New York American* editorial, quoted below, quoted in *Literary Digest* 24 (February 1, 1902): 138.

16. The Platt Amendment of March 2, 1901, is available in *Treaties and Other International Agreements,* vol. 8, 1116–17.

17. Peter Finley Dunne, *Mr. Dooley At His Best* (New York: C. Scribner's Sons, 1938), 73.

18. This first reference to the "open door" was made in McKinley's September 16, 1898, speech to the peace commissioners working on the treaty to formally end the Spanish American War; quoted in Gould, *Presidency of William McKinley,* 201.

19. Statistics from Diana Preston, *The Boxer Rebellion* (New York: Walker and Company, 1999, 2000), xiv and *passim.*

20. Alaska population statistics from Claus-M. Naske and Herman Slotnick, *Alaska,* 2nd ed. (Norman: University of Oklahoma Press, 1987), appendix F, 301.

21. *U.S. v. Wong Kim Ark,* 169 U.S. 649 (1898).

22. Robert Bremner, *From the Depths* (New York: New York University Press, 1956), 210. Veiller, housing reform, and the exhibition of 1900 are also discussed in Roy Lubov, *The Progressives and the Slums* (Pittsburgh: University of Pittsburgh Press, 1962), chap. 5.

23. Lillian Wald, *The House on Henry Street* (New York: Henry Holt, 1915), 84.

24. Quoted in Alan Brinkley, *American History,* 10th ed., vol. 2 (Boston: McGraw Hill College, 1999), 615.

25. Daniel Nelson, *Shifting Fortunes* (Chicago: Ivan R. Dee, 1997), 25.

26. Quote and Louisiana voting statistics, Franklin and Moss, *From Slavery to Freedom,* 288.

27. *Debates of the Constitutional Convention of Virginia, . . . June 12, 1901, to June 26, 1902,* excerpted in Richard Bardolph, ed., *The Civil Rights Record* (New York: Thomas Y. Crowell, 1970), 140–43; quote by speaker identified as Mr. Thom, 142.

28. Population statistics from Baird and Goble, *The Story of Oklahoma,* 284.

29. James Bryce, *The American Commonwealth,* vol. 1 (New York: Macmillan, 1888), 642. Brand Whitlock, *Forty Years of It* (New York: D. Appleton, 1914), 162.

30. Goodnow, "Political Parties and City Government," in National Municipal League, *A Municipal Program* (New York: Macmillan Company for the National Municipal League, 1900), 144–45.

31. Jones quoted online at "The Writings of Samuel 'Golden Rule' Jones," Toledo's Attic, URL: http://www.attic.utoledo.edu/att/jones/jones.html.

32. Woodruff, "The Movement for Municipal Reform," *North American Review* 167 (October 1898): 410–11.

33. Information and statistics on the election of U.S. senators by state legislatures from C. H. Hoebeke, *The Road to Mass Democracy* (New Brunswick, N.J.: Transaction Publishers, 1995), chap. 4, especially 89ff.

34. Dolan, *American Catholic Experience,* 326.

35. Information about Nation, including the quotes from Governor Stanley and Nation herself, is available online at Carry Nation, Kansas State Historical Society Online Exhibits (URL: http://hs4.kshs.org/exhibits/carry/)

36. Ruth Rosen, *The Lost Sisterhood* (Baltimore: Johns Hopkins University Press, 1982), 13. This account relies largely on Rosen's study.

37. Mark Thomas Connelly, *The Response to Prostitution in the Progressive Era* (Chapel Hill: University of North Carolina Press, 1980), chap. 4; statistics reviewed 70–71.

38. Hanna, letter to McKinley, June 25, 1900, quoted in Walter LeFeber, "Election of 1900," in *History of American Presidential Elections, 1789–2001,* vol. 5, 1888.

39. Wall's comment appears in his biography, *Andrew Carnegie* (Pittsburgh: University of Pittsburgh Press, 1970), 780.

40. Albert Fried, *Socialism in America* (Garden City, N.Y.: Doubleday, 1970), 380.

41. The complete text of the McKinley reciprocity speech is available in *Messages and Papers of the Presidents,* vol. 10 (New York: Bureau of National Literature and Art, 1908, c1897), 393ff.

42. Czolgosz quote available online at William McKinley Assassination, URL:http://www.crimelibrary.com/terrorists_spie/assassins/mckinley/2.html?sect=24. The Goldman-Czolgosz connection is discussed in more detail in Eric Rauchway, *Murdering McKinley* (New York: Hill and Wang, 2003), chap. 4 and *passim.*

43. According to H. H. Kohlstaat, publisher of the *Chicago Inter-Ocean,* Hanna made the comment to him aboard McKinley's funeral train. The comment has become part of historical lore, although some historians do not consider Kohlstaat an entirely reliable witness. Kohlstaat, *McKinley to Harding* (New York: C. Scribner's Sons, 1923), 100–101.

44. The statement was reported in newspapers coast to coast; for example, "Mr. Roosevelt Is Now The President," *New York Times,* September 16, 1901, page 1.

45. Roosevelt's First Annual Message, *Messages and Papers of the Presidents,* vol. 10, 417ff.

CHAPTER 4

1. Lincoln Steffens, *Autobiography* (New York: Harcourt, Brace and World, 1931), 502.

2. Steffens, *Autobiography,* 506. Historians usually assume that Steffens exaggerated the extent of his friendship with and influence on Roosevelt.

3. *Theodore Roosevelt: An Autobiography* (New York: Macmillan, 1913), 372.

4. Steffens, *Autobiography,* 502.

5. Louis Gould, *The Presidency of Theodore Roosevelt* (Lawrence: University Press of Kansas, 1991), 101.

6. The remodeling of the White House is described in William Seale, *The White House* (Washington DC: American Institute of Architects Press, 1992), chap. 6, and *The President's House,* vol. 2, (Washington, DC: White House Historical Association, 1986), chap. 29. Roosevelt's comment, made in a letter to Maria Longworth Storer, December 8, 1902, quoted in Gould, *Presidency of Theodore Roosevelt,* 102.

7. William Link and William Catton, *American Epoch,* vol. 1, 5th ed. (New York: Knopf, 1980), 33.

8. "We draw the line . . . ," Second Annual Message to Congress, December 2, 1902, complete text available online at URL: http://www.geocities.com/americanpresidencynet/1902.htm. Updated August 2, 2003. "When I became President . . . ," *Autobiography,* 439–40.

9. Morgan quoted in Gould, *Presidency of Theodore Roosevelt,* 51.

10. Baer letter reprinted in Caroline Lloyd, *Henry Demarest Lloyd* (New York: G. P. Putnam's Sons, 1912), 190.

11. Roosevelt, *Autobiography,* 422.

12. Letter to Silas McBee, February 3, 1903, quoted in Gould, *Presidency of Theodore Roosevelt,* 199.

13. Quoted in Edmund Morris, *Theodore Rex* (New York: Random House, 2001), 199.

14. Letter released to papers nationwide November 26, 1902, quoted in Gould, *Presidency of Theodore Roosevelt,* 120–21.

15. Immigration Act of March 3, 1903, *United States Statutes at Large,* 57th Congress, vol. 32, 1213ff.

16. Roosevelt, letter to Nicholas Murray Butler, October 9, 1901, quoted in Thomas Pitkin, *Keeper of the Gate* (New York: New York University Press, 1975), 35. This account relies on Pitkin's discussion in chaps. 3 and 4.

17. Williams quoted in Pitkin, *Keeper of the Gate,* 38.

18. Pitkin, *Keeper of the Gate,* 39.

19. Roosevelt commented candidly on his position in numerous letters to political and diplomatic figures; the phrases "did not have a leg to stand on" and "dangerously near blackmail" are from July 1902 letters to (respectively) John Stratchey, editor of the London *Spectator,* and Secretary of State John Hay; quoted in Thomas Bailey, "Shaking the Big Stick: TR and the Alaska Boundary," in *Interpreting Alaska's History,* ed. M. Mangusso and S. Haycox (Anchorage: Alaska Pacific University Press, 1989), 195. The phrase "six impartial jurists of repute" is language from the Hay-Herbert treaty between Canada and the United States agreeing to the tribunal, ratified by the Senate February 11, 1903. Roosevelt actually dispatched U.S. troops to southern Alaska in 1902 in case disturbances arose along the line; see Gould, *Presidency of Theodore Roosevelt,* 81ff.

20. Roosevelt, *Autobiography,* 540.

21. Roosevelt, *Autobiography,* 540; "to remove all misunderstandings. . . ." is language from the treaty with Columbia passed by the Senate April 20, 1921. The phrase replaced an expression of "sincere regret" appearing in the original version of the treaty, which was signed by the Wilson administration in 1914 but shelved by the Senate due to the strong opposition of Roosevelt and his supporters to any admission of wrongdoing. The treaty was not passed until "the relentless Rough Rider was safely in his grave," as historian Thomas Bailey puts it; *A Diplomatic History of the American People,* 10th ed. (Englewood Cliffs, N.J.: Prentice-Hall, 1980), 497.

22. Karsten, "Armed Progressives: The Military Reorganizes for the American Century," in *The Military in America,* ed. P. Karsten (New York: Free Press, 1980), 229–71. On the Root reforms see also articles available online at U.S. Army Center of Military History, 1901: Reforming the Army, URL: http://www.army.mil/cmh-pg/documents/1901/1901.htm. updated April 18, 2002, including William Donnelly, "The Root Reforms And the National Guard"; Terrence Gough, "The Root Reforms And Command"; Martin Kaplan, "Modernization in The Root Reform Era"; William Webb, "The Root Reforms And Army Schools And Branches"; and James Yarrison, "The U.S. Army in The Root Reform Era, 1899–1917."

23. Issued as Army General Orders, No. 107, July 20, 1903, reprinted in Root, *The Military and Colonial Policy of the United States,* ed. R. Bacon and J. Scott (Cambridge: Harvard University Press, 1916), 431–32.

24. Upton Sinclair, "What Life Means to Me," *Cosmopolitan* 41 (October 1906); and Peter Finley Dunne, "The Food We Eat," in *Dissertations by Mr. Dooley* (New York: Harper & Brothers, 1906); both available online at "The Jungle By Upton Sinclair, With Supplemental Readings on

the Beef Trust Scandal of 1906 and Its Outcome," BoondocksNet Editions, ed. Jim Zwick, URL:http://www.boondocksnet.com/editions/jungle/. Downloaded January 24, 2004.

25. William Riordon, *Plunkitt of Tammany Hall* (New York, McClure, Phillips, 1905), 17.

26. Johnson quoted in Steffens, *Autobiography,* 479.

27. Steffens cited in Frederic Howe, *Confessions of a Reformer* (New York: C. Scribner's Sons, 1925), 184.

28. Tom Johnson, *My Story,* ed. E. Hauser (New York: B.W. Huebsch, 1913), 194.

29. Mel Scott, *American City Planning Since 1890* (Berkeley: University of California Press, 1969), 80–81.

30. William Allen White, *Autobiography* (New York: Macmillan, 1946), 427.

31. Robert Bremner, *From the Depths* (New York: New York University Press, 1956), especially chap. 8. As Bremner points out, the idea that individuals are responsible for their own poverty (considered a conservative position by the end of the Progressive era) actually grew from a liberal if not revolutionary idea. When America was founded, class-bound Old World societies assumed that people were born to a station in life and remained there; by definition, the poor would always exist and were incapable of improving their position. Americans, on the other hand, began to embrace the idea that any individual could achieve a competency and therefore did not have to remain in poverty.

32. Robert Hunter, *Poverty* (New York: Macmillan, 1904, 1906); "too little . . . ," 5–6; "To live miserable . . . ," 2; estimate of the number of poor, 11 ff.

33. Walter Trattner, *Crusade for the Children* (Chicago: Quadrangle Books, 1970), 65. This account relies on Trattner's history of the campaign against child labor.

34. Adler quoted in Trattner, *Crusade,* 59.

35. Saloon statistics from Norman Clark, *Deliver Us From Evil* (New York: W.W. Norton, 1976); 50; consumption statistics from Thomas Pegram, *Battling Demon Rum,* 91–92.

36. James Timberlake, *Prohibition and the Progressive Movement, 1900–1920* (Cambridge: Harvard University Press, 1963), 39. *American Issue* circulation statistics, above, from Jack Blocker, *Retreat from Reform* (Westport, Conn.: Greenwood Press, 1976), 169.

37. W. E. B. DuBois, *The Souls of Black Folk* (Chicago: A. C. McClurg, 1903), 37–38; Booker T. Washington, *My Larger Education* (Garden City, N.Y.: Doubleday, Page, 1911), 224.

38. Union membership statistics from Philip Taft, *Organized Labor in American History* (New York: Harper and Row, 1964), 246.

39. Roosevelt, letter to George Cortelyou, July 13, 1903, quoted in Gould, *Presidency of Theodore Roosevelt,* 115.

40. For the chronology of hours legislation see Elizabeth Brandeis, "Labor Legislation," in *History of Labour in the United States,* vol. 4, ed. J. R. Commons, *et al.* (New York: Macmillan, 1935.) The 1898 Supreme Court case upholding restrictions on miners' hours is *Holden v. Hardy,* 169 US 366; citation for *Atkin v. Kansas,* 191 US 207.

41. On the history of flight, see Centennial of Flight, a comprehensive site developed by the U.S. Centennial of Flight Commission in honor of the 100th anniversary of the Wright brothers' first flight. URL: http://www.centennialofflight.gov.

42. Roosevelt's first recorded public use of the "big stick" phrase was in a speech at the Minnesota State Fair, September 2, 1901, *Works,* vol. 15, 334–35. The "bully pulpit" reference was a comment to George Haven Putnam, who had accused him of "preaching" during his first term of office, to which Roosevelt replied, "Yes, Haven, most of us enjoy preaching, and I've got such a bully pulpit!" Reported by Putnam in his introductory essay to volume 9 of Roosevelt, *Works,* x.

43. Roosevelt's Fourth Annual Message to Congress, December 6, 1904, *Works,* vol. 15, 257.

44. Quoted in Harbaugh, "Election of 1904," 1966.

45. Harbaugh, "Election of 1904," 1969.

46. Frick comment on Roosevelt reported by Oswald Garrison Villard, in his *Fighting Years* (New York: Harcourt, Brace, 1939), 181. Villard, who met with Frick before publishing a story in his *New York Evening Post,* was shocked when the business baron bluntly told him, "He got down on his knees to us. We bought the son-of-a-bitch and then he did not stay bought."

47. Quoted in Nathan Miller, *Theodore Roosevelt* (New York: William Morrow, 1992), 436.

48. The public announcement was widely reprinted in newspapers; for example, *New York Times,* November 9, 1904, page 1. See also Morris, *Theodore Rex,* 364; and Gould, *Presidency of Theodore Roosevelt,* 143–44.

CHAPTER 5

1. "Why, by interweaving our destiny with that of any part of Europe, entangle our peace and prosperity in the toils of European Ambition, Rivalship, Interest, Humour or Caprice?" asked Washington in his famous address of 1796; complete text available online at Papers of George Washington, URL: http://gwpapers.virginia.edu/farewell/transcript.html.

2. Convention of Algeciras in Malloy, ed., *Treaties, Conventions,* vol. 2, 2182–83.

3. "the total change . . . ," Fourth Annual Message, December 6, 1904, *Works,* vol. 15, 216; "Malefactors of great wealth," phrase in "The Puritan Spirit and the Regula-

tion of Corporations," speech at Provincetown, Massachusetts, August 20, 1907, *Works,* vol. 16, 84.

4. *Swift and Co. v. U.S.,* January 30, 1905, 196 U.S. 375; *U.S. v. E. C. Knight Co.,* January 21, 1895, 156 U.S. 1.

5. Hepburn Act, June 19, 1906, *U.S. Statutes at Large,* 59th Congress, vol. 34, part 1, 585ff.

6. In an 1896 advertisement in *National Druggist,* Coca-Cola Company openly advertised its "success in robbing both coca leaves and the kola nut of the . . . disagreeable taste while retaining their wonderful medicinal properties;" quoted in excerpt from Joseph Spillane, *Modern Drug, Modern Menace,* in Stephen Belenko, ed., *Drugs and Drug Policy in America* (Westport, Conn.: Greenwood, 2000), 23.

7. Roosevelt, Fifth Annual Message to Congress, December 5, 1905, *Works,* vol. 15, 326.

8. Roosevelt first used the figure at a speech to the Gridiron Club, March 17, 1906. It caused such a stir in official Washington that he determined to repeat it in a more public forum. He did so on April 14, 1906, in a speech at the cornerstone ceremony for the House Office Building, where it overshadowed his call for an inheritance tax on the wealthy and the most radical regulation of corporations he had yet proposed. See Gould, *Presidency of Theodore Roosevelt,* 161–62, and Morris, *Theodore Rex,* 439ff.

9. *Rassmussen v. U.S.,* April 10, 1905, 197 U.S. 516; complete text available online at Findlaw (URL: http://www.findlaw.com/casecode/supreme.html).

10. Population statistics for 1900 calculated at the United States Historical Census Browser, Geostat Center, University of Virginia Library, available online. URL: http://fisher.lib.virginia.edu/collections/stats/histcensus/, updated on January 8, 2004. The data in the browser is provided from the Inter-University Consortium for Political and Social Research, based on the decennial censuses of the United States. Adding together state data for "total number of Negro males" and "total number of Negro females" and dividing by "total population" gives the following percentages of *black* population in 1900: Alabama, 45 percent; Florida, 44 percent; Georgia, 47 percent; Louisiana, 47 percent; Mississippi, 59 percent; South Carolina, 58 percent.

11. In the words of historian John Ray Skates, "Vardaman was the most notorious racist in Mississippi history, excepting only his successor, Theodore Bilbo;" *Mississippi* (New York: W. W. Norton, 1979), 129.

12. In 1907 the population was 79 percent white; 12 percent black, and 9 percent Indian; Baird and Goble, *Story of Oklahoma,* 284.

13. James Scales and Danney Goble, *Oklahoma Politics* (Norman: University of Oklahoma Press, 1982), 23.

14. The complete text of the Oklahoma constitution is available online at Oklahoma Public Legal Research System, URL: http://oklegal.onenet.net/okcon.

15. *Arena,* June 1907, 742–43; Frederick U. Adams, "A Twentieth Century State Constitution," *Saturday Evening Post* 180 (November 16, 1907), 3.

16. Both quoted in the Oklahoma City *Daily Oklahoman*: Taft, August 25, 1907, page 1; Bryan September 6, 1907, page 1.

17. Roosevelt comment reported in the *Shawnee Herald,* September 6, 1907, quoted in Scales and Goble, *Oklahoma Politics,* 36. Taft later called the constitution's authors "a zoological garden of cranks;" quoted in H. Wayne Morgan and Anne Hodges Morgan, *Oklahoma, A History* (New York: Norton, 1977), 87.

18. Roosevelt quoted in Warren Beck, *New Mexico* (Norman: University of Oklahoma Press, 1962), 237.

19. For the chronology of primary election legislation see Charles Merriam and Louise Overaker, *Primary Elections,* rev. ed. (Chicago: University of Chicago Press, 1928), chap. 5.

20. For the chronology of the congressional battle over direct election, see C. H. Hoebeke, *The Road to Mass Democracy* (New Brunswick, N.J.: Transaction Publishers, 1995), chaps. 5–7.

21. *Lochner v. People of State of New York,* 198 U.S. 45, April 17, 1905; complete text including Holmes' dissent available online at Findlaw, URL: http://caselaw.lp.findlaw.com/scripts/getcase.pl?court=us&vol=198&invol=45.

22. Brandeis made the comment as a Supreme Court justice in his dissent to *Burns Baking v. Bryan,* 264 U.S. 504 (1924), available online at Findlaw, URL: http://www.findlaw.com/casecode/supreme.html.

23. The Brandeis brief in *Muller* is reprinted in Louis Brandeis and Josephine Goldmark, *Women in Industry* (1908; reprint, New York: Arno, 1969), 1ff. Most contemporary historians acknowledge Goldmark as the primary author of the factual section of the brief, research for which was done by National Consumer's League employees.

24. Trattner, *Crusade,* 106.

25. Trattner, *Crusade;* Kelley quoted 95 n. 1; Wald quoted 95.

26. Playground figures from Everett Bird Mero, *American Playgrounds* (Boston: American Gymnasia Co., 1908), 20–21.

27. North, "The Outlook for Statistical Science in the United States," presentation to the American Statistical Association, 1908, quoted in Fox, *Better City Government,* 77–78. This account of city budgeting and accounting relies on Fox, chap. 4.

28. Statistical information from Gladys Hansen, "Timeline of the San Francisco Earthquake," available online at

Museum of the City of San Francisco, URL: http://www.sfmuseum.org/hist10/06timeline.html. According to the Inflation Calculator, available online at URL: http://www.westegg.com/inflation, $500 million in 1906 would equal more than $9.7 billion in 2003.

29. Pardee quoted in Hansen, "Timeline," URL: http://www.sfmuseum.org/hist10/06timeline.html.

30. Kerr, *Organized for Prohibition,* 115.

31. Cherrington, *Evolution of Prohibition,* includes a detailed yearly chronology of liquor control legislation.

32. Blatch, speech to NAWSA's national convention in Buffalo, October 1908, Harper, ed., *History of Woman Suffrage,* vol. 5, 233.

33. Harriot Stanton Blatch and Alma Lutz, *Challenging Years* (New York: G. P. Putnam, 1940), 93. Blatch's comment referred to a 1907 meeting of young activists in New York.

34. Dorothy Schneider and Carl Schneider, *American Women in the Progressive Era, 1900–1920* (New York: Anchor Books, 1993), 168.

35. Information on Wisconsin clubs from Anne Firor Scott, *Natural Allies* (Urbana: University of Illinois Press, 1991), 163.

36. Scott speculates that the "curious absence" of information on municipal housekeeping is due to historians' attraction to situations of more evident conflict as well as a general cultural disposition to view women's groups as frivolous; *Natural Allies,* 157–58.

37. "They tell us . . .," speaker identified as Mrs. Gannett, a Unitarian minister's wife from Rochester, N.Y., Harper, ed., *History of Woman Suffrage,* vol. 5, 234; Breckinridge quote, 227. The 1908 NAWSA convention was held in Buffalo in October.

38. James Grossman, "A Chance to Make Good: 1900–1920," chap. 7 in *To Make Our World Anew,* ed. R. Kelley and E. Lewis (New York: Oxford University Press, 2000), 362.

39. In both Atlanta and Springfield, rioting was touched off by rumors that black men had attacked white women. In public discourse at the time, apologists for white supremacy constantly emphasized the threat to white women of the serious crime of sexual assault. Many whites came to believe that almost all lynchings were in retribution for sexual assault and defended vigilantism and rioting as justifiable responses to it. In fact, lynchings for sexual assaults represented only a minority of total lynchings. As Ida Wells Barnett first pointed out in the 1890s, the majority of lynching victims were accused of murder, assault (non-sexual), theft, or other offenses. See Wells-Barnett, *Mob Rule in New Orleans* [1900], in *On Lynchings* (1892, 1895, 1900; reprint, Amherst, N.Y.: Humanity Books, 2002), 201–03. A recent authoritative socio-historical study by Stewart

Tolnay and E.M. Beck, *A Festival of Violence* (Urbana: University of Illinois Press, 1995), determined that one-third of Southern lynching victims between 1880 and 1930 were accused of sexual assault or other sexual norm violations; the most frequent accusations were murder or nonsexual assault, which accounted for about 47 percent of all lynchings during the period overall. The percentage accused of rape was higher in the period 1880–1900 and declined markedly in the period 1900–1930, from 38 percent to 25 percent; see chap 2, especially Tables 2-6 and 2-7, 48–49.

40. DuBois, address to the second annual meeting of the Niagara Conference, Harpers Ferry, West Virginia, August 16, 1906. Available online at PBS's "Great American Speeches: 80 Years of Political Oratory." URL: http://www.pbs.org/greatspeeches/timeline/web_dubois_s.html.

41. Army report quoted in Gould, *Presidency of Theodore Roosevelt,* 239.

42. Roosevelt quoted in Gould, *Presidency of Theodore Roosevelt,* 238. This statement aroused great controversy in the black press.

43. Calculated from United States Bureau of the Census, *Historical Statistics of the United States,* Series C 89-119, Immigrants by Country, 1820–1970. See also Appendix C, Tables D and E, of this book.

44. Immigration Act of February 20, 1907, *United States Statutes at Large,* 59th Congress, vol. 34, 898ff.

45. Gompers to the AFL Convention, November 1906, *Samuel Gompers Papers,* ed. S. Kaufman *et al.,* vol. 7 (Urbana: University of Illinois Press, 1986), 140.

46. Forbes quoted in Chris Stirewalt, "Loss of Life Leads to Change," *West Virginia Daily Mail,* February 9, 1999, available online, URL: http://www.dailymail.com/static/specialsections/lookingback/lb0209.htm.

47. Haywood, speech at the First Convention of the Industrial Workers of the World (IWW), June 27, 1905, *Bill Haywood's Book* (1929; reprint, Westport, Conn: Greenwood Press, 1983), 181. IWW Preamble reprinted in *Bolshevik Propaganda* (Washington, D.C.: GPO, 1919), 1040.

48. J. Anthony Lukas, *Big Trouble* (New York: Simon and Schuster, 1997), 748. In his final chapter, however, Lukas suggests that Haywood and the other accused conspirators probably were responsible in the particular crime of Steunenberg's death. One of the attorneys representing the state at the trial was William Borah, later a prominent Republican Insurgent in the U.S. Senate.

49. Ryan, *A Living Wage* (New York: Macmillan, 1906), vii.

50. The early years of the Ford company are discussed in Douglas Brinkley, *Wheels for the World* (New York: Viking, 2003), chaps. 2–4: 1900–1908 auto totals, 118; Oldsmobile sales figures, 58; Model A sales figures, 68;

Model T price discussed, 110–11; Ford's famous quote (originally made probably in 1903), 113. The early advertised prices were stripped down base prices and most people chose to purchase add-ons. The name Model A was also given to a different and better known Ford in the later 1920s.

51. Eileen Bowser, *The Transformation of Cinema, 1907–1915* (Berkeley: University of California Press, 1990), 2.

52. Forest Reserve Act, March 3, 1891, *United States Statutes at Large,* 51st Congress, vol. 26, 1103.

53. Pinchot, *Breaking New Ground,* (1947; reprint, Washington, D.C.: Island Press, 1987), 259.

54. Roosevelt, special message to Congress, February 13, 1907, quoted in Samuel Hays, *Conservation and the Gospel of Efficiency* (1959; reprint, Pittsburgh: University of Pittsburgh Press, 1999), 85.

55. Roosevelt, *Autobiography,* 419.

56. Invitation dated November 11, 1907, quoted in Morris, *Theodore Rex,* 500.

57. Roosevelt, *Autobiography,* 563.

58. Taft quoted in Paola Coletta, "Election of 1908," in *History of American Presidential Elections, 1789–2001,* vol. 5 (Philadelphia: Chelsea House Publishers, 2001), 2062.

59. Coletta, "Election of 1908," 2078, 2082. By October 50,000 people had contributed about $250,000.

CHAPTER 6

1. *Inaugural Addresses of the Presidents of the United States* (Washington, DC: GPO, 1952), 213–14.

2. Tariff rates, Link and Catton, *American Epoch,* vol. 1, 97. Senator Robert La Follette of Wisconsin, Republican insurgent, reviewed tariff changes in Senate debate, June 3, 1909, *Congressional Record,* 61st Congress, 1st session, vol. 44, pp. 2682–2696. The following day lengthy schedules were introduced, pp. 2752–2832, summary table 2821.

3. Federal insurance on deposits in private banks was not established until the 1930s.

4. Roosevelt letter to Taft, June 8, 1910, quoted in Paolo Coletta, *The Presidency of William Howard Taft* (Lawrence: University Press of Kansas, 1973), 105.

5. George E. Mowry, "Election of 1912," in *History of American Presidential Elections, 1789–2001,* Vol. 6: *1912–1924,* ed. A. M. Schlesinger, Jr., and F. M. Israel (Philadelphia: Chelsea House Publishers, 2002), 2040.

6. Herbert Croly, *The Promise of American Life* (New York: Macmillan, 1909, 1912), 22.

7. Croly, *Promise,* 154.

8. Taft quoted in Mowry, "Election of 1912," 2141.

9. DePew, January 24, 1911, *Congressional Record,* 61st Congress, 3rd session, vol. 46, 1336.

10. The Hetch Hetchy controversy is described in Stephen Fox, *John Muir and his Legacy* (Boston: Little, Brown, 1981), chap. 4; Muir quoted 143, Phelan quoted 142.

11. Calculated from *Historical Statistics of the United States,* Series C 89–119, Immigrants by Country, 1820–1970; see also Appendix C, Tables D and E, of this volume.

12. United States Immigration Commission, *Abstracts of Reports of the Immigration Commission,* vol. 1 (Washington, D.C.: GPO, 1911), 24.

13. United States Immigration Commission, *Abstracts,* 44. Boas's study was entitled *Changes in Bodily Form of Descendants of Immigrants.*

14. United States Immigration Commission, *Abstracts,* 25.

15. United States Immigration Commission, "Recommendations," *Abstracts,* 45–48; quote from 47.

16. John Higham, *Strangers in the Land* (2nd ed.; New York: Atheneum, 1970), 187; this account draws on Higham's discussion of restrictionists and anti-restrictionists in chap. 7. James J. Hill quoted in Morris, *Theodore Rex,* 484; the comment was made to Finley Peter Dunne.

17. Burnham's motto was quoted in Charles Moore, *Daniel H. Burnham, Architect, Planner of Cities,* vol. 2 (Boston: Houghton Mifflin, 1921), 147, although its complete origins are unclear. See Thomas Hines, *Burnham of Chicago, Architect and Planner* (New York: Oxford University Press, 1974), 401, note 8.

18. W. E. B. DuBois, *Autobiography of W. E. B. DuBois* (N.p.: International Publishers, 1968), 258.

19. California statistics from Eleanor Flexner, *Century of Struggle,* rev. ed. (Cambridge: Harvard University Press, Belknap, 1959, 1975), 265.

20. *Women's Journal* quoted in Harper, *et al,* eds., *History of Woman Suffrage,* vol. 5, 332–33; Flexner, *Century of Struggle,* 265.

21. ICC estimate quoted in Pegram, *Battling Demon Rum,* 132.

22. *The Social Evil in Chicago* (Chicago: Gunthorp-Warren Printing Company, 1911; reprint, New York: Arno Press, 1970), 32–33.

23. The choice some women made to work as prostitutes is discussed in Rosen, *Lost Sisterhood,* especially chap. 8; and in Ruth Rosen and Sue Davidson, eds., introduction to *The Maimie Papers* (Old Westbury, N.Y.: Feminist Press, 1977).

24. Speech to the Society of Sanitary and Moral Prophylaxis, December 22, 1910, Edwin Seligman, ed., *The Social Evil,* 2nd ed. rev. (New York: G.P. Putman's Sons, 1912), 249–51.

25. Rosen, *The Lost Sisterhood,* 116, 133. Rosen discusses prostitutes' ethnicity in chap. 8; Connelly, *Response to Prostitution* discusses immigration, ethnicity, and procurers in chap. 3. On prostitution and the Jewish community, see Charlotte Baum, Paula Hyman, and Sonya

Michel, *The Jewish Woman in America* (New York: New American Library, 1975), 170–75; and Howard Sachar, *A History of the Jews in America* (New York: Alfred A. Knopf, 1992), 164–68.

26. "The Pittsburgh Survey," *Charities and the Commons* 22 (March 7, 1908): 1666.

27. Information on state laws and NCLC membership from Trattner, *Crusade,* 114–16.

28. Act establishing the Children's Bureau, April 9, 1912, *U.S. Statutes at Large,* 62nd Congress, vol. 37, part 1, 79–80.

29. About 1,000 children were institutionalized in 1890; by the early 1920s that number had grown to over 205,000, according to LeRoy Ashby, *Endangered Children* (New York: Twayne Publishers, 1997), 84.

30. "Letter to the President of the United States Embodying the Conclusions on the Conference on the Care of Dependent Children," reprinted in Robert Bremner *et al.,* eds., *Children and Youth in America,* vol. 2, part 1 (Cambridge, Mass.: Harvard University Press, 1971), 365.

31. "Letter to the President," Bremner *et al.,* eds., *Children and Youth,* 365.

32. The century-old Marine Hospital Service had been founded to prevent communicable diseases from being imported by merchant ships and later conducted medical inspections of immigrants. "Marine" in this case meant "sea-going," not a branch of the military.

33. Tuberculosis death statistics available online at Population Reference Bureau, URL: http://www.prb.org/Content/NavigationMenu/PRB/Educators/Human_Population/Health2/World_Health1.htm

34. Cooper Union was founded in the 19th century to offer what today would be called engineering degrees, to working people who had little access to traditional higher education. The People's Institute, under the direction of a former Columbia professor, was a reform initiative that offered a wide and vigorous program of educational, political, social, and even religious courses and forums. The buildings were also widely used for community meetings.

35. Market share information from Robert Sklar, *Movie-Made America* (New York: Random House, 1975), 37.

36. Bowser, *Transformation of Cinema,* chap. 10, especially 151–52, 162.

37. According to the United States Senate report on the disaster, the ship carried 2,223 passengers and crew, of which 706 were rescued: 60 percent of the first class passengers, 42 percent of the second class passengers, 25 percent of the third class or steerage passengers, and 24 percent of the crew. The official British report has slightly higher passenger totals, and calculates that 39 percent of third class passengers survived. Both official reports are available online at Titanic Inquiry Project, URL: http://www.titanicinquiry.org/index.html.

38. James Green, *The World of the Worker* (New York: Hill and Wang, 1980), 67.

39. Priscilla Murolo and A. B. Chitty, *From the Folks Who Brought You the Weekend* (New York: New Press, 2001), 145.

40. By 1913 single issue printings of the *Appeal* sometimes reached as high as 4.1 million; John Graham, ed., *"Yours for the Revolution"* (Lincoln: University of Nebraska University, 1990), x, 1, 12. Statistics on offices held, Maury Klein and Harvey Kantor, *Prisoners of Progress* (New York: Macmillan, 1976), 288.

41. Lemlich's words are quoted widely with variations; see, for example, "The Cooper Union Meeting," page 1 news report in *The Call,* a socialist newspaper in New York, November 23, 1909.

42. Green, *World of the Worker,* 71–72.

43. The most complete list of the victims is in David Von Drehle, *Triangle* (New York: Atlantic Monthly Press, 2003), 269–83. Von Drehle's count of casualties is 146, six of whom have never been identified.

44. Historians often call Lawrence the "Bread and Roses strike," in the belief that the popular labor slogan was first used there. That fact is now disputed. See Jim Zwick, "Bread and Roses: The Lost Histories of a Slogan and a Poem," available online at Bread and Roses (URL: http://www.boondocksnet.com/labor/history/bread-and-roses-history.html).

45. Taft, Message to Congress, February 2, 1912, *Messages and Papers of the Presidents* (Bureau of National Literature, 1917), vol. 16, 7727.

46. James Weinstein, *The Corporate Ideal in the Liberal State* (Boston: Beacon Press, 1968); thesis stated ix.

47. The term *disaster* is used for a mining accident that takes five or more lives. Statistics calculated from data available online at "Historical Mine Disasters," National Institute for Occupation Safety and Health, URL: http://www.cdc.gov/niosh/mining/data/disall.html#1890, updated December 28, 2001; other data at "Historical Data on Mine Disasters in the United States," Mine Safety and Health Administration, URL: http://www.msha.gov/mshainfo/factsheet/mshafct8.htm, downloaded September 1, 2003.

48. The Bureau of Mines received inspection authority in 1941; it was disbanded in 1996 as a cost-cutting measure.

49. Figures quoted in Weinstein, *Corporate Ideal,* 40.

50. Crystal Eastman, *Work Accidents and the Law* (New York: Charities Publication Committee, 1910), 165. NAM poll discussed in Weinstein, *Corporate Ideal,* 47.

51. Chronology of state employers' liability and workmen's compensation laws from Harry Weiss, "Employers' Lia-

bility and Workmen's Compensation," in *History of Labour in the United States,* vol. 4, ed. J. R. Commons, *et al.* (New York: Macmillan, 1935), 564–610.

52. Frederick W. Taylor, *The Principles of Scientific Management* (New York: Harper Brothers, 1911), 10.

53. Taylor, *Principles,* 140.

54. Taylor, *Principles,* 7.

55. New Mexico enabling act, also called the Hamilton Act, June 20, 1910, *United States Statutes at Large,* 61st Congress, vol. 36, part 1, 569–70.

56. Edwin M. Bacon and Morrill Wyman, *Direct Elections and Law-Making by Popular Vote* (Boston: Houghton Mifflin, 1912), 54.

57. Fred Wayne Catlett, "The Working of the Recall in Seattle," in *Initiative, Referendum, and Recall* (Philadelphia: American Academy of Political and Social Science, 1912), 230.

58. Thomas Cronin, *Direct Democracy* (Cambridge: Harvard University Press, 1989), 133.

59. Archbishop John Ireland, *Minneapolis Journal,* October 12, 1911, in *Selected Articles on the Recall,* ed. E. Phelps (White Plains, N.Y.: H. W. Wilson, 1913), 54.

60. Representative George Legaré, Democrat of South Carolina, debate over judicial recall in the Arizona constitution, May 16, 1911, *Congressional Record,* 62nd Congress, 2nd Session, vol. 48, 1252. Since 1920 only three more states have approved state wide recall and two more recall excluding judges, although a total of 36 permit some limited use of the recall device (in cities of certain size, for example); see table in Cronin, *Direct Democracy,* 126–27.

61. Taft, Special Message to Congress, January 26, 1911, *Canadian Reciprocity,* 61st Congress, 3rd session, Senate Doc. no. 787, vii.

62. Champ Clark, February 14, 1911, *Congressional Record,* 61st Congress, 3rd session, vol. 46, 2520.

63. Roosevelt made the comment February 21, 1912, to reporters in Cleveland, on his way to deliver a speech in Columbus where he announced his intentions more formally; quoted in Page Smith, *America Enters the World* (New York: McGraw-Hill, 1985), 302.

64. Thirteen states held presidential primaries in 1912 but the results of one of them, New York, are not available; see *Presidential Elections, 1789–1992* (Washington, D.C.: Congressional Quarterly, 1995), 148–150.

65. Mowry, "Election of 1912," 2145.

66. Arthur Link, *Woodrow Wilson and the Progressive Era* (New York: Harper and Row, 1954), 13.

67. Roosevelt's comment reported in William Allen White, *Autobiography* (New York: Macmillan, 1946), 482; White continues, "From that hour we, who followed in his train, were Bull Moosers, and proud of it."

68. Beveridge quoted in Smith, *America Enters the World,* 334.

69. Theodore Roosevelt, "Confession of Faith," delivered August 6, 1912, to the Progressive party convention, Chicago, *Works,* vol. 17, 254, 265, 299.

70. Resolution quoted in Salvatore, *Eugene V. Debs,* 255.

71. Woodrow Wilson, *The New Freedom* (New York: Doubleday, Page, 1913), 198.

Chapter 7

1. As part of that change Southerners, who dominated the Democratic Party at the time, held many high offices for the first time in over half a century. Wilson himself was born in Virginia and raised in the South; many of his cabinet members and advisers as well as the chief justice of the Supreme Court were southerners by birth.

2. Address of Wilson to Congress, April 8, 1913, *Congressional Record,* 63rd Congress, 1st session, vol. 50, 130ff.

3. Wilson's statement to the press, May 26, 1913, Associated Press Dispatch, reprinted in Commager, ed., *Documents of American History,* vol. 2, 87.

4. According to William Link and Arthur Link, the overall average of the Underwood duties was about 29 percent, as contrasted to 37 to 40 percent under the Payne-Aldrich Act. *American Epoch,* vol. 1, 7th ed. (New York: McGraw-Hill, 1993), 104.

5. Average income figures from Douglass, *Real Wages,* Table 147, n.p.; also see above, Chapter 2, note 2. The Bureau of Internal Revenue was given an appropriation to collect the tax and within a year had some 350 tax collectors at work. The first form, given the number 1040, was three pages long, with one additional page of instructions, numbered one through 20. The original 1913 form is available online at Tax History Project, URL: http://www.taxhistory.org/Articles/1913_form_1040.htm

6. Wilson to Mary Allen Hulbert, June 22, 1913; he continued, "Fortunately, my heart has formed no habit of failing." *The Papers of Woodrow Wilson,* ed. Arthur Link, 69 vols. (Princeton, N.J.: Princeton University Press, 1966–1994), vol. 27, 556.

7. Speech to join session of Congress, June 23, 1913, *Papers,* vol. 27, 572–73.

8. Section 6 of the Clayton Anti-Trust Act, October 15, 1914, *U.S. Statutes at Large,* 63rd Congress, vol. 38, 730ff.

9. Link, *Woodrow Wilson and the Progressive Era,* 64; Washingtons letter, August 10, 1913, quoted 65. Full text of letter, *Papers,* vol. 28, 186–88.

10. Editorial by Frank Cobb, November 13, 1914, quoted in Link, *Woodrow Wilson and the Progressive Era,* 65; the

World was owned by Oswald Garrison Villard, a founder of the NAACP. Wilson, raised in a genteel Southern ministerial family, shared in the paternalistic racial attitudes common to his class. In a letter to the editor of the influential Christian publication *Congregationalist,* for example, he stated the policy was "in the interest of the colored people, as exempting them from friction and criticism." Overall during his administration the number of black civil servants decreased from about 6 to 5 percent, although their actual number increased due to the overall growth of federal government. See Kendrick Clements, *The Presidency of Woodrow Wilson* (Lawrence: University Press of Kansas, 1992), 45–46.

11. This much-cited comment was made to E. G. Conklin, quoted in Ray Stannard Baker, *Woodrow Wilson: Life and Letters,* vol. 6 (Garden City, N.Y.: Doubleday, Page, 1927–39), 55.

12. John Milton Cooper, Jr., *Pivotal Decades: The United States, 1900–1920* (New York: W. W. Norton, 1900), 223.

13. Link defines missionary diplomacy in *Woodrow Wilson and the Progressive Era,* chap. 4, 81ff.; Wilson to Sir William Tyrrell, November 22, 1913, quoted 119.

14. Statistics from Nell Irvin Painter, *Standing at Armageddon* (New York: W. W. Norton, 1987), 285–6.

15. Baker, *Woodrow Wilson,* vol. 4, 242.

16. Barbara Rose, *American Art Since 1900* (Rev. ed.; New York: Praeger, 1975), 49.

17. Quoted in Rose, *American Art,* 52.

18. Theodore Roosevelt, "A Layman's Views of an Art Exhibition," *Outlook* 103 (March 29, 1913): 718.

19. Webb-Kenyon Act, March 1, 1913, *United States Statutes at Large,* 62nd Congress, vol. 37, 699.

20. Cherrington quoted in Austin Kerr, *Organized for Prohibition* (New Haven: Yale University Press, 1985), 137. Cherrington was general manager of the ASL's publications arm and one of the league's chief strategists.

21. This account relies on Kerr, *Organized for Prohibition,* pp. 187ff.

22. The resolution was drafted by ASL-affiliated lawyers and officials including Wayne Wheeler, the league's master lobbyist and best known public figure. In the House, it did not reach the necessary majority. In the Senate, it did not come to a vote before the 64th Congress ended in early 1917.

23. WCTU membership statistics from Kerr, *Organized for Prohibition,* 158–59; Blocker, *American Temperance Movements,* 116.

24. This account of the accumulating scientific and sociological evidence relies on Timberlake, *Prohibition,* chaps. 2 and 3; Massachusetts General Hospital statistics and psychiatrist's convention quoted 47.

25. Kerr discusses the industries in *Organized for Prohibition,* chap. 7; quote from 160.

26. *Women's Journal and Suffrage News,* Saturday, March 3, 1913, page 1; the *Journal* was published by NAWSA.

27. Schneider and Schneider, *American Women,* 180.

28. Article 2, Section 2, of the Constitution permits state legislatures to establish the manner in which presidential electors are selected. Electors, who meet formally as the electoral college to officially complete a presidential election, represent the electoral vote that each state can cast in a presidential election. Since the electors are decided by the electoral vote, which is in turn decided by the popular vote, suffragists argued that the state legislature had the right to pass a law permitting women to cast ballots in presidential elections. Like most industrial states east of the Mississippi, Illinois had not passed the direct democracy reform of initiative and referendum, which would have enabled citizens to demand a referendum on suffrage.

29. Progressive platform, Kirk Porter and Donald Johnson, eds, *National Party Platforms, 1840–1964* (Urbana: University of Illinois Press, 1966), 175ff.

30. This account of the Americanization movement relies on Edward Hartmann, *The Movement to Americanize the Immigrant* (New York: Columbia University Press, 1948), the most detailed history of the movement. New York bureau quote, State of New York, Bureau of Industries and Immigration, *First Annual Report . . . for the Twelve Months Ended September 30, 1911,* quoted in Hartmann, 69 n.

31. Series Q 148–162, Motor-Vehicle Factory Sales and Registration . . . 1900 to 1970, *Historical Statistics of the States of the United States,* vol. 2 (Westport, Conn.: Greenwood Press, 1993), 716.

32. Edward Steiner, *From Alien to Citizen* (New York: Fleming H. Revel, 1914), 285.

33. Comparative wage figures cited in Brinkley, *Wheels for the World,* 162–63.

34. Brinkley, *Wheels for the World,* 164.

35. Worker quoted in Brinkley, *Wheels for the World,* 173; from an oral history project conducted by Ford Museum and Library, Dearborn, Michigan.

36. Letter dated October 21, 1913, quoted online at The Rockefellers (URL: http://www.pbs.org/wgbh/amex/rockefellers/sfeature/sf 8.html).

37. "neutral in fact . . .", Message to the Senate, August 18, 1914, *Papers,* vol. 30, 393–94. Letter to his adviser Edward House, August 3, 1914, *Papers,* vol. 30, 336. Other neutral countries were Spain, Albania, Switzerland, Netherlands, and the Scandinavian nations.

38. Bryan quoted in Robert Cherny, *A Righteous Cause* (Boston: Little, Brown, 1985), 145.

39. The phrase "waging neutrality" is Thomas Bailey's, in *A Diplomatic History of the American People,* 10th ed. (Engle-

wood Cliffs, NJ: Prentice-Hall, 1980), where it is the title of chap. 38, 563ff.

40. Schneider and Schneider, *American Women,* 196–97; the quotations are from the preamble to the party's platform, written by Anna Garlin Spencer.

41. Millet and Malinowski, *For the Common Defense,* 324.

42. Letter of Bryan to Wilson, August 10, 1914, *Papers,* vol. 30, 372. The letter was in response to inquiry to the State Department by J.P. Morgan, asking if the government would object to loans to France.

43. Wilson's veto of the literacy test, January 28, 1915, *Congressional Record,* 63rd Congress, 3rd session, vol. 52, 2481–82.

44. On February 18, 1915, *The Birth of a Nation* was screened for the president, reportedly the first film ever shown in the White House. Wilson is widely quoted as having remarked, "It is like writing history with lightning. And my only regret is that it is all so terribly true." Today the comment even appears in most prints of the film. However, the source of the quote is uncertain and the president's secretary, Joe Tumulty, wrote to the Boston branch of the NAACP, "The President was entirely unaware of the nature of the play before it was presented and at no time has expressed his approbation of it." See film critic Robert Ebert's review, March 30, 2003, available online at *Chicago Sun-Times* (URL: http://www.suntimes.com/ebert/greatmovies/birthofanation.html).

45. David Levering Lewis, *W. E. B. DuBois* (New York: Henry Holt, 1993), 507. Protests resumed when the film was rereleased in the 1920s and 1930s. The major black roles in the film were actually played by white actors in blackface.

46. DuBois quoted in Lewis, *W. E. B. DuBois,* 507.

47. U.S. House of Representatives Report No. 1411, February 16, 1915, which reports that the Committee on Education unanimously recommended H.R. 14895, to create the Federal Motion Picture Commission.

48. *Mutual Film Corporation v. Ohio Industrial Commission,* February 23, 1915, 236 US 230, available online at Findlaw (URL: http://www.findlaw.com/casecode/supreme.html).

49. The 1952 movie censorship case, *Burstyn v. Wilson,* 343 U.S. 495 (often referred to as the *Miracle* case because it involved a film of that name) declared, "it cannot be doubted that the movies are a significant medium for communication of ideas." See Richard Randall, *Censorship of the Movies* (Madison: University of Wisconsin Press, 1968), chap. 1.

50. Note wired to James Watson Gerrard, ambassador in Berlin, February 10, 1915, under Bryan's signature; draft by Wilson, February 6, *Papers,* vol. 32, 195.

51. Draft of note, June 7, 1915, *Papers,* vol. 32, 359; the note was sent June 9 under the signature of Bryan's replacement as secretary of state, Robert Lansing.

52. Between 1914 and 1916 trade with the Central Powers declined from $169 million to $1.2 million, and with the Allied increased from $825 million to $3.2 billion according to William Link and Arthur Link, American Epoch, vol. 1, 7th ed. (New York: McGraw-Hill, 1993), 134.

53. An army reserve was first officially established by an act of Congress in the Reserve Act of 1912; a Medical Reserve Corps had been established earlier in 1908. The purpose of the 1912 act was to permit regulars to shorten their active term of service; two years later it had only sixteen members. See Millett and Maslowski, *For the Common Defense,* 314.

54. Wilson speech, May 10, 1915, *Papers,* vol. 33, 149. Although this speech is an eloquent defense of America as a nation of many peoples, it was delivered one week after the *Lusitania* incident and is most remembered for two sentences: "There is such a thing as a man being too proud to fight. There is such a thing as a nation being so right that it does not need to convince others by force that it is right." *Survey* article, "Americanization Day in 150 Communities," July 31, 1915, quoted in Hartmann, 121. The Federal Bureau of Naturalization was established in 1906 to standardize procedures throughout the nation, which at the time varied widely from state to state.

55. *The Passing of the Great Race* had multiple printings, new editions in 1918, 1920, and 1921, and translations into German, French, and Norwegian. Editions printed after America entered the war downplayed the Germanic roots of Anglo-Saxons.

56. Nearly half the money was used up in litigation and settlements with Leslie's relatives. The remainder became available at the beginning of 1917. Leslie, who died September 18, 1914, had made very small contributions to the suffrage cause previously but had not been notably active in it; see Flexner, *Century of Struggle,* 282. The will is reprinted in Harper, *et al,* eds., *History of Woman Suffrage,* vol. 5, 755.

57. Flexner, *Century of Struggle,* 283.

58. Figures from Link, *Woodrow Wilson and the Progressive Era,* 160.

59. Alfred Runte, *National Parks* (Lincoln: University of Nebraska Press, 1979), chap. 5; Soo brochure quoted 82.

60. Quoted in Barry Mackintosh, *Interpretation in the National Park Service,* 1986, chap. 1, available online at URL: http://www.cr.nps.gov/history/online_books/mackintosh2/index.htm Updated July 9, 2000.

61. Act to Establish a National Park Service, August 25, 1916, 39 Stat. 535, in Lary Dilsaver, ed., *America's*

National Park System (Lanham, Md.: Rowman & Little-field, 1994), available online at National Park Service History Online Books (URL: http://www.cr.nps.gov/history/online_books/anps/index.htm Updated October 25, 2000).

62. William Allen White, *Autobiography,* 513; the comment was made after the 1914 elections. Always the martial enthusiast, Roosevelt lost interest in reform as his interest in military preparedness increased, whether or not his fellow progressives did.

63. Arthur Link and William Leary, Jr., "Election of 1916," in *History of American Presidential Elections,* 1789–2001, vol. 6: 1912–1924, ed. A. M. Schlesinger, Jr., and F. M. Israel (Philadelphia: Chelsea House, 2002), 2261.

64. This account of the Keating-Owens bill relies on Trattner, *Crusade,* chap. 5, especially 122–132; vote tally 128. The only negative vote was a Republican congressman from New Jersey.

65. Party platforms in Porter and Johnson, eds., *National Party Platforms;* Democrats' comment on child labor in the "Labor" plank, 199; Republican statement favoring the enactment and rigid enforcement of a federal child labor law in "Labor Laws" plank, 207.

66. Letter dated July 19, 1916, *Papers,* vol. 37, 436.

67. *New York Tribune* quoted in Trattner, *Crusade,* 132. Wilson's speech, delivered at Long Branch, New Jersey, September 2, 1916, *Papers,* vol. 39, 127 and 130.

68. These commonly cited figures were published in Owen Lovejoy, "What Remains of Child Labor," *New Republic* 9 (November 11, 1916), 39.

69. On the Catholic hierarchy's opposition to Philippine independence see Link, 354; the Jones Act is discussed 350ff.

70. "assist the world," Democratic party platform "International Relations" plank, Porter and Johnson, eds., *National Party Platforms,* 196. Bryan quoted in Link and Leary, "Election of 1916," 2254.

71. Harding quoted in Link and Leary, "Election of 1916," 2249.

72. Statement in the Congressional Union's weekly publication *The Suffragist,* September 30, 1916, quoted in Flexner, *Century of Struggle,* 287.

73. The story is related in Flexner, *Century of Struggle,* 289.

Chapter 8

1. Comment made to Secretary of the Navy Josephus Daniels, quoted in Baker, *Life and Letters,* vol. 6, 258.

2. Wilson's note quoted in Bailey, *Diplomatic History,* 590.

3. Wilson's speech, Senate Document 685, 64th Congress, 2nd sess. Tillman quoted in Bailey, *Diplomatic History,* 590.

4. Bailey, *Diplomatic History,* 590.

5. Zimmermann telegram available online at Our Documents (URL: http://www.ourdocuments.gov/content.php?doc=60, downloaded March 15, 2004); Wilson's speech to Congress February 26, 1917, quoted in Baker, *Woodrow Wilson,* vol. 7, 476; Wilson's "willful men" comment quoted in Bailey, *Diplomatic History,* 592.

6. Address Delivered at Joint Session of the Two Houses of Congress, April 2, 1917, 65th Congress, 1st Session, Senate Doc. 5.

7. Historians have also disagreed about the reasons for America's entry into World War I. Many agree that America could have followed a stricter policy of neutrality and perhaps avoided the eventuality of war. But beyond that, explanations vary. Many historians conclude that German aggression and decisions on submarine warfare did precipitate, if they did not make inevitable, America's entry into the war. Some historians maintain that financial and economic interests, working through propaganda campaigns, drove the nation into war, or that Wilson himself chose to enter the war to protect them from loss since they were heavily invested in the Allies. Some historians focus on Wilson himself as the motive force. Some have seen him as a naive idealist and some have written off his noble sentiments as sheer propaganda. But others defend his strong conception of right and duty and his genuine belief that it was necessary to establish a new basis of world order in the 20th century.

8. Rankin quoted in Norma Smith, *Jeannette Rankin* (Helena: Montana Historical Society Press, 2002), 113. Rankin was defeated in the next election round, although probably less because of her stand on the war than her defense of Colorado workers in their battle with copper mining companies. In 1940, she was returned to the House and cast the sole "no" vote on the resolution to enter World War II, thus achieving the distinction of being the only Congressional representative to vote against both great conflicts of the 20th century.

9. Clark quoted in Cooper, *Pivotal Decades,* 271.

10. Statistics from Link and Link, *American Epoch,* 146.

11. Statistics from Link and Link, *American Epoch,* 152.

12. Baruch quoted in Cooper, *Pivotal Decades,* 291.

13. The Huns were a warlike tribe from Asia who invaded Europe in the fourth and fifth centuries, overrunning what remained of Roman civilization. Few Germans had lines of descent from the Huns, although modern Hungarians did. Prussia was the leading German-speaking state prior to and after the formation of the nation of Germany and was well known for its militarism.

14. Paul Murphy, *World War I and the Origin of Civil Liberties in the United States* (New York: Norton, 1979), 90.

15. The Supreme Court eventually overturned Berger's conviction on a technicality, and he was returned to

Congress for three more terms, despite the attempts of Congress to expel him. Debs' conviction was upheld—he ran for president from prison in 1920—but his sentence was commuted by President Warren G. Harding in 1921 and he was released.

16. Schenck v. United States, March 3, 1919, 249 U.S. 47; *Abrams v. United States,* November 10, 1919, 250 US 616, both available online at Findlaw (URL: http://www.findlaw.com/casecode/sgpreme.html).

17. American casualty totals from the Department of Defense, DIOR [Directorate of Information Operations and Reports], Table 2–23, Principal Wars in Which The United States Participated, available online at URL: http://webl.whs.osd.mil/mmid/mOl/SMS223R.HTM. The figures cover the period from April 1, 1917, to December 31, 1918, and include troops stationed in Russia. Statistics for other nations cited in Berkin, *et al., Making America,* 689.

18. Statistics from Link and Link, *American Epoch,* 146.

19. Statistics on African-American soldiers, Berkin, *et al., Making America,* 687.

20. Statistics on nurses, Lettie Gavin, *American Women in World War I* (Niwot: University Press of Colorado, 1997), 43–44 and 66–67, n. 1.

21. War department memo quoted in Mattie Treadwell, *The Women's Army Corps* (Washington, D.C.: Center of Military History, 1954, 1991, available online at URL: http://www.army.mil/cmh-pa/books/wwii/Wac/chOl.htm, page created August 23, 2002).

22. Statistics from Gavin, *American Women,* 2, 26.

23. Woodrow Wilson's Fourteen Points, address to Congress January 8, 1918, available online at Our Documents (URL: http://www.ourdocuments.gov/content.php?doc=62, downloaded April 3, 2004).

24. Alfred Crosby, Jr., *Epidemic and Peace, 1918* (Westport, Conn.: Greenwood Press, 1976): rates of infection in Spain, 26; incidence in American population and deaths among soldiers (for every one soldier who died in battle or of wounds or poison gas, 1.02 died of disease), 205–206. Other statistics from Molly Billings, "The Influenza Pandemic of 1918," available online at URL:http://www.stanford.edu/aroug/virus/uda/. Downloaded March 15, 2004.

25. This account of the CTCA relies on Connelly, *Response to Prostitution,* chaps. 7 and 8, 136–153; Baker quoted 139; "America is the land . . .," Edward Frank Allen, *Keeping our Fighters Fit to Fight* (New York: Century, 1918), 140–41.

26. Chamberlain-Kahn Act, July 9, 1918, *U.S. Statutes at Large,* 65th Congress, vol. 40, 886–87.

27. Prohibitionist quoted in Timberlake, *Prohibition, 179.*

28. *The Independent,* May 26, 1917, quoted in Timberlake, *Prohibition,* 174.

29. Wheeler, "The Inside Story of Prohibition's Adoption," *New York Times,* March 29, 1926, 21, one of seven serial articles "telling the Anti-Saloon League's version" of the Eighteenth Amendment's passage published in the *Times* and the *St. Louis Globe-Democrat* in March and April, 1926.

30. Carrie Chapman Catt and Nettie Rogers Shuler, *Woman Suffrage and Politics* (New York: Scribner's Sons, 1926), 317–18.

31. Doris Stevens. *Jailed for Freedom* (1920; new edition Troutdale, Oreg.: New Sage Press, 1995), 69.

32. Statistics from Flexner, *Century of Struggle, 295.*

33. The National Woman's Party claimed credit for the advances because the pickets inspired constant front page newspaper reports and kept the subject in the public eye. Carrie Chapman Catt remained publicly unsympathetic to the pickets and in private both NAWSA and members of Congress who supported suffrage, including Congresswoman Jeanette Rankin, believed it made their work more difficult.

34. Roosevelt's letter to the Republican National Committee was first reported in the *New York Times,* "Roosevelt Calls for Suffrage Amendment," January 4, 1918, 11; Wilson's statement, given to the press January 9, quoted in Baker, *Woodrow Wilson,* vol. 7, 458.

35. Rankin in the *Congressional Record,* quoted in Smith, *Jeannette Rankin,* 124.

36. Wilson address to the Senate, September 30, 1918, Congressional Record, 65th Congress, vol. 56, 2nd session, 10928–29.

37. Anne Firor Scott and Andrew Scott, *One Half the People* (Philadelphia: J.B. Lippincott, 1975), 25.

38. Catt quoted in Flexner, *Century of Struggle,* 311–12.

39. Quoted in Trattner, *Crusade,* 137.

40. *Bailey v. Drexel Furniture Company,* May 15, 1922, 259 US 42.

41. Roger Daniels, *Coming to America* (New York: Harper-Collins, 1990), 278.

42. Daniels, *Coming to America,* 278–79. Daniels notes that the limited effect was largely due to rising standards of literacy in Europe.

43. Statistics for residents in 1917, Higham, *Strangers in the Land,* 213; internment in America, Mitchel Yockelson, "The War Department: Keeper of Our Nation's Enemy Aliens During World War I," available online at URL: http://www.lib.byu.edu/-rdh/wwi/comment/yockel.htm; Canada, Alvin Finkel and Margaret Conrad, *History of the Canadian Peoples,* vol. 2 (2nd ed.; Toronto: Copp Clark, 1998), 210.

44. *Missionary Review of the World* 41 (1918): 803, quoted in Higham, *Strangers in the Land,* 217.

45. Higham, *Strangers in the Land,* 216.

46. Out-migration statistics, Stewart Tolnay and E.M. Beck, "Rethinking the Role of Racial Violence in the Great Migration," 20; city increases, Carole Marks, "Social and Economic Life of Southern Blacks During the Migration," 46, both in *Black Exodus,* ed. A. Harrison (Jackson: University Press of Mississippi, 1991). Other statistics from *Africana,* ed. K. A. Appiah and H. L. Gates, Jr. (New York: Basic Civitas Books, 1999), "The Great Migration," 869–72.

47. *The Survey,* 1919, quoted in Marks, "Social and Economic Life," 48.

48. Statistics, Link and Link, *American Epoch,* 177.

49. Strike total, Link and Link, *American Epoch,* 177. Union membership, Taft, *Organized Labor,* 319. Taft points out that there were actually more strikes in 1917 (4,450) than in 1919, but in 1919 the number of workers affected was about 3.5 times larger; *Organized Labor,* 341ff.

50. Coolidge statement to Gompers printed in "Gov. Coolidge's Reply to Samuel Gompers," *Boston Globe,* September 15, 1919, 1.

51. Chicago statistics, Link and Link, *American Epoch,* 182; Elaine, Arkansas, statistics, Tindall, *America,* 980.

52. Statistics, Link and Link, *American Epoch,* 182.

53. Statistics, Link and Link, *American Epoch,* 180. Since communists considered their theories to be a form of socialism, use of the two words in the late Progressive era can be confusing. Marx and Engels used the word *communism* to describe their program because at the time they wrote in the mid-19th century, the word *socialism* was also used generically to refer to any program of social and economic reform. But their followers usually used the term *scientific socialism* instead, until Lenin revived the word *communism.* Very generally, after that date communists held that all property should be held in common and all goods distributed on the basis of need; those who still called themselves socialists usually held that important productive facilities should be owned by society and that goods should be distributed "justly" in reward for the work performed.

54. Statistics, Link and Link, *American Epoch,* 179–80.

55. Bombing deaths, Cooper, *Pivotal Decades,* 330.

56. Taft and Roosevelt quoted in Harold Seymour, *Baseball,* vol. 2 (New York: Oxford University Press, 1971), 274. Veeck quoted in "Warned of Fixed Game, Says Veeck; Demands Inquiry," *Chicago Herald and Examiner,* October 5, 1920, 1–2; it was Veeck's demands for an inquiry into a Cubs-Phillies game that unearthed the evidence and confessions in the Black Sox scandal.

57. *Chicago Herald and Tribune,* September 30, 1920, quoted online at 1919 Black Sox (URL: http://www.1919blacksox.com/worldseries.htm); the story first appeared with variations in "Eight White Sox Indicted," *Chicago Herald and Examiner,* September 29, 1920, p. 1. Landis quoted in Seymour, *Baseball,* 323.

58. On the Water Power Act, see Hays, *Conservation,* 81, 239–40; on the Mineral leasing Act, 87–90, acreage statistic 90.

59. "Great and solemn referendum," quoted in Donald McCoy, "Election of 1920," in *History of American Presidential Elections, 1789–2001,* vol. 6, ed. A. M. Schlesinger, Jr., and F. M. Israel (Philadelphia: Chelsea House Publishers, 2002), 2354.

60. McAdoo quoted in Clements, *Presidency,* 222.

BIBLIOGRAPHY

"147 Dead, Nobody Guilty." *Literary Digest* 44 (January 6, 1912): 6–7.

1896: A Website of Political Cartoons. A Vassar College Website. Available online. URL: http://iberia.vassar.edu/1896/currency.html. Accessed March 2005.

"1919 Black Sox." Available online. URL: http://1919blacksox.com. Downloaded on April 12, 2004.

Abbot, Grace, ed. *The Child and the State.* Chicago: University of Chicago Press, 1938.

Abbott, Carl, Stephen J. Leonard, and David McComb. *Colorado: A History of the Centennial State.* Rev. ed. Boulder: Colorado Associated University Press, 1982.

Abbott, Lyman. "Anarchism: Its Cause and Cure," *Outlook* 70 (February 22, 1902): 465–71.

———. "Saving the Yosemite Park." *Outlook* 91 (January 30, 1909): 234–36.

Adams, Henry. *The Education of Henry Adams.* Boston, New York: Houghton Mifflin, 1918.

Adams, Samuel Hopkins. "The Great American Fraud." *Collier's* 36 (October 7, 1905): 14–29.

Addams, Jane. *A New Conscience and an Ancient Evil.* New York: Macmillan, 1912.

———. *Peace and Bread in Time of War.* 1922. New edition, intro. by John Dewey, Boston: G.K. Hall & Co., 1960. Available online at Dead Sociologists Society. URL: http://www2.pfeiffer.edu/~lridener/DSS/Addams/pbtoc.html. Downloaded on March 31, 2004.

———. "Recreation as a Public Function in Urban Communities." American Sociological Society, *Proceedings* 6 (1911): 35–39.

———. *The Spirit of Youth and the City Streets.* New York: Macmillan, 1909.

———. "Trade Unions and Public Duty." *American Journal of Sociology* 4 (January 1899): 448–60.

———. *Twenty Years at Hull-House, With Autobiographical Notes.* New York: Macmillan, 1910.

Adler, Mortimer, ed. *The Negro in American History.* Vol. 2, *A Taste of Freedom, 1854–1927.* N.p.: Encyclopedia Britannica Educational Corp., 1969.

"Aerial Flights." *Scientific American* 75 (October 31, 1896): 329.

"African American History of Western New York State." Available online. URL: http://www.math.buffalo.edu/~sww/0history/1900–1935.html.

"African American Perspectives: Pamphlets from the Daniel A. P. Murray Collection, 1818–1907." American Memory, Library of Congress. Available online. URL: http://memory.loc.gov/ammem/aap/aaphome.html. Page created on October 19, 1998.

"African American Odyssey." American Memory, Library of Congress. Available online. URL: http://memory.loc.gov/ammem/aaohtml/exhibit/aointro.html. Page dated on March 15, 2002.

Africana: The Encyclopedia of the African and African American Experience. Edited by Kwame Anthony Appiah and Henry Louis Gates, Jr. New York: Basic Civitas Books, 1999.

AfricanAmericans.com. Americans.Net. "The Negro National Anthem." Available online. URL: http://africanamericans.com. Downloaded March 31, 2004.

Aldrich, Thomas Bailey. *Unguarded Gates and Other Poems.* Boston: Houghton Mifflin, 1895.

Allen, Douglas. *Frederic Remington and the Spanish American War.* New York: Crown, 1971.

Allen, Frank Edward, with Raymond Fosdick. *Keeping Our Fighters Fit.* New York: Century, 1918.

AlohaQuest Hawaiian History Education. Available online. URL: http://www.AlohaQuest.com. Downloaded on June 7, 2002.

America; Great Crises in Our History Told by Its Makers. 12 vols. Chicago: Veterans of Foreign Wars of the United States, 1925.

"America and the League of Nations." *The New Republic* 17 (November 30, 1918): 116–18.

"The American Presidency." Speech Archive. Edited by Rick Matlick. Available online. URL: http://www.geocities.com/americanpresidencynet/archive.htm. Last updated on January 2, 2004.

"An American Time Capsule: Three Centuries of Broadsides and Other Printed Ephemera." American Memory Collection. Rare Book and Special Collection Division, Library of Congress. Available online. URL: http://memory.loc.gov/ammem/rbpehtml/pehome.html. Updated on November 22, 2002.

Andrews, E. Benjamin. "The Democracy Supreme." *Scribner's* 19 (April 1896): 469–90.

Andrews, John B. "Social Insurance." In *The Present Labor Situation: Compulsory Investigation and Arbitration,* 42–49. Philadelphia: American Academy of Political and Social Science, 1917.

Angle, Paul M. *The American Reader, from Columbus to Today.* New York: Rand McNally, 1958.

Annals of America. Vols. 11–14. Chicago: Encylopaedia Britannica, Inc., 1976.

"Annexation Agitation in Canada" *Literary Digest* 42 (March 4, 1911): 308–09.

Annotated Code of the General Statute Laws of the State of Mississippi. Edited by R. H. Thompson, George G. Dillard, and R. B. Campbell. Nashville: Marshall and Bruce, 1892.

"Anti-Annexation Documents." University of Hawaii at Manoa, Libraries, Special Collections. Available online. URL: http://libweb.hawaii.edu/libdept/hawaiian/annexation/protest.html.

"Anti-Imperialism in the United States, 1898–1935." Edited by Jim Zwick. Available online. URL: http://www.boondocksnet.com/ai/. Downloaded on January 3, 2003.

Appel, John J., ed. *The New Immigration.* New York: Pitman Publishing, Jerome S. Ozer, 1971.

Aptheker, Herbert, ed. *Documentary History of the Negro People in the United States.* Vol. 2, *From Reconstruction to the Founding of the N.A.A.C.P.* New York: Carol Publishing Group, Citadel Press, 1951, 1979.

"Army Nurse Corps History." Office of Medical History, Office of the Surgeon General. Available online. URL: http://history.amedd.army.mil/ANCWebsite/anchhome.html. Updated on August 22, 2002.

Ashby, Irene. "Child Labor in Southern Cotton Mills." *World's Work* 2 (October 1901): 1290–95.

Ashby, LeRoy. *Endangered Children: Dependency, Neglect, and Abuse in American History.* New York: Twayne Publishers, 1997.

"The Anti-Imperialistic Address." *The Outlook* 68 (July 13, 1901): 615–17.

Anti-Saloon League, 1893–1933. Westerville [Ohio] Public Library. Available online. URL: http//www.wpl.lib.oh.us/AntiSaloon. Downloaded on December 10, 2004.

Austin, Mary. *Earth Horizon.* Boston: Houghton Mifflin, 1932.

———. *Land of Little Rain.* Boston: Houghton Mifflin, 1903.

Bacon, Edwin M., and Morrill Wyman. *Direct Elections and Law-Making by Popular Vote: The Initiative, the Referendum, the Recall, Commission Governments for Cities, Preferential Voting.* Boston: Houghton Mifflin, 1912.

Bailey, Thomas A. *A Diplomatic History of the American People.* 10th ed. Englewood Cliffs, N.J.: Prentice-Hall, 1980.

———. "Shaking the Big Stick: TR and the Alaska Boundary." In *Interpreting Alaska's History: An Anthology.* Edited by M. Mangusso and S. Haycox. Anchorage: Alaska Pacific University Press, 1989.

Bair, Barbara. "Though Justice Sleeps: 1880–1900." In *To Make Our World Anew: A History of African Americans.* Edited by Robin D. G. Kelley and Earl Lewis. New York: Oxford University Press, 2000.

Bigelow, John, Jr. *Reminiscences of the Santiago Campaign.* New York: Harper, 1899.

Baird, W. David, and Danney Goble. *The Story of Oklahoma.* Norman: University of Oklahoma Press, 1994.

Baker, Abby Scott. "Letter to the Editor." *Outlook* 113 (August 23, 1916): 1002–04.

Baker, Newton D. *Frontiers of Freedom.* New York: George H. Doran, 1918.

Baker, S. Josephine. *Fighting for Life.* New York: Macmillan, 1939.

Baker, Ray Stannard. *American Chronicle, the Autobiography of Ray Stannard Baker.* New York: C. Scribner's Sons, 1945.

———. *Following the Color Line: An Account of Negro Citizenship in the American Democracy.* New York: Doubleday Page, 1908.

———. *Woodrow Wilson: Life and Letters.* 8 vols. Garden City, N.Y.: Doubleday, Page, 1927–39.

Balch, Emily Greene. *Beyond Nationalism: The Social Thought of Emily Greene Balch.* Edited by M. M. Randall. New York: Twayne, 1972.

———. *Our Slavic Fellow Citizens.* New York: Charities Publication Committee, 1910.

Bancroft, Hubert Howe. *The Book of the Fair.* Chicago: Bancroft Company, 1893.

Banks, Elizabeth L. "American 'Yellow Journalism.'" *The Living Age* 218 (September 3, 1898): 640–49.

Bannister, Robert C. *Ray Stannard Baker: The Mind and Thought of a Progressive.* New Haven: Yale University Press, 1966.

Bar Association of Erie County. "McKinley Trial Re-creation." Available online. URL: http://www.eriebar.org/about/pb.html. Downloaded on January 6, 2003.

Bardolph, Richard, ed. *The Civil Rights Record: Black Americans and the Law, 1849–1970.* New York: Thomas Y. Crowell, 1970.

Barker, Malcolm E., ed. *More San Francisco Memoirs: 1852–1899, The Ripening Years.* San Francisco: Londonborn Publications, 1996.

Baum, Charlotte, Paula Hyman, and Sonya Michel. *The Jewish Woman in America.* New York: New American Library, 1975.

Baxendall, Rosalyn, Linda Gordon, and Susan Reverby, eds. *America's Working Women: A Documentary History, 1600 to the Present.* New York: Vintage, Random House, 1979.

Beard, Charles A., and Mary R. Beard. *The Rise of American Civilization.* Vol. 2, *The Industrial Era.* New York: Macmillan, 1927, 1930.

Beard, Charles, and Birl E. Schultz, eds. *Documents on the State-Wide Initiative, Referendum, and Recall.* New York: Macmillan, 1912.

Beck, Warren A. *New Mexico: A History of Four Centuries.* Norman: University of Oklahoma Press, 1962.

Belenko, Stephen, ed., *Drugs and Drug Policy in America.* Westport, Conn.: Greenwood, 2000.

Bell, John C. "The Work of the Next Congress." *North American Review* 161 (December 1895): 662–67.

[Bellamy, Francis.] "National School Celebration of Columbus Day: The Official Program." *Youth's Companion* 65 (September 8, 1892): 446–47.

Berkin, Carol, et al. *Making America: A History of the United States.* Boston: Houghton Mifflin, 1995.

Berkman, Alexander. *Prison Memoirs of an Anarchist.* 1912. Reprint, New York: New York Review of Books, 1999.

Berry, Alice Edna Bush. *The Bushes and the Berrys.* Los Angeles: n.p., 1941.

Beveridge, Albert J. *The Meaning of the Times and Other Speeches.* Indianapolis: Bobbs-Merrill, 1908.

Billings, Molly. "The Influenza Pandemic of 1918." Available online at Human Virology at Stanford. URL: http://www.stanford.edu/aroug/virus/uda/. Created in June 1997.

Black, Martha Louise. *My Ninety Years.* Edited by F. Whyard. Anchorage: Alaska Northwest, 1976.

Black Sox Trial, 1921. UMKC [University of Missouri–Kansas City] Law School, Famous Trials. Edited by Douglas Linder. Available online. URL: http://www. law.umkc.edu/faculty/projects/ftrials/blacksox/blacksox.html. Downloaded on September 15, 2004.

Blatch, Harriot Stanton. *Mobilizing Woman-Power.* New York: Woman's Press, 1918. Also available online at Votes for Women: Selections from the National American Woman Suffrage Association Collection, 1848–1921. Library of Congress American Memory. URL: http://lcweb2.loc.gov/ammem/naw/nawshome.html. Created October 19, 1998.

Blatch, Harriot Stanton, and Lutz, Alma. *Challenging Years: Memoirs of Harriot Stanton Blatch.* New York: G. P. Putnam, 1940.

Blocker, Jack S., Jr. *American Temperance Movements: Cycles of Reform.* Boston: Twayne, 1989.

————. *Retreat from Reform: The Prohibition Movement in the United States, 1890–1913.* Westport, Conn.: Greenwood Press, 1976.

Blocker, Jack S., Jr., ed. *Alcohol, Reform, and Society: the Liquor Issue in Social Context.* Westport, Conn.: Greenwood Press, 1979.

Bogue, Donald Joseph. *The Population of the United States: Historical Trends and Future Projections.* New York: Free Press, 1985.

Bolshevik Propaganda. Hearings Before a Subcommittee of the Committee on the Judiciary, United States Senate. 65th Congress, 3rd session, February 11, 1919, to March 10, 1919. Washington, D.C.: GPO, 1919.

Bordin, Ruth. *Woman and Temperance: The Quest for Power and Liberty, 1873–1900.* Philadelphia: Temple University Press, 1981.

Bourne, Randolph. *The Radical Will: Selected Writings 1911–1918.* Edited by O. Hansen. New York: Urizen Books, 1977.

Bowser, Eileen. *The Transformation of Cinema, 1907–1915.* Berkeley: University of California Press, 1990.

Boyd, Herb, ed. *Autobiography of a People: Three Centuries of African American History Told by Those Who Lived It.* New York: Doubleday, 2000.

Brandeis, Elizabeth. "Labor Legislation." In *History of Labour in the United States.* Vol. 4. Edited by J. R. Commons, et al. New York: Macmillan, 1935.

Brandeis, Louis. *Other People's Money, and How the Bankers Use It.* New York: F. A. Stokes, 1914.

Brandeis, Louis Dembitz, and Josephine Goldmark. *Women in Industry; Decision of the United States Supreme Court . . . and Brief for the State of Oregon.* New York: National Consumers' League, 1908. Reprint, New York: Arno Press, 1969.

Brands, H. W. *The Reckless Decade: America in the 1890s.* New York: St. Martin's Press, 1995.

Bread and Roses: Poetry and History of the American Labor Movement. Edited by Jim Zwick. Available online. URL: http://www.boondocksnet.com/labor/history/index.html.

Breckinridge, Sophonisba Preston. *Madeline McDowell Breckinridge, A Leader in the New South.* Chicago: University of Chicago Press, 1921.

Breckinridge, William C. P. "Free Trade or Protection." *North American Review* 150 (April 1890): 505–27.

Bremner, Robert H. *From the Depths: The Discovery of Poverty in the United States.* New York: New York University Press, 1956.

Bremner, Robert H., et al., eds. *Children and Youth in America: A Documentary History.* Vol. 2, *1866–1932,* parts 1 and 2. Cambridge: Harvard University Press, 1971.

Breece, Hannah. *A Schoolteacher in Old Alaska: The Story of Hannah Breece.* Edited by Jane Jacobs. New York: Random House, 1995.

Brinkley, Alan. *American History: A Survey.* Vol 2, *Since 1865.* 10th ed. Boston: McGraw-Hill College, 1999.

———. *The Unfinished Nation: A Concise History of the American People.* New York: Alfred A. Knopf, 1997.

Brinkley, Douglas. *Wheels for the World: Henry Ford, His Company, and a Century of Progress, 1903–2003.* New York: Viking, 2003.

Browne, Waldo. R. *Altgeld of Illinois: A Record of His Life and Work.* New York: B. W. Huebsch, 1924.

Bryan, William Jennings. *The First Battle: A Story of the Campaign of 1896.* Chicago: B. Conkey Company, 1896.

Bryce, James. *The American Commonwealth.* 1888. Rev. ed. 2 vols. New York: Macmillan, 1921.

Buenker, John D., and Edward R. Kantowicz. *Historical Dictionary of the Progressive Era, 1890–1920.* New York: Greenwood Press, 1988.

Bunau-Varilla, Philippe. *The Great Adventure of Panama.* Garden City, N.J.: Doubleday, Page, 1920.

Burgoyne, Arthur G. *The Homestead Strike of 1892.* 1893. Reprint, Pittsburgh: University of Pittsburgh Press, 1979.

Burke, Emma M. "Woman's Experience of Earthquake and Fire." *Outlook* 83 (June 2, 1906): 273–77.

Burleson, A. S. "The Story of Our Air Mail." *Independent* 102 (April 3, 1920): 8.

Burrows, Edwin G., and Mike Wallace. *Gotham: A History of New York City to 1898.* New York: Oxford University Press, 1999.

Buswell, Leslie. *With the American Ambulance Field Service in France: The Personal Letters of a Driver at the Front.* Cambridge, Mass.: Riverside Press, 1915, 1916.

Butler, Elizabeth Beardsley. *Women and the Trades.* Vol. 1 of the Pittsburgh Survey. New York: Charities Publication Committee, 1909.

Butt, Archibald [Archie]. *Taft and Roosevelt: The Intimate Letters of Archie Butt, Military Aide.* Vol. 1. Garden City. N.Y.: Doubleday, Doran, 1930.

Byington, Margaret F. *Homestead: The Households of a Mill Town.* New York: Charities Publication Committee. Vol. 4 of the Pittsburgh Survey, 1910.

Calloway, Colin G., ed. *Our Hearts Fell to the Ground: Plains Indian Views of How the West Was Lost.* Boston: Bedford Books, St. Martin's Press, 1996.

Carnegie, Andrew. "Summing Up the Tariff Discussion." *North American Review* 51 (July 1890): 47–75.

Carry Nation. Kansas State Historical Society Online Exhibits. Available online. URL: http://hs4.kshs.org/exhibits/carry/. Downloaded on December 14, 2002.

Carver, George Washington. *George Washington Carver in His Own Words.* Edited by G. Kremer. Columbia: University of Missouri Press, 1987.

Cashman, Sean Dennis. *America in the Age of the Titans: The Progressive Era and World War I.* New York: New York University Press, 1988.

———. *America in the Gilded Age: From the Death of Lincoln to the Rise of Theodore Roosevelt.* New York: New York University Press, 1984.

Carter, Marion Hamilton. "The Vampire of the South." *McClure's* 33 (October 1909): 617–31.

Catt, Carrie Chapman, and Shuler, Nettie Rogers. *Woman Suffrage and Politics; the Inner Story of the Suffrage Movement.* New York: Scribner's Sons, 1926. Available online at Votes for Women: Selections from the National American Woman Suffrage Association Collection, 1848–1921. Library of Congress American Memory. URL: http://lcweb2.loc.gov/ammem/naw/nawshome.html. Created on October 19, 1998.

Cavallo, Dominik. *Muscles and Morals: Organized Playgrounds and Urban Reform, 1880–1920.* Philadelphia: University of Pennsylvania Press, 1981.

Centennial of Flight. U.S. Centennial of Flight Commission. Available online. URL: http://www.centennialofflight.gov. Downloaded on September 15, 2004.

Center for Public Education and Information on Polygamy. Available online. URL: http://www.polygamyinfo.com/. Updated June 16, 2000.

Center for the Study of the Pacific Northwest [CSPN], University of Washington Wired Outreach. Available online. URL: http://www.washington.edu/uwired/outreach/cspn/index.html. Downloaded December 11, 2002.

Chanute, Oscar. "Experiments in Flying, an Account of the Author's Own Inventions and Adventures," *McClure's* 15 (June 1900): 127–33.

Chase, Harvey S. "Municipal Accounting." *Annals of the American Academy of Political and Social Science* 28 (November 1906): 453–59.

Cherny, Robert W. *A Righteous Cause: The Life of William Jennings Bryan.* Boston: Little, Brown, 1985.

Cherrington, Ernest H. *The Evolution of Prohibition in the United States: A Chronological History.* Westerville, Ohio: American Issue Press, 1920.

Chew, Lew. "The Biography of a Chinaman." *Independent* 55 (February 19, 1903): 417–22.

Chicago Conference on Trusts. Chicago: Civic Federation of Chicago, 1900.

Child-labor Bill: Hearings . . . 64th Congress, 1st session, on H.R. 8234. Washington, D.C.: GPO, 1916.

Chronology and Documentary Handbook of the State of Arizona. Edited by E. L. Trover. Dobbs Ferry, N.Y.: Oceana Publications, 1972.

Chronology and Documentary Handbook of the State of Idaho. Edited by R. I. Vexler. Dobbs Ferry, N.Y.: Oceana Publications, 1978.

Chronology and Documentary Handbook of the State of Wyoming. Edited by R. I. Vexler. Dobbs Ferry, N.Y.: Oceana Publications, 1978.

Clanton, O. Gene. *Kansas Populism: Ideas and Men.* Lawrence: University Press of Kansas, 1969.

Clark, Norman H. *Deliver Us from Evil: An Interpretation of American Prohibition.* New York: W. W. Norton, 1976.

Clarke, Ida Clyde. *American Women and the World War.* New York: D. Appleton, 1918. Available online at World War I Document Archive. URL: http://www.lib.byu.edu/~rdh/wwi/comment/Clarke/Clarke10.htm. Downloaded on April 8, 2004.

Clements, J. C. "What Congress Has Done." *North American Review* 151 (November 1890): 530–33.

Clements, Kendrick A. *The Presidency of Woodrow Wilson.* Lawrence: University Press of Kansas, 1992.

Cohen, Rose Gallup. *Out of the Shadow.* New York: George H. Doran, 1918.

Coletta, Paolo E. "Election of 1908." In *History of American Presidential Elections, 1789–2001.* Vol. 5, *1892–1908.* Philadelphia: Chelsea House Publishers, 2001.

———. *The Presidency of William Howard Taft.* Lawrence: University Press of Kansas, 1973.

Commager, Henry Steele, ed. *Documents of American History.* 8th ed. 2 vols. New York: Appleton-Century-Crofts, 1968.

Commons, John R., et al. *History of Labour in the United States.* 4 vols. New York: Macmillan, 1918–1935.

"Comprehensiveness of Derangement in Business Affairs." *Commercial and Financial Advertiser* 57 (August 26, 1893): 321.

Congressional Quarterly's Guide to U.S. Elections. 4th ed. 2 vols. Edited by John L. Moore et al. Washington, D.C.: CQ Press, 2001.

Connelly, Mark Thomas. *The Response to Prostitution in the Progressive Era.* Chapel Hill: University of North Carolina Press, 1980.

Cooper, Anna Julia. *A Voice from the South.* 1892. New York: Oxford University Press, 1988.

Cooper, John Milton, Jr. *Pivotal Decades: The United States, 1900–1920.* New York: W.W. Norton, 1900.

Cott, Nancy F., et al., eds. *Root of Bitterness: Documents of the Social History of American Women.* 2nd ed. Boston: Northeastern University Press, 1996.

Covello, Leonard. *The Heart Is the Teacher.* New York: McGraw-Hill Book Company, 1958.

Cox, James M. "Improved Public Highways." In *Reducing the Cost of Food Distribution,* 35–37. Annals of the American Academy of Political and Social Science. Vol. 50. Philadelphia: American Academy of Political and Social Science, 1913.

Crawford, Richard. *America's Musical Life, A History.* New York: Norton, 2001.

Crane, Stephen. "In the Depths of a Coal Mine." *McClure's* 3 (August 1894): 195–209.

———. *Maggie, A Girl of the Streets (A Story of New York): An Authoritative Text.* Edited by T. Gullason. New York: W.W. Norton, 1979.

Creel, George. *How We Advertised America.* New York: Harper & Brothers, 1920.

Croly, Herbert. *Progressive Democracy.* New York: Macmillan, 1914.

———. *The Promise of American Life.* New York: Macmillan, 1909, 1912.

Cronin, Thomas E. *Direct Democracy: The Politics of Initiative, Referendum, and Recall.* Cambridge: Harvard University Press, 1989.

Crosby, Alfred W., Jr. *Epidemic and Peace, 1918.* Westport, Conn.: Greenwood Press, 1976.

Crosby, Ernest. *Swords and Ploughshares.* New York: Funk and Wagnalls, 1902.

Crunden, Robert. *Ministers of Reform: The Progressives' Achievement in American Civilization, 1889–1920.* Urbana: University of Illinois Press, 1984.

Currie, Barton W. "The Nickel Madness: The Amazing Spread of a New Kind of Amusement Enterprise . . ." *Harper's Weekly* 51 (August 24, 1907): 1246–47.

Daniels, Roger. *Coming to America: A History of Immigration and Ethnicity in American Life.* New York: HarperCollins, 1990.

———. *Not Like Us: Immigrants and Minorities in America, 1890–1924.* Chicago: Ivan R. Dee, 1997.

Davis, Allen F. *Spearheads for Reform: The Social Settlements and the Progressive Movement, 1890–1914.* New Brunswick, N.J.: Rutgers University Press, 1967, 1984.

Davis, Philip, ed. *Immigration and Americanization.* Boston: Ginn and Company, 1920.

Davis, Richard Harding. *Cuba in Wartime.* New York: R. H. Russell, 1897.

Daws, Gavan. *Shoal of Time: A History of the Hawaiian Islands.* New York: Macmillan, 1968.

Debs, Eugene V. *Debs: His Life, Writings and Speeches.* 3rd ed. St. Louis: P. Wagner, 1910.

———. *Gentle Rebel: Letters of Eugene V. Debs.* Edited by R. Constantine. Urbana: University of Illinois Press, 1995.

De Forest, Robert. "A Brief History of the Housing Movement in America." In *Housing and Town Planning,* 8–16. Philadelphia: American Academy of Political and Social Science, 1914.

De Forest, Robert W., and Lawrence Veiller, eds. *The Tenement House Problem.* 2 vols. New York: Macmillan, 1903.

De Novo, John A., et al., eds. *Selected Readings in American History.* Vol. 2, *Main Themes 1865 to the Present.* New York: Charles Scribner's Sons, 1969.

DeSantis, Vincent P. *The Shaping of America: 1877–1920.* 2nd ed. Arlington Heights, Ill.: Forum Press, 1989.

Dewey, Davis Rich. *National Problems, 1885–1897.* New York: Harper and Brothers, 1907. *The American Nation: A History.* Edited by Albert Bushnell Hart. Vol. 24.

Dewey, John. "Universal Service as Education." *New Republic* 6 (April 22, 1916): 309–10.

DeWitt, Benjamin Parke. *The Progressive Movement.* 1915. Reprint, Seattle: University of Washington Press, 1968.

Dilsaver, Lary M., ed. *America's National Park System: The Critical Documents.* Lanham, Md.: Rowman & Littlefield, 1994. Available online at National Park Service History: Online Books. URL: http://www.cr.nps.gov/history/online_books/anps/index.htm. Updated October 25, 2000.

Dixon, Thomas, Rev. "Booker T. Washington and the Negro: Some Dangerous Aspects of the Work at Tuskegee." *Saturday Evening Post* 178 (August 19, 1905): 1–3.

Doane, William Croswell, Right Rev. "Liquor and Law." *North American Review* 162 (March 1896): 292–96.

"Documenting the American South. The North Carolina Experience." University of North Carolina at Chapel Hill Libraries. Available online. URL: http://docsouth.unc.edu/nc/index.html. Last updated May 24, 2002.

Dodd, Don. *Historical Statistics of the States of the United States: Two Centuries of the Census, 1790–1990.* Westport, Conn.: Greenwood Press, 1993.

Dolan, Jay P. *The American Catholic Experience: A Social History from Colonial Times to the Present.* Garden City, N.Y.: Doubleday, 1985.

Donahue, M. Patricia. *Nursing, the Finest Art: An Illustrated History.* 2nd ed. St. Louis: Mosby, 1996.

Donnelly, William M. "The Root Reforms and the National Guard." Available online at U.S. Army Center of Military History, 1901: Reforming the Army. URL: http://www.army.mil/cmh-pg/documents/1901/Root-NG.htm. Page created on May 3, 2001.

Dos Passos, John. *The Fourteenth Chronicle: Letters and Diaries of John Dos Passos.* Edited by T. Ludington. Boston: Gambit, 1973.

Douglass, Paul. *Real Wages in the United States, 1890–1926.* Boston: Houghton Mifflin, 1930.

"Drinking in Dry Places: A Record of a Traveler's Experiences in Prohibition Communities." *American Magazine* 71 (January 1911): 370–77.

Dubofsky, Melvyn, and Dulles, Foster Rhea. *Labor in America: A History.* 6th ed. Wheeling, Ill.: Harlan Davidson, 1999.

DuBois, W. E. Burghardt. *Autobiography of W. E. B. Du Bois: A Soliloquy on Viewing My Life from the Last Decade of Its First Century.* N.p.: International Publishers, 1968.

———. "Editorial." *The Crisis* 1 (November 1910): 10–11.

———. "National Committee on the Negro." *Survey* 22 (June 12, 1909): 407–09.

———. "Returning Soldiers." *The Crisis* 18 (May 1919): 13–14.

———. *The Souls of Black Folk; Essays and Sketches.* Chicago: A. C. McClurg, 1903.

———. "The Talented Tenth." In *The Negro Problem, A Series of Articles by Representative American Negroes of Today.* New York: James Pott and Company, 1903.

Dunbar, Paul Laurence. *Lyrics of Lowly Life.* Introduction by W. D. Howells. New York: Dodd, Mead, 1896.

Dunne, Finley Peter. *Dissertations by Mr. Dooley.* New York: Harper and Brothers, 1906.

———. *Mr. Dooley At His Best.* New York: C. Scribner's Sons, 1938.

———. *Mr. Dooley: Now and Forever.* Edited by L. Filler. Stanford, Calif.: Academic Reprints, 1954.

Dwight, Frederick. "Automobiles: The Other Side of the Shield." *Independent* 65 (December 3, 1908): 1299–1303.

Early Adventures with the Automobile. EyeWitness to History. Available online. URL: www.eyewitnesstohistory.com. Downloaded on August 24, 2003.

Eastman. [Dr.] Charles A. (Ohiyesa). *From the Deep Woods to Civilization: Chapters in the Autobiography of an Indian.* Boston: Little, Brown, and Company, 1920.

Eastman, Crystal. *Work Accidents and the Law.* Vol. 2 of the Pittsburgh Survey. New York: Charities Publication Committee, 1910.

Eliot, Charles W. "A Study of American Liquor Laws." *Atlantic Monthly* 79 (February 1897): 177–88.

Elliott, Walter, Rev., C. S. P. "The Story of a Mission." *Catholic World* 67 (April 1898): 102–12.

Ellis, Richard N., ed. *New Mexico Historic Documents.* Albuquerque: University of New Mexico University 1975.

Ettling, John. *The Germ of Laziness: Rockefeller Philanthropy and Public Health in the New South.* Cambridge: Harvard University Press, 1981.

Eugene V. Debs Internet Archive. Available online. URL: http://www.marxists.org/archive/debs/works. Downloaded on April 2, 2004.

Evolution of the Conservation Movement, 1850–1920. American Memory, Library of Congress. Available online. URL: http://memory.loc.gov/ammem/amrvhtml/conshome.html. Revised May 3, 2002.

"Family Life Among the Mormons, by a Daughter of Brigham Young." *North American Review* 150 (March 1890): 339–351.

Fanning, C. E., ed. *Selected Articles on Direct Primaries.* 4th ed. rev. New York: H. W. Wilson, 1918.

Farman, Henry W. "Some Economic Aspects of the Liquor Problem." *Atlantic Monthly* 83 (May 1899): 644–54.

Farnsworth, Martha. *Plains Woman: The Diary of Martha Farnsworth, 1882–1922.* Edited by M. Springer and H. Springer. Bloomington: Indiana University Press, 1986.

Farrell, James. *My Baseball Diary.* Carbondale: University of Southern Illinois Press, 1957, 1988.

Fessenden, Helen M. *Fessenden, Builder of Tomorrows.* New York: Coward-McCann, 1940.

Findlaw. Cases and Codes, Supreme Court Decisions. Available online. URL: http://www.findlaw.com/casecode/supreme.html. Downloaded on September 15, 2004.

Finkel, Alvin, and Margaret Conrad. *History of the Canadian Peoples.* Vol. 2, *1867 to the Present.* 2nd ed. Toronto: Copp Clark, 1998.

Fiske, Admiral Bradley A. *War Time in Manila.* Boston: R. G. Badger, 1913.

Fitch, John A. *The Steel Workers.* Vol. 3 of the Pittsburgh Survey. New York: Charities Publication Committee, 1910.

Fite, Gilbert C. "Election of 1896." In *History of American Presidential Elections, 1789–2001.* Vol. 5, *1892–1908.* Philadelphia: Chelsea House Publishers, 2001.

Fleming, Thomas C. "Marcus Garvey Comes to Harlem." Reflections on Black History, Part 5. October 15, 1997. Available online at FreePress. URL: http://www.freepress.org/fleming/flemng05.html. Downloaded on September 16, 2004.

Fleming, Walter L., ed. *Documentary History of Reconstruction.* Vol. 2. Cleveland: Arthur H. Clark Company, 1906.

Flexner, Eleanor. *Century of Struggle: The Woman's Rights Movement in the United States.* Rev. ed. Cambridge: Harvard University Press, Belknap, 1959, 1975.

Flynn, Elizabeth Gurley. *I Speak My Piece: The Autobiography of "The Rebel Girl."* New York: Masses and Mainstream, 1955.

Foerster, Norman, and W. W. Pierson, Jr., eds. *American Ideals.* Boston: Houghton Mifflin, 1917.

Foner, Philip S. *The Spanish-Cuban-American War and the Birth of American Imperialism, 1895–1902.* 2 vols. New York: Monthly Review Press, 1972.

[Papers Relating to the] *Foreign Relations of the United States, Transmitted to Congress with the Annual Message of the President.* Washington, D.C.: GPO, 1870–1946.

Forsyth, Alastair, Sheila Jemima, and Donald Hyslop, eds. *Titanic Voices: Memories from the Fateful Voyage.* New York: St. Martin's Press, 1997.

Fosdick, Raymond B. *Chronicle of a Generation: An Autobiography.* New York: Harper and Brothers, 1958.

Foveaux, Jessie Lee Brown. *Any Given Day: The Life and Times of Jessie Lee Brown Foveaux, a Memoir of Twentieth Century America.* New York: Warner Books, 1997.

Fox, Kenneth. *Better City Government: Innovation in American Urban Politics, 1850–1937.* Philadelphia: Temple University Press, 1977.

Fox, Stephen. *John Muir and His Legacy: The American Conservation Movement.* Boston: Little, Brown, 1981.

Franklin, John Hope, and Alfred A. Moss, Jr. *From Slavery to Freedom: A History of African Americans.* 8th ed. New York: Alfred A. Knopf, 2000.

Freeman, Joshua, et al. *Who Built America? Working People and the Nation's Economy, Politics, Culture, and Society.* Vol. 2, *From the Gilded Age to the Present.* New York: Pantheon Books, 1992.

Fried, Albert. *Socialism in America: From the Shakers to the Third International.* Garden City, N.Y.: Doubleday, 1970.

Frost, Robert. *North of Boston.* New York: Henry Holt, 1914.

Frowne, Sadie. "The Story of a Sweatshop Girl." *Independent* 54 (September 25, 1902): 2279–82.

Galarza, Ernesto. *Barrio Boy.* Boston: Houghton Mifflin, 1993.

Garland, Hamlin. "Homestead and Its Perilous Trades—Impressions of a Visit." *McClure's* 3 (June 1894): 3–20.

———. *A Son of the Middle Border.* 1917. Reissue, New York: Grosset and Dunlap, 1927.

Gatewood, Willard B., Jr. *"Smoked Yankees" and the Struggle for Empire.* Urbana: University of Illinois Press, 1971.

Gauntier, Gene. "Blazing the Trail." *Woman's Home Companion* 55 (October 1928): 7–8, 181–86.

Gavin, Lettie. *American Women in World War I: They Also Served.* Niwot: University Press of Colorado, 1997.

Gibbons, Floyd Phillips. *"And They Thought We Wouldn't Fight."* New York: Doran, 1918.

Gibson, Arrell Morgan. *Oklahoma, a History of Five Centuries.* Norman: University of Oklahoma Press, 1981.

Giele, Janet Zollinger. *Two Paths to Women's Equality: Temperance, Suffrage, and the Origins of Modern Feminism.* New York: Twayne Publishers, 1995.

Gilman, Charlotte Perkins. *Women and Economics: A Study of the Economic Relation Between Men and Women as a Factor in Social Evolution.* Boston: Small, Maynard, 1898.

———. *The Yellow Wallpaper.* 1892. Edited. E. Hedges. Old Westbury, N.Y.: Feminist Press, 1973.

Gluck, Sherna, ed. *From Prison to Parlor: Five American Suffragists Talk About their Lives.* New York: Random House, Vintage Books, 1976.

Goble, Danney. *Progressive Oklahoma: The Making of a New Kind of State.* Norman: University of Oklahoma Press, 1980.

Godkin, E. L. "Diplomacy and the Newspaper." *North American Review* 160 (May 1895): 570–80.

Goldman, Emma. "The Traffic in Women." In *Anarchism and Other Essays.* New York, Mother Earth Publishing Association, 1910.

Gompers, Samuel. "Americanizing Foreign Workers." *American Federationist* 23 (August 1916): 689–90.

———. *The Samuel Gompers Papers.* Edited by S. Kaufman et al. Urbana: University of Illinois Press, 1986–.

Gough, Terrence J. "The Root Reforms and Command." Available online at U.S. Army Center of Military History, 1901: Reforming the Army. URL: http://www.army.mil/cmh-pg/documents/1901/Root-Cmd.htm. Page created May 3, 2001.

Gould, E. R. L. "The Housing Problem in Great Cities." *Quarterly Review of Economics* 14 (1899–1900): 378–393.

Gould, Louis L. *The Presidency of Theodore Roosevelt.* Lawrence: University Press of Kansas, 1991.

———. *The Presidency of William McKinley.* Lawrence: Regents' Press of Kansas, 1980.

Gould, Louis L., ed. *The Progressive Era.* Syracuse: Syracuse University Press, 1974.

Gracie, Archibald. *The Truth about the Titanic.* New York: M. Kennerly, 1913.

Graham, John, ed. *"Yours for the Revolution": The* Appeal to Reason, *1895–1922.* Lincoln: University of Nebraska University 1990.

Grant, Madison. *The Passing of the Great Race; Or, the Racial Basis of European History.* New York: Charles Scribner's Sons, 1916. Available online at The Xfiles: Xenophopia, Africa 2000 Media Group. URL: http://www.africa2000.com/XNDX/madgrant_intro.html

Grantham, Dewey W. *The South in Modern America: a Region at Odds.* New York: HarperCollins, 1994.

———. *Southern Progressivism: the Reconciliation of Progress and Tradition.* Knoxville: University of Tennessee Press, 1983.

Graves, Jackson A. *California Memories, 1857–1930.* Los Angeles: Times-Mirror Press, 1930.

Great American Speeches: 80 Years of Political Oratory. PBS. URL: http://www.pbs.org/greatspeeches/timeline/web_dubois_s.html. Downloaded on November 30, 2004.

Green, David. *The Language of Politics in America: Shaping Political Consciousness from McKinley to Reagan.* Ithaca, N.Y.: Cornell University Press, 1992.

Green, James R. *The World of the Worker: Labor in Twentieth-Century America.* New York: Hill and Wang, 1980.

Green, Robert P., Jr., ed. *Equal Protection and the African American Experience: A Documentary History.* Westport, Conn.: Greenwood Press, 2000.

Greene, Laurence, ed. *America Goes to Press; the News of Yesterday.* Indianapolis: Bobbs-Merrill Company, 1936.

Grossman, James. "A Chance to Make Good: 1900–1920." In *To Make Our World Anew: A History of African Americans.* Edited by Robin G. D. Kelley and Earl Lewis. New York: Oxford University Press, 2000.

———. *Land of Hope: Chicago, Black Southerners, and the Great Migration.* Chicago: University of Chicago Press, 1989.

Gulick, Luther Halsey. *The Healthful Art of Dancing.* New York: Doubleday, Page, 1910.

Hall, G. Stanley. *Adolescence: Its Psychology and Its Relations to Physiology, Sociology, Sex, Crime, Religion, and Education.* Vol. 1. New York: D. Appleton, 1904.

"Hannah Greenbaum Solomon." Jewish Women's Archive, Women of Valor Exhibit. Available online. URL: http://www.jwa.org/exhibits/wov/solomon/hs1.html. Downloaded on December 1, 2003.

Harbaugh, William H. "Election of 1904." In *History of American Presidential Elections, 1789–2001.* Vol. 5, *1892–1908.* Philadelphia: Chelsea House Publishers, 2001.

Harper, Ida Husted, Elizabeth Cady Stanton, Susan B. Anthony, and Mathilda Joslyn Gage, eds. *History of Woman Suffrage.* 6 vols. Rochester, N.Y.: 1881–1922.

Harriman, Florence Hurst [Mrs. J. Borden Harriman]. *From Pinafores to Politics.* New York: H. Holt, 1923. Available online at American Women, American Memory, Library of Congress. URL: http://memory.loc.gov/ammem/awhhtml/awgc1/firstacct.html.

Harris, Sherwood. *The First to Fly: Aviation's Pioneer Days.* Blue Ridge Summit, Pa.: Tab Aero, 1991.

Hartmann, Edward George. *The Movement to Americanize the Immigrant.* New York: Columbia University Press, 1948.

Haskell, Charles. "Governor Haskell Tells of Two Conventions." *Chronicles of Oklahoma* 14 (June 1936): 189–217.

Hart, Albert Bushnell, ed. *The American Nation: a History from Original Sources by Associated Scholars.* 28 vols. New York: Harper & Brothers, 1904–18.

Harvey, William Hope. *Coin's Financial School.* Chicago: Coin, 1894.

Hawaii Organic Act: Congressional Debates on Hawaii Organic Act, Together with Debates and Congressional Action on Other Matters Concerning the Hawaiian Islands. University of Hawaii at Manoa, Libraries, Special Collections. Available online. URL: http://libweb.hawaii.edu/libdept/hawaiian/annexation/organic.html. Revised June 25, 2002.

Haycox, Stephen. *Alaska, An American Colony.* Seattle: University of Washington Press, 2002.

Haynes, George E. *The Negro at Work in New York City: A Study in Economic Progress.* New York: Columbia University Press, 1912.

Hays, Samuel P. *Conservation and the Gospel of Efficiency: The Progressive Conservation Movement, 1890–1920.* 1959. Reprint, Pittsburgh: University of Pittsburgh Press, 1999.

———. *The Response to Industrialism, 1885–1914.* Chicago: University of Chicago Press, 1957.

Haywood, Big Bill [William D.] *Bill Haywood's Book: the Autobiography of William D. Haywood.* 1929. Reprint, Westport, Conn.: Greenwood Press, 1983.

Hendrick, Burton Jesse. *The Life and Letters of Walter H. Page.* 3 vols. Garden City, N.Y.: Doubleday, Page, 1922–25.

Henson, Matthew A. *A Negro Explorer at the North Pole: An Autobiographical Report by the Negro Who Conquered the Top of the World with Admiral Robert E. Peary.* 1912. Reprint, with the title *A Black Explorer at the North Pole.* New York: Walker Publishing, 1969.

Herron, George Davis. *Between Caesar and Jesus: A Course of Eight Monday-noon Lectures Given in Willard Hall, Chicago, for the Christian Citizenship League, upon the Subject of the Relation of the Christian Conscience to the Existing Social System, beginning October 24 and closing December 12, 1898.* 1899. Reprint, Westport, Conn.: Hyperion Press, 1975.

Higham, John. *Strangers in the Land: Patterns of American Nativism, 1860–1925*. 2nd ed. New York: Atheneum, 1970.

Hill, James Jerome. *The Natural Wealth of the Land and Its Conservation . . . Delivered White House, Washington at the Conference on the Conservation of Natural Resources, May 13–15, 1908*. Washington, D.C.?: 1908?

Hindus, Maurice. *Green Worlds, An Informal Chronicle.* New York: Doubleday, Doran, 1938.

Hine, Darlene Clark, ed. *Black Women in the Nursing Profession: A Documentary History.* New York: Garland Publishing, 1985.

Hines, Thomas S. *Burnham of Chicago, Architect and Planner.* New York: Oxford University Press, 1974.

"Historical Data on Mine Disasters in the United States." Mine Safety and Health Administration, United States Department of Labor. Available online. URL: http://www.msha.gov/mshainfo/factshet/mshafct8.htm. Downloaded September 1, 2003.

"Historical Mine Disasters." National Institute for Occupation Safety and Health. Available online. URL: http://www.cdc.gov/niosh/mining/data/disasters.html. Downloaded March 31, 2004.

History Buff. Available online. URL: www.historybuff.com. Downloaded on September 1, 2003.

HistoryMatters. American Social History Project / Center for Media and Learning (City University of New York, Graduate Center) and the Center for History and New Media (George Mason University). Available online. URL: http://historymatters.gmu.edu/. Downloaded on April 8, 2004.

Hobson, Richmond Pearson. *The Sinking of the "Merrimac."* 1899. Annapolis: Naval Institute Press, 1987.

Hoebeke, C. H. *The Road to Mass Democracy: Original Intent and the Seventeenth Amendment.* New Brunswick, N.J.: Transaction Publishers, 1995.

Hofstadter, Richard. *The Age of Reform: From Bryan to F.D.R.* New York: Alfred A. Knopf, 1955.

Holcombe, A. N. "The Effects of the Legal Minimum Wage for Women." In *The Present Labor Situation: Compulsory Investigation and Arbitration,* 34–41. Philadelphia: American Academy of Political and Social Science, 1917.

Horne, Charles F., ed. *Source Records of the Great War.* 7 vols. N.p.: National Alumni, 1923.

Hotchkiss, Willard E. "Chicago Traction: A Study in Evolution." *Annals of the American Academy of Political and Social Sciences* 28 (November 1906): 35–36.

House Committee on the Public Lands, Hetch Hetchy Dam Site. 63rd Congress, 1st session, 25–28 June 1913; 7 July 1913. Washington, D.C.: GPO, 1913.

"How a Dissolved Trust Prospers." *Literary Digest* 44 (March 23, 1912): 576–77.

"How to Stop Lynching." *The Women's Era* 2, no. 2 (1894): 8–9.

Howard, Major-General O. O. "The Menace of 'Coxeyism.'" *North American Review* 158 (June 1894): 687–706.

Howe, Frederic C. "The American City of To-Morrow." *Hampton's* 26 (May 1911): 573–84.

———. *Confessions of a Reformer.* New York: C. Scribner's Sons, 1925.

———. *Wisconsin: An Experiment in Democracy.* New York: Charles Scribner's Sons, 1912.

Howells, William Dean. *Impressions and Experiences.* New York: Harper and Brothers, 1896.

Hull-House Maps and Papers: A Presentation of Nationalities and Wages in a Congested District of Chicago, by Residents of Hull-House, a Social Settlement. New York: Thomas Y. Crowell, 1895.

Hunter, Ann Arnold. *A Century of Service: The Story of the DAR.* Washington, D.C.: National Society Daughters of the American Revolution, 1991.

Hunter, Robert. *Poverty.* New York: Macmillan, 1906.

Illinois Bureau of Labor Statistics. *Biennial Report.* Springfield: Office of the Bureau of Labor Statistics, 1881.

Illinois Factories Inspection Department. *Annual Report.* Vol. 15 (1906/1907)–Vol. 24 (1916/1917).

Illinois Inspector of Factories and Workshops. *Annual Report.* Vol. 1 (1893)–Vol. 14 (1905/1906).

Inaugural Addresses of the Presidents of the United States from George Washington 1789 to George Bush 1989. Bicentennial edition. Washington, D.C.: GPO, 1989.

The Inflation Calculator. Created by S. Morgan Friedman. Available online. URL: http://www.westegg.com/inflation. Downloaded on September 15, 2004.

"Influenza." Division of Medical Microbiology, University of Capetown, Faculty of Health Sciences. URL: http://web.uct.ac.za/depts/mmi/jmoodie/influen2.html#Pandemic%20influenza.

Interchurch World Movement, Commission of Inquiry. *Report on the Steel Strike of 1919 . . .* with the technical assistance of the Bureau of Industrial Research. New York: Harcourt, Brace, and Howe, 1920.

Investigation of the Department of the Interior and the Bureau of Forestry. 13 vols. Senate Document No. 719, 61st Congress, 3rd Session. Washington, D.C.: GPO, 1911.

Ives, Halsey C. *Dream City: A Portfolio of Photographic Views of the World's Columbian Exposition.* St. Louis, Mo.: N. D. Thompson Publishing Company, 1893–94.

Jackson, Kennell A. *America Is Me: 170 Fresh Questions and Answers on Black American History.* New York: HarperCollins, 1996.

James, William and Henry James. *William and Henry James: Selected Letters.* Edited by I. Skrupskelis and E. Berkeley. Charlottesville: University Press of Virginia, 1997.

Jensen, Carl Christian. *An American Saga.* Boston: Little, Brown, 1927.

Jensen, Joan M., ed. *With These Hands: Women Working on the Land.* New York: Feminist Press and McGraw-Hill, 1981.

Johnson, Elizabeth Sands. "Child Labor Legislation." In Vol. 4, *History of Labour in the United States.* New York: Macmillan, 1935.

Johnson, Tom L. *My Story.* Edited by E. Hauser. New York: B. W. Huebsch, 1913.

Jones, Eliot. *The Anthracite Coal Combination in the United States.* Vol. 11, Harvard Economic Studies. Cambridge: Harvard University Press, 1914.

Jones, Holway R. *John Muir and the Sierra Club: The Battle for Yosemite.* San Francisco: Sierra Club, 1965.

Jones, Mary Harris. *Autobiography of Mother Jones.* 1925. Available online at URL: http://womenshistory.about.com/library/etext/mj/bl_mj24.htm. Downloaded on April 7, 2004.

————. *Mother Jones Speaks: Collected Writings and Speeches.* Edited by P. Foner. New York: Monad Press, 1983.

"The Jungle By Upton Sinclair, With Supplemental Readings on the Beef Trust Scandal of 1906 and Its Outcome." Edited by Jim Zwick. BoondocksNet Editions. Available online. URL: http://www.boondocksnet.com/editions/jungle. Downloaded on January 24, 2004.

Kallen, Horace M. "Democracy Versus the Melting Pot [part 2]." *Nation* 100 (February 25, 1915): 217–20.

Kaplan, L. Martin. "Modernization in The Root Reform Era." Available online at U.S. Army Center of Military History, 1901: Reforming the Army. URL: http://www.army.mil/cmh-pg/documents/1901/Root-Mod.htm.

Karsten, Peter. "Armed Progressives: The Military Reorganizes for the American Century." In *The Military in America: From the Colonial Era to the Present.* New York: Free Press, 1980.

Kaztauskis, Antanas. "From Lithuania to the Chicago Stockyards." *Independent* 57 (August 4, 1904): 241–48.

Keating, Edward. *The Gentleman from Colorado: A Memoir.* Denver: Sage Books, 1964.

Kelley, Florence. "I Go to Work." *Survey* 58 (June 1, 1927): 271–74, 301.

Kellogg, Paul. "Pittsburgh Survey of the National Publication Committee of Charities and the Commons." *Charities and the Commons* 19 (March 7, 1908): 1665–70.

Kellor, Frances A. "The Intelligence Office as a Feeder for Vice." *Charities* 12 (March 5, 1904): 255–56.

Kerber, Linda K., and Jane Sherron De Hart, eds. *Women's America: Refocusing the Past.* 4th ed. New York: Oxford University Press, 1995.

Kerr, K. Austin. *Organized for Prohibition: A New History of the Anti-saloon League.* New Haven: Yale University Press, 1985.

Keyssar, Alexander. *The Right to Vote: The Contested History of Democracy in the United States.* New York: Basic Books, 2000.

Kimmel, Michael S., and Thomas E. Mosmiller, eds. *Against the Tide: Pro-feminist Men in the United States, 1776–1990: A Documentary History.* Boston, Mass.: Beacon Press, 1992.

"Kind Words for the McNamaras." *Literary Digest* 44 (January 6, 1912): 3–4.

Kindleberger, Dr. Charles P. "The Battle of Manila. The Destruction of the Spanish Fleet Described by Eye-Witness. Narrative of the Junior Surgeon of the Flag-Ship 'Olympia.'" *Century* 56 (August 1898): 620–24.

Kingdom of Hawai'i. Hawaiian Related Documents Before 1894. Available online. URL: http://www.pixi.com/~kingdom/before1894.html. Downloaded June 7, 2002.

Kipling, Rudyard. "The White Man's Burden." *McClure's* 12 (February 1899): 290–91.

Kirk, William S. "The History of the U.S. Bureau of Mines." Available online. United States Bureau of Mines Alumni Association. URL: http://www.bureauofmines.com/USBMAA.HTM. Updated on January 14, 2001.

Klein, Maury, and Harvey A. Kantor. *Prisoners of Progress: American Industrial Cities, 1850–1920.* New York: Macmillan, 1976.

Kohlsaat, Herman Henry. *From McKinley to Harding; Personal Recollections of Our Presidents.* New York: Charles Scribner's Sons, 1923.

Kohn, August. *The Cotton Mills of South Carolina.* Columbia, S.C.: n.p., 1907.

Krause, Paul. *The Battle for Homestead, 1880–1892: Politics, Culture, and Steel.* Pittsburgh: University of Pittsburgh Press, 1992.

Kroeger, Brooke. *Nellie Bly: Daredevil, Reporter, Feminist.* New York: Times Books, 1994.

La Follette, Robert Marion. *La Follette's Autobiography; A Personal Narrative of Political Experiences.* Madison, Wis.: Robert M. La Follette Co., 1913.

Lane, Franklin Knight. *The Letters of Franklin K. Lane, Personal and Political.* Edited by A. W. Lane and L. H. Wall. Boston: Houghton Mifflin, 1922.

Lansing, Robert. *War Memoirs of Robert Lansing, Secretary of State.* Indianapolis: Bobbs-Merrill, 1935.

Larson, T. A. *History of Wyoming.* 2nd ed. rev. Lincoln: University of Nebraska Press, 1978.

"The Law and the Lady." *Grip* 39 (September 1892): 202.

"The Lawrence Strike from Various Angles." *Survey* 28 (April 6, 1912): 65–82.

Lee, Mary Paik. *Quiet Odyssey: A Pioneer Korean Woman in America.* Edited by S. Chan. Seattle: University of Washington Press, 1990.

LeFeber, Walter. "Election of 1900." In *History of American Presidential Elections, 1789–2001.* Vol. 5, 1892–1908. Philadelphia: Chelsea House Publishers, 2001.

Lender, Mark Edward, and James Kirby Martin. *Drinking in America, a History.* New York: Free Press, 1982.

Leo XII, Pope. *Rerum Novarum.* Available online at Catholic Social Teaching, Archdiocese of St. Paul and Minneapolis Office for Social Justice. URL: http://www.osjspm.org/cst/rn.htm. Downloaded on September 15, 2004.

Lerner, Gerda, ed. *Black Women in White America: A Documentary History.* New York: Pantheon, 1972.

LeRoy, James A. *Americans in the Philippines: A History of the Conquest and First Years of Occupation with an Introductory Account of the Spanish Rule.* 2 vols. Boston: Houghton Mifflin, Riverside Press Cambridge, 1914.

Leupp, Constance D. "The Shirtwaist Makers' Strike." *The Survey* 23 (December 18, 1909): 383–86.

Lewis, David Levering. *W. E. B. DuBois: Biography of a Race, 1868–1919.* New York: Henry Holt, 1993.

Liliuokalani. *Hawaii's Story by Hawaii's Queen.* Boston: Lothrop, Lee and Shepard, 1898.

Link, Arthur S. *Wilson: Confusions and Crises, 1915–1916.* Princeton, N.J.: Princeton University Press, 1964.

———. *Wilson: The Struggle for Neutrality, 1914–1915.* Princeton, N.J.: Princeton University Press, 1960.

———. *Woodrow Wilson and the Progressive Era.* New York: Harper and Row, 1954.

Link, Arthur S.., and William B. Catton. *American Epoch: A History of the United States since 1900.* Vol. 1, *An Era of Economic Change, Reform, and World Wars, 1900–1945.* 5th ed. New York: Knopf, 1980.

Link, Arthur S., and William M. Leary, Jr. "Election of 1916." In *History of American Presidential Elections, 1789–2001.* Vol. 6: 1912–1924. Philadelphia: Chelsea House Publishers, 2002.

Link, Arthur S., and Richard L. McCormick. *Progressivism.* Wheeling, Ill.: Harlan Davidson, 1983.

Link, William A. *The Paradox of Southern Progressivism, 1880–1930.* Chapel Hill: University of North Carolina Press, 1992.

Link, William A., and Arthur S. Link. *American Epoch: A History of the United States since 1900.* Vol. 1, *War, Reform, and Society, 1900–1945.* 7th ed. New York: McGraw-Hill, 1993.

Linn, Brian McAllister. *The Philippine War, 1899–1902.* Lawrence: University Press of Kansas, 2000.

Lippmann, Walter. *Drift and Mastery: An Attempt to Diagnose the Current Unrest.* New York: Henry Holt, 1917.

———. "On Municipal Socialism, 1913." In *Socialism and the Cities.* Port Washington, N.Y.: Kennikat Press, National University Publications, 1975.

Litwack, Leon F. *Trouble in Mind: Black Southerners in the Age of Jim Crow.* New York: Knopf, 1998.

Lloyd, Caroline Augusta. *Henry Demarest Lloyd.* New York: G. P. Putnam's Sons, 1912.

Lloyd, Henry Demarest. *Wealth Against Commonwealth.* 1894. Reprint, edited by T. Cochran, Westport, Conn.: Greenwood Press, 1963.

Lodge, Henry Cabot. "The Federal Election Bill." *North American Review* 151 (September 1890), pp. 257–67.

———. "Our Blundering Foreign Policy." *Forum* 19 (March 1895): 8–17.

London, Jack. "The Story of an Eyewitness." Available online at Museum of the City of San Francisco. URL: http://www.sfmuseum.net/hist5/jlondon.html.

Love, Nat [Deadwood Dick]. *The Life and Adventures of Nat Love.* 1907. Reprint, New York: Arno Press, 1968.

Lovejoy, Owen R. "What Remains of Child Labor." *New Republic* 9 (November 11, 1916): 39–40.

Lovingood, R. S. "A Black Man's Appeal to His White Brothers." *The Crisis* 3 (March 1912): 196.

Lubov, Roy. *The Progressives and the Slums: Tenement House Reform in New York City, 1890–1917.* Pittsburgh: University of Pittsburgh Press, 1962.

Ludlow Massacre Curriculum. Colorado Bar Association. Available online. URL: http://www.cobar.org/group/index.cfm?category=673&EntityID=dpwfp. Downloaded on January 20, 2004.

Lukas, J. Anthony. *Big Trouble: A Murder in a Small Western Town Sets Off a Struggle for the Soul of America.* New York: Simon and Schuster, 1997.

Lynch, Jeremiah. *Three Years in the Klondike: A Gold Miner's Life in Dawson City, 1898–1901.* Santa Barbara, Calif.: The Narrative Press, 2001.

Mackintosh, Barry. *Interpretation in the National Park Service: A Historical Perspective.* 1986. Available online at National Park Service History: Online Books. URL: http://www.cr.nps.gov/history/online_books/mackintosh2/. Updated on July 9, 2000.

"Mademoiselle Miss"; Letters from an American Girl Serving with the Rank of Lieutenant in a French Army Hospital at the Front. Boston: W. A. Butterfield, 1916. Available online at The Medical Front. URL: http://www.ku.edu/carrie/specoll/medical/MMiss.htm. Downloaded on September 15, 2004.

Mahan, Alfred Thayer. *Retrospect and Prospect: Studies in International Relations, Naval and Political.* Boston: Little, Brown, 1902.

———. "The United States Looking Outward," *Atlantic Monthly* 66 (December 1890): 216–24.

Mallery, Otto T. "Field Day." *Playground* 2 (July 1908): 10–12.

Malloy, William M., ed. *Treaties, Conventions, International Acts, Protocols, and Agreements Between the United States of America and Other Powers.* 4 vols. Washington, D.C.: GPO, 1910–38.

Mangano, Antonio. "The Associated Life of the Italians in New York City." *Charities* 12 (May 7, 1904): 476–82.

"Mangled Bodies of Miners Recovered at Providence," *Crittenden [Kentucky] Record-Press,* December 1, 1910. Available online at RootsWeb. URL: http://www.rootsweb.com/~kywebste/mines/1910prov/1910prov.htm. Downloaded on September 15, 2003.

"Marianna Mine Disaster." Pennsylvania Bureau of Deep Mine Safety. Available online. URL: http://www.dep.state.pa.us/dep/deputate/minres/dms/records/marianna.htm. Downloaded on September 15, 2004.

Marcus, Jacob Rader, ed. *The Jew in the American World: A Source Book.* Detroit: Wayne State University Press, 1996.

Marks, Carole. "Social and Economic Life of Southern Blacks During the Migration." In *Black Exodus: The Great Migration from the American South.* Jackson: University Press of Mississippi, 1991.

Marsh, Benjamin Clarke. *An Introduction to City Planning; Democracy's Challenge to the American City.* New York: n.p., [1909].

Mast, Gerald. *A Short History of the Movies.* 4th ed. New York: Macmillan Publishing, 1986.

May, Dean L. *Utah: A People's History.* Salt Lake City: University of Utah Press, 1987.

Mayer, Melanie J. *Klondike Women: True Tales of the 1897–1898 Gold Rush.* N.p.: Swallow Press, Ohio University Press, 1989.

McAdoo, William. "What Congress Has Done, by Representative McAdoo." *North American Review* 151 (November 1890): 526–30.

McCall, Samuel W. "Representative as Against Direct Government." *Atlantic Monthly* 108 (October 1911): 554–66.

McClure, S. S. "Concerning Three Articles in this Number of *McClure's*." *McClure's* 20 (January 1903): 336.

McCoy, Donald R. "Election of 1920." In *History of American Presidential Elections, 1789–2001*. Vol. 6, 1912–1924. Philadelphia: Chelsea House Publishers, 2002.

"The McNamara Confessions." *Literary Digest* 43 (December 9, 1911): 1084–86.

McMath, Robert C. *American Populism: A Social History, 1877–1898*. New York: Hill and Wang, 1993.

McMillan, Neil R. *Dark Journey: Black Mississippians in the Age of Jim Crow*. Urbana: University of Illinois Press, 1989.

McMurray, Linda O. *George Washington Carver: Scientist and Symbol*. New York: Oxford University Press.

McPherson, Edward, ed. *A Handbook of Politics for 1892*. Washington, D.C.: J.J. Chapman, 1892.

M'Cumber, Porter J. "The Alarming Adulteration of Food and Drugs." *Independent* 58 (January 5, 1905): 28–31.

The Medical Front. World War I Document Archive. Available online. URL: http://www.ku.edu/carrie/specoll/medical/medtitle.htm. Updated December 28, 2003.

Meltzer, David, ed. *Reading Jazz*. San Francisco: Mercury House, 1993.

Meltzer, Milton, ed. *The Black Americans: A History in their Own Words, 1619–1983*. New York: Thomas Y. Crowell, 1984.

Mero, Everett Bird. *American Playgrounds, Their Construction, Equipment, Maintenance and Utility, with special contributions and extracts from . . . authorities*. Boston: American Gymnasia, 1908.

Merriam, Charles Edward, and Overaker, Louise. *Primary Elections*. Rev. ed. Chicago: University of Chicago Press, 1928.

Messages and Papers of the Presidents. Edited by J. Richardson. 20 vols. New York: Bureau of National Literature and Art, [1917].

Michelson, Miriam. "Many Thousands of Native Hawaiians Sign a Protest to the United States Government Against Annexation. Available online at Hawai'i Independent & Sovereign. URL: http://www.hawaii-nation.org/sfcall.html. Downloaded March 31, 2004.

Miller, Nathan. *Theodore Roosevelt, a Life*. New York: William Morrow, 1992.

Miller, Warner. "The Duty of The Hour." *North American Review* 163 (September 1896): 362–68.

Millett, Allan R., and Peter Maslowski. *For the Common Defense: A Military History of the United States of America.* New York: Free Press, 1984.

Mine Safety and Health Administration. United States Department of Labor. Available online. URL: www.msha.gov. Downloaded on September 1, 2003.

Minus, Paul M. *Walter Rauschenbusch: American Reformer.* New York: Macmillan, 1988.

Moloney, Deirdre. *American Catholic Lay Groups and Transatlantic Social Reform in the Progressive Era.* Chapel Hill: University of North Carolina Press, 2002.

Monahan, M., ed. *A Text-Book of True Temperance.* 2nd ed. rev. New York: United States Brewers' Association, 1911.

Mooney, James, "The Ghost-Dance Religion and the Sioux Outbreak of 1890." *14th Annual Report of the Bureau of American Ethnology, 1892–93.* Part 2. Washington, D.C.: U.S. GPO, 1896.

Moore, Charles. *Daniel H. Burnham, Architect, Planner of Cities.* 2 vols. Boston: Houghton Mifflin, 1921.

"More Slavery at the South." *Independent* 72 (January 25, 1912): 196–200.

Morgan, H. Wayne. "Election of 1892." In *History of American Presidential Elections, 1789–2001.* Vol. 5: 1892–1908. Philadelphia: Chelsea House Publishers, 2001.

Morgan, H. Wayne, and Anne Hodges Morgan. *Oklahoma, A History.* New York: Norton, American Association for State and Local History, 1977.

Morris, Edmund. *The Rise of Theodore Roosevelt.* New York: Coward, McCann, and Geoghegan, 1979.

———. *Theodore Rex.* New York: Random House, 2001.

Mowry, George E. "Election of 1912." In *History of American Presidential Elections, 1789–2001.* Vol. 6: 1912–1924. Philadelphia: Chelsea House Publishers, 2002.

Muir, John. "Features of the Proposed Yosemite National Park." *The Century,* vol. 40 (September 1890): 656–67.

———. *My First Summer in the Sierra.* Boston: Houghton Mifflin, 1911.

———. *The Yosemite.* New York: Century, 1912.

[Municipal Problems.] Annals of the American Academy of Political and Social Sciences. 28, no. 3 (November 1906). Philadelphia: American Academy of Political and Social Sciences, 1906.

"Municipal Reform Suggestions." *The Century* 47 (February 1894): 631–32.

Murolo, Priscilla, and A. B. Chitty. *From the Folks Who Brought You the Weekend: A Short, Illustrated History of Labor in the United States.* New York: New Press, 2001.

Murphy, Edgar Gardner. *Problems of the Present South: A Discussion of Certain of the Educational, Industrial, and Political Issues in the Southern States.* New York: Macmillan, 1904.

Murphy, Paul. *World War I and the Origin of Civil Liberties in the United States.* New York: Norton, 1979.

Museum of the City of San Francisco. Available online. URL: http://www.sfmuseum. org. Downloaded January 6, 2003.

Musser, Charles. *The Emergence of Cinema: The American Screen to 1907.* Berkeley: University of California Press, 1994.

"My Beloved Poilus." St. John, New Brunswick: Barnes, 1917. Available online at The Medical Front. URL: http://www.ku.edu/carrie/specoll/medical/canadian/ cnursmedtitle.htm.

Naske, Claus-M., and Herman E. Slotnick. *Alaska: A History of the 49th State.* 2nd ed. Norman: University of Oklahoma Press, 1987.

Nathan, Maud. *The Story of an Epoch-making Movement.* Garden City, N.Y.: Doubleday, Page, 1926.

Nation, Carry A. *The Use and Need of the Life of Carry A. Nation.* 1908. Available online at Electronic Text Center, University of Virginia. URL: http://etext.lib.virginia.edu/ toc/modeng/public/NatUsea.html.

National Archives and Records Administration (NARA) Digital Classroom. Teaching With Documents. Available online. URL: http://www.archives.gov/digital_classroom/ teaching_with_documents.html. Downloaded on September 15, 2004.

National Association of Manufacturers of the United States of America. *Proceedings of the Annual Convention,* No. 8. 1903.

National Child Labor Committee. *Proceedings of the Annual Meeting of the National Child Labor Committee, 1905, 1906.* Reprint, New York: Arno Press, 1974.

National Child Labor Committee. *Addresses at the Annual Meeting Held in New York City . . .* New York: National Child Labor Committee, 1905.

National Conference of Jewish Charities in the United States. *Proceedings of the Sixth Biennial Session.* Baltimore: Kohn and Pollock, 1910.

National Consumers' League. *The Consumer's Control of Production: The Work of the National Consumer's League.* Philadelphia: American Academy of Political and Social Science, 1909.

National Education Association. *Addresses and Proceedings, 1908.* Washington, D.C.: 1908.

National Municipal League. *A Municipal Program; Report of a Committee of the National Municipal League.* New York: Macmillan Company for the National Municipal League, 1900.

———. *Proceedings of the Second National Conference, December 1894 and the Third National Conference, May 1895.* Philadelphia: National Municipal League, 1895.

"The Naval Folly." *Nation* 76 (April 23, 1903): 324–25.

Nee, Victor G., and Brett De Bary Nee. *Longtime Californ': A Documentary Study of an American Chinatown.* New York: Pantheon, 1973.

"The New Order in New Jersey." *Literary Digest* 42 (May 6, 1911): 869–70.

Neihardt, John G. (Flaming Rainbow), ed. *Black Elk Speaks: Being the Life Story of a Holy Man of the Oglala Sioux.* 1932. Reprint, Lincoln: Bison Books, University of Nebraska Press, 1988.

Neimark, Peninah, and Peter Mott Rhoades, eds. *The Environmental Debate: A Documentary History.* Westport, Conn.: Greenwood Press, 1999.

Nelson, Daniel. *Shifting Fortunes: The Rise and Decline of American Labor from the 1820s to the Present.* Chicago: Ivan R. Dee, 1997.

Nevins, Allan, ed. *American Press Opinion, Washington to Coolidge: A Documentary Record of Editorial Leadership and Criticism, 1785–1927.* Boston: D.C. Heath, 1928.

"The New Slavery in the South—The Life Story of a Georgia Peon." *Independent 56* (February 25, 1904): 409–14.

Newcomb, Simon. "Is the Airship Coming?" *McClure's* 17 (September 17, 1901): 432–35.

New York Factory Investigating Commission. *Preliminary Report of the Factory Investigating Commission, 1912.* 3 vols. Albany, N.Y.: Argus Company, 1912.

Norris, Frank. "The Frontier Gone at Last." *World's Work* 3 (1902): 1728–31.

———. *The Octopus: A Story of California.* 1901. Cambridge, Mass.: R. Bentley, 1971.

Oates, William C. "The Homestead Strike. I. A Congressional View." *North American Review* 155 (September 1892): 355–76.

Oklahoma Public Legal Research System. Office of the Attorney General, State of Oklahoma. URL: http://oklegal.onenet.net/. Downloaded on March 31, 2004.

Okmulgee Historical Society. *History of Okmulgee, Oklahoma.* Tulsa: Historical Enterprises, 1985.

Olcott, Charles S. *The Life of William McKinley.* 2 vols. Boston: Houghton Mifflin, 1916.

Older, Fremont. *My Own Story.* San Francisco: Call Publishing, 1919. Available online. Library of Congress, "California as I Saw It": First-Person Narratives of California's Early Years, 1849–1900. URL: http://lcweb2.loc.gov/ammem/cbhtml/cbhome.html.

"One Farmer's Wife." *Independent* 58 (February 9, 1905): 294–99.

Osofsky, Gilbert. *The Burden of Race: A Documentary History of Negro-White Relations in America.* New York, Harper and Row, 1967.

Otken, Charles H. *The Ills of the South, or, Related Causes Hostile to the General Prosperity of the Southern People.* New York: G.P. Putnam, 1894.

Our Documents: 100 Milestone Documents. National Archives and Documents Administration. Available online. URL: http://www.ourdocuments.gov/content. php?page=milestone.

Paine, Ralph D. *Roads of Adventure.* Boston: Houghton Mifflin, 1922.

Painter, Nell Irvin. *Standing at Armageddon: The United States, 1877–1919.* New York: W.W. Norton, 1987.

Palmer, A. Mitchell. "The Case Against the Reds." *Forum* 63 (February 1920): 173–85.

Papers of George Washington. University of Virginia. Available online. URL: http://gwpapers.virginia.edu/index.html. Updated December 10, 2003.

Papke, David Ray. *The Pullman Case: The Clash of Labor and Capital in Industrial America.* Lawrence: University Press of Kansas, 1999.

Patterson, Joseph Medill. "The Nickelodeons: The Poor Man's Elementary Course in the Drama." *Saturday Evening Post* 180 (November 23, 1907): 10–11, 38.

Peffer, William Alfred. "The Mission of the Populist Party." *North American Review* 157 (December 1893): 665–79.

Pegram, Thomas R. *Battling Demon Rum: The Struggle for a Dry America, 1800–1933.* Chicago: Ivan R. Dee, 1998.

Perkins, Frank C. "Wireless Communication Between Santa Catalina Island and the Mainland." *Western Electrician* (June 27, 1903): 503.

Pershing, John, J. *My Experiences in the World War.* New York: Frederick A. Stokes, 1931.

Phelan, James. "Why Congress Should Pass the Hetch Hetchy Bill." *Outlook* 91 (February 13, 1909): 340–41.

Phelps, Edith M., ed. *Selected Articles on the Recall, Including the Recall of Judges and Judicial Decisions.* White Plains, N.Y.: H.W. Wilson, 1913.

Philip S. Hench Walter Reed Yellow Fever Collection. Health Sciences Library, University of Virginia. Available online. URL: http://yellowfever.lib.virginia.edu/reed/ and http://etext.lib.virginia.edu/etcbin/fever-browseprint?id=02262001.

Phillips, David Graham. *The Treason of the Senate.* 1906. Edited by G. Mowry and J. Grenier. Chicago: Quadrangle Books, 1964.

Pinchot, Gifford. *Breaking New Ground.* 1947. Reprint, Washington, D.C.: Island Press, 1987.

————. *The Fight for Conservation.* New York: Doubleday, Page, 1910.

Pingree, Hazen. "Detroit: A Municipal Study." *Outlook* 55 (February 6, 1897): 437–42.

Pitkin, Thomas M. *Keeper of the Gate: A History of Ellis Island.* New York: New York University Press, 1975.

Platforms of the Two Great Political Parties, 1856–1920 Inclusive. Compiled by G. Ellis . . . under the Direction of the Clerk, U.S. House of Representatives. Washington, D.C.: n.p., 1920.

Poll, Richard D., ed. *Utah's History.* Logan: Utah State University Press, 1989.

Poole, Earnest. "Waifs of the Streeet." *McClure's* 21 (May 1903): 40-44.

"Population Reference Bureau. Human Population, Health." Available online. URL: http://www.prb.org/Content/NavigationMenu/PRB/Educators/Human_Population/ Health2/World_ Health1.htm.

Porter, Kirk H., and Donald Bruce Johnson, eds. *National Party Platforms, 1840–1964.* Urbana: University of Illinois Press, 1966.

Powderly, T.V. "The Homestead Strike, III. A Knight of Labor's View." *North American Review* 155 (September 1892): 370–76.

Powell, E. P. "Call of Florida." *Independent* 85 (January 31, 1916): 156–58.

Pratt, Walter M. "The Lawrence Revolution." *New England Magazine* 41 (March 1912): 7–16.

Presidential Elections, 1789–1992. Washington, D.C.: Congressional Quarterly, 1995.

Preston, Diana. *The Boxer Rebellion: The Dramatic Story of China's War on Foreigners That Shook the World in the Summer of 1900.* New York: Walker, 2000.

Price, Eva Jane. *China Journal, 1889–1900: An American Missionary Family During the Boxer Rebellion.* New York: Charles Scribner's Sons, 1989.

Price, Homer C. "Effect of Farm Credits on Increasing Agricultural Production and Farm Efficiency." In *Reducing the Cost of Food Distribution, Annals of the American Academy of Political and Social Science,* (1913): 183–90.

"The Primary No Cure-All." *Nation* 87 (August 13, 1908): 131–32.

"Principal Wars in Which The United States Participated, U.S. Military Personnel Serving And Casualties," Table 2-23. U.S. Department of Defense, DIOR (Directorate of Information Operations and Reports). Available online. URL:http://web1.whs. osd.mil/mmid/m01/SMS223R.HTM.

Proceedings of a Conference of Governors in the White House . . . , May 13–15, 1908. Washington, D.C.: GPO, 1909.

Proceedings of the Conference on the Care of Dependent Children Held at Washington, D.C., January 25, 26, 1909. Washington, D.C.: GPO, 1909.

"The Race Problem—An Autobiography by a Southern Colored Woman." *Independent* 56 (March 17, 1904): 586–89.

Randall, Richard S. *Censorship of the Movies; the Social and Political Control of a Mass Medium.* Madison: University of Wisconsin Press, 1968.

Rauchway, Eric. *Murdering McKinley: The Making of Theodore Roosevelt's America.* New York: Hill and Wang, 2003.

Rauschenbusch, Walter. *Christianity and the Social Crisis.* New York: Macmillan, 1907.

Reed, John. *John Reed for* The Masses. Edited by J. Wilson. Jefferson, N.C.: McFarland, 1987.

Reed, Thomas B. "Reforms Needed in the House, by Hon. Thomas B. Reed." *North American Review* 150 (May 1890): 537–47.

"The Regulation of Films." *Nation* 100 (May 6, 1915): 486–87.

"Religious Views of the Titanic." *Literary Digest* 44 (May 4, 1912): 938–39.

Report of the Proceedings and Debates of the Constitutional Convention, State of Virginia, Held in the City of Richmond, June 12, 1901 to June 26, 1902. Vol. 2. Richmond, Va.: Hermitage Press, 1906.

"Report on Motion Picture Theatres of Greater New York." *Film Index* (March 22, 1911): 1–3. Available online at CinemaWeb. URL: http://www.cinemaweb.com/silentfilm/bookshelf/17_fi_3.htm.

Report on the Chicago Strike of June–July 1894. Washington, D.C.: GPO, 1895.

Republican National Committee. *Republican Campaign Text Book, 1896.* Edited by T. H. McKee. Washington, D.C., Hartman and Cadick, 1896.

Rhodes, James Ford. *The McKinley and Roosevelt Administrations, 1897–1909.* New York: Macmillan, 1922.

Richardson, James D., ed. *[A Compilation of the] Messages and Papers of the Presidents, 1789–1899.* 20 vols. New York: Bureau of National Literature and Art, [1917].

Rihbany, Abraham Mitrie. *A Far Journey.* New York: Houghton Mifflin, 1914.

Riis, Jacob A. *The Battle with the Slum.* New York: Macmillan, 1902.

———. *How the Other Half Lives: Studies Among the Tenements of New York.* London: Sampson Low, Marston, Searle, and Rivington, 1891.

———. "In the Gateway of Nations," *Century* 65 (March 1903): 674–82.

Riordon, William. *Plunkitt of Tammany Hall: A Series of Very Plain Talks on Very Practical Politics.* New York, McClure, Phillips, 1905.

Ritter, Lawrence S. *The Glory of Their Times: The Story of the Early Days of Baseball Told by the Men Who Played It.* New York: Macmillan, 1966.

The Rockefellers. American Experience, PBS. Available online. URL: http://www. pbs.org/wgbh/amex/rockefellers/index.html. Downloaded February on 15, 2004.

Roosevelt, Theodore. *Addresses and Presidential Messages.* New York: G. P. Putman's Sons, 1904.

———. "A Layman's Views of an Art Exhibition." *Outlook* 103 (March 29, 1913): 718–20.

———. *Letters of Theodore Roosevelt.* Edited by E. E. Morison, J. Blum, et al. 8 vols. Cambridge: Harvard University Press, 1951–54.

———. "Municipal Administration: The New York Police Force." *Atlantic Monthly* 80 (September 1897): 289–300.

———. *Progressive Principles; Selections from Addresses Made During the Presidential Campaign of 1912, Including the Progressive National Platform.* Edited by E. Youngman. New York: Progressive National Service, 1913.

———. *The Right of the People to Rule.* Washington, D.C.: GPO, 1919.

———. *The Rough Riders.* New York: Scribner, 1902. Reprint, New York: Da Capo Press, 1990.

———. *Selected Letters of Theodore Roosevelt.* Edited by H. W. Brands. New York: Cooper Square Press, 2001.

———. *Theodore Roosevelt, An American Mind, Selections from his Writings.* Edited by M. DiNunzio. New York: St. Martin's Press, 1994.

———. *Theodore Roosevelt: An Autobiography.* New York: Macmillan, 1913.

———. *The Works of Theodore Roosevelt.* National edition. 17 vols. New York: Charles Scribner's Sons, 1926.

Root, Elihu. *The Military and Colonial Policy of the United States: Addresses and Reports.* Edited by R. Bacon and J. Scott. Cambridge: Harvard University Press, 1916.

Rose, Barbara. *American Art Since 1900.* Rev. ed. New York: Praeger, 1975.

Rosen, Ruth. *The Lost Sisterhood: Prostitution in America, 1900–1918.* Baltimore: Johns Hopkins University Press, 1982.

Rosen, Ruth, and Sue Davidson, eds. *The Maimie Papers.* Old Westbury, N.Y.: Feminist Press, 1977.

Runte, Alfred. *National Parks: The American Experience.* Lincoln: University of Nebraska Press, 1979.

Russell, Charles Edward. *The Greatest Trust in the World.* New York: Ridgway-Thayer, 1905.

———. "The Tenements of Trinity Church." *Everybody's* 19 (July–December 1908): 45–57.

Ryan, John A. *A Living Wage: Its Ethical and Economic Aspects.* New York: Macmillan, 1906.

Sachar, Howard M. *A History of the Jews in America.* New York: Alfred A. Knopf, 1992.

Salvatore, Nick. *Eugene V. Debs, Citizen and Socialist.* Urbana: University of Illinois Press, 1982.

"Samuel Gompers Papers." A Project of University of Maryland–College Park, National Historical Publications and Records Commission, National Endowment for the Humanities, and AFL–CIO. Available online. URL: http://www.history.umd.edu/Gompers/index.html

Sandburg, Carl. *Always the Young Strangers.* New York: Harcourt, Brace, and World, 1953.

Sanger, Margaret. *Woman and the New Race.* New York: Brentano's, 1920.

Sarnecky, Mary T. *A History of the U.S. Army Nurse Corps.* Philadelphia: University of Pennsylvania Press, 1999.

Scales, James R., and Danney Goble. *Oklahoma Politics: A History.* Norman: University of Oklahoma Press, 1982.

Schlesinger, Arthur Meier, Fred L. Israel, and William P. Hansen, eds. *History of American Presidential Elections, 1789–2001.* 11 vols. Philadelphia: Chelsea House, 2001–2002.

Schneider, Dorothy, and Carl J. Schneider. *American Women in the Progressive Era, 1900–1920: Change, Challenge, and the Struggle for Women's Rights.* New York: Anchor Books, 1993.

Schurz, Carl. *Speeches, Correspondence and Political Papers of Carl Schurz.* Edited by F. Bancroft. 6 vols. New York: G. P. Putnam's Sons, 1913.

———. *The Policy of Imperialism.* Liberty Tract No. 4. Chicago: American Anti-Imperialist League, 1899.

Schwantes, Carlos A. *Coxey's Army: An American Odyssey.* Lincoln: University of Nebraska Press, 1985.

———. *In Mountain Shadows: A History of Idaho.* Lincoln: University of Nebraska Press, 1991.

Scidmore, Eliza Ruhamah. "Our New National Forest Reserves." *The Century* 6 (September 1893): 792–97.

Scott, Anne Firor. *Natural Allies: Women's Associations in American History.* Urbana: University of Illinois Press, 1991.

Scott, Anne Firor, and Andrew M. Scott. *One Half the People: The Fight for Women's Suffrage.* Philadelphia: J. B. Lippincott, 1975.

Scott, Mel. *American City Planning Since 1890.* Berkeley: University of California Press, 1969.

Scott, William R. *The Americans in Panama.* New York: Statler Publishing Company, 1912. Available online at Panama and Canal Zone. URL: http://www.czbrats. com/AmPan/index.htm. Downloaded on February 6, 2003.

Seale, William. *The President's House: A History.* 2 vols. Washington, D.C.: White House Historical Association, 1986.

————. *The White House: The History of an American Idea.* Washington, D.C.: American Institute of Architects Press, 1992.

Segale, Sister Blandina. *At the End of the Santa Fe Trail.* Columbus, Ohio: Columbian Press, 1932.

Seligman, Edwin R. A., ed. *The Social Evil, With Special Reference to Conditions Existing in the City of New York, A Report Prepared in 1902 Under the Direction of the Committee of Fifteen.* 2nd ed. rev. New York: G. P. Putman's Sons, 1912.

Senner, Dr. J[oseph] H. "Immigration from Italy." *North American Review* 162 (June 1896): 649–658.

"Sewerage at the World's Fair," *Manufacturer and Builder,* vol. 25, no. 6 (June 1893): 136.

Seymour, Harold. *Baseball. Vol. 1, The Early Years.* New York: Oxford University Press, 1960.

————. *Baseball. Vol. 2, The Golden Age.* New York: Oxford University Press, 1971.

Sheldon, Charles M. *In His Steps.* 1897. Available online at Kansas Collection Books. URL: http://www.kancoll.org/books/sheldon. Downloaded on September 15, 2004.

Shipman, David. *The Story of Cinema: A Complete Narrative History from the Beginnings to the Present.* New York: St. Martin's, 1982.

Simons, Geoff. *Cuba: From Conquistador to Castro.* New York: St. Martin's Press, 1996.

Sinclair, Upton. *The Jungle.* New York: Doubleday, Page, 1906.

Skates, John Ray. *Mississippi: A Bicentennial History.* New York: W. W. Norton, 1979.

Sklar, Robert. *Movie-Made America: A Social History of American Movies.* New York: Random House, 1975.

Smith, Norma. *Jeannette Rankin: America's Conscience.* Helena: Montana Historical Society Press, 2002.

Smith, Page. *The Rise of Industrial America: A People's History of the Post-Reconstruction Era.* Vol. 6. New York: McGraw-Hill, 1984.

————. *America Enters the World: A People's History of the Progressive Era and World War I.* Vol. 7. New York: McGraw-Hill, 1985.

"The Social Conscience of the Churches." *Outlook* 90 (December 19, 1908): 849–50.

The Social Evil in Chicago: A Study of Existing Conditions, with Recommendations by the Vice Commission of Chicago. Chicago: Gunthorp-Warren Printing Company, 1911. Reprint, New York: Arno Press, 1970.

Socolofsky, Homer E., and Allan B. Spetter. *The Presidency of Benjamin Harrison.* American Presidency Series. Lawrence: University Press of Kansas, 1987.

Spain, Daphne. *How Women Saved the City.* Minneapolis: University of Minnesota Press, 2002.

Spalding, Albert G. *America's National Game: Historic Facts Concerning the Beginning, Evolution, and Development and Popularity of Baseball.* New York: American Sports Publishing Company, 1911.

[Spalding, Albert G.] *Spalding's Official Base Ball Guide.* Chicago: A. G. Spalding and Brothers, 1878–1939.

Spanish American War Centennial Website. Available online. URL: http://www.spanamwar.com. Downloaded on December 9, 2002.

Spargo, John. *Americanism and Social Democracy.* New York: Harper and Brothers, 1918.

———. *The Bitter Cry of the Children.* New York: Macmillan, 1906.

Stave, Bruce M., ed. *Socialism and the Cities.* Port Washington, N.Y.: Kennikat Press, National University Publications, 1975.

Stave, Bruce M., John F. Sutherland, and Aldo Salerno, eds. *From the Old Country: An Oral History of European Immigration to America.* New York: Twayne, 1994.

Stead, W. T. (William Thomas). *If Christ Came to Chicago! A Plea for the Union of All Who Love in the Service of All Who Suffer.* Chicago: Laird and Lee, 1894.

"Steel Strike of 1919." Chicago Metro History Education Center. URL: http://www.uic.edu/orgs/cmhec/3_steel.html. Downloaded April 15, 2004.

Steffens, Lincoln. *The Autobiography of Lincoln Steffens.* New York: Harcourt, Brace, 1931.

———. *Letters of Lincoln Steffens.* Volume I: 1889–1919. Edited by E. Winter and G. Hicks. New York: Harcourt, Brace, 1938.

———. *The Shame of the Cities.* New York: McClure, Phillips, 1904.

Stein, Leon. *The Triangle Fire.* Philadelphia: Lippincott, 1962.

Steiner, Edward A. *The Confession of a Hyphenated American.* New York: Fleming H. Revell, 1916.

———. *From Alien to Citizen: The Story of My Life in America.* New York: Fleming H. Revel, 1914.

Stevens, Doris. *Jailed for Freedom.* New York: Boni and Liveright, 1920.

———. *Jailed for Freedom.* Edited by C. O'Hare. Troutdale, Oreg.: New Sage Press, 1995.

Stevenson, Robert Alston. "The Poor in Summer." *Scribner's* 30 (September 1901): 259–77.

Stewart, Frank Mann. *A Half Century of Municipal Reform: The History of the National Municipal League.* Berkeley: University of California Press, 1950.

Stratton, Joanna L., ed. *Pioneer Women: Voices from the Kansas Frontier.* New York: Simon and Schuster, 1981.

Street, Julian. *Abroad at Home.* New York: Century, 1914.

"Strike at Homestead." Available online. URL: http://www.history.ohio-state.edu/projects/HomesteadStrike1892. Downloaded on June 6, 2002.

"Strike at Homestead Mill: The Homestead Letters." Available online at PBS American Experience, Andrew Carnegie. URL: http://www.pbs.org/wgbh/amex/carnegie/sfeature/mh_letters.html. Updated in 1999.

The Strike at Lawrence, Massachusetts. Hearings Before the Committee on Rules of the House of Representatives on House resolutions 409 and 433, March 2–7, 1912. 62nd Congress, 2nd Session, House Document 671. Washington, D.C.: GPO, 1912.

Sullivan, Dean A., ed. *Early Innings: A Documentary History of Baseball, 1825–1908.* Lincoln: University of Nebraska Press, 1995.

———, ed. *Middle Innings: A Documentary History of Baseball, 1900–1948.* Lincoln: University of Nebraska Press, 1998.

Sullivan, Louis H. *The Autobiography of an Idea.* New York: Press of the American Institute of Architects, 1926.

Sullivan, Mark. *Our Times: America at the Birth of the Twentieth Century.* Edited by Dan Rather. 1926. Reprint, New York: Scribner's, 1996.

Sumner, Helen L. *History of Women in Industry in the United States.* Washington, D.C.: GPO, 1910.

Sumner, William Graham. *War and Other Essays.* Edited by A.G. Keller. New Haven: Yale University Press, 1911.

Supplement to the Messages and Papers of the Presidents Covering the Administration of William Howard Taft. Bureau of National Literature, 1917.

Supplement to the Messages and Papers of the Presidents Covering the First Term of Woodrow Wilson, March 4, 1913, to March 4, 1917. Bureau of National Literature, 1917.

"Suppress the Rebellion." *Harper's Weekly,* July 14, 1894. Available online at Railroad Extra. URL: http://catskillarchive.com/rrextra/sk94edit.Html. Downloaded on March 31, 2004.

Taft, Philip. *Organized Labor in American History.* New York: Harper and Row, 1964.

Tarbell, Ida. *All in the Day's Work: An Autobiography by Ida M. Tarbell.* New York: Macmillan, 1939.

———. *History of the Standard Oil Company.* 2 vols. New York: McClure, Phillips, 1904.

Tax History Project. Available online. URL: http://www.taxhistory.org. Downloaded on March 31, 2004.

Taylor, Frederick W. *The Principles of Scientific Management.* New York: Harper Brothers, 1911.

Taylor, Graham. *Chicago Commons Through Forty Years.* Chicago: Chicago Commons Association, 1936.

Terrell, Mary Church. "Lynching from a Negro's Point of View." *North American Review* 178 (June 1904): 853–68.

Tevis, Charles V. "A Ku-Klux Klan of To-day: The Red Record of Kentucky's 'Night Riders'." *Harper's Weekly* 52 (February 8, 1908): 14–16, 32.

Theodore Roosevelt Association. Available online. URL: http://www.theodoreroosevelt.org/index.htm. Downloaded on September 1, 2003.

Tifft, Wilton S. *Ellis Island.* Chicago: Contemporary Books, 1990.

Tillman, Benjamin R. "Causes of Southern Opposition to Imperialism." *North American Review* 171 (October 1900): 439–46.

Timberlake, James H. *Prohibition and the Progressive Movement, 1900–1920.* Cambridge: Harvard University Press, 1963.

Tindall, George Brown. *America, A Narrative History.* Vol. 2. New York: W. W. Norton, 1984.

Titanic Inquiry Project. Available online. URL: http://www.titanicinquiry.org/index.html. Downloaded on July 15, 2003.

Tolman, William Howe, ed. *Municipal Reform Movements in the United States.* New York: Fleming H. Revell, 1895.

Tolnay, Stewart E., and E. M. Beck. *A Festival of Violence: An Analysis of Southern Lynchings, 1882–1930.* Urbana: University of Illinois Press, 1995.

———. "Rethinking the Role of Racial Violence in the Great Migration." In *Black Exodus: The Great Migration from the American South.* Edited by A. Harrison. Jackson: University Press of Mississippi, 1991.

Toomy, Alice Timmons. "There is a Public Sphere for Catholic Women." *Catholic World* 57 (August 1893): 674–77.

Trachtenberg, Alan. *The Incorporation of America: Culture and Society in the Gilded Age.* New York: Hill and Wang, 1982.

Trattner, Walter I. *Crusade for the Children: A History of the National Child Labor Committee and Child Labor Reform in America.* Chicago: Quadrangle Books, 1970.

———. *From Poor Law to Welfare State: A History of Social Welfare in America.* 6th ed. New York: Free Press, 1999.

Treadwell, Mattie E. *The Women's Army Corps.* Washington, D.C.: Center of Military History, 1954, 1991. Also Available online at Center of Military History, U.S. Army. URL: http://www.army.mil/cmh-pg/books/wwii/Wac/index.htm#contents. Updated on February 3, 2003.

Treaties and Other International Agreements of the United States of America, 1776–1949. Vol. 8. Edited by C. I. Bevans. Washington, D.C.: GPO, 1971.

Turner, Frederick Jackson. *The Frontier in American History.* New York: Henry Holt, 1920.

Turner, George Kibbe. "The Daughters of the Poor." *McClure's* 34 (November 1909): 45–61.

Twain, Mark [Samuel Clemens]. *Mark Twain's Weapons of Satire: Anti-Imperialist on the Philippine-American War.* Edited by J. Zwick. Syracuse: Syracuse University Press, 1992.

Twombly, Robert. "Ellis Island: An Architectural History." In *Ellis Island: Echoes from a Nation's Past.* New York: Aperture Foundation in association with the National Park Service and Montclair State College, n.d.

Tumulty, Joseph P. *Woodrow Wilson as I Knew Him.* N.p.: Literary Digest, 1921.

"Unionism, Capitalism, and Dynamite." *Literary Digest* 42 (May 6, 1911): 867–68.

U.S. Army Center of Military History. 1901: Reforming the Army. Available online. URL: http://www.army.mil/cmh-pg/documents/1901/1901.htm. Updated on April 18, 2002.

U.S. Bureau of the Census. *200 Years of Census Taking: Population and Housing Questions, 1790–1990.* Washington, D.C.: Bureau of the Census, 1989.

———. *Historical Statistics of the United States, Colonial Times to 1970.* Washington D.C.: GPO, 1975.

U.S. Bureau of Corporations. *Report of the Commissioner of Corporations on the Petroleum Industry.* Part II. Washington, D.C.: GPO, 1907.

U.S. Commission on Industrial Relations. *Final Report and Testimony,* submitted to Congress by the Commission on Industrial Relations created by the act of August 23, 1912. 11 vols. 64th Congress, 1st sess. Senate Doc. 415.

U.S. Historical Census Data Browser. University of Virginia Geospatial and Statistical Data Center. Available online. URL: http://fisher.lib.virginia.edu/census/. Updated on February 21, 2003.

U.S. Immigration Commission. *Abstracts of Reports of the Immigration Commission, with Conclusions and Recommendations and the Views of the Minority.* 2 vols. Washington, D.C.: GPO, 1911.

———. *Dictionary of Races or Peoples.* Washington, D.C.: GPO, 1911.

U.S. Industrial Commission. *Preliminary Report on Trusts and Industrial Combinations.* Washington, D.C.: GPO, 1899.

U.S. Statutes at Large. 32 vols. Washington, D.C.: GPO, 1875–1936.

U.S. War Department. *Discharge of Enlisted Men of the Twenty-fifth United States Infantry.* Washington, D.C.: GPO, 1906.

"Utah's Road to Statehood." Available online. URL:http://www.archives.utah.gov/exhibits/Statehood/1896text.htm. Updated November 12, 2002.

Van Brunt, Henry. "Architecture at the Columbian Exposition [Part 1]." *The Century,* vol. 44, no. 1 (May 1892): 81–89.

Van Vorst, Mrs. John, and Marie Van Vorst. *The Woman Who Toils: Being the Experiences of Two Gentlewomen as Factory Girls.* New York: Doubleday, Page, 1903.

Vassar College. "1896: The Presidential Campaign, Cartoons and Commentary." Edited by Rebecca Edwards and Sarah DeFeo. Available online. URL: http://iberia.vassar.edu/1896/1896home.html.

Veblen, Thorstein. *The Theory of the Leisure Class.* 1899. Reprint, New York: Penguin Books, 1967.

Veiller, Lawrence. "The Tenement-House Exhibition." *Charities Review* 10 (1900–01): 19–25.

Vestal, Stanley, ed., *New Sources of Indian History, 1850–1891.* Norman: University of Oklahoma Press, 1934.

Villard, Oswald Garrison. *Fighting Years: Memoirs of a Liberal Editor.* New York: Harcourt, Brace, 1939.

———. "The Truth About the Peace Conference." *Nation* 108 (April 26, 1919): 646–47.

"Virtual Falmouth. Katherine Lee Bates Cybershrine, America the Beautiful!" Available online. URL: http://www.fuzzylu.com/falmouth/bates/america.html. Downloaded on October 12, 2003.

Von Drehle, David. *Triangle: The Fire That Changed America.* New York: Atlantic Monthly Press, 2003.

Wagenheim, Kal, and Olga Jimenez de Wagenheim, eds. *The Puerto Ricans: A Documentary History.* New York: Praeger Publishers, 1973.

Wald, Lillian D. *The House on Henry Street.* New York: Henry Holt, 1915.

Walker, C. S. "The Farmer's Movement." *Annals of the American Academy of Political and Social Science* 4 (1893–94) 94–102.

Wall, Joseph Frazier. *Andrew Carnegie.* Pittsburgh: University of Pittsburgh Press, 1989.

Wall, Joseph Frazier, ed. *The Andrew Carnegie Reader.* Pittsburgh: University of Pittsburgh Press, 1992.

Walling, William English. "A Children's Strike on the East Side." *Charities* 13 (1904–1905): 305.

————. "The Race War in the North." *Independent* 65 (September 3, 1908): 529–34.

Ward, Geoffrey C. *Jazz: America's Music.* New York: Knopf, 2000.

Ward, Geoffrey C., with Ken Burns. *Baseball, An Illustrated History.* New York: Alfred A. Knopf, 1994.

Ward, Robert De C. "An Immigration Restriction League." *The Century* 49 (February 1895): 639.

Washburn, Benjamin Earle. *As I Recall: the Hookworm Campaigns Initiated by the Rockefeller Sanitary Commission and the Rockefeller Foundation.* New York: Rockefeller Foundation, 1960.

Washington, Booker T. "The Awakening of the Negro." *Atlantic Monthly* 78 (September 1896): 322–28.

————. *My Larger Education; Being Chapters from My Experience.* Garden City, N.Y.: Doubleday, Page, 1911.

————. "My View of Segregation Laws." *New Republic* 5 (December 4, 1915): 113–14.

————. *Up from Slavery: An Autobiography.* New York: Doubleday, Page, 1901.

Watson, Thomas E. "The Negro Question in the South." *Arena* 6 (October, 1892): 540–550.

Weaver, James Baird. *A Call to Action: An Interpretation of the Great Uprising, Its Source and Causes.* Des Moines: Iowa Printing Company, 1892.

Webb, William J. "The Root Reforms And Army Schools And Branches." Available online at U.S. Army Center of Military History, 1901: Reforming the Army. URL: http://www.army.mil/cmh-pg/documents/1901/Root-Schools.htm.. Page created on May 3, 2001.

Weimann, Jeanne Madeline. *The Fair Women: The Story of the Women's Building, World's Columbian Exposition, Chicago 1893.* Chicago: Academy Chicago, 1981.

Weinstein, James. *The Corporate Ideal in the Liberal State.* Boston: Beacon Press, 1968.

Weiss, Harry. "Employers' Liability and Workmen's Compensation." In *History of Labour in the United States.* Vol. 4. Edited by J. R. Commons, et al. New York: Macmillan, 1935.

Welch, Richard E. *The Presidencies of Grover Cleveland.* Lawrence: University Press of Kansas, 1988.

Welch, Rodney. "The Farmer's Changed Condition." *The Forum* 10 (February 1891): 689–700.

Wells, Ida B. *Crusade for Justice: The Autobiography of Ida B. Wells.* Edited by A. Duster. Chicago: University of Chicago Press, 1970.

———. *On Lynchings: Southern Horrors, a Red Record, Mob Rule in New Orleans.* 1892, 1895, 1900. Reprint, Amherst, N.Y.: Humanity Books, 2002.

Wells, Ida B., et al., eds. *The Reason Why the Colored American Is Not in the World's Columbian Exposition.* Chicago: Ida B. Wells, 1893. Reprint, with an introduction by R. W. Rydell, Urbana: University of Illinois, 1999.

Welsh, Herbert. *The Other Man's Country: An Appeal to Conscience.* Philadelphia: J. B. Lippincott, 1900.

Werthner, William. "Personal Recollections of the Wrights." *Aero Club of America News.* June 1912. Available online at Wright Brothers Aeroplane Company. URL: http://www.first-to-fly.com/History/Wright%20Story/recollections. htm. Downloaded on March 1, 2003.

Wharton, Edith. *Fighting France, From Dunkerque to Belport.* New York: Charles Scribner's Sons, 1918.

White, Hervey. "Our Rural Slums." *Independent* 65 (October 8, 1908): 819–21.

White, Walter F. "Election by Terror in Florida." *New Republic* 25 (January 12, 1921): 195–97.

———. *A Man Called White: The Autobiography of Walter White.* New York: Viking, 1948.

White, William Allen. *The Autobiography of William Allen White.* New York: Macmillan, 1946.

———. *The Editor and His People: Editorials from the Emporia Gazette.* Edited by H. Mahin. New York: Macmillan, 1924.

Whitlock, Brand. *Forty Years of It.* New York: D. Appleton and Company, 1914.

Whitmarsh, H. Phelps. "The Steerage of To-Day." *Century* 55 (February 1898): 528–44.

William McKinley Assassination. Court TV's CrimeLibrary. Available online. URL: http://www.crimelibrary.com/assassins/mckinley/.

Wilson, Woodrow. *The New Freedom: A Call for the Emancipation of the Generous Energies of a People.* New York: Doubleday, Page, 1913.

———. *The Papers of Woodrow Wilson.* Edited by Arthur S. Link. 69 vols. Princeton, N.J.: Princeton University Press, 1966–1994.

"Wireless Telegraphy at the St. Louis Exposition." *Electrical Age* (September 1904): 161–167.

Wister, Owen. *The Virginian.* New York: Macmillan, 1902.

"Women and Social Movements in the United States, 1775–2000." URL: http://womhist.binghamton.edu/index.html. Downloaded June 12, 2002.

Wood, Mary I. Stevens. *The History of the General Federation of Women's Clubs.* New York: History Department, General Federation of Women's Club, 1912.

Wood, Maud Park. *Front Door Lobby.* Boston: Beacon Press, 1960. Available online at "Votes for Women: Selections from the National American Woman Suffrage Association Collection, 1848–1921." Library of Congress American Memory. URL: http://lcweb2.loc.gov/ammem/naw/nawshome.html. Created October 19, 1998.

Woodruff, Clinton Rogers. "The Movement for Municipal Reform." *North American Review* 167 (October 1898): 410–18.

Woodruff, Wilford. "Woodruff Manifesto." Center for Public Education and Information on Polygamy. Available online. URL: http://www.polygamyinfo.com/manfesto.htm. Updated on June 16, 2000.

Woods, Robert A. *The Neighborhood in Nation-Building: The Running Comment of Thirty Years at the South End House.* Boston: Houghton Mifflin 1923.

———, ed. *The City Wilderness: A Settlement Study.* Boston: Houghton, Mifflin, 1898.

———, et al. *The Poor in Great Cities.* New York: Charles Scribner's Sons, 1895. Reprint, New York: Arno Press, 1971.

Woodward, C. Vann. *The Strange Career of Jim Crow.* 3d rev. ed. New York: Oxford University Press, 1974.

Woodward, S. W. "A Businessman's View of Child Labor." *Charities and the Commons* 15 (March 3, 1906): 800–01.

World War I Document Archive. Available online. URL: http://www.lib.byu.edu/~rdh/wwi/index.html. Updated on February 2004.

"World's Columbian Exposition of 1893." Paul V. Galvin Library Digital History Collection, Illinois Institute of Technology. Available online. URL: http://columbus.iit.edu/index.html. Downloaded on June 13, 2002.

Wright, Frank Lloyd. "Louis H. Sullivan, His Work." *Architectural Record* 56 (July 1924): 28–32.

Wright, Wilbur, and Orville, Wright. "The Wright Brothers Aëroplane." *Century* 76 (September 1908): 641–50.

Wright Brothers Aeroplane Company and Museum of Pioneer Aviation. Available online. URL: http://www.first-to-fly.com. Downloaded on March 1, 2003.

"The Writings of Samuel 'Golden Rule' Jones." Toledo's Attic: A Virtual Museum of Toledo, Ohio. Available online. URL: http://www.attic.utoledo.edu/att/jones/jones.html. Downloaded on December 20, 2002.

Yans-McLaughlin, Virginia, and Marjorie Lightman. *Ellis Island and the Peopling of America.* New York: New Press, 1997.

Yarrison, James L. "The U.S. Army in The Root Reform Era, 1899–1917." Available online at U.S. Army Center of Military History, 1901: Reforming the Army. URL: http://www.army.mil/cmh-pg/documents/1901/Root-Ovr.htm. Page created on May 3, 2001.

Year Book of the Church and Social Service in the United States, Prepared for the Commission on the Church and Social Service of the Federal Council of the Churches of Christ in America. Edited by H. F. Ward. New York: Missionary Education Movement of the United States and Canada, 1916.

Yockelson, Mitchel. "The War Department: Keeper of Our Nation's Enemy Aliens During World War I." Presented to the Society for Military History Annual Meeting, April 1998. Available online at URL: http://www.lib.byu.edu/~rdh/wwi/comment/yockel.htm. Updated on May 17, 1998.

INDEX

Locators in *italics* indicate illustrations. Locators in **boldface** indicate main entries.
Locators followed by *m* indicate maps. Locators followed by *c* indicate tables.